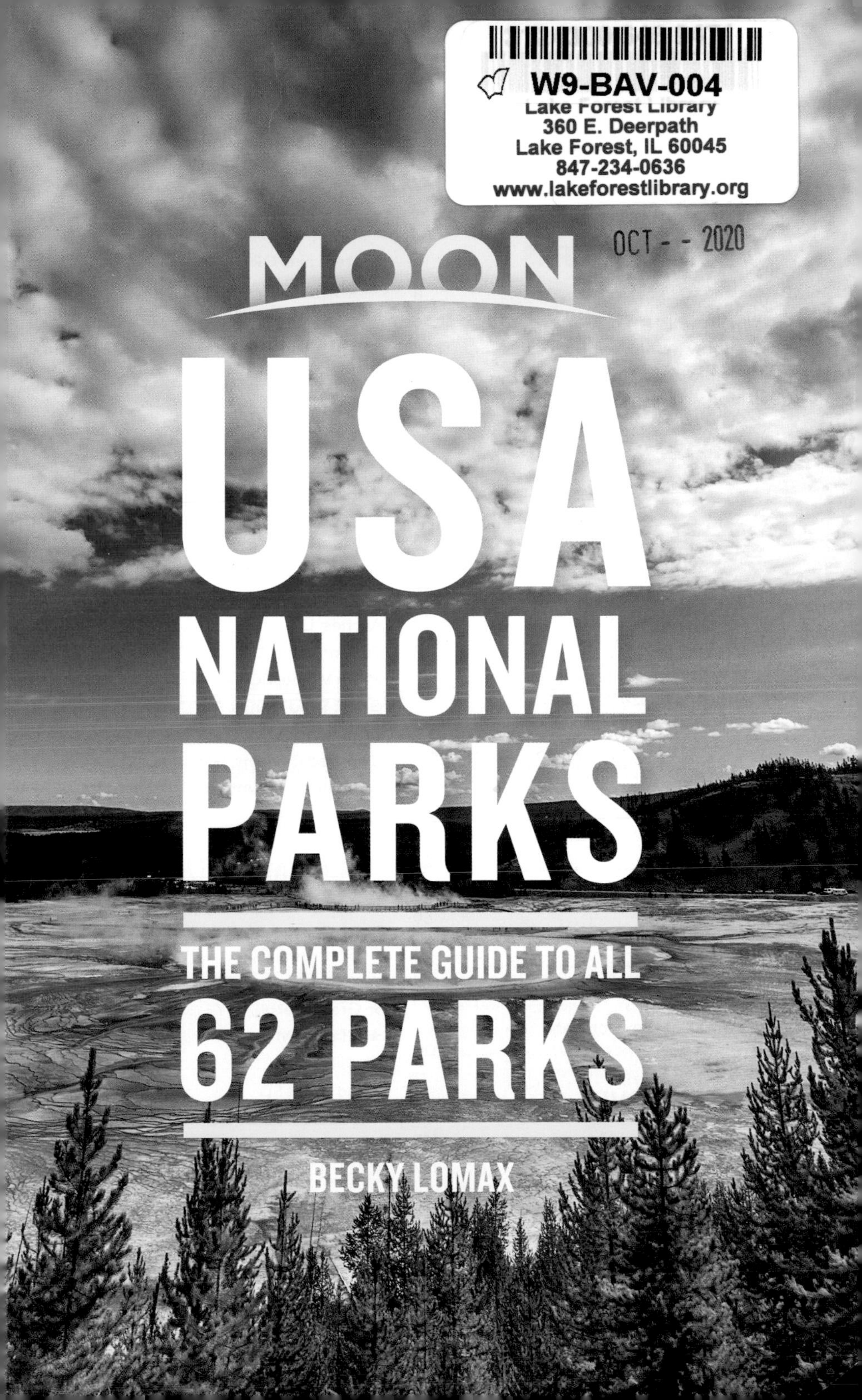

MOON

USA NATIONAL PARKS

THE COMPLETE GUIDE TO ALL 62 PARKS

BECKY LOMAX

CONTENTS

Although every effort was made to make sure the information in this book was accurate when going to press, research was impacted by the COVID-19 pandemic. Some things may have changed during this crisis and the recovery that followed. Be sure to confirm specific details when making your travel plans.

1: GRAND CANYON OF THE YELLOWSTONE, YELLOWSTONE
2: SOUTH RIM, CRATER LAKE
3: NEVADA FALL, YOSEMITE
4: SWIFTCURRENT VALLEY, GLACIER
5: BRYCE CANYON

DISCOVER THE USA NATIONAL PARKS

These 62 national parks are masterpieces spread across the United States. The artistry of nature paints their rainforests with mossy green, their lakes a vivid blue, and their canyons in shifting oranges and reds.

Their beauty is in their wildness. Cactus deserts bloom against the odds, and rugged mountains trap snow to feed rivers tumbling to oceans, where seascapes change with each tide. Wolves, grizzly bears, orcas, and eagles still rule the animal kingdom, much as they did when only Native Americans occupied these lands.

Their sights can only be described in superlatives: North America's highest peak, tallest waterfall, deepest lake, lowest elevation, biggest trees, and the world's first national park.

Our parks provide moments of connection: hearing birds chatter, smelling fragrant trees, feeling the spray of waterfalls, touching rocks smoothed over by the centuries, and staring up into dark skies. These are the moments that let nature wash through us; that offer renewal of the human spirit.

Your trip to any of these national parks can be the start of a longer, life-enriching journey. Let it begin here.

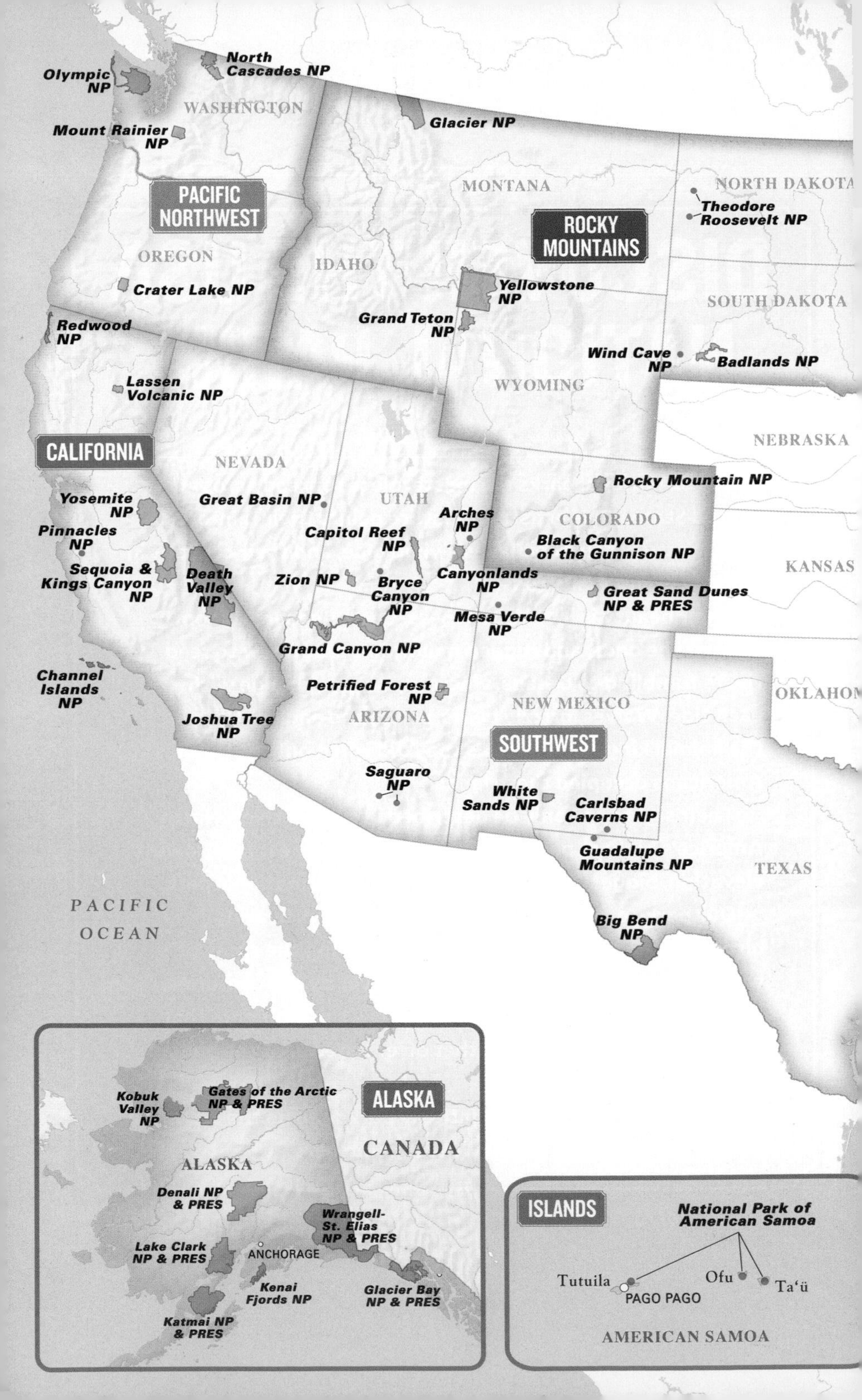

Olympic NP
North Cascades NP
WASHINGTON
Mount Rainier NP
Glacier NP
PACIFIC NORTHWEST
MONTANA
NORTH DAKOTA
Theodore Roosevelt NP
ROCKY MOUNTAINS
OREGON
IDAHO
Crater Lake NP
Yellowstone NP
SOUTH DAKOTA
Redwood NP
Grand Teton NP
Wind Cave NP
Badlands NP
Lassen Volcanic NP
WYOMING
CALIFORNIA
NEBRASKA
NEVADA
Rocky Mountain NP
Yosemite NP
Great Basin NP
UTAH
Arches NP
COLORADO
Pinnacles NP
Capitol Reef NP
Black Canyon of the Gunnison NP
KANSAS
Sequoia & Kings Canyon NP
Death Valley NP
Zion NP
Bryce Canyon NP
Canyonlands NP
Great Sand Dunes NP & PRES
Mesa Verde NP
Grand Canyon NP
Channel Islands NP
Petrified Forest NP
ARIZONA
NEW MEXICO
OKLAHOMA
Joshua Tree NP
SOUTHWEST
Saguaro NP
White Sands NP
Carlsbad Caverns NP
Guadalupe Mountains NP
TEXAS
PACIFIC OCEAN
Big Bend NP
Kobuk Valley NP
Gates of the Arctic NP & PRES
ALASKA
CANADA
ALASKA
Denali NP & PRES
Wrangell-St. Elias NP & PRES
Lake Clark NP & PRES
ANCHORAGE
Kenai Fjords NP
Glacier Bay NP & PRES
Katmai NP & PRES
ISLANDS
National Park of American Samoa
Tutuila
Ofu
Ta'ū
PAGO PAGO
AMERICAN SAMOA

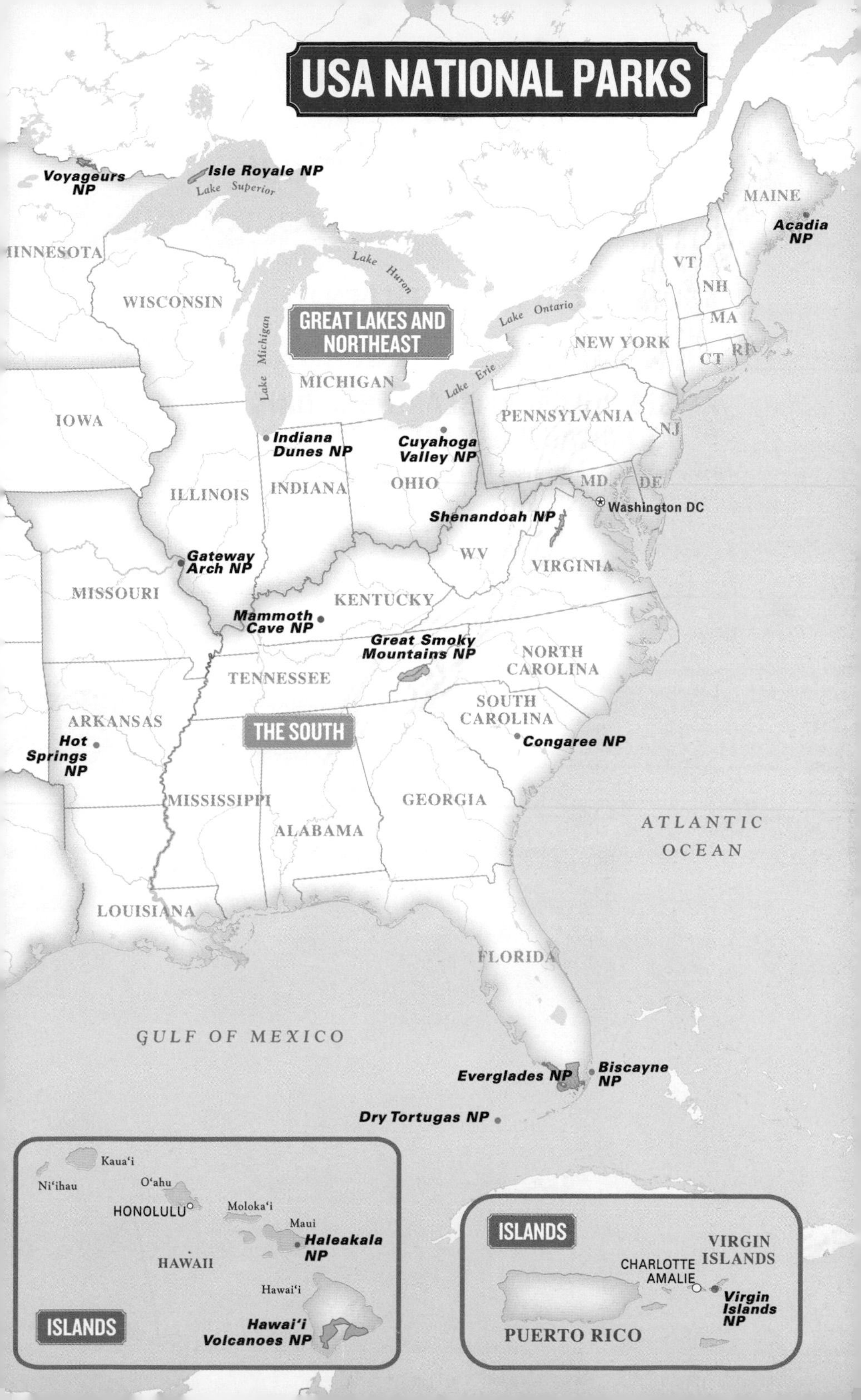
USA NATIONAL PARKS
Voyageurs NP
Isle Royale NP
Lake Superior
MAINE
Acadia NP
INNESOTA
Lake Huron
VT
NH
WISCONSIN
Lake Ontario
MA
GREAT LAKES AND NORTHEAST
Lake Michigan
NEW YORK
CT
RI
MICHIGAN
Lake Erie
IOWA
PENNSYLVANIA
NJ
Indiana Dunes NP
Cuyahoga Valley NP
ILLINOIS
INDIANA
OHIO
MD
DE
Washington DC
Shenandoah NP
Gateway Arch NP
WV
VIRGINIA
MISSOURI
KENTUCKY
Mammoth Cave NP
Great Smoky Mountains NP
NORTH CAROLINA
TENNESSEE
SOUTH CAROLINA
ARKANSAS
THE SOUTH
Hot Springs NP
Congaree NP
MISSISSIPPI
GEORGIA
ALABAMA
ATLANTIC OCEAN
LOUISIANA
FLORIDA
GULF OF MEXICO
Everglades NP
Biscayne NP
Dry Tortugas NP
Kaua'i
Ni'ihau
O'ahu
HONOLULU
Moloka'i
Maui
Haleakala NP
HAWAII
Hawai'i
ISLANDS
Hawai'i Volcanoes NP
ISLANDS
VIRGIN ISLANDS
CHARLOTTE AMALIE
Virgin Islands NP
PUERTO RICO

Top 10 Experiences

1 MARVEL AT ICE-LADEN DENALI

Feast your eyes on the immense icy wonder of crevassed glaciers plunging from the highest point in North America (page 43).

2 SEE VOLCANIC ISLAND-BUILDING AT HAWAII VOLCANOES

Newly active Kilauea spews lava into the ocean, expanding the island's footprint (page 695).

1

2

3 RAFT THROUGH THE GRAND CANYON

Synch with the rhythm of the Colorado River during 7-21 days of crashing white water and flatwater floats below the immense canyon walls (page 285).

4 TAKE A SCENIC DRIVE IN GREAT SMOKIES

Choose one of the many scenic drives in late fall to witness regal scarlets, oranges, and golds light up the forests (page 606).

4

5

6

5 GO UNDERGROUND AT MAMMOTH CAVE

Explore this labyrinth—part of the longest cave system in the world—under electric lights, with handheld lanterns, or crawling through tight squeezes (page 626).

6 SEE GEOLOGY IN ACTION IN YELLOWSTONE

Marvel at the radiance of geothermal features like Grand Prismatic Spring (page 458) and Old Faithful, the famous geyser that erupts roughly every 90 minutes (page 455).

7 CIRCLE CRATER LAKE

The ultra-clear water of the deepest lake in the United States yields a rich blue hue seen in few other places (page 217).

8 HIKE THE NARROWS IN ZION

Plod upstream in the rocky water of the North Fork of the Virgin River through a deep, narrow slot canyon of vertical cliffs (page 313).

9 TOUR ANCIENT CLIFF DWELLINGS IN MESA VERDE

Visit the wondrous cliffside homes of the Ancestral Pueblo people on ranger-led tours (page 376).

10 GAZE UP AT GIANT TREES IN SEQUOIA AND KINGS CANYON

Stand in awe at the base of giant sequoia trees—including the largest tree by volume in the world (page 141).

9

10

Where TO GO

ALASKA

Alaska contains some of the most rugged and wildest parks. In **Denali,** bus tours carry visitors deep into the park to see wolves, bears, moose, and the tallest peak in North America. Flightseeing gets visitors even closer to Denali mountain. See tidewater glaciers in **Glacier Bay** and **Kenai Fjords,** or fly above the Arctic Circle to **Gates of the Arctic and Kobuk Valley.** Watch brown bears fishing in **Katmai,** go fishing in **Lake Clark**, and hike to glaciers in **Wrangell-St. Elias.**

CALIFORNIA

The California parks span unique extremes: the marine environment of the **Channel Islands,** the desert badlands of **Death Valley,** and the bubbling mud pots of **Lassen Volcanic.** Two deserts collide in **Joshua Tree,** rocky spires shoot skyward in **Pinnacles,** and giant redwoods and sequoias pack into **Redwood** and **Sequoia-Kings Canyon.** The crowning park, **Yosemite,** shows off waterfalls in Yosemite Valley, far-reaching views from Glacier Point, and a cabled climb up the steep Half Dome.

PACIFIC NORTHWEST

Every one of the Pacific Northwest parks centers on mountains—from the volcano holding **Crater Lake** to high **Mount Rainier** spilling with glaciers to the icy peaks dominating the **North Cascades.** In **Olympic National Park**, you can drive into the alpine at Hurricane Ridge or go west to plunge into the lush Hoh Rain Forest and stroll rugged Ruby Beach.

SOUTHWEST

The parks of the Southwest show off nature's sculpture in the cliffs, fantastical hoodoos, and arches of **Bryce, Arches, Canyonlands,** and **Capitol Reef.** Belowground, the artistry continues with stalactites in **Carlsbad Caverns.** Even vegetation contains a rare beauty, with stately cacti in **Saguaro** and ancient bristlecones in **Great Basin.** Colors run rampant in the Painted Desert in the **Petrified Forest,** cliff dwellings of **Mesa Verde,** the giant dunes of **Great Sand Dunes,** glittering gypsum of **White Sands,** the Chisos Mountains of **Big Bend,** and the desert peaks of **Guadalupe Mountains.** Two parks stand out as Southwest royalty. **Zion** features the Narrows, Zion Canyon, and the Zion-Mount Carmel Highway. **Grand Canyon** has overlooks of the gaping chasm along Hermit Road and at Desert View Watchtower, while the inner canyon lures hikers and boaters.

ROCKY MOUNTAINS

In the Rocky Mountains, the large, famous parks often overshadow the smaller ones. But these modest parks enchant in their own right—the narrow slot of **Black Canyon of the Gunnison,** colorful erosion of **Badlands,** boxwork of **Wind Cave,** and beloved badlands of **Theodore Roosevelt.** The large parks have earned fame for their iconic attractions. **Rocky Mountain** has its elk, Longs Peak, and Trail Ridge Road, the highest paved road in the country. **Glacier** has the scenic Many Glacier area, and the cliff-hugging Going-to-the-Sun Road. **Grand Teton** has wildlife and Teton Park Road. And **Yellowstone** has wildlife-watching, the Grand Canyon of the Yellowstone, and the priceless Old Faithful Geyser.

GREAT LAKES AND NORTHEAST

In the northeast is **Acadia** with its Park Loop Road, Jordan Pond House, and historic Carriage Roads.

GRAND CANYON

Like no other region, the Great Lakes contain parks that focus on water. In **Cuyahoga Valley,** Ohio, the canals preserve one of the nation's early water highways. In **Voyageurs,** Minnesota, the lake acreage rivals the amount of land. Lake Superior holds the isolated **Isle Royale,** while **Indiana Dunes** anchors Lake Michigan.

THE SOUTH

From the Appalachian mountain parks such as **Shenandoah,** Virginia, to the coastal marine parks of **Biscayne** and **Dry Tortugas** in Florida, the national parks of the South include the subterranean world of **Mammoth Cave,** Kentucky; the free-standing **Gateway Arch,** Missouri; the swamps of **Congaree,** South Carolina; and the hot mineral springs of **Hot Springs,** Arkansas. Two jewels stand out: **Great Smoky Mountains** with Cades Cove, Cataloochee Valley, and Newfound Gap Road; and **Everglades** for wildlife-watching, canoeing or kayaking, and the Ten Thousand Islands.

ISLANDS

The Pacific Ocean and Caribbean Sea hold islands with lovely beaches. The **Virgin Islands** flank white-sand beaches with coral reefs and turquoise water. Located south of the equator, **American Samoa** likewise harbors impressive coral reefs. But in Hawaii, the national parks climb to great heights far above the beaches at **Haleakalā** and **Hawaiʻi Volcanoes.**

KEEPSAKE STAMPS ▼▼▼

Visitors can collect free cancellation stamps for each national park they tour. Each park has an individual stamp that serves as a record of your visit. A few stamps feature a park icon; most name the park, month, and year. More than 400 properties in the national park system, including historical parks, monuments, and historical trails, have stamps. You can usually get your stamp at the park's visitors centers.

You can use the space provided on the opening page of each chapter in this book to collect the stamp for each national park you visit. A passport-like booklet for collecting your park stamps is also available from the National Park Service (www.eparks.com).

Happy collecting!

Know BEFORE YOU GO

NATIONAL PARKS PASS

Most national parks charge an entrance fee that is usually valid for seven days. To get the most bang for your buck, consider buying the **Interagency Annual Pass** ($80), which is good for all national parks and federal fee areas. Interagency passes are free for fourth graders in the United States, disabled persons, and military personnel. Seniors have two interagency pass options: Annual ($20), which is valid for one year, and Lifetime ($80). Multiple parks are now offering the option to purchase your entry pass online (www.yourpassnow.com). **Print your pass at home** to zip through entrance stations faster.

FEE-FREE DAYS

Some national parks recognize several fee-free days annually, many of which fall on national or federal holidays. During fee-free days, the entrance fee for the national park is waived. Though dates may vary, most fee-free days include: Martin Luther King Day (Jan.), the first day of National Park Week (Apr.), National Park Service birthday (Aug.), National Public Lands Day (Sept.), and Veterans Day (Nov. 11).

RESERVATIONS

To stay overnight inside the parks, make reservations for peak seasons (usually summer) **one year in advance.** This is especially true for lodges in Great Smoky Mountains, Grand Canyon, Rocky Mountain, Yosemite, Yellowstone, Grand Teton, Glacier, Zion, Olympic, and Acadia, as accommodations in these parks book up fast.

Most **campgrounds** accept reservations up to **six months in advance;** they fill quickly at popular locations such as Yosemite. Make any dinner, tour, or other activity reservations when booking your room or campsite.

LOTTERIES

Some activities require **lotteries** or advance reservations. Lotteries operate differently throughout the parks; most occur in winter or spring for the upcoming season. Lottery events include the **synchronous fireflies** in **Great Smoky Mountains;** hiking **Half Dome** and backpacking to the **High Sierra Camps** in **Yosemite;** driving a private vehicle on **the park road in Denali; snowmobiling** in **Yellowstone;** and private **rafting trips** in the **Grand Canyon.** For commercial river trips in the Grand Canyon, book **1-2 years in advance.**

SEASONS

High Season

Summer is often the best time to visit the national parks. As the winter snows disappear and temperatures begin to warm, the tourist crowds thicken and visitor services are in full swing. Park roads start to open, though snow may bury high-elevation roads into **July** and often returns to dust mountain peaks at the end of **September.**

The parks of the Southwest, however, are best in **spring** and **fall;** time your visit then to avoid the triple-digit temperatures of summer.

Low Season

Winter is often the low season, when park lodges, campgrounds, and restaurants **close for the season,** leaving minimal services for visitors. Some national parks enjoy better weather and temperatures in winter thanks to their more moderate climates or tropical locales.

EATING IN THE PARKS

Before visiting a national park, check on food services first, so you can plan accordingly. Many parks have minimal or no food services. At parks with restaurants, expect to wait in line around mealtimes (very few accept reservations). Packing picnic meals helps avoid going hungry.

Collapsible soft-sided **coolers** keep lunches and water bottles cold. They pack well whether you're driving to the parks or flying into the nearest airport.

BEST MEALS IN THE PARKS

Here are the top restaurants in the parks. Each offers something special: dining with a view, a historic setting, a unique experience—or all of the above.

ACADIA: Enjoy afternoon tea at the rustic, recreated 19th-century **Jordan Pond House.**

CRATER LAKE: Feast on Pacific Northwest cuisine at the 1915 **Crater Lake Lodge.**

GLACIER: Enjoy lake views from the **Ptarmigan Dining Room** at the Many Glacier Hotel.

GRAND CANYON: Dine at the rustic but elegant **El Tovar** hotel.

GRAND TETON: See both murals and mountain views while dining at **Jackson Lake Lodge.**

SHENANDOAH: Dine on the terrace at **Big Meadows Lodge.**

YELLOWSTONE: The 1904 **Old Faithful Inn** epitomizes "parkitecture."

YOSEMITE: Even the elegant dining room at **The Ahwahnee** can't compete with the stellar valley views.

Take snacks while hiking and traveling inside the parks, in case you can't make it to a scheduled food service location.

Take at least one **refillable water bottle** per person. A larger water jug can refill individual bottles. Above all, do not purchase disposable plastic bottles which will end up in trash or recycling bins.

AVOID THE CROWDS

Our national parks are popular and rightly so. As visitation increases, however, so do the crowds. Here are some tips to avoid the mayhem.

VISIT IN SHOULDER SEASON

Summer is often peak season, when crowds are at their strongest. Time your visit for **spring** or **fall** instead, or consider visiting the park in **winter** when snowy solitude offers a quiet respite. If you must tour in summer, opt for some of the least-visited parks for a less harried experience. Visit on weekdays to avoid the influx of locals on weekends and holidays.

ARRIVE EARLY MORNING OR LATE AFTERNOON

Rush hour at park entrance stations is 10am-4pm. To claim a coveted parking spot at prime sights and trailheads, arrive **before 9am** (in the busiest, most visited parks or on weekends, arrive before 8am).

Tour the most popular sights and the best-loved trails in the early morning or late afternoon, which avoids the crowds common during the busiest part of the day. Aim first for park areas that may require more time or energy to reach.

SPEED THROUGH ENTRANCE STATIONS

To get through entrance stations faster, buy an **annual park pass.** Pay cash rather than using a credit card. You can also purchase an entrance pass to select parks **online in advance** (www.yourpassnow.com).

HAVE AN ALTERNATE PLAN

Be flexible with your itinerary to forgo a stop or hike if it is too crowded. Always have a second trailhead or sight in mind to visit instead.

SUSTAINABILITY TIPS

USE A WATER BOTTLE

Bring your own refillable water bottle. Don't needlessly add disposable plastic to the park refuse collection and recycling infrastructure.

STAY ON PATHS

Staying on designated paths and trails prevents erosion. This is especially crucial in alpine meadows and sensitive wild-flower zones. Take photos with your feet on a trail.

CARRY OUT YOUR TRASH

Bring a small bag or container to corral your trash to pack out rather than letting tidbits drop along a trail or road. Think ahead and bring food with little to no packaging.

GET OUT OF THE CAR

When possible, get around by walking, biking, or taking shuttles.

HIGHLINE TRAIL, GLACIER

WHAT'S NEW

PRINT YOUR PASS AT HOME. Multiple parks are now offering the option to purchase your entry pass online (www.yourpassnow.com) to zip through entrance stations faster.

During the busy summer season, **ACADIA NATIONAL PARK** is phasing in a timed entry by reservation system to alleviate congestion. Get an update from the park on timed entry reservation requirements before planning your trip.

Congress added more designated wilderness and acreage to **DEATH VALLEY NATIONAL PARK'S** north and south ends, making the largest U.S. national park outside of Alaska even bigger at 3.4 million acres (1.3 million ha).

In the **GREAT SMOKY MOUNTAINS,** a new section of Foothills Parkway has opened between Walland and Wears Valley, offering a new scenic drive for fall foliage.

In an act of island-building, Kīluaea Volcano sent lava flows into the ocean in 2018, adding 875 acres (354 ha) of new land to **HAWAI'I VOLCANOES NATIONAL PARK.**

JOSHUA TREE is acquiring new land in the Covington Flats area.

Flanking the shore of Lake Michigan, **INDIANA DUNES** is filled with ancient forested dunes and sandy beaches. Originally a national shore, it became the 61st national park in 2019.

GATEWAY ARCH celebrates the launch point for explorers and pioneers who followed the route of westward expansion, which started near St. Louis. Originally dedicated as a National Memorial, it became the 60th national park in 2018.

WHITE SANDS encompasses dunefields of white gypsum sand in New Mexico. This former National Monument became the 62nd national park in 2019.

Explore THE NATIONAL PARKS

Best HIKING

ACADIA

A bit of scrambling and aid from iron rungs, steps, and handrails on exposed segments gets you straight up to the apex of the **Beehive Loop Trail** for views of ocean and mountains.

ARCHES

Hike to the free-standing **Delicate Arch,** a natural work of art sculpted by wind and erosion.

GLACIER

This tiptoe along the top-of-the-world **Highline Trail**—full of wildflowers and mountain goats—goes to historic Granite Park Chalet for panoramic views.

KENAI FJORDS

The trail snuggles up to several viewpoints of **Exit Glacier** as it plunges from the Harding Icefield to melt into braided streams.

GRAND CANYON

From the rim to canyon depths, the **Bright Angel Trail** descends through eons of geology to the Colorado River.

GREAT SMOKY MOUNTAINS

Wooden steps, stone staircases, and elevated boardwalks make short work of the climb to **Andrews Bald,** a mountaintop meadow where views encompass the southern Smokies.

MOUNT RAINIER

At Paradise, the **Skyline** loops through sub-alpine wildflower meadows, waterfalls, and vistas of Nisqually Glacier tumbling from the ice cap of Rainier.

OLYMPIC

Wildflowers pave the path to the summit of **Hurricane Hill,** perched perfectly for views north of the Strait of Juan de Fuca into Canada and south into the icy Mount Olympus.

▼ DELICATE ARCH, ARCHES

SHENANDOAH

The switchback climb up **Old Rag** finishes by following blue markers with a hands-and-feet scramble under, over, and between boulders to reach the rocky summit.

YOSEMITE

Expect to be showered by waterfall mist on the **Mist Trail**'s scenery-laden ascent to thundering Vernal and Nevada Falls.

ZION

Zigzag your way up a series of short switchbacks to **Angels Landing,** where fixed chains assist you on the skinny shimmy between immense drop-offs to reach the summit.

FIND YOUR PARK

Which park is for you? If you want . . .

ACCESSIBILITY: Take the wheelchair-accessible shuttle and paths along the South Rim of **Grand Canyon.**

BACKPACKING: Hike the Teton Crest Trail in **Grand Teton** and circle the Wonderland Trail in **Mount Rainier.**

BIKING: Pedal the historic canal towpath in **Cuyahoga Valley.**

BOULDERING: Scale the rock piles at Hidden Valley in **Joshua Tree.**

CAVES: Tour the self-guided Natural Entrance to the Big Room in **Carlsbad Caverns.**

DIVING: Explore sunken wrecks off **Dry Tortugas.**

FALL FOLIAGE: Take an autumn drive along Skyline Drive in **Shenandoah.**

GLACIERS CALVING: Cruise on a boat into **Glacier Bay.**

HORSEBACK RIDING: Saddle up at Glacier Creek Stable in **Rocky Mountain.**

HOT SPRINGS: Soak your worries away at Buckstaff Baths in **Hot Springs.**

HOUSEBOATING: Rent a houseboat to tour the lakes at **Voyageurs.**

NORTHERN LIGHTS: Go aurora-watching at **Denali.**

PADDLING: Kayak the miles of inlets and islets around **Isle Royale** in Lake Superior.

RAINFORESTS: Sink into the lush greenery at the Hoh Rain Forest in **Olympic.**

REDWOODS: Walk amid old-growth giants in **Redwood National and State Parks.**

SAND: Sled or sandboard down dunes at **Great Sand Dunes** or **White Sands.**

SNORKELING: Swim through the coral reefs of the **Virgin Islands** or **American Samoa.**

SOLITUDE: Fly into **Gates of the Arctic** for the ultimate in wilderness.

SUNRISE: Catch the earliest dawn in the United States at Cadillac Mountain in **Acadia.**

SUNSET: Camp overnight on the **Channel Islands** to watch the sunset across the Pacific.

SWIMMING: Lounge on the sandy beaches of Lake Michigan at **Indiana Dunes.**

WATERFALLS: Get doused by waterfall spray in **Yosemite Valley** in spring.

Best FOR WILDLIFE

BIRDS IN BIG BEND

With year-round **birding**, Big Bend avians burst into song in spring, when tropical birds such as the Colima warbler arrive to nest.

BATS AT CARLSBAD CAVERNS

At dusk, sit in the amphitheater at the Natural Entrance to the caverns to watch thousands of **bats** take flight.

FIREFLIES AT CONGAREE AND GREAT SMOKY MOUNTAINS

In late spring, catch the mating ritual of **synchronous fireflies** in the evening as they light up together.

MARINELIFE IN THE CHANNEL ISLANDS

On these California islands in summer, **sea lions** and **northern fur seals** rear pups while **blue** and **humpback whales** surface offshore.

CARIBOU IN DENALI

From the bus tour on Denali Park Road, see a lone **wolf** cruising or a pack out hunting along river bottoms among herds of **caribou.**

CROCODILES IN THE EVERGLADES

You can bicycle or take a tram to see **crocodiles** and **alligators** in Shark Valley, plus scads of **egrets, ibis,** and **storks.**

▼ FIREFLIES, GREAT SMOKY MOUNTAINS

WHALES IN GLACIER BAY

On a summer boat tour in Glacier Bay, catch a **humpback whales, orcas,** or **bald eagles** drawn to the waters rich for feeding.

GRIZZLIES IN GLACIER

Bring binoculars to see **grizzly bears** claw through huckleberry bushes to feast on the succulent berries in Many Glacier.

MOOSE IN ISLE ROYALE

With willows galore, Isle Royale is home to giant, awkward-looking **moose** barely kept in check by waning **wolf** populations.

BEARS IN KATMAI

From special viewing platforms, watch **brown bears** capture fish in the tumbling waters at Brooks Camp.

DARK SKIES

City lights drown out the stars for more than three-fourths of the U.S. population. Designated International Dark Sky Parks offer places where you can still see the Milky Way. Moonless nights are best, and you'll need red flashlights rather than white light to let your eyes adjust to the darkness. Some parks offer telescopes for viewing the starry skies. In August, watch for the annual Perseid meteor shower.

International Dark Sky Parks

All International Dark Sky Parks have darks skies for astrophotography and self-guided night sky viewing in addition to public programs.

ARCHES: New Panorama Point built for stargazing and ranger telescope programs.

BADLANDS: Nightly telescope viewing at amphitheater, July astronomy festival

BIG BEND: Stargazing ranger programs

BLACK CANYON OF THE GUNNISON: June astronomy festival, weekly astronomy ranger programs

BRYCE CANYON: June astronomy festival; evening ranger talks and telescope viewing

CANYONLANDS: Night-sky programs with telescope viewing

CAPITOL REEF: October Heritage Starfest

DEATH VALLEY: Night-sky events in winter and spring, February astronomy festival

GLACIER: Logan Pass stargazing programs, after-dark telescope viewing at Apgar and St. Mary Visitor Centers

GRAND CANYON: June Star Party

GREAT BASIN: Star trains, astronomy programs, full moon hikes, September astronomy festival

GREAT SAND DUNES: Night sky programs

JOSHUA TREE: September night sky festival

OTHER PARKS WITH NIGHT SKY FESTIVALS: Acadia (Sept.), Lassen (Aug.), and Rocky Mountain (every two years)

PARKS WITH SPECIAL NIGHT SKY PROGRAMS: Pinnacles (spring night hikes), Petrified Forest (astronomy programs), Carlsbad Caverns (ranger-led star walks and full moon hikes), Voyageurs (Night Explorer Junior Ranger program), Olympic (Hurricane Ridge astronomy programs)

COW ELK HERD, ROCKY MOUNTAIN

CONDORS AT PINNACLES

Use telescopes near the visitors center or hike the High Peaks Trail in early morning or evening to view **condors.**

ELK IN ROCKY MOUNTAIN

In spring, newborn **elk** follow cows; and in fall, the park resounds with bugling as large-antlered bulls round up harems during the rut.

▼ WILD HORSES, THEODORE ROOSEVELT

WILD HORSES IN THEODORE ROOSEVELT

Through noisy **prairie dog** towns, **wild horses** run free. Visit in spring to see newborn colts prance.

BISON IN YELLOWSTONE

In spring, **bison** give birth to baby calves, known as "red dogs." See how the West once appeared with vast herds interspersed with **pronghorns.**

Best PARKS FOR KIDS

The National Park Service's **Junior Ranger Program** is one of the best activities for kids. The program includes a booklet, which children complete as they learn about each park and engage in fun activities (parents can participate). Kids then turn in their completed booklets at a visitors center to be sworn in as Junior Rangers and receive a national park badge or patch.

In addition to the Junior Ranger Program, specialty **naturalist programs** are great for kids. Look for **Wildlife Olympics** programs, where kids can test their physical skills and see how they stack up against animals. Check out **explorer backpacks** from the

BEST PARKITECTURE

National park lodges reflect the architecture of their surrounding landscape with stone and log work. Many are National Historic Landmarks not to be missed.

The Ahwahnee, Yosemite: This wood and granite palace features stained glass windows, two glorious stone fireplaces, Native American designs, and a three-story beamed ceiling in the dining room with floor-to-ceiling views of Yosemite Valley.

Grand Canyon Lodge, Grand Canyon: Perched on the North Rim, the lodge's dining room and sunroom offer dramatic overlooks of the immense canyon.

Many Glacier Hotel, Glacier: Restored to its former glory, Many Glacier boasts mountain views, a large fireplace, a double spiral staircase, and four-story lobby.

Old Faithful Inn, Yellowstone: The five-story lobby is ringed with knob-by-wood balconies centered on a stone fireplace equal in height.

Paradise Inn, Mount Rainier: The Paradise Inn features a steep-pitched roof and an immense lobby flanked by stone fireplaces.

Bryce Canyon Lodge, Bryce Canyon: The stone-and-wood edifice sports an expansive porch that invites a long look at the surrounding woods.

Crater Lake Lodge, Crater Lake: The lodge's first story is built of stone, then topped by wood and a shingled roof. The Great Hall and the back porch both overlook deep-blue Crater Lake.

Lake Crescent Lodge, Olympic: A glass-paned sunroom and dining room nearly pull Lake Crescent inside this lodge.

▼ MANY GLACIER HOTEL, GLACIER

SANDBOARD DOWN GREAT SAND DUNES

park visitors centers; each pack comes equipped with equipment for activities. The park visitors centers are filled with kids rooms, hands-on exhibits, and touchable learning programs.

ARCHES

Take the whole family on a guided walk through the rock-scrambling maze of the Fiery Furnace.

GREAT SMOKY MOUNTAINS

Join rangers to catch salamanders in Hen Wallow Falls.

ACADIA

Poke around tidepools to see the variety of creatures.

GLACIER

Gaze through special telescopes that let you look right at the sun.

GREAT SAND DUNES

Sandboard down the majestic dunes in this giant sandbox.

PETRIFIED FOREST

Touch fossilized plants and animals in the Junior Ranger Paleontologist program.

BISCAYNE

Don a mask and snorkel to be enchanted by this watery park.

Native American TRADITIONS

Many national parks are rooted in historic Native American lands. Some offer ways to connect with indigenous people and their culture. These are some of the best places to enrich your experience.

AMERICAN SAMOA

What better way to immerse yourself in an indigenous culture than staying with one! This national park works with local people to provide **homestays** where you participate in daily activities of fishing, gardening, or preparing meals.

GLACIER

Blackfeet drivers of **Sun Tours** buses share their heritage with visitors along Going-to-the-Sun Road. Campground amphitheaters also host **Native America Speaks** with local Blackfeet and Kootenai people sharing stories.

GLACIER BAY

The **Tlingit Huna House,** the Xunaa Shuká Hít, is a Tribal House that with daily interpretive programs that share traditional woodcraft and art including demonstrations of carving dugout canoes and dances.

GRAND CANYON

Inside **Desert View Watchtower,** Hopi artist Fred Kabotie painted murals incorporating Hopi symbols and stories. Today, the tower hosts cultural demonstrations by members of many tribes with ties to the park, including the Hopi, Navajo, and Puebloan.

HALEAKALA

Native Hawaiians from **Kīpahulu 'Ohana** lead cultural interpretive hikes with stops at a living farm, historic sites, and natural features like the Pools of 'Ohe'o.

TLINGIT HUNA HOUSE, GLACIER BAY

HAWAII VOLCANOES

Visit the **Volcano Art Center Gallery** on **Aloha Fridays** for demonstrations of traditional Hawaiian arts like ukulele, hula, and lei-making. Other programs include cultural forest walks, "talk stories."

▼ INTERIOR OF DESERT VIEW WATCHTOWER, GRAND CANYON

BEST FOR SOLITUDE

These parks offer some breathing room away from the crowds, with plenty of time to bask in the beauty of the landscape.

BLACK CANYON OF THE GUNNISON: The park's South Rim has popular overlooks, but the long drive to the North Rim means you might have the place to yourself.

CHANNEL ISLANDS: Most visitors arrive by boat and only stay for the day. Plan to camp overnight and you'll have nearly your own private island, especially on Anacapa (which has only seven campsites).

GATES OF THE ARCTIC: Access to this remote arctic park is only by air. Once you're dropped off, you can float or paddle a Wild and Scenic River or backpack through the trail-less wilderness.

GREAT BASIN: Few visit Great Basin, which means you can explore its caves or climb the trail to Wheeler Peak crowd-free.

GUADALUPE MOUNTAINS: Stand alone on the highest summit in Texas as you overlook the Chihuahuan Desert.

HALEAKALĀ: Visitors flock to the summit of this volcano to watch the sun rise. After that, parking spots open up and crowds dissipate. Come for sunset instead, when there are fewer people.

ISLE ROYALE: This park is set in the midst of Lake Superior, where only canoes and sea kayaks can reach its private bays tucked around the island's 337 miles of shoreline.

NORTH CASCADES: Pick up a backcountry permit and stay overnight in a shoreline camp on Ross Lake. Backpack into the mountains to put down some solitary miles.

THEODORE ROOSEVELT: Most visitors head for the park's South Unit, but you can find secluded nooks in the badlands of the North Unit or at Roosevelt's favorite, the Elkhorn Ranch.

VOYAGEURS: The largely water park has hundreds of boat-in campsites spread around the shorelines of multiple lakes.

WRANGELL-ST. ELIAS: The largest national park in the United States is home to millions of acres of solitude, especially along its less traveled Nabesna Road.

MESA VERDE

This park preserves more than 5,000 archeological sites that include surface and cliff dwellings from **Ancestral Puebloans,** the forebears of today's Puebloan people.

PETRIFIED FOREST

Kabotie's murals can also be appreciated inside the **Painted Desert Inn.** Local Native American artisans demonstrate traditional skills here.

REDWOOD

The Tolowa and Yurok tribes perform dance demonstrations periodically, including the annual **renewal dance,** called **Ne'-dosh,** in July.

Best SCENIC DRIVES

TRAIL RIDGE ROAD

The country's highest paved road climbs to a dizzying 12,183 feet (3,713 m) into alpine tundra among granite peaks that define **Rocky Mountain National Park.**

SKYLINE DRIVE

Skyline Drive winds through **Shenandoah**'s lush forests and across long ridgelines, surrounded by spring cherry blossoms or the golds, oranges, and reds of fall.

TIOGA ROAD, YOSEMITE

GOING-TO-THE-SUN ROAD

Amid sawtooth peaks and deep valleys, this National Civil Engineering Landmark cuts through **Glacier**'s cliffs to climb to its high point at Logan Pass.

BADLANDS LOOP DRIVE

In a landscape chiseled by water and wind, this scenic drive through the **Badlands** crawls between spires and sharp canyons banded in varied colors.

RIM DRIVE

This undulating loop circles the rim of **Crater Lake** to take in the intense blues of the deepest lake in the United States.

PAINTED DESERT RIM DRIVE

In **Petrified Forest National Park,** this road curves along the rim of pastel-hued badlands in the Painted Desert.

PARK LOOP ROAD

From rocky coast to forested lakes, this loop around **Acadia**'s Mount Desert Island stacks up scenery, from sunrise to sunset.

BADWATER BASIN

Take in colorful and stark landscapes on **Death Valley**'s scenic road, which drops below sea level to the lowest elevation in North America.

NEWFOUND GAP ROAD

Bisecting **Great Smoky Mountains,** this ridgetop route provides epic views of the Smokies, roadside stops, spring wildflowers, and autumnal colors.

TIOGA ROAD

Lined with subalpine lakes and granite peaks, **Yosemite**'s high-elevation road crests the Sierra through Tuolumne Meadows and Tioga Pass, with one of the best views of Half Dome.

Best BY PUBLIC TRANSIT

Ditch the car. Hop a plane, train, bus, or shuttle for your park visit. Here are the parks most accessible by public transit.

INDIANA DUNES

The electric **South Shore Line train** runs daily between Chicago and South Bend, with four stops inside the park. Some trains permit bicycles, and one stop is near the campground.

GATEWAY ARCH

Catch the **MetroLink Lightrail** from the St. Louis airport. It stops within a 10-minute walk from park.

ACADIA

Bus services connect airports in Bar Harbor and Boston with the park and the **Island Explorer shuttle.** Public ferries go to the islands.

CUYAHOGA VALLEY

Greater Cleveland Transit and **Cuyahoga Valley Scenic Railroad** both service the park from Cleveland.

GLACIER

Amtrak's Empire Builder goes to West or East Glacier where you can connect with **park shuttles** or tours.

YOSEMITE

From San Francisco or Sacramento, **Amtrak's San Joaquins train** connects

SHARE THE LOVE: THE BEST PICS IN THE PARKS

Look no further than these prime spots for the best photos to share on social media—they're guaranteed to make your friends jealous. Share your pics with other national park fans on Instagram at #nationalparks, #wildernessculture, #nps, and #travelwithmoon.

Glacier Point, Yosemite: This photo op makes it look as though you're on the top of an alpine peak . . . when you're really just three feet from the scenic walkway.

GLACIER POINT, YOSEMITE

Cadillac Mountain, Acadia: From the summit, capture the orange flames of sunrise or sunset with the golden glow glinting off water below amid pink granite slabs.

Watchman Overlook, Crater Lake: This overlook is the perfect spot for a top-of-the-world selfie backdropped by Wizard Island and the acute blue lake.

Mather Point, Grand Canyon: For the best color of Vishnu Temple and the immensity of the Grand Canyon, strike an early-morning pose at this promontory jutting above the abyss.

Zabriskie Point, Death Valley: Look like a total badass with a selfie taken in front of the craggy badlands. Go at sunrise to paint your pic with a depth of color.

Mormon Row, Grand Teton: These historic weathered barns stand in the foreground of the sawtooth Teton Mountains, offering timeless pics. The best lighting is in the morning.

Wonder Lake, Denali: In late evening, catch the reflection of North America's tallest peak in this subalpine lake—you'll be one of the few that do.

Grand Prismatic Overlook, Yellowstone: This is the place to capture the radiant fiery arms rimming the turquoise hot spring from above.

with Merced, where **buslines** cover the final stretch into the park. **Free shuttles** circle Yosemite Valley.

EVERGLADES AND BISCAYNE

Catch the local **Homestead Trolley** to these parks.

ISLE ROYALE

Indian Trails bus service runs from Green Bay, Wisconsin, to Houghton, Michigan. **Ferry service** connects Houghton and other mainland towns to the island.

GRAND CANYON

Arizona Shuttles operates buses from Flagstaff. Use the **free shuttles** inside the park.

DENALI

Alaska Railroad runs a summer train between Anchorage and Fairbanks, stopping at Denali, where you can tour the park road on buses.

SNOWCOACHES, YELLOWSTONE

Best IN THE OFF-SEASON

Visiting parks in the off-season gives you the chance for extraordinary experiences, plus you'll encounter fewer people.

YELLOWSTONE

Take a **snowcoach** into the **Old Faithful** area to spend the night. You'll be one of few spectators there to see the famous geyser erupt in the morning.

DENALI

While much of the park road closes with snow, you can reach some areas by **cross-country ski.** You may witness the sky dancing with the **Northern Lights.**

YOSEMITE

Head up to **Glacier Point** via **cross-country skis** for big views or opt for **downhill skiing** or **snowboarding** at Badger Pass.

OLYMPIC

Hurricane Ridge has it all: downhill skiing, snowboarding, cross-country skiing, snowshoeing, and sledding.

MAMMOTH CAVE, CARLSBAD CAVERNS, AND WIND CAVE

Caves maintain the same temperatures year-round, so they are great places to escape either summer heat or frigid winter temperatures on the surface.

DEATH VALLEY

February is one of the least visited months, but yields pleasant temperatures and in some years rampant **wildflower blooms.**

GRAND TETON

Teton Park Road is groomed for **Nordic skiing** and **snowshoeing.**

VOYAGEURS

Drive ice roads on frozen lakes, where you can try **ice fishing.** Go **sliding** at **Sphunge Island.**

JOSHUA TREE

Moderate winter temperatures make for pleasant **hiking**. Opt for January or February to avoid the crowds.

HOT SPRINGS

Soaking in a hot bath is the perfect antidote to cold winters.

The National Parks AT A GLANCE

NAME	STATE	WHY GO	HIGH SEASON	FEE (PER CAR)	VISITATION RANK	PAGE
Acadia ★	Maine	seacoast	May-Oct.	$15-30	7	544
Arches	Utah	arches	Mar.-Oct.	$15-30	17	350
Badlands	South Dakota	prairie badlands	June-Sept.	$30	27	512
Big Bend	Texas	the Rio Grande	Oct.-Dec., Feb.-May	$30	43	409
Biscayne	Florida	tropical waters	Mar.-June	none	29	668
Black Canyon of the Gunnison	Colorado	deep gorge	May-Sept.	$30	45	442
Bryce Canyon	Utah	hoodoos	Apr.-Oct.	$35	12	326
Canyonlands	Utah	canyon country	Mar.-Oct.	$30	28	360
Capitol Reef	Utah	cliffs, geology	Apr.-Oct.	$20	23	338
Carlsbad Caverns	New Mexico	caves	May-Sept.	$15 per person	44	397
Channel Islands	California	islands	June-Aug.	none	46	198
Congaree	South Carolina	old-growth forest	Mar.-June, Oct.	none	51	649
Crater Lake	Oregon	deepest lake	June-Sept.	$30	30	213
Cuyahoga Valley	Ohio	history	Mar.-Nov.	none	13	560
Death Valley	California	sand dunes, desert scapes	Mar.-May, Aug.-Sept.	$30	16	149
Denali	Alaska	Denali, the mountain	May-Sept	$15 per person	37	43
Dry Tortugas	Florida	coral and sand islands	Jan.-July	$15 per person	55	674
Everglades	Florida	subtropical wilderness	Nov.-Apr.	$30	24	654
Gateway Arch	Missouri	history	Mar., May-Aug.	$3 per person	15	634
Gates of the Arctic	Alaska	wilderness	June-Aug.	none	62	100

★ indicates one of the most-visited parks in the country.

NAME	STATE	WHY GO	HIGH SEASON	FEE (PER CAR)	VISITATION RANK	PAGE
Glacier ★	Montana	glaciers	June-Sept.	$35	10	490
Glacier Bay	Alaska	glaciers	May-Sept	none	32	91
Grand Canyon ★	Arizona	mile-deep canyon	Apr.-Oct.	$35	2	267
Grand Teton ★	Wyoming	mountains	May-Sept.	$35	8	472
Great Basin	Nevada	caves	June-Sept.	none	53	302
Great Sand Dunes	Colorado	sand dunes	May-Sept.	$25	40	381
Great Smoky Mountains ★	Tennessee/ North Carolina	Smoky Mountains	May-Oct.	none	1	599
Guadalupe Mountains	Texas	fossil reefs	Mar.-May, Oct.	$10 per person	49	403
Haleakalā	Hawaii	volcanic summit	Feb.-Sept., Dec.	$30	26	685
Hawai'i Volcanoes	Hawaii	volcanic activity	Dec.-Aug.	$30	21	695
Hot Springs	Arkansas	hot springs	Mar.-Nov.	none	19	640
Isle Royale	Michigan	freshwater island	June-Sept.	$7 per person	59	577
Joshua Tree	California	Joshua trees	Oct.-Apr.	$15-30	11	160
Indiana Dunes	Indiana	beaches	Mar., June-Sept.	free-$6	14	634
Katmai	Alaska	brown bears	July-Aug.	none	54	74
Kenai Fjords	Alaska	fjords, glaciers	June-Aug.	none	47	60
Kings Canyon	California	scenic byways	May-Sept.	$35	34	137
Kobuk Valley	Alaska	caribou, sand dunes	June-Aug.	none	61	100
Lake Clark	Alaska	wilderness	June-Sept.	none	60	69
Lassen Volcanic	California	volcanic land	June-Oct.	$30	41	174
Mammoth Cave	Kentucky	cave	Apr.-Aug	none	39	626
Mesa Verde	Colorado	cliff dwellings	May-Oct.	$30	38	372
Mount Rainier	Washington	glacial peak	June-Sept.	$30	19	240
National Park of American Samoa	American Samoa	tropical forests, coral reef	Mar.-May, Oct.-Nov.	none	57	714
North Cascades	Washington	glacial scenery	June-Sept.	none	58	251

NAME	STATE	WHY GO	HIGH SEASON	FEE (PER CAR)	VISITATION RANK	PAGE
Olympic ★	Washington	rain forest	May-Sept.	$30	9	223
Petrified Forest	Arizona	petrified trees	Mar.-Oct.	$25	33	289
Pinnacles	California	volcanic peaks, talus caves	Mar.-June	$30	50	191
Redwood	California	coast redwoods	May-Sept.	varies	42	182
Rocky Mountain ★	Colorado	high peaks, wildlife	May-Sept.	$35	3	425
Saguaro	Arizona	saguaros	Nov.-Mar.	$25	25	295
Sequoia	California	giant sequoias	May-Oct.	$35	22	137
Shenandoah	Virginia	Blue Ridge mountains	May-Oct.	$30	20	616
Theodore Roosevelt	North Dakota	wildlife, badlands	May-Sept.	$30	31	529
Virgin Islands	U.S. Virgin Islands	coral reefs	Oct.-Dec., Apr.-June	none	52	705
Voyageurs	Minnesota	watery wilderness	May-Sept.	none	48	584
Wind Cave	South Dakota	caves	Apr.-Sept.	none	35	520
White Sands	New Mexico	gypsum dunes	Mar.-July	$25	36	389
Wrangell-St. Elias	Alaska	largest national park	June-Aug.	none	56	81
Yellowstone ★	Wyoming	geysers, volcanic scapes	May-Sept.	$35	6	449
Yosemite ★	California	waterfalls, granite	May-Oct.	$35	5	115
Zion ★	Utah	canyons	May-Sept.	$35	4	309

▼ KENNICOTT GLACIER, WRANGELL-ST. ELIAS

ALASKA

Steep-walled fjords, charismatic bears, soaring eagles, and glaciers that creep down mountainsides into the sea: Alaska's national parks enchant with stunning scenery and wildlife. The eight parks may be a challenge to reach, with some only accessible by boat or air, but the rewards more than make up for the effort to see them. Within their vast wildernesses, you can find solitude amid stark beauty.

Crowning the state, Denali bests all other mountains as the tallest summit in North America. Blanketed year-round in ice, the immense peak reflects in Wonder Lake in Denali National Park. In many of Alaska's parks, visitors can spot wolves, grizzly bears, caribou, moose, and in the coastal parks, whales and sea otters. These animals figure prominently in the culture and survival of indigenous peoples. Immense mountains, wildlife, and cultural experiences await in this Land of the Midnight Sun.

◂ SLOPE MOUNTAIN, LAKE CLARK

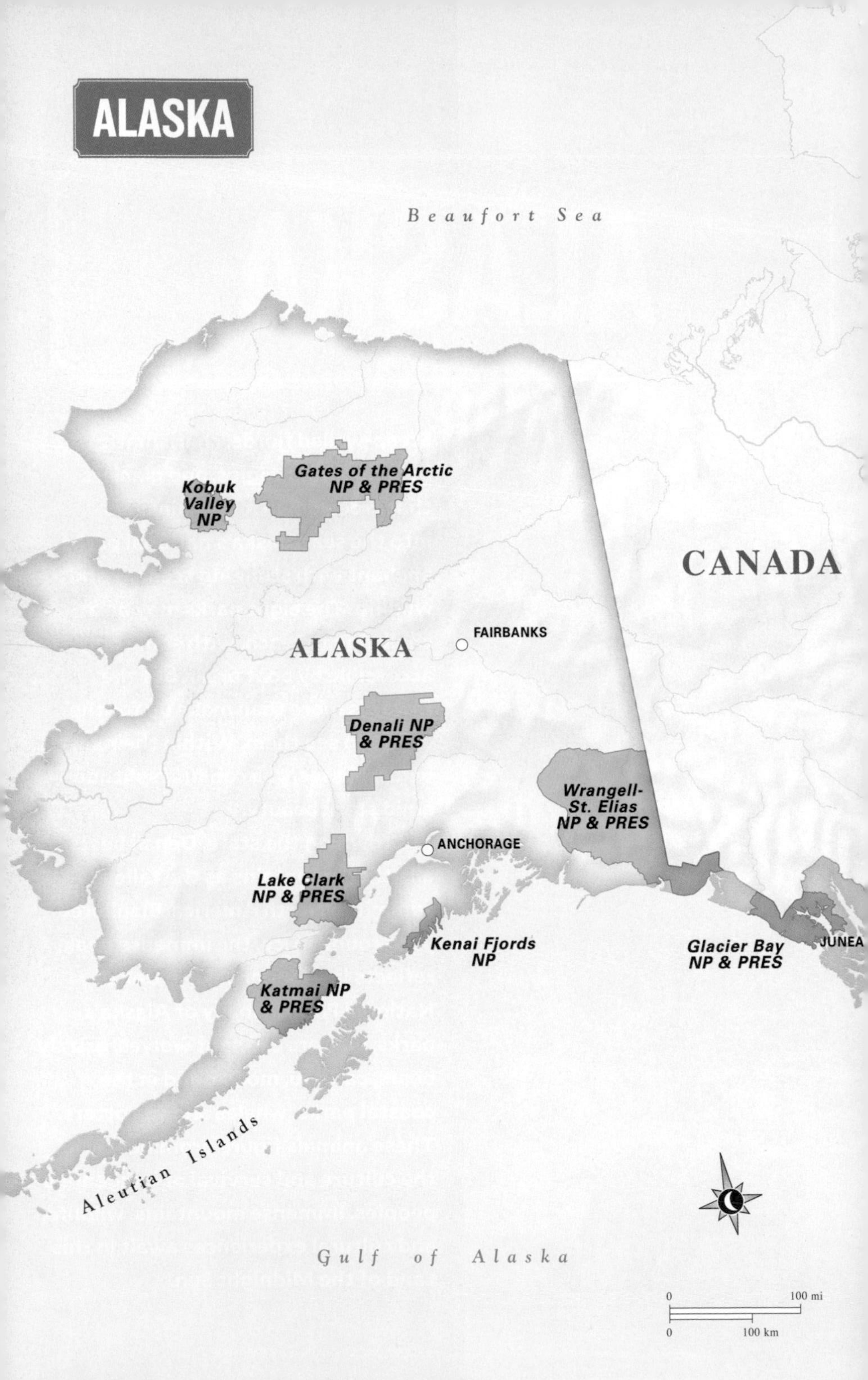

ALASKA
Beaufort Sea
Gates of the Arctic NP & PRES
Kobuk Valley NP
CANADA
FAIRBANKS
ALASKA
Denali NP & PRES
Wrangell-St. Elias NP & PRES
ANCHORAGE
Lake Clark NP & PRES
Kenai Fjords NP
Glacier Bay NP & PRES
JUNEA
Katmai NP & PRES
Aleutian Islands
Gulf of Alaska
0
100 mi
0
100 km

The National Parks of ALASKA

DENALI
This sweeping wilderness is great for wildlife-viewing and spotting the tallest peak in North America (page 43).

KENAI FJORDS
The immense Harding Icefield spills with some 40 glaciers, some that reach the sea in fjords (page 60).

LAKE CLARK
This roadless park defines wilderness with brown bear-viewing and fly-fishing, plus large lakes that serve as floatplane highways (page 69).

GLACIER BAY
Ice only vacated much of the bays in the past 300 years, and glaciers still carve down rugged mountains through temperate rainforest into fjords (page 91).

KATMAI
Home to 2,200 brown bears, Katmai is the state's most iconic destination for bear-viewing (page 74).

WRANGELL-ST. ELIAS
It's a magnet for mountaineers, birders, wildlife-watchers, backcountry hikers, and ghost town fans (page 81).

GATES OF THE ARCTIC
This vast, untouched wilderness spans the Brooks Range with no established roads, trails, or campgrounds (page 100).

KOBUK VALLEY
Charter a small plane to Kobuk Valley National Park and its staggering sand dunes (page 100).

1: CARIBOU, DENALI
2: CYLINDRICAL PINNACLES OF ICE, GLACIER BAY
3: GREAT KOBUK SAND DUNES, KOBUK VALLEY

Best OF THE PARKS

Flightseeing: Take a flightseeing trip around 20,310-foot (6,191-m) Denali (page 47).

Bear-viewing: View bears at Brooks Camp in Katmai, in Denali, and at Lake Clark (page 78).

Exit Glacier and Harding Icefield: Hike to the toe of Exit Glacier or up a mountainside overlooking the Harding Icefield (page 64).

McCarthy and Kennecott: Visit a quirky and isolated town that is joined by a neighboring "ghost mine town" (page 85).

Valley of Ten Thousand Smokes: Tour the desolate, ash-covered landscape created by the largest volcanic eruption of the 20th century (page 78).

▲ BEARS NEAR SILVER SALMON CREEK, LAKE CLARK

PLANNING YOUR TRIP

Because Alaska is so big and the logistics of transport are challenging, plan at least **three weeks** to tour the national parks. Make lodging and campground **reservations** for in-park lodges a year in advance.

High season is **mid-June** through **early September.** You'll have the best weather, the richest landscape, the most touring and wildlife-viewing opportunities, and the most services available—along with the highest prices.

While you can drive to Denali, Kenai Fjords, and Wrangell-St. Elias, touring them may require shuttles, buses, and boat transportation. To visit Katmai, Lake Clark, Kobuk Valley, and Gates of the Arctic, you'll need to fly. To see Glacier Bay, take a ferry or plane to Gustavus and then head into the park via boat.

Anchorage offers the most accessible airport to the Alaskan parks.

Road Trip

Pound down some wild miles in this epic road trip that links Alaska's three road-accessible national parks. Fly into **Ted Stevens Anchorage International Airport** in Anchorage and **rent a car** capable of driving **gravel roads.**

In Anchorage, gain an understanding of Alaskan culture by visiting the **Anchorage Museum** (625 C St., 907/929-9200, www.anchoragemuseum.org, 9am-6pm daily May-Sept., shorter hours and days winter, $9-18) and the Alaska Native Heritage Center (8800 Heritage Center Dr., 907/330-8000, www.alaskanative.net, 9am-5pm daily mid-May-mid-Sept., $17-25), which concentrates on the indigenous people of Alaska through art, dance, movies, and game demonstrations.

NEAR HOLGATE GLACIER

Kenai Fjords

135 miles (217 km) / 2.5 hours

From Anchorage, drive south on the Seward Highway (AK 1) for 2.5 hours to the east side of the Kenai Peninsula. At 87 miles (140 km), continue straight onto AK 9. In **Seward,** take Exit Glacier Road (aka Herman Leirer Rd.) to enter the park to see **Exit Glacier** and **Exit Glacier Nature Center.** From your two-night lodging accommodations in Seward, hop a full-day **boat tour** to see a tidewater glacier in **Aialik Bay.** Depart the following morning, unless you

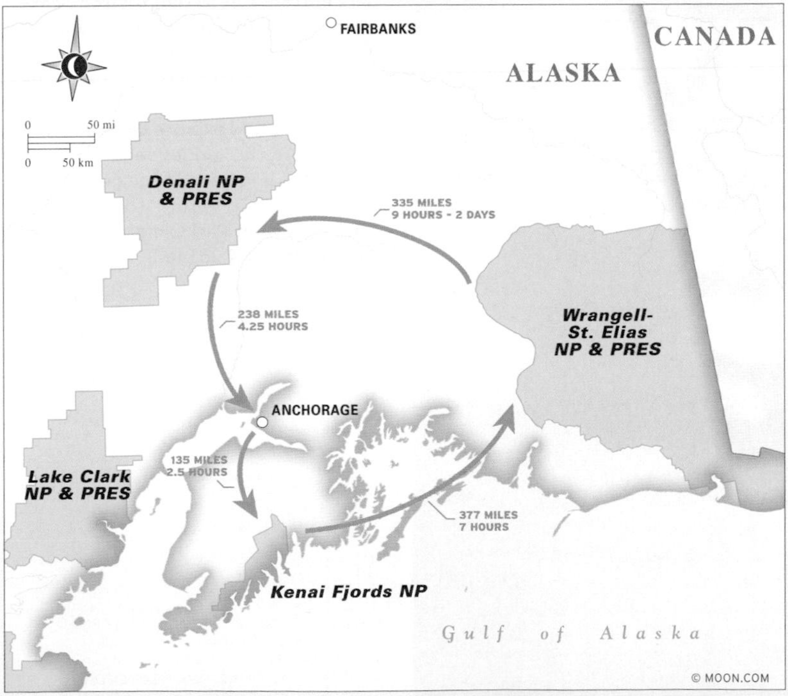

want to tack on the climb to the **Harding Icefield.**

Wrangell-St. Elias

380 miles (610 km) / 7 hours

From Kenai Fjords, the route to Wrangell-St. Elias retraces the drive to Anchorage on the Seward Highway (AK 1) before following the Glenn Highway (AK 1) east to the Richardson Highway (AK 4) and the **Copper Center Visitor Center.** Overnight at a motel on the Richardson Highway. The next morning, take the Edgerton Highway east to enter Wrangell-St. Elias on the unpaved **McCarthy Road.** At the bumpy road's terminus, walk into **McCarthy** to explore the funky town. Catch the shuttle and spend two nights at **Kennicott Glacier Lodge.** The next day, explore the **ghost mine** and hike to **Kennicott Glacier.**

Denali

335 miles (540 km) / 9 hours or 2 days

From Wrangell-St. Elias, regain the Richardson Highway (AK 4) north to the **Denali Highway (AK 8)** a mostly gravel 134-mile (216-km) trek through the Alaska Range. At Cantwell, turn north on Parks Highway (AK 3) to the park entrance at **Denali Visitor Center.** Plan to overnight at one of the entrance hotels, then catch your transport the next morning to relax at **North Face Lodge** for several nights. En route, look for **wildlife** and explore **Eielson Visitor Center.** At the lodge, paddle **Wonder Lake,** hike, and gaze at the great mountain **Denali.** To return to Anchorage, drive south on Parks Highway for 240 miles (385 km, 4.25 hrs.).

1: DIXIE PASS, NEAR THE MCCARTHY ROAD, WRANGELL-ST. ELIAS
2: LYNX, DENALI
3: DENALI NATIONAL PARK NEAR EIELSON

DENALI NATIONAL PARK AND PRESERVE

Alaska

KEEPSAKE STAMPS ▼▼▼

WEBSITE:
www.nps.gov/dena

PHONE NUMBER:
907/683-9532

VISITATION RANK:
37

WHY GO:
See Denali, the highest peak in North America.

▲ THOROFARE RIDGE

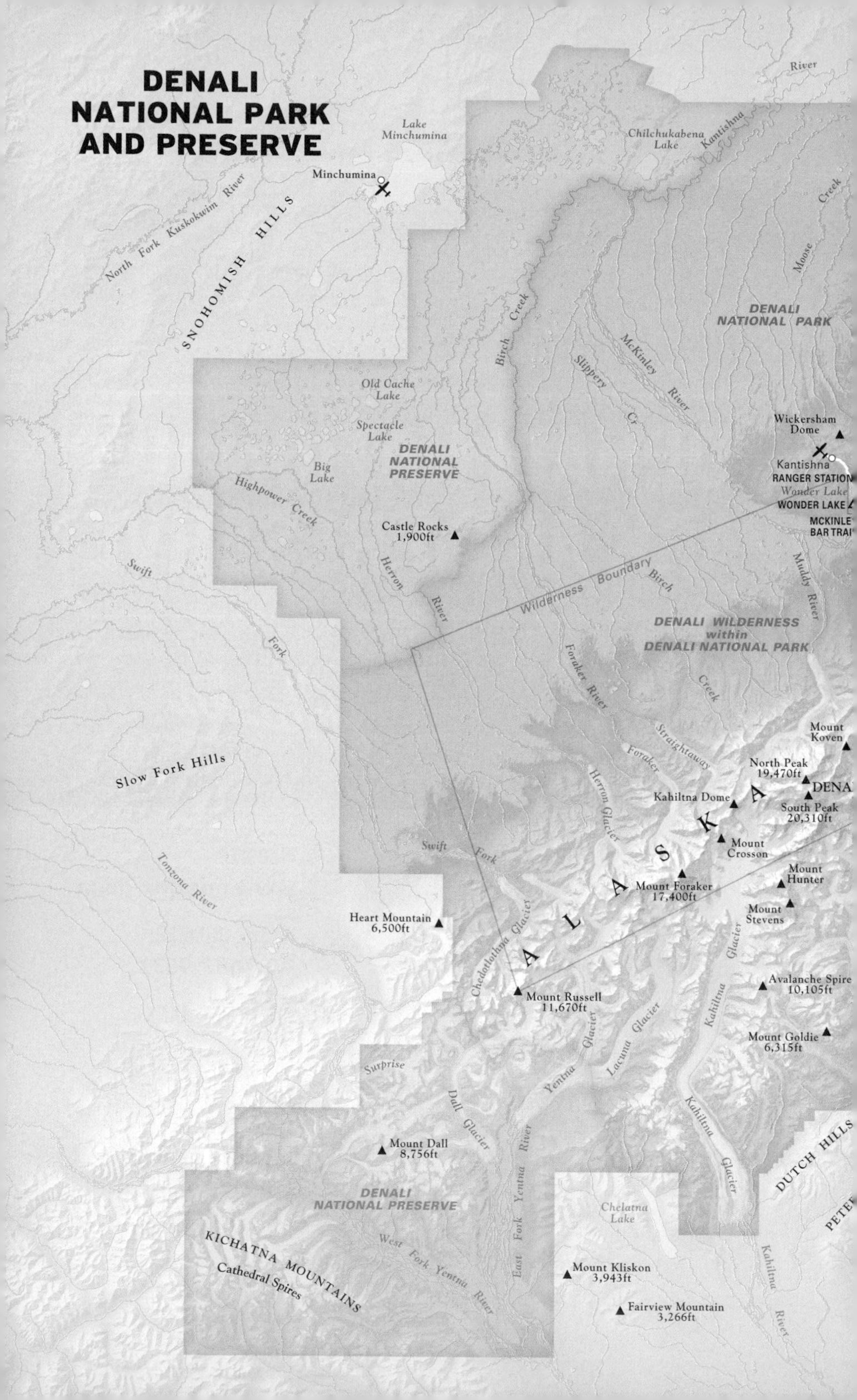
DENALI
NATIONAL PARK
AND PRESERVE
Lake
Minchumina
Minchumina
River
Chilchukabena
Lake
Kantishna
Creek
Moose
North Fork Kuskokwim River
SNOHOMISH HILLS
Birch Creek
McKinley River
Slippery Cr
DENALI
NATIONAL PARK
Old Cache
Lake
Spectacle
Lake
Big
Lake
DENALI
NATIONAL
PRESERVE
Highpower Creek
Wickersham
Dome
Kantishna
RANGER STATION
Wonder Lake
WONDER LAKE
Castle Rocks
1,900ft
Herron
River
Swift
Fork
Wilderness Boundary
Birch
Muddy River
DENALI WILDERNESS
within
DENALI NATIONAL PARK
Foraker River
Creek
Straightaway
Foraker
Mount
Koven
North Peak
19,470ft
Slow Fork Hills
Herron Glacier
Kahiltna Dome
South Peak
20,310ft
Mount
Crosson
Swift
Fork
Tonzona River
Mount Foraker
17,400ft
Mount
Hunter
Mount
Stevens
ALASKA
Heart Mountain
6,500ft
Chedotlothna Glacier
Glacier
Avalanche Spire
10,105ft
Mount Russell
11,670ft
Kahiltna
Lacuna Glacier
Yentna Glacier
Mount Goldie
6,315ft
Surprise
Dall Glacier
Kahiltna
East Fork Yentna River
Mount Dall
8,756ft
DUTCH HILLS
Glacier
DENALI
NATIONAL PRESERVE
Chelatna
Lake
KICHATNA MOUNTAINS
Cathedral Spires
West Fork Yentna River
Mount Kliskon
3,943ft
Kahiltna
Fairview Mountain
3,266ft
River

To Fairbanks
ALASKA RAILROAD
Nenana River
Healy
Chitsia Mountain 3,862ft
Toklat River
Sushana
KANTISHNA HILLS
East Fork Toklat
River
Teklanik R
Savage R
Sugar Loaf Mtn
Mount Healy
SAVAGE RIVER LOOP TRAIL
SAVAGE ALPINE TRAIL
PARK HEADQUARTERS
SANCTUARY RIVER
SAVAGE RIVER
MOUNTAIN VISTA
Yanert Fork
Triple Lakes
TEKLANIKA RIVER
WYOMING HILLS
Stony Creek
Toklat River
Kankone Peak
Spruce Peak
IGLOO CREEK
Sable Mountain 6,002ft
Polychrome Mountain 5,790ft
Sable Pass
Teklanik R
Fang Mountain 6,736ft
TOKLAT RIVER
Highway Pass
Divide Mtn 5,195ft
Panorama Mountain 5,778ft
EIELSON ALPINE TRAIL
RK ROAD (RESTRICTED)
Thorofare Pass
GORGE CREEK TRAIL
EIELSON VISITOR CENTER
RANGE
Foggy Pass
Mount Pendleton 7,840ft
Cantwell
Nenana River
DENALI HIGHWAY
To Paxson
rtle Hill
Easy Pass
Red Mountain 7,165ft
Sunset
Scott Peak 8,828ft
Summit Lake
Broad Pass
Anderson Pass
Muldrow Glacier
Wilderness Boundary
ount Brooks 11,940ft
Mount Mather 12,123ft
Lookout Mountain 2,965ft 904m
Mount Deception
Brooks
EAST FORK REST AREA
Mount Eldridge 10,433ft
Mount Silverthrone 13,220ft
Ohio Cr
Chulitna River
GEORGE PARKS HIGHWAY
Don Sheldon Amphitheater
Eldridge Glacier
Buckskin Glacier
The Great Gorge
Mooses Tooth 10,335ft
DENALI VIEW NORTH
LITTLE COAL CREEK TRAILHEAD
DENALI NATIONAL PARK
ERMINE HILL TRAILHEAD
Susitna River
VISITOR INFORMATION
ALASKA VETERANS MEMORIAL
BYERS LAKE CAMPGROUND
Ruth Glacier
Tokosha Mountains
Denali State Park
Susitna River
UPPER TROUBLESOME CREEK TRAILHEAD
LOWER TROUBLESOME CREEK
DENALI VIEWPOINT SOUTH
K'ESUGI KEN
Talkeetna River
etersville
Chulitna River
ALASKA RAILROAD
CHULITNA REST AREA
To Anchorage
Trapper Creek
Talkeetna
PETERSVILLE ROAD
TALKEETNA HISTORICAL MUSEUM
RAILROAD DEPOT
0 25 mi
0 25 km
© MOON.COM

Colossal **DENALI NATIONAL PARK AND PRESERVE** contains pristine lakes, braided rivers, and tundra set against the backdrop of the Alaska Range and 20,310-foot (6,191-m) Denali, the highest mountain in North America, whose name means "Tall One" in the indigenous Koyukon language. This vast swath of wilderness is renowned for stellar opportunities to see bears, moose, caribou, and wolves in an intact, protected ecosystem. A single rough road runs just 92 miles into a park that measures almost 9,500 square miles (24,605 sq km). Private vehicles are allowed on only the first few miles while buses tour the rest. Those looking to soak up an experience of a lifetime will overnight in the park's remote interior.

PLANNING YOUR TIME

The rugged, 92-mile **Denali Park Road** is the sole entrance into the park. You can only drive the first 15 miles (24 km) of it. Beyond that, restricted access makes planning ahead imperative. Shuttles or tour buses require advance reservations to go beyond the first 15 miles (24 km).

Peak season (late May-mid-Sept.) is when services throughout the road system are fully operational. Once mid-September rolls around, many visitor-oriented activities and services—chief among them the "town" just outside the entrance to Denali National Park—shut down almost completely.

Advance reservations are required for shuttle, tour, and camper buses. For specific travel dates in peak season, make these reservations in December or January. If you have time and flexibility, you can book later, but if you wait to make shuttle reservations until your arrival at the park, you'll be put on a two-day waiting list. Reservations are also required for park lodges and campgrounds beyond the first 15 miles (24 km) of road. Make these in December or January also.

ENTRANCE AND FEES

There is only one entrance to Denali, located at Mile 237 between Healy and Cantwell on George Parks Highway (AK 3). The entrance fee is $15 per person and good for seven days. The fee is collected during reserving bus tickets and campsites; if you're not riding the bus or camping, pay the fee in person at the Denali Visitor Center.

VISITORS CENTERS

Denali has three main visitors centers and a couple of secondary visitor stations. Most are open from mid-May to mid-September; visitors centers deeper inside the park may open later. During the summer, public restrooms are available in all the park's visitors centers, with public-use pit toilets (basically, permanent outhouses) in the campgrounds.

The **Backcountry Information Center** (8am-6pm daily mid-May-mid-Sept.) and **Denali Bus Depot** (5am-7pm daily mid-May-mid-Sept. for bus departures and coffee, 7am-7pm for tickets) are both at Mile 1 of the Park Road. If you're here for a backcountry permit, head to the Backcountry Information Center; for bus tickets, to board a bus, or to arrange a stay in a campground, go to the Wilderness Access Center. If you need tickets or to check into a campground after hours, you can do so at the **Riley Creek Mercantile** (Mile 0.5 Park Rd.) until 11pm.

Denali Visitor Center

The **Denali Visitor Center** (Mile 1.5 Park Rd., 8am-6pm daily mid-May-mid-Sept.) is the main welcome center, with many ranger-led activities, an Alaska Geographic bookstore and gift shop, a luggage check, the only restaurant in the park, and beautiful exhibits

Top 3

1 FLY OVER DENALI

FLIGHTSEEING IN DENALI

Any trip into Denali National Park will be a phenomenal sightseeing adventure. But to see much of the park—and Denali, the mountain—up close, take a **flightseeing** trip. Even the most jaded Alaskan will subside into awe when "the High One" is front and center in the windshield. Many flightseeing operations also include a landing on a nearby glacier, so you can get out and walk on ice that only the world's most intrepid explorers have ever reached by other means. It's a worthy splurge.

2 TOUR THE PARK BY BUS

With the exception of the road lottery and the early shoulder season, you can only drive to Mile 15 of the Park Road. If you want to go farther than that, you must take a bus. Most of the road is very narrow, with graded gravel and no shoulder, so it's a relief to let someone else do the driving while you keep an eye out for wildlife and scenery. Buses run into Denali National Park from mid-May to mid-September. The buses that go all the way to **Kantishna,** at the end of the road, usually don't start until June. Take along a day pack, lunch, and water with additional clothing layers for changeable weather.

3 WATCH WILDLIFE

Even if Denali, the mountain, is hiding behind the clouds, the park offers unparalleled views of dramatic scenery—from the towering, snow-clad Alaska Range to high tundra and swift-flowing glacier-fed streams—and great opportunities to see wildlife. Many visitors treat the bus ride into the park as a photo safari and come back with scads of wildlife shots.

To help find the specific animals that interest you, direct your eyes—or binoculars—to a few specific places. Spot **moose** on the first 15 miles (24 km) of the roadway, especially near streams; see **caribou** near mileposts 13-15; watch for **Dall sheep** on rocky areas above tree line; and look for **grizzly bears** everywhere, but especially above tree line. There are black bears in Denali National Park, too, but they tend to stay below tree line and aren't often seen. **Wolf** sightings are unpredictable, but this remains one of the best places in Alaska to view them.

DALL SHEEP

ONE DAY IN DENALI

If you only have one day in Denali, hop aboard the **shuttle bus** along Denali Park Road. The early morning bus takes four hours to travel to **Eielson Visitor Center,** stopping en route for wildlife-watching. Upon reaching the visitors center, tour the exhibits and then join a ranger on the **Eielson Stroll** or opt for a more strenuous adventure on the **Eielson Alpine Trail.** If Denali is visible, you'll burn through plenty of photos before your evening return. For the trip, pack a few warm layers of clothing, lunch, snacks, water—and a camera.

showcasing Denali's landscapes, wildlife, and natural history. The Alaska Railroad train depot is just a short walk away.

Murie Science and Learning Center

The **Murie Science and Learning Center** (Mile 1.4 Park Rd., 9:30am-5pm daily year-round) acts as the primary welcome center except for summer when it is only open for family programs (daily 1pm-3pm). The science center also runs small-group interactive learning opportunities. Many of those programs are intended for local students, but if you plan ahead, you might be able to send young visitors on an experiential field expedition through the **Alaska Geographic Field Institute** (www.akgeo.org).

Eielson Visitor Center

With million-dollar views of Denali (when it is visible), the **Eielson Visitor Center** (Mile 66 Park Rd., 9am-5:30pm daily June-mid-Sept.) offers services deep within the park, including daily ranger-led walks, interpretive exhibits, and a small art gallery. Many visitors make this their destination on the Park Road and hike one of the three nearby trails. Eielson Visitor Center has water, but no food services. Sights

SIGHTS

DENALI, THE MOUNTAIN

At a whopping 20,310 feet in elevation (6,191 m), **Denali** is the tallest peak in North America. On clear days,

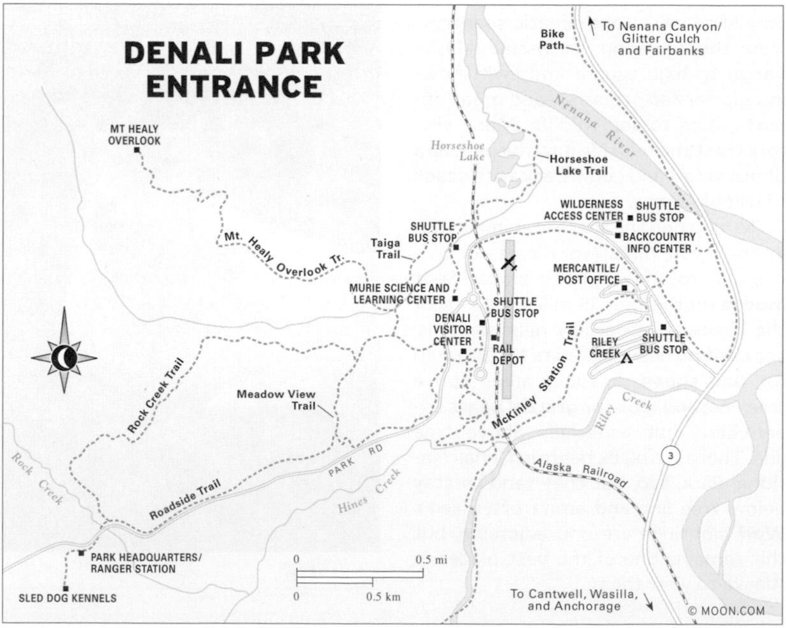

SLED DOG DEMONSTRATIONS

it is visible from Anchorage, Fairbanks, and Talkeetna, although you can't see it from the park entrance because terrain is in the way! Once you're past Mile 9 of the Park Road, however, you have a chance of viewing the mountain—if it's "out." If you take a bus all the way to Mile 66 of the Park Road and the Eielson Visitor Center, where there won't be any folds of land between you and *the* mountain, you might even get stunning vistas of Denali (weather permitting).

The skies around Denali are often clear during the winter, but the mountain generates its own clouds during the summer, so on average, it may only be fully visible one day out of three. Don't give up, though—it's worth taking a chance to see it, and you have a better than 50-50 chance of getting at least a partial view of the mountain peeking out of the clouds. Alaska's climate is changing, but you have a slightly better chance of seeing the mountain in the early summer rather than later in the year.

Here's one thing that you shouldn't do: Don't march up to the Denali National Park rangers and announce that you'd like to hike the mountain itself. Plainly put, most people can't; any trip up Denali is a high-level mountaineering expedition that requires technical skill, equipment, and quite a good level of fitness. If you don't have the requisite skills, you can enlist the aid of a professional guiding service like the locally run **Alaska Mountaineering School** (13765 E. 3rd St., Talkeetna, 907/733-1016, www.climbalaska.org)—but you need to be willing to work hard, put in a lot of preparation beforehand, and learn a new skill set that might just save your life or those of your fellow climbers.

WONDER LAKE

Wonder Lake is one of the most photogenic places for reflection pictures of Denali and the Alaska Range. The road that circles part of the 2.7-mile-long (4.3-km) lake allows you the closest view of the mountain. Even if clouds preclude seeing the reflection, the lake provides good wildlife-watching for moose and waterfowl. Even grizzlies swim across the lake. Swarms of mosquitoes cling to boggy ground in the area, so bring bug spray or head nets. To get to Wonder Lake requires an **11-hour round-trip shuttle ride.** The best views, made famous by photographs from the likes of Ansel Adams, are from the north end.

SLED DOG DEMONSTRATIONS

Denali is the only national park with a working kennel of sled dogs. You can tour the park kennels and visit the working huskies in free, 30-minute tours given several times daily (June-Aug., limited schedule May and Sept.). The only catch is getting there. There's no parking at the kennels, so you have to either walk 1.5 miles (2.4 km, mostly uphill) or take the **Sled Dog Demonstration Shuttle** from the Denali Visitor Center bus stop, departing at least 40 minutes before each demonstration begins.

The kennels are also open year-round to visits (generally 9am-4:30pm) even if a tour isn't scheduled. During the winter, the kennels may be almost vacant when the dog teams are out working. Do not bring your pets—this would not be a fun bonding experience for them or for the sled dogs.

SCENIC DRIVE

DENALI PARK ROAD

When snowplowing is complete (late Mar. or early Apr.), the 92-mile **Denali Park Road** opens. In summer, rich patchworks of green forests and tundra flank broad braided rivers in gravel bars, while late August brings on yellows and reds. The road closes when winter returns (Sept.-Oct.).

Touring the first 15 miles (24 km) of paved road to Savage River Rest Area will take about an hour without stops. This is as far as cars can go, with the exception of those with reservations at Teklanika Campground. Even though the mountain Denali is 70-plus miles away, you can still nab views through breaks in the taiga. When weather permits, you can spot it at **Mile 9** where the taiga breaks into tundra, again about 1.5 miles (2.4 km) farther, and around **Savage River.** For wildlife, keep your eyes peeled for caribou and Dall sheep near the last 2 miles (3.2 km).

For those with **camping reservations at Teklanika Campground,** pass through the checkpoint at Savage River and continue another 14 miles (23 km) beyond the pavement on the bumpy gravel road. Stop in early summer to look at wildflowers at **Primrose Ridge** (Mile 16) and scan for sheep. The road parallels the Teklanika River for several miles before the campground.

For those lucky ones who won the **road lottery**, permits allow driving as far as conditions allow. The narrow and shoulderless gravel road includes washboards and potholes. After crossing Sable Pass, brilliant green and orange colors flank hillsides from **Polychrome Overlook** (Mile 46). The braided **Toklat River** (Mile 52) spreads wide across the valley floor, often home to herds of caribou, before the road climbs over Highway Pass to **Stony Dome** (Mile 56) for a closer view of Denali. After popping over Thorofare Pass, the views of Denali only get bigger at **Eielson Visitor**

▼ TOKLAT RIVER

WINNING THE ROAD LOTTERY

The 92-mile road running into Denali National Park is only open to private vehicles until Mile 15—unless you're lucky enough to win the yearly road lottery. Anybody (including visitors from out of state or out of country) can apply for the lottery. The lucky winners can drive their own cars as far into the park as conditions permit.

The **lottery entry period** runs from May 1 to May 31 every year (www.recreation.gov) and the winning tickets are drawn in mid-June; if you win, you'll be notified by email and your credit card will be charged a $25 fee for the road permit. The driving period runs for four days, usually in September, and you're automatically assigned a day that your permit is valid. It's up to you to cover travel costs and logistics and to provide the car.

Many rental car companies won't allow you to take their vehicles on gravel highways (including the Park Road), but **Alaska Auto Rental** (907/457-7368, www.alaskaautorental.com), which is based out of Fairbanks with a second office in nearby Healy, will. They also rent to drivers under 25 years of age.

Center (Mile 66) and **Wonder Lake** (Mile 85).

HIKING

Most of the maintained trails in Denali National Park are short, and the trails nearest the visitors centers are often crowded (by Alaska standards, anyway). But what these trails lack in length and sometimes privacy, they make up for in their beauty and scenic variety. If you want some company on the trail, rangers often lead hikes on the maintained paths and "Discovery Hikes" that go off-trail.

Hikers can access a few maintained trails off the paved section of **Denali Park Road.** (Vehicles are permitted on this section, so you can hit the trailhead whenever you want.) A free shuttle also runs to Savage River. A family-friendly trail, the mostly level **Savage River Loop** (1.7 mi./2.7 km rt., 1 hr.) starts from the Savage River Day Use Area. Through the glacier-carved river valley, the tundra trail goes downstream, crosses the river on a bridge,

HIKING IN DENALI

Best Hike

EIELSON ALPINE TRAIL

1.6 MILES (2.6 KM) ROUND-TRIP
DURATION: 1.5 hours
ELEVATION CHANGE: 1,010 feet (308 m)
DIFFICULTY: strenuous
TRAILHEAD: Eielson Visitor Center; access via park shuttle to Mile 66

The views just get bigger and bigger on this trail that climbs Thorofare Ridge north from Eielson Visitor Center. Three long switchbacks ascend steeply to gain elevation. But soon, the trail departs the tundra to enter talus slopes and a seemingly barren alpine world, where tiny wildflowers such as pink moss campion thrive tucked in the rocks. When Denali is visible, hikers often forget to look elsewhere, but the ridge overlooks the giant McKinley River that widens along the valley floor. The high alpine tundra harbors Dall sheep and grizzly bears along with marmots. While you can zip up and down, exploring the wide-open summit with 360-degree views is worth the additional time.

and returns. Or you can take the more strenuous 4-mile (6.4 km, one-way) **Savage Alpine Trail,** which goes up and over tundra slopes to the Savage River Campground.

The **Horseshoe Lake Trail** (3.2 mi./5.3 km rt., 1.5 hrs., from Denali Visitor Center) loops around a pretty lake of the same name. The trailhead is less than 1 mile (1.6 km) into the park (near the railroad tracks) and goes to an overlook before dropping steeply to circle the lake. An additional 0.5-mile (0.8-km) loop at the north end leads to the Nenana River.

Beyond the pavement on the Park Road, shuttle buses access other trailheads and let hikers hop on and off anywhere. At Mile 85, near Wonder Lake Campground, the level **McKinley River Bar Trail** (4.8 mi./7.7 km rt., 2.5 hrs.) goes through boggy meadows and spruce trees to terminate at the broad gravel expanse of the river bar.

SAVAGE CANYON

RECREATION

BACKPACKING

Venturing off established trails and into the backcountry is one of the most glorious ways to see Denali. Due to the remote location and challenging terrain, which often involves crossings of swift, glacier-fed creeks, treat even a simple day trip as a serious backcountry expedition.

To backpack in Denali—sleeping in a tent somewhere off in the tundra, with the midnight sun or a spangle of stars and aurora borealis glimmering overhead—you'll need a permit. First-come, first-served **backcountry permits** (free) are issued in person only at the **Backcountry Information Center** (Mile 1 Park Rd., 8am-6pm daily mid-May-mid-Sept.) 24 hours before your departure date. You will also receive a loaner bear-resistant food container, which is required while in the

BACKPACKING IN DENALI

backcountry; return it within 48 hours of departing the backcountry.

The permit process takes about an hour and must be completed, in person, by all members of your party. To help you speed through the process, watch the wilderness safety video in the **Wilderness Access Center** (Mile 1 Park Rd.), which opens at 7am—an hour before the Backcountry Information Center opens. Then grab a copy of the worksheet from the back door of the Backcountry Information Center and fill it out in advance. Once the Backcountry Information Center opens, talk to a ranger, be assigned your unit number, buy maps, and purchase any bus tickets needed.

FLIGHTSEEING

Only a few carriers are authorized to make glacier landings in Denali National Park. They are:

Fly Denali (907/683-2359, www.flydenali.com) is the only provider that can depart straight from the park entrance (they base their aircraft in Anchorage, Talkeetna, and Healy).

Talkeetna Air Taxi (departing from Talkeetna; 800/533-2219, www.talkeetnaair.com)

Sheldon Air Service (departing from Talkeetna; 907/733-2321, www.sheldonairservice.com)

K2 Aviation (departing from Talkeetna; 800/764-2291, www.flyk2.com)

Kantishna Air Taxi (departing from Kantishna; 907/644-8222 June-Sept., 303/449-1146 Oct.-May, www.katair.com) provides air taxi services between Kantishna and the park entrance.

Temsco Air (907/683-0683, http://temscoair.com) also offers glacier landing tours to a glacier near the park and helicopter-supported hiking within the park. Small planes are an amazing adventure, but helicopters are even better: They can go closer, lower, and slower to terrain than a plane, and they can easily land in places that a plane pilot would never consider.

BIKING

You can only drive the entirety of the Park Road if you're lucky enough to win the road lottery. But you can travel the entire Park Road—all 92 miles of it—on two wheels anytime you like. You can rent a bike from most lodges near or inside the park, or use nearby **Denali Outdoor Center** (Mile 238.9 Parks Hwy., 888/303-1925 or 907/683-1925, www.denalioutdoorcenter.com). Make sure you bring proof that you paid your

TOKLAT RIVER

entrance fee at the Denali Visitor Center, or you may not get past Savage River at Mile 15.

If you want to overnight anywhere along the road, you'll need to book at one of the pricey all-inclusive lodges along the way, stay in one of the park's six bike rack-equipped campgrounds, or rough it like a backpacker (permit required). If you go the backpacking route, you'll be required to carry a bear-resistant food container and conceal your bike off the road; if you lose your bike in the bushes, park officials won't help you hunt for it.

To extend your reach on a day trip, take a bus into the park to bike as far as you like on the road, then hop on a bus coming back. You can only take your bike on shuttle buses—not the narrated tour buses. Not all shuttles can take bikes, and those that do are limited to just two bikes at a time, so it's best to make **reservations** (www.reservedenali.com) or at least verify scheduling with a call to the shuttle operator (800/622-7275 or 907/272-7275).

RAFTING

Denali's swift, restless creeks make for dangerous crossings on foot—but that also translates to lots of fun for rafters. At Denali, rafting is on the Nenana River, which borders the park. **Denali Raft Adventures** (888/683-2234 or 907/683-2234, www.denaliraft.com) offers trips all the way from calm Class I water to boiling Class IV rapids. You choose between oar rafts (in which only the guide paddles) and paddle rafts (where every client pitches in, following commands from the guide).

Denali Outdoor Center (888/303-1925 or 907/683-1925, www.denalioutdoorcenter.com) runs oar or paddle rafts down Class III-IV rapids, plus guides lake and white-water kayaking trips.

WHERE TO STAY

INSIDE THE PARK

There are various bed-and-breakfasts and lodges near the entrance to Denali National Park but only a few lodges within the park. Most offer all-inclusive rates, with no TVs, no phones, and limited satellite Wi-Fi (if any). People come here to unplug or to splurge on a basecamp experience that lets them hike, bike, or paddle deep into the park without having to take a long bus ride or secure a backcountry camping permit. To overnight at private lodges requires taking a bus or flying to Kantishna, the airstrip at the road's terminus.

Denali Backcountry Lodge (Mile 92 Park Rd., 800/808-8068, www.

alaskacollection.com, from $560) is unique because it has no minimum stay. The rate includes lodgings, three meals, twice-daily shuttle runs to nearby Wonder Lake, and extra activities like gold panning, mountain biking, morning yoga classes, and lake fishing. Ask for a room near the creek. If you want to avoid crowds of day-trippers, eat lunch early.

The **North Face Lodge** (907/683-2290, www.campdenali.com, from $1,920/3 nights) is the closest facility to the very popular backcountry camping destination of Wonder Lake, just 1.5 miles (2.4 km) away on bicycle or by foot. The 15 hotel-style rooms all have electricity, private bathrooms, and running water, and an outdoor patio provides beautiful views of the Alaska Range. The all-inclusive rate covers meals, lodgings, transportation from the railroad depot, day and night programs that are heavy on hiking, and the use of outdoor gear, including canoes, bikes, and fishing equipment. There's a fixed schedule for arrivals, with only three-, four-, or seven-night stays allowed.

The same company runs **Camp Denali** (907/683-2290, www.campdenali.com, from $1,920/3 nights), where you pay the same rate to stay in rustic cabins lit by propane lamps and woodstoves, with outhouses instead of flush toilets. A modern, shared bathroom and shower facility is available, but you'll have to take a five-minute walk to get there. Bonus: The camp sits right at tree line and has some amazing views, including Denali when it's "out."

There's just one real restaurant in Denali National Park: **Morino Grill** (Mile 1.5 Park Rd., 8am-6pm daily mid-May-mid-Sept., limited hours during the shoulder season) is about 30 yards (27 m) from the Denali Visitor Center. It offers boxed takeaway lunches and coffee all day long, plus made-to-order lunch and dinner.

You can purchase a limited selection of snacks at the **Wilderness Access Center** (Mile 1 Park Rd.), which also has a small coffee stand. The **Riley Creek Mercantile** (Mile 0.5 Park Rd., 907/683-9246) sells sandwiches, snacks, and limited groceries, along with camp fuel.

Camping

There are six established campgrounds within Denali National Park. **Reservations** (800/622-7275 or 907/272-7275, www.reservedenali.com) are recommended for Riley Creek and Teklanika Campgrounds, located right inside the park entrance on either end of the paved section of the park road. **Riley Creek** has 147 campsites and an RV

GRIZZLY BEARS

WHERE TO STAY IN DENALI

NAME	LOCATION	PRICE	SEASON	AMENITIES
Denali Backcountry Lodge	Kantishna	$560 and up	June-Sept.	lodge rooms, dining, shuttle
North Face Lodge	end of Denali Park Rd.	$1,900 and up	June-Sept.	hotel rooms, dining, transportation
Camp Denali	end of Denali Park Rd.	$1,900 and up	June-Sept.	cabins, pit toilets, shared bath
Riley Creek	Mile 0.25	$15-30	May-Sept.	tent and RV sites
Savage River	Mile 13	$30-46	May-Sept.	tent, RV, and group sites
Sanctuary River	Mile 23	$15	May-Sept.	tent sites; camper bus
Teklanika River	Mile 29	$25	May-Sept.	tent and RV sites
Igloo Creek	Mile 35	$15	May-Sept.	tent sites; camper bus
Wonder Lake	Mile 85	$16	June-Sept.	tent sites; camper bus

dump station (summer only), as well as cell and Internet reception. Camping is free in winter, when services are limited. One of the most coveted campgrounds in the park, **Teklanika River** has 53 campsites for tents or RVs. Book a three-night minimum stay so that you can drive to the campground. Then use the shuttle to hike or sightsee farther up the Park Road.

Savage River is reached by car or via the Savage River Shuttle. The campground has 32 tent and RV sites that can book up.

Three campgrounds can only be accessed via the **camper shuttle bus. Wonder Lake,** with 28 tent-only campsites, is the most popular regardless of its healthy mosquito population. Reservations (800/622-7275, www.reservedenali.com, $16 per site plus $6 reservation fee) are accepted. **Sanctuary River** and **Igloo Creek** (both first come, first served) have seven tent-only campsites.

Basic camping items are available at **Riley Creek Mercantile** (Mile 0.5 Park Rd., 907/683-9246). To rent or buy backpacking equipment, contact **Denali Mountain Works** (Mile 239 Parks Hwy., 907/683-1542, http://denalimountainworks.com), 1.5 miles (2.4 km) north of the park entrance along the Parks Highway. You can also rent gear from REI, which has locations in Fairbanks and Anchorage.

OUTSIDE THE PARK

Outside the park, on George Parks Highway (AK 3), a small community of seasonal visitor services and lodges clusters around the **entrance to Denali National Park.** Twelve miles (19 km) north, **Healy** is the closest year-round town to the park entrance.

GETTING THERE

AIR

Alaska Airlines (800/252-7522, www.alaskaair.com) offers daily flights to Anchorage and Fairbanks. In Anchorage, **Ted Stevens Anchorage International Airport** (ANC, 5000 W. International Airport Rd., www.dot.state.ak.us/anc) receives year-round service from Alaska Airlines, Delta, United, and Iceland Air, with seasonal service from JetBlue and Condor.

RAIL

Unless you're planning to drive the Park Road or stay outside the park, taking the **Alaska Railroad** (800/544-0552, www.alaskarailroad.com) to Denali is one of the best rides in the state. The trip takes about 4 hours from Fairbanks or 7.5 hours from Anchorage.

CAR

Talkeetna, Anchorage, and Fairbanks are connected by the Parks Highway

TOUR DENALI BY BUS.

(AK 3), which merges into the Glenn Highway as it nears Anchorage. If you're coming to Denali by car, the trip is 240 miles (385 km) from Anchorage, theoretically a little more than four hours, but leave yourself at least five to make it up the Parks Highway, which is often congested by Alaska standards. The drive from Fairbanks is 124 miles (200 km) or just over two hours if you don't run into construction or slow RVs.

Year-round gas stations are available in Cantwell (30 mi./48 km south of the park entrance) and Healy (12 mi./19 km north of the entrance). During the summer, you can also get gas at a seasonal station 1 mile (1.6 km) north of the park entrance.

BUS

You can get to Denali on the **Park Connection** (800/266-8625, www.alaskacoach.com), one of the most established bus services in the state, with service all the way from Seward to Denali.

GETTING AROUND

DRIVING

You can only drive to Mile 15 of the Park Road. Fortunately, you don't really need a car to get around once you've made it to the park. Most housing comes with a free shuttle that will pick you up from the train depot, airport, or bus stop, and if you're taking a tour, most tour operators will happily pick you up from your hotel or from one of the free shuttle bus stops near the park entrance.

TOURS AND SHUTTLE BUSES

Tickets (800/622-7275 or 907/272-7275, www.reservedenali.com) for both tour buses and shuttle buses are sold through the park concessionaire and can be ordered as early as December 1 of the preceding year. This is also when the ticket prices, which fluctuate every year, are set. Get tickets online or at the **Wilderness Access Center** (Mile 1 Park Rd., 5am-7pm for bus departures and coffee, 7am-7pm for tickets). About two-thirds of shuttle reservations are sold in advance.

Narrated tour buses ($100-237) are guided by the drivers, who are also trained naturalists. They do stop for photo opportunities, but don't let people hop on and off the bus. Trips range 5-12 hours, depending on how far each bus goes into the park. Bus schedules fluctuate throughout the summer, but the staff at the Wilderness Access Center can fill you in. Lunch, snacks, and water are included.

Shuttle buses ($64 round-trip to Kantishna) aren't narrated, but they do stop for wildlife-viewing and to let people hop on and hop off along the road.

SAVAGE RIVER AREA

Schedules and where the buses start and stop vary quite a bit, so always double-check to make sure you don't miss the last bus back! Bring along food, snacks, and water.

Finally, the **camper bus** ($43 round-trip) is available only to people who are staying at an established campground or in the backcountry.

COURTESY BUSES

There are three courtesy buses near the park entrance—not to be confused with the tours that run deeper into the park. The entrance shuttles all operate daily during the summer season (roughly mid-May-mid-Sept.), and they're all free and wheelchair-accessible.

The **Savage River Shuttle** (marked "Woo Hoo!", 2 hrs. rt.) travels between the Denali Visitor Center, the Wilderness Access Center, and the Savage River area (Mile 15 Park Rd.). This is also the shuttle to the Savage River Campground. The round-trip takes about two hours.

The **Riley Creek Loop Shuttle** (marked "Nom Nom Nom!", 30 min. rt.) travels a loop between all the visitors centers near the park entrance, the Riley Creek Campground, and the Horseshoe Lake/Mount Healy Trailhead.

The **Sled Dog Demonstration Shuttle** leaves from the Denali Visitor Center bus stop, departing at least 40 minutes before each demonstration begins.

THE DENALI HIGHWAY

If you just can't get enough of Alaska's glorious alpine scenery, there is no drive better than the **135-mile (217-km) Denali Highway,** which runs east-west between the small community of Cantwell, on the Parks Highway, and the minuscule community of Paxson on the Richardson Highway. The road is mostly gravel and very rough in places, but tour buses navigate it—so if you're careful and go slow, it is almost always drivable in passenger vehicles. Because most of the road is above tree line, you'll be treated to nonstop views of glaciers, lakes, and the skirts of dense green trees that are slowly creeping higher on the peaks as the state warms. Wildlife sightings include moose, bear, and waterfowl.

THE NORTHERN LIGHTS

Fairbanks, Alaska, is one of the very best places for viewing the northern lights, or the aurora borealis. The lights, which are caused by electrically charged particles from the sun colliding with earth's atmosphere, can be seen directly overhead in Fairbanks, as opposed to down low on the horizon as you'd see them from the southern part of Alaska. One study showed that if you spend three nights actively looking for the northern lights in Fairbanks from September to April—when it's dark enough to actually see them—you have an 80 percent chance of success.

Visitors are sometimes disappointed to find that summer—Alaska's most hospitable season by far—is the worst possible time for seeing the aurora borealis. The sky just isn't dark enough. If the aurora is your thing, plan a trip to Fairbanks, Nome, or any community at similar latitude **September-April,** when skies are dark and the northern lights are more active.

There's no guarantee you'll see them while you're here—but if you take three or four days and use the following tips, you'll have better odds:

Plan to visit Nome, Fairbanks, or a community farther north (like Barrow); all three are at a high-enough latitude to see the lights overhead. You might still see the lights in more southerly parts of Alaska, but they're more likely to shine low on the horizon and may even be blocked by mountains.

Get as far away as you can from the city lights and any other light pollution. The darker the sky, the clearer your view of the lights will be. Chena Hot Springs is good place for viewing the northern lights: It's 60 miles outside of Fairbanks and offers heated viewing areas where you can watch for the lights all night long.

Ask for a wake-up call. Most hotels under the "aurora oval" (the latitude at which the aurora shines overhead) will happily let you know if the aurora comes out. You can also check the University of Alaska Fairbanks Geophysical Institute's aurora forecast at www.gi.alaska.edu/auroraforecast.

Be patient. The northern lights don't shine every night, but if you spend three nights under the aurora oval—when it's dark enough to see them—and you're actively looking for them, you have at least an 80 percent chance of seeing them.

KENAI FJORDS NATIONAL PARK

Alaska

WEBSITE:
www.nps.gov/kefj

PHONE NUMBER:
907/422-0500

VISITATION RANK:
47

WHY GO:
Explore Alaskan fjords and the glaciers that shaped them.

▲ BEAR GLACIER BERG

KEEPSAKE STAMPS ▼▼▼

KENAI FJORDS NATIONAL PARK encompasses the traditional lands of the Sugpiaq or Alutiiq, whose descendants still live along its coastline. It gets its name from the deep, steep-walled inlets that were gouged by 38 glaciers, who now spill east and west from the immense Harding Icefield. These shrinking and thinning glaciers reveal the effects of climate change, despite the maritime weather that dumps 35 feet (11 m) of snow annually on the ice field.

The collision of the marine fjord and ice field environment makes this national park unique. Its marine zone bounces with wildlife that includes puffins, bald eagles, black oystercatchers, Dall's porpoises, Steller's sea lions, and black bears. In the mountains above, creatures such as marmots, wolverines, moose, snowshoe hares, and mountain goats adapt to the cold. An added bonus are the humpback and gray whales that pass through during their March-mid-May migration.

Taking to the water—or to the air—is the easiest way to absorb the high drama of this park.

PLANNING YOUR TIME

Kenai Fjords National Park is just outside the town of Seward on the Kenai Peninsula in south-central Alaska. There are three easy ways to explore the park: **by air** on a flightseeing trip; **on foot,** via some of the state's most spectacular hiking trails; or **by tour boat** into the fjords. Most of the park is roadless wilderness, so you'll need to combine various modes of exploration.

June-August is the peak season for visiting. Services are reduced in May and September. Be prepared for cool, rainy weather in summer, though temperatures can climb to the low 70s (21°C and up). October-April offers cross-country skiing on the Exit Glacier Road, but rough seas preclude boat tours of the fjords.

ENTRANCE AND FEES

From Seward Highway (AK 9), the main vehicle entrance is via **Exit Glacier Road** (signed as Herman Leirer Rd.), 3 miles (4.8 km) north of Seward. This is the only road that enters Kenai Fjords National Park. It takes about 20 minutes to drive to its end at the Exit Glacier Nature Center, where trails head to Exit Glacier, the closest glacier to reach on foot, and the Harding Icefield. There is no entrance fee.

VISITORS CENTERS

The **Kenai Fjords National Park Visitor Center** (1212 4th Ave., Seward, 907/422-0535, 9am-7pm daily Memorial Day-Labor Day, 9am-5pm daily mid-May-mid-Sept.) is in Seward, outside the park. It contains interpretive displays and an auditorium where the national park's many films are shown.

The modest **Exit Glacier Nature Center** (Herman Leirer Rd., 9am-5pm daily in summer) has a small selection of natural history displays. Ranger naturalists give daily talks and guide walks to Exit Glacier. Parking can be limited 10:30am-3:30pm; plan to arrive in the morning or afternoon, when the light will make the glaciers appear bluer.

RECREATION

HIKING

When the weather is nice, strong hikers can tackle the **Harding Icefield Trail** (8.2 mi./13.2 km rt., 6-8 hrs.). The path climbs above Exit Glacier to the

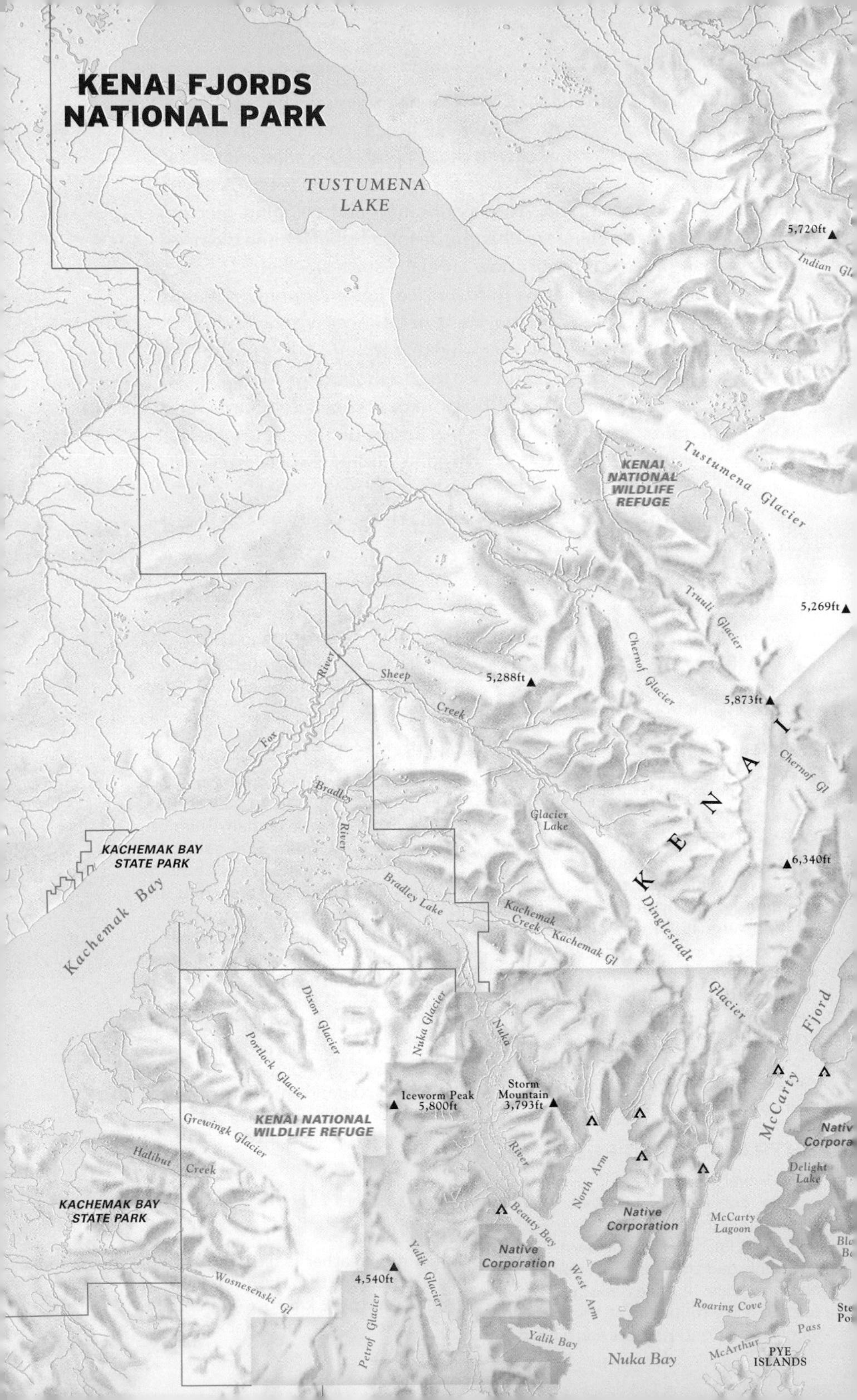

KENAI FJORDS NATIONAL PARK
TUSTUMENA LAKE
5,720ft
Indian Gl
KENAI NATIONAL WILDLIFE REFUGE
Tustumena Glacier
Truuli Glacier
5,269ft
Chernof Glacier
5,288ft
5,873ft
Sheep Creek
River
Fox
Chernof Gl
KENAI
Bradley River
Glacier Lake
6,340ft
KACHEMAK BAY STATE PARK
Kachemak Bay
Bradley Lake
Kachemak Creek
Kachemak Gl
Dinglestadt Glacier
McCarty Fjord
Dixon Glacier
Nuka Glacier
Nuka River
Portlock Glacier
Iceworm Peak 5,800ft
Storm Mountain 3,793ft
KENAI NATIONAL WILDLIFE REFUGE
Grewingk Glacier
Halibut Creek
North Arm
Native Corporation
Delight Lake
KACHEMAK BAY STATE PARK
Beauty Bay
McCarty Lagoon
Native Corporation
Yalik Glacier
4,540ft
Wosnesenski Gl
West Arm
Roaring Cove
Petrof Glacier
Yalik Bay
Pass
Nuka Bay
McArthur
PYE ISLANDS

Skilak Glacier
Placer Creek
Resurrection River
Martin
Lowell Gl
5,005ft
Mount Ascension
5,710ft
Lost Lake
Lost Lake Trail
SEWARD HIGHWAY
9
To Anchorage
Paradise Peak
Bear Lake
EXIT GLACIER NATURE CENTER
EXIT GLACIER
Exit Glacier
HERMAN LEIRER ROAD
NASH RD
Paradise Creek
Phoenix Peak
5,155ft
Marathon Mountain
4,603ft
VISITOR CENTER
SEWARD
Mount Alice
5,265ft
Godwin Glacier
5,355ft
5,912ft
5,197ft
MOUNTAINS
Harding Icefield
Resurrection Bay
Coastal Trail
Caines Head State Rec Area
Callisto Peak
3,223ft
Caines Head
Bear Glacier
Skee Glacier
KENAI FJORDS NATIONAL PARK
Aialik Glacier
Addison Gl
5,641ft
3,768ft
AIALIK PENINSULA
RESURRECTION PENINSULA
Humpy Cove
Day Harbor
Fox Island
Eldorado Narrows
2,904ft
Driftwood Bay
Callisto Head
Bulldog Cove
Bear Glacier Point
Hive Island
Native Corporation
Pedersen Glacier
Northwestern Glacier
Holgate Glacier
Coleman Bay
AIALIK BAY RANGER STATION
Rugged Island
Barwell Island
HARRIS PENINSULA
Holgate Arm
Porcupine Cove
Harding Gateway
Aialik Bay
Highest point in park)
6,450ft
4,430ft
Bear Cove
Agnes Cove
Cheval Island
Northwestern Fjord
GULF OF ALASKA
Harris Bay
Cliff Bay
1,109ft
4,734ft
Chat Cove
No Name Island
Aialik Cape
Crater Bay
Chat Island
Harbor Island
Dora Passage
Petes Pass
Granite Passage
Native Corporation
Paguna Arm
Sandy Bay
Harris Point
1,615ft
Natoa Island
Aligo Point
Granite Island
Surok Point
Two Arm Bay
Taroka Arm
Granite Cape
Matushka Island
CHISWELL ISLANDS
Cloudy Mountain
1,810ft
ALASKA MARITIME NATIONAL WILDLIFE REFUGE
Lone Rock
Seal Rocks
0
10 mi
0
10 km
© MOON.COM

Top 3

HIKER AT EXIT GLACIER

1 GAZE AT EXIT GLACIER

Exit Glacier is the only drive-to glacier in the park. Visit the **Exit Glacier Nature Center** to learn about glaciers, how they shape the landscape, and their glacial retreat. Then follow the wheelchair-accessible pavement-and-gravel **Glacier View Loop** (1 mi./1.6 km rt.), where a spotting scope allows viewing the ice which is 0.4 mile (0.6 km) away. As Exit Glacier has melted, it has retreated back up the valley. Trail signs mark its size at various years of its retreat. In early summer, some of the ice will still be covered with winter snow. To see the exposed blue ice and crevasses, plan a late summer trip.

Exit Glacier is accessed via Exit Glacier Road (early May-mid-Nov.). In summer, avoid the clogged parking area and take the hourly **Exit Glacier Shuttle** from Seward. Rangers also lead daily walks in the area.

2 FLY OVER HARDING ICEFIELD

Atop the Kenai Mountains, the Harding Icefield covers half of the park. You can see it in two ways. **Flightseeing** with local air charters based in the Seward Airport allows for aerial viewing of fjords, marine and mountain environments; you can see crevasses, icefalls, and arms of glaciers extending miles from the ice field. Strong hikers can grunt up the **Harding Icefield Trail.** From the Exit Glacier area, the steep route climbs up to a viewpoint overlooking the expanse of ice.

3 TOUR THE FJORDS BY BOAT

Boat tours are one-way to see some of the more than 400 miles (645 km) of magical coastline in Kenai Fjords. Tides, waves, winds, storms, and glaciers pummel the coast into a rugged work of art containing caves, arches, and standing rocks called stacks. As tectonic plates pull the Kenai Fjords landmass down into the sea, the coastline forests sink into the seawater. You can see plenty in a half-day tour of **Resurrection Bay**—including seabird rookeries of cormorants, harlequin ducks, and kittiwakes—but the best tours visit a tidewater glacier in **Aialik Bay.**

HOLGATE GLACIER

ONE DAY IN THE KENAI FJORDS

Exit Glacier is an easy day trip by car. Follow Exit Glacier Road to the trailhead and hike 1-2.2 miles (1.6-3.5 km) along the **Exit Glacier Trails** to peer at the ice. Fit hikers with more time can extend their trek to gaze at the **Harding Icefield.** From Seward, you can take a half-day **boat tour** of Resurrection Bay or visit a tidewater glacier in Aialik Bay.

ice field. Start on the Glacier View Loop to reach the signed junction for the Harding Icefield. The steep trail gains 3,300 feet (1,006 m) in elevation on its way to overlooks of the massive sheet of ice and snow that spawns 38 glaciers. Be ready for common black bear encounters, sun glare from the ice, and quick-changing weather.

If you want to hike on a glacier, book a trip with the trained guides from **Exit Glacier Guides** (907/224-5569, www.exitglacierguides.com). They offer ice climbing on Exit Glacier plus multiday or heli-assisted ice climbing adventures, guided hikes, and camping trips.

KAYAKING

With the proper guidance, almost anybody can manage a stable sea kayak in the waters of Resurrection Bay. One of the best outfitters for both tours and equipment rental is **Sunny Cove Sea Kayaking Co.** (1304 4th Ave., Seward, 907/224-4426, www.sunnycove.com). **Liquid Adventures** (1013 3rd Ave., Seward, 907/224-9225, www.liquid-adventures.com) offers both paddling and stand-up paddleboard adventures and rentals.

DOGSLEDDING

Many of the flightseeing services that will take you into Kenai Fjords National Park offer some sort of a glacier dogsled adventure, including **Ididaride Sled Dog Tours** (12820 Old Exit Glacier Rd., 907/224-8607, www.ididaride.com, mid-May-mid-Sept.). You can tour the kennels, cuddle puppies, and take a 2-mile (3.2-km) cart or sled ride.

▼ HARBOR SEALS

Best Hike

EXIT GLACIER OVERLOOK TRAIL

2.2 MILES (3.5 KM) ROUND-TRIP
DURATION: 1.5 hours
ELEVATION CHANGE: 470 feet (143 m)
DIFFICULTY: moderately strenuous
TRAILHEAD: Exit Glacier Nature Center

From a junction at the west end of the Glacier View Loop Trail, the **Exit Glacier Overlook Trail** (also called Edge of the Glacier Trail) climbs a steeper path up bedrock to the Exit Glacier Overlook to the north side of the glacier. This closer overlook allows for photographing the blue ice and crevasses. En route, two spurs also descend to the Outwash Plain where you may be able to pluck a route over the rocky cobble and braided streams to the **Toe of the Glacier** (Add about 0.6 mi./1 km rt. and an hour for this trail-less route, and check conditions with rangers first as flooding and icefalls may close the area).

WHERE TO STAY

INSIDE THE PARK

Set amid the Pedersen Lagoon Sanctuary on Aialik Bay, **Kenai Fjords Glacier Lodge** (800/334-8730, www.kenaifjordsglacierlodge.com, late May-early Sept., from $875 pp for 2 days and 1 night) is a modern eco-lodge with 16 private cabins featuring full baths, electricity, and heat. The cabins are connected via boardwalks to the main lodge, which houses a dining room and lobby overlooking Pedersen Glacier. Transportation is by boat from Seward to the lodge. Stays include all meals, activities, and lodgings.

Those willing to rough it in the wilderness can reap huge rewards of solitude, wildlife-watching, and scenery. Two rustic public-use cabins are located in Aialik Bay. Situated at the head of the bay in a spruce forest, the **Aialik Bay Cabin** sleeps four people in two wooden beds. Across the bay, Aialik Glacier plunges to the water. Below the cabin, you can explore the rocky beach at low tide. In Holgate Arm off Aialik Bay, the **Holgate Cabin** sleeps six people in six wooden bunks. From the deck, you can stare right at Holgate Glacier and listen to the sounds of calving ice.

The cabins are equipped with a table, chairs, and a propane heater; there is no electricity and no running water (bring your own). Both cabins are surrounded by blueberries and salmonberries, which attract bears. Reaching the cabins means taking a boat (2 hrs.)

BLACK BEAR

or seaplane (30-35 min.) to get there. Competition is keen—book **reservations** in early January (877/444-6777, www.recreation.gov, Memorial Day-Labor Day, $75 per night, 3-night max).

The **Exit Glacier Campground** (first come, first served, free) is a walk-in, tent-only campground located 0.25 mile (0.4 km) before the Exit Glacier Nature Center. There are 12 sites and a central storage area for food and cooking items. Drinking water and pit toilets are available.

OUTSIDE THE PARK

Seward (www.seward.com) is the gateway to spectacular Kenai Fjords National Park. Just outside the park, it has motels, campgrounds, restaurants, boat tours, flightseeing, and visitor services. It is also the site of the Kenai Fjords National Park Visitor Center.

GETTING THERE

AIR

The closest international airport is **Ted Stevens Anchorage International Airport** (ANC, 5000 W. International Airport Rd., www.dot.state.ak.us/anc), which receives year-round service from Alaska Airlines, Delta, United, and Iceland Air, with seasonal service from JetBlue and Condor. Car rentals are available at the airport.

BOAT

Many cruise lines use Seward as their port of call for Anchorage. If you're a ferry buff, you're out of luck; this is one of the few port cities the Alaska Marine Highway System does not serve.

RAIL

You can travel between Seward and Anchorage on the **Alaska Railroad** (800/544-0552, www.alaskarailroad.com). A one-way ticket for "adventure class" (coach class) starts at $156 for adults.

CAR

The scenic drive from Anchorage to Seward is 127 miles (204 km, 2.5 hrs.). From Anchorage, head southeast on the Seward Highway/AK 1 to curve around Turnagain Arm, which separates the Kenai Peninsula from the mainland. In 87 miles (140 km), AK 1 exits right to Homer; continue straight which becomes AK 9 to its terminus 39 miles (63 km) later in Seward. The year-round route is known as the Seward Highway, a National Scenic Byway.

BEAR GLACIER

BEAR GLACIER

BUS

Several bus services ply the roads up and down the Kenai Peninsula. The best deal is from **Seward Bus Lines** (888/420-7788 or 907/563-0800, www.sewardbuslines.net, May-mid-Sept., from $50 one-way to Anchorage or Whittier), with two departures from Seward to Anchorage daily.

GETTING AROUND

The only road in the park is Exit Glacier Road (signed as Herman Leirer Rd.), 3 miles (4.8 km) north of Seward. The road terminates in 8.4 miles (13.5 km) at Exit Glacier Nature Center.

FLIGHT TOURS

Local air charters include **Seward Helicopter Tours** (2210 Airport Rd., 888/476-5589 or 907/202-8390, www.sewardhelicopters.com), **Marathon Helicopters** (2210-B Airport Rd., 907/224-3616, www.marathonhelicopters.com), and **AA Seward Air Tours** (2300 Airport Rd., 907/362-6205, www.sewardair.com), which uses small planes. All tour operators are based from the airport in Seward. Planes do not land inside the park.

BOAT TOURS

Two popular day-cruise operators are **Major Marine Tours** (1302-B 4th Ave., Seward, 800/274-7300 or 907/274-7300, www.majormarine.com) and **Kenai Fjords Tours** (888/478-3346, www.alaskacollection.com). Late March-late September, they run a similar series of half-day sightseeing cruises and full-day adventures. However, Kenai Fjords Tours is the only company that sets foot onto Fox Island in the heart of the bay. All boat tours depart from the harbor in Seward.

SHUTTLES

From Seward, the **Exit Glacier Shuttle** (call for reservations 907/224-5569 or 907/224-9225, www.exitglaciershuttle.com, $15 round-trip) offers hourly trips to and from the Exit Glacier Nature Center. **Alaska Shuttle Service** (907/947-3349, www.alaskashuttleservice.com) offers taxi, shuttle, and tour service up and down the Kenai Peninsula, usually with a four-person minimum.

TAXIS

Land, air, and water taxis service the community of Seward. Air taxis licensed through the park service can get you to remote locations in Kenai Fjords, dropping you off one day and picking you up at a scheduled time and place. Water taxis vary according to season due to rough seas in winter. **Seward Ocean Excursions** (907/599-0499, www.sewardoceanexcursions.com) is the only water taxi that offers year-round service. **Alaska Coastal Safari/Seward Water Taxi** (907/362-4101, www.sewardwatertaxi.com) is a one-man operation with a three-person minimum for each trip.

LAKE CLARK NATIONAL PARK AND PRESERVE

Alaska

KEEPSAKE STAMPS ▼▼▼

WEBSITE:
www.nps.gov/lacl

PHONE NUMBER:
907/644-3626

VISITATION RANK:
60

WHY GO:
Experience big wilderness.

▲ ILIAMNA VOLCANO

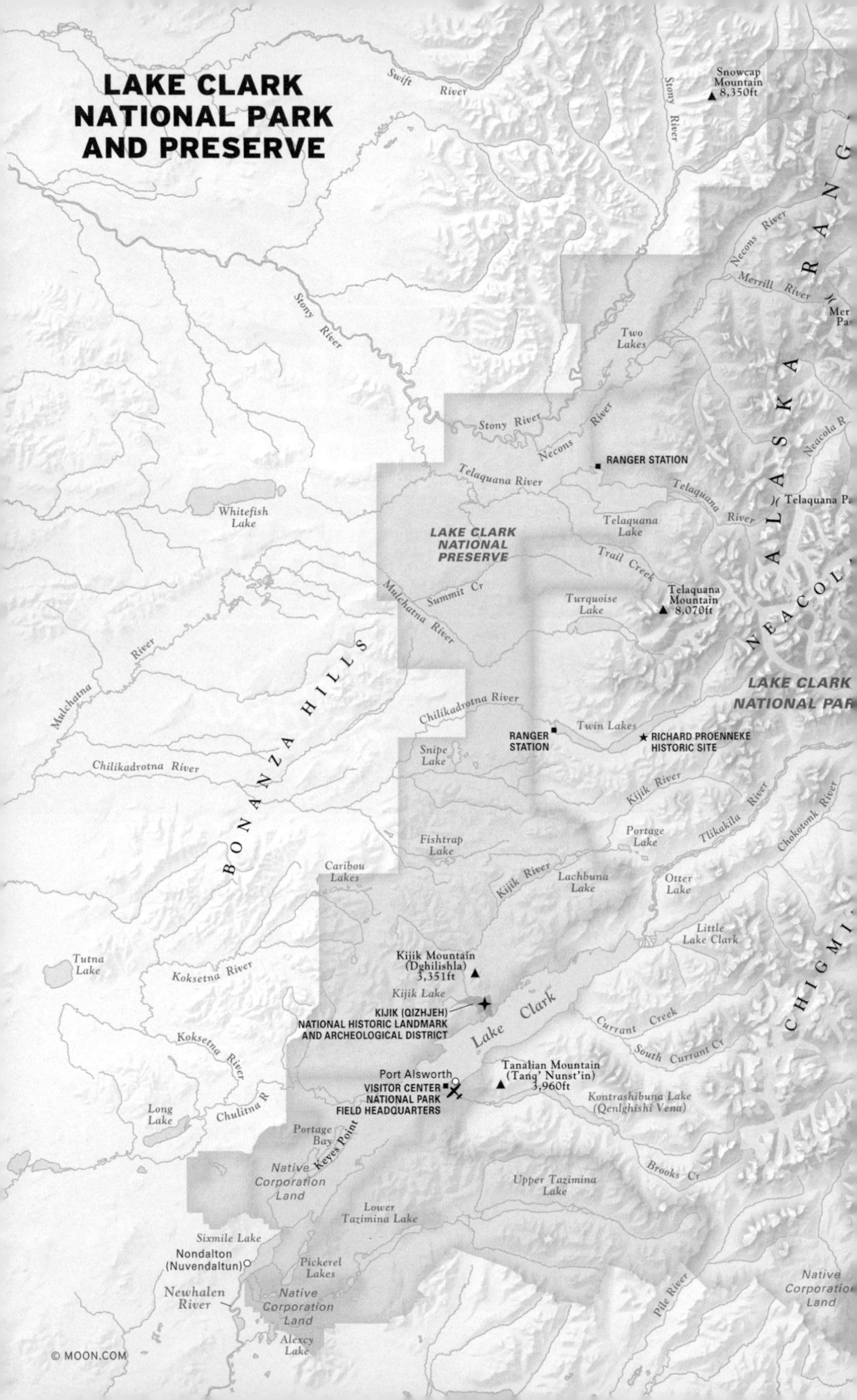
LAKE CLARK NATIONAL PARK AND PRESERVE
Swift River
Stony River
Snowcap Mountain 8,350ft
Stony River
Necons River
Merrill River
Two Lakes
ALASKA RANGE
Stony River
Necons River
RANGER STATION
Telaquana River
Telaquana River
Telaquana Lake
Whitefish Lake
LAKE CLARK NATIONAL PRESERVE
Trail Creek
Summit Cr
Mulchatna River
Turquoise Lake
Telaquana Mountain 8,070ft
NEACOLA
Neacola R
LAKE CLARK NATIONAL PARK
Mulchatna River
BONANZA HILLS
Chilikadrotna River
RANGER STATION
Twin Lakes
RICHARD PROENNEKE HISTORIC SITE
Snipe Lake
Chilikadrotna River
Kijik River
Tlikakila River
Chokotonk River
Portage Lake
Fishtrap Lake
Caribou Lakes
Kijik River
Lachbuna Lake
Otter Lake
Little Lake Clark
CHIGMIT
Tutna Lake
Koksetna River
Kijik Mountain (Dghilishla) 3,351ft
Kijik Lake
KIJIK (QIZHJEH) NATIONAL HISTORIC LANDMARK AND ARCHEOLOGICAL DISTRICT
Lake Clark
Currant Creek
South Currant Cr
Koksetna River
Tanalian Mountain (Tang' Nunst'in) 3,960ft
Port Alsworth
VISITOR CENTER NATIONAL PARK FIELD HEADQUARTERS
Kontrashibuna Lake (Qenlghishi Vena)
Long Lake
Chulitna R
Portage Bay
Keyes Point
Native Corporation Land
Brooks Cr
Upper Tazimina Lake
Lower Tazimina Lake
Sixmile Lake
Nondalton (Nuvendaltun)
Pickerel Lakes
Newhalen River
Native Corporation Land
Pile River
Native Corporation Land
Alexcy Lake
© MOON.COM

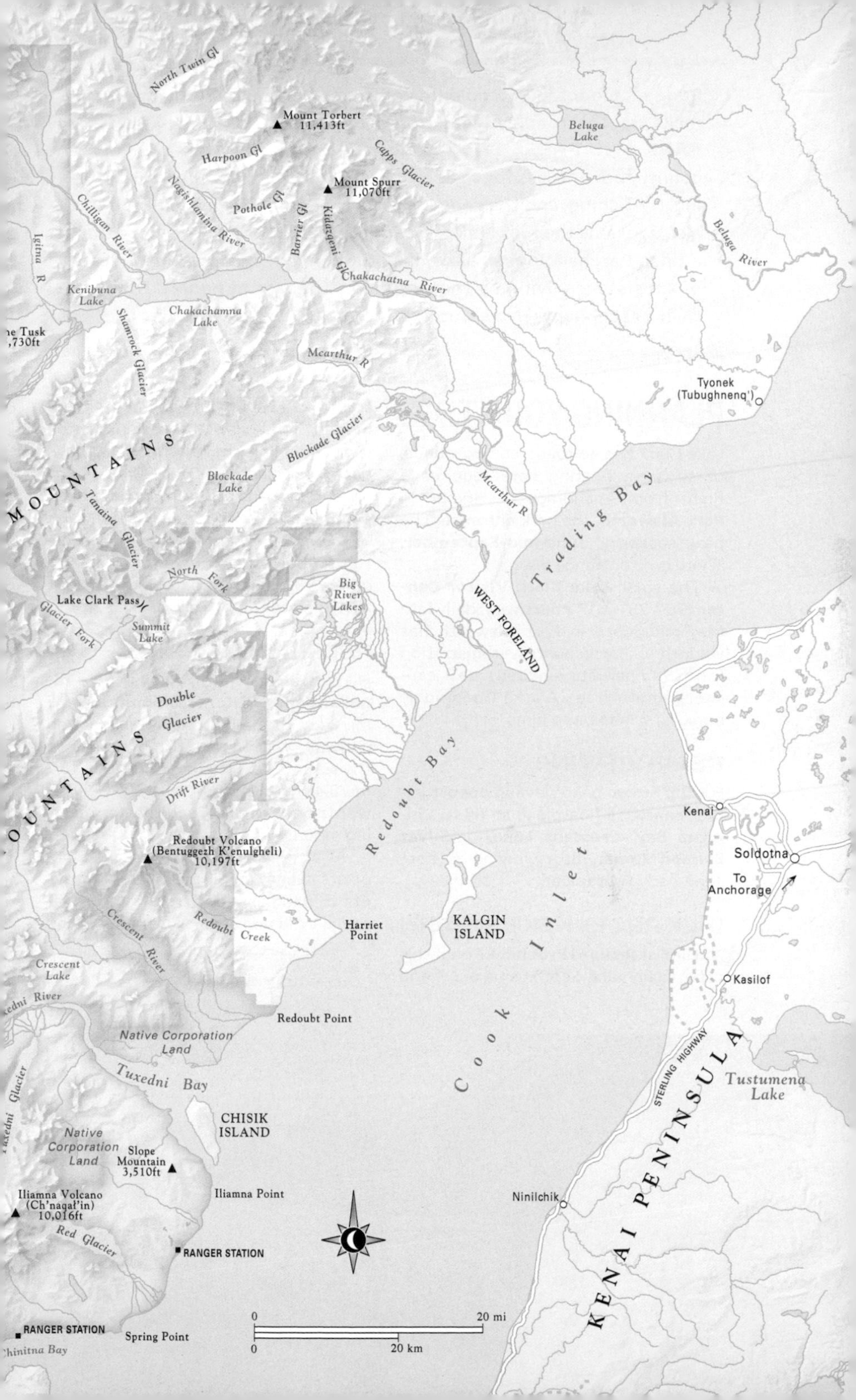
North Twin Gl
Mount Torbert
11,413ft
Harpoon Gl
Capps Glacier
Mount Spurr
11,070ft
Beluga
Lake
Nagishlamina River
Pothole Gl
Barrier Gl
Kidazqeni Gl
Chilligan River
Igitna R
Beluga River
Chakachatna River
Kenibuna
Lake
Chakachamna
Lake
Shamrock Glacier
Mcarthur R
Tyonek
(Tubughnenq')
Blockade Glacier
MOUNTAINS
Blockade
Lake
Mcarthur R
Trading Bay
Tanaina
Glacier
North Fork
Big
River
Lakes
WEST FORELAND
Lake Clark Pass
Glacier Fork
Summit
Lake
Double
Glacier
MOUNTAINS
Drift River
Redoubt Bay
Kenai
Soldotna
To
Anchorage
Redoubt Volcano
(Bentuggezh K'enulgheli)
10,197ft
Crescent River
Redoubt Creek
Harriet
Point
KALGIN
ISLAND
Cook Inlet
Crescent
Lake
Kasilof
Redoubt Point
Native Corporation
Land
Tuxedni Bay
STERLING HIGHWAY
Tustumena
Lake
CHISIK
ISLAND
Native
Corporation
Land
Slope
Mountain
3,510ft
Iliamna Point
Iliamna Volcano
(Ch'naqał'in)
10,016ft
Ninilchik
KENAI PENINSULA
Red Glacier
RANGER STATION
RANGER STATION
Spring Point
0
20 mi
0
20 km

Rugged mountains, smoking volcanoes, and pristine waterways make up the roadless wilderness of **LAKE CLARK NATIONAL PARK AND PRESERVE**. The undeveloped park offers only backcountry adventures for the hardy. It is famous for brown bear-viewing, fly-fishing, and the cabin of naturalist Richard Proenneke. But it also contains the Kijik National Historic Landmark where more than a dozen archaeological sites, including villages, show 2,000 years of subsistence living by the Dena'ina Athabascan people. Many of their descendants live around the southern end of Lake Clark.

PLANNING YOUR TIME

Lake Clark has no roads, campgrounds, or services. Getting here requires a flight from Anchorage or Homer to **Port Alsworth,** the park entrance. The peak season is **June-mid-September.** There is no entrance fee.

The small **Lake Clark Visitor Center** (907/781-2117, hours vary, daily late May-mid-Sept.) in Port Alsworth has voluntary backcountry registration forms (no permits required), bear canister rentals (free), Alaska Geographic books and maps, and films.

BEAR-VIEWING

For top brown bear-viewing opportunities, charter a floatplane to fly to **Chinitna Bay, Crescent Lake,** or **Silver Salmon Creek.** Bear-viewing is best June-early September.

DICK PROENNEKE'S CABIN

Naturalist **Richard Proenneke** built this cabin (daily June-Sept.) using only hand tools and lived in it for 30 years with no modern conveniences. He documented the building process in videos that have been collected in a DVD, *Alone in the Wilderness,* and his journals have been published in book form as *One Man's Wilderness.* Park rangers give cabin tours upon request. Getting here requires a 30-minute floatplane from Port Alsworth to Upper Twin Lake.

RECREATION

Hiking trails leave Port Alsworth for **Tanalian Falls** and **Kontrashibuna Lake** (5 mi./8 km rt., 2.5 hrs). At a trail junction midway, a strenuous climb shoots to the summit of **Tanalian Mountain** (5.2 mi./8.4 km rt., 2.5 hrs.), with big-view rewards of Lake Clark and the surrounding mountains.

At 42 miles (68 km) long, Lake Clark offers plenty of shoreline for **kayakers** to paddle, and there are three National Wild and Scenic Rivers for skilled

▼ KONTRASHIBUNA LAKE FROM THE SLOPES OF HOLEY MOUNTAIN

THE TANALIAN RIVER

white-water rafting (Class III): the Tlikakila, Mulchatna, and Chilikadrotna. The rafting season runs June-September; trips span 70-230 miles (113-370 km).

Crescent Lake and Silver Salmon Creek are the top fishing spots, where you may cast for salmon in the company of bears. For guided fishing trips, contact **Redoubt Mountain Lodge** (866/733-3035, www.redoubtlodge.com) on Crescent Lake or **Silver Salmon Creek Lodge** (888/872-5666, www.silversalmoncreek.com) at Silver Salmon Creek. Fishing season runs May-October.

In Port Alsworth, **Tulchina Adventures** (907/782-4720, www.tulchinaadventures.com) rents camping gear, paddling equipment, and motorized skiffs. It also maintains a campground and cabin rentals. For guided hiking, backpacking, kayaking, or rafting trips from Anchorage, contact **Alaska Alpine Adventures** (877/525-2577 or 907/351-4193, www.alaskaalpineadventures.com).

WHERE TO STAY

Lodges in Lake Clark are all privately owned and cater as much to fishing and kayaking as to bear-viewing. A full list is available online. **Silver Salmon Creek Lodge** (888/872-5666, www.silversalmoncreek.com, from $1,050) offers transport from Homer and Anchorage. **Redoubt Mountain Lodge** (866/733-3034, www.redoubtlodge.com, from $2,895, two-night min) offers transport from Anchorage. Rates include use of gear.

Reservations and an air taxi are required to stay at the historic **Woodward Cabin at Priest Rock** (877/444-6777, www.recreation.gov, $65) on Lake Clark. It offers a rustic stay for six people with no electricity or running water.

Backcountry camping is permitted throughout the park. Primitive campsites at **Hope Creek** (free) are first come, first served. Other backcountry sites include **Upper** and **Lower Twin Lakes.**

For accommodations and services, stay outside the park in tiny **Port Alsworth** on the shore of Lake Clark.

GETTING THERE AND AROUND

Alaska Airlines (800/252-7522, www.alaskaair.com) services **Ted Stevens Anchorage International Airport** (ANC, 5000 W. International Airport Rd., www. dot.state.ak.us/anc). From Anchorage, take an air taxi to Lake Clark National Park and Preserve.

Air taxis require reservations. From Anchorage, contact **Lake Clark Air** (907/278-2054 or 888/440-2281, www.lakeclarkair.com) and **Lake and Peninsula Air** (907/345-2228, www.lakeandpenair.com). From Homer, contact **Adventure Airways** (907/299-7999, www.adventureairways.com), **Beluga Air** (907/235-8256, www.belugaair.com), or **Northwind Aviation** (907/235-7482, www.northwindak.com). **Lake Clark Air** (888/440-2281) and **Lake and Peninsula Air** (907/781-2228) maintain offices in Port Alsworth.

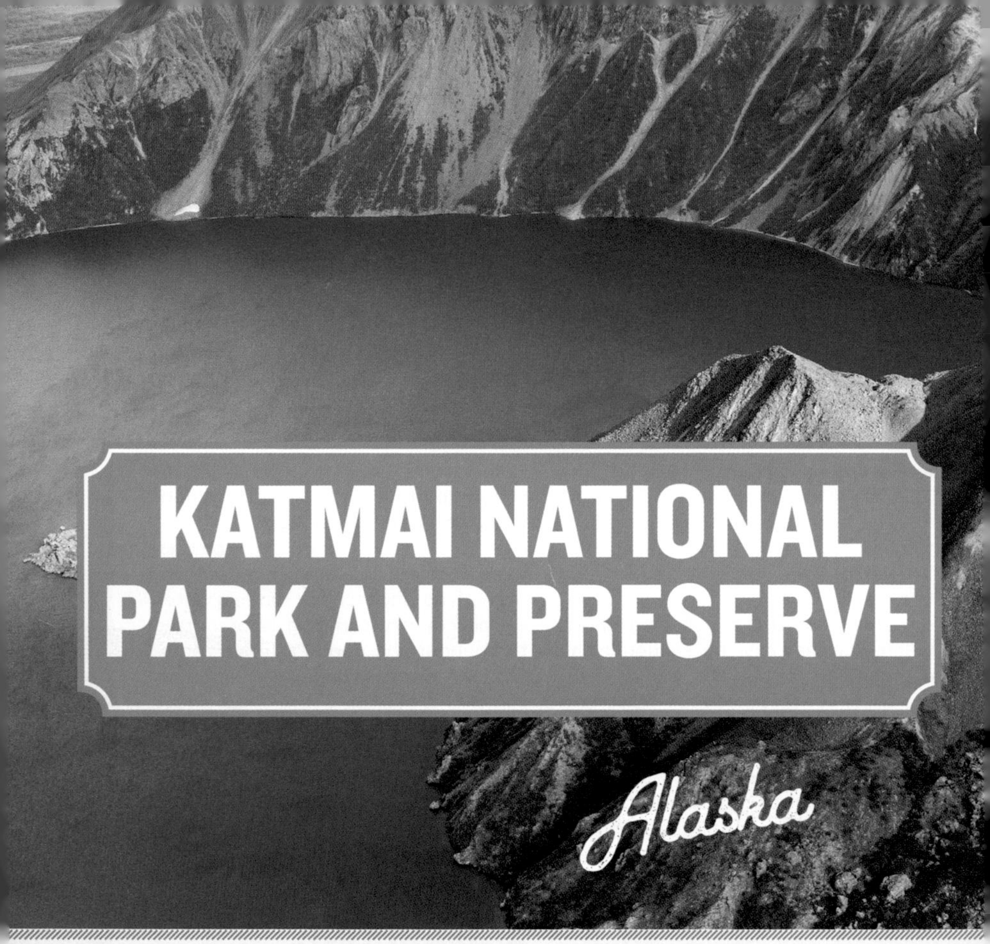

KATMAI NATIONAL PARK AND PRESERVE

Alaska

WEBSITE:
www.nps.gov/katm

PHONE NUMBER:
907/246-3305

VISITATION RANK:
54

WHY GO:
Watch brown bears fish for salmon.

▲ SWIKSHAK, KATMAI COAST

KEEPSAKE STAMPS ▼▼▼

Stretching southwest from the bottom of the mainland, the Alaska Peninsula fractures into the volcanic Aleutian Islands. The biggest attraction here is bear-viewing at **KATMAI NATIONAL PARK AND PRESERVE**. While Katmai may be the best-known bear-viewing location in the world, this park also includes phenomenal sea kayaking, world-class fishing, and one of the most stunning sights you'll ever see: the Valley of Ten Thousand Smokes. An archaeological district contains hundreds of depressions along the Brooks River, where the Alutiiq people lived for thousands of years.

PLANNING YOUR TIME

Inaccessible by road, Katmai National Park requires **air travel** to reach its remote wonders. Flights from **Anchorage** go to **King Salmon,** the service community outside the park. From King Salmon, floatplanes head to Brooks Camp to watch bears catch fish in the river.

July and August are the nicest months to visit; limited travel and visitor services start in June and continue into September. Bear-viewing is best July and September, while fishing is better in the shoulder seasons.

ENTRANCE AND FEES

The town of King Salmon serves as the jumping-off point into Katmai. Floatplanes depart here for **Brooks Camp,** the point of entry for most visitors. No roads go into the park, and there is no entrance fee.

MOUNT GRIGGS

VISITORS CENTERS

The **King Salmon Visitor Center** (King Salmon Airport Bldg. 1, King Salmon, 907/246-4250, www.fws.gov/refuge/Becharof, 8am-5pm daily in summer) serves as the park headquarters with information, a bookstore, and educational displays on the Alaska Peninsula's Native cultures and traditions, wildlife, and fishing.

The **Brooks Camp Visitor Center** (June-mid-Sept.) serves as the campground check-in and provides backcountry information for those heading beyond Brooks Camp. Books and maps are available at the center's Alaska Geographic Association store. Rangers lead daytime and evening programs, as well as an orientation on bear safety.

In the Valley of Ten Thousand Smokes, 23 miles (37 km) southeast of Brooks Camp, the small outpost of **Robert F. Griggs Visitor Center** (summer only) overlooks the ash and pumice valley, fallout from the 1912 eruption of Novarupta. Rangers lead daily hikes to the valley floor with a steep climb on the return.

SIGHTS

From Brooks Camp Visitor Center, ranger-led cultural walks (2pm daily early June-mid-Sept.) go to **archaeological sites** of the Alutiiq people. More than 900 depressions made by their ancient homes still remain. The program finishes at a partially reconstructed Alaska Native home.

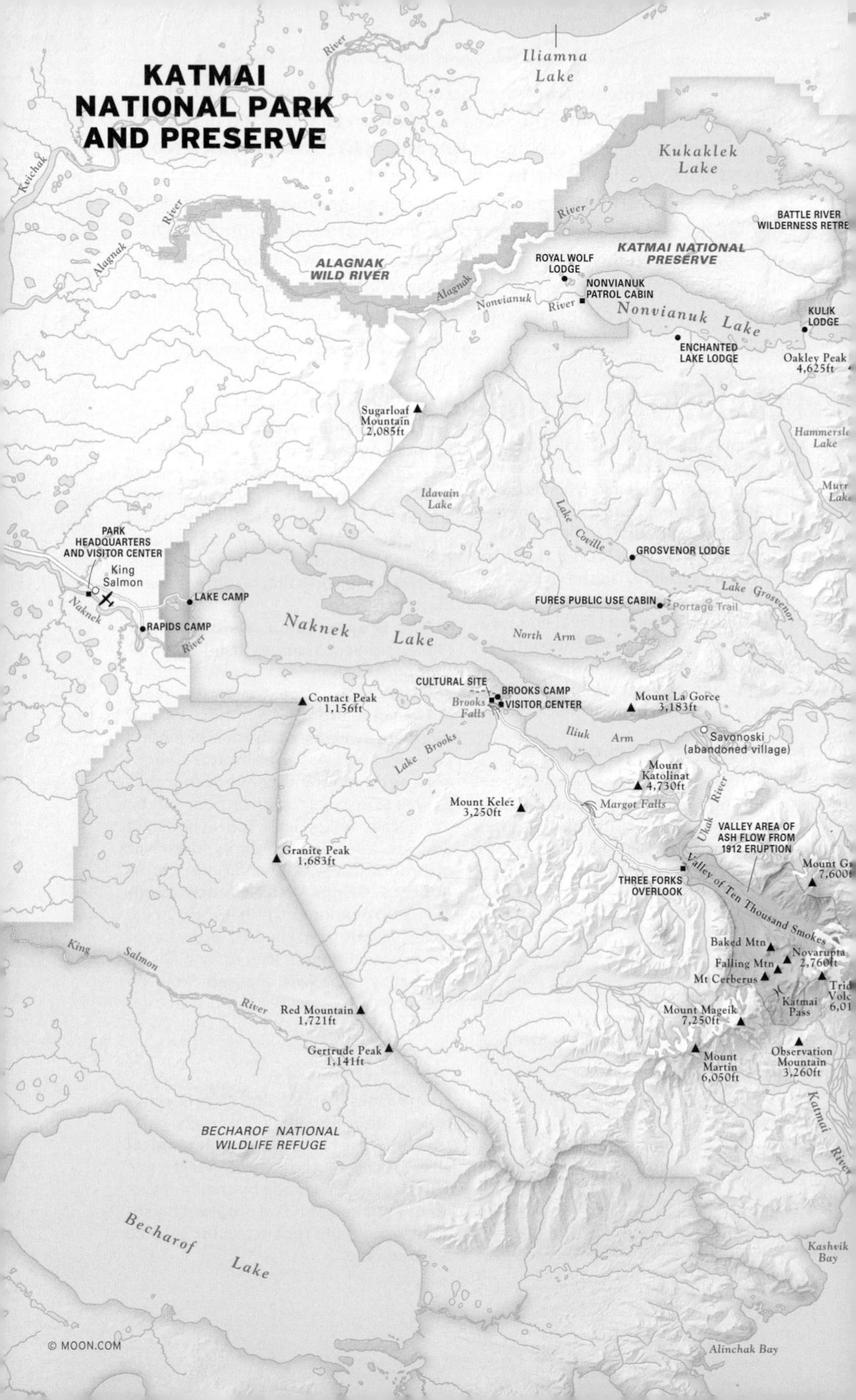
KATMAI NATIONAL PARK AND PRESERVE
Iliamna Lake
Kukaklek Lake
River
Kvichak
Alagnak
River
ALAGNAK WILD RIVER
Alagnak
River
KATMAI NATIONAL PRESERVE
BATTLE RIVER WILDERNESS RETRE
ROYAL WOLF LODGE
NONVIANUK PATROL CABIN
Nonvianuk
River
Nonvianuk Lake
KULIK LODGE
ENCHANTED LAKE LODGE
Oakley Peak 4,625ft
Sugarloaf Mountain 2,085ft
Hammersle Lake
Idavain Lake
Lake Coville
GROSVENOR LODGE
Lake Grosvenor
PARK HEADQUARTERS AND VISITOR CENTER
King Salmon
Naknek
LAKE CAMP
RAPIDS CAMP
River
FURES PUBLIC USE CABIN
Portage Trail
Naknek Lake
North Arm
CULTURAL SITE
BROOKS CAMP
VISITOR CENTER
Brooks Falls
Contact Peak 1,156ft
Mount La Gorce 3,183ft
Iliuk Arm
Savonoski (abandoned village)
Lake Brooks
Mount Katolinat 4,730ft
Mount Kelez 3,250ft
Margot Falls
Ukak River
VALLEY AREA OF ASH FLOW FROM 1912 ERUPTION
Granite Peak 1,683ft
THREE FORKS OVERLOOK
Valley of Ten Thousand Smokes
Baked Mtn
Novarupta 2,760ft
Falling Mtn
Mt Cerberus
Katmai Pass
King Salmon River
Red Mountain 1,721ft
Mount Mageik 7,250ft
Gertrude Peak 1,141ft
Mount Martin 6,050ft
Observation Mountain 3,260ft
Katmai River
BECHAROF NATIONAL WILDLIFE REFUGE
Becharof Lake
Kashvik Bay
Alinchak Bay
© MOON.COM

Kamishak Bay
COOK INLET
Mcneil Falls
Mcneil Cove
River
Akumwarvik Bay
Mcneil
Mcneil Lake
Pirate Lake
McNEIL RIVER STATE GAME SANCTUARY
KAMISHAK SPECIAL USE AREA (STATE OF ALASKA)
Creek
River
River
Douglas
Spotted Gl
Mount Douglas 7,063ft
Sukoi Bay
Cape Douglas
Strike
Kamishak
Fourpeaked Gl
Fourpeaked Mountain 6,903ft
KATMAI NATIONAL PARK
Big River
Kaguyak Crater
SWIKSHAK PATROL CABIN
Swikshak Bay
HALLO BAY WILDERNESS CAMPS
Wolverine Falls
Devils Desk 6,411ft
Kukak Volcano 6,700ft
Hook Glacier
Mount Steller 7,300ft
Mount Denison 7,606ft
Hallo Glacier
Ninagiak Island
Hallo Bay
Serpent Tongue Glacier
KATMAI WILDERNESS LODGE
Snowy Mountain 7,090ft
Kukak Bay
Kaflia Bay
Hidden Harbor
Kuliak Bay
Missak Bay
Kinak Bay
AMALIK BAY PATROL CABIN
Takli Island
Katmai Village (abandoned)
Dakavak Bay
SHELIKOF STRAIT
AFOGNAK ISLAND
Kupreanof Strait
KODIAK ISLAND
0 10 mi
0 10 km

Top 3

BROOKS RIVER, KATMAI

1 WATCH BROWN BEARS

If you're going bear-viewing, the most popular destination in Katmai is **Brooks Camp.** This National Historic Landmark includes the park visitors center, a campground, an auditorium where rangers lead nightly chats in addition to their daytime guided hikes, and, if you want to spend the night within four walls, **Brooks Lodge.** From here you can hike to Brooks Falls and the three bear-viewing platforms lining the Brooks River, where brown bears feed on sockeye salmon. In 2019, the park service replaced the seasonal floating bridge with a $6 million permanent bridge and elevated boardwalks over the Brooks River. It offers easier access to the bear-viewing platforms and another place from which to enjoy the bears. When the Falls Platform maxes out with people during prime seasons in July and September, you may need to wait for space, and rangers limit viewing time to one hour per person.

2 TOUR THE VALLEY OF TEN THOUSAND SMOKES

EXTINCT FUMAROLE NEAR KNIFE CREEK GORGE, VALLEY OF TEN THOUSAND SMOKES

The desolate, ash-covered **Valley of Ten Thousand Smokes** was created by the largest volcanic eruption of the 20th century. In 1912, the Novarupta volcano erupted for 60 hours, transforming the fertile Ukak River valley into the smoking landscape you see today.

To visit the valley, book the daylong Natural History Tour with park concessionaire **Katmailand** (907/243-5448, www.katmailand.com, daily early June-mid-Aug., advance reservations required, $51-96 pp). From Brooks Camp, a narrated tour bus travels 23 miles (37 km) to the Overlook Cabin, where you'll stop for lunch, wildlife-viewing, and a guided trek 1,000 feet (305 m) down to the valley floor (3.4 mi./5.5 km rt., 1.7 hrs., strenuous).

For a guided backpacking trip through the valley, hire **Alaska Alpine Adventures** (877/525-2577 or 907/351-4193, www.alaskaalpineadventures.com), based in Anchorage.

3 FISH FOR SALMON

During the June-September fishing season, the Brooks River is one of the hottest spots for fishing. **Brooks Lodge** and **Grosvenor Lodge** offer 3- to 7-day guided fishing packages that include meals, lodgings, and air travel from Anchorage. Cast your line for five species of salmon, plus rainbow trout, char, and arctic grayling.

THE VALLEY OF TEN THOUSAND SMOKES

RECREATION

A bewildering number of guide services are authorized to operate within Katmai. If you want to narrow it quickly and ensure a good experience, stick with **Brooks Camp** or **Brooks Lodge** (907/243-5448, www.katmailand.com) for right-at-the-camp lodging and fishing opportunities. From Anchorage, use **Alaska Alpine Adventures** (877/525-2577 or 907/351-4193, www.alaskaalpineadventures.com) for other activities such as hiking, backpacking, and paddling.

HIKING

Katmai has less than 5 miles (8 km) of maintained trails. From Brooks Camp Visitor Center, a wheelchair-accessible trail leads to **Brooks Falls** (2.4 mi./3.9 km rt., 1.2 hrs.), where two viewing platforms provide a way to watch brown bears fishing for sockeye salmon. The third platform is at the mouth of Brooks River. The more ambitious trail to **Dumpling Mountain** (3 mi./4.8 km rt., 1.5 hrs.) climbs 800 feet (244 m) in elevation to views of Lake Brooks, Naknek Lake, the Brooks River, and Brooks Camp below.

KAYAKING AND CANOEING

At Brooks Camp you can canoe or kayak **Naknek Lake.** Experienced sea kayakers go for the inland **Savonoski Loop.** Starting and finishing at Brooks Camp, the 86-mile (138-km) route links two large lakes and two rivers. The route requires excellent skills to paddle the swift-moving wave trains, avoid obstacles in the Savonoski River, and portage kayaks 1 mile (1.6 km). Most paddlers do the loop in 4-7 days. Fure's Cabin provides an overnight option in the Bay of Islands in the North Arm of Naknek Lake.

WHERE TO STAY

INSIDE THE PARK

Most visitors will want to stay in Brooks Camp, where **Brooks Lodge** (800/544-0551, www.katmailand.com, June-mid-Sept., from $208) has 16 modern guest rooms with baths. Breakfast, lunch, and dinner are served buffet-style in the lodge dining room, which overlooks Naknek Lake. Bear-viewing platforms are nearby. The lodge offers daily tours to the Valley of Ten Thousand Smokes.

Grosvenor Lodge (800/544-0551, www.katmailand.com, June-mid-Sept., package rates apply), a fishing lodge on Grosvenor Lake, accommodates 4-6 guests in three cabins (with heat and electricity), a separate bathhouse, and a kitchen and dining area. The main lodge holds a lounge and bar.

Brooks Camp Campground (877/444-6777, www.recreation.gov, $12 June-Sept., $6 May and Oct.) accommodates 60 tent campers and fills quickly. Reservations open in early January for the summer; July reservations book fast for the peak bear-viewing periods. Facilities include cooking shelters, fire rings, food storage boxes, water, and vault toilets. The campground

MCNEIL RIVER STATE GAME SANCTUARY

Tucked outside the northern edge of Katmai National Park, **McNeil River State Game Sanctuary** was established in 1967 to protect the highest concentration of wild brown bears in the world. As you can imagine, that leads to some amazing bear-viewing opportunities. Guides and researchers have counted more than 70 brown bears near the McNeil River at one time. Bear-viewing is best in July and mid-August, when chum salmon congregate at McNeil River Falls. A smaller number of bears swarm an early sockeye run up nearby Mikfik Creek.

A permit program limits visits to McNeil River Falls. Only 10 guided viewing permits are issued per day from early June to late August. **Permits** (907/267-2189, www.adfg.alaska.gov, $30 for lottery, $525 for non-Alaska resident permit) are assigned by lottery, which starts on March 2 of the prior year and ends on March 1 of the viewing year. Each permit is valid for four days. It's a four-mile (6.4 km, 2 hrs.) round-trip hike to reach the falls.

If you don't win the permit lottery, apply for a camp-standby permit ($262 non-Alaska resident), which is also valid for four days. The camp-standby permit allows you to stay in the sanctuary campground (tents only) and view bears from the campground and beach area. If somebody no-shows for a guided viewing trip, you can then take their spot.

This roadless sanctuary has no roads or modern amenities. Access is by chartered flight from Anchorage or Homer.

has no designated sites—the open, grassy area is protected from bears by an electric fence.

Backcountry camping in the Valley of Ten Thousand Smokes can be arranged with a one-way drop-off from Katmailand; some sites fringe the valley. Alternatively, hike 12 miles (19.3 km, one-way) from Valley Road to the primitive **Baked Mountain Huts** (first come, first served, free). No permits are required, and there are no services.

In the Bay of Islands of Naknek Lake, rustic **Fure's Cabin** (877/444-6777, www.recreation.gov, June-Sept., $45) is a one-room, wood-heated cabin with no electricity. It sleeps six. Make reservations starting in early January.

THE VALLEY OF TEN THOUSAND SMOKES

OUTSIDE THE PARK

Services are located in the town of **King Salmon,** which has one hotel: the **Antlers Inn** (Mile 1 Alaska Peninsula Hwy., 888/735-8525 or 907/246-8525, www.antlersinnak.com, from $175).

GETTING THERE AND AROUND

King Salmon sits 290 miles (465 km) southwest of Anchorage on the Alaska Peninsula, just off the west flank of Katmai National Park. You can only get here by plane. In summer, **Alaska Airlines** (800/252-7522, www.alaskaair.com) offers flights daily from Anchorage to King Salmon. **PenAir** (800/448-4226, www.penair.com) offers five or six flights from Anchorage in summer.

Upon arrival in King Salmon, take an air taxi with **Katmai Air** (800/544-0551, www.katmaiair.com, reserve in advance) into the park at Brooks Camp. Katmai Air also provides floatplane charters to other locations in the park.

Katmai has no public transportation. To get around, you'll need a boat or kayak, or to book a floatplane or tour bus to the Valley of Ten Thousand Smokes.

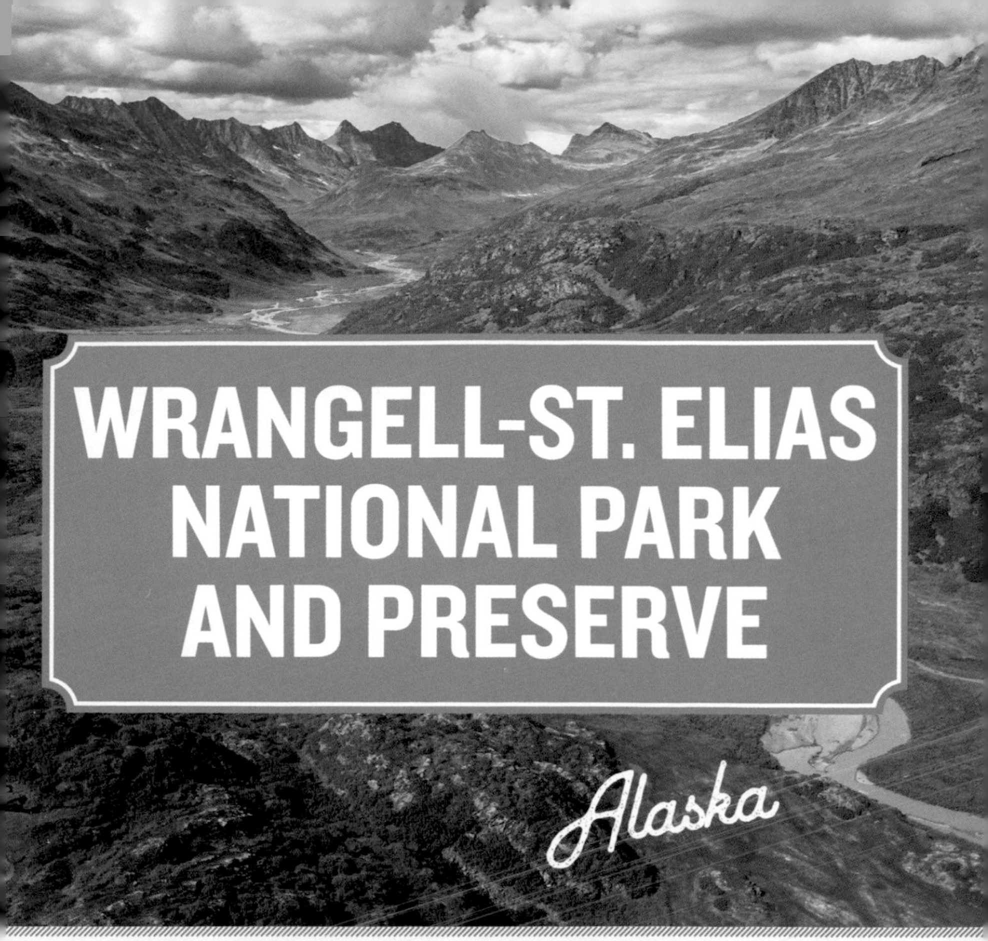

WRANGELL-ST. ELIAS NATIONAL PARK AND PRESERVE

KEEPSAKE STAMPS ▾▾▾

WEBSITE:
www.nps.gov/wrst

PHONE NUMBER:
907/822-5234

VISITATION RANK:
56

WHY GO:
Visit the largest national park in the United States.

▲ FALLS CREEK, CHUGACH

To Delta Junction and Fairbanks
DISTRICT RANGER STATION
Slana
MENTASTA MOUNTAINS
NABESNA ROAD
To Tok
Fish Lake
Chistochina
Copper River
TOK CUTOFF GLENN HIGHWAY
WRANGELL-ST. ELIAS NATIONAL PRESERVE
Ewan Lake
Crosswind Lake
Gulkana River
Capital Mountain 7,731ft
Jack Lake
Copper Lake
Tanada Lake
Nabesna
Nabesna River
Gulkana
Gakona
Tanada Peak 9,358ft
Mt Sanford 16,237ft
Jacksina Creek
Cooper Pass
WRANGELL MOUNTAINS
Glennallen
To Anchorage
Mt Drum 12,010ft
Klawasi R
Copper Gl
Mt Gordon 9,040ft
MAIN PARK VISITOR CENTER
Tazlina Lake
Mt Zanetti 13,009ft
Mt Jarvis 13,421ft
Mt Wrangell 14,163ft
Copper Center
Nabesna Glacier
St. Anne Lake
Klutina River
Chisana Pass
Willow Lake
Kenny Lake
Klutina Lake
EDGERTON HIGHWAY
Tonsina
Mt Blackburn 16,390ft
Atna Peaks
Regal Mountain 13,845ft
Donoho Peak 6,696ft
Liberty Falls
Dixie Pass
Kennicott Glacier
Root Glacier
Chitina
RANGER STATION (SUMMER ONLY)
Kotsina
Strelna
Chitina River
Tonsina Lake
Chokosna
KENNECOTT MIN
KENNECOTT VISITOR CENTER
McCarthy
MCCARTHY ROAD
Nizina R
DAN CRE
MAY CREEK
Valdez Glacier
Tonsina Glacier
Spirit Mountain 7,287ft
Nelson Mountain 5,457ft
Hanagita River
Chitina River
RICHARDSON HIGHWAY
Thompson Pass
Valdez
Lowe River
Tebay Lakes
Tasnuna River
Tana River
Hanagita Peak 8,504ft
CHUGACH MOUNTAINS
Bremner River
GRANIT
Rude River
Allen Glacier
Wernicke Glacier
Granite
Tana Glacier
Scott Glacier
Childs Glacier
Sherman Glacier
Miles Lake
Mt Hawkins 10,395ft
Mt Tom White 11,210ft
CHUGACH NATIONAL FOREST
Cordova
Bagl
Martin River Glacier
Mt Steller 10,617ft
Copper River Delta
Bering Glacier
ROBINSO
Katalla
Cape Suckling
0
20 mi
20 km
Kayak Island
Gulf of Alask
© MOON.COM

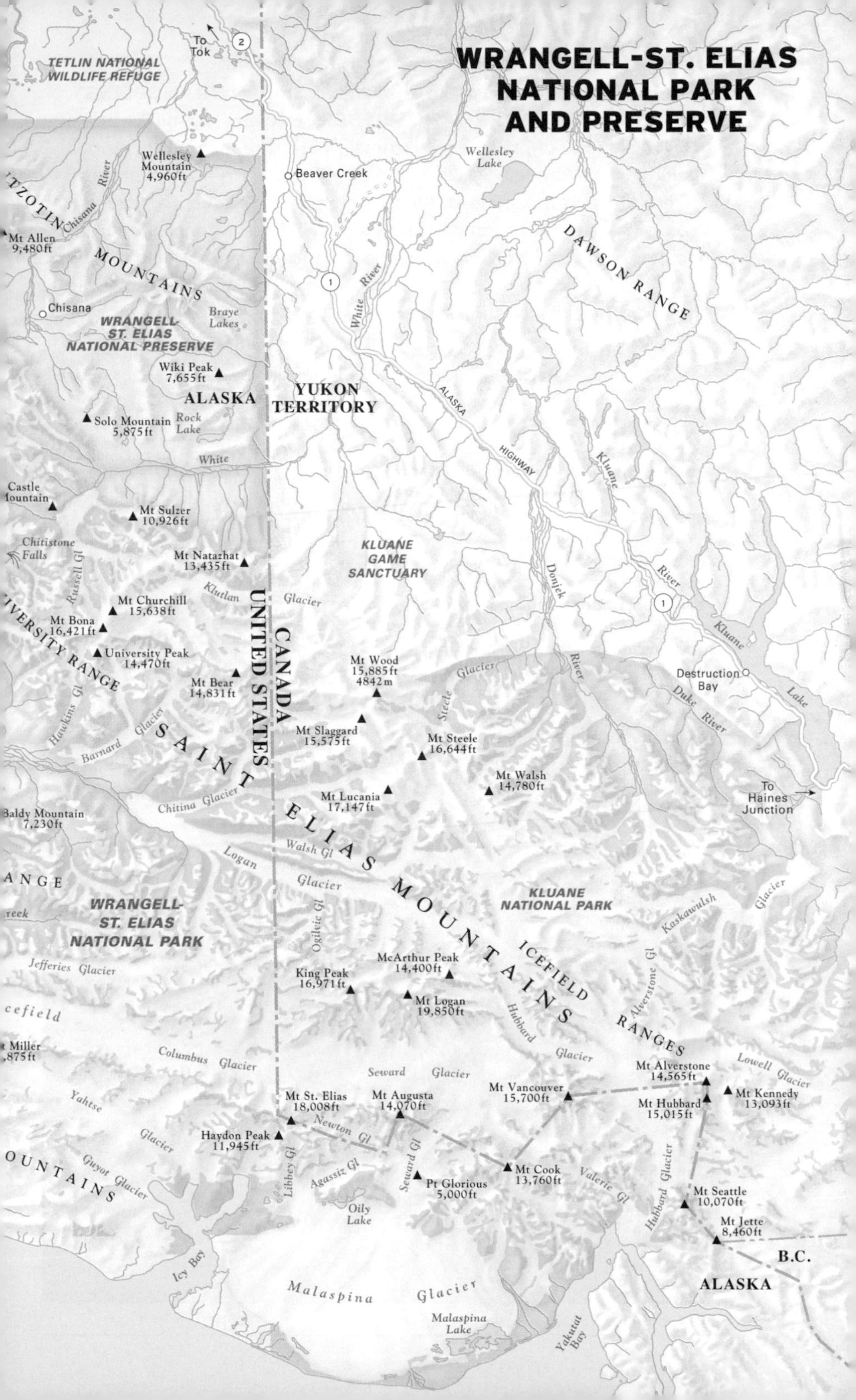

WRANGELL-ST. ELIAS NATIONAL PARK AND PRESERVE
To Tok
2
TETLIN NATIONAL WILDLIFE REFUGE
Wellesley Mountain 4,960ft
Wellesley Lake
Beaver Creek
Chisana River
Mt Allen 9,480ft
MOUNTAINS
DAWSON RANGE
1
White River
Chisana
Braye Lakes
WRANGELL-ST. ELIAS NATIONAL PRESERVE
Wiki Peak 7,655ft
ALASKA
YUKON TERRITORY
ALASKA HIGHWAY
Solo Mountain 5,875ft
Rock Lake
White
Kluane
Castle
Mt Sulzer 10,926ft
Chitistone Falls
KLUANE GAME SANCTUARY
Mt Natazhat 13,435ft
Russell Gl
Klutlan
Glacier
Donjek
River
Mt Churchill 15,638ft
UNITED STATES
CANADA
Mt Bona 16,421ft
Kluane
University Peak 14,470ft
Mt Wood 15,885ft 4842m
Glacier
River
Destruction Bay
Mt Bear 14,831ft
Steele
Duke River
Lake
Hawkins Gl
Glacier
Mt Slaggard 15,575ft
SAINT ELIAS MOUNTAINS
Mt Steele 16,644ft
Barnard
Mt Walsh 14,780ft
To Haines Junction
Mt Lucania 17,147ft
Chitina Glacier
Baldy Mountain 7,230ft
Walsh Gl
Logan
Glacier
KLUANE NATIONAL PARK
WRANGELL-ST. ELIAS NATIONAL PARK
Kaskawulsh
Glacier
Ogilvie Gl
ICEFIELD RANGES
McArthur Peak 14,400ft
King Peak 16,971ft
Mt Logan 19,850ft
Alverstone Gl
Jefferies Glacier
Hubbard
Columbus Glacier
Glacier
Mt Alverstone 14,565ft
Lowell Glacier
Seward
Glacier
Mt Vancouver 15,700ft
Mt Kennedy 13,093ft
Mt Hubbard 15,015ft
Yahtse
Mt St. Elias 18,008ft
Mt Augusta 14,070ft
Newton Gl
Haydon Peak 11,945ft
Glacier
Guyot Glacier
Libbey Gl
Agassiz Gl
Seward Gl
Pt Glorious 5,000ft
Mt Cook 13,760ft
Valerie Gl
Hubbard Glacier
Mt Seattle 10,070ft
Mt Jette 8,460ft
Oily Lake
Icy Bay
B.C.
ALASKA
Malaspina Glacier
Malaspina Lake
Yakutat Bay

The largest national park in the United States, **WRANGELL-ST. ELIAS NATIONAL PARK AND PRESERVE** covers 13.2 million acres (5.3 million ha) of pristine wilderness where three mountain ranges collide (the Wrangell, St. Elias, and Chugach). With huge peaks and rivers of ice, it is a magnet for mountaineers. Serious backpackers come for solitude at turquoise lakes while wildlife-watchers hone binoculars on bears, bison, mountain goats, and wolves. It is also a place where the indigenous Ahtna, Upper Tanana, Eyak and Tlingit people pass on the skills of subsistence living to their future generations. Only two roads penetrate the interior of this rugged wilderness.

PLANNING YOUR TRIP

Wrangell-St. Elias National Park and Preserve sits snug against the Canadian border, 190 miles (305 km) east of Anchorage. Paved roads skirt the park's western boundary, providing access to the gateway communities of Glennallen, Copper Center, Kenny Lake, and Chitina. Inside the park, most visitors beeline for the historic mining towns of **McCarthy** and **Kennecott,** accessible only by a long and difficult dirt road.

The best time to visit is **June-August,** when balmy summers peak with highs in the 70s (21-26°C) by July.

ENTRANCE AND FEES

The main entrance to the park is south of Glennallen along the paved **Richardson Highway** (AK 4), which runs through the town of Copper Center. There is no entrance station and no entrance fee.

VISITORS CENTERS

The **Copper Center Visitor Center** (Copper Center, mile 106.8 Richardson Hwy. at Glenn Hwy., 907/822-7250, 9am-6pm daily mid-May-mid-Sept., reduced spring/fall hours, closed winter) is 10 miles (16 km) south of Glennallen. As the main park visitors center, it has exhibits, backcountry information,

KENNICOTT GLACIER AND STAIRWAY ICEFALL

Top 3

1 SCENIC DRIVE ON MCCARTHY ROAD

McCarthy Road stretches 60 miles (97 km) from Chitina to McCarthy, taking 2-3 hours one-way on the rugged dirt road. Stop to marvel at the **Kuskulana Bridge** (mile 17), a 775-foot (236-km) expanse made even more impressive because it was built in 1910—and because you have to drive across it! Stop again at the huge **Gilahina Trestle** (mile 29) to admire its construction. Just before reaching the parking area, look for the Kennicott Glacier. The road terminates at the **Kennicott River Footbridge.**

The road is legendary for being narrow, rough, and full of sharp rocks and railroad spikes just waiting to puncture tires. Fill up on gas at Kenny Lake (AK 4) before making the trip.

2 EXPLORE ROOT GLACIER

Descending from Mount Blackburn, **Root Glacier** is one of Alaska's easiest glaciers to access. Join a guided day trek with **St. Elias Alpine Guides** (888/933-5427 or 907/231-6395, www.steliasguides.com, daily mid-May-mid-Sept. $95) to step out onto the ice to see brilliant turquoise pools, ice canyons, and crevasses. No experience is necessary for this adventure; you just need to be able to hike up to 6 miles (10 km), which includes the trail to get to the glacier. The company supplies the expert guide, crampons, and gear. It'll give you a taste of what mountaineers experience.

ROOT GLACIER

3 EXPLORE KENNECOTT MINING TOWN

A 5-mile (8-km) road connects McCarthy with the ghost town of **Kennecott,** whose historic, bright red mine buildings are an eye-catching sight backdropped by the snowy Wrangell Mountains. In summer, **St. Elias Alpine Guides** (888/933-5427 or 907/231-6395, www.steliasguides.com) lead tours into the **Kennecott Mill** buildings, part of the Kennecott Mines National Historic Landmark**.** Most of the equipment is in surprisingly good condition and still works. With no private vehicle access, you must hike or bike to get here—or hop aboard the shuttle van from McCarthy.

KENNECOTT

Best Hike

ROOT GLACIER

4-8 MILES (6.4-12.9 KM) ROUND-TRIP
DURATION: 2.5-4 hours
ELEVATION CHANGE: 263-900 feet (80-274 m)
DIFFICULTY: easy to moderate
TRAILHEAD: Kennecott Visitor Center

Favored by hikers and bears, this trail parallels the toe of Kennicott Glacier to reach the toe of Root Glacier. Both look like ice rivers coursing down from Mount Blackburn. The spectacular Stairway Icefall appears in the distance. The trail begins on a road to a fork where the left trail weaves through lateral moraines. At the junction past the Jumbo Creek Footbridge, turn left to drop to the toe of Root Glacier. Use caution: slick ice, collapsing ice bridges, frigid water, and falling ice can be dangerous. Return the way you came, or back on the main trail, continue for another 2 miles (3.2 km) paralleling the glacier for more views.

a bookstore, theater, and ranger talks. Next door, the **Ahtna Cultural Center** (907/822-3535, year-round, hours vary) is a native heritage museum with a hand-built fish wheel. Outside, short paths visit scenic overlooks, and rangers lead guided walks.

McCarthy Road has several spots for obtaining visitor information. Outside the park, stop at **Chitina Ranger Station** (mile 33, Edgerton Hwy., Chitina, 907/823-2205, 10am-4:30pm Thurs.-Sun. Memorial Day-Labor Day) for an update on road conditions. At the upper end of McCarthy Road, the unstaffed **McCarthy Road Info Station** (mile 59) has an orientation kiosk. Five miles (8 km) north of McCarthy in a historic schoolhouse, **Kennecott Visitor Center** (907/205-7106, 9am-5pm daily in summer) has ranger programs, exhibits, films, a bookstore, and backcountry information.

WRANGELL MOUNTAINS

FLOATPLANE

At the entrance to rugged Nabesna Road, stop at **Slana Ranger Station** (mile 0.5, 907/822-7401, 8am-5pm daily in summer) to find out road conditions. The station also has exhibits, a film, ranger programs, and backcountry information.

SIGHTS

MCCARTHY

A remote Alaskan homestead miles from pavement, **McCarthy** once supplied the mining district with necessities and services. Today, you'll find lodgings, dining, a museum, and railroad memorabilia lining its 0.1-mile (0.2-km) main street. McCarthy is a launch point for backcountry exploration, flightseeing, and guided trips, with hiking trails to glaciers and mines. Visitors are restricted to one access point—a wide footbridge over the Kennicott River with a 0.5-mile (0.8-km) walk into town. Learn about the history of the area at the **McCarthy-Kennicott Historical Museum** (hours vary late May-early Sept.) in the old red depot building with the railcar outside.

SCENIC DRIVES

Two rugged dirt roads reach into the Wrangell-St. Elias interior. While the roads are open year-round, they are full of potholes and washboards—if you drive too fast or have bald tires, expect a few flat tires. Fuel up in advance and bring a full-size inflated spare, jack, patch kit or Fix-a-Flat, and air compressor.

The challenging **McCarthy Road** (60 mi./97 km one-way) is the better of the two roads. To drive rugged **Nabesna Road** (3 hrs. rt.), fuel up in Slana (Tok Cutoff Rd., AK 1) for the 42-mile (68-km) drive into the north side of the park. Between miles 15 and 18, the rugged Wrangell Mountains come into view and you may spot **Mount Wrangell,** the park's only active volcano. **Kendesnii Campground,** at mile 28, is where many drivers turn around because the remaining road is rougher. Stop at the Slana Ranger Station for road updates, as washouts are frequent.

RECREATION

HIKING

To see the **Kennicott Glacier** (1.5 mi./2.4 km one-way, 0.8 hr.), hike the trail from the museum in McCarthy to the meltwater lake at the toe of the glacier. A lengthy river of ice, Kennicott Glacier carries mounds of debris: boulders, rocks, gravel, and silt. Most people

WRANGELL MOUNTAINS

expect to see white or blue ice, but much of the toe of the glacier is covered by brown and gray debris.

St. Elias Alpine Guides (888/933-5427 or 907/231-6395, www.steliasguides.com) leads hikes, ice climbing, ice caving, backpacking, air-assisted hiking trips, river rafting, and mountaineering expeditions.

FLIGHTSEEING

In McCarthy, air taxis offer expeditions into the park. Go flightseeing with **Copper Valley Air Day Tours** (866/570-4200 or 907/822-4200, www.coppervalleyairservice.com) or **Wrangell Mountain Air** (800/478-1160 or 907/554-4411, www.wrangellmountainair.com).

RAFTING

The silt-colored Kennicott River churns and boils beneath the footbridge toward McCarthy. **McCarthy River Tours & Outfitters** (907/302-0688, www.raftthewrangells.com, mid-May-mid-Sept.) specializes in these turbulent waters, with single-day and multiday trips in the Copper River Valley. They also offer calmer paddleboarding and kayaking trips in the lake at the toe of Kennicott Glacier.

WHERE TO STAY

INSIDE THE PARK

For those seeking solitude, the park maintains 14 fly-in or snowmobile-in **backcountry cabins** (most first come, first served; four require reservations) in remote locations.

McCarthy

The **McCarthy Lodge** (101 Kennicott Ave., 907/554-4402, www.mccarthylodge.com) has two accommodation options: the old boardinghouse of **Ma Johnson's Hotel** (from $229) and the **Lancaster Backpacker Hotel** (from $139). Bathrooms are shared. The lodge bistro serves local yak meat and wild-caught Copper River sockeye salmon. The **Golden Saloon,** where the town goes to socialize, serves pub fare. The lodge store sells ready-made sandwiches, ice cream, liquor, hardware, and limited groceries.

Kennecott

The nicest accommodations are at the **Kennicott Glacier Lodge** (15 Kennicott Millsite, 800/582-5128, www.kennicottlodge.com, late May-mid-Sept., from $205). Guest rooms are in two buildings: 24 rooms in the lodge have shared baths and 20 rooms in the south wing

MA JOHNSON'S HOTEL

have private baths. The dining room serves family-style breakfast, lunch, and dinner fare that some term "wilderness gourmet." Common areas are lined with historical artifacts from the Kennecott copper mine.

For a cozier experience, reserve one of the five **Blackburn Cabins** (907/231-6227, www.blackburncabins.com, year-round, from $169), which have two full beds, propane heaters, kitchens, and running water. Bike rentals, guided hikes and trips and snow machine rentals are also available.

Camping

McCarthy Road has two private campgrounds before the footbridge at McCarthy. Only the aptly named **Glacier View Campground** (mile 58.9, McCarthy, 907/441-5737, www.glacierview-campground.com, June-mid-Sept., $15) accepts reservations. It has a small open-air café and a bare-bones camp store.

At mile 27.8 on Nabesna Road, the primitive **Kendesnii Campground** (year-round, free) has 10 first-come, first-served campsites, but no drinking water. It is the only park service campground in the park. You can also camp at pullouts (free) along the road.

OUTSIDE THE PARK

The gateway communities of **Glennallen, Copper Center, Kenny Lake,** and **Chitina** have limited services. Small motels, cabins, and campgrounds dot **Richardson Highway** (AK 4), **Glenn Highway** (AK 1), and **Tok Cutoff Road** (AK 1).

BACKPACKERS

MT. DRUM

GETTING THERE

AIR

The closest international airport is **Ted Stevens Anchorage International Airport** (ANC, 5000 W. International Airport Rd., www.dot.state.ak.us/anc). Car rentals are available at the airport.

CAR

From Anchorage, it is a 180-mile (290-km) drive on Glenn Highway (AK 1) to Glennallen. Three miles (4.8 km) east of Glennallen, turn south onto Richardson Highway (AK 4); from there it's 10 miles (16 km) to the Copper Center Visitor Center.

To reach McCarthy and Kennecott, continue south on Richardson Highway (AK 4) from Copper Center for 23 miles (37 km). Turn left (east) onto Edgerton Highway (AK 10) and drive 33 miles (53 km) to the pavement's end at Chitina, the park entrance, and the McCarthy Road.

If Slana and Nabesna Road are your destination, follow Glenn Highway (AK 1) north from Glennallen for 76 miles (122 km).

SHUTTLE

From Anchorage, **Wrangell-St. Elias Tours** (907/390-0369, www.alaskayukontravel.com) runs a van shuttle to Glennallen, Chitina, and McCarthy. **Interior Alaska Bus Line** (800/770-6652, www.interioralaskabusline.com) travels to Glennallen.

GETTING AROUND

AIR

Wrangell Mountain Air (800/478-1160 or 907/554-4411, www.wrangellmountainair.com) operates twice-daily flights in summer from Chitina to McCarthy.

CAR

Prepare for rugged dirt roads inside the park. From the park entrance at Chitina, **McCarthy Road** (60 mi./97 km, 2-3 hrs. one-way) goes to McCarthy and Kennecott. From the Tok Cutoff Road (AK 1), the rougher Nabesna Road (42 mi./68 km, 1.5 hrs. one-way) leads north of the mountains.

SHUTTLES

The **Kennicott Shuttle** (907/822-5292, www.kennicottshuttle.com, summer only, reservations required) picks up guests outside the park in Glennallen, Copper Center, Kenny Lake, or Chitina with transportation to McCarthy and Kennicott. **Wrangell-St. Elias Tours** (907/390-0369, www.alaskayukontravel.com) runs a shuttle van twice daily between Chitina and McCarthy.

At the Kennicott River, shuttles stop at the footbridge for the walk into McCarthy.

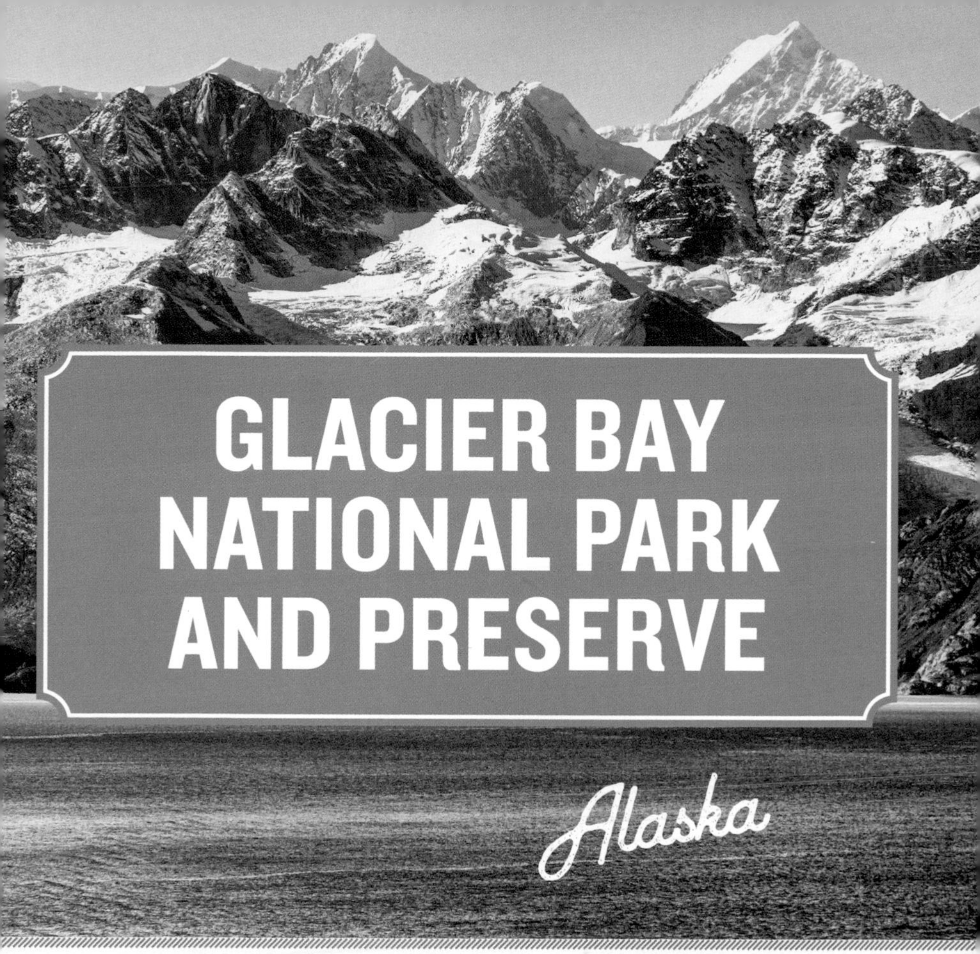

GLACIER BAY NATIONAL PARK AND PRESERVE

Alaska

KEEPSAKE STAMPS ▼▼▼

WEBSITE:
www.nps.gov/glba

PHONE NUMBER:
907/697-2230

VISITATION RANK:
32

WHY GO:
Watch tidewater glaciers calve.

▲ GLACIER BAY NATIONAL PARK

GLACIER BAY NATIONAL PARK AND PRESERVE
CANADA
UNITED STATES
Tatshenshini River
Novatak Glacier
Brabazon Range
Alsek River
SAINT ELIAS MOUNTAINS
Konamoxt Gl
Towagh Glacier
Tsiatka Gl
ALSEK RANG
Tikke Glacier
Melburn Glacier
Hay Glacier
Mount Hay 8,870ft
Alsek Glacier
Alsek Lake
Alsek River
DRY BAY RANGER STATION
Dry Bay
GLACIER BAY NATIONAL PRESERVE
Grand Pacific Glacier
Deception Hills
Mount Lodge 10,530ft
Mount Barna 8,214ft
Ferris Glacier
Grand Plateau Glacier
Gulf of Alaska
Mount Root 12,860ft
FAIRWEATHER RANGE
Margerie Glacier
Mount Fairweather 15,300ft
Mount Quincy Adams 13,650ft
Johns Hopkins Glacier
Mount Salisbury 12,000ft
Fairweather Glacier
Cape Fairweather
Lituya Mountain 11,750ft
Mount A 8,750
Mount Orville 10,495ft
Lituya Glacier
Mount Bertha 10,204ft
North Crillon Glacier
Lituya Bay
Mount Crillon 12,726ft
Mount La Perouse 10,728ft
Crillon Lake
La Perouse Glacier
PACIFIC OCEAN
Icy Point
Palma Bay
Astro Poi
0 10 mi
0 10 km

Mount McDonnell
5,481ft
3
7
Chilkat
CHILKOOT TRAIL
To Whitehorse
98
Skagway
WHITE PASS &
YUKON ROUTE RAILROAD
Klehini
River
Klukwan
Buckwell Glacier
Tsirku Glacier
Glacier
Tsirku
River
River
Taiya
Inlet
Mount Harris
5,177ft
Takhin
River
Haines
BRITISH
COLUMBIA
TAKHINSHA
MOUNTAINS
Mount Krause
6,978ft
Chilkoot
Inlet
Chilkat
Inlet
Muir Glacier
Morse Glacier
Riggs Glacier
ALASKA
Cushing Glacier
Carroll Glacier
Rendu Glacier
Sitth-gha-ee Peak
5,870ft
Mcbride Glacier
Chilkat
Peninsula
Davidson Glacier
Casement Glacier
Mount Rice
5,658ft
Lynn Canal
Mount
Abdallah
5,964ft
Rendu
Inlet
Wachusett
Inlet
Queen Inlet
Sullivan
Island
Mount Merriam
5,083ft
Muir
Inlet
Adams
Inlet
Endicott Gap
900ft
Reid Glacier
Gilbert
Peninsula
Endicott
River
Mount
Wright
5,139ft
BEARTRACK MTS
Tlingit
Point
North Sandy
Cove
Glacier Bay
Beartrack
River
CHILKAT RANGE
GLACIER BAY
NATIONAL PARK
BRADY ICEFIELD
Drake
Island
Excursion
Geikie Inlet
Beartrack Cove
Willoughby
Island
EXCURSION
RIDGE
Wood
Lake
Lake
Seclusion
Sitakaday
River
Abyss
Lake
Bartlett
River
BEARDSLEE
ISLANDS
Brady
Glacier
Dundas
River
VISITOR CENTER
GLACIER BAY LODGE
Bartlett
Cove
Narrows
Gustavus
Icy Passage
Excursion
Inlet
Point
Gustavus
Pleasant
Island
Dundas
Bay
Icy Strait
Taylor
Bay
Point Adolphus
Lemesurier
Island
Graves Harbor
Inian
Islands
Eagle Point
Mud Bay
Cape
Spencer
Elfin Cove
Cross Sound
CHICHAGOF ISLAND
© MOON.COM

GLACIER BAY NATIONAL PARK AND PRESERVE encompasses some 3.3 million acres (1.3 million ha) of land and water. Its craggy, snowcapped mountains, towering spruce and cedar trees, calving glaciers, and rich waters are hardly unique in Alaska, but this park is remarkable for several reasons.

The first is the pristine nature of the waters and lands; the waters, in particular, are some of the richest on earth, and Glacier Bay is one of the largest protected biosphere preserves in the world. Second, the solitude—cruise ships do visit the bay, but they never dock, and access is controlled during peak months.

Third, an enormous thick glacier covered much of the park until nearly 300 years ago, when a fast series of glacial advances and retreats melted out the bay. Today, active tidewater glaciers from the Little Ice Age still push into the bay, but are receding at an alarming rate.

Finally, Glacier Bay is an integral part of the Tlingit Alaska Native tradition. In collaboration between the park and the Tlingit clans, the new Xunaa Shuká Hít (Huna House) clan house became the first permanent clan house in the area since Tlingit villages were destroyed by a rapid glacier advance more than 250 years ago.

PLANNING YOUR TIME

Glacier Bay is virtually roadless. The park encompasses a 65-mile-long (105-km) saltwater bay with multiple fjords hunkering between ice-laden mountains draped with glaciers that plunge into the tidewater. To see the glaciers requires **travel by air or water,** plus the logistics of several trip legs to get there. From **Juneau,** getting to the park entrance requires a ferry or a flight to **Gustavus,** a service town just outside the park that is unreachable by road. From Gustavus, taxis travel the short distance to Bartlett Cove, inside the park. From Gustavus or Bartlett Cove, boat tours enter Glacier Bay.

May-September is high season, with services in Gustavus and Bartlett Cove open. Despite moderate summer temperatures, erratic maritime weather systems deliver pervasive rains, especially around Bartlett Cove, which sees up to 70 inches (178 cm) annually. Bring rain gear and warm, quick-dry layers, including hat and gloves. For less rain, go in May or June.

ENTRANCE AND FEES

The park has no entrance station, but the official entrance is Bartlett Cove. There is no entrance fee.

VISITORS CENTERS

In Bartlett Cove, **Glacier Bay National Park Visitor Center** (Glacier Bay Lodge, 2nd fl., 907/697-2661, 11am-8pm daily late May-early Sept.) contains an Alaska Geographic bookstore and exhibits, including an underwater listening station and a kids corner. The theater has nightly educational programs, and ranger-guided walks depart for beachcombing or rainforest tours.

To go boating or camping in Glacier Bay, stop at the **Visitor Information Station** (Bartlett Cove, 907/697-2627, hours vary daily May-Sept.), adjacent to the public dock in Bartlett Cove. Pick up permits, maps, tide tables, and nautical charts, and attend an orientation covering the rigors of wilderness boating and camping.

Top 3

1 CRUISE GLACIER BAY

MCBRIDE GLACIER

Visitors can travel up the Main Channel or tour Glacier Bay's West Arm to view the tidewater glaciers. The only scheduled day tour in the park is the **Glacier Bay Tour** out of **Glacier Bay Lodge** (179 Bartlett Cove, 888/229-8687, www.visitglacierbay.com, daily in summer). National Park Service rangers narrate the eight-hour tour on high-speed catamarans. The tour takes in wildlife and the tidewater Grand Pacific and Margerie Glaciers. Lunch is included.

Cruise ships depart from West Coast and Alaskan cities to tour Glacier Bay. Two ships per day are allowed up the West Arm to spend four hours in the glacier areas. Cruise ships do not dock; sightseeing is only from the boat. Tour operators in Gustavus also offer day trips and longer overnight expeditions into Glacier Bay.

2 GO WHALE-WATCHING

From mid-June through August, whale-watching for humpback whales is phenomenal in the waters of Glacier Bay. Two of the best whale-watching tours are the half-day, naturalist-narrated **The Taz Cross-Sound Express** (888/698-2726 or 907/321-2303, www.tazwhalewatching.com), which also offers water-taxi services for kayakers and backpackers (the deck is large enough to handle large groups of kayaks), and the half-day **Wild Alaska Charters** tour (855/997-2704 or 907/697-2704, www.glacierbay.biz), limited to six passengers at a time.

3 KAYAK THE OPEN WATERS

Sea kayaking Glacier Bay is a bucket-list adventure. **Glacier Bay Sea Kayaks** (Bartlett Cove, 907/697-2257, www.glacierbayseakayaks.com) guides full- and half-day trips in the park and also provides gear rentals and trip-planning assistance to paddlers experienced enough to go without a guide. Two destinations are favored by kayakers: The **Beardslee Islands** have great beach camping and wildlife-viewing, and **Muir Inlet** restricts motorized boats, making this a prime place for quiet and solitude. Kayakers can use the daily Glacier Bay Tour boat as a water taxi to cut days off paddling time; they can also bring their own boats on the ferry from Juneau.

For multiday longer guided kayak tours, go with **Alaska Mountain Guides** (based in Haines, 800/766-3396 or 907/313-4422, www.alaskamountainguides.com) or **Spirit Walker Expeditions** (800/529-2537, www.seakayakalaska.com).

ONE DAY IN GLACIER BAY

If you must pack your Glacier Bay visit into one day, charter an early morning flight from Juneau to Gustavus. Spend that night at **Glacier Bay Lodge,** then take the **Glacier Bay Tour** into Glacier Bay—it's the only way to see the wildlife and tidewater glaciers. The eight-hour tour boat returns in time to catch a late afternoon flight back to Juneau.

SIGHTS

BARTLETT COVE

Bartlett Cove is Glacier Bay National Park's headquarters. Nestled at the south end of the bay, the enclave houses **Glacier Bay Lodge,** which contains the visitors center, hotel rooms, and a restaurant. The cove also has the **Huna Tribal House,** docks with boat services, kayak rentals, the **Visitor Information Station,** and a walk-in campground. Low tide is the perfect time to explore the intertidal zone around the cove, which is teeming with seaweed, algae, crabs, mollusks, and birds.

HUNA TRIBAL HOUSE

The **Huna Tribal House** (noon-5:30pm Mon.-Sat.) pays tribute to the Tlingit culture, which has a rich history in the lower bay. The building sports carvings and paintings that portray the history of Tlingit clans. Interpretive presentations (20 min.) are offered several times daily; weekly programs include guided walks and demonstrations on making dugout canoes. The house sits on the shoreline trail of Bartlett Cove, adjacent to Glacier Bay Lodge.

WHALE EXHIBIT

Stop at the outdoor pavilion near the Visitor Information Station to see the **Whale Exhibit,** home to the largest humpback whale skeleton in the United States. Known as Snow, this humpback whale was a regular summer resident in the bay for 26 years. Her 3,729-pound (1,691-kg) skeleton is more than 45 feet long (14 m).

MARGERIE GLACIER

HIKER AND GLACIER

GLACIER BAY

There are three main areas to tour in Glacier Bay. The **Main Channel** contains the Marble Islands, where you might spot cliff-dwelling seabirds, sea lions, or summering humpback whales. At Tlingit Point, the waterways divide into two main arms.

The smaller **Muir Inlet** (sometimes called East Arm) contains multiple glaciers that are mostly terrestrial; McBride Glacier still reaches the tidewater, but Muir Glacier has melted with speedy recession back onto land.

The larger arm is **Glacier Bay,** known also as West Arm, where motorized boats and cruises can go. This arm holds the 35-mile-long (56 km) Grand Pacific Glacier and the smaller Margerie Glacier, which calve off icebergs into the bay. Johns Hopkins and Gilman Glaciers produce submarine calving, where ice breaks off underwater to explode to the surface.

RECREATION

HIKING

Glacier Bay has only 10 miles (16 km) of designated hiking trails, including an easy forested shoreline stroll on the **Tlingit Trail** (0.5 mi./0.8 km rt., 0.3 hr.) to the Huna Tribal House. A 0.25-mile (0.4-km) trail goes along the beach to the Bartlett Cove Campground.

The **Forest Trail** (1 mi./1.6 km rt., 0.5 hr.) is a wheelchair-accessible boardwalk trail that leads to two viewing decks overlooking a pond. Past the pond, a dirt trail continues to the campground and the beach before looping back to the starting point. Park rangers lead daily hikes on this trail.

Bartlett River Trail (4 mi./6.4 km rt., 4 hrs.) explores an intertidal lagoon, forest, and river estuary. The **Bartlett Lake Trail** (9.4 mi./15.1 km rt., 7-8 hrs.) climbs over moraine to tour spruce forests on its way to Bartlett Lake.

BOATING

Glacier Bay has 700 miles (1,130 km) of shoreline for boaters to explore. June-August, private boat owners must secure a free permit (available online) to enter the waters of **Glacier Bay** and **Bartlett Cove.** Permits are good for up to seven days; apply within 60 days of your planned arrival date. Don't dillydally, though—permits often run out quickly from mid-June to early August. Motorized boats are limited to 25 craft per day in Glacier Bay. The public dock at Bartlett Cove has boater services.

SEA LIONS

FISHING

The waters of Glacier Bay and Icy Straits are enormously productive—this is one of the best places in the world for fishing—and the isolated location means you won't have to battle crowds. Book an all-inclusive, multiday fishing trip with **Glacier Bay Sportfishing** (907/697-3038, www.glacierbaysportfishing.com, lodgings at the Annie Mae Lodge) or opt for a half-day to five-day trip with **Taylor Charters** (801/647-3401, www.taylorchartersfishing.com). Glacier Bay Lodge rents fishing gear and sells licenses.

WHERE TO STAY

INSIDE THE PARK

The only accommodations inside the park are at **Glacier Bay Lodge** (179 Bartlett Cove, 888/229-8687, www.visitglacierbay.com, mid-May-early Sept., from $208). The facility has 48 small, rustic guest rooms with private baths. The lodge restaurant serves breakfast, lunch, and dinner; entrées specialize in Alaskan seafood. Bicycle rentals, fishing gear rentals, fishing licenses, and a laundry are available.

Bartlett Cove Campground (free, permit required, May-Sept.) offers serene tent camping with fantastic views over the water. It's a 0.25-mile (0.4-km) walk to the 33-site campground; facilities include bear-resistant food caches, outhouses, and a warming shelter. Register at the Visitor Information Station near the private docks, follow an orientation, and then pick up your free camping permit. Campers can shower at Glacier Bay Lodge.

OUTSIDE THE PARK

Accommodations and dining options can be found in the picturesque community of **Gustavus,** 8 miles (13 km) from the park entrance.

GETTING THERE

AIR

Alaska Airlines (800/252-7522, www.alaskaair.com, June-Aug.) offers seasonal service via a 30-minute flight from Juneau to Gustavus. From the airport in Gustavus, it's about 8 miles (13 km) to the entrance of Glacier Bay National Park.

▼ SUNRISE ON THE FAIRWEATHER RANGE

A CRUISE SHIP APPROACHES MARGERIE GLACIER

Small planes, including seaplanes, hop between towns in southeast Alaska. They provide transportation, plus flightseeing trips. **Alaska Seaplanes** (907/789-3331, www.flyalaska-seaplanes.com) is based in Gustavus and Juneau. **Admiralty Air Service** (907/796-2000, www.admiraltyairservice.com) and **Ward Air** (907/789-9150, http://wardair.com) are based in Juneau.

BOAT

Cruise ships enter the bay but don't dock. The **Alaska Marine Highway System Ferry** (800/642-0066, www.dot.state.ak.us/amhs) has cut back service to 4-5 sailings per month, June-September, between Juneau and Gustavus, a 4.5-hour trip.

GETTING AROUND

Glacier Bay Lodge and most lodges in Gustavus provide shuttles from the airport or ferry terminal to the hotel. Taxis link the communities of Gustavus and Bartlett Cove; call **TLC Taxi** (907/697-2239, www.glacierbaytravel.com/tlctaxi.htm) for service. The only road is the 10-mile (16-km) link between Gustavus and Bartlett Cove, but if you need to rent a car, contact **Bud's Rent-a-Car** (907/697-2403).

GLACIER BAY NATIONAL PRESERVE

Glacier Bay is a remote and special place—so much so that UNESCO recognized it as a World Heritage Site and a Biosphere Reserve. That designation is thanks in part to **Glacier Bay National Preserve,** a small portion of the park tucked in the northeast corner. Bounded by the Gulf of Alaska and the Alsek River, this unique area is rich in wildlife. Recreation includes fishing, hunting, river rafting, and 60 miles (97 km) of designated ATV trails.

To reach the remote preserve requires chartering an air taxi from Yakutat to one of two airstrips on the preserve. Visitors can camp in the wilderness (free) or reserve a small cabin rented by the Yakutat Ranger Station (907/784-3295, $25). Three small lodges operate concessions.

GATES OF THE ARCTIC AND KOBUK VALLEY NATIONAL PARKS

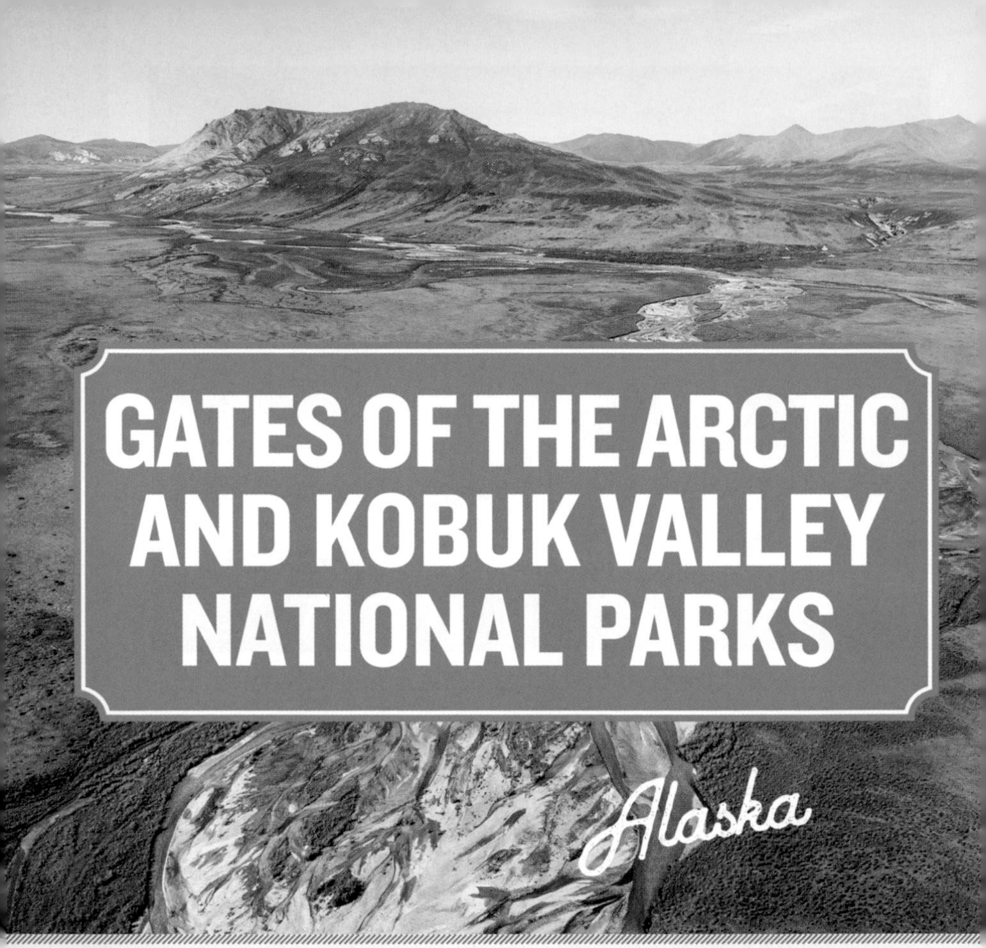

GATES OF THE ARCTIC

WEBSITE:
www.nps.gov/gaar

PHONE NUMBER:
907/692-5494

VISITATION RANK:
62

WHY GO:
Visit a remote, raw wilderness.

KOBUK VALLEY

WEBSITE:
www.nps.gov/kova

PHONE NUMBER:
907/442-3890

VISITATION RANK:
61

WHY GO:
See sand dunes and migrating caribou.

KEEPSAKE STAMPS ▼▼▼

▲ WESTERN BROOKS RANGE

Two remote national parks claim places above Alaska's Arctic Circle. These roadless wildernesses see very few visitors. Most of the human footprints belong to the Inupiat people who still hunt caribou here as their ancestors did. The larger **GATES OF THE ARCTIC NATIONAL PARK AND PRESERVE** contains the wild Brooks Range, spilling with glaciers, huge rivers, tundra, and boreal forests.

The smaller **KOBUK VALLEY NATIONAL PARK** gains its fame from sand dunes made from ice age glaciers. Both have immense herds of caribou, plus tundra swans, musk ox, moose, wolves, and grizzly bears. The weather and the animals still rule here; we are simply transient visitors.

PLANNING YOUR TIME

These wilderness parks are devoid of trails, roads, campgrounds, lodgings, visitors centers, and services. There are no entrance fees—or even entrances! All access is on foot or by bush plane. It's this very wildness that is the draw.

Winters are unforgivingly harsh and long. The best months to travel are **June-August.** Even during summer's short, mild weather, temperatures can drop well below freezing. Expect high winds, mosquitoes, and changeable weather.

Fairbanks is the jumping-off point for driving the Dalton Highway (AK 11), a rough dirt-road trek to the small service towns east of Gates of the Arctic. Fly-in guided trips depart from Anchorage, Fairbanks, Kotzebue, or Bettles. For visitors aiming to check off all U.S. national parks, the right outfitter can get

THE NOATAK RIVER

GATES OF THE ARCTIC AND KOBUK VALLEY NATIONAL PARKS

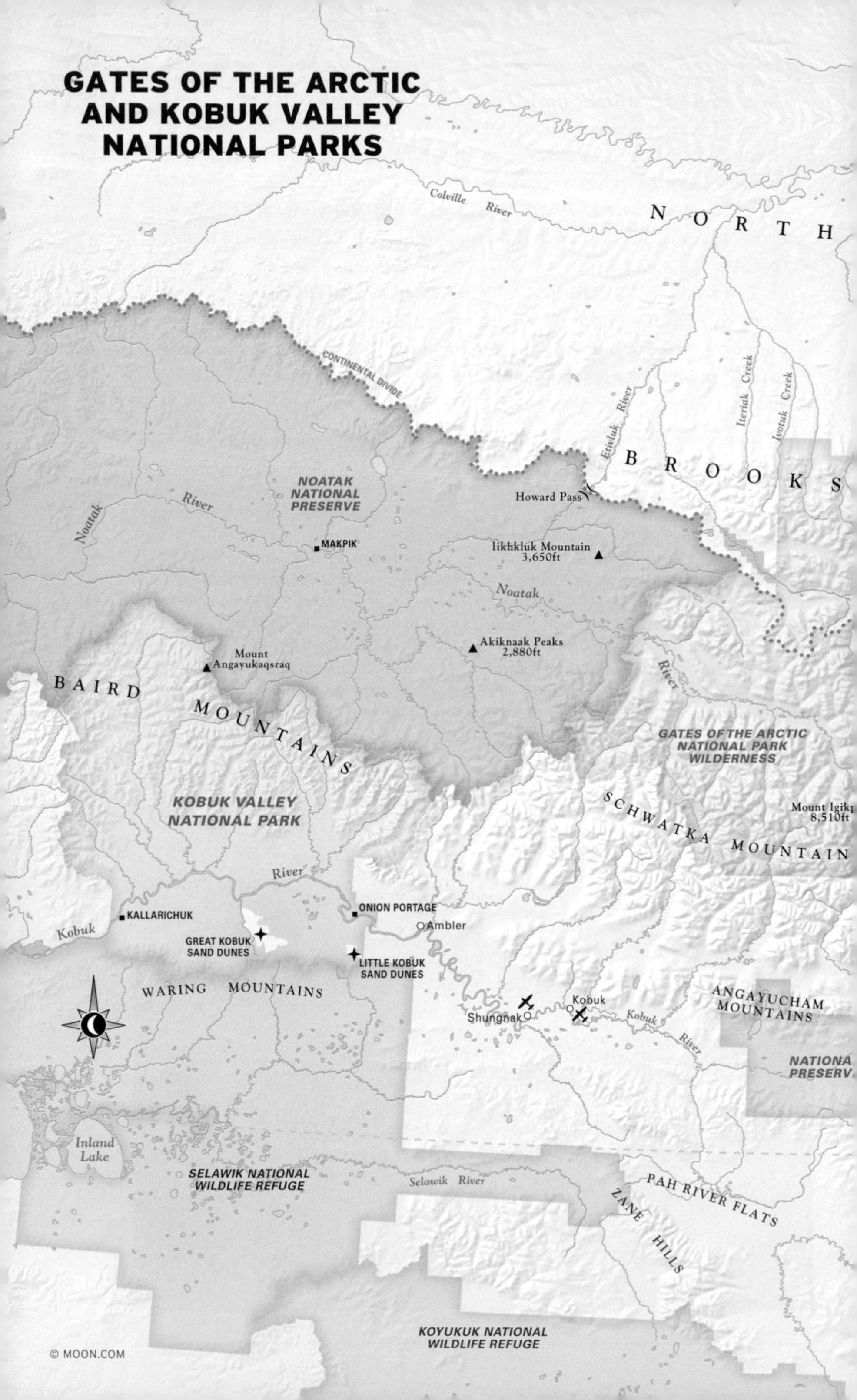

Colville River
NORTH
BROOKS
CONTINENTAL DIVIDE
Etivluk River
Iteriak Creek
Ivotuk Creek
NOATAK NATIONAL PRESERVE
Noatak River
Howard Pass
MAKPIK
Iikhkluk Mountain 3,650ft
Noatak
Akiknaak Peaks 2,880ft
Mount Angayukaqsraq
BAIRD MOUNTAINS
River
GATES OF THE ARCTIC NATIONAL PARK WILDERNESS
SCHWATKA MOUNTAIN
Mount Igik
8,510ft
KOBUK VALLEY NATIONAL PARK
River
ONION PORTAGE
KALLARICHUK
Ambler
Kobuk
GREAT KOBUK SAND DUNES
LITTLE KOBUK SAND DUNES
WARING MOUNTAINS
Shungnak
Kobuk
Kobuk River
ANGAYUCHAM MOUNTAINS
NATIONA PRESERV
Inland Lake
SELAWIK NATIONAL WILDLIFE REFUGE
Selawik River
PAH RIVER FLATS
ZANE HILLS
KOYUKUK NATIONAL WILDLIFE REFUGE

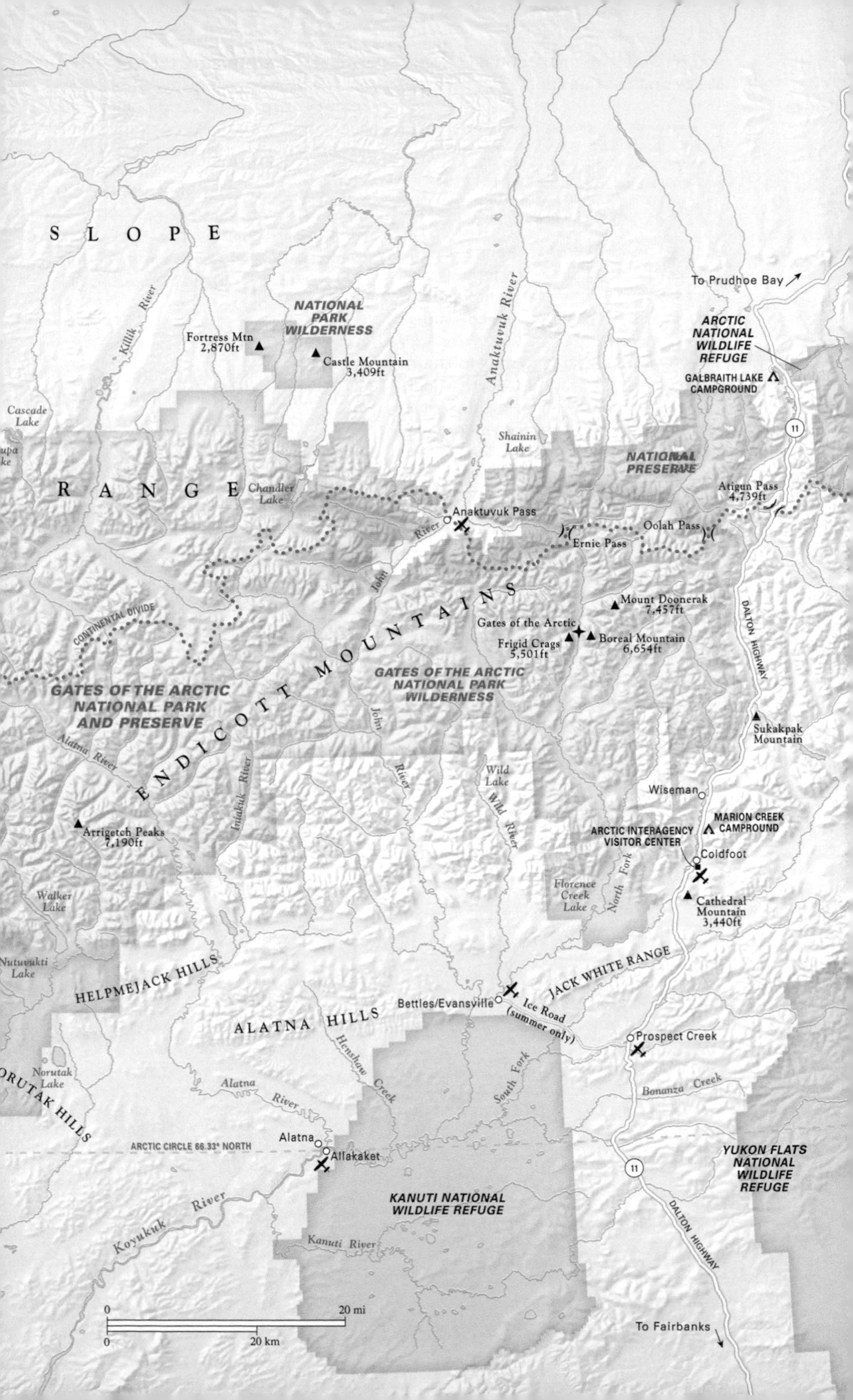

SLOPE
RANGE
ENDICOTT MOUNTAINS
NATIONAL PARK WILDERNESS
Fortress Mtn 2,870ft
Castle Mountain 3,409ft
Killik River
Anaktuvuk River
To Prudhoe Bay
ARCTIC NATIONAL WILDLIFE REFUGE
GALBRAITH LAKE CAMPGROUND
11
Cascade Lake
Shainin Lake
NATIONAL PRESERVE
Chandler Lake
Atigun Pass 4,739ft
Anaktuvuk Pass
John River
Oolah Pass
Ernie Pass
DALTON HIGHWAY
Mount Doonerak 7,457ft
CONTINENTAL DIVIDE
Gates of the Arctic
Frigid Crags 5,501ft
Boreal Mountain 6,654ft
GATES OF THE ARCTIC NATIONAL PARK WILDERNESS
GATES OF THE ARCTIC NATIONAL PARK AND PRESERVE
Sukakpak Mountain
Alatna River
Wild Lake
Wild River
Wiseman
Arrigetch Peaks 7,190ft
Itkillik River
MARION CREEK CAMPROUND
ARCTIC INTERAGENCY VISITOR CENTER
Coldfoot
Walker Lake
Florence Creek Lake
North Fork
Cathedral Mountain 3,440ft
Nutuvukti Lake
HELPMEJACK HILLS
JACK WHITE RANGE
Bettles/Evansville
Ice Road (summer only)
ALATNA HILLS
Prospect Creek
Henshaw Creek
Norutak Lake
ORUTAK HILLS
Alatna River
South Fork
Bonanza Creek
ARCTIC CIRCLE 66.33° NORTH
Alatna
Allakaket
YUKON FLATS NATIONAL WILDLIFE REFUGE
KANUTI NATIONAL WILDLIFE REFUGE
Koyukuk River
Kanuti River
0
20 mi
20 km
To Fairbanks

you to Gates of the Arctic and Kobuk Valley on the same trip.

GATES OF THE ARCTIC NATIONAL PARK AND PRESERVE

Located in the Brooks Range at the foot of the needlelike Arrigetch Peaks, Gates of the Arctic National Park and Preserve is a vast, untouched wilderness that spans 8.4 million acres (3.4 million ha). Containing the northernmost mountain range in North America, it stretches west from the Dalton Highway through country where wildlife far outnumbers humans. Dense vegetation, marshes, frequent water crossings, glacial lakes, and soaring granite peaks make travel very challenging but beautifully remote.

PLANNING YOUR TIME

The closest "town" is the tiny hub of Bettles (population 12), accessible only by air or snow machine on the winter ice road.

Outside the park are three visitors centers. The **Arctic Interagency Visitor Center** (mile 175 Dalton Hwy., Coldfoot, 907/658-5209, hours vary daily, summer only) updates road conditions on the Dalton Highway, offers backcountry trip registration, and rents bear canisters. It also has films, exhibits, and a bookstore with maps.

Reachable only by air, the small **Bettles Ranger Station and Visitor Center** (in Bettles, summer only, 907/692-5494) has exhibits. The backcountry **Anaktuvuk Ranger Station** (summer only, 907/661-3520) has an outdoor information kiosk.

RECREATION

Gates of the Arctic has flightseeing, remote camping, backpacking, pack rafting, river float trips, paddling, photography, fishing, and hunting; hire a guide for all activities. In addition to guides licensed for both parks, two companies provide guide services from Anchorage into Gates of the Arctic:

Alaska Alpine Adventures (877/525-2577 or 907/351-4193, www.alaskaalpineadventures.com) guides hiking, backpacking, and rafting trips.

Expeditions Alaska (770/952-4549, www.expeditionsalaska.com) owner Carl Donohue guides photography, backpacking, and pack rafting trips.

▼ ARCTIC DIVIDE NEAR ANAKTUVUK PASS

GATES OF THE ARCTIC NATIONAL PARK AND PRESERVE

WHERE TO STAY

Outside the park, **Bettles Lodge** (Bettles, 907/692-5111, http://bettleslodge.com, year-round) has guest rooms, dining, flightseeing, guided backpacking and fishing, aurora viewing, and dogsledding.

On the Dalton Highway, small communities such as **Coldfoot** also have a few lodging and outfitter options.

GUIDE SERVICES

For most visitors, access is by bush plane. Professional guide services offer a safe (although pricey) way to experience the wonder of these Arctic parks.

Bettles Lodge (907/692-5111, http://bettleslodge.com) books flightseeing in both parks.

From Bettles airstrip, **Brooks Range Aviation** (800/692-5443 or 907/692-5444, http://brooksrange.com) offers flightseeing in both parks and guides backpacking, river floating, remote camping, hunting, and fishing trips.

From Fairbanks, **Arctic Wild** (907/479-8203, www.arcticwild.com) guides backpacking, pack rafting, hiking, and remote camping in Gates of the Arctic.

Campgrounds are at Galbraith Lake and Marion Creek.

GETTING THERE

From Fairbanks or Anchorage, **Ravn Alaska** (907/266-8394, www.flyravn.com) flies air taxis via Kotzebue to Bettles or Anaktuvuk Pass. **Wright's Air Service** (907/474-0502, www.wrightairservice.com) flies from Fairbanks to Bettles and Coldfoot.

KOBUK VALLEY NATIONAL PARK

The 1.75-million-acre (708,000-ha) Kobuk Valley National Park gains its fame from its 30 square miles (78 sq. km) of massive sand dunes made by glaciers that ground their way through the land. Some dunes tower 100 feet (30 m) high. More than a half-million caribou migrate through the dunes, many crossing the Kobuk River at Onion Portage where indigenous people still gather to harvest the animals much as they did 8,000 years ago.

PLANNING YOUR TIME

Kotzebue is the gateway for visiting Kobuk Valley. The multiagency **Northwest Arctic Heritage Center** (171 3rd Ave., 907/442-3890, 9am-6:30pm Mon.-Fri., 10am-6:30pm Sat., June-Aug.) serves as the visitors center, nature center, and museum, plus headquarters for the park. Educational programs include classes in traditional native crafts. Spend an hour taking in the exhibits to learn about the parks.

RECREATION

These are the largest active dunes in the North American Arctic, wind-shaped relics that show how the grinding power of ancient glaciers continue to change, even as grasses gain footholds in the sand. **Flightseeing** is the easiest way to see the dunes—on a flyover or landing to walk the sand.

To see the **Onion Portage caribou migration,** plan a trip around Labor

CAMPING ALONG THE SALMON RIVER

GREAT KOBUK SAND DUNES

Day to the Kobuk River. Charter a bush plane to get there, set up camp, and climb a hill to watch the show.

From Kotzebue, fly with **Arctic Backcountry Flying Service** (907/442-3200, www.arcticbackcountry.com) for flightseeing or guided fishing, backpacking, and float trips.

WHERE TO STAY

Outside the park, Kotzebue houses the modern, European-inspired **Nullaġvik Hotel** (306 Shore Ave., 907/442-3331, www.nullagvikhotel.com, from $279), whose name means "a place to sleep" in Inupiaq. Guest rooms have private baths and touches of Alaska Native art. One of the upper floors has an observation room overlooking Kotzebue Sound.

GETTING THERE

To reach Kobuk Valley, book a flight from Anchorage or Fairbanks to Kotzebue (there is no road access). From Kotzebue, charter a flight into the park. In summer, **Alaska Airlines** (800/252-7522, www.alaskaair.com) has daily flights from Anchorage. From Fairbanks or Anchorage, **Ravn Alaska** (907/266-8394, www.flyravn.com) flies to Kotzebue and then connects with Bettles. From Bettles, charter flights into Kobuk Valley are available from Ravn or **Bering Air** (800/478-3943 or 907/442-3943, www.beringair.com).

ARCTIC NATIONAL WILDLIFE REFUGE

Established in 1960, the **Arctic National Wildlife Refuge** (ANWR, U.S. Fish and Wildlife Service, Fairbanks, 800/362-4546 or 907/456-0250) includes 19.64 million acres (7.9 million ha) of land and water, more than 200,000 caribou, an unthinkable horde of mosquitoes, and one human settlement—the Inupiat village of **Kaktovik** (population 250).

Bordered by Canada to the east, the Arctic Ocean to the north, and the Dalton Highway to the west, ANWR is so large that it spans varied ecological regions: boreal forest, alpine, coastal plain tundra, and coastal marine. It is home to grizzly bears, polar bears, musk oxen, and the highest concentration of nesting golden eagles in Alaska.

Only 1,500 people visit the refuge annually. ANWR remains a vast, largely trackless wilderness, an undisturbed spectrum of Arctic ecosystems that most human beings will never see in their lifetime.

CALIFORNIA

From redwood forests to snowcapped mountains, the California landscape is filled with overwhelming natural beauty and wide-open wilderness. The national parks here excel in superlatives: the tallest mountain in the continental United States, the lowest point in North America, and the highest waterfall in North America. They are a testament to powerful, earth-shaping forces that left their diverse handiwork across the region.

In Yosemite, waterfalls feather down faces of granite. Groves of giant sequoias tower above the trails in Sequoia and Kings Canyon. Along the Pacific coast, lush forests fill with coastal sequoias and islands harbor endemic marinelife. In between, active volcanoes, bone-dry deserts, and craggy alpine peaks beg for exploration.

◂ VALLEY VIEW, YOSEMITE

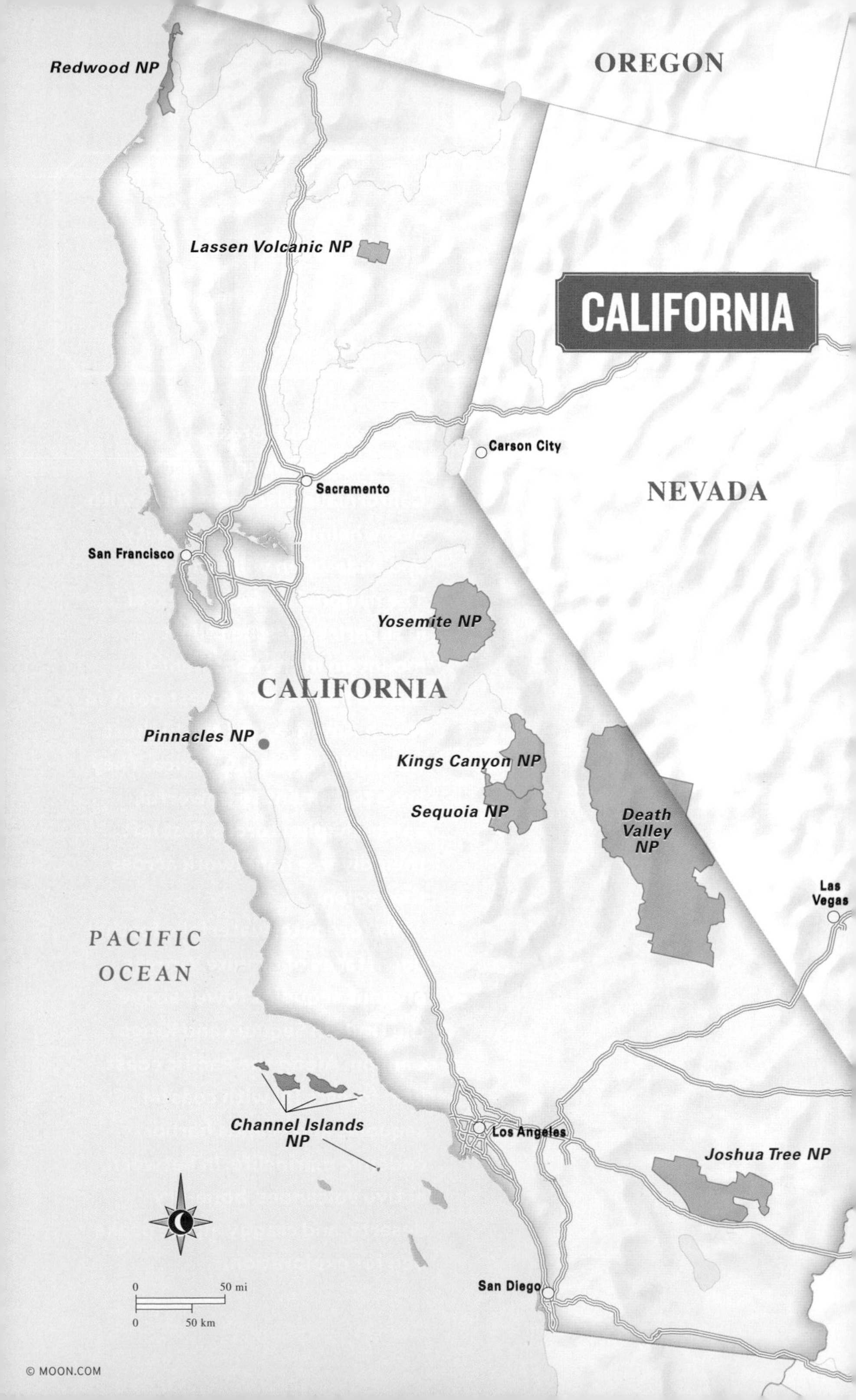

OREGON
Redwood NP
Lassen Volcanic NP
CALIFORNIA
Carson City
Sacramento
NEVADA
San Francisco
Yosemite NP
CALIFORNIA
Pinnacles NP
Kings Canyon NP
Sequoia NP
Death Valley NP
Las Vegas
PACIFIC OCEAN
Channel Islands NP
Los Angeles
Joshua Tree NP
San Diego
0
50 mi
0
50 km
© MOON.COM

The National Parks of CALIFORNIA

YOSEMITE

Granite monoliths and plunging waterfalls are the hallmarks of this Sierra park that lures hikers, backpackers, and big-wall climbers (page 115).

SEQUOIA AND KINGS CANYON

These joined parks boast giant sequoia groves, numerous hiking trails, thriving wildlife, and smaller crowds than their more famous neighbor (page 137).

DEATH VALLEY

Sculpted sand dunes, crusted salt flats, and polished marble canyons pervade this park, which has both the Western Hemisphere's lowest and hottest spots (page 149).

JOSHUA TREE

The park's namesake trees and surreal appeal draw wildflower hounds, serious hikers, and hard-core rock climbers (page 160).

LASSEN VOLCANIC

Geologic wonders include boiling mud pots, fumaroles, and a 10,457-foot (3,187-m) volcano (page 174).

REDWOOD NATIONAL AND STATE PARKS

A series of state and national parks line the California coast, filled with groves of primordial giant redwoods (page 182).

PINNACLES

Climbers, hikers, and campers can't get enough of the huge rock formations, deep caves, and vertical topography in this smaller treasure (page 191).

CHANNEL ISLANDS

This series of islands has undeveloped beauty, stellar coastal views, and stunning sea caves for exploring by kayak (page 198).

1: BRIDGE OVER WOODS CREEK, KINGS CANYON
2: CINDER CONE, LASSEN
3: BALCONIES CAVE TRAIL, PINNACLES

Best OF THE PARKS

Yosemite Valley: Go to Yosemite's heart for El Capitan, Half Dome, and Bridalveil Fall (page 120).

Badwater Basin: Drive this scenic road for the best of Death Valley, including North America's lowest elevation (page 153).

Keys Ranch: Tour the well-preserved ruins of this former homestead, listed on the National Register of Historic Places (page 165).

General Sherman Tree: Admire the largest tree known on earth (page 141).

Lassen Peak: Climb to the summit of this active volcano (page 178).

PLANNING YOUR TRIP

California's best feature is its all-season appeal. Time your trip for **summer** and **early fall,** when Tioga Pass opens across the Sierra between Yosemite and Death Valley. Be aware that summer brings the most visitors, which will not only add to the crowds, but also to the traffic. To avoid the crowds, visit in **spring** when Yosemite's waterfalls are at their peak and fewer people populate the trails. In **winter,** some of Yosemite's roads are closed, including CA 120 and the Tioga Pass. Snow can blanket the California mountains anytime between November and April.

The easiest places to fly into are **San Francisco** and **Los Angeles.** Book **hotels** and **rental cars** in advance for the best rates and availability, especially in the high season of summer. Reservations are essential for **campgrounds.**

1: GENERAL SHERMAN TREE, SEQUOIA
2: EL CAPITAN, YOSEMITE

Road Trip

YOSEMITE, DEATH VALLEY, AND SEQUOIA & KINGS CANYON

Start your trip in the Bay Area where you can fly into **San Francisco International Airport** and **rent a car. Oakland International Airport** may be a cheaper alternative. This route is best traveled between **early summer** or **late fall** (June-Oct.), when Yosemite's Tioga Road (CA 120) is open. If Tioga Road is closed, visit Sequoia and Kings Canyon before traveling south to enter Death Valley.

UPPER YOSEMITE FALL

Yosemite

167 miles (269 km) / 4 hours

Leave San Francisco at 8am to reach Yosemite by noon. The drive to the **Big Oak Flat Entrance** takes at least four hours; however, traffic, especially in summer and on weekends, can make it much longer. From San Francisco International Airport, take US 101 South followed by CA 92 East. Merge onto I-880 North, then I-238 East. Continue on to I-580 East, then I-205 East followed by I-5 North. Then, take CA 120 East, CA 99 North, and CA 120 East.

Spend a day touring **Yosemite Valley,** seeing **Half Dome**, **El Capitan,** and **Yosemite Falls,** and then hike the **Mist**

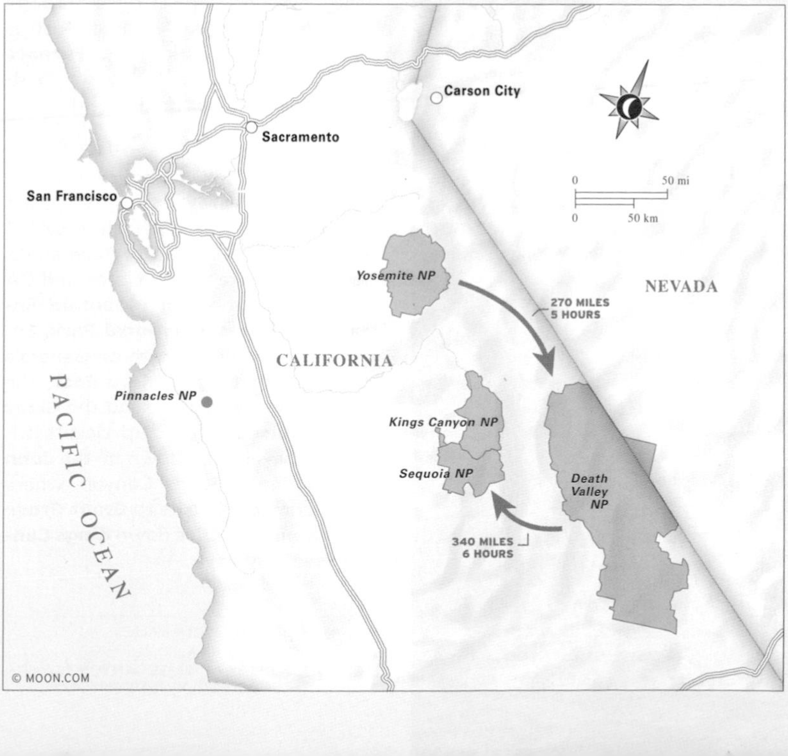

Trail to Vernal Fall. Spend a night under the stars at one of the park's campgrounds or indoors at **The Ahwahnee Hotel** (make reservations well in advance). In summer, go higher on the scenic Tioga Road and plan a hike at **Tuolumne Meadows** before overnighting there at the lodge or campground. Exit the park over Tioga Pass.

Death Valley

221 miles (372 km) / 4.5 hours

Cross Yosemite's **Tioga Pass** heading east on CA 120, then onto US 395 South. Geology fans will love two optional side trips with 30-minute walks: the **Tufa Trail** at **Mono Lake** (add 12 mi./19 km rt., 25 min.) and the Devils Postpile Trail to columns of basalt rocks at **Devils Postpile National Monument** (west on CA 203; add 78 mi./126 km rt., 2 hrs). Another side trip is the **Ancient Bristlecone Pine Forest** (east on CA 168 past Bishop; add 2 hrs. rt., 760/873-2400, www.fs.usda.gov, 6am-10pm daily mid-May-Nov.), which contains the oldest tree in the world, the Methuselah Tree, dated 4,750 years old. Farther south along US 395 South is the Wild West town of **Lone Pine.**

At US 190, head east to enter Death Valley National Park. Cruise through **Panamint Springs.** An hour east is the aptly named park hub of **Furnace Creek,** a perfect base for touring **Badwater Road** and **Zabriskie Point.**

Sequoia and Kings Canyon

326 miles (524 km) / 6 hours

Cross Death Valley on US 190 West and drive US 395 South, then CA 14 South, and CA 58 West to Bakersfield. From there, take CA 99 North and CA 65 North to the **Ash Mountain Entrance** of **Sequoia National Park.** Enjoy the scenic drive north on Generals Highway, stopping at **Moro Rock,** the **General Sherman Tree,** and the **Giant Forest Museum** (pick up tickets for **Crystal Cave!**). Bed down at the **John Muir Lodge** in Kings Canyon, where you're primed for visits to **Grant Grove** and the winding drive down **Kings Canyon Scenic Byway.**

1: ZABRISKIE POINT, DEATH VALLEY
2: MORO ROCK, SEQUOIA
3: REDWOOD CREEK AT KINGS CANYON SCENIC BYWAY, HIGHWAY 180, KINGS CANYON

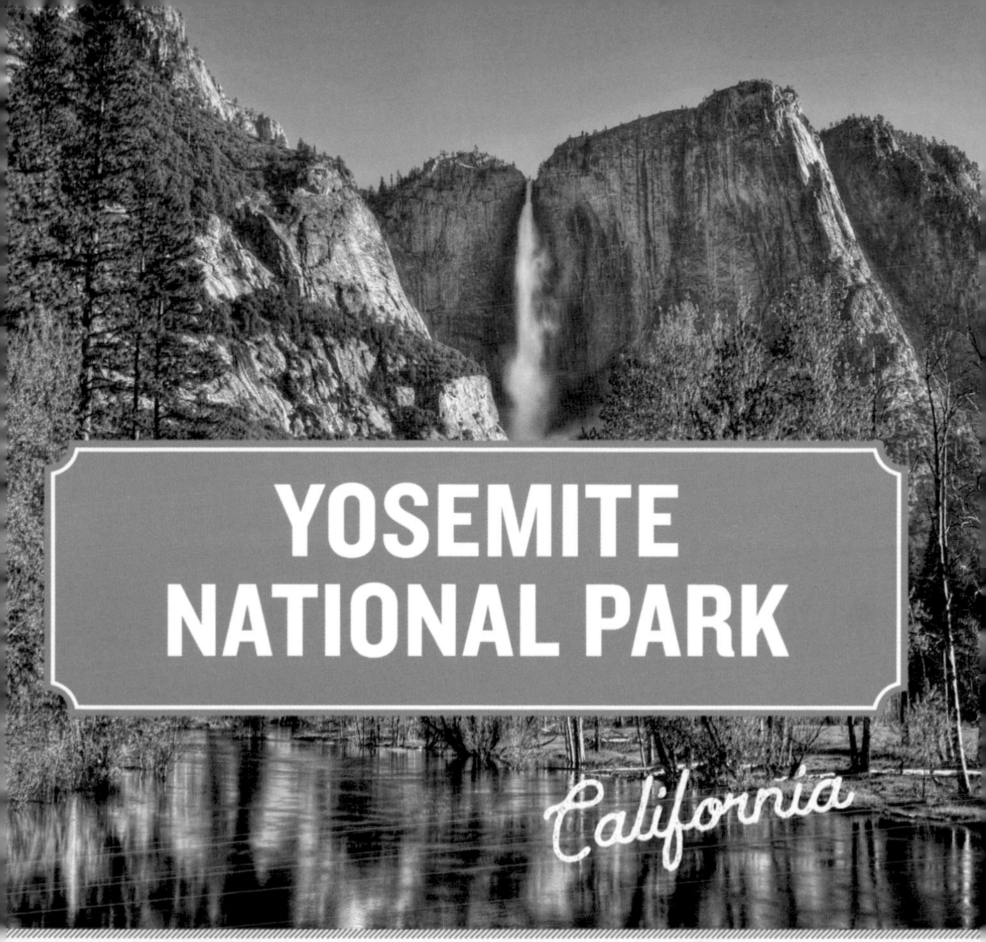

▲ MERCED RIVER AND YOSEMITE FALLS

YOSEMITE NATIONAL PARK

California

KEEPSAKE STAMPS ▼▼▼

WEBSITE:
www.nps.gov/yose

PHONE NUMBER:
209/372-0200

VISITATION RANK:
5

WHY GO:
Admire waterfalls and granite cathedrals.

YOSEMITE NATIONAL PARK
Wilma Lake
Kibbie Lake
JACK MAIN CANYON
TILTILL MOUNTAIN
Piute Mountain 10,541 ft
Lake Eleanor
Laurel Lake
Mount Gibson
Benson Lake
Table Lake
Pettit Peak 10,788 ft
LAKE ELEANOR
TILTILL VALLEY
RANCHERIA MOUNTAIN
GRAND CANYON OF T
HETCH HETCHY BACKPACKERS CAMP
Hetch Hetchy Reservoir
Smith Peak 7,751 ft
PATE VALLEY
Tuolumne River
River
HETCH HETCHY ROAD
HETCH
YOSEMITE WILDERNESS
Harden Lake
Tuolumne
Mather
HETCH HETCHY ENTRANCE
Grant Lakes
Tuolumne Peak 10,845 ft
WHITE WOLF
Middle Tuolumne
Bald Mountain 7,261 ft
Lukens Lake
May Lake
EVERGREEN ROAD
ASPEN VALLEY
TIOGA ROAD
Siesta Lake
Mount Hoffmann 10,850 ft
120
To Manteca
INFORMATION STATION
BIG OAK FLAT ENTRANCE
HODGDON MEADOW
South Fork
YOSEMITE NATIONAL PARK
YOSEMITE CREEK
PORCUPINE FLAT
OLMSTED POINT
Yosemite Creek
Mount Watkins
Tenaya Creek
TENAYA
BIG OAK FLAT ROAD
TAMARACK FLAT
YOSEMITE VALLEY VISITOR CENTER
CRANE FLAT
Half Dome
El Capitan
TUNNEL
VALLEY VIEW
GLACIER POINT
BIG OAK FLAT RD
TUNNEL VIEW
YOSEMITE VALLEY
LITTLE YOSEMITE VALLEY
Dewey Point
Mount Starr King 9,092 ft
Moss Creek
STANISLAUS NATIONAL FOREST
To Merced
ARCH ROCK ENTRANCE
EL PORTAL RD
El Portal
Illilouette
GLACIER POINT RD
140
Merced River
BRIDALVEIL CREEK
YOSEMITE SKI & SNOWBOARD AREA
HENNESS RIDGE
Yosemite West
Bridalveil Creek
OSTRANDER SKI HUT
YOSEMITE WILDERNESS
South Fork Merced River
WAWONA ROAD
HORSE RIDGE
Alder Creek
TURNER RIDGE
Buena Vista Peak 9,709 ft
SIERRA NATIONAL FOREST
Royal Arch Lake
Crescent Lake
BUCK CAMP
Wawona Dome
WAWONA
WAWONA VISITOR CENTER
PIONEER YOSEMITE HISTORY CENTER
South Fork Merced River
MARIPOSA GROVE ROAD
SOUTH ENTRANCE
To Fresno
41
MARIPOSA GROVE
Fish Camp

Virginia Pass
Summit Lake
Virginia Lakes
To Carson City
167
Lundy Lake
395
MONO LAKE
INYO NATIONAL FOREST
Upper McCabe Lake
Creek
VIRGINIA CANYON
Return
COLD CANYON
Pacific Crest Trail
North Peak
Saddlebag Lake
Roosevelt Lake
Mount Conness 12,590 ft
Gardisky Lake
MONO BASIN SCENIC AREA VISITOR CENTER
Lee Vining
White Mountain
Tioga Peak 11,526 ft
Ellery Lake
120
Creek
Ragged Peak
Conness
Gaylor Peak
Granite Lakes
Tioga Lake
TIOGA PASS ENTRANCE
Creek
Delaney
120
Mount Dana 13,057 ft
Pothole Dome
Lembert Dome
Mount Gibbs 12,764 ft
Fairview Dome
TUOLUMNE MEADOWS VISITOR CENTER
Medlicott Dome
Mammoth Peak 12,117 ft
Mono Pass 10,604 ft
Cathedral Peak 10,940 ft
Johnson Peak
LYELL CANYON
KUNA CREST
Parker Pass
Echo Peaks
CATHEDRAL RANGE
Pacific Crest Trail and John Muir Trail
395
June Lake Junction
Koip Peak 12,962 ft
Potter Point
Amelia Earhart Peak
Emeric Lake
Ireland Lake
June Lake
Vogelsang Peak
Donohue Peak 12,023 ft
Waugh Lake
To Mammoth Lakes
Bernice Lake
Donohue Pass
MERCED LAKE
Mount Maclure
Merced Lake
Mount Florence 12,561 ft
Mount Lyell 13,114 ft
Washburn Lake
Mount Ansel Adams 11,760 ft
Banner Peak 12,936 ft
Mount Clark 11,522 ft
Foerster Peak 12,057 ft
Mount Ritter 13,142 ft
Long Mountain 11,502 ft
CLARK RANGE
Isberg Peak
Isberg Pass
Merced Peak 11,726 ft
Triple Divide Peak
Post Peak Pass
ANSEL ADAMS WILDERNESS
SIERRA NEVADA
Fernandez Pass
Breeze Lake
Gale Peak 10,693 ft
Sing Peak 10,552 ft
SIERRA NATIONAL FOREST
0
5 mi
0
5 km
© MOON.COM

Of all the natural wonders California has to offer, few are more iconic than this national park nestled in the Sierra Nevada and the historic lands of the Miwok people. **YOSEMITE NATIONAL PARK** is a natural playground that has been immortalized in the photographs of Ansel Adams. Naturalist John Muir called it "the grandest of all the special temples of Nature I was ever permitted to enter." It was Muir who lobbied for national park designation in 1890 and then introduced its wonders to President Theodore Roosevelt in 1903. If this is your first visit, prepare to be awed.

PLANNING YOUR TIME

The first place most people go is Yosemite Valley (CA 140, Arch Rock Entrance), the most visited region in the park, filled with sights, hikes, and services. Park in the Yosemite Village day-use lot and use the **park shuttle** (7am-10pm daily year-round, free) to get around. Plan at least 2-3 days just in **Yosemite Valley,** with an excursion to Glacier Point. With a week or more, explore Tuolumne Meadows (summer only) or Wawona.

Reservations for camping and lodgings, as well as any permits, should be obtained up to **one year in advance.** It takes advance planning to score an overnight reservation in Yosemite Valley. **Curry Village** is your best bet for last-minute tent cabins, or you can try one of the first-come, first-served campgrounds.

Summer is high season, when traffic jams and parking problems plague the park. Use the free shuttles to reach popular sights and trailheads. Tuolumne Meadows and the Eastern Sierra are less congested, making them good summer options. **Spring** is best for waterfalls and wildflowers, and there are fewer crowds, as in **fall.** In **winter,** roads close and crowds are minimal. Chains may be required on any park road at any time.

ENTRANCES AND FEES

Yosemite is open daily year-round, though some roads close in winter. The entrance fee is $35 per vehicle ($30 motorcycle, $20 individual) and is valid for seven days. You can **buy your pass online** (www.yourpassnow.com) from home to speed through entrance stations faster. There are **five park entrances**:

Arch Rock (CA 140): The main entrance accesses Yosemite Valley from the west (San Francisco, Sacramento). Once inside the park, CA 140 becomes El Portal Road. Long lines form at this busy entrance station May-October; plan to arrive before 9am or after 5pm.

Big Oak Flat (CA 120): This entrance accesses Yosemite Valley and Tuolumne Meadows (summer only) from the north (San Francisco, Sacramento). Inside the park, CA 120 becomes Big Oak Flat Road.

South (CA 41): This entrance goes to Wawona from the south (Fresno, Los Angeles). Inside the park, CA 41 becomes Wawona Road.

Tioga Pass (CA 120): This High Sierra route is on the east side of Yosemite, 12 miles (19 km) west of US 395. Tioga Road accesses Tuolumne Meadows and the Eastern Sierra in summer. Tioga Pass is **closed in winter** (usually Oct.-May or early June).

Hetch Hetchy (off CA 120): This is the only access to the Hetch Hetchy Reservoir and region. The entrance and Hetch Hetchy Road are open 7am-9pm year-round.

VISITORS CENTERS

Valley Visitor Center

The **Valley Visitor Center** (Yosemite Village, 209/372-0299, shuttle stops 5 and 9, 9am-5pm daily year-round) has an interpretive museum in addition to information, books, maps, and

Top 3

HALF DOME

1 SCALE HALF DOME

One of Yosemite's most recognizable features rises high above the valley floor—**Half Dome.** This piece of a narrow granite ridge was polished to its smooth dome-like shape millions of years ago by glaciers, giving it the appearance of half a dome. Hikers summit the dome with the assistance of a cable route first installed in 1919; it's terrifying to some and has been deadly for a few. Instead of climbing, view the iconic granite dome from the safety of the park road by taking the shuttle to **Mirror Lake,** where you can admire the giant from its base. Other good viewpoints include **Stoneman Meadow, Tunnel View** (CA 41), and **Glacier Point.**

For those who are prepared, the most nontechnical climb requires a monumental day on **Half Dome** (14-16 mi./23-25 km rt., 10-12 hrs., late May-early Oct. only, shuttle stop 16). The trail follows the Mist Trail to Nevada Fall and then is signed for Half Dome. Its 4,800-foot (1,463-m) gain and descent are grueling. The final ultrasteep, 400-foot (122-m) ascent is via metal hand cables that see a lineup of climbers. Once you stagger to the top, you'll find a restful expanse of stone on which to enjoy the scenery.

Do not attempt this trail lightly! It is not for young kids, anyone out of shape, or those unaccustomed to lengthy and strenuous high-altitude hikes. You must begin the trail *before sunrise* and turn around by 3:30pm. Do not climb the dome when the cables are down or when the trail is closed.

A **permit** (877/444-6777, www.recreation.gov, $10 reservation, $10 per person) is required. The park distributes 300 permits per day through an online lottery that starts in March.

2 TOUR YOSEMITE VALLEY

Most people go first to the floor of **Yosemite Valley.** It's the most visited spot in Yosemite, home to the towering granite walls of **El Capitan** and **Half Dome** and the plunging **Bridalveil Fall** and **Yosemite Falls.** It's also the starting point of many hikes, including the popular **Mist Trail.** From the valley floor, you can check out the visitors center, theater, galleries, museum, hotels, and outdoor historical exhibits. Tour it by car, shuttle, bicycle, or foot although the last three are best in summer.

3 VIEW THE VALLEY FROM GLACIER POINT

In 1903, naturalist John Muir brought President Theodore Roosevelt to **Glacier Point**, igniting the president's passion for Yosemite. A drive or shuttle bus up Glacier Point Road (16 mi./26 km one-way, open June-Oct.) leads to a short, paved, wheelchair-accessible path with epic vistas across Yosemite Valley and the High Sierra. Pose for a photo op in the footsteps of Muir and Roosevelt, then return to the valley floor via the Four-Mile Trail (4.8 mi./7.7 km one-way, 3-4 hrs.). Be aware that Glacier Point Road will be closed for reconstruction in 2021 and have construction delays in 2022. When the road is closed or snowbound, you can still hike up and back from the valley floor or cross-country ski (10.5 mi one-way) from Badger Pass Ski Area to Glacier Point and back.

ONE DAY IN YOSEMITE

With only one day, concentrate on the sights in Yosemite Valley, which is accessible year-round. Enter Yosemite National Park through the **Big Oak Flat** or **Arch Rock Entrances.** Once in Yosemite Valley, hop aboard the **Valley Shuttle** for a scenic exploration of **Bridalveil Fall, El Capitan,** and **Half Dome.** The best way to experience Yosemite's beauty is on one of its many trails. Enjoy a leisurely stroll around **Mirror Lake,** scale a waterfall on the **Mist Trail,** or test your powers of endurance on the way to **Upper Yosemite Fall.**

schedules of ranger-led walks and talks. The complex includes the **Yosemite Museum** (9am-5pm daily, free), the **Ansel Adams Gallery** (9am-6pm daily summer, 10am-5pm daily winter), and the all-important public restrooms. A short walk from the visitors center leads to the re-created **Indian Village of the Ahwahnee,** home to structures made by the Miwok tribe.

Behind the visitors center, the **Yosemite Theater** (Northside Dr., 7pm daily mid-May-Oct., adults $10, children 12 and under free) presents programs and films, including the **John Muir Performances** starring Lee Stetson, Yosemite's resident actor.

Wawona Visitor Center at Hill's Studio

The **Wawona Visitor Center at Hill's Studio** (Wawona, 209/375-9531, 8:30am-5pm daily May-Oct.) is housed in the former studio and gallery of Thomas Hill, a famous landscape painter from the 1800s. You can see his floor-to-ceiling paintings, gather information, get wilderness permits, and rent bear-proof canisters.

Tuolumne Meadows Visitor Center

The **Tuolumne Meadows Visitor Center** (Tioga Rd., 209/372-0263, 9am-6pm daily late May-late Sept.) is in a rustic building near the campground and Tuolumne Meadows Store. Ranger talks are held in the parking lot through summer. Pick up permits and rent bear canisters at the **Tuolumne Meadows Wilderness Center** (8am-5pm daily mid-May-mid-Oct.) along the road to Tuolumne Meadows Lodge (shuttle stop 3).

SIGHTS

YOSEMITE VALLEY

Bridalveil Fall

Bridalveil Fall (0.5 mi./0.8 km rt., 20 min.) is a 620-foot (189-m) cascade running year-round. Accompanied by a roar, its mist sprays most powerfully in the spring—expect to get wet! By autumn, the waterfall thins. Slated to be rebuilt in 2020 with a new trailhead, boardwalks, interpretive signs, wheelchair accessibility, and viewing areas, the main parking area is at the beginning of the Wawona Road or from Southside Drive east of the junction with Wawona Road.

Yosemite Falls

Yosemite Falls (shuttle stop 6, Northside Dr.) is actually three separate waterfalls—Upper Fall, Lower Fall, and the middle cascades. This dramatic formation together creates one of the highest waterfalls in the world.

MIRROR LAKE

EL CAPITAN

The best time to visit is in **spring,** when snowmelt swells the falls and the thundering water throws mist like rain (bring rain gear!). Walk to **Lower Yosemite Fall** (1 mi./1.6 km rt., 30 min., easy) to enjoy the wondrous views of both Upper and Lower Yosemite Falls.

Mirror Lake

Mirror Lake (shuttle stop 17, end of Southside Dr., no vehicles) offers a stunningly clear reflection of the already spectacular views of Tenaya Canyon and the ubiquitous Half Dome. A short, level **hiking and biking path** (5 mi./8 km rt., 2.5 hr., easy) leads to the lake.

El Capitan

The province of world-class climbers, **El Capitan** (Northside Dr., west of El Capitan Bridge) rises as a massive hunk of Cretaceous granite soaring in vertical cliffs nearly 3,600 feet (1,100 m) above the floor of Yosemite Valley. Most big-wall climbers use ropes and technical gear, but Alex Honnold free-soloed the face, the only person to do so. From **El Capitan picnic area** or roadside pullovers, most visitors prefer to gape with binoculars at climbing teams and the portaledges where they sleep. You can also hear climbers call back and forth. Be cautious about walking to the base without a helmet as rockfall can be dangerous.

WAWONA

The tiny village of **Wawona**, 4 miles (6.4 km) from the South Entrance, is home to a historical district with a hotel and restaurant, outdoor exhibits, and even a golf course.

Pioneer Yosemite History Center

The **Pioneer Yosemite History Center** (open daily year-round) is a rambling outdoor display area with an array of historic vehicles and original buildings from the park. Pass through the covered bridge to an uncrowded stretch of land where informative placards describe the history of Yosemite National Park. In summer, take a 10-minute tour by **horse-drawn carriage** (adults $5, kids $4), or check the *Yosemite Guide* for listings of living-history programs and live demonstrations.

TIOGA ROAD

Tuolumne Meadows

The waving grasses of **Tuolumne Meadows** offer a rare peak at a fragile subalpine meadow that supports a variety of wildlife. Park at the visitors center or Lembert Dome Trailhead (shuttle stop 4 and 6) to walk across the Tuolumne River, past carbonated **Soda Springs,** and see historical **Parsons Memorial Lodge** (1.5 mi./2.4 km rt., 1 hr., easy). The lodge opens 10am-4pm daily

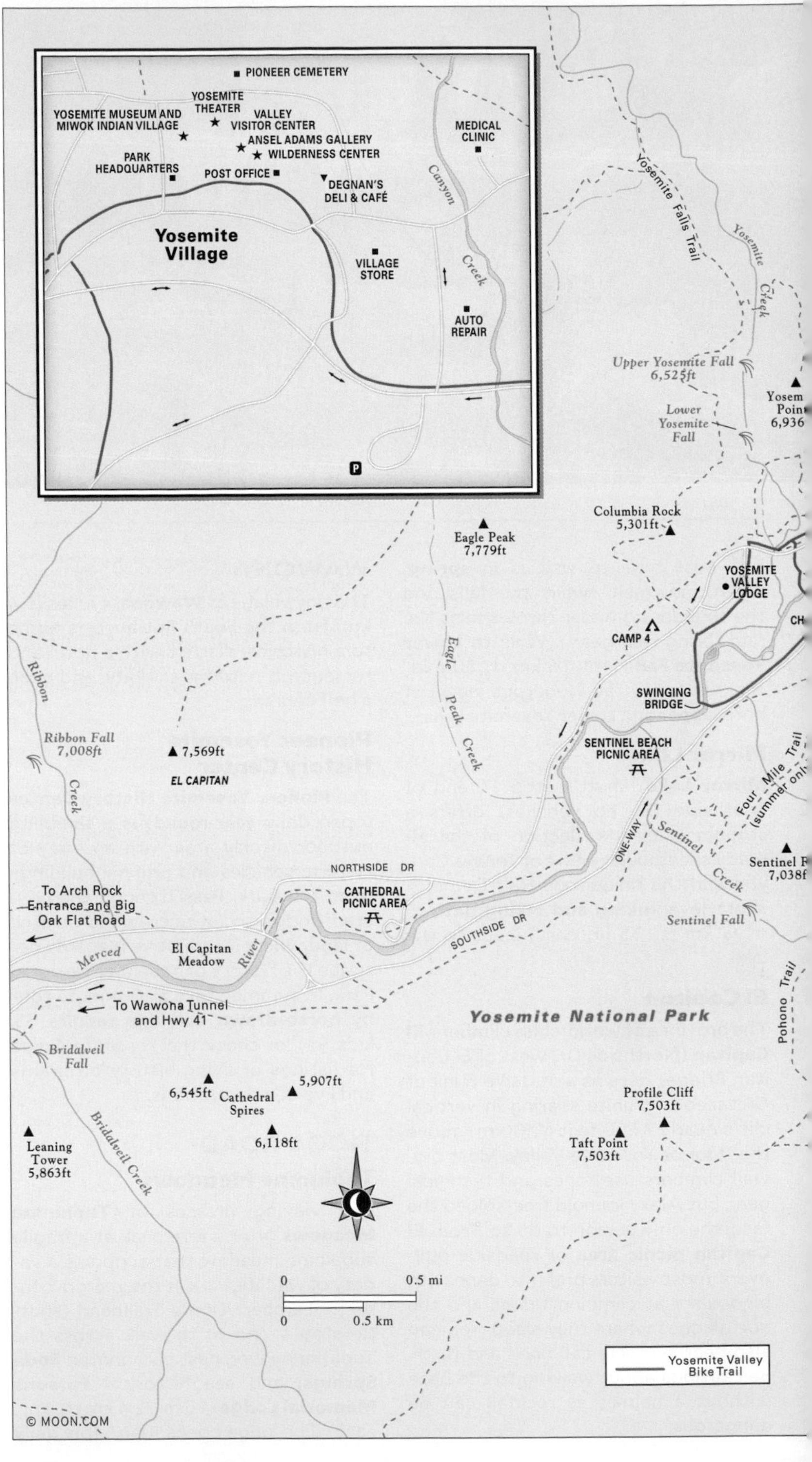
PIONEER CEMETERY
YOSEMITE THEATER
YOSEMITE MUSEUM AND MIWOK INDIAN VILLAGE
VALLEY VISITOR CENTER
ANSEL ADAMS GALLERY
WILDERNESS CENTER
MEDICAL CLINIC
PARK HEADQUARTERS
POST OFFICE
DEGNAN'S DELI & CAFÉ
Canyon
Yosemite Village
VILLAGE STORE
Creek
AUTO REPAIR
Yosemite Falls Trail
Yosemite
Creek
Upper Yosemite Fall 6,525ft
Lower Yosemite Fall
Columbia Rock 5,301ft
Eagle Peak 7,779ft
YOSEMITE VALLEY LODGE
CAMP 4
Eagle
Peak
Creek
SWINGING BRIDGE
SENTINEL BEACH PICNIC AREA
Ribbon
Ribbon Fall 7,008ft
7,569ft
EL CAPITAN
Creek
NORTHSIDE DR
CATHEDRAL PICNIC AREA
ONE-WAY
Sentinel
Creek
Sentinel Fall
To Arch Rock Entrance and Big Oak Flat Road
Merced
El Capitan Meadow
River
SOUTHSIDE DR
To Wawona Tunnel and Hwy 41
Yosemite National Park
Pohono Trail
Bridalveil Fall
6,545ft
Cathedral Spires
5,907ft
6,118ft
Profile Cliff 7,503ft
Taft Point 7,503ft
Leaning Tower 5,863ft
Bridalveil Creek
0
0.5 mi
0
0.5 km
Yosemite Valley Bike Trail
© MOON.COM

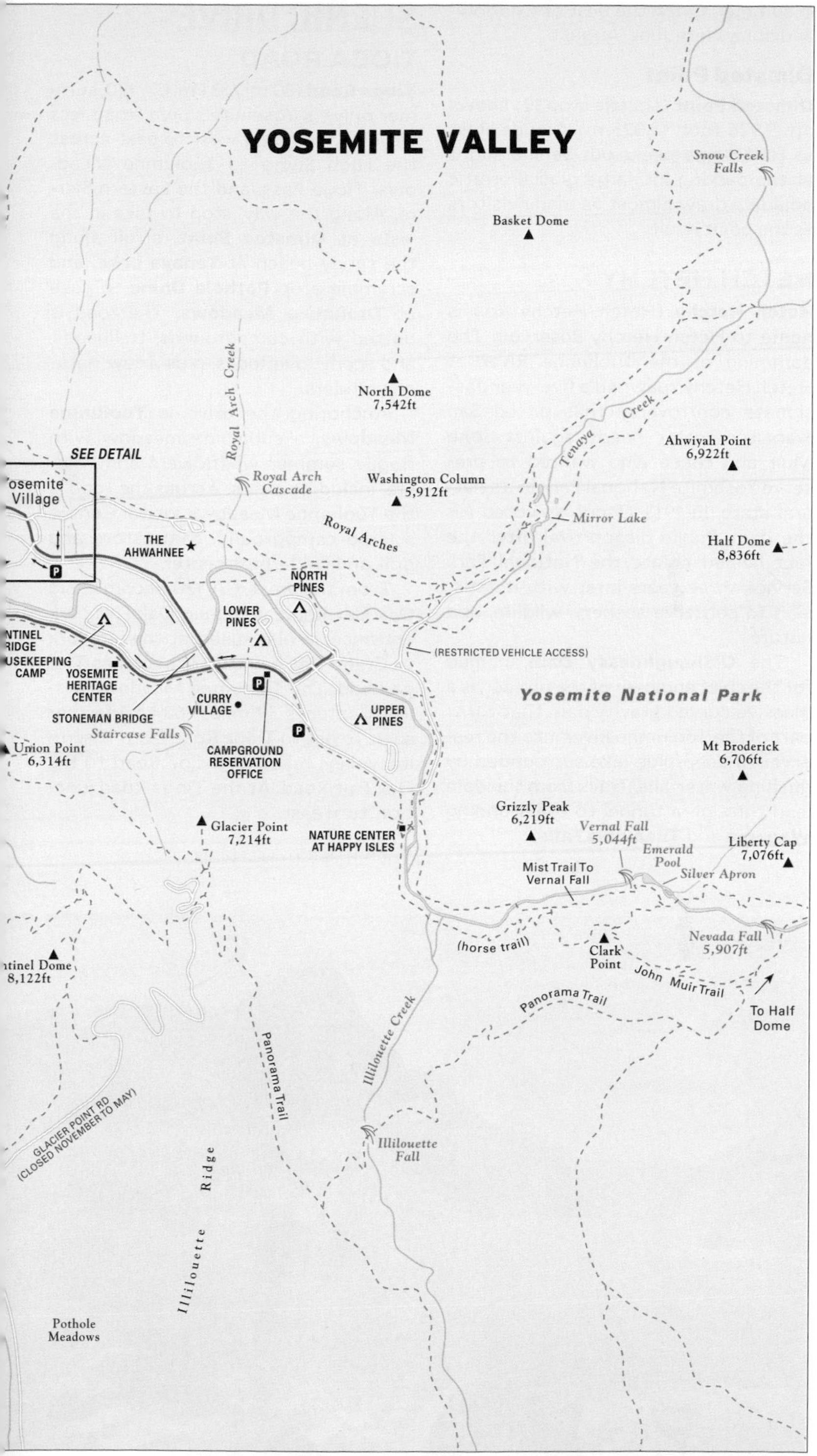
YOSEMITE VALLEY
Snow Creek Falls
Basket Dome
North Dome 7,542ft
Royal Arch Creek
Tenaya Creek
Ahwiyah Point 6,922ft
SEE DETAIL
osemite Village
Royal Arch Cascade
Washington Column 5,912ft
Mirror Lake
Royal Arches
Half Dome 8,836ft
THE AHWAHNEE
NORTH PINES
LOWER PINES
NTINEL IDGE
USEKEEPING CAMP
YOSEMITE HERITAGE CENTER
(RESTRICTED VEHICLE ACCESS)
Yosemite National Park
CURRY VILLAGE
UPPER PINES
STONEMAN BRIDGE
Staircase Falls
Union Point 6,314ft
CAMPGROUND RESERVATION OFFICE
Mt Broderick 6,706ft
Grizzly Peak 6,219ft
Glacier Point 7,214ft
NATURE CENTER AT HAPPY ISLES
Vernal Fall 5,044ft
Emerald Pool
Liberty Cap 7,076ft
Mist Trail To Vernal Fall
Silver Apron
Nevada Fall 5,907ft
(horse trail)
Clark Point
tinel Dome 8,122ft
John Muir Trail
Panorama Trail
To Half Dome
Illilouette Creek
Panorama Trail
GLACIER POINT RD (CLOSED NOVEMBER TO MAY)
Illilouette Fall
Illilouette Ridge
Pothole Meadows

in summer. Catch the best of wildflower displays late June-August.

Olmsted Point

Olmsted Point (shuttle stop 12) shows off 9,926-foot (3,025-m) Clouds Rest as Half Dome peeks out behind. Right at the parking lot, large glacial erratic boulders draw almost as many visitors as the point itself.

HETCH HETCHY

Hetch Hetchy (Hetch Hetchy Rd.) is home to Hetch Hetchy Reservoir. The damming of the Tuolumne River at Hetch Hetchy spawned a five-year passionate controversy that pitted San Francisco water needs against John Muir and those who wanted to preserve Yosemite National Park in its natural state. In 1913, Congress voted for the dam. Public disapproval after the fact helped create the National Park Service three years later with its mission to conserve scenery, wildlife, and nature.

The **O'Shaughnessy Dam**, named for the chief engineer of the project, is a massive curved gravity dam that turns part of the Tuolumne River into the reservoir, a deep-blue lake surrounded by gushing waterfalls. Trails from the dam lead through a tunnel to the stunning **Wapama** and **Tueeulala Falls.**

SCENIC DRIVE

TIOGA ROAD

Tioga Road (39 mi./63 km, CA 120, summer only) is Yosemite's own "road less traveled," winding west to east across the High Sierra to Tuolumne Meadows, Tioga Pass, and the Eastern Sierra. Along the way, stop to take in the vista at **Olmsted Point,** stroll along the sandy beach at **Tenaya Lake,** and scramble atop **Pothole Dome** to gaze at **Tuolumne Meadows.** The road is dotted with campgrounds, trailheads, and scenic overlooks, plus a few natural wonders.

Anchoring the drive is **Tuolumne Meadows,** a subalpine meadow with fragile summer wildflowers and wildlife, including bears. Across the road is the Tuolumne Meadows Visitor Center, a large campground, camp store and grill, and wilderness center.

From the west, CA 120 becomes Big Oak Flat Road at the Big Oak Flat park entrance. In nine miles, at the left fork to Crane Flat junction, it becomes Tioga Road. The Tuolumne Meadows Visitor Center is 39 miles (63 km) farther east. To get to Tioga Road from Yosemite Valley, take Northside Road to Big Oak Flat Road. At the Tioga Road junction, turn east.

▾ HETCH HETCHY RESERVOIR

TUOLUMNE MEADOWS

HIKING

YOSEMITE VALLEY

Cook's Meadow

Soak in quintessential Yosemite Valley views from **Cook's Meadow Loop** (1 mi./ 1.6 km rt., 30 min., easy, shuttle stop 5 or 9). From the trailhead at the visitors center, you'll observe Ansel Adams's famous view of Half Dome from Sentinel Bridge and also the **Royal Arches** and Glacier Point. You can extend the hike into a bigger loop (2.25 mi./3.6 km rt., 1 hr.) by circling both Cook's and Sentinel Meadows. Trail signs, and the plethora of other hikers, make it easy to find the turns.

Upper Yosemite Fall

One of the most strenuous, yet most rewarding, treks is **Upper Yosemite Fall** (7.2 mi./11.6 km rt., 6-8 hrs., shuttle stop 7). From the trailhead at Camp 4, the climb steepens right away—2,700 vertical feet (823 m) in just three miles. For a shorter climb with plenty of switchbacks, you'll reach **Columbia Rock** (2 mi./3.2 km rt., 1,000 vertical ft./305 m, 2-3 hours), with plummeting views of the valley below. Continuing farther up about 0.75 mile, you can grab a good view of Upper Yosemite Fall after two downhill switchbacks lead to a traverse along a sparsely treed ledge that heads toward the fall's base. Turning north and climbing back into the forest, the wet, slippery trail assumes a stack of relentless stone-step switchbacks with occasional railings to reach the lip of the fall. Bring plenty of water and snacks to replenish energy for the potentially tricky climb down.

GLACIER POINT

The road to Glacier Point is open late May-November, depending on snow. For one-way hikes from Glacier Point to the valley floor, make shuttle reservations with **Glacier Point Tour** (888/413-8869, www.travelyosemite.com). Reconstruction will close the road in 2021, but you can still hike trails up to Glacier Point and back from the valley floor.

Sentinel Dome and Taft Point

A choice of two spectacular viewpoints 2,000 feet (610 m) above the valley floor await from the trailhead 1 mile (1.6 km) west of Glacier Point. At the junction shortly after starting, turn right to walk through the forest to **Sentinel Dome** (2.2 mi./3.5 km rt., 2-3 hrs., moderate). Below the dome, a spur trail departs left for a steep but quick climb to the top. To go instead to **Taft Point** (2 mi./3.2 km rt., 1 hr., moderate), go left at the first junction after the trailhead to pop over a small hill and descend to the point. You'll see unusual rock formations en route, fissures at the point, and stare straight across at El Capitan.

Best Hike

MIST TRAIL

DISTANCE: 2.4-5.4 miles (3.9-8.7 km) round-trip
DURATION: 3-6 hours
ELEVATION CHANGE: 1,050-2,000 feet (320-610 m)
EFFORT: moderate
TRAILHEAD: Happy Isles

From the Happy Isles Nature Center (shuttle stop 16), the moderately strenuous **Mist Trail** climbs over steep, slick granite—including more than 600 stairs, most of which are wet with mist—to the top of **Vernal Fall** (2.4 mi./3.9 km rt., 3 hrs.). In spring and June, bring rain jackets and pants to avoid getting drenched. From lip of the fall, views take in the valley below where mist can create a rainbow. Climb another two miles of switchbacks to the top of **Nevada Fall** (5.4 mi./8.7 km rt., 5-6 hrs.) and return via the **John Muir Trail.** This popular trail is **closed in winter** due to ice and snow and can be dangerous in spring, when the river is at its peak. To get here, park in the day-use parking lot at Curry Village and board the free Yosemite Valley shuttle bus to Happy Isles.

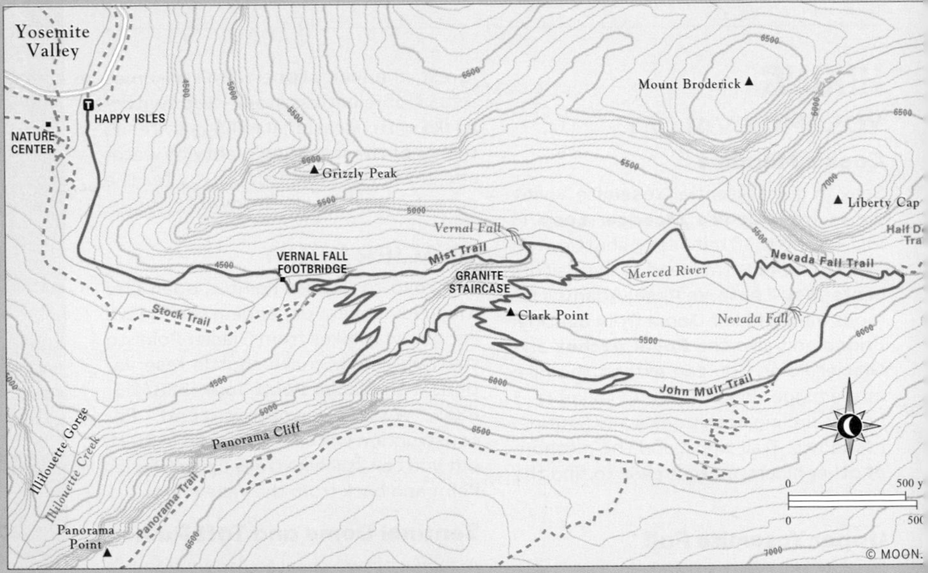

HIKING IN YOSEMITE'S HIGH SIERRA

Panorama Trail

The **Panorama Trail** (8.5 mi./13.6 km one-way, 6-8 hrs., strenuous) runs from the Glacier Point Trailhead to Yosemite Valley, with a 700-foot (213-m) ascent and a 3,200-foot (975-m) descent. Along the way, you'll see Illilouette Fall and Panorama Point, with views of Half Dome, Upper and Lower Yosemite Falls, and a sweeping vista of Yosemite Valley. The route finishes on the Mist Trail, picking up at Nevada and Vernal Falls.

VERNAL FALL, MIST TRAIL

Four-Mile Trail

Take a shuttle to Glacier Point to descend to Yosemite Valley via the **Four-Mile Trail** (4.8 mi./7.7 km one-way, 3-4 hrs., strenuous). The climb down affords views of Yosemite Falls and the valley that grow more impressive with each switchback.

WAWONA

Mariposa Grove of Giant Sequoias

From the Mariposa Grove parking area near the South Entrance, hop the free wheelchair-accessible shuttle bus (8am-8pm, hours shorten spring and late fall, mid-Mar.-Nov., depending on weather) to reach the trailhead for this famous grove of giant sequoias. Parking usually fills by midmorning, but cars are allowed in as spaces free up. Bicyclists can ride and drivers with disability placards can drive up to the grove trailhead where **Big Trees Loop** (0.3 mi /0.5 km rt., 45 min., easy) is wheelchair accessible. **Grizzly Giant Loo**p (2 mi./3.2 km rt., 1.5 hrs., moderate) climbs to the famous California Tunnel Tree and 3,000-year-old Grizzly Giant. The **Guardians Loop** (6.5 mi./10.5 km rt., 4 hrs., strenuous) takes in parts of the lower loops and climbs farther to Telescope Tree and Wawona Tunnel Tree.

TUOLUMNE MEADOWS AND TIOGA PASS

When Tioga Road opens (late May-June, depending on snow), the **Tuolumne Meadows Hikers Bus** (mid-June-mid-Sept., $2-23) offers car-free access to some trailheads.

Tenaya Lake

You can see the water from Tioga Road, but the loop trail around **Tenaya Lake** (2.5 mi./4 km rt., 1.5 hrs., easy, shuttle stop 9) takes you to sunny beaches on the east end and possibly the most picturesque views in all of Yosemite. The only difficult part is fording the chilly and sometimes deep outlet stream at the west end of the lake.

May Lake and Mount Hoffman

May Lake (2.4 mi./3.9 km rt., 1 hr., moderate, shuttle stop 11) sits peacefully at the base of the sloping granite of Mount Hoffman. The trail up to the lake gains a steady and steep 500 feet (153 m). For energetic hikers, a more difficult trail grunts 2,000 feet (610 m) higher to the top of **Mount Hoffman** (6 mi./9.7 km rt., 3-4 hrs., strenuous). Much of this walk is along granite slabs and rocky paths, but you'll have clear views of Cathedral Peak, Mount Clark, Half Dome, and Clouds Rest.

▼ FALLEN MONARCH IN MARIPOSA GROVE

TENAYA LAKE

North Dome

For an unusual look at a Yosemite classic, take the **North Dome Trail** (9 mi./14.5 km rt., 4-5 hrs., strenuous) from the trailhead at Porcupine Creek through the woods and out to the dome. Getting to stare right at the face of Half Dome and Clouds Rest at what feels like eye level makes the effort worth it.

Clouds Rest

Strong hikers often prefer **Clouds Rest** (14.5 mi./23 km rt., 7 hrs., strenuous, shuttle stop 10) to Half Dome due to fewer people, no permits, less elevation gain, and a higher summit. The 1,775 vertical feet (540 m) packs into switchbacks about 30 minutes into the hike. At Clouds Rest, stupendous 360-degree views take in the plunge to Yosemite Valley surrounded by North Dome, Sentinel Dome, and Half Dome. You can hone your binoculars on climbers on the cables.

Cathedral Lakes

The trail to **Cathedral Lakes** (7 mi./11.3 km rt., 4-6 hrs., strenuous, shuttle stop 7) climbs more than 800 feet (244 m) to picture-perfect lakes that show off crystalline waters, surrounding lodgepole pines, and dramatic alpine peaks. You'll encounter backpackers as the route is part of the John Muir Trail. These high-elevation lakes may test your lung capacity, but will reward with Instagram pictures.

Gaylor Lakes

From the Tioga Pass Entrance, the less crowded **Gaylor Lakes Trail** (3 mi./4.8 km rt., 2 hrs., easy) starts at a thin-air 10,000 feet (3,048 m) and climbs a steep 600 vertical feet (180 m) up the pass to the Gaylor Lakes valley. Once in the valley, you can wander around five lovely lakes, stopping to admire the mountain views or visit the abandoned 1870s mine site above Upper Gaylor Lake.

HETCH HETCHY

Wapama and Tueeulala Falls

Begin the hike to thundering **Wapama Falls** (5 mi./8 km rt., 2 hrs., moderate) by crossing O'Shaughnessy Dam, then following the Wapama Falls Trail through a tunnel and along the shore of the reservoir. Along the way, the ribbon **Tueeulala Falls** plunges from cliffs above.

CLIMBERS ON EL CAPITAN

RECREATION

BACKPACKING

Yosemite has bucket list backpacking routes, including the north end of the 210-mile (340-km) **John Muir Trail** and 70 miles (113 km) of the **Pacific Crest Trail.** A **wilderness permit** ($5 reservation, $5 pp) is required. Reserve a permit in advance online or pick up first-come, first-served permits one day in advance at a permit issuing station. Bear canisters are required.

Yosemite's **High Sierra Camps** (888/413-8869, www.travelyosemite.com, July-early Sept.) offer tent cabins with amenities, breakfast and dinner in camp, and a sack lunch. Stay at **Merced Lake, Vogelsang, Glen Aulin, May Lake,** or **Sunrise Camp**—or visit all the camps in one 49-mile (78.8 km) loop. Reservations are by lottery; applications are accepted in October for the following summer.

ROCK CLIMBING

El Capitan boasts a reputation as one of the world's seminal big-face climbs, a challenge that draws experienced rock climbers. But Yosemite also has other significant rock faces for climbers. For gear rental and guided rock climbing, use **Yosemite Mountaineering School** (209/372-8344, www.travelyosemite.com, 8:30am daily Mar.-Nov.). They also have beginner, intermediate, and advanced rock climbing classes for adults and children.

BICYCLING

Yosemite Valley has 12 miles (19 km) of paved bike trails, mostly scenic areas on the Valley Loop Trail. Bicycles can also use the road, especially routes closed to cars at the east end of the valley. **Rentals** (www.travelyosemite.com, 10am-6pm) are available at **Yosemite Valley Lodge** (209/372-1208, mid-Apr.-mid-Nov.) and **Curry Village** (209/372-8323, mid-Apr.-Oct.). Glacier Point Road allows bicycles for a few days each May before opening to vehicles.

HORSEBACK RIDING

Big Trees Lodge Stable (Pioneer Yosemite History Center, Wawona Rd., 209/375-6502, www.travelyosemite.com, 7am-5pm daily mid-May-Sept.) has sedate two-hour horseback rides on a historical wagon trail. More strenuous trips go into the mountains. Reservations are recommended.

WINTER SPORTS

Yosemite Ski & Snowboard Area (Glacier Point Rd., 209/372-8430, www.travelyosemite.com, 9am-4pm daily mid-Dec.-Mar.) has rentals, lessons, and plenty of beginner downhill ski runs with enough intermediate runs to keep it interesting. The **Cross-Country Ski School** runs classes, rents gear, and guides cross-country ski tours, including an overnight trip to **Glacier Point Ski Hut.** A free **shuttle** runs between Yosemite Valley and the ski area twice daily in season.

THE AHWAHNEE HOTEL

Curry Village (Southside Dr., 209/372-8333, 3:30pm-9pm Mon.-Fri., noon-9:30pm Sat.-Sun. mid-Nov.-mid-Mar.) has an outdoor ice-skating rink in winter with skate rentals.

WHERE TO STAY

INSIDE THE PARK

All Yosemite lodgings book quickly—up to one year in advance. Lodging **reservations** (888/413-8869, www.travelyosemite.com) for overnight accommodations are essential. Rates vary seasonally.

Yosemite Valley

Yosemite Valley is where everyone wants to be: It has the most services, lodging options, campgrounds, and restaurants.

Yosemite Valley Lodge (shuttle stop 8, year-round, from $278) has motel-style rooms and lodge rooms with king beds and balconies overlooking the valley. Enjoy the heated pool in the summer and free shuttles to the Glacier Point ski area in winter. Food services include the **Mountain Room Restaurant** (5pm-8pm daily), **Mountain Room Lounge** (4:30pm-11pm Mon.-Fri., noon-11pm Sat.-Sun.), and **Base Camp Eatery** (6:30am-9:30pm daily).

Built as a luxury hotel in the early 1900s, **The Ahwahnee** (shuttle stop 3, year-round, from $518), formerly the Yosemite Majestic Hotel, includes cottages and hotel rooms dripping with sumptuous appointments and Native American decor. A bonus is the elegant **Dining Room** (7am-10am, 11:30am-3pm, and 5:30pm-9pm Mon.-Sat., 7am-3pm and 5:30pm-9pm Sun.) with expansive ceilings, wrought-iron chandeliers, and a stellar valley view. Make reservations for all meals; dinner attire is resort style (long pants, collared shirts or blouses, dresses).

Curry Village (shuttle stop 13, Mar.-Nov. and Dec.-Jan., Sat.-Sun. Jan.-Mar., from $145), formerly Half Dome Village, has more rustic options. Canvas tent cabins come with or without heat and shared community bathrooms. The **Yosemite Cabins** and **Stoneman Cottage** rooms have heat, private baths, and daily cleaning service. The three-sided tent cabins at **Housekeeping Camp** have cement walls, white canvas roofs, and a white canvas curtain separating the bedroom from a covered patio and shared community baths.

In Curry Village, the Curry **Village Pavilion** (7am-10am and 5:30pm-8:30pm mid-April-Oct.) serves breakfast and dinner. Other eateries include the

CURRY VILLAGE

Coffee Corner (6am-11pm daily Apr.-Nov.), **Curry Village Bar** (11am-10pm daily May-Oct.), **Pizza Patio** (11am-10pm daily Apr.-Nov.), and **Meadow Grill** (11am-8pm daily summer).

Yosemite Village has no lodgings, only dining options. **The Loft at Degnan's** (11:30am-9pm daily year-round) serves pizza, Mexican fare, and Asian rice bowls. **Degnan's Kitchen** (7am-6pm daily year-round) has sandwiches, salads, and baked goods. The **Village Grill Deck** (11am-6pm daily Mar.-Oct.) has standard burgers and grilled food.

Wawona

Formerly the Big Trees Lodge, the **Wawona Hotel** (Apr.-Nov. and mid-Dec.-early Jan., from $150) opened in 1879 and still maintains its white-washed look and historic charm. Rooms (with bath and without) come with Victorian wallpaper, antique furniture, and a lack of in-room TVs and telephones. In summer, the lodge runs shuttles to the Mariposa Grove Trailhead for guests.

The **dining room** (209/375-1425, 7am-10am, 11am-3pm, and 5pm-9pm) serves upscale California cuisine. Reservations are not accepted, so expect to wait for a table on weekends and in summer. The common area offers seating, drinks, and live piano (Tues.-Sat.).

Tuolumne Meadows and Tioga Pass

White Wolf Lodge (White Wolf Rd. off Tioga Rd., mid-June-Sept., from $125) rents 24 heated canvas tent cabins and four wood cabins. The wood cabins include a private bath, limited electricity, and daily cleaning service, while the tent cabins share a central restroom and shower facility; all cabins include linens and towels. Amenities are few, but the scenery is breathtaking.

Tuolumne Meadows Lodge (Tioga Rd., early June-mid-Sept., from $125) offers charming wood-frame tent cabins with no electricity in a gorgeous subalpine meadow setting. Central facilities include restrooms, hot showers, and a **dining room** (209/372-8413, breakfast and dinner daily early June-mid-Sept.); dinner reservations are required.

Camping

Campground reservations (877/444-6777, www.recreation.gov, $26-50) are imperative. At 7am (Pacific time) on the 15th of each month, campsites become available for booking five months in advance. If you need a reservation for a specific day, get up early to call or check online diligently starting at 7am. If you're in the valley and don't have a campsite reservation, call the **campground**

status line (209/372-0266) for a recording of what's available that day.

Yosemite Valley has three ultrapopular campgrounds with fierce competition for reservations: **Upper Pines** (238 sites), **Lower Pines** (60 sites), and **North Pines** (81 sites). Competition for the first-come, first-served sites at **Camp 4** (35 shared walk-in sites, tents only) is heavy spring-fall; a line forms long before the 8:30am registration at the kiosk opens.

Bridalveil Creek Campground (110 sites, first come, first served) is midway up Glacier Point Road, a 45-minute drive from the valley. Its location along Bridalveil Creek makes it an appealing spot.

North of Wawona, the forested **Wawona Campground** (93 sites) has scenic sites along the Tuolumne River. Reservations are accepted April-September (sites are first come, first served Oct.-Mar.).

Along Tioga Road, campgrounds for **Crane Flat** (166 sites), **Hodgdon Meadow** (105 sites, reservations accepted mid-Apr.-mid-Oct.), and **Tuolumne Meadows** (304 sites) book far in advance for summer. The remaining campgrounds are first come, first served: **Tamarack Flat** (52 sites), **White Wolf** (74 sites), **Yosemite Creek** (75 sites), and **Porcupine Flat** (52 sites).

OUTSIDE THE PARK

Gateway towns cluster the park entrances, offering accommodations, campgrounds, dining, and services. **Groveland** (CA 120) is 24 miles (39 km) from the Big Oak Flat Entrance. One mile (1.6 km) outside the Hetch Hetchy Entrance, the **Evergreen Lodge** (33160 Evergreen Rd., Groveland, 209/379-2606, www.evergreenlodge.com) rents cabins.

El Portal (CA 140) is less than 4 miles (6.4 km) from the Arch Rock Entrance and 15 miles (24 km) from Yosemite Valley, making it one of the closest places to overnight. **Mariposa** (CA 140) lies about 30 miles (48 km) from the Arch Rock Entrance and about 40 miles (64 km) from Yosemite Valley.

Oakhurst (CA 41) lies 16 miles from the South Entrance. **Fish Camp** (CA 41) is 40 miles (64 km) from Yosemite Valley via the South Entrance, a little over an hour's drive.

The resort town of **Mammoth Lakes** (U.S. 395) has upscale lodging 40 minutes south of Yosemite's east entrance. YARTS shuttles run from Mammoth into the park.

GETTING THERE

AIR

The closest international airports are **San Francisco International Airport** (SFO, US 101, San Mateo, 650/821-8211

1: HALF DOME FROM SENTINEL BRIDGE
2: SEQUOIAS IN MARIPOSA GROVE
3: TAFT POINT

NAME	LOCATION	PRICE	SEASON	AMENITIES
Camp 4	Yosemite Valley	$6pp + $10 lottery fee	year-round	tent sites
Upper Pines	Yosemite Valley	$26	year-round	tent and RV sites
North and Lower Pines	Yosemite Valley	$26	Mar.-Nov.	tent and RV sites
Curry Village	Yosemite Valley	$145 and up	year-round	motel rooms, wooden cabins, tent cabins, dining
Housekeeping Camp	Yosemite Valley	$90	Apr.-Oct.	duplex camp units, showers
Yosemite Valley Lodge	Yosemite Valley	from $278	year-round	hotel rooms, dining
The Ahwahnee Hotel	Yosemite Valley	from $518	year-round	hotel rooms, cottages, suites, dining
Bridalveil Creek	Wawona	$18	July-Sept.	tent and RV sites
Wawona	Wawona	$26	year-round	tent and RV sites
Wawona Hotel	Wawona	$150	Apr.-Dec.	hotel rooms, dining
Tamarack Flat	Tuolumne Meadows	$12	June-Oct.	tent sites
Yosemite Creek	Tuolumne Meadows	$12	June-Sept.	tent sites
Porcupine Flat	Tuolumne Meadows	$12	July-Oct.	tent and RV sites
White Wolf	Tuolumne Meadows	$18	June-Sept.	tent and RV sites
Hodgdon Meadow	Tuolumne Meadows	$26	year-round	tent and RV sites
Crane Flat	Tuolumne Meadows	$26	July-Oct.	tent and RV sites
Tuolumne Meadows	Tuolumne Meadows	$26	June-Sept.	tent and RV sites
White Wolf Lodge	Tuolumne Meadows	$125	June-Sept.	wooden cabins, tent cabins, dining
Tuolumne Meadows Lodge	Tuolumne Meadows	$125	June-Sept.	tent cabins, dining

ARCH ROCK ENTRANCE

or 800/435-9736, www.flysfo.com), **Oakland International Airport** (OAK, 1 Airport Dr., 510/563-3300, www.oaklandairport.com), **Sacramento International Airport** (SMF, 6900 Airport Blvd., 916/929-5411, www.sacramento.aero/smf), and **Reno-Tahoe International Airport** (RNO, 2001 E. Plumb Ln., Reno, NV, 775/328-6400, www.renoairport.com). Car rentals are available at all airports.

CAR

From the San Francisco Bay Area, it's a 4-5-hour drive to the park's west entrances of Arch Rock and Big Oak Flat for the quickest access to Yosemite Valley. Take I-580 east and continue east to I-205 and I-5 near Manteca. From Manteca, follow CA 120 east through Groveland and the **Big Oak Flat Entrance** on the west side of the park. From Big Oak Flat, it's a 45-minute drive to Yosemite Valley.

Alternatively, from I-5 south take CA 140 east through Merced to reach the **Arch Rock Entrance.** From Arch Rock, it's a 30-minute drive to the valley. This is the **most popular and most crowded entrance** to Yosemite Valley. Plan to arrive before 9am or after 5pm to avoid long entrance lines.

◂ DOGWOOD IN SPRING, YOSEMITE VALLEY

From points south, enter the park through the **South Entrance** via CA 41, a 1.5-hour drive north from Fresno. In 4 miles (6.4 km), CA 41 becomes Wawona Road. From Wawona, it's another 1.5 hours to Yosemite Valley.

TRAIN AND BUS

From San Francisco or Sacramento, **Amtrak** (www.amtrak.com) connects with Merced and Fresno, where **buses** with the **Yosemite Area Regional Transportation System** (YARTS, 877/989-2787, www.yarts.com) travel the final stretch into the park. You can buy tickets on the bus; no reservations are necessary. Buses run more frequently in summer. From **Merced,** YARTS buses goes to Yosemite Valley, where free shuttles circle the valley. From **Fresno,** YARTS buses go to the South Entrance of Yosemite.

GETTING AROUND

DRIVING

Driving in **Yosemite Valley** can be a crowded, congested experience. Parking lots and roadside pullouts fill early. Plan to arrive by 9am and leave your car in one of the three parking lots (Yosemite Village, Yosemite Falls, Curry Village), and then navigate the valley via the park's free shuttle.

EL CAPITAN

There are no **gas stations** in Yosemite Valley. The closest stations are in El Portal and at Crane Flat.

Glacier Point Road

Glacier Point is about an hour's drive from Yosemite Valley. From the Valley Visitor Center, drive 14 miles (23 km) south to Chinquapin junction and turn left onto **Glacier Point Road** (closed Nov.-May) for 16 miles (26 km). In winter (Dec.-Mar.), the first 5 miles (8 km) of the road are plowed up to Badger Pass Ski Area; chains may be required. Reconstruction from Badger Pass to Glacier Point will close the road during 2021 and cause delays in 2022.

Tioga Road

Tioga Road (CA 120) stretches from Crane Flat east to Tioga Pass, the east entrance to the park, where it becomes Tioga Pass Road. **The road is open only in summer.** To check weather conditions and road closures, call 209/372-0200. When the road is closed, there is no access to Tuolumne Meadows.

SHUTTLE BUS

In summer—especially on weekends—traffic and parking in Yosemite Valley can be stressful. Park your car at the Yosemite Village day-use lot and use the **Yosemite Valley shuttle** (7am-10pm daily year-round, free) to get around. Shuttles run every 10-20 minutes, stopping at Yosemite Valley Lodge, Valley Visitor Center, Curry Village, all campgrounds, and Happy Isles Trailhead.

The **Glacier Point Tour** (888/413-8869, www.travelyosemite.com, 8:30am and 1:30pm daily May-Nov., $26-52) meets at Yosemite Valley Lodge to travel to Glacier Point Road when the road is open. This tour will not operate in 2021 when the road is closed for reconstruction.

The summer-only **Tuolumne Meadows Hikers Bus** (209/372-1240, mid-June-Sept., $2-23) runs along Tioga Road between Olmsted Point and the Tuolumne Meadows Lodge. Service varies seasonally.

The **Mariposa Shuttle** (8am-8pm, hours shorten spring and late fall, mid-Mar.-Nov., depending on weather, free) goes from the Mariposa parking area to the grove trailhead.

SIGHTS NEARBY

Mono Lake (CA 120 and US 395, www.monolake.org), east of Tioga Pass, is a saline and alkaline lake with strange-looking tufa towers. The 1-mile (1.6-km) interpretive South Tufa Trail ($3) winds through spectacular limestone towers that originally formed underwater.

SEQUOIA AND KINGS CANYON

California

KEEPSAKE STAMPS ▼▼▼

WEBSITE:
www.nps.gov/seki

PHONE NUMBER:
559/565-3341

VISITATION RANK:
22 (Sequoia) and
34 (Kings Canyon)

WHY GO:
Explore giant sequoias, underground caves, and scenic byways.

▲ SEQUOIA NATIONAL PARK

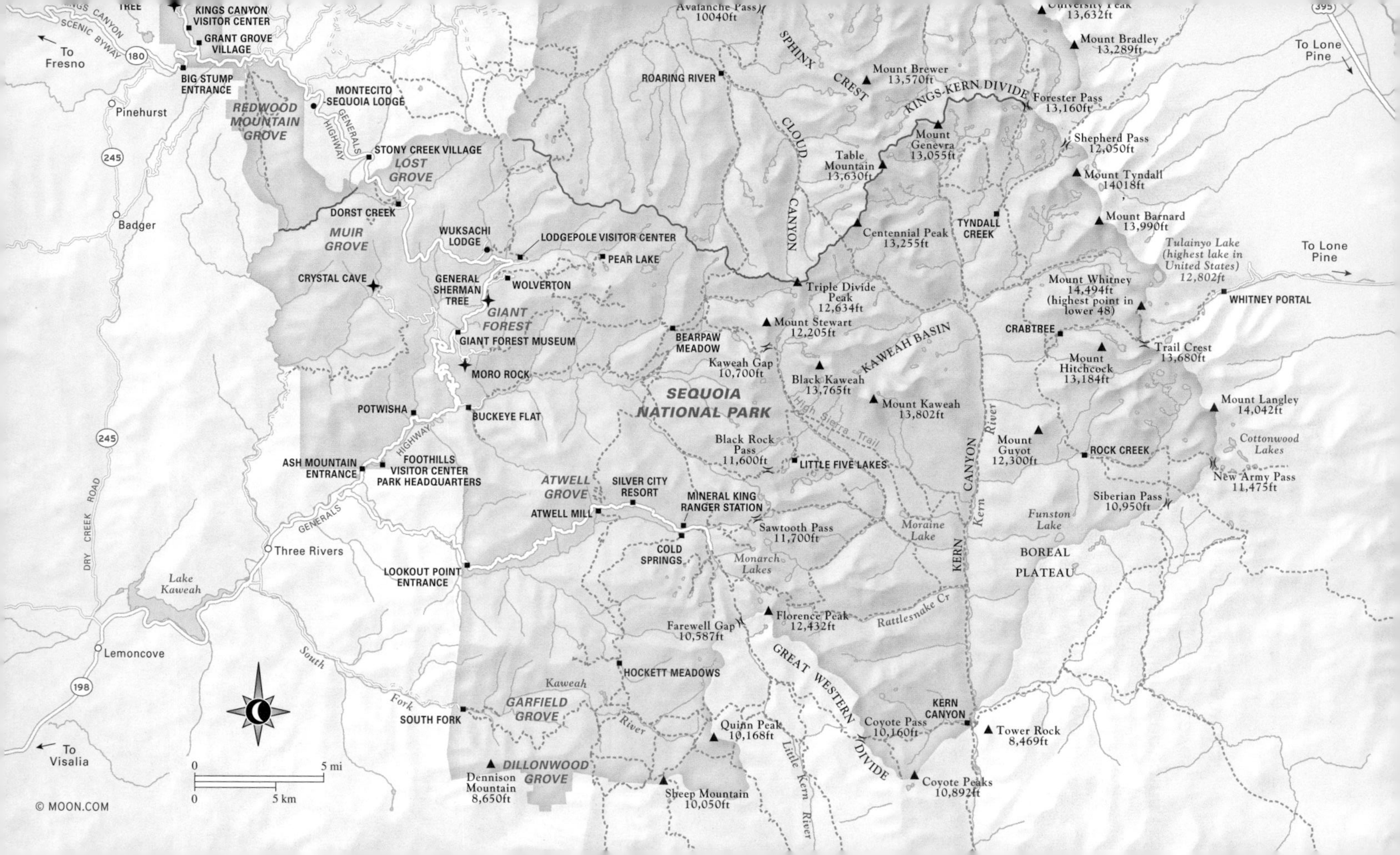

KINGS CANYON VISITOR CENTER
GRANT GROVE VILLAGE
SCENIC BYWAY
180
To Fresno
BIG STUMP ENTRANCE
MONTECITO SEQUOIA LODGE
REDWOOD MOUNTAIN GROVE
GENERALS HIGHWAY
Pinehurst
245
STONY CREEK VILLAGE
LOST GROVE
DORST CREEK
Badger
MUIR GROVE
WUKSACHI LODGE
LODGEPOLE VISITOR CENTER
PEAR LAKE
CRYSTAL CAVE
GENERAL SHERMAN TREE
WOLVERTON
GIANT FOREST
GIANT FOREST MUSEUM
MORO ROCK
POTWISHA
BUCKEYE FLAT
ASH MOUNTAIN ENTRANCE
FOOTHILLS VISITOR CENTER PARK HEADQUARTERS
HIGHWAY
ATWELL GROVE
SILVER CITY RESORT
ATWELL MILL
MINERAL KING RANGER STATION
GENERALS
DRY CREEK ROAD
Three Rivers
COLD SPRINGS
LOOKOUT POINT ENTRANCE
Lake Kaweah
Lemoncove
198
To Visalia
South Fork
SOUTH FORK
Kaweah River
GARFIELD GROVE
HOCKETT MEADOWS
DILLONWOOD GROVE
Dennison Mountain 8,650ft
Sheep Mountain 10,050ft
Quinn Peak 10,168ft
Farewell Gap 10,587ft
0 5 mi
0 5 km
© MOON.COM
Avalanche Pass 10040ft
ROARING RIVER
SPHINX CREST
CLOUD CANYON
Mount Brewer 13,570ft
KINGS-KERN DIVIDE
Forester Pass 13,160ft
University Peak 13,632ft
Mount Bradley 13,289ft
395
To Lone Pine
Mount Genevra 13,055ft
Table Mountain 13,630ft
Shepherd Pass 12,050ft
Mount Tyndall 14018ft
TYNDALL CREEK
Centennial Peak 13,255ft
Mount Barnard 13,990ft
Tulainyo Lake (highest lake in United States) 12,802ft
To Lone Pine
Triple Divide Peak 12,634ft
Mount Whitney 14,494ft (highest point in lower 48)
WHITNEY PORTAL
Mount Stewart 12,205ft
BEARPAW MEADOW
KAWEAH BASIN
CRABTREE
Trail Crest 13,680ft
Kaweah Gap 10,700ft
Black Kaweah 13,765ft
Mount Hitchcock 13,184ft
SEQUOIA NATIONAL PARK
High Sierra Trail
Mount Kaweah 13,802ft
Mount Langley 14,042ft
Black Rock Pass 11,600ft
LITTLE FIVE LAKES
Mount Guyot 12,300ft
ROCK CREEK
Cottonwood Lakes
New Army Pass 11,475ft
Kern River
KERN CANYON
Siberian Pass 10,950ft
Sawtooth Pass 11,700ft
Moraine Lake
Funston Lake
Monarch Lakes
BOREAL PLATEAU
Florence Peak 12,432ft
Rattlesnake Cr
GREAT WESTERN DIVIDE
Little Kern River
KERN CANYON
Coyote Pass 10,160ft
Tower Rock 8,469ft
Coyote Peaks 10,892ft

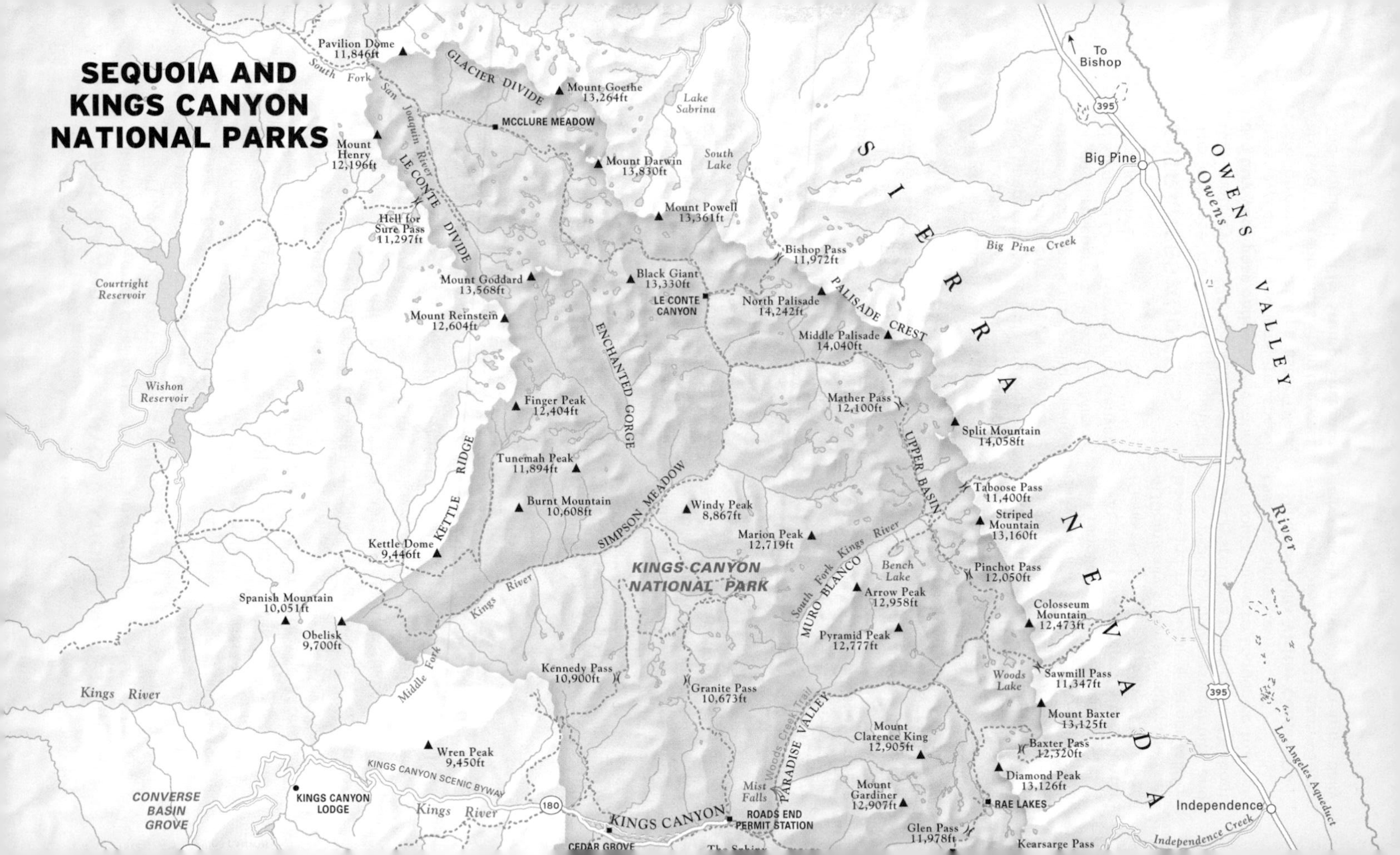
SEQUOIA AND KINGS CANYON NATIONAL PARKS
Pavilion Dome 11,846ft
South Fork
San Joaquin River
GLACIER DIVIDE
Mount Goethe 13,264ft
Lake Sabrina
MCCLURE MEADOW
Mount Henry 12,196ft
LE CONTE DIVIDE
Mount Darwin 13,830ft
South Lake
Hell for Sure Pass 11,297ft
Mount Powell 13,361ft
Bishop Pass 11,972ft
Big Pine Creek
Big Pine
To Bishop
395
Owens
OWENS VALLEY
SIERRA NEVADA
Courtright Reservoir
Mount Goddard 13,568ft
Black Giant 13,330ft
LE CONTE CANYON
North Palisade 14,242ft
PALISADE CREST
Middle Palisade 14,040ft
Mount Reinstein 12,604ft
ENCHANTED GORGE
Wishon Reservoir
Finger Peak 12,404ft
Mather Pass 12,100ft
Split Mountain 14,058ft
KETTLE RIDGE
Tunemah Peak 11,894ft
UPPER BASIN
SIMPSON MEADOW
Taboose Pass 11,400ft
Burnt Mountain 10,608ft
Windy Peak 8,867ft
Striped Mountain 13,160ft
Marion Peak 12,719ft
Kettle Dome 9,446ft
South Fork Kings River
River
KINGS CANYON NATIONAL PARK
Bench Lake
Pinchot Pass 12,050ft
Kings River
MURO BLANCO
Arrow Peak 12,958ft
Spanish Mountain 10,051ft
Colosseum Mountain 12,473ft
Obelisk 9,700ft
Pyramid Peak 12,777ft
Kennedy Pass 10,900ft
Sawmill Pass 11,347ft
Woods Lake
Middle Fork
Granite Pass 10,673ft
Kings River
Mount Baxter 13,125ft
Woods Creek Trail
PARADISE VALLEY
Mount Clarence King 12,905ft
Baxter Pass 12,320ft
Wren Peak 9,450ft
Diamond Peak 13,126ft
Los Angeles Aqueduct
KINGS CANYON SCENIC BYWAY
Mist Falls
Mount Gardiner 12,907ft
CONVERSE BASIN GROVE
KINGS CANYON LODGE
RAE LAKES
Independence
Kings River
180
KINGS CANYON
ROADS END PERMIT STATION
Glen Pass 11,978ft
Independence Creek
CEDAR GROVE
Kearsarge Pass

SEQUOIA AND KINGS CANYON NATIONAL PARKS have two claims to fame: some of the tallest and oldest trees on earth and the 14,494-foot (4,418-m) summit of Mount Whitney, the highest peak in the contiguous United States. When combined with their shared boundary, these parks stretch across a huge acreage larger than Yosemite but with the benefit of smaller crowds. They are part of a larger ecosystem that includes Sequoia National Forest, Giant Sequoia National Monument, and historic lands of the Monache, Yokuts, and Tubatulabal.

Much of the landscape is wild Sierra Nevada backcountry. From the immense vertical in the north, the terrain plunges into glacier-carved deep canyons and soars to alpine peaks. Most is accessible only by hiking paths, including the John Muir Trail and Pacific Crest Trail. To the south, the forest hosts acres of giant sequoia and redwood groves as well as a unique cave system. Together, this pair will delight you.

PLANNING YOUR TIME

Located in central California, Sequoia and Kings Canyon are accessed by road only from the west side of the Sierra. *No roads enter the park from the Eastern Sierra, and there is no way to drive across the Sierra from either park.*

Exploring the large parks takes time and requires long drives. Plan to stay 3-4 days to take some of the many walks through scenic redwood groves. In the main campgrounds, vacationers often set up a tent for one or two weeks and use the camp as a base for exploring the parks.

Due to vast elevation differences, weather varies with extremes. **Summer** is high season, when snow melts from cooler high-elevation trails and hot temperatures pervade the foothills. Winter dumps snow on the mountains, often closing park roads and making driving treacherous. Roads in Mineral King and Cedar Grove Kings Canyon close in winter.

ENTRANCES AND FEES

The entrance fee is $35 per vehicle ($30 motorcycle, $20 individual). You can **buy your pass online** (www.yourpassnow.com) from home to speed through entrance stations faster. There are two main entrances. From the west and north, the **Big Stump Entrance** (CA 180) is the most direct route with the closest access to Kings Canyon National Park, Grant Grove, and Generals Highway. From the south, the **Ash Mountain Entrance** (CA 198) enters Sequoia National Park, where CA 198 becomes Generals Highway.

VISITORS CENTERS

The **Kings Canyon Visitor Center** (83918 CA 180 E., 559/565-3341, 9am-5pm daily summer, 9am-4pm daily winter) is in Grant Grove Village near the Big Stump Entrance. This is the place to get maps and information on camping, hiking, wilderness permits, weather conditions, and road closures. Rangers offer interpretive programs, including snowshoe walks in winter.

Near Cedar Grove Village in Kings Canyon, the **Cedar Grove Visitor Center** (CA 180, 559/565-3793, 9am-5pm daily summer) has books, maps, and park rangers to answer questions.

At the **Lodgepole Visitor Center** (Generals Hwy., 559/565-4436, 8am-4:30pm daily summer) visitors can get books and maps, join a ranger talk or walk, pick up wilderness permits, and buy Crystal Cave tour tickets. It's about an hour's drive to Lodgepole from either park entrance.

The **Foothills Visitor Center** (Generals Hwy., 559/565-3341, 8am-4:30pm daily mid-Mar.-Nov., 9am-4pm daily

Top 3

1 GAZE UP AT THE "GENERALS"

GENERAL GRANT TREE, KINGS CANYON

By sheer volume of wood, the Generals are the two largest trees on earth. At 275 feet high (84 m) and 106 feet (32 m) in circumference at the base, the 2,000-year-old **General Sherman Tree** (Wolverton Rd., off Generals Hwy.) is the largest. From the parking lot or shuttle stop at Wolverton Road, a 1-mile (1.6-km) round-trip trail with interpretive signs leads down stairs and walkways to the viewing area, where summer crowds swarm to get a look at the giant. Visit on a weekday or early in the morning for a quieter experience. A wheelchair-accessible trailhead with a shorter trail is on Generals Highway (south of Wolverton Rd.).

The **General Grant Tree** (north of Kings Canyon Visitor Center) may be the second-largest tree and the nation's only living war memorial. The 1,700-year-old giant sequoia is 268 feet (92 m) tall with a diameter of 33 feet (10 m). The paved **General Grant Tree Trail** (0.5 mi./0.8 km rt., 20 min., easy) leads to its namesake tree and the **Fallen Monarch,** an immense tree lying on its side and hollowed out in the middle. It also passes the 1872 **Gamlin Cabin,** the former living quarters of the grove's first ranger, and the **Centennial Stump,** which once hosted whole Sunday school classes on top of it.

2 LEARN ABOUT SEQUOIAS AT THE GIANT FOREST MUSEUM

The **Giant Forest Museum** (Generals Hwy., 9am-6pm daily summer, hours shorten fall, winter, and spring) has touchable and interactive exhibits that provide context to these fast-growing trees. Learn about the importance of fire in the life of a giant sequoia, how the park used to look, and why many of the buildings have been removed to make way for more trees. This is a great stop for families. From the museum, numerous hikes branch out into the surrounding Giant Forest Sequoia Grove, which contains 8,000 of these special trees.

3 GO UNDERGROUND AT CRYSTAL CAVE

Magical **Crystal Cave** (Cave Rd., near Giant Forest, May-Sept.) is one of the most beautiful of the 275 natural caves in the park. Its immense underground rooms fill with sparkling stalagmites and stalactites made of limestone that has metamorphosed over time into marble.

Access to the cave is by **guided tour only** (877/444-6777, www.recreation.gov, adults $16-25, kids $5-8). Tours range from 45 minutes to two hours, with longer adventures for serious spelunkers ($140, six hours). Tickets are *not* sold at the cave entrance; purchase them in advance at the visitors centers or online. Day-of tickets go quickly; pick them up in early morning.

The long, winding drive to the cave parking lot can take more than an hour and reaching the cave requires a steep and strenuous 0.5-mile walk; bring a warm layer of clothing for the 50-degree temperatures (10°C) inside.

ONE DAY IN SEQUOIA & KINGS CANYON

Those short on time should head for the giant trees. Start with a walk around **General Grant Grove.** Then drive down Generals Highway to the **General Sherman Tree** and tour the **Giant Forest Museum.** If time permits, drive **Kings Canyon Scenic Byway** to Cedar Grove. Stop at canyon overlooks and hike the short **Zumwalt Meadow Trail.**

Dec.-mid-Mar.), 1 mile (1.6 km) north of the Ash Mountain Entrance, serves as the park headquarters with a bookstore, exhibits, and ranger talks and walks. You can also buy Crystal Cave tickets or get a wilderness permit.

The **Mineral King Ranger Station** (559/565-3768, 8am-4pm daily summer) is near the end of Mineral King Road. It has park information and wilderness permits.

SIGHTS

GIANT SEQUOIA NATIONAL MONUMENT

Giant Sequoia National Monument (www.fs.usda.gov) sits encased within the two parks. In fact, most visitors are unaware that it is officially national forest rather than national park. The monument is home to 13 giant sequoia groves. Along Kings Canyon Scenic Byway east of Grant Grove, the **Converse Basin Grove** may have once held the largest grove of sequoias but it was logged in the late 1800s. A wheelchair-accessible path also goes to the **Chicago Stump** (0.5-mi. loop/0.8 km, easy), a 20-foot-high (6-m) stump that remains from the 3,200-year-old General Noble Tree cut down in chunks to ship to Chicago for the 1893 World's Columbian Exposition. **Boole Tree Loop** (2.5 mi./4 km rt., moderate) takes in immense stumps and a post-logging second-growth forest that includes the Boole Tree.

SCENIC DRIVE

KINGS CANYON SCENIC BYWAY

North of Grant Grove Village, CA 180 becomes the **Kings Canyon Scenic Byway** (35 mi./56 km) as it continues east through Cedar Grove. It crosses through Giant Sequoia National Monument and Converse Basin. From its start at 6,400 feet (1,951 m), the road weaves down several thousand feet before climbing back up along the South Fork Kings River and terminating at Roads End. Ample roadside pullouts make it easy to stop and take in the tremendous views of the vast canyons that give the park its name.

The best stop is **Canyon View** 1 mile (1.6 km) east of Cedar Grove Village. Look for the U-shaped canyon carved by glaciers, lodged between the soaring peaks flanking the Kings River. One mile (1.6 km) farther east, walk a short path to the small, picturesque **Knapp's Cabin,** built in the 1920s by businessman George Knapp. The wheelchair-accessible **Roaring River Falls Trail** (0.5 mi./0.8 km rt.) travels under a cool canopy of trees to water gushing through rock slots.

Cowering between North Dome and Grand Sentinel, **Roads End** is the end of the road in Kings Canyon. Beyond Roads End, the park is trails, canyons, forests, and lakes.

RECREATION

HIKING

Grant Grove

General Grant Grove is home to dozens of giant sequoias, the largest of which is the General Grant Tree. From the parking lot, take the **North Grove Loop Trail** (1.5 mi./2.4 km rt., 1 hr., easy) along an old park road through the sequoia forest.

North of the Big Stump Entrance, the **Big Stump Trail** (2 mi./3.2 km rt., 1 hr., easy) travels through a grove that was heavily logged in the late 19th century. Today, it is reclaiming its true nature as a sequoia grove. The route passes the **Mark Twain Stump,** the remains of a 26-foot-wide (8-m) tree that was cut in 1891.

Redwood Mountain Grove (in

HIKER IN KINGS CANYON

Redwood Canyon) is home to the largest grove of giant sequoias in the world. Walk down a short old roadbed to a trail junction and turn left to begin the **Hart Tree and Fallen Goliath Loop** (6.5 mi./10.5 km rt., 3-4 hrs., moderate) across Redwood Creek and past the former logging site of Barton's Post Camp. About halfway around the loop, you'll come to a short spur trail that takes you to the **Hart Tree,** the largest in the grove and the 25th largest known in the world. **Fallen Goliath,** a little farther along, is another impressive sight. To reach the trailhead from Grant Grove, drive five miles (8 km) south on Generals Highway to Quail Flat; turn right and drive 1.5 miles (2.4 km) to Redwood Saddle. Turn left at the fork for the trailhead.

The trail to **Buena Vista Peak** (2 mi./3.2 km rt., 2 hrs., moderate) makes a 450-foot (137-m) ascent to the peak for views of the Western Divide, Mineral King, and Farewell Gap. The Buena Vista Trailhead is 6 miles (9.7 km) south of Grant Grove.

The **Big Baldy Trail** (4.4 mi./7.1 km rt., 2.5 hrs., moderate) climbs 600 feet (183 m) to the granite summit of Big Baldy for views into Redwood Canyon. The trailhead is 8 miles (13 km) south of Grant Grove.

Cedar Grove

Kings Canyon Scenic Byway leads to trailheads for family-friendly hikes and big mountain adventures. One mile (1.6 km) west of Roads End, the **Zumwalt Meadow Trail** (1.5 mi./2.4 km rt., 1 hr., easy) leads through the lush meadow and continues through a grove of heavenly smelling incense cedar and pine trees along the Kings River.

From the Roads End Trailhead, the **Mist Falls Trail** (8 mi./13 km rt., 4-5 hrs., moderate) begins with a sandy, dusty path to a granite junction. Turn north to climb steep switchbacks 600 vertical feet (183 m) to the refreshing falls.

Giant Forest and Lodgepole

Along the Generals Highway, short trails lead to big views and giant trees. From the Little Baldy Trailhead, the 790-foot (241-m) ascent up 8,044-foot (2,452-m) **Little Baldy** (3.4 mi./5.5 km rt., 2-3 hrs., moderate) reaches the top of the granite dome to look down into the Giant Forest.

From the General Sherman Tree Trailhead, the wheelchair-accessible **Congress Trail** (2 mi./3.2 km rt., 1 hr., easy) passes many of the park's most famous giant sequoias—Chief Sequoyah, General Lee, and President McKinley—as well as the House and Senate Groups.

Best Hike

MORO ROCK

DISTANCE: 0.5 mile (0.8 km) round-trip
DURATION: 30 minutes
ELEVATION CHANGE: 380 stairs
EFFORT: strenuous
TRAILHEAD: Moro Rock/ Crescent Meadow Rd.

The granite dome of **Moro Rock** stands starkly alone amid the landscape, providing an amazing vantage point for much of Sequoia. Park in the lot at the base of the rock and climb the nearly 400 steps to the top, holding on to the handrails for support. At the top, views extend into the canyons of the Great Western Divide and across the peaks of the Sierra Nevada. In summer, the road is closed to vehicles weekends and holidays, so take the free shuttle (9am-6pm).

At the Giant Forest Museum, the level **Big Trees Loop** (1.2 mi./1.9 km rt., 1 hr., easy) circles Round Meadow. Interpretive panels make this a fun walk for kids and the paved boardwalk is wheelchair-accessible.

From Crescent Meadow parking lot, the **Crescent Meadow-Log Meadow Loop** (1.6 mi./2.6 km rt., 1 hr., easy) lets hikers experience wildflowers as the trail passes Tharp's Log, the park's oldest cabin.

Foothills and Mineral King

At the southern entrance of Sequoia National Park, the Foothills area offers vigorous adventure with a big payoff. The **Marble Falls Trail** (7.4 mi./12 km rt., 4 hrs., strenuous) starts from Potwisha Campground on a forest road before winding upward through the woods 2,150 feet (655 m) to sweeping views of the canyons and the water below. At a large slab that looks like white marble, you see the dramatic Marble Falls.

▼ TRAIL UP MORO ROCK

Hikes in the remote Mineral King area (Lookout Point Entrance, May-Nov.) are demanding and strenuous. The exception is the **Cold Springs Nature Trail** (2.4 mi./3.9 km rt., 1 hr.), an easy walk from the campground along the Kaweah River.

BACKPACKING

The premier backpacking trip in Kings Canyon is the **Rae Lakes Loop** (42 mi./68 km rt., 5-7 days). From Roads End, the trail varies from flat and pleasant to mettle-testing rock scrambling, rugged switchbacks, and stream crossings. Along the way, you'll gain about 7,000 feet (2,134 m) of elevation to reach 11,978-foot (3,651-m) **Glen Pass** (snow covered until July) and the sparkling blue Rae Lakes; many hikers spend at least two nights here. The loop also takes in a portion of the John Muir and Pacific Crest Trails.

Wilderness permits ($15 late May-late Sept.) are required, available from the visitors center or the **Roads End Permit Station** (7am-3:30pm daily late May-late Sept.). Permit quotas are enforced during high season and bear canisters are required.

HORSEBACK RIDING

In summer, saddle up with **Grant Grove Stables** (559/335-9292) or **Cedar Grove Pack Station** (Cedar Grove Village, 559/565-3464 or 559/337-2413). Cedar Grove also guides customized backcountry overnight trips.

WHERE TO STAY

INSIDE THE PARK

All park lodgings and campgrounds fill on weekends, holidays, and June-early September. Make reservations in advance.

Grant Grove

Lodging reservations at Grant Grove fill 4-6 months in advance. **Grant Grove Cabins** (866/807-3598, www.visitsequoia.com, year-round, from $100) are rustic timber structures and tent cabins with private bathrooms or a shared central facility with public showers. The attractive yet simple **John Muir Lodge** (866/807-3598, www.visitsequoia.com, year-round, from $210) is cedar lodges with motel-style rooms built in 1999. Nearby, **Grant Grove Restaurant** (Grant Grove Village, 7am-9pm daily) serves meals.

RAE LAKES

Montecito Sequoia Lodge (63410 Generals Hwy., 559/565-3388 or 800/227-9900, www.mslodge.com, year-round, from $249) is a rustic full-service resort with lodge rooms and cabins. In summer, Montecito operates primarily as a family camp, but rooms are available to non-campers. Rates are all-inclusive. The dining room (hours vary daily year-round) serves breakfast, lunch, and dinner; reservations are accepted for hotel guests.

Cedar Grove

Cedar Grove Lodge (Cedar Grove Village, 866/807-3598, www.visitsequoia.com, May-Oct., from $150) has 21 guest rooms with private baths and air-conditioning. Services include a **snack bar** (7:30am-9pm daily May-Oct.), gift shop, mini-mart, laundry, showers, and an ATM.

Lodgepole

The **Wuksachi Lodge** (64740 Wuksachi Way, 866/807-3598, www.visitsequoia.com, year-round, from $226) offers upscale accommodations with facilities built in 1999. The on-site **Peaks Restaurant** (559/625-7700, 7am-10pm daily year-round) features sweeping forest views and serves three meals daily, plus the lodge has a new pizza deck.

SEQUOIA TREE

Lodgepole Village contains a large visitors center, market, the **Lodgepole Café** (8am-8pm daily May-Oct.) with a full menu or grab-and-go, a gift shop, coin laundry, an ATM, shuttle services, and a post office. Many facilities close in winter.

Stony Creek Village has the **Stony Creek Lodge** (Generals Hwy., 877/828-1440, www.sequoia-kingscanyon.com, May-early Oct., from $160) with a **restaurant** (lunch and dinner), market/gift shop, an ATM, and a gas station (credit card, 24 hours daily).

The **Sherman Shack** (11am-5pm summer, weather dependent), a solar-powered food cart in the General Sherman Tree parking lot, has grab-and-go snacks and lunches.

Mineral King

At Mineral King, the **Silver City Resort** (559/242-3510, www.silvercityresort.com, May-mid-Oct., from $195) has chalets and cabins. Reaching the Mineral King area (Mineral King Rd., 25 mi./40 km east of CA 198) requires driving a narrow, 22-mile (35-km) road that takes at least 1.5 hours in good weather. Trailers and RVs are not recommended on the road.

Camping

For **campground reservations** (877/444-6777, www.recreation.gov, $22-60), book up to six months in advance. Sunset, Sentinel, Lodgepole, Dorst Creek, Stony Creek, Upper Stony Creek, Potwisha, and Buckeye take reservations; a few others takes reservations only for group campsites.

Three campgrounds cluster near Grant Grove Village: **Sunset** (157 sites, May-Sept.), **Azalea** (110 sites, year-round), and **Crystal Springs** (36 sites, late May-early Sept.).

Cedar Grove Village has **Sheep Creek** (111 sites, late May-mid-Sept.), **Sentinel** (82 sites, May-mid-Nov.), and **Moraine** (121 sites, late June-early Sept.). **Canyon View** (late May-Sept., $40-60) has group sites by reservation.

Near Lodgepole, **Lodgepole Campground** (214 sites, May-Sept.) is along the Kaweah River, and **Dorst Creek Campground** (218 sites, late June-Labor

GRANITE PEAKS IN KINGS CANYON

Day, $22-60) sits along Generals Highway north of Wuksachi Village. Shuttles stop at both campgrounds. Near Stony Creek Lodge, **Stony Creek Campground** (50 sites, May-Oct.) and **Upper Stony Creek Campground** (23 sites, mid-May-mid-Sept.) are U.S. Forest Service sites.

At Foothills, **Potwisha Campground** (42 sites, year-round) and tent-only **Buckeye Flat** (28 sites, early Apr.-late Sept.) sit on the Kaweah River. The primitive **South Fork Campground** (South Fork Dr., 10 sites, year-round, $6) is 13 miles (21 km) off CA 198 near Three Rivers. There are pit toilets, but no drinking water.

Two tent-only campgrounds (May-Oct., $12) are at Mineral King: **Atwell Mill** (21 sites) and **Cold Springs** (40 sites).

OUTSIDE THE PARK

Visalia and **Three Rivers** have visitor services, lodgings, and a summer shuttle into the park. The Hume Lake Ranger District of the Sequoia National Forest/Giant Sequoia National Monument (www.fs.fed.us) manages nearby campgrounds. Reservations are accepted for **Princess Campground** (CA 180, June-Sept.) and **Hume Lake** (Generals Hwy., May-Sept.), 10 miles (16 km) northeast of Grant Grove. **Tenmile** (Generals Hwy., May-Sept., $23-50), **Landslide** (Generals Hwy., summer only, $23), and **Convict Flat** (CA 180, summer only, free) are first come, first served.

GETTING THERE

AIR

The closest international airport is **Fresno Yosemite International** (FAT, 559/621-4500, www.flyfresno.com), a 1- to 2-hour drive to either park entrance. Rental cars are available. From **Los Angeles International Airport** (LAX, 1 World Way, 424/646-5252, www.flylax.com), it's a 4- to 5-hour drive to the park, most of it on I-5.

CAR

From Fresno, take **CA 180** to enter Kings Canyon National Park or go to Sequoia National Park from the west. For the south entrance to Sequoia, take **CA 99 South** to Visalia and turn east onto **CA 198.** Both park entrances are linked by the slow, winding Generals Highway, which may close in winter due to snow.

MOUNT WHITNEY

One of the most famous backpacking trips in Northern California is the trek to **Mount Whitney.** At 14,494 feet (4,418 m), Whitney is the highest peak in the continental United States, and this must-do trek draws intrepid hikers and climbers from around the world. Whitney also marks the southern end of the **John Muir Trail** and makes for a dramatic end or beginning for hikers doing the whole route.

Mount Whitney is at the far eastern edge of Sequoia National Park, just west of the town of Lone Pine. You can see the impressive peak from a few places in the backcountry of Sequoia and Kings Canyon, but you can't drive there from within the parks as **no road crosses the parks from west to east.** If you're coming from the west, you have to drive around the parks and enter from the eastern side.

Although Mount Whitney is a very challenging climb, with an elevation gain of more than 6,100 feet (1,859 km), it is not technical. You can climb the 10.7 miles (17.2 km) of switchbacks all the way to the top of Mount Whitney and back in one day if you're in good shape and prepare properly for the journey. It's important to plan ahead, start early, and bring all the right safety gear for extreme weather.

Permits (760/873-2483, www.fs.fed.us/r5/inyo) are required for anyone entering the Mount Whitney Zone—even day hikers. Permit reservations are issued by lottery application (submitted Feb.-mid-Mar., 877/444-6777, www.recreation.gov).

The nearest campground is **Whitney Portal** (end of Whitney Portal Rd., 6 mi./9.7 km west of Lone Pine, 47 sites, late Apr.-late Oct., $26-80) in the Inyo National Forest 7 miles (11 km) from the trailhead. Make reservations (877/444-6777, www.recreation.gov). If you're planning to climb the summit, stay even closer at 25 walk-in sites located near the **Mount Whitney Trailhead** (first come, first served, one-night limit) to wake up in the wee hours and start your ascent.

GETTING AROUND

DRIVING

Park roads may require chains at any time due to snow. Check online or call the park for road conditions.

Grant Grove is located in Kings Canyon National Park, 3 miles (4.8 km) east of the Big Stump Entrance on CA 180. **Cedar Grove** is 30 miles (48 km) northeast of Grant Grove on Kings Canyon Scenic Byway (CA 180); only the first 6 miles (10 km) of the road are open in winter (Oct.-Apr.).

Lodgepole is on Generals Highway, 22 miles (35 km) north of the Ash Mountain Entrance and 27 miles (43 km) south of the Big Stump Entrance, about an hour's drive from either entrance. Wuksachi Village is 3 miles (4.8 km) northwest of Lodgepole.

From CA 198, the Ash Mountain Entrance accesses the **Foothills** area. To reach **Mineral King,** turn right onto Mineral King Road (2 mi./3.2 km before the Ash Mountain Entrance) and drive 25 miles east (40 km/1.5 hrs.). The narrow and winding road does not permit RVs or trailers. Pass through the Lookout Point Entrance (May-Oct., gate locked Nov.-Apr.) and pay the entrance fee at a self-serve kiosk.

No **gas** is sold in the national parks, but **Stony Creek Village** (Generals Hwy., 24 hrs. daily summer only) has gas pumps and accepts credit cards.

SHUTTLES

Sequoia National Park provides free summer **shuttle service** (9am-6pm daily late May-Sept.), stopping at Giant Forest Museum, Lodgepole Visitor Center, and Moro Rock, plus Dorst and Lodgepole Campgrounds. The **Visalia Shuttle** (reservations required, 877/287-4453, www.sequoiashuttle.com, late May-early Sept., $20 rt.) runs from Visalia and Three Rivers to Giant Forest Museum; the park entrance fee is included.

DEATH VALLEY NATIONAL PARK

California

KEEPSAKE STAMPS ▼▼▼

WEBSITE:
www.nps.gov/deva

PHONE NUMBER:
760/786-3200

VISITATION RANK:
16

WHY GO:
See sculpted sand dunes, hidden oases, and geologic discoveries.

▲ ZABRISKIE POINT

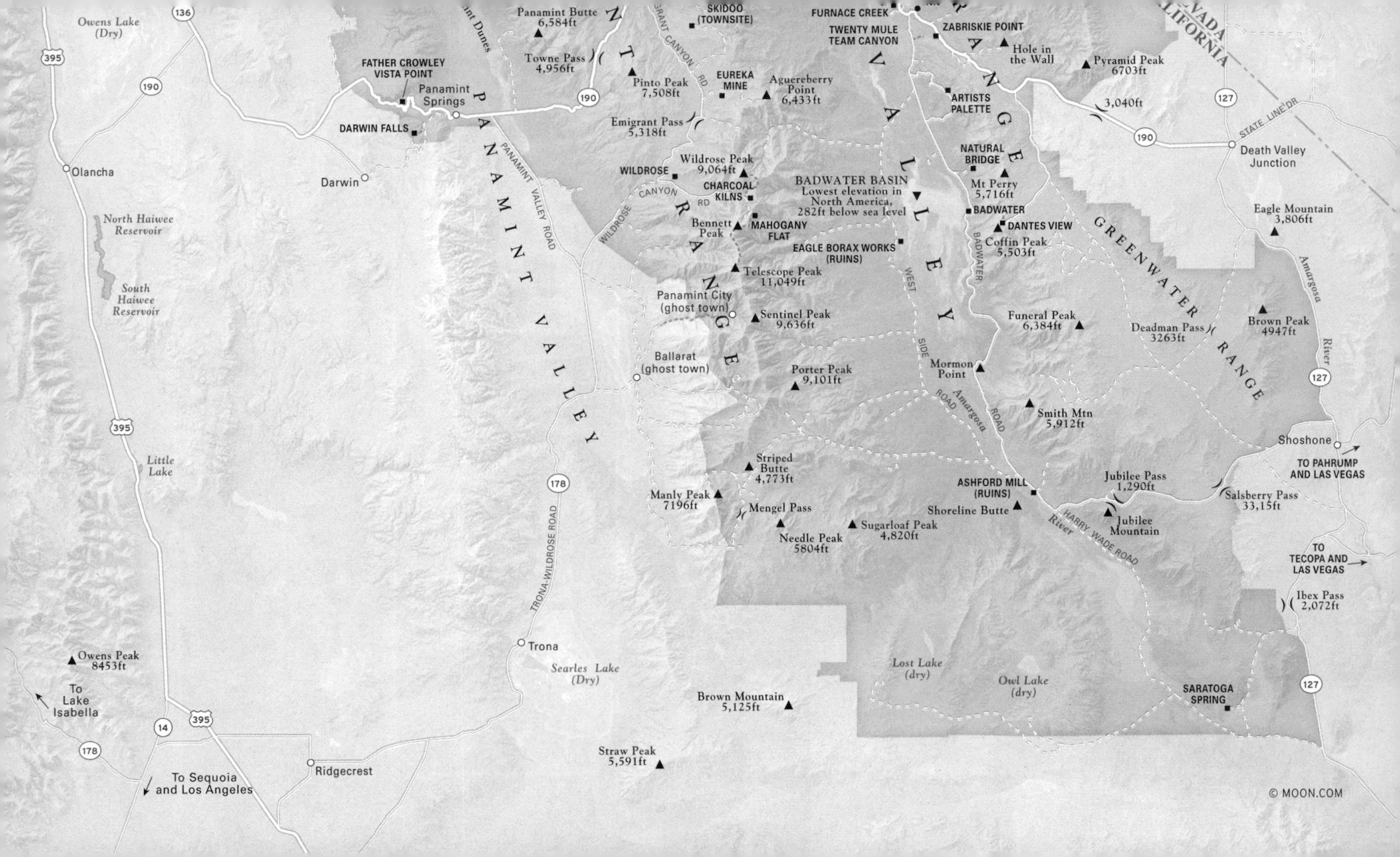

Owens Lake (Dry)
Olancha
North Haiwee Reservoir
South Haiwee Reservoir
Little Lake
Owens Peak 8453ft
To Lake Isabella
To Sequoia and Los Angeles
Ridgecrest
Darwin
DARWIN FALLS
FATHER CROWLEY VISTA POINT
Panamint Springs
Panamint Butte 6,584ft
Towne Pass 4,956ft
Pinto Peak 7,508ft
Emigrant Pass 5,318ft
PANAMINT VALLEY
PANAMINT VALLEY ROAD
PANAMINT RANGE
SKIDOO (TOWNSITE)
GRANT CANYON RD
EUREKA MINE
Aguereberry Point 6,433ft
WILDROSE
WILDROSE CANYON RD
Wildrose Peak 9,064ft
CHARCOAL KILNS
Bennett Peak
MAHOGANY FLAT
Telescope Peak 11,049ft
Panamint City (ghost town)
Sentinel Peak 9,636ft
Ballarat (ghost town)
Porter Peak 9,101ft
Striped Butte 4,773ft
Manly Peak 7196ft
Mengel Pass
Needle Peak 5804ft
Sugarloaf Peak 4,820ft
Trona
TRONA-WILDROSE ROAD
Searles Lake (Dry)
Brown Mountain 5,125ft
Straw Peak 5,591ft
FURNACE CREEK
TWENTY MULE TEAM CANYON
ZABRISKIE POINT
Hole in the Wall
Pyramid Peak 6703ft
ARTISTS PALETTE
NATURAL BRIDGE
Mt Perry 5,716ft
BADWATER BASIN
Lowest elevation in North America, 282ft below sea level
BADWATER
DANTES VIEW
Coffin Peak 5,503ft
EAGLE BORAX WORKS (RUINS)
DEATH VALLEY
WEST SIDE ROAD
BADWATER ROAD
Mormon Point
Amargosa ROAD
Funeral Peak 6,384ft
Smith Mtn 5,912ft
ASHFORD MILL (RUINS)
Shoreline Butte
HARRY WADE ROAD
River
Jubilee Pass 1,290ft
Jubilee Mountain
Lost Lake (dry)
Owl Lake (dry)
SARATOGA SPRING
GREENWATER RANGE
Deadman Pass 3263ft
Brown Peak 4947ft
3,040ft
NEVADA
CALIFORNIA
STATE LINE DR
Death Valley Junction
Eagle Mountain 3,806ft
Amargosa River
Shoshone
TO PAHRUMP AND LAS VEGAS
Salsberry Pass 33,15ft
TO TECOPA AND LAS VEGAS
Ibex Pass 2,072ft
395
190
136
14
178
127
© MOON.COM

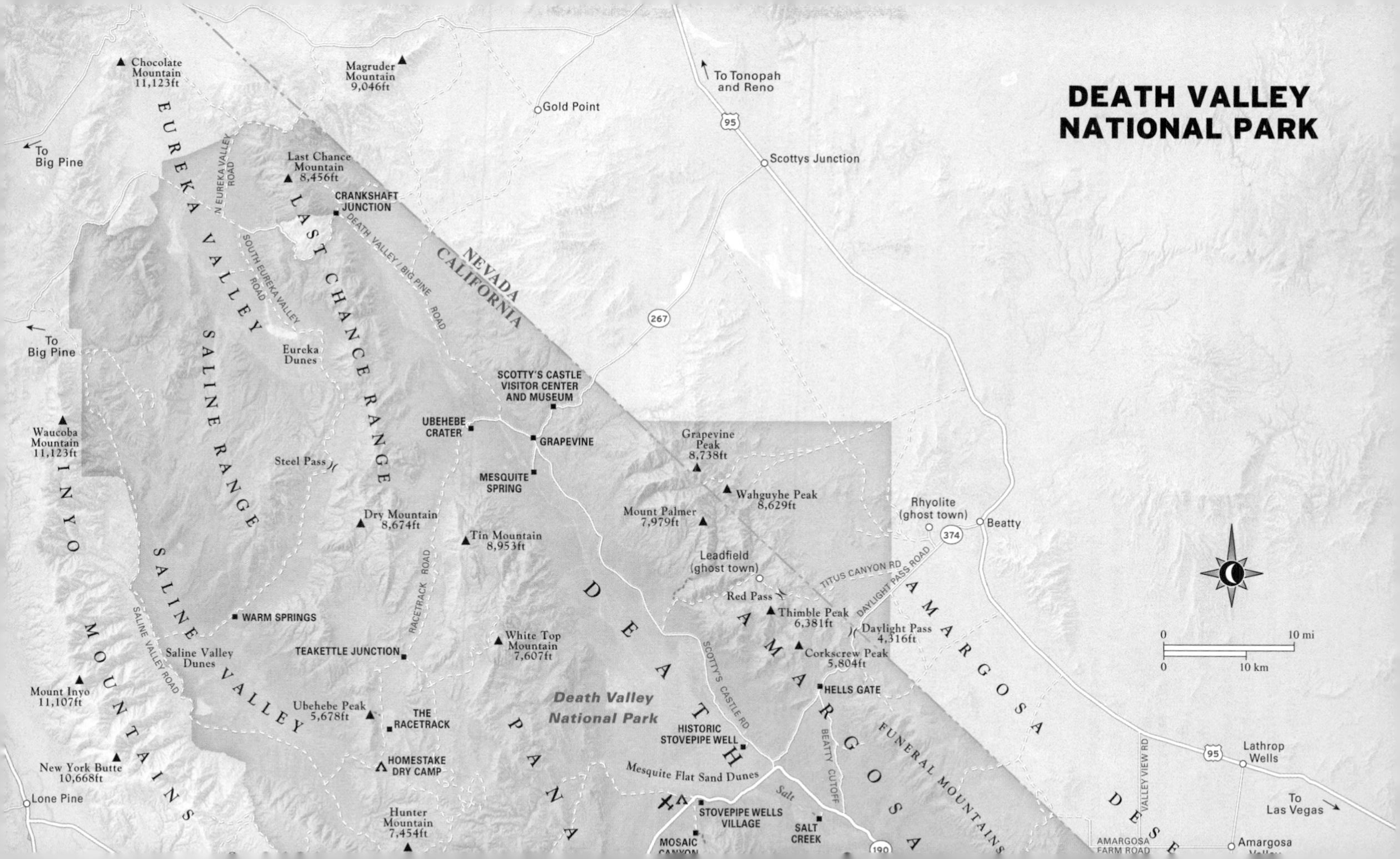
DEATH VALLEY NATIONAL PARK
Death Valley National Park
NEVADA
CALIFORNIA
EUREKA VALLEY
SALINE RANGE
LAST CHANCE RANGE
SALINE VALLEY
INYO MOUNTAINS
DEATH
PANAMINT
AMARGOSA
AMARGOSA RANGE
FUNERAL MOUNTAINS
AMARGOSA DESERT
Chocolate Mountain 11,123ft
Magruder Mountain 9,046ft
Gold Point
To Tonopah and Reno
Scottys Junction
To Big Pine
To Big Pine
Last Chance Mountain 8,456ft
CRANKSHAFT JUNCTION
N EUREKA VALLEY ROAD
SOUTH EUREKA VALLEY ROAD
DEATH VALLEY / BIG PINE ROAD
Eureka Dunes
SCOTTY'S CASTLE VISITOR CENTER AND MUSEUM
UBEHEBE CRATER
GRAPEVINE
MESQUITE SPRING
Waucoba Mountain 11,123ft
Steel Pass
Dry Mountain 8,674ft
Tin Mountain 8,953ft
Grapevine Peak 8,738ft
Wahguyhe Peak 8,629ft
Mount Palmer 7,979ft
Rhyolite (ghost town)
Beatty
Leadfield (ghost town)
TITUS CANYON RD
DAYLIGHT PASS ROAD
Red Pass
Thimble Peak 6,381ft
Daylight Pass 4,316ft
Corkscrew Peak 5,804ft
HELLS GATE
WARM SPRINGS
RACETRACK ROAD
SALINE VALLEY ROAD
Saline Valley Dunes
TEAKETTLE JUNCTION
White Top Mountain 7,607ft
Mount Inyo 11,107ft
Ubehebe Peak 5,678ft
THE RACETRACK
SCOTTY'S CASTLE RD
HISTORIC STOVEPIPE WELL
BEATTY CUTOFF
New York Butte 10,668ft
HOMESTAKE DRY CAMP
Mesquite Flat Sand Dunes
Salt
Lone Pine
Hunter Mountain 7,454ft
STOVEPIPE WELLS VILLAGE
SALT CREEK
MOSAIC CANYON
VALLEY VIEW RD
AMARGOSA FARM ROAD
Lathrop Wells
To Las Vegas
Amargosa
0
10 mi
0
10 km
95
267
374
190

Located within the northern Mojave Desert, **DEATH VALLEY** boasts extremes as both the hottest place on earth and the lowest national park in the United States. From the glaring salt flats below sea level to its snowcapped tallest peak, this arid park reveals a complex geology of seas, volcanoes, tectonic forces, and fault lines.

Battered by wind or watered by secret oases, the landscape is flecked with hidden springs, mining camps, ghost towns, petroglyphs, and sacred spots of the indigenous Timbisha Shoshone people who call the valley home. Get out of the car to walk its twisting canyons, cool off near its waterfalls, and listen to its wilderness.

PLANNING YOUR TIME

Death Valley National Park is in southeastern California, with a small slice crossing the border into Nevada. Most of the park is accessible year-round. **CA 190** bisects it east to west, passing through the main park hub of Furnace Creek, an outpost of comfort and civilization.

Spring, fall, and **winter** are popular times to visit. Reservations for the few accommodations and campgrounds around Furnace Creek can be hard to come by; make lodging arrangements several months in advance. Summer is the off-season, with temperatures topping 120°F (49°C). Winter brings snow to the higher elevations and some roads may close, but the valley areas are pleasant and cool. In spring (Feb.-Apr.), the desert explodes with **wildflower blooms.**

Services are limited at Furnace Creek, Stovepipe Wells, and Panamint Springs. Before entering the park, stock up on food, gas, supplies, and especially water (2 g/7.6 l of water per person per day).

ENTRANCES AND FEES

CA 190 is the most efficient way to enter the park from east or west, and it accesses the most popular sights. The entrance fee is $30 per vehicle ($25 motorcycle, $15 individual) and valid for seven days. Pay the entrance fee at self-pay kiosks or at ranger stations.

VISITORS CENTERS

The **Furnace Creek Visitor Center** (Furnace Creek, CA 190, 8am-5pm daily) has exhibits, drinking water, information on park sights and activities, ranger programs, camping, and hiking. Buy park passes, permits, and park books from the on-site **Death Valley Natural History Association** (http://dvnha.org). Designated an International Dark Sky Park, the park hosts astronomy events and ranger-led stargazing programs in winter and spring.

Stovepipe Wells has a small ranger station with general park and backcountry information.

SIGHTS

DANTE'S VIEW

Dante's View (Dante's View Rd.) provides spectacular panoramic views of Death Valley. The Panamint Range rises dramatically from the stiflingly low Badwater Basin salt flats 282 feet (86 m) below sea level to 11,049-foot (3,368-m) Telescope Peak, which is snowcapped much of the year.

TWENTY MULE TEAM CANYON

The graded dirt **Twenty Mule Team Canyon Road** (CA 190, east of Furnace Creek, 3 mi./4.8 km one-way) loops through a mudstone canyon past badlands and the site of historical mining prospects at **Twenty Mule Team Canyon.** When the road veers to the right, look to the left to see the site of the **Monte Blanco assay office,** a large wooden house built in 1883 to serve miners.

Top 3

1 FEEL THE BURN AT FURNACE CREEK

SUNRISE AT ZABRISKIE POINT

Furnace Creek (CA 190) provides a good introduction for first-time visitors and includes access to many of the park's highlights: Zabriskie Point, Badwater Basin, and Artist's Drive. **The Oasis at Death Valley** is home to a cabin and motel complex as well as restaurants, a general store, saloon, post office, golf course, horse stables, a **gas station,** restrooms, park headquarters, and a **visitors center.**

Constructed in 1883, the building that now houses the **Borax Museum** (760/786-2345, www.oasisatdeathvalley.com, 9am-9pm daily, donation) was once the assay office for the Monte Blanco Mine in what is now Twenty Mule Team Canyon. It has exhibits on Native Americans, mining history, and the history of borax, the "white gold" of the valley. Outdoor exhibits include a 60-ton (54 metric ton) oil-burning locomotive that hauled borate.

Two miles (3.2 km) north of Furnace Creek, a short, paved path leads to the site of **Harmony Borax Works.** A 20-mule team wagon, the remains of a borax refinery, and interpretive signs tell the history of the site as a base for the 1883-1888 borax mining and processing operations. Faint, eroded remains of **borax haystacks** flank a 1.5-mile (2.4-km) walk across the salt pan.

2 SPY HIGH FROM ZABRISKIE POINT

Iconic **Zabriskie Point** (CA 190, 5 mi./8 km south of Furnace Creek) overlooks otherworldly and eroded badlands from a high vantage point. A popular stop for photographers and other visitors, the colors kindle at sunrise and sunset, capturing the magnificent desolation of the valley.

3 SINK LOW AT BADWATER BASIN

Badwater Basin (Badwater Rd., 15 mi./24 km south of Furnace Creek) is a Death Valley classic. The lowest point in North America at 282 feet (86 m) below sea level, these vast salt flats encapsulate the mesmerizing yet unforgiving landscape of Death Valley. Walk out onto the salt flats to feel the sea of air and look for delicate salt-crystal formations. The blinding glare, emanating heat, and scale of humans next to the surrounding Black Mountains put our existence into perspective.

BADWATER BASIN

ONE DAY IN DEATH VALLEY

CA 190's paved route along **Badwater Road** makes for a perfect tour of the park. Stop at **Badwater Basin, Mesquite Flat Dunes,** and **Zabriskie Point** and make time for a short hike off **Artist's Drive** or to **Darwin Falls.** Plan in advance for overnight accommodations in the Furnace Creek area.

NIGHT SKIES

As an International Dark Sky Park, Death Valley has places with minimal light pollution to impede night views of stars and the Milky Way. The park holds an annual Dark Sky Festival in late February and the Oasis at Death Valley hosts star parties. Both have telescope-viewing and astronomers to tell you what you are seeing. On your own, you can also go out to stargaze on moonless nights around Harmony Borax Works, Mesquite Flat Sand Dunes, or Badwater Basin. Bring binoculars and red flashlights as white flashlights makes seeing stars more difficult.

ARTIST'S DRIVE

Named for its shifting palette of colors, the one-way loop **Artist's Drive** (Badwater Rd.) rises along an alluvial fan fed by the Black Mountains. The colors, caused by the oxidizing of different metals on the volcanic rock, proffer a chaotic jumble of hues, including green, rose, yellow, purple, and red. Stop midway at **Artist's Palette** for a scenic viewpoint. The lovely paved 9-mile loop (15 km, one-way) starts on Badwater Road, 5 miles (8 km) south of Furnace Creek.

DEVIL'S GOLF COURSE

Admire the controlled chaos of the **Devil's Golf Course** (Badwater Rd., 10 mi./16 km south of Furnace Creek) on the northern end of the eerie, stark salt flats of Badwater Basin. Devil's Golf Course is filled with spiky salt crystals—as groundwater seeps to the surface, it prompts the jagged pinnacles. Drive the graded dirt road to a small parking lot, where you can see the formations at closer range.

STOVEPIPE WELLS

Stovepipe Wells (CA 190, www.deathvalleyhotels.com), a touring outpost built in 1926, still sits on the toll road that officially kicked off tourism in Death Valley. The road was originally built to join Stovepipe Wells with Lone Pine in the Sierra Nevada and now serves as the park hub for this region, with a campground, hotel, restaurant, and gas station.

East of Stovepipe Wells, the wind-sculpted **Mesquite Flat Dunes** rise above the desert floor to catch the light of the sky in smooth, unbroken crests and lines.

At **Devil's Cornfield,** mounded clumps of arrowweed plants stretch in neat rows along the sandy desert floor. The effect of the carefully plotted lines of salt-tolerant plants against the backdrop of the Funeral Mountains is surreal. In the spring, the haystacks blossom with blue tops.

As CA 190 curves south, the Salt Creek area appears. A weathered, wheelchair-accessible boardwalk loop follows the miraculous **Salt Creek,** winding 0.5 mile (0.8 km, one-way) toward pale, eroded mud hills through an expanse of pickleweed. This tiny riparian environment supports the endemic **Salt Creek pupfish.**

SCOTTY'S CASTLE

Scotty's Castle (Scotty's Castle Rd. at CA 267) is an unlikely sight in this desert. The Spanish Colonial-style mansion was built in 1922 by millionaires Albert and Bessie Johnson at the urging of Walter Edward Scott, better known as **Death Valley Scotty.** Scotty was an infamous Death Valley character who spun wild tales of gold deposits in the valley to lure investors. Ultimately his colorful personality proved to be the real investment.

The elaborate complex features a two-story house with stucco walls, a Spanish tile roof, and tiled walkways, plus an annex and a clock tower. The

MESQUITE FLAT DUNES

interior was fully furnished with the Johnsons' original possessions, including 1920s period furnishings, rich tapestries, mosaic tile work, arched doorways, and a spiral staircase.

Scotty's Castle is an hour's drive from Furnace Creek and Stovepipe Wells. It closed in 2015 after a flash flood caused $47 million in damages to the historic buildings and roads. By advance reservation, ranger-led walking tours can see the repairs (www.dvnha.org, Sun. early Dec.-mid-Apr., 9:30am, 1pm, 2 hrs., $25). Following completion of repairs, Scotty's Castle is slated to reopen in fall 2021.

UBEHEBE CRATER

Perhaps 300 years ago, a powerful volcanic explosion created this colorful crater that measures 600 feet (183 m) deep and 0.5 mile (0.8 km) across. Park at the end of the paved access road to see **Ubehebe Crater** (Scotty's Castle Rd.). A rim hike (1.5 mi./2.4 km rt.) allows you to peer down into the colorful depths of Ubehebe Crater, Little Hebe Crater, and other smaller craters.

THE RACETRACK

Despite its remoteness, many visitors make the long and difficult drive to **The Racetrack** (Racetrack Valley Rd.), an eerily dry lake bed scattered with the faint trails of rocks that skate across its surface. (Thin ice sheets cover the ground, acting as sails in a light wind, enough to propel the rocks across the surface and create the mysterious tracks.)

From the start of Racetrack Valley Road, it's a long but scenic haul along 26 miles (42 km) of rutted, rocky washboard. You'll know you're getting close when you pass **Teakettle Junction** (19.4 mi./31 km). A high-clearance vehicle is usually adequate, but a 4WD vehicle may be necessary. Many people stay in Furnace Creek or Stovepipe Wells and turn the adventurous, 3- to 4-hour drive into a long day trip.

EUREKA DUNES

Isolated in the park's remote north, the beautiful and pristine **Eureka Dunes** (South Eureka Rd.) rise from the valley floor to cover an area 3 miles (4.8 km) long and 1 mile (1.6 km) wide. They are the tallest sand dunes in California, towering more than 680 feet (207 m) from the enclosed valley floor. From their base, a climb into the dunes goes 0.5-2.5 miles (0.8-4 km) and ascends 300-600 feet (91-183 m). Upon reaching the ridgeline, you are rewarded with sculpted dunes and sweeping views of the valley.

AGUEREBERRY POINT

Prospector Pete Aguereberry established Harrisburg camp in 1905, working what would become the **Eureka Mine.** Today, you can explore the

WILDROSE CHARCOAL KILNS

original camp, visible from **Aguereberry Point Road.** Explore the remains of the Eureka Mine and Aguereberry's cabins just over the hill to the south behind the camp. The road continues toward epic views at **Aguereberry Point.**

WILDROSE CHARCOAL KILNS

The **Wildrose Charcoal Kilns** (Wildrose Canyon Rd.) are made of cut limestone, quarried locally and cemented with gravel, lime, and sand. They stand approximately 25 feet (7.6 m) tall, their walls curving gracefully inward to form a beehive shape. The Modock Consolidated Mining Company built them in 1877 to fuel the smelters of lead-silver mines in the Argus range to the west. Open, arched doorways lead to the interior of the now-defunct kilns; stomp around on the floors of each one to capture their hollow echoes.

SCENIC DRIVE

TITUS CANYON ROAD

From CA 374 (Daylight Pass Rd.), 6 miles (10 km) south of Beatty, the dirt and gravel **Titus Canyon Road** (27 mi./43 km one-way, 3 hrs.) sweeps through rugged rock formations, hangs over canyon views, skirts past **petroglyphs,** and even rolls through a **ghost town,** eventually passing through the grand finale: the canyon narrows. The narrows tower overhead, barely letting cars squeeze through before they open wide to reveal the barren Death Valley floor. A **high-clearance** vehicle is usually fine, but a 4WD vehicle may be needed in inclement weather.

RECREATION

HIKING

Off Badwater Road, **Golden Canyon** (3 mi./4.8 km rt., 1.5 hrs., easy) has gentle grades that lead to sheer red walls with majestic creases. The mouth of the canyon begins along a gravel wash through short narrows with sedimentary and volcanic rocks on the passage walls. Then the canyon opens up to a gold corridor of badlands, both bright and

▼ TITUS CANYON ROAD

Best Hike

DARWIN FALLS

DISTANCE: 2 miles (3.2 km) round-trip
DURATION: 1.5 hours
ELEVATION CHANGE: 220 feet (67 m)
EFFORT: easy
TRAILHEAD: CA 190, west of Panamint Springs

The marvel of **Darwin Falls** is that they exist at all. The hike to the first falls is an easy and quick detour from Panamint Springs. A short gravelly walk along a canyon creek leads to several creek crossings, surprising in the desert. As the canyon narrows, you come to a sight to behold: actual water streaming over slanted bedrock. The 20-foot (6-m) waterfall flows year-round.

desolate. At a fork about 1 mile in, go another 0.25 mile to the **Red Cathedral.** Some hikers make a loop by continuing all the way to **Zabriskie Point** (6 mi./9.7 km rt., 3 hrs., moderate) and returning via **Gower Gulch.**

Farther south on Badwater Road, **Natural Bridge** (1 mi./1.6 km rt., 1 hr., easy) is one of the few natural bridges in the park. You'll share this trail with plenty of hikers. Natural Bridge spans a red-wall canyon that contrasts with the bright sky above. Look back toward Badwater Basin to see Telescope Peak in the distance.

Wildrose Canyon Road goes to two peak-bound trailheads. Near Wildrose Charcoal Kilns, a signed trail leads to **Wildrose Peak** (8.4 mi./13.5 km rt., 5 hrs., moderate). The trail is intermittently steep up to the saddle, where you have sweeping views of Death Valley.

Near Mahogany Flat, the hike up the highest peak in Death Valley—**Telescope Peak** (14 mi./23 km rt., 8 hrs., strenuous)—is worth every switchback. The path climbs to 11,049 feet (3,368 m) above Badwater Basin. Expect sweeping views of Death Valley to the east and Panamint Valley to the west.

BIKING

A paved bicycle path (2 mi./3.2 km rt.) travels from Furnace Creek to Harmony Borax Works. More difficult rides include the hilly paved loop of **Artist's Drive** (9 mi./14.5 km one-way) and the exposed gravel loop of the **West Side Road** (up to 40 mi./64 km) running along the valley floor. Mountain bikers can ride all 4WD roads. **Furnace Creek Ranch General Store** (760/786-3371, www.oasisatdeathvalley.com) rents mountain bikes; pickup and drop-off are at the gas station.

GOLF

At 214 feet (65 m) below sea level, **Furnace Creek Golf Course** (CA 190, 760/786-3373, www.oasisatdeathvalley.com) claims to be the lowest-elevation golf course in the world. Dotted with water, this 18-hole course is lined with palm and tamarisk trees.

WHERE TO STAY

INSIDE THE PARK

In Furnace Creek, lodgings (CA 190, Death Valley, 800/236-7916, www.oasisatdeathvalley.com, year-round) are at **The Inn at Death Valley** (from $319) with new casitas built in 2018 and the **Ranch at Death Valley** (from $179), both with outdoor swimming pools. The **Inn Dining Room** (760/786-3385, breakfast 7:30am-10:30am, lunch 11:30pm-2:30pm, dinner 5pm-9pm Oct.-Apr. and 6pm-10pm May-Sept.) takes advance dinner reservations for hotel guests and requires resort attire. At the Ranch, the **Ranch 1849 Buffet** (7am-7pm) rotates self-serve options for breakfast, lunch, and dinner, and the **Last Kind Words Saloon** (760/786-3335, 11am-10pm), a steakhouse, takes reservations. The Ranch also has a general store with convenience foods.

Stovepipe Wells Village (51880 CA 190, Death Valley, 760/786-7090, www.deathvalleyhotels.com, from $179) has

SCENIC FOUR-WHEEL DRIVES

Hundreds of miles of unmaintained 4WD roads provide access to remote destinations in Death Valley. **Farabee's Jeep Rentals** in Furnace Creek rents 4WD vehicles and has up-to-date backcountry road information.

Cottonwood Canyon Road: West of Stovepipe Wells, this 8.5-mile (14-km) primitive road travels deep into the Cottonwood Mountains. The road starts off spitting through semi-deep sand, eventually becoming more solid on washboard and gravel. It gets much rougher as it enters Cottonwood Canyon wash.

Echo Canyon to Inyo Mine: Between Furnace Creek and Zabriskie Point, this popular 20-mile (32-km) round-trip road tours a scenic, winding canyon and ghost camp ruins. It requires a high-clearance vehicle for the first 3 miles (4.8 km) to the canyon mouth and 4WD beyond to the mining camp.

Pleasant Canyon to Rogers Pass: From Panamint Valley Road, this rugged 4WD trek goes through Pleasant Canyon. You will drive directly in the creek en route to backcountry cabins and historic mining camps in the Western Panamint Mountains.

Racetrack Valley Road: High-clearance vehicles can make the long, white-knuckle drive 28 rocky miles (45 km) into the Racetrack Valley from Ubehebe Crater, but 4WD may be necessary due to flooding and washouts. At **Teakettle Junction** at 19.4 miles (31 km), go west and south for 7 miles (11 km) to **The Racetrack,** an eerily dry lake bed scattered with the faint trails of rocks that skate across its surface. Day trips take four hours; multiday trips can add on **Ubehebe Peak,** hidden mining camps like **Ubehebe Mine, Lost Burro Mine, Lippincott Mine,** and the **Goldbelt Mining District,** and even the occasional canyon.

Saline Valley Road: This rough yet graded dirt road travels 78 lonely miles (126 km) from Death Valley-Big Pine Road near Big Pine to CA 190, west of Panamint Springs. Although a high-clearance vehicle is suitable during good weather, 4WD is preferred to access the remote **Saline Valley** that contains sand dunes and Salt Lake. To drive the road takes the better part of a day without stops; for time to explore, allow at least three days, and camp at the centrally located, primitive **Warm Springs Camp.** The best times to visit are spring and fall. Summer sees blazing temperatures; in winter, rain and snow can render the Saline Valley Road impassable.

Warm Spring Canyon to Butte Valley: The lower canyon is easily accessible, following a good graded road the first 11 miles (18 km) to Warm Springs Camp. The upper canyon is harder to reach and requires 4WD into Butte Valley.

a hotel with an outdoor swimming pool. Dining is in the **Toll Road Restaurant** (7am-10am and 5:30pm-9pm daily) and **Badwater Saloon** (11:30am-close daily). The RV Park (from $40) has hookups.

Panamint Springs Resort (40440 CA 190, Panamint Springs, 775/482-7680, www.panamintsprings.com) has motel rooms (from $164), camping (tents $10, RV hookups $40, tent cabins from $55), a restaurant (7am-9pm), and a general store.

There are nine national park campgrounds. **Furnace Creek** (136 sites, year-round, $16-$60) is the only park campground that accepts **reservations** (877/444-6777, www.recreation.gov, Oct. 15-Apr. 15). From mid-April to mid-October, sites are first come, first served.

All other campgrounds are first come, first served, but not all are open year-round. Along CA 190, find **Texas Springs** (92 sites, Nov.-May, $16), **Sunset** (270 sites, Nov.-May, $14), **Emigrant** (10 tent sites, year-round, free), and **Stovepipe Wells** (190 sites, mid-Sept.-mid-May, $14). **Mesquite Spring** (30 sites, year-round, $14) is nearest Scotty's Castle. **Thorndike** (6 sites, Mar.-Nov., free), **Wildrose** (23 sites, year-round, free), and **Mahogany Flat** (10 sites, Mar.-Nov., free) are on Emigrant Canyon Road (no vehicles over 25 ft./7.6 m, high-clearance needed for Thorndike and Mahogany Flats).

All campgrounds can get very windy at night. If tent camping, stake all items properly. If relying on RV electrical hookups, don't be surprised by electricity surges and power outages.

OUTSIDE THE PARK

The gateway towns of **Lone Pine, Big Pine, Bishop, Ridgecrest,** and **Beatty, Nevada,** have limited accommodations and restaurants.

GETTING THERE AND AROUND

AIR

The closest international airports are **Los Angeles International Airport** (LAX, 1 World Way, 855/463-5252, www.flylax.com) and **McCarran International Airport** (LAS, 5757 Wayne Newton Blvd., Las Vegas, 702/261-5211, www.mccarran.com). The airports have car rentals.

CAR

From **Los Angeles,** take I-5 north toward Palmdale and Lancaster to CA 14. Drive 120 miles (19s3 km) north on CA 14 to Indian Wells to join US 395. Continue north on US 395 for 42 miles (68 km) to the town of Olancha. Turn right (east) onto CA 190 and continue 45 miles (72 km) to Panamint Springs. Stovepipe Wells lies 29 miles (47 km) east of Panamint Springs; Furnace Creek is 53 miles (85 km) east of Panamint Springs.

From **Las Vegas,** I-15 intersects with US 95 north of the airport. Take US 95 north for 88 miles (142 km) to Lathrop Wells, Nevada. Turn left (south) onto NV 373 and drive 24 miles (39 km) southwest. NV 373 becomes CA 127 when it crosses into California. At the tiny outpost of Death Valley Junction, turn right (west) onto CA 190 and continue west for 30 miles (48 km) to the park hub at Furnace Creek.

The park has no shuttles or public transportation—bring **your own vehicle**. For back-road excursions, rent 4WD rigs through **Farabee's** (Furnace Creek, 760/786-9872, http://farabeejeeps.com, mid-Sept.-mid-May); advance reservations are recommended.

Gas is sold inside the park, but prices are expensive. Fill up at one of the gateway towns instead.

SIGHTS NEARBY

Amargosa Opera House and Hotel (CA 127, Death Valley Junction, 760/852-4441, www.amargosa-opera-house.com, 7am-10:30pm daily) is a historic (and haunted) hotel and restaurant still hosting live performances.

Rhyolite is a ghost town that dates to 1904. Located off NV 374, just 7 miles (11 km) outside the park boundary, the town's ruins include a beautiful mission-style train station, cemetery, mine ruins, and a house made of glass bottles.

◂ COLORFUL CANYONS

JOSHUA TREE NATIONAL PARK

California

WEBSITE:
www.nps.gov/jotr

PHONE NUMBER:
760/367-5500

VISITATION RANK:
11

WHY GO:
Explore a desert landscape filled with jumbled boulders and Joshua trees.

▲ YUCCA VALLEY

KEEPSAKE STAMPS ▼▼▼

JOSHUA TREE's stunning, alien landscape both startles and charms. Powerful geologic forces have whipped the rocks here into twisted shapes and scrambled boulder piles. Among the eroded chaos, spiky Joshua trees reach out in unpredictable angles, forming jagged, moody backdrops to the dusty desert roads. Farther south, the landscape straddles the boundary between the Mojave and Colorado Deserts. The lower Colorado sits austere and arid, with wide alluvial fans guarding mountain canyons. Instead of Joshua trees, creosote bushes and spindly ocotillos dot the wilderness.

The park lures spring wildflower hounds, serious hikers, and hardcore rock climbers. For many city dwellers who visit, the landscape looks empty; for the indigenous people—the Cahuilla, Chemehuevi, Serrano, and Mojave—who traditionally relied on what the land provided, it is ripe with fruits, seeds, berries, and animal life.

PLANNING YOUR TIME

Joshua Tree is in Southern California, east of Los Angeles and northeast of Palm Springs. Its location near these major urban centers brings scads of day-trippers. Most visitors arrive via CA 62 to enter the park on the west side near the town of Joshua Tree. From Joshua Tree, Park Boulevard connects with Twentynine Palms, the north entrance on CA 62. Short spurs from CA 62 take in the park's sights. The two tiny park border towns are filled with quirky outsider art and alien-inspired feats of aeronautical engineering.

Visit during the cooler, but crowded, months of **October-April**; weekdays offer fewer people. The weather is gorgeous in spring and fall, but brutal in summer with average temperatures topping 100°F (38°C). In winter, the park is dusted by snow. For spring flowers, visit in late February-May.

Camping is the only overnight option inside the park. You'll need a **car,** a full tank of gas, and **water** (at least 2 g/7.6 l per person per day), as there are no services inside the park.

ENTRANCES AND FEES

The entrance fee is $30 per vehicle ($25 motorcycle and $15 individual), which is good for seven days. All roads and entrance stations are open year-round, weather permitting. The park has three entrance stations:

West Entrance (CA 62 and Park Blvd.) is in the town of Joshua Tree, south of the Joshua Tree Visitor Center. It sees the heaviest visitation; expect midday lines during peak season.

North Entrance (CA 62 and Utah Trail) is in the town of Twentynine Palms near the Oasis Visitor Center.

South Entrance (exit 168 off I-10) accesses the park's Colorado Desert and the less visited Cottonwood Spring.

VISITORS CENTERS

The park's four visitors centers have information, exhibits, maps, natural history bookstores, water, and restrooms. Rangers lead patio talks and chats; you can also get schedules of ranger-led walks throughout the park.

Joshua Tree Visitor Center (6554 Park Blvd., Joshua Tree, 760/366-1855, 8am-5pm daily) is near the park's West Entrance. It has a bookstore with guides, maps, and gifts. There is also a restroom and a café (760/366-8200, 8am-5pm daily).

Black Rock Nature Center (9800 Black Rock Canyon Rd., Yucca Valley, 760/367-3001, 8am-4pm Sat.-Thurs., 8am-8pm Fri. Oct.-May) is a small visitors center in the Black Rock Canyon Campground area.

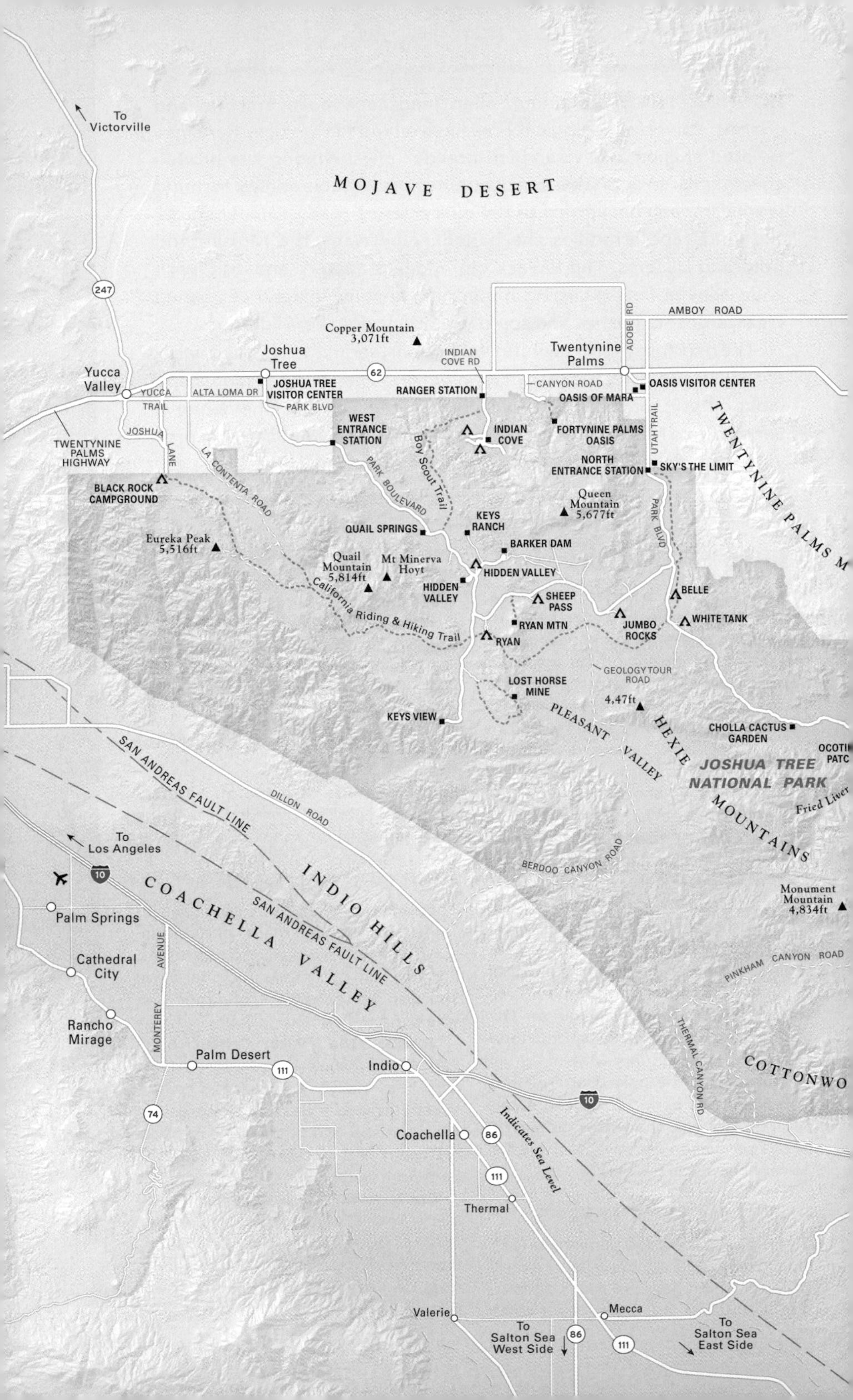

To Victorville
MOJAVE DESERT
247
Copper Mountain 3,071ft
Joshua Tree
62
INDIAN COVE RD
Twentynine Palms
ADOBE RD
AMBOY ROAD
Yucca Valley
YUCCA TRAIL
ALTA LOMA DR
JOSHUA TREE VISITOR CENTER
PARK BLVD
RANGER STATION
CANYON ROAD
OASIS VISITOR CENTER
OASIS OF MARA
TWENTYNINE PALMS HIGHWAY
JOSHUA LANE
WEST ENTRANCE STATION
Boy Scout Trail
INDIAN COVE
FORTYNINE PALMS OASIS
UTAH TRAIL
TWENTYNINE PALMS M
NORTH ENTRANCE STATION
SKY'S THE LIMIT
LA CONTENTA ROAD
BLACK ROCK CAMPGROUND
PARK BOULEVARD
Queen Mountain 5,677ft
KEYS RANCH
QUAIL SPRINGS
PARK BLVD
Eureka Peak 5,516ft
BARKER DAM
Quail Mountain 5,814ft
Mt Minerva Hoyt
HIDDEN VALLEY
HIDDEN VALLEY
California Riding & Hiking Trail
SHEEP PASS
BELLE
JUMBO ROCKS
WHITE TANK
RYAN MTN
RYAN
GEOLOGY TOUR ROAD
LOST HORSE MINE
4,47ft
KEYS VIEW
PLEASANT VALLEY
HEXIE MOUNTAINS
CHOLLA CACTUS GARDEN
OCOTI PATC
JOSHUA TREE NATIONAL PARK
Fried Liver
SAN ANDREAS FAULT LINE
DILLON ROAD
To Los Angeles
10
INDIO HILLS
COACHELLA VALLEY
SAN ANDREAS FAULT LINE
BERDOO CANYON ROAD
Monument Mountain 4,834ft
Palm Springs
Cathedral City
MONTEREY AVENUE
PINKHAM CANYON ROAD
Rancho Mirage
THERMAL CANYON RD
COTTONWO
Palm Desert
111
Indio
10
74
Indicates Sea Level
Coachella
86
111
Thermal
Valerie
Mecca
To Salton Sea West Side
86
111
To Salton Sea East Side

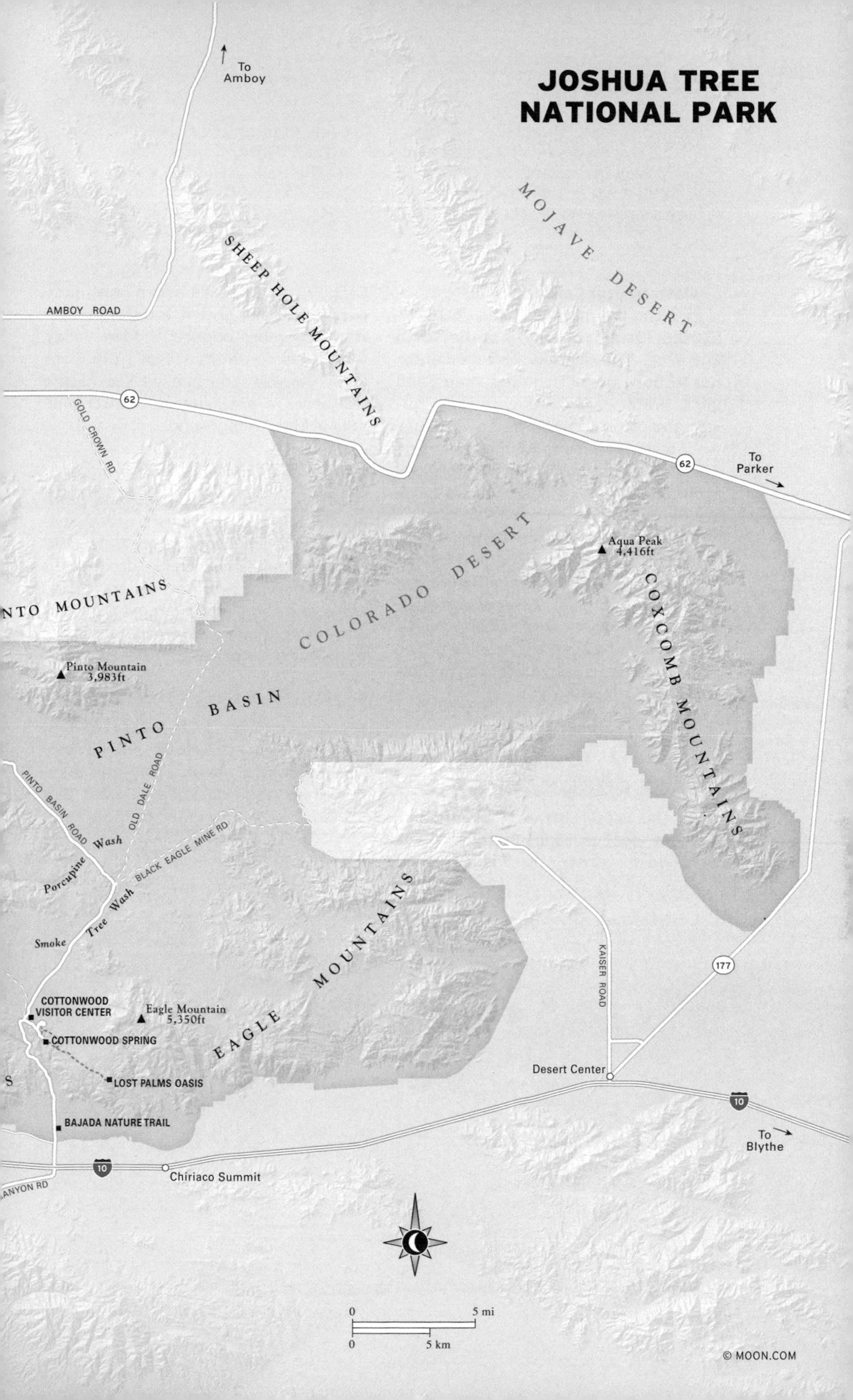
JOSHUA TREE
NATIONAL PARK
To Amboy
AMBOY ROAD
SHEEP HOLE MOUNTAINS
MOJAVE DESERT
62
GOLD CROWN RD
To Parker
COLORADO DESERT
Aqua Peak 4,416ft
NTO MOUNTAINS
COXCOMB MOUNTAINS
Pinto Mountain 3,983ft
PINTO BASIN
OLD DALE ROAD
PINTO BASIN ROAD
Porcupine Wash
BLACK EAGLE MINE RD
Smoke Tree Wash
EAGLE MOUNTAINS
KAISER ROAD
177
COTTONWOOD VISITOR CENTER
Eagle Mountain 5,350ft
COTTONWOOD SPRING
LOST PALMS OASIS
Desert Center
BAJADA NATURE TRAIL
10
To Blythe
Chiriaco Summit
ANYON RD
0
5 mi
0
5 km
© MOON.COM

ONE DAY IN JOSHUA TREE

If time is short, spend the day driving a scenic loop on the park road. From CA 62, start with an introduction at **Joshua Tree Visitor Center.** Then cruise along **Park Boulevard**, stopping to hike one of the trails in **Hidden Valley,** such as **Skull Rock** or **Cap Rock**. Finish your auto tour at the **Oasis Visitor Center** with a walk to the **Oasis of Mara.**

Oasis Visitor Center (74485 National Park Dr., Twentynine Palms, 760/367-5500, 8:30am-5pm daily) is at the North Entrance. The staffed visitors center has a bookstore with guides, maps, and gifts. Water, restrooms with flush toilets, and picnic tables are also available. An interpretive loop (0.5 mi./0.8 km rt., 30 min.) leads to the **Oasis of Mara,** a historic fan palm oasis with a large standing pool.

Cottonwood Visitor Center (Cottonwood Spring Rd., 8:30am-4pm daily) is at the South Entrance. There is a bookstore with guides, maps, and gifts. Water, restrooms with flush toilets, and picnic tables are also available. The visitors center is convenient to the Cottonwood Campground.

SIGHTS

BLACK ROCK CANYON

Near the West Entrance, **Black Rock Canyon** (Joshua Lane) huddles in the northwest corner of Joshua Tree. Craggy rolling peaks and piñons, junipers, and oaks give it a different feel from the more popular Hidden Valley, which has no direct access from Black Rock Canyon. You can walk a nature trail, tour a small nature center, and stay at the campground.

COVINGTON FLATS

A series of lightly traveled and graded dirt roads in the park's northwestern corner tour **Covington Flats** (10.9 mi./17.5 km). This scenic drive leads to a sweeping overlook, several hiking trails, and some of the largest stands of Joshua trees, junipers, and piñons in the park. Access is off La Contenta Road.

EUREKA PEAK OVERLOOK

Follow signs to 5,521-foot (1,683-m) **Eureka Peak Overlook** for sweeping panoramic views. From the summit, the Coachella Valley, Desert Hot Springs, and the San Jacinto Mountains

▼ COVINGTON FLATS

Top 3

1 CRUISE ALONG PARK BOULEVARD

From the West Entrance near the town of Joshua Tree, **Park Boulevard** delves deep into the Hidden Valley to emerge in the town of Twentynine Palms 25 miles (40 km) later. This scenic drive takes in the most popular regions of the park, with access to Hidden Valley's **campgrounds, trailheads,** and **sights.**

BOARDED-UP WELL AT KEYS RANCH

2 TOUR THE RUINS OF KEYS RANCH

From 1917 to 1969, homesteader, rancher, and miner Bill Keys carved out a desert domain that included a ranch house, schoolhouse, store, and workshop. Today, park rangers lead guided 90-minute tours of **Keys Ranch** (daily Oct.-May, adults $10, kids $5, under 6 free), the well-preserved ruins of the Desert Queen Ranch, a historic homestead near the Hidden Valley Campground. The tour is popular; purchase tickets on the day of the tour in person at Oasis Visitor Center (starting at 8:30am). Allow 40 minutes to drive the 22 miles (35 km) from the visitors center to the ranch gate to meet your guide.

3 ROCK CLIMB IN HIDDEN VALLEY

From beginners to rock stars, climbers of all levels seek the park's vast array of traditional-style crack, slab, and steep-face climbing. More than 400 climbing formations and more than 8,000 recognized climbs make it a world-class destination. Plenty of rock climbing guides are in the area if you want hire one to try the sport. Some good places to watch climbers in action are the **Quail Springs** picnic area, **Hidden Valley Campground,** the **Wonderland of Rocks, Cap Rock, Jumbo Rocks, Indian Cove, Ryan Campground, Split Rock,** and **Live Oak.**

CAP ROCK

DESERT QUEEN MINE

lie southwest, while views to the north take in the Morongo Valley.

HIDDEN VALLEY

Wonderland of Rocks

Dubbed the **Wonderland of Rocks,** this region contains a wildly eroded maze of striking granite rock formations studded with secret basins, gorgeous views, and history. The Wonderland of Rocks covers the area between Indian Cove Campground and Hidden Valley Campground. When you drive along Park Boulevard, its compelling rock formations are visible to the northeast. To go into the belly of the beast, walk the **Barker Dam Nature Trail** (Park Blvd.) and stay at **Indian Cove Campground** (Indian Cove Rd.).

Ryan Ranch

The homestead ruins of the **Ryan Ranch** (Park Blvd. near Ryan Campground) date to 1896. A 1-mile (1.6 km, rt., 30 min.) interpretive stroll leads to the remains of the ranch, adobe bunkhouse, windmill, and outbuildings. Further exploring reveals a pioneer cemetery and evidence of Native American grinding stones.

Keys View

For impressive vistas, the paved, wheelchair-accessible **Keys View** (Keys View Rd.) is a windswept observation point in the Little San Bernardino Mountains. Take in a panorama that stretches to the Salton Sea, Santa Rosa Mountains, San Andreas Fault, Palm Springs, San Jacinto Peak, and San Gorgonio Peak.

QUEEN VALLEY

The **Queen Valley** is a cross section of Joshua Tree's greatest hits, with Joshua trees, mining ruins, Native American villages, scenic hikes, and views. A series of short dirt roads crisscrosses Queen Valley through one of the largest pockets of Joshua trees in the park. Mining ruins range from Desert Queen Mine, a large gold operation, to the humble, rusty remains of tent encampments. Hiking trails follow old mining roads to **Desert Queen Mine, Lucky Boy Vista,** and **Wall Street Mine.** To reach the Queen Valley area, follow the unpaved Queen Valley Road or Desert Queen Mine Road east to Pine City.

CHOLLA CACTUS GARDEN

Driving through the endless landscape of the Pinto Basin, the **Cholla Cactus Garden** (Pinto Basin Rd.) appears like an army of prickly planted teddy bears. Their sheer numbers impress in this surreal landscape. A 0.25-mile (0.4 km, rt.) interpretive trail tours this strange flora.

COTTONWOOD SPRING

At the South Entrance, **Cottonwood Spring** (Cottonwood Spring Rd.) is a fan palm oasis. Its name comes from a surprising crop of native cottonwood trees that mix into the luxuriant vegetation surrounding the spring.

NIGHT SKIES

Designated an International Dark Sky Park, Joshua Tree has minimal light pollution letting moonless nights bring out the Milky Way. You can go out on your own to stargaze from campgrounds or road pullouts. The Pinto Basin Road between Cottonwood and Cholla Cactus Garden has minimal light and traffic. Use a red flashlight; white lights impinge seeing the stars. Year-round, rangers in tandem with park partners offer Night Sky Programs, with telescopes for viewing planets and nebulae. The Night Sky Festival happens annually around the fall equinox. Tickets go on sale in June (www.nightskyfestival.org).

SCENIC DRIVE

GEOLOGY TOUR ROAD

The **Geology Tour Road** (18 mi./29 km) is a backcountry drive that descends south into the broad Pleasant Valley and an ancient dry lake. Enjoy views of the unique geologic phenomena, which include dramatic erosion and uplifts. Pick up a free interpretive pamphlet from the Joshua Tree Visitor Center, which details the route with 16 numbered points of interest (also available from a small metal box at the start of the drive).

The first 5 miles (8 km) of graded dirt road to Squaw Tank are passable by most cars (no RVs) in dry weather. Beyond Squaw Tank, the road is **4WD only** due to deep ruts, sand, and steep grades. Past Squaw Tank, the road completes a one-way loop clockwise along the Hexie Mountain foothills and through Pleasant Valley. You're committed to the two-hour drive once you start the loop.

RECREATION

HIKING

Joshua Tree has top-notch hiking in an otherworldly landscape. But watch for dehydration, the biggest danger. Always carry at least **2 gallons (7.6 l) of water per person per day.** Hike during cooler times of the day, such as early morning or late afternoon. Never hike in summer or in midday heat.

▼ BARKER DAM

Best Hike

BARKER DAM AND WALL STREET MILL

DISTANCE: 1.3-2.2 miles (2.1-3.5 km) round-trip
DURATION: 1-1.5 hours
ELEVATION CHANGE: negligible
EFFORT: easy
TRAILHEAD: Barker Dam

From one trailhead, you can tackle two unique trails. The popular **Barker Dam Trail** (1.1 mi./1.8 km rt., 1 hr., easy) loops through boulders to a small pond, a watering hole for migrating birds, and bighorn sheep.

Marked with stone trail boundaries and occasional arrows, the **Wall Street Mill Trail** (2.2 mi./3.5 km rt., 1.5 hrs., easy) veers east passing abandoned cars and mining artifacts. A pink building marks the remains of the **Wonderland Ranch.** At the end of the trail are the **Desert Queen Well** ruins. A tall windmill, once used to pump water, still stands over piles of weathered timbers and an old tank.

Black Rock Canyon

Hike the interpretive **Hi-View Nature Trail** (1.3 mi./2.1 km rt., 1.5 hrs., moderate) clockwise to take in sweeping views of the Yucca Valley, Black Rock Canyon, and San Bernardino Mountains, including the snowcapped 11,503-foot (3,506 m) San Gorgonio Mountain.

SKULL ROCK

Hidden Valley

Trails around Hidden Valley are the **most popular in the park.** Arrive early as parking lots fill up.

The wheelchair-accessible, hard-packed sandy **Cap Rock Trail** (0.4 mi./0.6 km rt., 20 min., easy) leads through whimsically eroded boulder formations to a flat, cap-like rock balanced on top of a spectacular formation.

Anthropomorphically named for its gaunt eye socket-like depressions, **Skull Rock** (1.7 mi./2.7 km rt., 1.5 hrs., easy) is a loop trail that winds through the boulder- and plant-strewn landscape to Jumbo Rocks Campground. The trail follows the campground road until it crosses Park Boulevard to loop back through more boulders with desert views.

The **Hidden Valley Loop** (1 mi./1.6 km rt., 45 min., easy) passes through granite boulders to emerge in scenic Hidden Valley, a small, enclosed valley with tempting bouldering opportunities.

The trail to **Ryan Mountain** (3 mi./4.8 km rt., 2.5 hrs., strenuous) climbs more than 1,000 feet (305 m) in its ascent to the summit, where you are rewarded with panoramic views from the wind-scoured 5,457-foot (1,663-m) vantage point.

A weathered stamp mill and the surrounding ruins (rock house foundations, equipment, and mining tunnels)

LOST HORSE MINE

are the highlight of **Lost Horse Mine Trail** (4 mi./6.4 km rt., 2-3 hrs., moderate). Go counterclockwise to climb the stark Lost Horse Mountain through Joshua trees, yucca, and juniper, passing **Optimist Mine,** where a stone chimney and scattered artifacts remain. Then, the trail climbs precipitously, with sweeping views and **Lost Horse Mine** below. Although the mill and tunnels are fenced off, remains of rock houses and artifacts make for fun exploration.

Indian Cove

A flinty landscape hides **49 Palms Oasis** (3 mi./4.8 km rt., 2-3 hrs., moderate) until you are close enough to see it nestled against the jagged hills. The path climbs over a ridge and down through arid hills to the oasis of native fan palms secluded in a rocky canyon.

Cottonwood Spring

Two trails depart from Cottonwood Spring parking area. **Mastodon Peak Loop** (3 mi./4.8 km rt., 2 hrs., moderate) affords dramatic desert views to the Salton Sea. The nature trail heads northwest to a junction; turn right to pass concrete foundations of the old **Winona Mill.** At the foothills, the trail climbs toward the peak for sweeping views of the Cottonwood Mountains and the remains of the **Mastodon Mine**. The loop drops to a fork; turn right to finish.

Lost Palms Oasis Trail (7.5 mi./12 km rt., 5-6 hrs., strenuous) undulates down an exposed trail to a secluded canyon and the largest collection of fan palms in the park. The steep-walled canyon holds boulders, and the oasis, a watering hole for bighorn sheep and other wildlife.

CHOLLA CACTUS ALONG PINTO BASIN ROAD

ROCK CLIMBING IN JOSHUA TREE

BIKING

The paved **Park Boulevard** (25 mi./40 km) offers prime cycling through the park's most spectacular scenery between the West Entrance in Joshua Tree to the North Entrance near Twentynine Palms. **Pinto Basin Road** (30 mi./48 km), the other paved park road, cuts through the Pinto Basin's open desert with scenery that's less rewarding than Park Boulevard, but also more lightly traveled.

Bike rentals are outside the park's West Entrance in the town of Joshua Tree at **Joshua Tree Bicycle Shop** (6416 Hallee Rd., Joshua Tree, 760/366-3377, www.joshuatreebicycleshop.com, 10am-6pm Mon.-Sat.).

ROCK CLIMBING OUTFITTERS

Joshua Tree lures rock climbers. Four trails (Barker Dam Loop, Boy Scout Trail, Willow Hole, and Wonderland Wash) knife short distances into the **Wonderland of Rocks,** where rock climbing trails are signed and established.

Climbers Coffee (Hidden Valley Campground, 8am-10am Sat.-Sun. mid-Oct.-Apr.) offers the opportunity to meet Joshua Tree's climbing ranger and glean information from other climbers.

WILLOW HOLE TRAIL

To get in on the action, take a group class or a private, guided climb through one of several outfitters:

Joshua Tree Rock Climbing School (760/366-4745, www.joshuatreerockclimbing.com) offers year-round rock climbing classes and private guided outings.

Cliffhanger Guides (760/401-5033, www.cliffhangerguides.com) specializes in custom guided rock climbing half-day and full-day adventures.

Vertical Adventures (800/514-8785, www.vertical-adventures.com) has 1- to 5-day courses, private instruction, and guided climbing.

Climbing Life Guides (760/780-8868, www.theclimbinglifeguides.com) lead rock climbing and teach technical climbing.

To gear up for your rock climbing adventure, check out one of the three outfitters located on the main drag in Joshua Tree:

Nomad Ventures (61795 Twentynine Palms Hwy., Joshua Tree, 760/366-4684, www.nomadventures.com)

Coyote Corner (6535 Park Blvd., Joshua Tree, 760/366-9683, www.jtcoyotecorner.com)

Joshua Tree Outfitters (61707 Twentynine Palms Hwy., Joshua Tree, 760/366-1848, http://joshuatreeoutfitters.com)

WHERE TO STAY

INSIDE THE PARK

There are no accommodations or food inside the park. The only option is camping. Black Rock, Jumbo Rocks, Indian Cove, and Cottonwood accept **reservations** (877/444-6777, www.recreation.gov, $15-20) six months in advance for October-May. The remaining campgrounds are first come, first served and open year-round. Campgrounds start to fill by Thursday most weekends **October-May**. In summer, all campgrounds are first come, first served.

Black Rock Campground (reservations Oct.-May), in the northwest corner of Joshua Tree, is a good choice for first-time visitors, with 99 sites.

JUMBO ROCKS CAMPGROUND

Drinking water is available, and the location offers easy access to Yucca Valley for supplies.

Hidden Valley, on the south end of the Wonderland of Rocks, is popular with rock climbers—and everyone else. The 44 sites are at a premium.

CACTUS FLOWER

Jumbo Rocks is the largest campground in the park. Its 124 sites fill quickly at this convenient location along Park Boulevard. Nearby **Belle** and **White Tank**, off Pinto Basin Road, are both first come, first served.

Indian Cove (reservations Aug.-June) has 101 sites, with options for both groups and RVs, on the north edge of the Wonderland of Rocks. Access is from CA 62.

Cottonwood Campground (reservations Oct.-May) has 62 sites near the South Entrance to the park, off I-10.

Sheep Pass (reservation only) is a tent-only campground with 6 group sites, off Park Boulevard, between **Ryan** and Jumbo Rocks.

OUTSIDE THE PARK

Outside the park, find lodging and dining in **Yucca Valley,** the town of **Joshua Tree,** and **Twentynine Palms.** Backcountry camping is permitted on BLM land, and the town of Joshua Tree has a private RV park.

GETTING THERE

AIR

The closest airport is **Palm Springs Airport** (PSP, 3400 E. Tahquitz Canyon Way, 760/318-3800, www.palmspringsca.gov). International travelers

WHERE TO CAMP IN JOSHUA TREE

NAME	LOCATION	PRICE	SEASON	SITES	AMENITIES
Black Rock	Black Rock Canyon	$20	year-round; reserve Oct.-May	99	tent/RV and horse sites, flush toilets, drinking water, dump station
Hidden Valley	Hidden Valley	$15	year-round	44	tent/RV sites, vault toilets
Ryan	Hidden Valley	$15	year-round	31	tent and horse sites, vault toilets
Sheep Pass	Hidden Valley	$25-50	year-round	6	group tent sites, vault toilets
Jumbo Rocks	Hidden Valley	$15	year-round; reserve Oct.-May	124	tent/RV sites, vault toilets
Belle	Hidden Valley	$15	Oct.-May	18	tent sites, vault toilets
White Tank	Hidden Valley	$15	year-round	15	tent/RV sites, vault toilets
Indian Cove	Indian Cove	$20	year-round; reserve Oct.-May	101	tent/RV sites and group sites, vault toilets
Cottonwood	Cottonwood Spring	$20	year-round; reserve Oct.-May	62	tent/RV and group sites, flush toilets, drinking water, dump station

can fly into **Los Angeles International Airport** (LAX, 1 World Way, 424/646-5252, www.flylax.com) or **Las Vegas's McCarran International Airport** (LAS, 5757 Wayne Newton Blvd., 702/261-5211, www.mccarran.com).

CAR

From **Palm Springs,** it's an hour's drive. Yucca Valley is the best place to fuel up before entering the park. The small town has several major car rental agencies available. From **Los Angeles,** it's roughly a 3-hour drive east via CA 91.

The **West Entrance** (CA 62) to Joshua Tree is located 50 miles (81 km, 1.25 hr.) north of Palm Springs and 145 miles (233 km, 3-4 hrs.) east of Los Angeles. From I-10 near Palm Springs, head north on CA 62 for 30 miles (48 km) to the town of Joshua Tree. Turn south on Park Boulevard and follow the road into the park.

The **North Entrance** (CA 62) is farther east near Twentynine Palms. From Joshua Tree, drive 16 miles (26 km) east along CA 62 then turn south on Utah Trail. From **Las Vegas,** it's roughly a 4-hour drive southwest via I-15 to the North Entrance.

The **South Entrance** (I-10) is about 65 miles (105 km, 1.25 hr.) east of Palm Springs along I-10 and 160 miles (257 km, 4 hrs.) east of Los Angeles. From I-10, turn north on Cottonwood Spring Road to enter the park.

GETTING AROUND

Gas up before you go into the park. Most visitors drive into the park from the West Entrance and follow the main Park Boulevard to sights and trailheads in the Hidden Valley. In peak season, congestion at trailheads and parking areas may be a problem.

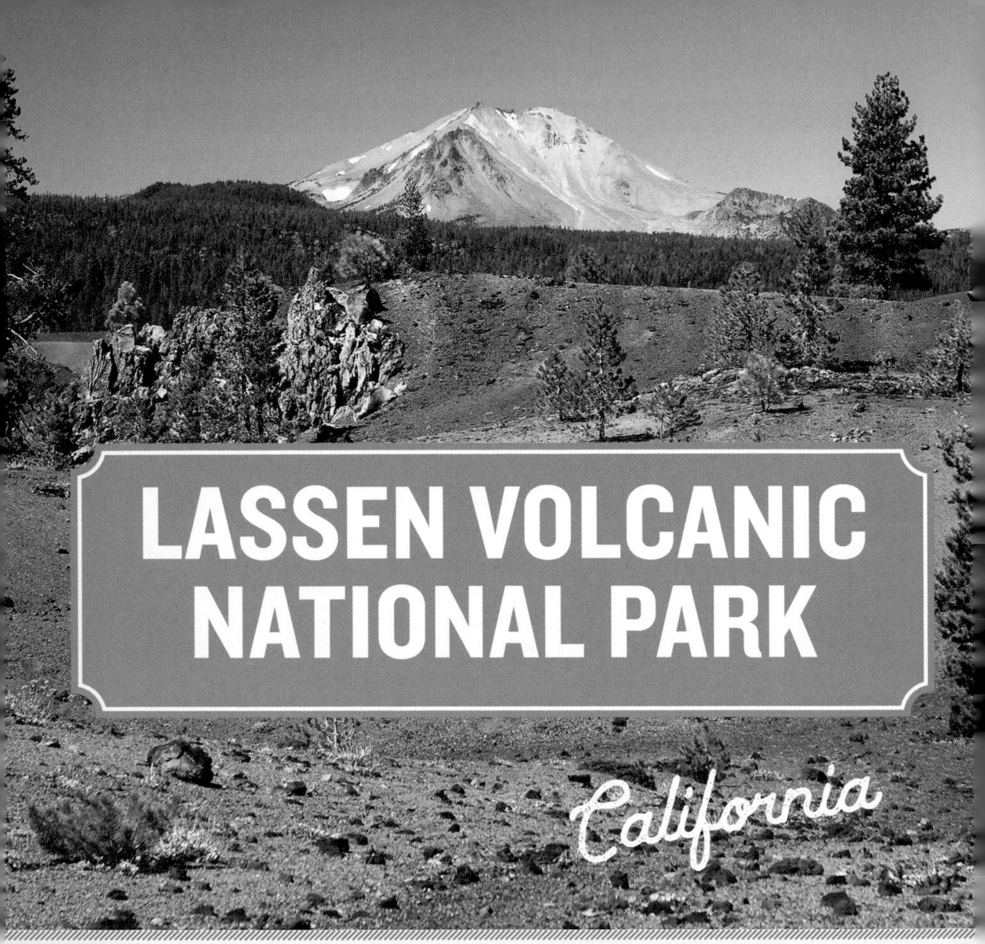

LASSEN VOLCANIC NATIONAL PARK

California

WEBSITE:
www.nps.gov/lavo

PHONE NUMBER:
530/595-4480

VISITATION RANK:
41

WHY GO:
Explore a volcanic landscape.

▲ LASSEN PEAK AND PAINTED DUNES

KEEPSAKE STAMPS ▼▼▼

Due to rugged weather and geographic distance from California's urban centers, **LASSEN VOLCANIC NATIONAL PARK** is preserved as largely unspoiled wilderness, much as it was when four local tribes harvested and hunted through the these valleys. Encased within the park is Mount Lassen, an active volcano with a history of eruptions, the last of which took place 1914-1917. As in Yellowstone, hydrothermals pushing to the surface still shape the landscape, which clusters with fumaroles, mud pots, and hot springs. A partial loop drive through the park follows the stark slopes and jagged rocks of the most recent eruption to an enormous volcano crater. Plentiful hiking trails, ponds, and campsites welcome visitors to enjoy the panorama.

PLANNING YOUR TIME

Located in Northern California, this high-elevation park is only accessible **June** into **October** when snow melts and daytime temperatures rise to the 80s and 90s (upper 20s and lower 30s Celsius). Snow chokes the area October-June, closing the main road through the park. Most visitors arrive **July** through **September.** Those short on time stick to the park's paved loop road.

ENTRANCES AND FEES

There are two park entrances, both located on CA 89. The **northwest entrance** (summer only) is at the junction of CA 89 and CA 44 near Manzanita Lake. The **southwest entrance** (open year-round) is accessed from CA 36 and travels north through the park from the Kohm Yah-mah-nee Visitor Center. In winter, the park road is closed after the visitors center.

The entrance fee is $30 per vehicle ($25 motorcycle, $15 individual) and good for seven days.

VISITORS CENTER

The **Kohm Yah-mah-nee Visitor Center** (21800 Lassen National Park Hwy., Mineral, 530/595-4480, 9am-5pm daily May-Oct., 9am-5pm Wed.-Sun. Nov.-Mar.) has interactive exhibits, a café, a souvenir shop, and a bookstore. Outside, strategically placed benches offer gorgeous views of the mountains and a short interpretive trail tours the paved walkways. Rangers lead programs, including snowshoe walks in winter.

SULPHUR WORKS

SIGHTS

SULPHUR WORKS

The **Sulphur Works** boardwalk leads to loud boiling mud pots and a small steaming stream that sends up occasional bursts of boiling water. From the southwest entrance station, drive along the park road to the parking area north of the Kohm Yah-mah-nee Visitor Center.

SUMMIT LAKE

Lassen is dotted with tiny lakes. One of the most popular (and most easily accessible) is **Summit Lake.** The bright

LASSEN VOLCANIC NATIONAL PARK
VOLCANO ADVENTURE YOUTH CAMP
LOST CREEK GROUP CAMP
LASSEN NATIONAL FOREST
Hat Creek
Badg
Table Mountain 6,919ft
Nobles Emigrant Trail
Lost Creek
To Redding
Dwarf Forest
Chaos Jumbles
CHAOS CRAGS AND CHAOS JUMBLES
Reflection Lake
ENTRANCE STATION
Manzanita Lake
MANZANITA LAKE CAMPGROUND
HOT ROCK
Anklin Meadows
Raker Peak 7,483ft
Crags Lake
Lava
CHAOS CRAGS
8,530ft
Manzanita Creek
Hat Creek
DEVASTATED AREA
Devastated Area
HAT CREEK TRAILHEAD
Dersch Meadows
Hat Mounta 7,695ft
Crescent Crater 8,645ft
LASSEN NATIONAL FOREST
LASSEN VOLCANIC WILDERNESS
Paradise Meadows
SUMMIT LAKE TRAILHEAD
SUMMIT LAKE NORTH
Summit Lake
SUMMIT LAKE SOUTH
North Fork
Loomis Peak 8,658ft
Crescent Cliff
LASSEN PEAK 10,457ft
Bailey Creek
Blue Lake Canyon
Shadow Lake
Eagle Peak 9,222ft
ROAD'S HIGH POINT 8,512FT
Soda Lake
LASSEN PEAK TRAILHEAD
Cliff Lake
Reading Peak
Lake Helen
Pilot Pinnacle 8,886ft
Emerald Lake
Mount Diller 9,087ft
BUMPASS TRAILHEAD
Upper Meadow
Bumpass Mountain 8,753ft
Kings Creek Falls
Kings
KINGS CREEK PICNIC AREA
KINGS CREEK TRAILHEAD
Ridge Lakes
Little Hot Springs Valley
Hydrothermal Areas
Diamond Pk 7,968ft
SULPHUR WORKS
Sifford Lakes
Brokeoff Mountain
Bumpass Cr
Crumbaugh Lake
Mill Creek Falls
Forest Lake
Conard Meadows
LASSEN VOLCANIC WILDERNESS
Devils Kitchen
SOUTHWEST
KOHM YAH-MAH-NEE VISITOR CENTER
ENTRANCE STATION
Twin Meadows
Panther Creek
Mount Conard 8,204ft
Drake Lake
Mill Creek
Ridge Lake
Huckleberry Lake
Blue Lake
LASSEN NATIONAL FOREST
To Mineral

To Hwy 44
Butte Creek
Prospect Peak 8,338ft
Bathtub Lake
BUTTE LAKE
Butte Lake
Lava
Sunrise Peak 7,139ft
Pacific Crest Trail
Soap Lake
Cinder Cone 6,907ft
Fantastic Lava Beds
Nobles Emigrant Trail
Emigrant Lake
Widow Lake
Cluster Lakes
Big Bear Lake
Silver Lake
Feather Lake
Little Bear Lake
Lava
Ash Butte 7,577ft
Fairfield Peak 7,272ft
Snag Lake
Teal Lake
Lower Twin Lake
Rainbow Lake
LASSEN VOLCANIC WILDERNESS
Upper Twin Lake
Swan Lake
Echo Lake
Mount Hoffman 7,883ft
Red Cinder Cone 8,008ft
Hidden Lake
LASSEN VOLCANIC NATIONAL PARK
Crater Butte 7,267ft
Cameron Meadow
Creek
Grassy
Jakey Lake
Inspiration Point
Grassy Swale
Horseshoe Lake
Corral Meadow
Crystal Cliffs 7,548ft
Pilot Mountain 7,175ft
Kings
Crystal Lake
Saddle Mountain 7,638ft
Indian Lake
Juniper Lake
Glen Lake
Island Lake
Flatiron Ridge
Creek
East Lake
DRAKESBAD GUEST RANCH
WARNER VALLEY
JUNIPER LAKE
Bonte Peak 7,777ft
WARNER VALLEY TRAILHEAD
Hot Springs Creek
Boiling Springs Lake
Pacific Crest Trail
MOUNT HARKNESS FIRE LOOKOUT TOWER
Hydrothermal Areas
Terminal Geyser
Warner Valley
ford Mountain 7,408ft
Kelly Mountain
Little Willow Lake
Willow Lake
0
1 mi
0
1 km
To Chester
To Chester
© MOON.COM

Top 3

BUMPASS HELL

1 TOUR LASSEN VOLCANIC SCENIC BYWAY

From the southwest entrance, the **park road** (CA 89, open June-early Oct., snow depending) twists and turns for 30 miles (48 km) through a volcanic landscape. The stunning drive climbs to 8,512 feet (2,595 m) below the summit of Lassen Peak. Scenic pullouts en route offer places for viewing and photographing the scenery, including volcanic features. South of Lassen Peak, the road has multiple switchbacks; north of the peak, there are fewer curves. Bicyclists can ride the road car-free in spring between snowplows freeing the pavement and the opening to vehicles. In winter, cross-country skiers can also tour the route, but be aware of avalanche dangers.

2 WALK THROUGH BUMPASS HELL

North of the Sulphur Works, **Bumpass Hell** is packed with hydrothermal activity. Walk the boardwalks and paths, reconstructed in 2018-2020, along the **Bumpass Nature Trail** (3 mi./4.8 km rt., 2 hrs., moderate) allow peeks at boiling mud pots, fumaroles, steaming springs, and bubbling pools. The strong smell of sulfur proves that this volcano is far from extinct. If you can't get to Yellowstone, this is a close cousin.

3 ADMIRE LASSEN PEAK

Majestic **Lassen Peak** stretches 10,457 feet (3,187 m) into the sky. The craggy and broken mountain peak is all that's left after the 1915 eruption—hence the lack of vegetation. Climb 2.5 miles (4 km) to the summit or simply settle for multiple views of its raw landscape from pullouts on the park road. The Lassen Peak Parking Area and Viewpoint offers the closest look.

LASSEN PEAK

Best Hike

LASSEN PEAK TRAIL

DISTANCE: 5 miles (8 km) round-trip
DURATION: 3-5 hours
ELEVATION CHANGE: 1,957 feet (597 m)
EFFORT: strenuous
TRAILHEAD: Lassen Peak

The **Lassen Peak Trail** is the park's must-do hike. From the Lassen Peak Trailhead, this loose rock path climbs 1,957 feet (597 m) to the highest point on Lassen Peak via a starkly beautiful, unusual trail. Long views extend across the park and beyond. Along the way, exhibits explain the fascinating scenery of volcanic remains, lakes, wildlife, and rock formations. Due to the high elevation, the trail tends to be cool even in summer heat; sea-level visitors may feel winded.

and shining small lake attracts campers to its two campgrounds, and an easy walk navigates its waters and the plantlife. Follow one of the small trails down to the edge of the water to eke out a spot on the miniscule beach.

DEVASTATED AREA

When Lassen Peak blew its top in 1915, the eruption destroyed a tremendous part of the mountain. Boiling mud and explosive gases tore off the side of the peak, killing all the vegetation in the area. A hail of lava rained down, creating new rocks ranging in size from gravel to boulders across the north side of the mountain. Today, the **Devastated Area** north of Summit Lake offers an interpretive, wheelchair-accessible walk (0.5 mi./0.8 km rt.) through a small part of the disrupted mountainside to see some of the world's youngest rocks, plus renewing vegetation.

CHAOS CRAGS AND JUMBLES

In the northwest corner of the park, a massive rock avalanche about 300 years ago created the broken **Chaos Jumbles.** The avalanche was so big and came down so fast that it trapped a pocket of air underneath. The regrowth of the living landscape has allowed a greater variety of competing plants to get a foothold. Today, visitors can enjoy the broader-than-average variety of coniferous trees at the park road pullout.

LOOMIS MUSEUM

Near the northwest entrance is the **Loomis Museum** (530/595-6140, 9am-5pm Fri.-Sun. mid-May-mid-June, 9am-5pm daily mid-June-Oct., 9am-5pm Fri.-Sun. Oct., free). The interpretive museum shows the history of Mount Lassen, focusing heavily on the 1914-1915 eruptions photographed by B. F. Loomis. The photos offer a rare chance to see the devastation and following stages of regrowth on the volcanic slopes.

RECREATION

HIKING

Trailheads line the paved park road. The **Kings Creek Falls Trail** (2.3 mi./3.7 km rt., 2 hrs., moderate) treks downhill to waterfalls. Admire the small cascade and pool before beginning the 700-foot (213-m) climb back up. Find the trailhead 13 miles (21 km) north of the southwest entrance.

From the Summit Lake Trailhead, a forested path runs the length of Summit Lake to **Echo Lake** (4.4 mi./7.1 km rt., 2-3 hrs., moderate). With a gentle elevation gain, the pleasant walk reaches Echo Lake and its views of Lassen Peak.

The Brokeoff Mountain Trail (7.4 mi./11.9 km rt., 5-7 hrs., strenuous) grunts up a 2,600-foot (793-m) ascent from a more than mile-high starting point for one of the toughest hikes. But the reward is big panoramic views. Locate the trailhead south of the southwest entrance station.

For hiking instead in the remote northeast corner of the park and a radical change of scenery, take the **Cinder Cone Trail** (4-5 mi./6.4-8 km rt., 3 hrs. moderate) that rises 800 vertical

ONE DAY IN LASSEN

Visitors short on time can enjoy most of the park's sights by cruising along the 30-mile (48-km) **Lassen Volcanic Scenic Byway.** Pick up the park's road guide from the visitors center, stop at interpretive pullovers, and marvel at the volcanic wonders.

feet (244 m) to overlook dunes and lava fields. To lengthen the hike, walk down the south side of the cone. Geology and photography buffs will like this hike, which shows off some of the park's less seen volcanic features. Find the trailhead at Butte Lake at the end of a gravel road (CA 44).

BACKPACKING

Lassen offers backpacking through a volcanic landscape pockmarked with scenic lakes. Wilderness permits are required on the **Pacific Crest Trail** (available at the visitors center, bear canister required). For families and beginning backpackers, an 11-mile (17.7 km) loop from the Summit Lake Trailhead takes in seven lakes; short side trips add more lakes.

WHERE TO STAY

INSIDE THE PARK

Lassen has few in-park accommodations, most of them campgrounds (one with cabins). Four developed campgrounds are accessible via the paved park road; the remaining primitive campgrounds are via dirt roads. **Reservations** (877/444-6777, www.recreation.gov) are highly recommended six months in advance for **Manzanita Lake, Summit Lake,** and **Butte Lake.** All campsites have picnic tables and fire pits.

Near the northwest entrance, **Manzanita Lake** May-Oct., $26) is the largest campground with 179 sites, flush toilets, potable running water, an RV dump station, and showers. Trailers and campers up to 35 feet (11 m) are allowed. Reservations go fast for the rustic cabins ($70-95) that line the north shore of the lake. The **Manzanita Lake Camper Store** (8am-6pm daily mid-May-Sept., hours vary seasonally) sells hot food and snacks.

At 7,000 feet (2,134 m), **Summit Lake North and South** (late June-Sept., $22-24) are split on either side of the

▼ BROKEOFF MOUNTAIN

water, with scenery and prime hiking. The two developed campgrounds have 94 sites with flush toilets; bring water for drinking and washing.

Near the Kohm Yah-mah-nee Visitor Center, **Southwest Walk-In** (first come, first served, year-round, $10-16) has 21 tent-only campsites that are reached via a short, paved walk from the parking area (RVs can park in the lot). In summer, there are flush toilets and drinking water; fees are reduced in winter when the water is shut off.

The **Lassen Cafe & Gift** (Kohm Yah-mah-nee Visitor Center, 530/595-3555, 11am-2pm Sat.-Sun. mid-Oct-mid-May, 9am-5pm mid-May-mid-Oct.) sells burgers, pizza, coffee, and ice cream.

In the park's remote northeast corner, accessed from CA 44, a gravel road reaches the 6,100-foot (1,859-m) **Butte Lake** (June-Sept., $22). The large campground has pit toilets, but no drinking water. Trailers and RVs are limited to 35 feet (11 m). The nearby Butte Lake has a boat launch and hiking trails.

On the park's east side, a rough dirt road leads to **Juniper Lake** (north of Chester, June-Oct., $12). At 6,700-foot (2,042-m) Juniper Lake, the campground has 17 sites, with pit toilets but no drinking water. A boat launch sits about 1.5 miles (2.4 km) north. Hiking trails circle the lake.

LASSEN VOLCANIC NATIONAL PARK

North of Chester, a dirt road accesses small **Warner Valley** (June-Sept., $16), which has 17 sites, pit toilets, and drinking water. Trailers are not allowed. Nearby hiking trails showcase volcanic features.

Near the southwest entrance station, the **Drakesbad Guest Ranch** (14423 Chester Warner Valley Rd., Chester, 866/999-0914, www.lassenlodging.com, June-mid-Oct., from $220) is an all-inclusive ranch with horseback riding, swimming, and fishing.

OUTSIDE THE PARK

The nearest lodgings are about 9 miles (14.5 km) south in **Mineral** and in the tiny town of **Chester,** 29 miles (47 km) east of the southwest entrance on CA 89/36.

GETTING THERE AND AROUND

AIR

The closest international airport is **Sacramento International Airport** (SMF, 6900 Airport Blvd., 916/929-5411, www.sacramento.aero/smf), where car rentals are available.

CAR

Lassen Volcanic National Park is 150-175 miles (242-280 km, 3 hrs.) north of Sacramento. Take I-5 north to Red Bluff, then follow CA 36 east for 43 miles (69 km) past Mineral. Turn left onto CA 89, which leads to the southwest park entrance.

CA 89 becomes the main road through the park; the visitors center, campgrounds, trailheads, and lakes cluster along it. It is closed from late October to May, June, or July, depending on weather and snowfall.

The park has no public transportation; exploration requires a vehicle. Manzanita Lake Camper Store has the only **gas station.** Otherwise, gas up en route in Red Bluff, Chester, or Susanville.

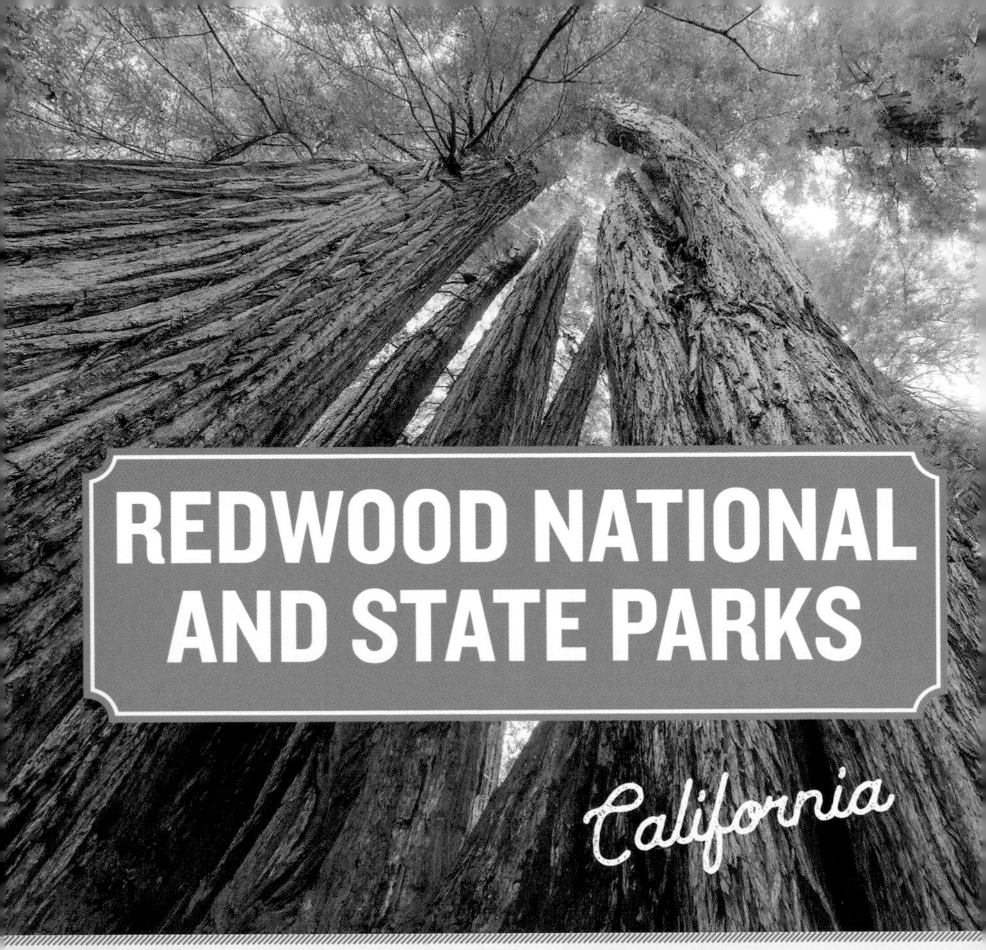

REDWOOD NATIONAL AND STATE PARKS

California

WEBSITE:
www.nps.gov/redw

PHONE NUMBER:
707/464-6101

VISITATION RANK:
42

WHY GO:
Feel small beneath coast redwoods.

▲ TALL TREES GROVE

KEEPSAKE STAMPS ▼▼▼

Along California's rugged north coast, these towering redwoods inspire pure awe. *Sequoia sempervirens* define the verdant landscape. It's easy to imagine ancestors of the Tolowa and Yurok people collecting berries and hunting wild game here. The best places to explore the natural groves of these gargantuan treasures are in the **REDWOOD NATIONAL AND STATE PARKS**, which line the coast from Eureka to Crescent City. Along US 101, the cluster of state and national parks lure travelers with numerous hiking trails, forested campgrounds, kitschy tourist stops, and some of the tallest and oldest trees on the continent.

PLANNING YOUR TIME

The Redwood National and State Parks meander 40 miles (64 km) along the Northern California coast between Crescent City in the north and the old logging town of Eureka in the south. In addition to **Redwood National Park,** this parkland includes three state parks—**Prairie Creek Redwoods, Del Norte Coast Redwoods,** and **Jedediah Smith Redwoods.** Combined, the region encompasses most of California's northern redwood forests.

May through **September** are the busiest months, with cool temperatures in the 40s-60s (4-16°C), fog, and damp weather. Fall, winter, and early spring (Oct.-Apr.) can deliver copious rain.

ENTRANCES AND FEES

US 101 connects the multiple park entrances. Redwood National Park has no entrance fee; however, Prairie Creek Redwoods, Del Norte Coast Redwoods, and Jedediah Smith Redwoods State Parks collect entrance and day-use fees.

VISITORS CENTERS

Four visitors centers offer information, exhibits, maps, ranger-led talks and walks, and restrooms.

Thomas H. Kuchel Visitor Center (US 101, Orick, 707/465-7765, 9am-5pm daily spring-fall, 9am-4pm daily winter) is the largest facility, with a ranger station, maps, advice, permits for backcountry camping, and books. In the summer, rangers lead talks and coast walks.

Prairie Creek Visitor Center (Newton B. Drury Scenic Pkwy., 707/488-2039, 9am-5pm daily summer, 9am-4pm daily fall-spring) includes a small interpretive museum that describes the history of the California redwood forests. A tiny bookshop adjoins the museum.

Hiouchi Visitor Center (US 199, Hiouchi, 707/458-3294, 9am-5pm daily summer, 9am-4pm daily winter) has backcountry permits, a park movie, and a picnic area.

Jedediah Smith Visitors Center (US 199, Hiouchi, 707/458-3496, 9am-5pm daily summer) has information and materials about all of the nearby parks.

SIGHTS

REDWOOD NATIONAL PARK

This iconic park harbors old-growth groves of coastal redwoods. These sacred places spur the imagination with their verdant beauty and lush undergrowth of moss, ferns, and rhododendrons. On the coast, tidepools await for exploring, and rangers lead tours to see the creatures in the tidal zone. Bring the binoculars to watch whales migrate (Nov.-Dec. and Mar.-Apr.).

PRAIRIE CREEK REDWOODS STATE PARK

Prairie Creek Redwoods State Park (Newton B. Drury Scenic Pkwy., 707/488-2039, www.parks.ca.gov, sunrise-sunset daily, day use $8) has miles of wild beach, roaming wildlife, and a popular hike through a one-of-a-kind

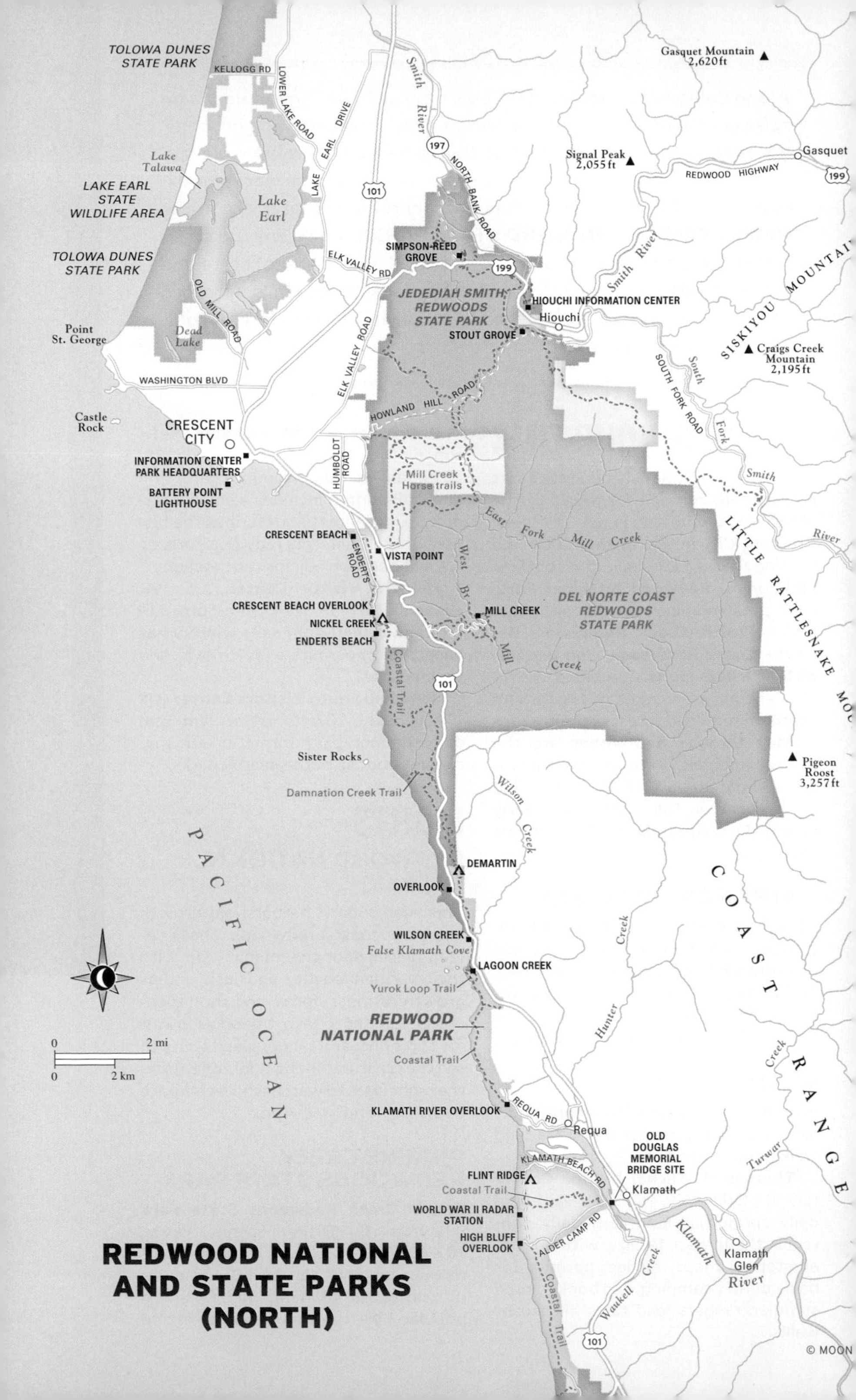
REDWOOD NATIONAL AND STATE PARKS (NORTH)
TOLOWA DUNES STATE PARK
KELLOGG RD
LOWER LAKE ROAD
LAKE EARL DRIVE
Smith River
197
NORTH BANK ROAD
Gasquet Mountain 2,620ft
Signal Peak 2,055ft
Gasquet
REDWOOD HIGHWAY
199
Lake Talawa
LAKE EARL STATE WILDLIFE AREA
Lake Earl
101
SIMPSON-REED GROVE
ELK VALLEY RD
TOLOWA DUNES STATE PARK
JEDEDIAH SMITH REDWOODS STATE PARK
HIOUCHI INFORMATION CENTER
Hiouchi
Smith River
SISKIYOU MOUNTAINS
OLD MILL ROAD
Dead Lake
ELK VALLEY ROAD
STOUT GROVE
Point St. George
SOUTH FORK ROAD
South Fork Smith
Craigs Creek Mountain 2,195ft
WASHINGTON BLVD
HOWLAND HILL ROAD
Castle Rock
CRESCENT CITY
INFORMATION CENTER PARK HEADQUARTERS
BATTERY POINT LIGHTHOUSE
HUMBOLDT ROAD
Mill Creek Horse trails
East Fork Mill Creek
LITTLE RATTLESNAKE MOUNTAIN
River
CRESCENT BEACH
ENDERTS ROAD
VISTA POINT
West Br
DEL NORTE COAST REDWOODS STATE PARK
CRESCENT BEACH OVERLOOK
NICKEL CREEK
MILL CREEK
ENDERTS BEACH
Mill Creek
Coastal Trail
101
Sister Rocks
Damnation Creek Trail
Pigeon Roost 3,257ft
Wilson Creek
PACIFIC OCEAN
COAST RANGE
DEMARTIN
OVERLOOK
WILSON CREEK
False Klamath Cove
Creek
LAGOON CREEK
Yurok Loop Trail
REDWOOD NATIONAL PARK
Hunter Creek
0 2 mi
0 2 km
Coastal Trail
Creek
KLAMATH RIVER OVERLOOK
REQUA RD
Requa
OLD DOUGLAS MEMORIAL BRIDGE SITE
KLAMATH BEACH RD
Turwar
FLINT RIDGE
Coastal Trail
Klamath
WORLD WAR II RADAR STATION
HIGH BLUFF OVERLOOK
ALDER CAMP RD
Klamath River
Klamath Glen
Waukell Creek
Coastal Trail
101
© MOON

REDWOOD NATIONAL AND STATE PARKS (SOUTH)
Coastal Trail
101
AH-PAH
PRAIRIE CREEK REDWOODS STATE PARK
NEWTON B. DRURY SCENIC PKWY
Prairie Creek
FERN CANYON
GOLD BLUFFS BEACH
BIG TREE WAYSIDE
PRAIRIE CREEK VISITOR CENTER
ELK PRAIRIE
Gold Bluffs
DAVISON RD
May Creek
PACIFIC OCEAN
COAST RANGE
Klamath River
HOLTER RIDGE
LOST MAN CREEK
Lost Man Cr
ELK MEADOW
Trillium Falls Trail
Berry Glen Trail
LADY BIRD JOHNSON GROVE
REDWOOD CREEK TRAILHEAD
KUCHEL VISITOR CENTER
Orick
ORICK HORSE TRAILHEAD
REDWOOD CREEK
Freshwater Lagoon
BALD HILLS ROAD
STONE LAGOON
ELAM CAMP
REDWOOD CREEK OVERLOOK
HUMBOLDT LAGOONS STATE PARK
Stone Lagoon
McArthur Creek
INFORMATION
DRY LAGOON BEACH
44 CAMP
Dolason Prairie Trail
DOLASON PRAIRIE
HARRY A. MERLO STATE RECREATION AREA
REDWOOD HIGHWAY
TALL TREES GROVE
Tall Trees Trail
Emerald Ridge Trail
REDWOOD NATIONAL PARK
Big Lagoon
Rodgers Peak 2,745 ft
Bridge Creek
BRIDGE CREEK RIDGE
Redwood Creek
Schoolhouse Peak 3,097 ft
LYONS RANCH
PATRICK'S POINT STATE PARK
PATRICKS POINT DR
To Eureka
0
2 mi
2 km

Top 3

1 CRUISE NEWTON B. DRURY SCENIC PARKWAY

Gorgeous **Newton B. Drury Scenic Parkway** parallels US 101 through the redwoods. Along the parkway, old-growth redwoods line the road and offer an up-close view of the forest ecosystem, with a grove or a trailhead every 100 yards (91 m) for further exploration. The north entrance is 4 miles (6.4 km) south of Klamath; the south entrance is 6 miles (9.7 km) north of Orick.

NEWTON B. DRURY SCENIC PARKWAY

2 STROLL ALONG GOLD BLUFFS BEACH

Gold Bluffs Beach is truly wild. Lonely waves pound the shore, a spikey grove of Sitka spruce tops the nearby bluffs, and herds of Roosevelt elk frequently roam the wide, salt-and-pepper-colored beach. Look for whales migrating in early spring and late fall. Prospectors found gold flakes here in 1850, giving the beach its name. The beach, part of Prairie Creek Redwoods State Park, is accessible via Davison Road off US 101 at Elk Meadow.

3 GAZE UP AT GIANTS IN STOUT MEMORIAL GROVE

In **Jedediah Smith Redwoods State Park,** a pristine forest of old-growth redwoods sits along the Smith River. The **Stout Memorial Grove** is home to some of the biggest and oldest trees on the North Coast that were somehow spared the loggers' saws. This grove is very quiet and less populated than others, since its far-north latitude makes it harder to reach than some of the other big redwood groves in California.

STOUT MEMORIAL GROVE IN JEDEDIAH SMITH REDWOOD STATE PARK

Best Hike

LADY BIRD JOHNSON GROVE

DISTANCE: 1.4 mile (2.3 km) round-trip
DURATION: 1 hour
ELEVATION CHANGE: 1,425 feet (434 m)
EFFORT: easy
TRAILHEAD: Lady Bird Johnson Grove Trailhead on Bald Hills Road

The most popular place to get close to the redwoods is the **Lady Bird Johnson Grove Nature Trail** in Redwoods National Park. It can be otherworldly with fog floating in from the ocean along the trail lined with lush ferns and mossy fallen logs. Early June visitors get treated to rhododendron blooms. The gradual uphills and downhills on a lollipop loop provides an intimate view of the redwood-fir ridgetop forests that define this region. Pick up an interpretive brochure at the trailhead.

fern-draped canyon. Prairie Creek offers a sampler platter of the best natural elements of California's North Coast.

Stop at the **Big Tree Wayside,** home to the 304-foot-high (123-m) **Big Tree.** Its life was almost cut short by a homesteader who wanted to cut it down to use the stump as a dance floor. Follow the short, five-minute loop trail near the Big Tree to see other neighboring giants.

Look for a herd of **Roosevelt elk** at Elk Prairie, a stretch of open grassland along the southern end of the parkway. This subspecies of elk stands up to 5 feet high (1.5 m) and weighs up to 1,000 pounds (454 kg). The best times to see the elk are early morning and around sunset. During the mating season (Aug.-Oct.), the bugling of the bulls fills the air.

DEL NORTE COAST REDWOODS STATE PARK

South of Crescent City, **Del Norte Coast Redwoods State Park** (Mill Creek

▼ ROOSEVELT ELK

PRAIRIE CREEK BRIDGE

Campground Rd. off US 101, 707/464-6101, www.parks.ca.gov, day use $8) encompasses a variety of ecosystems, including 8 miles (13 km) of wild coastline, second-growth redwood forest, and virgin old-growth forests. Del Norte State Park has no visitors center, but you can get information from the **Crescent City Information Center** (1111 2nd St., Crescent City, 707/465-7306, 9am-5pm daily spring-fall, 9am-4pm Thurs.-Mon. winter).

JEDEDIAH SMITH REDWOODS STATE PARK

The **Jedediah Smith Redwoods State Park** (US 199, 9 mi./15 km east of Crescent City, 707/464-6101, www.parks.ca.gov, day use $8) is the northernmost of the redwoods parks. It preserves a pristine forest of old-growth redwoods along the Smith River in the **Stout Memorial Grove.** Each July, the Tolowa Tribe performs a demonstration of the renewal dance at the campground.

RECREATION

HIKING

Redwood National Park

The cool, dark **Trillium Falls Trail** (Davison Rd. at Elk Meadow, 2.5 mi./4 km rt., 1.5 hrs., easy-moderate) has striking redwoods and a small, moss-flanked waterfall that is lovely anytime, but best in spring when the water volume peaks. The trail is named for the white trillium that bloom in spring.

The **Lost Man Creek Trail** (east of Elk Meadow, 1 mile (1.6 km) off US 101, 1-22 mi./1.6-35 km rt., easy-difficult) has it all. The first 0.5 mile (0.8 km) is perfect for wheelchairs and families with small children. But as the lush redwood-and-fern-lined trail rolls along, grades get steeper and more challenging. To reach the Lost Man Creek picnic grounds at 11 miles (18 km) requires ascending more than 3,000 feet (914 m) of elevation and crossing several streams. Bikes are permitted on this trail.

To sink into a full day of enchantment in this moist forest, hike the **Redwood Creek Trail** (Bald Hills Rd. spur off US 101, 8-14 mi./13-23 km rt., 7-9 hrs., strenuous), which follows Redwood Creek to the **Tall Trees Grove.** Two bridges over the river are installed in summer only (May-Sept.) along the route.

Prairie Creek Redwoods State Park

Near Gold Bluffs Beach, **Fern Canyon Loop** (0.7 mi./1.1 km rt., 30 min., easy) runs through a narrow canyon carved by Home Creek. Ferns, moss, and other water-loving plants grow thick up the sides of the canyon, creating a beautiful vertical carpet of greenery (scenes from *Jurassic Park 2* and *Return of the Jedi* were filmed here).

The **James Irvine Loop** (12.4 mi./20 km rt., 7 hrs., moderate) starts from the visitors center on the **James Irvine**

ONE DAY IN THE REDWOODS

A drive along US 101 on the Redwood Highway gets you up close to the looming trees. Make your first stop at the **Thomas H. Kuchel Visitor Center** to learn about the giant trees, then take a walk to the beach. Stroll the **Lady Bird Johnson Grove Nature Trail** in Redwoods National Park then drive north to the otherworldly **Newton B. Drury Scenic Parkway** in Prairie Creek Redwoods State Park

Trail and reaches the beach. Return on the **Miners' Ridge Trail.** As you head out, bear right when you can, following the trail through enormous trees until it joins Fern Canyon Trail. Turn left when you get to the coast and walk along Gold Bluffs Beach for 1.2 miles (1.9 km) to the campground, turning east to head back on the more demanding trail toward the visitors center.

Del Norte Coast Redwoods State Park

In summer, Mill Creek Campground is the trailhead for several trails (access is from US 101 when the campground is closed). The **Trestle Loop Trail** (1 mi./1.6 km rt., 30 min., easy) trots along a defunct railroad route from the logging era with trestles and other artifacts along the way. It's a good place to tour second-growth redwoods. A leisurely walk on the **Nature Loop Trail** (1 mi./1.6 km rt., 30 min., easy) educates visitors with interpretive signage about the unique redwood trees and ecosystem.

Jedediah Smith Redwoods State Park

A shady hike beneath 1,000-year-old redwoods, the **Simpson-Reed Trail** (1 mi./1.6 km rt., 30 min., easy) descends to the banks of the Smith River, where fallen trees create pools for fish. Look for red-legged frogs on the damp forest floor.

From the Hiouchi Visitor Center and Jedediah Smith Campground, paths cross a summer footbridge over the turquoise Smith River to access several trailheads. To hike north along the river, take the **Hiouchi Trail** (2 mi./3.2 km rt., 1 hr., moderate) through old-growth redwoods into a streamside environment of wild berries and Pacific madrone.

For a more aggressive trek along a salmon stream, follow the **Mill Creek Horse Trail** (7.75 mi./12.5 km rt., 4 hrs., strenuous) upstream through old-growth redwoods to unpaved Howland Hill Road. Fall brings on reds and golds of big-leaf maples along the clear stream.

The **Boy Scout Tree Trail** (Howland Hill Rd., 5.6 mi./9 km rt., 3 hrs., moderate) is usually quiet with few hikers, and its gargantuan forest will make you feel truly tiny. A spur at the end of the trail leads to a double-trunked redwood tree. The trail ends at Fern Falls.

BACKPACKING

Hikers can don an overnight pack on the Redwood Creek Trail for a 2- to 3-day trip. Designated campsites are at **Elam Camp** (3 sites) and **44 Camp** (4 sites), plus a segment along the river with large gravel bars that has dispersed camping. The northern section of the **California Coastal Trail** (CCT, www.californiacoastaltrail.info) runs through Redwood National Park and has primitive backcountry sites. The trail is reasonably well marked with signs featuring the CCT logo.

Backcountry camping is allowed by permit (free), available in person from the visitors centers.

WHERE TO STAY

INSIDE THE PARKS

Redwood National Park has no designated campgrounds, but several state park campgrounds take **reservations** (800/444-7275, www.reservecalifornia.com, mid-May-Sept., $35) during the busy summer season. Book reservations six months in advance to guarantee a spot. Outside of summer, campgrounds are first come, first served. Sites include picnic tables, firepits, flush toilets, showers, and food storage lockers, but no hookups.

Tucked under ancient redwoods, **Elk Prairie Campground** (Prairie Creek Redwoods, 127011 Newton B. Drury Scenic Pkwy., year-round) has 75 sites for tents and RVs. A campfire area is an easy walk north of the campground, with evening programs hosted by rangers and volunteers.

Gold Bluffs Beach Campground (Prairie Creek Redwoods, Davison Rd., year-round) has 26 beachfront sites for tents only with wide ocean views.

Mill Creek Campground (Del Norte Redwoods, US 101, mid-May-Sept.) has 145 sites for tents and RVs spread beneath young redwoods.

Jedediah Smith Campground (Jedediah Smith Redwoods, US 199, Hiouchi, year-round) has 86 sites for tents and RVs under old-growth redwoods on the banks of Smith River. Most sites are near the River Beach Trail. Reservations are advised, especially for summer.

OUTSIDE THE PARKS

Small towns dot the coast along US 101. Look for accommodations and restaurants in **Crescent City, Trinidad, Garberville, Eureka,** and **Arcata.**

GETTING THERE AND AROUND

The Redwood National and State Parks line 40 miles (64 km) of US 101. There is no public transportation; a vehicle is required for exploration.

AIR

The closest airport is the small regional **Del Norte County Airport/Jack McNamara** (CEC, 1650 Dale Rupert Rd., Crescent City, 707/464-7288, http://flycrescentcity.com). The closest international airports are **San Francisco International Airport** (SFO, US 101, San Mateo, 800/435-9736 or 650/821-8211, www.flysfo.com) and **Sacramento International Airport** (SMF, 6900 Airport Blvd., 916/929-5411, www.sacramento.aero/smf), both a six-hour drive from the parks.

CAR

From **San Francisco,** take US 101 north to Leggett, where it meets with CA 1. Follow US 101 north to Orick, where you'll find the Thomas H. Kuchel Visitor Center.

From **Sacramento,** take I-5 north to CA 299 West, which ends in Arcata. Turn north on US 101 to Orick. The 330-mile (530-km) drive will take about 5-6 hours.

Prairie Creek Redwoods is 6 miles (10 km) north of Orick on US 101. The Newton B. Drury Scenic Parkway parallels US 101 as an alternate route.

Del Norte Coast Redwoods is on US 101, 19 miles (31 km) north of Prairie Creek Redwoods. The park entrance is on Hamilton Road, east of US 101.

To reach Jedediah Smith Redwoods State Park, follow north along US 101 to US 199. Turn left onto US 199 and continue east for 9 miles (15 km).

SIGHTS NEARBY

More sights await along US 101. **Humboldt Redwoods State Park** (17119 Avenue of the Giants, Weott, 707/946-2263, www.parks.ca.gov or www.humboldtredwoods.org, visitors center 9am-5pm daily Apr.-Oct., 10am-4pm daily Nov.-Mar.) houses the **Avenue of the Giants** (CA 254, between Weott and Myers Flat), which parallels US 101 and the Eel River for 32 miles (52 km) between Garberville and Scotia.

Patrick's Point State Park (4150 Patrick's Point Dr., Trinidad, 707/677-3570, www.parks.ca.gov, day use $8) is a rambling coastal park with campgrounds, trails, and beaches.

Richardson Grove State Park (1600 US 101, 707/247-3318, www.parks.ca.gov, daily sunrise-sunset, day use $8) is the first of the old-growth redwoods heading north on US 101. It has a visitors center and campground.

Trees of Mystery (15500 US 101 N., 707/482-2251 or 800/638-3389, www.treesofmystery.net, daily 8am-7pm June-Aug., daily 8:30am-6:30pm Sept.-Oct., daily 9am-4:30pm Nov.-May, $18), a roadside tourist stop, offers a SkyTrail gondola ride through the old-growth redwoods, a palatial gift shop, and a little-known gem: a Native American museum.

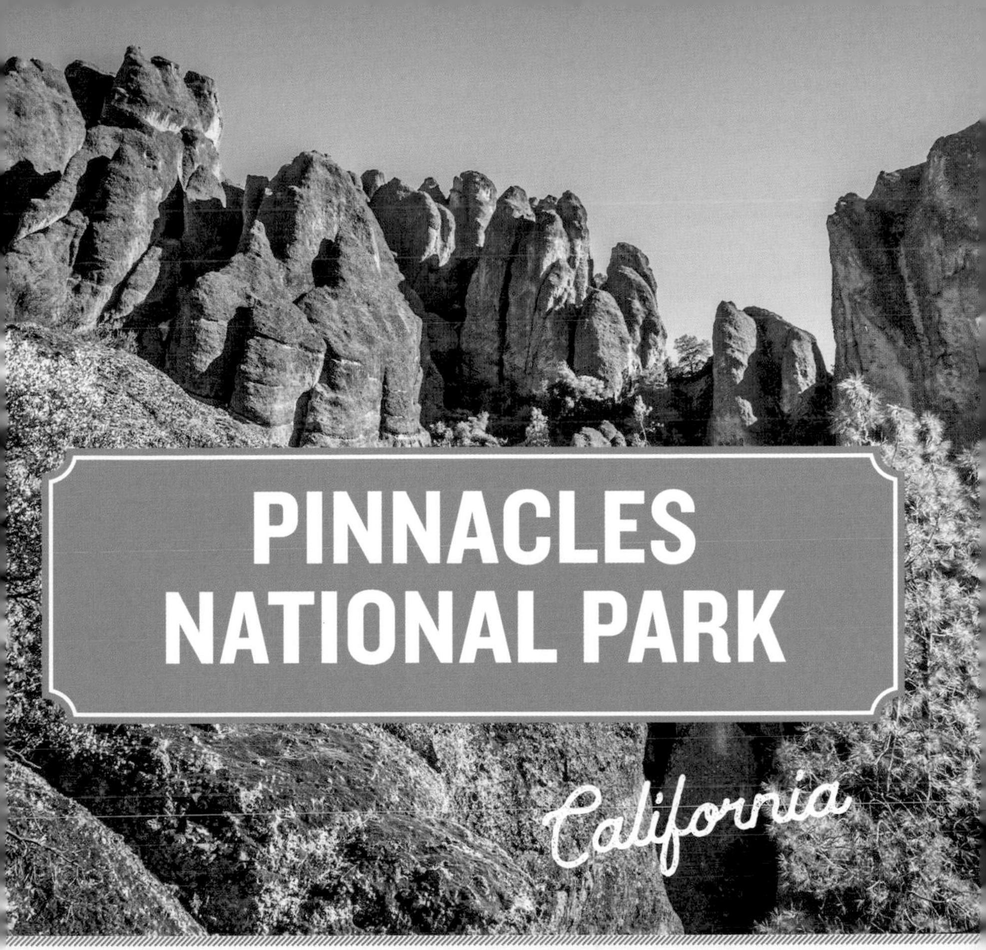

PINNACLES NATIONAL PARK

California

KEEPSAKE STAMPS ▾▾▾

WEBSITE:
www.nps.gov/pinn

PHONE NUMBER:
831/389-4485 visitors center, 831/389-4486 park headquarters

VISITATION RANK:
50

WHY GO:
Scramble through talus caves and up volcanic peaks.

▲ PINNACLES NATIONAL PARK

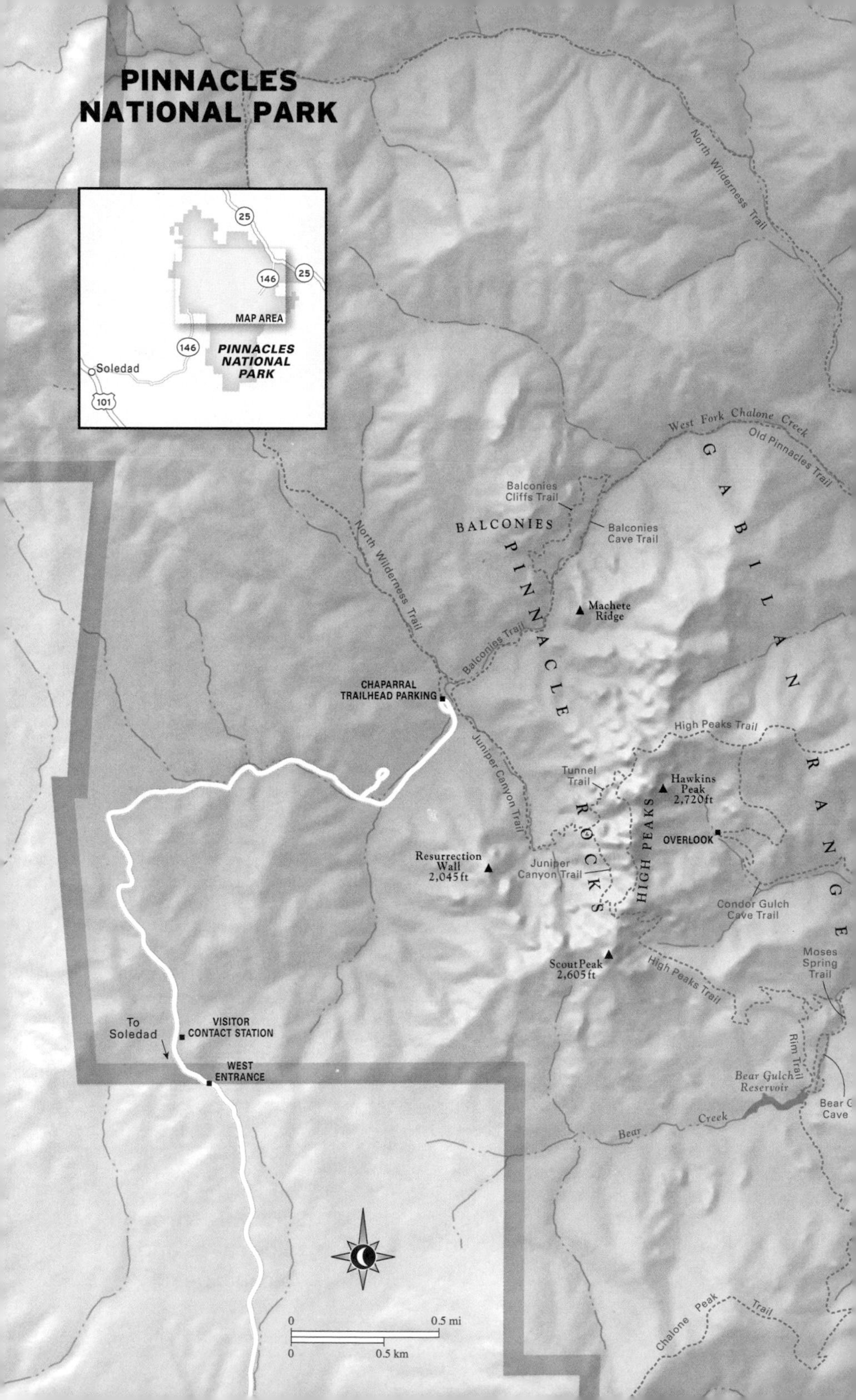

PINNACLES NATIONAL PARK
25
146
25
MAP AREA
146
PINNACLES NATIONAL PARK
Soledad
101
North Wilderness Trail
West Fork Chalone Creek
Old Pinnacles Trail
GABILAN RANGE
Balconies Cliffs Trail
BALCONIES
Balconies Cave Trail
North Wilderness Trail
PINNACLE ROCKS
Machete Ridge
Balconies Trail
CHAPARRAL TRAILHEAD PARKING
Juniper Canyon Trail
High Peaks Trail
Tunnel Trail
Hawkins Peak 2,720 ft
HIGH PEAKS
OVERLOOK
Resurrection Wall 2,045 ft
Juniper Canyon Trail
Condor Gulch Cave Trail
Moses Spring Trail
Scout Peak 2,605 ft
High Peaks Trail
To Soledad
VISITOR CONTACT STATION
WEST ENTRANCE
Rim Trail
Bear Gulch Reservoir
Bear Creek
0
0.5 mi
0
0.5 km
Chalone Peak Trail

To Hollister
EAST ENTRANCE
To King City
McCABE CANYON
Willow Spring
PINNACLES NATIONAL PARK
Creek
Sandy
Old Pinnacles Trail
BEAR VALLEY
OLD PINNACLES TRAILHEAD PARKING
PINNACLES VISITOR CENTER
Bench
High Peaks Trail
PINNACLES CAMPGROUND
EAST ENTRANCE STATION
Trail
BEAR GULCH
Bear Gulch Cave Trail
PEAKS VIEW
EAR GULCH
Bench
Trail
South
GRASSY CANYON
LE PINNACLES
Wilderness
FROG CANYON
Mt. Defiance 2657ft
Trail
Chalone
Creek
© MOON.COM

Rising above the Gabilan Mountains on the east side of the Salinas Valley, **PINNACLES NATIONAL PARK** is filled with the walls, spires, and towers of rock castles. A natural wonder created by volcanic activity, Pinnacles holds some of the world's largest talus caves, created when boulders became lodged in narrow canyons. Its intricate geology is best explored on hiking trails and along rock faces, where climbers ascend cracks and nubbins. After extinction in the wild, California condors have returned to Pinnacles, thrilling biologists, birders, and the Amah Mutsun people, whose mythology celebrates the condor as the escorts to the afterlife.

PLANNING YOUR TIME

East of the Salinas Valley, in the parched hills of the Gabilan Mountains, Pinnacles National Park (5000 CA 146, Paicines) attracts hikers, rock climbers, cave explorers, and birders. True to its name, the park is studded with huge rock formations jutting into the sky.

The weather is generally warm and dry throughout the year, but blazing hot in summer. **Spring** (Mar.-June) is high season, when visitors flood the park for rare access to the upper and lower Bear Gulch Caves. Regardless of when you visit, it is essential to bring plenty of water with you on the trails.

ENTRANCES AND FEES

Pinnacles National Park has two entrances, both accessed via CA 146. No roads connect the two entrances. The **east entrance** accesses the park campground and popular Bear Gulch Day Use Area, with multiple trail options. On the **west side** is a ranger station parking area that closes at night. The west entrance is only accessible when the park gate is open (7:30am-8pm daily). There are no services or campgrounds on the west side.

The entrance fee is $30 per vehicle ($25 pp on motorcycle, $15 on foot or bicycle).

VISITORS CENTERS

On the east side of the park, the **Pinnacles Visitor Center** (831/389-4485, 9:30am-5pm daily) is the main source of information for visitors and campers. Inquire about the status of the caves here. The **Bear Gulch Nature Center** (10am-4pm Sat.-Sun. Jan.-May) in the Bear Gulch Day Use Area has wildlife and nature exhibits.

The west entrance hosts the **West Pinnacles Visitor Contact Station** (831/389-4427, 9am-4:30pm daily), where you can pay the entrance fee; however, there are no services.

RECREATION

HIKING

One of the best ways to experience the geology of Pinnacles is via the west side's **Juniper Canyon Loop** (4.3 mi./6.9 km rt., 2-3 hrs., strenuous), which leads hikers through a steep, narrow traverse of the High Peaks. From the Chaparral Parking Area, begin on the Juniper Canyon Trail to climb 2,605-foot (794 m) Scout Peak, where you may spot a condor soaring overhead. The loop then swings through High Peaks before returning to the trailhead.

From the east side Bear Gulch Day Use Area, hikers can take the **Moses Spring to Rim Loop Trail** (2.2 mi./3.5 km rt., 1.5 hrs., moderate) to Bear Gulch Reservoir. For a longer hike, the **Chalone Peak Trail** (9 mi./14.5 km rt., 4-5 hrs., strenuous) continues from the reservoir to North Chalone Peak.

ROCK CLIMBING

Most of the park's best rock climbing is on the east side, where routes range from beginner to advanced, but the rock here is volcanic breccia and prone to weakness. The **Tourist Trap** and the

Top 3

1 SCRAMBLE UP BEAR GULCH CAVE

BEAR GULCH CAVE

From the Bear Gulch Day Use Area, a series of well-signed, connected trails leads to **Bear Gulch Cave** (2.2 mi./3.5 km rt., 1.5 hrs., moderate). The high rocky walls of this talus cave slope inward as the 0.7-mile (1.1 km) self-guided path meanders past lodged boulders and along Bear Creek. You'll need a flashlight or headlamp to see in the dark, and you may splash through a little water in places as the cavern route follows a tumbling creek. The climb through the cave goes up stairways, scrambles through a few slots, and you'll need to duck a few times to avoid hitting your head. Exiting the upper portion of the cave, the trail climbs to scenic **Bear Gulch Reservoir,** a convenient spot to catch your breath and enjoy a quick lunch.

To start, head out on the **High Peaks Trail;** turn left onto the **Moses Spring Trail** to reach the entrance to the **Bear Gulch Cave Trail.** The return loop follows the **Rim Trail** back to the High Peaks Trail; turn right to return to the day-use area or left to scale the High Peaks Trail.

Mid-May to mid-July, Bear Gulch Cave closes to protect the large colony of Townsend's big-eared bats raising young. Access to both upper and lower Bear Gulch Cave is open to hikers for only a few weeks in March and October. Otherwise, the lower part opens with the exit trail cutting back to the Moses Spring Trail. Check online or at the visitors center for closure schedules.

2 CRAWL THROUGH BALCONIES CAVE

Balconies Cave offers a fun, self-guided, 0.4-mile (0.6 km) scramble through a series of stacked boulders, the shorter but more tactile and hands-on exploration of the park's talus caves. Bring a flashlight or headlamp to see in darkness as you climb over stones, crawl under chockstones, and squeeze through slots. You also may wade through water.

Before planning a trip to the cave, check online or with the visitors center about its status. Rainstorms can close it, as does the annual spring-summer schedule to protect the maternity colony of Townsend's big-eared bats.

To get to Balconies Cave takes more work than Bear Gulch Cave. From the west side Chaparral Parking Area, the **Balconies Cliffs-Cave Loop** (5.3 mi./8.5 km rt., 3 hrs., moderate) is the shortest route. The trail ascends to the south junction where you can opt to climb through the cave first or over the top on Balconies Cliff first. Either way, the loop returns to the junction. From the east side at the Old Pinnacles Trailhead parking area, hike the **Old Pinnacles Trail** (7 mi./11.3 km) up the West Fork of Chalone Creek to the north junction of the Balconies Cliffs-Cave Loop. Opt for either way as the loop returns to the junction.

3 WATCH CONDORS

Impressive California condors inhabit Pinnacles year-round. The endangered species reached extinction in the wild, but Pinnacles National Park serves as the only NPS release site for transitioning captive birds back into the wild. With binoculars, you can see condors with radio transmitters and plastic identification tags, which help biologists monitor the birds. Watch for condors soaring on thermals near High Peaks and the ridge south of the campground. Look for them roosting in trees, too. Spotting scopes are on the Bench Trail near the visitors center for looking for condors. Rangers often do 30-minute Condor Talks on weekends at Bear Gulch Day Use Area.

Discovery Wall are the closest climbs from the Bear Gulch Day Use Area. For more information, visit **Friends of Pinnacles** (www.pinnacles.org), an organization dedicated to climbing at Pinnacles.

WHERE TO STAY

INSIDE THE PARK

The **Pinnacles Campground** (877/444-6777, www.recreation.gov, year-round, tents $30, RVs $40) is at the east entrance and has 99 tent sites, 36 RV sites, and 14 group sites. Most are shaded by oaks and all come with a picnic table, fire ring, and bathrooms, with showers nearby. There is a dump station to accommodate RVs, and all sites have electrical hookups. The camp store sells food and necessities.

OUTSIDE THE PARK

Accommodations and dining options are located in **Salinas, Soledad,** and **King City.**

GETTING THERE

AIR

The closest international airports are **Mineta San Jose International**

BALCONIES CAVE TRAIL

Best Hike

HIGH PEAKS TRAIL

DISTANCE: 7.2 miles (11.6 km) round-trip
DURATION: 5 hours
ELEVATION CHANGE: 1,425 feet (434 m)
EFFORT: strenuous
TRAILHEAD: Bear Gulch Day Use Area

The star loop trail in the park is the **High Peaks Trail,** a tough haul to the top of the park's volcanic pinnacles with views across multiple counties. At the top, a 0.7-mile (1.1 km) portion of the trail climbs across the steep rock-strewn ridgeline via steps carved into the rock with handrails for support. It's almost like a beginner's version of Yosemite's famed Half Dome hike. Multiple trails connect with the High Peaks Trail. With more mileage and time, you can add on Bear Gulch Cave. For a shorter loop, link High Peaks with **Condor Gulch Trail** (5.3 mi./8.5 km rt., 4 hrs., strenuous).

Airport (SJC, 1701 Airport Blvd., San Jose, 408/392-3600, www.flysanjose.com) and **San Francisco International Airport** (SFO, US 101, San Mateo, 800/435-9736 or 650/821-8211, www.flysfo.com). From either airport, it's roughly a two-hour drive south to the park via US 101.

CAR

Pinnacles has two entrances, but no roads connect them—making the drive from one to the other a two-hour endeavor.

To reach the **east entrance** from the north, take US 101 to CA 25 through the town of Hollister. After another 30 miles (48 km), turn right on CA 146 to the park entrance. From San Francisco, the trip is more than 130 miles (209 km) and takes nearly 3 hours. From Monterey, it is 79 miles (127 km) and 1.5 hours.

For the **west entrance,** continue south on US 101, past Salinas, to CA 146 in Soledad. Take CA 146 east for a very slow 14 miles (23 km). There are no services at this entrance. The trip from Monterey, via CA 68, is 54 miles (87 km), taking a little over an hour.

GETTING AROUND

There is limited parking on both the east and west side lots. On weekends, a free **shuttle** stops at the East Pinnacles Visitor Center and the Bear Gulch Day Use Area on the east side of the park. Plan to board the shuttle early (before 10am) to avoid the hour-plus wait on weekends.

CALIFORNIA CONDORS

With wings spanning 10 feet (3 m) from tip to tip, California condors are some of the area's most impressive natural treasures. The largest flying bird in North America, their presence here is a story of hope and testament to the success of conservation efforts. In the early 1980s, the condor population had dropped to a low of 22 raptors, due to their susceptibility to lead poisoning and through deaths caused by electric power lines, habitat loss, and hunting. A captive breeding program was initiated for this endangered species and, after more than 30 years, there are now more than 400 California condors.

The jutting spires of Pinnacles are home to about 86 California condors bred in captivity and then released into the wild. The park has also seen the first chick fledge in the wild. If you're lucky, you might even spy one flying overhead on one of the park's rugged hiking trails. (Look for a tracking tag on the bird's wing to determine that you are actually looking at a California condor and not a big turkey vulture, plentiful in the park.)

CHANNEL ISLANDS NATIONAL PARK

California

WEBSITE:
www.nps.gov/chis

PHONE NUMBER:
805/658-5730

VISITATION RANK:
46

WHY GO:
Paddle and hike an island sanctuary.

▲ ANACAPA ISLAND

KEEPSAKE STAMPS ▼▼▼

Off the California coast, the remote **CHANNEL ISLANDS** are only accessible by air or sea. Boats travel routes once paddled in dugout canoes by the indigenous Chumash people to reach the islands. On even the most visited islands, hardy souls are rewarded with uncrowded trails, isolated beaches, and an extensive marine sanctuary. Kelp forests offshore sway in the ocean's surge as the California state fish, the pumpkin-colored garibaldi, swim past rocks dotted with multicolored sea urchins. Onshore, rare species, including the island fox and the island scrub-jay, roam freely. Day-trippers can kayak, snorkel, and even scuba dive, while campers can enjoy solitude and dark skies.

PLANNING YOUR TIME

The five Channel Islands lie off the central California coast, accessible by boat or plane from Santa Barbara and Ventura. The most visited islands are tiny **Anacapa,** a dramatic 5-mile (8-km) spine jutting out from the sea and closest to the mainland, and **Santa Cruz,** California's largest island at 24 miles (39 km) long and 6 miles (10 km) wide. The second-largest island, **Santa Rosa,** is difficult to access because of consistently strong winds. The smaller **San Miguel** is accessible spring-fall by permit only. **Santa Barbara** is the smallest and southernmost of the islands.

You can visit Anacapa, Santa Cruz, and to a lesser degree Santa Rosa on day trips (boats depart roughly 8:30am-10am, return at 4pm); only trips to Santa Cruz and Anacapa are available year-round.

Summer (June-Aug.) is high-season for recreational activities such as snorkeling, diving, and kayaking. Wildlife migrations take place in **spring** and **fall.** Sailing to the islands takes 1-4 hours, and tough winds can crop up on the open water. While weather varies daily, daytime temperatures hang in the mid-60s (16-21°C) with nights dropping by only 10-15 degrees (6-9°C).

ENTRANCES AND FEES

There is no entrance fee to visit Channel Islands; however, you must buy a ticket on a boat or plane departing from Santa Barbara or Ventura.

VISITORS CENTERS

There is no main visitors center. Instead, go to the **Robert J. Lagomarsino Channel Islands National Park Visitor Center** (1901 Spinnaker Dr., Ventura, 805/658-5730, www.nps.gov/

▼ MARINELIFE ABOUNDS IN THE CHANNEL ISLANDS.

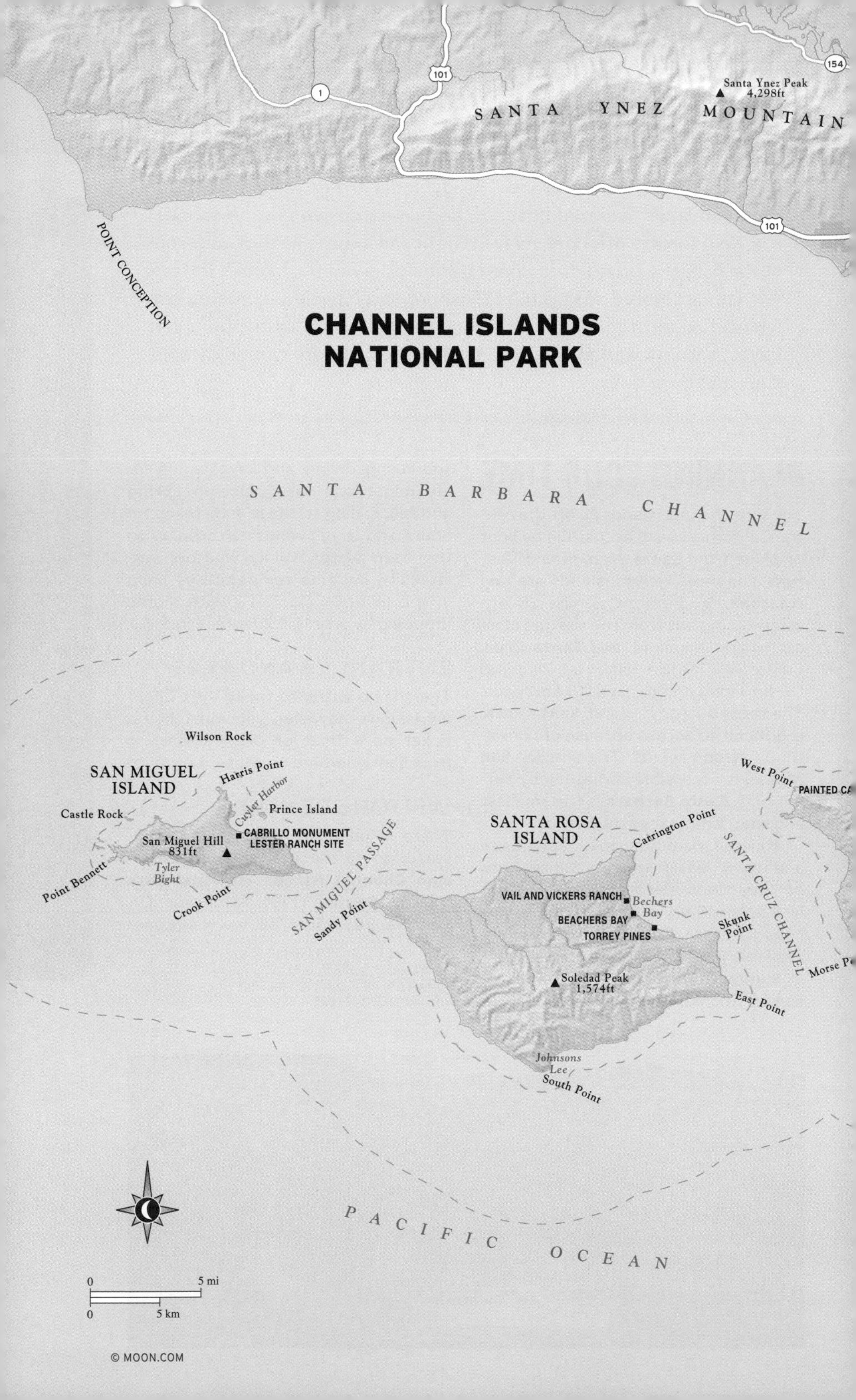
CHANNEL ISLANDS NATIONAL PARK
1
101
154
Santa Ynez Peak 4,298ft
SANTA YNEZ MOUNTAIN
101
POINT CONCEPTION
SANTA BARBARA CHANNEL
Wilson Rock
SAN MIGUEL ISLAND
Harris Point
Cuyler Harbor
Prince Island
Castle Rock
CABRILLO MONUMENT
LESTER RANCH SITE
San Miguel Hill 831ft
Tyler Bight
Point Bennett
Crook Point
SAN MIGUEL PASSAGE
Sandy Point
SANTA ROSA ISLAND
Carrington Point
West Point
PAINTED CA
SANTA CRUZ CHANNEL
VAIL AND VICKERS RANCH
Bechers Bay
BEACHERS BAY
TORREY PINES
Skunk Point
Morse P
Soledad Peak 1,574ft
East Point
Johnsons Lee
South Point
PACIFIC OCEAN
0
5 mi
0
5 km
© MOON.COM

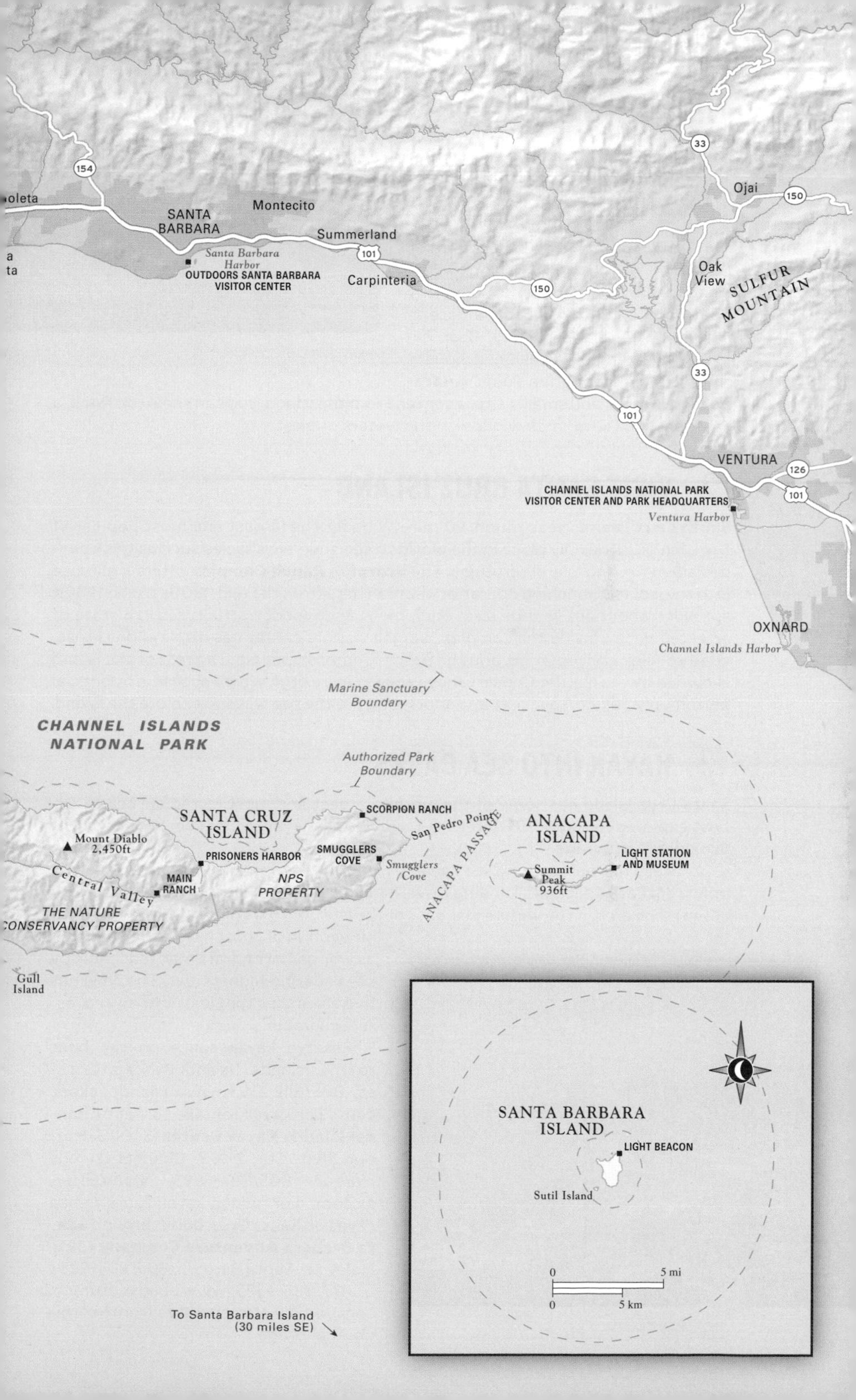

oleta
a
ta
154
SANTA BARBARA
Montecito
Summerland
Santa Barbara Harbor
OUTDOORS SANTA BARBARA VISITOR CENTER
101
Carpinteria
150
33
Ojai
150
Oak View
SULFUR MOUNTAIN
33
101
VENTURA
126
101
CHANNEL ISLANDS NATIONAL PARK VISITOR CENTER AND PARK HEADQUARTERS
Ventura Harbor
OXNARD
Channel Islands Harbor
Marine Sanctuary Boundary
CHANNEL ISLANDS NATIONAL PARK
Authorized Park Boundary
SANTA CRUZ ISLAND
SCORPION RANCH
San Pedro Point
ANACAPA ISLAND
Mount Diablo 2,450ft
PRISONERS HARBOR
SMUGGLERS COVE
Smugglers Cove
ANACAPA PASSAGE
LIGHT STATION AND MUSEUM
Summit Peak 936ft
Central Valley
MAIN RANCH
NPS PROPERTY
THE NATURE CONSERVANCY PROPERTY
Gull Island
SANTA BARBARA ISLAND
LIGHT BEACON
Sutil Island
0
5 mi
0
5 km
To Santa Barbara Island (30 miles SE)

Top 3

ANACAPA LIGHTHOUSE

1 DAY TRIP TO ANACAPA ISLAND

Tiny **Anacapa** has three islets on the east end of the main island, West Anacapa. Boats (year-round, 90 min. by boat) land on **East Anacapa,** a desert-like island with steep cliffs. Best explored by hiking or kayaking, it houses the stunning Inspiration Point, **Anacapa Lighthouse,** and small visitors center. From the island, you can see **Arch Rock,** a 40-foot-high (12-m) rock window in the waters offshore.

2 VISIT SANTA CRUZ ISLAND

Santa Cruz Island (year-round, 90 min. by boat), the largest and most popular of the islands, is the only place in the world to see endemic species such as the Channel Island fox and island scrub-jay. The **Scorpion Ranch Complex** offers a glimpse into the isolated ranching operation that ran here from the mid-1800s to the 1980s; sprinkled about are various farm equipment and wooden structures in a state of arrested decay. Inside the complex, a small visitors center has displays on threatened species, conservation, and the native Chumash people. The rest of the island is owned by the Nature Conservancy (www.nature.org), where access is by special permit only. Hiking, kayaking, and snorkeling are the top ways to explore the island.

3 KAYAK INTO SEA CAVES

Santa Cruz Island has some of the world's largest and most incredible sea caves, best explored by kayak. To find easy-to-reach sea caves, paddle northwest out of **Scorpion Anchorage.**

Anacapa has outstanding sea kayaking, but due to rugged cliffs, water access is only from East Anacapa's Landing Cove. Paddle out to **Arch Rock,** the 40-foot-high (12-m) rock arch in the waters just east of the islet, or to **Cathedral Cove.** This scenic section of coast has **Cathedral Arch** as well as **Cathedral Cave,** reachable by kayak during higher tides. The cave has five entrances that lead into an impressive chamber.

ANAPACA ISLAND

Reserve kayak space on the boat to the islands (Island Packers Cruises, 805/642-1393, www.islandpackers.com). For kayak rentals, contact **Channel Islands Kayak Center** (3600 S. Harbor Blvd., Ste. 2-108, Channel Islands Harbor, 805/984-5995, www.cikayak.com). For guided kayak tours to sea caves on Santa Cruz, book through **Santa Barbara Adventure Company** (32 E. Haley St., Santa Barbara, 805/884-9283 or 877/885-9283, www.sbadventureco.com), which also operates from Scorpion Anchorage.

Best Hike

INSPIRATION POINT

DISTANCE: 1.5 miles (2.4 km) round-trip
DURATION: 1 hour
EFFORT: easy
TRAILHEAD: Landing Cove, East Anacapa

If you have seen a photo of the Channel Islands on a calendar or postcard, most likely that is the spectacular view from **Inspiration Point** on Anacapa Island**.** On the way, the trail includes stops at Pinniped Point and Cathedral Cove, where you can view sea lions stacked like sandbags on pocket beaches hundreds of feet down. From this high vantage point on the west end of the island, Middle Anacapa Island and West Anacapa Island rise out of the ocean like a giant sea serpent's spine. Below, the healthy blue-green ocean is spotted with rust-colored kelp forests. Overhead and below, gulls soar and do aerial acrobatics. In the distance, the large mass of Santa Cruz Island bulges out from behind the other Anacapa Islands. With a bench, Inspiration Point is a place to sit and soak in the view and the solitude of the Channel Islands. In a word, Inspiration Point is inspiring.

chis, 8:30am-5pm daily) in Ventura Harbor Village before heading to the islands. It has a bookstore, displays of marinelife, exhibits, and a 25-minute introductory film on the islands. The **Outdoors Santa Barbara Visitor Center** (113 Harbor Way, Santa Barbara, 805/456-8752, http://outdoorsb.sbmm.org, 11am-5pm Sun.-Fri., 9am-3pm Sat.) also has information about the national park and the Channel Islands National Marine Sanctuary.

SANTA ROSA ISLAND

Fewer visitors reach the rugged and windy **Santa Rosa Island** (Apr.-early Nov., 3 hrs. by boat), whose mountainous spine rises to 1,592-foot (485-m) Soledad Peak with views of neighboring Santa Cruz Island and the mainland coastline. The island's white-sand beaches and coastal lagoons seem virtually untouched, as is the Torrey pine forest, home to some of the rarest pines in the world.

SAN MIGUEL

The westernmost island in the chain, **San Miguel Island** (Apr.-early Nov., 4 hrs. by boat) has exceptional wildlife, especially at **Point Bennett,** where an estimated 30,000 seals and sea lions reside. Most visitors arrive at **Cuyler Harbor,** a large half-moon bay on the northeast side. Tidepools await at the east end of the scenic 2-mile-long (3.2-km-long) white-sand beach. Western gulls, California brown pelicans, cormorants, and Cassin's auklets nest on Prince Island, which sits in the mouth of the harbor. On a bluff above the harbor, an inscribed stone cross is dedicated to Juan Rodríguez Cabrillo, the Portuguese explorer who anchored here in 1542.

SANTA BARBARA

At one square mile, **Santa Barbara** (Apr.-early Nov., 3 hrs. by boat) is the smallest of the islands and a rare stop. This southernmost island has warm water for swimming, diving, snorkeling, and kayaking, and is home to impressive seabird colonies, including one of the world's largest colonies of Scripps's murrelets.

RECREATION

HIKING

Anacapa is home to the flat **Inspiration Point Loop** (1.5 mi./2.4 km rt., 1 hr., easy), which circles the island. The **Lighthouse Trail** (0.5 mi./0.8 km rt., 20 min., easy) climbs to a viewpoint.

Santa Cruz Island can't be beat for coastal scenery, cliff-top views to the mainland, and whale-watching. **Cavern Point Loop** (2 mi./3.2 km rt., 2 hrs., moderate) provides a vantage to spot whales. The **Smugglers Cove Trail** (7.5 mi./12.1 km rt., 4 hrs., strenuous) follows an old ranch road across the eastern interior to a south-facing beach. Even if you don't find the elusive island scrub-jay on **Scorpion Canyon Loop** (4.5 mi./7.2 km rt., 3 hrs., moderate), you'll tour a unique canyon followed by a series of stunning vistas.

On Santa Rosa Island, the **Water Canyon Beach Trail** (3 mi./4.8 km rt., 1.5 hrs., easy) leads to a white-sand beach. The **East Point Trail** (16 mi./25.7 km rt., 8 hrs., strenuous) takes in the Torrey pine forest and beaches of Santa Rosa Island. The **Lobo Canyon Trail** (9 mi./14.5 km rt., 5 hrs., strenuous) leads to a water-sculpted canyon resembling those in the Southwest.

On San Miguel, hike inland from Cuyler Harbor through a canyon with native vegetation to the **Lester Ranch Site** (2 mi./3.2 km rt., 1 hr., moderate) to see the remains of a cistern, root cellar, and the living-room chimney in a rubble pile.

On Santa Barbara Island, hike the **Arch Point Trail** (1 mi./1.6 km rt., 30 min., moderate) to view the 130-foot-high (40-m) arch on the island's northern tip. For wildlife, walk to **Elephant Seal Cove** (2.5 mi./4 km rt., 1.5 hrs., moderate) or **Sea Lion Rookery** (2 mi./3.2 km rt., 1 hr., moderate), where steep cliffs overlook sea mammal colonies. To view the whole island, take the **Signal Peak Trail** (2.5 mi./4 km rt., 1.5 hrs., moderate) to the island apex at 634 feet (193 m).

SNORKELING AND SCUBA DIVING

Santa Cruz Island offers fine snorkeling and scuba diving in Scorpion Harbor. The kelp east and west of the Scorpion Anchorage Pier are rich in sealife, while the wreck of the **USS *Peacock***, a World War II minesweeper 50 yards (46 m) off Scorpion Rocks in 40-60 feet (12-18 m) of water, captivates divers. Rent snorkel gear from **Santa Barbara Adventure Company** (805/884-9283 or 877/885-9283, www.sbadventureco.com) in Scorpion Harbor.

To dive the island's other spots, you'll need your own boat or to a charter dive boat. Schedule diving trips from Ventura Harbor with **Peace Dive Boat** (1691 Spinnaker Dr., G Dock, 805/650-3483, www.peaceboat.com) or Santa Barbara Harbor with **Truth Aquatics** (301 W. Cabrillo Blvd., 805/962-1127, http://truthaquatics.net).

WHERE TO STAY

INSIDE THE PARK

There are no accommodations, food, or services on the Channel Islands. **Camping** (877/444-6777, www.recreation.gov, $15) is the only overnight option.

▼ SANTA CRUZ ISLAND

ANACAPA ISLAND

All campsites have picnic tables and access to pit toilets.

On Santa Cruz Island, **Scorpion Ranch Campground** is a 0.5- to 1-mile (0.8-1.6-km) walk from the pier at Scorpion Anchorage. The lower campground (22 sites) sits in a eucalyptus-shaded canyon, while the upper loop (3 sites, 6 group sites) is spread in a meadow—but it's twice as far to lug your camping gear. The campgrounds have drinking water and food storage boxes. From Prisoners Harbor, a strenuous 3.5-mile (5.6 km) hike goes to the **Del Norte Backcountry Campsite,** a remote spot in an oak grove.

The other islands have primitive campgrounds with no drinking water; bring water with you. A 0.5-mile (0.8-km) hike on East Anacapa includes 157 stairs to reach the **Anacapa Island Campground** (7 sites), which is quite sun- and wind-exposed. A steep one-mile hike uphill reaches **San Miguel Island Campground** (9 sites). From the visitors center, a steep 0.5-mile (0.8-km) hike connects with the seasonal **Santa Barbara Island Campground** (10 sites). On Santa Rosa, a level 1.5-mile (2.4-km) hike accesses the **Water Canyon Campground** (15 sites), where backcountry beach camping (mid-Aug.-Dec.) is allowed on the undeveloped coastline.

OUTSIDE THE PARK

Accommodations and restaurants are plentiful in **Ventura** and **Santa Barbara.**

GETTING THERE

AIR

The closest major airport is **Los Angeles International Airport** (LAX, 1 World Way, 424/646-5252, www.flylax.com). There are also regional airports in the Greater LA area. It's roughly a two-hour drive north via US 101 to reach Ventura, the gateway to the Channel Islands.

Channel Island Aviation (305 Durley Ave., Camarillo, 805/987-1301, www.flycia.com) has flights to Santa Rosa Island.

BOAT

Most visitors reach Channel Islands National Park by hopping a boat run by **Island Packers Cruises** (1691 Spinnaker Dr., Ste. 105B, Ventura Harbor, 805/642-1393, www.islandpackers.com). Schedules change seasonally. The crossing time ranges 1-4 hours, based on distance and conditions. Some landings require climbing steel ladders to docks and then stairs to reach the island tops.

Anacapa: By boat (year-round, 90 min.), Anacapa requires debarking by climbing up a steel ladder and then ascending stairs to the island top.

Santa Cruz: The two primary points of entry onto Santa Cruz are at **Scorpion Anchorage** and **Prisoners Harbor.** After a 90-minute boat ride from Ventura, travelers off-load either by climbing a steel ladder to a short shore pier or via skiff landings.

Santa Rosa: Boats debark at Santa Rosa, where visitors must climb a 20-foot (6.1-m) steel-rung ladder to reach flat land. Year-round flights to the island take 25 minutes.

San Miguel: Boat trips can experience potentially rough seas and skiff landings require waterproof gear.

Santa Barbara: Boat travel requires a skiff transfer with a climb up a steel-rung ladder, then laboriously trudging up 0.25 mile (0.4 km) of steps to crest the island top.

PACIFIC NORTHWEST

Oregon's only national park, Crater Lake pits startlingly blue water against a rim of steep rock cliffs.

Washington's three national parks are home to glaciers clinging to rugged mountains.

Around its mountainous interior, Olympic National Park contains rainforests, enormous old-growth trees, and rocky tidepools on the Pacific coast.

Looming above Seattle, 14,411-foot (4,392-m) Mount Rainier lures climbers to scale its summit while hikers waltz through wildflower meadows and backpackers circle the peak on the Wonderland Trail.

Explore hiking trails, a scenic highway, and the fjord-like Lake Chelan in the wild country of North Cascades National Park.

◂ OLYMPIC NATIONAL PARK

CANADA
North Cascades NP
Olympic NP
PACIFIC OCEAN
Seattle
Olympia
WASHINGTON
Mount Rainier NP
Portland
Salem
PACIFIC NORTHWEST
OREGON
Crater Lake NP
0
50 mi
0
50 km
© MOON.COM

The National Parks of THE PACIFIC NORTHWEST

CRATER LAKE, OR

The caldera from a catastrophic volcanic eruption 7,700 years ago now contains the nation's deepest and bluest lake (page 213).

OLYMPIC, WA

Wet, lush, and wild, the park fills with a rugged coastline, rainforests housing world-record trees, and a mountain range that begs hiking (page 223).

MOUNT RAINIER, WA

The king of the Cascades, this volcanic peak is crowned with the largest number of glaciers on any mountain in the Lower 48 states (page 240).

NORTH CASCADES, WA

These jagged peaks comprise one of the wildest places in the Lower 48. Get a taste of the scenery on the beautiful North Cascades Highway (page 251).

1: JAMES ISLAND, RIALTO BEACH, OLYMPIC
2: MOUNT RAINIER GLACIER
3: CRATER LAKE LODGE, CRATER LAKE

Best OF THE PARKS

Crater Lake Rim Drive: Circle the rim of this lake-filled caldera (page 217).

Hoh Rain Forest: Walk under some of the tallest trees in the world in this rainforest (page 227).

Hurricane Ridge: Take in majestic alpine views that get even more impressive if you continue on one of several hiking trails (page 227).

Ruby Beach: Enjoy a winning combination of beauty and accessibility at this Pacific beach (page 227).

Wildflowers at Paradise: Relish icy Mount Rainier framed by fields of wildflowers in summer (page 244).

North Cascades Highway: Navigate the beautiful curves, reservoirs, forests, and peaks of this scenic mountain highway (page 255).

PLANNING YOUR TRIP

You'll need at least **two weeks** to tour all four parks or **7-10 days** for the Washington parks. To stay inside the parks, make advance **reservations:** one year for lodges, six months for campgrounds. **Winter** closes many of the roads in this region, with limited access to a handful of locations and services.

Summer is prime time for Washington and Oregon. From June to September, the days are long and the temperatures seldom climb above the mid-80s (upper 20°C). Snow melts from mountain passes and high-altitude hiking trails, usually by July. The sunny, mild days are great for kayaking.

Seattle provides the most central access to Olympic, Mount Rainier, and North Cascades National Parks.

1: SUNSET AT HURRICANE RIDGE
2: NORTH CASCADES HIGHWAY

Road Trip

MOUNT RAINIER, OLYMPIC, AND NORTH CASCADES

BENCH LAKE, MOUNT RAINIER

Launching from **Seattle,** this road trip makes a grand loop that includes a ferry ride across Puget Sound. The route spans the mountains to the coast for a rich taste of Washington's best.

Mount Rainier

165 miles (265 km) / 4.75 hours

From **Seattle,** get an early start for the two-hour drive to the **White River Entrance** in the northeast corner of Mount Rainier National Park. In Seattle, take I-5 south to exit onto WA 18 heading east to Auburn, where WA 164 heads east to Enumclaw. Go east and then south on WA 410 into the park, turning right onto Sunrise Park Road to reach the entrance station. A winding road climbs to **Sunrise**, a hub of park activity and the highest point on the mountain accessible by car. Get your bearings at the visitors center, have lunch at the cafeteria, and then head out for a couple of hours of alpine hiking.

Drive down Sunrise Park Road to WA 410, where a right turn follows the highway southward until it becomes WA 123. Turn right onto Stevens Canyon Road to climb through switchbacks up to Paradise for dinner and overnighting at **Paradise Inn.** In the morning, tour the visitors center, explore the wildflower meadows, and hike to **Bench Lake** or **Plummer Peak.** The next day, exit the park via **Longmire** and the **Nisqually River Entrance.**

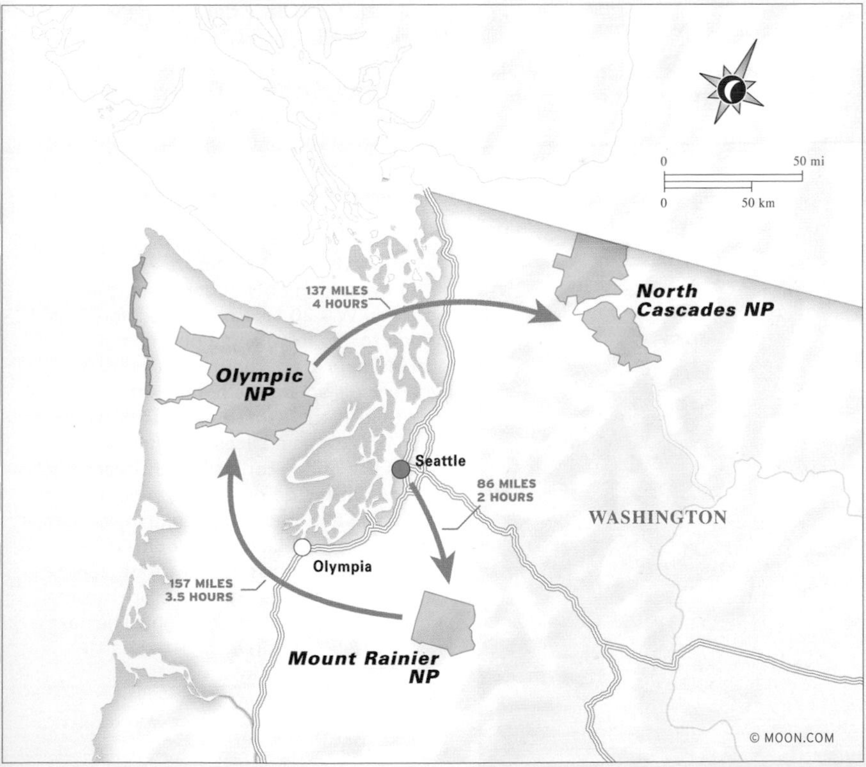

Olympic

300 miles (485 km) / 6 hours

Say goodbye to Rainier as you head west on WA 706 toward Olympic National Park. In Elbe, continue northwest on WA 7 to connect with WA 702 heading west. In McKenna, take WA 507 west to Yelm and continue northwest on WA 510 to reach I-5. Go southwest to reach Olympia, exiting onto US 101 going northwest. Take WA 8 west to Elma, then US 12 west to Aberdeen and then US 101 north.

Stop at **Lake Quinault,** at the southwestern end of the park, where you'll experience the lush, primordial forest. Drive up the coast on US 101 to dine and overnight at **Kalaloch Lodge**.

In the morning, drive north to **Ruby Beach,** a classic example of Washington's misty, pebble-strewn coastline. Continue north on US 101 to glacier-carved **Lake Crescent.** Spend the afternoon floating on its tranquil, turquoise-green waters before overnighting at **Lake Crescent Lodge** or in Port Angeles.

The next morning, drive from Port Angeles up Hurricane Ridge Road to the only part of the Olympic Mountains accessible by car: **Hurricane Ridge.** Stop at **Hurricane Ridge Visitor Center** and walk to **Hurricane Hill** for expansive views. Depart the Olympics in the early afternoon to drive east on US 101 to Discovery Bay and then north on WA 20 to Port Townsend (1 hr.) to catch the 35-minute ferry (fee, reservations required) across Puget Sound to Whidbey Island.

North Cascades

154 miles (248 km) / 4 hours

After debarking on Whidbey Island, drive north on WA 20 to cross Deception Pass Bridge to the mainland. Your next stop is **Marblemount,** two hours east on WA 20, where you'll spend the night. In the morning, follow the **North Cascades Highway** (WA 20) as it slices 30 miles (48 km) across the park. Stop at **North Cascades Visitor Center** before taking a boat tour of **Diablo Lake.** Back on the highway, head east to visit **Ross Lake Overlook.** Go as far as **Washington Pass** for views of Liberty Bell and Early Winter Spires before returning to your lodging for the night. The next day, it's a 2.5-hour drive back to Seattle.

1: VIEWS INTO OLYMPIC NATIONAL PARK
2: KAYAKING ON CRESCENT LAKE
2: DIABLO LAKE TRAIL, NORTH CASCADES

CRATER LAKE NATIONAL PARK

Oregon

KEEPSAKE STAMPS ▼▼▼

WEBSITE:
www.nps.gov/crla

PHONE NUMBER:
541/594-3000

VISITATION RANK:
30

WHY GO:
Visit a sapphire-blue lake in the heart of a sunken volcano.

▲ CRATER LAKE

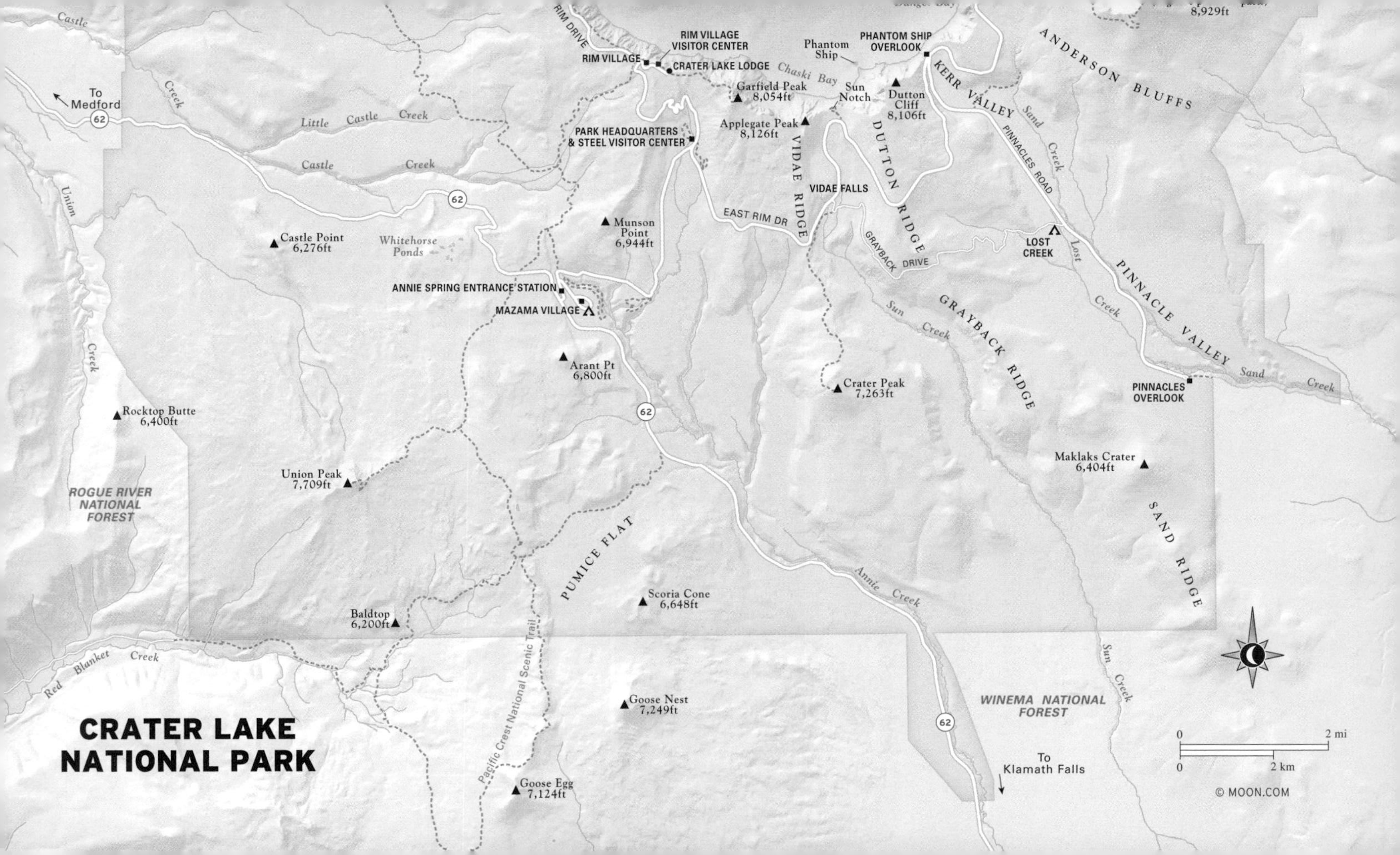
CRATER LAKE NATIONAL PARK
To Medford
62
Castle Creek
Little Castle Creek
Castle Creek
Union Creek
RIM DRIVE
RIM VILLAGE
RIM VILLAGE VISITOR CENTER
CRATER LAKE LODGE
Chaski Bay
Phantom Ship
PHANTOM SHIP OVERLOOK
Garfield Peak 8,054ft
Sun Notch
Dutton Cliff 8,106ft
Applegate Peak 8,126ft
PARK HEADQUARTERS & STEEL VISITOR CENTER
VIDAE RIDGE
VIDAE FALLS
DUTTON RIDGE
EAST RIM DR
KERR VALLEY
ANDERSON BLUFFS
8,929ft
PINNACLES ROAD
Sand Creek
Castle Point 6,276ft
Whitehorse Ponds
Munson Point 6,944ft
GRAYBACK DRIVE
LOST CREEK
Lost Creek
PINNACLE VALLEY
ANNIE SPRING ENTRANCE STATION
MAZAMA VILLAGE
Sun Creek
GRAYBACK RIDGE
Arant Pt 6,800ft
Crater Peak 7,263ft
PINNACLES OVERLOOK
Sand Creek
Rocktop Butte 6,400ft
Union Peak 7,709ft
ROGUE RIVER NATIONAL FOREST
Maklaks Crater 6,404ft
SAND RIDGE
PUMICE FLAT
Scoria Cone 6,648ft
Annie Creek
Baldtop 6,200ft
Red Blanket Creek
Pacific Crest National Scenic Trail
Goose Nest 7,249ft
Sun Creek
WINEMA NATIONAL FOREST
To Klamath Falls
Goose Egg 7,124ft
0
2 mi
0
2 km
© MOON.COM

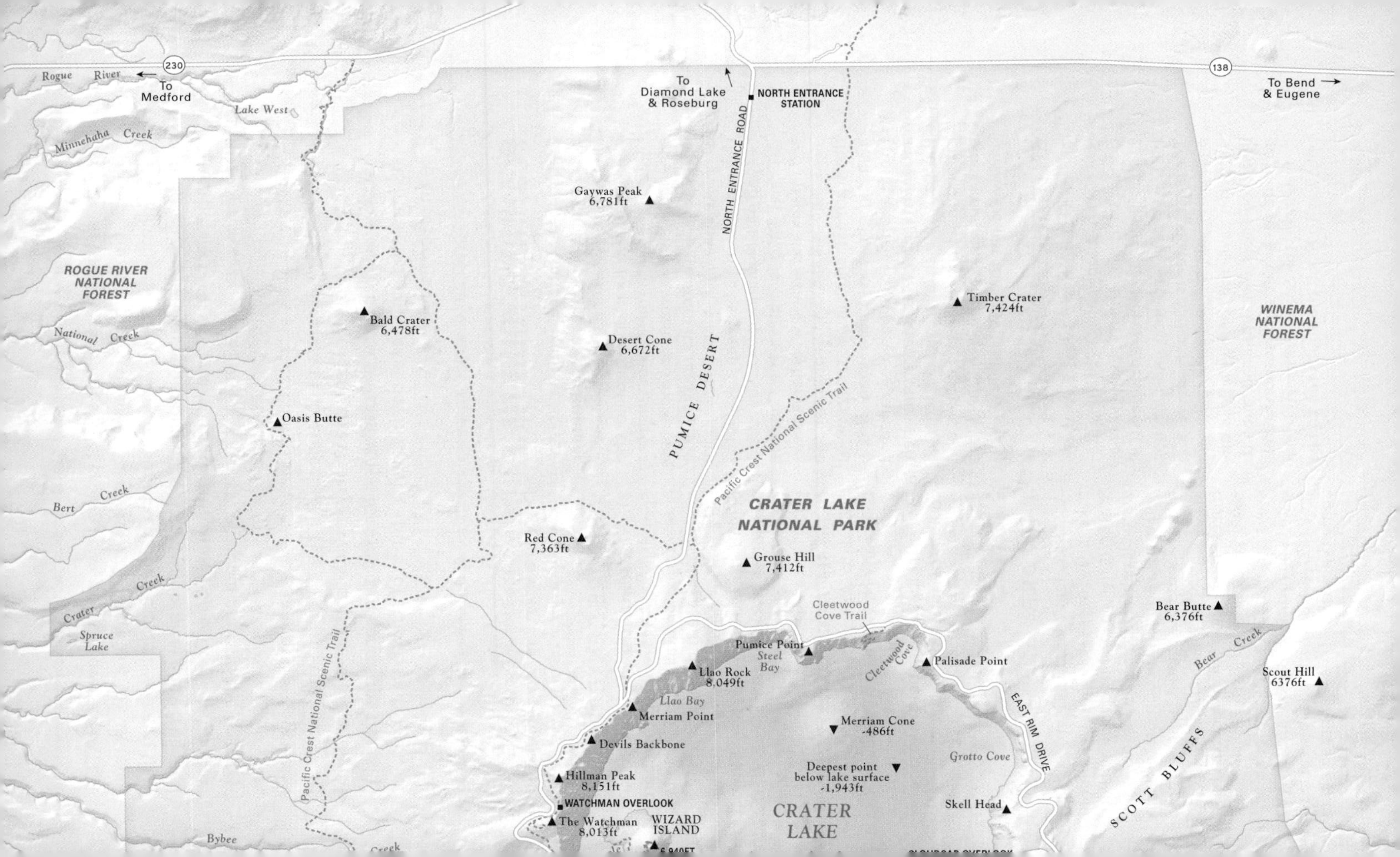

230
Rogue River
To Medford
Lake West
Minnehaha Creek
ROGUE RIVER NATIONAL FOREST
National Creek
Bert Creek
Crater Creek
Spruce Lake
Bybee
To Diamond Lake & Roseburg
NORTH ENTRANCE STATION
NORTH ENTRANCE ROAD
138
To Bend & Eugene
Gaywas Peak 6,781ft
Bald Crater 6,478ft
Desert Cone 6,672ft
Oasis Butte
PUMICE DESERT
Timber Crater 7,424ft
WINEMA NATIONAL FOREST
Pacific Crest National Scenic Trail
CRATER LAKE NATIONAL PARK
Red Cone 7,363ft
Grouse Hill 7,412ft
Cleetwood Cove Trail
Bear Butte 6,376ft
Bear Creek
Scout Hill 6376ft
Pumice Point
Steel Bay
Cleetwood Cove
Palisade Point
Llao Rock 8,049ft
Llao Bay
Merriam Point
Devils Backbone
Hillman Peak 8,151ft
WATCHMAN OVERLOOK
The Watchman 8,013ft
WIZARD ISLAND
Merriam Cone -486ft
Deepest point below lake surface -1,943ft
Grotto Cove
EAST RIM DRIVE
Skell Head
CRATER LAKE
SCOTT BLUFFS

High in the Cascades lies the crown jewel of Oregon: **CRATER LAKE,** the country's deepest lake at 1,943 feet (592 m). Its surface glimmers like a polished sapphire hidden inside a volcano that erupted, then collapsed thousands of years ago, an event witnessed by the ancestors of the Klamath tribes and Cow Creek Umpquas. Today, we know it as one of the first national parks in the country, preserving a pristine aquatic habitat.

Crater Lake's extraordinary hues are the result of the depth and clarity of the water, which absorbs all the colors of the spectrum visible to our eyes except the shortest wavelengths—blue and violet. As you crest into the crater for the first time and spot the lake, its immense, azure expanse hits with a burst of stark beauty. "Wow" is an afterthought.

PLANNING YOUR TIME

Crater Lake National Park is southern Oregon's top destination. **Summer** (June-Sept.) weekends are peak season, when the loop drive around the caldera clogs with traffic. Most visitors schedule their trip when the whole loop is open to drive—from its opening late May-late June until winter snows bury the road starting between mid-October and mid-November.

Crater Lake is high in the Cascade Mountains and erratic weather is prevalent. July, August, and September see the warmest and sunniest days with highs in the 60s (more than 16°C). Spring and fall yo-yo between rain and snow. In winter, wet snowstorms pelt the park—which averages 43 feet (13 m) of annual snowfall—and clouds can block your view of the lake. Check the park webcams to verify visibility.

ENTRANCES AND FEES

The park's **South** and **West Entrances** (OR 62) are open year-round; a pay station for both is at Annie Creek near Mazama Village. The **North Entrance** (OR 138) is open mid-June-mid-October. The entrance fee is $30 per vehicle, $25 per motorcycle, $15 per individual, valid for seven days. You can **buy a pass online** (YourPassNow.com) in advance to go through the entrance station faster.

In winter, the South Entrance is the only way to reach the south rim to see the lake; the North Entrance, East Rim Drive, and West Rim Drive are closed by snow.

VISITORS CENTERS

The tiny **Rim Visitor Center** (9:30am-5pm daily late May-late Sept., shorter hours spring and fall) is in Rim Village near Crater Lake Lodge. It has a few exhibits and a bookstore. A rock stairway behind the building leads to **Sinnott Memorial Overlook,** with one of the best views of the lake and daily ranger talks.

The **Steel Visitor Center** (9am-5pm daily late Apr.-early Nov., 10am-4pm daily early Nov.-late Apr.) is below Rim Village near park headquarters. It has a film, exhibits, information, maps, backcountry permits, and a bookstore.

SIGHTS

THE LAKE

At 1,943 feet deep (592 m), Crater Lake is the deepest lake in the United States. It has no inlet or outlet, with its water level maintained by snow, rain, and evaporation. Although Crater Lake often records the coldest temperatures in the Cascades, the lake itself has only frozen over once since records have been kept. Deeper water in the lake stays around 38°F (3°C), although scientists have discovered hot spots 1,400 feet (427 m) below the lake's surface. Some types of mosses and green algae

Top 3

1 CIRCLE THE LAKE ON THE RIM DRIVE

BICYCLISTS RIDE THE RIM LOOP

The 33-mile (53-km) scenic **Rim Drive** (mid-June-early Nov.), divided into a longer East Rim and a shorter West Rim, offers a scenic cruise around the glistening lake. If you're seeing Crater Lake for the first time, drive into the park from the north for the most dramatic perspective. After crossing through a pumice desert, the road climbs to higher elevations until it overlooks the blue lake.

From the North Junction, follow **East Rim Drive,** stopping at pullovers along the way to the park headquarters and Steel Visitor Center. East Rim Drive finishes at the park headquarters and Steel Visitor Center.

From park headquarters, continue your tour on **West Rim Drive,** which takes in the historic **Crater Lake Lodge** and **Watchman Overlook,** for picture-perfect views of Wizard Island.

If you enter from the north, drive East Rim followed by West Rim; for entering from park headquarters, drive West Rim followed by East Rim. This clockwise circling of the lake makes pulling off at more than 30 viewpoints easier. Plan at least three hours for the curvy drive.

2 TAKE A BOAT TOUR TO WIZARD ISLAND

Due to the caldera's steep, avalanche-pruned slopes, only one trail leads down to the lake itself, and it is the only way to reach the tour boat. **Crater Lake Hospitality** (866/292-6720, www.travelcraterlake.com, daily July-mid-Sept.) launches a narrated cruise to Wizard Island, with three hours of exploration on the tiny dot of land. A boat shuttle offers access for self-explorers as well. All boats depart from Cleetwood Cove, accessible only by the steep trail.

3 BIKE THE RIM

The 33-mile (53-km) paved **Rim Drive** (summer and fall only) around Crater Lake is a cyclist's dream ride. But it's no lazy pedal nor family-friendly riding. Flying downhills swoop immediately into steep, long uphill climbs as the rolling road circles the lake. Elevation gain for the entire loop nearly reaches 4,000 feet (1,219 m), and minimal shoulders on the narrow road make the ride only for cyclists experienced with cars at their elbows. Most cyclists opt for a clockwise loop from park headquarters to get the monster climbs done first.

Two times offer prime cycling. September usually has two car-free days on the East Rim (registration recommended, https://ridetherimoregon), and cyclists are permitted to ride portions of the road still closed to cars in June after the plows have removed snow. Bring your own bicycle; the closest rentals are in Ashland, 89 miles (143 km) away.

ONE DAY IN CRATER LAKE

Thanks to the scenic **Rim Drive,** visitors who only have one day can circle the entire loop. Stop at overlooks to enjoy the lake for various vantages and squeeze in at least one short hike to **Sun Notch** or **Watchman Peak.**

grow more than 400 feet (122 m) below the lake's surface, a world record for these freshwater species. See the lake from all sides via Rim Drives.

WIZARD ISLAND

Wizard Island, a large cinder cone that rises 760 feet (201 m) above the surface of the lake, offers evidence of volcanic activity since the caldera's formation. The true crater at the top of the island is the source of the lake's name. See the island from overlooks on East Rim and West Rim Drives, or for up close inspection, take the tour boat over to hike on it and see its 800-year-old trees.

BEST EAST RIM DRIVE OVERLOOKS

On the east side of **East Rim Drive**, check out three overlooks within about 4 miles (6.4 km) of each other just north of Pinnacles Road. **Cloudcap Overlook** has its own signed spur road (2 mi. rt./3.2 km), Oregon's highest paved road. Spotted with wind- and snow-battered whitebark pines, the overlook affords a panoramic view of the crater and lake. At the **Pumice Castle Overlook**, spot the bright orange "castle" on the cliff wall. It's especially vibrant in the early evening, when the sun lights it up. At the **Phantom Ship Overlook,** try to spy the tiny island in this big lake. Formed from lava, it is 170 feet tall (52 m). Be aware that East Rim Drive will be undergoing reconstruction during summers 2021 and 2022.

BEST WEST RIM DRIVE SIGHTS

West Rim Drive has historic and scenic overlooks. At the junction above park headquarters, go right to visit the **Sinnott Memorial Overlook** and historic **Crater Lake Lodge.** Return to the junction to continue north on West Rim Drive. In about 1 mile (1.6 km), stop at **Discovery Point** (a great sunrise location), where a gold prospector stumbled upon the lake while riding his mule. Farther along West Rim Drive, **Watchman Overlook** offers good views of Wizard Island and an outstanding sunset location.

RECREATION

HIKING

West Rim Drive

Just east of Crater Lake Lodge, the **Garfield Peak Trail** (3.4 mi./5.5 km rt., 2-3 hrs., strenuous) climbs an imposing ridge with wildflower displays of phlox, Indian paintbrush, and lupine, as well as frequent sightings of eagles and hawks. The route tops out at Garfield Peak, which provides a 360-degree view of the crater and the lake 1,888 feet (575 m) below.

GARFIELD PEAK TRAIL

Best Hike

WATCHMAN PEAK

DISTANCE: 1.4 miles (2.3 km) round-trip
DURATION: 1.5 hours
ELEVATION CHANGE: 420 feet (128 m)
EFFORT: moderately strenuous
TRAILHEAD: Watchman Overlook (3.8 mi./6.1 km northwest of Rim Village)

From the trailhead, the route to **Watchman Peak** starts on the Pacific Crest Alternate Trail until the trail splits at a signed intersection. Here, the Watchman trail bolts up a series of switchbacks to reach a fire lookout watching over Crater Lake. Wizard Island is in the foreground, almost at your feet. Park rangers often lead sunset hikes to the top.

East Rim Drive

A half mile east of park headquarters, the **Castle Crest Wildflower Loop** (0.4 mi./0.6 km rt., 20 min., easy) is one of the best places to view the mid-July-mid-August flora. A short loop with lots of visual punch goes to **Sun Notch** (0.5 mi./0.8 km rt., 45 min., easy), 4.4 miles (7.1 km) east of park headquarters. This loop climbs 150 feet (46 m) through a meadow to overlook the Phantom Ship and Crater Lake.

From the Pinnacles Road, a well-graded dirt path goes through old-growth forest to **Plaikni Falls** (2 mi./3.2 km rt., 1 hr., easy), a cascade that rolls down a glacier-carved cliff. To view the falls at the end requires a short, steep grunt uphill.

Only the **Cleetwood Cove Trail** (2.2 mi./3.5 km rt., 1.5 hrs., strenuous) cuts through Crater Lake's plunging rim to reach the lakeshore. Near the boat dock, you can swim in the crystal clear lake water. But be ready for frigid cold and a return climb that gains nearly 700 feet (213 m) in elevation. A hike to **Wizard Island Summit** (2.3 mi./3.7 km rt., 2 hrs., strenuous) requires a boat ride (fee) and a 770-foot (235-km) climb. Once at the top, you can peer into the crater while circumnavigating the rim on a flat trail. Drop-offs are steep, but the views go all directions.

From a trailhead 14 miles (23 km) east of park headquarters, a trail ascends to the top of 8,926-foot (2,721-m) **Mount Scott** (5 mi./8 km rt., 3 hrs.,

CLEETWOOD COVE FOR SWIMMING AND BOAT TOURS

CRATER LAKE LODGE

strenuous), the highest peak in the park. Lake views and perspectives on a dozen Cascade peaks are the rewards at the end of the trek that gains 1,152 feet (351 m).

WINTER SPORTS

When snow buries the park in winter, services and activities are cut to a minimum. However, many cross-country skiers, snowshoers, and winter campers enjoy this solitude. Park rangers lead **snowshoe hikes** (1pm daily mid-Dec.-mid-Apr., weather permitting). Ski and snowshoe rentals are available at Rim Village.

Winter trekkers must be prepared to blaze their own cross-country trails and contend with frequent snowstorms. Inquire about trail, avalanche, and weather conditions at the visitors center before embarking. Circling the lake takes two or three days, even in good weather. Only highly skilled winter hikers or skiers should attempt this 33-mile (53-km) route, which requires a beacon, probe, and shovel for traversing avalanche paths.

WHERE TO STAY

INSIDE THE PARK

Lodging is concentrated on the southern edge of the lake at **Rim Village;** opening and closing dates vary. Most services are open mid-May to mid-October. Make lodging and camping **reservations** (866/292-6720, www.travelcraterlake.com) one year in advance.

Crater Lake Lodge (late May-mid-Oct., from $202) is hewn of local wood and stone with massive picture windows of the lake and decor echoing its 1915 origins. Many of the 71 rooms have expansive views of the lake, while less expensive rooms face Upper Klamath Lake and Mount Shasta. The lobby's large stone fireplace serves as a gathering spot on chilly evenings. The **dining room** (7am-10am, 11am-3pm, and 5pm-9:30pm daily, hours vary seasonally, dinner reservations advised) serves Pacific Northwest cuisine. A bar menu offers drinks and appetizers in the lobby or on the porch overlooking the lake.

At Mazama Village (7 mi./11 km south of Rim Village), the **Cabins at Mazama Village** (late May-late Sept., $164) have rooms with 1-2 queen beds and a bath; there are no TVs, phones, or air-conditioning. The **Annie Creek Restaurant** (7am-10:30am, 11am-4pm, and 5pm-9pm daily mid-June-Labor Day, shorter hours spring and fall) serves American-style comfort food.

Mazama Campground (Mazama Village, June-late Sept., $21-42) accepts reservations for some of its more than 200 sites; all other sites are first come, first served. Facilities include drinking water, flush toilets, and showers (fee). **Lost Creek Campground** (Pinnacles

CRATER LAKE WITH WIZARD ISLAND

Rd., July-Oct., first come, first served, $5) has 16 tent-only sites with drinking water and vault toilets.

The **Rim Village Cafe** (9am-8pm daily mid-June-Labor Day, shorter hours fall-spring) is open year-round and sells grab-and-go sandwiches, salads, and rice bowls.

OUTSIDE THE PARK

Accommodations, restaurants, and services are available in **Ashland.** Several national forests surrounding Crater Lake have campgrounds and lodges, including **Diamond Lake** in Umpqua National Forest north of Crater Lake.

GETTING THERE

AIR

The closest international airport is **Rogue Valley International-Medford Airport** (MFR, 1000 Terminal Loop Pkwy., Medford, 541/772-8068, www.jacksoncountyor.org), served by United, Horizon, and Allegiant. Car rentals are available at the airport.

TRAIN

Amtrak (800/872-7245) has a station 70 miles east at Klamath Falls (KFS, 1600 Oak Ave., 541/884-2822). The **Crater Lake Trolley** (541/882-1896, www.craterlaketrolley.net) runs a shuttle from the Amtrak station to Rim Village (July-early Oct.).

CAR

The only year-round access to Crater Lake is from the south via **OR 62.** To reach Crater Lake from Grants Pass, head for Gold Hill and take OR 234 until it meets OR 62. As you head up OR 62, the road makes a horseshoe bend through the Cascades, starting at Medford and ending 20 miles (32 km) north of Klamath Falls.

The northern route via **OR 138** (Roseburg to US 97, south of Beaver Marsh)

TAKE A BOAT RIDE ON CRATER LAKE.

THE GEOLOGY OF CRATER LAKE

Crater Lake lies in a caldera, which is produced when the center of a volcano caves in on itself. The cataclysm occurred 7,700 years ago with the destruction of formerly 12,000-foot-high (3,657-m) Mount Mazama. Klamath Native American legend tells of a fierce battle between the chiefs of the underworld and the world aboveground causing explosions and ashfall. The story parallels the scientific explanation for Crater Lake's formation.

Following the volcanic activity, the caldera filled with water over thousands of years. The lake is self-contained, fed only by snow and rain, with no outlets other than evaporation and seepage.

This great eruption left huge, deep drifts of ash and pumice. The pumice deserts to the north of the lake and the deep ashen canyons to the south are the most dramatic examples. These reddish pockets of bleakness in the otherwise green forest are so porous that water percolates through too rapidly for plants to survive. In the southern canyons, hot gases bubbling up through the ash created the eerie gray hoodoos that hardened into rocklike towers to withstand centuries of erosion.

is usually closed by snow mid-October-July, as is the park's north entrance.

GETTING AROUND

There is no public transportation within the park. Most visitors tour the 33-mile (53-km) Rim Drive in private vehicles.

BOAT TOURS

Crater Lake Hospitality (866/292-6720, www.travelcraterlake.com, daily July-mid-Sept.) offers narrated tours on the lake. Tickets are sold up to 24 hours in advance via touch-screen kiosks in Crater Lake Lodge or Annie Creek Gift Shop in Mazama Village. Kiosk sales shut down two hours before departure; after that, you can pick up any remaining tickets at the Cleetwood Cove Trailhead until 45 minutes before departure. A limited number of tickets are available by **reservation requests** online. Choose between two boat tours:

Two-hour narrated excursions (6 departures daily, 9:30am-3:45pm, adults $44, kids $30) cruise counterclockwise around the perimeter of the lake and do not stop at Wizard Island.

Five-hour narrated cruises (departs 9:45am and 12:45pm daily, adults $55, kids $37) make a three-hour stop for hiking at Wizard Island.

If you just want to get to Wizard Island for three hours of self-guided exploration, take the **boat shuttle** (departs 8:30am and 11:30am daily, adults $28, kids $18).

Allow 90 minutes to drive the 12 miles (19 km) from Rim Village to the Cleetwood trailhead. Prepare to hike the **Cleetwood Trail** (1.1 mi./1.8 km one-way, 30-45 min., strenuous) 700 feet (213 m) down to **Cleetwood Cove dock,** where boat tours depart. Dress warmly, as the lake is cool.

TROLLEY TOURS

The **Crater Lake Trolley** (541/882-1896, www.craterlaketrolley.net, 10am-3pm daily July-mid-Oct., tours vary June and Sept.-Oct., $26-29 adults, $18 kids) takes a two-hour tour along Rim Drive with stops at scenic viewpoints. The natural gas-powered trolleys are ADA-compliant and feature commentary by a guide. Purchase tickets in advance from a trolley parked by the Community House at Rim Village, near the Crater Lake Lodge.

SIGHTS NEARBY

En route from Redwood National Park to Crater Lake, it's worth a stop at **Oregon Caves National Monument** (OR 46, 541/592-2100, www.nps.gov/orca, hours vary spring and fall), to see stalactites and stalagmites deep inside a mountain.

OLYMPIC NATIONAL PARK

Washington

KEEPSAKE STAMPS ▼▼▼

WEBSITE:
www.nps.gov/olym

PHONE NUMBER:
360/565-3130

VISITATION RANK:
9

WHY GO:
Wander amid old-growth temperate rain forests.

▲ HALL OF MOSSES, OLYMPIC NATIONAL PARK

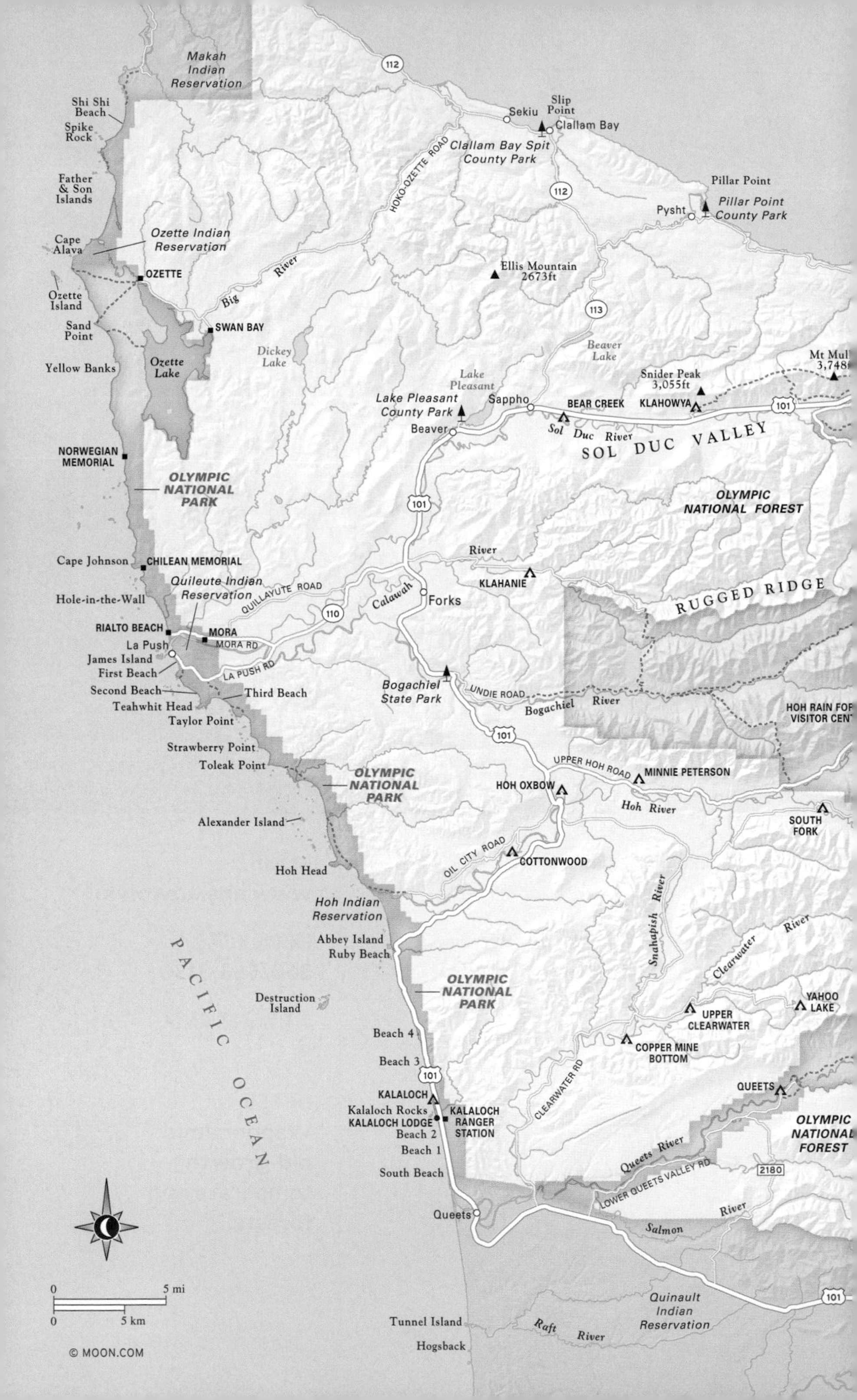

Makah Indian Reservation
Shi Shi Beach
Spike Rock
Father & Son Islands
Cape Alava
Ozette Island
Sand Point
Yellow Banks
Ozette Indian Reservation
OZETTE
SWAN BAY
Ozette Lake
Big River
HOKO-OZETTE ROAD
112
Sekiu
Slip Point
Clallam Bay
Clallam Bay Spit County Park
Pillar Point
Pysht
Pillar Point County Park
Ellis Mountain 2673ft
113
Dickey Lake
Beaver Lake
Lake Pleasant
Lake Pleasant County Park
Sappho
Beaver
BEAR CREEK
KLAHOWYA
Snider Peak 3,055ft
Mt Mull 3,748ft
101
Sol Duc River
SOL DUC VALLEY
NORWEGIAN MEMORIAL
OLYMPIC NATIONAL PARK
OLYMPIC NATIONAL FOREST
Cape Johnson
CHILEAN MEMORIAL
Quileute Indian Reservation
Hole-in-the-Wall
QUILLAYUTE ROAD
110
Calawah River
Forks
KLAHANIE
RUGGED RIDGE
RIALTO BEACH
MORA
MORA RD
La Push
James Island
First Beach
LA PUSH RD
Second Beach
Third Beach
Teahwhit Head
Taylor Point
Bogachiel State Park
UNDIE ROAD
Bogachiel River
HOH RAIN FOREST VISITOR CENTER
Strawberry Point
Toleak Point
UPPER HOH ROAD
MINNIE PETERSON
HOH OXBOW
Hoh River
SOUTH FORK
Alexander Island
OIL CITY ROAD
COTTONWOOD
Hoh Head
Hoh Indian Reservation
Abbey Island
Ruby Beach
Snahapish River
Clearwater River
PACIFIC OCEAN
Destruction Island
YAHOO LAKE
UPPER CLEARWATER
COPPER MINE BOTTOM
Beach 4
Beach 3
CLEARWATER RD
KALALOCH
Kalaloch Rocks
KALALOCH LODGE
KALALOCH RANGER STATION
Beach 2
Beach 1
South Beach
QUEETS
Queets River
LOWER QUEETS VALLEY RD
2180
Queets
Salmon River
0
5 mi
5 km
Quinault Indian Reservation
Tunnel Island
Raft River
Hogsback
© MOON.COM

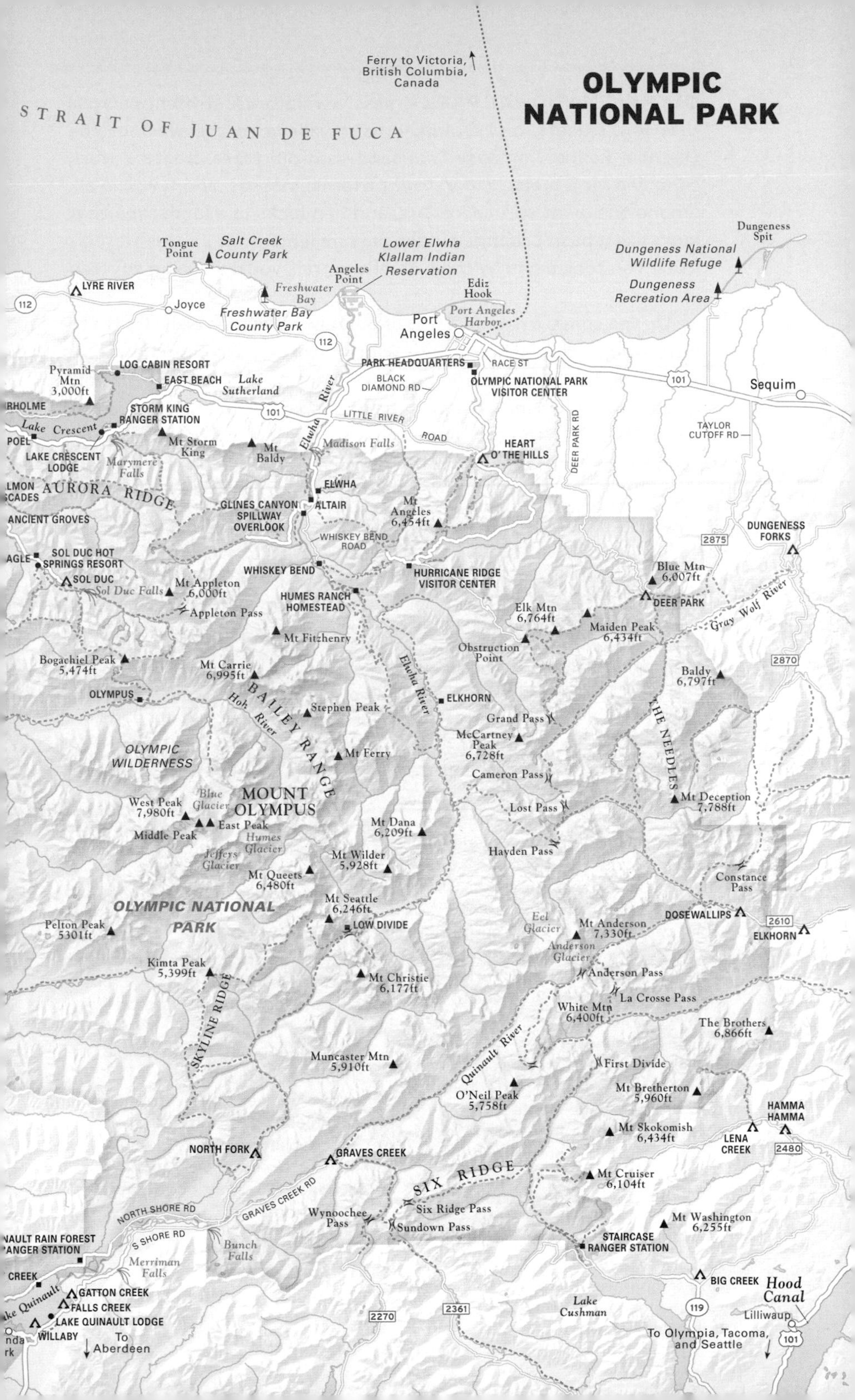
OLYMPIC NATIONAL PARK
Ferry to Victoria, British Columbia, Canada
STRAIT OF JUAN DE FUCA
Tongue Point
Salt Creek County Park
Lower Elwha Klallam Indian Reservation
Angeles Point
Ediz Hook
Dungeness Spit
Dungeness National Wildlife Refuge
Dungeness Recreation Area
LYRE RIVER
Freshwater Bay
Joyce
Freshwater Bay County Park
Port Angeles Harbor
Port Angeles
112
PARK HEADQUARTERS
RACE ST
OLYMPIC NATIONAL PARK VISITOR CENTER
BLACK DIAMOND RD
101
Sequim
Pyramid Mtn 3,000ft
LOG CABIN RESORT
EAST BEACH
Lake Sutherland
Elwha River
LITTLE RIVER ROAD
DEER PARK RD
TAYLOR CUTOFF RD
STORM KING RANGER STATION
Lake Crescent
Mt Storm King
Mt Baldy
Madison Falls
HEART O' THE HILLS
LAKE CRESCENT LODGE
Marymere Falls
AURORA RIDGE
ELWHA
ALTAIR
GLINES CANYON SPILLWAY OVERLOOK
Mt Angeles 6,454ft
ANCIENT GROVES
WHISKEY BEND ROAD
DUNGENESS FORKS
2875
SOL DUC HOT SPRINGS RESORT
WHISKEY BEND
HURRICANE RIDGE VISITOR CENTER
Blue Mtn 6,007ft
SOL DUC
Sol Duc Falls
Mt Appleton 6,000ft
Appleton Pass
HUMES RANCH HOMESTEAD
DEER PARK
Gray Wolf River
Elk Mtn 6,764ft
Maiden Peak 6,434ft
Mt Fitzhenry
Obstruction Point
Bogachiel Peak 5,474ft
Mt Carrie 6,995ft
2870
Baldy 6,797ft
OLYMPUS
Elwha River
ELKHORN
BAILEY RANGE
Hoh River
Stephen Peak
Grand Pass
THE NEEDLES
OLYMPIC WILDERNESS
McCartney Peak 6,728ft
Mt Ferry
Cameron Pass
MOUNT OLYMPUS
Blue Glacier
West Peak 7,980ft
East Peak
Middle Peak
Lost Pass
Mt Deception 7,788ft
Mt Dana 6,209ft
Humes Glacier
Jeffers Glacier
Hayden Pass
Mt Wilder 5,928ft
Mt Queets 6,480ft
Constance Pass
Mt Seattle 6,246ft
OLYMPIC NATIONAL PARK
Pelton Peak 5301ft
LOW DIVIDE
Eel Glacier
Mt Anderson 7,330ft
Anderson Glacier
DOSEWALLIPS
2610
ELKHORN
Kimta Peak 5,399ft
Mt Christie 6,177ft
Anderson Pass
SKYLINE RIDGE
La Crosse Pass
White Mtn 6,400ft
The Brothers 6,866ft
Quinault River
Muncaster Mtn 5,910ft
First Divide
O'Neil Peak 5,758ft
Mt Bretherton 5,960ft
HAMMA HAMMA
Mt Skokomish 6,434ft
LENA CREEK
2480
NORTH FORK
GRAVES CREEK
SIX RIDGE
Mt Cruiser 6,104ft
GRAVES CREEK RD
NORTH SHORE RD
Wynoochee Pass
Six Ridge Pass
Sundown Pass
Mt Washington 6,255ft
S SHORE RD
Bunch Falls
STAIRCASE RANGER STATION
Merriman Falls
BIG CREEK
Hood Canal
GATTON CREEK
FALLS CREEK
LAKE QUINAULT LODGE
Lake Cushman
2270
2361
119
Lilliwaup
WILLABY
To Aberdeen
To Olympia, Tacoma, and Seattle
101

OLYMPIC NATIONAL PARK's massive rainforest stretches across the Hoh, Queets, and Quinault river valleys to the west of the Olympic Range. Immense thousand-year-old trees create a thick canopy over a moist understory of ferns, mosses, and fungi. Walk among the giant spruce, cedars, and hemlocks in a landscape that looks like it hasn't changed in the past millennium. It's so lush it feels like if you took a nap by the side of the trail, you'd wake up covered in moss.

On the coast, a narrow strip of parkland provides easy access to mist-shrouded beaches where winter storm-watching is a recreational activity. From sea level to 7,980 feet (2,432 m) at the glaciated summit of Mount Olympus, the park spans a breadth of ecosystems. These rich forests, mountains, and beaches provided plentiful food for the ancestors of eight tribes who still feel a deep connection to this place.

PLANNING YOUR TIME

This more than 1,400-square-mile (3,734-sq.-km) park lies in the center of the Olympic Peninsula and includes a 73-mile (118-km) stretch of the Pacific coastline. With multiple entrance points placed far apart, the easiest access is via US 101, which loops nearly around the park. Most of the park's interior is inaccessible by car, keeping it the province of hikers, backpackers, and climbers.

With a lot of driving, **four days** will get you to the main sights. Plan 7-10 days to soak up the area's riches. Lodging in the park is limited, so most visitors make use of the surrounding gateway towns: **Port Angeles, Port Townsend, Sequim,** and **Forks.** Book summer **reservations** in these areas one year in advance.

The park is open year-round. **May-September** is the most popular time to visit, when it's dry and temperatures range 75-85 degrees (24-29°C). Avoid the big summer crowds by visiting in off-season or hiking in remoter locations.

Fall-spring, some roads, campgrounds, and facilities close and the threat of rain is ever-present—bring rain gear. Come winter, low-elevation temperatures stay above freezing while upper elevations like Hurricane Ridge amass snow.

ENTRANCES AND FEES

The entrance fee is $30 per vehicle ($25 motorcycle, $15 individual) and good for seven days. Purchase a pass in advance online (YourPassNow.com) to go through the entrance station faster. There is no fee to enter parts of the park crossed by US 101, such as at Lake Crescent and along the coastline south from Ruby Beach.

Five entrance stations are staffed daily May-September: **Hurricane Ridge** (Hurricane Ridge Rd., weekends and holidays in winter), **Hoh** (Upper Hoh Rd.), **Ozette** (Hoko-Ozette Rd.), **Sol Duc** (Sol Duc Rd.), and **Staircase** (Staircase Rd.).

Entrance stations are unstaffed in the off-season (Sept.-May); use the self-serve pay stations instead.

VISITORS CENTERS

Olympic National Park has four visitors centers with exhibits, information and schedules, maps, and bookstores. Kids can choose from two Junior Ranger booklets (free) or pick up a **Discovery Backpack** ($5 donation) for in-the-field explorations.

Olympic National Park Visitor Center

The **Olympic National Park Visitor Center** (3002 Mount Angeles Rd., Port Angeles, 360/565-3130, 7:30am-6pm

Top 3

1 STEP INTO THE HOH RAIN FOREST

The **Hoh Rain Forest** is the best place to explore the park's lush rainforest environment. A drive up the Hoh River proffers views of the dark canopy and shaded understory, but walking through the rainforest yields a vastly different experience—damp woods, earthy scents, fields of moss, and every shade of green imaginable. Explore the short trails around the Hoh Visitor Center.

HOH RAIN FOREST

2 GO HIGH ON HURRICANE RIDGE

Hurricane Ridge is the only car-accessible route to high vistas inside the Olympic Mountains. From Port Angeles, **Hurricane Ridge Road** (daily May-mid-Oct., Fri.-Sun. Nov.-Mar., chains required in winter) snakes up the mountainside for 17 picturesque miles (27 km) at an easy 7 percent grade. The road climbs amid big scenery to alpine trails, fields bursting with wildflowers, and shrieking marmots. As the road nears the summit, you'll reach the **Hurricane Ridge Visitor Center,** which has an observation deck for peak-gazing. To the south lie ice-draped citadels and Mount Olympus, the park's highest peak.

3 EXPLORE TIDEPOOLS AT RUBY BEACH

Sea stacks and driftwood decorate **Ruby Beach,** which transitions from rocky ground to red sand as waves crash on the shore. From the parking area overlook, the paved **Ruby Beach Trail** (0.5 mi./0.8 km rt., 20 min.) leads through woods and tall undergrowth down to the tidal zone. Come at low tide, when you have clear passage up and down the beach to explore tidepools full of mussels, starfish, and urchins and observe sea otters in the water. Look for the famous hole in a sea stack next to Cedar Creek.

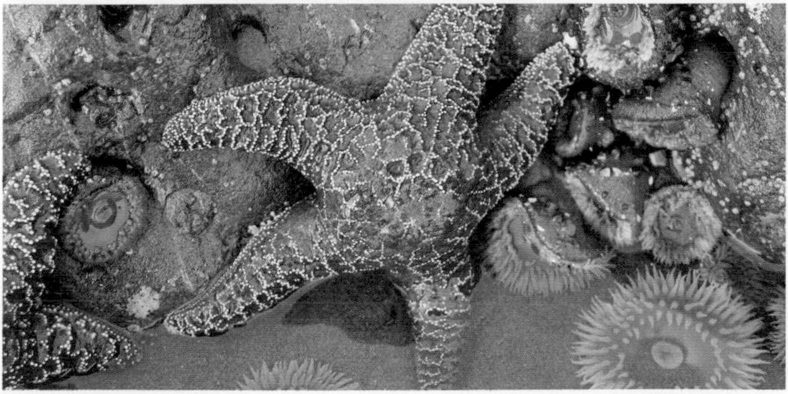

STARFISH, RUBY BEACH

ONE DAY IN OLYMPIC

Spend the night in **Port Angeles** so you can get an early start for your one day in the park. Start with a drive up to **Hurricane Ridge,** followed by a stop for lunch at **Crescent Lake Lodge.** Then cruise through the **Hoh Rain Forest** and finish with a stroll along **Ruby Beach.**

daily summer, hours vary fall-spring) has park-wide information, hands-on exhibits for kids, and a park film. The **Wilderness Information Center** (360/565-3100, daily Apr.-Oct.) has weather updates, trail reports, overnight permits, and bear canisters.

Hurricane Ridge

The **Hurricane Ridge Visitor Center** (Hurricane Ridge Rd., 9am-6pm daily late June-Sept., hours and days vary Oct.-May) has an observation deck, self-guided nature trails, and ranger-led walks in summer. It is located 17 miles (27 km) south of Port Angeles on the south slope of Hurricane Ridge.

Hoh Rain Forest

The **Hoh Rain Forest Visitor Center** (360/374-6925, 9am-5pm daily mid-May-Sept., hours and days vary May-Oct.) has a bookstore, an information desk, and ranger-led interpretive walks and presentations. It is located at the end of the Upper Hoh Road, 31 miles (50 km) southeast of Forks.

Kalaloch

The small **Kalaloch Ranger Station** (156954 US 101, Forks, 360/962-2283, hours vary daily late June-Sept., Tues.-Sat. mid-May-late June) is the best resource for the Olympic coast.

SIGHTS

ELWHA VALLEY

The **Elwha Valley** has seen a major transformation due to removal of two dams to return the Elwha River to free-flowing. Since the removal of the dams in 2011-2014, the water is being

HURRICANE RIDGE

KAYAKING ON LAKE CRESCENT

coaxed back to its old channels, and salmon now swim upstream.

From US 101 about 11 miles (18 km, 20 min.) southwest of Port Angeles, follow Olympic Hot Springs Road (Elwha River Road) south into the park. Due to a washout on the road, access now terminates at a gate just inside the park boundary. Here, the paved, wheelchair-accessible 200-foot (61-m) path leads to **Madison Falls.** To see the river transformation, you can hike or bike the closed road and bypass trail that goes around the washout to get to **Glines Canyon Overlook** (6.8 mi./10.9 km rt.).

BULL ELK

LAKE CRESCENT

Lake Crescent is the place to go for tranquil beauty. Follow US 101 south as it cuts into the park along the 12-mile-long (19-km) glacier-carved lake. Set in a trough of steep old-growth forest, Lake Crescent is more than 600 feet (183 m) deep. The translucent turquoise-green water is startlingly clear; at some points, visibility on the lake's surface extends to 60 feet (18 m), making it a popular spot for paddlers and anglers. Boat tours (888/896-3818, www.olympicnationalparks.com, 3-4 times Thurs.-Sun. mid-June-mid-Sept., 90-min., $13-27) cruise on Lake Crescent. Enjoy the lake from its three picnic areas, a campground, the **Crescent Lake Lodge, Log Cabin Resort,** or two **boat launches.**

An environmental education center with a facility near the lodge, **NatureBridge** (415/992-4700, www.naturebridge.org) has weekend family programs (spring-summer) and two-week science camps for teens (summer).

SOL DUC VALLEY

West of Lake Crescent on US 101, paved **Sol Duc Hot Springs Road** (pronounced "Saul Duck") leads into the park along the Sol Duc River. Old-growth forest looms on either side of the road, and hiking feels like something out of a fairy tale, with beams of sunlight breaking through high tree branches to dapple the forest floor.

At 5 miles (8 km), **Salmon Cascades** has a viewing platform for watching steelhead trout in spring and coho salmon in fall as they fly through the air, struggling to migrate upstream.

Near the end of the road, **Sol Duc Hot Springs Resort** (12076 Sol Duc Rd., 888/896-3818, www.olympicnationalparks.com, Apr.-mid-Oct., day passes $11-15 adults, $11 kids) feels like a suburban rec center plopped down in the middle of the woods. Soak in three cement pools with temperatures ranging 99-104°F (37-40°C) (bathers often go au naturel). One large, nonthermal swimming pool offers shared space for sunbathers, swimmers, and kids.

LAKE OZETTE

Lake Ozette is the third-largest natural lake in Washington. The area from its eastern shore to the coastline is part of the national park and includes a picnic area, boat launch, and campground on the north shore.

KALALOCH

The name **Kalaloch** (CLAY-lock) derives from a Quinault term meaning "sheltered landing." This coastal portion of Olympic National Park stretches between the Hoh Indian Reservation and the Quinault Reservation, providing easy access to beaches that maintain a wild feel.

Seven points along US 101 can get you down to the water. Stop first at the north-end viewpoint to overlook **Ruby Beach.** From here, six numbered points access the beach from south to north. **Beach Four** is good for tidepooling, and in summer park rangers conduct guided tours of the tidepools. Next up is **Kalaloch Beach,** 7.6 miles (12 km) south of Ruby. Between Kalaloch Campground and Kalaloch Lodge, Kalaloch Creek enters the ocean where the **Kalaloch Rocks** sit offshore. **South Beach** is the southernmost beach in the park.

QUEETS RAIN FOREST

South of Kalaloch, the paved and gravel Upper Queets Valley Road leads 27 miles (43 km) into the **Queets Rain Forest.** This off-the-beaten-path region of the park is the province of campers, hikers, and anglers casting into the Queets River. At the road's terminus is the huge **Queets Sitka Spruce**—the largest spruce in the world by volume. The

WILLABY CREEK FLOWS INTO LAKE QUINAULT

Best Hike

HURRICANE HILL

DISTANCE: 3.2 miles (5.2 km) round-trip
DURATION: 2 hours
ELEVATION CHANGE: 700 feet (213 m)
EFFORT: moderate
TRAILHEAD: Hurricane Hill Road parking lot, 1 mile (1.6 km) west of Hurricane Ridge Visitor Center

The **Hurricane Hill Trail** waltzes through summer fields of wildflowers, where you may have to fight the impulse to throw your arms wide and belt out the opening bars of "The Sound of Music." With interpretive signs, the paved, wide trail climbs out of the forest into high alpine meadows and mountain goat terrain. The path steepens the farther you go. At the ridge, immense views spread to the south, including glaciers flanking Mount Olympus, the highest peak in the park. To the north, look straight down on Port Angeles and the Strait of Juan de Fuca, which separates the United States from Canada. Plan to arrive by 9am, as parking lot fills.

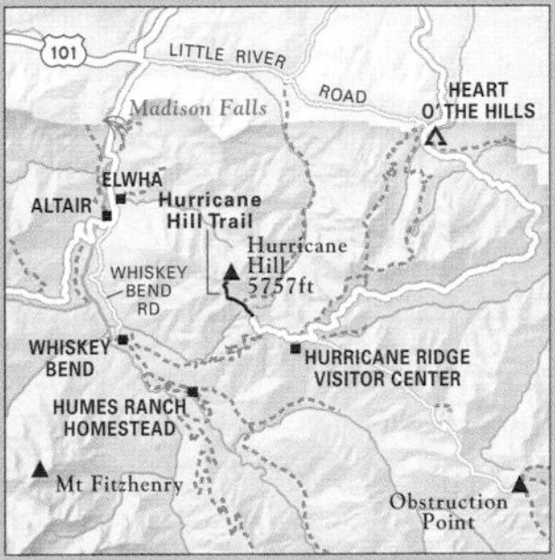

248-foot-tall (77.6-m) wonder is almost 15 feet (4.6 m) in diameter at its base.

QUINAULT RAIN FOREST

The **Quinault Rain Forest** is just as rainy and impressive as the Hoh. Its forest includes some huge trees, like the **Quinault Lake Spruce,** the world's largest Sitka spruce by girth on the **Big Sitka Spruce Tree Trail** (0.6 mi./1 km rt., 30 min., easy), located on the South Shore Road. However, the most impressive trees are on the North Shore on the **Big Cedar Trail** (0.4 mi./0.6 km rt., 20 min., easy).

At the center of the rainforest sits **Lake Quinault,** a glacier-fed natural reservoir of the Quinault River. The lake harbors **Lake Quinault Lodge** (on the South Shore), which is listed on the National Register of Historic Places. You can boat, fish, and swim in summer or just hang out watching the rain the rest of the year. Boat tours (888/896-3818, www.olympicnationalparks.com, three times daily June-Sept., 90-min., $25-35) cruise on Lake Quinault.

Hikers and campers follow the **Quinault Rain Forest Loop Drive** (31 mi./50 km) to access trailheads and campsites. The road travels around the lake and up one side of the Quinault River and back down the other. The upper portions of North Shore and South Shore Roads are dirt.

HIKING

HURRICANE RIDGE AND THE NORTH SIDE

Opposite the visitors center, easy paths let you absorb the beauty. Two wheelchair-accessible paved trails go to **Big Meadow** (0.5 mi./0.8 km rt., 20 min.) for mountain views and **Cirque Rim** (1 mi./1.6 km rt., 45 min., wheelchair assistance may be needed) to overlook the Strait of Juan de Fuca. The partly paved **High Ridge Loop** (1 mi./1.6 km rt., 30 min.) climbs to Sunrise Point for views in all directions.

Klahhane Ridge

From the Hurricane Ridge Visitor Center, an out-and-back traverse to **Klahhane Ridge** (7.6 mi./12.2 km rt., 4 hrs., strenuous) packs in big views in both directions, scads of wildflower meadows, and resident mountain goats and marmots. After passing the Switchback Trail, the last mile steepens to climb more than 700 feet (213 m) to the ridge.

Grand Valley

From the end of Obstruction Point Road, an upside-down trail descends into **Grand Valley** with four destinations. All demand a strenuous 1,800-foot (549-m) climb back up on the return. The route starts with a stunning high traverse south on Lillian Ridge before dropping into the valley cradling three lovely lakes—**Moose Lake** (8.2 mi./13.2 km rt.), **Grand Lake** (8.3 mi./13.4 km rt.), and **Gladys Lake** (9.2 mi./14.8 km rt.), the last above the tree line. Talus and wildflower meadows line the trail that culminates at **Grand Pass** (13 mi./20.9 km rt.) for big views.

Royal Basin

The Upper Dungeness Trail enters the park to reach **Royal Lake** (14.4 mi./23.2 km rt., 8 hrs., strenuous), tucked below the craggy Needles and Mount Deception. The trail follows Royal Creek into the rugged Royal Basin, a glaciated bowl of forest, meadows, talus slopes, and waterfalls. The **Upper Dungeness Trailhead** is located outside the park, south of Sequim. You'll need an America the Beautiful Pass or Northwest Forest Pass ($5, www.discovernw.org) and an early start to park at the crowded trailhead parking lot.

LAKE CRESCENT

Marymere Falls

From Storm King Ranger Station, a gentle walk in the woods culminates at the 90-foot (27-m) **Marymere Falls** (1.8 mi./2.9 km rt., 1 hr., easy).

Spruce Railroad Trail

From East Shore Road, the **Spruce Railroad Trail** (2-8 mi./3.2-12.9 km rt., 1-4 hrs., easy) takes a lakeside route along the north shore of Lake Crescent on a repurposed railroad track that goes through a tunnel. Bikes are allowed. For a short destination on the trail, **Devil's Punchbowl** (1 mi./1.6 km from the trailhead) is a calm cove surrounded by tall bluffs. A bridge with a postcard-worthy view of Mount Storm King crosses the cove, a popular swimming hole.

SOL DUC VALLEY

Drive to the terminus of Sol Duc Road to hike to roaring **Sol Duc Falls** (1.6 mi./2.6 km rt., 1 hr., easy) that makes a two-level, 50-foot (15-m) drop. Find the best viewing at the bridge, where you'll get spritzed with a gentle mist. From Sol Duc Hot Springs Resort, the **Lover's Lane Trail** (5.8 mi./9.3 km rt., 3 hrs., easy) follows Sol Duc River to the falls.

WATERFALL VIEWS INTO OLYMPIC NATIONAL PARK

HOH RAIN FOREST

HOH RAIN FOREST

From the visitors center, follow the **Mini-Trail** (0.1 mi./0.2 km), a wheelchair-accessible loop with interpretive signage. The evocatively named **Hall of Mosses Trail** (0.8 mi./1.3 km rt., 30 min.) arcs past giant firs, big-leaf maples festooned with moss, and licorice ferns that carpet the forest floor. The **Spruce Nature Trail** (1.2 mi./1.9 km rt., 45 min.) goes through the forest to the Hoh River.

LAKE OZETTE AND THE COAST

Shi Shi Beach

Head through the Makah Reservation to **Shi Shi Beach** (4-8 mi./6.4-12.9 km rt., 2-5 hrs., easy, purchase $10 pass in Neah Bay), pronounced "shy shy." A partial boardwalk path cuts through damp woods to a steep, rope-assisted descent to the sand and driftwood beach. The 2.5-mile (4 km) beach, best at low tide for tidepools of starfish and sea urchins, terminates at **Point of Arches,** massive intricate sea stacks.

To reach the trailhead, take Cape Flattery Road west of Neah Bay for 2.5 miles (4 km) and turn south onto Hobuck Beach Road. After crossing the Sooes River the road becomes Sooes Beach Road to reach the trailhead.

Cape Alava

From the Lake Ozette **Ranger Station** (360/565-3130, daily June-Sept.) at the end of Hoko-Ozette Road, two routes diverge to go to the coastline. **Cape Alava** (6.2 mi./10 km rt., 3.5 hrs., easy) plods on a cedar boardwalk through forest and wet prairie to the westernmost point of the Lower 48, passing the site of a **Makah village.** The **Sand Point Trail** (5.6 mi./9 km rt., 3 hrs., easy) travels mostly over boardwalk to reach the beach at a southern point.

The **Ozette Triangle** (9 mi./14.5 km rt., 5 hrs., easy) connects the Cape Alava Trail to the Sand Point Trail, adding 3 miles (4.8 km) of walking along the beach strewn with rocks and driftwood, plus the **Wedding Rocks,** with Indian petroglyphs depicting whales, fertility figures, and a European ship.

EAST SIDE

Upper Lena Lake

The trail to Lena Lake crowds with weekend hikers, but those who hike to **Upper Lena Lake** (14 mi./22.5 km rt.,

BACKPACKING IS A POPULAR ACTIVITY IN THE PARK.

7-8 hrs., strenuous) will find plenty of breathing room along with subalpine wildflowers, huckleberries, and views of the Brothers, a pair of rugged peaks. From US 101 north of Hoodsport, take the Hamma Hamma River Road (#25) to the trailhead.

Staircase Rapids Loop

From the Staircase Ranger Station, at the end of the twisting dirt road, the **Staircase Rapids Trail** (2 mi./3.2 km rt., 1 hr., easy) combines with **North Fork of the Skokomish River Trail** to make a loop on both sides of the river and connected by a bridge. The route passes Pacific rhododendrons, vibrant mossy old growth, a big fallen cedar tree, and waterfalls.

RECREATION

BACKPACKING

Beaches, long forested valleys, and stunning subalpine passes with a riot of colorful wildflowers define backpacking trips. The best two- or three-day trips head to the **Ozette Triangle** (9 mi./14.5 km rt.), **Royal Basin** (14.4 mi./23.2 km rt.), **Grand Valley** (8.2-13 mi./13.2-20.9 km rt.), and **Seven Lakes Basin-High Divide Loop** (18.2 mi./29.2 km rt.) that takes a goat-trail traverse across Bogachiel Peak with spectacular views of Mount Olympus and Blue Glacier.

On the west side, the most popular backpacking trips last 3-5 days. The **Hoh River Trail** (34.8 mi./56 km rt.) combines a gentle rainforest walk with a climb to Glacier Meadows, where wildflowers intersperse among glacial moraine below Mount Olympus. For long beach treks, watch the tides for **Rialto Beach to Cape Alava** (44 mi./70.8 km rt.) or **Third Beach to Hoh River** (32 mi./51.5 km rt.).

Permits are required. Pick them up 24 hours in advance from the **Wilderness Information Center** (3002 Mount Angeles Rd., 360/565-3100, daily Apr.-Oct., $8 pp per night plus $6 permit fee). Make advance **reservations** (www.recreation.gov) online starting six months in advance. Bear canisters, required in some locations, are available first come, first served.

CLIMBING

The end of the Hoh River Trail is the most popular launching point for experienced mountaineers to scale 7,980-foot (2,432-m) **Mount Olympus** (late

June-early Sept.), the tallest peak in the park. It's a technically demanding scramble over glaciers and a rock spire at the summit, requiring ice axes, harnesses, ropes, and crampons. Permits are not required for climbing, but are required for backcountry camping.

Mountain Madness (800/328-5925, www.mountainmadness.com) and **International Mountain Guides** (360/569-2609, www.mountainguides.com) lead climbing trips.

KAYAKING AND RAFTING

Several lakes make for exceptional paddling. Lake Crescent, Lake Ozette, and Lake Quinault have boat launches for watercraft. **Lake Crescent Lodge** and **Log Cabin Resort** rent kayaks, rowboats, canoes, and paddleboards for Lake Crescent. **Adventures Through Kayaking** (2358 US 101, 360/417-3015, www.atkayaking.com) leads kayak or paddleboard tours on Lake Crescent and provide lessons and rentals. For Lake Quinault, **Lake Quinault Lodge** rents kayaks, paddleboards, canoes, and rowboats.

Guided trips raft the rivers. **Rainforest Paddlers** (360/374-5254) leads trips down the Hoh, Sol Duc, and Elwha Rivers. They also guide kayak trips on the Hoh and in an estuary near La Push.

FISHING

Lake Crescent contains Beardslee rainbows, Crescenti cutthroats, and abundant kokanee runs May-October (no license needed). The **Sol Duc River** has steelhead and salmon (Washington Catch Cards required).

WINTER SPORTS

With 400 inches (1,016 cm) of annual snow, **Hurricane Ridge** becomes a winter playground December-March. You can downhill ski, cross-country ski, snowboard, tube, and snowshoe. Hurricane Ridge Road is open to uphill traffic Friday-Sunday (9am-4pm), weather permitting (carry tire chains).

For downhill skiing and snowboarding, **Hurricane Ridge Ski and Snowboard Area** (848/667-7669, www.hurricaneridge.com, 10am-4pm Sat.-Sun. Dec.-Mar., pass required) operates two rope tows and a Poma lift and rents tubes for sliding. A gift shop rents downhill skis, cross-country skis, and snowshoes.

Ranger-led **snowshoe walks** (2pm Sat.-Sun. mid-Dec.-Mar., adults $7, children $3) last 1.5 hours and include snowshoes. Sign up 30 minutes before the start time at the Hurricane Ridge Visitor Center.

▼ HIKING AT RIALTO BEACH

SNOWSHOEING ON HURRICANE RIDGE

WHERE TO STAY

INSIDE THE PARK

For summer stays, make **reservations** (888/896-3818, www.olympicnationalparks.com) one year in advance at four lodges.

Lake Crescent

The historic **Lake Crescent Lodge** (416 Lake Crescent Rd., 360/928-3253, May-Nov., from $152) has cabins with fireplaces, motel rooms, and lodge rooms with shared baths. The lodge **restaurant** (7:30am-10:30am, 11am-2:30pm and 5pm-9pm daily, May-mid-Oct.) overlooks the lake and has a bar and gift shop.

At the north end of Lake Crescent, the **Log Cabin Resort** (3183 E. Beach Rd., 360/928-3325, late May-Sept., from $110) has cabins, a few large chalets, and an RV campground. The modest on-site **restaurant** (8am-11am, noon-9pm daily) serves breakfast, lunch, and dinner.

Sol Duc

Sol Duc Hot Springs Resort (12076 Sol Duc Rd., 360/327-3583, Mar.-Oct., from $210) consists of RV campsites and 32 no-frills cabins next to the hot springs complex; some rooms have kitchens. The resort's **Springs Restaurant** (7:30am-10am, 11am-4pm, and 5pm-9pm daily) and **Espresso Bar & Lounge** (7:30am-9pm daily) serve cafeteria-style breakfast, lunch, and dinner.

Lake Quinault

Built in 1926, **Lake Quinault Lodge** (345 South Shore Rd., 360/288-2900, year-round, from $249) is a classic national park hotel with rooms in the original lodge, a newer building with larger rooms, or a small annex. The lodge's **Roosevelt Dining Room** (7:30am-11am, 11:30am-2pm, and 5pm-8pm daily) serves breakfast, lunch, and dinner.

Kalaloch

Kalaloch Lodge (157151 US 101, 360/962-2271, www.thekalalochlodge.com, year-round, from $210) sits on a bluff overlooking the ocean. Accommodations include Bluff Cabins, smaller Kalaloch Cabins, and guest rooms in the main lodge. The lodge's **Creekside Restaurant** (8am-8pm daily winter, 7am-9pm summer) serves breakfast, lunch, and dinner, with reservations essential in summer.

WHERE TO STAY IN OLYMPIC NATIONAL PARK

NAME	LOCATION	PRICE	SEASON	AMENITIES
Heart O' the Hills	Hurricane Ridge	$20	year-round	tent and RV sites
Fairholme	Lake Crescent	$20	May-Oct.	tent and RV sites
Lake Crescent Lodge	Lake Crescent	$152	May-Nov.	cabins, motel and lodge rooms, dining
Log Cabin Resort	Lake Crescent	$110	May-Sept.	cabins, chalets, RV sites, dining
Sol Duc	Sol Duc	$28	Mar.-Oct.	tent and RV sites
Sol Duc Hot Springs Resort	Sol Duc	from $210	Mar.-Oct.	cabins, RV sites, dining
Ozette	Lake Ozette	$20	year-round	tent and RV sites
Hoh	Hoh Rain Forest	$20	year-round	tent and RV sites
Lake Quinault Lodge	Lake Quinault	$249	year-round	lodge rooms, dining
Kalaloch Campground	Kalaloch	$22		tent and RV sites
Kalaloch Lodge	Kalaloch	$200	year-round	cabins, lodge rooms, dining
Mora	Rialto Beach	$20	year-round	tent and RV sites
Staircase	Staircase	$20	May-Oct.	tent and RV sites

KALALOCH

MOUNTAIN VIEWS OF OLYMPIC NATIONAL PARK

Campgrounds

Only two campgrounds accept **reservations** (877/444-6777, www.recreation.gov, $20-$22) in summer. **Sol Duc Campground** (82 sites) near Sol Duc Hot Springs and popular **Kalaloch Campground** (170 sites) on the ocean. All remaining campgrounds are first come, first served: **Heart O' the Hills Campground** (105 sites) near Hurricane Ridge, **Fairholme Campground** (88 sites) near a noisy highway, **Hoh Campground** (78 sites) near the Hoh Visitor Center, **Ozette Campground** (15 sites), **Mora Campground** (94 sites) 2 miles (3.2 km) from Rialto Beach, and **Staircase** (49 sites) on the Skokomish River.

Primitive campgrounds (no drinking water, $15) include: **Deer Park** (Deer Park Rd., June-mid-Oct., 14 tent-only sites), **South Beach** (mid-May-Sept., 55 sites), **Graves Creek** (year-round, 30 tent-only sites), **North Fork** (North Shore Rd., year-round, 9 tent-only sites), and **Queets** (Upper Queets River Rd., year-round, 20 sites).

OUTSIDE THE PARK

Port Angeles, Port Townsend, and **Sequim** serve as gateway towns for the north side of Olympic National Park. Tiny **Forks** and **Kalaloch** are bases for exploring the park's coastal side. **Hoodsport** is a small eastside base with minimal services.

GETTING THERE

AIR

The closest international airport is **Seattle-Tacoma International Airport** (SEA, 800/544-1965 or 206/787-5388, www.portseattle.org/sea-tac). Car rentals are at the airport.

BUS

Olympic Bus Lines (360/417-0700, http://olympicbuslines.com) operates the Dungeness Line between Sea-Tac airport and Port Angeles, with three stops in Seattle. The four-hour ride travels twice eastbound and twice westbound per day.

CAR

From Seattle, drive south on I-5 through Tacoma, then turn north on WA 16 to Bremerton. From Bremerton, take WA 3 north to WA 104 where it meets up with US 101 north to Port Townsend and Port Angeles. Port Angeles is on US 101, 20 miles (32 km) north of the Hurricane Ridge Visitor Center in Olympic National Park. Plan 4 hours for the drive of 185 miles (300 km).

FERRY

From Seattle, **Washington State ferries** (206/464-6400, www.wsdot.wa.gov) depart for Bainbridge Island and Bremerton. Both connect by highways to US 101.

GETTING AROUND

Driving along US 101 will give you plenty of views of trees with snippets of the beach, but you'll see little of the mountains and rainforest in the heart of the park. Lots of driving is required between park regions and you'll need to take paved spur roads to visit them. Check the park's road and weather hotline (360/565-3131) for travel conditions.

From Port Angeles, **Hurricane Ridge** is 20 miles (32 km, 45 min.) south of downtown, where Race Street becomes Mount Angeles Road and then Hurricane Ridge Road. West of Port Angeles, US 101 reaches the southern side of **Lake Crescent** in 22 miles (35 km, 30 min.) and the **Sol Duc** entrance in 30 miles (48 km, 1 hr.) via Sol Duc Road.

To reach **Lake Ozette,** turn off WA 112 just west of Sekiu onto Hoko-Ozette Road and drive 21 miles (34 km) south to the road's end.

To get to the **Hoh Rain Forest,** take US 101 to Upper Hoh Road and drive 18 miles (29 km) to the visitors center. It's about 90 miles (145 km, 2 hrs.) from Port Angeles.

Along US 101 on the coast, **Kalaloch** is 90 miles (145 km, 2.5 hrs.) south of Port Angeles. **Ruby Beach** is on the northernmost point of the Kalaloch coast, 8 miles (13 km) north of Kalaloch Lodge and 27 miles (43 km) south of Forks.

US 101 skirts the western edge of **Lake Quinault** 32 miles (52 km, 45 min.) south of Kalaloch. The Quinault Rain Forest is accessed off the North Shore or South Shore Roads. It's a 120-mile drive (193-km, 3.3 hrs.) from Port Angeles.

SIGHTS NEARBY

At the north end of WA 112, **Museum at the Makah Cultural and Research Center** (Makah Indian Reservation, 1880 Bayview Ave., Neah Bay, 360/645-2711, http://makahmuseum.com, 10am-5pm daily, $5) features artifacts from the Lake Ozette archaeological site.

SUNLIGHT STREAMS THROUGH SOL DUC

MOUNT RAINIER NATIONAL PARK

Washington

WEBSITE:
www.nps.gov/mora

PHONE NUMBER:
360/569-2211

VISITATION RANK:
19

WHY GO:
Visit the most glaciated peak in the contiguous United States.

KEEPSAKE STAMPS ▼▼▼

▲ MOUNT RAINIER NATIONAL PARK

MOUNT RAINIER NATIONAL PARK is named for the most impressive geographical landmark in the Pacific Northwest. At 14,411 feet (4,392 m), this volcano is the tallest peak in the Cascade Mountains, which stretch from Canada to California. Glaciers tumble from its icy cone, the most of any peak in the Lower 48. Towering "Takhoma," as it was called by the six indigenous tribes who lived on its flanks for thousands of years, dominates the horizon, making it an icon of Washington state's identity.

At the two highest car-accessible points—Paradise and Sunrise—the icy summit feels within your grasp, just one flower-filled meadow away. But it looms 8,000-9,000 feet (2,438-2,743 m) overhead. Its lower elevations cradle nooks of old-growth forests, serene alpine lakes, and plunging waterfalls.

PLANNING YOUR TIME

About 100 miles (161 km) south of Seattle, Mount Rainier beckons. Visitors come to explore the park's five developed areas. In the center of the park, **Paradise** tucks south of Rainier's peak while **Sunrise** lies northeast. Both offer elevated locations with big views, visitors centers, and trailheads. South of Paradise is **Longmire,** with a hotel, restaurant, and museum. In the southeast corner, near the Stevens Canyon Entrance, **Ohanapecosh** has a visitors center and campground. In the rainy northwest corner, **Carbon/Mowich** gets very little traffic; it's where hikers, bikers, and campers go to escape the crowds.

The majority of visitors come during the mild **summer** season (June-Sept.) when temperatures hang in the 60s and 70s (16-21°C). July-August sees long midday lines at the Nisqually and White River Entrances, and parking lots fill at Sunrise, Paradise, and popular trailheads. Plan to go early in the day or on a weekday for more solitude. Fall and spring are rainy and cool; in winter, snow closes park roads, except for Nisqually Entrance Station to Paradise.

ENTRANCES AND FEES

There are three entrance stations: the **Nisqually Entrance** (open year-round) at the southwest corner, the **Stevens Canyon Entrance** (late May-mid-Sept.) at the southeast corner, and the **White River Entrance** (late June-mid-Oct.) in the northeast. For the remote **Carbon River/Mowich Lake** area, pay fees in a drop box or at the ranger station.

The entrance fee is $30 per vehicle ($25 motorcycle, $15 individual) and good for seven days. Purchase a pass in advance online (YourPassNow.com) to go through the entrance station faster.

VISITORS CENTERS

At Paradise, the **Henry M. Jackson Memorial Visitor Center** (360/569-6571, 10am-5pm daily May-mid-June and Oct., 10am-7pm daily mid-June-Sept., shorter hours and days Oct.-mid-June) is a modern take on traditional alpine design. Inside, watch an introductory park film, see exhibits, and have a bite at the snack bar. The center is the starting point for ranger-led daily nature walks in summer and weekend snowshoe treks in winter.

At Sunrise, the historic log cabin **Sunrise Visitor Center** (360/663-2425, 10am-6pm daily July-early Sept.) houses natural history displays and has telescopes to check out Mount Rainier's glaciers. Rangers answer questions and lead daily nature walks. Across the parking lot, **Sunrise Day Lodge** has a gift shop and a cafeteria.

CARBON RIVER ENTRANCE
CARBON RIVER TRAIL
CARBON RIVER
To Wilkeson
Tirzah Peak 5,208ft
Adelaide Lake
Pigeon Peak
Wallace Peak
Oliver Lake
Green Lake
IPSUT CREEK
Carbon River
Chenuis Lakes
Lake Ethel
Florence Peak 5,508ft
Arthur Peak 5,483ft
Wonderland Trail
Natural Bridge
Howard Peak 5,683ft
Eunice Lake
Redstone Peak
Windy Gap
Ipsut Pass
Castle Peak 6,110ft
Crescent Lake
Sluiskin Mountain
Mowich Lake
SEATTLE PARK
Pacific Point
MOWICH LAKE
Hessong Rock 6,385ft
Mount Pleasant 6,454ft
Paul Peak 4,800ft
Mowich River
Mystic Lake
Mineral Mountain 6,500ft
Echo Rock 7,870ft
Observation Rock
PTARMIGAN RIDGE
Russell Glacier
Carbon Glacier
Winthrop Glacier
BURROUGHS
Golden Lakes
North Mowich Glacier
Inter Gl
Puyallup River
Wonderland Trail
Steamboat Prow 9,702ft
CAMP SCHURMAN
Edmunds Glacier
Liberty Cap 14,122ft
South Mowich Gl
MOUNT RAINIER
Columbia Crest 14,410ft
Little Tahoma Peak 11,138ft
Klapatche Point 4,120ft
Puyallup Glacier
PUYALLUP CLEAVER
Point Success 14,153ft
Ingraham
Gibraltar Rock
Tahoma Glacier
Tokaloo Rock 7,684ft
CAMP MUIR
SUCCESS CLEAVER
South Tahoma Glacier
Success Gl
Kautz Gl
Van Trump Glacier
Wilson Glacier
Nisqually Glacier
Anvil Rock 9,584ft
Paradise Gl
Muir Snowfield
GLACIER VIEW WILDERNESS
(FORMER ROAD)
Pyramid Peak 6,937ft
McClure Rock 7,385ft
Mildred Point
Panorama Point 6,800ft
Round Pass 3,900ft
Goat Lake
Iron Mountain 6,283ft
HENRY M. JACKSON MEMORIAL VISITOR CENTER
PARADISE INN
Mount Ararat 6,010ft
Creek
Lake George
Satulick Mountain 5,577ft
Lake Allen
Tahoma
COUGAR ROCK
Creek
Rampart Ridge Trail
Reflection Lakes
To Elbe & Ashford
WESTSIDE ROAD
Lane Peak
Eagle Peak 5,958ft
Cliff Lake
Tumtum Peak 4,678ft
Trail of the Shadows
WILDERNESS INFORMATION CENTER
Plummer Peak 6,370ft
706
2023ft
NATIONAL PARK INN
Kautz Creek Trail
Kautz
Wahpenayo Peak 6,231ft
LONGMIRE MUSEUM
NISQUALLY ENTRANCE
Twin Firs Trail
52
Nisqually River
Johnson Lake
0 2 mi
0 2 km

MOUNT RAINIER NATIONAL PARK
MT. BAKER-SNOQUALMIE NATIONAL FOREST
Scarface 6,108ft
Lake Eleanor
Slide Mountain 6,339ft
White River
410
Brown Peak 6,322ft
SOURDOUGH MOUNTAINS
Marcus Peak 6,962ft
Forest Lake
Clover Lake
SUNRISE RIDGE
MATHER MEMORIAL PARKWAY
CRYSTAL MOUNTAIN SKI AREA AND RESORT
Pacific Crest National Scenic Trail
Frozen Lake
SUNRISE DAY LODGE
Dege Peak 7,008ft
SUNRISE VISITOR CENTER
EMMONS VISTA
Shadow Lake
WHITE RIVER
WHITE RIVER ENTRANCE
White River
Crystal Lake
Placer Lake
MATHER MEMORIAL PARKWAY
410
River
Baker Point
GOAT ISLAND MOUNTAIN
GOVERNORS RIDGE
Deadwood Lakes
American
Tamanos Mountain 6,790ft
Ghost Lake
Chinook Pass 5,432ft
WENATCHEE NATIONAL FOREST
Owyhigh Lakes
Cayuse Pass 4,694ft
Tipsoo Lake
Barrier Peak 6,514ft
Dewey Lake
Servant Glaciers
Panhandle Gap 6,800ft
123
Seymour Peak 6,337ft
Swamp Lake
Double Peak 6,199ft
Chinook Creek
Ohanapecosh River
Shriner Peak 5,834ft
American Lake
Pacific Crest National Scenic Trail
Cougar Lake
COWLITZ DIVIDE
Wonderland Trail
Fan Lake
Bald Rock 5,411ft
Crag Lake
Grove of the Patriarchs Trail
Three Lakes
Marsh Lakes
BOX CANYON
Bench Lake
STEVENS CANYON ENTRANCE
Creek
Carlton
Stevens Peak 6,510ft
Blue Lake
Muddy Fork Cowlitz River
OHANAPECOSH VISITOR CENTER
River
Ohanapecosh
Jug Lake
GIFFORD PINCHOT NATIONAL FOREST
123
To Packwood
© MOON.COM

Top 3

VIEW NISQUALLY GLACIER FROM PARADISE TRAILS

1 SOAK IN THE PARADISE VIEWS

At 5,400 feet (1,646 m), with glacier-clad Rainier standing before you, gorgeous **Paradise** is the most crowded place in the park with the large parking lot packing out on weekends and holidays. Late July and August is prime time for viewing the peak framed by fields of wildflowers, but year-round access allows for visitors to revel in snowy winter beauty, too. Tour the **Henry M. Jackson Memorial Visitor Center** (360/569-6571, 10am-7pm daily mid-June-Sept., shorter hours and days Oct.-mid-June). Built in 1916, **Paradise Inn** (mid-May-Sept.) is an imposing wooden lodge with classic "parkitechture." The impressive lobby soars with high ceilings, stone fireplaces, and mountain views. A stay here is a step back in time with no TVs, phones, or Wi-Fi. Just views for days. Access Paradise from Longmire or the Stevens Canyon Road.

2 GAZE AT MOUNT RAINIER FROM SUNRISE

The **Sunrise** area occupies a subalpine plateau with spectacular views of the northeast side of Mount Rainier—the towering summit feels just beyond your grasp. It's one of the most popular destinations within the park, but the window for visiting is narrow (late June or early July-early Sept.). Hiking trails depart from the visitors center, and a walk-in picnic area is the perfect place for alfresco dining. Watch for elk herds in summer and fall.

VIEW OF MOUNT RAINIER FROM SUNRISE

3 DRIVE SCENIC STEVENS CANYON ROAD

The 19-mile (31-km) **Stevens Canyon Road** (open June-Oct., RV height limited due 12.5-ft.-high/3.8-m tunnel) packs with scenery. From WA 123 on the east side of the park, it links the Stevens Canyon Entrance with Paradise.

The road starts deep within old-growth forests of Douglas fir and western hemlock at an elevation of 2,200 feet (670 m). At **Box Canyon,** a trail (0.3 mi/0.5km rt, 20 min., easy) leads to a footbridge spanning the deep, narrow gorge created by the **Muddy Fork of the Cowlitz River.** From here, the road cuts across the slopes of Stevens Canyon to follow Stevens Creek uphill.

A pullout along the way offers side views of multitiered **Martha Falls,** which end with a 121-foot (37-m) plunge. For a closer look, pull off the road where it intersects with the **Wonderland Trail,** 0.5 mile (0.8 km) west of the falls pullout. Take the trail to the bridge at the falls' base.

At the top of the climb, a pullover spot lets you absorb the views at **Reflection Lakes,** which mirror the icy Rainier in their waters. At the junction with the Longmire-Paradise Road, turn right to reach Paradise.

Best Hike

SKYLINE TRAIL

DISTANCE: 5.5 miles (8.8 km) round-trip
DURATION: 4.5 hours
ELEVATION CHANGE: 1,700 feet (518 m)
EFFORT: strenuous
TRAILHEAD: Paradise Visitor Center

For impressive views of Rainier and thick wildflower meadows, the **Skyline Trail** climbs above timberline for massive views of its rock clefts and tumbling glaciers. Drawing scads of hikers, it starts by ascending stone steps etched with words from John Muir. The loop grunts up to Panorama Point with up close views of Nisqually Glacier before dropping into Paradise Valley and passing Myrtle Falls. With some exposure and steep snowfields that linger on the upper part into July, this trail is not for acrophobes. Check conditions in the visitors center before hiking.

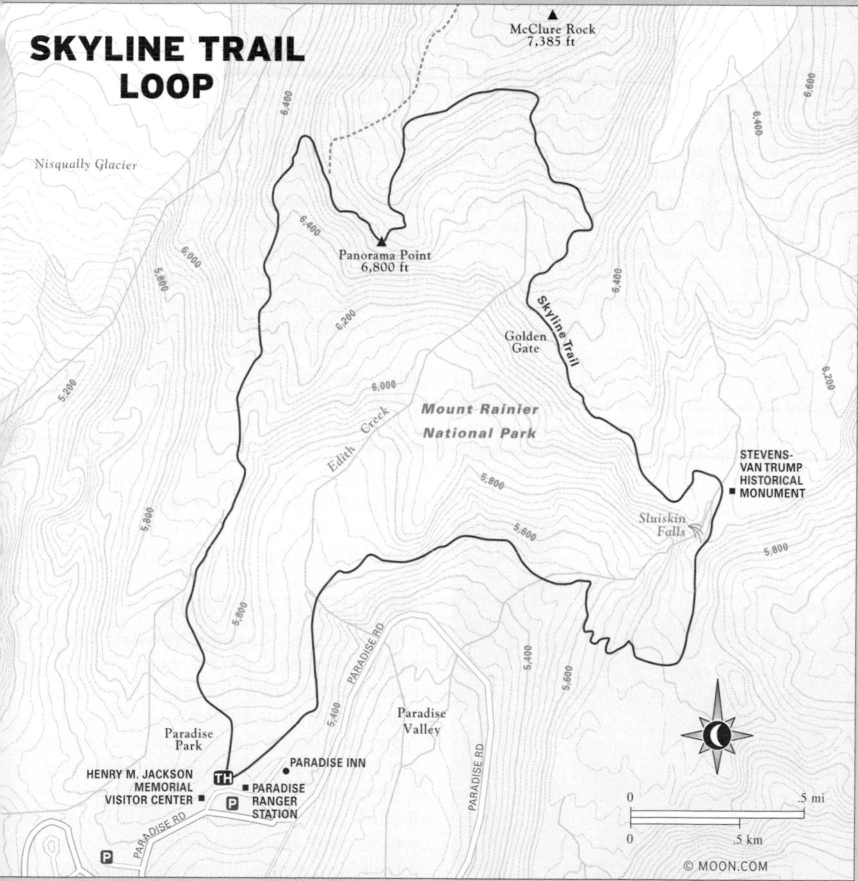

At the Stevens Canyon Entrance is the tiny **Ohanapecosh Visitor Center** (360/569-6581, hours vary June-Sept.) with trail maps and information. In summer, rangers lead nature walks several times a week.

At Longmire's **Wilderness Information Center** (360/569-6650, 7:30am-5pm daily mid-May-mid-Oct.) you can get passes for and information about backcountry hiking and camping.

ONE DAY IN MOUNT RAINIER

Drive the scenic park road to **Paradise** or **Sunrise** and concentrate your time there. Stop at scenic pullouts en route, tour the visitors centers, and tackle a hike to soak up the mountain's splendor.

SCENIC DRIVES

LONGMIRE TO PARADISE

Open year-round, the 12-mile (19-km) drive from Longmire to Paradise ascends through evergreen forests where periodic openings provide down-valley and up-mountain vistas. Three miles (4.8 km) before Paradise, stop at the overlook for **Narada Falls,** where a steep trail leads to the plunge pool at its base. After passing the turnoff to the Stevens Canyon Road, you'll reach the parking lot at Paradise with the visitors center, hiking trails, and Paradise Inn, a National Historic Landmark. In summer, you can drive the one-way downhill Paradise Valley Road.

The Nisqually Entrance Station west of Longmire sees long lines on weekends and holidays; plan to arrive before 9am. In winter, the gates at Longmire close at night, and the plowed road opens 9am-5pm. You are required to carry chains and may need to put them on to reach Paradise; check on conditions before driving as the road can have delayed opening or be closed during storms.

PINNACLE SADDLE

SUNRISE PARK ROAD

At 6,400 feet (1,951 m), **Sunrise Park Road** (late June or early July-early Sept.) pops to the highest point in the park reachable by car—and getting there is part of the fun. From the **White River Entrance station** off WA 410, the road climbs for 14 miles (23 km) on switchbacks lacing through evergreen forests to emerge into meadows with all-encompassing vistas. The subalpine plateau has spectacular views of Rainier's two largest glaciers (Emmons and Winthrop), and large numbers of **elk** congregate during summer and fall. The road terminates at the visitors center, trailheads, and picnic area.

The White River Entrance may close when parking lots fill up, allowing one car in when one departs; plan to arrive before 9am or you may have a long wait in line, especially on weekends and holidays. Due to the steepness and sharp curves, RVs and trailers longer than 25 feet (7.6 m) are not recommended beyond White River Campground.

CARBON/MOWICH

The remote **Carbon/Mowich** area tucks into the park's rainforest-like northwest corner that sees fewer visitors. Reach it by taking WA 165 south from Buckley to Carbonado and crossing the Carbon River Gorge Bridge to a junction. The left fork onto Carbon River Road goes to the park's border, where the washed-out road becomes a trail for 6 miles (10 km) of walking or biking. The right fork ventures 17 potholed gravel miles (27 km) on Mowich Lake Road to **Mowich Lake** (open mid-July-mid-Oct.), the largest and deepest body of water in the park. The lake has a picnic area, tent-only campground, and several trails.

SIGHTS

LONGMIRE

Longmire is home to the **Longmire Museum** (360/569-6575, 9am-4:30pm daily June, 9pm-5pm July-Sept., off-season hours vary). The small facility, located in the original park headquarters, contains displays on the park's natural history, along with exhibits of basketry, a small totem pole, and photos from the park's early days. It's 7 miles (11 km) from the Nisqually Entrance in the park's southwest corner.

OHANAPECOSH

The Ohanapecosh area consists of a visitors center, hiking trails, and campground along the Ohanapecosh River. Old-growth forests provide a thick canopy overhead in this southeast corner of the park.

RECREATION

HIKING

The prime hiking season runs July-September after most of the snow is gone. Wildflowers usually peak late July-August.

Longmire

Across the road from Longmire National Inn, the **Trail of the Shadows** (0.7 mi./1.1 km rt., 30 min., easy) takes a stroll around the meadow where Longmire's resort once stood. Cutting off from this trail, a longer loop continues up **Rampart Ridge Trail** (4.6 mi./7.4 km rt., 2.5 hrs., moderate) to a majestic view over the Nisqually River far below, then joins the Wonderland Trail. Go clockwise for better views of Rainier.

With a 1,200-foot (366-m) ascent partly on log steps across a rocky face comes the reward of **Comet Falls** (3.8 mi./6.1 km rt., 2 hrs., strenuous), a 301-foot-tall (92-m) ribbon. Locate the trailhead halfway between Longmire and Paradise west of Christine Falls.

Paradise

For flamboyant florals and subalpine forest, the **Nisqually Vista Trail** (1.2 mi./1.9 km rt., 45 min., moderate) overlooks the Nisqually River and Glacier.

Between Paradise and Stevens Canyon, the **Pinnacle Peak Trail** (2.6 mi./4.2 km rt., 2 hrs., strenuous) starts at the Reflection Lakes parking lot to climb a saddle between Pinnacle and Plummer Peaks. Retaining snow into July, the trail gains 1,050 feet (320 m) to the saddle for huge Rainier views. From a trailhead 1 mile (1.6 km) east of Reflection Lakes, an easier trail filled with bear grass and flowers cruises to **Bench and Snow Lakes** (2.4 mi./3.9 km rt., 1.5 hrs., moderate).

Ohanapecosh

West of the Stevens Canyon Entrance station, the **Grove of the Patriarchs Trail** (1.1 mi./1.8 km rt., 1 hr., easy) crosses the crystalline Ohanapecosh River via a suspension bridge onto an island

LUPINE ON SOURDOUGH RIDGE TO DEGE PEAK

VIEW OF MT. RAINIER FROM SUMMERLAND

of virgin old-growth trees. These thousand-year-old Douglas firs, western hemlocks, and western red cedars tower over ferns.

From Ohanapecosh Campground, the **Silver Falls Trail** (2.7 mi./4.3 km rt., 1.5 hrs., easy) follows the river through old-growth forest to the 75-foot (23-m) Silver Falls.

A rigorous grind up a steep, shadeless ridge goes to **Shriner Peak Lookout** (8 mi./12.9 km rt., 5 hrs., strenuous). Big 360-degree views from the peak make it worth the elevation gain (3,400 ft./1,036 m). Find the trailhead 3.5 miles (5.6 km) north of the Stevens Canyon Entrance on WA 123.

Sunrise

From the Sunrise Visitor Center parking lot, trails gain views of Rainier's biggest glaciers. The **Sunrise Nature Trail** (1.5 mi./2.4 km rt., 1 hr., easy) takes a self-guided loop. The **Shadow Lake Loop** (3 mi./4.8 rt., 1.5 hrs., moderate) drops to a rim overlooking the White River valley, follows the ridge to Shadow Lake, and returns via Frozen Lake and Sourdough Ridge. The trail to 7,317-ft. (2,230-m) **Mount Fremont Lookout** (5.6 mi./9 km rt., 3 hrs., strenuous) trots up Sourdough Ridge to Frozen Lake before branching off north to mountain goat terrain. A gentler climb to **Dege Peak** (3.4 mi./5.5 km rt., 2 hrs., moderate) goes east on Sourdough Ridge for views north of Mount Baker and south of Mount Adams.

From the White River Campground, the **Glacier Basin Trail** (7 mi./11.3 km rt., 6 hrs., strenuous) pops out of the forest into an idyllic basin of meadows cradling a glacial tarn. Views take in the Wedge and Mount Ruth on Rainier. A side spur (1 mi./1.6 km rt.) goes up the moraine to see Emmons Glacier, the largest of Rainier's glaciers.

The trail along Fryingpan Creek switchbacks up to **Summerland** (8.4 mi./13.5 km rt., 4.5-5 hrs., strenuous) to reach prolific wildflower meadows below Little Tahoma and Rainier. The trailhead is 3 miles (4.8 km) west of the White River Entrance; arrive by 8am for a spot in the parking lot.

Carbon/Mowich

To escape crowds, drive the 17-mile (27-km), rough-graveled Mowich Lake Road (located near Carbonado on WA 165 south of Buckley) to Mowich Lake. Climbing to **Spray Park** (6 mi./9.7 km rt., 4 hrs., moderate) takes in Spray Falls on a short spur trail and wildflower meadows with a backdrop of the ice-capped Rainier. The less demanding trail to **Tolmie Peak Lookout** (6.5 mi./10.5 km rt., 4 hrs., moderate) passes Eunice Lake before zipping up switchbacks to a big view of Rainier.

BACKPACKING

A 93-mile (149.6-km) loop circling Mount Rainier, the **Wonderland Trail** traverses passes, forests, streams, and alpine meadows—all with changing views of the icy mountain. The strenuous trail has copious ups and downs (22,000 ft./6,705 m of elevation gain). Backpackers need 10-14 days for the entire loop. You can start at multiple trailheads and choose from 18 designated trailside camps and three front-country campgrounds for overnighting.

Wilderness permits are required. Due to heavy competition for permits, get **reservations** ($20) online starting March 15. For first-come, first-served permits on your day of departure, go early in person to the Longmire or White River Wilderness Information Centers, Jackson Visitor Center, or Carbon River Ranger Station. Most of the route is snow-free **late June to mid-October**.

CLIMBING

For climbers, Mount Rainier is a premier summit and training peak, where raging winds, whiteouts, avalanches, hidden crevasses, rockfall, and altitude increase the hazard. About 10,000 people attempt the summit every year; less than half succeed. DIY trips require fluency in rock climbing, navigation, glacier travel, and crevasse rescue. Ropes, harnesses, crampons, and ice axes are vital. Most climbs launch from Paradise to overnight at Camp Muir before clambering via Disappointment Cleaver and Ingraham Glacier to the highest point at the Columbia Crest. A second common route goes from White River Campground onto the Inter and Emmons Glaciers to overnight at Camp Schurman before ascending the Emmons and Winthrop Glaciers.

Climbing the peak usually requires two days. Fees include a **climbing cost recovery fee** ($35-50) and a reservation for a **wilderness permit for overnighting** ($20). Once in the park, you must also obtain a **climbing permit** (free) from the Paradise Climbing Information Center or White River Wilderness Information Center within 24 hours of departure.

For guided climbs, contact **Alpine Ascents International** (206/378-1927, www.alpineascents.com), **International Mountain Guides** (360/569-2609, www.mountainguides.com), or **Rainier Mountaineering Inc.** (888/892-5462, www.rmiguides.com).

WINTER SPORTS

In winter, most visitors head to **Paradise** (Dec.-Apr.) to play in a supervised **snow-play** area. Bring your own soft sliding toys, such as inner tubes. **Cross-country skiers** and **snowshoers** tour ungroomed roads or trails to Nisqually Vista, Narada Falls, or Reflection Lakes.

Rent skis, avalanche beacons, snowshoes, and other winter gear from the **Longmire General Store** (360/569-2275, 9am-8pm daily mid-June-Aug., 10am-5pm daily Sept.-mid-June). You can also arrange ski lessons and tours.

From Jackson Visitor Center, rangers lead **snowshoe walks** (free) on winter weekends and holidays. Snowshoes are free to use during these walks.

WHERE TO STAY

INSIDE THE PARK

With limited lodging, **reservations** (855/755-2275, www.mtrainierguestservices.com) are mandatory; book one year ahead for summer stays.

In Longmire, the **National Park Inn** (360/569-2411, year-round, from $138) has 25 guest rooms; some share

WONDERLAND TRAIL CIRCLING MT. RAINIER

bathrooms. The **dining room** (7am-11am, 11:30am-4:30pm, and 5pm-7:30pm) serves three meals daily.

Erected in 1916 at Paradise and renovated in 2018-19, **Paradise Inn** (360/569-2413, mid-May-Sept., $123-185), a National Historic Landmark, is an imposing timber lodge with an impressive lobby, high ceilings, hand-painted lampshades, stone fireplaces, and mountain views. Some small guest rooms share bathroom facilities; others have private bathrooms. The **dining room** (7am-9:30am, noon-2:30pm, and 5:30pm-8pm daily) serves breakfast, lunch, and dinner.

There are small eateries at **Paradise Camp Deli** (Jackson Visitor Center, 10am-6:45pm daily mid-June-mid-Sept., 11am-4pm Sat.-Sun. Oct.-Apr.) and **Sunrise Day Lodge Snack Bar** (10am-7pm daily late June-early Sept., 11am-3pm, Sat.-Sun. Sept.). **Longmire General Store** (360/569-2275, 9am-8pm daily mid-June-Aug., 10am-5pm daily Sept.-mid-June) sells snacks.

Two campgrounds accept **reservations** (877/444-6777, www.recreation.gov) up to six months in advance. **Cougar Rock** (late-May-late-Sept., $20), between Longmire and Paradise, has 173 tent and RV sites. **Ohanapecosh** (late-May-late Sept., $20), south of the Stevens Canyon Entrance, has 188 tent and RV sites. Amenities include drinking water, flush toilets, and dump stations, but no hookups.

Two campgrounds are first come, first served. **White River** (late June-late Sept., $20), along the road to Sunrise, has 112 tent and RV sites. The primitive **Mowich Lake Campground** (mid-July-early Oct., free) has 10 walk-in tent platforms.

OUTSIDE THE PARK

The surrounding towns of **Ashford, Greenwater,** and **Enumclaw** have limited amenities. More options lie farther north in **Seattle** or **Tacoma.**

GETTING THERE

AIR

Seattle-Tacoma International Airport (SEA, 800/544-1965 or 206/787-5388, www.portseattle.org/sea-tac), served by about two dozen airlines, is closest to the park. **Portland International Airport** (PDX, 7000 NE Airport Way, 877/739-4636, www.flypdx.com) is farther from the park, just across the Oregon border. Both airports have car rentals.

CAR

From Seattle (85 mi./137 km, 2 hrs.), drive south on I-5 to exit 127. Go east on WA 512. Turn south on WA 7 to Elbe and turn east on WA 706 to Ashford and the **Nisqually Entrance** (open year-round), the busiest entrance. To reach the **White River Entrance** (summer only), the closest entrance to Seattle, drive to Enumclaw and WA 410. **Stevens Canyon** (usually open May-Nov.) is farthest from the Seattle area.

From Portland (144 mi./232 km, 2.5 hrs.), drive north on I-5 to exit 68. Go east on US 12 to Morton, then north on WA 7 to Elbe. Go east on WA 706 to Ashford and the **Nisqually Entrance.**

GETTING AROUND

The park has no public transportation and **no gasoline.** You'll need a car gassed up to get around.

In winter, most of the park roads close due to snow (Oct. or Nov.-May or June). The road from Nisqually Entrance through Longmire to Paradise remains open year-round. In winter, vehicles are required to carry tire chains, and the road to Paradise closes nightly and can remain closed during the day due to storms.

SIGHTS NEARBY

The next volcano south of Rainier in the Cascades chain is **Mount St. Helens** (Rte. 504, 360/274-0962, http://parks.state.wa.us, 9am-5pm daily mid-May-mid-Sept., hours and days shorten in spring, fall, and winter). It has a visitors center with exhibits about the 1980 volcanic eruption and trails through the barren blast zone. It's roughly a four-hour drive south via I-5.

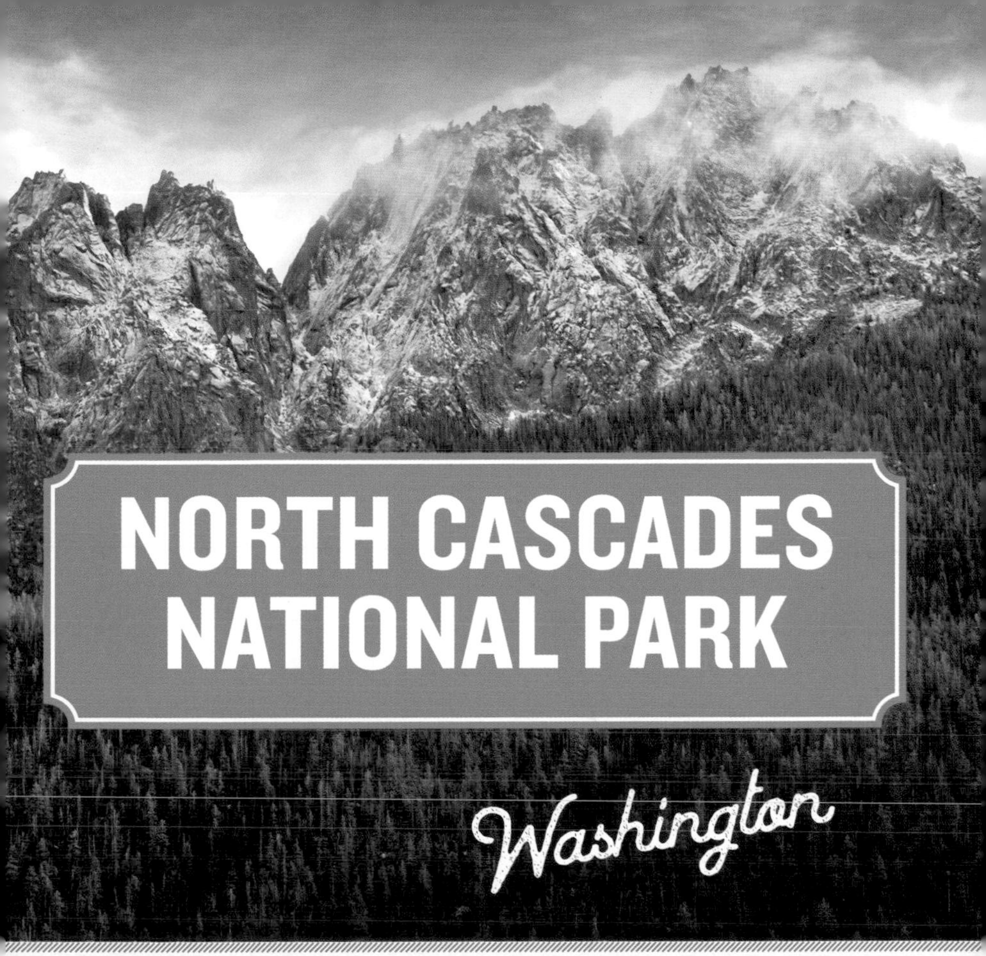

NORTH CASCADES NATIONAL PARK

Washington

KEEPSAKE STAMPS ▼▼▼

WEBSITE:
www.nps.gov/noca

PHONE NUMBER:
360/854-7200

VISITATION RANK:
58

WHY GO:
Rugged glaciated scenery.

▲ THE NORTH CASCADES HIGHWAY

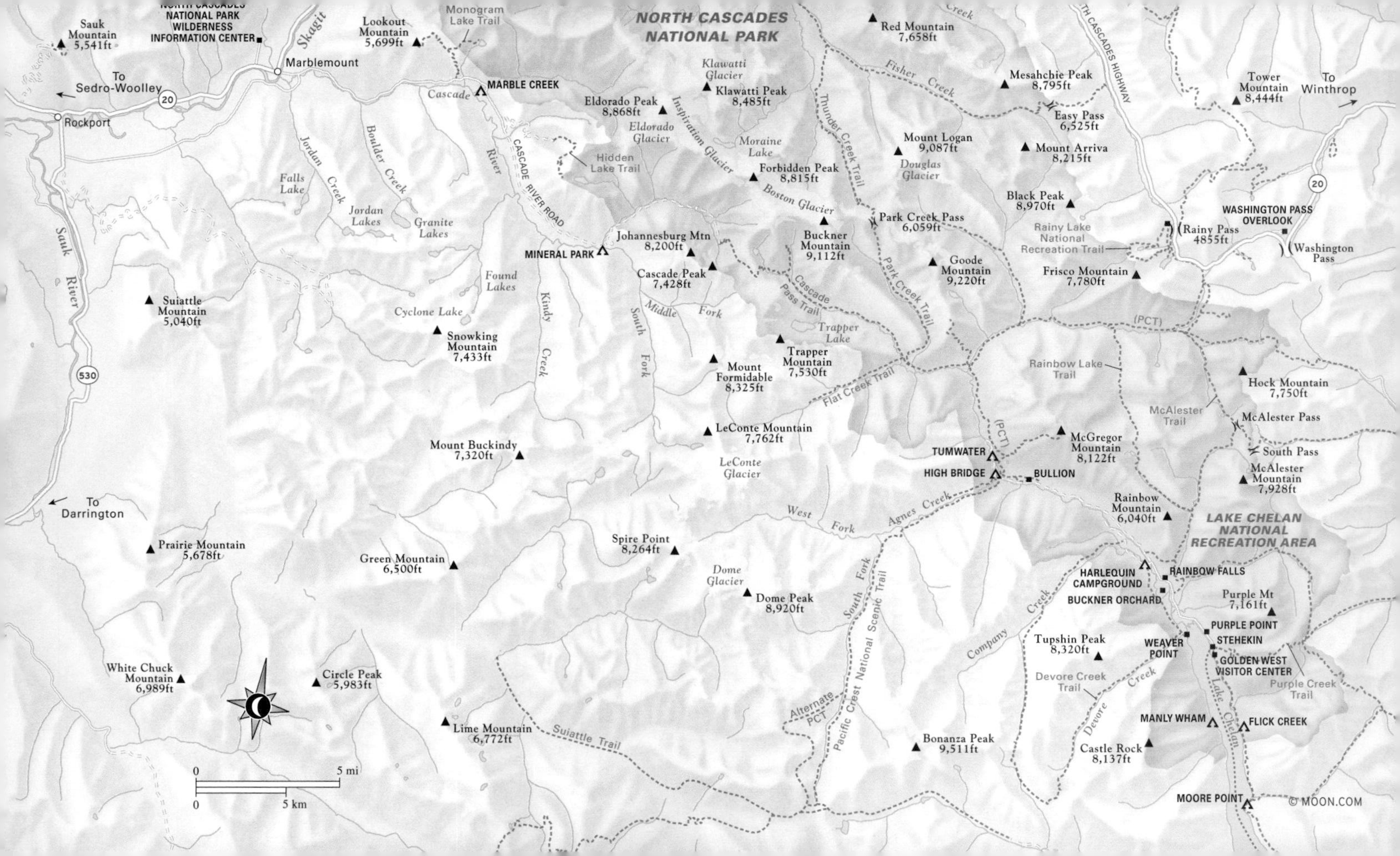
NORTH CASCADES NATIONAL PARK
NATIONAL PARK WILDERNESS INFORMATION CENTER
Sauk Mountain 5,541ft
Lookout Mountain 5,699ft
Monogram Lake Trail
Skagit
Marblemount
To Sedro-Woolley
20
Rockport
MARBLE CREEK
Cascade River
Red Mountain 7,658ft
Klawatti Glacier
Klawatti Peak 8,485ft
Eldorado Peak 8,868ft
Eldorado Glacier
Inspiration Glacier
Fisher Creek
Thunder Creek Trail
Mesahchie Peak 8,795ft
Easy Pass 6,525ft
Tower Mountain 8,444ft
To Winthrop
NORTH CASCADES HIGHWAY
Jordan Creek
Boulder Creek
Falls Lake
Jordan Lakes
Granite Lakes
Hidden Lake Trail
CASCADE RIVER ROAD
Moraine Lake
Forbidden Peak 8,815ft
Mount Logan 9,087ft
Douglas Glacier
Mount Arriva 8,215ft
Boston Glacier
Black Peak 8,970ft
Park Creek Pass 6,059ft
WASHINGTON PASS OVERLOOK
Rainy Pass 4855ft
Washington Pass
Rainy Lake National Recreation Trail
Sauk River
Johannesburg Mtn 8,200ft
MINERAL PARK
Buckner Mountain 9,112ft
Goode Mountain 9,220ft
Frisco Mountain 7,780ft
Found Lakes
Cascade Peak 7,428ft
Cascade Pass Trail
Park Creek Trail
Suiattle Mountain 5,040ft
Cyclone Lake
Kindy Creek
South Fork
Middle Fork
Snowking Mountain 7,433ft
Trapper Lake
Trapper Mountain 7,530ft
(PCT)
Rainbow Lake Trail
530
Mount Formidable 8,325ft
Flat Creek Trail
Hock Mountain 7,750ft
McAlester Trail
McAlester Pass
LeConte Mountain 7,762ft
Mount Buckindy 7,320ft
TUMWATER
McGregor Mountain 8,122ft
South Pass
LeConte Glacier
HIGH BRIDGE
BULLION
McAlester Mountain 7,928ft
To Darrington
West Fork
Agnes Creek
Rainbow Mountain 6,040ft
LAKE CHELAN NATIONAL RECREATION AREA
Prairie Mountain 5,678ft
Spire Point 8,264ft
Green Mountain 6,500ft
Dome Glacier
HARLEQUIN CAMPGROUND
RAINBOW FALLS
BUCKNER ORCHARD
Dome Peak 8,920ft
South Fork
Pacific Crest National Scenic Trail
Company Creek
Purple Mt 7,161ft
PURPLE POINT
STEHEKIN
Tupshin Peak 8,320ft
WEAVER POINT
GOLDEN WEST VISITOR CENTER
White Chuck Mountain 6,989ft
Circle Peak 5,983ft
Devore Creek Trail
Devore Creek
Purple Creek Trail
Alternate PCT
Lime Mountain 6,772ft
Suiattle Trail
MANLY WHAM
FLICK CREEK
Lake Chelan
Bonanza Peak 9,511ft
Castle Rock 8,137ft
0 5 mi
0 5 km
MOORE POINT
© MOON.COM

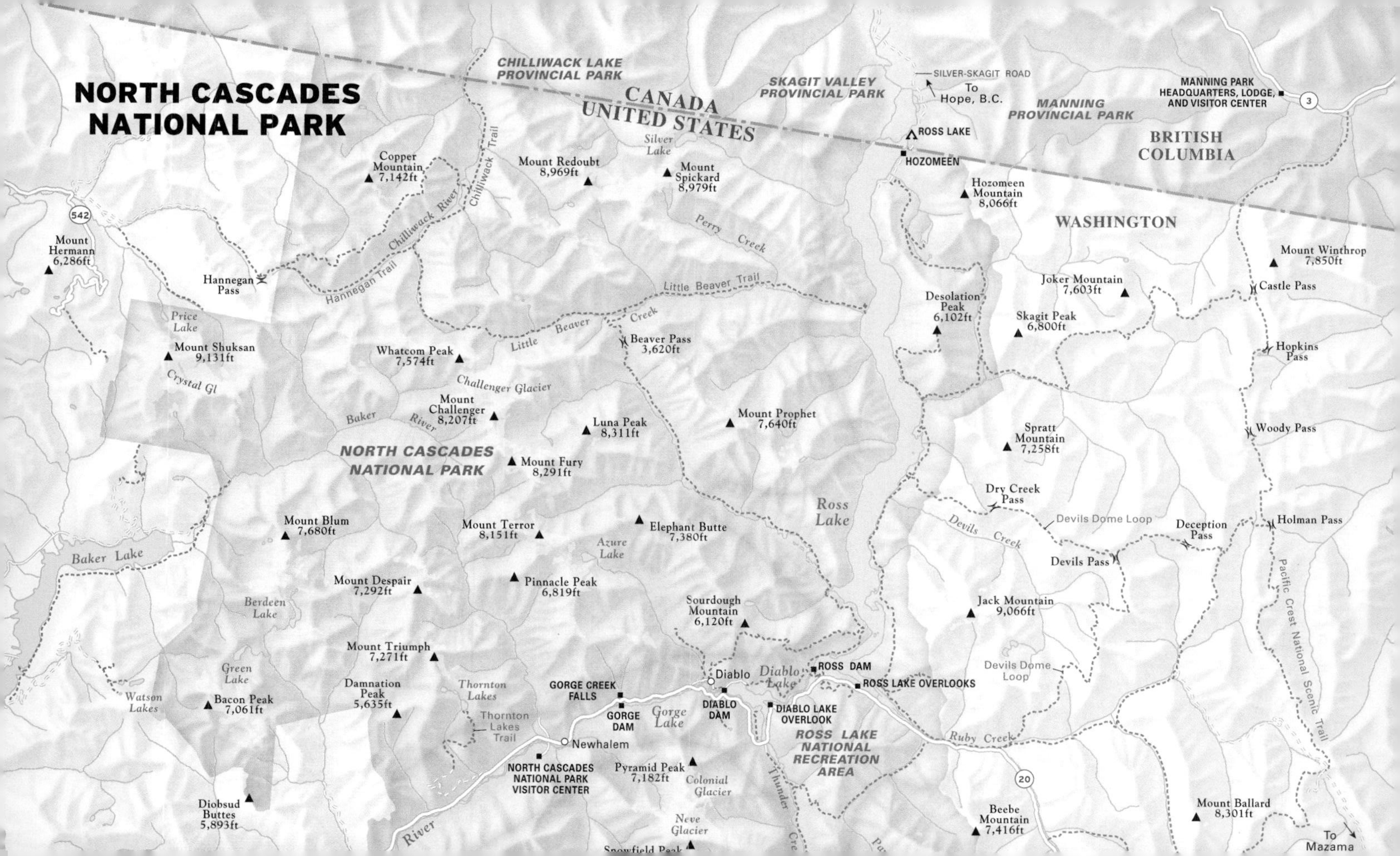
NORTH CASCADES NATIONAL PARK
CHILLIWACK LAKE PROVINCIAL PARK
SKAGIT VALLEY PROVINCIAL PARK
MANNING PROVINCIAL PARK
CANADA
UNITED STATES
BRITISH COLUMBIA
WASHINGTON
SILVER-SKAGIT ROAD
To Hope, B.C.
MANNING PARK HEADQUARTERS, LODGE, AND VISITOR CENTER
ROSS LAKE
HOZOMEEN
Hozomeen Mountain 8,066ft
Mount Winthrop 7,850ft
Castle Pass
Joker Mountain 7,603ft
Desolation Peak 6,102ft
Skagit Peak 6,800ft
Hopkins Pass
Woody Pass
Spratt Mountain 7,258ft
Dry Creek Pass
Devils Dome Loop
Deception Pass
Holman Pass
Devils Creek
Devils Pass
Pacific Crest National Scenic Trail
Jack Mountain 9,066ft
Devils Dome Loop
Ruby Creek
Beebe Mountain 7,416ft
Mount Ballard 8,301ft
To Mazama
Copper Mountain 7,142ft
Chilliwack Trail
Chilliwack River
Mount Redoubt 8,969ft
Silver Lake
Mount Spickard 8,979ft
Perry Creek
Mount Hermann 6,286ft
Hannegan Pass
Hannegan Trail
Little Beaver Trail
Little Beaver Creek
Beaver Pass 3,620ft
Price Lake
Mount Shuksan 9,131ft
Crystal Gl
Whatcom Peak 7,574ft
Challenger Glacier
Mount Challenger 8,207ft
Baker River
Luna Peak 8,311ft
Mount Prophet 7,640ft
NORTH CASCADES NATIONAL PARK
Mount Fury 8,291ft
Ross Lake
Mount Blum 7,680ft
Mount Terror 8,151ft
Elephant Butte 7,380ft
Azure Lake
Baker Lake
Mount Despair 7,292ft
Pinnacle Peak 6,819ft
Berdeen Lake
Sourdough Mountain 6,120ft
Mount Triumph 7,271ft
Green Lake
Watson Lakes
Bacon Peak 7,061ft
Damnation Peak 5,635ft
Thornton Lakes
Thornton Lakes Trail
GORGE CREEK FALLS
GORGE DAM
Gorge Lake
Diablo
DIABLO DAM
Diablo Lake
ROSS DAM
ROSS LAKE OVERLOOKS
DIABLO LAKE OVERLOOK
ROSS LAKE NATIONAL RECREATION AREA
Newhalem
NORTH CASCADES NATIONAL PARK VISITOR CENTER
Pyramid Peak 7,182ft
Colonial Glacier
Thunder Cre
Diobsud Buttes 5,893ft
River
Neve Glacier
542
20
3

More than 300 glaciers still cling to the mountains within **NORTH CASCADES NATIONAL PARK**, by far the greatest concentration in the Lower 48. But climate change with its melting glaciers and more frequent fires is rapidly altering the landscape.

Today, most visitors reach the park by car, driving the North Cascades Highway. But beyond is a vast wilderness of ice-chewed peaks and turquoise lakes that includes Ross Lake and Lake Chelan. Access is via foot or boat, just as it was for the Lake Chelan and Upper Skagit indigenous people who used Cascade Pass as their trade route.

PLANNING YOUR TIME

North Cascades National Park lies north of Seattle and east of Bellingham. Most visitors spend their time at three destinations: the **North Cascades Highway,** which bisects the park; **Ross Lake**; and upper **Lake Chelan.**

Late June-September is the prime time to visit when North Cascades Highway is open, and temperatures are in the 60s-90s (16-32°C). Fall colors arrive in October-early November. Late November-April, snow pounds the park, closing 44 miles (71 km) of North Cascades Highway.

ENTRANCES AND FEES

Most visitors access the park via WA 20 east from **Marblemount** or west from Winthrop. The park has no official entrance stations and no entrance fee.

VISITORS CENTERS

North Cascades Visitor Center (WA 20, milepost 120, 206/386-4495, 9am-5pm daily mid-May-Sept., 9am-5pm Sat.-Sun. mid-Apr.-mid-May and Oct.), near the town of Newhalem, contains exhibits, a bookstore, theater, and wheelchair-accessible trails.

SIGHTS

ROSS LAKE

The 540-foot-high (165-m) **Ross Lake Dam** holds back 23-mile-long (37-km) **Ross Lake.** You can see the lake from **Ross Lake Overlook** (milepost 135) on the North Cascades Highway. The only road to **Ross Lake National Recreation Area** is via Hope, British Columbia, on a 40-mile (64-km) route to **Hozomeen Campground** and **boat launch.**

Near the lake's south end, **Ross Lake Resort** (206/386-4437, www.rosslakeresort.com, mid-June-Oct.) rents canoes, kayaks, motorboats, and fishing gear to day-trippers. It also has lodging and a water taxi service to trailheads and lakeshore campsites. To get to the resort takes about one hour in three stages: Diablo Lake Ferry, a resort land shuttle ($10), and a short boat ride up-lake.

LAKE CHELAN

Lake Chelan National Recreation Area adjoins the park's south end, which includes the upper 4 miles of the lake and lower 10 miles (16 km) of Stehekin Valley. Only hikers and boaters can reach the isolated hamlet of **Stehekin** (steh-HEE-kin), 50 miles (81 km) up Lake Chelan. Most Stehekin day visitors arrive on the **Lady of the Lake** or **Lady Express** (509/682-4584, http://ladyofthelake.com, daily May-mid-Oct., 3-5 days weekly mid-Oct.-Apr., 8:30am-2:45pm or 6pm, adults $36-61, kids half price) to have lunch.

RECREATION

HIKING

The **Sourdough Mountain Trail** (10.4 mi./16.7 km rt., 6 hrs., strenuous) gains 4,870 feet (1,484 m) on a switchback-loaded climb to the summit, where sumptuous views take in lakes and peaks. From the North Cascades

Top 3

DIABLO LAKE

1 CRUISE ON TURQUOISE DIABLO LAKE

Turquoise **Diablo Lake** glistens behind Diablo Dam on the Skagit River. From the **North Cascades Environmental Learning Center** (1940 Diablo Dam Rd., 360/854-2599, www.ncascades.org) on the lake's north shore, **lake tours** (360/854-2589, www.seattle.gov, July-mid-Sept., adults $30-45, kids half price, reservations required) on a glass-ceilinged boat frequently sell out. The **Diablo Lake Lunch Tour** (10:15am check-in Thurs.-Mon., 4 hrs.) and **Diablo Lake Afternoon Cruise** (1pm check-in Fri.-Sun., 2.5 hrs.) take in waterfalls, peaks, and two dams.

2 DRIVE SCENIC NORTH CASCADES HIGHWAY

The **North Cascades Highway** (WA 20, May-late Nov.) slices across the park. Most visitors drive the 21 miles (34 km) from the west entrance to Washington Pass Overlook before turning around. In winter (late Nov.-Apr.), snow and avalanches close the road from Ross Dam to east of Washington Pass (mileposts 134-178).

From Marblemount, go east past **North Cascades Visitor Center** to **Newhalem.** Next to **Skagit General Store** (milepost 120) is **Old Number Six,** a 1928 Baldwin steam locomotive that hauled passengers and supplies to the Skagit River dams in pre-highway days. The **Trail of the Cedars Nature Walk** (0.3 mi./0.5 km rt., 30 min., easy) tours 1,000-year-old trees.

East of Newhalem, the highway climbs along the three dams and reservoirs of Gorge, Diablo, and Ross. Stop at three overlooks: See **Gorge Creek Falls** plunging into the gorge, peer down on the turquoise waters of **Diablo Lake,** and gaze at **Ross Lake,** the centerpiece of **Ross Lake National Recreation Area.**

After the road exits the national park, it climbs through Okanogan National Forest to crest **Rainy Pass** (4,860 ft./1,481 m) and **Washington Pass** (5,483 ft./1,671 m). From the latter pass, a short, paved trail goes to viewpoints of 7,720-foot (2,353-m) **Liberty Bell**—the symbol of the North Cascades Highway—and **Early Winter Spires.** From the passes, the highway spins down into the Methow Valley to Winthrop, 30 miles (48 km) eastward.

3 OVERNIGHT AT STEHEKIN

No road nor cell phone service reaches **Stehekin** (steh-HEE-kin), located 50 miles (81 km) up Lake Chelan. This tiny community revels in backcountry assets: breathing room, hiking, kayaking, horseback riding, and biking. Wheelchair-accessible shuttle buses cart visitors along about 15 miles (24 km) of road, which connect the boat dock with lodgings and trailheads. The most popular destination is the 312-foot-high (95-m) Rainbow Falls, reached via an accessible trail. In summer, rangers put on evening naturalist presentations and lead guided walks on weekends to the Buckner Homestead National Historic District and orchards.

Most Stehekin visitors arrive on the **Lady of the Lake** or **Lady Express** (509/682-4584, http://ladyofthelake.com, daily May-mid-Oct., 3-5 days weekly mid-Oct.-Apr., 8:30am-2:45pm or 6pm, adults $36-61, kids half price). A hearty few come by foot over Cascade Pass, just like Native American traders did, while even fewer come by helicopter from Chelan. Overnighting at Stehekin (three rustic lodges or camping) allows you to soak up the solitude—and the night sky ablaze with stars.

CASCADE PASS

Environmental Learning Center, the **Diablo Lake Trail** (7.6 mi./12.2 km rt., 4 hrs., moderate) leads to Ross Dam; you can chop the mileage in half by returning via the Diablo Lake Ferry.

From the North Cascades Highway at Rainy Pass (pay Northwest Forest Passes fee at parking lot, $5), one trailhead leads to three destinations. A flat, wheelchair-accessible paved trail goes to glacier-fed **Rainy Lake** (2 mi./3.2 km rt., 1 hr., easy). The **Lake Ann Trail** (3.4 mi./5.5 km rt., 2 hrs., moderate) reaches a cirque lake rimmed by larches that turn gold in fall. The **Maple Pass Loop** (7.2 mi./11.6 km rt., 4 hrs., strenuous) gains 2,200 feet (670 m) for a ridgeline traverse. From a trailhead between Rainy and Washington Passes, the **Blue Lake Trail** (4.4 mi./7.1 km rt., 2.5 hrs., moderate) traipses through subalpine meadows to emerald waters surrounded by a trio of spectacular summits: Liberty Bell, Whistler Mountain, and Cutthroat Peak.

DIABLO LAKE TRAIL

BACKPACKING

A two-day trip (13.4 mi./21.6 km rt.) climbs to wildflower-strewn Cascade Pass and farther up **Sahale Arm** to **Sahale Glacier**, where camps tuck into rocks and the views claim glaciers and peaks for miles. For a 4- to 5-day loop (35 mi./56 km rt.), tackle a portion of the Pacific Northwest Trail to cross **Hannegan Pass,** traverse **Copper Ridge,** drop to the **Chilliwack River,** and return over the pass; camp at Boundary, Copper Lake, Indian Creek, and Copper Creek.

Best Hike

CASCADE PASS

DISTANCE: 7.4 miles (11.9 km) round-trip
DURATION: 5 hours
ELEVATION CHANGE: 1,800 feet (549 m)
EFFORT: strenuous
TRAILHEAD: From Marblemount, follow the rugged gravel Cascade River Road (check conditions at the Wilderness Information Center before driving) for one hour (24 mi./39 km) to Cascade Pass Trailhead.

More than 30 switchbacks help you gain the elevation to ascend from old-growth forest to **subalpine meadows** at Cascade Pass. After the switchbacks, the trail crosses talus slopes, home to marmots and pikas; this steep area can still retain snow into July. Upon reaching the pass, a 360-degree view spreads out with summer wildflower meadows full of glacier lilies or pink mountain heather in the foreground and backdropped by peaks and glaciers.

Backcountry permits are free in advance from the **North Cascades Wilderness Information Center** (7280 Ranger Station Rd., Marblemount, 360/854-7245, 7am-6pm daily July-Aug., 8am-5pm daily May-June and Sept.). Apply March 15-May 15 for an **advance reservation** ($20) for summer and fall.

WHERE TO STAY

INSIDE THE PARK

Spend the night at rustic resorts for a serious dose of peace and quiet. Make reservations a year in advance for these prized getaways that are only accessible by boat or on foot.

▼ LAKE CHELAN

NORTH CASCADES NATIONAL PARK

Ross Lake Resort (206/386-4437, www.rosslakeresort.com, mid-June-Oct., from $240) has cabins and bunkhouses that float on the water. Cabins have full kitchens with shared barbecue grills. The resort rents motorboats, kayaks, and canoes and has a water taxi service to trailheads and campsites along the lakeshore.

At the head of Lake Chelan, Stehekin has three lodging options. The **North Cascades Lodge at Stehekin** (855/685-4167, https://lodgeatstehekin.com, from $214) has lodge rooms (May-Oct.) and units with kitchens (year-round). Amenities include a convenience store, kayak rentals, and a **restaurant** that serves three meals daily (mid-May-mid-Oct.). Nine miles (15 km) up the valley, **Stehekin Valley Ranch** (800/536-0745 or 509/682-4677, stehekinvalleyranch.com, mid-June-early Oct., from $110 per adult per night) operates its cabins, wagons, and tent cabins won solar power with all meals and shuttle transportation included. Two miles (3.2 km) from the boat dock, **Stehekin Pastry Company** (509/682-7742, https://stehekinpastry.com, early May-late Oct.) serves breakfast, lunch, pastries, and pies plus rents two log cabins (from $240).

Along North Cascades Highway, the only food is at **Skagit General Store** (milepost 120, Newhalem, 206/386-4489, 7:30am-5pm Mon.-Fri., 10am-5pm Sat.-Sun.).

Several campgrounds line North Cascades Highway. Most have potable water and pit or flush toilets, but no showers or hookups. Make **reservations** (877/444-6777, www.recreation.gov) up to six months in advance for **Newhalem Creek** (milepost 120, mid-May-mid-Oct., 109 sites, $16) and **Colonial Creek** (milepost 130, mid-May-mid-Oct., 142 sites, $16).

Find first-come, first-served campgrounds at **Goodell Creek** (milepost 119, year-round, 19 sites, small RVs only, $16) and tiny, primitive **Gorge Lake** (milepost 126, year-round, 8 sites, free).

Accessible only from British Columbia, **Hozomeen Campground** (Silver/Skagit Rd., first come, first served, mid-May-Oct., 75 sites, free) sits at the north end of Ross Lake. The 40-mile (64-km) rough, graveled Silver/Skagit Road goes south from Hope, British Columbia, to this remote campground in the United States.

The park has **boat-in backcountry campsites** on Diablo Lake (launch at Colonial Creek), Ross Lake (launch at Hozomeen Campground), and Lake

Chelan near Stehekin (launch at Chelan or 25-Mile Creek State Park). Pick up backcountry camping permits (free) 24 hours before departure from the **North Cascades Wilderness Information Center** (7280 Ranger Station Rd., Marblemount, 360/854-7245, 7am-6pm daily July-Aug., 8am-5pm daily May-June and Sept.) or the nearest ranger station. Make **reservations** (Mar. 15-May 15, $20) for summer.

OUTSIDE THE PARK

Accommodations, food, and services are in **Bellingham, Burlington, Mount Vernon, Sedro-Wooley, Concrete,** and **Marblemount.** To the east, look for services in **Winthrop, Twisp,** and **Chelan.**

GETTING THERE AND AROUND

AIR

The closest international airport is **Seattle-Tacoma International Airport** (SEA, 800/544-1965 or 206/787-5388, www.portseattle.org/sea-tac). The airport has car rentals.

CAR

A car is essential for getting around and across the North Cascades. It's a 126-mile (203 km, 3 hrs.) drive from Seattle to the North Cascades Visitor Center in Newhalem. From Seattle, drive 65 miles (105 km) north on I-5 to Burlington. Exit onto WA 20 and continue 60 miles (97 km) east to the park entrance.

BOATS

Hikers, backpackers, and campers make use of boats as shuttles on lakes. On Diablo Lake, the **Diablo Lake Ferry** (daily 8:30am and 3pm, $20) carts hikers and day-trippers up-lake. On Lake Chelan, the **Lady of the Lake** (509/682-4584, http://ladyofthelake.com, daily May-mid-Oct., 3-5 days weekly mid-Oct.-Apr., 8:30am-2:45pm or 6pm, adults $36-61, kids half price) goes from Chelan and 25-Mile to Stehekin. On Ross Lake, **Ross Lake Resort** (206/386-4437, www.rosslakeresort.com, mid-June-Oct.) runs a water taxi service to trailheads and lakeshore campsites. Take the Diablo Lake Ferry to connect with the resort's land shuttle ($10), and then shuttles up Ross Lake.

NORTH CASCADES HIGHWAY

SOUTHWEST

Across the Southwest, cliffs and canyons dominate the mysterious landscape. Here, the national parks range from red-rock spires to river-cut canyons, water pockets, and arches. You can even slide down sand dunes and explore underground caves. This land of variety is littered with unique sights: petrified trees in badlands, giant saguaros in desert, and ancient bristlecone pines in mountains.

Three prominent canyons top the parks. Zion tucks a narrow slot into soaring, colorful walls. In Bryce Canyon, a geologic fairyland of rock spires rises beneath high cliffs. At the Grand Canyon, layers of geologic history transport visitors back in time millions of years. Through all of them, rich colors vie for your attention, lit up by sunrises and sunsets.

◀ THE NARROWS, ZION NATIONAL PARK

NV
Salt Lake City
WYOMING
Cheyenne
Great Basin NP
UTAH
Denver
COLORADO
Arches NP
Capitol Reef NP
Canyonlands NP
Bryce Canyon NP
Zion NP
Great Sand Dunes NP & PRES
Mesa Verde NP
Grand Canyon NP
Santa Fe
Albuquerque
Petrified Forest NP
ARIZONA
Phoenix
NEW MEXICO
White Sands NP
Saguaro NP
Carlsbad Caverns N
El Paso
Guadalupe Mountains N
SOUTHWEST
TEXAS
Big Bend NP
0
50 mi
0
50 km

The National Parks of THE SOUTHWEST

GRAND CANYON, AZ

The massive, mile-deep canyon is a wonder. Hike its rim or descend into the inner canyon (page 267).

PETRIFIED FOREST, AZ

A scenic drive tours pastel badlands strewn with petrified wood (page 289).

SAGUARO, AZ

The Sonoran Desert houses unique forests with saguaros that live longer than humans (page 295).

GREAT BASIN, NV

You can hike high among ancient bristlecones on Wheeler Peak or dive underground into the Lehman Caves (page 302).

ZION, UT

Sheer cliffs and monoliths frame large canyons and tighten into narrow slots (page 309).

BRYCE, UT

Unique red and pink hoodoos shoot up from a steep mountainside (page 326).

CAPITOL REEF, UT

Waterpocket Fold rises from the desert in an enormous wrinkle of rock (page 338).

ARCHES, UT

Delicate rock arches create windows in the scenery (page 350).

CANYONLANDS, UT

Expansive vistas, trails, and scenic back roads take in hundreds of miles of canyon country (page 360).

MESA VERDE, CO

The park's geometric stone-and-mortar cliff dwellings echo the area's long human history (page 372).

GREAT SAND DUNES, CO

This park holds the continent's tallest sand dunes in one immense sandbox (page 381).

CARLSBAD CAVERNS, NM

Expansive underground caves contain delicate, lacy stalactites (page 397).

WHITE SANDS, NM

White gypsum sand dunes stretch for miles, looking like snow and even requiring plowing for its wind-blown drifts on roads (page 389)

GUADALUPE MOUNTAINS, TX

The summit of the highest point in Texas overlooks multihued canyons and desert (page 403).

BIG BEND, TX

This mountain, canyon, and desert park yields colorful cacti, tropical birds, and views into Mexico (page 409).

1: BLUE MESA, PETRIFIED FOREST
2: SAGUARO CACTUS, SAGUARO
3: DUNES, WHITE SANDS

Best OF THE PARKS

Inner Canyon: Descend into the Grand Canyon on foot, by mule, or on a raft to gaze up at the immense, colorful walls (page 271).

Desert View Watchtower: See one of architect Mary Colter's finest accomplishments—a rock tower standing tall on the edge of the Grand Canyon (page 271).

The Narrows: Hike the bed of the Virgin River in Zion between high, fluted walls—only 20 feet (6 m) apart in some places—where little sunlight penetrates and mysterious side canyons beckon (page 313).

Sunrise and Sunset Points: Walk a stretch of the Rim Trail between these two viewpoints for stunning views of Bryce Canyon (page 330).

Delicate Arch: Admire this fragile, freestanding rock formation, which rises from a slickrock bluff in Arches (page 357).

Grand View Point: Perch yourself on top of 1,000-foot (305-m) cliffs at this dramatic vista, with Canyonlands spread out beneath your feet (page 365).

Cliff Dwelling Tours: Tour North America's largest cliff dwellings at Mesa Verde for a spectacular glimpse into the lives of the Ancestral Puebloans (page 376).

Big Room: Take a self-guided tour through the Big Room at Carlsbad Caverns to experience the intricacies in the largest single-room cave in North America (page 400).

PLANNING YOUR TRIP

Plan at least **one week** to tour a selection of Southwest parks; to hit all of the parks, you'll need 2-3 weeks. Make advance **reservations** for inside the park: one year for lodging and six months for campgrounds. Summer temps bake this region into an arid crisp, but the shoulder seasons of **spring** and **fall** offer more pleasant temperatures, along with slightly fewer people. Winter **closes the road** between Zion and Bryce, the East Entrance and North Rim of Grand Canyon, part of Mesa Verde, and higher elevations of Great Basin.

Salt Lake City and Las Vegas provide the best access to many Southwest national parks.

▲ DESERT VIEW WATCHTOWER

Road Trip

VIRGIN RIVER VALLEY, ZION NATIONAL PARK

You can visit the major national parks of the Southwest by driving a loop of roughly 1,000 miles (1,610 km). Fly into **Las Vegas, Nevada,** and then rent a car and hit the road! Make reservations well in advance for all park lodges or campgrounds.

Zion and Bryce

255 miles (410 km) / 4.5 hours

From Las Vegas, drive 165 miles (265 km, 3 hrs.) northeast on I-15 and cut east on UT 9 to **Zion** where barren, towering rock walls surround a verdant oasis. Explore iconic attractions like **Court of the Patriarchs,** the **Emerald Pools,** and the **Narrows.** Spend the night in the **Zion Lodge.**

For the 87-mile (140 km, 1.5 hrs.) drive to **Bryce Canyon,** exit Zion via the Zion-Mt. Carmel Highway (UT 9) and turn north onto US 89, east onto UT 12/63, and south onto UT 63 to reach the canyon of red and pink hoodoos—delicate fingers of stone rising from a steep mountainside. Explore the rim at spots like **Inspiration Point,** take a short hike below the rim on the **Queen's Garden Trail,** and watch the sun set over the canyon. Stay the night at the **Lodge at Bryce Canyon.**

Capitol Reef

133 miles (214 km) / 2.5 hours

Leave Bryce going north on UT 63 by 8am for the drive to Capitol Reef. Continue north onto UT 22 and north again onto UT 62. In Koosharem, turn east onto UT 24 which goes south and then

east to Capitol Reef, where the Fremont River carves a magnificent canyon through **Waterpocket Fold.** Take the **21-mile scenic drive** (34 km, 1.5 hrs.) to **Capitol Gorge** to see the petroglyphs, pioneer register, and natural water tanks.

Arches and Canyonlands

170 miles (275 km) / 2.5 hours

From Capitol Reef, continue east on UT 24 for 144 miles (232 km, 2.5 hrs.) to I-70, where driving east meets with US 191 going south toward **Moab,** gateway to Arches and Canyonlands. Just north of Moab, turn north into **Arches** to drive the park road to see windows through the solid rock. Stop to walk to four arches at **The Windows** and hike to **Delicate Arch.**

In vast **Canyonlands,** the Colorado River tunnels through an otherworldly landscape of sandstone. Drive 25 miles (40 km, 40 min.) north on US 191 and southwest on UT 313 to the **Island in the Sky District** to explore viewpoints like **Shafer Canyon Overlook.** Stop at the visitors center and hike the short **Grand View Trail,** overlooking Monument Basin before returning to Moab.

Mesa Verde

151 miles (243 km) / 3 hours

From Moab, drop south on US 191 and turn east onto US 491 into Colorado. In Cortez, take US 160 east to reach Mesa Verde. Get tickets online in advance for a ranger-led tour of one of the cliff dwellings: **Cliff Palace, Balcony Palace,** or **Long House.** If time permits, drive to Wetherill Mesa to walk through several archaeological sites or visit **Chapin Mesa Archeological Museum.** Overnight at **Far View Lodge.**

Grand Canyon

300 miles (485 km) / 5.5 hours

From Mesa Verde, head west on US 160 to US 89 in Arizona. Go south on US 89 and west on AZ 64 to reach the South Rim of Grand Canyon. Enter the park at the **East Entrance** to stop at **Desert View Watchtower** and **Grandview Point** for your first views of the immense canyon before driving to Grand Canyon Village and touring the visitors center. Catch the sunset from **Yavapai Point** and spend the night at **El Tovar** or **Bright Angel Lodge.** In the morning, take the shuttle to **Hermit's Rest** and walk the rim between two viewpoints on the return before driving from Grand Canyon south on AZ 64 to I-40 West and then US 93 Northwest and becoming I-11 to return to Las Vegas (280 mi./450 km, 4.5 hrs.).

1: SHAFER CANYON OVERLOOK, ISLAND IN THE SKY DISTRICT, CANYONLANDS
2: LONG HOUSE ON WETHERILL MESA, MESA VERDE
3: DESERT VIEW WATCHTOWER, GRAND CANYON

GRAND CANYON NATIONAL PARK

Arizona

KEEPSAKE STAMPS ▾▾▾

WEBSITE:
www.nps.gov/grca

PHONE NUMBER:
928/638-7888

VISITATION RANK:
2

WHY GO:
Enjoy rim-side views, inner canyon trails, and rafting the Colorado.

▲ SOUTH RIM DRIVE, GRAND CANYON NATIONAL PARK

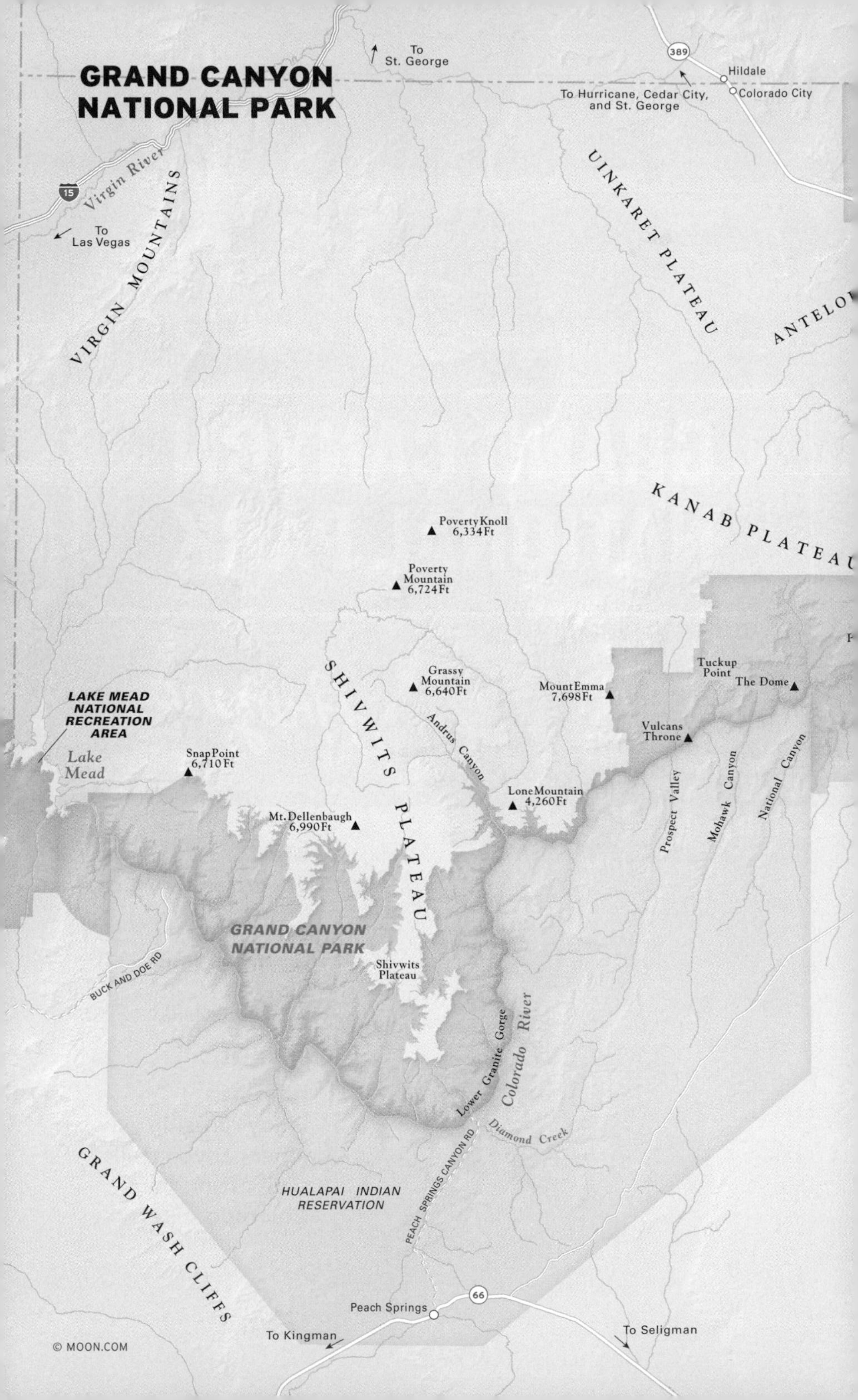

GRAND CANYON NATIONAL PARK
To St. George
389
Hildale
Colorado City
To Hurricane, Cedar City, and St. George
15
Virgin River
To Las Vegas
VIRGIN MOUNTAINS
UINKARET PLATEAU
ANTELO
KANAB PLATEAU
Poverty Knoll 6,334 Ft
Poverty Mountain 6,724 Ft
Grassy Mountain 6,640 Ft
Mount Emma 7,698 Ft
Tuckup Point
The Dome
Vulcans Throne
SHIVWITS PLATEAU
Andrus Canyon
LAKE MEAD NATIONAL RECREATION AREA
Lake Mead
Snap Point 6,710 Ft
Lone Mountain 4,260 Ft
Mt. Dellenbaugh 6,990 Ft
Prospect Valley
Mohawk Canyon
National Canyon
GRAND CANYON NATIONAL PARK
Shivwits Plateau
BUCK AND DOE RD
Colorado River
Lower Granite Gorge
Diamond Creek
PEACH SPRINGS CANYON RD
GRAND WASH CLIFFS
HUALAPAI INDIAN RESERVATION
66
Peach Springs
To Kingman
To Seligman
© MOON.COM

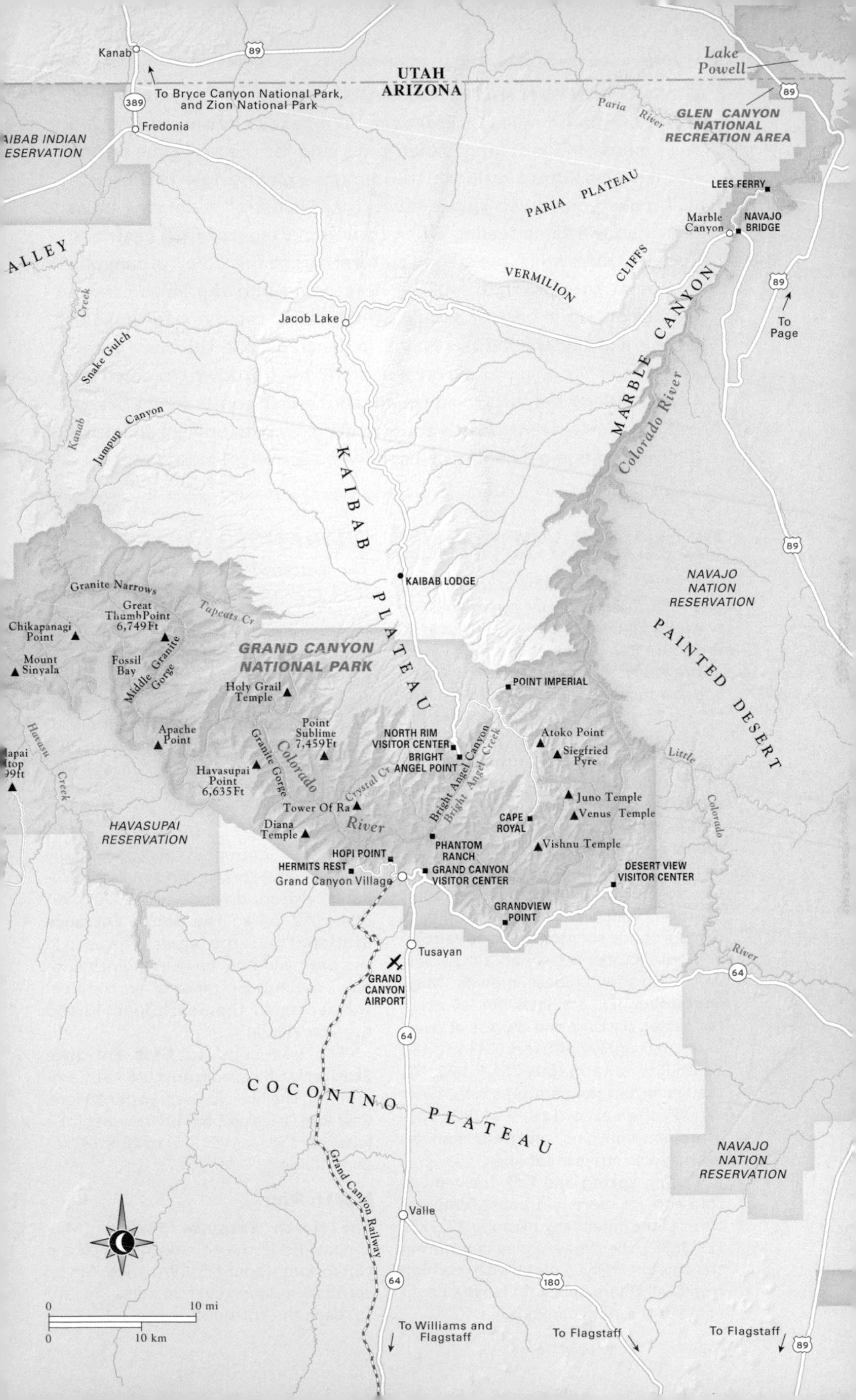

Kanab
89
UTAH
ARIZONA
To Bryce Canyon National Park,
and Zion National Park
389
Fredonia
AIBAB INDIAN
ESERVATION
Lake
Powell
89
Paria River
GLEN CANYON
NATIONAL
RECREATION AREA
PARIA PLATEAU
LEES FERRY
Marble
Canyon
NAVAJO
BRIDGE
ALLEY
VERMILION CLIFFS
MARBLE CANYON
89
To
Page
Kanab Creek
Snake Gulch
Jacob Lake
Jumpup Canyon
KAIBAB PLATEAU
Colorado River
89
KAIBAB LODGE
NAVAJO
NATION
RESERVATION
PAINTED DESERT
Granite Narrows
Great
Thumb Point
6,749 Ft
Tapeats Cr
Chikapanagi
Point
Mount
Sinyala
Fossil
Bay
Middle Granite
Gorge
GRAND CANYON
NATIONAL PARK
Holy Grail
Temple
POINT IMPERIAL
Apache
Point
Point
Sublime
7,459 Ft
NORTH RIM
VISITOR CENTER
BRIGHT
ANGEL POINT
Bright Angel Canyon
Bright Angel Creek
Atoko Point
Siegfried
Pyre
Little Colorado River
Havasu Creek
Havasupai
Point
6,635 Ft
Granite Gorge
Colorado River
Crystal Cr
Tower Of Ra
Juno Temple
Venus Temple
CAPE
ROYAL
HAVASUPAI
RESERVATION
Diana
Temple
PHANTOM
RANCH
Vishnu Temple
HOPI POINT
HERMITS REST
GRAND CANYON
VISITOR CENTER
Grand Canyon Village
DESERT VIEW
VISITOR CENTER
GRANDVIEW
POINT
Tusayan
64
GRAND
CANYON
AIRPORT
64
COCONINO PLATEAU
NAVAJO
NATION
RESERVATION
Grand Canyon Railway
Valle
64
180
0
10 mi
0
10 km
To Williams and
Flagstaff
To Flagstaff
To Flagstaff
89

GRAND CANYON NATIONAL PARK must be seen to be believed. It is more than 1 mile (1.6 km) deep, 18 miles (29 km) wide, and 275 river miles (445 km) long. When you stand for the first time on one of the South Rim's overlooks, the immense, gaping gash in the earth will make your pulse skip a beat. The Ancestral Puebloans must have had the same feeling when contemplating its brash vastness. Today's tribes still have strong cultural ties to this colorful canyon.

Get a more intimate look by descending into the inner canyon by foot or on the back of a mule. Strong hikers climb rim-to-rim with an overnight at the famous Phantom Ranch deep in the inner gorge. Rafters can hire a guide for a once-in-a-lifetime trip down the down the Colorado River, riding its roiling rapids and camping on its serene beaches. From rim to river, sunrises and sunsets glow with brilliant shades of pink and orange, a reminder of just how mutable this landscape is.

PLANNING YOUR TIME

The Grand Canyon runs across northern Arizona, practically straddling the border with Utah. Most visitors head to the South Rim (open year-round), where 2-3 days is enough time to see the sights, watch a sunset, and day-hike. To visit the North Rim (open mid-May-mid-Oct.), add 1-2 days and plan for a five-hour drive between the two rims. Arizona does not observe daylight saving time but stays on Mountain Standard Time year-round.

It's vital to book reservations **13 months in advance** to stay one of the inside-the-park lodges or enter the lottery **15 months in advance** to stay at Phantom Ranch. Make reservations at campgrounds **six months in advance**.

April-October is the park's busy season, with the biggest crowds **May-September.** Expect lines for shuttles, congested parking, and crowds at overlooks. At roughly 7,000 feet (2,134 m), the South Rim is warm (60s-70s F, 16-21°C) in summer, but temperatures in the inner canyon often exceed 110°F (43°C). Late afternoon lightning and thundershowers may also strike in summer.

During **spring** and **fall**, the crowds thin and are more laid-back. Temperatures in the inner canyon range 80-97°F (27-36°C); the rims are pleasant during the day, but chilly at night with morning frost. Fall colors appear in November in some of the inner canyons.

ENTRANCES AND FEES

The entrance fee is $35 per vehicle ($30 motorcycle, $20 individual) and good for seven days to both the North and South Rims. You can **buy your pass online** (www.yourpassnow.com) from home to speed through entrance stations faster. There are two entrances on the South Rim and one on the North Rim. It is a five-hour drive (220 mi./355 km) between the South Rim and the North Rim.

South Rim

South Rim entrances are open daily year-round, 24 hours per day. From Williams, visitors drive 63 miles (101 km) along AZ 64 to the **South Entrance Station.** This is the busiest entrance in the park and may have long lines midday. The South Entrance offers the closest access to the South Rim's Grand Canyon Village.

The less crowded **East Entrance Station** is accessed from US 89 at Cameron (on the Navajo Reservation). Here, East Rim Drive (AZ 64) heads west for a leisurely 33 miles (53 km) to Grand Canyon Village.

North Rim

The **North Entrance Station** (May 15-Oct. 15) is the sole entrance to the North Rim. From US 89A, take AZ 67 south from Jacob Lake 36 miles (58 km) to reach the entrance.

Top 3

1 TOUR HERMIT ROAD

HERMIT'S REST

On the South Rim, the Hermit Road (7 mi./11 km) viewpoints are some of the best in the park, especially for sunsets. The park's **free shuttle** (5am-sunset daily Mar.-Nov., 2 hrs. rt.) travels along Hermit Road from Grand Canyon Village to **Hermit's Rest.** It stops at eight viewpoints along the way; return buses stop only at Hermit's Rest, Mohave, Pima, and Powell Points. Catch the shuttle at the **Hermit's Rest Transfer Stop,** west of the Bright Angel Lodge. When Hermit Road opens to cars in winter (Dec.-Feb.), you can drive your vehicle to most viewpoints.

2 DESCEND INTO THE INNER CANYON

Spending time inside the canyon offers unparalleled intimacy with diurnal changes of color, blooming cacti, crawly creatures, and rugged terrain cut by the roaring Colorado River. While you can **day-hike** or **ride a mule** below the rim, other options invite grander exploration: overnight stay at **Phantom Ranch (**enter the lottery 15 months in advance); backpack the canyon's rugged trails, overnighting at **designated backcountry campsites** like Cottonwood, Bright Angel, and Indian Garden (apply for permit online during an 11-day window 4 months prior to trip month, $8 pp per night and $10 reservation fee); or **float the Colorado River** on a guided raft trip.

Note: Descending to the river and back to the rim in one day is *not advised.*

NORTH KAIBAB TRAIL IN INNER CANYON

3 GAZE OUT FROM DESERT VIEW WATCHTOWER

One of Mary Colter's greatest constructions is this Puebloan-inspired structure along Desert View Drive, a 25-mile (40-km) drive east from the village. **Desert View Watchtower** (9am-5pm daily, hours vary seasonally) is an artful homage to smaller towers built by Ancestral Puebloans throughout the Four Corners region. You reach the tower's high, windy deck by climbing the twisting, steep steps curving around the open middle, past walls painted with visions of Hopi lore and religion by Hopi artist Fred Kabotie. (Pick up *The Watchtower Guide* in the gift shop on the bottom floor for interpretations of the figures and symbols.) From the top of the watchtower, the South Rim's highest viewpoint, the whole arid expanse opens up, and you feel something like a lucky survivor at the very edge of existence, even among the crowds.

ONE DAY IN GRAND CANYON

One day at Grand Canyon will only taunt you to return for longer. Plan to tour the South Rim by entering through the East Entrance. Check out the **Desert View** sights, then drive to **Grand Canyon Village** and have lunch at **El Tovar.** After lunch, hop the **Hermit Road Shuttle,** getting off to hike a segment of the **South Rim Trail.** If you can, linger until sunset to catch the color from **Hopi Point.**

VISITORS CENTERS

South Rim

The South Rim has two main visitors centers. Both have bookstores, information, maps, and brochures. Ranger programs change seasonally. Kids can also participate in the educational Junior Ranger Program. **Grand Canyon Visitor Center** (Grand Canyon Village, 8am-6pm daily summer, hours vary seasonally) is the park's main welcome and information center. The visitors center's theater screens a 20-minute orientation film about the canyon. **Desert View Visitor Center** (9am-5pm daily) sits on Desert View Point about 25 miles (40 km) east of Grand Canyon Village. This is the stop for those entering the park from the East Entrance.

South Rim also has two other information stations. **Verkamp's Visitor Center** (Grand Canyon Village, 8am-7pm daily, hours vary seasonally) has an information desk and park exhibits in addition to crafts and park souvenirs. **Canyon View Information Plaza** (9am-5pm daily), near Mather Point, has outdoor displays on the history of the canyon.

North Rim

The **North Rim Visitor Center** (8am-6pm daily May 15-Oct. 15) is near Grand Canyon Lodge and Bright Angel Point. Stop here for park maps, brochures, and exhibits on North Rim science and history. A bookstore is on-site, and rangers offer a full program of talks and guided hikes.

SIGHTS

SOUTH RIM

The South Rim is the most developed portion of Grand Canyon National Park. It is home to **Grand Canyon Village Historic District,** a small assemblage of hotels, restaurants, gift shops, and lookouts that offer some of the best viewpoints of the canyon. You can also see some of Arizona's most evocative buildings, all of them National Historic Landmarks.

The South Rim Road has 19 named viewpoints, from the eastern Desert View to the western Hermit's Rest. The best and easiest way to see the canyon viewpoints is to park your car and take

▼ DESERT VIEW WATCHTOWER

MATHER POINT

the park's free shuttle or walk along the **Rim Trail.**

Mather Point

Mather Point is named for the first National Park Service director, Stephen T. Mather. Walking out onto the two railed-off rocks will make you feel like you're hovering on the edge of the canyon's abyss. The point can get busy, especially in the summer. From Mather Point, leave your car at the large parking area and walk along the **Rim Trail** west to Yavapai Point and Geology Museum.

Yavapai Point and Geology Museum

First opened in 1928, **Yavapai Point and Geology Museum** (8am-8pm daily summer, 8am-6pm daily winter, free) is a limestone-and-pine museum designed by architect Herbert Maier. The site for the stacked-stone structure was handpicked by canyon geologists as best for viewing the various strata. Inside are displays about canyon geology and a huge topographic relief map of the canyon.

Hopi House

Designed by architect Mary Colter, the 1905 **Hopi House** (928/638-2631, 8am-5pm daily, hours vary seasonally) used Hopi workers and local materials to build what is now a gift shop and Native American arts museum. The Harvey Company even hired the famous Hopi-Tewa potter Nampeyo to live here with her family while demonstrating her artistic talents and Hopi lifeways to tourists. This is one of the best places in the region for viewing and buying Hopi, Navajo, and Pueblo art (though most of the art is quite expensive), and even items made by Nampeyo's descendants are on view and for sale here.

El Tovar Hotel

El Tovar was the South Rim's first great hotel. Designed in 1905 by Charles Whittlesey for the Santa Fe Railroad, El Tovar has the look of a Swiss chalet and a log-house interior, watched over by the wall-hung heads of elk and buffalo; it is at once rustic, cozy, and elegant. This Harvey Company jewel has hosted dozens of rich and famous canyon visitors over the years, including George Bernard Shaw and presidents Teddy Roosevelt and William Howard Taft. Inside you'll find two gift shops, a cozy lounge, and El Tovar's restaurant, the best in the park.

Bright Angel Lodge

Off the lobby of the rustic **Bright Angel Lodge** is a small History Room (7am-10pm daily) with fascinating exhibits about Fred Harvey, architect

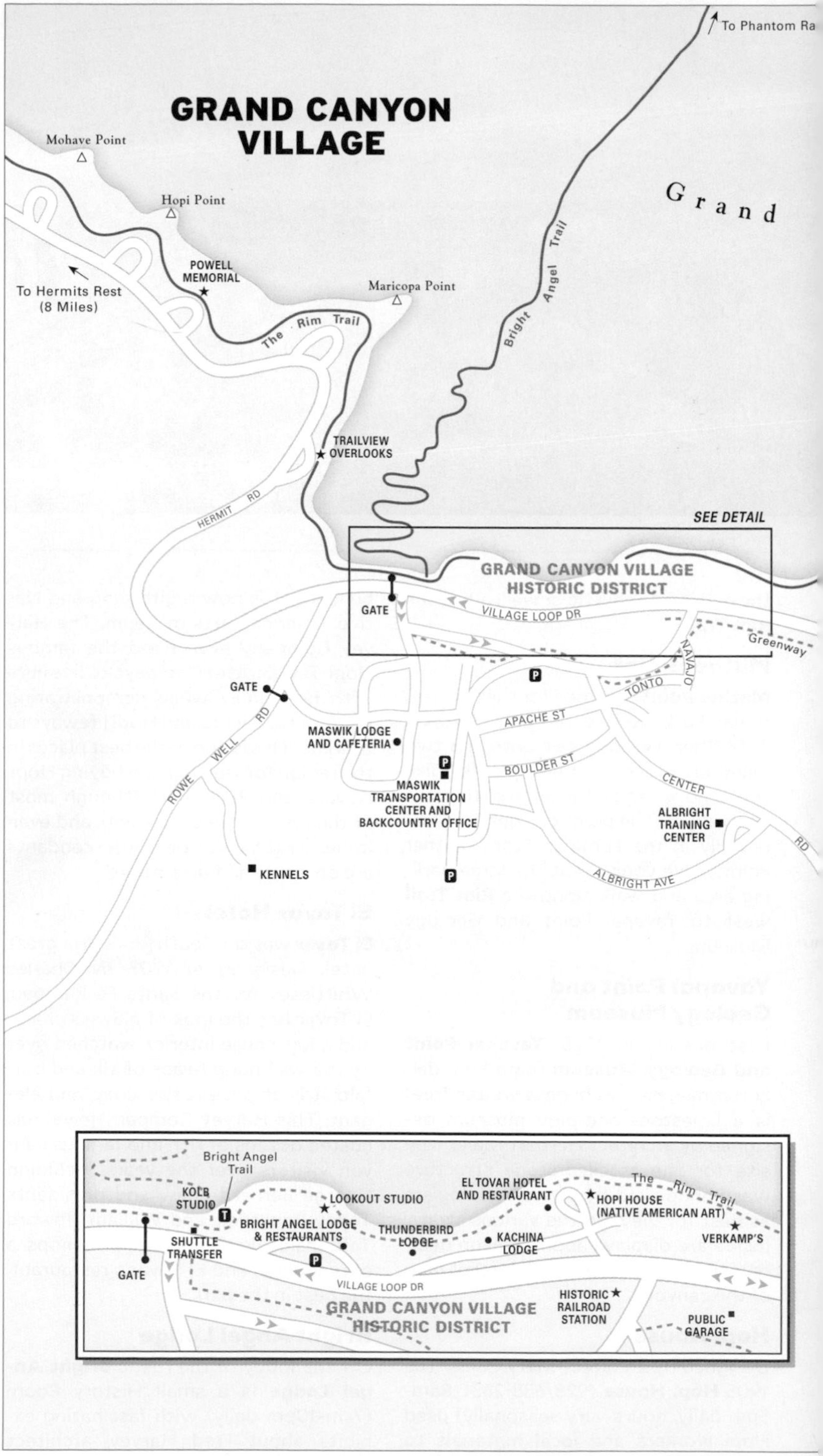
GRAND CANYON VILLAGE
To Phantom Ranch
Grand
Mohave Point
Hopi Point
POWELL MEMORIAL
To Hermits Rest (8 Miles)
Maricopa Point
The Rim Trail
Bright Angel Trail
TRAILVIEW OVERLOOKS
HERMIT RD
SEE DETAIL
GRAND CANYON VILLAGE HISTORIC DISTRICT
GATE
VILLAGE LOOP DR
Greenway
NAVAJO
TONTO
GATE
APACHE ST
ROWE WELL RD
MASWIK LODGE AND CAFETERIA
BOULDER ST
CENTER RD
MASWIK TRANSPORTATION CENTER AND BACKCOUNTRY OFFICE
ALBRIGHT TRAINING CENTER
KENNELS
ALBRIGHT AVE
Bright Angel Trail
KOLB STUDIO
LOOKOUT STUDIO
EL TOVAR HOTEL AND RESTAURANT
HOPI HOUSE (NATIVE AMERICAN ART)
The Rim Trail
BRIGHT ANGEL LODGE & RESTAURANTS
THUNDERBIRD LODGE
KACHINA LODGE
VERKAMP'S
SHUTTLE TRANSFER
GATE
VILLAGE LOOP DR
GRAND CANYON VILLAGE HISTORIC DISTRICT
HISTORIC RAILROAD STATION
PUBLIC GARAGE

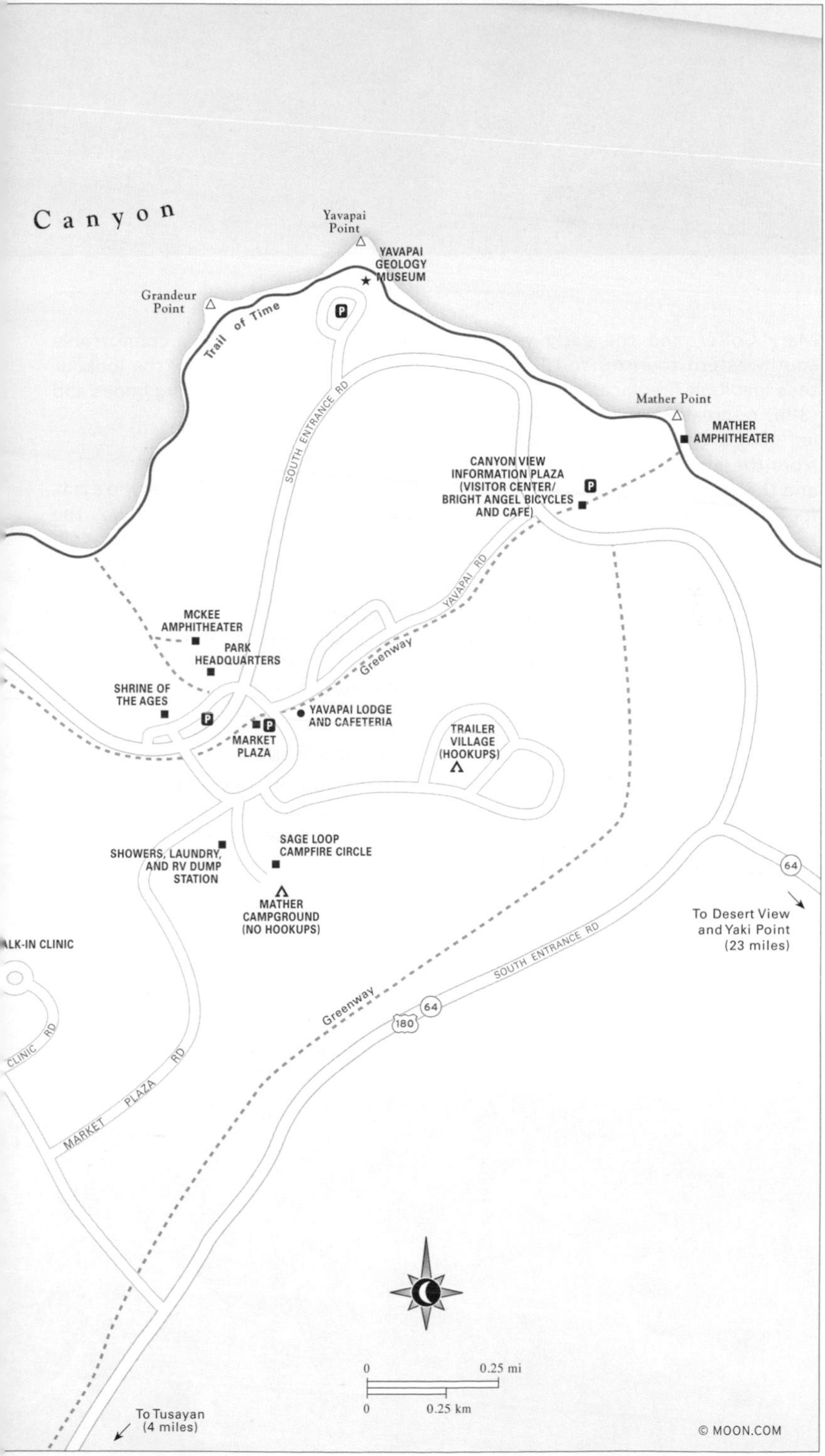
Canyon
Yavapai Point
YAVAPAI GEOLOGY MUSEUM
Grandeur Point
Trail of Time
P
SOUTH ENTRANCE RD
Mather Point
MATHER AMPHITHEATER
CANYON VIEW INFORMATION PLAZA (VISITOR CENTER/ BRIGHT ANGEL BICYCLES AND CAFE)
YAVAPAI RD
MCKEE AMPHITHEATER
PARK HEADQUARTERS
Greenway
SHRINE OF THE AGES
YAVAPAI LODGE AND CAFETERIA
MARKET PLAZA
TRAILER VILLAGE (HOOKUPS)
SHOWERS, LAUNDRY, AND RV DUMP STATION
SAGE LOOP CAMPFIRE CIRCLE
MATHER CAMPGROUND (NO HOOKUPS)
LK-IN CLINIC
CLINIC RD
64
To Desert View and Yaki Point (23 miles)
SOUTH ENTRANCE RD
Greenway
180
64
MARKET PLAZA RD
0
0.25 mi
0
0.25 km
To Tusayan (4 miles)
© MOON.COM

HERMIT'S REST

Mary Colter, and the early years of southwestern tourism. You'll see Colter's "geologic fireplace," a 10-foot-high (3-m) re-creation of the canyon's varied strata. The stones were collected from the inner canyon by a geologist and then loaded on the backs of mules for the journey out. The fireplace's strata appear exactly like those stacked throughout the canyon walls, equaling a couple of billion years of earth-building from bottom to rim. The lodge includes a collection of small cabins just to the west of the main building. The cabin closest to the rim was once the home of **Bucky O'Neill,** an early canyon resident and prospector.

Lookout Studio

Mary Colter designed the **Lookout Studio** (8am-8pm daily summer, hours vary seasonally), a little stacked-stone watchhouse that seems a mysterious extension of the rim. The stone patio jutting out over the canyon is a popular place for photos and canyon gazing. Built in 1914 to provide a comfortable but "indigenous" building, the lookout now contains a store selling books and souvenirs.

Kolb Studio

Built in 1904 right on the canyon's rim, **Kolb Studio** (8am-7pm daily) was the home and studio of the famous Kolb Brothers, pioneer canyon photographers, moviemakers, river rafters, and entrepreneurs. Inside are a gift shop, gallery, and display about the brothers, who in 1912 rode the length of the Colorado in a boat with a movie camera rolling.

Hermit's Rest

Hop on and off the park's free shuttle bus (5am-sunset daily Mar.-Nov.) to tour the 7 scenic miles (11 km) along Hermit Road, from Grand Canyon Village to Hermit's Rest. Along the way, epic vistas await.

▼ FOOTPATH TO POWELL POINT

CAPE ROYAL ON THE NORTH RIM

Trailview Overlook is the first stop, with views of Bright Angel Trail twisting down into the canyon and across the plateau to overlook the Colorado River.

Maricopa Point provides a vast, mostly unobstructed view of the canyon all the way to the river. To the west, look for the rusted remains of the Orphan Mine.

Powell Point holds a memorial to explorer and writer John Wesley Powell, who led the first and second river expeditions through the canyon in 1869 and 1871. The point is a good spot for sunset views.

Hopi Point offers sweeping views of the western canyon. It is the most popular viewing point for sunsets. North across the canyon is Isis Temple and the Temple of Osiris.

Mohave Point peers down into the Colorado River. Also visible are the 3,000-foot (914-m) red-and-green cliffs named **The Abyss.** Below the viewpoint you can see the red-rock mesa called the Alligator.

Pima Point is the last viewpoint, with wide-open views to the west and the east.

The final stop on the Hermit Road is the enchanting rest house called **Hermit's Rest** (9am-5pm daily, hours vary seasonally). Inside the low-slung stone cabin, a huge, yawning fireplace dominates the warm, rustic front room, outfitted with a few chairs and a Navajo blanket or two splashing color against the gray stone. Outside, the views of the canyon and down the Hermit Trail are spectacular.

Tusayan Museum and Ruin

The **Tusayan Museum** (9am-5pm daily, free) has a small exhibit on the canyon's early human settlers. Find the museum 3 miles (4.8 km) west of Desert View and 22 miles (35 km) east of Grand Canyon Village, located near an 800-year-old Ancestral Puebloan ruin with a self-guided trail and regularly scheduled ranger walks.

NORTH RIM

It's all about the scenery here at 8,000 feet (2,438 m) on the North Rim. The often-misty canyon and thick, old-growth forest along its rim command attention. Stop at three developed viewpoints, each offering a slightly different look at the canyon.

Bright Angel Point looks over Bright Angel Canyon with a view of Roaring Springs, the source of Bright Angel Creek and fresh water for the North Rim and inner canyon. At 8,803 feet (2,683 m), **Point Imperial** is the highest point on the North Rim with the best all-around view of the canyon. **Cape Royal,** at the end of a 23-mile (37 km) one-way drive, takes in the South Rim and its landmarks.

Grand Canyon Lodge

Perched on the edge of the North Rim, **Grand Canyon Lodge** (www.grandcanyonforever.com) is a rustic log-and-stone structure built in 1927-1928. Its warm Sun Room frames the canyon through huge picture windows. At sunset, head out to the back patio to watch the sun sink over the canyon. Right near the door leading out to the patio is sculptor Peter Jepson's charming life-size bronze of **Brighty,** a famous canyon burro and star of the 1953 children's book *Brighty of the Grand Canyon* by Marguerite Henry.

SCENIC DRIVES

DESERT VIEW DRIVE

The South Rim's **Desert View Drive** (25 mi./40 km) heads east of Grand Canyon Village to exit via the park's East Entrance. Along the way, canyon viewpoints offer scenic vistas with fewer crowds. Take a side road to reach **Grandview Point.** The site where the original canyon lodge once stood takes in a sweeping bend in the Colorado River. To the east, look for the monument called the Sinking Ship, and to the north look for Horseshoe Mesa.

Moran Point, east of Grandview, offers impressive views of the canyon and the river. (The point is named for the great painter Thomas Moran.) Directly below, you'll see Hance Rapid, one of the largest on the river. Next you'll come to **Lipan Point,** with its wide-open vistas and the best view of the river from the South Rim. At **Desert View,** climb the namesake watchtower to catch a faraway glimpse of sacred Navajo Mountain near the Utah-Arizona border, the most distant point visible from within the park.

CAPE ROYAL SCENIC DRIVE

On the North Rim, **Cape Royal Scenic Drive** (23 mi./37 km) boasts dramatic views. From Grand Canyon Lodge to Cape Royal, the paved road wends through mixed conifer and aspen forests on the **Walhalla Plateau.** Short trails go to stunning viewpoints of the canyon. Plan at least half a day for the drive and bring water and snacks.

Leave the lodge just before dawn to watch the sun rise from **Point Imperial,** a 3-mile (4.8-km) side road at the beginning of Cape Royal Road. Continue along the drive to **Vista Encantadora** (Charming View) as it rises above Nankoweap Creek. Just beyond is **Roosevelt Point,** where you can hike the easy 0.2-mile (0.3-km) **Roosevelt Point Trail** to a view worthy of the man who saved the Grand Canyon.

The drive terminates at **Cape Royal.** To see an expansive and unbounded view of the canyon, walk the **Cape Royal Trail** (0.6 mi./1 km rt., 20 min.). On a clear day, you can spot the South Rim's Desert View Watchtower way across the gorge and the river far below. Along

▼ LIPAN POINT

SOUTH KAIBAB TRAIL

the trail, you'll pass the rock arch called **Angel's Window.**

HIKING

This is arid country. Avoid hiking midday (10am-4pm) and carry at least one gallon of water per person per day. All canyon trails descend—which means it will take twice as long to climb back up. Hiking to the canyon bottom and back in one day *is not advised.*

SOUTH RIM

South Kaibab Trail

Steep and shadeless with three destinations, the **South Kaibab Trail** has fewer crowds. You may also spot bighorn sheep, deer, and California condors. **Ooh Aah Point** (1.8 mi./2.9 km rt., 1-2 hrs., moderate) lets you peer into the canyon from steep switchbacks. **Cedar Ridge** (3 mi./4.8 km rt., 2-4 hrs., strenuous) grabs views of O'Neill Butte and Vishnu Temple. The limit for a one-day hike, **Skeleton Point** (6 mi./9.7 km rt., 4-6 hrs., strenuous) overlooks the Colorado River. The trailhead is near Yaki Point accessed via the Kaibab Trail Route shuttle bus.

Hermit Trail

The moderate **Hermit Trail** (7 mi./11.3 km rt., 3-4 hrs., strenuous) leads to some less visited areas of the canyon, especially secluded **Dripping Springs.** For mid-level to expert hikers, the route plunges down the Hermit Trail's steep, rocky, almost stair-like switchbacks to the **Dripping Springs Trailhead** in 1.5

YAKI POINT

Best Hike

BRIGHT ANGEL TRAIL

DISTANCE: 3-9.5 miles (4.8-15.3 km) round-trip
DURATION: 2-9 hours
ELEVATION GAIN: 3,060 feet (933 m)
EFFORT: moderate to strenuous
TRAILHEAD: Grand Canyon Village on the South Rim

The **Bright Angel Trail** is the most popular trail into the Grand Canyon. Many visitors walk a short stretch down Bright Angel just to get a feeling of what it's like below the rim. Hiking down, you quickly leave behind the crowded rim and enter a sharp, arid landscape, twisting down switchbacks on a path that is sometimes rocky underfoot. The trail is steep, and it doesn't take long for the rim to look very far away and those rim-top people to look like scurrying ants.

The hike to **Mile-and-a-Half Resthouse** (3 mi./4.8 km rt., 2-4 hrs.) offers a good introduction to the steep, twisting trail. A little farther on is **Three-Mile Resthouse** (6 mi./9.7 km rt., 4-6 hrs.). Both rest houses have water (available seasonally). A rather punishing day hike, beautiful **Indian Garden** (9 mi./14.5 km rt., 6-9 hrs.) is a cool, green oasis in the arid inner canyon. *Due to heat, this route is not recommended in the summer.*

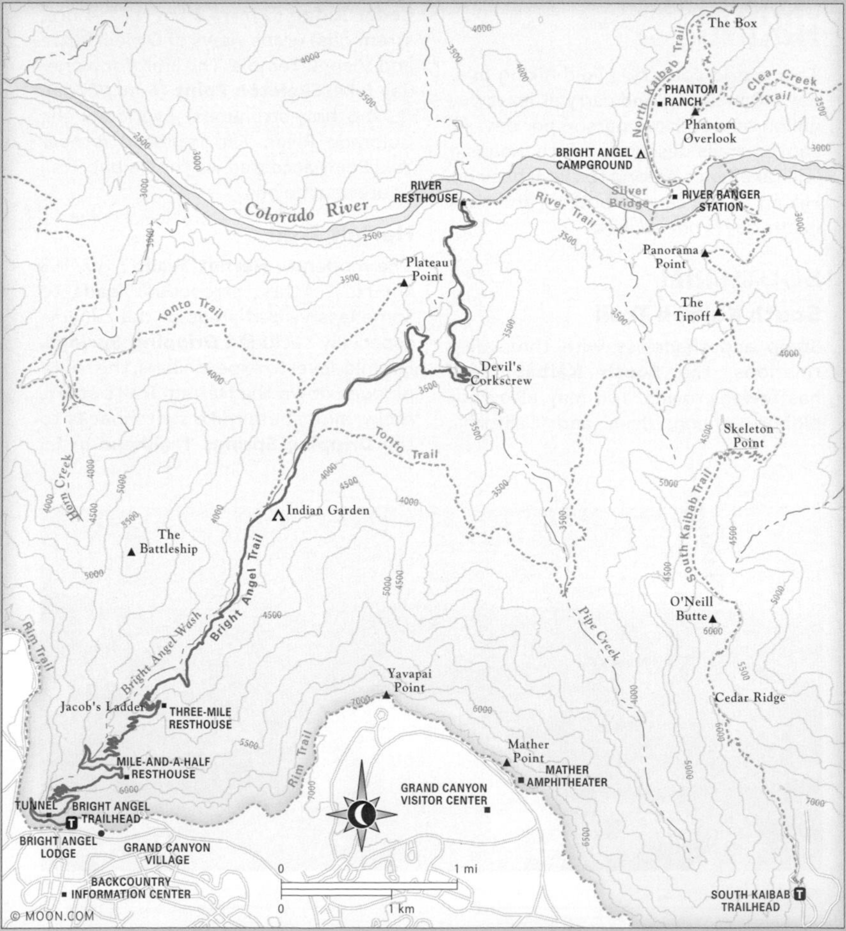

BRIGHT ANGEL TRAIL

miles (2.4 km). Veer left along a ridgeline across Hermit Basin with awe-inspiring unobstructed views. At the junction with the Boucher Trail, continue west for 0.5 mile (0.8 km) up a side canyon to Dripping Springs, a shock of fernlike greenery off a rock overhang with spring water trickling into a small collecting pool. The hike back up is punishing, and there's no water on the trail.

Rim Trail

The **Rim Trail** (12.8 mi./21 km one-way, 5-7 hrs., easy-moderate) is the best way to see the South Rim. The mostly paved trail runs from **South Kaibab Trailhead** and through Grand Canyon Village, ending at **Hermit's Rest.** It hits major sights and overlooks along the way.

With 13 **shuttle stops,** you can hop on and off the trail at your pleasure. Past the Bright Angel Trailhead, the path becomes a dirt single-track between Powell Point and Monument Creek Vista. **Yavapai Point** (0.7 mi./1.1 km one-way, 1 hr.) has stunning canyon views from the Yavapai Observation Station. Grand Canyon Village to **Hopi Point** (0.8 mi./1.3 km one-way, 1 hr.) is best at sunset.

NORTH RIM

It's cool on the high, forested North Rim, making hiking in summer less of a chore. From Grand Canyon Lodge, **Transept Trail** (3 mi./4.8 km rt., 1.5 hrs., easy) travels through forest to the

NORTH KAIBAB CANYON BELOW SUPAI TUNNEL

TONTO TRAIL

campground and provides a good introduction to the North Rim.

Uncle Jim Trail

The **Uncle Jim Trail** (5 mi./8 km rt., 2.5 hrs., easy) winds through old stands of spruce and fir, sprinkled with quaking aspen, to Uncle Jim Point, where you can let out your best roar into the canyon known as Roaring Springs.

Widforss Trail

The mostly flat **Widforss Trail** (10 mi./16 km rt., 5 hrs., easy) leads along the Transept Canyon through ponderosa pine, fir, and spruce, with a few stands of aspen mixed in, to Widforss Point, where you can stare across the great chasm. For a shorter interpretive hike, follow the first half of the trail using the guide available at the visitors center.

North Kaibab Trail

The **North Kaibab Trail** is the only North Rim route into the inner canyon and the Colorado River. A short jog down to **Coconino Overlook** (1.5 mi./2.4 km rt., 1-2 hrs., moderate) offers views of the San Francisco Peaks and the South Rim. Lower destinations include **Supai Tunnel** (4 mi./6.4 km rt., 3-4 hrs., strenuous), which was blasted out of the rock in the 1930s by the Civilian Conservation Corps, and **Redwall Bridge** (5.2 mi./8.4 km rt., 4-6 hrs., strenuous), which was built in 1966 after a flood.

Strong hikers can descend the North Kaibab to **Roaring Springs** (9.4 mi./15 km rt., 6-8 hrs., strenuous). The springs fall headlong out of the cliff to spray mist and rainbows into the hot air. Start your hike early and bring plenty of water. The 3,000-foot (914-m) climb back out of the canyon is grueling. In summer, there is water at the trailhead, Supai Tunnel, and Roaring Springs.

The North Kaibab Trailhead is a few miles north of Grand Canyon Lodge. Take the **hiker's shuttle** (twice daily) from the lodge. Purchase tickets 24 hours in advance.

RECREATION

BACKPACKING

The inner canyon beckons backpackers with rugged trails and a number of **designated backcountry campsites** including Cottonwood, Bright Angel, and

▸ NORTH KAIBAB TRAIL

BACKPACKING RIM-TO-RIM

This classic journey begins on the South Rim at the **Bright Angel** or **South Kaibab Trailhead** to cross the Colorado River and connect with the North Rim via the **North Kaibab Trailhead.** Most backpackers plan 3-4 days for the trip and rely on **Trans-Canyon Shuttle** (928/638-2820, www.trans-canyonshuttle.com, twice daily each direction, May 15-Oct. 15, $90) for the five-hour return drive back to the starting rim. Advanced planning and physical preparation are imperative for this trip.

The Bright Angel and North Kaibab Trails have three developed backcountry campgrounds with restrooms, drinking water, and campsites with picnic tables, pack poles, and food storage bins. From the South Rim, the Bright Angel Trail descends 9.5 miles (15 km, 4,380 ft./1,335 m) to **Bright Angel Campground** near the Colorado River and Phantom Ranch. A much steeper plunge, South Kaibab Trail drops 7 miles (11 km) over 4,780 feet (1,457 m) to the same point.

From the North Rim, the **North Kaibab Trail** cruises 14 miles (22.5 km) into the canyon with the greatest elevation change (5,761 ft./1,756 m). The most common rim-to-rim route connects the Bright Angel and North Kaibab Trails, with a two-night stay at Bright Angel Campground to explore and rest.

For hikers climbing out of Bright Angel Campground, a predawn start is a must. Due to the extreme elevation gains, many choose to break the uphill grunt into two days by camping at **Indian Garden** on the Bright Angel Trail or at **Cottonwood** on the North Kaibab Trail. (The South Kaibab Trail has no camping. Due to its steep, waterless pitch, it is recommended only for descents.)

A **permit** ($10, plus $8 pp per night) is required and it's not easy to get. The park receives 30,000 requests for backcountry permits annually, but issues only 13,000. To apply for a permit, visit the park website for an application, submission dates (usually four months in advance), and regulations. For more information, contact the South Rim Backcountry Information Center (928/638-7875, 8am-5pm daily).

BRIGHT ANGEL TRAIL

Indian Garden. Designated campsites also flank the Kaibab Trail and Tonto Plateau between Indian Garden and Hermit Trail. Permits are required.

BIKING

When **Hermit Road** (7 mi./11 km one-way, Mar.-Nov.) closes to cars, it remains open to cyclists who can ride from Grand Canyon Village to Hermit's Rest. To make a loop, opt for the paved **Hermit Road Greenway Trail** (2.8 mi./4.5 km one-way), a portion of the Rim Trail from Monument Creek Vista to Hermit's Rest.

Near the Grand Canyon Visitor Center, **Bright Angel Bicycles and Café** (928/679-0992, www.bikegrandcanyon.com, 6am-7pm daily May-mid-Sept., 7am-6pm daily mid-Sept.-Apr.) rents bikes, safety equipment, and

▼ RAFTING THE COLORADO

MULE RIDES

trailers. They also offer guided bike tours of the South Rim.

RIVER TRIPS

River rafters place the trip along the Colorado River through the Grand Canyon at the top of their bucket lists. Huge white-water rapids alternate with placid turquoise pools. At night, star-filled evenings accompany campers as owls hoot deep in the gorge. Rafting season runs **April-October.** Guided river trips range from three days to three weeks on dories, motorized rafts, oared rafts, or paddle rafts. Some trips include a hike down one of the corridor trails to the river. Book 6-12 months in advance.

The best place to start is the **Grand Canyon River Outfitters Association** (www.gcroa.org), a nonprofit group of about 16 licensed river outfitters monitored and approved by the National Park Service. Each has a good safety record and similar rates.

MULE RIDES

Grand Canyon mules have been dexterously picking along the skinny trails, loaded with packs and people, for generations. Weight and age restrictions apply. On the South Rim, **Xanterra** (303/297-2757 or 888/297-2757, www.grandcanyonlodges.com) leads mule rides along the **East Rim** (3 hrs., $145) or down the Bright Angel Trail into the canyon to overnight at **Phantom Ranch** (1-2 nights, $605-875 pp, meals included). Make reservations 13 months in advance.

On the North Rim, **Canyon Trail Rides** (435/679-8665, www.canyonrides.com, May 15-Oct. 15, 3 hrs., $90) go to Uncle Jim Point. You can also take a mule down into the canyon along the North Kaibab Trail to the Supai Tunnel.

WHERE TO STAY

INSIDE THE PARK

South Rim

Xanterra (303/297-2757 or 888/297-2757, www.grandcanyonlodges.com) operates five lodges in Grand Canyon Village. Make reservations 13 months in advance for stays April-October and 6 months in advance in other seasons.

El Tovar (from $300) is a 1905 National Historic Landmark near the rim with 78 rooms and suites. The hotel's **restaurant** (928/638-2631,

NAME	LOCATION	PRICE	SEASON	AMENITIES
Mather Campground	South Rim	$18	year-round	tent sites
Trailer Village	South Rim	$49	year-round	RV sites
Bright Angel Lodge	South Rim	from $108	year-round	hiker rooms, hotel rooms, cabins, dining
Maswik Lodge	South Rim	from $245	year-round	motel rooms, cabins, dining
Yavapai Lodge	South Rim	from $185	year-round	motel rooms, dining
Kachina Lodge	South Rim	from $249	year-round	motel rooms
Thunderbird Lodge	South Rim	from $249	year-round	motel rooms
El Tovar Hotel	South Rim	from $300	year-round	hotel rooms, dining
Desert View Campground	East Rim	$12	May-mid-Oct	tent sites
North Rim Campground	North Rim	$18-25	May 15-Oct. 31	tent sites
Grand Canyon Lodge	North Rim	from $148	May 15-Oct. 15	cabins, motel rooms, dining
Indian Garden	Inner Canyon	permit required	year-round	hike-in tent sites
Bright Angel	Inner Canyon	permit required	year-round	hike-in tent sites
Cottonwood	Inner Canyon	permit required	year-round	hike-in tent sites
Phantom Ranch	Inner Canyon	$61-169	year-round	hike-in dorms, cabins, food

6:30am-10:30am, 11:15am-2pm, and 4:30pm-9:30pm daily, reservations recommended) serves some of the best food in Arizona. Off the log-cabin lobby is a cocktail lounge with a window on the canyon, a mezzanine sitting area overlooks lobby, and a gift shop with Native American art and crafts.

Bright Angel Lodge (from $108) retains a rustic character that fits perfectly with the wild canyon just outside. Most lodge rooms have only one bed and no TVs. Utilitarian "hiker" rooms have refrigerators and share showers. The lodge's cabins have private baths, TVs, and sitting rooms. The **Arizona Steakhouse** (928/638-2631, 11:30am-3pm and 4:30pm-9:30pm daily Mar.-Dec.) serves southwestern dishes in a stylish yet casual atmosphere, and the **Harvey House Cafe** (928/638-2631, 6:30am-10:30am, 11:30am-3:30pm, and 4:30-10pm daily) plates standard rib-sticking food.

Kachina Lodge and **Thunderbird Lodge** (both from $249) both offer basic rooms with TVs, safes, private baths, and refrigerators.

Maswik Lodge (303/297-2757, www.grandcanyonlodges.com, from $245) has motel-style rooms with TVs, private baths, and refrigerators. (The lodge's south section is under construction.) The hotel has the cafeteria-style **Maswik Food Court** (928/638-2631, 6am-9pm daily) and a sports bar.

Delaware North (877/404-4611, www.visitgrandcanyon.com) operates **Yavapai Lodge** (11 Yavapai Lodge Rd., from $185) near Market Plaza. The basic motel has air-conditioning, refrigerators, and TVs.

PHANTOM RANCH

The west section has no air-conditioning but is pet-friendly. The lodge **restaurant** (7am-9pm daily) has a limited menu of hot and cold sandwiches. The **Canyon Village Market & Deli** (8am-8pm daily, hours vary seasonally) sells groceries, camping supplies, and deli foods.

North Rim

Built in the late 1930s, the **Grand Canyon Lodge** (928/638-2611 or 877/386-4383, www.grandcanyonforever.com, mid-May-mid-Oct., from $148) is the only hotel on the North Rim. It has several small, comfy lodge rooms and dozens of cabins with private bathrooms; some have gas fireplaces.

The rustic log-and-stone lodge has a large central lobby, a **Dining Room** (6:30am-10am, 11:30am-2:30pm, and 4:30pm-9:30pm daily mid-May-mid-Oct., dinner reservations required), deli, saloon, gift shop, general store, and gas station.

Inner Canyon

Designed in 1922 by Mary Colter for the Fred Harvey Company, **Phantom Ranch** (888/297-2757, www.grandcanyonlodges.com, dorms $65, cabin $169) has the only accommodations inside the canyon. Located near the mouth of Bright Angel Canyon, the complex is shaded by cottonwoods that were planted in the 1930s by the Civilian Conservation Corps. Phantom Ranch has several rustic, air-conditioned cabins and dormitories, one for men and one for women; both offer restrooms with showers.

The lodge's Phantom Ranch Canteen sells beer and lemonade (with air-conditioning!). The Canteen offers two meals daily: breakfast (eggs, pancakes, and bacon) and dinner, with a choice of steak, stew, or vegetarian. It also offers a boxed lunch with a bagel, fruit, and salty snacks. Meal reservations are required.

Reservations are on a lottery system (www.grandcanyonlodges.com/lodging/phantom-ranch/lottery). Lottery reservations begin 15 months in advance.

Camping

The South Rim has three campgrounds. For RVers, **Trailer Village** (Delaware North, 877/404-4611, www.visitgrandcanyon.com, $49) has hookups.

Mather Campground (877/444-6777, www.recreation.gov, 327 sites, $18) has coin-operated showers and laundry. Grand Canyon Village is a 15-minute walk and a shuttle stop is nearby. The campground typically fills by noon in summer. Make reservations six months in advance for March-mid-November. One loop stays open in winter with limited services.

Near the park's East Entrance, **Desert View Campground** (May-mid-Oct., 50 sites, $12) is for tents and small RVs with first-come, first-served sites.

The **North Rim Campground** (877/444-6777, www.recreation.gov, mid-May-Oct., 90 sites, $18-25) has campsites near the rim, with showers and a coin-operated laundry. Reserve sites six months in advance.

OUTSIDE THE PARK

Plentiful accommodations, restaurants, and services are available in **Tusayan, Williams,** and **Flagstaff.**

GETTING THERE

AIR

Most visitors fly into **Phoenix Sky Harbor International Airport** (PHX, 3400 E. Sky Harbor Blvd., 602/273-3300, www.skyharbor.com), rent a car, and drive about 3.5 hours north to the South Rim. Flying into **Las Vegas's McCarran International Airport** (LAS, 5757 Wayne Newton Blvd., 702/261-5211, www.mccarran.com) places you within five hours' drive of the park. **Grand Canyon Airlines** (www.grandcanyonairlines.com) has flights from Boulder City, Nevada, near Las Vegas, to **Grand Canyon Airport** (GCN) at Tusayan. However, car rentals are not available at the Grand Canyon GC Airport.

BUS

Arizona Shuttles (928/350-8466, www.groometransportation.com) offers service from Flagstaff to the Grand Canyon (daily Mar.-Oct., $68 rt.). Connections also go between Phoenix's Sky Harbor Airport and Flagstaff ($49 one-way) several times a day.

From Tusayan, a free **shuttle** (8am-9:30pm daily Mar. 1-Sept. 30) runs from the National Geographic IMAX theater into the park to the Grand Canyon Visitor Center. Purchase your entrance ticket at the IMAX before getting on the shuttle.

TRAIN

From Williams, the **Grand Canyon Railway** (800/843-8724, www.thetrain.com, $67-226 rt.) takes about 2.5 hours to reach the South Rim Depot. Fiddlers often stroll through the restored historic cars; some trips stage a mock train robbery with bandits on horseback.

CAR

Most visitors drive to the park's South Rim from **Flagstaff** or **Williams,** entering through the south or east gates. The **South Entrance** is the busiest; traffic backs up during summer. The quickest way to the South Entrance is via AZ 64 from Williams (55 mi./89 km). From Flagstaff, take US 180 through the forest past the San Francisco Peaks to merge with AZ 64 at Valle (80 mi./129 km) to get to the entrance.

To reach the **East Entrance,** take US 89 north from Flagstaff to Cameron, then take AZ 64 west to the entrance. Entering through the East Entrance lands you at Desert View, Desert View Watchtower, and Tusayan Museum and Ruin.

GETTING AROUND

SOUTH RIM

Driving is unnecessary on the South Rim thanks to the park's shuttle service and the walkable Rim Trail. When visiting in the summer, park your vehicle early in the day and use the park's shuttle system to get around. The **Backcountry Information Center** has a large parking lot; the southern portion can accommodate RVs and trailers. If you're just visiting for the day, drive into the village and park your car in El Tovar parking lot or the large lot at **Market Plaza.**

The park operates free **shuttle service** with buses fueled by compressed natural gas. The shuttle runs from sunrise until about 9pm; however, there is no shuttle that travels east from Grand Canyon Village to the East Entrance.

NORTH RIM

The drive from the South Rim to the North Rim is 215 miles (345 km, 5 hrs.). AZ 67 from Jacob Lake to the North Rim typically closes to vehicles from late November until May.

The **Trans-Canyon Shuttle** (928/638-2820, www.trans-canyonshuttle.com, $90 one-way, reservations required) makes a twice-daily round-trip excursion between the North and South Rims.

To get from the Grand Canyon Lodge to the North Kaibab Trailhead, take the **Hikers Shuttle** ($4-7), which leaves the lodge twice daily in early morning. Buy tickets the day before at the lodge.

SIGHTS NEARBY

Hualapai Skywalk (888/868-9378 or 928/769-2636, www.grandcanyonwest.com), at Eagle Point on the Hualapai Reservation, extends 4,000 feet above the Grand Canyon floor on a glass-bottom viewing bridge.

PETRIFIED FOREST NATIONAL PARK

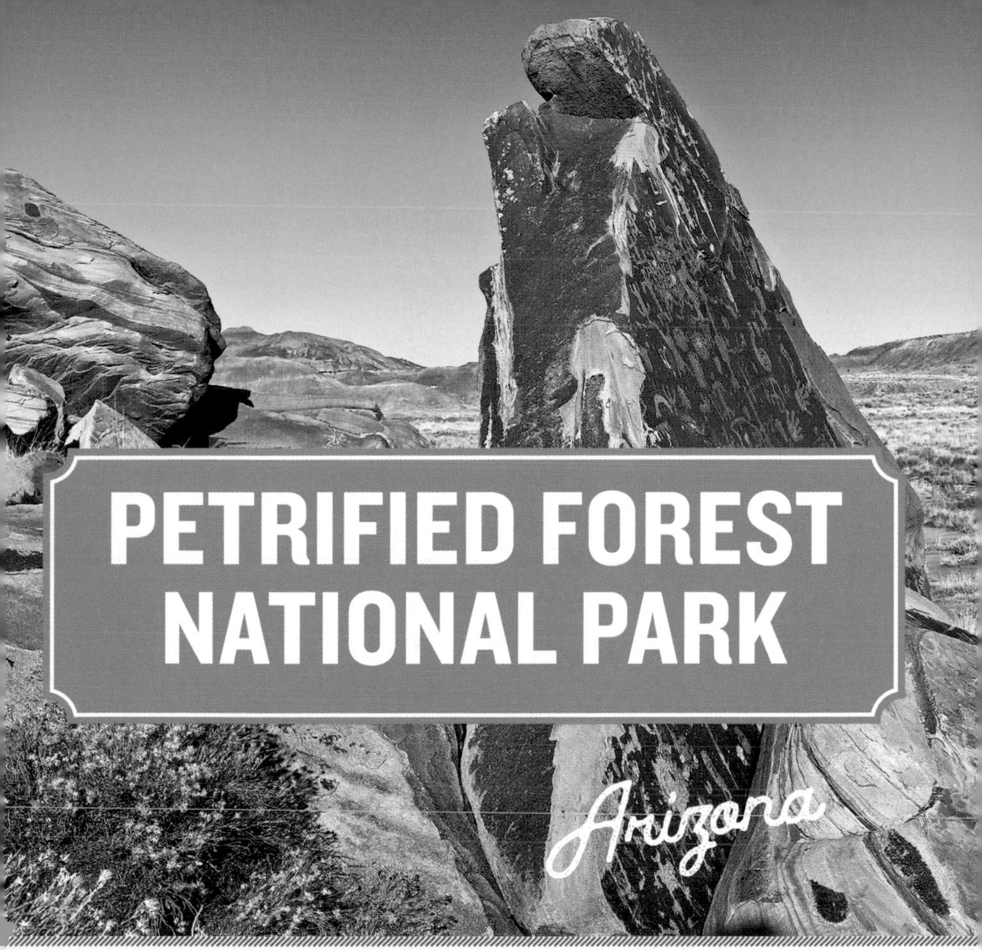

KEEPSAKE STAMPS ▼▼▼

WEBSITE:
www.nps.gov/pefo

PHONE NUMBER:
928/524-6228

VISITATION RANK:
33

WHY GO:
See petrified trees loaded with colorful quartz crystal.

▲ FLATIRON PETROGLYPH PANEL, PETRIFIED FOREST NATIONAL PARK

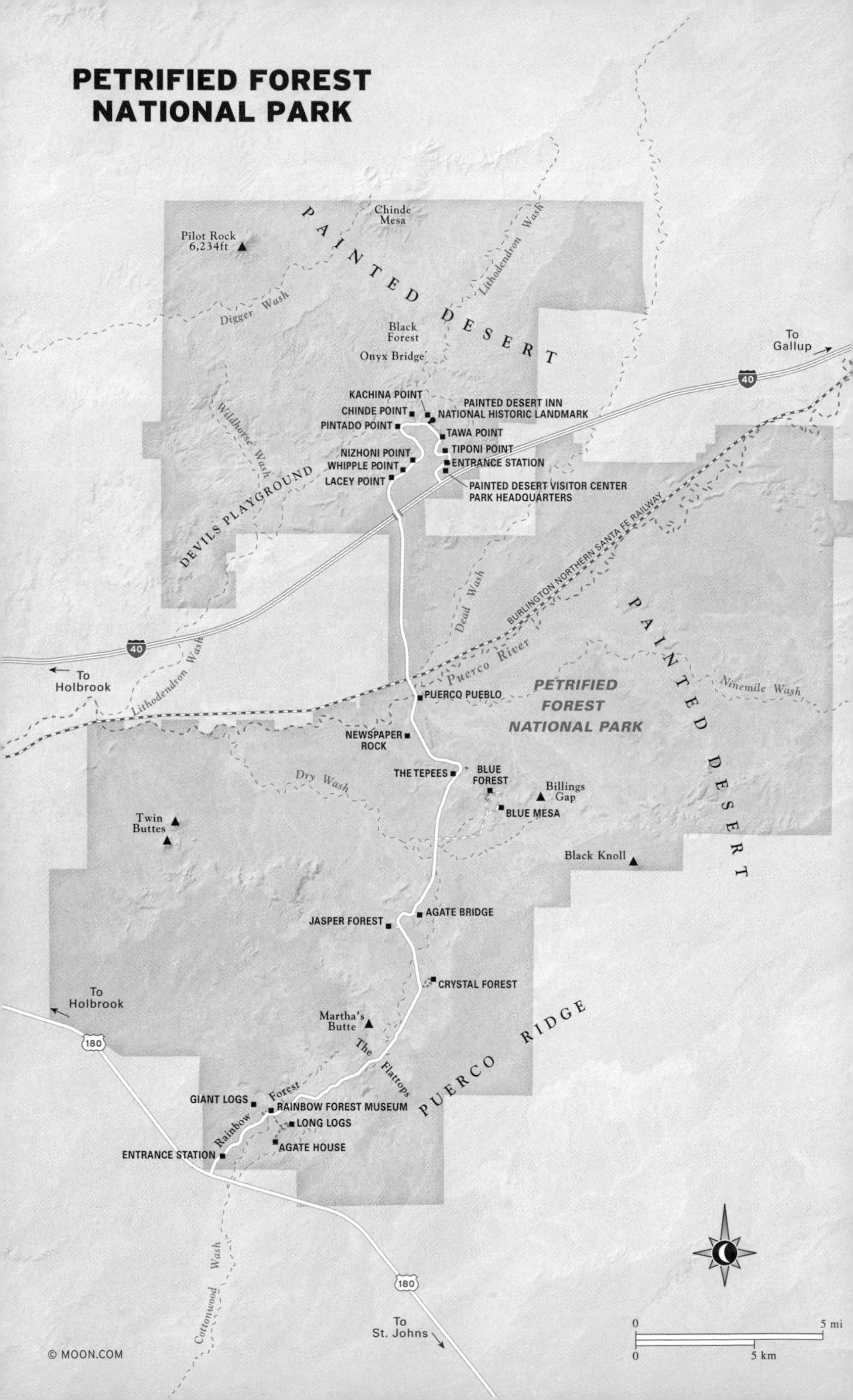

PETRIFIED FOREST NATIONAL PARK
Pilot Rock 6,234ft
Chinde Mesa
PAINTED DESERT
Lithodendron Wash
Digger Wash
Black Forest
Onyx Bridge
To Gallup
40
KACHINA POINT
CHINDE POINT
PINTADO POINT
PAINTED DESERT INN NATIONAL HISTORIC LANDMARK
TAWA POINT
TIPONI POINT
ENTRANCE STATION
NIZHONI POINT
WHIPPLE POINT
LACEY POINT
PAINTED DESERT VISITOR CENTER PARK HEADQUARTERS
Wildhorse Wash
DEVILS PLAYGROUND
Dead Wash
BURLINGTON NORTHERN SANTA FE RAILWAY
PAINTED DESERT
To Holbrook
Lithodendron Wash
Puerco River
PUERCO PUEBLO
PETRIFIED FOREST NATIONAL PARK
Ninemile Wash
NEWSPAPER ROCK
THE TEPEES
BLUE FOREST
Billings Gap
BLUE MESA
Dry Wash
Twin Buttes
Black Knoll
AGATE BRIDGE
JASPER FOREST
CRYSTAL FOREST
To Holbrook
180
Martha's Butte
The Flattops
PUERCO RIDGE
GIANT LOGS
Rainbow Forest
RAINBOW FOREST MUSEUM
LONG LOGS
AGATE HOUSE
ENTRANCE STATION
Cottonwood Wash
To St. Johns
0
5 mi
5 km

What was once a swampy forest frequented by ancient oversize reptiles is now **PETRIFIED FOREST NATIONAL PARK**, a blasted scrubland strewn with quartz-wrapped trees some 225 million years old. Each petrified log reveals a smooth, multicolored splotch or swirl on the interior where tree rings would be. The ancient Puebloans used their petrified fragments to build tools and houses.

Drive between the north and south entrances on the park road to take in pastel-hued badlands of the Painted Desert. Orange and rusty hues color the badlands at the north end while blue, purple, gray, and white form the layers at the Tepees and Blue Mesa in the central zone. Along the way, this desert shouts in shifting colors.

PLANNING YOUR TIME

Petrified Forest National Park is in northeast Arizona, approximately 116 miles (187 km) east of Flagstaff. **Spring** (Feb.-May) is the best time to be in Arizona's lowland deserts. The weather hangs in the high 70s and 80s (21-32°C). Typically, triple-digit heat smothers the park June through October; yet crowds visit March-October. By November the weather cools off, and winter settles on the desert with sometimes freezing temperatures and dustings of snow.

The park is bisected by I-40. For a one-day visit, follow the paved, 26-mile (42-km) road between the north and south entrances. Hours for opening the park road vary throughout the year: 7am-7pm mid-April-August (until 7:30pm mid-May-early Aug.), 7am-6pm September 1-14, 8am-5pm mid-September-mid-April. The road is gated at night.

Note that Arizona does not observe daylight saving time. The park stays on Mountain Standard Time year-round.

ENTRANCES AND FEES

The entrance fee is $25 per vehicle ($20 motorcycle, $15 individual) and valid for seven days. Two entrances access the park. The **north entrance** is just beyond Painted Desert Visitor Center off I-40 (exit 311). The **south entrance** is off US 180.

VISITORS CENTERS

The park has two visitors centers with maps of all the sightseeing stops, park films, restrooms, and bookstores. At the north entrance, **Painted Desert Visitor Center** (8am-6pm daily summer, shorter hours fall-spring) has hands-on exhibits and backcountry permits. The historic **Rainbow Forest Museum** (8am-6pm daily summer, shorter hours fall-spring) is at the south entrance. It contains fossils and displays about the dinosaurs that once ruled this land.

SIGHTS

PAINTED DESERT

The **Painted Desert** sprawls on the north end of the park lighting up with hues of orange, yellow, and pink. Eight viewpoints on the park road north of the visitors center allow places to stop to absorb the colors. Interpretive signs fill you in on the geology and formations. Tiponi Point provides the best orientation to the Painted Desert. Tawa Point lets you gaze straight down at formations. Pintado Point allows for long views across the Painted Desert wilderness. Use the park map to locate the overlooks.

PUERCO PUEBLO RUIN

In the central area of the park road, **Puerco Pueblo** is a collection of ruins that were occupied 700-800 years ago. You can see the foundations of a kiva and several rooms. A collection of rocks contains petroglyphs, and a modern stone building has interpretive information. From the Puerco Pueblo parking area, take the paved **Puerco Pueblo**

Loop (0.3 mi./0.5 km rt., 45 min., easy) to tour the site.

DARK SKY

With little humidity to clog visibility, Petrified Forest National Park is designated as an International **Dark Sky Park.** For the best stargazing, go backpacking into the Painted Desert wilderness on a moonless night (free permit required) to sleep under the Milky Way. Rainbow Forest Museum hosts nighttime astronomy programs periodically throughout the year. Petrified Forest Field Institute (www.petrifiedforestinstitute.org) leads full moon and Milky Way photo expeditions.

PALEONTOLOGY LAB

At the **Painted Desert Visitor Center** complex, the Paleontology Lab offers a demonstration program (9am-3pm Wed.) to see fossils from the Triassic period found in the park being preserved. Junior Rangers can also do a Junior Paleontologist Program by picking up a book at either visitors center to earn a special paleontology badge. Also, Petrified Forest Field Institute (www.petrifiedforestinstitute.org) offers hands-on fossil digs for adults and special fossil work for kids.

SCENIC DRIVE

To see this understated masterpiece of a national park, drive the **26-mile (42-km) park road** (open 7am-7:30pm daily summer, shorter hours fall-spring), stopping at the pullouts. Start at the north entrance and the **Painted Desert Visitor Center,** where the road enters the Painted Desert. You'll pass several viewpoints, including **Tawa Point,** where the views are long, subtle, colorful, and barren.

Two miles (3.2 km) from the north entrance, stop at the **Painted Desert Inn** (Kachina Point, 9am-4pm daily) to see the National Historic Landmark. Past the inn is **Pintado Point,** offering one of the best views of this strange landscape. As the road turns south, look for the rusted husk of a **1932 Studebaker** sitting alone off the side of the road. This artifact marks the line that old Route 66 once took through the park, roughly visible now in the alignment of the power lines stretching west behind the car.

Cross I-40 and continue south to the **Newspaper Rock** petroglyphs; some of the 650 petroglyphs are viewable through spotting scopes from a spur road to the overlook. Farther on, the **Puerco Pueblo ruin** preserves the cultural legacy of the people that once lived and thrived on this high-desert plain. Continuing south, look out for the hard-to-miss red-and-gray formations aptly named **The Tepees.** Farther south, **Blue Mesa Scenic Road** departs eastward. Then, the **Agate Bridge** pullout features a 110-foot-long (34-m) bridge made of petrified logs. In the next stretch are two fallen petrified

PAINTED CANYON

Top 3

1 PAINTED DESERT INN

PAINTED DESERT INN

Two miles (3.2 km) north of the north entrance, **Painted Desert Inn** (9am-4pm daily) is a National Historic Landmark perched on Kachina Point. With its original walls built from petrified wood and native stone, the inn launched as a restaurant and hotel for travelers in the 1920s, before the National Park Service purchased the building. Later, it serviced drivers on Route 66. Following World War II, the Fred Harvey Company operated a restaurant and store in the inn redesigned by Mary Colter, the genius of southwestern style and elegance. Her vision and color scheme turned the inn into a Pueblo Revival-style structure for modern visitors. She commissioned Hopi artist Fred Kabotie to paint murals full of Hopi mythology and symbolism on the inside walls.

Docent-led tours are available upon request (daily, summer). Local Native American artisans often share their heritage through skill demonstrations (10am-3pm, Wed.-Mon.). Outside, you can see one of the most dramatic petroglyphs in the state—a large, stylized mountain lion etched into a slab of rock.

2 BLUE MESA

About midway on the park road, Blue Mesa rises from the desert floor in layered shades of purple, blue, gray, and white. These badlands of bentonite clay are littered with petrified wood, and paleontologists have unearthed buried fossils here. **Blue Mesa Scenic Road** (5.2 mi./8.4 km rt.) loops around the top of Blue Mesa with several stops at overlooks. From the Blue Mesa Sun Shelter, follow the paved and gravel **Blue Mesa Loop** (1 mi./1.6 km rt., 45 min., moderate), also called the Blue Forest Trail, into the bowels of the blue bentonite clay cliffs, worn and sculpted into fantastic shapes. Prepare for a steep descent and a climb on the return hike.

3 CRYSTAL FOREST

Crystal Forest is no vertical grove of trees. It's a forest of fallen petrified giants around 225 million years old. Petrification happens when trees are buried and over time, groundwater replaces their organic matter with inorganic minerals. Here, you can see petrified bark on the outside and brilliant crystallized interiors where the logs have split. Walk from the Crystal Forest parking area on the paved **Crystal Forest Loop** (0.75 mi./1.2 km rt., 30 min., easy) to see trees and their shiny rounds of maroon, yellow, and white crystal. Remember: these trees are protected.

CRYSTALIZED PETRIFIED WOOD

forests: drive through a barren loop to see **Jasper Forest** and stop to walk the paved loop through **Crystal Forest.** The scenic road tour terminates at the **Rainbow Forest Museum.**

RECREATION

HIKING

Accessible from the park's scenic road are several short side hikes that offer a deeper connection with the landscape. Between Tawa Point and Kachina Point, you can walk the unpaved **Painted Desert Rim Trail** (1 mi./1.6 km rt., 30 min., easy) for views of this exotic and colorful landscape.

Several short hikes depart from the Rainbow Forest Museum. For a short walk on a paved trail, take the **Giant Logs Trail** (0.4 mi./0.6 km rt., 30 min., easy) to visit the park's largest petrified trees. The partially paved **Long Logs Loop** (2.6 mi./4.2 km rt., 1 hr., easy) heads south of the road to see some of the park's longest and most numerous petrified trees in a logjam. A spur trail goes to **Agate House**, a pueblo built from petrified wood about 700 years ago.

BICYCLING

Cyclists can ride the 26-mile (42 km) park road, but must exercise caution—many drivers are staring at the views instead of the road. Mountain bikers can ride a section of sagebrush-covered Old Route 66 that lacks pavement and the first portion of the Long Logs Loop.

WHERE TO STAY

INSIDE THE PARK

There are no campgrounds or lodgings inside the park. Backcountry camping is permitted in the park's wilderness area (free permit required). The only place to get a meal is the south entrance's Fred Harvey Company restaurant, **Painted Desert Diner** (928/524-3756, 9am-4pm daily), which serves fried chicken, Navajo tacos, burgers, and other road-food favorites in a cool Route 66 retro dining room. The south entrance visitors center sells snacks.

BLUE MESA PETRIFIED WOOD

OUTSIDE THE PARK

Accommodations and restaurants are available in the nearby towns of **Holbrook** and **Winslow;** however, **Flagstaff** offers the best variety of each and the most services.

GETTING THERE AND AROUND

There is no public transportation to or within the park. Only one road traverses the park, running 26 miles (42 km) between the north and south entrances.

AIR

The closest international airport is **Phoenix Sky Harbor International Airport** (PHX, 3400 E. Sky Harbor Blvd., 602/273-3300, www.skyharbor.com). From Phoenix, you'll need to rent a car and drive almost four hours to the park entrance. **Flagstaff Pulliam Airport** (FLG, 6200 S. Pulliam Dr., 928/213-2930, www.flagstaff.az.gov) is serviced by American Eagle Airlines. The drive from Flagstaff takes two hours to reach either park entrance.

CAR

Approaching Petrified Forest National Park by car from the west, take I-40 toward Holbrook (exit 285 or 286) and continue through the small town's dilapidated downtown. From Holbrook, take US 180 for 21 miles (34 km) to the south entrance. From the east, take I-40 to exit 311 and the north entrance.

SAGUARO NATIONAL PARK

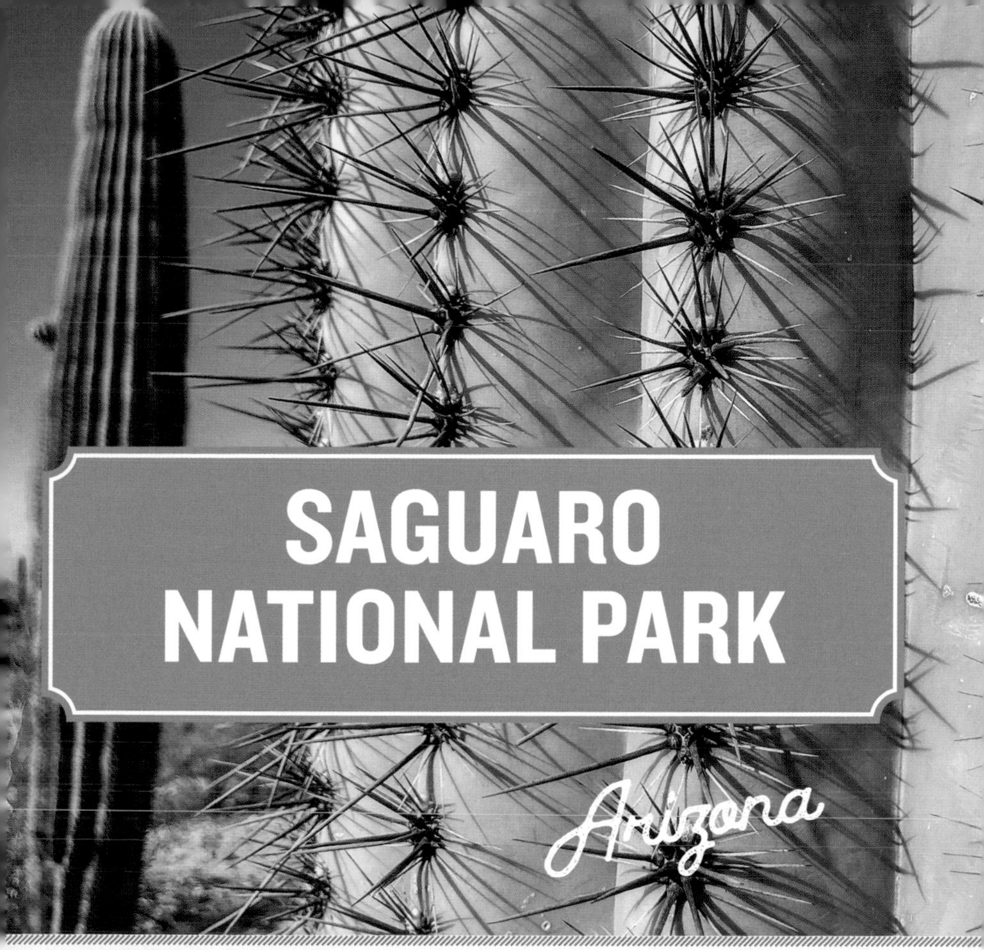

KEEPSAKE STAMPS ▾▾▾

WEBSITE:
www.nps.gov/sagu

PHONE NUMBER:
520/733-5100

VISITATION RANK:
25

WHY GO:
See stately saguaros in the Sonoran Desert.

▲ SAGUARO NATIONAL PARK

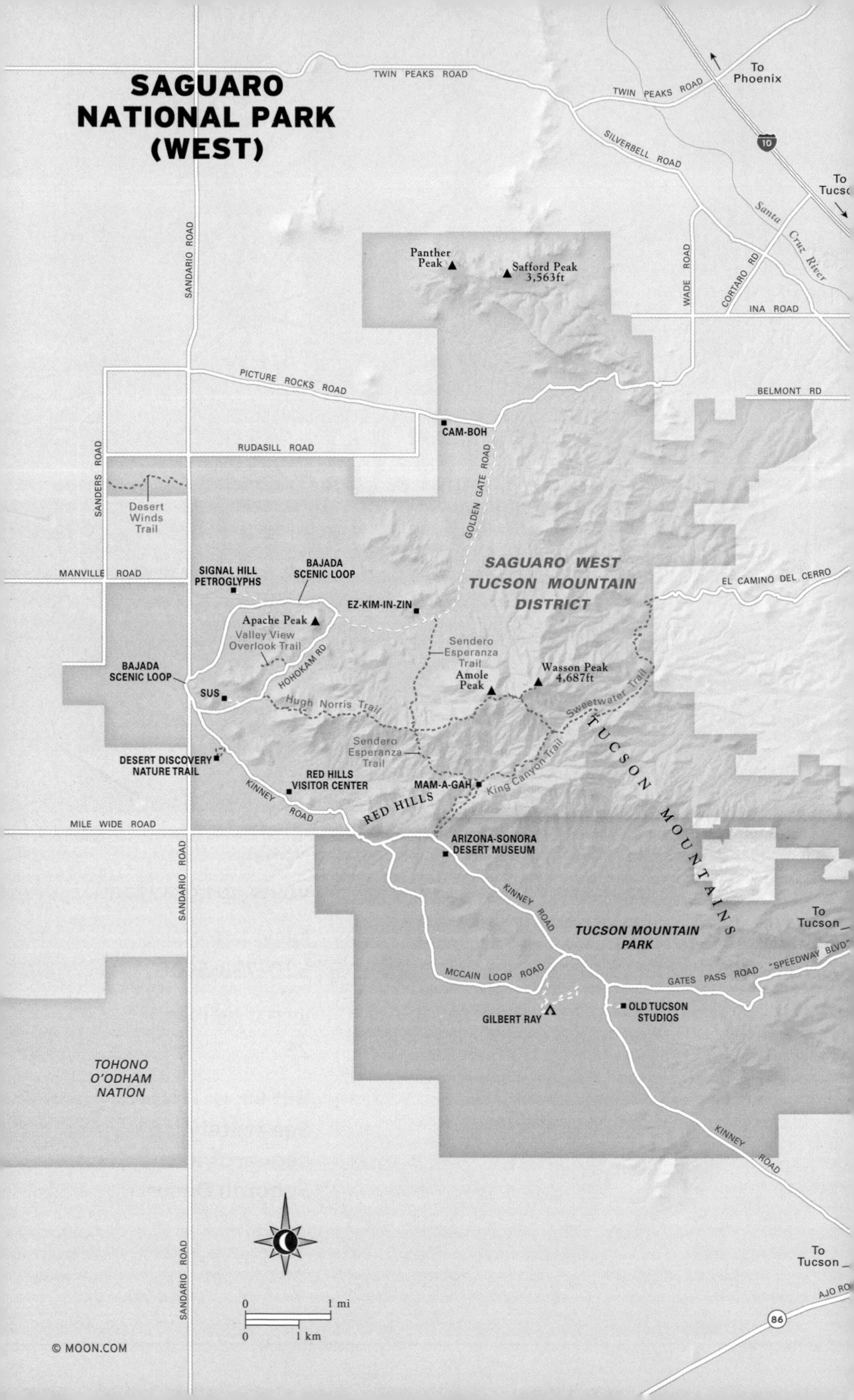

SAGUARO NATIONAL PARK (WEST)
TWIN PEAKS ROAD
TWIN PEAKS ROAD
To Phoenix
10
SILVERBELL ROAD
To Tucson
Santa Cruz River
WADE ROAD
CORTARO RD
INA ROAD
SANDARIO ROAD
Panther Peak
Safford Peak 3,563ft
PICTURE ROCKS ROAD
BELMONT RD
CAM-BOH
RUDASILL ROAD
SANDERS ROAD
GOLDEN GATE ROAD
Desert Winds Trail
SAGUARO WEST TUCSON MOUNTAIN DISTRICT
MANVILLE ROAD
SIGNAL HILL PETROGLYPHS
BAJADA SCENIC LOOP
EL CAMINO DEL CERRO
EZ-KIM-IN-ZIN
Apache Peak
Valley View Overlook Trail
HOHOKAM RD
Sendero Esperanza Trail
BAJADA SCENIC LOOP
Wasson Peak 4,687ft
Amole Peak
SUS
Hugh Norris Trail
Sweetwater Trail
TUCSON MOUNTAINS
Sendero Esperanza Trail
DESERT DISCOVERY NATURE TRAIL
King Canyon Trail
RED HILLS VISITOR CENTER
MAM-A-GAH
KINNEY ROAD
RED HILLS
MILE WIDE ROAD
ARIZONA-SONORA DESERT MUSEUM
KINNEY ROAD
To Tucson
TUCSON MOUNTAIN PARK
"SPEEDWAY BLVD"
MCCAIN LOOP ROAD
GATES PASS ROAD
GILBERT RAY
OLD TUCSON STUDIOS
TOHONO O'ODHAM NATION
KINNEY ROAD
To Tucson
AJO RD
86
0
1 mi
0
1 km
© MOON.COM

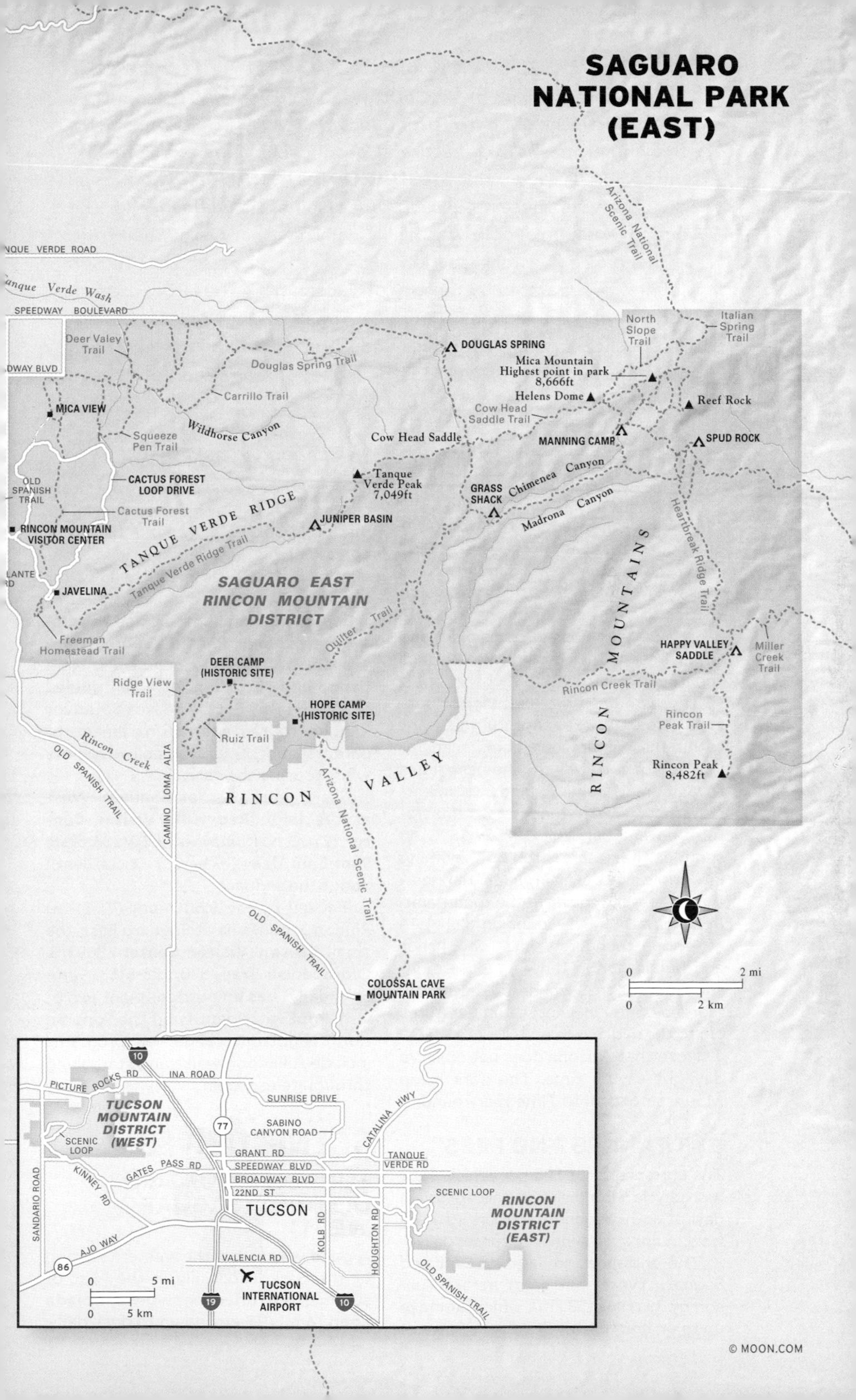

SAGUARO NATIONAL PARK (EAST)
NQUE VERDE ROAD
anque Verde Wash
SPEEDWAY BOULEVARD
DWAY BLVD
Deer Valley Trail
Douglas Spring Trail
DOUGLAS SPRING
Carrillo Trail
Wildhorse Canyon
MICA VIEW
Squeeze Pen Trail
OLD SPANISH TRAIL
CACTUS FOREST LOOP DRIVE
Cactus Forest Trail
RINCON MOUNTAIN VISITOR CENTER
TANQUE VERDE RIDGE
Tanque Verde Ridge Trail
JAVELINA
LANTE RD
Freeman Homestead Trail
Tanque Verde Peak 7,049ft
JUNIPER BASIN
Cow Head Saddle
Cow Head Saddle Trail
Helens Dome
Mica Mountain Highest point in park 8,666ft
North Slope Trail
Italian Spring Trail
Reef Rock
MANNING CAMP
SPUD ROCK
GRASS SHACK
Chimenea Canyon
Madrona Canyon
Arizona National Scenic Trail
SAGUARO EAST RINCON MOUNTAIN DISTRICT
Quilter Trail
Heartbreak Ridge Trail
RINCON MOUNTAINS
HAPPY VALLEY SADDLE
Miller Creek Trail
Rincon Creek Trail
Rincon Peak Trail
Rincon Peak 8,482ft
DEER CAMP (HISTORIC SITE)
HOPE CAMP (HISTORIC SITE)
Ridge View Trail
Ruiz Trail
Rincon Creek
OLD SPANISH TRAIL
CAMINO LOMA ALTA
RINCON VALLEY
COLOSSAL CAVE MOUNTAIN PARK
0 2 mi
0 2 km
10
PICTURE ROCKS RD
INA ROAD
SUNRISE DRIVE
TUCSON MOUNTAIN DISTRICT (WEST)
77
SABINO CANYON ROAD
CATALINA HWY
SCENIC LOOP
GRANT RD
TANQUE VERDE RD
GATES PASS RD
SPEEDWAY BLVD
BROADWAY BLVD
KINNEY RD
22ND ST
SANDARIO ROAD
TUCSON
KOLB RD
HOUGHTON RD
SCENIC LOOP
RINCON MOUNTAIN DISTRICT (EAST)
AJO WAY
VALENCIA RD
86
0 5 mi
0 5 km
TUCSON INTERNATIONAL AIRPORT
19
10
OLD SPANISH TRAIL

This is where the icon of the Southwest holds court. The country's largest cacti, the saguaro (pronounced sa-WAH-ro), grow slowly, achieving arms and full stature at around 125 years old. Some extend to 50 feet (15 m) tall. **SAGUARO NATIONAL PARK** serves as a sanctuary for these regal cacti that also have significance for the Tohono O'odham people, who historically have harvested their fruit.

The park's western section sits at the base of the Tucson Mountains, separated by the city of Tucson from the larger eastern section along the Rincon Mountains. Together, they protect a magnificent slice of forest with thick underbrush of ocotillo, prickly pear, cholla, mesquite, and palo verde. This is the Sonoran Desert at its best.

PLANNING YOUR TIME

Saguaro National Park is split by the city of Tucson in southern Arizona. A one-hour drive apart, both Saguaro East (Rincon Mountains) and Saguaro West (Tucson Mountains) sections are worth visiting. If you have time only for one, choose Saguaro East, which is older and larger. Despite their proximity to Tucson, you'll need a car to visit either section.

The park has two **peak visitor seasons** (Nov.-Dec., Feb.-Apr.) If you want to hit the wildflower blooms, plan for late February or March. The best times to visit are March-May and September-November, when moderate temperatures hover around 85-95°F (29-35°C). In summer, the desert is too hot, zooming into triple digits even in shade. Temperatures are a bit cooler in the mountains. In July and August, count on daily late afternoon thunderstorms. Though hot and humid during the day, these monsoon months are a wonderful time to see more blooms. In winter, temperatures dip to the mid-50s to mid-70s (13-24°C).

Note that Arizona does not observe daylight saving time. The park is on Mountain Standard Time year-round.

ENTRANCES AND FEES

The entrance fee is $25 per vehicle ($20 motorcycle, $15 individual), valid for seven days at both sections of the park. Park entrances are open sunrise to sunset daily.

The entrances to Saguaro East and Saguaro West split apart across Tucson by 33 miles (53 km), which can take up to an hour to drive.

VISITORS CENTERS

Each section of the park has a visitors center with exhibits, maps and information, bookstores, and a film that narrates the Native American connection with the desert. Schedules for ranger-led walks and talks vary year-round, but generally take place November-May. Junior Ranger Programs are available for kids and include earning a badge and checking out a self-guided Discovery Day Pack. The Not So Junior Ranger Program adds a fun element for parents and seniors to collect points while touring the park.

Start your tour of Saguaro West at the large **Red Hills Visitor Center** (2700 N. Kinney Rd., 520/733-5158, 9am-5pm daily), where you can learn about the saguaro.

Backed by the 8,600-foot (2,621-m) Rincon Mountains at Saguaro East, the small **Rincon Visitor Center** (3693 S. Old Spanish Trail, 520/733-5153, 9am-5pm daily) has an outdoor plant exhibit, helpful with identifying the Sonoran flora. Nighttime ranger-led programs include full moon walks and stargazing through telescopes.

SCENIC DRIVES

TUCSON MOUNTAIN DISTRICT (SAGUARO WEST)

A good way to see the western section of the park, especially in the heat of summer, is to drive the two-way **Bajada Loop** (6 mi./9.7 km, dawn to dusk daily,

Top 3

1 PEER AT PETROGLYPHS

In Saguaro West, a walk from the **Signal Hill Picnic Area** on Bajada Loop Drive climbs the **Signal Hill Petroglyphs Trail** (0.3 mi./0.5 km rt., 20 min., easy). Its boulder-topped hill has several petroglyphs—symbols carved in the rock—above the trail on the way up. At the top, some petroglyphs are right next to the trail railing while dozens decorate the sides of rock slabs. These petroglyphs, stories from the Hohokam people, date from 450-1450 CE.

PETROGLYPHS ON SIGNAL HILL

2 TOUR DESERT DISCOVERY NATURE TRAIL

From a parking area on Kinney Road 1 mile (1.6 km) north of the Red Hills Visitor Center at Saguaro West, the **Desert Discovery Nature Trail** (0.5 mi./0.8 km rt., 20 min., easy) is a wheelchair-accessible paved interpretive pathway that loops through a saguaro forest. Signs identify cacti and plants, and many older saguaros tower high overhead, with barrel cactus and prickly pear at their feet.

3 CYCLE CACTUS FOREST LOOP

Cyclists flock to the paved **Cactus Forest Loop Drive** (8 mi./12.9 km one-way) in Saguaro East below the Rincon Mountains. The road is not family-friendly but an intermediate to expert road cyclist's delight. The rolling route swoops down gullies only to climb up again and has a steep ascent on the east side. Tucson has several rental bike companies; some will deliver to the visitors center.

CYCLISTS ON CACTUS FOREST LOOP

SAGUARO BUDS

RVs and trailers are not recommended) through a thick saguaro forest. The route is graded dirt and can get dusty, but you can also walk or bike the loop. This loop accesses several picnic areas, plus short trails to **Valley View Overlook** and the **Signal Hill Petroglyphs.**

RINCON MOUNTAIN DISTRICT (SAGUARO EAST)

The easiest way to see the eastern section of the park is to drive very slowly along the **Cactus Forest Loop Drive** (8 mi./13 km one-way, dawn to dusk daily, no oversize vehicles). The route begins at the visitors center and winds up across the bajada. The desert here is gorgeous, especially after a rainstorm or early in the morning during the wildflower bloom months. On the loop's east side, stop at two overlooks to see the **Sonoran Desert** and the **Cactus Forest.** Take a break to loop the wheelchair-accessible paved **Desert Ecology Trail** (0.25 mi./ 0.4 km, 15 min., easy) to learn about life in the desert. As the road climbs below the mountains, stop at the **Rincon Mountain Overlook** to take in the views.

RECREATION

HIKING

Both sections of Saguaro National Park offer superior desert hiking. In Saguaro West, the trail to **Valley View Overlook** (0.8 mi./1.3 km rt., 30 min., easy) offers a big payoff for little effort. A short drop into Bajada Wash leads to a gentle climb across a hillside with a few stone steps to the top, where you can rest on a bench to view saguaros and the Sonoran Desert spreading out across the Avra Valley.

In Saguaro East, the **Freeman Homestead Trail** (0.9 mi./1.4 km rt., 1 hr., easy) adds interpretive signs for kids on this route that loops past a homestead site, large saguaros, and a desert wash. The **Cactus Forest Trail** (2-2.5 mi./3.2-4 km

SAGUARO WITH VERTICAL ARMS

Best Hike

WASSON PEAK

DISTANCE: 8 miles round-trip (12.9 km)
DURATION: 3-4 hours
ELEVATION GAIN: 1,800 feet (549 m)
EFFORT: strenuous
TRAILHEAD: Kings Canyon Trailhead in Saguaro West

In Saguaro West, a strenuous but beautiful hike goes up 4,687-foot (1,428 m) **Wasson Peak**, the highest in the Tucson Mountains. Start by picking up the **King Canyon Trail** just across Kinney Road near the Arizona-Sonora Desert Museum. It's about 3.5 miles (5.6 km) to the top of the peak, hiking on switchbacks through typical bajada desert. Then, make a loop by heading down the **Hugh Norris Trail** to its junction with the **Sendero Esperanza Trail** and taking the **Gold Mine Trail** back to the car.

rt., 1 hr., easy) is a mostly flat trail that goes to two lime kilns. Start at the north or south trailhead to walk among the green-armed giants.

MOUNTAIN BIKING

In Saguaro West, the gravel **Bajada Loop** (6 mi./9.7 km) offers an opportunity to pedal through a forest thick with saguaros. The only downside is contending with copious dust kicked up from cars. In Saguaro East, mountain bikers can ride the **Cactus Forest Trail** (2.5 mi./4 km), a single-track, two-way path that bisects Cactus Forest Loop Drive.

WHERE TO STAY

There are no developed campgrounds within the park. Backcountry camping is permitted at six primitive campgrounds in the **Saguaro Wilderness Area of Saguaro East;** a permit ($8) is required. The closest developed campground is the **Gilbert Ray Campground** (8451 W. McCain Loop, off Kinney Rd., 520/883-4200, $10-20) in Tucson Mountain Park near Saguaro West. The city of **Tucson** is filled with plentiful accommodations, restaurants, and services.

GETTING THERE AND AROUND

AIR

Tucson International Airport (TUS, 7250 S. Tucson Blvd., 520/573-8100, www.flytucson.com) hosts eight airlines (including American, Delta, Southwest, and Alaska Airlines) flying to 18 destinations with daily nonstop flights throughout the United States.

CAR

To reach the park's **Saguaro West** from I-10, take Speedway Boulevard west to Kinney Road. Turn right and drive 4 miles (6.4 km). At the junction with Mile Wide Road, veer right to continue on Kinney Road. The Red Hills Visitor Center will appear in 1 mile (1.6 km).

To reach **Saguaro East** from I-10, exit the freeway east onto Houghton Road. Drive 8 miles (13 km) north to Escalante Road and turn right for 2 miles (3.2 km). At Old Spanish Trail, turn left to reach the park entrance road.

PUBLIC TRANSPORTATION

For public transportation to Tucson, **Greyhound** (801 E. 12th St. near Broadway and Euclid, 520/792-3475, www.greyhound.com) and **Amtrak** (400 N. Toole Ave., 800/872-7245, www.amtrak.com) both have stations downtown. Amtrak lines include Sunset Limited and Texas Eagle.

The city of Tucson operates **Sun Tran** (4220 S. Park Ave., 520/792-9222, www.suntran.com, 6am-7pm Mon.-Fri., 8am-5pm Sat.-Sun.) bus line with stops all over Tucson. But routes do not extend to the parks.

No public transportation is available from Tucson to the parks or inside the parks.

WEBSITE:
www.nps.gov/grba

PHONE NUMBER:
775/234-7331

VISITATION RANK:
53

WHY GO:
Explore ancient bristlecone pines and limestone caves.

▲ BRISTLECONE-PINE TRAIL

KEEPSAKE STAMPS ▼▼▼

Carved out of Humboldt National Forest, **GREAT BASIN NATIONAL PARK** drapes its mountainous slopes with groves of 4,000-year-old bristlecone pines, one of the oldest living organisms on the planet. Their longevity comes from their ability to survive an arid, harsh climate and poor soil. Underground, the quartzite limestone corridors of the Lehman Caves are even older, carved by water over millions of years.

You can drive on the highest road in Nevada to camp near 10,000 feet (3,048 m) on Wheeler Peak. With minimal light pollution, the dark skies ignite with brilliant stars, seen today just as they have been by the five indigenous tribes who have inhabited this land for centuries.

PLANNING YOUR TIME

Great Basin National Park straddles the Nevada-Utah state line near the end of US 50, "the Loneliest Road" in east-central Nevada. It's a remote park far from anywhere else. Many visitors treat the park as a day trip, viewing the caves and driving to the peak before continuing on their way elsewhere. Those who spend a few days here can acclimate for the hike to the 13,063-foot (3,981-m) summit of Wheeler Peak.

The park crowds with visitors on **summer** (June-Sept.) weekends, when the weather is mild, with highs of 85°F (29°C) and lows of 55°F (13°C). Mosquito season runs June-July. Make reservations for cave tours or risk being turned away. Fall and spring can be cool but pleasant, while winter brings snow to the mountain peaks.

BRISTLECONE PINE

ENTRANCE AND FEES

The entrance to the park is along NV 488 (Lehman Caves Rd.), which ends at the Lehman Caves Visitor Center. The park has no entrance station and no entrance fee.

VISITORS CENTERS

At **Lehman Caves Visitor Center** (5500 W. NV 488, 775/234-7510, 8am-5pm daily summer, 8am-4pm fall through spring), you can purchase same-day cave tour tickets, peruse exhibits, watch an orientation film, and pick up park information.

Located outside the park, the **Great Basin Visitor Center** (57 N. NV 487, Baker, 775/234-7520, 8am-5:30pm daily Apr.-Oct.) shows a film, and features exhibits on park flora, fauna, and cave formations.

SIGHTS

NIGHT SKY

Due to little light pollution, Great Basin has stunning night skies. In summer, evening **astronomy programs** (8:30pm Sat., free) include a ranger presentation at the visitors center followed by telescope-viewing of celestial objects. When the full moon brightens the sky,

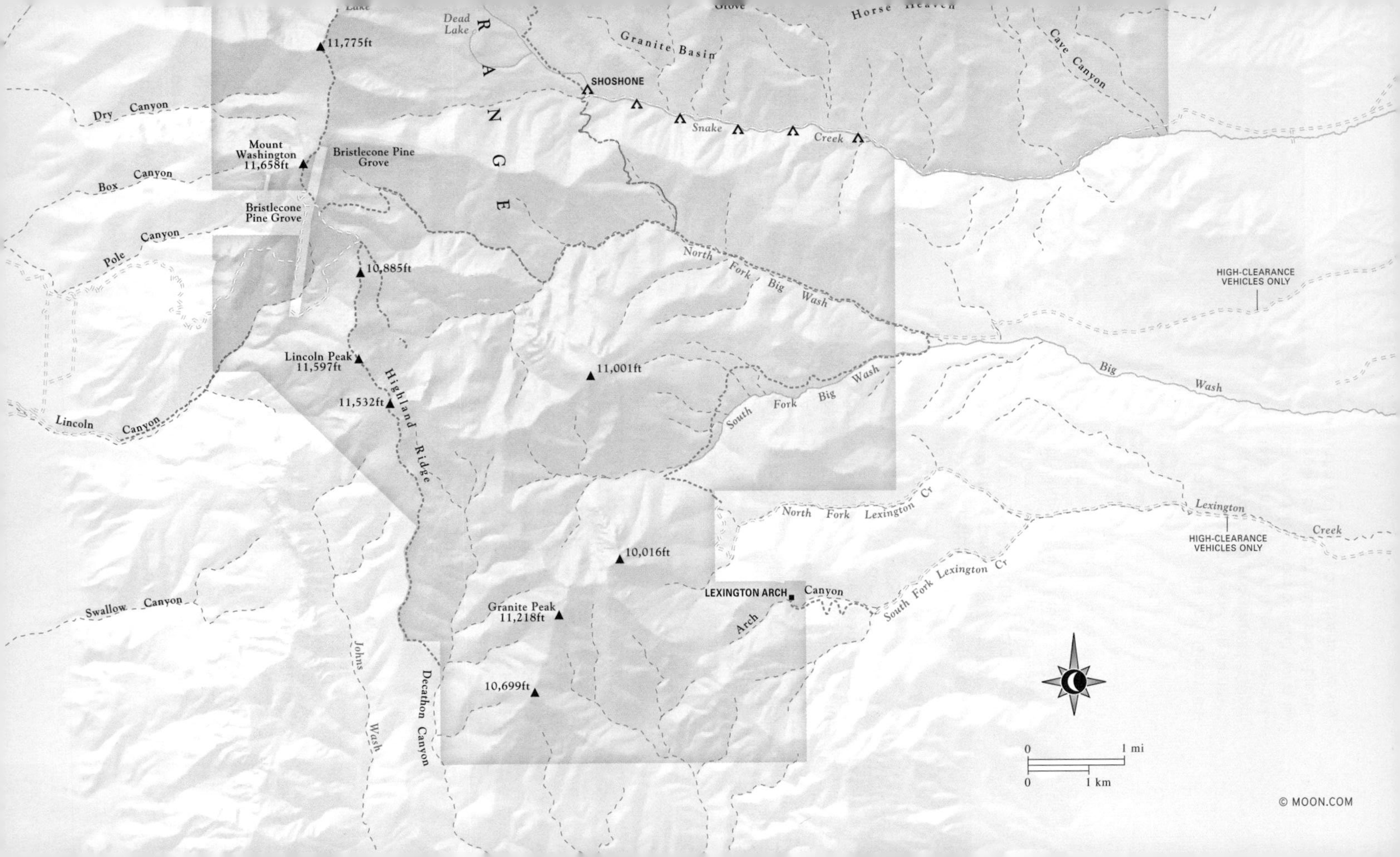

11,775ft
Dead Lake
R A N G E
Horse Heaven
Granite Basin
Cave Canyon
SHOSHONE
Snake Creek
Dry Canyon
Mount Washington 11,658ft
Bristlecone Pine Grove
Box Canyon
Bristlecone Pine Grove
Pole Canyon
10,885ft
North Fork Big Wash
HIGH-CLEARANCE VEHICLES ONLY
Lincoln Peak 11,597ft
11,532ft
Highland Ridge
11,001ft
Big Wash
South Fork Big Wash
Lincoln Canyon
North Fork Lexington Cr
Lexington Creek
HIGH-CLEARANCE VEHICLES ONLY
10,016ft
LEXINGTON ARCH
Canyon
Arch
South Fork Lexington Cr
Swallow Canyon
Granite Peak 11,218ft
Johns Wash
Decathon Canyon
10,699ft
0
1 mi
0
1 km

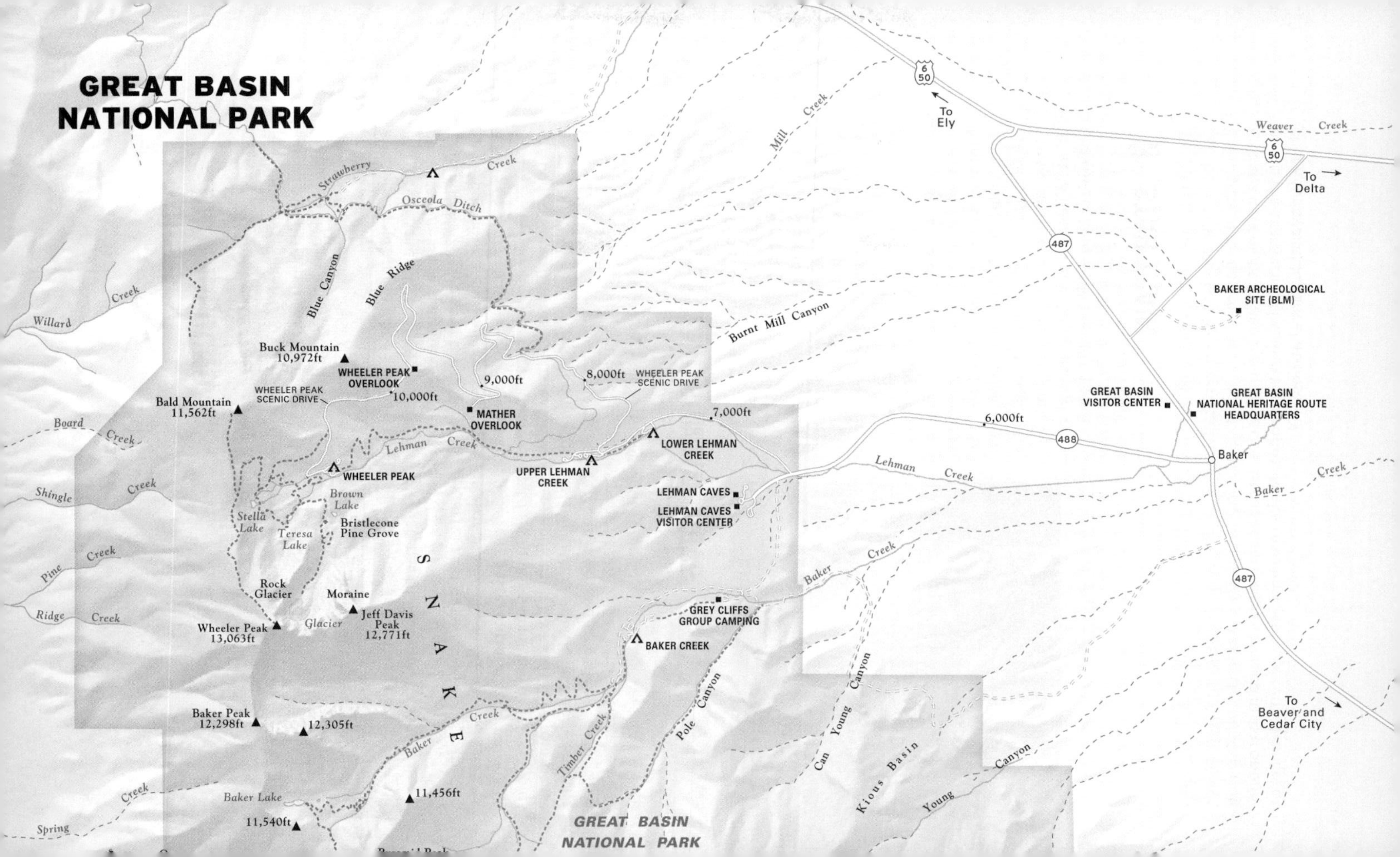
GREAT BASIN
NATIONAL PARK
Strawberry
Creek
Osceola Ditch
Blue Canyon
Blue Ridge
Willard
Creek
Buck Mountain
10,972ft
WHEELER PEAK
OVERLOOK
9,000ft
8,000ft
WHEELER PEAK
SCENIC DRIVE
10,000ft
Bald Mountain
11,562ft
MATHER
OVERLOOK
7,000ft
Board
Creek
Lehman
Creek
LOWER LEHMAN
CREEK
WHEELER PEAK
UPPER LEHMAN
CREEK
Shingle
Brown
Lake
Stella
Lake
Teresa
Lake
Bristlecone
Pine Grove
LEHMAN CAVES
LEHMAN CAVES
VISITOR CENTER
Pine
Rock
Glacier
Moraine
S
N
A
K
E
Ridge
Jeff Davis
Peak
12,771ft
Glacier
Wheeler Peak
13,063ft
GREY CLIFFS
GROUP CAMPING
BAKER CREEK
Baker Peak
12,298ft
12,305ft
Baker
Timber Creek
Pole Canyon
Can Young Canyon
Kious Basin
Young
Canyon
Baker Lake
11,456ft
11,540ft
Spring
GREAT BASIN
NATIONAL PARK
Mill
Burnt Mill Canyon
6
50
To
Ely
Weaver
To
Delta
487
BAKER ARCHEOLOGICAL
SITE (BLM)
GREAT BASIN
VISITOR CENTER
GREAT BASIN
NATIONAL HERITAGE ROUTE
HEADQUARTERS
6,000ft
488
Baker
To
Beaver and
Cedar City

Top 3

1 TOUR UNDERGROUND CAVES

LEHMAN CAVES

Five hundred million years ago, Nevada sat under a shallow sea, teeming with creatures like the ichthyosaur (now Nevada's official state fossil). Eons of pressure changes, incessant heating and cooling cycles, erosion, and calcification acted on that primordial seabed—pushing it into mountain ranges, changing sandstone into marble, and cutting deep gashes in the rock. The result, countless calcite dribbles later, is the **Lehman Caves,** with ornate stalagmites, stalactites, and "soda straws."

Rangers lead two **cave tours** (summer departing daily every two hours between 9am-3pm, spring and fall twice daily, winter once per day Fri.-Sun., adults $9-11, ages 5-15 and seniors $4.50-$6, kids under 5 free). **Reservations** (877/444-6777, www.recreation.gov) are recommended up to six months in advance. The 60-minute **Lodge Room Tour** is 0.4 mile (0.6 km) long and perfect for kids. The tour passes through three main cave rooms—the Gothic Palace, the Music Room, and the Lodge Room. The 90-minute **Grand Palace Tour** is limited to children older than five. The 0.6-mile (1-km) tour includes the Lodge Room Tour with additional access to the Grand Palace, which holds the Parachute Shield.

2 TAKE A SCENIC SUMMIT DRIVE

Wheeler Peak Scenic Drive (June-Oct., weather permitting, no vehicles or trailer combos over 24 ft./7.3 m permitted) switchbacks 12 miles (19 km) along Lehman Creek toward 13,063-feet (3,981-m) Wheeler Peak. This extraordinary drive curves at 8,500 feet (2,591 m) where Wheeler Peak comes into prime view. Stop at **Mather Overlook,** at 9,000 feet (2,743 m), where the views are even better. The road keeps climbing, with the peak ahead and the vast valley behind, until reaching the parking lot for the Summit Trail. The scenic drive ends 1 mile (1.6 km) later at Wheeler Peak Campground at a breath-sucking 9,886 feet (3,013 m).

WHEELER PEAK SCENIC DRIVE

3 STAR TRAIN

This International Dark Sky Park features a unique ranger-led experience. At sunset, board the **Nevada Northern Railway** (777/289-2085, https://nnry.com, select Fri. nights mid-May-mid-Sept., adults $42, kids $41) in Ely outside the park to ride into the dark night. When the train stops, Great Basin rangers trained in astronomy guide the stargazing through telescopes. Make reservations a year in advance, or check for available cancellations.

Best Hike

WHEELER PEAK SUMMIT

DISTANCE: 8.6 miles (13.8 km) round-trip
DURATION: 5-6 hours
ELEVATION CHANGE: 2,900 feet (853 m)
EFFORT: strenuous
TRAILHEAD: Wheeler Peak Trail Parking Area

Hardy hikers set their sights on Wheeler Peak, though its trails are usually snow-buried until mid-June. From the trailhead near Wheeler Peak Campground, the **Wheeler Peak Summit Trail** climbs to the top of the 13,063-foot (3,981-m) peak. Start by 7am to avoid getting caught in midafternoon thunderstorms, which are common and treacherous on the mountain. The route ascends gently through forest interrupted by periodic wildflower meadows. After 2 miles (3.2 km), it will steepen and exit the forest. Most of the route switchbacks up a windy, rock-strewn ridge that yields bigger and bigger views until taking in the full 360-degree panorama at the summit.

rangers guide **moonlight hikes** instead (free, tickets at visitors center). The park's sky programs culminate in a three-day **Astronomy Festival** (late Sept.).

HIKING

At the visitors center, the **Mountain View Nature Trail** (0.3 mi./0.5 km, 20 min., easy) is a gentle stroll that passes **Rhodes Cabin,** a historical exhibit. Pick up a trail guide at the visitors center to learn about flora and geology.

On **Wheeler Peak,** two trails at higher elevation, best June-September, depart near the campground. The **Bristlecone and Glacier Trail** (4.6 mi./7.4 km rt., 2-3 hr., strenuous) links an interpretive trail circling a sanctuary of bristlecone pines with Great Basin's only remnant glacier. Past the temple of the pines, the Glacier Trail becomes steep and rocky over the next mile. Soon you enter a cirque, a valley carved by the extant glacier at the head, bookended by sheer cliffs, with the summit of Wheeler Peak in full view. The **Alpine Lakes Loop Trail** (2.7 mi./4.3 km rt., 2 hrs., moderate) passes Teresa and Stella Lakes with easy grades and views of mighty peaks.

At the end of Baker Creek Road is the trailhead for the steep **Baker Lake and Johnson Lake Loop Trail** (13.1 mi./21.1 km rt., 7 hrs., strenuous). Reach scenic Baker Lake in 5 miles (8 km). Continuing to Johnson Lake requires a 1-mile (1.6-km) climb over the 10,800-foot (3,292-m) Johnson Pass below Pyramid Peak. Several points on the trail provide 360-degree vistas, including inspiring looks at Baker Peak and Wheeler Peak. Just before Johnson Lake are the remains of the Johnson Lake Mine, now reduced to a few cabin ruins, discarded mining equipment, and an aerial tramway.

TRAIL TO WHEELER PEAK

WHEELER PEAK ON THE SUMMIT TRAIL

WHERE TO STAY

INSIDE THE PARK

Great Basin has no lodging accommodations, but it does have five developed **campgrounds** ($15) with vault toilets, picnic tables, drinking water, and tent pads. Most sites are first come, first served; only one accepts reservations.

Three campgrounds are accessed via the paved Wheeler Peak Road with Lehman Creek options at lower elevations. Trailers and RVs favor **Lower Lehman Creek** (11 sites) for its easy year-round access while **Upper Lehman Creek Campground** (24 sites, May-Oct.) has better scenery. At 9,886 feet (3,013 m) is **Wheeler Peak Campground** (37 sites, May-Oct., vehicle length limited to 24 ft./7.3 m); due to the altitude, some people find difficulty sleeping and breathing here.

The gravel Baker Creek Road has two campgrounds: **Baker Creek Campground** (38 sites, May-Oct.) has loops along the creek while **Grey Cliffs Campground** (16 sites, May-early Sept.) has sites available by reservation (877/444-6777, www.recreation.gov, $15-30) six months in advance.

Primitive campsites with fire grates and picnic tables (no water) line the dirt **Snake Creek Road** (year-round, free). The sites are difficult to reach, muddy in spring, and snow-covered in winter.

Inside the visitors center, the **Great Basin Café and Gift Shop** (8am-5pm daily Apr.-Oct., shorter hours spring and fall) serves breakfast and lunch.

OUTSIDE THE PARK

The tiny town of **Baker,** 6 miles (9.7 km) from the park entrance, has a couple of accommodation and dining options. **Ely,** 67 miles (108 km) northwest, is the largest nearby town with more services.

GETTING THERE AND AROUND

AIR

The nearest major international airports are **Salt Lake City International Airport** (SLC, 776 N. Terminal Dr., 801/575-2400, www.slcairport.com), 235 miles (380 km) northeast in Salt Lake City, Utah, and **McCarran International Airport** (LAS, 5757 Wayne Newton Blvd., 702/261-5211, www.mccarran.com), 305 miles (490 km) south in Las Vegas, Nevada. Car rentals are available at both airports.

CAR

There is no public transportation into or within the park; a car is necessary. Access is via US 50, also known as "the Loneliest Road." From the junction of US 50, NV 487 heads south for 5 miles (8 km) to the town of Baker. At Baker, take NV 488 (Lehman Caves Rd.) west for 6 miles (9.7 km) into the park.

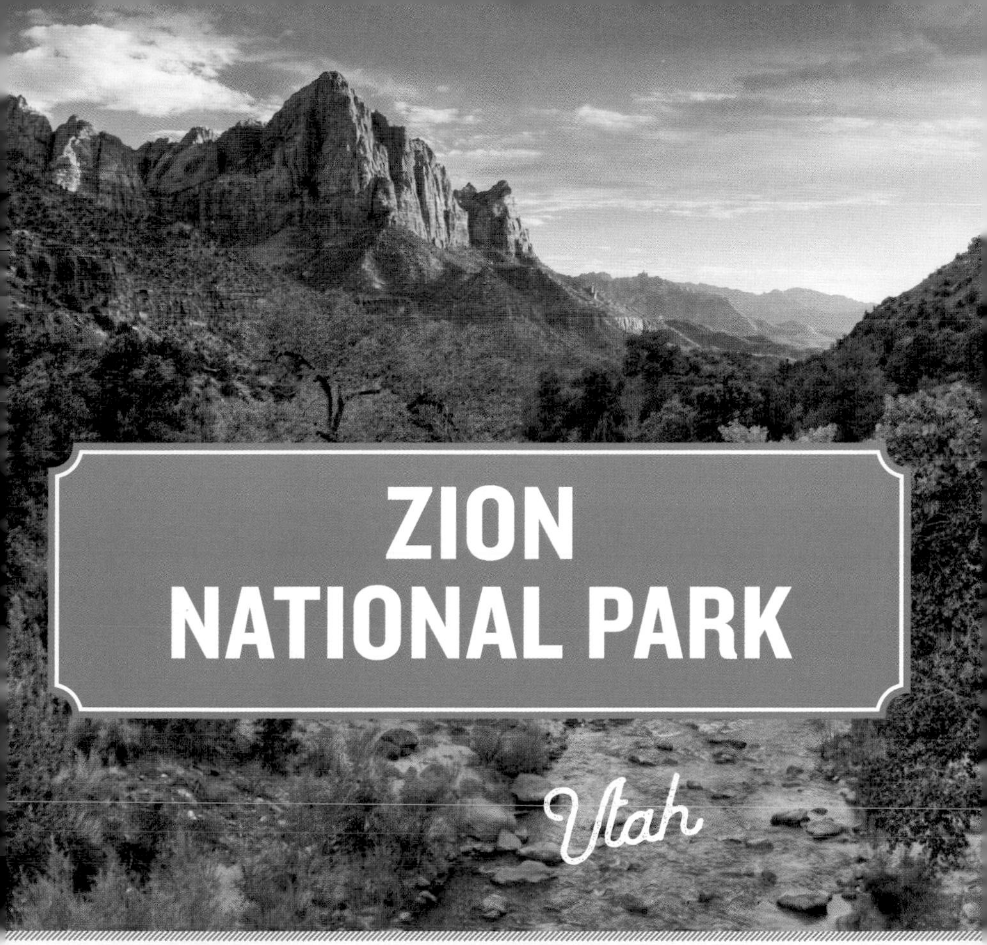

▲ VIRGIN RIVER, ZION NATIONAL PARK

ZION NATIONAL PARK

Utah

KEEPSAKE STAMPS ▼▼▼

WEBSITE:
www.nps.gov/zion

PHONE NUMBER:
435/772-3256

VISITATION RANK:
4

WHY GO:
Explore one of the West's most impressive canyons.

To Cedar City, and Salt Lake City
15
Camp Creek
Horse Ranch Mountain 8,726ft
Taylor Creek
Taylor Cr Trail
KOLOB CANYONS VISITOR CENTER
KOLOB CANYONS ROAD
LEE PASS TRAILHEAD
KOLOB CANYONS VIEWPOINT
Nagunt Mesa 7,785ft
Timber Creek Overlook Trail
KOLOB CANYONS
KOLOB ARCH
Bear Trap Canyon
La Verkin Creek Trail
Chasm Lake
Kolob Reservoir
Gregory Butte 7,705ft
La Verkin Creek Trail
Kolob Arch Trail
Langston Mountain 7,408ft
The Hardscrabble
Kolob Peak 8,933ft
UPPER KOLOB PLATEAU
La Verkin Creek
Hop Valley Trail
Hop Valley
Burnt Mountain 7,682ft
Blue Springs Reservoir
LAVA POINT RD
WEST TRAIL
LAVA POINT
LAVA POINT OVERLOOK
HURRICANE CLIFFS
LOWER KOLOB PLATEAU
KOLOB TERRACE ROAD
Firepit Knoll 7,265ft
Wildcat Canyon Trail
HOP VALLEY TRAILHEAD
Connector Trail
WILDCAT CANYON TRAILHEAD
Northgate Peaks Trail
SMITH MESA
Cave Valley
Lee Valley
VIEWPOINT
North Guardian Angel 7,395ft
Left Fork
Keyhole Falls
15
HURRICANE MESA
La Verkin Creek
Tabernacle Dome 6,430ft
South Guardian Angel 7,140ft
To St George and Las Vegas
LEFT FORK TRAILHEAD
Double Falls
GRAPEVINE TRAILHEAD
RIGHT FORK TRAILHEAD
Right Fork
ZION NATIONAL PARK
Toquerville
Creek
Cougar Mountain
17
North
KOLOB TERRACE ROAD
OILWELL (RUINS)
Altar of Sacrifice 7,505ft
The West Temple 7,810ft
La Verkin
9
Crater Hill 5,192ft
Virgin
9
Mount Kinesava 7,285ft
Virgin River
Hurricane
Chinle Trail
To St. George
COALPITS WASH
Grafton (ghost town)
Rockville
9
CHIN TRAIL
59
To Grand Canyon National Park
0
2 mi
0
2 km
GRAFTON RD
SMITHSONIAN BUTTE SCENIC BACKWAY
© MOON.COM

ZION NATIONAL PARK

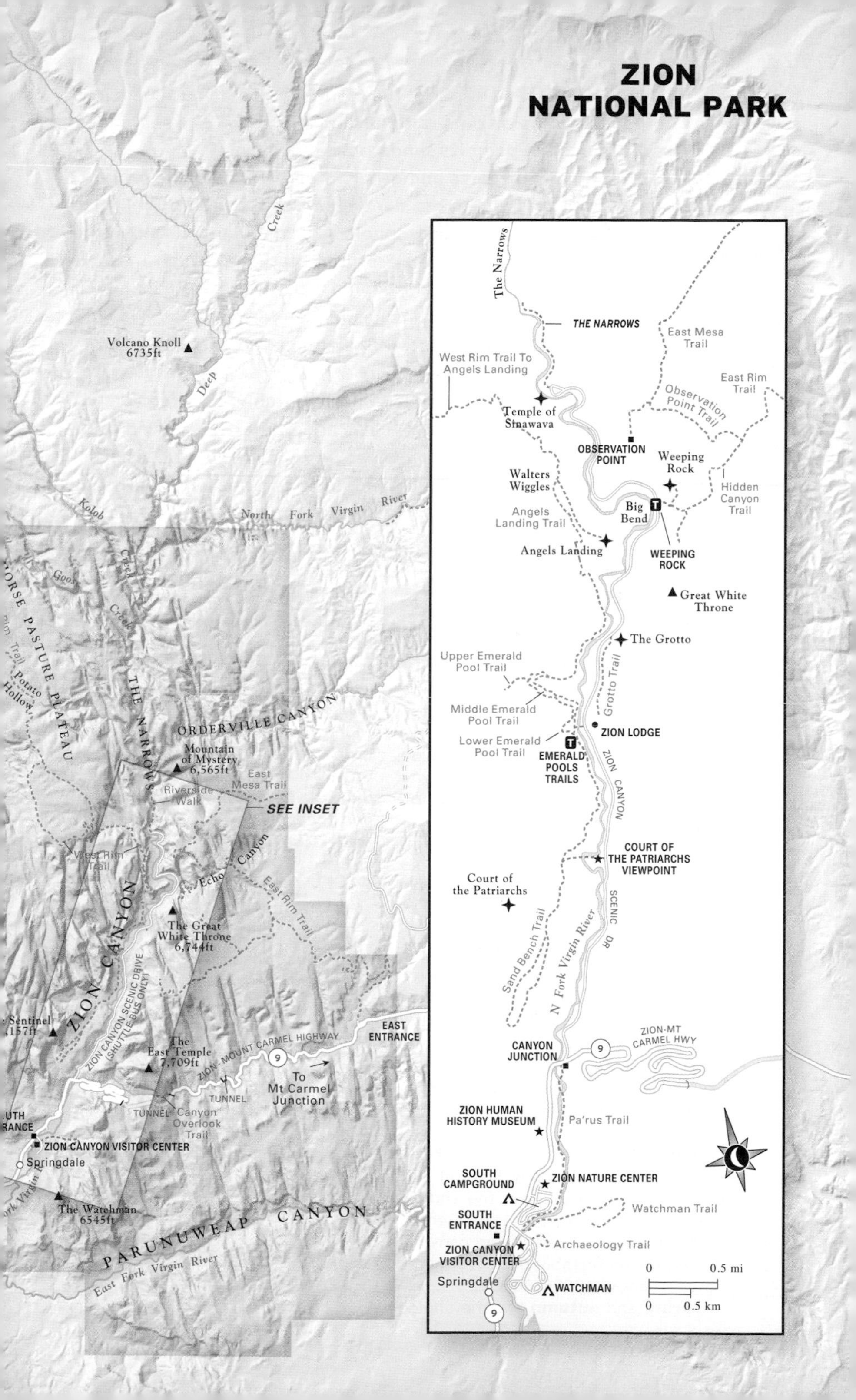

Volcano Knoll
6735ft
Deep
Creek
Kolob
North Fork Virgin River
HORSE PASTURE PLATEAU
Goose Creek
Potato Hollow
THE NARROWS
ORDERVILLE CANYON
Mountain of Mystery
6,565ft
East Mesa Trail
Riverside Walk
SEE INSET
West Rim Trail
Echo Canyon
East Rim Trail
The Great White Throne
6,744ft
ZION CANYON
ZION CANYON SCENIC DRIVE (SHUTTLE BUS ONLY)
Sentinel
The East Temple
7,709ft
ZION-MOUNT CARMEL HIGHWAY
9
EAST ENTRANCE
To Mt Carmel Junction
TUNNEL
Canyon Overlook Trail
ZION CANYON VISITOR CENTER
Springdale
The Watchman
6545ft
PARUNUWEAP CANYON
East Fork Virgin River
The Narrows
THE NARROWS
East Mesa Trail
West Rim Trail To Angels Landing
East Rim Trail
Observation Point Trail
Temple of Sinawava
OBSERVATION POINT
Weeping Rock
Walters Wiggles
Hidden Canyon Trail
Big Bend
Angels Landing Trail
Angels Landing
WEEPING ROCK
Great White Throne
The Grotto
Upper Emerald Pool Trail
Grotto Trail
Middle Emerald Pool Trail
ZION LODGE
Lower Emerald Pool Trail
EMERALD POOLS TRAILS
ZION CANYON
COURT OF THE PATRIARCHS VIEWPOINT
Court of the Patriarchs
Sand Bench Trail
N Fork Virgin River
SCENIC DR
ZION-MT CARMEL HWY
CANYON JUNCTION
ZION HUMAN HISTORY MUSEUM
Pa'rus Trail
SOUTH CAMPGROUND
ZION NATURE CENTER
Watchman Trail
SOUTH ENTRANCE
Archaeology Trail
ZION CANYON VISITOR CENTER
Springdale
WATCHMAN
0
0.5 mi
0
0.5 km

ZION NATIONAL PARK packs the wonders of the Southwest into a compact area. Color runs rampant: pale yellows, pinks, oranges, reds, and chocolate paint its sandstone landscape.

Here, energetic streams and other forces of erosion have created finely sculptured rock, from slender slot canyons through which you can barely squeeze to the monolith-flanked canyons along the Virgin River. Little trickles of water percolating through massive chunks of sandstone have left behind surprisingly rich habitats, where a variety of plants find niches in lush fern grottos. This has also been home to the Ancestral Puebloans, Fremont people, and more recently the Southern Paiute.

When you visit Zion, the first thing to catch your attention will be the sheer 2,000-foot (610-m) cliffs and great monoliths of Zion Canyon. After that, the park's intricacies will tickle your eyes: freestanding arches, the patterned sandstone of Checkerboard Mesa, and a petrified forest. It's a place that enchants.

PLANNING YOUR TIME

Zion National Park is in southwest Utah, 86 miles (138 km) southwest of Bryce Canyon National Park. Visitors usually drop in at the visitors center, travel the Zion Canyon Scenic Drive, and take short walks on the Riverside Walk Trail. A stay of 2-4 days lets you take in more of the grand scenery and hike other inviting trails.

Crowds come February-late November into Zion Canyon. If you can, avoid Easter weeks, Memorial and Labor Day weekends, and Utah schools break in October.

Many people check off Zion Canyon as "seeing the park." But as impressive as it is, Zion Canyon is only a small slice of this national park. Roads venturing into other sections—Kolob Canyons and Kolob Terrace Road to Lava Point—see far fewer people, have breathing room, and offer equally enchanting scenery.

Summer (May-Sept.) is the busiest season, with midday lines at the entrance to Zion Canyon, the shuttle stops, and Zion Canyon Visitor Center. Summer temperatures in the canyons can be uncomfortably hot, with highs hovering above 100°F (38°C).

Spring and **autumn** are the choice seasons for the most pleasant temperatures. They are also good for the best chances of seeing wildlife and wildflowers. Mid-October-early November, cottonwoods and other trees blaze with color.

In **winter,** nighttime temperatures drop to near freezing, and weather tends to be unpredictable. Snow may block some of the high-country trails and the road to Lava Point, and some trails close for safety from ice falls.

ENTRANCE AND FEES

Two entrances reach the Zion Canyon section of the park. From **Springdale,** enter the south end of Zion Canyon near the visitors center and the Zion Canyon shuttle bus stops. During high season, this entrance backs up with long lines; take the free shuttle from Springdale instead.

From the east, enter via the **Zion-Mount Carmel Highway,** passing through a long tunnel, and then popping into Zion Canyon a few miles north of the visitors center. Large RVs and bicycles must heed special regulations for the long tunnel.

The entrance fee is $35 per vehicle ($30 motorcycle, $20 individual) and valid for seven days.

Top 3

NIGHTFALL IN ZION CANYON

1 EXPLORE ZION CANYON

Zion Canyon Scenic Drive winds along the floor of the canyon, cut by the North Fork of the Virgin River. Both canyon walls rise with immense cliffs. The drive terminates at the Temple of Sinawava, where the wheelchair-accessible **Riverside Walk** (2.2 mi./3.5 km rt, 1.5 hrs., easy) follows the river to the Narrows. During spring-fall, a **shuttle bus** ferries visitors along this route to nine stops; you can drive it in winter. Hiking trails branch off to lofty viewpoints and narrow side canyons.

2 RIVER-HIKE THE NARROWS

Hike *inside* the Virgin River, below high, fluted walls. You'll be wading much of the time in knee- to chest-deep water. From shuttle stop 9 and the end of **Riverside Walk** (2.2 mi./3.5 km rt., 1 hr., easy), the shortest route follows the Narrows upstream to **Orderville Canyon** (3 mi./4.8 km, rt., 3-4 hrs., moderate, no permit needed), then back downstream. To hike the **entire Narrows** (16 mi./26 km one-way, strenuous, 12 hrs. to 2 days, permit required), consider going with a guide. Early summer and early fall are the best times to go. Savvy hikers rent canyoneering shoes, walking sticks, neoprene socks, dry bags, and dry suits for cool weather.

3 DRIVE ZION-MOUNT CARMEL HIGHWAY

Built in the late 1920s, the **Zion-Mount Carmel Highway** (UT 9, 10 mi./16 km one-way, 1-2 hrs. in summer traffic) features unique road engineering amid geological wonders. It's worth driving both directions between the East Entrance Station and Zion Canyon, but the westbound route yields a spectacular descent via two tunnels and six switchbacks into the canyon. On the eastern plateau, the road tours sandstone slickrock, hoodoos, the White Cliffs, and photo-worthy Checkerboard Mesa, a weathered mound riddled with vertical and horizontal fractures.

While the route is open 24/7, RVs can only access the long tunnel when traffic control rangers are present (8am-8pm daily May-Aug., shorter hours rest of the year, $15, pay at entrance station) closing down travel for one-way driving when necessary to allow RVs, buses, trailers, and some truck-campers to pass.

THE VIRGIN RIVER

ONE DAY IN ZION

Park your car at **Zion Canyon Visitor Center.** Enjoy the exhibits, then jump on the **free park shuttle** for a stroll on the **Riverside Walk** or **Weeping Rock.** Jump off the shuttle at Zion Lodge for lunch at the **Red Rock Grill.** Then take a longer hike: **Watchman Trail** for big views or the **Emerald Pools** for an easier stroll. **Springdale** is just a short walk or shuttle bus ride from the park entrance, and it has restaurants, shops, and galleries.

VISITORS CENTERS

Zion Canyon

Located between the Watchman and South Campgrounds, **Zion Canyon Visitor Center** (8am-6pm daily mid-Apr.-late May and Sept.-early Oct., 8am-7pm daily late May-Aug., 8am-5pm daily early Oct.-mid-Apr.) has information about trails, weather, shuttles, and ranger programs. The bookstore has an excellent selection of books and topographic and geologic maps. During summer, the visitors center entrance can have long waiting lines; go early or late for fewer crowds.

The **backcountry desk** (opens at 7am daily late Apr.-late Nov.) issues permits for backpacking and canyoneering. A backcountry shuttle board allows hikers to coordinate transportation between trailheads, and a list of authorized concessionaire shuttles is available to get to and from remote trailheads.

Kolob Canyons

The **Kolob Canyons Visitor Center** (8am-5pm daily mid-Mar.-mid-Oct., 8am-4:30pm daily mid-Oct.-mid-Mar.) has information on exploring the Kolob region. Hikers can learn current trail conditions and obtain the permits required for overnight trips and Zion Narrows day trips. The visitors center is just off I-15 (exit 40) at the start of Kolob Canyons Road.

SIGHTS

ZION NATURE CENTER

Zion Nature Center (shuttle stop 2, 1pm-6pm Sun.-Fri., 10am-6pm Sat. late May-mid-Aug.) houses natural history programs for kids, including Junior Ranger activities for ages 6-12. It's at the northern end of South Campground, an easy walk along the Pa'rus Trail from the Zion Canyon Visitor Center or the Human History Museum.

ZION HUMAN HISTORY MUSEUM

The **Zion Human History Museum** (shuttle stop 2, 10am-6pm daily mid-Apr.-late May, 9am-6pm daily late May-early Oct., 10am-5pm early Oct.-mid.-Apr.) focuses on southern Utah's cultural history, with a film introducing the park plus exhibits on Native American and Mormon history. It's the first shuttle stop after the visitors center.

COURT OF THE PATRIARCHS

The **Three Patriarchs** (shuttle stop 4), a trio of peaks to the west, overlook

KOLOB CANYONS

Birch Creek. They are known as (from left to right) Abraham, Isaac, and Jacob. Mount Moroni, the reddish peak on the far right, partly blocks the view of Jacob.

NORTH FORK OF THE VIRGIN RIVER

The North Fork of the **Virgin River** cuts through Zion Canyon. You'll see it from shuttle stops and trails. For strolls along the river, the paved wheelchair-accessible **Pa'rus Trail** (3.5 mi./5.6 km rt., 2 hrs., easy, shuttle stops 1, 2 & 3) runs from the visitors center and South Campground to the museum and Canyon Junction, crossing the Virgin River several times. It is also open to bicycles and pets.

WEEPING ROCK

Weeping Rock (shuttle stop 7) is home to hanging gardens and many moisture-loving plants, including the striking Zion shooting star. The rock "weeps" because this is a junction between porous Navajo sandstone and denser Kayenta shale. Water trickles down through the sandstone and, when it can't penetrate the shale, moves laterally to the face of the cliff. The paved but steep **Weeping Rock Trail** (0.4 mi./0.6 km rt., 20 min., easy) climbs to this dripping alcove. Rockfall in 2019 closed this trail; check on status.

BIG BEND

Big Bend (shuttle stop 8) is where you'll see rock climbers on the towering walls. Pull out your binoculars to watch their moves on the face of the vertical walls.

TEMPLE OF SINAWAVA

The last shuttle stop is at the **Temple of Sinawava** (shuttle stop 9), where 2,000-foot-tall (610-m) rock walls stretch skyward from the Virgin River. The paved interpretive **Riverside Trail** (2.2 mi./3.5 km rt., 1 hr., easy) winds upstream along the river to the Virgin River Narrows with the first half of the trail wheelchair-accessible. From the Virgin Narrows, a place where the canyon becomes too narrow for even a sidewalk to squeeze alongside, hikers wade up the **Narrows.**

SCENIC DRIVES

KOLOB CANYONS ROAD

Kolob Canyons Road (I-15, exit 40, 5 mi./8 km) is in the northwestern corner of the park. From the Kolob Canyons Visitor Center, the paved scenic drive winds past the dramatic Finger Canyons of the Kolob to the terminus

ZION-MT. CARMEL HIGHWAY

at Kolob Canyons Viewpoint. The road has many pullouts where you can stop to admire the scenery as it climbs in elevation. The first part of the drive follows the 200-mile-long (320-km) Hurricane Fault that forms the west edge of the Markagunt Plateau. Look for the tilted rock layers deformed by friction as the plateau rose nearly 1 mile (1.6 km). After crossing Lee Pass, the road ends at a climb to the 6,369-foot (1,949-m) **Timber Creek Overlook** (1 mi./1.6 km rt., moderate), where views take in the Pine Valley Mountains, Zion Canyon, and distant Mount Trumbull.

KOLOB TERRACE ROAD

From the town of Virgin on UT 9, the paved **Kolob Terrace Road** (23 mi./37 km, early June-early Nov.) accesses a high plateau roughly parallel to and west of Zion Canyon. The steep road runs north through ranchland and up a narrow tongue of land, with drop-offs on either side. After reaching a high plateau, the land widens. The Hurricane Cliffs rise from the gorge to the west, and the back side of Zion Canyon's big walls are to the east.

At Lava Point Road, turn right and follow the dirt road 1.8 miles (3 km) east through aspen, ponderosa pine, Gambel oak, and white fir to reach 7,900-foot (2,408-m) **Lava Point** and its tiny, primitive campground. A panorama takes in the Cedar Breaks area, Pink Cliffs, Zion Canyon Narrows and tributaries, the monoliths of Zion Canyon, and Mount Trumbull on the Arizona Strip to the south. Lava Point is a good place to cool off in summer—temperatures are about 20°F (12°C) cooler than in Zion Canyon. Expect the trip from Virgin to Lava Point to take about one hour.

HIKING

ZION CANYON

Watchman Trail

SHUTTLE STOP: Zion Canyon Visitor Center

From a trailhead north of Watchman Campground, the **Watchman Trail** (3.3 mi./5.3 km rt., 2 hrs., easy) climbs to a bench below Watchman Peak, where views encompass lower Zion Canyon and the town of Springdale.

Sandbench Trail

SHUTTLE STOPS: Court of the Patriarchs and Zion Lodge

The **Sandbench Trail** (7.6 mi./12.2 km rt., 4 hrs., moderate) has good views of the Three Patriarchs, the Streaked Wall, and other monuments of lower Zion Canyon. You'll most likely meet horses on this trail (Mar.-Oct.).

Emerald Pools Trails

SHUTTLE STOP: Zion Lodge

Spring-fed pools, small waterfalls, and views of Zion Canyon make this climb to the **Emerald Pools** (1-3 hrs., easy-moderate) worthwhile, but don't expect solitude on these popular trails. From the footbridge at Zion Lodge, three trails diverge. Turn right for the paved, wheelchair-accessible trail to the **Lower Pool** (1.2 mi./1.9 km rt.), a recessed alcove with hanging gardens and misty falls. Turn left at the footbridge to go to the pair of **Middle Pools** (1.8 mi./2.9 km rt.) at the base of small waterfalls. A trail also connects Lower Pool and Middle Pools to link the two routes. From Middle Pool, a steep up-and-back 0.4-mile (0.6 km) spur trail leads to **Upper Emerald Pool** (2.6 mi./4.2 km rt.), a magical spot with a white-sand beach below towering cliffs.

Observation Point Trail

SHUTTLE STOP: Weeping Rock

This highly scenic trail climbs 2,148 feet (655 m) to **Observation Point** (8 mi./12.9 km rt., 4-6 hrs., strenuous) on the edge of Zion Canyon. Switchbacks begins a short way up from the trailhead to eventually enter sinuous Echo Canyon. At the halfway point, turn left onto the **East Rim Trail** to climb slickrock slopes above Echo Canyon on a path cut right into the cliffs in the 1930s by the Civilian Conservation Corps. At the rim, an easy jaunt through a forest of piñon pine, juniper, Gambel oak, manzanita, sage, and ponderosa pine goes to Observation Point. Surrounded by mountains and mesas, you'll peer down into Zion Canyon. Check on trail status: rockfall closed the trail in 2019, but the park

TEMPLE OF SINAWAVA

plans to stabilize the slopes and reopen the trail.

Hidden Canyon

SHUTTLE STOP: Weeping Rock

Inside narrow **Hidden Canyon** (5 mi./8 km rt., 3-4 hrs., strenuous), high walls block sunlight except for a short time at midday. At the signed junction about 20 minutes up the trail, turn right to traverse to the canyon entrance, where heavy rains and spring runoff form a small waterfall. Inside the 1-mile-long (1.6-km) canyon, the fun begins: walking on loose sand, using chains for handholds, and stepping in rock footholds to bypass deep pools. About halfway, look for the arch on the right. Check on trail status: rockfall closed the trail in 2019, but the park plans to stabilize the slopes and reopen the trail.

ZION-MOUNT CARMEL HIGHWAY

From the small parking lot east of the tunnel, the **Canyon Overlook Trail** (1 mi./1.6 km rt., 1 hr., moderate) has great views from the heights without the stiff climbs found on most other Zion trails. The trail winds in and out along the ledges (some fenced) of Pine Creek Canyon. Panoramas at trail's end take in lower Zion Canyon, Bridge Mountain, Streaked Wall, and East Temple. The immense Great Arch of Zion—termed a blind arch because it's open on only one side—lies below.

KOLOB CANYONS ROAD

You're likely to have the trails to yourself in this quiet section of the park. Access these hikes from the Kolob Canyons Road, which begins off I-15 (exit 40).

Starting 2 miles (3.2 km) east from the Kolob Canyons Visitor Center, **Taylor Creek Trail** (5 mi./8 km rt., 2.5-4 hrs., moderate) heads upstream into the canyon of the Middle Fork of Taylor Creek to Double Arch Alcove and a dry fall that blocks the way (water flows over it during spring runoff and after rains).

The 287-foot (87-m) span on **Kolob Arch** makes it one of the world's largest arches. From Lee Pass, **La Verkin Creek Trail** (14 mi./22.5 km rt., 7-8 hrs., strenuous) drops into Timber Creek, then pops over hills to the year-round La Verkin before turning up side canyons to the arch. The return climb back to the trailhead can be hot and tiring.

KOLOB TERRACE ROAD

From the Lava Point Trailhead, the **West Rim Trail** (June-early Nov.) offers two hiking options. You can walk the trail as an out-and-back trek into **Potato Hollow** (13 mi./21 km rt., 6-7 hrs., strenuous) to overlook Wildcat Canyon. Or hike the trail one-way (13.3 mi./21.4 km, 6-8 hrs., strenuous) beyond Potato Hollow southeast into Zion Canyon. Many hikers do this as a point-to-point hike by setting up a shuttle (contact the visitors center backcountry desk). While the total route drops 3,600 feet (1,097 m) in elevation, two-thirds of that plunges in a knee-pounding descent in the last 4.7 miles (7.6 km) to the Grotto.

RECREATION

BACKPACKING

For two-day backpacking trips, **Kolob Arch** (14 mi./22.5 km) makes a great destination. The **West Rim Trail** offers a point-to-point (13 mi./21 km) trip from Lava Point Trailhead to Zion Canyon.

The Narrows

Hands down, the best two-day trip is on the **Narrows** (16 mi./26 km). The "top down" route starts at Chamberlain's Ranch and hikes downstream to the Riverside Walk. Only one-night stays are allowed. No camping is permitted below Big Springs. Opt to go when water levels are lowest and weather has fewer thunderstorms causing flash flooding (May-June, Sept.-Oct.).

▼ SUNSET OVER THE WATCHMAN

THE EAST RIM TRAIL

For hiking the Narrows, the following Springdale outfitters rent specially designed river-hiking boots, neoprene socks, walking sticks, and dry suits. They also lead tours and provide shuttle service to Chamberlain's Ranch.

Zion Adventure Company (36 Lion Blvd., Springdale, 435/772-1001, www.zionadventures.com)

Zion Outfitter (7 Zion Park Blvd., Springdale, 435/772-5090, www.zionoutfitter.com)

Zion Guru (795 Zion Park Blvd., Springdale, 435/632-0432, www.zionguru.com)

Zion Rock and Mountain Guides (1458 Zion Park Blvd., Springdale, 435/772-3303, www.zionrockguides.com)

Permits

Overnight hikers must obtain **backcountry permits** (https://zionpermits.nps.gov, $15-25, $5 reservation fee) in person one day in advance from the visitors center or by reservation online three months in advance. Competition for Narrows' permits is cutthroat: apply for a reservation at 10am Mountain Time on the fifth day of the month when permits release. To nab a remaining permit in person, be in line before the backcountry office opens at 7am the day before your hike. For backcountry trailheads outside Zion Canyon, shuttles are available from **Zion Rock and Mountain Guides** (435/772-3303, www.zionrockguides.com) and **Zion Adventure Company** (435/772-1001, www.zionadventures.com).

BIKING

Between the park entrance and Canyon Junction, the paved **Pa'rus Trail** is open to cyclists for easy family pedaling. Bike parking is plentiful at the visitors center, Zion Lodge, and most trailheads. Outside the Zion Canyon area, **Kolob Terrace Road** is a good place

ECHO CANYON

Best Hike

WEST RIM TRAIL TO ANGELS LANDING

DISTANCE: 5.4 miles (8.7 km) round-trip
DURATION: 4-5 hours
ELEVATION CHANGE: 1,488 feet (453 m)
EFFORT: strenuous
TRAILHEAD: The Grotto

Not for acrophobes, the trail up to Angels Landing tiptoes along a narrow rib with cliff drop-offs on both sides. But for those up for the challenge, it's a hike full of entertainment with huge rewards. The finale puts you on a high-elevation point in the middle of Zion Canyon with 360-degree views, including the Great White Throne and the Organ. Some days, hundreds of people hike this trail; you may have to wait in places for people to pass or descend pitches where there's only room for one hiker.

After crossing the bridge over the North Fork of the Virgin River, the route heads north along 2 miles (3.2 km) of pavement on the West Rim Trail. As the hot trail ascends the narrow Refrigerator Canyon between Angels Landing and Cathedral Mountain, the air cools a bit. Then, Walter's Wiggles, a feat of trail engineering, zigzags for 21 short switchbacks up to Scout Lookout. From the lookout saddle, turn off the West Rim Trail toward Angels Landing to climb a 0.5 mile (0.8 km) along the top of the rib. Along steeper pitches and narrow stairsteps, chains bolted into the rock serve as handholds. The rib plunges vertically off both sides, leading to the last skinny ramps to the summit.

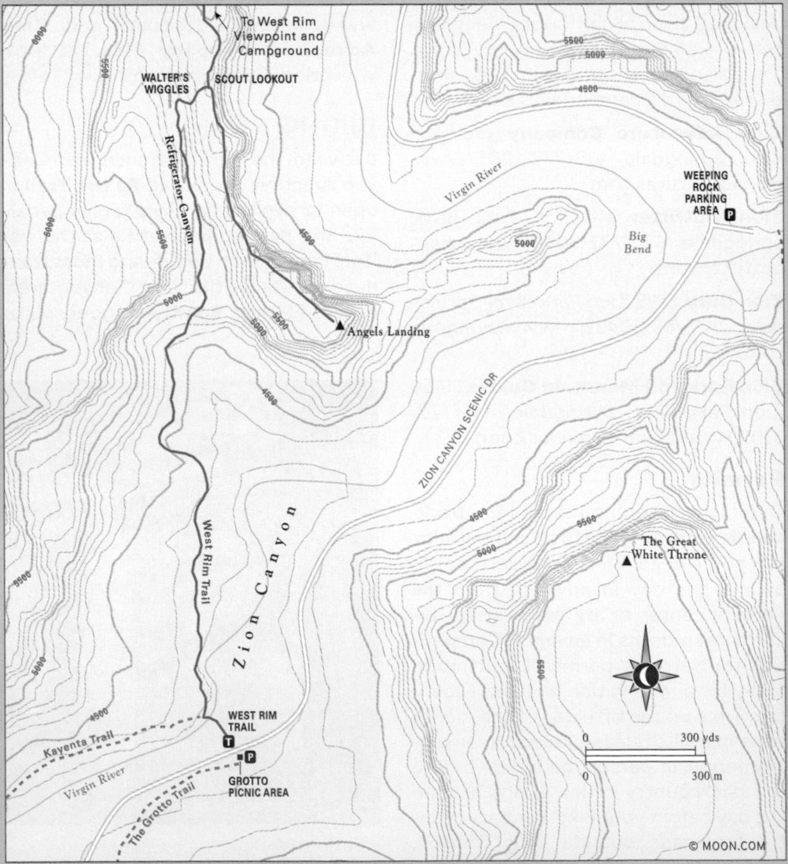

ANGELS LANDING

for cyclists to pound down the miles to Kolob Reservoir (44 mi./71 km rt.). Bike rentals and maps are available in Springdale at **Zion Outfitter** (7 Zion Park Blvd., 435/772-5090, www.zion-outfitter.com).

HORSEBACK RIDING

Trail rides on horses and mules leave from the corral near **Zion Lodge** (435/679-8665, www.canyonrides.com, mid-Mar.-Oct., $45-$95) and head down the Virgin River. A one-hour trip goes to the Court of the Patriarchs, and a half-day ride follows the Sandbench Trail.

THE WEST RIM TRAIL

WHERE TO STAY

INSIDE THE PARK

Zion Lodge

Within the park, lodging is limited to Zion Lodge and the three park campgrounds. Rustic **Zion Lodge** (shuttle stop 5, 888/297-2757, www.zionlodge.com, year-round, from $225) has accommodations in hotel rooms near the main lodge or in cute cabins (gas fireplaces but no TV). Reservations can be made up to 13 months in advance, and they book fast for April-October.

The lodge's **Red Rock Grill** (435/772-7760, 6:30am-10:30am, 11:30am-3pm, and 5pm-10pm daily, dinner reservations required) offers a southwestern and Mexican-influenced menu for breakfast, lunch, and dinner. The **Castle Dome Café** serves decent fast food, including salads and coffee.

Camping

Two campgrounds lie inside the south entrance to Zion Canyon. **Watchman Campground** (877/444-6777, www.recreation.gov, year-round, 176 sites, $20-30) has some sites with electrical hookups and takes reservations six months in advance. **South Campground** (Mar.-Nov., 117 sites, $20-$50) is first-come, first-served. Both campgrounds have drinking water, but no showers, and they fill on major holidays and in summer. Plan to arrive by 8am to score a spot. Campers have access, via the park's free shuttles, to restaurants and showers in Springdale.

Up Kolob Terrace Road, primitive **Lava Point Campground** (May-Sept., free) has six first-come, first-served sites with pit toilets, but no drinking water. The campground is a 80-minute drive from Zion Canyon.

OUTSIDE THE PARK

Near the park's south entrance are several small towns with good services for travelers. **Springdale** has the widest range of services, including excellent lodgings and restaurants; **Rockville** has a few B&Bs; and **Hurricane** is a hub for less expensive chain motels. **St. George** offers many places to stay and eat.

GETTING THERE

AIR

McCarran International Airport (LAS, 5757 Wayne Newton Blvd., 702/261-5211, www.mccarran.com) in Las Vegas, Nevada, is the closest airport at 170 miles (275 km) from the park. Major domestic airlines and smaller or "no-frills" carriers serve McCarran. **Salt Lake City International Airport** (SLC, 776 N. Terminal Dr., 801/575-2400, www.slcairport.com), better for travelers who want to make a road-trip loop through all of Utah's parks, is more than 300 miles (485 km) north of Zion. Both airports have car rentals.

CAR

To get to the south entrance of Zion National Park from Las Vegas, drive 119 miles (192 km) northeast on I-15 to St. George and turn east on UT 9 for 42 miles (68 km), a two-hour route. From Salt Lake City, take I-15 south, UT 17 southeast, and UT 9 east for 300 miles (485 km); the driving time is about four hours.

For Kolob Canyons entrance and Kolob Canyons Road, take I-15 to exit 40. For the Kolob Terrace Road, take UT 9 to Virgin and turn north.

For driving from Bryce Canyon National Park, take US 89 south and UT 9 west on the Zion-Mount Carmel Highway to the east entrance.

▼ KOLOB ARCH

WATERFALLS NEAR KOLOB ARCH

GETTING AROUND

DRIVING

Zion Canyon Scenic Drive is only open to private vehicles mid-November-early February, excluding December holidays. The road may close when parking spots fill.

February-mid-November, Zion Canyon Scenic Drive is closed to private vehicles and access is via shuttle bus. In summer, visitors park at Zion Canyon Visitor Center, where the small lot usually fills by 8am. To avoid congestion, park in Springdale and take the free shuttle into the park.

The Kolob Canyons area in the park's northwest corner has its own entrance. Reach this area via **Kolob Canyons Road,** which begins just off I-15 at exit 40.

To visit a less traveled part of the park, take UT 9 north to the tiny town of Virgin on the **Kolob Terrace Road.** The road goes to backcountry sites and Lava Point, but has no entrance station or visitors center.

SHUTTLE BUS

Two separate **free shuttles** (daily: 7am-7:45pm Mar.-late May, 6am-8:30pm late May-late Sept., 7am-6:45pm late Sept.-Oct., 7am-6pm early Nov., additional service Feb. weekends and Dec. holidays) run throughout Zion. The **Springdale buses** stop at nine locations outside the park in Springdale and go to the pedestrian entrance station

CANYONEERS SCALE ZION'S WALLS AND CLIFFS.

near Zion Canyon Visitor Center. The **Zion Canyon shuttle buses** stop at nine locations inside the park including scenic overlooks, trailheads, and Zion Lodge. You can transfer between the two shuttle systems at Zion Canyon Visitor Center. The buses, which run every 7-10 minutes, are wheelchair-accessible; pets are not allowed.

Mid-November-February, excluding December holidays, the buses are out of service, and private vehicles are allowed into Zion Canyon.

ZION-MOUNT CARMEL TUNNEL

On Zion-Mount Carmel Highway, most RVs (including buses, trailers, fifth wheels, and some truck-campers) will require oncoming traffic to be stopped to allow one-way travel through the 1-mile-long (1.6-km) tunnel. Drivers must time their trips for when traffic control rangers are present (8am-8pm daily May-early Sept., shorter hours rest of the year).

RVs are measured at the entrance station where, if you are within the vehicle limits, a **permit** ($15) will be issued for travel through the tunnel while rangers manage one-way traffic for your passage. The fee is good for two trips through the tunnel within seven days. Height, width, and length restrictions will ban access for the largest RVs, forcing alternate routes into the park. Bicycles and pedestrians are not allowed in the tunnel.

TOURS

The **Zion Canyon Field Institute** (435/772-3264, www.zionpark.org) runs educational programs ranging from animal tracking to photography to archaeology.

THE NARROWS

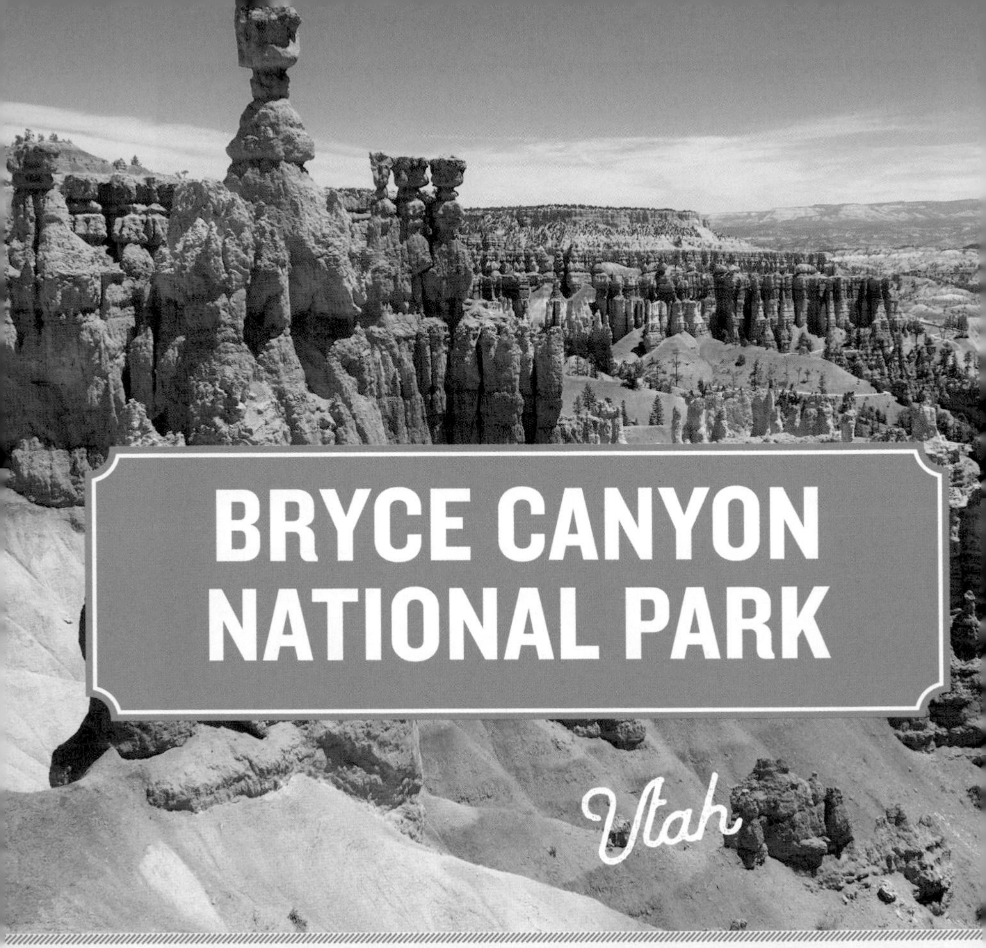

WEBSITE:
www.nps.gov/brca

PHONE NUMBER:
435/834-5322

VISITATION RANK:
12

WHY GO:
Spy sculpted hoodoos and colorful hues.

▲ BRYCE CANYON NATIONAL PARK

KEEPSAKE STAMPS ▼▼▼

In **BRYCE CANYON NATIONAL PARK**, a geologic fairyland of spires rises below the high cliffs of the Paunsaugunt Plateau. In a series of massive amphitheaters, this intricate maze, eroded from a soft limestone, glows with warm shades of reds, oranges, pinks, yellows, and creams. The rocks provide a continuous show of changing color throughout the day as the sun's rays and cloud shadows move across the landscape. The hoodoos seem to form shapes; the Paiute, who came through on seasonal hunting or gathering expeditions, attributed them to the Legend People transformed by Coyote into rocks. Today's visitors see the natural rock sculptures as Gothic castles, Egyptian temples, subterranean worlds inhabited by dragons, or the vast armies of a lost empire.

You can gaze at the sculpted hoodoos from viewpoints and trails on the plateau rim. But a whole different world awaits you when you hike down the steep trails among the magical spires.

PLANNING YOUR TIME

Bryce Canyon is in southern Utah, between Zion National Park and Grand Staircase-Escalante National Monument. Allow a full day to tour the park, stopping at visitors centers, cruising the scenic drive, and taking a few short walks. Sunsets and sunrises reward overnight visitors, while moonlit nights reveal yet another spectacle. Those staying at least three days can hike into the amphitheaters on longer trails.

September-October are choice hiking months—the weather is at its best and the crowds are at their smallest, although nighttime temperatures in late October can dip well below freezing. The park's elevation ranges 6,600-9,100 feet (2,012-2,773 m), so it's usually much cooler here than at Utah's other national parks. Expect pleasantly warm days in summer, frosty nights in spring and autumn, and snow at almost any time of year. The visitors center, scenic drive, and a campground stay open year-round, but snow can close some trails and the Scenic Drive at 3 miles (4.8 km) past the visitors center. The busy season is **April-October;** make advance reservations for lodging and camping.

ENTRANCE AND FEES

The entrance fee is $35 per vehicle ($30 motorcycle, $20 individual) and good

▼ THE SNOW-COVERED AMPHITHEATER

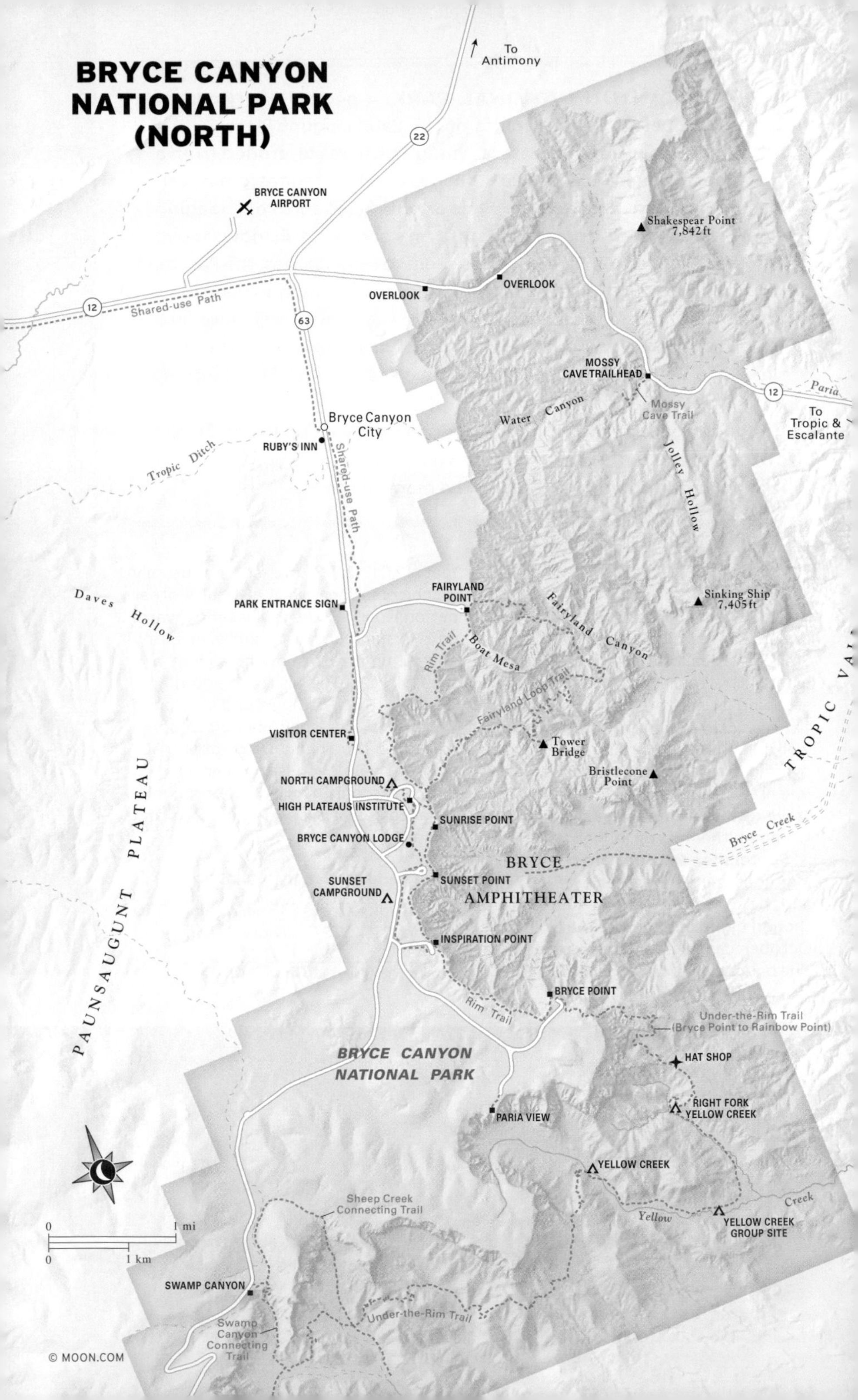
BRYCE CANYON NATIONAL PARK (NORTH)
To Antimony
22
BRYCE CANYON AIRPORT
Shakespear Point 7,842 ft
OVERLOOK
OVERLOOK
12
Shared-use Path
63
MOSSY CAVE TRAILHEAD
Mossy Cave Trail
Paria
12
To Tropic & Escalante
Water Canyon
Jolley Hollow
Bryce Canyon City
RUBY'S INN
Tropic Ditch
Shared-use Path
Daves Hollow
FAIRYLAND POINT
PARK ENTRANCE SIGN
Sinking Ship 7,405 ft
Fairyland Canyon
Rim Trail
Boat Mesa
Fairyland Loop Trail
TROPIC VA
VISITOR CENTER
Tower Bridge
Bristlecone Point
NORTH CAMPGROUND
HIGH PLATEAUS INSTITUTE
SUNRISE POINT
BRYCE CANYON LODGE
Bryce Creek
BRYCE AMPHITHEATER
SUNSET POINT
SUNSET CAMPGROUND
PAUNSAUGUNT PLATEAU
INSPIRATION POINT
BRYCE POINT
Rim Trail
Under-the-Rim Trail (Bryce Point to Rainbow Point)
HAT SHOP
BRYCE CANYON NATIONAL PARK
RIGHT FORK YELLOW CREEK
PARIA VIEW
YELLOW CREEK
Sheep Creek Connecting Trail
Yellow Creek
YELLOW CREEK GROUP SITE
0 1 mi
0 1 km
SWAMP CANYON
Under-the-Rim Trail
Swamp Canyon Connecting Trail
© MOON.COM

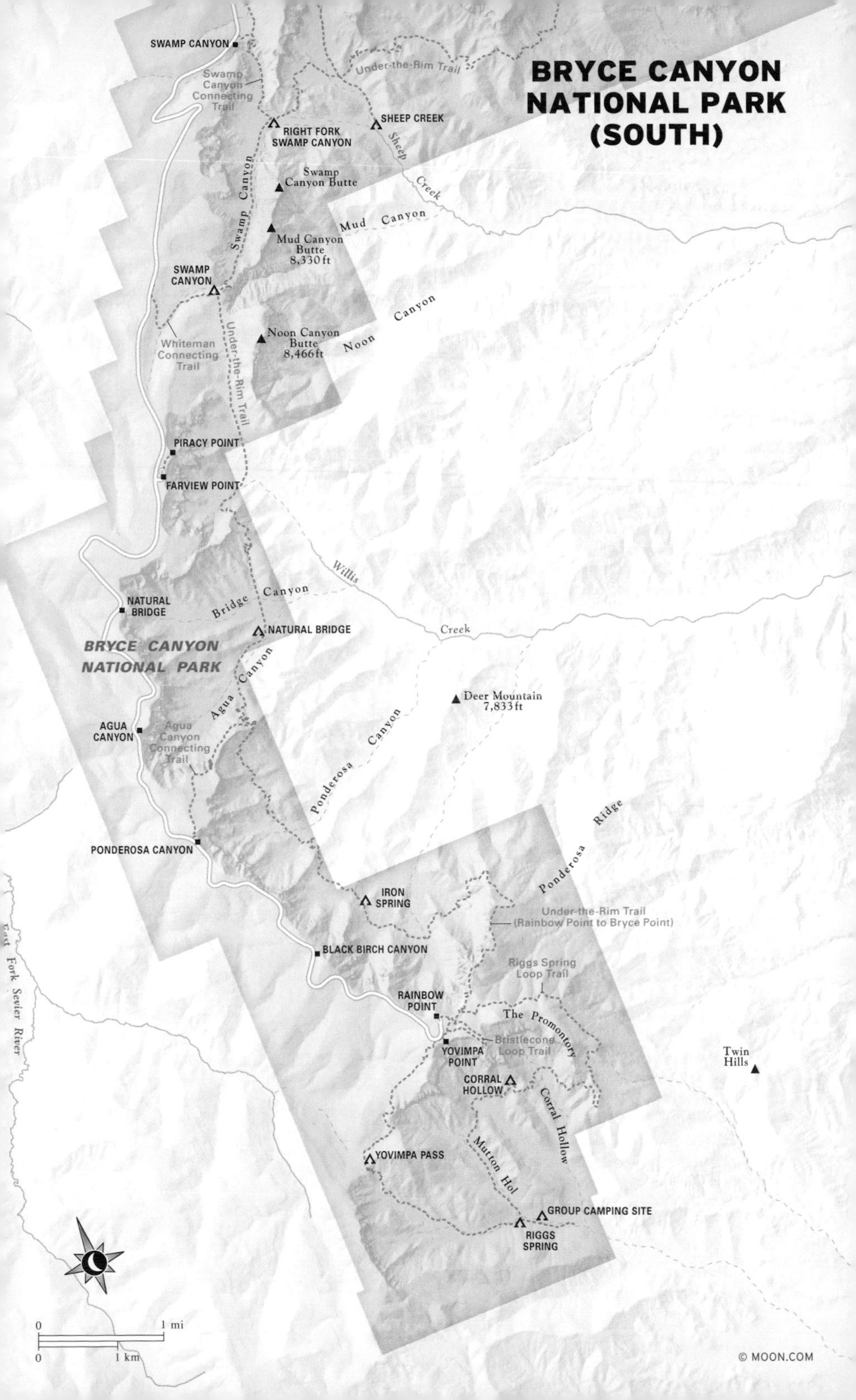

BRYCE CANYON NATIONAL PARK (SOUTH)
SWAMP CANYON
Swamp Canyon Connecting Trail
Under-the-Rim Trail
RIGHT FORK SWAMP CANYON
SHEEP CREEK
Sheep Creek
Swamp Canyon Butte
Swamp Canyon
Mud Canyon
Mud Canyon Butte 8,330 ft
SWAMP CANYON
Noon Canyon
Noon Canyon Butte 8,466 ft
Whiteman Connecting Trail
Under-the-Rim Trail
PIRACY POINT
FARVIEW POINT
Willis Creek
Bridge Canyon
NATURAL BRIDGE
NATURAL BRIDGE
BRYCE CANYON NATIONAL PARK
Agua Canyon
Deer Mountain 7,833 ft
AGUA CANYON
Agua Canyon Connecting Trail
Ponderosa Canyon
Ponderosa Ridge
PONDEROSA CANYON
IRON SPRING
Under-the-Rim Trail (Rainbow Point to Bryce Point)
East Fork Sevier River
BLACK BIRCH CANYON
Riggs Spring Loop Trail
RAINBOW POINT
The Promontory
Bristlecone Loop Trail
YOVIMPA POINT
Twin Hills
CORRAL HOLLOW
Corral Hollow
Mutton Hol
YOVIMPA PASS
GROUP CAMPING SITE
RIGGS SPRING
0
1 mi
0
1 km
© MOON.COM

Top 3

1 TAKE IN PANORAMAS FROM SUNRISE AND SUNSET POINTS

Sunrise and Sunset Points overlook stunning canyon scenery all through the day, but their names indicate when best to visit for photographing the colors below. About 1 mile (1.6 km) south of the visitors center on side spur roads, the points are connected by a paved section of the Rim Trail (1 mi./1.6 km rt., 30 min., easy). Panoramas from each point take in large areas of Bryce Amphitheater and beyond. The lofty Aquarius and Table Cliff Plateaus rise along the skyline to the northeast. At Sunset Point, rangers also give geology talks (30 min., times vary, summer).

VIEW FROM SUNSET POINT

2 VIEW HOODOOS FROM INSPIRATION POINT

Weathering along vertical joints has cut many rows of narrow gullies, some more than 200 feet (61 m) deep. The result is a fantastical maze of hoodoos in the Silent City. To overlook this wonder, drive south on the park road (no trailers) about 2 miles (3.2 km), turning left onto Bryce Point Road and then left again to reach **Inspiration Point.** A short but steep walk ascends **Upper Inspiration Point** (0.4 mi./0.6 km rt., 15 min., easy).

HOODOO ROCK FORMATIONS

3 TOP OUT AT YOVIMPA AND RAINBOW POINTS

The land drops away in rugged canyons and fine views at the end of the scenic drive (17 mi./27 km south of the visitors center, no trailers). At an elevation of 9,115 feet (2,778 m), this is the highest area of the park. **Rainbow Point** is a few footsteps north of the parking lot; walk south of the parking lot to **Yovimpa Point** (0.2 mi./0.3 km rt., 10 min., easy). Both have striking vistas of different amphitheaters.

VIEW OF THE VALLEY FROM BRISTLECONE LOOP TRAIL, RAINBOW POINT

ONE DAY IN BRYCE CANYON

Get up early and catch the free park shuttle so you don't miss the scene at **Sunrise Point.** If you don't want to hike down (and climb back up), take a walk along the **Rim Trail.** Catch the shuttle to **Rainbow Point,** at the end of the parkway, for a picnic with views over much of southern Utah. After lunch, descend from the rim on the **Navajo Loop Trail.** At the bottom of the loop, turn onto the **Queen's Garden Trail** and follow that back up to the rim. The Rim Trail connects the two trailheads.

for seven days. The park entrance is on UT 63 past Ruby's Inn; fee stations are inside the park adjacent to the visitors center.

VISITORS CENTERS

At the **visitors center** (435/834-5322, 8am-8pm daily May-Sept., 8am-6pm daily Apr. and Oct., 8am-4:30pm daily Nov.-Mar.), geologic exhibits illustrate how the land was formed and how it has changed. Historical displays interpret the Paiute people, early explorers, and the first settlers. Rangers guide short hikes (mid-May-early Sept.), give daily geology talks (winter), and lead full moon hikes among the hoodoos (tickets by lottery, dates vary). As an International Dark Sky Park, Bryce hosts an annual Astronomy Festival (4 days, June) and gives summer night sky presentations often with telescope-viewing. On UT 63, follow signs; the visitors center is adjacent to the park entrance fee station.

SCENIC DRIVE

The 19-mile (31 km, one-way, no trailers south of Sunset Point Campground) park road is a scenic drive with spurs shooting eastward to impressive overlooks that also serve as trailheads into the canyons (overlooks are listed north to south).

FAIRYLAND POINT

From **Fairyland Point,** whimsical forms line Fairyland Canyon a short distance below, beckoning you to descend into the "fairyland." To reach the turnoff, drive south 0.3 mile (0.5 km) inside the park boundary, then turn east and go 1 mile (1.6 km).

▼ SUNRISE AT BRYCE POINT

BRYCE POINT

A spectacular sunrise location, **Bryce Point** overlooks the south end of Bryce Amphitheater with a full view of its intricate geology. It also yields expansive scenery to the north and east. At **Paria View**, cliffs drop precipitously into the headwaters of Yellow Creek, a tributary of the Paria River. Look for a section of the Under-the-Rim Trail winding up a hillside near the mouth of the amphitheater below. Distant views take in the Paria River Canyon, White Cliffs (of Navajo sandstone), and Navajo Mountain. Drive 1.7 miles (2.7 km) south of the visitors center and turn left on Bryce Point Road for 2 miles (3.2 km) to reach Bryce Point. Backtrack 0.5 mile (0.8 km) and turn left for 0.4 miles (0.6 km) for Paria View.

FARVIEW POINT

The sweeping panorama of **Farview Point** takes in levels of the Grand Staircase that include the Aquarius and Table Cliff Plateaus to the northeast, Kaiparowits Plateau to the east, and White Cliffs to the southeast. Look beyond the White Cliffs to see a section of the Kaibab Plateau that forms the North Rim of the Grand Canyon in Arizona. The point is over 9 miles (14.5 km) south of the visitors center.

NATURAL BRIDGE

This large **Natural Bridge** spans 54 feet (16.5 m) and is 95 feet (29 m) high. Despite its name, the arch was formed by weathering from rain and freezing water, not by stream erosion like a true natural bridge. Once the opening reached ground level, runoff began to enlarge the hole and dig a gully through it. It is just off the road to the east, 1.9 miles (3.1 km) past Farview Point.

AGUA AND PONDEROSA CANYONS

You can admire sheer cliffs and hoodoos from the **Agua Canyon Overlook** (1.4 mi./2.3 km south of Natural Bridge). With a little imagination, you may be able to pick out the Hunter and the Rabbit below. The **Ponderosa Canyon Overlook** (1 mi./1.6 km south of Agua

▼ A RED SANDSTONE NATURAL BRIDGE

STUNNING CHINA WALL

Canyon Overlook) offers a panorama similar to that at Farview Point.

RECREATION

HIKING

The **Rim Trail** (11 mi./17.7 km rt., 5-6 hrs., easy) follows the edge of Bryce Amphitheater for 5.5 miles (8.8 km) between Fairyland and Bryce Points. Most people just walk sections of it on leisurely strolls or use the trail to connect with other routes. The 0.5-mile (0.8-km) section near the lodge between Sunrise and Sunset Points is paved and nearly level; other parts are gently rolling.

The **Fairyland Loop Trail** (8 mi./12.9 km rt., 4-5 hrs., strenuous) winds in and out of colorful rock spires in the northern part of Bryce Amphitheater and

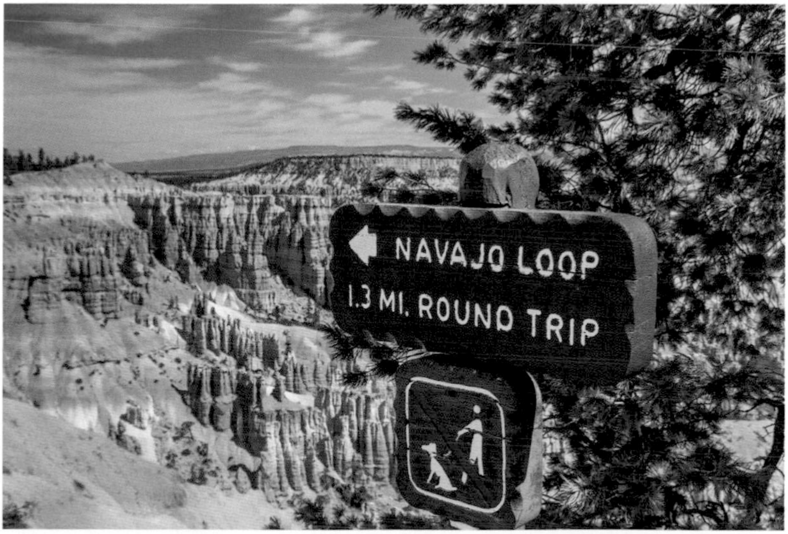

HIKE THE NAVAJO LOOP TRAIL.

Best Hike

QUEEN'S GARDEN TRAIL

DISTANCE: 1.8 miles (2.9 km) round-trip
DURATION: 1.5 hours
ELEVATION CHANGE: 357 feet (109 m)
EFFORT: easy-moderate
TRAILHEAD: Sunrise Point

For the easiest down-and-back up excursion below the rim, Queen's Garden Trail drops from Sunrise Point through impressive features in the middle of Bryce Amphitheater. At the end of a short spur trail stands a hoodoo resembling a portly Queen Victoria. For the most popular loop route, combine the Queen's Garden Trail with the **Navajo Loop** and **Rim Trails** (3.5 mi./5.6 km rt.), descending the steeper Navajo and climbing out on Queen's Garden. Trails also connect with the **Peekaboo Loop Trail.**

includes views of Tower Bridge. The route gains and loses elevation several times, including the climb to exit to the rim (2,309 ft./704 m), making the trail feel much longer. You can start the loop from Fairyland Point or Sunrise Point, connecting the two via the Rim Trail.

HOODOOS

From Sunset Point, you'll plunge down the **Navajo Loop Trail** (1.3 mi./2.1 km rt., 1.5 hrs., moderate, closed in winter) through a narrow canyon. At the bottom, the loop leads into deep, dark **Wall Street**—an even narrower long canyon—and then the climb back to the rim.

From Bryce Point, **Peekaboo Loop Trail** (6.5 mi./10.5 km rt., 3-4 hrs., strenuous) is full of surprises at every turn—and there are lots of turns. The trail tours the southern part of Bryce Amphitheater, which has some of the most striking rock features. You can also start from Sunset Point (5.5 mi./8.8 km rt. via Navajo Loop Trail) or from Sunrise Point (7 mi./11.3 km rt. via Queen's Garden Trail).

The **Bristlecone Loop Trail** (1 mi./1.6 km rt., 30 min., easy) begins from either Rainbow or Yovimpa Point and goes to ancient bristlecone pines—some 1,800 years old—along the rim. Viewpoints include the Four Corners.

HORSEBACK RIDING

Canyon Trail Rides (Lodge at Bryce Canyon, 435/679-8665, www.canyonrides.com, Apr.-Oct.) offers guided two-hour and half-day rides near Sunrise Point. Both rides descend to the canyon floor; the longer ride follows the Peekaboo Loop Trail. **Ruby's Horseback Adventures** (435/834-5358 or 866/782-0002, www.horserides.net, Apr.-Oct.) offers horseback riding in and near Bryce Canyon with 1.5-hour, half-day, and full-day trips.

WHERE TO STAY

INSIDE THE PARK

Travelers may have a hard time finding accommodations and campsites April-October. Advance reservations at lodges, motels, and the park campground are imperative.

The **Lodge at Bryce Canyon** (877/386-4383, http://brycecanyonforever.com, Apr.-Oct., rooms from $223, cabins $231), a National Historic Landmark, is the only lodge inside the park. Accommodations include lodge suites, motel-style guest rooms, and lodgepole pine cabins. Activities include horseback rides, park tours, evening entertainment, and ranger talks; a gift shop sells souvenirs. Make reservations 13 months in advance.

The lodge's **dining room** (7am-10am, 11:30am-3pm, and 5pm-10pm daily Apr.-Oct., $13-34) is classy and atmospheric, with a large stone fireplace and white tablecloths. A short walk from the main lodge is **Valhalla Pizzeria and Coffee Shop** (noon-8 pm daily mid-May-mid-Sept.).

The park has two campgrounds. The **North Campground** is just past the visitors center; the best sites are a few yards downhill from the Rim Trail. The **Sunset Campground** is about 1.4 miles (2.3 km) farther on the right, across the road from Sunset Point. **Reservations** (877/444-6777, www.recreation.gov, May-Sept., $20 tents, $30 RVs) are accepted for some sites six months in advance. The remaining sites are first come, first served; arrive by late morning to claim a spot.

Backcountry camping is available on the Under-the-Rim and Riggs Spring Loop Trails. Not for novice backpackers, the Under-the-Rim Trail is rugged and may require route-finding skills in places. A permit is required ($5) from the visitors center.

OUTSIDE THE PARK

On UT 63 north of the park boundary, **Best Western Ruby's Inn** (26 S. Main St., 435/834-5341 or 866/866-6616, www.rubysinn.com, from $80) offers year-round services including a hotel, dining, and a general store, as well as recreational outfitters, entertainment, and shopping. Many tour bus groups bed down here.

The town of **Tropic** has a cache of motels lining Main Street (UT 12) and

▼ HIKE AMID NATURAL SPIRES.

THE HOODOOS

About 60 million years ago, sediments filtered into a large body of water, named Lake Flagstaff by geologists. Silt, calcium carbonate, and other minerals settled on the lake bottom. These sediments consolidated and became the Claron Formation, a soft, silty limestone with some shale and sandstone. Lake Flagstaff had long since disappeared when the land began to rise as part of the Colorado Plateau uplift about 16 million years ago. Uneven pressures beneath the plateau caused it to break along fault lines into a series of smaller plateaus at different levels, collectively known as the Grand Staircase. Bryce Canyon National Park occupies part of one of these plateaus—the Paunsaugunt.

The spectacular Pink Cliffs on the park's east edge contain the famous erosional features known as hoodoos, carved in the Claron Formation. Variations in hardness of the rock layers result in these strange features. Water flows through cracks, wearing away softer rock around hard, erosion-resistant caps. When a cap becomes so undercut that the overhang allows water to drip down, a "neck" of rock is left below the harder cap. Iron and manganese provide the distinctive coloring.

The hoodoos continue to change—new ones form and old ones ebb away. Wind plays little role in creating this landscape; it's the freezing and thawing, snowmelt, and rainwater that dissolve weak layers, pry open cracks, and carve out the forms. The plateau cliffs, meanwhile, recede at a rate of about 1 foot (0.3 m) every 50-65 years; look for trees on the rim that now overhang the abyss. Listen, and you might hear pebbles plinking away down the steep slopes.

▲ HOODOOS OF BRYCE CANYON

several pleasant B&Bs. **Panguitch** is a stopover on the road between Zion and Bryce Canyon National Parks, with reasonably priced motels and good dining. The Dixie National Forest has three Forest Service campgrounds.

GETTING THERE

AIR

Delta and all other major airlines have regular flights into **Salt Lake City International Airport** (SLC, 776 N. Terminal Dr., 801/575-2400, www.slcairport.com). It is a four-hour drive (275 mi./445 km) via I-15 south to the park. **McCarran International Airport** (LAS, 5757 Wayne Newton Blvd., 702/261-5211, www.mccarran.com) in Las Vegas, Nevada, is another option, with a four-hour drive via I-15 north to the park. Both airports have car rentals.

BRYCE'S HOODOOS

CAR

Two scenic routes go to Bryce, both with captivating scenery. To reach the park from Bryce Junction (7 mi./11 km south of Panguitch at the intersection of US 89 and UT 12), head 14 miles (23 km) east on UT 12 to the park turnoff. From Escalante, it's 46 miles (74 km) west on UT 12 to the turnoff for Bryce. From UT 12 between Bryce Junction and Tropic, turn south onto UT 63 for the final 4 miles (6.4 km) into the park (winter snows occasionally close this section).

GETTING AROUND

You can drive your own vehicle into Bryce Canyon National Park. However, trailers cannot go past Sunset Campground. For day visitors, trailer parking is available at the visitors center. For free **parking** to catch shuttles, park at the visitors center or near Ruby's Inn, outside the park entrance.

SHUTTLE BUS

During the summer, the National Park Service runs the **Bryce Canyon Shuttle** (every 15-20 min. 8am-8pm daily mid-May-Sept., shorter hours off-season, free) from the shuttle parking and boarding area at the intersection of UT 12 and UT 63 to the visitors center, with stops at Ruby's Inn and Ruby's Campground. From the visitors center, the shuttle travels to the park's developed areas, including all the main amphitheater viewpoints, Sunset Campground, and Bryce Canyon Lodge.

TOURS

Free **shuttle bus tours** (435/834-5290, 9am and 1:30pm daily mid-Apr.-mid-Oct., reservations required at Ruby's Inn, Ruby's Campground, or the shuttle parking area) of the park go all the way to Rainbow Point. **Ruby's Inn** (26 S. Main St., 866/866-6616, www.rubysinn.com) is filled with recreational outfitters, along with vendors who organize hayrides, barn dances, and chuckwagon dinners.

Bryce Canyon Airlines (Ruby's Inn, 435/834-8060) offers scenic flightseeing tours by plane and helicopter.

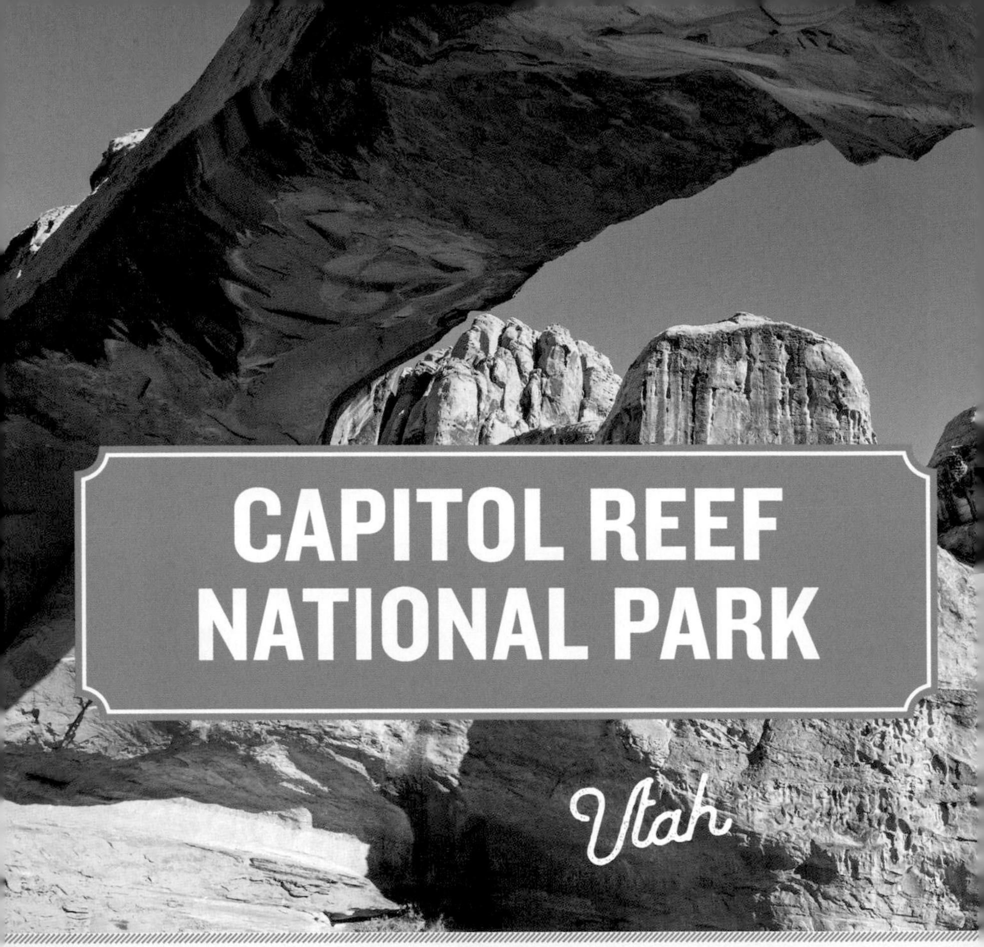

WEBSITE:
www.nps.gov/care

PHONE NUMBER:
435/425-3791

VISITATION RANK:
23

WHY GO:
See spectacular cliffs and colorful geology.

▲ HICKMAN BRIDGE, CAPITOL REEF NATIONAL PARK

KEEPSAKE STAMPS ▾▾▾

Named for its white Navajo sandstone, **CAPITOL REEF NATIONAL PARK** receives less attention than Utah's other parks. However, it is special in its own right, a place where sculpted rock layers in a rainbow of colors put on a fine show.

The Waterpocket Fold—so named for the many small pools of water trapped by the tilted strata—extends 100 miles (161 km) between Thousand Lake Mountain in the north and Lake Powell in the south. Its most spectacular cliffs and rock formations form Capitol Reef.

Roads and hiking trails provide access to the colorful rock layers. You'll also see remnants of human history—petroglyphs and storage bins of the Fremont people and Ancestral Puebloans, and a schoolhouse and other structures built by Mormon pioneers. Like these people who lived off the land, you can soak up the glittering stars here in the dark night skies.

PLANNING YOUR TIME

Capitol Reef National Park flanks UT 24, a major east-west road south of I-70 in south-central Utah. Travelers short on time will enjoy a quick stop at the visitors center and a drive on UT 24 through an impressive cross section of Capitol Reef cut by the Fremont River.

You can see more of the park, hike trails, and experience the night sky with a stay of 2-4 days. Visiting the park's remote north or south require several more days. Crowds show up April-October. Make reservations at Fruita Campground six months in advance.

In **summer** (May-Sept.), expect hot days (highs in the upper 80s and low 90s/upper 20s to low 30s C) and cool nights. Late afternoon thunderstorms are common in July-August; impending storms are warnings for flash flooding. Winter brings cool days (highs in the 40s/4°C) and night temperatures in the low 20s and teens (-6°C and below). Snow accents the colored rocks while rarely hindering traffic on the main highway. Snow may halt winter travel on the back roads and trails, but it soon melts when the sun comes out.

ENTRANCES AND FEES

The entrance fee is $20 per vehicle ($15 motorcycle, $10 individual). The entrance fee is only collected for vehicles on the Scenic Drive; a self-pay kiosk is just past the campground. Though UT 24 bisects Capitol Reef National Park, driving the road is free.

VISITORS CENTER

At the **Capitol Reef Visitors Center** (Hwy. 24/52 West Headquarters Dr., Torrey, 8am-6pm daily mid-May-Sept., 8am-4:30pm daily Oct.-May), a 15-minute film introduces Capitol Reef's history, wildlife, and geology. Hikers can pick up trail maps and checklists of plants, birds, mammals, and wildlife. Easter through October, rangers offer geology talks, evening programs, Junior Ranger Programs, and dark sky programs on moonless nights. The visitors center is at the turnoff for Fruita Campground and the Scenic Drive.

SIGHTS

TWIN ROCKS, CHIMNEY ROCK, AND THE CASTLE

From the west, **UT 24** drops from the broad mountain valley near Torrey to Sulphur Creek, with dramatic rock formations soaring to the horizon. A huge amphitheater of stone rings the basin, with formations such as **Twin Rocks, Chimney Rock,** and the **Castle** glowing in deep red and yellow tones. Ahead,

CAPITOL REEF NATIONAL PARK (NORTH)
OIL WELL BENCH ROAD
HIGH CLEARANCE RECOMMENDED
BAKER RANCH RD
Little Black Mountains
MONOLITHS
GYPSUM SINKHOLE
MIDDLE DESERT
CATHEDRAL VALLEY
HIGH CLEARANCE RECOMMENDED
CATHEDRAL VALLEY
UPPER CATHEDRAL VALLEY OVERLOOK
POLK CREEK ROAD
UPPER SOUTH DESERT OVERLOOK
Black Mountain 6,308ft
HARTNET ROAD
TEMPLE OF THE SUN
TEMPLE OF THE MOON
WOOD BEN
CATHEDRAL ROAD
THE HARTNET
Polk Creek
Deep Creek
LOWER SOUTH DESERT OVERLOOK
HIGH CLEARANCE RECOMMENDED
SOUTH DESERT
WATERPOCKET FOLD
HARTNET ROAD
CAPITOL REEF NATIONAL PARK
Spring Canyon
Deep Creek
North Blue Flats
Red Desert
Sulphur
24
TWIN ROCKS
ORIENTATION PULLOUT
CHIMNEY ROCK
To Bicknell
PANORAMA POINT
Creek
Torrey
GOOSENECKS OVERLOOK
SUNSET POINT
HIGH CLEARANC RECOMMENDE
VISITOR CENTER
Fruita
Fremont River
ORIENTATION PULLOUT
BEHUNIN CABIN
12
Fremont River
CASSIDY ARCH
SCENIC DRIVE
FERNS NIPPLE
To Hanksvill
Creek
Notom
Grover
GOLDEN THRONE
Capitol Gorge
Miners Mountain
Pleasant
Burro Wash
0 4 mi
0 4 km
SINGLETREE
South Draw
Cottonwood Wash
Sand
12
HIGH CLEARANCE RECOMMENDED
BOULDER MOUNTAIN
LARB HOLLOW OVERLOOK
Pleasant Creek
NOTOM-BULLFROG
PLEASANT CREEK
Lower Bowns Reservoir
Sheets Gulch
OAK CREEK
Oak Creek
Oak Creek Reservoir
ROAD
Sandy Creek Benches
STEEP CREEK OVERLOOK
HOMESTEAD OVERLOOK
© MOON.COM

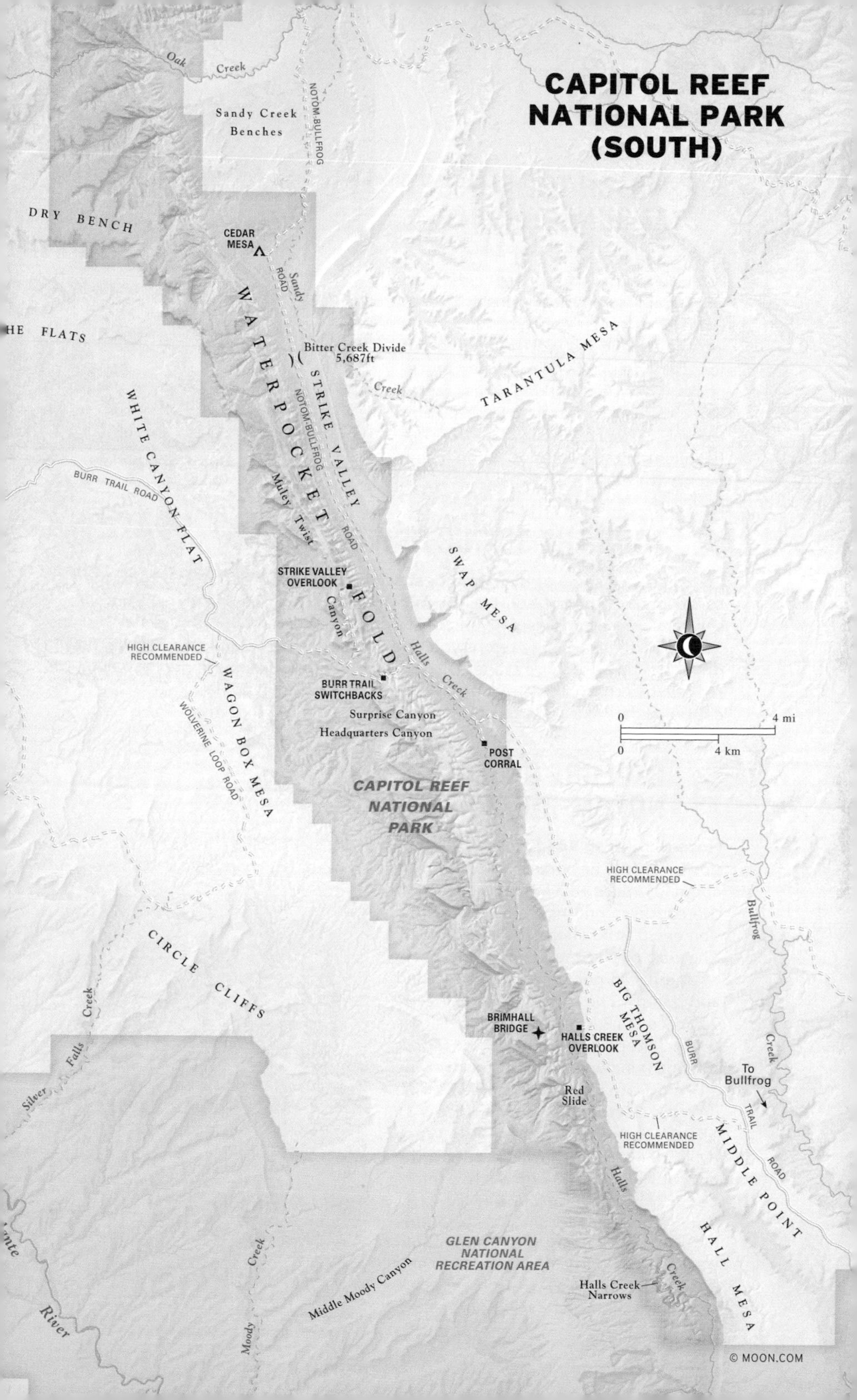

CAPITOL REEF NATIONAL PARK (SOUTH)
Oak Creek
Sandy Creek Benches
NOTOM-BULLFROG
DRY BENCH
CEDAR MESA
Sandy
ROAD
WATERPOCKET FOLD
HE FLATS
Bitter Creek Divide 5,687ft
TARANTULA MESA
Creek
STRIKE VALLEY
NOTOM-BULLFROG
ROAD
WHITE CANYON FLAT
BURR TRAIL ROAD
Muley Twist
SWAP MESA
STRIKE VALLEY OVERLOOK
Canyon
Halls Creek
HIGH CLEARANCE RECOMMENDED
WAGON BOX MESA
WOLVERINE LOOP ROAD
BURR TRAIL SWITCHBACKS
Surprise Canyon
Headquarters Canyon
0
4 mi
0
4 km
POST CORRAL
CAPITOL REEF NATIONAL PARK
HIGH CLEARANCE RECOMMENDED
Bullfrog
CIRCLE CLIFFS
Creek
BIG THOMSON MESA
BRIMHALL BRIDGE
HALLS CREEK OVERLOOK
BURR
TRAIL
ROAD
Creek
To Bullfrog
Falls
Silver
Red Slide
HIGH CLEARANCE RECOMMENDED
MIDDLE POINT
Halls
HALL MESA
GLEN CANYON NATIONAL RECREATION AREA
Creek
Middle Moody Canyon
Moody
Halls Creek Narrows
Creek
River
© MOON.COM

Top 3

1 WATCH THE SUN SET AT SUNSET POINT

Enjoy panoramic views of the Fremont River gorge, the Capitol Reef cliffs, and the distant Henry Mountains at **Sunset Point.** Plan your evening around viewing the sunset; it's worth hanging out for the whole show. From the Goosenecks Overlook parking area, waltz along the slickrock trail to Sunset Point (0.8 mi./1.3 km rt., 20 min., easy). Bring a flashlight and use caution when hiking back in the dark.

SUNSET FROM SUNSET POINT

2 TOUR THE SCENIC DRIVE

To experience some of the park's best scenery, turn south from **UT 24** at the visitors center for the out-and-back **Scenic Drive** (16-21 mi./26-34 km rt., 1.5 hrs.). You'll see spires, escarpments, canyons, buttes, mud cracks, and ripple marks at 11 stops. Several hiking trails may tempt you to extend your stay. Before embarking on the drive, pick up a brochure at the visitors center for descriptions of geology along the road. While the Scenic Drive is paved, side roads have gravel surfaces. Due to exceptional dark skies, stargazing is best at the end of Scenic Drive.

3 EXPLORE GEOLOGY ALONG NOTOM-BULLFROG ROAD

Notom-Bullfrog Road crosses some of the younger geologic layers of the **Waterpocket Fold.** The northernmost 10 miles (16 km) of the road have been paved, and about 25 miles (40 km) are paved on the southern end near Bullfrog, a settlement on the shores of Lake Powell. The rest of the road is dirt and gravel, and it can get pretty washboarded and bumpy. The turnoff from UT 24 is 9.2 miles (14.8 km) east of the visitors center. Stops along the drive (north to south) include: **Notom Ranch** (Mile 4.1), a private ranch; **Burro Wash** (Mile 8.1); and **Cottonwood Wash** (Mile 9.3). The pavement ends at **Five Mile Wash** (Mile 10.4). The dirt road reenters the park at Mile 20 with options to explore **Cedar Mesa Campground** (Mile 22.3), **Burr Trail Road** (Mile 34.1), and **Surprise Canyon** (Mile 36). Notom-Bullfrog Road exits the park at Mile 37.5 to end at Bullfrog Marina in Glen Canyon National Recreation Area (Mile 70).

GEOLOGIC FORMATIONS ON THE NOTOM-BULLFROG ROAD, THE WATERPOCKET FOLD

the canyon narrows as the Fremont River slips between the cliffs to carve its chasm through Waterpocket Fold.

PANORAMA POINT

Take in the sweeping view from **Panorama Point** (2.6 mi./4.2 km west of the visitors center). To reach the point, follow signs south to Panorama Point. Enjoy views of Capitol Reef, the distant Henry Mountains to the east, and looming Boulder Mountain to the west. The point also makes a good stargazing location on moonless nights

GOOSENECKS OVERLOOK

The Goosenecks of Sulphur Creek are located on a gravel road 1 mile (1.6 km) south of Panorama Point. A walk (0.2 mi./0.3 km rt., 5 min., easy) leads to the **Goosenecks Overlook** on the rim with dizzying views of the creek below. The overlook at **Sunset Point** (0.8 mi./1.3 km rt., 20 min., easy) views Capitol Reef cliffs and distant Henry Mountains.

FRUITA

The Fruita area contains a breadth of history stretching along the narrow Fremont River canyon. On the north side of UT 24 is the **Fruita Schoolhouse,** a one-room log structure from 1896. The school closed in 1941 due to a lack of students. Although the schoolhouse is locked, you can peer inside the windows.

Just east, on a northside pullout, are panels of the **Fremont petroglyphs**; several mountain sheep and human figures with headdresses decorate the cliff. Rangers give daily talks about the Fremont people (times vary, May-Oct., free). View more petroglyphs by walking left and right along the cliff face.

Farther east, another northside pullout shows where Elijah Cutler Behunin used blocks of sandstone to build the **Behunin Cabin** around 1882. For several years, Behunin, his wife, and 11 of their 13 children shared this sturdy but small cabin (the kids slept outside). Peek through the window to see the dirt-floored structure, but no furnishings remain.

In the **Fruita Rural Historic District,** south of the visitors center on Scenic Drive, you'll pass orchards and several of Fruita's buildings. A **blacksmith shop** displays tools, harnesses, farm machinery, and Fruita's first tractor. **Ripple Rock Nature Center** has activities and exhibits for kids, many centering on pioneer life. Typical of rural

AUTUMN IN THE FRUITA HISTORIC DISTRICT

THE WATERPOCKET FOLD

About 65 million years ago, well before the Colorado Plateau uplifted, sedimentary rock layers in south-central Utah buckled, forming a steep-sided monocline, a rock fold with one very steep side in an area of otherwise nearly horizontal layers. A monocline is a "step-up" in the rock layers along an underlying fault. The rock layers on the west side of the Waterpocket Fold have been lifted more than 7,000 feet (2,134 m) higher than the layers to the east. The 100-mile-long (161-km) fold was then subjected to millions of years of erosion, which slowly removed the upper layers to reveal the warped sedimentary layers at its base. Continued erosion of the sandstone has left many basins, or "water pockets," along the fold. These seasonal water sources, often called "water tanks," are used by desert animals, and they were a water source for prehistoric people. Erosion of the tilted rock layers continues today, forming colorful cliffs, massive domes, soaring spires, stark monoliths, twisting canyons, and graceful arches. Getting a sense of the Waterpocket Fold requires some off-pavement driving. The best viewpoint is along **Burr Trail Road,** which climbs up the fold between Boulder and Notom-Bullfrog Road.

NATURAL WATER TANKS ABOVE CAPITOL GORGE

Utah farmhouses of the early 1900s, the **Gifford Homestead** houses cultural demonstrations; handmade baked goods, gifts and a picnic area are also available. Rangers conduct evening Star Talks here (30 min., dates and times vary, free).

CATHEDRAL VALLEY

Only the most adventurous travelers enter the remote canyons and desert country of the park's northern district of Cathedral Valley. Four-wheel-drive roads lead through stately sandstone monoliths, volcanic remnants, badlands country, many low mesas, and vast sand flats. The district's two main roads—**Hartnet Road** and **Cathedral Road** (aka Caineville Wash Rd.)—combine with a short stretch of UT 24 to form a loop, with a campground at their junction. Sights include the Temples of the Sun and Moon.

SCENIC DRIVE

GRAND WASH

The Scenic Drive leaves the Fremont River valley and climbs up a desert slope, with the rock walls of the Waterpocket Fold rising to the east. Turn eastward off the pavement to explore **Grand Wash,** a dry channel etched through the sandstone. A dirt road follows the twisting gulch for 1 mile (1.6 km), with sheer rock walls rising along the sandy streambed. The road terminates at the Cassidy Arch Trailhead.

Back on the paved road, continue south past **Slickrock Divide**, to where the rock lining the reef deepens into a ruby red and erosion forms odd columns and spires that resemble statuary. The **Egyptian Temple** is one of the most striking and colorful features with its white-topped red rock.

CAPITOL GORGE

From the end of the pavement, this eastward gravel road tours the narrow, twisting **Capitol Gorge,** the route of the main state highway through south-central Utah for 80 years. The Capitol Gorge Trail departs from the terminus.

PLEASANT CREEK ROAD

Near the beginning of the Capitol Gorge Road, the dirt **Pleasant Creek Road** (high-clearance vehicles recommended) heads south below the face of the reef. After 3 miles (4.8 km), the road ends at Pleasant Creek. The creek's perennial waters begin high on Boulder

◂ GRAND WASH IN THE WATERPOCKET FOLD

HICKMAN BRIDGE

Mountain to the west and cut a scenic canyon completely through Capitol Reef.

HIKING

UT 24

From 3 miles (4.8 km) west of the visitors center on the north side of UT 24, **Chimney Rock Loop Trail** (3.6 mi./5.8 km rt., 2 hrs., moderate) ascends 590 feet (180 m) in elevation to a ridge overlooking Chimney Rock, a fluted spire of dark red rock capped by a block of hard sandstone.

From 2 miles (3.2 km) west of the visitors center, **Hickman Bridge Trail** (1.8 mi./2.9 km rt., 1 hr., moderate) follows the Fremont River's green banks a short distance before climbing a dry wash shaded by cottonwood, juniper, and piñon trees. The trail terminates under the 133-foot (40-m) natural bridge, eroded from the Kayenta Formation.

For a longer option, take the Hickman Bridge Trail for 0.25 mile (0.4 km), then turn right at the signed fork. A splendid overlook above Fruita beckons hikers to climb 1,100 feet (335 m) on the **Rim Overlook Trail** (4.6 mi./7.4 km rt., 3.5 hrs., strenuous). Panoramic views take in the Fremont River valley below, the great cliffs of Capitol Reef above, the Henry Mountains to the southeast, and Boulder Mountain to the southwest.

Continue another 2.2 miles (3.5 km) to reach **Navajo Knobs** (9.4 mi./15.1 km rt., 4-5 hrs., strenuous), a 1,620-foot (494-m) ascent from the trailhead. Rock cairns lead the way over slickrock

CHIMNEY ROCK

Best Hike

GRAND WASH TRAIL

DISTANCE: 4.4 miles (7.1 km) round-trip
DURATION: 2-3 hours
ELEVATION CHANGE: 200 feet (61 m)
EFFORT: easy
TRAILHEAD: 4.5 miles (7.2 km) east of the visitors center on UT 24

One of only five canyons cutting completely through the reef, Grand Wash offers easy hiking, great scenery, and an abundance of wildflowers. There's no trail—just follow the dry riverbed. (Flash floods can occur during storms.) Only a short distance from UT 24, canyon walls rise 800 feet (244 m) above the floor and narrow to as little as 20 feet (6 m) in width; this stretch of trail is known as the Narrows. After the Narrows, the wash widens, and wildflowers grow everywhere. The Cassidy Arch Trailhead is 2 miles (3.2 km) from UT 24.

along the rim of the Waterpocket Fold. A magnificent panorama at trail's end takes in much of southeastern Utah.

FRUITA

From the Fruita blacksmith shop, the **Fremont Gorge Overlook** trail (4.6 mi./7.4 km rt., 2.5 hrs., strenuous) crosses a lovely native prairie on Johnson Mesa and steeply climbs 1,090 feet (332 m) to the overlook above the Fremont River.

Across the road from the Fruita Campground, **Cohab Canyon Trail** (3.4 mi./5.5 km rt., 2 hrs., moderate) follows steep switchbacks during the first 0.25 mile (0.4 km), with gentler grades to the top. Turn right at the top on the **Frying Pan Trail** (5.8 mi./9.3 km rt., 2 hrs., moderate) to Cassidy Arch.

From the Fruita Campground amphitheater, the **Fremont River Trail** (2 mi./3.2 km rt., 1 hr., moderate) passes orchards along the Fremont River. The trail climbs sloping rock strata to a

GRAND WASH

GIFFORD HOMESTEAD

viewpoint on Miners Mountain where sweeping views take in Fruita, Boulder Mountain, and the reef.

SCENIC DRIVE

Off Grand Wash Road, the **Cassidy Arch Trail** (3.4 mi./5.5 km rt., 2-3 hrs., strenuous) climbs the north wall of Grand Wash, then winds across slickrock to a vantage point close to the arch.

The **Old Wagon Trail Loop** (3.8 mi./6.1 km rt., 2 hrs., moderate) crosses a wash, then ascends steadily through piñon and juniper woodland on a wagon road on Miners Mountain to a high knoll for the best views of Capitol Reef. Look for the trailhead on the west side of the Scenic Drive 0.7 mile (1.1 km) south of Slickrock Divide, between Grand Wash and Capitol Gorge.

At the end of Scenic Drive, Capital Gorge Road terminates at a trailhead for two routes. On the **Capitol Gorge Trail** (2 mi./3.2 km rt., 1 hr., easy), Fremont petroglyphs appear at a left turn after 0.1 mile (0.2 km). The narrows of Capitol Gorge close in at 0.3 mile (0.5 km). In 0.5 mile (0.8 km), look for a pioneer register on the left to see the names and dates of early travelers and ranchers scratched in the canyon wall. At 0.75 mile (1.2 km), look left for natural water tanks typical of those in the Waterpocket Fold. The **Golden Throne Trail** (4 mi./6.4 km rt., 4 hrs., strenuous) turns left to climbs 1,100 feet (335 m) in a steady grade to a viewpoint of the Golden Throne, a massive monolith of

▼ CASSIDY ARCH

A BOARDWALK-LINED TRAIL THROUGH THE GORGE

yellow-hued Navajo sandstone capped by a thin layer of red Carmel Formation.

WHERE TO STAY

INSIDE THE PARK

There are no accommodations or restaurants inside the park. Camping is the only overnight option. Campgrounds have picnic tables and fire rings or grates, but no showers or hookups.

Surrounded by orchards and lush grass, **Fruita Campground** (year-round, 71 sites, $20) has drinking water (May-Oct.) and restrooms. Reserve sites (877/444-6777, www.recreation.gov) six months in advance for March-October, but they are first-come, first-served November-February.

Two year-round, primitive campgrounds (free) have first-come, first-served sites, but no water. In the southern district, **Cedar Mesa Campground** (5 sites) is 23 miles (37 km) south on Notom-Bullfrog Road. In the northern district, **Cathedral Valley Campground** (6 sites) is near the Hartnet Junction, about 30 miles (48 km) north of UT 24.

Backcountry camping is allowed in the park; obtain a free backcountry permit at the visitors center.

OUTSIDE THE PARK

At the junction of UT 12 and UT 24, 11 miles (18 km) west of the visitors center, the town of **Torrey** has several lodging options and a restaurant. Several Forest Service campgrounds are south of Torrey on Boulder Mountain along UT 12.

GETTING THERE AND AROUND

AIR

The closest international airport is **Salt Lake City International Airport** (SLC, 776 N. Terminal Dr., 801/575-2400, www.slcairport.com), 225 miles (360 km) north via I-15 to US 50 and UT 24. Rental cars are available.

CAR

There is no public transportation into or within the park; you'll need a car. Travelers coming from Zion and Bryce should head north on UT 12 from the town of Boulder. Twisty UT 12 will take you over Boulder Mountain to UT 24 at the town of Torrey; Capitol Reef is just 11 miles (18 km) east.

ARCHES NATIONAL PARK

Utah

WEBSITE:
www.nps.gov/arch

PHONE NUMBER:
435/719-2299

VISITATION RANK:
17

WHY GO:
Hike amid natural sandstone arches.

▲ DELICATE ARCH, ARCHES NATIONAL PARK

KEEPSAKE STAMPS ▼▼▼

ARCHES NATIONAL PARK

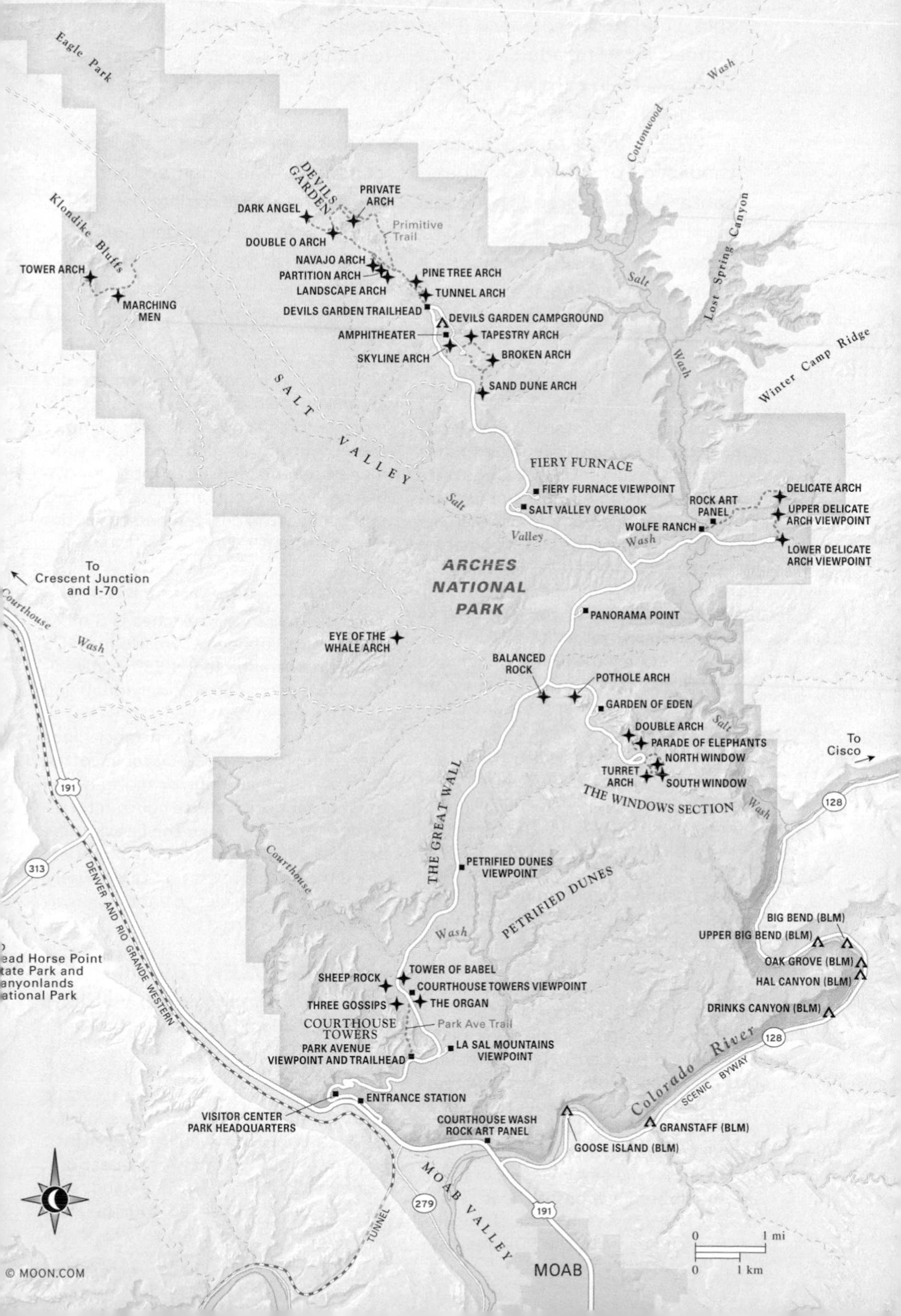

Eagle Park
Klondike Bluffs
TOWER ARCH
MARCHING MEN
DEVILS GARDEN
PRIVATE ARCH
DARK ANGEL
Primitive Trail
DOUBLE O ARCH
NAVAJO ARCH
PARTITION ARCH
LANDSCAPE ARCH
PINE TREE ARCH
TUNNEL ARCH
DEVILS GARDEN TRAILHEAD
DEVILS GARDEN CAMPGROUND
AMPHITHEATER
TAPESTRY ARCH
SKYLINE ARCH
BROKEN ARCH
SAND DUNE ARCH
SALT VALLEY
Cottonwood Wash
Lost Spring Canyon
Salt Wash
Winter Camp Ridge
FIERY FURNACE
FIERY FURNACE VIEWPOINT
SALT VALLEY OVERLOOK
Salt Valley Wash
ROCK ART PANEL
WOLFE RANCH
DELICATE ARCH
UPPER DELICATE ARCH VIEWPOINT
LOWER DELICATE ARCH VIEWPOINT
To Crescent Junction and I-70
Courthouse Wash
ARCHES NATIONAL PARK
PANORAMA POINT
EYE OF THE WHALE ARCH
BALANCED ROCK
POTHOLE ARCH
GARDEN OF EDEN
DOUBLE ARCH
PARADE OF ELEPHANTS
NORTH WINDOW
TURRET ARCH
SOUTH WINDOW
THE WINDOWS SECTION
To Cisco
191
128
313
DENVER AND RIO GRANDE WESTERN
THE GREAT WALL
PETRIFIED DUNES VIEWPOINT
PETRIFIED DUNES
Courthouse Wash
ead Horse Point
tate Park and
anyonlands
ational Park
BIG BEND (BLM)
UPPER BIG BEND (BLM)
OAK GROVE (BLM)
HAL CANYON (BLM)
DRINKS CANYON (BLM)
TOWER OF BABEL
SHEEP ROCK
COURTHOUSE TOWERS VIEWPOINT
THREE GOSSIPS
THE ORGAN
COURTHOUSE TOWERS
Park Ave Trail
PARK AVENUE VIEWPOINT AND TRAILHEAD
LA SAL MOUNTAINS VIEWPOINT
Colorado River
SCENIC BYWAY
ENTRANCE STATION
VISITOR CENTER PARK HEADQUARTERS
COURTHOUSE WASH ROCK ART PANEL
GRANSTAFF (BLM)
GOOSE ISLAND (BLM)
MOAB VALLEY
279
TUNNEL
MOAB
0 1 mi
0 1 km

More than 2,000 rock arches have formed within the maze of red sandstone fins at **ARCHES NATIONAL PARK.** It's the densest concentration of natural arches in the world. Balanced rocks and tall spires add to the splendor. These features formed from sands that bonded into Entrada Sandstone, then bulged upward into domes and cracked in parallel lines. Rain and wind erosion added the final touches of artistry.

While Ancestral Puebloans seasonally farmed the park area thousands of years ago, their descendants—the Acoma, Cochiti, Santa Clara, Taos, and the Hopi—still find the park's rock art speaking their history. The Ute also find their past in the large petroglyph panel near Wolfe Ranch, which documents acquisition of horses from the first Spanish in the area.

PLANNING YOUR TIME

Located in southeastern Utah about four hours from Salt Lake City, Arches is easy to reach via US 191. Due to its proximity to Island in the Sky in Canyonlands National Park, most visitors go to both on the same trip. Its position just outside Moab gives it loads of options for lodgings, camping, and dining; make reservations, as the town packs out in spring and fall. With no food services inside the park, bring a lunch and water. To visit all the stops on the park road and hike a few short trails takes all day.

March through October is high season; expect long entrance lines, congestion on the park road, and full parking lots at all sights and trailheads. Be flexible to return to locations later in the day, if parking is not available. Better yet, visit in early morning or late afternoon and evening. If possible, avoid the weeks around Easter, Memorial Day weekend, Fourth of July, Labor Day Weekend, and Utah schools break usually the third week of October. Unless you are camping inside the park, RV and trailer drivers are better off leaving rigs at campgrounds in Moab and renting a car if necessary to tour the park as oversize parking options are minimal.

Fall and **spring** are the most popular times to visit, as daytime temperatures are moderate. Real desert heat sets in during late May-early June. Temperatures then soar into the 90s and 100s (32-38°C) at midday, although the dry air makes the heat more bearable. Early morning is the choice time for summer travel. Autumn begins after late summer rains end and lasts into November or even December; days are bright and sunny with ideal temperatures, but nights become cold.

ENTRANCES AND FEES

The sole entrance to Arches is 5 miles (8 km) north of downtown Moab on US 191. The entrance fee is $30 per vehicle ($25 motorcycle, $15 individual) and good for seven days.

Be aware that long entrance lines form 8am-3pm March-October, often with waits of an hour or more. If you must enter during those hours, hit a restroom prior to joining the line as none are available. If the park fills, rangers close the entrance station temporarily, only allowing vehicles to enter again after enough depart.

VISITORS CENTERS

Past the park entrance, the **visitors center** (7:30am-6pm daily Mar.-Sept., 8am-5:30pm daily Oct., 8am-4:30pm daily Nov., 9am-4pm daily Dec.-Feb.) provides a good introduction to the area. Exhibits cover rock layers, geology, human history, wildlife, and plants. Staff members can answer questions, issue backcountry permits, and sign you up for a ranger-led tour of Fiery Furnace.

Top 3

1 EXPLORE THE WINDOWS

The Windows (12 mi./19 km from the entrance) area holds four massive arches. From the Windows parking area, a series of short easy trails lead to the arches. Take the Windows Trailhead to walk below **North Window, South Window,** and **Turret Arch. Double Arch,** a short walk from the second trailhead, has two arches framing a large opening overhead. On the way back to the main park road, stop at **Garden of Eden Viewpoint** for a panorama of the Salt Valley.

SOUTH WINDOW

2 WRIGGLE THROUGH THE FIERY FURNACE

A labyrinth of red sandstone, the **Fiery Furnace** is open only to those joining a **ranger-led hike** (3 hrs., twice daily May-Sept., adults $10, kids $5) or to experienced hikers with **permits** (adults $6, kids $3). The trailless hike is moderately strenuous with steep ledges, squeezing through narrow cracks, a couple of jumps, and hoisting yourself up off the ground. There is no turning back once the hike starts, so make sure you're physically prepared and properly equipped. **Reservations** (877/444-6777, www.recreation.gov) for the ranger-led hike are accepted up to six months in advance and often fill.

3 CATCH THE SUNSET AND NIGHT SKY

Arrive an hour before sunset to join the hordes of photography fans waiting to snap photos of the sunset framed through **Delicate Arch.** Other features such as **Balanced Rock** and the reds of **Fiery Furnace** also light up at sunset. Then, after dark, this **International Dark Sky Park** is prime for viewing the Milky Way at the night sky viewing area at **Panorama Point,** a 30-minute drive from the visitors center. Located away from lights and in a wide-sky zone, the viewing area has backless seats specifically for stargazing, and on select summer nights, rangers offer telescope-viewing. Other outstanding night sky viewing locations include **Balanced Rock Picnic Area** and **The Windows** area. For night sky viewing, use red lights to protect your night vision and allow 30 minutes for your eyes to become accustomed to the dark.

DELICATE ARCH

BALANCED ROCK

SIGHTS

MOAB FAULT

A pullout for **Moab Fault** offers an amazing view of Moab Canyon and its huge fault. The rock layers on this side of the canyon have slipped down more than 2,600 feet (792 m) in relation to the other side.

PARK AVENUE

Great sandstone slabs form a skyline on each side of **Park Avenue,** a dry wash version of the famed New York City street. The large rock monoliths of **Courthouse Towers** rise on the west, followed by the sandstone towers forming the **Three Gossips.** You can also see these from the road at Courthouse Towers Viewpoint.

BALANCED ROCK

The gravity-defying **Balanced Rock** is a boulder more than 55 feet (17 m) high that rests precariously atop a 73-foot (22-m) pedestal. For a closer peek, take the 0.3-mile (0.5-km) trail that encircles it.

FIERY FURNACE

A viewpoint off the park road offers a look into the **Fiery Furnace,** closely packed pink, orange, and red sandstone fins that form a maze of deep slots with many arches and at least one natural bridge. The Fiery Furnace gets its name from sandstone fins that can turn flaming red at sunrise or sunset.

▼ COURTHOUSE TOWERS

SKYLINE ARCH

SCENIC DRIVE

Arches has one **main park road** (36 mi./58 km rt.) that cruises past fantastical monoliths and the artistry of weathered red rocks. From the visitors center, the road begins a long but well-graded climb up the cliffs to the northeast. After cresting onto the mesa top, you'll gaze out onto a landscape loaded with geological sights thrusting up from the sagebrush desert. Short, paved spurs turn off to sightseeing features and trailheads. The road terminates at Devils Garden Trailhead and campground.

Between March and October, expect traffic congestion and full parking lots, which may force bypassing some sights. Go before 8am or after 3pm for less traffic.

RECREATION

HIKING

Park Avenue

Great sandstone slabs form a skyline on each side of **Park Avenue** (1 mi./1.6 km one-way, 30 min., moderate) a dry wash version of the famed New York City street. From the South Park Avenue Trailhead, the path drops down the wash as the large rock monoliths of **Courthouse Towers** rise on the west, followed by the sandstone towers forming the **Three Gossips** to end at the North Park Avenue Trailhead.

SAND DUNE ARCH

ONE DAY IN ARCHES

With the park's scenic drive and short hikes, even those who have only one day can explore its easily accessed arches. Drive the main park road to The Windows area, where you can walk to **North Window** and **South Window.** Stop to walk a little of **Park Avenue** before driving to the trailhead for the park and Utah icon—the freestanding **Delicate Arch.**

Sand Dune and Broken Arches

From the Sand Dune Arch parking area, a walk on red sand leads to the small, ground-level **Sand Dune Arch** (0.3 mi./0.5 km rt., 20 min., easy) tucked within fins. The loop trail to **Broken Arch** (2 mi./3.2 km rt., 1 hr., easy), which isn't really broken, also goes through sand dunes, fins, and slickrock.

Skyline Arch

From the Skyline Arch parking area, **Skyline Arch Trail** (0.4 mi./0.6 km rt., 20 min., easy) trots to the base of the arch. In 1940, a giant boulder fell from its opening, doubling the size of the arch in just seconds.

Delicate Arch View

For distant views of the park's iconic arch, drive 1.2 miles (1.9 km) on Wolfe Ranch Road beyond Wolfe Ranch to **Delicate Arch Viewpoints** for a short wheelchair-accessible trail (300 ft./91 m rt., easy, 10 min.) and a steeper trail (0.5 mi./0.8 km rt., 30 min., easy).

DOUBLE O ARCH

Devils Garden Loop

A full walk of **Devils Garden** (7.2 mi./11.6 km rt., 4 hrs., moderate) leads to eight arches, but you can also do a short hike with three arches. From Devils Garden Trailhead, where you can pick up a trail guide, you'll see two arches off a side spur to the right: **Tunnel Arch** has a symmetrical opening, and **Pine Tree Arch** once had a piñon pine growing inside. Continue on the main trail to the 306-foot (93-m) **Landscape Arch,** which is one of the longest unsupported rock spans in the world. Turn around at Landscape Arch for a shorter hike (1.6 mi./2.6 km rt., 1 hr., easy).

Beyond Landscape Arch, the trail narrows to reach the remains of **Wall Arch,** which collapsed in 2008. Beyond

THE FIERY FURNACE

Best Hike

DELICATE ARCH TRAIL

DISTANCE: 3 miles (4.8 km) round-trip
DURATION: 2 hours
ELEVATION CHANGE: 500 feet (152 m)
EFFORT: strenuous
TRAILHEAD: Wolfe Ranch

Hiking to the base of **Delicate Arch** is a highlight. Shortly after the trailhead at Wolfe Ranch, a spur trail leads to some Ute petroglyphs depicting horses, their riders, and a few bighorn sheep. The first stretch of the main trail is broad, flat, and not especially scenic, except for displays of spring wildflowers. Soon, the trail climbs steeply up onto the slickrock and the views open up of the park and the distant La Sal Mountains. The arch sits in a magnificent setting atop gracefully curving slickrock. Expect to see crowds at the arch, especially at sunset.

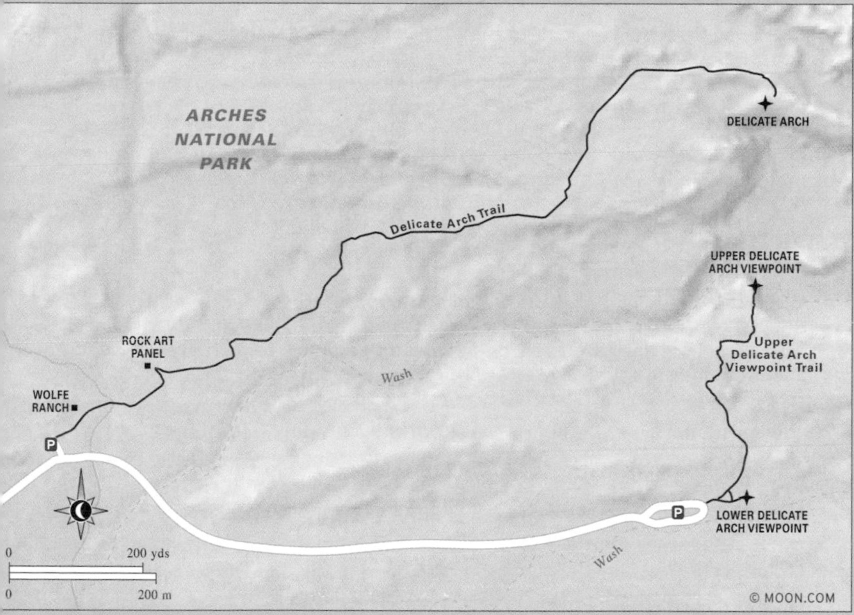

Wall Arch, a short side trail branches off to the left to **Partition Arch** and **Navajo Arch.** The main trail continues northwest and ends at **Double O Arch,** with a large, oval-shaped opening and a smaller hole underneath. **Dark Angel** is a distinctive rock pinnacle 0.25 mile (0.4 km) northwest; cairns mark the way. Beyond Double O, a primitive trail loops back to Landscape Arch via Fin Canyon and adds 1 mile (1.6 km).

BIKING

The rolling terrain of the main park road appeals to road cyclists. Relatively fit mountain bikers can go for the 24-mile (39-km) ride to **Tower Arch** and back via a dirt road. From the Devils Garden parking area, take Salt Valley Road for about 7.5 miles (12 km). Turn left onto a jeep road that leads to the "back door" to Tower Arch.

ROCK CLIMBING

Rock climbers find plenty of drool-worthy cracks and nubbins in the park. Most go for the sheer stone faces of **Park Avenue** or **Owl Rock,** the small, owl-shaped tower on the Windows Road. Stop by the visitors center for

MOAB

The largest town in southeastern Utah, **Moab** makes an excellent base for exploring Arches and Canyonlands National Parks and the surrounding canyon country. The slickrock canyons seem made for exploration by bike, and people come from all over the world to pedal the backcountry. River trips on the Colorado River are nearly as popular, and a host of other outdoor recreational diversions—from horseback riding to 4WD jeep exploring—combine to make Moab one of the most popular destinations in Utah.

The **Moab Information Center** (25 E. Center St., 435/259-8825, www.discovermoab.com, 8am-7pm Mon.-Sat., 9am-6pm Sun.) is the best source for information about the area's recreational options. **Canyonlands Field Institute** (435/259-7750 or 800/860-5262, http://cfimoab.org) leads weekend day hikes (mid-Apr.-mid-Oct., from $40, including transportation and fees) at various locations near Moab; join one of these to learn the area's natural history.

Mountain Biking

Most people come to Moab to mountain bike **mid-March-late May** or **mid-September-October.** The interconnected **MOAB Brand Trails,** with loops and spur paths, form a trail system with several options that are good for beginners or riders who are new to slickrock. Several bicycle rental shops offer daylong mountain bike excursions in addition to rentals: **Rim Tours** (1233 S. US 191, 435/259-5223, www.rimtours.com), **Magpie Cycling** (435/259-4464, www.magpiecycling.com), **Western Spirit Cycling** (478 Mill Creek Dr., 435/259-8732, www.westernspirit.com), and **Escape Adventures** (Moab Cyclery, 391 S. Main St., 800/596-2953, www.escapeadventures.com).

Rafting

Outfitters offer laid-back and exhilarating day trips, plus multiday trips. Rafting season runs **April-September.** Most do-it-yourself river-runners obtain their permits by applying in January-February for a March drawing; the Moab Information Center's BLM ranger can advise on this process. The following outfitters offer a variety of rafting options:

Adrift Adventures (378 N. Main St., 800/874-4483, www.adrift.net)

Canyonlands Field Institute (800/860-5262, http://cfimoab.org)

Canyon Voyages (211 N. Main St., 435/363-3793, www.canyonvoyages.com)

Moab Adventure Center (225 S. Main St., 866/904-1163, www.moabadventurecenter.com)

Navtec Expeditions (321 N. Main St., 800/833-1278, www.navtec.com)

Red River Adventures (1140 S. Main St., 877/259-4046, www.redriveradventures.com)

Sheri Griffith Expeditions (2231 S. US 191, 435/259-8229 or 800/332-2439, www.griffithexp.com)

Tag-A-Long Expeditions (378 N. Main St., 435/259-8594 or 800/874-4483, www.tagalong.com)

Camping

There are 26 **BLM campgrounds** ($20) in the Moab area. Although these spots can't be reserved, sites are abundant enough that campers can usually get a spot. The campgrounds are concentrated on the banks of the Colorado River—along Highway 128 toward Castle Valley, along Highway 279 toward the potash factory, and along Kane Creek Road—and at the Sand Flats Recreation Area near the Slickrock Bike Trail. Only a few of these campgrounds can handle large RVs; none have hookups, and few have piped water. For a full list of BLM campgrounds and facilities, visit www.discovermoab.com.

DEVILS GARDEN CAMPGROUND

a free **permit** (https://archespermits.nps.gov). **Pagan Mountaineering** (59 S. Main St., Moab, 435/259-1117, www.paganclimber.com) rents and sells climbing gear.

WHERE TO STAY

INSIDE THE PARK

Come prepared with a picnic lunch; there are no accommodations or food inside the park.

Devils Garden Campground (877/444-6777, www.recreation.gov, year-round, $25) tucks some sites under rock formations while others offer great views—but it's extremely popular. Plan to reserve a site well in advance for stays March-October; campers without reservations are out of luck. A camp host is on-site, and firewood is available ($5). In winter, 24 sites are available first come, first served.

OUTSIDE THE PARK

Moab is the gateway for accommodations, food, services, and camping. Bureau of Land Management (BLM) campsites are on Route 313, just west of US 191, on the way to Canyonlands National Park's Island in the Sky District, and along the Colorado River on Route 128, which runs northeast from US 191 at the north end of Moab.

GETTING THERE AND AROUND

AIR

Salt Lake City International Airport (SLC, 776 N. Terminal Dr., 801/575-2400, www.slcairport.com) is 235 miles (380 km) north of Moab. The four-hour drive follows I-15, US 6, I-70, and US 191. Rental cars are available.

CAR

Arches National Park is 27 miles (43 km) south of I-70 and 5 miles (8 km) north of Moab, both off US 191. If you're driving from Moab, allow 15 minutes to reach the park, slow-moving RV traffic often crowds the route.

Parking for oversize vehicles inside Arches is limited. If possible, leave the RV or trailer at your campground.

TOUR

Canyonlands Field Institute (800/860-5262 or 435/259-7750, http://cfimoab.org) guides one-day and multiday educational adventures and programs in Arches.

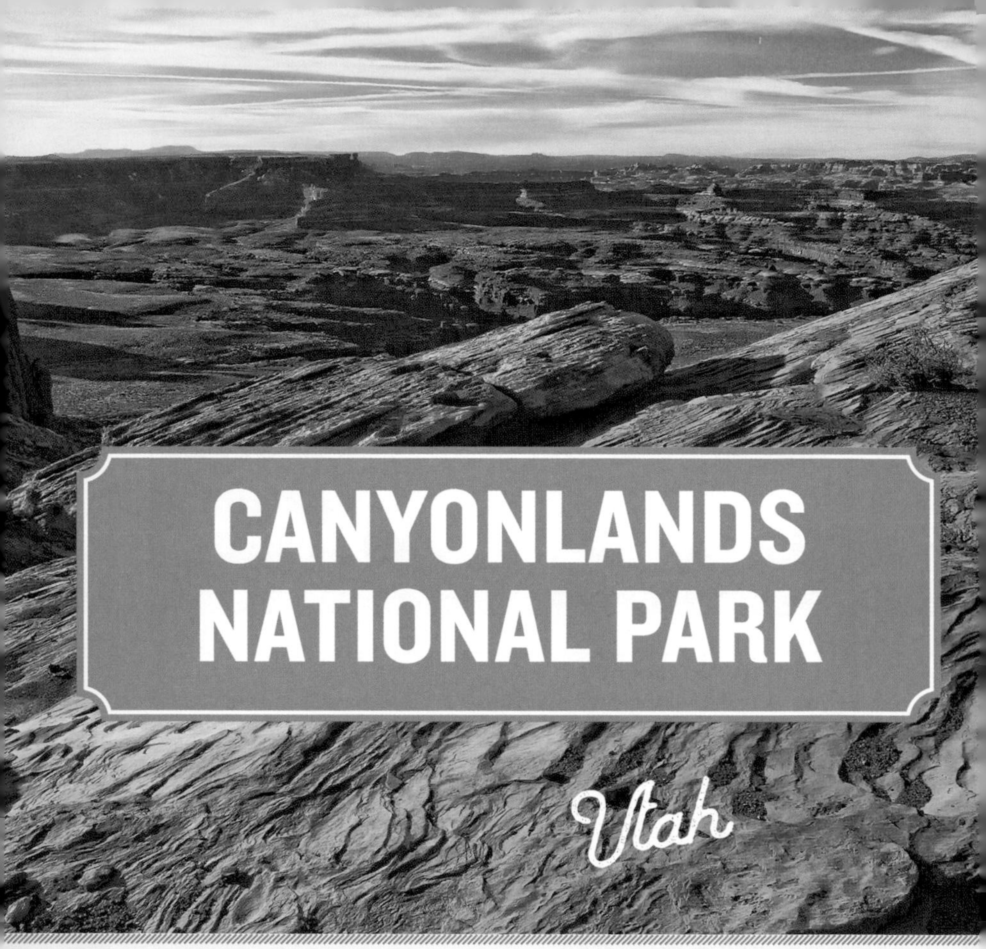

CANYONLANDS NATIONAL PARK

Utah

WEBSITE:
www.nps.gov/cany

PHONE NUMBER:
435/719-2313

VISITATION RANK:
28

WHY GO:
Explore Utah's canyon country.

▲ WHITECRACK OFF THE WHITE RIMROAD, CANYONLANDS NATIONAL PARK

KEEPSAKE STAMPS ▼▼▼

Utah's canyon country puts on a supreme performance in this vast park. The deeply entrenched Colorado and Green Rivers collide at its heart, then rage south as the mighty Colorado roars through tumultuous Cataract Canyon. The rivers split the park into distinct districts full of serrated cliffs, spires, boulders, and colorful rock that lights up at sunrise and sunset. Desert mesas plunge thousands of feet into canyon webs, some of which have seen little to no human exploration. In places, petroglyphs pay tribute to Ancestral Puebloans and the Fremont people, forebearers of the Ute, Paiute, and Navajo.

You won't find elaborate park facilities—most of **CANYONLANDS NATIONAL PARK** remains a primitive backcountry park prized by hikers, backpackers, mountain bikers, 4WD explorers, and river rafters. In fact, paved roads only reach limited places in two districts. This is a wilderness with breathing space, beauty, and a dark night sky spread with a zillion stars.

PLANNING YOUR TIME

Canyonlands is divided into separate districts. The Colorado and Green Rivers form the **Rivers** district and divide Canyonlands National Park into three other regions. **Island in the Sky** lies between the Colorado and Green Rivers; it is the quickest to visit with limited time. To the southwest, **The Maze** is for backcountry travelers on rough roads suitable only for 4WD vehicles. To the southeast, **The Needles** attracts campers, hikers, and backpackers. The small **Horseshoe Canyon Unit,** farther west, preserves astounding petroglyphs and ancient rock paintings. To sink into the wondrous solitude and canyon backcountry, plan a multiday trip (backpacking, four-wheel-drive touring, river-running, or bicycling), self-supported or guided from companies in Moab.

No roads directly connect the districts. Visitors must leave the park to drive from one district to another (2-4 hrs.). Due to Canyonlands' proximity to Arches National Park, most visitors combine visits to the two national parks.

March-October sees the most visitors, but **spring** (Mar.-May) and **fall** (Sept.-Oct.) are the best times to visit. In summer, temperatures can climb to more than 100°F (38°C). Winter days tend to be bright and sunny, with nighttime temperatures in the teens or below zero; snow and ice may close roads and trails.

ENTRANCES AND FEES

Each district has its own entrance. The entrance fee is $30 per vehicle ($25 motorcycle, $15 individual) and good for seven days.

A variety of **permits** (435/259-4351, https://canypermits.nps.gov) are required for backcountry exploration. **Day-use permits** (free) are required for 4WD vehicles, motorcycles, and bicycles on the White Rim Road and Elephant Hill. Day-use permits are available online one day in advance.

Overnight backcountry permits ($30 for 5-15 people) are required for any overnight excursions into Canyonlands' backcountry on foot, bike, or a 4WD vehicle. Reservations are recommended. Apply online up to four months in advance. For spring backpacking in The Needles and fall or spring White Rim Road trips, competition demands reserving online at midnight Mountain Time.

River permits ($30 fee, $20 pp) are required for day trips through Cataract Canyon and all overnights by rafters, kayakers, and canoers. Permits are first come, first served. Reserve online or at

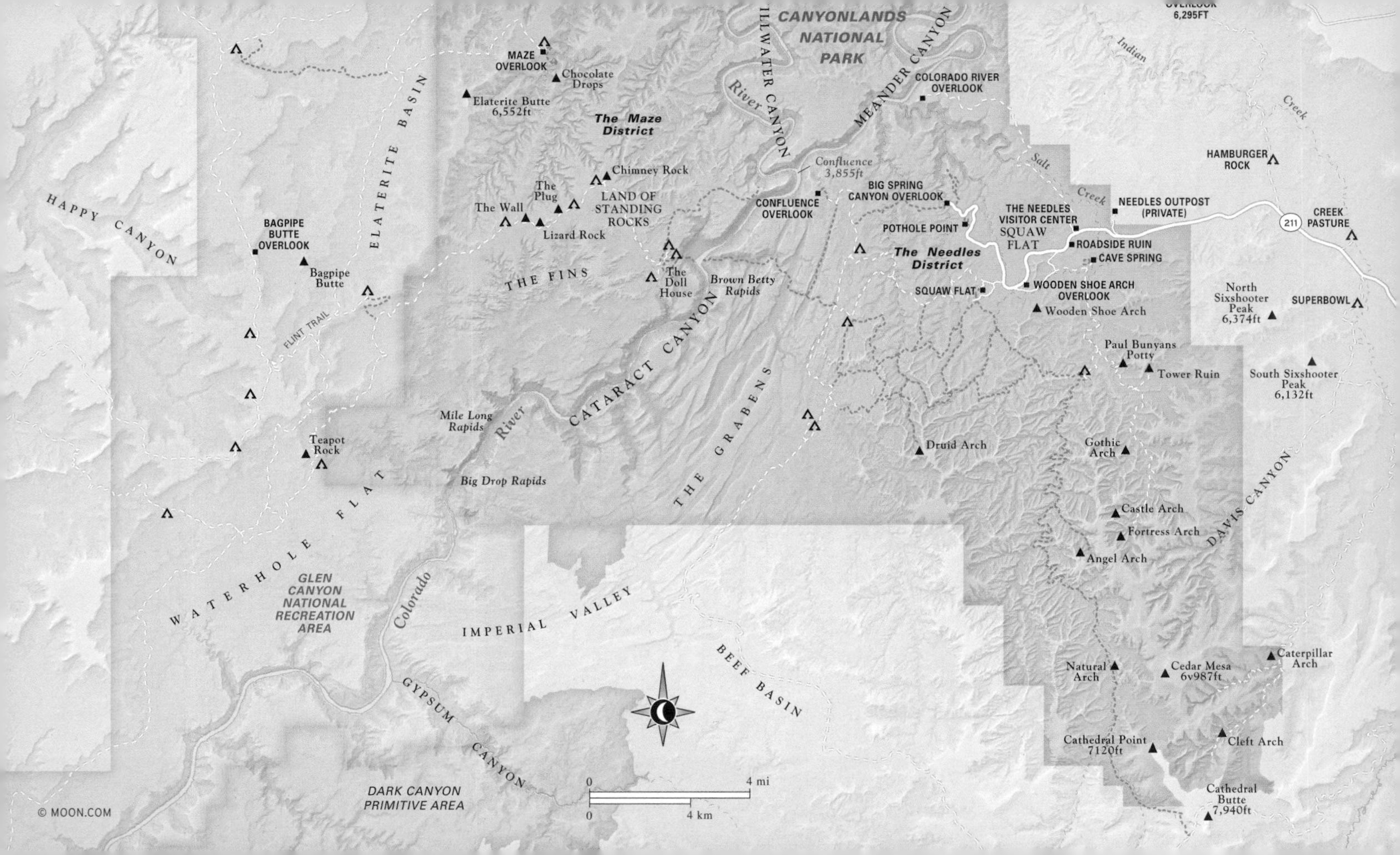
CANYONLANDS NATIONAL PARK
6,295FT
Indian
Creek
MAZE OVERLOOK
Chocolate Drops
Elaterite Butte 6,552ft
The Maze District
ILLWATER CANYON
River
MEANDER CANYON
COLORADO RIVER OVERLOOK
Salt
Creek
HAMBURGER ROCK
Confluence 3,855ft
Chimney Rock
The Plug
The Wall
LAND OF STANDING ROCKS
Lizard Rock
HAPPY CANYON
ELATERITE BASIN
BAGPIPE BUTTE OVERLOOK
Bagpipe Butte
CONFLUENCE OVERLOOK
BIG SPRING CANYON OVERLOOK
THE NEEDLES VISITOR CENTER
NEEDLES OUTPOST (PRIVATE)
211
CREEK PASTURE
POTHOLE POINT
SQUAW FLAT
ROADSIDE RUIN
CAVE SPRING
The Needles District
The Doll House
Brown Betty Rapids
THE FINS
SQUAW FLAT
WOODEN SHOE ARCH OVERLOOK
Wooden Shoe Arch
North Sixshooter Peak 6,374ft
SUPERBOWL
FLINT TRAIL
CATARACT CANYON
Paul Bunyans Potty
Tower Ruin
South Sixshooter Peak 6,132ft
Mile Long Rapids
River
Teapot Rock
THE GRABENS
Druid Arch
Gothic Arch
Big Drop Rapids
DAVIS CANYON
Castle Arch
Fortress Arch
Angel Arch
WATERHOLE FLAT
GLEN CANYON NATIONAL RECREATION AREA
Colorado
IMPERIAL VALLEY
BEEF BASIN
Natural Arch
Cedar Mesa 6v987ft
Caterpillar Arch
GYPSUM CANYON
Cleft Arch
Cathedral Point 7120ft
DARK CANYON PRIMITIVE AREA
0
4 mi
0
4 km
Cathedral Butte 7,940ft
© MOON.COM

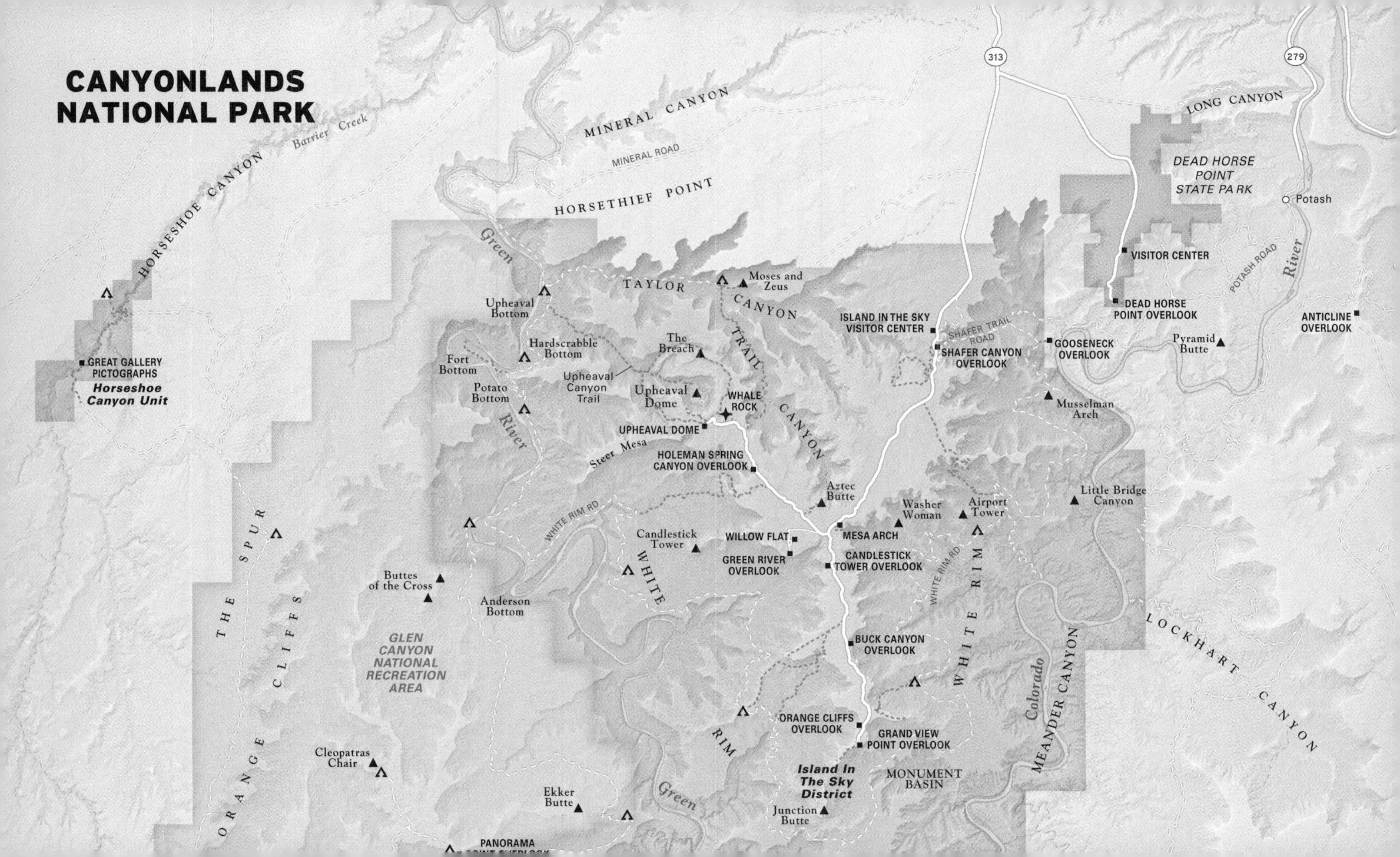

CANYONLANDS NATIONAL PARK
HORSESHOE CANYON
Barrier Creek
MINERAL CANYON
MINERAL ROAD
HORSETHIEF POINT
LONG CANYON
DEAD HORSE POINT STATE PARK
Potash
313
279
GREAT GALLERY PICTOGRAPHS
Horseshoe Canyon Unit
Green
River
Upheaval Bottom
TAYLOR CANYON
Moses and Zeus
Hardscrabble Bottom
Fort Bottom
Potato Bottom
Upheaval Canyon Trail
The Breach
Upheaval Dome
WHALE ROCK
TRAIL CANYON
UPHEAVAL DOME
Steer Mesa
HOLEMAN SPRING CANYON OVERLOOK
ISLAND IN THE SKY VISITOR CENTER
SHAFER TRAIL ROAD
SHAFER CANYON OVERLOOK
GOOSENECK OVERLOOK
VISITOR CENTER
DEAD HORSE POINT OVERLOOK
POTASH ROAD
ANTICLINE OVERLOOK
Pyramid Butte
Musselman Arch
Aztec Butte
Washer Woman
Airport Tower
Little Bridge Canyon
MESA ARCH
WILLOW FLAT
GREEN RIVER OVERLOOK
CANDLESTICK TOWER OVERLOOK
Candlestick Tower
WHITE RIM RD
WHITE RIM
THE SPUR
ORANGE CLIFFS
Buttes of the Cross
Anderson Bottom
GLEN CANYON NATIONAL RECREATION AREA
BUCK CANYON OVERLOOK
Colorado
MEANDER CANYON
LOCKHART CANYON
ORANGE CLIFFS OVERLOOK
GRAND VIEW POINT OVERLOOK
Island In The Sky District
MONUMENT BASIN
Junction Butte
Cleopatras Chair
Ekker Butte
PANORAMA

ONE DAY IN CANYONLANDS

Begin your day at the **Island in the Sky Visitor Center,** which overlooks an 800-foot-deep (244-m) natural amphitheater. After a 6-mile (9.7-km) drive south, you'll find the trail for the easy walk to **Mesa Arch,** which rewards you with one of the most dramatic vistas in Utah: an arch on the edge of a giant cliff. For lunch, hit the picnic area at **Grand View Point,** another 6 miles (9.7 km) south, for astonishing views over red-rock canyons. After lunch, hike Grand View Point Trail to a second vista before touring overlooks of **Upheaval Dome.**

a visitors center up to four months in advance.

VISITORS CENTERS

While the **Moab Information Center** (25 E. Center St., Moab, 435/259-8825, www.discovermoab.com, 8am-7pm Mon.-Sat., 9am-6pm Sun.) is outside the national park, it's the best place to get oriented due to its central location between Island in the Sky, Needles, and Arches National Park. The center has brochures, maps, and books as well as someone to answer questions.

The **Island in the Sky Visitor Center** (8am-6pm daily late Apr.-mid-Sept., limited hours spring and fall, Fri.-Tues. Jan.-early-Mar.) is located just before the neck crosses to Island in the Sky. It has maps, a bookstore, exhibits, a short park film, and permits. Rangers offer programs spring-fall with intermittent stargazing events.

Stop at the **Needles Visitor Center** (west end of UT 211, 8:30am-4:30pm daily July-Aug., hours vary spring and fall) for information on hiking, back roads, permits, maps, brochures, books, and a film. When the office is closed, you'll find information posted outside.

The Maze is served by the tiny **Hans Flat Ranger Station** (8am-4:30pm daily year-round).

ISLAND IN THE SKY

Island in the Sky is a triangle of mesas and canyons between the Green and Colorado Rivers. Paved roads lead to impressive overlooks along the upper mesa rim, while trails access geologic features. Below the rim, the White Rim 4WD Road makes a loop above the rivers on a route favored by mountain bikers. To reach Island in the Sky from Moab (40 min.), drive 32 miles (51 km) north on UT 191 and southwest on Route 313 to the visitors center.

▼ SHAFER CANYON ROAD

Top 3

1 WATCH SUNRISE BENEATH MESA ARCH

MESA ARCH AT SUNRISE

The Island in the Sky district's **Mesa Arch** (0.5 mi./0.8 km rt., 30 min., easy) follows an easy loop to a Navajo sandstone arch perched on the rim of a sheer 800-foot (244-m) cliff. For the best photo op, arrive by sunrise and watch the glowing orb peek between the narrow arch's gap.

2 GAZE OUT FROM GRAND VIEW POINT

VIEW FROM THE GRAND VIEW POINT

Island in the Sky's Grand View Point Road tours 12 miles (19 km) of overlooks like Candlestick Tower, Buck Canyon, and Orange Cliffs. The road's terminus holds the best view at **Grand View Point,** a perch overlooking Monument Basin, countless canyons, Colorado River, The Needles, and mountain ranges in the distance. Rangers give periodic geology talks at the viewpoint, and you can walk Grand View Point Trail (2 mi./3.2 km rt., 1.5 hrs., easy) to a second overlook. Grand View Point is also the best place for stargazing, on your own or with periodic ranger-led telescope-viewing programs.

3 ADMIRE PICTOGRAPHS IN HORSESHOE CANYON

THE GREAT GALLERY AT HORSESHOE CANYON

An outstanding day trip, **Horseshoe Canyon** contains exceptional prehistoric rock art. Ghostly life-size pictographs in the **Great Gallery** and rock art left by the subsequent Fremont people and Ancestral Puebloans provide an intriguing look into the past. The **Horseshoe Canyon Trail** (7 mi./11.3 km rt., 5-6 hrs., strenuous) drops from the canyon rim on a path to a long, sandy wash slog to the gallery. Rangers sometimes guide hikes to the gallery. From UT 24, a dirt, washboarded 2WD road to goes east to Horseshoe Canyon (32 mi./52 km). It's 2.5 hours from Moab (do not use a GPS).

GREEN RIVER

SCENIC DRIVES

Shafer Canyon Road

From the visitors center, the road heads south (6 mi./9.7 km one-way). First, turn into **Shafer Canyon Overlook** to look down on the twisting Shafer Trail Road that goes to the White Rim 4WD Road 1,200 feet (366 m) below. Continuing south, the mesa squeezes into a narrow land bridge just wide enough for the road.

Upheaval Dome Road

From the main park road, turn north on **Upheaval Dome Road** (10 mi./16 km rt.). The best viewpoint is on the dirt spur road that goes 1.5 miles (2.4 km) to **Green River Overlook.** Views plunge thousands of feet to the river oxbows below. Back on the main road, you can drive to the terminus to see **Upheaval Dome,** which requires hiking.

White Rim Road

White Rim Road lies below the sheer cliffs of Island in the Sky. Travel along the winding road presents a constantly changing panorama of rock, canyons, river, and sky. You'll see all three levels of Island in the Sky: high plateaus, the White Rim, and the rivers.

Only 4WD vehicles with high clearance can make this **100-mile trip** (161 km, 2-3 days), camping by permit along the way. Driving is slow and winding; a few steep, single-lane, rocky, or sandy sections pose white-knuckled driving. The road has no services or developed water sources, so have plenty of fuel and water with some to spare. From the visitors center on Route 313, the east entrance is Shafer Trail Road 1 mile (1.6 km) north, and the west entrance is Mineral Bottom Road, aka Horsethief Trail, 9 miles (14.5 km) north.

HIKING

Grand View Point Road

From White Rim Overlook Picnic Area, the **White Rim Overlook Trail** (1.8 mi./2.9 km rt., 1 hr., easy) trots east along a peninsula to an overlook of canyons and the La Sal Mountains.

Upheaval Dome Road

From the Aztec Butte Trailhead, **Aztec Butte Trail** (2 mi./3.2 km rt., 1 hr., moderate) climbs a dome that contains ruins of Puebloan granaries.

At the road's terminus, trails go for views of Upheaval Dome, a geological curiosity of a rocky crater about 3 miles (4.8 km) across and 1,200 feet (366 m) deep. The **Crater View Trail** (1.8 mi./2.9 km rt., 1 hr., easy) leads to two overlooks on the rim while the **Syncline Loop Trail** (8.3 mi./13.4 km rt., 5-7 hrs., strenuous) circles up and down completely around the dome. Halfway around, the **Upheaval Dome Canyon Trail** (add 3 mi./4.8 km rt., 2 hrs.) goes into the crater itself.

Best Hike

MESA ARCH TRAIL

DISTANCE: 0.5 mile (0.8 km) round-trip
DURATION: 30 minutes
ELEVATION CHANGE: 80 feet (24 m)
EFFORT: easy
TRAILHEAD: Grand View Point Road

In Island in the Sky, this trail leads to a spectacular arch on the rim of the mesa. On the way, the road crosses the grasslands and scattered juniper trees of Gray's Pasture. A trail brochure available at the start describes the ecology of the mesa. The sandstone arch frames views of rock formations below and the La Sal Mountains in the distance. Photographers come here to catch the sun (or moon) rising through the arch.

MOUNTAIN BIKING

Mountain bikers rank the **White Rim Road** as one of the region's best routes. Endurance riders do the 100-mile (161-km) loop in one epic day, but most prefer to tour the route in 3-4 days (self-supported or with vehicle support to haul water and gear). Be prepared to handle emergencies and flat tires on your own. **Permits** are required for both single-day and overnight trips. Bike shops, rentals, and guides are based in Moab.

THE NEEDLES

The Needles district showcases some of the finest rock sculptures in Canyonlands National Park. Spires, arches, and monoliths appear in almost any direction you look. Prehistoric ruins and rock art exist in a greater variety and quantity than anywhere else in the park. A paved road, several 4WD roads, and many hiking trails offer a variety of ways to explore the Needles. From Moab, reach the Needles (2 hrs.) by

BIKING THE WHITE RIM TRAIL, ISLAND IN THE SKY DISTRICT

traveling south on US 191 for 40 miles (64 km) and then turning right on Route 211 and going 34 miles (55 km) to the visitors center.

SCENIC DRIVES

From the visitors center, the paved park road into the Needles (6.4 mi./10.3 km one-way) doesn't have the giant views like Island in the Sky, but rather short walks to sights.

Stops go to **Roadside Ruin** (0.3 mi./0.5 km rt., 10 min., easy) to see the well-preserved granary left by Ancestral Puebloan people, **Cave Spring Trail** (0.6 mi./1 km rt., 20 min., easy) for a clockwise interpretive loop that provides an introduction to the park's geology, and **Pothole Point Trail** (0.6 mi./1 km rt., 20 min., easy) to visit dissolved sandstone holes. The road terminates at **Big Spring Canyon Overlook.**

Salt Creek Canyon Road

For high-clearance 4WD rigs, the dirt **Salt Creek Canyon Road** (26 mi./42 km rt.) begins near Cave Spring Trail, crosses sage flats, and then heads deep into this spectacular canyon; included is a side trip to 150-foot-high (46-m) Angel Arch. Salt Canyon is frequently closed due to quicksand after flash floods in summer and shelf ice in winter. **Horse Canyon Road** (13 mi./21 km rt., permit required) turns left shortly before the mouth of Salt Canyon for a side trip to Tower Ruin.

Colorado Overlook Road

Starting at the visitors center, the dirt and slickrock **Colorado Overlook Road** (14 mi./23 km rt., 4WD rigs only) follows Salt Creek west to Lower Jump Overlook. It then bounces across slickrock to a view of the Colorado River. The road is very rough the last 1.5 miles (2.4 km).

HIKING

The Needles has outstanding day hiking and backpacking (overnight trips require permits for preassigned

▼ POTHOLE POINT

THE NEEDLES, CHESLER PARK

campsites; ask about water sources). Interconnected trails loop through Lost, Squaw, Big Springs, and Elephant Canyons with routes including sandy washes, slickrock passes and ramps, cairned routes, exposed ledges, rock-hewn foot holes, and ladders. The best routes make loops, which you can do in either direction.

Squaw Flat Trailhead

From the Squaw Flat Trailhead, the **Squaw Canyon-Lost Canyon Loop** (8.7 mi./14 km rt., 4-6 hrs., moderate) climbs over a slickrock pass. Most of the trail goes through vegetated washes, where you may need to wade. You can also loop the other direction to connect **Squaw Canyon to Big Spring Canyon** (7.5 mi./12.1 km rt., 3-4 hrs., moderate) via a steep slickrock climb over red and white sandstone.

Elephant Hill Trailhead

The desert meadow of **Chesler Park** contrasts with the surrounding red and white spires that gave the Needles its name. **Chesler Park Trail** (6 mi./9.7 km rt., 3-4 hrs., moderate) winds through sand and slickrock before ascending a small pass through spires to overlook Chesler Park and return on the same route. Starting on the same trail, **Chesler Park Loop** (11 mi./17.7 km rt., 5-7 hrs., strenuous) circles the park and tours the **Joint Trail,** which squeezes through a long narrow crack.

Druid Arch Trail (11 mi./17.7 km rt., 6-7 hrs., strenuous) climbs into Elephant Canyon flanked with large white-domed red rocks and ascends to a viewpoint of the freestanding arch.

THE MAZE

Only the rivers, a handful of 4WD roads, and hiking routes provide access to the Maze. Due to the difficulty of travel, most visitors come for three days minimum, camping in primitive sites; **backcountry permits are required** ($30) for overnight trips. This district has no cell service, no reliable GPS, **no developed water sources,** and no services. All travelers must be able handle emergencies (flat tires, medical, and equipment malfunctions) and must be self-sufficient (carry water, read topographical maps, and be proficient with navigation)**. Gas up** before reaching the Maze.

Getting here from Moab (3.5 hrs.) involves 134 miles (216 km) of driving via I-70, Route 24, and a 46-mile (74 km) 2WD dirt road to **Hans Flat Ranger Station** (435/259-2652, 8am-4:30pm daily) before driving 2-6 hours to your destination.

COLORADO RIVER

SCENIC DRIVES

Only 4WD, high-clearance rigs should tackle the slow, rough roads of the Maze. Check road conditions first at the ranger station. Avoid travel during or after rains, due to slippery rocks and clay.

Fourteen miles (23 km) south of the ranger station, the narrow, single-lane **Flint Trail Road** (2.8 mi./4.5 km one-way) descends switchbacks, but stop first at the signed overlook to scout for vehicles headed up. A rough, rocky trek with switchbacks, drop-offs, and steep pitches leads to the **Maze Overlook** (60 mi./97 km rt., 6 hrs., 2 campsites) for canyon views. A second route goes to the **Land of Standing Rocks** (74 mi./119 km rt., 10 hrs., 3 campsites) to see the Wall, Standing Rock, and Chimney Rock or farther to the tall, rounded spires of **The Doll House** (add on 10 mi./16 km rt., 2 hrs., 3 campsites). Be prepared for extremely rough road after Teapot Rock Camp; carry extra gas and vehicle repair gear.

HIKING

Experienced, self-sufficient hikers can explore the Maze on unmarked strenuous routes of cairned paths from the mesa to canyon bottoms and slogs through sandy washes. A few places require using hands and feet to climb or descend boulders; bring a 25-foot (7.6-m) rope to haul packs up or down. Due to the remoteness, most hikers get required permits to camp in designated zones for several days. Consult with rangers about potential water sources.

From the Maze Overlook, the **Maze Overlook Trail** (2 mi./3.2 km rt., 2 hrs.) drops over a Class IV boulder into the South Fork of Horse Canyon, where a sandy wash goes to the prehistoric Harvest Scene (add 3 mi./4.8 km rt., 2 hrs.) pictographs. Two miles (3.2 km) east of the bottom of the Flint Trail Road, the steep **Golden Stairs** (4 mi./6.4 km rt., 3-4 hrs.) descends to the Land of Standing Rocks Road for views of Ernies Country and the Fins. From the Doll House, the **Spanish Bottom Trail** (2.4 mi./3.9 km rt., 2-3 hrs.) plunges 1,260 vertical feet (384 m) to Spanish Bottom beside the Colorado River.

THE RIVERS

The Rivers district includes long stretches of the **Green** and **Colorado Rivers.** River-floating provides one of the best ways to experience the inner depths of the park. Above the confluence, the rivers have flat water for paddlers in canoes, sea kayaks, and rafts. Below the confluence, the volume of water squeezes through 14-mile (22-km) Cataract Canyon with Class III-V white water. Boaters need permits.

For ease, commercial trips take care of everything. The following outfitters in Moab are authorized by the National Park Service. Most offer single-day and multiday trips.

Adrift Adventures (378 N. Main St., 435/259-8594 or 800/874-4483, www.adrift.net)

Sheri Griffith Expeditions (2231 S. UT 191, 435/259-8229 or 800/332-2439, www.griffithexp.com)

Tag-A-Long Expeditions (378 N. Main St., 435/259-8594 or 800/874-4483, www.tagalong.com)

Western River Expeditions (225 S. Main St., 801/942-6669 or 866/904-1160, www.westernriver.com)

WHERE TO STAY

INSIDE THE PARK

Developed park campgrounds have picnic tables, toilets, and fire rings, but no RV hookups.

Island in the Sky

On Murphy Point Road, the **Willow Flat Campground** (year-round, 12 sites, $15) is available first-come, first-served; sites fill up early in all seasons except winter. Get drinking water at the visitors center.

The Needles

Located 3 miles (4.8 km) south of the visitors center, **Squaw Flat Campground** (year-round, 26 sites, $20) snuggles under the slickrock. Rangers present evening programs at the campfire circle spring-autumn. Make reservations six months in advance for spring-fall (877/444-6777, www.recreation.gov); otherwise, they are first-come, first-served. Potable water is available spring-fall.

The Maze

The Maze has **nine primitive camping locations**. A backcountry permit ($30) is required. Expect to share your site with others, especially in spring.

OUTSIDE THE PARK

With scads of lodging, restaurants, and services, **Moab** is a tourist town. Book reservations for spring and fall six months in advance.

Near the Island in the Sky District, the year-round campground at **Dead Horse Point State Park** (800/322-3770, www.reserveamerica.com, book four months in advance) fills daily February-November. Primitive Bureau of Land Management (BLM) campsites flank Route 313. Its hiking trails lead to spectacular canyon and Colorado River overlooks.

Just outside the Needles district, **Needles Outpost** (435/459-0777, www.needlesoutpost.com, mid-Mar.-late Oct.) has campsites without hookups. Nearby BLM land also offers a number of places to camp, including two first-come, first-served campgrounds in the Canyon Rims Special Recreation Management Area.

GETTING THERE AND AROUND

The closest airport is **Salt Lake City International Airport** (SLC, 776 N. Terminal Dr., 801/575-2400, www.slcairport.com), 235 miles (380 km) north of Moab. The four-hour drive follows I-15, US 6, I-70, and US 191. Rental cars are available; however, 4WD vehicles with high clearance are preferred.

CAR

Island in the Sky

From Moab, drive 11 miles (18 km) north on US 191 and turn left (west) onto Route 313. If you are coming in from I-70, drive 20 miles (32 km) south on US 191 from exit 182 to reach the junction. Continue on this paved road for 22 miles (35 km) west, and then south, to reach the park entrance. From Moab, allow 45 minutes to reach the park.

The Needles

To reach the Needles district, drive 40 miles (64 km) south from Moab (or 14 mi./23 km north from Monticello) on US 191, and then turn west onto UT 211 for 38 miles (61 km).

The Maze and Horseshoe Canyon

South of I-70, Route 24 and Route 95 access dirt roads to the western canyons. The easiest way in is the dirt, washboarded 2WD road from Route 24 to Hans Flat Ranger Station (46 mi./74 km). Beyond there, a 2WD dirt road goes north to Horseshoe Canyon (32 mi./52 km), and extremely rugged 4WD, high-clearance roads go to Maze destinations (30-47 mi./48-76 km).

TOURS

Canyonlands Field Institute (800/860-5262 or 435/259-7750, http://cfimoab.org) guides one-day and multiday educational adventures and programs.

MESA VERDE NATIONAL PARK

Colorado

WEBSITE:
www.nps.gov/meve

PHONE NUMBER:
970/529-4465

VISITATION RANK:
38

WHY GO:
Marvel at ancient Pueblo cliff dwellings.

▲ CLIFF PALACE, MESA VERDE NATIONAL PARK

KEEPSAKE STAMPS ▾▾▾

Nearly 5,000 archaeological sites spread across **MESA VERDE NATIONAL PARK.** They contain ruins of Ancestral Puebloan people who once farmed the mesa tops and lived in tiny mud-brick rooms. After living on the mesa for nearly 600 years, they began building pueblos beneath the impressive overhanging cliffs. Some 600 intricate, multistory cliff dwellings are tucked into enormous sandstone alcoves and can be visited today. The structures range greatly in size, from one-room storage areas to entire villages. These remnants offer keen insight into the lives of the ancient Puebloans.

One of the first things modern visitors notice is how cramped the rooms feel. At that time, the average man stood 5 feet, 4 inches (1.6 m) tall and the average woman was about 5 feet (1.5 m) tall. Petroglyphs offer further hints of their culture, which lasted about 700 years until they vacated the sites within just a generation or so. Today, 26 tribes maintain special connections with the remarkable history of Mesa Verde.

PLANNING YOUR TIME

Mesa Verde National Park is situated in southwestern Colorado, near the Four Corners of Colorado, Utah, Arizona, and New Mexico. It's easy to link a visit to Mesa Verde with several nearby national monuments. The region boasts impressive ruins and acre upon acre of gorgeous slickrock scenery, where crimson and white sandstone monoliths tower above vegetation and secluded archaeological sites.

The park's main draw is its remarkable cliff dwellings. **Balcony House, Cliff Palace,** and **Long House** can only be visited on ranger-guided tours. In summer, it's not always possible to visit both Balcony House and Cliff Palace on the same day due to high demand for tours. Consider staying 2-3 days, or visit **Long House** (road open May-mid-Oct.), the park's second-largest dwelling, instead.

Tour season runs May-mid-October although most crowds arrive May-September. Tours are not offered in winter. Book tickets for tours six months in advance online; two days in advance in person.

This area can be hot in summer with temperatures in the 90s (32°C and above); summer afternoon thunderstorms can dole out lightning. Spring and fall, when 60-75°F (16-24°C) is the norm, are ideal times to visit. In spring, the cottonwoods along the sparse creeks begin to leaf out. In autumn, their leaves turn gold and the distant mountaintops are dusted with fresh snow. Winter nights are chilly, but the daytime temperatures are usually pleasantly cool. Expect snowstorms November-April.

ENTRANCE AND FEES

The park entrance is accessed via one clearly signed road that branches south from US 160. Upon turning onto the park entrance road, the visitors center appears on the left; this is where you'll pay the entrance fee January-March. The actual park entrance station is 0.5 mile (0.8 km) farther down the park road; pay the entrance fee here late March-December.

The entrance fee is $30 per vehicle ($25 motorcycle, $15 individual). All entrance fees are valid for seven days.

VISITORS CENTER

The **Mesa Verde Visitor and Research Center** (7:30am-7pm daily late May-early Sept., shorter hours in winter) is housed in a scenic LEED building. Pick up tour tickets and view exhibits on the Ancestral Puebloan people,

491
160
Cortez
To Dove Creek
To Shiprock
MESA VERDE NATIONAL PARK
MONTEZUMA VALL OVERLOOK
PARK POINT OVERLOOK
NORTH RIM
GEOLOGIC OVERLOOK
WINDOW TO THE PAST
FIRE RECOVERY VIEWPOINT
FAR VIEW TERRACE
FAR VIEW LODGE
MESA VERDE NATIONAL PARK
MCELMO CANYON VIEW
Long Canyon
West Fork
East Fork
FAR VIEW SITES
WETHERILL MESA
CHAPIN MESA
ROCK CANYON TOWER VIEW
ROCK TOWER
WETHERILL MESA ROAD
Soda Canyon
School Section Canyon
Moccasin Canyon
Spruce Canyon
Navajo Canyon
Wickiup Canyon
CEDAR TREE TOWER
Farming Terrace Trail
Park Mesa
STEP HOUSE
CHAPIN MESA ARCHEOLOGICAL MUSEUM
BADGER HOUSE COMMUNITY
NORDENSKIÖLD SITE #16
LONG HOUSE
SPRUCE TREE TERRACE
AMPHITHEATER
Soda Canyon
UTE MOUNTAIN UTE INDIAN RESERVATION
LONG HOUSE LOOP
Spruce Canyon Trail
SPRUCE TREE HOUSE
Wildhorse Mesa
Long Canyon
KODAK HOUSE
KODAK HOUSE OVERLOOK
MESA TOP LOOP
CLIFF PALACE LOOP
Petroglyph Point Trail
Rock Canyon
PIT HOUSE
SUN TEMPLE
CLIFF PALACE
Soda Canyon Overlook Trail
NAVAJO CANYON VIEW
SODA CANYON OVERLOOK
SQUARE TOWER HOUSE
BALCONY HOUSE
PIT HOUSES AND VILLAGES
SUN POINT VIEW
HEMENW HOUS
© MOON.COM

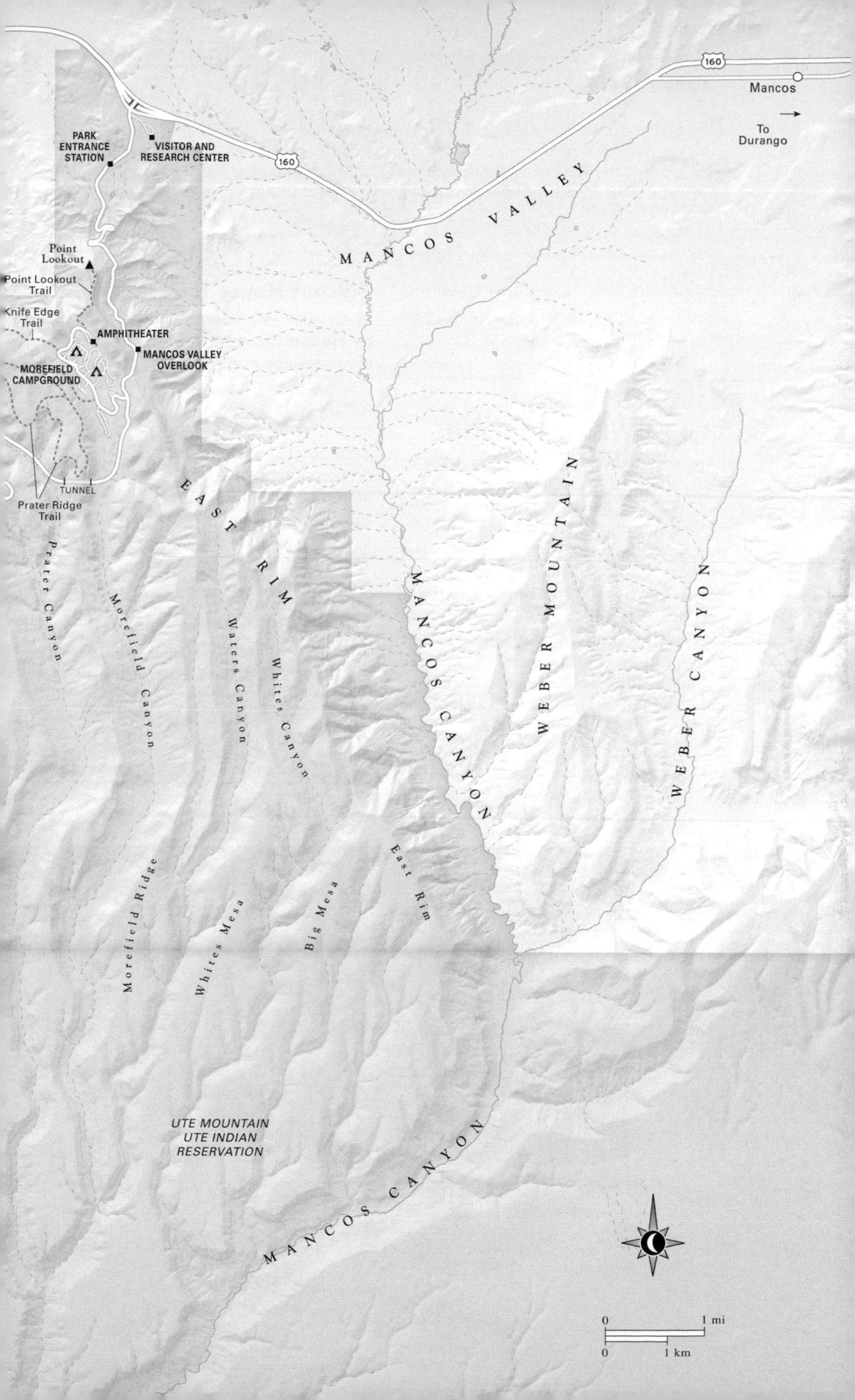

160
Mancos
To Durango
PARK ENTRANCE STATION
VISITOR AND RESEARCH CENTER
MANCOS VALLEY
Point Lookout
Point Lookout Trail
Knife Edge Trail
AMPHITHEATER
MANCOS VALLEY OVERLOOK
MOREFIELD CAMPGROUND
TUNNEL
Prater Ridge Trail
EAST RIM
Prater Canyon
Morefield Canyon
Waters Canyon
Whites Canyon
MANCOS CANYON
WEBER MOUNTAIN
WEBER CANYON
East Rim
Big Mesa
Whites Mesa
Morefield Ridge
UTE MOUNTAIN UTE INDIAN RESERVATION
MANCOS CANYON
0
1 mi
0
1 km

ONE DAY IN MESA VERDE

If you only have half a day, drive the park road south to the Chapin Mesa area, where you can see some of the mesa-top sites at **Far View** and take a tour of either **Cliff Palace** or **Balcony House.** If you can spend a full day, add in an afternoon at **Chapin Mesa Archeological Museum** and walk the **Petroglyph Point Trail.**

original art, and sculptures. Facilities include a bookstore, restrooms, and Wi-Fi.

SIGHTS

CLIFF DWELLING TOURS

Ranger-led tours are the only way to visit some of the cliff dwellings. For Cliff Palace, Balcony House, or Long House, purchase **tickets** ($5) in person up to two days in advance at the visitors center. The **Durango Welcome Center** (802 Main Ave., Durango, 800/525-8855, www.durango.org, 10am-6pm daily mid-Apr.-late Oct.) also sells tickets. Limited tickets are available at **Chapin Mesa Archeological Museum** (20 mi./32 km south of the park entrance, roughly 9am-5pm, limited hours in winter). Book **reservations** up to six months in advance (877/444-6777, www.recreation.gov, $10-25).

Balcony House Tour

With just 40 rooms, nearby **Balcony House** (daily May-Oct.) is an intermediate-size complex. To access their mesa-top gardens, the villagers used hand- and footholds carved into the sandstone, as well as tall wooden ladders. You'll climb a 32-foot (10-m) modern version of this during the tour. This adventurous outing involves climbing down a 100-foot (30-m) staircase into the canyon and clambering through a 12-foot-long (3-m), 18-inch-wide (46-cm) tunnel.

Long House Tour

The park's second-largest cliff dwelling is **Long House** (daily May-mid-Oct. weather permitting). Excavated between 1959 and 1961, the Long House includes about 150 rooms and 21 kivas

▼ BALCONY HOUSE

Top 3

CLIFF PALACE

1 TOUR CLIFF PALACE

The largest of the under-the-rim dwellings, **Cliff Palace** (daily May-mid-Sept., $5) has more than 150 rooms and 23 circular kivas—distinctive circular pits used for performing cultural ritual). Considering that three-quarters of the park's 600 cliff dwellings contain just 1-5 rooms, Cliff Palace is exceptionally big, a neighborhood where an estimated 100 people once lived. Visits are only possible on ranger-led tours; consider the **Twilight Tour**. You must be able to climb several ladders, the highest of which is 15 feet tall (4.6 m). Purchase tickets up to two days in advance at the visitors center or the **Durango Welcome Center** (802 Main Ave., Durango, 800/525-8855, www.durango.org, 10am-6pm daily mid-Apr.-late Oct.). Book reservations up to six months in advance (877/444-6777, www.recreation.gov, $10-25). You can also look down at Cliff Palace from a Mesa Top Loop Road overlook.

2 EXPLORE CHAPIN MESA ARCHEOLOGICAL MUSEUM

A National Historic Landmark, the **Chapin Mesa Archeological Museum** (roughly 9am-5pm, limited hours in winter, free) contains artifacts from the Ancestral Puebloan people who used to inhabit Mesa Verde. It shows a 25-minute orientation film and has educational exhibits that include dioramas and other cultural items. Nearby, rangers give daily talks at overlooks of **Spruce Tree House.** The museum is located on Chapin Mesa, 21 miles (34 km) south of park entrance.

SPRUCE TREE HOUSE

3 DRIVE NORTH RIM ROAD

The curvy **North Rim Road** (12 mi./19 km one-way) skims along canyon rims between Morefield Campground and Far View Lodge. It goes through a tunnel and passes three overlooks: Montezuma Valley, Park Point, and Geologic Overlook, each offering a different take on the rugged mesa-and-canyon scenery. Of the three, **Park Point** at 8,572 feet (2,613 m) is the highest point in the park, with a 360-degree view where you can see the four states of the Four Corners. This road accesses Chapin Mesa and Mesa Top Loop Roads plus Wetherill Mesa Road.

Best Hike

PETROGLYPH POINT

DISTANCE: 2.4 miles (3.9 km) round-trip
DURATION: 1.5 hours
ELEVATION CHANGE: 300 feet (91 m)
EFFORT: moderate
TRAILHEAD: Gated trailhead near Chapin Mesa Archeological Museum

The crowded **Petroglyph Point Loop** accesses close-up views of ancient rock art, including hunting scenes, spirals, and dainty handprints. The rocky, narrow path follows a canyon wall with steep drop-offs, and you may need to use your hands to help climb a steep stone stairway. The last portion of the loop is a flat forest walk. Entrance to the trail is through a gated trailhead (check with a ranger for current open hours). Register to hike at the trailhead or Chapin Mesa Archeological Museum, where an interpretive brochure is also available.

whose beams date to 1145 CE. Archaeologists believe that 150-175 people once lived beneath the shadow of its 300-foot-long (91-m) alcove. Of special note is a well-preserved, triangular tower rising four stories from floor to ceiling at the western end of the alcove. Visiting the site requires walking 2.3 miles (3.7 km) round-trip from Wetherill Mesa Kiosk, and you'll climb two 15-foot (4.6-m) ladders as part of the tour.

Other Cliff Dwelling Tours

Book other tours up to six months in advance (877/444-6777, www.recreation.gov, $10-25). These include the **Twilight Tour of Cliff Palace** and **Sunrise Tour of Balcony House** and tours through **Oak Tree House, Yucca House,** and **Mug House.**

FAR VIEW

A self-guided stroll to **Far View House** (8am-sunset, 1.2 mi./1.9 km rt., 1-2 hrs., easy) visits several pueblo villages, including eye-catching spiral petroglyphs at the **Pipe Shrine House.** Far View is 4 miles (6.4 km) north of the Chapin Mesa Archeological Museum.

SCENIC DRIVES

MESA TOP LOOP ROAD

Mesa Top Loop Road (daily 8am-sunset, 6 mi./10 km) tours several overlooks such as **Navajo Canyon** and **Sun Point,** which offer plunging views down adjacent canyons. Twelve self-guided stops include several pit houses, an overlook of **Cliff Palace,** and the ceremonial **Sun Temple,** which may have been an astronomical observatory. Mesa Top Loop Road is 21 miles (34 km) south of the park entrance, beyond the Chapin Mesa Archeological Museum.

WETHERILL MESA

Wetherill Mesa Road (8am-6pm daily May-Oct. weather permitting) tours a long, protruding peninsula of land bordered by impressive canyons whose sandstone cliffs host many natural alcoves. Ancestral Puebloans took advantage of many of these landmarks to build storage buildings and homes in their protective shadows. Stop at overlooks to take in **McElmo Canyon** and **Rock Canyon Tower.** At the road's terminus at Wetherill Mesa Kiosk, you can hike to Step House or Badger House. The road is on the west side of the park, 27 miles (43 km) from the visitors center.

RECREATION

HIKING

From Morefield Campground, the **Knife Edge Trail** (2 mi./3.2 km rt., 1 hr., moderate) follows a steep bluff along the original entrance road built in 1914 to an overlook of Montezuma Valley.

On Chapin Mesa, **Spruce Canyon Trail** (2.4 mi./3.9 km rt., 1.5 hrs.,

PETROGLYPH POINT TRAIL

strenuous) descends into the canyon to cross a seasonal trickle of a stream on small bridges before climbing about 500 feet (152 m) back up. Registration to hike is required at the Chapin Mesa Archeological Museum or the nearby gated trailhead; check with the museum for current hours. On Cliff Palace Loop Road, the **Soda Canyon Overlook Trail** (1.2 mi./1.9 km rt., 45 min., easy) descends to the canyon rim for views of archaeological sites, including Balcony House, in the canyon below. Find the trailhead 1 mile (1.6 km) north of the Balcony House parking area.

From the Wetherill Mesa Kiosk at the terminus of Wetherill Mesa Road (daily May-Oct. weather permitting), two trails go to archaeological sites which you can explore via self-guided tours. A winding trail descends to **Step House** (9am-4pm, 1 mi./1.6 km rt., 1 hr., moderate), where you can walk around a cliff dwelling and see a pit house and petroglyphs before climbing back up. The **Badger House Trail** (2.3 mi./3.7 km rt., 1.5-2 hrs., easy) visits four mesa-top archaeological sites on a graveled and paved trail.

BICYCLING

Cyclists enjoy the thrill of the park's curvy roads and their steep climbs and descents, but they come with challenges: narrow roadways, no shoulders, broken pavement, and congested traffic. Riding early or late in the day is a more pleasant experience. All roads in the park permit bicycles, with the exception of Wetherill Mesa Road.

WHERE TO STAY

INSIDE THE PARK

Located 15 miles (24 km) south of the park entrance, **Far View Lodge** (970/529-4421 or 800/449-2288, www.visitmesaverde.com, mid-Apr.-mid-Oct., from $160) is the only lodging option in the park. It has 150 southwestern-styled rooms that lack TVs but have sweeping views and free Wi-Fi. Rates include a full breakfast; dinner is available at the **Metate Room Restaurant** (5pm-9:30pm daily in season); reservations are strongly recommended.

The 267-site **Morefield Campground** (970/529-4421 or 800/449-2288, www.visitmesaverde.com, mid-Apr.-mid-Oct., $33) is 4 miles (6.4 km) south of the park entrance. Some sites can be reserved in advance. Amenities include flush toilets, showers, a camp store, laundry, and a dump station.

The casual, self-service **Far View Terrace Café** (0.25 mi./0.4 km south of Far View Lodge, 7am-10am, 11am-3pm, 5pm-7pm daily mid-Apr.-early Oct.) has reasonably priced food, including Navajo tacos. Farther up the road, near the Chapin Mesa Archeological Museum, the **Spruce Tree Terrace Café** (9am-6:30pm daily June-mid-Aug., limited hours other seasons) serves barbecue. Near the Morefield Campground, the **Knife Edge Café** (7am-10am daily May-Sept., 11am-6pm daily June-Aug., 11am-2pm daily Aug.-Sept.) is known for its pancake-and-sausage breakfasts.

OUTSIDE THE PARK

Located 10 miles (16 km) from the park entrance, the small town of **Cortez** offers basic services in between the area's many monuments.

GETTING THERE

AIR

The closest international airport is **Denver International Airport** (DEN, 8500 Peña Blvd., Denver, 303/342-2000, www.flydenver.com). **Durango-La Plata County Airport** (DRO, 1000 Airport Rd., Durango, 970/382-6050, www.durangogov.org) offers daily service by United Airlines and American Airlines, including nonstop service to Denver. Car rentals are available.

Animas Transportation (2023 Main Ave., Durango, 970/259-1315, www.animastransportation.com) will shuttle a carload to the park on a per-mile basis, which works out to about $150 one-way.

CAR

The east-west US 160 connects Mesa Verde National Park with Durango, 35 miles (56 km) east of the park entrance, and Cortez, 10 miles (16 km) west.

GETTING AROUND

There is no public transportation within the park. You'll need a car to get around, and the roads are steep, extremely curvy, and narrow with no shoulders. **Gas** is available at the campground. Inside the park (about 15 mi./24 km south of US 160), the road splits: one branch turns west toward Wetherill Mesa (May-Oct. only), while the main road continues south to Chapin Mesa, the location of Balcony House and Cliff Palace.

Guided bus tours (Aramark, 800/449-2288, www.visitmesaverde.com, twice daily mid-Apr.-mid-Oct, $75) are an option for touring the park. The 700 Years Tour takes in the Cliff Palace and other sites. The Far View Tour climbs Park Point and goes to the Sun Temple and Spruce Tree Overlook. Purchase tickets in advance online or in person at the visitors center. Morefield Campground, or Far View Lodge are an option for touring the park. The 700 Years Tour takes in the Cliff House and other sites. The Far View Tour climbs Park Point and goes to the Sun Temple and Spruce Tree Overlook. Purchase tickets in advance online or in person at the visitors center, Morefield Campground, or Far View Lodge.

SIGHTS NEARBY

Anasazi Heritage Center (27501 Hwy. 184, Dolores, 970/882-5600, www.blm.gov, 9am-5pm daily Mar.-Oct., 10am-4pm daily Nov.-Feb.), 10 miles north of Cortez, serves as an introduction to the region's archaeological attractions and an information center for Canyons of the Ancients National Monument.

Canyons of the Ancients National Monument (27501 Hwy. 184, Dolores, 970/882-5600, www.blm.gov, 9am-5pm daily Mar.-Oct., 10am-4pm daily Nov.-Feb., free), southwest of Cortez, is a relatively untouched wilderness of flat-topped mesas and twisting canyons whose sandstone walls harbor the largest concentration of archaeological sites in the country.

Four Corners Monument (U.S. 160, 38 miles south of Cortez, 928/206-2540, www.navajonationparks.org, 8am-8pm daily late May-mid-Sept.) marks the only spot in the United States where four states—Colorado, New Mexico, Arizona, and Utah—meet.

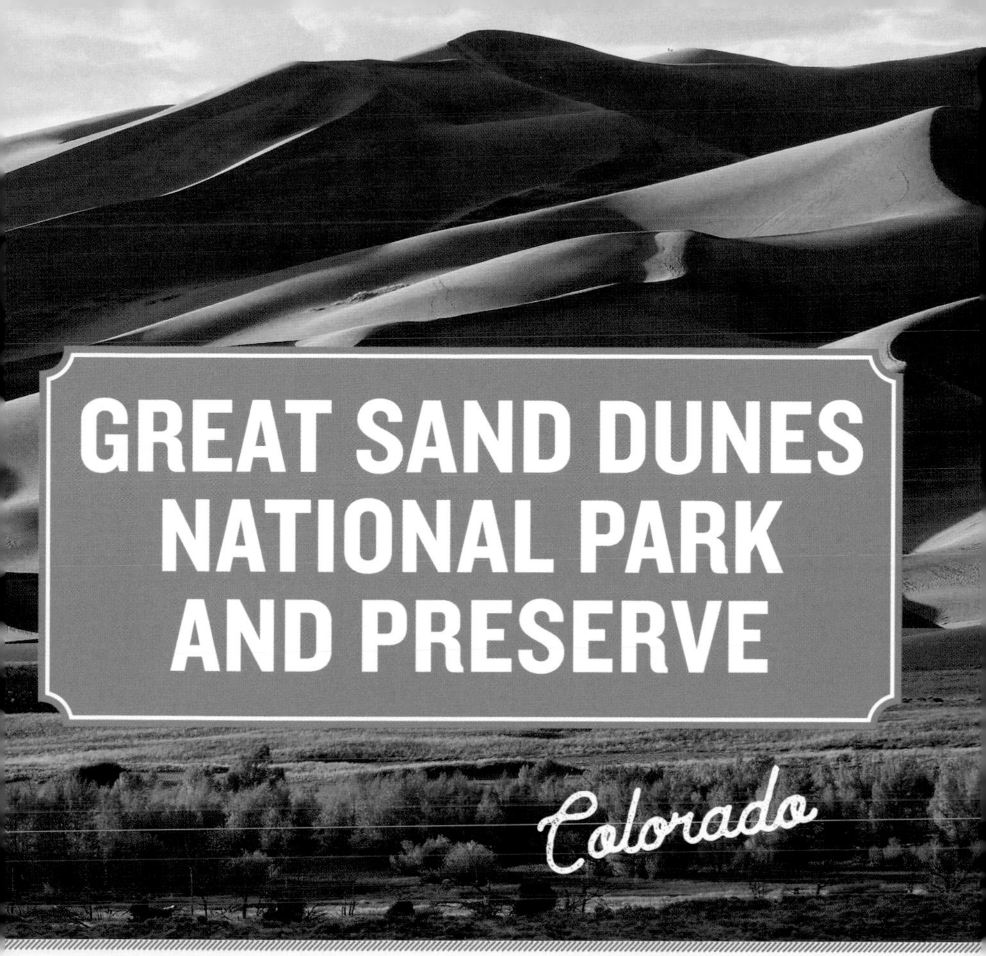

GREAT SAND DUNES NATIONAL PARK AND PRESERVE

Colorado

KEEPSAKE STAMPS ▼▼▼

WEBSITE:
www.nps.gov/grsa

PHONE NUMBER:
719/378-6395

VISITATION RANK:
40

WHY GO:
Slide down the tallest sand dunes in North America.

▲ GREAT SAND DUNES NATIONAL PARK

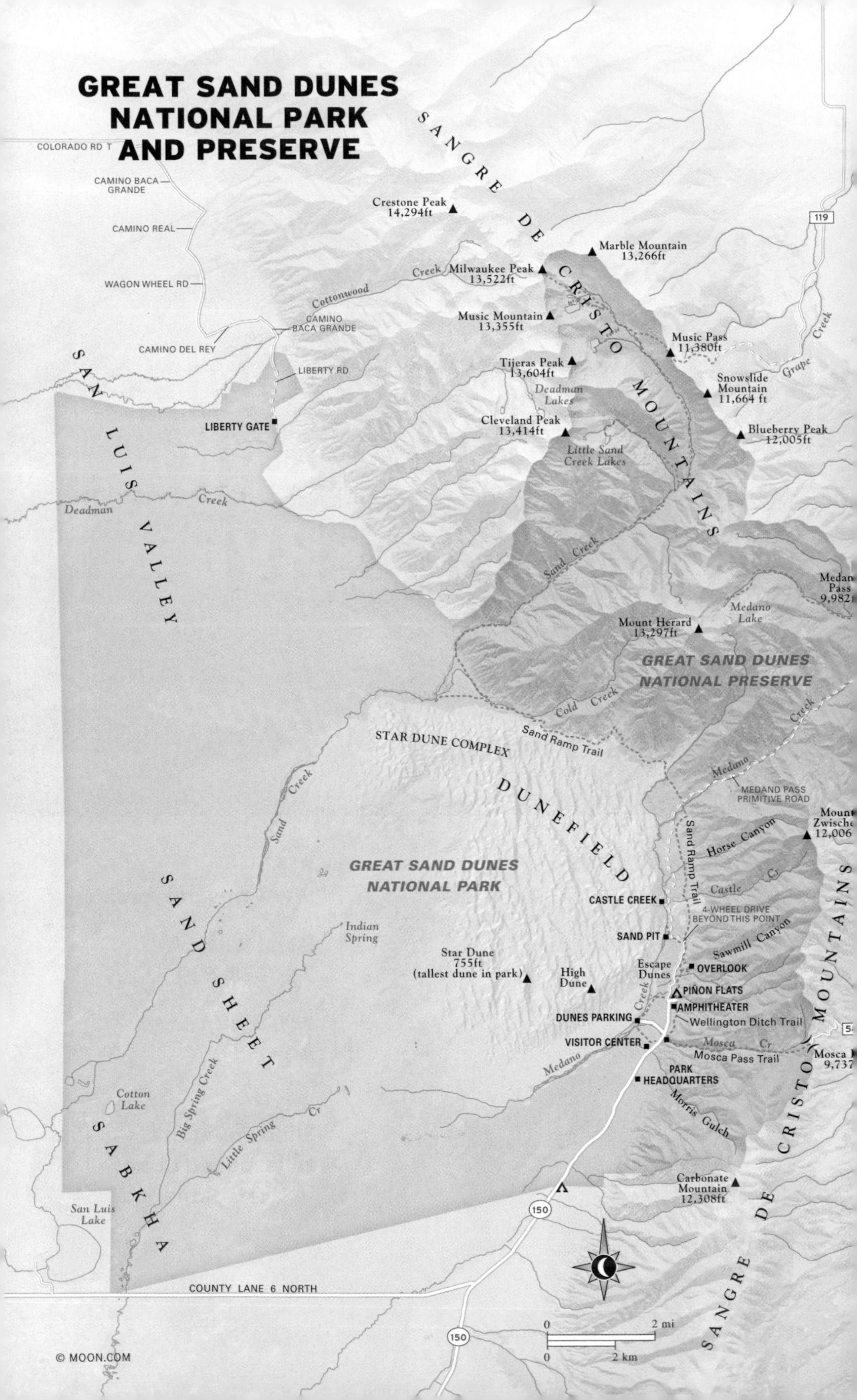

GREAT SAND DUNES NATIONAL PARK AND PRESERVE
SANGRE DE CRISTO MOUNTAINS
COLORADO RD T
CAMINO BACA GRANDE
CAMINO REAL
WAGON WHEEL RD
CAMINO BACA GRANDE
CAMINO DEL REY
LIBERTY RD
LIBERTY GATE
Crestone Peak 14,294ft
Marble Mountain 13,266ft
Milwaukee Peak 13,522ft
Cottonwood Creek
Music Mountain 13,355ft
Music Pass 11,380ft
Tijeras Peak 13,604ft
Deadman Lakes
Snowslide Mountain 11,664 ft
Grape Creek
Cleveland Peak 13,414ft
Blueberry Peak 12,005ft
Little Sand Creek Lakes
119
SAN LUIS VALLEY
Deadman Creek
Sand Creek
Medano Pass 9,982
Medano Lake
Mount Herard 13,297ft
GREAT SAND DUNES NATIONAL PRESERVE
Cold Creek
Sand Ramp Trail
STAR DUNE COMPLEX
DUNEFIELD
Medano Creek
MEDANO PASS PRIMITIVE ROAD
Mount Zwischen 12,006
Horse Canyon
Sand Ramp Trail
Castle Cr
GREAT SAND DUNES NATIONAL PARK
CASTLE CREEK
4-WHEEL DRIVE BEYOND THIS POINT
SAND PIT
Sawmill Canyon
Indian Spring
Star Dune 755ft (tallest dune in park)
High Dune
Escape Dunes
OVERLOOK
PIÑON FLATS
AMPHITHEATER
DUNES PARKING
Wellington Ditch Trail
VISITOR CENTER
Mosca Cr
Mosca Pass Trail
Mosca Pass 9,737
PARK HEADQUARTERS
Morris Gulch
SAND SHEET
Big Spring Creek
Cotton Lake
Little Spring Cr
SABKHA
Carbonate Mountain 12,308ft
150
San Luis Lake
COUNTY LANE 6 NORTH
150
0 2 mi
0 2 km
© MOON.COM

Along the eastern edge of Colorado's San Luis Valley is a vast, high-elevation basin almost as large as the state of New Jersey. Tucked into this valley, **GREAT SAND DUNES NATIONAL PARK AND PRESERVE** holds a remarkable dunefield with mounds of sand up to 750 feet (228 m) high. While these are the tallest dunes in North America, they are utterly dwarfed by their incredible backdrop—the long line of the jagged Sangre de Cristo Mountains. Water flowing from the mountains surrounds the dunes with braided streams. Contrary to other geological formations that alter more slowly with time, the dunes change daily. Shifting sands move with wind, water, and gravity, creating a fluid landscape that always seems to be in motion.

PLANNING YOUR TIME

Great Sand Dunes National Park is in southern Colorado, less than 65 miles (105 km) north of the state line with New Mexico and about four hours south of Denver. This is the arid Southwest, although the Sangre de Cristos form a reminder of Colorado's northern high mountains.

Elevations span 7,515-13,604 feet (2,290-4,146 m), which keep temperatures in the 50-80°F (10-27°C) range during the day May-September: This is the crowded season. Winter temperatures range 30-45°F (-1-7°C), sometimes with a few inches of snowfall. Year-round, the arid desert weather often has blue skies, but nighttime temperatures can plunge to cool and even frigid zones. Summer can produce afternoon lightning storms.

Despite the temperature, the surface of the sand heats up in summer; during midday, the sand can exceed 150°F (66°C). Plan for early morning or evening excursions on foot. During windstorms, which are frequent in spring, wear protective glasses.

ENTRANCE AND FEES

The entrance fee is $25 per vehicle ($20 motorcycle and bicycle, $15 individual) and good for seven days. The entrance station is on CO 150 at the park headquarters.

VISITORS CENTER

Located 0.7 mile (1.1 km) beyond the entrance station, the **Great Sand Dunes Visitor Center** (11999 CO 150, Mosca, 8:30am-5pm daily summer, 9am-4:30pm daily fall-spring) has interactive exhibits, park information, a bookstore, and a Junior Ranger Program. View the dunes through spotting scopes on the back porch. Ranger programs (May-fall, schedules vary weekly) are held at the visitors center or campground amphitheater and guided hikes are also offered. At this International Dark Sky Park, several nighttime programs include full moon dune walks, stargazing, and viewing nocturnal migrations of salamanders and frogs. Visitors with disabilities can use the special sand-friendly wheelchairs.

ONE DAY IN GREAT SAND DUNES

A visit to Great Sand Dunes is all about the dunes. If you only have one day to explore its wonders, choose from a quick cruise to **scenic viewpoints,** a longer **hike** to the tip of the dunes themselves, or rent a **sandboard** and ride down the slopes for a speedy rush.

Top 3

STAR DUNE

1 DRIVE TO SCENIC VIEWPOINTS

Bordered on the north by Sand Creek and to the east and south by Medano Creek, the **dunefield** resembles a sea of sand waves. The tallest dune is 755-foot (230-m) **Star Dune;** the second tallest is 699-foot (213-m) **High Dune.** For the closest views, drive to the Dunes Parking Lot at the end of a spur road just past the visitors center. The shifting back and forth of the wind keeps the dunes relatively in place. Though the dunefield covers 30 square miles (78 sq. km)—an area estimated to contain five billion cubic meters of sand—it is only 10 percent of the total sand in the area.

2 GO SAND SLEDDING AND BOARDING

Specifically designed gear is used for sledding or boarding on the sand dunes. Near the park entrance, the **Oasis Restaurant and Store** (7800 CO 150 N., Mosca, 719/378-2222, www.greatdunes.com, May-mid-Oct., $20) rents sandboards and sand sleds. From the Dunes Parking Lot, wade Medano Creek to access the closest slopes with a good pitch for sliding.

3 SPLASH IN MEDANO CREEK

The shallow and wide Medano Creek provides a short seasonal family splash and float place. Bring the inflatable float toys for kids to enjoy the small surge waves that come a couple times each minute downstream. Water flow reaches its peak late May-early June, when weekends pack out beaches with families playing in the sand near Dunes Parking Lot, Sand Pit Picnic Area, and Castle Creek Picnic Area. The creek usually dries up August-March.

SOLITARY HIKER ON THE DUNES

Best Hike

HIGH DUNE

DISTANCE: 2.5 miles (4 km) round-trip
DURATION: 2-3 hours
ELEVATION CHANGE: 699 feet (213 m)
EFFORT: strenuous
TRAILHEAD: Dunes Parking Lot

Hiking the **High Dune on First Ridge** is a grunt: each footstep sinks into the sand as you make slow headway up. Start by crossing Medano Creek, and then follow the ridge up. Sometimes zigzagging up the ridge helps. Footsteps from previous hikers may disappear as winds shift sands, so stick to the ridge. The view from the top of the dune spreads across the entire dunefield with the Sangre de Cristo Mountains rising above.

SCENIC DRIVE

For high-clearance 4WD vehicles only, **Medano Pass Primitive Road** (22.4 mi./36 km rt., closed in winter) climbs into Great Sand Dunes National Preserve in the **Sangre de Cristo Mountains.** Check road conditions first at the visitors center before driving north to the road entrance to ascend to 10,040 feet (3,060 m) at Medano Pass. You may need to deflate tire pressure to handle the sand, rocks, and stream crossings on this rugged unpaved road, but can refill on your return at the air station at the pavement end. Fall is best for leaf color. Jeep rentals and tours are available through **Pathfinders 4X4** (719/496-6288, http://pathfinders4x4.com).

HIKING

From Loop 2 in Piñon Flats Campground, a trail goes to **Dunes Overlook** (2.3 mi./3.7 km rt., 1.5-2.5 hrs., moderate) with a 450-foot (137-m) ascent occurring in switchbacks at the end where you can take in the dunefield across Medano Creek drainage.

Near the visitors center at the Montville-Mosca Pass Trailhead, hikers have the option of a short forest trail with views of the first dune ridge on the **Montville Nature Trail** (0.5 mi./0.8 km rt., 30 min., easy) or the tougher **Mosca Pass Trail** (7 mi./11.3 km rt., 3.5-4 hrs., strenuous), which climbs 1,400 feet (427 m) in elevation along the trickling Mosca Creek through the forest to

TUBING MEDANO CREEK

COTTONWOODS ALONG MEDANO CREEK

HOW THE SAND DUNES FORM

The formula for creating the sand dunes is simple: wind and water deposit the sand in piles. It's an ongoing process that forms and reshapes the dunes, causing some to shift several feet in a week. The sand comes from surrounding mountains—the San Juan Mountains to the west and the Sangre de Cristo Mountains to the east. Originally, a lake on the valley floor trapped sand blowing in from the San Juans and washing down the creeks that flow from the Sangre de Cristos. The lake has long since dried up, but the dunes continue to grow. Winds and water also recycle escaping sands back into the dunes.

The **sabkha** are wetlands of dried white mineral beds that flank the western portion of the dunes. The dunes' midsection contains 90 percent of the sand. The large **sand sheet** is mostly covered by grassland and swept over by prevailing winds that are responsible for building the dunes. Fields of yellow sunflowers show up in August. You can view both of these features while driving along the park's south boundary on County Lane 6 (between Mosca and CO 150) and at several pullouts along the park entrance road.

9,737-foot (2,968-m) Mosca Pass in the Sangre de Cristo Mountains.

From the Point of No Return parking area, a trail reaches to two picnic areas on Medano Creek on the edge of the dunes. These are prime destinations for families where kids can frolic in the creek and play on the sand. The **Sand Pit** (1.5 mi./2.4 km rt., 1 hr., easy) has gentle sand slopes, while **Castle Creek** (3 mi./4.8 km rt., 1.5-2 hrs., moderate) has a 400-foot (122-m) dune that you can slide down and into a creek.

RECREATION

FAT TIRE BIKING

Bring your own fat tire bikes (not mountain bikes) to handle the sand, rocks, and creeks on the challenging Medano Pass Primitive Road (22.4 mi./36 km rt., closed in winter). The route, lined with primitive campsites, climbs to 10,040 feet (3,060 m) at **Medano Pass** in the Sangre de Cristo Mountains.

▼ ASPEN ABOVE THE DUNES

SUNSET OVER THE DUNES

HIKER ON TOP OF HIGH DUNE

WHERE TO STAY

INSIDE THE PARK

Some of the 88 sites at the park's **Piñon Flats Campground** (877/444-6777, www.recreation.gov, Apr.-Oct., $20) can be reserved up to six months in advance. The remaining 44 sites are first come, first served. Amenities include flush toilets and drinking water. On **Medano Pass Primitive Road** (4WD only) primitive campsites (21 sites, first come, first served, free) have bear boxes and fire rings.

OUTSIDE THE PARK

The **Oasis Restaurant and Store** (7800 CO 150 N., Mosca, 719/378-2222, www.greatdunes.com, May-mid-Oct.) has a restaurant, convenience store, motel, campground, and gas station just outside the park entrance. The town of **Alamosa,** 34 miles (55 km) south, has limited services. Nearby lodging options include the primitive **Zapata Falls Campground** (BLM Monte Vista office, 719/852-7074) and motel rooms at **Great Sand Dunes Lodge** (719/378-2900, www.gsdlodge.com, Mar.-Oct.). Located 7.8 miles (15 min.) from the park entrance, **Zapata Ranch** (5305 CO-150, Mosca, 719/ 378-2356, www.zranch.org, $1,530-2,765 for 3-7 nights) is a working cattle ranch with horseback riding, educational programs, and all-inclusive accommodations. It's the only licensed provider of horseback rides into the park.

GETTING THERE AND AROUND

AIR

The closest airports are **Denver International Airport** (DEN, 8500 Peña Blvd., 303/342-2000, www.flydenver.com) and the smaller **Colorado Springs Airport** (COS, 7770 Milton E. Proby Pkwy., 719/550-1900, https://coloradosprings.gov/flycos). Car rentals are available at both.

CAR

Great Sand Dunes National Park is 255 miles (410 km) south of Denver and 170 miles (275 km) south of Colorado Springs via I-25 South and US 160 West. From US 160 near Alamosa, take CO 150 north for 20 miles (32 km) to the visitors center. There is no public transportation to or within the park.

WHITE SANDS NATIONAL PARK

New Mexico

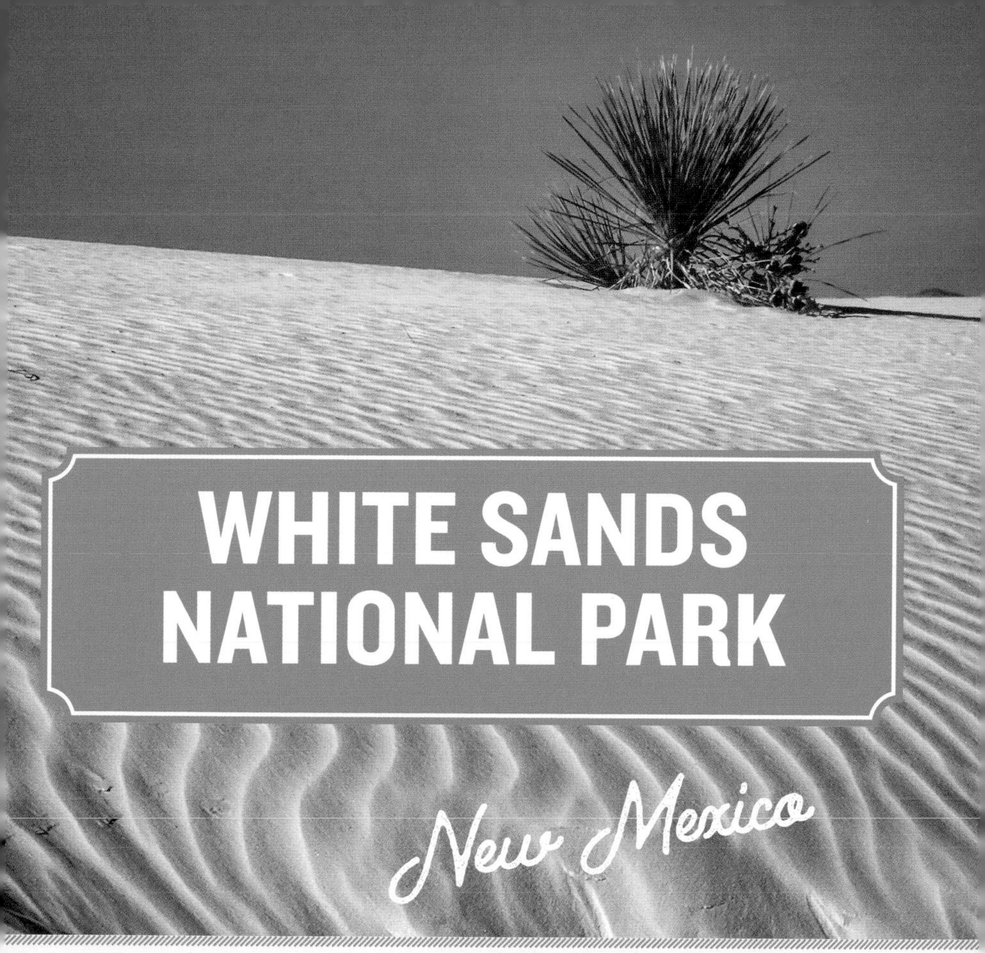

KEEPSAKE STAMPS ▾▾▾

WEBSITE:
www.nps.gov/whsa

PHONE NUMBER:
575/479-6124

VISITATION RANK:
36

WHY GO:
Walk in the world's largest gypsum dunefield.

▲ WHITE SAND DUNE

WHITE SANDS NATIONAL PARK

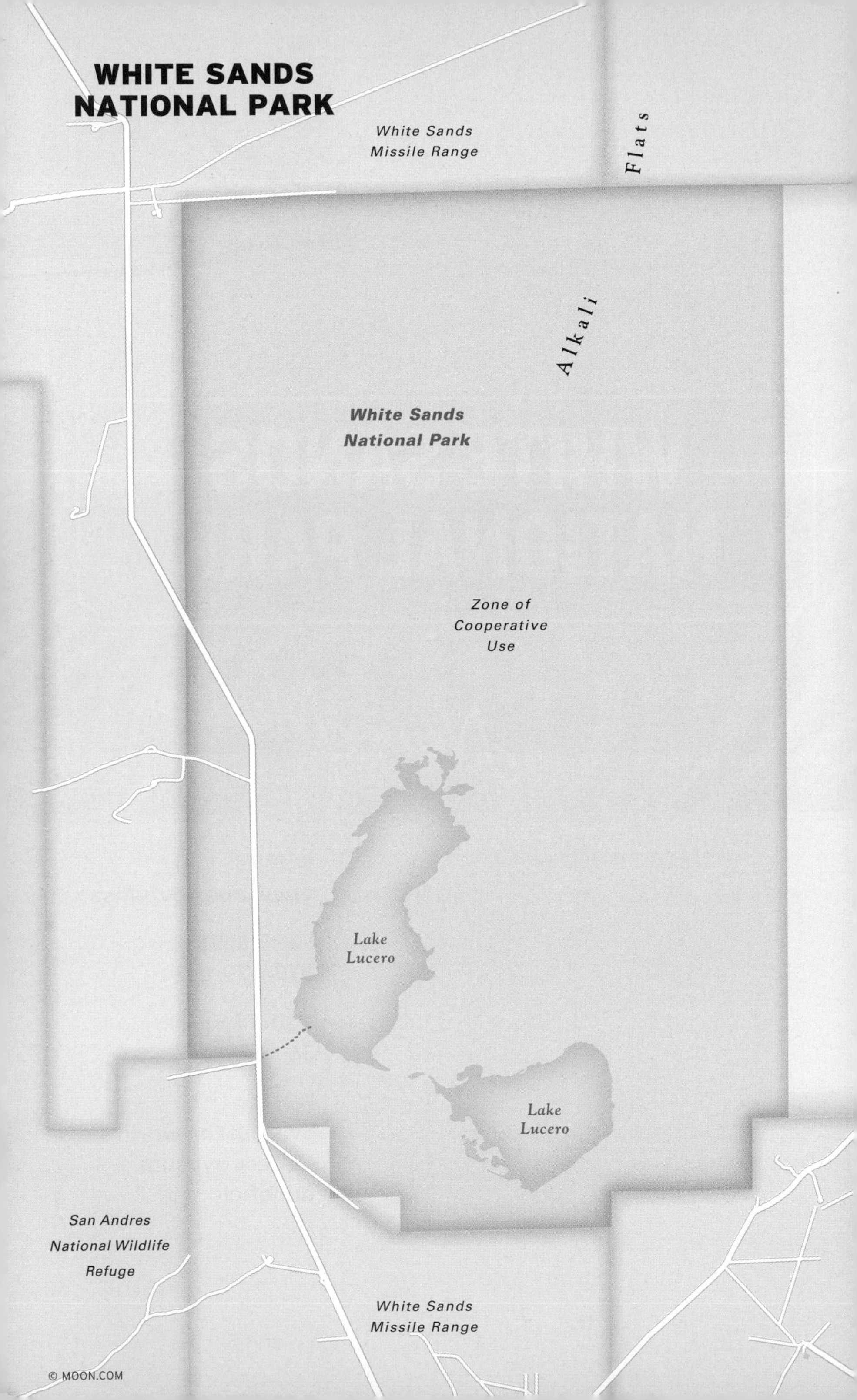

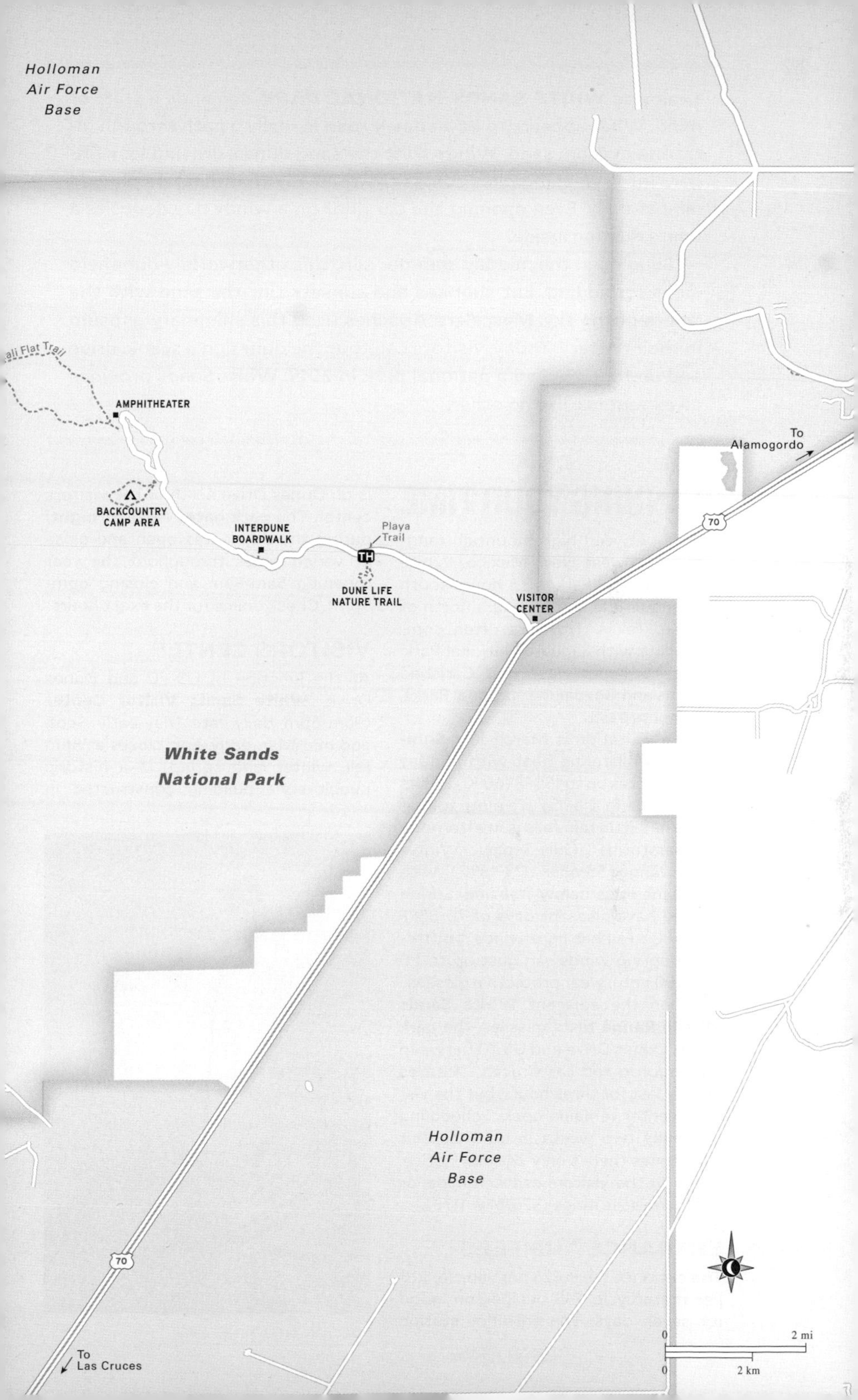

Holloman Air Force Base
Alkali Flat Trail
AMPHITHEATER
BACKCOUNTRY CAMP AREA
INTERDUNE BOARDWALK
Playa Trail
TH
DUNE LIFE NATURE TRAIL
VISITOR CENTER
To Alamogordo
70
White Sands National Park
Holloman Air Force Base
70
To Las Cruces
0
2 mi
0
2 km

Exploring **WHITE SANDS NATIONAL PARK** demands a shift of mind. What appears to be a snowy road is really a path through ultrafine gypsum sand. Winds shift the sand dunes, drifting lacy fingers into sweeping piles across the roadway that must be plowed almost daily. Even opening the car door on a windy day deposits a white dusting inside.

Blinding in the midday summer sun, this otherworldly dunefield looks forbidding. But sunrises and sunsets tint the sand with the colors of the sky. Mescalero Apaches used this shimmery gypsum in their pottery. Today, visitors can tour the dunes on a scenic drive and on foot. Named a national park in 2019, White Sands provides an experience like no other.

PLANNING YOUR TIME

Tucked between high mountain ranges in southwest New Mexico, White Sands National Park is 3.5 hours south of Albuquerque and 1.5 hours north of El Paso, Texas. Travelers often combine visits with Saguaro National Park, about 4.5 hours west, and Carlsbad Caverns and Guadalupe National Parks, 3.5-4 hours east.

High visitation is March-July. **Summer** sees blistering heat with midday temperatures up to 150°F (66°C). Visits early or late in the day are more tolerable. What little rain falls is in afternoon thunderstorms (July-Sept.). Winter highs range 55-65°F (13-18°C) with nighttime lows below freezing. Spring and fall have pleasant days of 70-85°F (21-29°C). Fall has light winds, but frequent spring winds can gust up to 50 mph (80 kph); wear protective glasses.

When the adjacent **White Sands Missile Range** tests missiles, the park closes Dunes Drive and US 70 between Alamogordo and Las Cruces. Closures usually last for three hours, but the visitors center remains open. Scheduling is usually two weeks in advance, but sometimes there's only 24-hour notice. Check in the visitors center, online, or call the missile range (575/678-1178).

ENTRANCE AND FEES

The entrance fee is $25 per vehicle, $20 per motorcycle, $15 per person, good for seven days. The entrance station is on Dunes Drive north of the visitors center. The **park gates close at night;** during the day, gates open and close at varied times throughout the year (opening 5am-8am and closing 6pm-9pm). Check online for the exact hours.

VISITORS CENTER

At the junction of US 70 and Dunes Drive, **White Sands Visitor Center** (9am-6pm daily late May-early Sept. and mid-Mar.-early Apr., closes at 5pm fall, winter, and spring) is a historic pueblo-style building constructed in

YUCCA IN INTERDUNES AREA

Top 3

DUNES DRIVE SAND ROAD

1 TOUR DUNES DRIVE

Dunes Drive (16 mi./26 km rt., 45 min.) goes north from the visitors center on pavement surrounded by thick desert scrub. But soon the vegetation thins and white dunes become more prominent with yucca anchored into the sand. Wind blows sand drifts over the road margins. At 5 miles (8 km), the pavement is replaced by packed sand that is plowed daily with berms on the side that look like snow. Be ready to encounter washboards, potholes, and larger drifts of sand along the curves amid dunes of brilliant white gypsum. Pullouts have exhibits, picnic areas have vault toilets, and parking areas allow you to walk amid the dunes. Don't stray out of visual distance from the road unless you are on a marked trail.

2 REVEL IN THE FULL MOON

Visit at night to delight in the moonlight glinting off gypsum dunes. Rangers lead **Full Moon Hikes** (www.recreation.gov, 877/444-6777, Apr.-Oct., 1.5 hrs., $8 pp) on the Dune Life Nature Trail once a month on the night before the full moon. Reservations, which can be made up to 30 days in advance, are required. **Full Moon Nights** (1-2 hrs., May-Oct., free) take place at the natural dune amphitheater near the end of Dunes Drive once a month with live music, ranger talks, or artists. Bring a camp chair or blanket for sitting.

3 CAMP OVERNIGHT

Camping allows you to watch the sunrise and sunset smear color across the sparkling sand, but it is only permitted in one location. With orange trail markers, the **Backcountry Camping Trail** (2 mi./3.2 km rt., 1.5 hrs., moderate) climbs several steep dunes to reach the 10 primitive backcountry campsites among the white gypsum. They have no shade, toilets, or water. Plan to bring a tent and carry 1 gallon (3.8 l) of water per person per day. Pick up first-come, first-served **permits** ($3 adults, $1.50 kids) at the visitors center. The trailhead is 6 miles (9.7 km) north on Dunes Drive and has a vault toilet.

GYPSUM SAND DUNES

Best Hike

ALKALI FLATS

DISTANCE: 5 miles (8 km) round-trip
DURATION: 3 hours
ELEVATION CHANGE: 94 feet (29 m)
EFFORT: strenuous
TRAILHEAD: Alkali Flats Trailhead at the end of Dunes Drive

Don't be fooled by the "flats" in the name. **Alkali Flat Trail** (4.6 mi./7.4 km, 3 hrs., strenuous) vaults up and down over the shade-less gypsum dunes in the heart of the park. Each step sinks into the sand on this loop. With one white dune looking like the next and wind filling in footprints, it's easy to get lost. Follow the orange markers; if you can't see the next trail marker, turn around. The trail looks over the dry bed that once housed ice-age Lake Otero.

TRAILHEAD FOR ALKALI FLATS

the 1930s. It offers park information, interactive exhibits, a film, and a bookstore. Outside is a native plant garden. A gift shop sits behind the visitors center.

HIKING

Since shifting sands erase footprints, routes in the sand are lined with trail markers, each within spotting distance of the last one. If you can't see the next marker, turn around as it's unsafe to continue. Spring winds often reduce visibility. In the shifting sands, even short walks will feel like a slog.

In the vegetated gypsum dunes, follow green markers and interpretive signs on the **Playa Trail** (Dunes Drive, 0.5 mi./0.8 km rt., 30 min., easy) to a depression that collects rainfall into a temporary lake.

Dune Life Nature Trail (Dunes Drive, 1 mi./1.6 km rt., 45 min., moderate), with blue trail markers, climbs to the top of a partially vegetated dune to make a loop in soft sand, passing 14 interpretive signs.

The wheelchair-accessible **Interdune Boardwalk** (Dunes Drive, 0.4 mi./0.6 km rt., 20 min., easy) is an interpretive trail with a variety of desert vegetation and an elevated boardwalk for easier walking.

Lake Lucero (1.5 mi./2.4 km, 3 hrs., moderate) is a dry lake bed filled with

ONE DAY IN WHITE SANDS

For a one-day trip, tour **Dunes Drive.** Follow the easy, accessible **Interdune Boardwalk** to learn about this unique desert. For a real adventure, hike out on the dunes to experience the feel of the fine gypsum sand beneath your feet.

selenite crystals, some up to 2 feet (0.6 m) long and the source of the gypsum feeding the dunes. You can only hike down along the lake bed on a ranger-led trip, offered once a month. It starts with a caravan in your own car across the neighboring missile range to the trailhead for the hike down a steep gully to the lake. Required reservations can be made up to 30 days in advance (www.recreation.gov, 877/444-6777, Nov.-Apr., $8 adults, $4 kids).

RECREATION

BIKING

Bring your own fat tire or mountain bikes to handle the sand on Dunes Drive. Drifting sand and washboards add to the challenge of this unique ride.

SAND SLIDING

Bring your own plastic saucer or buy one from the gift shop behind the visitors center to go sand sliding. Then

PICNIC TABLE WITH WINDSCREEN

GYPSUM DUNES

White Sands is estimated to contain 4.5 billion tons of gypsum. Similar to salt, gypsum dissolves in water but re-crystallizes when dry. This mineral, which is used in toothpaste, makes up 98 percent of the dunes in White Sands. About 12,000 years ago, after the last ice age, rain and melting snow washed the dissolved gypsum down from the surrounding mountains into the large Lake Otero, which eventually dried up to form dunes. Today, the mineral still washes down from the mountains to pool seasonally at Lake Lucero. When the water evaporates, it leaves fragile selenite crystals to be broken down by wind and water blowing across the dunes.

head for the bare dunes along the second half of Dunes Drive. Look for a clear runout away from the road.

WHERE TO STAY

INSIDE THE PARK

No lodgings or camping is available inside the park, with the exception of backcountry camping in one location. The park plows sand to create several picnic areas that resemble large sandy parking lots. They have tables with wind screens, raised grills, and vault toilets. The gift shop behind the visitors center carries convenience foods.

OUTSIDE THE PARK

The closest lodgings, dining, and services are in **Alamogordo** 15 miles (24 km) from the park, but there are more plentiful options in **Las Cruces,** which is roughly a one-hour drive. The nearest campgrounds are 30-45 minutes away.

GETTING THERE AND AROUND

AIR

The closest airport is **El Paso International Airport** (ELP, 6701 Convair Rd., 915/212-0330, www.elpasointernationalairport.com). Car rentals are available.

CAR

You'll need a car to get to and explore White Sands. The nearest gas station is in Alamogordo, 15 miles (24 km) east of the park.

From El Paso, Texas, drive north on I-10, then take I-25 to US 70 East to reach the park (95 mi./153 km, 1.5 hrs.).

From Albuquerque, drive south on I-25, east on US 380, and south on US 54 to Alamogordo and then east on US 70 to the park (225 mi./360 km, 3.5 hrs.).

From Carlsbad Caverns National Park, drive north on US 285 and west on US 82 to Alamogordo to catch US 70 West to reach the park (190 mi./305 km, 3.5 hrs.).

▼ INTERDUNES BOARDWALK TRAIL

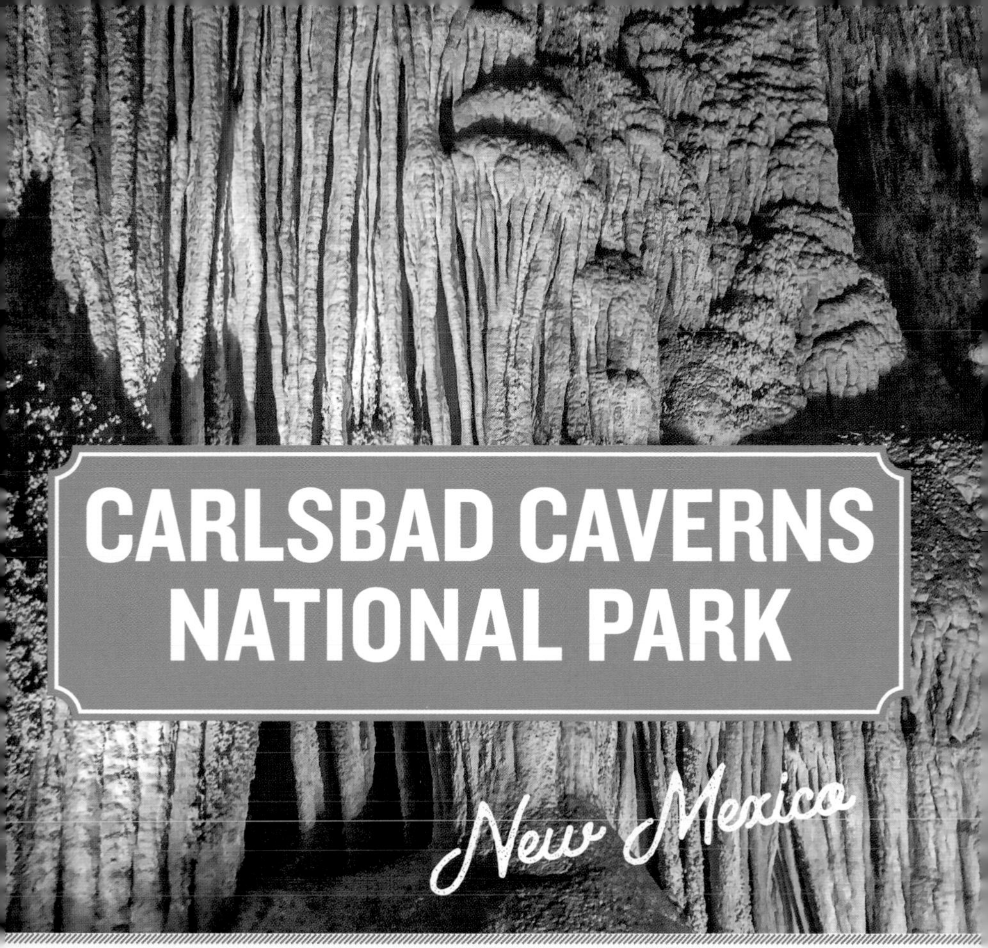

KEEPSAKE STAMPS ▼▼▼

WEBSITE:
www.nps.gov/cave

PHONE NUMBER:
575/785-2232

VISITATION RANK:
44

WHY GO:
Tour underground limestone caves.

▲ FLOWSTONES, CARLSBAD CAVERNS NATIONAL PARK

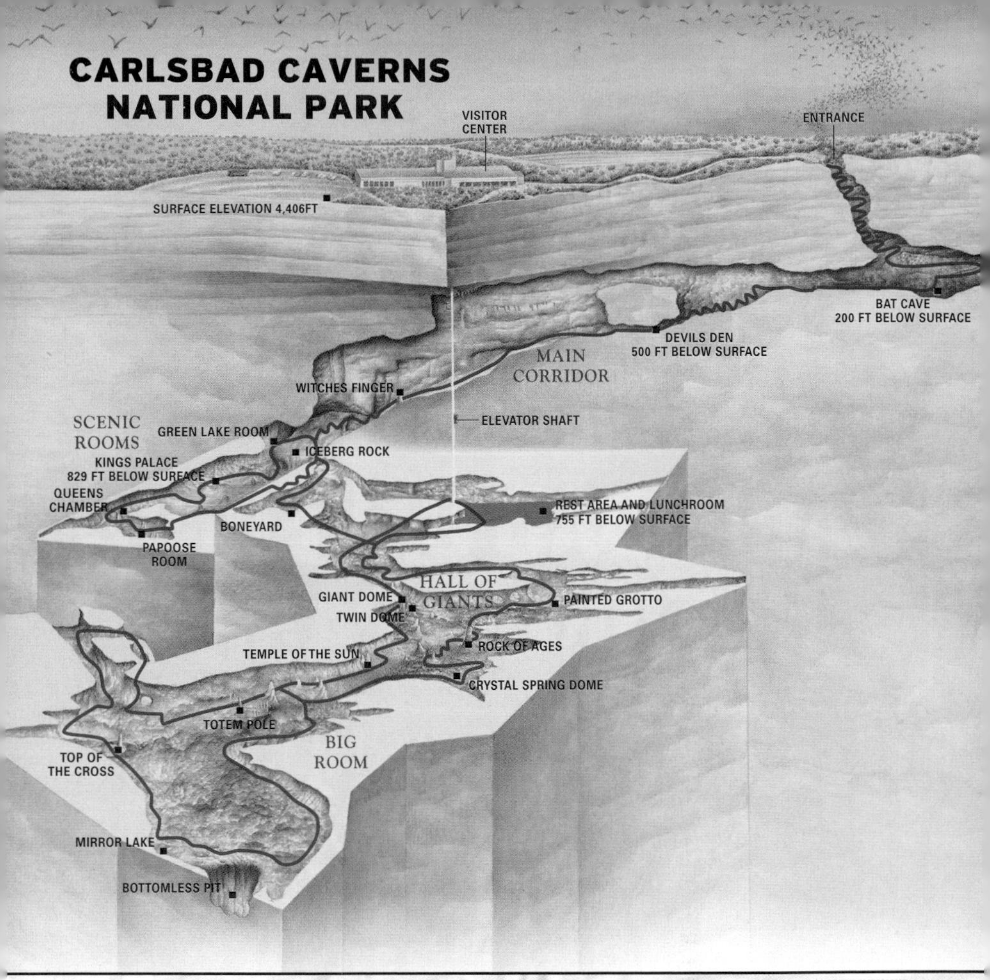
CARLSBAD CAVERNS NATIONAL PARK
VISITOR CENTER
ENTRANCE
SURFACE ELEVATION 4,406FT
BAT CAVE
200 FT BELOW SURFACE
DEVILS DEN
500 FT BELOW SURFACE
MAIN CORRIDOR
WITCHES FINGER
ELEVATOR SHAFT
SCENIC ROOMS
GREEN LAKE ROOM
ICEBERG ROCK
KINGS PALACE
829 FT BELOW SURFACE
QUEENS CHAMBER
BONEYARD
PAPOOSE ROOM
REST AREA AND LUNCHROOM
755 FT BELOW SURFACE
HALL OF GIANTS
GIANT DOME
TWIN DOME
PAINTED GROTTO
ROCK OF AGES
TEMPLE OF THE SUN
CRYSTAL SPRING DOME
TOTEM POLE
BIG ROOM
TOP OF THE CROSS
MIRROR LAKE
BOTTOMLESS PIT

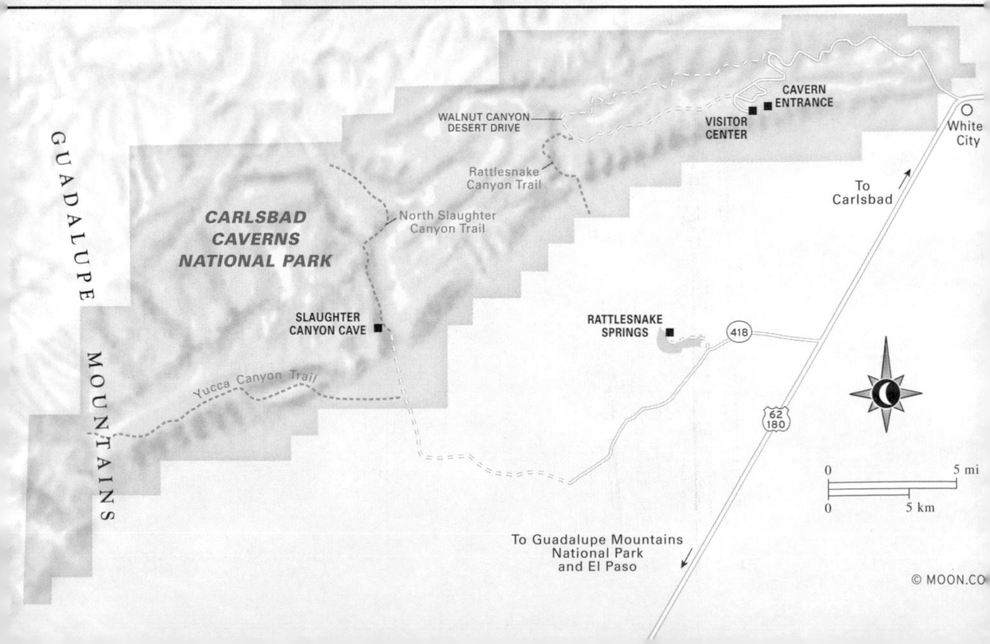
CAVERN ENTRANCE
VISITOR CENTER
WALNUT CANYON DESERT DRIVE
White City
Rattlesnake Canyon Trail
To Carlsbad
North Slaughter Canyon Trail
CARLSBAD CAVERNS NATIONAL PARK
GUADALUPE MOUNTAINS
SLAUGHTER CANYON CAVE
RATTLESNAKE SPRINGS
418
Yucca Canyon Trail
62
180
0
5 mi
0
5 km
To Guadalupe Mountains National Park and El Paso
© MOON.CO

CARLSBAD CAVERNS NATIONAL PARK is mesmerizing—one of the country's most awesome natural marvels. Scientists theorize that these cave systems began to form more than 20 million years ago, as the petroleum deposits under the Guadalupe Mountains reacted with groundwater to create sulfuric acid, which ate through the stone to form vast hollow spots under the ground. These spaces started to fill with stalagmites and stalactites about 500,000 years ago, and now the intricate formations—still growing—range from hulking towers that ripple like clay to delicate needles that look more like icicles than stone.

Belowground, you can enjoy the park's wonders via a stroll around the aptly named Big Room—a vast cavern dripping with stalactites. Or spend several days visiting the park's more obscure underground worlds, 119 caves in all. At more than 136 miles (219 km), Lechuguilla is the longest cave in the park, loaded with rare gypsum and sulfur formations. Aboveground, the Chihuahuan Desert is studded with flowering cacti that feed a colony of Brazilian free-tailed bats, whose flight at dusk wows visitors.

PLANNING YOUR TIME

Reaching Carlsbad Caverns requires a long drive to southern New Mexico near the border with Texas. Plan at least one day to explore the caverns, though the smaller, more adventurous group tours are worth a second day. **May-September** is high season with a full tour schedule, and lines inside and outside the cave may mean a long wait. For greater solitude, visit in **December** (before the holidays) or **January-February.** Though not all tours operate in winter, you'll have the place to yourself in near ghostly silence.

While temperatures may soar aboveground in summer, cave temperatures hover at 56°F (13°C) year-round. Bring a sweater or warm coat and

THE NATURAL ENTRANCE AT CARLSBAD CAVERNS

Top 3

CHANDELIER DRAPERIES IN THE BIG ROOM

1 ZOOM DOWN INTO THE BIG ROOM

The **Big Room** (elevator entry/exit 8:30am-6:45pm daily late May-early Sept., 8:30am-4:45pm daily early Sept.-late May) is the largest cave by volume in the Carlsbad complex. An elevator whisks visitors 754 feet (229 m) down to the cavern floor. Lit with tasteful white lights, the Big Room glows like a natural cathedral: The ceiling soars into darkness within the immense chamber. Along the 1.25-mile (2-km) path, look for features such as the **Hall of Giants** and the **Bottomless Pit.** Plan 1.5 hours to complete the **Big Room Self-Guided Trail.**

2 HIKE DOWN THE NATURAL ENTRANCE

Descend into the cavern on foot via the **Natural Entrance** (entry/exit 8:30am-5pm daily late May-early Sept., 8:30am-3:30pm daily Sept.-late May), which drops about 800 feet (244 m) through the **Main Corridor** along a strenuous 1.25-mile (2 km) trail dense with switchbacks. Walking down the Natural Entrance conveys the scale of this underground cave system: At one point, you have to hike for about 30 minutes around **Iceberg Rock,** a 200,000-ton (181,437-metric ton) boulder. The paved route has several steep sections with handrails and the path may be slippery. Plan one hour to complete the **Natural Entrance Self-Guided Trail.** The path ends at the entrance to the Big Room and the elevators, which you can take back up.

3 MARVEL AT BATS IN FLIGHT

Late May-mid-October, hundreds of thousands of bats rush out from the depths of the caverns and into the bug-filled twilight. Half an hour before sunset at an amphitheater at the top of the Natural Entrance Trail, rangers give a short talk about the bats (ask at the visitors center for times). When the **Bat Flight** begins, you hear the soft flapping of their wings and feel the rush of air as they pass overhead.

AN OUTDOOR AMPHITHEATER PROVIDES SEATING FOR THE BAT FLIGHT.

pack a lunch too, as the park cafeteria is pretty institutional. Hiking boots are the best footwear for slick trail and rocky surfaces.

Due to the park's proximity to **Guadalupe Mountains National Park** (about 40 min.), many visitors link a trip to the caverns with a visit to Guadalupe.

ENTRANCE AND FEES

From Carlsbad, it takes about 45 minutes to reach the visitors center. From Whites City, the visitors center is 7 miles (11 km) to the west on Carlsbad Caverns Highway. In the summer months, allow an extra hour's wait at the visitors center. The entrance ticket is $15 per adult (age 16 and older) and good for three days.

VISITORS CENTER

The **visitors center** (727 Carlsbad Caverns Hwy., 8am-7pm daily late May-early Sept., 8am-5pm daily early Sept.-late May) is at the end of Carlsbad Caverns Highway, the park entrance road. This is where you can pick up cave tour tickets and park information. For both of the self-guided trails, you can rent an **audio tour** ($5). At the bottom of the elevators and Natural Cave Entrance Trail, the cave floor has a snack bar and restrooms hidden behind rock formations.

RANGER-GUIDED TOURS

Small-group tours offer an alternative to the crowds in the Big Room: It's quieter and you'll see a lot more of the caverns. **Reservations** (877/444-6777, www.recreation.gov) are required and can be booked between 48 hours and six months in advance. When available, first-come, first-served tickets are sold on the day of tours at the visitors center. Be sure to ask what time to arrive; some tours require hour-long hikes to the departure point.

KING'S PALACE

King's Palace (daily year-round, 1 mi./1.6 km, 1.5 hrs., adults $8, children age 4 and older $4) is the deepest part of the caves open to the public. Limited to 75 participants, the tour passes giant formations as well as tiny details such as a bat's skeleton grown into a stalagmite. Best of all, it includes a few minutes with the lights turned off, when you get to stand in the cool, smothering black. Unlike the other ranger-led tours, the paved trail is only steep at the entrance and exit.

LEFT HAND TUNNEL

Left Hand Tunnel (daily year-round, 0.5 mi./0.8 km, 2 hrs., adults $7, children age 6 and older $3.50) is best for a sheer sense of discovery. A small group of 15 visitors carries flickering lanterns through fantastic rock formations—made all the more bizarre as they loom out of the darkness.

LOWER CAVE

Lower Cave (four times a week year-round, 1 mi./1.6 km, 3 hrs., adults $20, children age 12 and older $10) requires some exertion, as the path starts with a clamber down 60 feet (18 m) of rope and narrow ladders. Formations include toothpick-like stalactites and the perfectly round and white formations called "cave pearls."

THE BIG ROOM

SLAUGHTER CANYON CAVE

Slaughter Canyon Cave (once weekly year-round, 1 mi./1.6 km, 5.5 hrs., adults $15, children age 8 and older $7.50) is located 5 miles (8 km) south of Whites City off a well-signed county road. After a steep 0.5-mile (0.8-km) hike to the cave entrance, the walk inside isn't too difficult. Look for formations like the glittering, crystal-covered column dubbed the Christmas Tree.

HALL OF THE WHITE GIANT & SPIDER CAVE

For those who aren't afraid of tight spaces, the **Hall of the White Giant** and **Spider Cave** (once weekly in summer, 1 mi./1.6 km, 4 hrs., adults $20, children age 12 and older $10) are strenuous but rewarding trips. Expect to wiggle through some very narrow tunnels and to get muddy in the process.

NIGHT SKY PROGRAMS

Nighttime aboveground is magical. These June-October free ranger-led programs take place on select dates following the bat flight program. Dates vary for these nocturnal adventures. Register on the morning of the program to be one of the 25 people on a **Star Walk** (0.5 mi./0.8 km rt.) or **Full Moon Hike** (1.5 mi./2.4 km rt.). **Star Parties** (no registration needed) on select no-moon nights take place at the Bat Flight Amphitheater.

POOL OF WATER IN BIG ROOM

WHERE TO STAY

INSIDE THE PARK

There are no accommodations or campgrounds inside the park. **Primitive backcountry camping** is allowed with a permit (free) available at the visitors center. Inside the visitors center, the **Carlsbad Caverns Trading Company** sells a limited menu of to-go snacks and drinks.

OUTSIDE THE PARK

Guadalupe Mountains National Park (915/828-3251, www.nps.gov/gumo) is where people usually camp when visiting Carlsbad Caverns. It's 35 miles (56 km) south of Whites City on US 62/180. **Carlsbad,** 27 miles (43 km) north of the park on US 62/180, has accommodations, though they are often overpriced. **Roswell** has a selection of national chain hotels.

GETTING THERE AND AROUND

AIR

The closest airport is **El Paso International Airport** (6701 Convair Rd., 915/212-0330, www.elpasointernationalairport.com) in Texas. From there, drive east on US 62/180 to NM 7 to reach Whites City, New Mexico (138 mi./222 km, 2.5 hrs.).

CAR

From Carlsbad, New Mexico, drive 20 miles (32 km) south on US 62/180 to reach Whites City. Fill your gas tank in Carlsbad to avoid being at the mercy of the one pricey station in Whites City.

From Whites City, drive 7 miles (11 km) west on winding Carlsbad Caverns Highway. Plan 45 minutes to reach the visitors center, due to the curvy road and slow vehicles. Watch for wildlife darting onto the road.

GUADALUPE MOUNTAINS NATIONAL PARK

Texas

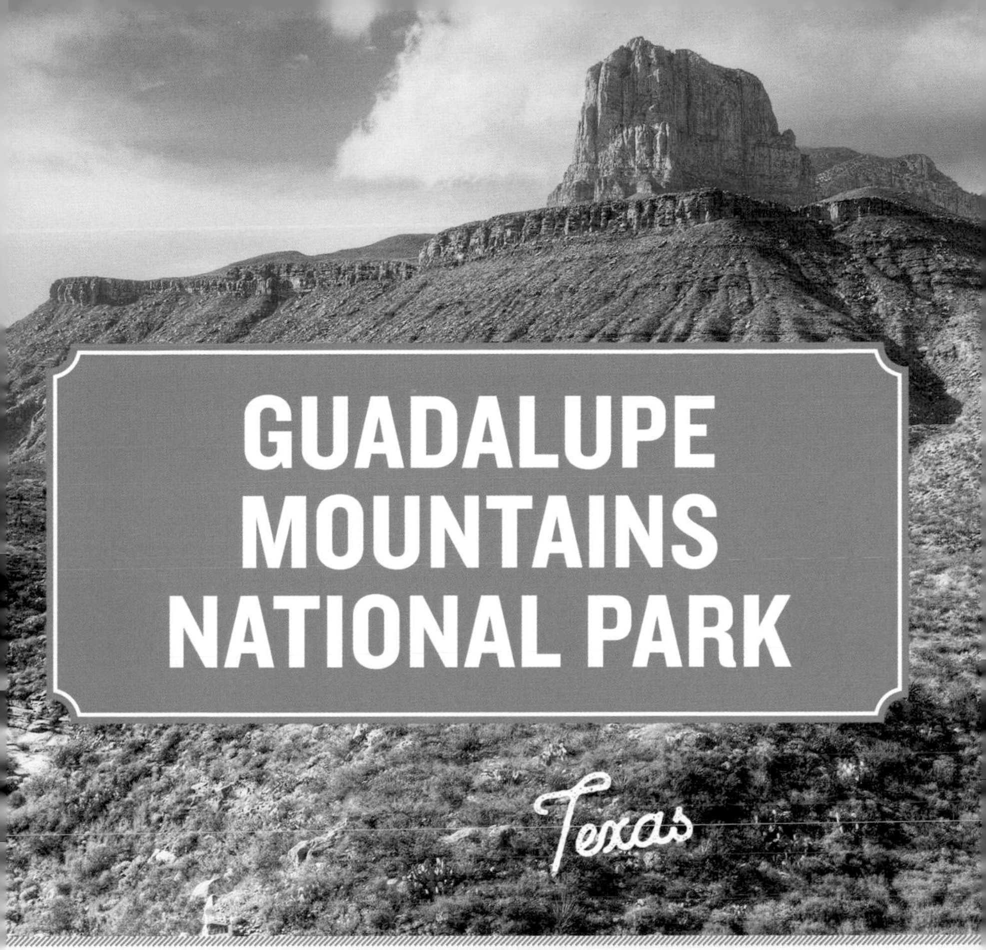

KEEPSAKE STAMPS ▼▼▼

WEBSITE:
www.nps.gov/gumo

PHONE NUMBER:
915/828-3251

VISITATION RANK:
49

WHY GO:
Hike ancient fossil reefs.

▲ EL CAPITAN, GUADALUPE MOUNTAINS NATIONAL PARK

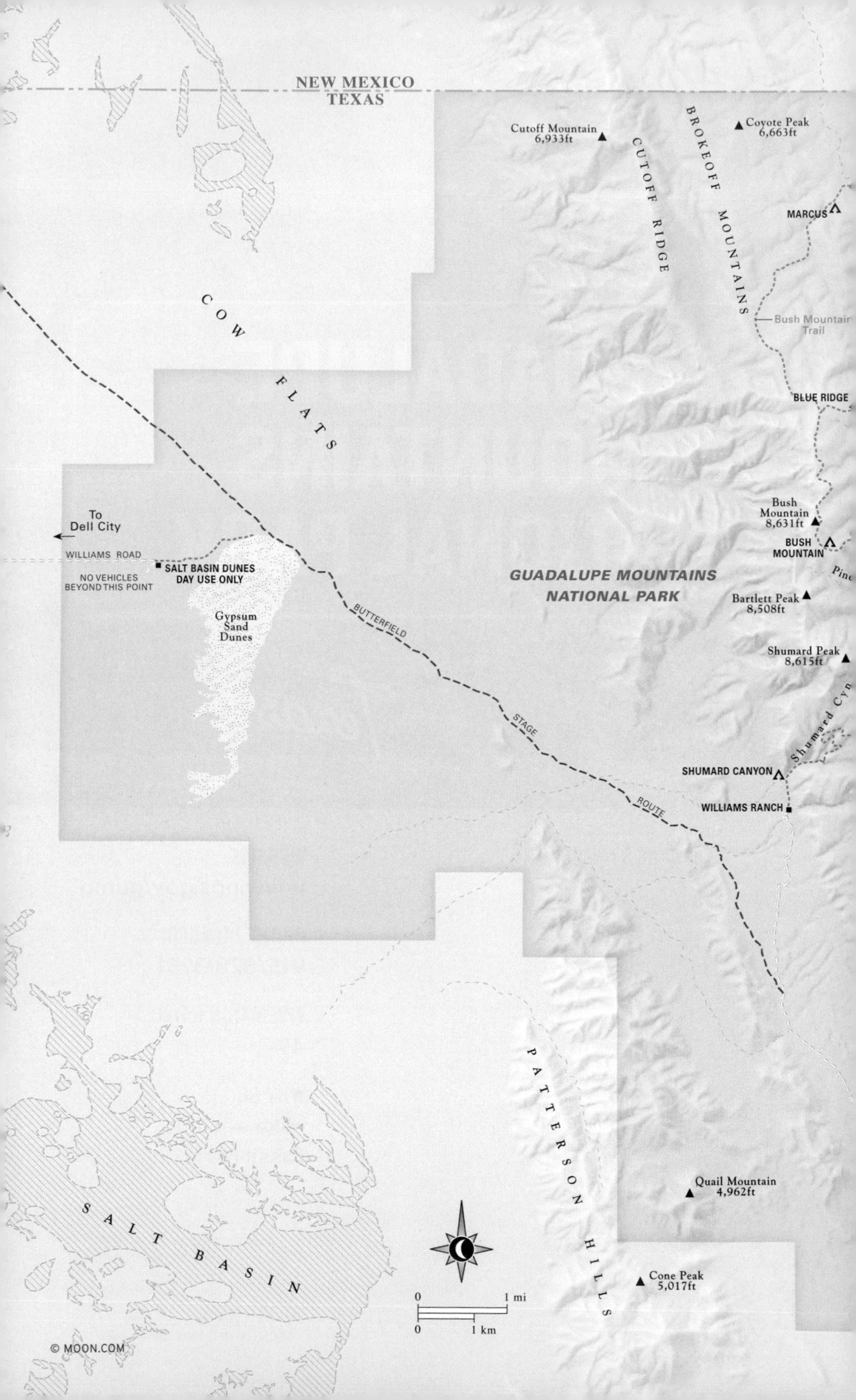

NEW MEXICO
TEXAS
Cutoff Mountain
6,933ft
CUTOFF RIDGE
BROKEOFF MOUNTAINS
Coyote Peak
6,663ft
MARCUS
COW FLATS
Bush Mountain Trail
BLUE RIDGE
To Dell City
WILLIAMS ROAD
NO VEHICLES BEYOND THIS POINT
SALT BASIN DUNES DAY USE ONLY
Gypsum Sand Dunes
Bush Mountain
8,631ft
BUSH MOUNTAIN
GUADALUPE MOUNTAINS NATIONAL PARK
Bartlett Peak
8,508ft
Shumard Peak
8,615ft
BUTTERFIELD STAGE ROUTE
Shumard Cyn
SHUMARD CANYON
WILLIAMS RANCH
PATTERSON HILLS
Quail Mountain
4,962ft
SALT BASIN
Cone Peak
5,017ft
0
1 mi
0
1 km

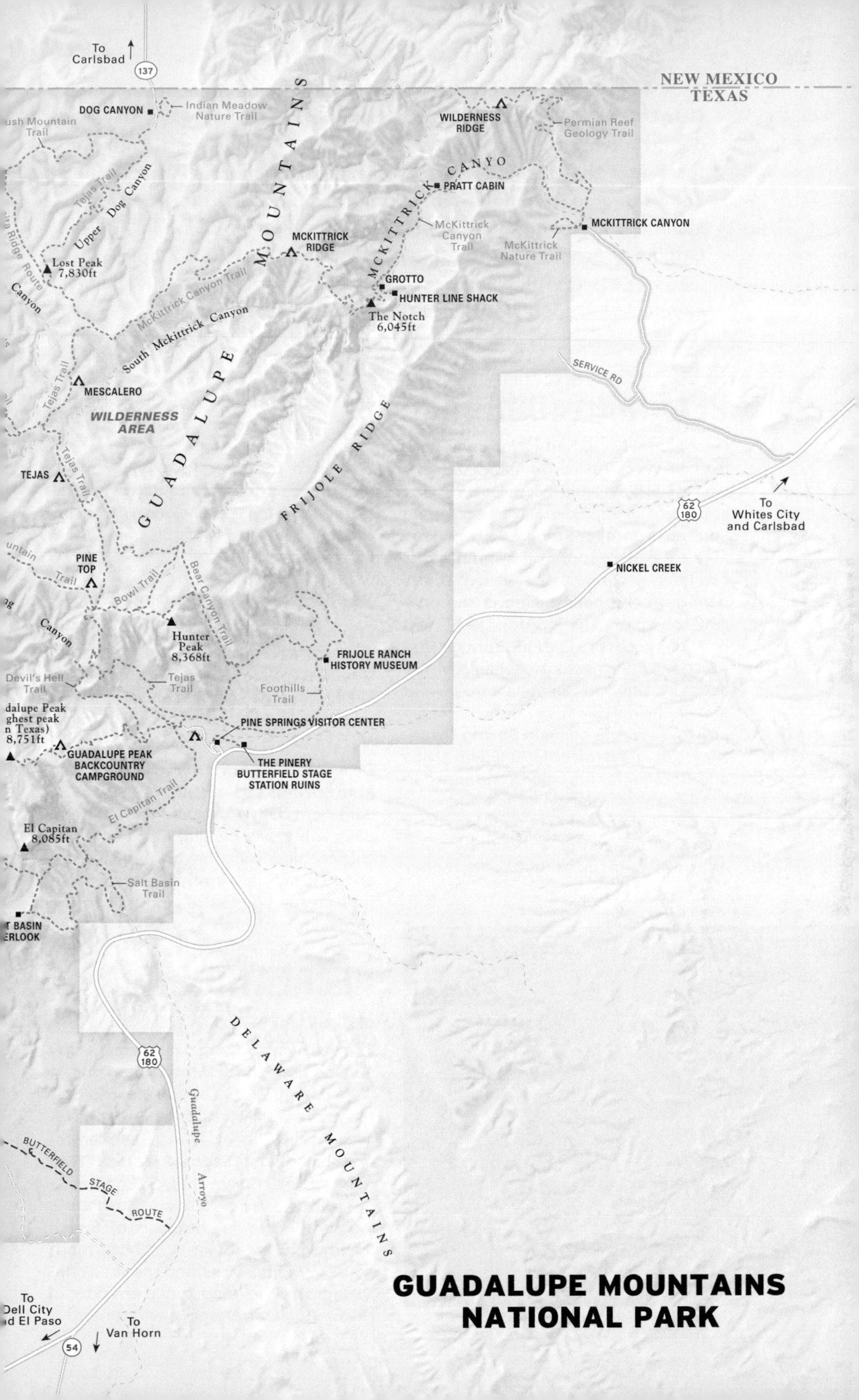

To Carlsbad
137
NEW MEXICO
TEXAS
DOG CANYON
Indian Meadow Nature Trail
Bush Mountain Trail
WILDERNESS RIDGE
Permian Reef Geology Trail
GUADALUPE MOUNTAINS
MCKITTRICK CANYON
PRATT CABIN
Tejas Trail
Upper Dog Canyon
MCKITTRICK RIDGE
McKittrick Canyon Trail
MCKITTRICK CANYON
McKittrick Nature Trail
Lost Peak 7,830ft
McKittrick Canyon Trail
GROTTO
HUNTER LINE SHACK
The Notch 6,045ft
South Mckittrick Canyon
SERVICE RD
MESCALERO
WILDERNESS AREA
FRIJOLE RIDGE
TEJAS
62 180
To Whites City and Carlsbad
PINE TOP
NICKEL CREEK
Bowl Trail
Bear Canyon Trail
Hunter Peak 8,368ft
FRIJOLE RANCH HISTORY MUSEUM
Devil's Hell Trail
Tejas Trail
Foothills Trail
PINE SPRINGS VISITOR CENTER
8,751ft
GUADALUPE PEAK BACKCOUNTRY CAMPGROUND
THE PINERY BUTTERFIELD STAGE STATION RUINS
El Capitan Trail
El Capitan 8,085ft
Salt Basin Trail
DELAWARE MOUNTAINS
62 180
Guadalupe Arroyo
BUTTERFIELD STAGE ROUTE
To Van Horn
54

GUADALUPE MOUNTAINS NATIONAL PARK

Beckoning high in the distance from the Chihuahuan Desert, the **GUADALUPE MOUNTAINS** are an underappreciated natural wonder straddling the Texas-New Mexico border. Built from a marine fossil reef that formed under tropical waters more than 260 million years ago, the mountains extend from desert floor to craggy summits, including Guadalupe Peak, the highest point in Texas. Originally occupied by the Nde (Mescalero Apache) people, this landscape is a compelling destination for hikers, backpackers, and campers who appreciate solitude and rugged terrain.

PLANNING YOUR TIME

Guadalupe Mountains National Park is in far West Texas, 114 miles (183 km) east of El Paso and 55 miles (89 km) south of Carlsbad, New Mexico. While you can drop in for a single day, you'll be able to explore more on a multi-night camping excursion. No paved roads penetrate the park; hiking is the only way to explore the interior. US 62/180 provides access to the Pine Springs Visitor Center in the south, while NM 137 accesses the Dog Canyon campground area in the north.

Most visitors come in **Spring** (Mar.-May) for days of 60F-90°F (16-27°C) and October for fall color. **Summers** can be slightly warmer while fall and winter see cool and windy conditions. The park, visitors center, and campground are open year-round, but some higher elevations can see snow on the trails (Dec.-Jan.) and winds can howl up to 70 mph (112 kph).

OVERLOOKING PINE SPRINGS

Due to the park's proximity (a 40-min. drive) to **Carlsbad Caverns National Park** in New Mexico, many visitors combine a tour of this park with a trip to the caverns.

ENTRANCE AND FEES

The entrance fee is $10 per person and valid for seven days. There are no entrance stations; pay the fee at trailhead kiosks or in the visitors center.

VISITORS CENTER

Drop by the park's visitors center at **Pine Springs** (US 62/180, 915/828-3251, 8am-6pm daily Apr.-Oct., 8am-4:30pm daily winter) to pick up maps and brochures, find out the current weather forecast, view interpretive exhibits, browse the bookstore, and talk to the knowledgeable park staff.

RECREATION

HIKING

The best way to appreciate the park is by putting boot to rocky terrain on one of its hiking trails. For self-guided interpretive trails, walk **McKittrick Canyon Nature Trail** (0.9 mi./1.4 km rt., moderate) or the **Indian Meadows Nature Trail** (0.6 mi./1 km rt., easy) at Dog Canyon.

From the Frijole Ranch Museum, a loop trail goes to the oasis of **Smith Springs** (2.3 mi./3.7 km rt., 1-2 hrs., moderate). Wildlife, birds, and the shady oasis indicate the importance of water in the Chihuahuan Desert environment.

Top 3

EL CAPITAN

1 SPY EL CAPITAN

For those approaching the park from the west or south, **El Capitan** (8,751 ft./2,667 m) is the most prominent peak in view. While not the highest peak, its limestone vertical cliffs, reminiscent of a far more popular peak in Yosemite by the same name, mark the southern end of the exposed marine fossil reef. You can best see it from US 62/180 between the two picnic areas outside the park south of Pine Springs Visitor Center. For up close views, the **El Capitan Trail** (11.3 mi./18.2 km rt., 6-8 hrs.) tours below the cliffs.

2 HIKE THE PINERY NATURE TRAIL

From the visitors center, tour the wheelchair-accessible paved **Pinery Nature Trail** (0.7 mi./1.1 km rt., 20 min., easy) to the fragile rock-walled ruins of a stagecoach station that once served the Butterfield Mail Coach and mule trains. The limestone structure was the place to get fresh horses and repair wagons. Interpretive signs on the path introduce you to the flora that thrives in the arid Chihuahuan Desert.

3 VISIT A HISTORIC RANCH

At an oasis 1.5 miles (2.4 km) northeast of the visitors center, the **Frijole Ranch Museum** (8am-4:30 daily based on volunteer staffing) contains exhibits about the Mescalero Apache and early ranchers who eeked out livings here in the Chihuahuan Desert. Adjacent to the museum is a one-room schoolhouse and a spring house. A paved wheelchair-accessible trail goes to **Manzanita Spring** (0.4 mi./0.6 km rt., 15 min., easy), a haven for birds.

PINERY NATURE TRAIL

Best Hike

DEVIL'S HALL

DISTANCE: 3.8 miles (6.1 km) round-trip
DURATION: 2.5 hours
ELEVATION GAIN: 550 feet (168 m)
EFFORT: moderately strenuous
TRAILHEAD: Pine Springs Campground

Beginning at Pine Springs Campground, the **Devil's Hall Trail** follows a maintained path for 1 mile (1.6 km) before the fun begins. Hikers must navigate the trail by scrambling over boulders in a wash to reach a pour-over known as Hiker's Staircase. After climbing the natural staircase, the route squeezes into a narrow, steep-walled canyon where the sides look like layers of pancaked rock.

To experience the majesty of McKittrick Canyon, allow most of the day to reach the high ridges. Start at the McKittrick Canyon contact station to descend the **McKittrick Canyon Trail** (2.4-7.6 mi./3.9-12.2 km one-way) before reaching the first milestone—Pratt Cabin, the 1929 structure of geologist and land donator Wallace Pratt. Another 1.1 miles (1.8 km) leads to Grotto Picnic Area, one of the canyon's most scenic areas. With enough time and stamina, continue 4.1 more miles (6.6 km) to McKittrick Ridge for views of colorful canyon walls and rugged outcroppings. McKittrick Canyon is known for fall color.

From Pine Springs Campground, the **Guadalupe Peak Trail** (8.5 mi./13.7 km rt., 6-8 hrs.) leads to stunning views atop the highest point in Texas. With a 2,906-foot (886-m) ascent, the trek climbs at a moderate clip to 8,751 feet (2,667 m), where huge views take in the expansive desert and mountain surroundings. The summit contains a large obelisk installed by American Airlines. At 1 mile (1.6 km) before the summit is a backcountry campsite.

BACKPACKING

There are nine remote **wilderness sites** (backcountry permit required, free). Due to the isolated nature of these sites, it's essential to bring at least 1 gallon (3.8 l) of water per person per day, ample food (open fires are prohibited), and emergency gear. First-come, first-served permits are available from the Pine Springs Visitor Center or Dog Canyon Campground.

WHERE TO STAY

The park's two campgrounds ($15) are first come, first served. Both have drinking water and flush toilets (no showers). Near the park's headquarters and visitors center, **Pine Springs** is the larger of the two, with 20 graveled tent sites among junipers and 19 RV sites in a big ol' paved parking lot. The nearby trailhead goes to Guadalupe Peak and Devil's Hall.

Sitting at 6,280 feet, **Dog Canyon Campground** is in a secluded, tree-filled canyon on the north side of the park. Its higher elevation and sheltered location beneath steep cliff walls result in cooler temperatures than Pine Springs. The canyon also protects the area from strong winds that blast through in winter and spring. The campground has nine tent sites and four RV sites. Cooking grills are available for charcoal fires.

GETTING THERE AND AROUND

The nearest international airport is in **El Paso** (ELP, 6701 Convair Rd., 915/212-0330, www.elpasointernationalairport.com), 114 miles (184 km) west of the Guadalupe Mountains via US 62/180. Rental cars are available.

For those arriving from the east, take either I-20 or I-10 to Van Horn. Then, head north for about an hour on TX 54, one of the most scenic drives in the state, to reach the park.

There is no public transportation into or within the park. The nearest gas station is 35 miles (56 km) away in Dell City, so gas up before you arrive.

BIG BEND NATIONAL PARK

Texas

KEEPSAKE STAMPS ▼▼▼

WEBSITE:
www.nps.gov/bibe

PHONE NUMBER:
432/477-2251

VISITATION RANK:
43

WHY GO:
Experience the Rio Grande.

▲ SANTA ELENA CANYON, BIG BEND NATIONAL PARK

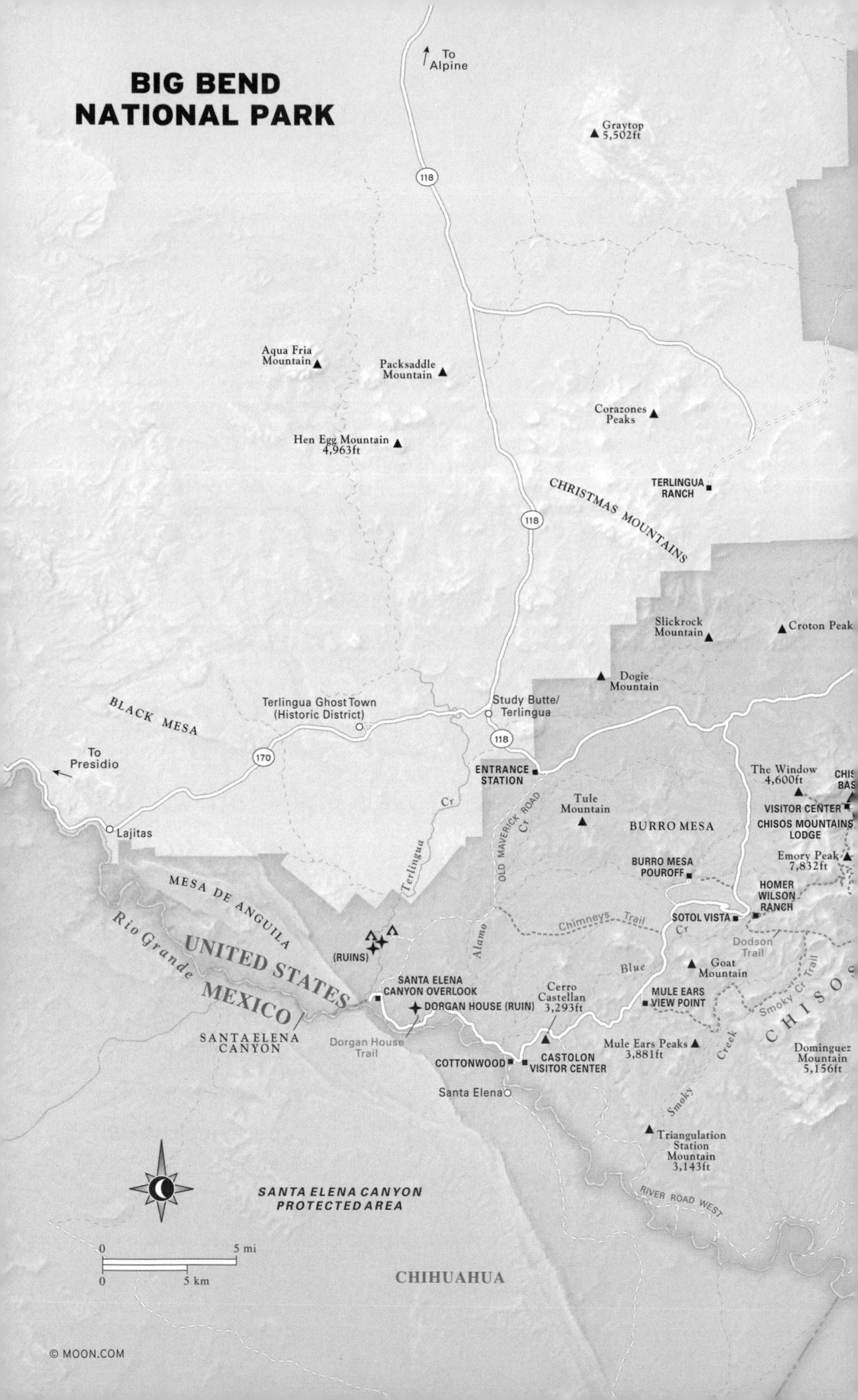
BIG BEND
NATIONAL PARK
To
Alpine
Graytop
5,502ft
118
Aqua Fria
Mountain
Packsaddle
Mountain
Corazones
Peaks
Hen Egg Mountain
4,963ft
TERLINGUA
RANCH
CHRISTMAS MOUNTAINS
118
Slickrock
Mountain
Croton Peak
Dogie
Mountain
BLACK MESA
Terlingua Ghost Town
(Historic District)
Study Butte/
Terlingua
118
To
Presidio
170
ENTRANCE
STATION
The Window
4,600ft
VISITOR CENTER
CHISOS MOUNTAINS
LODGE
Tule
Mountain
BURRO MESA
OLD MAVERICK ROAD
Cr
Lajitas
Terlingua
BURRO MESA
POUROFF
Emory Peak
7,832ft
HOMER
WILSON
RANCH
MESA DE ANGUILA
Chimneys Trail
SOTOL VISTA
Rio Grande
Alamo
Dodson
Trail
UNITED STATES
(RUINS)
Goat
Mountain
Blue
SANTA ELENA
CANYON OVERLOOK
Cerro
Castellan
3,293ft
MULE EARS
VIEW POINT
Smoky Cr Trail
MEXICO
DORGAN HOUSE (RUIN)
CHISOS
SANTA ELENA
CANYON
Dorgan House
Trail
Mule Ears Peaks
3,881ft
Creek
Dominguez
Mountain
5,156ft
COTTONWOOD
CASTOLON
VISITOR CENTER
Santa Elena
Smoky
Triangulation
Station
Mountain
3,143ft
SANTA ELENA CANYON
PROTECTED AREA
RIVER ROAD WEST
0
5 mi
0
5 km
CHIHUAHUA
© MOON.COM

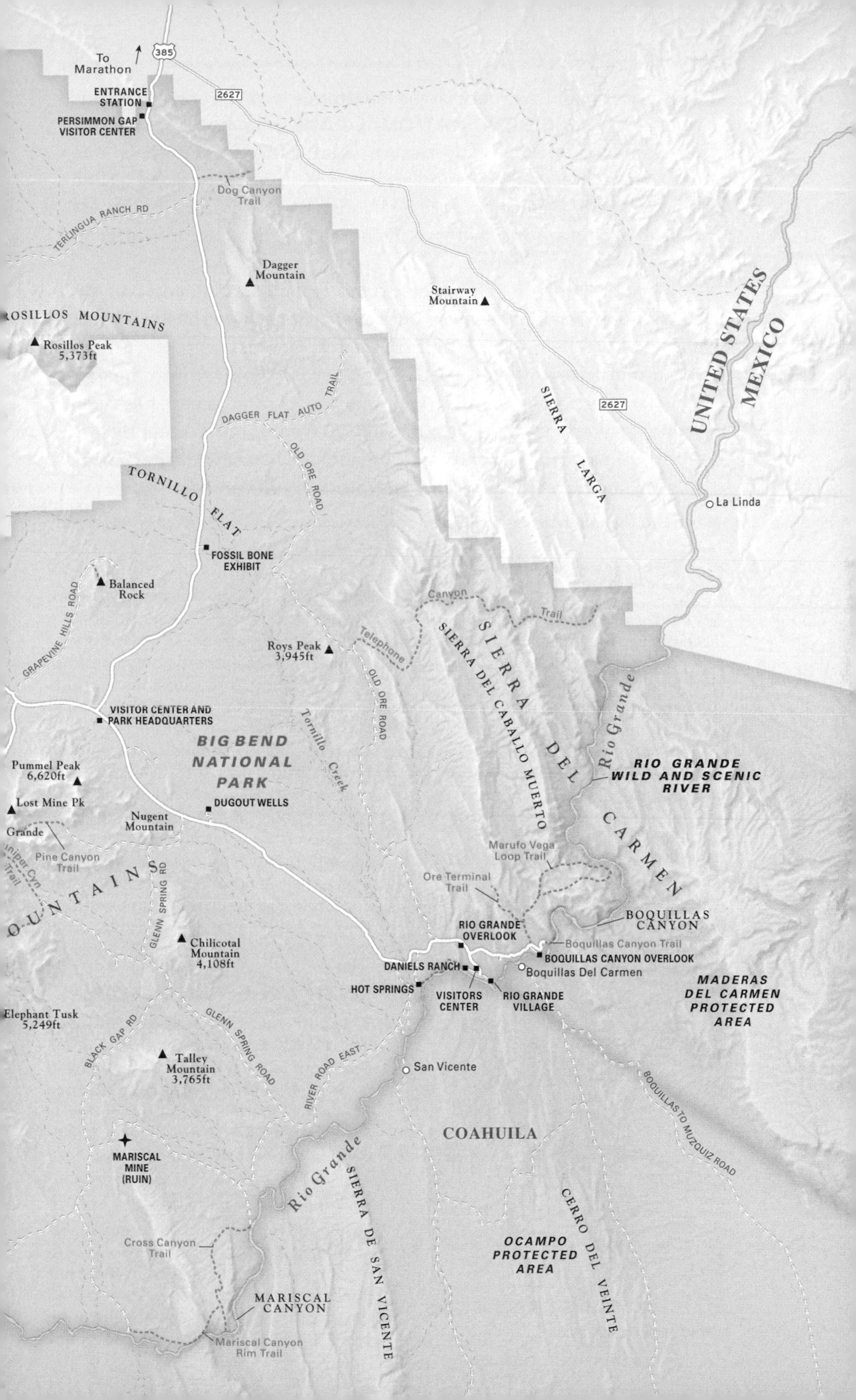

To Marathon
385
2627
ENTRANCE STATION
PERSIMMON GAP VISITOR CENTER
Dog Canyon Trail
TERLINGUA RANCH RD
Dagger Mountain
Stairway Mountain
ROSILLOS MOUNTAINS
Rosillos Peak 5,373ft
DAGGER FLAT AUTO TRAIL
OLD ORE ROAD
SIERRA LARGA
UNITED STATES
MEXICO
La Linda
TORNILLO FLAT
FOSSIL BONE EXHIBIT
Balanced Rock
GRAPEVINE HILLS ROAD
Canyon Trail
Telephone
Roys Peak 3,945ft
SIERRA DEL CABALLO MUERTO
SIERRA DEL CARMEN
Rio Grande
VISITOR CENTER AND PARK HEADQUARTERS
BIG BEND NATIONAL PARK
Tornillo Creek
RIO GRANDE WILD AND SCENIC RIVER
Pummel Peak 6,620ft
Lost Mine Pk
DUGOUT WELLS
Nugent Mountain
Grande
Pine Canyon Trail
Juniper Cyn Trail
MOUNTAINS
GLENN SPRING RD
Marufo Vega Loop Trail
Ore Terminal Trail
BOQUILLAS CANYON
RIO GRANDE OVERLOOK
Boquillas Canyon Trail
BOQUILLAS CANYON OVERLOOK
Chilicotal Mountain 4,108ft
DANIELS RANCH
Boquillas Del Carmen
HOT SPRINGS
VISITORS CENTER
RIO GRANDE VILLAGE
MADERAS DEL CARMEN PROTECTED AREA
Elephant Tusk 5,249ft
BLACK GAP RD
GLENN SPRING ROAD
Talley Mountain 3,765ft
RIVER ROAD EAST
San Vicente
BOQUILLAS TO MUZQUIZ ROAD
COAHUILA
MARISCAL MINE (RUIN)
Rio Grande
SIERRA DE SAN VICENTE
CERRO DEL VEINTE
OCAMPO PROTECTED AREA
Cross Canyon Trail
MARISCAL CANYON
Mariscal Canyon Rim Trail

This park's namesake bend in the Rio Grande isn't the only enormous feature here. **BIG BEND NATIONAL PARK** encompasses spectacular canyons, mesmerizing desert, awe-inspiring mountains, and unexpected temperate woodlands teeming with birdsong. High mountain cliffs house peregrine falcons; colorful tropical birds nest here in spring; and birds from the north migrate here in winter to enjoy the warm climate.

Ancient limestone cliffs flank steep-walled Santa Elena Canyon, formations that lend a sacred aura to the slot where the Rio Grande slices its way toward the Gulf of Mexico. Downstream, the Chisos Mountains rise with views extending across the river into Mexico. This landscape of canyons, river, mountains, and desert has been home to Native Americans for 10,000 years, most recently the Chisos, Mescalero Apache, and Comanche. They saw the dark skies above yielding a brilliant Milky Way. Today, you can, too.

PLANNING YOUR TIME

Big Bend National Park sits in an isolated pocket of southwest Texas. With driving times and distances considerable, a car is the only means of access. Advanced planning is required: make reservations for lodging and camping six months in advance for visits in peak season—**February-May** and **October-December.**

PRICKLY PEAR CACTUS

Plan to spend 2-5 days in Big Bend National Park. Some visitors never leave the scenic drives, but hiking or camping is the best way to soak up its variety.

Big Bend's weather is only comfortable October-April. Summer is ridiculously hot—this *is* the Chihuahuan Desert—and despite the increased elevation and low humidity, triple-digit temperatures are brutal. May and June are the hottest months. Later in summer, periodic rainstorms along with occasional heavy thunderstorms and flash flooding help ease the intensity of the heat. Winter is the most volatile season in Big Bend; mild temperatures through extremes are possible, from 85°F (29°C) to periods of light snow.

ENTRANCES AND FEES

The park has two entrance stations: The **North Entrance Station** (via US 385 from Marathon) and the western gate at **Maverick Junction Entrance Station** (TX 118). The entrance fee is $30 per vehicle ($25 motorcycle, $15 individual) and good for seven days.

VISITORS CENTERS

Big Bend National Park has several visitors centers. The main visitors center is the park headquarters at **Panther Junction** (9am-5pm daily), 26 miles (42 km) from the North Entrance Station and 25 miles (40 km) from the Maverick

Top 3

CHISOS VILLAGE IN THE CHISOS MOUNTAINS

1 EXPLORE THE CHISOS MOUNTAINS

From Panther Junction, the Chisos Mountains rise like a forested island above the arid Chihuahuan Desert. This unique mixed forest fills with a cacophony of birdsong in spring. The mountains are topped by **Emory Peak.** To see them up close, drive steep **Chisos Basin Road** (6 mi./9.7 km one-way, RV limit 24 ft./7.3 m, trailer limit 20 ft./6.1 m) up dramatic hairpin turns (10 mph/16 kph limit) to **Chisos Mountains Lodge** and **Chisos Basin Visitor Center.** From Chisos Basin, trails depart for hikers and backpackers to explore the forest, cliffs, and vistas into Mexico.

2 CRUISE ALONG ROSS MAXWELL SCENIC DRIVE

The western portion of Big Bend contains **Ross Maxwell Scenic Drive** (30 mi./48 km one-way). The vast desert slowly shifts into volcanic rock formations reminiscent of an otherworldly scene from *Star Trek*. Stop at **Mules Ear Overlook** to see the striking peaks before driving through the volcanic ash of Tuff Canyon**.** Drop by the historic village of **Castolon** for an hour to explore the exhibits in the century-old military structures. From the Castolon/Santa Elena Junction, continue west to the road terminus at the must-see **Santa Elena Canyon Overlook,** where immense cliffs pinch the Rio Grande.

3 RAFT THE RIO GRANDE

Famed as the international boundary between the United States and Mexico, the Rio Grande provides rafting opportunities amid the steep walls of **Santa Elena Canyon.** Expect 13 miles (21 km) of easy desert paddling and 7 miles (11 km) of huge Class IV rapids, where the river funnels through the towering cliffs overhead.

Downstream, the designated **Rio Grande Wild and Scenic River** flows past giant limestone cliffs of **Mariscal Canyon** (10 mi./16 km) and froths with Class II-III rapids. For a multiday float for canoes or rafts, **Boquillas Canyon** (33 mi./53 km) is tamer with Class I-II rapids.

Permits ($12) are required for overnight rafting trips, available in person at Panther Junction Visitor Center. To book guided river trips, rent gear, or hire shuttles, contact **Big Bend River Tours** (800/545-4240, www.bigbendrivertours.com), **Desert Sports** (888/989-6900, www.desertsportstx.com), or **Far Flung Outdoor Center** (432/371-2633, www.bigbendfarflung.com).

RIVER RAFTING ON THE RIO GRANDE

ONE DAY IN BIG BEND

If you only have one day to spend in the park, stop at **Panther Junction Visitor Center** before taking a scenic drive into the **Chisos Mountains** to **Chisos Basin Visitor Center.** Follow that with the **Ross Maxwell Scenic Drive** out to **Santa Elena Canyon Overlook** to see the **Rio Grande** spilling from the huge slot. If you have time, hike the short trail into the canyon.

Junction Entrance Station. This visitors center offers interpretive exhibits and scores of books, brochures, and maps. You can also get schedules for **free ranger-led programs** (varies weekly) that include guided walks and evening amphitheater programs. If you can catch a night sky telescope program, you'll be treated to brilliant sights unseen around city lights, an attribute that makes Big Bend an **International Dark Sky Park.**

Entering from the North Entrance Station, you will first pass through the seasonal visitors center at **Persimmon Gap** (10am-4pm daily Nov-Apr.). The park's smaller visitors centers include **Chisos Basin** (8:30am-4pm daily year-round), **Castolon** (10am-4pm daily Nov.-Apr.) in the Garlick House, and **Rio Grande Village** (9am-4pm daily Nov.-Apr.).

SCENIC DRIVES

OLD MAVERICK ROAD

High-clearance vehicles can tackle the dirt-and-gravel **Old Maverick Road** (14 mi./23 km one-way). The road completes the loop between Ross Maxwell Scenic Drive, Santa Elena Canyon Overlook, and Maverick Junction. Speckled with historical sites, such as the **Terlingua Abaja** ruins, it slices across the Terlingua Creek Badlands. Plan one hour for the washboard drive.

SIGHTS

FOSSIL DISCOVERY EXHIBIT

Off the Persimmons Gap Entrance Road (US 385, 8 mi./13 km north of Panther Jct.), the roadside **Fossil Discovery**

RUINS OFF OLD MAVERICK ROAD

Best Hike

LOST MINE TRAIL

DISTANCE: 4.8 miles (7.7 km) round-trip
DURATION: 3-4 hours
EFFORT: moderate
TRAILHEAD: Chisos Basin Road, mile 5.1

The **Lost Mine Trail** offers an ideal combination of moderate grades, varied vegetation, multiple vantage points, and an interpretive brochure at the trailhead. Views take in nearby Casa Grande and Juniper Canyon at a saddle about 20 minutes up the trail. Then, after ascending through the oak and pine forest, the trail tops out with a panoramic view of the Sierra del Carmen in Mexico.

Exhibit (http://fossildiscoveryexhibit.com, dawn-dusk daily, not recommended for RVs or trailers, free) is the best place to learn about the dinosaurs that inhabited Big Bend up to 130 million years ago and some of the 1,200 fossils unearthed in the park. The accessible site contains large murals, tactile displays, dinosaur bones, shaded picnic area, fossil playground for kids, and an interpretive trail (0.2 mi./0.3 km rt., 10 min., moderate) to see geologic points.

CASTOLON HISTORIC DISTRICT

History of isolated life on the border is preserved at **Castolon Historic District,** a collection of buildings from the 20th century. Castolon Visitors Center (10am-4pm daily, Nov.-Apr.) is housed in the historic Garlick House. Magdalena House has exhibits of the early days in this two-nation, bicultural community. Some buildings, including the store, are from the military installation here while others later served La Harmonia Ranch. (Castolon suffered fire damage in 2019, but moved into a temporary facility, with plans to return to its original location in spring 2020.)

RECREATION

HIKING

In the Chisos Mountains, two trails depart from Chisos Basin Trailhead. The **Window Trail** (5.6 mi./9 km rt., 3-4 hrs., moderate) goes downhill to the top of an often-dry pour-over (no railings) through a slot with a western vantage of the desert; the return is uphill. To climb the highest peak, take the **Emory Peak Trail** (10.5 mi./16.9 km rt., 5-6 hrs., strenuous) which starts on the Pinnacles Trail before turning off on the steep spur to the summit for those 360-degree views.

Find short trails at Rio Grande Village. From the campground at site 18, **Rio Grande Village Nature Trail** (1 mi./1.6 km rt., 1 hr., easy) starts with a boardwalk across a natural spring wetland followed by a climb to the top of a

RIO GRANDE RUNNING INTO BOQUILLAS CANYON

cactus and scrub hill with sweeping vistas of the Rio Grande and Mexico. From the Hot Springs Parking Lot where you can pick up an interpretive brochure, **Hot Springs Historic Trail** (1 mi./1.6 km rt., 45 min., easy) takes in old resort and homestead ruins, pictographs, and an historic hot springs pool (105°F/41°C). Check conditions first before planning to soak.

Two river trails on opposite sides of the park take in mighty canyon walls. From the end of Ross Maxwell Scenic Drive, the **Santa Elena Canyon Trail** (1.7 mi./2.7 km rt., 1-2 hrs., moderate) climbs switchbacks, concrete steps, and a rocky path before descending into the canyon below sheer cliffs 1,500 feet (457 m) high on each side of the narrow gap forged by the Rio Grande. From the Boquillas Canyon Spur Road, **Boquillas Canyon Trail** (1.4 mi./2.3 km rt., 1 hr., moderate) ascends to overlook the Rio Grande before dropping to the sandy shore as the canyon walls pinch in.

Two desert hikes lead to geologic features. From Grapevine Hills Road, the **Grapevine Hills Trail** (2.2 mi./3.5 km rt., 1.5 hrs., easy) trots through a gravel wash before finishing with a steep climb to see Balanced Rock, a large boulder wedged between two towering rocks. To stand below a 100-foot-tall (30-m) water-smoothed pour-over, walk to **Lower Burro Mesa Pour-off** (1 mi./1.6 km rt., 30 min., easy) on a spur off Ross Maxwell Scenic Drive.

BACKPACKING

Almost 20 miles (32.2 km) of trails loop through the **Chisos Mountains** for prime backpacking routes. Forested canyons with colorful birds warbling in song lead to high scenic rim walks overlooking the Rio Grande thousands of feet below. Spread throughout the loops are 42 designated campsites with food storage lockers; four junctions include compost toilets.

Most hikers limit trips to 2-3 days due to unreliable water sources. **Required permits** ($10) are available first come, first served up to 24 hours in advance from Panther Junction Visitor Center.

▼ BALANCED ROCK ON THE GRAPEVINE HILLS TRAIL

WHERE TO STAY

INSIDE THE PARK

The only accommodations in the park are at **Chisos Mountains Lodge** (432/477-2291 or 877/386-4383, www.chisosmountainslodge.com, from $145). Situated nearly 1 mile (1.6 km) high in a basin surrounded by mountains, the complex offers a no-frills experience of hotel, motel, and lodge rooms. Book one year in advance for holidays and for the five coveted historic Roosevelt Stone Cottages.

The **Chisos Mountains Lodge Restaurant** (7am-10am, 11am-4pm, and 5pm-8pm daily, $8-20) serves Tex-Mex fare, standard dishes, hearty breakfasts, and to-go hiker lunches.

Three year-round **campgrounds** ($14) have drinking water, picnic tables, grills, and flush toilets, but no hookups. **Reservations** (877/444-6777, www.recreation.gov, $14) up to six months in advance are available for mid-November-May at Rio Grande Village and Chisos Basin. Located in the mountains, **Chisos Basin** (60 sites, 26 reservable) is best for tents and small RVs (RV limit 24 ft./7.3 m, trailer limit 20 ft./6.1 m). **Rio Grande Village** (100 sites, 56 reservable) is on the Rio Grande on the eastern edge of the park. Set in a cottonwood oasis between Castolon and Santa Elena Canyon, **Cottonwood** (24 sites) has pit toilets instead of flush.

ROAD TO RIO GRANDE VILLAGE

Rio Grande Village RV Campground (877/386-4383, 25 sites, accepts reservations, $33) has full hookups for RVs.

Big Bend has dozens of primitive **backcountry campsites** (permit required, $12, first come, first served), typically consisting of only a flat gravel pad. Many are only accessible by high-clearance vehicles or four-wheel drives.

OUTSIDE THE PARK

A few motels and campgrounds are outside the park in **Terlingua/Study Butte** For more choices, stay in **Marathon.**

GETTING THERE AND AROUND

AIR

The closest airport is **Midland International Air & Space Port** (MAF, 9506 Laforce Blvd., 432/560-2200, www.flymaf.com), four hours from Big Bend. An alternative is **El Paso International Airport** (ELP, 6701 Convair Rd., 915/212-0330, www.elpasointernationalairport.com), which offers a few more flights but is five hours from the park. Both have rental cars.

CAR

From Midland, drive south on US 385 for 230 miles (370 km, 3.5 hours) to the park visitors center. There is no public transportation available to Big Bend or inside the national park.

Big Bend has three types of roads (all marked on the park map you can pick up at the entrance station): paved, graveled dirt, and primitive. Paved roads are mostly narrow with skimpy shoulders and some curvy parts; watch your speed as javelina, deer, and jackrabbits can run out in front of vehicles. Most high-clearance vehicles can handle the graveled dirt roads that may have potholes and washboards. The rough primitive roads are only for high-clearance four-wheel-drive rigs.

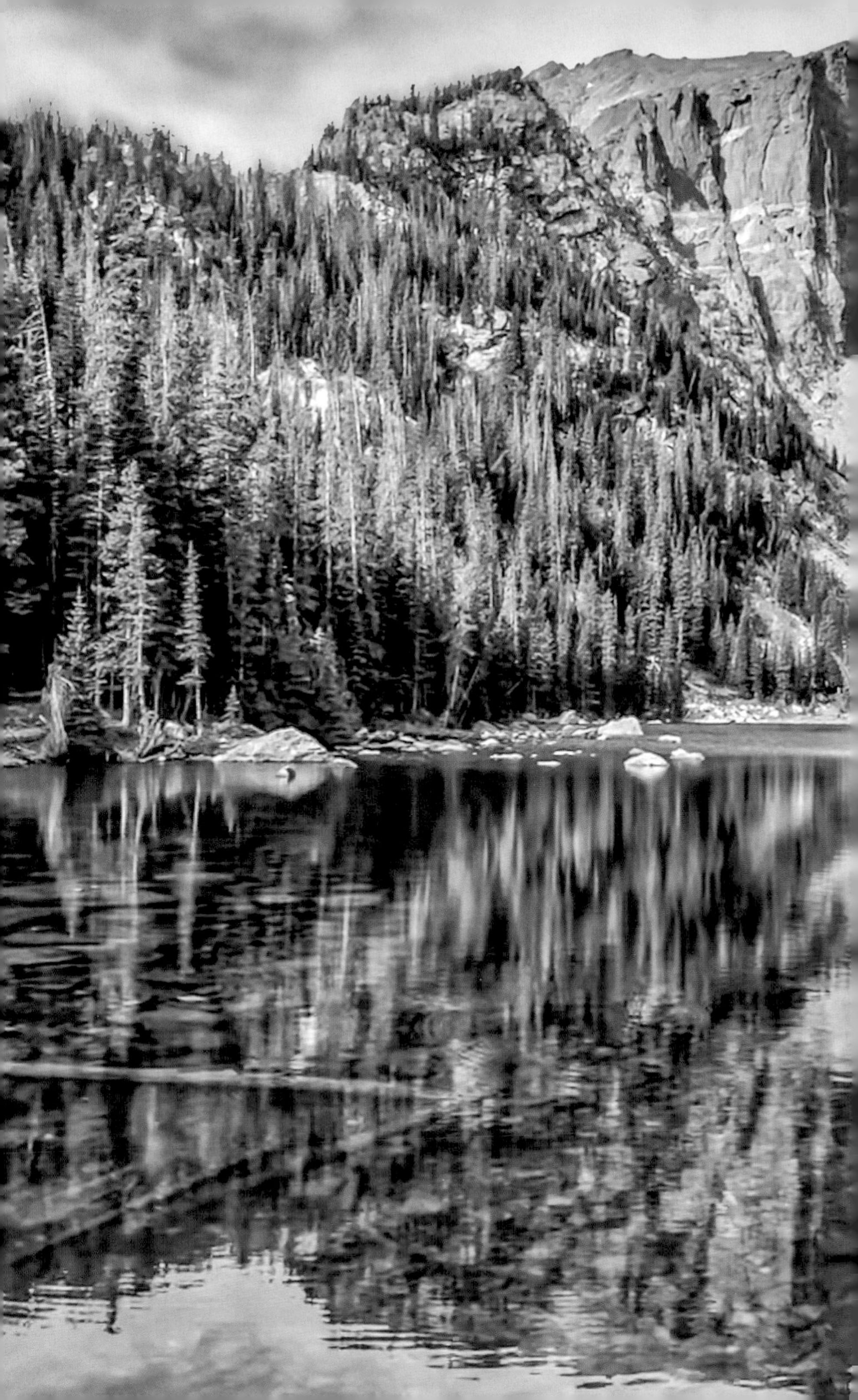

ROCKY MOUNTAINS

The Rocky Mountains climb along the backbone of the Continental Divide. In Rocky Mountain National Park, the hairpin bends of Trail Ridge Road reveal snowcapped peaks and alpine tundra. Farther south, the Black Canyon of the Gunnison squeezes through a narrow fissure.

Anchoring the middle are a pair of parks in a landscape rife with bison. Yellowstone sputters with geysers, mud pots, and hot springs while Grand Teton struts a line of sawtooth peaks.

In the north, Glacier rises with jagged arêtes and glacier-carved basins, sliced through by Going-to-the-Sun Road.

To the east, these rugged mountains give way to prairies of the Great Plains. Colorful Badlands and Theodore Roosevelt National Parks break up grasslands, while Wind Cave hides underground.

◄ EMERALD LAKE, ROCKY MOUNTAINS

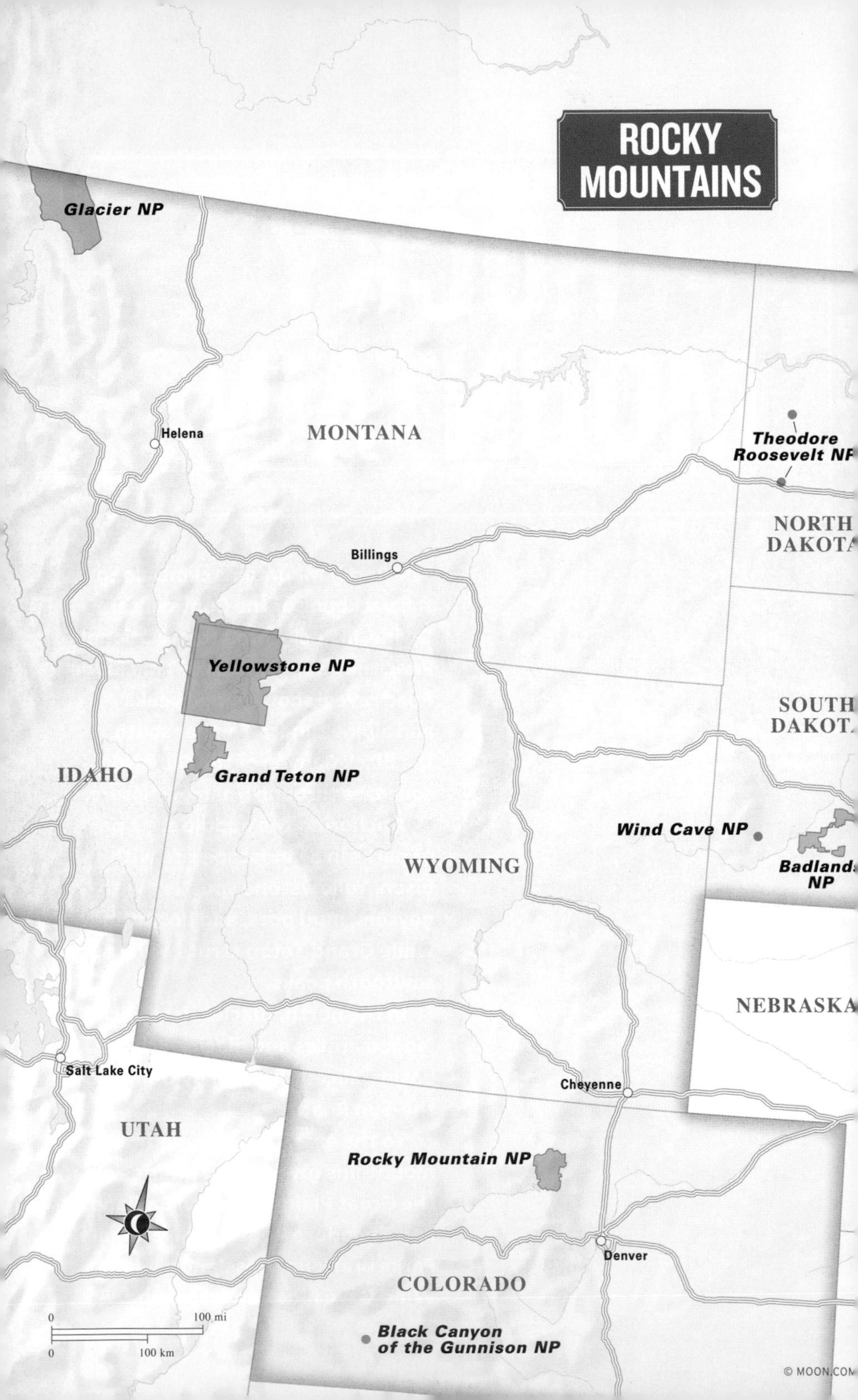

ROCKY MOUNTAINS
Glacier NP
Helena
MONTANA
Theodore Roosevelt NP
NORTH DAKOTA
Billings
Yellowstone NP
SOUTH DAKOTA
IDAHO
Grand Teton NP
Wind Cave NP
Badlands NP
WYOMING
NEBRASKA
Salt Lake City
Cheyenne
UTAH
Rocky Mountain NP
Denver
COLORADO
0
100 mi
0
100 km
Black Canyon of the Gunnison NP
© MOON.COM

The National Parks of THE ROCKY MOUNTAINS

ROCKY MOUNTAIN, CO

Alpine lakes, lush meadows teeming with elk, and a glaciated landscape of deep valleys beneath soaring summits create awe-inspiring splendor (page 425).

BLACK CANYON OF THE GUNNISON, CO

This narrow, deep chasm cuts through black volcanic rock to create one of the country's most dramatic canyons (page 442).

YELLOWSTONE, WY

Our first national park remains one of the finest, with gushing geysers, thundering waterfalls, and epic wildlife (page 449).

GRAND TETON, WY

A craggy spine of peaks laced with hiking trails spills into glacial lakes and historic Jackson Hole ranches (page 472).

GLACIER, MT

Captivating scenery, wondrous trails, huge lakes, and scenic drives fill this park that shares a border with Canada (page 490).

BADLANDS, SD

A wall of tall spires, grassy buttes, and colorful eroding cliffs present an otherworldly landscape (page 512).

WIND CAVE, SD

Beneath the ground's surface is the seventh-longest cave in the world (page 520).

THEODORE ROOSEVELT, ND

This badland and grassland landscape projects a raw beauty favored by Theodore Roosevelt (page 529).

1: MORMON ROW, GRAND TETON
2: SCENIC DRIVE, BADLANDS
3: BISON, THEODORE ROOSEVELT

Best OF THE PARKS

Going-to-the-Sun Road: Drive the only road bisecting Glacier on a skinny cliff shimmy to Logan Pass (page 494).

Old Faithful Geyser: Watch one of the most regular geysers erupt (page 455).

Wildlife-Watching: Pull out binoculars in Lamar Valley in Yellowstone, on Moose-Wilson Road in Grand Teton, and throughout Rocky Mountain National Park (pages 455, 478, and 429).

Trail Ridge Road: Drive the winding, hairpin curves on this scenic traverse across the Continental Divide in Rocky Mountain (page 429).

Badlands Loop Road: Tour this road through South Dakota's Badlands, dotted with scenic turnouts and dramatic vistas (page 516).

▲ GOING-TO-THE-SUN ROAD, GLACIER

PLANNING YOUR TRIP

Plan at least **two weeks** to tour the national parks of the Rockies. Make advance **reservations** for inside Glacier, Yellowstone, Grand Teton, and Rocky Mountain: 12-13 months for lodging and 6-12 months for camping. Winter buries these parks in snow, so first-timers prefer **summer** when visitors centers and services are open and the weather is pleasantly warm.

High Season

Summer (May-October) is high season in the Rockies, when the parks see the most visitors. July and August see the big crowds and the best weather. Summer heralds the opening of the high-elevation scenic drives—pending weather conditions and snow removal—such as Trail Ridge Road in Rocky Mountain and Going-to-the-Sun Road in Glacier.

Low Season

In **winter** (Nov.-Apr.), deep snows turn the parks white, and many park roads close for the season. Even though winter sees fewer people, it's the time for snow sports. In Yellowstone, visitors go to Old Faithful on snowcoaches or snowmobiles, while roads in Glacier and Grand Teton become snowshoeing and cross-country skiing paths.

Road Trip

GRAND TETON, YELLOWSTONE, AND GLACIER

String together these three iconic parks in a **one-week** road trip. Fly into **Jackson Hole Airport, Wyoming,** rent a car, and enjoy the park on the same day. Make reservations for historic in-park lodges up to 13 months in advance. Fly out of **Glacier International Airport,** Kalispell, Montana.

JENNY LAKE, GRAND TETON

Grand Teton

48 miles (77 km) / 1.5 hours

Drive north on US 26/89/191 to Moose. Turn left onto Teton Park Road, stopping to tour the **Craig Thomas Discovery and Visitor Center.** Farther north, enjoy views of the Tetons from **Jenny Lake,** with a walk along the lakeshore overlooks. If time permits, hop the boat shuttle to hike to **Hidden Falls** and **Inspiration Point.** Continue north on Teton Park Road and US 89/191/287 to **Jackson Lake Lodge.** Spend the night, dine in the **Mural Room,** and go **horseback riding** the next morning. Then, drive north along Jackson Lake on US 89/191/287 and pass through **John D. Rockefeller Jr. Parkway.**

Yellowstone

147 miles (237 km) / 4 hours

Drive the South Entrance Road to **West Thumb Geyser Basin** and walk the boardwalk to see **Yellowstone Lake.**

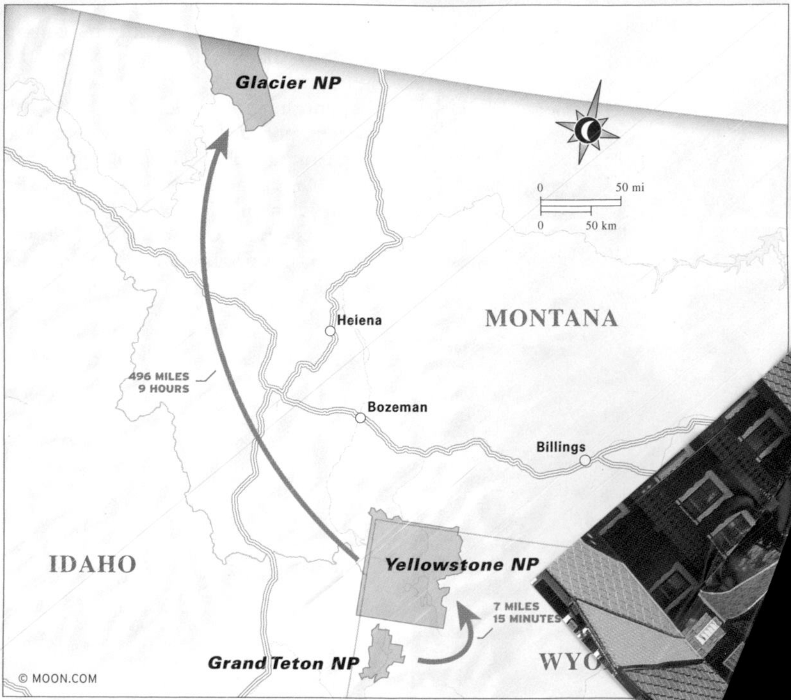

Then, head west on Grand Loop Road (US 89) to pop over the Continental Divide to watch **Old Faithful Geyser** and tour the Upper Geyser Basin. Spend the night at historic **Old Faithful Inn.** In the morning, continue north on Grand Loop Road (US 89) through Madison Junction to Norris Junction to walk through **Norris Geyser Basin.** Then, go east on Norris-Canyon Road and head south on Grand Loop Road to explore several overlooks on the North Rim of **Grand Canyon of the Yellowstone.** Go north on Grand Loop Road to Tower Junction where the Northeast Entrance Road (US 212) goes to **Lamar Valley** for wildlife-watching. Return to Grand Loop Road heading west to end your day at **Mammoth Hot Springs** and overnight at **Mammoth Hot Springs Hotel.**

Glacier

500 miles (805 km) / 10 hours

Hit the road by 8am for this long haul up the Rocky Mountains. Take US 89 north, I-90 west, US 12/287 north, and I-15 north. Exit onto US 287 northward, followed by US 89 and US 2 along the Rocky Mountain Front to Browning. Head north on MT 464 and US 89, and west on Many Glacier Road to enter Glacier. You should arrive just in time to dine amid mountain scenery at **Many Glacier Hotel** and watch the sun set over the Continental Divide. In the morning, take a boat ride on **Swiftcurrent** and **Josephine Lakes** to hike to **Grinnell Lake.** The following day, drive Many Glacier Road east and US 89 south for a cliffside drive west on the **Going-to-the-Sun Road.** Stop at **Logan Pass** to soak up the splendor before descending west and aiming for the airport on US 2.

1: PORCELAIN BASIN, NORRIS, YELLOWSTONE
2: LOWER FALL, GRAND CANYON OF THE YELLOWSTONE, YELLOWSTONE
3: MANY GLACIER HOTEL & MT. GOULD, GLACIER

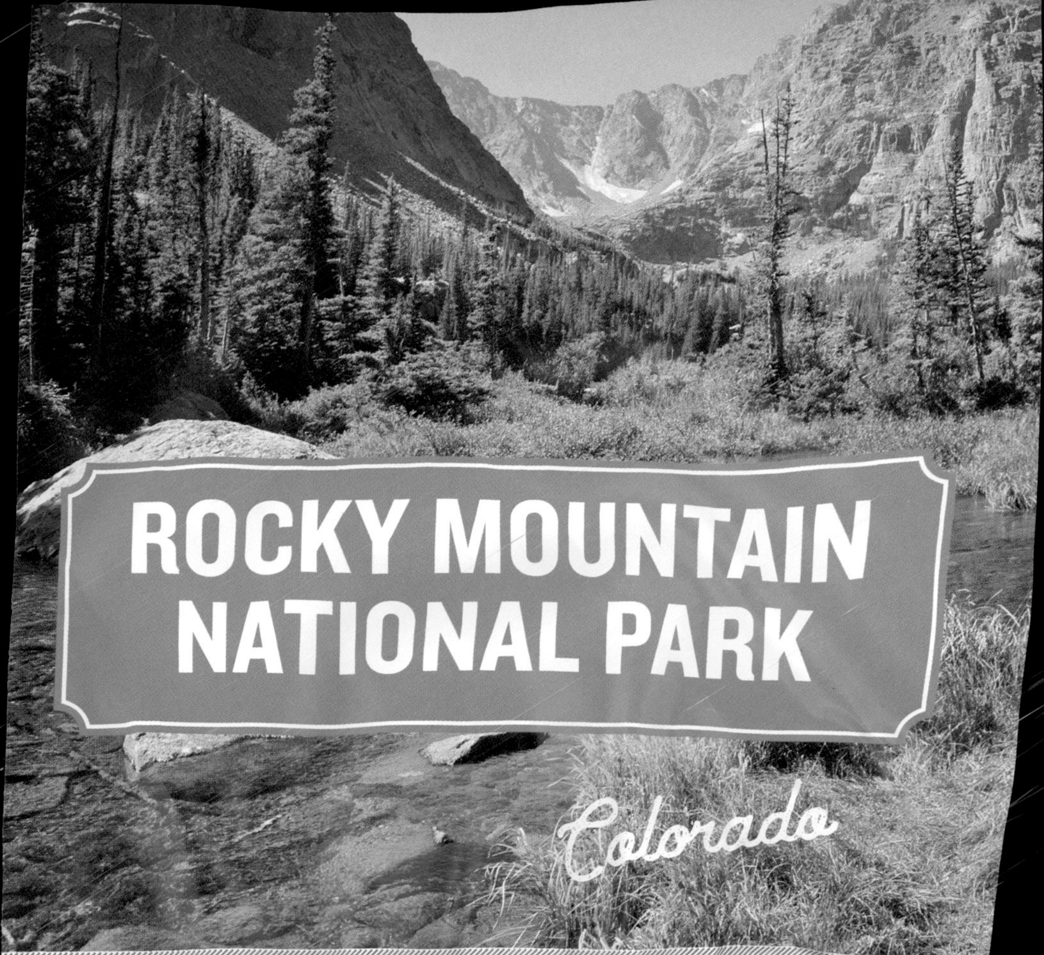

KEEPSAKE STAMPS ▼▼▼

WEBSITE:
www.nps.gov/romo

PHONE NU[illegible]ER:
970/5[illegible]-1206

VI[illegible]ION RANK:

[illegible]HY GO:
Explore [illegible]igh peak[illegible]
and [illegible]atch wildl[illegible]

▲ DREAM LA[illegible]

72

12,216ft
HOLLOWELL PARK TRAILHEAD
Gabletop Mtn 11,821ft
Knobtop Mtn 12,336ft
GLACIER BASIN
EAST PORTAL TRAILHEAD
BIERSTADT LAKE TRAILHEAD
SPRAGUE LAKE
Ptarmigan Point 12,270ft
BEAR LAKE TRAILHEAD/ EMERALD LAKE TRAILHEAD
STORM PASS TRAILHEAD
LILY LAKE TRAILHEAD
GREEN MOUNTAIN TRAILHEAD
Flattop Mtn 12,362ft
GLACIER GORGE TRAILHEAD
TWIN SISTERS TRAILHEAD
Hallett Pk 12,599ft
Otis Pk 12,484ft
Estes Cone
Twin Sisters Peaks 11,428ft
HARBISON MEADOWS
GRAND LAKE ENTRANCE STATION
KAWUNEECHE VISITOR CENTER
Taylor Pk 13,143ft
GLACIER GORGE
LONGS PEAK
LONGS PEAK TRAILHEAD
Powell Pk 13,176ft
McHenrys Pk 13,242ft
TONAHUTU TRAILHEAD
Alva B. Adams Tunnel (water diversion tunnel)
Grand Lake
Longs Peak 14,259ft
Mount Meeker 13,911ft
Grand Lake
EAST SHORE TRAIL/ ANRA TRAILHEAD
EAST INLET TRAILHEAD
Mount Alice 13,310ft
Shadow Mountain Lake
CONTINENTAL DIVIDE
SANDBEACH LAKE TRAIL
Allenspark
7
EAST SHORE TRAIL/ SHADOW MOUNTAIN DAM TRAILHEAD
WILD BASIN TRAILHEAD
34
GREEN RIDGE
Isolation Peak 13,118ft
CUTTHROAT BAY
Ogalalla Peak 13,138ft
Lake Granby
0
0
© MOON.COM

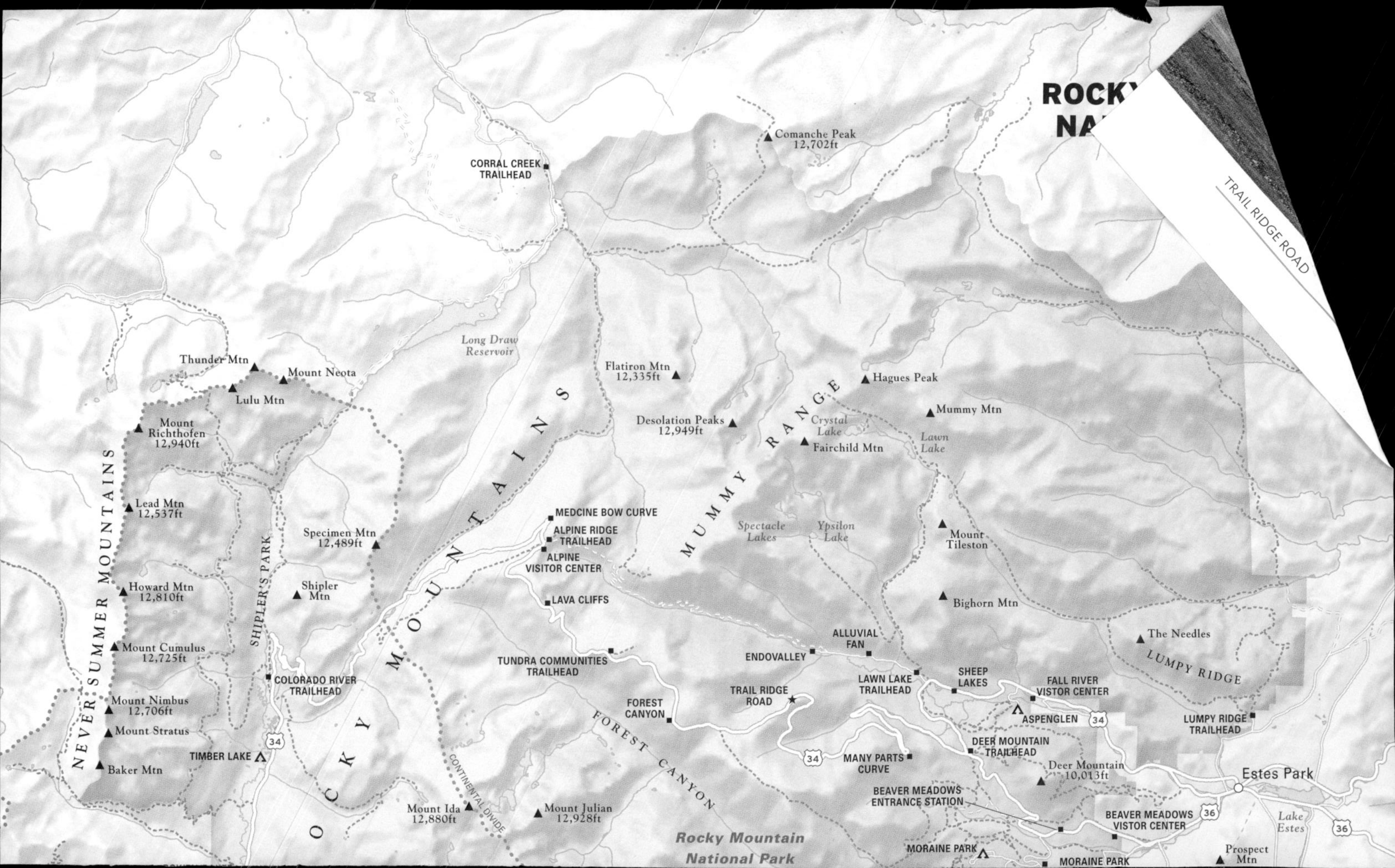

ROCKY
NA
TRAIL RIDGE ROAD
CORRAL CREEK TRAILHEAD
Comanche Peak 12,702ft
Long Draw Reservoir
Thunder Mtn
Mount Neota
Lulu Mtn
Mount Richthofen 12,940ft
Lead Mtn 12,537ft
Specimen Mtn 12,489ft
Howard Mtn 12,810ft
Shipler Mtn
Mount Cumulus 12,725ft
Mount Nimbus 12,706ft
Mount Stratus
Baker Mtn
NEVER SUMMER MOUNTAINS
SHIPLER'S PARK
COLORADO RIVER TRAILHEAD
TIMBER LAKE
34
ROCKY MOUNTAINS
CONTINENTAL DIVIDE
Mount Ida 12,880ft
Mount Julian 12,928ft
Flatiron Mtn 12,335ft
Desolation Peaks 12,949ft
Hagues Peak
Mummy Mtn
Crystal Lake
Fairchild Mtn
Lawn Lake
MUMMY RANGE
MEDCINE BOW CURVE
ALPINE RIDGE TRAILHEAD
ALPINE VISITOR CENTER
LAVA CLIFFS
Spectacle Lakes
Ypsilon Lake
Mount Tileston
Bighorn Mtn
The Needles
LUMPY RIDGE
TUNDRA COMMUNITIES TRAILHEAD
ENDOVALLEY
ALLUVIAL FAN
LAWN LAKE TRAILHEAD
SHEEP LAKES
FALL RIVER VISTOR CENTER
TRAIL RIDGE ROAD
FOREST CANYON
FOREST CANYON
ASPENGLEN
LUMPY RIDGE TRAILHEAD
MANY PARTS CURVE
DEER MOUNTAIN TRAILHEAD
Deer Mountain 10,013ft
Estes Park
BEAVER MEADOWS ENTRANCE STATION
BEAVER MEADOWS VISTOR CENTER
36
Lake Estes
Rocky Mountain National Park
MORAINE PARK
MORAINE PARK
Prospect Mtn

At **ROCKY MOUNTAIN NATIONAL PARK**, rugged scenery is guaranteed. Meadows, forests, and lakes butt up against a backdrop of sheer cliffs and soaring peaks that dominate the Continental Divide. You'll find some of the highest summits in the Lower 48 and the highest paved road in the United States.

From low valleys to 14,259-foot-high (4,346-m) Longs Peak, the enormous changes in elevation create a mosaic of ecosystems that top out in alpine tundra. A thick blanket of snow drapes the mountains in winter, but summer heralds the opening of Trail Ridge Road, the signature scenic drive, a winding ribbon of hairpin bends. Its corridor follows a Ute seasonal hunting path to travel across the mountains. When aspen change to bright gold in fall, the air resounds with elk bugles and bighorn rams banging horns. This park captivates all senses.

PLANNING YOUR TIME

Rocky Mountain National Park is separated by the Continental Divide into east and west sides. These sides are only connected when **Trail Ridge Road** (US 34, Memorial Day-mid-Oct.) is open. When the road is closed (mid-Oct.-Memorial Day), **Estes Park** offers the main driving access into the park.

Rocky Mountain is one of the country's busiest national parks, and **summer** (May-Sept.) booms with visitors, and July sees the biggest crowds. Due to extreme elevation differences, the weather is changeable and unpredictable—even in summer. You might leave Denver's lowland heat to arrive in chilling winds at 12,000 feet (3,658 m). Summer afternoons frequently bring thunderstorms. Spring and fall offer a mix of warm sun, rain, or snow; fall tends toward blue skies. For elk calving season, visit late May-early June. To listen to bugling bull elk, go in fall. Winter (Dec.-Mar.) pummels the mountains with snow.

Rocky Mountain has no inside park lodges, but make reservations 9-12 months in advance for lodgings in Estes Park or Grand Lake. Make reservations six months in advance for campgrounds inside the park.

ENTRANCES AND FEES

The bustling east side has two entrances open year-round: **Fall River Entrance Station** (US 34) and **Beaver Meadows Entrance Station** (US 36). The gateway town of **Estes Park** provides access to both roads. Access the west side through the **Grand Lake Entrance Station** (US 34, year-round), north of the town of Grand Lake.

The entrance fee is $35 per vehicle ($30 motorcycle, $20 individual) and good for seven days.

VISITORS CENTERS

Beaver Meadows Visitor Center

The **Beaver Meadows Visitor Center** (US 36, 8am-6pm daily in summer, 8am-4:30pm daily in winter) is the park's primary access point. It has an information desk, bookstore, nature exhibits,

Road Trip

GRAND TETON, YELLOWSTONE, AND GLACIER

String together these three iconic parks in a **one-week** road trip. Fly into **Jackson Hole Airport, Wyoming,** rent a car, and enjoy the park on the same day. Make reservations for historic in-park lodges up to 13 months in advance. Fly out of **Glacier International Airport,** Kalispell, Montana.

JENNY LAKE, GRAND TETON

Grand Teton

48 miles (77 km) / 1.5 hours

Drive north on US 26/89/191 to Moose. Turn left onto Teton Park Road, stopping to tour the **Craig Thomas Discovery and Visitor Center.** Farther north, enjoy views of the Tetons from **Jenny Lake,** with a walk along the lakeshore overlooks. If time permits, hop the boat shuttle to hike to **Hidden Falls** and **Inspiration Point.** Continue north on Teton Park Road and US 89/191/287 to **Jackson Lake Lodge.** Spend the night, dine in the **Mural Room,** and go **horseback riding** the next morning. Then, drive north along Jackson Lake on US 89/191/287 and pass through **John D. Rockefeller Jr. Parkway.**

Yellowstone

147 miles (237 km) / 4 hours

Drive the South Entrance Road to **West Thumb Geyser Basin** and walk the boardwalk to see **Yellowstone Lake.**

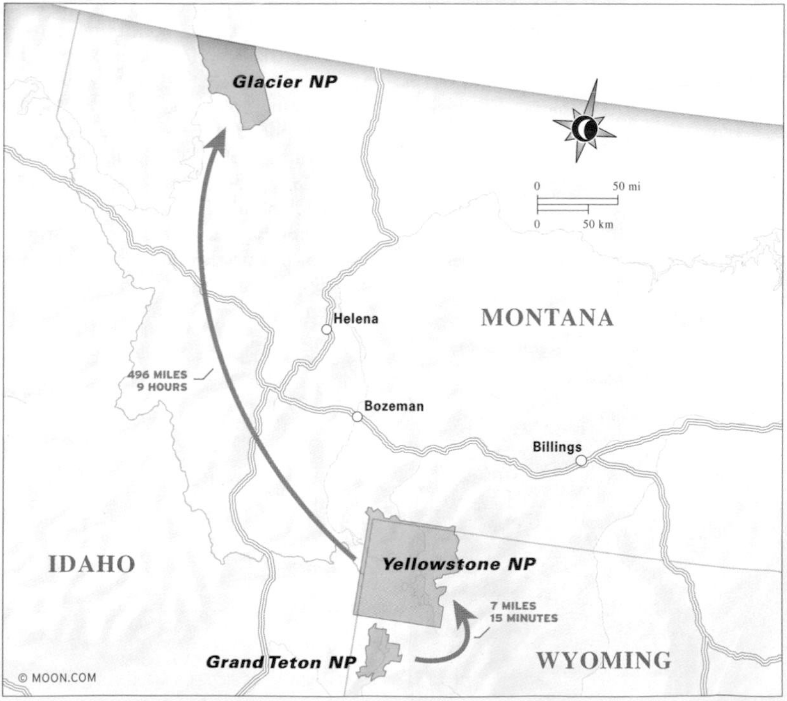

Then, head west on Grand Loop Road (US 89) to pop over the Continental Divide to watch **Old Faithful Geyser** and tour the Upper Geyser Basin**.** Spend the night at historic **Old Faithful Inn.** In the morning, continue north on Grand Loop Road (US 89) through Madison Junction to Norris Junction to walk through **Norris Geyser Basin.** Then, go east on Norris-Canyon Road and head south on Grand Loop Road to explore several overlooks on the North Rim of **Grand Canyon of the Yellowstone.** Go north on Grand Loop Road to Tower Junction where the Northeast Entrance Road (US 212) goes to **Lamar Valley** for wildlife-watching. Return to Grand Loop Road heading west to end your day at **Mammoth Hot Springs** and overnight at **Mammoth Hot Springs Hotel.**

Glacier

500 miles (805 km) / 10 hours

Hit the road by 8am for this long haul up the Rocky Mountains. Take US 89 north, I-90 west, US 12/287 north, and I-15 north. Exit onto US 287 northward, followed by US 89 and US 2 along the Rocky Mountain Front to Browning. Head north on MT 464 and US 89, and west on Many Glacier Road to enter Glacier. You should arrive just in time to dine amid mountain scenery at **Many Glacier Hotel** and watch the sun set over the Continental Divide. In the morning, take a boat ride on **Swiftcurrent** and **Josephine Lakes** to hike to **Grinnell Lake.** The following day, drive Many Glacier Road east and US 89 south for a cliffside drive west on the **Going-to-the-Sun Road.** Stop at **Logan Pass** to soak up the splendor before descending west and aiming for the airport on US 2.

1: PORCELAIN BASIN, NORRIS, YELLOWSTONE
2: LOWER FALL, GRAND CANYON OF THE YELLOWSTONE, YELLOWSTONE
3: MANY GLACIER HOTEL & MT. GOULD, GLACIER

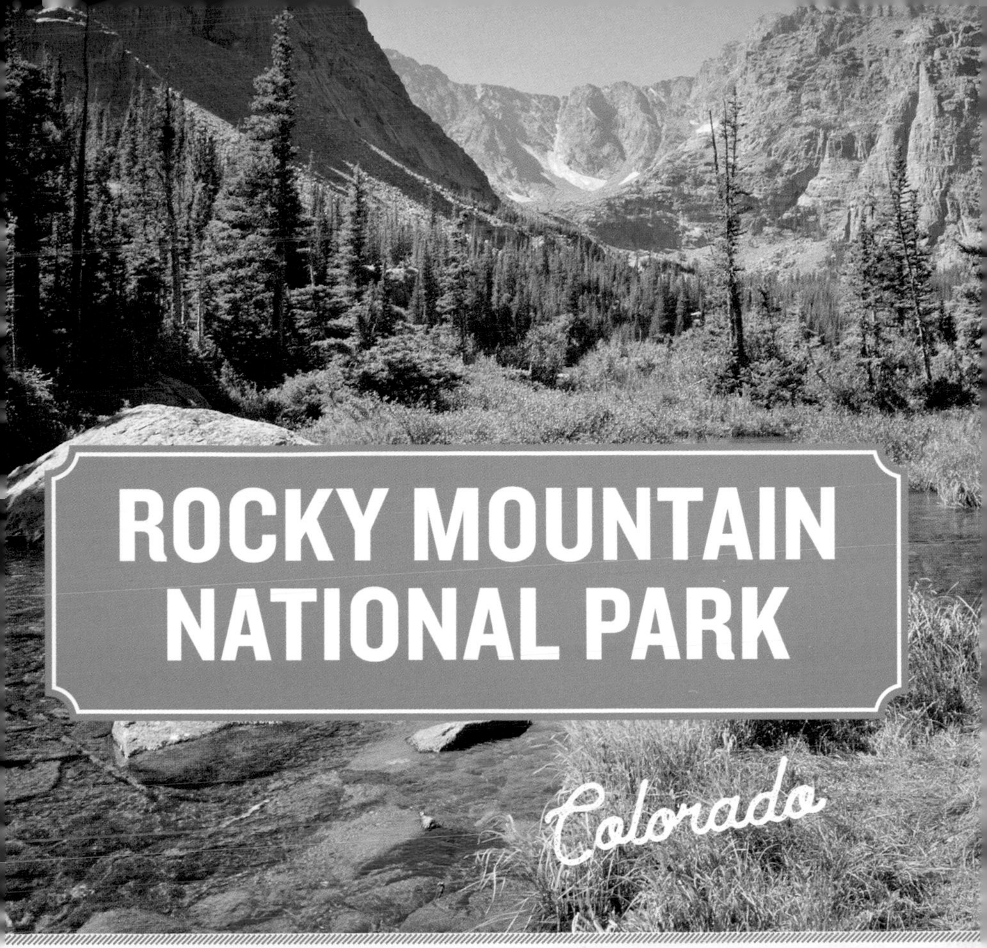

KEEPSAKE STAMPS ▼▼▼

WEBSITE:
www.nps.gov/romo

PHONE NUMBER:
970/586-1206

VISITATION RANK:
3

WHY GO:
Explore high peaks and watch wildlife.

▲ DREAM LAKE

12,216ft
Gabletop Mtn
11,821ft
Knobtop Mtn
12,336ft
Ptarmigan Point
12,270ft
Flattop Mtn
12,362ft
Hallett Pk
12,599ft
Otis Pk
12,484ft
Taylor Pk
13,143ft
Powell Pk
13,176ft
McHenrys Pk
13,242ft
Longs Peak
14,259ft
Mount Meeker
13,911ft
Mount Alice
13,310ft
Isolation Peak
13,118ft
Ogalalla Peak
13,138ft
Estes Cone
Twin Sisters Peaks
11,428ft
GLACIER GORGE
CONTINENTAL DIVIDE
Alva B. Adams Tunnel
(water diversion tunnel)
HOLLOWELL PARK TRAILHEAD
GLACIER BASIN
EAST PORTAL TRAILHEAD
BIERSTADT LAKE TRAILHEAD
SPRAGUE LAKE
STORM PASS TRAILHEAD
BEAR LAKE TRAILHEAD/
EMERALD LAKE TRAILHEAD
GLACIER GORGE TRAILHEAD
LILY LAKE TRAILHEAD
TWIN SISTERS TRAILHEAD
LONGS PEAK
LONGS PEAK TRAILHEAD
GREEN MOUNTAIN TRAILHEAD
HARBISON MEADOWS
GRAND LAKE ENTRANCE STATION
KAWUNEECHE VISITOR CENTER
TONAHUTU TRAILHEAD
Grand Lake
Grand Lake
EAST SHORE TRAIL/
ANRA TRAILHEAD
EAST INLET TRAILHEAD
Shadow Mountain Lake
EAST SHORE TRAIL/
SHADOW MOUNTAIN DAM TRAILHEAD
GREEN RIDGE
34
CUTTHROAT BAY
Lake Granby
Meeker Park
SANDBEACH LAKE TRAILHEAD
WILD BASIN TRAILHEAD
Allenspark
7
72
0
5 mi
0
5 km
© MOON.COM

ROCKY MOUNTAIN NATIONAL PARK

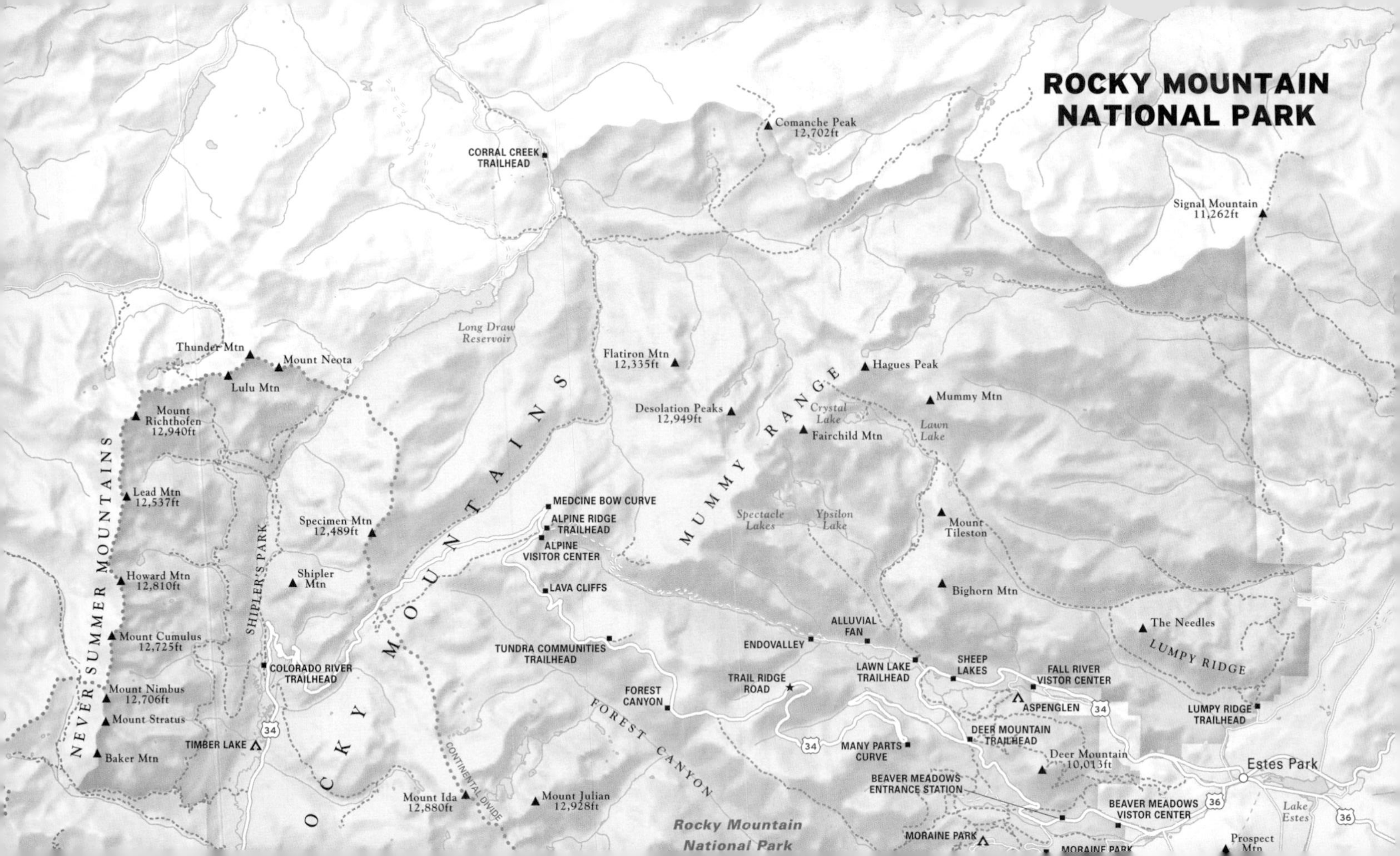

At **ROCKY MOUNTAIN NATIONAL PARK**, rugged scenery is guaranteed. Meadows, forests, and lakes butt up against a backdrop of sheer cliffs and soaring peaks that dominate the Continental Divide. You'll find some of the highest summits in the Lower 48 and the highest paved road in the United States.

From low valleys to 14,259-foot-high (4,346-m) Longs Peak, the enormous changes in elevation create a mosaic of ecosystems that top out in alpine tundra. A thick blanket of snow drapes the mountains in winter, but summer heralds the opening of Trail Ridge Road, the signature scenic drive, a winding ribbon of hairpin bends. Its corridor follows a Ute seasonal hunting path to travel across the mountains. When aspen change to bright gold in fall, the air resounds with elk bugles and bighorn rams banging horns. This park captivates all senses.

PLANNING YOUR TIME

Rocky Mountain National Park is separated by the Continental Divide into east and west sides. These sides are only connected when **Trail Ridge Road** (US 34, Memorial Day-mid-Oct.) is open. When the road is closed (mid-Oct.-Memorial Day), **Estes Park** offers the main driving access into the park.

Rocky Mountain is one of the country's busiest national parks, and **summer** (May-Sept.) booms with visitors, and July sees the biggest crowds. Due to extreme elevation differences, the weather is changeable and unpredictable—even in summer. You might leave Denver's lowland heat to arrive in chilling winds at 12,000 feet (3,658 m). Summer afternoons frequently bring thunderstorms. Spring and fall offer a mix of warm sun, rain, or snow; fall tends toward blue skies. For elk calving season, visit late May-early June. To listen to bugling bull elk, go in fall. Winter (Dec.-Mar.) pummels the mountains with snow.

TRAIL RIDGE ROAD

Rocky Mountain has no inside park lodges, but make reservations 9-12 months in advance for lodgings in Estes Park or Grand Lake. Make reservations six months in advance for campgrounds inside the park.

ENTRANCES AND FEES

The bustling east side has two entrances open year-round: **Fall River Entrance Station** (US 34) and **Beaver Meadows Entrance Station** (US 36). The gateway town of **Estes Park** provides access to both roads. Access the west side through the **Grand Lake Entrance Station** (US 34, year-round), north of the town of Grand Lake.

The entrance fee is $35 per vehicle ($30 motorcycle, $20 individual) and good for seven days.

VISITORS CENTERS

Beaver Meadows Visitor Center

The **Beaver Meadows Visitor Center** (US 36, 8am-6pm daily in summer, 8am-4:30pm daily in winter) is the park's primary access point. It has an information desk, bookstore, nature exhibits,

Top 3

YOUNG BULL ELK

1 WATCH ELK AND BIGHORN SHEEP

Hearing the eerie sounds of a 700-pound (318-kg) **bull elk** echoing through the autumn air is a quintessential Rocky Mountain experience. During **fall breeding season** (mid-Sept-mid-Oct.), anxious males round up their harems and bugle a loud noise that begins with a deep resonance, then rises to a high-pitched squeal, before ending in grunts. Catch this rutting ritual at dusk and dawn, on roads around **Moraine** and **Horseshoe Parks** and **Upper Beaver Meadows.**

Sheep Lakes (US 34) are the best place to look for **bighorn sheep,** often seen in late spring between 9am and 3pm. At the **Bighorn Crossing Zone** in Horseshoe Park, rangers toting stop signs control traffic to allow sheep to move in and out of the meadow, while also providing great photo ops for visitors.

2 DRIVE TRAIL RIDGE ROAD

The 48-mile (77-km) paved **Trail Ridge Road** (US 34, late May-mid-Oct.) is the only road crossing the park between Estes Park and Grand Lake. Topping out at 12,183 feet (3,713 m), it is the country's highest paved road. From lush montane forests in deep valleys, the road quickly climbs above tree line into a harsh windswept tundra, home to tiny wildflowers and wildlife. Because the road is open 24/7, it offers high-elevation night sky viewing for stars.

Pullouts along the way offer safe places to stop for photos and enjoy the forever views. On the east side, top viewpoints include **Hidden Valley, Many Parks Curve,** and **Rainbow Curve.** Farther west, walk the interpretive **Tundra Communities Nature Trail** (1.1 mi./1.8 km rt., 30 min., easy) before crossing road's unmarked high point to the **Alpine Visitor Center,** where steps climb the **Alpine Ridge Trail** (0.6 mi./1 km rt., 30 min., moderate), nicknamed "Huffer's Hill."

On the west side, Trail Ridge Road crosses the **Continental Divide** at **Milner Pass.** Below that, **Farview Curve** overlooks the Colorado River and Kawuneeche Valley.

3 CLIMB LONGS PEAK

The 14,259-foot (4,356-m) **Longs Peak** is the highest peak in Rocky Mountain National Park with a distinct flat-topped summit and east face (the Diamond). About 30,000 mountaineers and technical rock climbers attempt to summit its difficult and challenging routes each summer.

The **Keyhole Route** (15 mi./24 km rt., 10-15 hrs., strenuous) ascends nearly 5,000 vertical feet (1,524 m) of scrambling, steep drop-offs, and extreme exposure to the fast-changing alpine weather. The climb requires a predawn start from the Longs Peak Trailhead and campground, located south of Estes Park via CO 7.

CLIMBING LONGS PEAK

Fortunately, you don't *have* to climb Longs Peak to admire it. See it from the easily accessible northern shore of **Bear Lake.**

and public Wi-Fi. Beginning in mid-April, rangers also offer a variety of **programs**. The **Backcountry Permit Office** (970/586-1242), where you can obtain backcountry permits on a space-available basis, is below the center.

Fall River Visitor Center

Just east of the Fall River Entrance Station is the **Fall River Visitor Center** (US 34, 9am-5pm daily late May-mid-Oct., closed winter except select holidays), with brochures, maps, and a bookstore.

Alpine Visitor Center

The **Alpine Visitor Center** (Trail Ridge Rd., 970/586-1222, 9am-5pm daily late May-mid-Oct.) has one of the best views in Colorado, a panorama looking down Fall River Canyon toward Longs Peak and Estes Park far below. The center has exhibits, restrooms, and the **Trail Ridge Store,** the only place in the park where you can grab food or snacks.

Kawuneeche Visitor Center

The west side of Rocky Mountain National Park has just one entrance that leads to **Kawuneeche Visitor Center** (16018 US 34, Grand Lake, 970/627-3471, 8am-6pm daily in summer, 8am-4:30pm daily in winter), where you can pick up maps, peruse exhibits, hop on public Wi-Fi, and reserve backcountry campsites.

SIGHTS

MORAINE PARK

The large meadow west of the Beaver Meadows Entrance Station is **Moraine Park** (US 36), one of the best places to spot wildlife, especially **elk.** Moraine Park stretches from **Bear Lake Road** to **Deer Ridge Junction** (US 36/34). You can obtain great views of the meadow from both roads, as well as from the two side roads that pierce the meadow's eastern side to access several trailheads, picnic areas, and the Moraine Park Stables.

Housed in a historic log-and-stone building, the seasonal **Moraine Park Discovery Center** (Bear Lake Rd., 970/586-1363, 9am-4:30pm daily late May-mid-Oct.) has a natural history exhibit describing how the park's distinctive landscape formed, a 0.5-mile (0.8-km) nature trail, and a gift shop and bookstore.

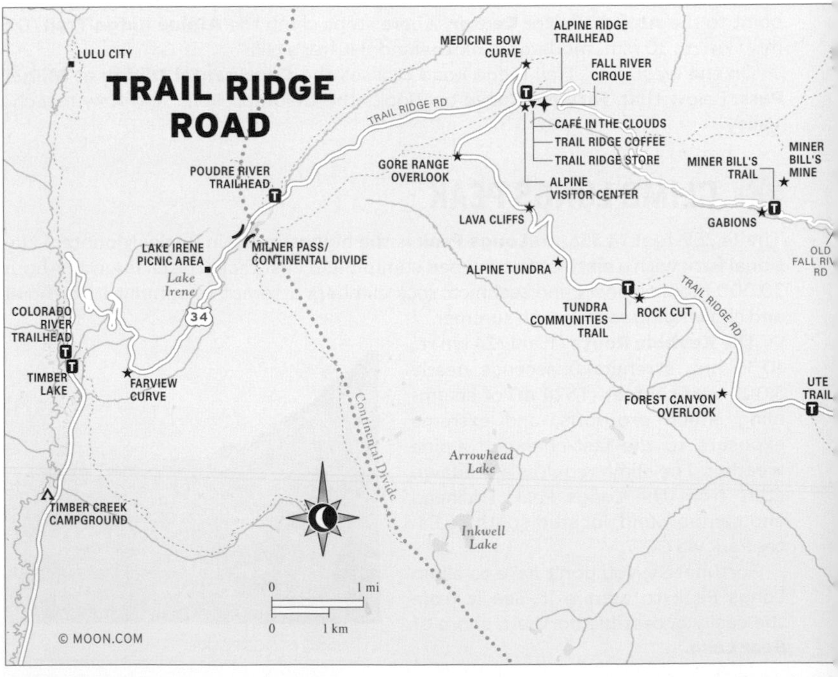

AVOID THE CROWDS

Crowds fill parking lots, visitors centers, roads, and trailheads in summer 10am-3pm. To avoid the crowds, hit the trails close to **sunrise** or later in the **evening.** Ride the earliest hiker shuttles from Estes Park to the Park & Ride on Bear Lake Road. Visit the **west side** midday, when crowds clog the east side. Take the free **shuttle buses** whenever possible to avoid traffic during one of the inevitable "elk jams."

BEAR LAKE

The shimmering, cobalt-blue waters of **Bear Lake** (shuttle 7am-7:30pm daily late May-mid-Oct., free) are nestled beneath the soaring summit of Hallett Peak, with many impressive mountains, including Longs Peak, rising to the south and east. The best way to experience its beauty is by strolling the interpretive **Bear Lake Nature Trail (**0.5 mi./0.8 km rt., 30 min., easy). From the shore, you'll enjoy great views of Longs Peak and other towering peaks while walking through spruce, lodgepole pine, and fir trees. Bear Lake also launches extended hikes and offers picnicking with stunning views.

ALLUVIAL FAN

The prominent, treeless scar on the northern flank of **Horseshoe Park** was created in just a few hours when, on July 15, 1982, the Lawn Lake Dam collapsed, sending 129 million gallons (488 million l) of water racing down Roaring River and knocking down every tree in its path. When the water reached flat Horseshoe Park, it slowed dramatically and dropped the debris it was carrying, creating a distinct cone of sand, gravel, and boulders called an alluvial fan. From the west or east **Alluvial Fan Parking Areas** (Endovalley Rd. off Old Fall River Rd.), walk the **Alluvial Fan Trail** (0.4 mi./0.6 km rt., 20 min., easy) over the debris.

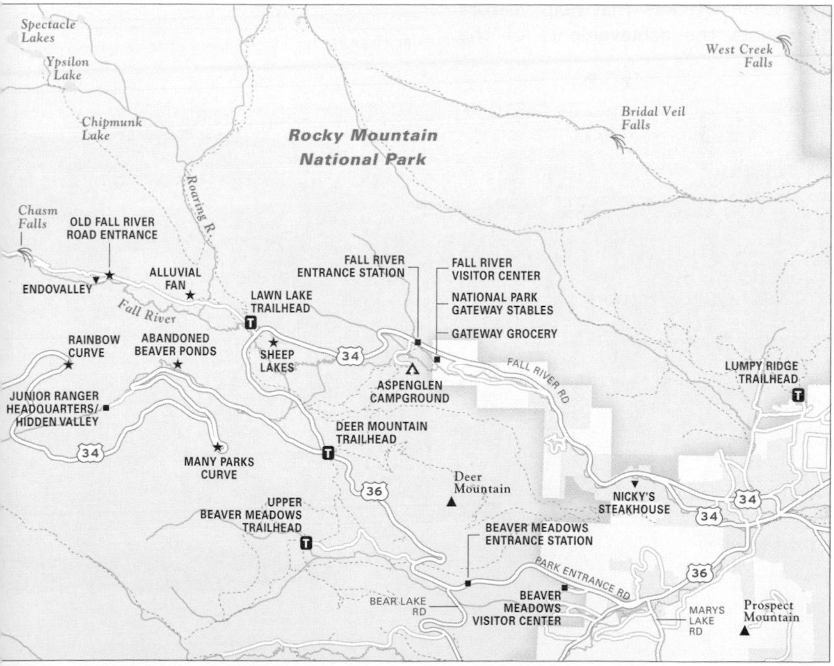

ONE DAY IN ROCKY MOUNTAIN

Start with a morning visit to **Bear Lake** for a stroll around its turquoise waters. Then drive up **Trail Ridge Road,** stopping at pullovers to enjoy the views. Picnic up on Trail Ridge with a sack lunch at an overlook of your choice. Walk the Alpine Communities Trail, visit the **Alpine Visitor Center,** and climb to Alpine Ridge Trail (known as Huffer's Hill) for 360-degree views and a selfie with the elevation sign that says "12,005 feet."

LILY LAKE

At the toe of the Twin Sisters Peaks, **Lily Lake** is one of Rocky Mountain's most accessible alpine lakes. Lying just feet from CO 7 about 7 miles (11 km) south of Estes Park, this turquoise lake is a popular place to picnic and stroll along the shoreline. The flat **wheelchair-accessible trail** (0.8 mi./1.3 km rt., 30 min., easy) makes a great walk for families and visitors not yet acclimated to the elevation.

ENOS MILLS CABIN MUSEUM

Housed in a wooden cabin built in 1885, the small **Enos Mills Cabin Museum** (6760 Hwy. 7, 970/586-4706, www.enosmills.com, tour reservations required) has old photographs, letters, and other artifacts that help visitors appreciate the achievements of the "Father of Rocky Mountain National Park." The highlights are the gorgeous scenery and the opportunity to learn about the family's history from one of Mills's relatives.

WILD BASIN

Tucked into the park's southeastern corner on a narrow gravel road, beautiful **Wild Basin** (parking lot fills by 9:30am in summer) is home to a series of waterfalls and gorgeous wildflowers, including clusters of Colorado blue columbine, the state flower. Crowds are often smaller in this outlying park zone that is primarily a hiking destination. But **Lower Copeland Falls** (0.6 mi./1 km rt., 20 min., easy) spills over a ledge for those wanting a short destination.

▼ BEAR LAKE

LILY LAKE

MILNER PASS

Contrary to what one would expect, **Trail Ridge Road** (late May-mid-Oct.) crosses the Continental Divide at Milner Pass, at 10,759 feet (3,279 m) several thousand feet lower than Alpine Visitor Center. Small **Poudre Lake** tucks into the meadow, and you can walk five minutes or so on the **Ute Trail** along the lake before it climbs into the forest.

KAWUNEECHE VALLEY

The main entrance to the park's west side is on **Trail Ridge Road** (US 36). While the full road only opens summer and fall (late May-mid-Oct.), a seasonal gate closure below Farview Curve allows for year-round visits to the lower elevations of Kawuneeche Valley.

Descending the western side of Trail Ridge Road, you're treated to spectacular views of the craggy peaks of the Never Summer Range, the upper Colorado River valley, lush meadows in Kawuneeche Valley, dense pine forests, and glimpses of the shimmering blue waters of Grand Lake. **Farview Curve,** a large pullout, takes in the best views.

On the valley floor, the **Holzwarth Historic Site** is the site homesteaded by German immigrant John Holzwarth Sr. From the parking area, walk the smooth **trail** (1.3 mi./2.1 km rt., 45 min., easy) that crosses the Colorado River before looping through the historic hand-hewn wooden cabins. Although visitors can only go inside the buildings in summer (mid-June-Labor Day), you can walk around the site year-round.

Harbison Meadows is the former site of two more homesteads belonging to sisters Annie and Kitty Harbison, who along with their family migrated here from Kansas in the late 1800s. Today, the empty grass meadows are a beautiful spot to enjoy a picnic lunch and watch for wildlife.

SCENIC DRIVES

OLD FALL RIVER ROAD

Built between 1913 and 1920, **Old Fall River Road** (July-Sept., closed in winter) is one of the park's signature scenic drives. From US 34, at the bend between Sheep Lakes and Horseshoe Park, the road heads northwest from the Endovalley to the Alpine Visitor Center on Trail Ridge Road. After leaving the valley, the rugged road climbs steadily through thick evergreen forest. About 1 mile (1.6 km) from its start, a five-minute walk drops from a small pullout on the left side down a stone pathway to **Chasm Falls.** From this stop, the road continues beneath the looming hulk of 12,454-foot (3,796-m) Mount Chapin. After passing **Willow Park,** where you can often spot elk, Old Fall River Road crosses into the treeless alpine tundra. Near the crest at **Fall River Pass,** the road contours around the **Fall River Cirque,** a giant cookie bite that a glacier sculpted out of the hard rock, before joining Trail Ridge Road at the Alpine Visitor Center.

Although the dirt surface is frequently graded and accessible to regular passenger vehicles, it's intended as a leisurely scenic drive, with a **15 mph (24 kph)** speed limit, no guardrails, and 16 tight switchbacks. Because it's too narrow and winding for cars to safely pass, the **11-mile route (18-km)** is a **one-way drive.**

HIKING

Most trailhead parking lots fill early. Use the park shuttle bus (7am-7:30pm daily late May-mid-Oct.) to avoid the

HOLZWARTH HISTORIC SITE

DREAM LAKE

anxiety of parking. You'll want to return from your destination before the afternoon thunderstorms begin to hurtle lightning, especially on hikes above tree line.

EAST SIDE

Lawn Lake

To explore the Mummy Range in the park's northeastern corner, **Lawn Lake Trail** (Lawn Lake Trailhead, Endovalley Rd., 12.4 mi./20 km rt., 6-7 hrs., strenuous) follows the path of the Roaring River up to Lawn Lake, surrounded by wildflower meadows and glaciated rock. Crystal Lake sits 1.5 mile (2.4 km) beyond Lawn Lake.

Deer Mountain

At the start of Trail Ridge Road, **Deer Mountain** (Deer Ridge Junction, US 34/36, 6 mi./9.7 km rt., 3-4 hrs., strenuous) makes a good first summit at 10,013 feet (3,052 m). It is usually accessible by late spring.

Fern Lake

The **Fern Lake Trail** (Fern Lake Rd. near Moraine Park Campground, 7.6 mi./12.2 km rt., 4-5 hrs., easy, shuttle stop) follows a creek through a deep and shady valley past several pretty waterfalls to narrow Fern Lake, rimmed with lily pads.

Bear Lake

Bear Lake Trailhead (parking lot fills by 8:30am in summer, shuttle stop) is the start of many hikes. The **shoreline stroll** (0.5 mi./0.8 km rt., 20 min., easy) around Bear Lake suits most visitors. On the northeast side of the lake, strong hikers take off at a junction to reach the historic **Flattop Mountain Trail** (8.8 mi./14.2 km rt., 5 hrs., strenuous). After turning left at two more junctions, the trail climbs to the summit of 12,324-foot (3,756-m) Flattop Mountain, located on the Continental Divide. En route, the trail passes overlooks of Dream and Emerald Lakes, plus views of Longs and Hallett Peaks.

A few feet up the Bear Lake Trail is the **Emerald Lake Trailhead,** which goes south and west to a string of deep-blue lakes. The shortest destination is spritely **Nymph Lake** (1 mi./1.6 km rt., 30 min., easy), after which the trail climbs steeply to celestial **Dream Lake** (2.2 mi./3.5 km rt., 1.5 hrs., moderate). Just before Dream Lake, the trail forks at a junction to go on either side of Hallett Peak. Turn left to ascend to sparkling **Lake Haiyaha** (4.2 mi./6.8 km rt., 2.5 hrs., moderate) with views up Chaos Canyon. The right fork goes to **Emerald Lake** (3.6 mi./5.8 km rt., 2 hrs., moderate) at the base of Tyndall Gorge.

Best Hike

LUMPY RIDGE

DISTANCE: 5.2 miles (8.4 km) round-trip
DURATION: 2.5 hours
ELEVATION CHANGE: 1,000 feet (305 m)
DIFFICULTY: moderate
TRAILHEAD: Lumpy Ridge/ Gem Lake

The climb up Lumpy Ridge goes through evergreen forest and ancient granite, which ice, wind, and rain have sculpted over millions of years into the ridge's distinctive knobs. From the trailhead, go left to ascend below the captivating **Twin Owls** rock outcrop. At the main trail, a right turn marches below the owls and past the next junction through aspen trees, that turn brilliant golds in early autumn. After ascending several small switchbacks, you'll reach a distinctive rock formation called **Paul Bunyan's Boot** (note the hole in the "sole"). From here, the final climb is steep, but distant views take in Longs Peak, Mount Meeker, and Estes Park. At **Gem Lake,** several rocky outcrops and a small, sandy beach make ideal lunch spots. On the return, turn left at the first junction to reach the trailhead more directly.

Glacier Gorge

The **Glacier Gorge Trailhead** (east of Bear Lake, parking lot fills by 6am in summer, shuttle stop) is the starting point for several destinations. The first is the three-story **Alberta Falls** (1.6 mi./2.6 km rt., 1 hr., easy) before the climb ramps up through two signed junctions. At the second junction, turn south for **Mills Lake** (5.6 mi./9 km rt., 3 hrs., moderate) and **Black Lake** (10 mi./16.1 km rt., 5-6 hrs., strenuous) tucked into Glacier Gorge. Continue straight instead to switchback up to **Loch Vale** (5.6 mi./9 km rt., 3 hrs., moderate) and on to Timberline Falls where some scrambling using hands is required to reach **Sky Pond** (9.8 mi./15.8 km rt., 5-6 hrs., strenuous), with its stunning backdrop and crystal-clear waters.

South of Estes Park

South of Estes Park, CO 7 leads to spur roads to access trailheads. No shuttles access these.

From the top of **Twin Sisters Peaks** (gravel road opposite Lily Lake, 7.4 mi./11.9 km rt., 4 hrs., strenuous), the 360-degree views take in Estes Park, the national park, and the Great Plains. The trail leads through the forest, past a landslide, and up switchbacks. A long, straight slope through granite slabs reaches the saddle between the two peaks, the higher of which is the 11,428-foot (3,483-m) eastern peak.

Tucked at the base of Longs Peak, **Chasm Lake** (Longs Peak Rd., 8.5 mi./13.7 km rt., 4.5 hrs, strenuous) sits in a rocky basin at 11,823 feet (3,604

▼ LUMPY RIDGE

CHASM LAKE

m). From the Longs Peak Trailhead, the path switchbacks up through the forest to reach the rocky tundra. It sweeps over a ridge and traverses a cliff walk to enter a hanging basin where a scramble with some use of hands goes up a boulder moraine to the lake.

In the southeastern corner of the park, the **Wild Basin Trailhead** (Wild Basin Rd., parking lot fills by 9:30am in summer) accesses several waterfalls, beginning with **Copeland Falls** (0.9 mi./1.4 km rt., 30 min., easy). A bridge crosses the long **Calypso Cascades** (3.6 mi./5.8 km rt., 2 hrs., moderate) where it spills through the forest. **Ouzel Falls** (5.4 mi./8.7 km rt., 3 hrs., moderate) spits down a rock face.

WEST SIDE

Colorado River to Lulu City

The **Colorado River Trail** (Colorado River Trailhead, Trail Ridge Rd., 6.2 mi./10 km rt., 3 hrs., easy) wanders through Shipler Park at the base of the Never Summer Range to **Lulu City,** a mining town built in 1879 that, at its peak, had about 200 residents. Only the foundations from a couple of cabins remain.

North Inlet Trail

North of Grand Lake, the **North Inlet Trail** (Road 663) goes to the gushing **Cascade Falls** (7 mi./11.3 km rt., 3.5 hrs., moderate) and the Big Pool (9.6 mi./15.4 km rt., 5 hrs., moderate), a swimming hole.

East Inlet Trail

On Grand Lake's east side, the **East Inlet Trail** leads to **Adams Falls** (West Portal Rd., 0.6 mi./1 km rt., 20 min. easy), a short stroll that showcases a pretty cascade of water tumbling down the final steep pitch before mixing with the smooth waters of Grand Lake.

RECREATION

BACKPACKING

Many of the day hikes in Rocky Mountain can be extended to two days, such as the hike to **Lawn Lake** (12.4 mi./20 km rt.) in the Mummy Range on the east side. On the west side, the **East Inlet Trail** leads to **Lone Pine Lake** (11 mi./17.7 km rt.).

By setting up shuttles, you can tackle point-to-point trails. Hike a portion of the 3,100-mile (4,988-km) **Continental Divide Scenic Trail** (30 mi./48.3 km one-way, 2-3 days) by starting in Arapaho National Forest on the Bowen Pass Spur Trail and hiking through the Never Summer Wilderness before entering the park to loop with the Tonuhutu Creek Trail and finish at North Inlet

ALBERTA FALLS

HIKING TRAILS CURVE AROUND ROCKY PEAKS.

Trailhead. From the North Inlet Trailhead, you can hike over the Continental Divide to Flattop Mountain (12 mi./19.3 km one-way) and Bear Lake (17 mi./27.4 km one-way).

Backpackers must obtain a **permit** (970/586-1242, www.pay.gov, $26) for designated campsites in advance or in person from one of the **Backcountry Permit Offices.** Applications begin March 1 for the upcoming season.

ROCK CLIMBING

Rocky Mountain National Park is well known for its world-class technical rock climbing and mountaineering. **Lumpy Ridge**'s granite walls feature almost 400 trad routes, but the park's most famous multi-pitch technical route ascends the Diamond, the sheer, diamond-shaped alpine wall on **Longs Peak**'s upper east face. Many climbing routes on Lumpy Ridge are closed March-July for nesting birds of prey. The **Colorado Mountain School** (341 Moraine Ave., Estes Park, 720/387-8944, http://coloradomountainschool.com) offers classes and guided rock climbing trips.

HORSEBACK RIDING

Two stables within the park offer more than a dozen rides daily: **Moraine Park Stables** (970/586-2327, www.sombrero.com) and **Glacier Creek Stable** (970/586-3244, www.sombrero.com).

FISHING

The park's lakes and streams delight anglers. Two great locations for catch-and-release fishing are **Fern Lake** and **Lawn Lake,** both of which host native greenback cutthroat trout. To fly-fish for brown and cutthroat trout, go for the clear, rushing **Colorado River.** Lower Trail Ridge Road offers several access points, including the Holzwarth Historic Site.

WHERE TO STAY

INSIDE THE PARK

There are no lodgings available within Rocky Mountain National Park; camping is the only overnight option and it's very popular, with only a small number of sites available. All campgrounds include drinking water, picnic tables, fire grates, food storage lockers, and vault or flush toilets. No hookups are available for RVs.

Make **reservations** (877/444-6777, www.recreation.gov) six months in advance for tent and RV camping.

Moraine Park Campground (year-round, 244 sites, $18-26) sits about 2.5

THE STANLEY HOTEL

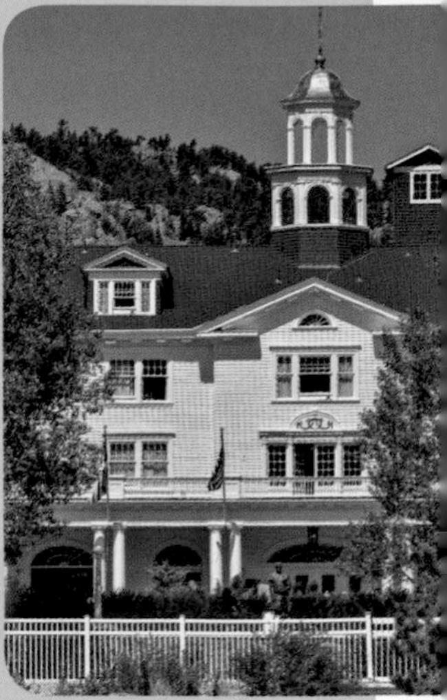

STANLEY HOTEL, ESTES PARK

As you drive into **Estes Park,** you can't help but notice the enormous, gleaming-white building with the bright red roof perched high on a hill in front of the dramatic granite outcrops of Lumpy Ridge. This is **The Stanley Hotel** (333 Wonderview Ave., 800/976-1377, tours 970/577-4111, www.stanleyhotel.com, $249-449), the most distinctive building in Estes Park and one of the oldest. Built in 1909 by F. O. Stanley, famous for the Stanley Steamers, the grand Colonial Revival-style hotel had modern innovations like electricity. Completion of the original 48-room Stanley Hotel in 1909 spurred the local economy, as did Stanley's efforts to improve and pave the roads from the Front Range up to Estes Park.

Today, the 140-room hotel is known for its amazing views from every window and for hosting horror writer Stephen King and serving as the inspiration for the terrifying Overlook Hotel in his best-selling novel *The Shining*. Reputedly one of the nation's most active sites for paranormal activity, the hotel is infamous for its ghostly guests, including Stanley and his wife Flora, who apparently enjoys playing her antique piano in the middle of the night.

Take a **Night Tour** through the hotel's most haunted areas. To learn more about its history, architecture, and famous (live) guests, sign up for **The Stanley Tour.**

miles (4 km) south of the Beaver Meadows Entrance Station. Facilities include a dump station and shuttle stops. In winter, toilets and drinking water are not available; sites are first come, first served.

- **Glacier Basin Campground** (June-Sept., 150 sites, $26) is about 6 miles (9.7 km) south of the Beaver Meadows Entrance Station. A park shuttle stop is nearby.
- **Aspenglen Campground** (late May-late Sept., 52 sites, $26) is located on a hillside near the Fall River Visitor Center.
- **Longs Peak Campground** (June-Sept., 26 sites, $26) is the best place to stay if you're planning on an early start to climb Longs Peak. The sites are for tents only.
- **Timber Creek** (late May-early Nov., 98 sites, $26) is on Trail Creek Road adjacent to the Colorado River. It's the only campground on the east side.

OUTSIDE THE PARK

Estes Park serves as the gateway to the park's east side, providing easy access to Bear Lake and Moraine Park. Most restaurants and accommodations surround the junction of US 34 and US 36. **Grand Lake** is the west side's tourist hub, but accommodations are limited. Book ahead for May-September, the busiest season.

GETTING THERE

AIR

Denver International Airport (DEN, 8500 Peña Blvd., 303/342-2000, www.flydenver.com) is the nearest airport and serviced by all major American airlines. Rental cars are available. **Estes Park Shuttle** (1805 Cherokee Dr., 970/586-5151, www.estesparkshuttle.com) offers year-round, scheduled, door-to-door service from the Denver airport to all Estes Park venues.

LONGS PEAK FROM TRAIL RIDGE ROAD

CAR

To reach Estes Park from Denver, take I-25 north to US 36 West, following signs for Boulder. Continue west on US 36 for about 65 miles (105 km). At the junction with US 34, turn left to remain on US 36 (called Moraine Ave.), which passes through Estes Park before arriving at the Beaver Meadows Entrance Station. In good weather and traffic conditions, this trip typically takes about two hours.

GETTING AROUND

DRIVING

From Beaver Meadows, US 36 continues west and then north, passing Bear Lake Road which heads south to connect Moraine Park and Bear Lake. At the Deer Ridge Junction, the road splits: Trail Ridge Road climbs west, while US 34 drops north to meet Old Fall River Road before veering west to the Fall River Visitor Center.

Trail Ridge Road

The Fall River Visitor Center on US 34 offers convenient access to both Trail Ridge and Fall River Roads (open seasonally). In summer, Trail Ridge Road is accessible from the east side at the junction of US 34 and US 36. Trail Ridge Road (US 34, open May-mid-Oct.) is the only road into the park's west side. In winter, the road closes and the west side must be accessed through the Grand Lake Entrance Station.

SHUTTLES

Both Estes Park and the national park run free summer shuttles. From the Estes Park Visitor Center (500 Big Thompson Ave.), the park's **Hiker Shuttle Route** (7:30am-10pm daily late June-mid-Sept., 7:30am-8pm Sat.-Sun. mid-Sept.-mid-Oct., free) runs to the large **Park & Ride** (Bear Lake Rd., fills by 10am in summer). Two additional **park shuttles** (7am-7:30pm daily, late May-mid-Oct.) are the orange **Bear Lake Route** that runs every 10-15 minutes along Bear Lake Road and the green **Moraine Park Route** that runs every 30 minutes between Bear Lake Road and Fern Lake.

There is no public transport or shuttle service to the west side of Rocky Mountain National Park, on Trail Ridge Road, or in the Fall River area.

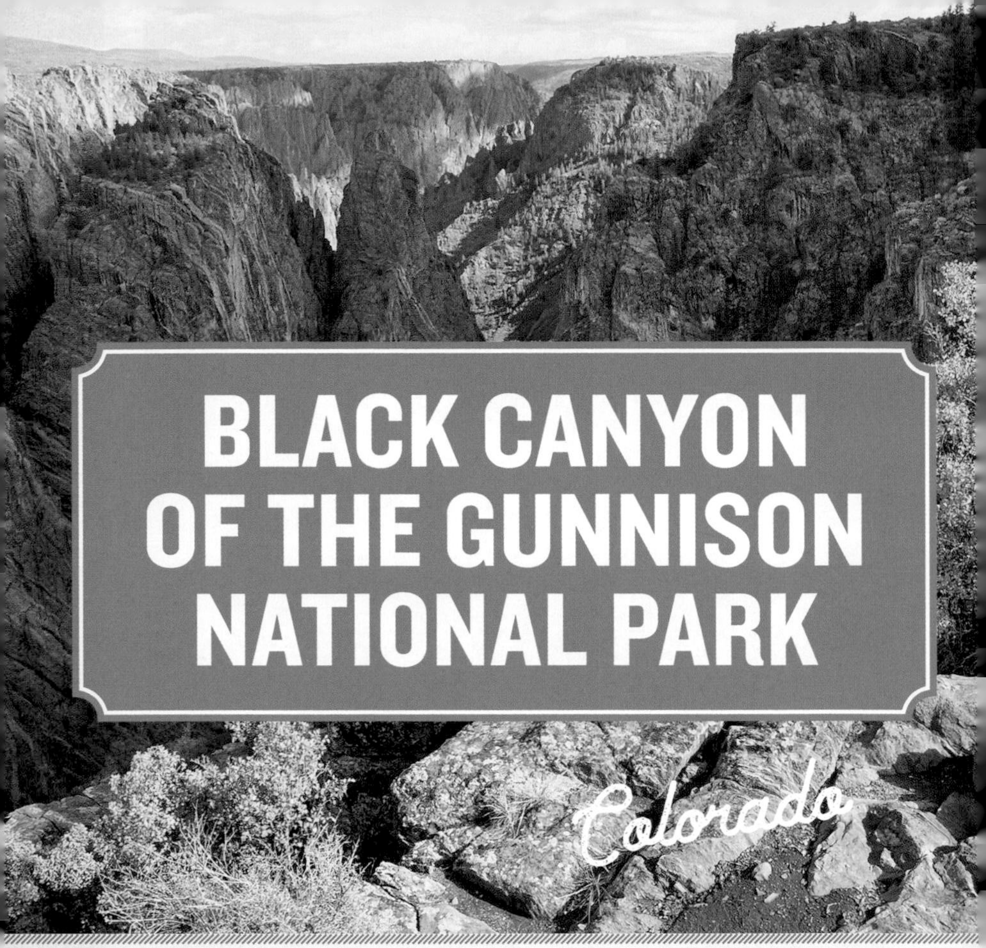

BLACK CANYON OF THE GUNNISON NATIONAL PARK

Colorado

WEBSITE:
www.nps.gov/blca

PHONE NUMBER:
970/641-2337, ext. 205

VISITATION RANK:
45

WHY GO:
Peer down into the thin slice of this deep, dark, steep-walled gorge.

▲ CROSS FISSURES OVERLOOK

KEEPSAKE STAMPS ▼▼▼

Millions of years ago, the powerful Gunnison River first chewed through soft volcanic rock like a saw blade, creating the slot for the **BLACK CANYON OF THE GUNNISON.** Once the river had carved this initial channel, it remained there, chipping away at the hard metamorphic rock below. The vertical canyon walls are so tough that they barely retreated. Archaeological evidence of the early Ute people only appears high above, on the rims.

While the canyon isn't the longest or deepest in the country, it is narrow, deep, and dark. The canyon's sheer walls are higher than Chicago's Willis Tower, and its inner gorge is so narrow—only 1,100 feet (335 m) across at its thinnest—that it receives only minutes of sunlight each day. Below the Chasm View overlook at the Gunnison River, the canyon shrinks to a narrow slot of only 40 feet (12 m) where the river gushes with monster rapids.

PLANNING YOUR TIME

In western Colorado, the Black Canyon of the Gunnison sits southeast of Grand Junction between Montrose and Gunnison. The park's North and South Rims are only 0.25 mile (0.4 km) apart in places; however, to get from one rim to the other takes 2-3 hours of driving. The park is open year-round, with all roads open mid-April to mid-November. In winter, roads close with the exception of the South Rim Road to Gunnison Point. Due to more difficult accesses for the North Rim and East Portal Roads, most visitors only go to the **South Rim.**

Peak visitation is in **summer** (May-Sept.) when days range 55-90°F (13-32°C) and frequent afternoon thunderstorms appear. Winter days see 15-40°F (-9-5°C) as the norm, with varied snow depths on the ground. Temperatures can fluctuate radically in one day; bring layers of clothing.

ENTRANCES AND FEES

The main entrance to the park is through the South Rim via **CO 347.** The North Rim entrance is south of Crawford, where you can pay fees at the ranger station or a self-pay kiosk. The entrance fee is $25-30/vehicle, $20-25 motorcycle, $15 individual) and valid for seven days.

VISITORS CENTER

Located at Gunnison Point, the **South Rim Visitor Center** (CO 347, 8am-6pm daily late May-early Sept., reduced hours off-season) has exhibits, a film, maps, a bookstore, backcountry permits, and Junior Ranger Programs. Rangers lead geology walks, Chasm View talks, and night sky talks, constellation tours, and telescope-viewing.

SCENIC DRIVES

NORTH RIM ROAD

From the park entrance for the North Rim, take the gravel **North Rim Road** (14 mi./23 km rt., mid-Apr.-mid-Nov.) to six viewpoints, including **The Narrows View,** which overlooks the canyon's narrowest point (40 ft./12 m wide at river level).

EAST PORTAL ROAD

Between the South Rim entrance and campground, the **East Portal Road** (14 mi./23 km rt., mid-Apr.-mid-Nov.) begins a steep descent to the river. It plunges with a 16 percent grade and tight, sharp switchbacks to the bottom of the Black Canyon of the Gunnison and into Curecanti National Recreation Area at **Crystal Dam.** (No vehicles longer than 22 ft./6.7 m permitted, including trailer combos.)

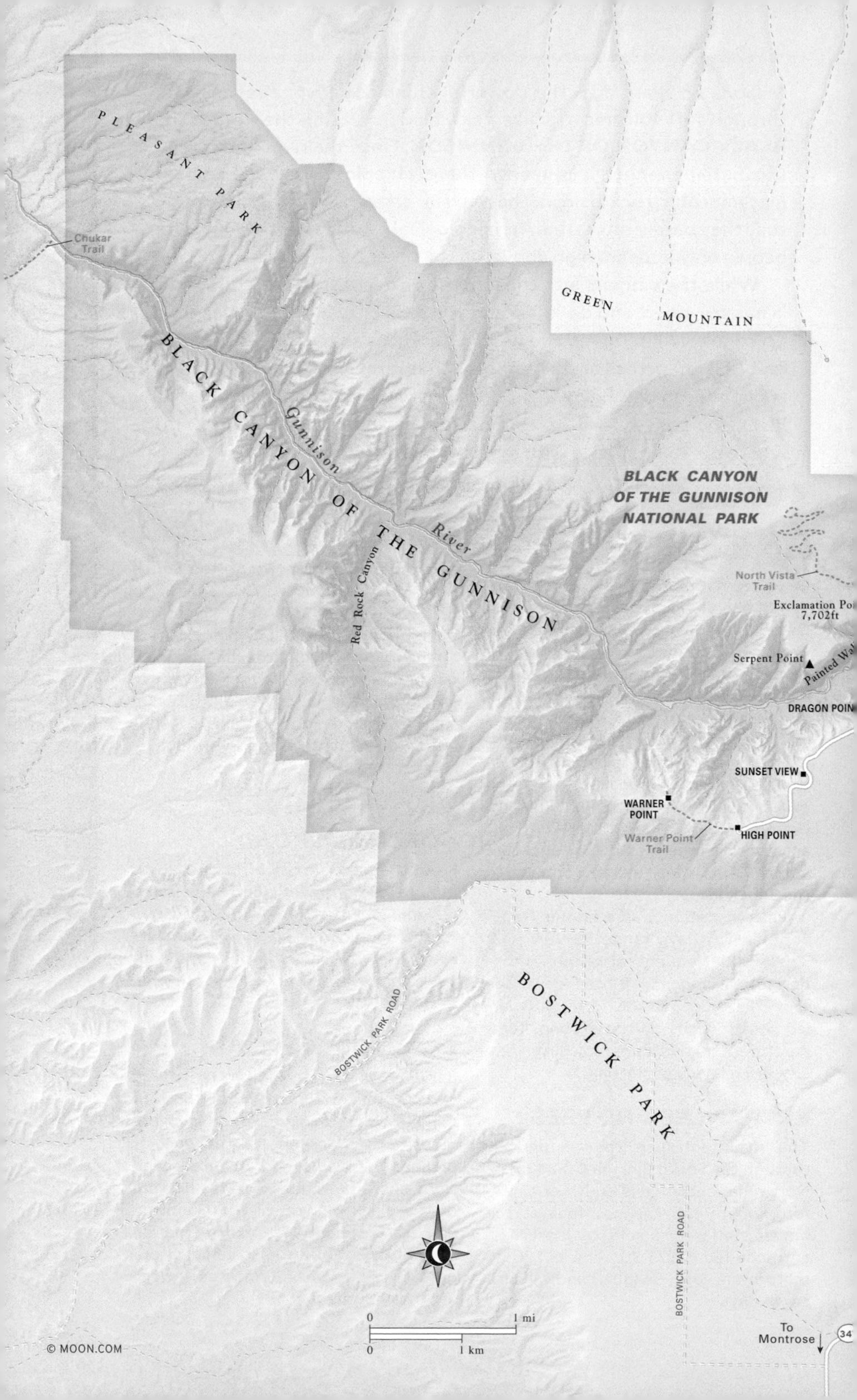
PLEASANT PARK
Chukar Trail
GREEN
MOUNTAIN
BLACK CANYON OF THE GUNNISON
Gunnison
River
Red Rock Canyon
BLACK CANYON
OF THE GUNNISON
NATIONAL PARK
North Vista Trail
Exclamation Po
7,702ft
Serpent Point
Painted Wa
DRAGON POIN
SUNSET VIEW
WARNER POINT
Warner Point Trail
HIGH POINT
BOSTWICK PARK
BOSTWICK PARK ROAD
BOSTWICK PARK ROAD
0
1 mi
0
1 km
To Montrose
347
© MOON.COM

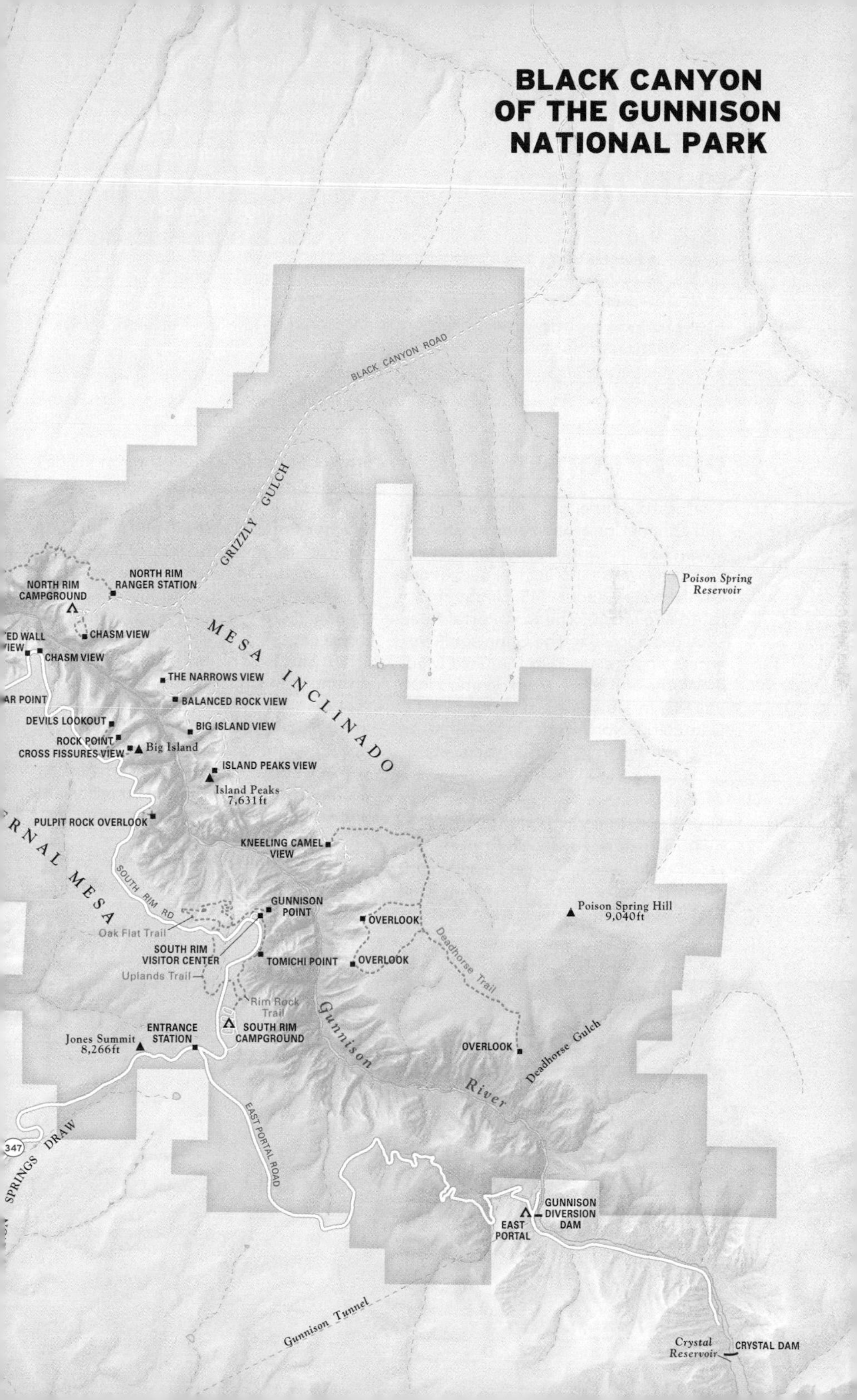
BLACK CANYON
OF THE GUNNISON
NATIONAL PARK
BLACK CANYON ROAD
GRIZZLY GULCH
NORTH RIM
RANGER STATION
NORTH RIM
CAMPGROUND
CHASM VIEW
ED WALL
IEW
CHASM VIEW
MESA INCLINADO
THE NARROWS VIEW
BALANCED ROCK VIEW
AR POINT
DEVILS LOOKOUT
BIG ISLAND VIEW
ROCK POINT
CROSS FISSURES VIEW
Big Island
ISLAND PEAKS VIEW
Island Peaks
7,631ft
PULPIT ROCK OVERLOOK
RNAL MESA
KNEELING CAMEL
VIEW
SOUTH RIM RD
GUNNISON
POINT
OVERLOOK
Oak Flat Trail
SOUTH RIM
VISITOR CENTER
TOMICHI POINT
OVERLOOK
Uplands Trail
Deadhorse Trail
Rim Rock
Trail
Gunnison River
Jones Summit
8,266ft
ENTRANCE
STATION
SOUTH RIM
CAMPGROUND
OVERLOOK
Deadhorse Gulch
Poison Spring
Reservoir
Poison Spring Hill
9,040ft
347
SPRINGS DRAW
EAST PORTAL ROAD
GUNNISON
DIVERSION
DAM
EAST
PORTAL
Gunnison Tunnel
Crystal
Reservoir
CRYSTAL DAM

Best Hike

NORTH VISTA TRAIL

DISTANCE: 3 miles (4.8 km) round-trip
DURATION: 1.5 hours
ELEVATION CHANGE: 370 feet (113 m)
DIFFICULTY: moderate
TRAILHEAD: near the North Rim Ranger Station

On the North Rim, saunter the flat and gently rolling **North Vista Trail.** The trail picks up several stunning views into the Black Canyon of the Gunnison, but nothing compared to the view at Exclamation Point Overlook. From the point, cliffs plunge vertically to the river below (watch your footing), and the view looks straight upriver through the narrow slot of the inner canyon.

RECREATION

Visitors bike the rim roads in spring and summer or **cross-country ski** and **snowshoe** in winter. The park's sheer vertical walls attract expert **rock climbers** for about 145 climbs, most rated above 5.10. The East Portal Road provides access to the Gunnison River, where anglers can **fish** the Gold Medal Water and Wild Trout Water (200 yd./183 m downstream from Crystal Dam to the North Fork of the Gunnison River) within the steep canyon walls.

HIKING

From South Rim Visitor Center, the sunny **Rim Rock Nature Trail** (1 mi./1.6 km rt., 30 min., easy) is a level, self-guided interpretive path. The steep **Oak Flat Loop Trail** (2 mi./3.2 km rt., 1 hr., strenuous) drops below the rim inside the canyon, but not to the river.

At South Rim Road's terminus, the **Warner Point Nature Trail** (1.5 mi./2.4 km rt., 45 min., moderate) wanders through piñon-juniper forest with views of the San Juan Mountains. Pick up a guide to the trail's flora at the visitors center.

On the North Rim from the campground loop, **Chasm View Nature Trail** (0.4 mi./0.6 km rt., 15 min., easy) starts in a piñon-juniper forest to wander near the rim for a look across the canyon at Chasm View on the South Rim. A second overlook takes in Painted Wall and Serpent Point. Watch for peregrine falcons.

Green Mountain Trail (7 mi./11.3 km rt., 3.5 hrs., strenuous) begins on the

▼ THE GUNNISON RIVER

Top 3

1 DRIVE SOUTH RIM ROAD

CLIFF-SIDE VIEW INTO THE CANYON

The paved **South Rim Road** (14 mi./23 km rt., Apr.-mid-Nov.) has a dozen overlooks between the visitors center and **High Point,** the road's end. The following four overlooks are the best: From two viewpoints at **Gunnison Point,** orange lichen cliffs plunge down to the Gunnison River while vertical light-colored dikes slice the broken North Rim wall. At **Chasm View,** the depth drops by 1,820 feet (556 m) to the river in one of the narrowest sections, making ultrasteep walls where you might spot expert rock climbers. You can walk from Chasm View to **Painted Wall View,** which gets its name from layers of lighter rock amid the black across Colorado's highest cliff. With picnic tables, **Sunset View** is the best place to eat while soaking up the immense canyon.

2 CATCH THE SUN, MOON, AND STARS

North Rim overlooks are prime for **sunrise,** but on the South Rim, from Cedar Point you can catch first light on the Painted Wall. Farther on the South Rim, the west-facing **Sunset View** is best for watching the sun drop over the canyon. At night, pull out your astrophotography skills for shooting the Milky Way in this **International Dark Sky Park.** In summer, the Milky Way moves directly overhead in late night but in fall earlier. Due to minimal light interference, the best South Rim viewpoints for stargazing are Chasm View, Dragon Point, and Sunset View. On the North Rim, try Chasm View Nature Trail or Kneeling Camel View. Use red lights (not white) for walking, and give your eyes 30 minutes to adjust to the darkness.

3 SCRAMBLE INTO THE INNER CANYON

With no trails from rim to river, six scrambling routes dive into the inner canyon. Only for strong and fit hikers, they require using hands and feet on boulders, exposed roots, steep ledges, and loose rock in ultrasteep ravines. At the visitors center, consult a ranger about your route (six available) and get a free wilderness permit for day or overnight hiking. Most first-timers do the **Gunnison Route** (2 mi./3.2 km rt., 4-5 hrs., strenuous), a Class III gully with 1,800 feet (549 m) elevation drop and a grueling crawl straight back up. Be cautious of poison ivy and rockfall.

SUNSET OVER THE CANYON

ONE DAY IN BLACK CANYON OF THE GUNNISON

Stop at the **South Rim Visitor Center** and stretch your legs on the **Rim Rock Nature Trail** to gaze into the canyon's abyss. Then, spend your day cruising the paved **South Rim Road,** stopping at the overlooks between the visitors center and High Point, the road's end.

North Vista Trail and can be combined with hiking to Exclamation Point. But the route continues on farther for 360-degree views of Grand Mesa, the Uncompahgre Plateau, and a different perspective peering down into the canyon.

WHERE TO STAY

INSIDE THE PARK

With no lodgings inside the park, camping is the only option. Drinking water is trucked in during summer; off-season, campers should bring their own. On South Rim Road, **reservations** (877/444-6777, www.recreation.gov) are accepted in summer at the **South Rim Campground** (year-round, 88 sites, $16-22). Sites are first come, first served outside the summer season, and 23 have electrical hookups. Nearby is the Night Sky Viewing and Telescope Site.

Two other campgrounds are first come, first served. The smaller **North Rim Campground** (Apr.-mid-Nov., 13 sites, $16) is on the North Rim Road. The **East Portal Campground** (mid-Apr.-mid.-Nov., 15 sites, $16) is 5 miles (8 km) down the steep and hairpin East Portal Road.

OUTSIDE THE PARK

Accommodations and food are available in the towns of **Gunnison, Grand Junction,** and **Montrose.**

GETTING THERE AND AROUND

AIR

The closest international airport is **Denver International Airport** (DEN, 8500 Peña Blvd., 303/342-2000, www.flydenver.com). Small regional airports include the **Gunnison-Crested Butte Airport** (GUC, 711 Rio Grande Ave., Gunnison, 970/641-2304, www.flygunnisonairport.com), the **Montrose Regional Airport** (MTJ, 2100 Airport Rd., 970/249-3203, wwwflymontrose.com), and the **Grand Junction Regional Airport** (GJT, 2828 Walker Field Dr., 970/244-9100, www.gjairport.com). All airports have rental cars.

CAR

From **Denver,** the Black Canyon of the Gunnison is 5-6 hours' drive via I-70, US 285, and US 50.

To reach the **South Rim,** take US 50 west from Gunnison for about 62 miles (100 km) or east from Montrose for 14 miles (23 km). Turn onto CO 347, which becomes the paved South Rim Road.

To access the **North Rim,** follow US 50 east. Turn left onto CO 92 and drive west and then north until just before the Crawford State Park entrance. Turn left onto Black Canyon Road and follow signs for the next 12 miles (19 km) to reach the park's North Rim. The paved road becomes gravel for 7 miles (11 km) in the park. Plan at least 2-3 hours to drive from rim to rim.

In winter (mid-Nov.-mid-Apr) the park roads close except for South Rim Road, which remains open from the visitors center to Gunnison Point. There is no public transit in the park.

SIGHTS NEARBY

Bordering the Black Canyon of the Gunnison National Park, **Curecanti National Recreation Area** (www.nps.gov/cure) has a series of three dam reservoirs (Blue Mesa, Morrow Point, and Crystal Reservoir) that offer campgrounds, boating, fishing, and a ranger-led boat tour (970/641-2337, ext. 205, 10am and 12:30pm Wed.-Mon. early June-early Sept., 1.5 hrs., hiking required to reach boat dock, reservations required).

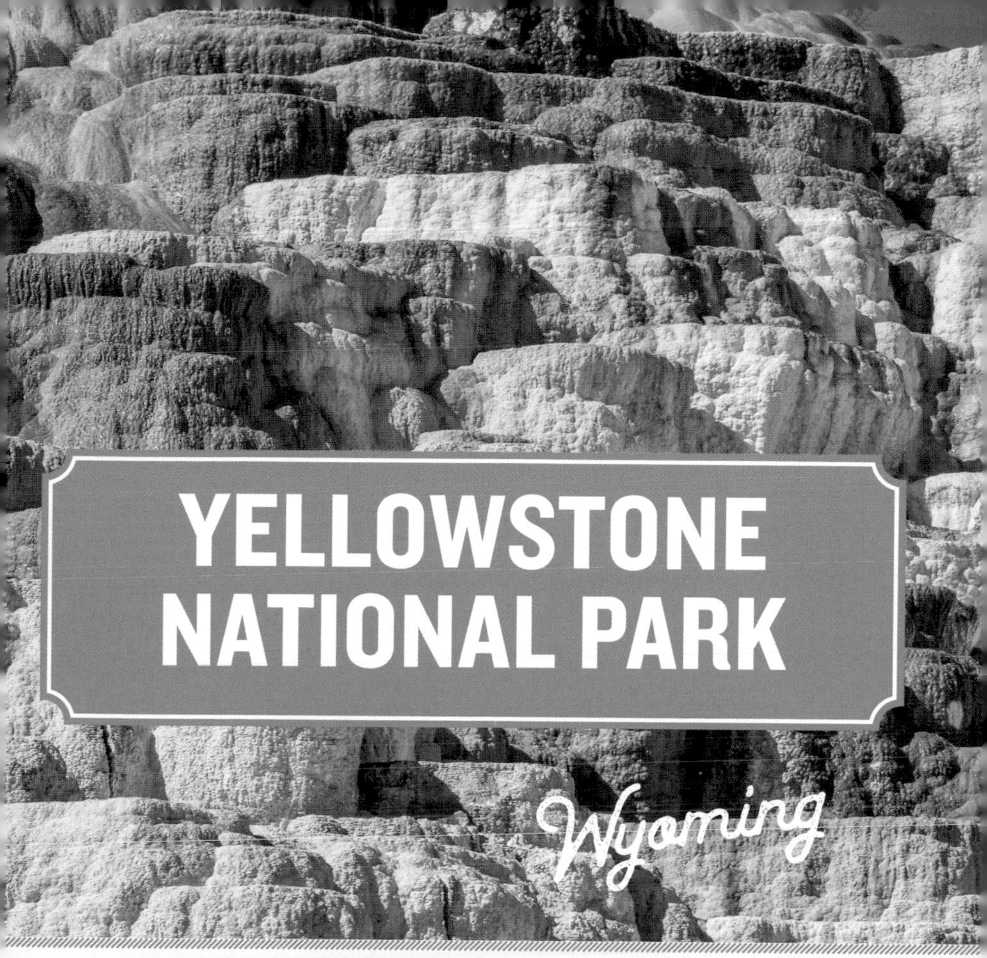

YELLOWSTONE NATIONAL PARK

Wyoming

KEEPSAKE STAMPS ▼▼▼

WEBSITE:
www.nps.gov/yell

PHONE NUMBER:
307/344-7381

VISITATION RANK:
6

WHY GO:
Watch wildlife, geysers, and volcanic wonders.

▲ PALETTE SPRING, MAMMOTH HOT SPRINGS

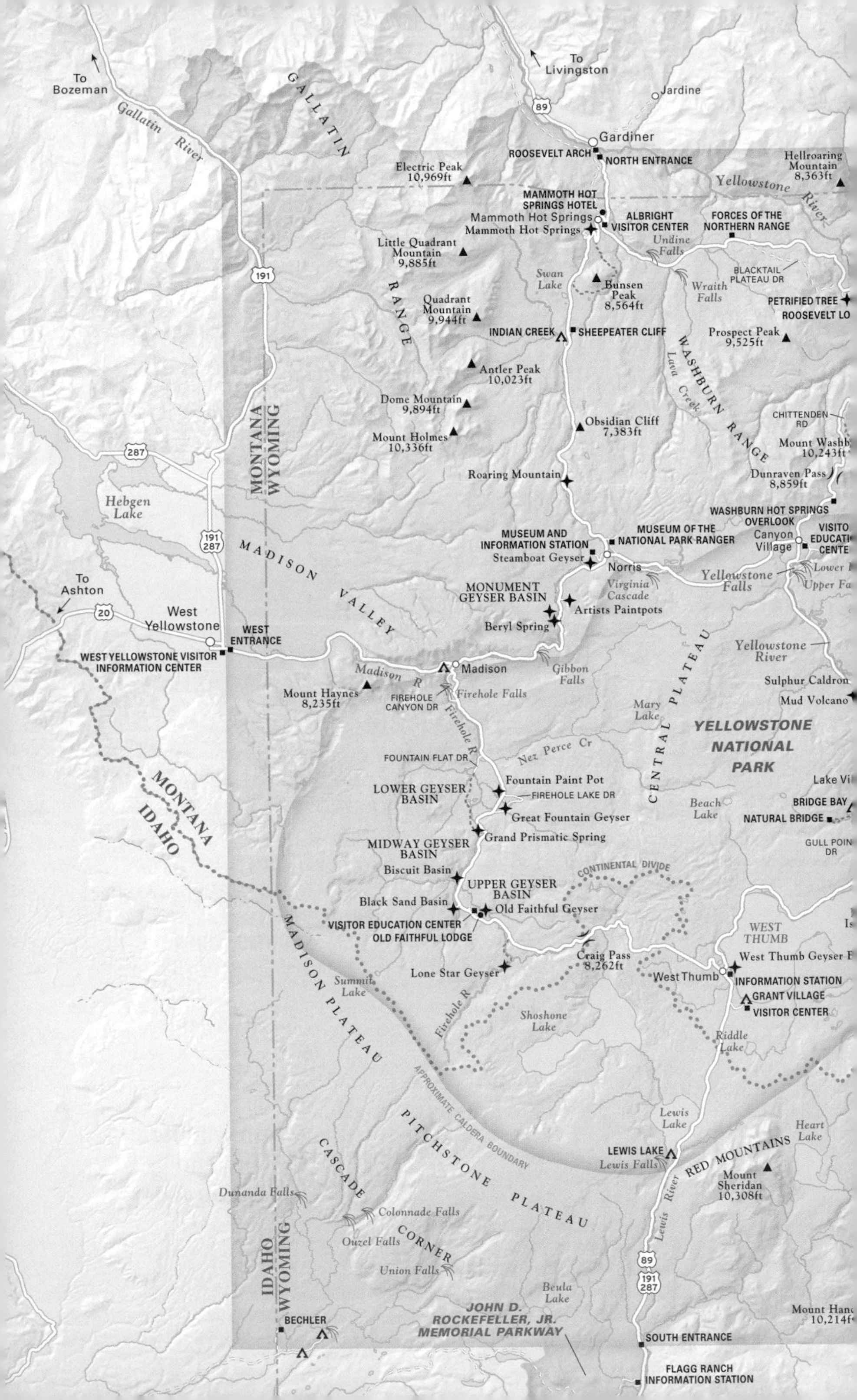

To Bozeman
To Livingston
Jardine
Gardiner
GALLATIN
RANGE
Gallatin River
ROOSEVELT ARCH
NORTH ENTRANCE
Electric Peak 10,969ft
Hellroaring Mountain 8,363ft
Yellowstone River
MAMMOTH HOT SPRINGS HOTEL
Mammoth Hot Springs
Mammoth Hot Springs
ALBRIGHT VISITOR CENTER
FORCES OF THE NORTHERN RANGE
Little Quadrant Mountain 9,885ft
Undine Falls
Swan Lake
Bunsen Peak 8,564ft
BLACKTAIL PLATEAU DR
Wraith Falls
PETRIFIED TREE
ROOSEVELT LO
Quadrant Mountain 9,944ft
INDIAN CREEK
SHEEPEATER CLIFF
Prospect Peak 9,525ft
WASHBURN RANGE
Lava Creek
Antler Peak 10,023ft
Dome Mountain 9,894ft
Obsidian Cliff 7,383ft
CHITTENDEN RD
Mount Holmes 10,336ft
Mount Washb 10,243ft
MONTANA
WYOMING
191
287
Hebgen Lake
Roaring Mountain
Dunraven Pass 8,859ft
WASHBURN HOT SPRINGS OVERLOOK
MUSEUM OF THE NATIONAL PARK RANGER
MUSEUM AND INFORMATION STATION
Canyon Village
VISITO EDUCATI CENTE
Steamboat Geyser
Norris
MADISON VALLEY
Lower F
Yellowstone Falls
Upper Fa
To Ashton
20
West Yellowstone
WEST ENTRANCE
MONUMENT GEYSER BASIN
Virginia Cascade
Artists Paintpots
Beryl Spring
WEST YELLOWSTONE VISITOR INFORMATION CENTER
Madison
Madison R
Gibbon Falls
Yellowstone River
Mount Haynes 8,235ft
FIREHOLE CANYON DR
Firehole Falls
Sulphur Caldron
Mud Volcano
Firehole R
Mary Lake
CENTRAL PLATEAU
YELLOWSTONE NATIONAL PARK
FOUNTAIN FLAT DR
Nez Perce Cr
MONTANA
IDAHO
Fountain Paint Pot
LOWER GEYSER BASIN
FIREHOLE LAKE DR
Lake Vi
Beach Lake
BRIDGE BAY
Great Fountain Geyser
NATURAL BRIDGE
Grand Prismatic Spring
GULL POIN DR
MIDWAY GEYSER BASIN
CONTINENTAL DIVIDE
Biscuit Basin
UPPER GEYSER BASIN
Black Sand Basin
Old Faithful Geyser
VISITOR EDUCATION CENTER
OLD FAITHFUL LODGE
WEST THUMB
Craig Pass 8,262ft
West Thumb Geyser B
West Thumb
INFORMATION STATION
MADISON PLATEAU
Lone Star Geyser
GRANT VILLAGE
VISITOR CENTER
Summit Lake
Firehole R
Shoshone Lake
Riddle Lake
APPROXIMATE CALDERA BOUNDARY
Lewis Lake
Heart Lake
PITCHSTONE PLATEAU
LEWIS LAKE
Lewis Falls
RED MOUNTAINS
Mount Sheridan 10,308ft
CASCADE CORNER
Lewis River
Dunanda Falls
Colonnade Falls
Ouzel Falls
Union Falls
IDAHO
WYOMING
89
191
287
Beula Lake
JOHN D. ROCKEFELLER, JR. MEMORIAL PARKWAY
Mount Hanc 10,214f
BECHLER
SOUTH ENTRANCE
FLAGG RANCH INFORMATION STATION

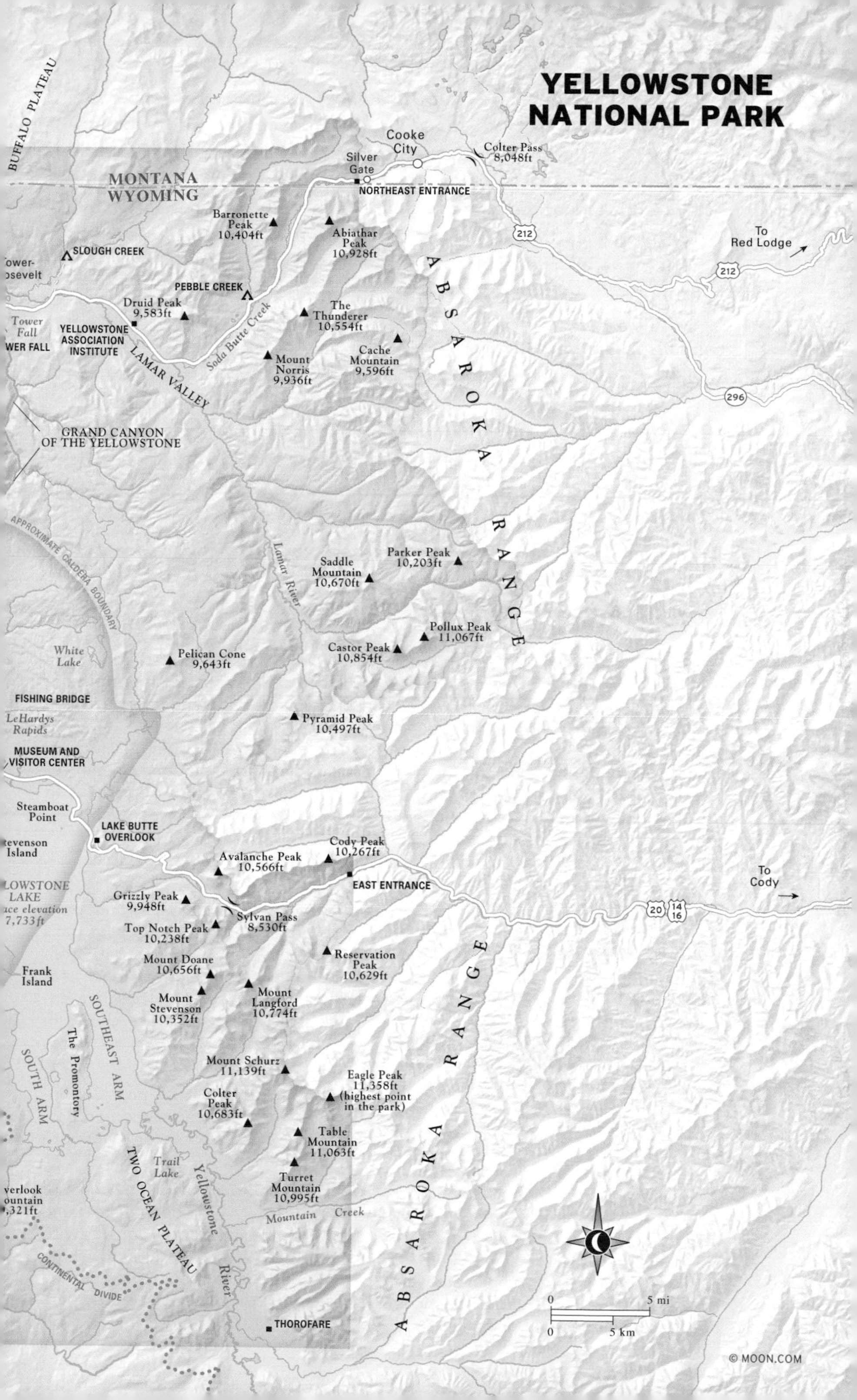
YELLOWSTONE NATIONAL PARK
BUFFALO PLATEAU
MONTANA
WYOMING
Cooke City
Silver Gate
Colter Pass 8,048ft
NORTHEAST ENTRANCE
212
To Red Lodge
Barronette Peak 10,404ft
Abiathar Peak 10,928ft
SLOUGH CREEK
PEBBLE CREEK
Druid Peak 9,583ft
The Thunderer 10,554ft
Tower Fall
YELLOWSTONE ASSOCIATION INSTITUTE
Soda Butte Creek
Cache Mountain 9,596ft
Mount Norris 9,936ft
LAMAR VALLEY
ABSAROKA RANGE
296
GRAND CANYON OF THE YELLOWSTONE
APPROXIMATE CALDERA BOUNDARY
Lamar River
Parker Peak 10,203ft
Saddle Mountain 10,670ft
Pollux Peak 11,067ft
Castor Peak 10,854ft
White Lake
Pelican Cone 9,643ft
FISHING BRIDGE
LeHardys Rapids
Pyramid Peak 10,497ft
MUSEUM AND VISITOR CENTER
Steamboat Point
LAKE BUTTE OVERLOOK
Cody Peak 10,267ft
Avalanche Peak 10,566ft
Island
EAST ENTRANCE
To Cody
20
14 16
Grizzly Peak 9,948ft
Sylvan Pass 8,530ft
Top Notch Peak 10,238ft
Reservation Peak 10,629ft
Mount Doane 10,656ft
Frank Island
Mount Langford 10,774ft
Mount Stevenson 10,352ft
SOUTHEAST ARM
The Promontory
SOUTH ARM
Mount Schurz 11,139ft
Eagle Peak 11,358ft (highest point in the park)
Colter Peak 10,683ft
Table Mountain 11,063ft
Turret Mountain 10,995ft
TWO OCEAN PLATEAU
Trail Lake
Yellowstone River
Mountain Creek
CONTINENTAL DIVIDE
THOROFARE
0 5 mi
0 5 km
© MOON.COM

In **YELLOWSTONE NATIONAL PARK**, rumblings of a supervolcano boil to the surface—spewing, spitting, oozing, and bubbling. Steam rolls from vividly colored pools, muddy cauldrons burp sulfurous gases, and blasts of hot water shoot high into the air. This cantankerous landscape contains some of the world's most active hydrothermal features, gushing from spouters like iconic Old Faithful, while minerals create artful travertine terraces at Mammoth Hot Springs.

Yellowstone is also home to the biggest remaining wild herds of bison in the country. Several Native American tribes partner with the park to manage their numbers and migrations outside Yellowstone. Bison jams are common on park roads. Bears, elk, pronghorn, wolves, and bighorn sheep also wander the landscape. So many wild animals cluster in Lamar Valley that it has gained fame as "America's Serengeti." Yellowstone itself has become famous as America's first national park.

PLANNING YOUR TIME

Yellowstone National Park tucks into the northwest corner of Wyoming, its north and west borders spilling over into Montana and Idaho.

Summer (May-Sept.) sees the most visitors, with July and August luring the biggest crowds. All park lodges, campgrounds, and visitors centers are open, as are most park roads. Temperatures range 60-80°F (16-27°C), depending on elevation, and afternoon thundershowers are common.

In **winter,** deep snows turn the park white. Park roads close (early Nov.-late Apr.), except for the road between Yellowstone's North and Northeast Entrances. Tours are via guided snowcoaches or snowmobiles (mid-Dec.-early Mar.). Lodgings are available at Mammoth Hot Springs and Old Faithful.

Spring (Mar.-May) offers car-free bicycling on park roads that won't open to vehicles until late April or May. Come in May for bison-calving season, or in June to spot bighorn sheep ewes with newborn lambs and grizzly bears foraging along Yellowstone Lake. By May, most park roads start to open and visitor services return. Weather bounces between blue skies, rain, and snow.

In **fall** (Sept.-Nov.), cooler days yield pleasant hiking with fewer crowds. Sporadic snowstorms can temporarily close park roads until winter descends in early November. Services are limited.

To guarantee lodging, camping, tour, or dinner reservations any time of year, make reservations **13 months in advance.**

ENTRANCES AND FEES

The entrance fee is $35 per vehicle ($30 motorcycle, $20 individual) and good for seven days. You can **buy your pass online** (www.yourpassnow.com) from home to speed through entrance stations faster. Yellowstone has five entrance stations; several are closed in winter. Drive times between entrances can take several hours.

- **North Entrance** (US 89, near Gardiner, MT) is open year-round and provides the closest access to Mammoth Hot Springs.
- **Northeast Entrance** (US 212, west of Silver Gate, MT) is open year-round and links the Beartooth Highway with the Lamar Valley. Winter snow shuts the roads east of Cooke City, but access remains open between the park entrance and Cooke City.

ONE DAY IN YELLOWSTONE

Drive Lower Grand Loop Road to walk the boardwalks in **Midway Geyser Basin** and **Upper Geyser Basin** before catching **Old Faithful** as it erupts. Then cruise across the Continental Divide to drive along **Yellowstone Lake** into **Hayden Valley** to see bison and elk. Finish by gazing from **Artist Point** into the **Grand Canyon of the Yellowstone.**

- **West Entrance** (US 20, West Yellowstone, MT), the busiest entrance in the park, is open mid-April to early November. In winter, it admits only snowcoaches and snowmobiles.
- **East Entrance** (US 20), between Fishing Bridge and Cody, Wyoming, is open mid-May to early November.
- **South Entrance** (US 89/191/287), on the border between Yellowstone and Grand Teton, is open mid-May to early November. In winter, it admits only snowcoaches and snowmobiles.

VISITORS CENTERS

Inside the park, visitors centers offer exhibits, park maps, bookstores, road conditions, trail information, Junior Ranger Program booklets, and naturalist talks and walks.

Old Faithful Visitor Education Center (307/344-2751, 8am-8pm daily June-Sept., 9am-5pm daily Oct.-March, seasonal closures occur) has exhibits on geysers, hot springs, mud pots, and fumaroles. Geyser eruption predictions are available, and the theater rotates park films.

Albright (Mammoth) Visitor Center (Mammoth Hot Springs, 307/344-2263, 8am-6pm daily June-Sept., 9am-5pm daily Oct.-May) has exhibits on historic Fort Yellowstone. The **backcountry office** (8am-4:30pm daily June-Aug.) issues permits for backcountry camping, boating, and fishing.

Canyon Visitor Education Center (Canyon Village, 307/344-2550, 8am-6pm daily May-mid-Sept., hours vary other seasons) features films, murals, and geology exhibits and contains a **backcountry office** (8am-4:30pm daily June-Aug.).

Fishing Bridge Visitor Center (Yellowstone Lake, 307/344-2450,

OLD FAITHFUL VISITOR EDUCATION CENTER

AVOID THE CROWDS

Avoid July, which sees the heaviest visitation.

Visit in **June** or **September** when crowds thin in comparison to midsummer, in **May** for newborn bison and elk calves, or in **October** for fall colors, bear activity, and elk bugling.

Go in **winter** for the beauty of the icy landscape and prolific steam in geyser basins.

Avoid midday (10am-4pm), when most of the crowds are out in force. Utilize the **early morning** and **late afternoon-evening** hours instead.

Hit **Midway** and the **Lower Geyser Basins** in early morning en route to Norris Geyser Basin **by 10am.**

Visit the **Upper Geyser Basin** (Old Faithful, Black Sands, Biscuit) at **sunset** (8pm-9:30pm in summer).

Visit Old Faithful at sunrise (5am-6:30am in summer).

Go wildlife-watching in the **morning** and **evening,** when animals are more active.

Park early. Plan to be at your trailhead parking lot by **8am-9am** or earlier.

Stop at picnic areas for restroom breaks; geyser basins and Canyon Village restrooms usually have lengthy lines.

8am-7pm daily late May-early Sept., hours vary other seasons) showcases bird and waterfowl specimens and has an outdoor amphitheater for naturalist presentations.

Grant Visitor Center (Grant Village, 307/344-2650, 8am-7pm daily late May-early Oct., hours vary other seasons) has exhibits on fire and a park film.

In West Yellowstone, **West Yellowstone Visitor Information Center** (30 Yellowstone Ave., 307/344-2876, 8am-8pm daily late May-early Sept., shorter hours in spring, fall, and winter) has information and **backcountry permits** (8am-4:30pm daily June-Aug.).

SIGHTS

MAMMOTH HOT SPRINGS

Raised boardwalks and stairways loop through the Mammoth Hot Springs, where sulfur fills the air and limestone creates travertine terraces and calcium carbonate sculptures.

To explore the **Lower Terraces,** park and stroll the boardwalk to **Liberty Cap,** a 37-foot-tall (11-m) dormant hot springs cone, then visit **Palette Spring,** where orange and brown thermophiles color the sinter. The main boardwalk circles the striking travertine sculptures of **Minerva Terrace. Cleopatra, Mound,** and **Jupiter Terraces** flank the stairs to the overlook at the Upper Terrace Drive parking lot. At the top, a boardwalk leads to brilliant orange and white **Canary Spring.** Three parking lots access the lower terraces south of Mammoth Village.

FISHING BRIDGE

Top 3

1 MARVEL AT OLD FAITHFUL

When **Old Faithful Geyser** erupts, it shoots up to 8,400 gallons (31,797 l) of hot water as high as 185 feet (56 m). It's one of the most regular geysers in the park, erupting every 90 minutes. Often it sputters for 20 minutes before an eruption, which lasts a few minutes. In summer, massive crowds fill the benches surrounding the geyser 30 minutes in advance.

Old Faithful is behind the Old Faithful Visitor Education Center, which has exhibits that explain the geyser's inner workings. Eruption times are posted at the visitors center or on the park's geyser app.

OLD FAITHFUL GEYSER

2 WATCH WILDLIFE

Wildlife captivates in Yellowstone. The massive **Lamar Valley** is America's Serengeti thanks to its hefty numbers of abundant wildlife. The Lamar River flows through the sagebrush valley where immense herds of **bison** feed. Between herds, look for **pronghorn, bighorn sheep, elk, bears, coyotes,** and **wolves.** In late fall, listen for bighorn sheep butting heads or elk bugling.

Sliced by the Yellowstone River, the bucolic **Hayden Valley** contains prime wildlife-watching with frequent bison jams. Watch for **coyotes, moose, elk, raptors, grizzly bears, trumpeter swans, wolves,** and hordes of **Canada geese.**

Along the **Madison River,** pullouts aid viewing of **bison, elk, deer,** and **raptors.** In fall, bull elk often round up harems, with the bulls' bugling echoing across the valley.

3 GAZE INTO THE GRAND CANYON OF THE YELLOWSTONE

The Yellowstone River cuts a colorful deep and narrow swath through the **Grand Canyon of the Yellowstone.** The river crashes over the **Upper Falls** before thundering down the **Lower Falls,** the park's tallest and most famous waterfall. Three roads access overlooks surrounding the 20-mile-long (32-km) canyon. Trails trot along the rim, while switchbacks and stairways plunge into the canyon for closer views (but require strenuous return climbs).

LOWER FALL, GRAND CANYON OF THE YELLOWSTONE

The one-way **Upper Terrace Drive** (1 mi./1.6 km, mid-May-early Nov.) tours a paved loop of older formations such as **Orange Spring Mound.** The entrance is 2 miles (3.2 km) south of Mammoth Village on the road toward Norris.

Fort Yellowstone

In the pre-National Park Service decades, the village of Mammoth was **Fort Yellowstone,** which housed the U.S. Army unit that managed the park 1891-1916. A self-guided walking tour sees the **Bachelor Officers' Quarters** (Albright Visitor Center), **parade ground,** red-roofed **officers' quarters,** and other buildings.

Roosevelt Arch

In Gardiner, the original park entrance road crosses under the 1903 stone-and-mortar **Roosevelt Arch** dedicated to President Theodore Roosevelt. Passenger vehicles can drive through the narrow entrance, or you can park on Park Street to walk through the arch and **Arch Park.**

LIBERTY CAP

TOWER FALL

Tower Fall (2.3 mi./3.7 km south of Tower Jct.) plunges from its brink between rhyolite spires, dropping from a hanging valley into a ribbon that spews in a long freefall. An overlook near the Tower Fall parking lot offers the best view.

NORRIS GEYSER BASIN

Interpretive boardwalks and paths loop through two hydrothermal basins at

▾ MAMMOTH TERRACES

ROOSEVELT ARCH

Norris Geyser Basin. At 459°F (237°C) below the surface, it is the hottest geyser basin and also the oldest geothermal basin. **Norris Geyser Basin Museum & Information Station** (307/344-2812, 9am-5pm daily late May-mid-Oct.) has exhibits and ranger-led walks into the basin.

TOWER FALL

Back Basin

Back Basin (1.5 mi./2.4 km rt., 1 hr., easy) houses the blue **Emerald Spring** and **Steamboat Geyser,** the world's tallest geyser. The route loops past blue-green **Cistern Spring** and the red-orange-rimmed pool of **Echinus Geyser,** the world's largest acidic geyser. A collection of fumaroles, hot springs, mud pots, roiling **Porkchop Geyser,** and spitting **Minute Geyser** finish the loop.

Porcelain Basin

The acidic **Porcelain Basin** (0.75 mi./1.2 km rt., 30 min. easy), which contains the park's highest concentration of silica, has **Crackling Lake** bubbling along its edges. While **Pinwheel Geyser** is defunct, active **Whirligig Geyser** spills into a stream of orange iron oxide and green thermophiles. **Hurricane Vent** roars steam, and **Porcelain Springs** contains blue pools.

LOWER GEYSER BASIN

Between Madison Junction and Old Faithful, the Lower Geyser Basin houses **Fountain Paint Pot** (8 mi./13 km south of Madison Jct.) and **Firehole Lake Drive** (9.3 mi./15 km south of Madison Jct.).

An interpretive boardwalk loops around **Fountain Paint Pot** (0.5 mi./0.8

km, 30 min. easy) that includes all four hydrothermal features: geysers, mud pots, hot springs, and fumaroles.

The one-way **Firehole Lake Drive** (3 mi./4.8 km) passes eight thermal features. Brown **Firehole Lake** is the road's largest hot spring. **Great Fountain Geyser** shoots a high spray every 10-14 hours for up to an hour.

MIDWAY GEYSER BASIN

At 10 miles (16 km) south of Madison Junction, **Midway Geyser Basin** (0.7 mi./1.1 km, 30 min., easy) loops a boardwalk across the Firehole River. The dormant crater of **Excelsior Geyser** contains a steaming turquoise pool spilling into the river. **Grand Prismatic Spring,** the third-largest hot spring in the world, radiates fiery arms of orange, gold, and brown thermophiles from the yellow-rimmed, blue hot pool.

OLD FAITHFUL AREA

Old Faithful Inn

Built in 1903-1904, **Old Faithful Inn** epitomizes "parkitecture." With a steep-pitched roof and gabled dormers, the lobby vaults five stories high. It centers on a giant stone fireplace and handcrafted clock built from wood, copper, and iron. Daily **tours** (hours vary, daily early May-early Oct., free) are available.

Upper Geyser Basin

Maps at the visitors center aid in navigating interconnected loops of **Upper Geyser Basin** (4.5 mi./7.2 km, 3 hrs., easy). Walk as many or as few loops in this largest of the geyser basins. The visitors center and the NPS Geyser App let you know predictions for notable geyser eruptions.

From the Old Faithful viewing area behind the visitors center, cross the Firehole River to reach **Geyser Hill,** where **Beehive Geyser** is the largest geyser. The smaller **Anemone Geyser** erupts every 10 minutes while **Plume Geyser** spouts hourly. Clear-blue **Heart Spring** sits near the **Lion Geyser Group,** a family of sputtering geysers.

At **Castle Geyser,** a cone geyser built into the largest sinter formation in the world, the **Firehole River Loop** crosses two bridges to reach **Grand Geyser,** a fountain geyser. Just north are a pair of colorful hot springs, **Beauty Pool** and **Chromatic Pool.**

PORCELAIN SPRINGS, NORRIS GEYSER BASIN

GRAND PRISMATIC SPRING

At the west end of the basin, **Grotto Geyser** squirts water from its odd-shaped cone. **Riverside Geyser** shoots an arc of water over the river at six-hour intervals. The striking green, orange, and yellow **Morning Glory Pool** marks the turnaround point.

A spur loop to the south, **Daisy Geyser Basin** arcs past **Daisy Geyser** that erupts every 2-3 hours. Turn around at **Punch Bowl** that boils in its raised sinter bowl.

Biscuit Basin

Located 3.5 miles (5.6 km) north of Old Faithful, a bridge crosses the Firehole River to reach **Biscuit Basin** (0.7 mi./1.1 km rt., 30 min., easy). Three hot springs bring on color: **Black Opal Pool, Wall Pool,** and **Sapphire Pool** with crystal blue water. The upper loop passes yellow **Mustard Spring** and **Jewel Geyser,** which spits every 10 minutes.

Black Sand Basin

Two miles (3.2 km) northwest of Old Faithful, **Black Sand Basin** (0.6 mi./1 km, 20 min. easy) takes in **Cliff Geyser** and two boardwalk spurs. One goes to **Sunset Lake,** named for its yellow-orange rim, and the other to see **Emerald Pool,** colored from algae.

GRAND CANYON OF THE YELLOWSTONE

North Rim

The one-way **North Rim Drive** (1.2 mi./1.9 km south of Canyon Jct.) visits overlooks of the canyon and the Lower Falls. **Brink of the Lower Falls** has a paved walkway to an upper overlook and a trail (1 mi./1.6 km, 30 min., moderate) that switchbacks to a platform at the lip of the Lower Falls. **Lookout Point** has an upper overlook facing the falls and a stairway that plunges to **Red Rock Point** (0.6 mi./1 km, 20 min., moderate) for a closer perch. **Grand View Overlook** takes in the canyon and Lower Falls. At the end of North Rim Drive, turn right onto the two-lane road to reach **Inspiration Point** for four platforms (several are wheelchair-accessible) overlooking the colorful canyon and river below.

From the **Brink of the Upper Falls Road** (0.4 mi./0.6 km south of North Rim Dr.), a short walk follows the river upstream to a viewing platform at the

MORNING GLORY POOL, UPPER GEYSER BASIN

Brink of the Upper Falls (0.4 mi./0.6 km, 20 min., easy), which mesmerizes with a powerful hurtle downstream.

South Rim

From **South Rim Drive** (2.2 mi./3.5 km south of Canyon Jct.), cross the Chittenden Bridge to two parking areas. **Uncle Tom's Point** has a paved walkway to face the **Upper Falls** and a trail that drops on switchbacks and 328 steel stairs on **Uncle Tom's Trail** (0.7 mi./1.1 km, 30 min., strenuous) for the closest view of the **Lower Falls. Artist Point** has the classic view of the canyon and Lower Falls.

YELLOWSTONE LAKE

Yellowstone Lake is the largest high-elevation freshwater lake in North America. Roads tour the western and northern shores, with multiple picnic areas for access. **Steamboat Springs** puffs on the north side, while historic Fishing Bridge crosses the outlet, the beginning of the Yellowstone River**.** Boat tours go out from Bridge Bay daily in summer.

West Thumb Geyser Basin

Northeast of West Thumb Junction, **West Thumb Geyser Basin** (0.8 mi./1.3 km, 30 min., easy) offers loops past three geysers and 11 hot springs, plus fumaroles and mud pots. The lower loop goes to Yellowstone Lake where visitors once cooked fish in **Fishing Cone. Black Pool** spills with colorful

▼ PUNCH BOWL, UPPER GEYSER BASIN

BISCUIT BASIN

thermophiles and **Abyss Pool** may be one of the deepest in the park.

SCENIC DRIVE

GRAND LOOP ROAD

Most drivers split the 142-mile (229-km) **Grand Loop Road** into 2-3 days, as a one-day push (5-8 hrs.) limits the amount of time to stop at sights. Different segments open annually late April through late May.

At **Mammoth Hot Springs,** join the Grand Loop Road (US 89) heading south toward **Norris, Madison Junction,** and **Old Faithful** (52 mi./84 km, 2 hrs., late Apr.-early Nov.). The road climbs south through hoodoos and crawls along the cliffs of **Golden Gate** before topping out at **Swan Lake Flat.** It passes **Obsidian Cliff,** a site of geological and Native American significance, and hissing **Roaring Mountain,** pumping out steam. After going by **Norris Geyser Basin,** a hotbed of geothermal activity, the road drops into the supervolcano caldera, passing blue **Beryl Springs** and **Gibbon Falls** to reach Madison Junction. From this low point in the caldera, begin climbing along the **Firehole River** toward the geyser basins: **Lower**, **Midway**, and **Upper**, the last home to **Old Faithful Geyser.**

From the geyser basins, the road bounces eastward twice over the Continental Divide to **West Thumb Junction** (17 mi./27 km, 45 min., mid-May-early Nov.). Turn left to stop at **West Thumb Geyser Basin.**

Aim north toward **Canyon Village** (36 mi./58 km, 1.5 hrs., mid-May-early Nov.) along **Yellowstone Lake,** passing **Bridge Bay** and **Lake Village,** which houses the historic **Lake Yellowstone Hotel.** After the junction at **Fishing Bridge,** the road hugs the **Yellowstone River** flowing north to sulfur-smelling **Mud Volcano** and wildlife-rich **Hayden Valley,** where you may get caught in a bison jam. At **Grand Canyon of the Yellowstone,** turn off on the South Rim Drive to stop at **Artist Point** before continuing to Canyon Junction.

At Canyon Junction, climb north over **Dunraven Pass** and drop through curves down to **Tower Fall** and **Tower Junction** (19 mi./31 km, 45 min., late May-early Nov.). Then, continue west to return to **Mammoth Hot Springs** (18 mi./29 km, 45 min., year-round). Take in **Petrified Tree** and **Undine Falls** before closing the loop.

▼ BRINK OF THE LOWER FALL

WEST THUMB GEYSER BASIN

HIKING

MAMMOTH HOT SPRINGS

Bunsen Peak and Osprey Falls

From the Old Bunsen Peak Road Trailhead (4.8 mi./7.7 km south of Mammoth) the trail to **Bunsen Peak** (4.6 mi./7.4 km rt., 3 hrs., strenuous) winds back and forth up the mountain, passing Cathedral Rock en route. Steep switchbacks lead across talus slopes to the 8,564-foot (2,610-m) summit. Return the way you came, or drop eastward 1.4 steep miles (2.3 km) to the Old Bunsen Peak Road, turning right to circle 3 gentle miles (4.8 km) around the peak's base (6.6 mi./10.6 km rt., 4 hrs.). Lengthen the loop with a descent and return climb to 150-foot (46-m) **Osprey Falls** (11.6 mi./18.7 km rt., 7 hrs.) on the Gardner River.

Wraith Falls

The trail to **Wraith Falls** (1 mi./1.6 km rt., 1 hr., easy) travels through a sagebrush-scented meadow to 79-foot (24-m) Wraith Falls as it cascades down a wide-angled rock face squeezed into a canyon.

TOWER JUNCTION

Lost Lake Loop

Hikers have plenty of things to see on the **Lost Lake Loop** (4 mi./6.4 km rt., 2 hrs., moderate): a waterfall, the small lake, Petrified Tree, and views of the Absaroka Mountains. From Roosevelt Lodge, take the left spur to the **Lost Creek Falls Trail** to climb a pine-shaded ravine to the falls. Return to the junction and continue on **Lost Lake Trail** to reach the bridge at the lake's outlet. The trail rims the lake until it heads west through another ravine to **Petrified Tree.** From the Petrified Tree parking lot, the trail mounts a hill to the east before dropping behind Tower Ranger Station and back to Roosevelt Lodge.

Trout Lake

Trout Lake (1.2 mi./1.9 km rt., 1.5 hrs., strenuous) is an idyllic little lake sitting at about 7,000 feet (2,134 m) in elevation in the Absaroka Mountains. From the trailhead (Northeast Entrance Rd.) the path catapults vertically through a Douglas fir forest to circle the lake.

OLD FAITHFUL AREA

For a different vantage point of Old Faithful, circle the 0.7-mile (1.1-km) loop around the geyser or climb to **Observation Point** (1.6 mi./2.6 km rt.).

Lone Star Geyser

Lone Star Geyser (4.8 mi./7.7 km rt., 2-3 hrs., easy) is tucked away from the busy Upper Geyser Basin. The 12-foot-tall (4-m) pink and gray sinter cone spouts up to 40 feet (12 m) in the air, erupting about every three hours with spurts lasting 30 minutes. From the Lone Star Geyser Trailhead (2.5 mi./4 km east of Old Faithful), walk south along the old asphalt service road through conifers along the meandering Firehole River. After a large meadow (scout for wildlife), ascend a gentle hill to the geyser basin.

WRAITH FALLS

Mystic Falls

From the Biscuit Basin parking lot, a boardwalk loop provides access to the trailhead for **Mystic Falls** (2.4 mi./3.9 km rt., 1.5 hr., moderate). Turn right and hike 0.4 mile (0.6 km) to a junction. Take the left fork and ascend 0.5 mile (0.8 km) to Mystic Falls, a 70-foot (21-m) waterfall that feeds a series of cascades.

CANYON AREA

Mount Washburn Lookout

At 10,243 feet (3,107 m), the **Mount Washburn Lookout** yields a panoramic 360-degree view from the highest peak in Yellowstone. A strenuous trail climbs in a steady plod on a former road to the summit. From Dunraven Pass (4.5 mi./7.2 km north of Canyon Jct.), the **Dunraven Pass Trail** (6 mi./9.7 km rt., 4 hrs.) traverses meadows and forest to crest a ridge, where a scenic walk finishes with a 360-degree circle to Mount Washburn Lookout. From the end of Chittenden Road (10.3 mi./16.5 km north of Canyon Jct.), the steeper **Chittenden Trail** (5.8 mi./9.3 km rt., 4 hrs., bikes permitted) has a bit more elevation gain in its meadowed switchbacks up the slope to the summit.

Cascade Lake

From Cascade Picnic Area north of Canyon Junction, the trail cuts through forest, wildflower meadows, and marshes to reach the idyllic **Cascade Lake** (4.4 mi/7 km rt, 2.5 hrs., easy). Cradled in a basin surrounded by meadows, the lily-padded lake can house trumpeter swans.

RECREATION

BACKPACKING

Backpackers must obtain **permits** ($3 pp per night) in person 48 hours in advance from the backcountry offices. To guarantee a trip, use the advanced reservation application online (submit starting Jan. 1, $25).

Point-to-point backpacking trips in the **Black Canyon of the Yellowstone** (16.5 mi./26.5 km, 3 days) go from **Hellroaring Creek Trailhead** to **Blacktail Creek Trailhead.** Choose from 19

Best Hike

GRAND PRISMATIC OVERLOOK AND FAIRY FALLS

DISTANCE: 1.2 or 6.7 miles (1.9-10.7 km) round-trip
DURATION: 1 or 3 hours
ELEVATION CHANGE: 52 or 129 feet (16-39 m)
EFFORT: easy
TRAILHEAD: Fairy Falls parking area

At 200 feet (61 m), Fairy Falls is the park's fourth-highest waterfall, and it provides a scenic year-round destination for hikers, bikers, and skiers. In 2017, a spur trail added an overlook of Grand Prismatic Spring to see the cobalt hot spring and fiery arms of thermophiles. The trail is closed in spring until late May because of bear activity.

From **Fairy Falls Trailhead,** cross the Firehole River and hike the abandoned road. To climb to the new overlook of **Grand Prismatic Spring** (1.2 mi./1.9 km rt.), take the signed 0.5-mile (0.8 km) spur to ascend 105 feet (32 m) in elevation to the platform. After returning to the trail, the route westward reaches the junction with the **Fairy Falls Trail** at 1.1 miles (1.8 km). Turning west, hike 1.5 miles (2.4 km) through a young lodgepole forest to the base of the falls. In summer, the falls plunge ribbon-like into a pool; in winter, it's an ice sculpture. With the spur to Grand Prismatic Overlook, the round-trip distance is 6.7 miles (10.7 km) to the falls.

campsites with the best flanking the Yellowstone River.

From the Lone Star Geyser Trailhead, the **Bechler River Trail** (30 mi./48.3 km, 3-5 days) descends into the land of waterfalls with the best campsites at Ouzel, Colonnade, and Albright Falls. Due to annual flooding, permit reservations are only available from July 15 onward.

BIKING

In spring (late Mar.-mid-Apr.), roads between Mammoth and West Yellowstone open to bicyclists but remain closed to vehicles for quiet, car-free cycling. Bring your own bike, as rentals are only available in West Yellowstone.

Several side roads permit bikes in both directions while cars are limited to one-way travel. The **Old Gardiner Road** (10 mi./16.1 km rt.) connects Gardiner with Mammoth Hot Springs. **Blacktail Plateau Drive** (12 mi./19.3 km rt.) rolls through higher-elevation terrain with wildlife.

Only a handful of trails allow bikes, including Lone Star Geyser, Fountain Freight Road, and Old Faithful to Morning Glory Pool. In Gardiner, the level, kid-friendly **Abandoned Railroad Bed Bike Trial** (8 mi./12.9 km rt.) parallels the Yellowstone River. More challenging, the **Chittenden Trail** (5.8 mi./9.3 km rt.) climbs to Mount Washburn Lookout.

HORSEBACK RIDING

Wranglers lead one-hour and two-hour **Saddle Up** (Xanterra, 307/344-7311, www.yellowstonenationalparklodges.com, daily June-early Sept.) horseback tours from the corrals at Roosevelt and Canyon.

BOATING AND FISHING

Yellowstone Lake attracts boaters for sightseeing, cruising, angling, sailing, and paddling. **Bridge Bay Marina** (Xanterra, 307/344-7311, www.yellowstonenationalparklodges.com, late May-Oct. for boat launch, daily mid-June-early Sept.) has a boat launch, marina services, and rentals. Located on the West Thumb, **Grant Village Marina** (mid-June-Oct.) has a boat launch, but no services.

TROUT LAKE TRAIL

In Yellowstone, fly-fishing is the epitome of fishing. Inside the park, the **Firehole, Madison,** and lower **Gibbon Rivers** offer prime fly-fishing for rainbow and brown trout. Portions of the **Yellowstone River** offer an outstanding trout fly-fishery with parts accessible from Grand Loop Road. **Yellowstone Lake** and **Lewis Lake** work for shoreline fishing, float-tube fishing, spin-casting, fly-fishing, and fishing from motorboats or rowboats.

WINTER SPORTS

In winter (mid-Dec.-early Mar.), visitors can explore groomed trails on snowshoes or cross-country skis and tour the snow-buried roads of Yellowstone in heated snowcoaches. Led by interpretive guides, snowcoaches stop at sights for photos and wildlife. Tours depart from **Mammoth Hot Springs** and **Old Faithful Snow Lodge** (reservations 307/344-7311, www.yellowstonenationalparklodges.com) and from companies in West Yellowstone, Gardiner, and Flagg Ranch. Reservations are required. Guided snowmobile tours are also available.

WHERE TO STAY

INSIDE THE PARK

Make **reservations** (307/344-7311, www.yellowstonenationalparklodges.com) for lodges, restaurants, and campgrounds **13 months in advance**. In winter, **dinner reservations** are required at Mammoth Hotel Dining Room and Snow Lodge.

In summer, reservations are mandatory for the Old West Dinner Cookout and are highly recommended for Old Faithful Inn, M66 Grill at Canyon Village, Grant Village Dining Room, and Lake Hotel Dining Room. Restaurant hours shorten spring, fall, and winter.

Mammoth Hot Springs

Mammoth Hot Springs Hotel (2 Mammoth Hotel Ave., late Apr.-Oct. and mid-Dec.-early Mar., from $112) has hotel rooms and cabins. It is the only winter hotel accessible by private vehicle.

MYSTIC FALLS

LONE STAR GEYSER

BIKING GRAND LOOP ROAD

Eateries include **Mammoth Hotel Dining Room** (6:30am-10am, 11:30am-2:30pm, 5pm-10pm daily) and **Mammoth Terrace Grill** (7am-9pm daily).

Tower Junction

Roosevelt Lodge and Cabins (Grand Loop Rd., early June-early Sept., from $104) has cabins with wood-burning stoves and private or shared bathrooms. The 1920s lodge has a **dining room** (7am-10am, 11:30am-9:30pm daily). For the **Old West Dinner Cookout** (reservations required), guests saddle up or ride a wagon from the corrals to the cookout.

Old Faithful

The most requested lodge in the park, **Old Faithful Inn** (early May-mid-Oct., from $227) is a National Historic Landmark with 10 room styles, a five-story log lobby, and a **Dining Room** (6:30am-10am, 11:30am-2:30pm, and 4:30pm-10pm daily) and the **Bear Paw Deli** (6:30am-7pm).

Old Faithful Lodge (mid-May-early Oct., from $174) has small motel-style rooms in duplex or fourplex cabins with private baths or a communal bathroom and shower cabin. The lodge has a **Bake Shop** (6:30am-9pm daily) and a **Cafeteria** (11am-9pm daily).

Snow Lodge (late Apr.-mid-Oct. from $246, mid-Dec.-Feb. from $159) has modern lodge rooms and cabins located a short walk from the lodge. Restaurants include the **Obsidian Dining Room** (6:30am-10:30am, 11:30am-3pm, 5pm-10:30pm daily) and the **Geyser Grill** (10:30am-9pm daily).

Canyon Village

Canyon Lodge and Cabins (late May-late Sept., from $364) has the newest lodgings. Hotel rooms are in multistory lodges and motel-style rooms in cabins. The complex includes the **Canyon Lodge M66 Bar and Grill** (6:30am-10:30am, 5pm-10pm daily mid-May-early Sept.) and **Canyon Lodge Eatery** (6:30am-10am, 11:30am-3pm, 4:30am-9pm daily mid-May-mid-Oct.).

Yellowstone Lake

A National Historic Landmark, **Lake Yellowstone Hotel and Cabins** (mid-May-early Oct., from $209) is a striking colonial-style structure with renovated hotel rooms and suites, motel rooms in an older lodge, and cabins. Restaurants include a **Dining Room** (6:30am-10am, 11:30am-2:30pm, 5pm-10pm daily), a bar, and a deli.

Set back from the shore of Yellowstone Lake, **Lake Lodge Cabins** (early June-late Sept., from $162) has rustic cabins with private baths. The lodge has a **cafeteria** (6:30am-9:30pm daily) and a bar.

On West Thumb Bay, **Grant Village Lodge** (Grant Village, late May-late Sept., from $277) has hotel rooms with private baths. The **Dining Room** (6:30am-10am, 11:30am-2:30pm, 5pm-10pm daily) overlooks the lake. A short walk leads to the **Grant Village Lake House Restaurant** (6:30am-10:30am, 5-9pm daily).

Camping

With more than 2,000 campsites, Yellowstone has 12 campgrounds. The largest five accept **reservations** (307/344-7311, www.yellowstonenationalparklodges.com) 13 months in advance. **Madison** (May-mid-Oct., $27), **Canyon** (late May-late Sept., showers, $32), **Bridge Bay** (mid-May-early Sept., $27), and **Grant Village** (early June-mid-Sept., showers, $32) do not have hookups. Fishing Bridge RV Park (May-Sept., $79) has full hookups and showers.

The park's smaller campgrounds are **first come, first served**: Mammoth (year-round, $20), Indian Creek (mid-June-mid-Sept., $15), Norris (mid-May-Sept., $20), Tower Fall (early June-early Sept., $15), Slough Creek (mid-June-mid-Oct., $15), Pebble Creek (mid-June-Sept., $15), or Lewis Lake (mid-June-Oct., $15).

OUTSIDE THE PARK

Find lodgings, restaurants, and services in **West Yellowstone, Gardiner,** and **Silver Gate-Cooke City.**

GETTING THERE

AIR

Bozeman Yellowstone International Airport (BZN, 406/388-8321, 850 Gallatin Field Rd., Belgrade, MT, www.bozemanairport.com) is closest to the park entrances at West Yellowstone and Gardiner. From Bozeman, it takes roughly 2 hours to drive to the park, depending on which entrance you use. Jackson Hole Airport (JAC, 1250 E. Airport Rd., Jackson, 307/733-7682, www.jacksonholeairport.com) is closest to the south entrance, which is about an hour's drive. **Billings Logan International Airport** (BIL, 1901 Terminal Circle, Billings, MT, 406/247-8609, www.flybillings.com) works for summer access (late May-mid-Oct.) to the park's north and east roads. All airports have rental cars.

CAR

I-90 crosses east-west through Montana north of Yellowstone. Between Billings and Butte, multiple routes drop south to reach the park's **West, North,** and **Northeast Entrances.** East of Bozeman, drivers can take US 89 south through Gardiner to the North Entrance. West of Bozeman, US 191 drops south to the park entrance at West Yellowstone.

The most scenic approach is the **Beartooth Highway** (US 212, late May-mid-Oct., weather depending), which travels 111 miles (179 km) from Red

▼ LAKE YELLOWSTONE HOTEL

OLD FAITHFUL INN

Lodge, Montana, to the Northeast Entrance. Plan three hours for the drive and check road and weather conditions.

From the west, US 14 enters the park's East Entrance via **Cody, Wyoming.** Yellowstone's **South Entrance** straddles the border with Grand Teton National Park on US 89/191/287.

GETTING AROUND

There is no park shuttle. In summer, you'll need a vehicle to get around. In winter, visitors can ride snowcoaches or snowmobiles from West Yellowstone or Mammoth to Old Faithful or the Grand Canyon of the Yellowstone.

DRIVING

Two-lane roads are the standard in Yellowstone. Throw in curves, wildlife, and scenery, and drivers need to pay attention—use pullouts for sightseeing and wildlife-watching. Driving between park areas can take 35-45 minutes due to wildlife jams and crowds. On summer afternoons, traffic gets extremely congested on the North Rim and South Rim Drives of the Grand Canyon of the Yellowstone. To avoid the mayhem, visit earlier or later in the day.

The Grand Loop Road from Mammoth Village east to Tower Junction and the Northeast Entrance Road are the only roads that are open year-round. All other roads close in winter.

PARKING

Parking lots in the park fill 10am-5pm (and restroom lines are long, too). RVs will find limited parking. At trailheads, claim a parking spot before 9am.

Two giant parking lots are available at Old Faithful, and they pack out in summer. The smaller parking lot is between Snow Lodge and Old Faithful Inn. The larger parking lot is southwest of Old Faithful Lodge.

TOURS

Xanterra (307/344-7311, www.yellowstonenationalparklodges.com) operates wildlife-watching, geyser basin, and winter snowcoach tours. Reservations are required. **Yellowstone Forever Institute** (406/848-2400, www.yellowstone.org) offers expert-led educational tours year-round. Multiple companies in West Yellowstone, Gardiner, and Jackson also run full-day sightseeing tours.

WHERE TO STAY IN YELLOWSTONE

NAME	LOCATION	PRICE	SEASON	AMENITIES
Mammoth Campground	Mammoth Hot Springs	$20	year-round	campsites
Mammoth Hot Springs Hotel	Mammoth Hot Springs	from $112	Apr.-Oct., Dec.-Mar.	hotel rooms, cabins, dining
Tower Fall Campground	Tower-Roosevelt	$15	early June-early Sept.	campsites
Roosevelt Lodge and Cabins	Tower-Roosevelt	from $104	early June-early Sept.	cabins, dining
Slough Creek Campground	Northeast Entrance	$15	mid-June-mid-Oct.	campsites
Pebble Creek Campground	Northeast Entrance	$15	mid-June-Sept.	campsites
Madison Campground	Madison	$27	May-mid-Oct.	campsites
Indian Creek Campground	Mammoth/Norris	$15	June- Sept	campsites
Norris Campground	Norris	$20	May-Sept.	campsites
Old Faithful Lodge	Old Faithful	from $174	May-Oct.	cabins, dining
Snow Lodge	Old Faithful	from $246	Apr.-Oct., Dec.-Feb.	hotel rooms, cabins, dining
Old Faithful Inn	Old Faithful	from $227	May-Oct.	hotel rooms, dining
Canyon Campground	Canyon Village	$32	late May-late Sept.	campsites, showers
Canyon Lodge and Cabins	Canyon Village	from $364	May-Sept.	hotel rooms, cabins, dining
Fishing Bridge RV Park	Fishing Bridge	$79	May-Sept.	RV hookups
Bridge Bay Campground	Lake Village	$27	mid-May-early Sept.	campsites, marina
Lake Lodge Cabins	Lake Village	from $162	June-Sept.	motel rooms, cabins, dining
Lake Yellowstone Hotel and Cabins	Lake Village	from $209	May-Oct.	hotel rooms, cabins, dining
Grant Village Campground	Grant Village	$32	June-Sept.	campsites
Grant Village Lodge	Grant Village	from $277	May-Sept.	hotel rooms, dining
Lewis Lake Campground	South Entrance Road	$15	June-Oct.	campsites

GRAND TETON NATIONAL PARK

Wyoming

WEBSITE:
www.nps.gov/grte

PHONE NUMBER:
307/739-3300

VISITATION RANK:
8

WHY GO:
Bask in the beauty of the Tetons.

KEEPSAKE STAMPS ▼▼▼

▲ GRAND TETON NATIONAL PARK

In **GRAND TETON NATIONAL PARK,** sawtooth spires claw the sky in one of the youngest mountain ranges in the Rockies. Towering thousands of feet culminating in the Grand Teton itself, these mountains dwarf the wildlife that roams across the floor of Jackson Hole. These peaks were likely first summited by Native Americans, who gave them spiritual value. The Snake River people—Northern Paiute, Bannock, and Shoshone—named the trio of Grand, Middle, and South Tetons the "Hoary-headed Fathers."

Snuggled at the base of the peaks, glacial lakes string along the valley floor, offering picturesque places to hike, paddle, and fish. Boating on Jackson Lake, floating the Wild and Scenic Snake River, pedaling paved pathways, and skiing winter slopes are all enjoyed beneath the skyscraping grandeur of the Tetons.

PLANNING YOUR TIME

Grand Teton National Park is in Wyoming, sandwiched between the town of Jackson and Yellowstone National Park. **Summer** (May-Sept.) is high season when visitors centers, campgrounds, lodges, marinas, and services are open; most **roads are open May-mid-November.** Lower-elevation trails are snow-free in June, while higher-elevation trails don't melt out until mid-July.

In summer, warm days in the 70s-80s (21-26°C and above) can evolve into afternoon thunderstorms, especially in the mountains. Spring and fall yo-yo between sunny days and rain or high-elevation snow. Winter snows blanket the ground late November through April.

Most visitor services **close in winter.** Teton Park Road closes **November-April,** from Signal Mountain Lodge to Taggart Lake Trailhead, and is groomed for cross-country skiing and snowshoeing. **US 26/89/191** provides year-round access to the park.

To guarantee lodgings, RV camping, tours, or dinner, make reservations at least **one year in advance.**

ENTRANCES AND FEES

Grand Teton has three entrance stations that are open year-round. The **Moran Entrance** (US 26/89/191 and US 26/287) offers access from the east. The **Granite Canyon Entrance** is the south entrance to the Moose-Wilson Road, north of Teton Village. The **Moose Entrance** (Teton Park Rd.) accesses Teton Park Road.

The entrance fee is $35 per vehicle ($30 motorcycle, $20 individual) and valid for seven days.

VISITORS CENTERS

Craig Thomas Discovery and Visitor Center

Craig Thomas Discovery and Visitor Center (Moose, 307/739-3399, 8am-7pm daily June-Sept., shorter hours spring and fall) has natural history exhibits, wildlife sculptures, a 30-foot (9-m) climbing wall, kids' exhibits, and a topographic map that shows wildlife migration and glacier progression. The information desk has maps, schedules of ranger programs and hikes, current weather, and permits for backcountry camping and boating. A large bookstore sells field guides and books on wildlife, human history, and geology.

Jenny Lake Visitor Center

At South Jenny Lake, **Jenny Lake Visitor Center** (Moose, 307/739-3392, 8am-7pm daily June-early Sept., 8am-5pm daily mid-May-early June and Sept.) has activity schedules, ranger program information, maps, and a small bookstore. **Jenny Lake Ranger Station** (307/739-3343, 8am-5pm daily early June-early Sept.) has information on trail conditions and mountain climbing

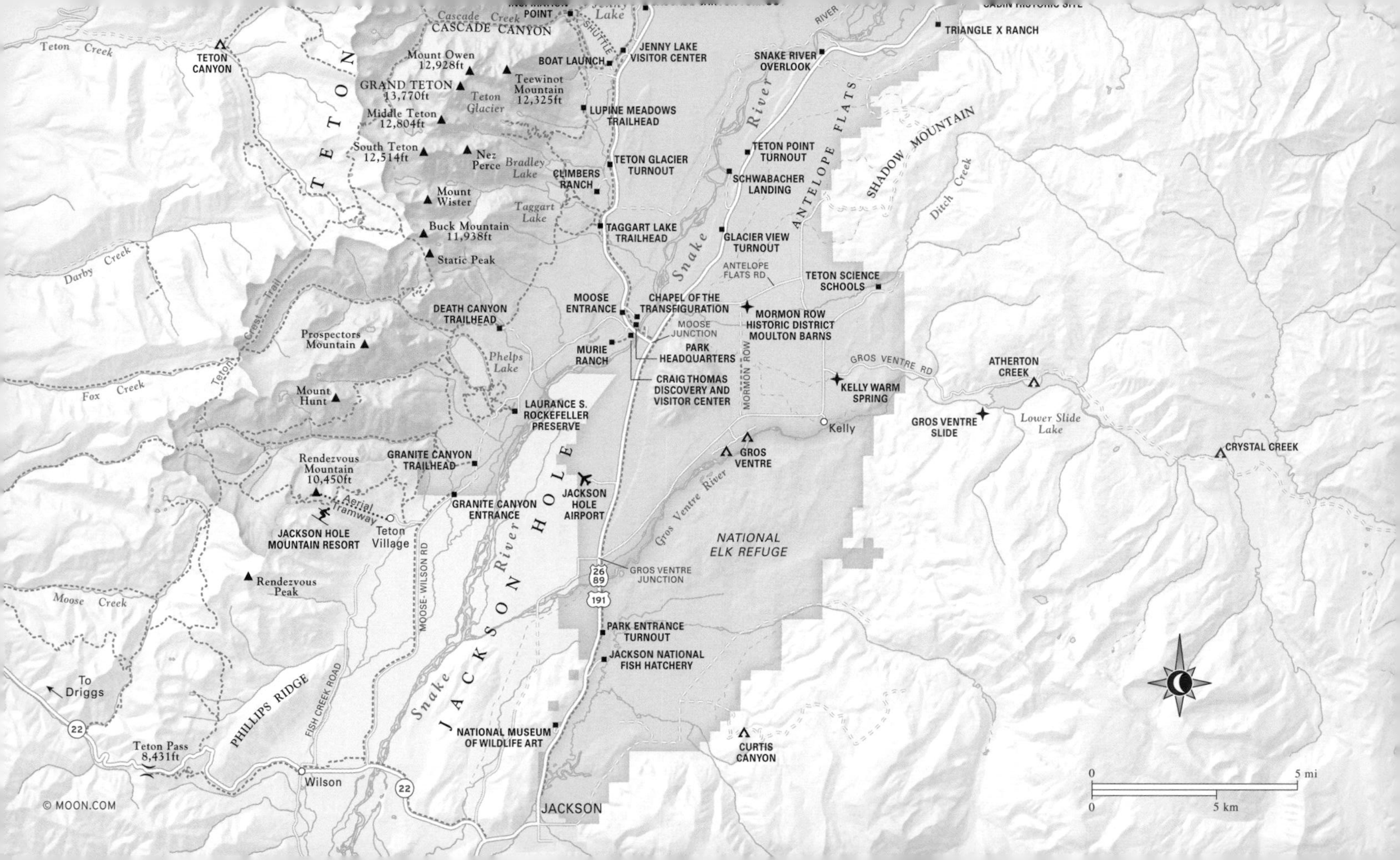
TETON
Teton Creek
TETON CANYON
Cascade Creek
CASCADE CANYON
Mount Owen 12,928ft
GRAND TETON 13,770ft
Teton Glacier
Teewinot Mountain 12,325ft
Middle Teton 12,804ft
South Teton 12,514ft
Nez Perce
Bradley Lake
Mount Wister
Taggart Lake
Buck Mountain 11,938ft
Static Peak
Darby Creek
Crest Trail
Teton
Prospectors Mountain
Fox Creek
Mount Hunt
Phelps Lake
Rendezvous Mountain 10,450ft
Aerial Tramway
JACKSON HOLE MOUNTAIN RESORT
Teton Village
Rendezvous Peak
Moose Creek
To Driggs
22
Teton Pass 8,431ft
PHILLIPS RIDGE
FISH CREEK ROAD
Wilson
MOOSE-WILSON RD
Snake River
JACKSON HOLE
JACKSON
© MOON.COM
Lake
SHUTTLE
BOAT LAUNCH
JENNY LAKE VISITOR CENTER
LUPINE MEADOWS TRAILHEAD
TETON GLACIER TURNOUT
CLIMBERS RANCH
TAGGART LAKE TRAILHEAD
DEATH CANYON TRAILHEAD
MOOSE ENTRANCE
CHAPEL OF THE TRANSFIGURATION
MOOSE JUNCTION
MURIE RANCH
PARK HEADQUARTERS
CRAIG THOMAS DISCOVERY AND VISITOR CENTER
LAURANCE S. ROCKEFELLER PRESERVE
GRANITE CANYON TRAILHEAD
GRANITE CANYON ENTRANCE
JACKSON HOLE AIRPORT
26
89
191
GROS VENTRE JUNCTION
PARK ENTRANCE TURNOUT
JACKSON NATIONAL FISH HATCHERY
NATIONAL MUSEUM OF WILDLIFE ART
TRIANGLE X RANCH
RIVER
SNAKE RIVER OVERLOOK
TETON POINT TURNOUT
SCHWABACHER LANDING
GLACIER VIEW TURNOUT
ANTELOPE FLATS
ANTELOPE FLATS RD
SHADOW MOUNTAIN
Ditch Creek
TETON SCIENCE SCHOOLS
MORMON ROW HISTORIC DISTRICT MOULTON BARNS
MORMON ROW
GROS VENTRE RD
KELLY WARM SPRING
Kelly
GROS VENTRE
Gros Ventre River
NATIONAL ELK REFUGE
ATHERTON CREEK
GROS VENTRE SLIDE
Lower Slide Lake
CRYSTAL CREEK
CURTIS CANYON
0
5 mi
0
5 km

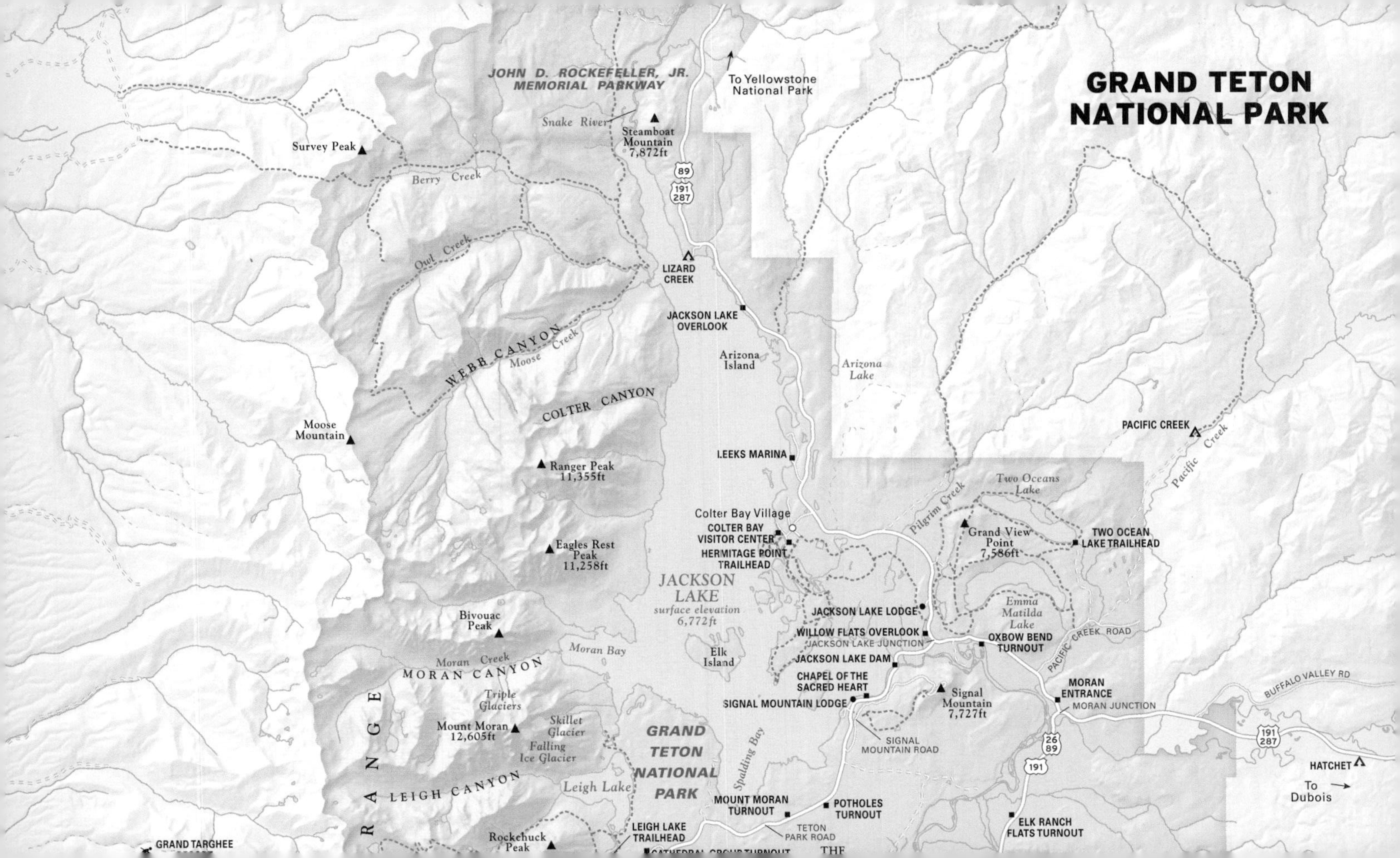
GRAND TETON NATIONAL PARK
JOHN D. ROCKEFELLER, JR. MEMORIAL PARKWAY
To Yellowstone National Park
Snake River
Steamboat Mountain 7,872ft
Survey Peak
Berry Creek
Owl Creek
LIZARD CREEK
JACKSON LAKE OVERLOOK
WEBB CANYON
Moose Creek
COLTER CANYON
Arizona Island
Arizona Lake
Moose Mountain
PACIFIC CREEK
Pacific Creek
Ranger Peak 11,355ft
LEEKS MARINA
Two Oceans Lake
Pilgrim Creek
Colter Bay Village
COLTER BAY VISITOR CENTER
HERMITAGE POINT TRAILHEAD
Grand View Point 7,586ft
TWO OCEAN LAKE TRAILHEAD
Eagles Rest Peak 11,258ft
JACKSON LAKE
surface elevation 6,772ft
Emma Matilda Lake
JACKSON LAKE LODGE
Bivouac Peak
WILLOW FLATS OVERLOOK
JACKSON LAKE JUNCTION
OXBOW BEND TURNOUT
PACIFIC CREEK ROAD
Moran Bay
Elk Island
JACKSON LAKE DAM
Moran Creek
MORAN CANYON
CHAPEL OF THE SACRED HEART
MORAN ENTRANCE
MORAN JUNCTION
BUFFALO VALLEY RD
Triple Glaciers
Signal Mountain 7,727ft
SIGNAL MOUNTAIN LODGE
Skillet Glacier
Mount Moran 12,605ft
Falling Ice Glacier
GRAND TETON NATIONAL PARK
Spalding Bay
SIGNAL MOUNTAIN ROAD
HATCHET
To Dubois
RANGE
LEIGH CANYON
Leigh Lake
MOUNT MORAN TURNOUT
POTHOLES TURNOUT
TETON PARK ROAD
ELK RANCH FLATS TURNOUT
LEIGH LAKE TRAILHEAD
Rockchuck Peak
GRAND TARGHEE

ONE DAY IN GRAND TETON

Pair up two activities for a taste of the Tetons. In the morning, explore **Jenny Lake** by sauntering the interpretive plaza and lake overlooks, hopping the boat shuttle across the lake, and hiking to **Hidden Falls** and **Inspiration Point.** In the afternoon, relax on a float trip down the **Snake River** as the twisting waterway shifts your viewpoint of the skyscraping **Teton Mountains**.

routes plus backcountry camping and boating permits.

Colter Bay Visitor Center

Colter Bay Visitor Center (Colter Bay Village, Moran, 307/739-3594, 8am-7pm daily June-early Sept., 8am-5pm daily May-early June and Sept.-Oct.) has maps and information on hiking, boating, weather, backcountry permits, activities, and a bookstore. In summer, join in interpretive programs, see craft demonstrations, and tour the Indian Arts Museum.

North of Colter Bay, tiny **Flagg Ranch Information Station** (John D. Rockefeller Jr. Memorial Parkway, US 89/191/287, 307/543-2372, 9am-4pm daily early June-early Sept.) has information on trails, road conditions, and weather, and sells maps and books.

SIGHTS

MORMON ROW

Mormon Row is a treat for history buffs, photographers, and wildlife lovers. Originally a Mormon ranch settlement that started in the 1890s, the tract grew to 27 homesteads. Today, its six clusters of buildings are on the National Register of Historic Places, including the famous **Moulton Barn** that appears in the foreground of so many photos of Grand Teton. Mormon Row is in the southeast corner of the park, off Antelope Flats Road.

MORMON ROW

LAURANCE S. ROCKEFELLER PRESERVE CENTER

The **Laurance S. Rockefeller Preserve Center** (Moose-Wilson Rd., 307/739-3654, 9am-5pm daily early June-late Sept.) sits in a 1,000-acre (405-ha) preserve that was once a Rockefeller family ranch. The preserve's LEED-certified building contains exhibits, nature videos, and natural soundscapes. Rangers lead daily programs, talks, hikes, sunrise strolls, and evening walks. The parking lot usually fills 9am-4pm; visit early in the morning or late in the afternoon.

MENOR'S FERRY HISTORIC DISTRICT

North of the Moose Entrance, **Menor's Ferry Historic District** (Teton Park Rd., Moose) preserves buildings from the 1890s. In summer, rangers guide afternoon walks or you can take a self-guided tour of the site's cabins, barns, smokehouse, farm implements, wagons, replica ferry, and **general store** (9am-4:30pm daily late May-late Sept.). The **Chapel of the Transfiguration** holds the famous clear window over the altar that frames Grand Teton.

THE MURIE RANCH

At the north end of Moose-Wilson Road, the **Murie Center** (Teton Science School, 1 Murie Ranch Rd., Moose, 307/732-7752, www.tetonscience.org,

Top 3

1 GAZE AT GRAND TETON

GRAND TETON (LEFT) AND TETON GLACIER

The Teton Mountains are dominated by their highest peak—the 13,775-foot (4,198-km) **Grand Teton.** Carved by erosion from ice, water, and wind, the Grand Teton spirals into a pinnacle. A lure for climbers, the Grand serves as a notch in the belts of mountaineers who summit its vertical cliffs. The best way to enjoy the peak is by hiking to **Bradley Lake, Amphitheater Lake, Hurricane Pass,** or **Lake Solitude.** For the best car-accessible peeks at the peak, eyeball its crags through binoculars at the **Teton Glacier Turnout** on Teton Park Road. For photo ops, head to the **Chapel of the Transfiguration** or **Mormon Row.**

2 CRUISE TETON PARK ROAD

Teton Park Road (24 mi./39 km May-Oct.) is all about getting views of the Tetons. From Craig Thomas Discovery and Visitor Center in Moose, drive north through the Moose Entrance Station and turn right to see the **Menor's Ferry Historic District** and the small log **Chapel of the Transfiguration.** Continue north to **Teton Glacier Turnout,** where you can spot small **Teton Glacier** and towering **Grand Teton.** Stop at **South Jenny Lake** to walk from the visitors center to overlooks of the idyllic waters.

From North Jenny Lake, turn left for a detour on **Jenny Lake Road** (4 mi./6.4 km one-way). Stop at the **Cathedral Group Pullout** for views of three prominent peaks.

Continue north on Teton Park Road, stopping at the **Mount Moran turnout** to examine the black dike and small glaciers in the mountain's upper cliffs. Next, **Signal Mountain Summit Road** (10 mi./16 km rt.) climbs to Jackson Overlook for sweeping Teton views. At Jackson Lake Dam, walk the paved path to the shore of **Jackson Lake.**

3 ENJOY JENNY LAKE

Tucked below the Grand Teton, **Jenny Lake** beckons photographers to capture its grandeur. Early morning often offers reflections in smooth water. To see the lake, stroll the new wheelchair-accessible **Discovery Loop** (0.5 mi./0.8 km rt., 30 min., easy) from the interpretive plaza to several lake overlooks and benches for soaking up scenery. You can also explore the small visitors center, ranger station, store, scenic boat tours, paddle, hike, or camp.

JENNY LAKE

AVOID THE CROWDS

To avoid the crowds of summer, visit in the quieter **spring** and **fall,** although weather can be erratic. If lower-elevation hiking and sightseeing are on your agenda, the shoulder seasons are the perfect time, with snow-clad peaks standing out against a blue sky. Most roads are open, and wildlife is active. **Spring** brings the chance to see bison and pronghorn newborns, and during fall, the air fills with the sound of elk bugling. **Fall** also brings outstanding hiking, with warm bug-free days and cool nights. During early spring or late fall, you may need to stay in Jackson or Teton Village when in-park facilities are closed.

9am-5pm daily mid-May-mid-Oct., free) is a National Historic Landmark. Pick up a self-guided walking tour guide on the Muries' front porch or take a docent-led **tour** (2:30pm Mon.-Fri. in summer) inside one of the ranch cabins.

SIGNAL MOUNTAIN

At 7,720 feet (2,353 m) high, **Signal Mountain** (Signal Mountain Summit Rd., 10 mi./16 km rt., May-Oct., no trailers or large RVs) cowers below the massive Tetons. Two forested routes climb steeply to reach the summit: drive or bike the paved road or hike the trail (6.8 mi./10.9 km rt., 4 hrs., moderate). The summit has two overlooks: **Jackson Point Overlook** on the south with majestic Teton Mountain views and **Emma Matilda Overlook** on the north facing the Absarokas.

MENOR'S FERRY HISTORIC DISTRICT

JACKSON LAKE LODGE

With views of Mount Moran and Jackson Lake, **Jackson Lake Lodge** (307/543-3100, www.gtlc.com, mid-May-early Oct.) is a National Historic Landmark. Windows frame the Teton Mountains, which compete for attention with the 10 "Rendezvous Murals" by Carl Roters, a late-20th-century American artist. John D. Rockefeller Jr. hand-selected the location on **Lunch Tree Hill** for its unobstructed mountain views. Commissioned by Rockefeller and built in 1955, the three-story lodge blends modern international architecture with artful takes on western and Native American elements. It also houses a small selection of Native American artifacts.

COLTER BAY

Colter Bay (US 89/191/287) is one of those do-everything places with sights galore. To see the offshore islands, take a scenic cruise or rent a boat, canoe, or kayak. A maze of hiking trails loops the peninsulas, passing tiny lakes. Bikes can go on the trail to the jetty. Around Colter Bay, Jackson Lake often reflects Mount Moran and the Teton Mountains at sunrise or sunset.

WILDLIFE-WATCHING

Moose-Wilson Road

Moose-Wilson Road (16 mi./26 km, mid-May-Oct.), a shoulderless, bumpy shortcut between Teton Village and Jenny Lake, snuggles into the southern base of the Teton Mountains. This narrow paved and gravel road weaves through beaver, porcupine, bear, and moose habitat, especially at **Sawmill Ponds** and the **Laurance S. Rockefeller Preserve.**

Antelope Flats Road

Antelope Flats Road (US 89/191/287, 1.1 mi./1.8 km north of Moose Junction) is a habitat for bison, pronghorn, moose, coyotes, and raptors such as northern harriers or American kestrels. In spring, look for migrating elk and newborns of bison and pronghorn.

Blacktail Ponds Overlook

Stop at **Blacktail Ponds Overlook** (US 89/191/287, 1.3 mi./2.1 km north of Moose Junction) to see moose that often feed here. The habitat also attracts ospreys, waterfowl, and songbirds. Active beavers maintain the dams that keep the ponds in water.

Oxbow Bend

With slow-moving convolutions of water, **Oxbow Bend** (US 89/191/287, 1 mi./1.6 km east of Jackson Lake Junction) has river otters, beavers, and muskrats. Look for moose foraging on willows. Squawking American pelicans add to the cacophony from songbirds, and ospreys and bald eagles hunt for fish.

HIKING

MOOSE

Phelps Lake

At the Laurance S. Rockefeller Preserve (Moose-Wilson Rd., park by 9am), the **Lake Creek-Woodland Trail Loop** (3 mi./4.8 km rt., 1.5 hrs., moderate) is the most direct route through moose country to Phelps Lake. **Phelps Lake Loop** (6.2 mi./10 km rt., 3.5 hrs., moderate) climbs via Lake Creek to circle the lake for a changing perspective on the Teton Mountains.

Phelps Lake Overlook & Static Peak Divide

From the Death Canyon Trailhead (Moose-Wilson Rd.), the trail ascends to a saddle overlooking **Phelps Lake** (2 mi./3.2 km rt., 1.5 hrs., moderate). Strong hikers out for 5,100 feet (1,554 m) of climbing go farther into Death Canyon before shooting up a rocky scree and cliff ridge to **Static Peak Divide** (16.3 mi./26.2 km rt., 9-12 hrs., strenuous), where a short path zips up to the summit for a view of Grand Teton.

TETON PARK ROAD

Taggart and Bradley Lakes

Get an early start in order to claim a parking spot at the popular Taggart Lake Trailhead (Teton Park Rd.) to hike to this pair of idyllic lakes. **Taggart Lake** (3 mi./4.8 km rt., 1.5 hrs., moderate) is perfect for families and wading. Make the full loop that includes **Bradley Lake** (5.9 mi./9.5 km rt., 3-4 hrs.), which sits below Grand Teton.

Surprise and Amphitheater Lakes

From the Lupine Meadows Trailhead (Teton Park Rd.), the trail to **Surprise and Amphitheater Lakes** (10.1 mi./16.3 km rt., 6 hrs., strenuous) climbs to a junction with the Taggart Lake Trail before piling on the switchbacks to reach a small hanging valley cradling Surprise Lake. The trail ascends about 10 more minutes into a second basin housing Amphitheater Lake, tucked below Disappointment Peak.

Lake Solitude

Ride the Jenny Lake shuttle boat (fee) to the west shore boat dock and trailhead for **Lake Solitude** (15.3 mi./24.6 km rt., 8 hrs., strenuous). Follow the trail to Hidden Falls and Inspiration Point before joining Cascade Canyon Trail. At the Forks of Cascade Canyon, turn right to climb out of the forest into vast wildflower meadows surrounding blue Lake Solitude.

Holly Lake and Paintbrush Divide

Holly Lake (13 mi./20.9 km rt., 7 hrs., strenuous) sits in an alpine cirque populated by pikas. From String Lake Trailhead, cross the outlet and hike north along the base of Rockchuck Peak to reach Paintbrush Canyon. Climb west through forest, avalanche slopes, and huge boulders into a hanging basin to reach the lake. Strong hikers grunt up further through scree and across steep snowfields to top 10,720-foot (3,267-m) **Paintbrush Divide** and a 4,100-foot (1,250-m) elevation gain. But

JACKSON POINT OVERLOOK ON SIGNAL MOUNTAIN

once there, most descend via **Paintbrush-Cascade Loop** (19 mi./30.6 km rt., 10-13 hrs., strenuous), a bucket list route to Lake Solitude and Cascade Canyon to connect with the Jenny Lake Trail back to the trailhead.

Leigh Lake-Rockchuck Loop

Walk the **Leigh Lake-Rockchuck Loop** (3.7 mi./6 km rt., 2 hrs., moderate) counterclockwise for big views of Jenny Lake and the Tetons. From the Leigh Lake Trailhead, hike along String Lake and the creek to a junction near Leigh Lake. Cross a bridge and climb to a second junction, where a left turn breaks onto the open slopes of Rockchuck Peak to descend to the foot of String Lake to catch the Jenny Lake Trail that finishes at the String Lake Trailhead.

JACKSON LAKE

Heron Pond and Hermitage Point

From the Hermitage Point Trailhead at Colter Bay Village, **Heron Pond Trail** (3 mi./4.8 km rt., 2 hrs., moderate) takes in a variety of views on a gently rolling path. At each junction, turn right to reach Jackson Lake Overlook and lily-padded **Heron Pond** with the Tetons reflected in the water. After Heron Pond, turn left to loop to Swan Lake for the return to the trailhead.

To continue on to **Hermitage Point** (9.7 mi./15.6 km rt., 5 hrs., moderate) after Heron Pond, turn right at all junctions along the peninsula's west side where views span Jackson Lake and Mount Moran. At the point, curve along the east side of the peninsula. At the next junction, turn left to return to the trailhead via Swan Lake.

Emma Matilda and Two Ocean Lakes

Two glacially carved lakes are located 1 mile (1.6 km) apart in a maze of forest and meadow trails. From the trailhead at Two Ocean Lake, hike a counterclockwise loop around **Two Ocean Lake** and **Emma Matilda Lake** (6.4-10.7 mi./10.3-17.2 km rt., 4-6 hrs., moderate). The loop takes in the higher **Grand View Point** for outstanding views of

MOOSE COW AND CALF

the Tetons and the lakes. To just hike up to **Grand View Point** (6 mi./9.7 km rt., 3 hrs., moderate), start at Jackson Lake Lodge.

RECREATION

BACKPACKING

The king of backpacking trips is the **Teton Crest Trail** (38-58 mi./61-93 km), a high-elevation romp with major elevation gains and descents. The route crosses Fox Creek Pass, Death Canyon Shelf, Mount Meek Pass, Alaska Basin, Hurricane Pass, and Paintbrush Divide at 9,600-10,720 feet (2,926-3,267 m). The **38-mile (61-km) point-to-point** route requires a shuttle between trailheads, or you can complete the loop by adding 20 miles (32.2 km) on the Valley Trail (**58-mi./93-km loop**). Many hikers gain elevation by starting at Jackson Hole Mountain Resort's aerial tram (fee), reducing the total distance to 34 miles (55 km). Along the Teton Crest, you can camp at Marian Lake, Death Canyon Shelf, South Fork Cascade, and Upper Paintbrush. Shorter two- three-day routes go up Paintbrush, Cascade, Death, and Granite Canyons to the crest and back down as loops or the same trail of ascent.

Bear canisters and backcountry **permits** ($35) are required. They are available from **Jenny Lake Ranger Station** (307/739-3343, 8am-5pm daily early June-early Sept.) or Craig Thomas Discovery and Visitor Center. Apply online (www.recreation.gov, early Jan.-mid-May, $45/trip) to guarantee your permit in advance.

BIKING

The **Multi-Use Pathway** (29 mi./47 km dawn-dusk) is a mostly level, paved cycling and walking path that parallels the roads between Jenny Lake, Moose, Antelope Flats Road, and Jackson. For the most scenic ride, the Moose-Jenny Lake segment (7.7 mi./12.4 km) skims just below the Tetons. The section from Jackson to Gros Ventre Junction closes November-April for migrating elk. Rent bikes from Dornan's **Adventure Sports** (12170 Dornan Rd., Moose, 307/733-2415, http://dornans.com, 8am-6pm daily early May-late Sept.).

ROCK CLIMBING

To reach Teton summits demands technical climbing skills and the gear for rock or ice routes. Climbing the **Grand Teton** involves 14 miles (22.5 km) of hiking and 6,545 feet (1,995 m) of ascent and descent. More than 35 climbing

TAGGART LAKE

routes lead to its summit, with countless variations. The most popular and famous route for climbing the Grand is the exposed Upper Exum Ridge. Mid-July-August offers the best weather.

Exum Mountain Guides (South Jenny Lake, 307/733-2297, http://exumguides.com) leads individual and group climbs, plus offers climbing instruction and camps. **Jenny Lake Ranger Station** (307/739-3343, 8am-5pm daily early June-early Sept.) is the only place for current climbing conditions and information and to pick up a backcountry camping **permit**.

HORSEBACK RIDING

Grand Teton Lodging Company (reservations 307/543-2811, www.gtlc.com, daily June-early Sept., $48-78) offers one- and two-hour horseback rides from corrals at Colter Bay Village, Jackson Lake Lodge, and Flagg Ranch.

BOATING AND FISHING

Jenny Lake

Boating on **Jenny Lake** (boat launch on Lupine Meadows Rd.) is a quiet, idyllic experience; only hand-propelled boats or motorboats with 10 horsepower or less are permitted. North of Jenny Lake, **String Lake** has a canoe and kayak launch site (North Jenny Lake Rd.). The lake connects via a portage to **Leigh Lake,** where paddlers can overnight in solitude at eight prime backcountry campsites (permit required).

AMPHITHEATER LAKE

LAKE SOLITUDE

Jenny Lake Boating (Jenny Lake boathouse, 307/734-9227, www.jennylakeboating.com, 7am-7pm daily mid-June-mid-Sept., shorter hours in fall) rents kayaks and canoes. Dornan's **Adventure Sports** (12170 Dornan Rd., Moose, 307/733-2415, http://dornans.com, 8am-6pm daily early May-late Sept.) rents canoes, kayaks, and paddleboards. Acquire boating permits and fishing licenses at **Colter Bay Visitor Center** (307/739-3594, 8am-7pm daily early June-early Sept).

Jackson Lake

Fifteen islands inhabit **Jackson Lake,** and their boat-accessible backcountry campsites (permit required) are perfect destinations for boaters and paddlers. Three marinas offer launch sites late May-late September: **Leek's Marina** and **Signal Mountain Lodge** (contact for both at 307/543-2831, www.signalmountainlodge.com), and **Colter Bay Marina** (Grand Teton Lodging Company, 307/543-2811, www.gtlc.com). Rent motorboats, canoes, and kayaks from Colter Bay Marina and Signal Mountain Lodge.

Rafting the Snake River

Rafts, kayaks, and canoes can float the **Wild and Scenic Snake River** below Jackson Lake Dam. Start at Jackson Lake Dam or Cattleman's Bridge Site to take out at Pacific Creek. Only experienced paddlers should put in at Deadman's Bar and take out at Moose Landing (10 mi./16 km, 2 hrs.), an advanced section with strong currents, waves, logjams, and a maze of braided streams.

Guided scenic float trips (mid-May-Sept.) on the Snake River depart from **Jackson Lake Lodge** (Grand Teton Lodging Company, 307/543-2811, www.gtlc.com), **Signal Mountain Lodge** (307/543-2831, www.signalmountainlodge.com), and Moose through **Barker-Ewing Scenic Float Trips** (307/733-1800 or 800/365-1800, www.barkerewing.com) or **Triangle X-National Park Float Trips** (307/733-5500, http://nationalparkfloattrips.com). Guided Snake River fishing trips are offered through **Snake River Angler** (10 Moose St., Moose, 307/733-3699, www.snakeriverangler.com) and **Triangle X** (307/733-2183, www.trianglex.com).

Best Hike

HIDDEN FALLS AND INSPIRATION POINT

DISTANCE: 2.2-7.2 miles (3.5-11.6 km) round-trip
DURATION: 1.5-4 hours
ELEVATION CHANGE: 1,250 feet (381 m)
EFFORT: moderately strenuous
TRAILHEAD: Jenny Lake Visitor Center

Hidden Falls is a tall tumbler in Cascade Canyon, and Inspiration Point, a rocky knoll squeeze between Mount Teewinot and Mount St. John. Hordes of hikers clog this trail, except in early morning or late in the day. The boat shuttle (fee) reduces this hike to a 2.2-mile (3.5-km) loop from the west boat dock.

From the visitors center, head west toward the east boat dock and cross the bridge at the outlet of Jenny Lake at Cottonwood Creek. Arc west along the south shore of Jenny Lake, passing the boat launch and two junctions for Moose Pond Loop to take the scenic lakeshore to the lake's west side. Ascending Cascade Creek, follow the well-signed junctions to **Hidden Falls** Overlook**.** To continue to Inspiration Point, cross the two upper bridges below the falls to climb south-facing switchbacks to Lower and Upper **Inspiration Point.**

WHERE TO STAY

INSIDE THE PARK

Moose

On the Snake River, **Dornan's Spur Ranch Cabins** (307/733-2415, www.dornans.com, May-Oct. and Dec.-Mar., from $225) have full kitchens. Their eateries include **Pizza Pasta Company** (11:30am-9:30pm daily, shorter hours in winter), the **Chuckwagon** (307/733-2415, hours and days vary, mid-June-early Sept.) in a covered outdoor pavilion with picnic tables, and **Moose Trading Post & Deli** (9am-5pm daily winter, 8am-8pm daily summer).

Jenny Lake

Built in 1920, **Jenny Lake Lodge** (400 Jenny Lake Loop, 307/543-3100, www.gtlc.com, June-early Oct., from $776) offers rustic luxury in 37 log cabins. Reserve a year in advance. **Reservations** (307/543-3351) are recommended for breakfast and lunch and required for dinner, along with a dress code.

The **Grand Teton Climber's Ranch** (Teton Park Rd., 307/733-7271 summer, 303/384-0110 fall-spring, http://americanalpineclub.org, early June-mid-Sept., $17-27) offers small, hostel-style coed log cabins with wooden bunks. Facilities include sex-separated bathrooms and shower houses and an outdoor cook shelter. Bring your own sleeping bag, pad, cooking gear, food, and towels.

Jackson Lake

Jackson Lake Lodge (307/543-3100, www.gtlc.com, mid-May-early Oct., from $346) is a National Historic Landmark built in 1955 with a commanding Teton panoramic view, an outdoor swimming pool, and horseback riding. Rooms are in the main lodge, separate two-story lodges, or in cabins. Reserve a year in advance. The complex includes four restaurants: the upscale **Mural Room** (7am-9:30am, 11:30am-1:30pm, and 5:30pm-9pm daily), the café-style **Pioneer Grill** (6am-10pm daily), the **Blue Heron** (11am-midnight daily) with back patio service, and the **Pool Cantina and BBQ** (11am-4pm and 5:30pm-8pm daily mid-June-mid-Aug.). **Reservations** (307/543-3463) for the Mural Room and BBQ are accepted starting in late May.

Signal Mountain Lodge (1 Inner Park Rd., 307/543-2831, www.signalmountainlodge.com, mid-May-mid-Oct., from $292) sits on Jackson Lake with stunning Teton views. The lodge

LOWER INSPIRATION POINT

has a variety of different room options and is so popular that it takes **reservations 16 months out.** The complex has two restaurants: **Peaks Restaurant** (5:30pm-10pm daily) and **Trapper Grill** (7am-10pm daily). Up the road at Leek's Marina, **Leek's Pizzeria** (307/543-2494, 11am-10pm daily late May-mid-Sept.) serves pizza and pasta.

At Colter Bay, where water and hiking activities abound, **Colter Bay Cabins** (Colter Bay Village, 307/543-3100, www.gtlc.com, late May-early Oct., from $175) come in three sizes. **Colter Bay Tent Village** (late May-early Sept., from $76) has partial log and canvas cabins with communal bathrooms. Reserve a year in advance. Eateries include **Café Court Pizzeria** (11am-10pm daily late May-early Sept.) and the **Ranch House** (6:30am-10:30am, 11:30am-1:30pm, 5:30-9pm daily late May-Sept.). **Colter Bay Cookouts** (reservations required) offer outdoor dining around a western-style campfire via **Cookout boat cruises** (307/543-2811, June-mid-Sept.) and **Cookout horseback** or **wagon rides** (307/543-3100, Sun.-Fri. early June-early Sept.).

Flagg Ranch

Closest to Yellowstone, **Headwaters Lodge & Cabins at Flagg Ranch** (John D. Rockefeller Jr. Memorial Parkway, 307/543-2861, www.gtlc.com, June-Sept., from $240) has three room types. Reserve a year in advance. **Sheffields Restaurant & Bar** (6:30am-10am, 11:30am-2pm, 5:30-9:30pm daily June-Sept.) has the only dining. In the adjacent campground, tiny **camper cabins** ($78) help those on a budget.

Triangle X Ranch

Triangle X Ranch (2 Triangle X Ranch Rd., 307/733-2183, http://trianglex.com, mid-May-mid-Oct. and late Dec.-mid-Mar.) is a dude ranch with lodgings in cabins. Early June-late August is peak season (from $1,957 pp weekly), with shorter stays in the off-season (mid-May-early June and Sept.-Oct., from $266 pp per day).

Camping

Grand Teton's six campgrounds are all first come, first served: **Gros Ventre** (May-mid-Oct., 314 sites $30, 36

▼ GRAND VIEW POINT

CLIMBING PAINTBRUSH DIVIDE ON PAINTBRUSH-CASCADE CANYON LOOP

electrical hookups $55) is nearest to Jackson. Popular **Jenny Lake** (May-Sept., 49 sites, $29) is for tents only. **Signal Mountain** (early May-mid-Oct., 81 sites, $33) and **Colter Bay** (late May-Sept., 335 sites, $32) both flank Jackson Lake with marinas and rentals. **Lizard Creek** (mid-June-early Sept., 60 sites, $30) tucks on the quiet north end of Jackson Lake. **Headwaters** (Flagg Ranch, mid-May-Sept., 141 sites, $39) is closest to Yellowstone. Most campgrounds fill by noon in summer.

Colter Bay RV Park (Colter Bay Village, 307/543-3100, www.gtlc.com, early May-early Oct., $73-83) and **Headwaters Campground & RV Park** (Flagg Ranch, 307/543-2861, www.gtlc.com, mid-May-Sept., $75) accommodate RV campers and accept reservations a year in advance.

OUTSIDE THE PARK

Jackson and **Teton Village** offer lodgings, restaurants, and amenities.

GETTING THERE

AIR

Jackson Hole Airport (JAC, 1250 E. Airport Rd., Jackson, 307/733-7682, www.jacksonholeairport.com) is actually inside Grand Teton National Park, just north of Jackson. It's a 15-minute drive north to the park's main visitors center and the Moose Entrance. **Idaho Falls Regional Airport** (IDA, 2140 N. Skyline Dr., 208/612-8221, www.idahofallsidaho.gov) may have cheaper flights, but it's more than a two-hour drive to the park. Both airports have rental cars.

CAR

US 89/191/287 (open year-round) exits Yellowstone south to immediately enter John D. Rockefeller Jr. Memorial Parkway and Grand Teton National Park. The road stretches south to Moran Junction, the park's east entrance, and links with the Outside Road (US 26/89/191) and Inside Road (Teton Park Rd.).

From the south, **US 26/89/191** leads north from the town of Jackson to the park's Moose and Moran Entrances.

From Idaho, **ID 33/WY 22** crosses over Teton Pass to Jackson, Wyoming, connecting with US 89/191/287 north into the park.

From eastern Wyoming, drivers from I-80 can take **US 189 or 191** toward Jackson. From I-25 East, the route goes over Togwotee Pass (US 26) for a stunning descent to Moran Junction.

Winter weather can make for whiteouts and icy roads. Check conditions for park roads by calling 307/739-3682.

BOAT SHUTTLE IN JENNY LAKE

GETTING AROUND

DRIVING

US 26/89/191 (Outside Road) is open year-round from Moran to Moose and Jackson. **US 89/191/287** opens year-round from Moran to Flagg Ranch and Yellowstone's South Entrance.

Teton Park Road (Inside Road) is fully open May-November. The segment from Taggart Lake Trailhead to Signal Mountain Lodge closes in winter. **Moose-Wilson Road** is a narrow paved and seasonal dirt road that closes in winter.

During July and August, **parking** lots at trailheads pack out. Plan to arrive around 8am to claim a spot.

SHUTTLES

On Jenny Lake, **Jenny Lake Boating** (307/734-9227, www.jennylakeboating.com, daily mid-May-late Sept., 7am-7pm early June-early Sept., shorter hours early and late season, $8-18) runs shuttles from the boat dock near the visitors center across the lake to trailheads.

TOURS

From Jackson Lake Lodge, scenic **bus tours** (Grand Teton Lodging Company, 307/543-2811, www.gtlc.com, 8:30am Mon., Wed., and Fri., late May-early Oct., 4 hrs., $52-92) offer guided narration and travel to the Tetons, Jenny Lake Overlook, the Chapel of the Transfiguration, and Oxbow Bend.

From Colter Bay Marina, **Jackson Lake boat tours** (Grand Teton Lodging Company, 307/543-2811, www.gtlc.com, daily late May-Sept., $20-74) soaks up the lustrous views of Mount Moran on daytime and campfire meal cruises. Reservations are required; hours and times vary.

On Jenny Lake, **Jenny Lake Boating** (South Jenny Lake, 307/734-9227, www.jennylakeboating.com, daily mid-May-late Sept., $15-25) guides one-hour interpretive tours. Reservations by credit card are highly recommended.

The **Teton Science School** (700 Coyote Canyon Rd., Jackson, 307/733-1313, www.tetonscience.org, daily year-round) leads educational wildlife-watching expeditions.

SIGHTS NEARBY

At the southern edge of the park, **Jackson Hole Mountain Resort** (3395 Cody Ln., Teton Village, 307/733-2292 or 888/333-7766, www.jacksonhole.com, daily late May-early Oct. and late Nov.-early Apr.) has summer activities, including an ultrascenic ride to the 10,450-foot (3,185-m) summit of Rendezvous Mountain via their Aerial Tram, and skiing and snowboarding in winter.

WHERE TO STAY IN GRAND TETON

NAME	LOCATION	PRICE	SEASON	AMENITIES
Grassy Lake Road	John D. Rockefeller, Jr. Memorial Parkway	free	June-Sept.	tent sites
Lizard Creek	John D. Rockefeller, Jr. Memorial Parkway	$30	June-Sept.	tent sites
Headwaters Campground & RV	John D. Rockefeller, Jr. Memorial Parkway	$75	June-Sept.	tent and RV sites, camping cabins
Headwaters Lodge & Cabins at Flagg Ranch	John D. Rockefeller, Jr. Memorial Parkway	from $240	June-Sept.	motel rooms, cabins, camper cabins, dining
Colter Bay	Colter Bay	$32	mid-May-Oct.	tent and RV sites
Colter Bay RV Park	Colter Bay	$73-83		RV sites
Colter Bay Tent Village	Colter Bay	from $76	May-Sept.	tent cabins
Colter Bay Cabins	Colter Bay	from $175	May-Oct.	cabins
Jackson Lake Lodge	Jackson Lake	rom $346	May-Oct	hotel rooms, cottages, dining
Signal Mountain	Signal Mountain	$33	May-Oct.	tent sites
Signal Mountain Lodge	Signal Mountain	from $292	May-Oct.	motel rooms, cabins, dining
Jenny Lake	Jenny Lake	$29	May-Sept	tent sites
Jenny Lake Lodge	Jenny Lake	from $776	June-Oct.	cabins, dining
Grand Teton Climber's Ranch	Teton Park Road	$17-27		dorm bunks
Gros Ventre	Moose	$30	May-Oct.	tent and RV sites
Dornan's Spur Ranch Cabins	Moose	from $225	May-Oct., Dec.-Mar.	cabins, dining
Triangle X Ranch	Moose/ Moran	rates vary	May-Oct., Dec.-Mar.	dude ranch

WEBSITE:
www.nps.gov/glac

PHONE NUMBER:
406/888-7800

VISITATION RANK:
10

WHY GO:
See glaciers and wildlife along scenic drives.

▲ GRINNELL LAKE AND ANGEL WING

KEEPSAKE STAMPS ▼▼▼

GLACIER NATIONAL PARK is the crown of the continent. The Blackfeet called these mountains the "Backbone of the World." It's a place where the earth's forces have left their imprints on the landscape with jagged arêtes, red pinnacles, and glacier-carved basins built on some of the oldest rock in North America. It's home to grizzly bears, wolves, mountain goats, wolverines, and bighorn sheep, animals once hunted by the Blackfeet and Kootenai. Amid it all, a handful of glaciers cling to high elevations, struggling to survive in their last decades of life.

The Continental Divide splits Glacier into west and east sides. Slicing through the park's heart, the historic Going-to-the-Sun Road twists and turns on a narrow cliff climb. Tunnels, arches, and bridges lead sightseers over precipices where seemingly no road could go. Glacier preserves one of the nation's most amazing historic and natural landscapes, a place to visit before the warming climate further alters the landscape forever.

PLANNING YOUR TIME

In northwest Montana on the Canadian border, Glacier is a remote location, but popular enough to clog during its short summer season. Make **reservations 13 months in advance** for in-park lodgings and **six months** for camping. Only one route bisects the entire park: Going-to-the-Sun Road. Rush hour on this road is 8am-5pm seven days a week July-August. Plan for an early start, as the Logan Pass parking lot fills by 8:30am.

Summer (June-Sept.) attracts crowds when lodges, campgrounds, and trails are open. Barring deep snows, Going-to-the-Sun Road is open **mid-June-mid-October,** with peak visitation and the best weather in July-August. Snow buries some trails into July.

Although saddled with unpredictable weather, the off-season **fall, winter,** and **spring** offer less hectic visits. Low-elevation trails are usually snow-free, but **minimal commercial services** are **open.** Peak-top snows descend in September. **Going-to-the-Sun Road** is **closed to vehicles** in spring and fall. In winter, snow closes most park roads, which become quiet snowshoeing and cross-country ski trails.

BIGHORN SHEEP

ENTRANCES AND FEES

The entrance fee is $35 vehicle, $30 motorcycle, $20 individual and good for seven days. You can **buy your pass online** (www.yourpassnow.com) from home to speed through entrance stations faster. Glacier National Park is split along the Continental Divide, with several entrances on each side:.

East Entrances

- **Two Medicine** (Two Medicine Rd. off MT 49, open late May-Oct.) leads to Two Medicine Lake on the east side.

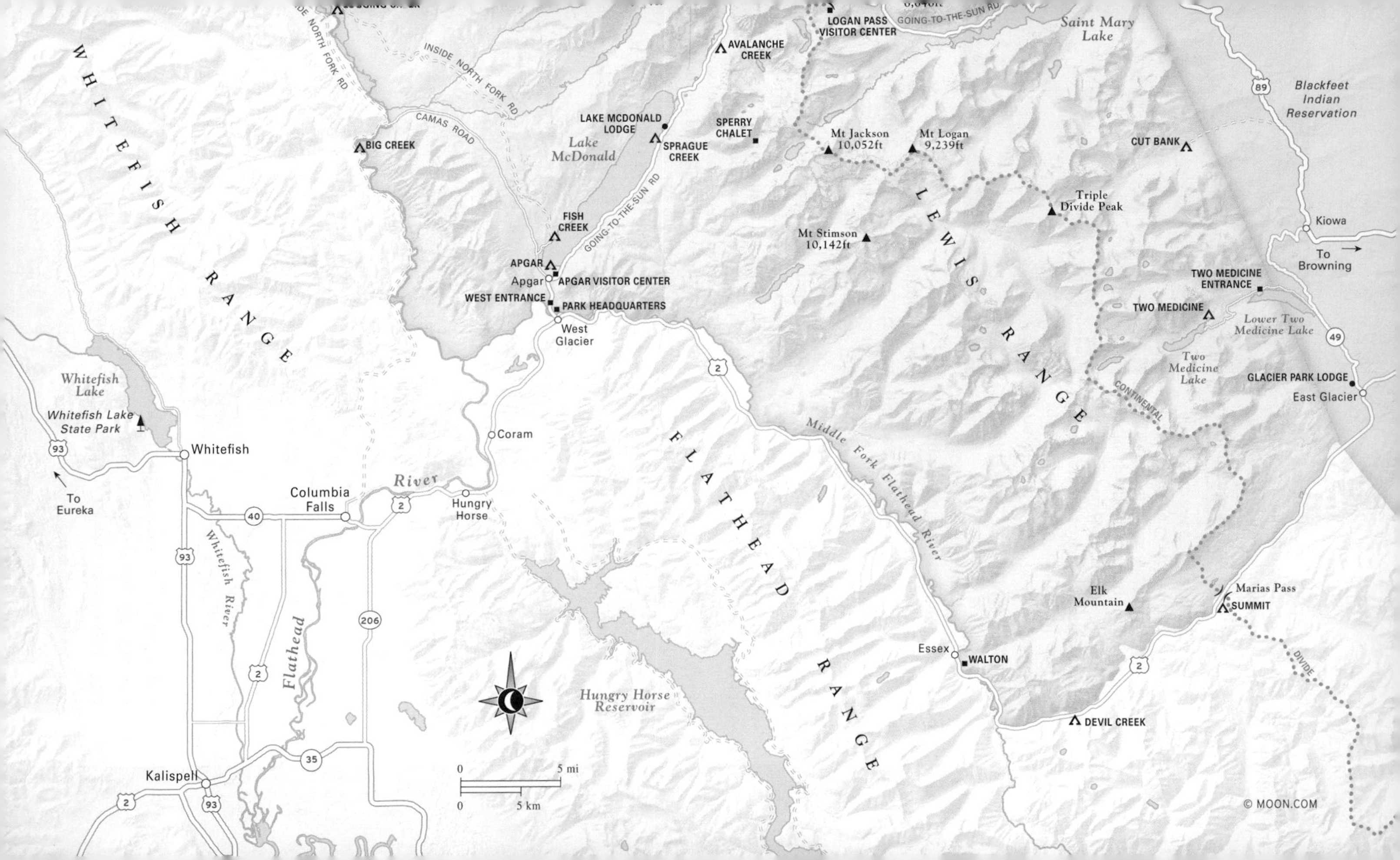
WHITEFISH RANGE
LOGAN PASS VISITOR CENTER
GOING-TO-THE-SUN RD
Saint Mary Lake
INSIDE NORTH FORK RD
AVALANCHE CREEK
CAMAS ROAD
LAKE MCDONALD LODGE
SPERRY CHALET
Mt Jackson 10,052ft
Mt Logan 9,239ft
Blackfeet Indian Reservation
89
CUT BANK
BIG CREEK
Lake McDonald
SPRAGUE CREEK
Triple Divide Peak
LEWIS RANGE
FISH CREEK
Mt Stimson 10,142ft
Kiowa
To Browning
APGAR
Apgar
APGAR VISITOR CENTER
WEST ENTRANCE
PARK HEADQUARTERS
West Glacier
TWO MEDICINE ENTRANCE
TWO MEDICINE
Lower Two Medicine Lake
49
Two Medicine Lake
GLACIER PARK LODGE
East Glacier
CONTINENTAL
DIVIDE
Whitefish Lake
Whitefish Lake State Park
Coram
FLATHEAD RANGE
Middle Fork Flathead River
93
Whitefish
To Eureka
River
Columbia Falls
Hungry Horse
40
Whitefish River
206
Flathead
Hungry Horse Reservoir
Elk Mountain
Marias Pass
SUMMIT
Essex
WALTON
DEVIL CREEK
35
Kalispell
0 5 mi
0 5 km
© MOON.COM

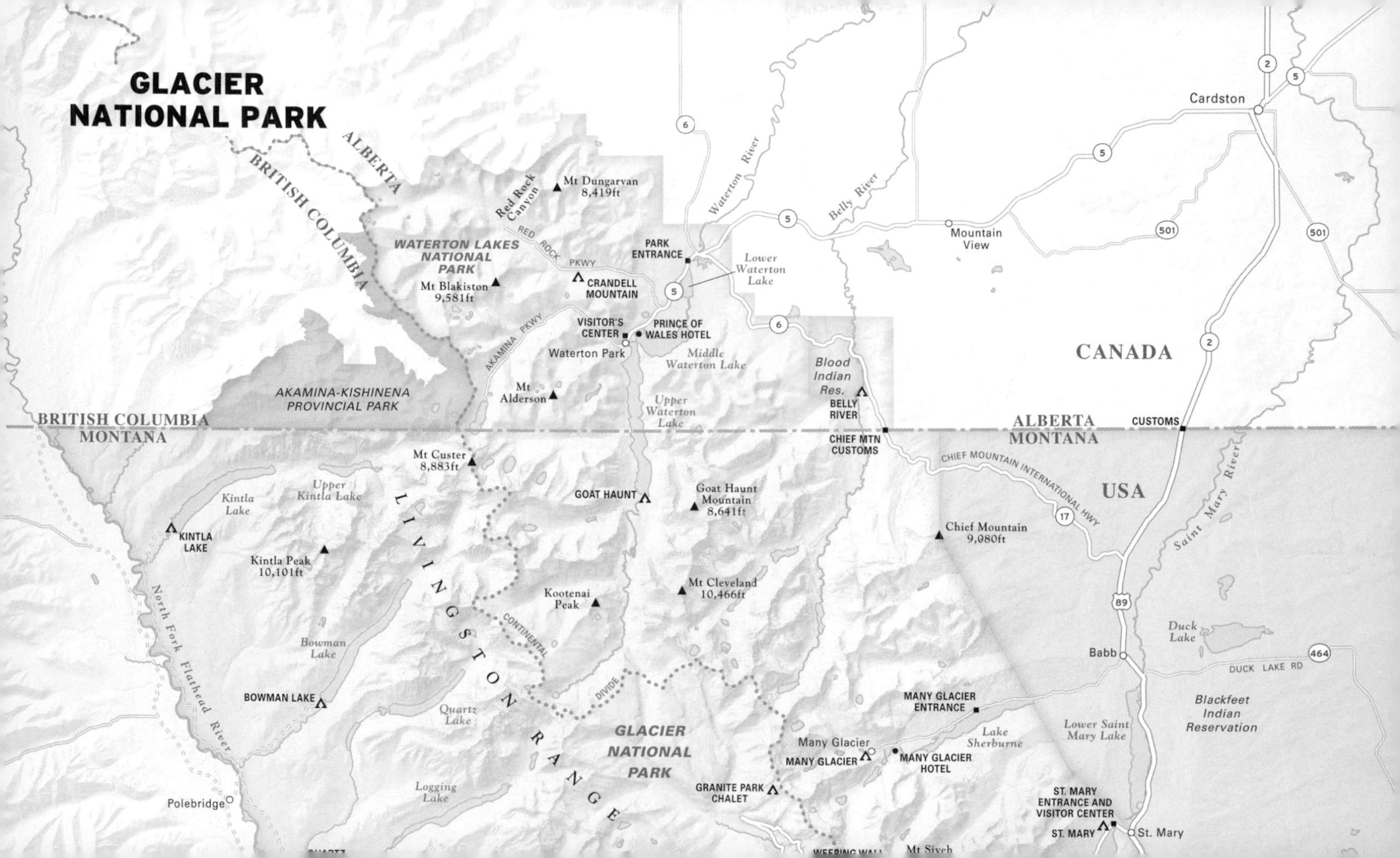
GLACIER NATIONAL PARK
ALBERTA
BRITISH COLUMBIA
Mt Dungarvan 8,419ft
Red Rock Canyon
RED ROCK PKWY
WATERTON LAKES NATIONAL PARK
Mt Blakiston 9,581ft
CRANDELL MOUNTAIN
PARK ENTRANCE
Lower Waterton Lake
Waterton River
Belly River
Mountain View
Cardston
VISITOR'S CENTER
PRINCE OF WALES HOTEL
Waterton Park
AKAMINA PKWY
Middle Waterton Lake
Mt Alderson
AKAMINA-KISHINENA PROVINCIAL PARK
Upper Waterton Lake
Blood Indian Res.
BELLY RIVER
CANADA
BRITISH COLUMBIA
MONTANA
ALBERTA
MONTANA
CUSTOMS
CHIEF MTN CUSTOMS
CHIEF MOUNTAIN INTERNATIONAL HWY
USA
Mt Custer 8,883ft
GOAT HAUNT
Goat Haunt Mountain 8,641ft
Kintla Lake
Upper Kintla Lake
KINTLA LAKE
Kintla Peak 10,101ft
LIVINGSTON RANGE
Chief Mountain 9,080ft
Saint Mary River
Mt Cleveland 10,466ft
Kootenai Peak
CONTINENTAL DIVIDE
North Fork Flathead River
Bowman Lake
BOWMAN LAKE
Quartz Lake
Duck Lake
Babb
DUCK LAKE RD
MANY GLACIER ENTRANCE
Blackfeet Indian Reservation
GLACIER NATIONAL PARK
Lake Sherburne
Lower Saint Mary Lake
Many Glacier
MANY GLACIER
MANY GLACIER HOTEL
Logging Lake
Polebridge
GRANITE PARK CHALET
ST. MARY ENTRANCE AND VISITOR CENTER
ST. MARY
St. Mary
Mt Siyeh

ONE DAY IN GLACIER

Glacier's biggest attraction is the 50-mile (81 km) **Going-to-the-Sun Road.** A tour of the road over Logan Pass yields a small taste of the park's grandeur, with waterfalls, immense glacier-carved valleys, and serrated peaks. Plan to drive the road to **Logan Pass** and hike to **Hidden Lake Overlook, Avalanche Lake,** or **St. Mary Falls.** If you can, squeeze in a **boat tour** on St. Mary Lake.

- **St. Mary** (off US 89, open May-Oct.) is the east portal for Going-to-the-Sun Road.
- **Many Glacier** (on Many Glacier Rd. off US 89, open mid-May-early Nov.) leads to Many Glacier and Swiftcurrent on the east side.
- **Cut Bank** (US 89, open June-Sept.) has a dirt road that leads to Cut Bank Campground and trailheads.

West Entrances

- **West Glacier** (off US 2, open year-round) is the west portal for Going-to-the-Sun Road and Lake McDonald.
- **Polebridge** (Outside North Fork Rd., open late May-Oct.) accesses Bowman and Kintla Lakes.
- **Camas** (Outside North Fork Rd., open mid-May-Oct.) connects to Apgar and West Glacier.

VISITORS CENTERS

Glacier National Park has three small visitors centers with shuttle stops lining Going-to-the-Sun Road. They have maps, information, bookstores, and backcountry desks for permits. Because the park is an International Dark Sky Park, they offer night astronomy programs.

Two ranger stations can also provide trail information and backcountry permits: **Many Glacier Ranger Station** (milepost 12.4, Many Glacier Rd., 406/888-7800, 8am-5pm daily late May-mid-Sept.) and **Two Medicine Ranger Station** (Two Medicine Rd., 406/888-7800, 7am-5pm daily summer).

Apgar Visitor Center

Apgar Visitor Center (406/888-7800, daily mid-May-mid-Oct., Sat.-Sun. spring, fall, and winter) anchors the west entrance of Going-to-the-Sun Road. It has a shuttle stop and large parking lot for leaving your car all day. A five-minute walk goes to the **Apgar Backcountry Permit Office** (Apgar, 406/888-7859 May-Oct., 406/888-7800 Nov.-Apr., 7am-4:30pm daily June-Sept., 8am-4pm daily May

▼ ST. MARY LAKE

Top 3

1 TOUR GOING-TO-THE-SUN ROAD

GOING-TO-THE-SUN ROAD

Going-to-the-Sun Road (mid-June-mid-Oct.) stands in a class by itself. The 50-mile (81 km) historic transmountain highway bisects Glacier's heart, with tight curves that hug cliff walls producing scary, white-knuckle driving. Yet its beauty, diversity, color, flora, fauna, and raw wildness will leave an impression like no other. Although you can drive its length in less than two hours, most visitors take all day, driving over and back for different views. Early mornings and early evenings offer less crowded times for driving. Shuttles stop at lodges, campgrounds, and trailheads; tour buses stop at sights.

2 GAZE AT GLACIERS

Glacier National Park's glaciers are melting rapidly. So where can you see them while they still exist? On Going-to-the-Sun Road, **Jackson Glacier Overlook** offers the best views of Jackson and Blackfoot Glaciers. In Many Glacier, hike to **Grinnell Glacier,** the most accessible glacier. On the jagged wall above the lake perch the tiny **Salamander Glacier** and **Gem Glacier,** both shrunken to static snowfields. From Siyeh Bend on Going-to-the-Sun Road, hike Siyeh Pass Trail to see **Piegan Glacier** while climbing to the pass and **Sexton Glacier** while descending to Sunrift Gorge. A hefty climb to Comeau Pass accesses the scoured basin that cradles **Sperry Glacier.**

SPERRY GLACIER

3 EXPLORE MANY GLACIER

Jagged parapets rim **Many Glacier,** where you can park the car and hike for days. Five valleys loaded with hiking trails and scenic lakes radiate from the core, which holds a campground, picnic area, cabins, and **Many Glacier Hotel,** a National Historic Landmark. Tour the restored hotel and sit on the deck to watch bears and bighorn sheep through binoculars.

An easy walking trail circles **Swiftcurrent Lake,** a mountain-rimmed pool preferred by moose. Paddlers can rent kayaks and rowboats or ride a **tour boat** on Swiftcurrent and Josephine Lakes, which shortens the walk to milky turquoise **Grinnell Lake.** At the end of the day, take in the sunset over the Continental Divide and watch on moonless nights for a sky full of stars and the northern lights.

MANY GLACIER HOTEL, SWIFTCURRENT LAKE, MT. GOULD

and Oct.) is the main office for overnight backpacking. Rush hour is the first 2-3 hours of each morning in July and August; lines begin forming at 6am.

Logan Pass Visitor Center

Logan Pass Visitor Center (406/888-7800, daily mid-June-Sept.) perches at the apex of Going-to-the-Sun Road. It's a seasonal outpost with a few displays. The parking lot crowds by 8:30am, and it has a shuttle stop.

St. Mary Visitor Center

St. Mary Visitor Center (406/888-7800, daily late May-early Oct.), at the East Entrance Station, has the most exhibits, shows films, and offers Native American programs. A night-sky observatory containing a powerful telescope projects live images of celestial objects on large screens in the parking lot.

SIGHTS

NORTH FORK

Outside the park, **Polebridge** is the hub of the remote North Fork—a backwoods place lacking electricity, flush toilets, and cell service. The historic, red-planked **Polebridge Mercantile** (265 Polebridge Loop, 406/888-5105, http://polebridgemerc.com, daily Apr.-Oct.) sells bakery goods. Next door, the tiny log **Northern Lights Saloon** (255 Polebridge Loop, 406/888-9963, 11am-9pm Mon.-Thurs., 11am-10pm Fri.-Sat. late May-mid-Sept.) packs in diners, with extras spilling outside onto picnic tables.

From Polebridge, potholed dirt roads launch bouncing rides into the park to two remote lakes with campgrounds and trails. **Bowman Lake** sits in a narrow, glacier-scoured trough. Secluded **Kintla Lake** tucks deep in the trees. Drop in a canoe, kayak, or paddleboard to tour the quiet shorelines.

LAKE MCDONALD

Catching water from Glacier's longest river, **Lake McDonald** stretches 10 miles (16 km) long, 1.5 miles (2.4 km) wide, and 472 feet (144 m) deep to be the park's largest and deepest lake. Visitors fish, boat, paddle, and swim in its cold blue water. Access the lakeshore via three picnic areas, many pullouts along Going-to-the-Sun Road, or historic **Lake McDonald Lodge,** where scenic **boat tours** launch daily. At the lake's foot, **Apgar** crowds in summer due to its restaurant, camp store, two inns, a boat ramp, swimming beach, paddling and boat rentals, campground, and picnic area.

▼ BOWMAN LAKE

AVOID THE CROWDS

Glacier sees crowds in summer. Parking fills up at Logan Pass and trailheads, a few overcrowded trails see long lines of hikers, and shuttles pack out with riders. So what can you do to have a more enjoyable trip?

Use the Glacier Information Display. Online and visitors centers have the Glacier Information Display that shows current weather at Logan Pass (which can be vastly different from lower elevations) and fill status for parking lots and campgrounds for the day and previous day. Use it to make decisions on crowds.

Visit in June or September. Avoid between July 4 and Labor Day. June still has high-elevation snow, which may preclude access to Logan Pass and some trails; plan for potential limitations pending road plowing and weather. September brings more breathing space with access to Logan Pass. But be ready for schizophrenic weather bouncing between warm temperatures and snow.

Drive Going-to-the-Sun Road early or late. Once open, you can drive Going-to-the-Sun Road 24/7. Catch the sunrise or sunset, and you'll encounter fewer people. Plus, early morning and evening yield better lighting for photography.

Spend the Evening at Logan Pass. Avoid the daytime parking mayhem at Logan Pass; arrive around 5pm to hike Hidden Lake Overlook and back before dusk. Then, hang out in the parking lot after dark to soak up the Milky Way from this location with minimal light pollution.

Hike off the beaten path. Avoid the heavily used trails along the Going-to-the-Sun Road corridor and in Many Glacier. Instead, hike trails in Two Medicine, Cut Bank, or the North Fork.

Camp and stay put. Rather than fighting for a new campsite in a new campground every morning, select a campground to use as home base. Then, drive to other locations as day trips. Make reservations six months ahead for campgrounds at St. Mary, Fish Creek, and Many Glacier.

GOING-TO-THE-SUN ROAD

Rush hour on Going-to-the-Sun Road is 8am-5pm seven days a week July-August; plan for an early start, as the Logan Pass parking lot fills by 8:30am during those months. Early mornings and early evenings offer less crowded times for driving. The shuttle goes to trailheads, and interpretive bus tours stop at sights.

West Side

From Apgar, the Going-to-the-Sun Road cruises along **Lake McDonald**, the largest lake in the park, which has the historic **Lake McDonald Lodge** at its upper end. The road follows **McDonald Creek,** the longest river in the park, with stops to see its tumbling rapids and waterfalls before reaching Avalanche, where the **Trail of the Cedars** runs through a rainforest, the easternmost in the country.

When the road swings north, its path climbs through engineering feats that garnered the road's designation as a National Civil Engineering Landmark. Its **West Tunnel** has two stunning alcoves framing Heavens Peak, and **The Loop** is the only hairpin.

Above the Loop, the road cuts through cliffs with views of the ribbonlike **Bird Woman Falls** and stair-step **Haystack Falls.** The **Weeping Wall** wails profusely in June, enough to douse cars driving the inside lane, but in August, drips slow to a trickle.

After **Big Bend,** drive slowly uphill to see **Triple Arches** (no pullout) at the very narrow S-turns. As the road arcs up the final mile to the pass, a wheelchair-accessible path goes to **Oberlin Bend Overlook,** the best spot for photographing the road's west side and the

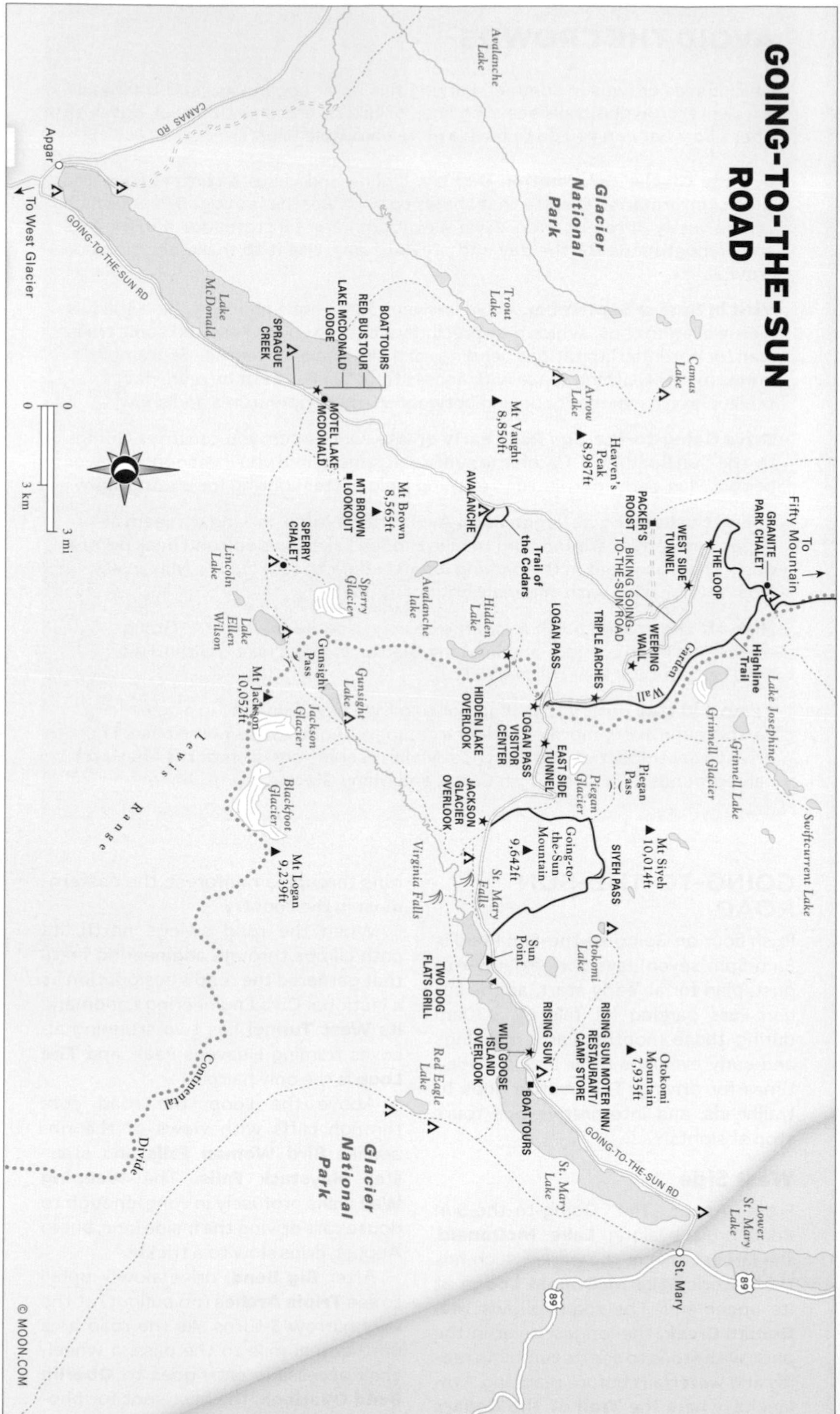
GOING-TO-THE-SUN ROAD
Glacier National Park
Glacier National Park
Apgar
To West Glacier
CAMAS RD
GOING-TO-THE-SUN RD
Avalanche Lake
Trout Lake
Camas Lake
Arrow Lake
Lake McDonald
BOAT TOURS
RED BUS TOUR
LAKE MCDONALD LODGE
SPRAGUE CREEK
MOTEL LAKE MCDONALD
Mt Vaught 8,850ft
Heaven's Peak 8,987ft
Mt Brown 8,565ft
MT BROWN LOOKOUT
AVALANCHE
Trail of the Cedars
PACKER'S ROOST
BIKING GOING-TO-THE-SUN ROAD
To Fifty Mountain
GRANITE PARK CHALET
THE LOOP
WEST SIDE TUNNEL
WEEPING WALL
TRIPLE ARCHES
Highline Trail
Garden Wall
LOGAN PASS
SPERRY CHALET
Sperry Glacier
Avalanche lake
Hidden Lake
Lincoln Lake
Lake Ellen Wilson
Gunsight Pass
Gunsight Lake
Mt Jackson 10,052ft
Jackson Glacier
HIDDEN LAKE OVERLOOK
LOGAN PASS VISITOR CENTER
EAST SIDE TUNNEL
Lake Josephine
Grinnell Glacier
Grinnell Lake
Swiftcurrent Lake
Piegan Pass
Piegan Glacier
Mt Siyeh 10,014ft
SIYEH PASS
Going-to-the-Sun Mountain 9,642ft
JACKSON GLACIER OVERLOOK
Blackfoot Glacier
Mt Logan 9,239ft
Lewis Range
Virginia Falls
St. Mary Falls
Sun Point
Otokomi Lake
TWO DOG FLATS GRILL
RISING SUN
RISING SUN MOTER INN/ RESTAURANT/ CAMP STORE
Otokomi Mountain 7,935ft
WILD GOOSE ISLAND OVERLOOK
BOAT TOURS
Red Eagle Lake
Continental Divide
St. Mary Lake
GOING-TO-THE-SUN RD
Lower St. Mary Lake
St. Mary
89
89
0 3 mi
0 3 km
© MOON.COM

HAYSTACK FALLS

knifelike **Garden Wall** on the Continental Divide.

Logan Pass

Sitting atop the Continental Divide at 6,646 feet (2,026 m), **Logan Pass** rules an alpine wonderland of wildflower meadows, snowfields, and mountain goats. In June, high walls of snow rim the parking lot; July brings on wildflowers, and late summer turns meadows golden. Explore the small **visitors center** and scan surrounding slopes for goats, bighorn sheep, and bears. A boardwalk trail climbs to **Hidden Lake Overlook.**

The parking lot packs out 8:30am-5pm. If the lot is full, you may need to drive to other sights and return at a later time. Moonless nighttime visits to the pass yield ultraclear skies full of stars.

East Side

From Logan Pass, the road drops by the cascades of **Lunch Creek,** a good place to sit on the rock wall to look up at **Piegan Mountain.** Below, the **East Side Tunnel,** dug out entirely by hand, pops with a downhill view of **Going-to-the-Sun Mountain.**

After **Siyeh Bend,** the route drops into the trees for a peekaboo look through binoculars at **Jackson Glacier** 6 miles (9.7 km) away.

Along **St. Mary Lake,** a short uphill stroll goes to **Sunrift Gorge,** a narrow canyon cut by Baring Creek. **Sun Point** (5 min. walk) marks the site of the park's Going-to-the-Sun Chalets atop the rock promontory jutting into the lake. Midway down the lake, the road arrives at one of the most photographed spots, where sharp peaks dwarf tiny **Wild Goose Island.**

Around a bluff, **Rising Sun** has visitor services, including a boat tour, while **Two Dog Flats** lures elk, coyotes, and bears to grassland meadows bordered by aspen groves. The Going-to-the-Sun Road terminates in the town of **St. Mary.**

ST. MARY

Turquoise **St. Mary Lake,** at nearly 10 miles (16 km) long the second-largest lake in the park, flanks the east side of Going-to-the-Sun Road. Often windy, peaks pinch its upper end, while the small seasonal town of **St. Mary** anchors its east end with visitor services. Midway, **Rising Sun** has a campground, motel, picnic area, boat launch, and scenic **boat tours.** To overlook the lake, hike from **Sun Point to Baring Falls** (1.6 mi./2.6 km rt., 1 hr., easy).

TWO MEDICINE

Two Medicine Lake is the highest road-accessible lake in Glacier at

MOUNTAIN GOAT

almost 1 mile high (1.6 km). Peaks rich in Blackfeet history flank the lake. En route, a trail goes to **Running Eagle Falls** (0.6 mi./1 km rt., 20 min., easy), where part of the falls runs underground and spits out through a cavern halfway down the cliff face. At the lake, jump on the historic **Sinopah tour boat** or rent a kayak or small motorboat to go fishing. The National Historic Landmark dining hall now operates as the **Two Medicine Campstore**. Two Medicine has trails to lakes, passes, and scenic overlooks.

RUNNING EAGLE FALLS

WATERTON LAKES NATIONAL PARK

Bordering Glacier in Canada, Waterton Lakes National Park serves as the entrance to Glacier's remote north country. Together, the two national parks are the world's first International Peace Park and International Dark Sky Park. They are also a Biosphere Reserve and World Heritage Site. In summer 2017, the Kenow Fire burned 47,700 acres (19,394 ha) of the park, which included many trails, a campground, backcountry campsites, picnic areas, and roads, but not Waterton Townsite, which houses motels, restaurants, a campground, boat tours, and visitor services.

The **Waterton Lakes Visitor Information Centre** (403/859-5133, www.pc.gc.ca) provides information, maps, permits, and licenses. The entrance gate is open 24/7 year-round (staffed early May-early Oct.). To enter, purchase a **Parks Canada day pass** (C$7-20, May-Oct.).

Sights and Activities

Chief Mountain International Highway: This two-nation scenic road circles Chief Mountain, sacred to the Blackfeet, and crosses through Glacier and Waterton.

Boat Tour: Hop aboard the historic *MV International* for a ride on the deepest lake in the Canadian Rockies. You'll float across the international boundary to Goat Haunt, USA, in Glacier.

Goat Haunt, USA: Accessible only by boat or on foot, Goat Haunt is a launchpad onto Glacier's remote northern trails.

Prince of Wales Hotel: This 1927 hotel maintains British ambience thanks to kilt-wearing bellhops and afternoon high tea.

Bison Paddock: In a tribute to the great wild herds that once roamed the prairies, Parks Canada maintains a small herd of bison.

Crypt Lake: A boat ride leads to the trailhead, where switchbacks ascend to what looks like impassable cliffs. A hidden tunnel curls into a hanging valley holding an alpine lake cowering below peaks in Glacier.

Getting There

North of Babb, Montana, **Chief Mountain International Highway** (30 mi./48 km) connects Glacier with Waterton. Its season and hours are linked to the Canadian and U.S. immigration and customs stations at the border (open daily mid-May-Sept., 7am-10pm June-Labor Day, 9am-6pm May and Sept.). At the north terminus, turn west onto Highway 5 and south into Waterton.

TRAIL OF THE CEDARS

HIKING

Ranger-led hikes go to multiple destinations; check at visitors centers or online for schedules. **Glacier Guides** (11970 US 2 E., West Glacier, 406/387-5555, www.glacierguides.com, mid-May-Sept.) leads day hikes and backpacking trips.

GOING-TO-THE-SUN ROAD

Sperry Chalet and Sperry Glacier

From the trailhead at Lake McDonald Lodge, the **Sperry Trail** (12.4 mi./20 km rt., 6-7 hrs., strenuous) climbs to historic **Sperry Chalet** (Belton Chalets, 406/387-5654 or 888/345-2649, www.sperrychalet.com, July-early Sept.) for lodgings and meals. Make reservations in early January; they go fast. With an overnight stay, you can add on the trail up to **Sperry Glacier** (6.6 mi./10.6 km rt., 4 hrs., strenuous).

Trail of the Cedars and Avalanche Lake

Adjacent to Avalanche Campground, a boardwalk loops through a lush rainforest of cedars, hemlocks, and cottonwoods on the **Trail of the Cedars** (0.7 mi./1.1 km rt., 30 min., easy). Departing from the loop's southeast end, the trail to **Avalanche Lake** (4.6 mi./7.4 km rt., 2.5 hrs., moderate) turns uphill along Avalanche Gorge before climbing steadily through woods littered with glacial erratics into a cliff-rimmed cirque with waterfalls.

Hidden Lake Overlook

From Logan Pass, the trail to **Hidden Lake Overlook** (2.7 mi./4.3 km rt., 1.5 hrs., moderate) climbs a boardwalk through alpine meadows with mountain goats and bighorn sheep. Then the path cuts around a moraine top out on the Continental Divide overlooking blue Hidden Lake.

HIDDEN LAKE OVERLOOK TRAIL

Best Hike

HIGHLINE TRAIL AND GRANITE PARK CHALET

DISTANCE: 11.4 miles (18.3 km) point-to-point
DURATION: 5-6 hours
ELEVATION CHANGE: 1,300 feet (396 m) up; 3,700 feet (1,128 m) down
EFFORT: strenuous
TRAILHEADS: Logan Pass and the Loop

Beginning at **Logan Pass,** this point-to-point walk along the **Highline Trail** (mid-July-mid-Oct.) tiptoes along the Continental Divide to historic **Granite Park Chalet** before dropping to the **Loop.** Wildflowers peak mid-July-early August.

The trail starts with a cliff walk above the Going-to-the-Sun Road before crossing a flowering land that gave the Garden Wall arête its name. At 3 miles (4.8 km), more than half the total elevation gain is packed into one climb interrupted with a break at the saddle below Haystack Butte. After the high point, the trail drops and swings through several large bowls before passing Bear Valley to reach Granite Park Chalet atop a knoll at 6,680 feet (2,036 m).

At the rustic stone-and-log **Granite Park Chalet,** hikers cuddle up to the fire on cold days or picnic outside to take in the panoramic view. Overnighting at the chalet (Belton Chalets, 406/387-5654 or 888/345-2649, www.graniteparkchalet.com, July-early Sept.) requires reservations. **Online bookings for the upcoming summer go fast, starting in early January.**

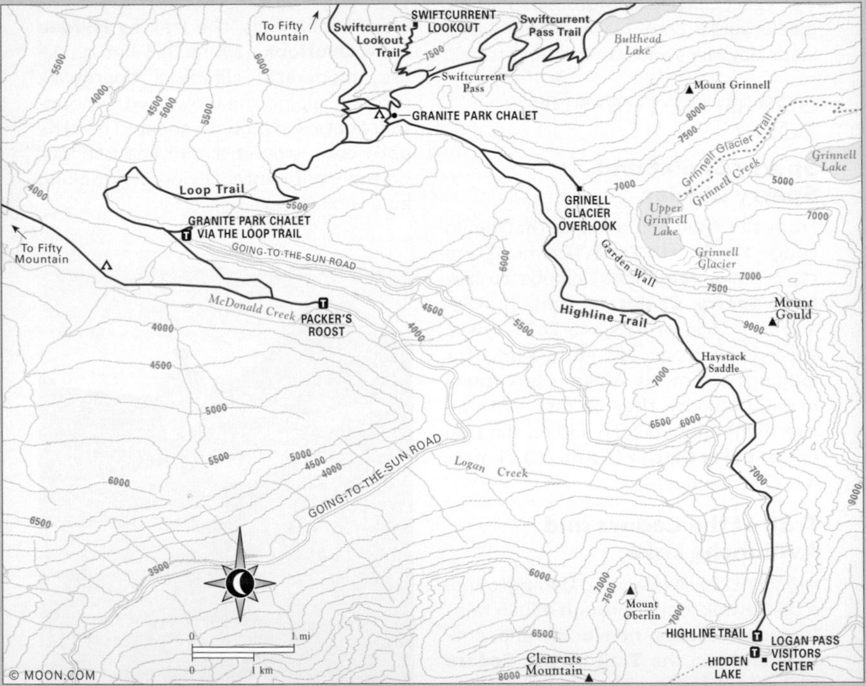

HEAVENS PEAK FROM THE HIGHLINE TRAIL

Piegan and Siyeh Passes

From Siyeh Bend on Going-to-the-Sun Road, a trail climbs to the wildflower meadows of **Preston Park,** where a junction separates into two trails. Go left for **Piegan Pass** (9 mi./14.5 km rt., 4-5 hrs., moderate); the route swings around a basin to the pass and returns on the same trail. Go right for **Siyeh Pass** (10 mi./16.1 km one-way, 6 hrs., strenuous) to switchback up to the pass and down Baring Creek to Sunrift Gorge. Use the shuttle to return to your vehicle.

St. Mary and Virginia Falls

The trail to **St. Mary Falls** (1.6 mi./2.6 km rt., 1 hr., easy) and **Virginia Falls** (3.2 mi./5.2 km rt., 2 hrs., moderate) sees a constant stream of people. The west trailhead descends from the shuttle stop while the east trailhead launches from the vehicle parking lot with both trails connecting onto the main trail. At St. Mary Falls, a wooden bridge crosses blue-green pools. Then, the trail switchbacks up to Virginia Falls, a broad waterfall spewing mist.

MANY GLACIER

Grinnell Lake and Grinnell Glacier

From Swiftcurrent Picnic Area or Many Glacier Hotel, circle Swiftcurrent Lake to reach Josephine Lake and walk the trail along the lake's north shore to signed junctions on the west end. Taking the boat shuttle (fee) to the west end of Josephine Lake shortens both routes. For **Grinnell Lake** (2.2 mi./3.5

GRINNELL GLACIER

ICEBERG LAKE

km rt., 1.5 hrs. plus boat shuttle; full trail 7.4 mi./11.9 km rt., 4 hrs., easy), head west from Josephine to cross a river on a swinging bridge to reach the turquoise lake backed by a large waterfall. For **Grinnell Glacier** (7.8 mi./12.6 km, 4 hrs. plus boat shuttle; full trail 10.6 mi./17.1 km rt., 6 hrs., strenuous), climb uphill from Josephine's northwest inlet through wildflowers, waterfalls, cliffs, and moraine to reach the shrinking glacier with a large lake at its snout.

Iceberg Lake and Ptarmigan Tunnel

From behind Swiftcurrent Motel, the trail to **Iceberg Lake** (9.6 mi./15.4 km rt., 5 hrs., moderate) shoots up a short, steep jaunt, then maintains an easy railroad grade to the lake that retains icebergs until late summer. At the signed junction after Ptarmigan Falls, a turnoff for the **Ptarmigan Tunnel Trail** (10.6 mi./17.1 km rt., 6 hrs., strenuous) ascends above tree line passing Ptarmigan Lake and switchbacking up to the historic tunnel.

TWO MEDICINE

Scenic Point

From Two Medicine Road, **Scenic Point** (7.8 mi./12.6 km rt., 4-5 hrs., strenuous) is a short climb up switchbacks with big

▼ SCENIC POINT OVERLOOKING TWO MEDICINE LAKE

GUNSIGHT PASS

scenery. Above tree line, the trail traverses a talus slope before descending to Scenic Point and views of the plains.

Twin Falls and Upper Two Medicine Lake

Hop the tour boat (fee) to hike to **Twin Falls** (2 mi./3.2 km rt., 1 hr., easy), a double waterfall. Continuing farther climbs to **Upper Two Medicine Lake** (4.6 mi./7.4 km rt., 3 hrs., moderate), a subalpine lake tucked below Lone Walker Peak.

RECREATION

BACKPACKING

Glacier National Park's backpacking is unrivaled, with miles of well-marked scenic trails. Sixty-six designated backcountry campgrounds spread campers out to avoid crowds, and **permits** ($7 pp per night) guarantee solitude. Pick up permits 24 hours in advance at Apgar Backcountry Office or other permit locations; submit advance reservations online starting March 15 ($40). Go for popular trails such as **Gunsight Pass** (28 mi./45.1 km, including Sperry Glacier), or head for something remote like **Boulder Pass** (33 mi./53.1 km). Bring rope for hanging food.

BIKING

Going-to-the-Sun Road is an unforgettable bicycle trip. While the 3,500-foot (1,067-m) climb up the west side seems intimidating, it's not steep . . . just a constant uphill grind amid stunning scenery. Cycling begins in early April as snowplows free the pavement. Without cars on the road, riders climb as far as plowing permits. By May, free bicycle-carrying shuttles run from Lake McDonald Lodge to Avalanche. After the road opens to cars, cyclists may continue to ride, but due to heavy traffic, the west side closes to bikes 11am-4pm.

GOING-TO-THE-SUN ROAD

TWO MEDICINE LAKE

BOATING

Glacier's lakes provide stunning backdrops, but the threat to the pristine lakes posed by invasive species has forced the park to adopt stringent boating guidelines. Check with the park on current regulations.

On the west side, paddlers can ply the waters of **Lake McDonald, Bowman Lake,** and **Kintla Lake.** On the east side, **Two Medicine Lake, St. Mary Lake,** and **Swiftcurrent Lake** also attract paddlers. All have boat launches. Lake McDonald also permits launching from pullouts along Going-to-the-Sun Road. Use caution on St. Mary Lake, as winds there kick up fast.

Glacier Park Boat Company (406/257-2426, www.glacierparkboats.com, daily mid-June-mid-Sept.) rents canoes, kayaks, small motorboats, and rowboats at Apgar, Lake McDonald Lodge, Many Glacier, and Two Medicine. **North Fork Recreation** (80 Beaver Dr., Polebridge, 406/888-9853, http://northforkrecmt.com) rents paddleboards, kayaks, and canoes for Bowman and Kintla.

FISHING

Glacier is a trout fishery. To fish the large lakes like **Lake McDonald** and **Two Medicine Lake,** anglers have more success tossing in a line from a boat rather than fishing from shore. **Many Glacier Valley** has lots of fishing holes: Grinnell, Josephine, Swiftcurrent, Red Rock, and Bullhead Lakes support trout populations.

Pick up free fishing permits and regulations at visitors centers or ranger stations. Rent fishing gear at **Glacier Outfitters** (196 Apgar Loop Rd., Apgar, 406/219-7466, www.goglacieroutfitters.com, 8am-8pm daily mid-May-late Sept., shorter hours in shoulder seasons).

RAFTING

Glacier has two boundary rivers for rafting—the Wild and Scenic **Middle Fork** and **North Fork of the Flathead River.** The rafting season runs May-September, with water levels usually peaking in late May. By late August, both rivers are at their lowest levels.

West Glacier houses four rafting companies that offer scenic floats and white-water thrills. Contact **Glacier Raft Company** (106 Going-to-the-Sun Rd., 406/888-5454 or 800/235-6781, www.glacierraftco.com), **Great Northern Whitewater** (12127 US 2 E., 406/387-5340 or 800/735-7897, www.greatnorthernresort.com), **Montana Raft Company** (11970 US 2 E., 406/387-5555 or 800/521-7238, www.glacierguides.com), or **Wild River**

LAKE MCDONALD

Adventures (11900 US 2 E., 406/387-9453 or 800/700-7056, www.riverwild.com).

Glacier Outdoor Center (406/888-5454 or 800/235-6781, www.glacierraftco.com) offers vehicle shuttle services and rents rafts and inflatable kayaks.

WHERE TO STAY

INSIDE THE PARK

Advance **reservations** for all in-park lodgings are imperative, especially July-August. Book **13 months in advance** (Xanterra, 855/733-4522, www.glaciernationalparklodges.com) for Many Glacier Hotel, Lake McDonald Lodge, Rising Sun Motor Inn, Swiftcurrent Motor Inn, and Village Inn Motel.

For Apgar Village Lodge and Motel Lake McDonald, make **reservations** (Pursuit Glacier Park Collection, 844/868-7474, www.glacierparkcollection.com) **one year in advance.**

Lake McDonald

In Apgar, **Apgar Village Lodge** (33 Apgar Loop Rd., late May-late Sept., from $150) clusters small motel rooms and rustic cabins within a few steps of Lake McDonald. On Lake McDonald's beach, every one of the 36 guest rooms in the **Village Inn Motel** (62 Apgar Loop Rd., late May-mid-Sept., from $179) wakes up to an unobstructed million-dollar view.

Near the upper end of Lake McDonald, historic **Lake McDonald Lodge** (288 Lake McDonald Lodge Loop, late May-late Sept., from $115) has four types of accommodations: main lodge rooms, cabin rooms, suites, and budget rooms with shared bathrooms. **Russell's Fireside Dining Room** (6:30am-10am, 11:30am-2pm, and 5pm-9:30pm daily) serves breakfast, lunch, and dinner with no reservations. The cozy **Lucke's Lounge** (11:30am-10pm daily) has a limited menu. **Jammer Joe's Grill and Pizzeria** (11am-9pm daily) serves cafeteria style.

In the Lake McDonald Lodge complex, **Motel Lake McDonald** (3 Lake McDonald Lodge Loop, mid-June-mid-Sept., from $165) is an old 1950s-style two-story motel.

St. Mary Lake

On the east side of Going-to-the-Sun Road, **Rising Sun Motor Inn** (2 Going-to-the-Sun Rd., mid-June-mid-Sept., from $175) has cabin rooms and motel units, the **Two Dog Flats Grill** (6:30am-10pm daily), and a store.

Many Glacier

On Swiftcurrent Lake, **Many Glacier Hotel** (milepost 11.5, Many Glacier Rd.,

NAME	LOCATION	PRICE	SEASON	AMENITIES
Apgar	Apgar	$20	Apr.-Oct.	tent and RV sites
Fish Creek	Apgar	$23	June-Sept.	tent and RV sites
Apgar Village Lodge	Apgar	from $150	May-Sept.	motel rooms, cabins
Village Inn Motel	Apgar	from $179	May-Sept.	motel rooms
Logging Creek	North Fork	$10	July-Sept.	tent sites
Quartz Creek	North Fork	$10	July-Nov.	tent sites
Bowman Lake	North Fork	$15	May-Sept.	tent sites
Kintla Lake	North Fork	$15	June-Sept.	tent sites
Avalanche Campground	Going-to-the-Sun Road	$20	June-Sept.	tent and RV sites
Rising Sun	Going-to-the-Sun Road	$20	May-Sept.	tent and RV sites
Sprague Creek	Going-to-the-Sun Road	$20	May-Sept.	tent and RV sites
Lake McDonald Lodge	Going-to-the-Sun Road	from $115	May-Sept.	hostel, lodge, cottage rooms, dining
Motel Lake McDonald	Going-to-the-Sun Road	from $165	June-Sept.	motel rooms
Rising Sun Motor Inn	Going-to-the-Sun Road	from $175	June-Sept.	cabins, motel rooms, dining
Granite Park Chalet	Going-to-the-Sun Road	$82-115 pp	July-Sept.	backcountry hostel
St. Mary	St. Mary	$23	May-Sept.	tent and RV sites
Many Glacier	Many Glacier	$23	May-Sept.	tent and RV sites
Swiftcurrent Motor Inn	Many Glacier	from $115	June-Sept.	cabins, motel rooms, dining
Many Glacier Hotel	Many Glacier	from $211	June-Sept.	hotel rooms, dining
Cut Bank	Two Medicine	$10	June-Sept.	tent and RV sites
Two Medicine	Two Medicine	$20	May-Sept.	tent and RV sites

mid-June-mid-Sept., from $211) is the largest and most popular of the park's historic lodges. Rooms and suites facing the lake have outstanding views. **Ptarmigan Dining Room** (6:30am-10am, 11:30am-2:30pm, and 5pm-9:30pm daily) serves breakfast, lunch, and dinner. The adjacent **Swiss Lounge** (11:30am-10pm daily) offers small bites.

At Many Glacier Road's terminus, **Swiftcurrent Motor Inn** (2 Many Glacier Rd., mid-June-mid-Sept., from $115) has cabins with or without bathrooms and motel rooms. **Nell's at Swiftcurrent Restaurant** (6:30am-10pm daily) crowds at mealtimes.

Camping

Most of Glacier's 13 campgrounds are first come, first served. **Make reservations six months in advance** (877/444-6777, www.recreation.gov) for Fish Creek, St. Mary, and Many Glacier.

Apgar (194 sites, Apgar Loop Rd., Apr.-Nov., $20), **Fish Creek** (178 sites, Fish Creek Rd., June-early Sept., $23), and **Sprague Creek** (25 sites, Going-to-the-Sun Rd., mid-May-mid-Sept., $20) flank Lake McDonald. **Avalanche** (87 sites, Going-to-the-Sun Rd., mid-June-early Sept., $20) is the closest west-side campground to Logan Pass.

Near St. Mary Lake, **Rising Sun** (84 sites, Going-to-the-Sun Rd., late May-mid-Sept., $20) and **St. Mary** (148 sites, Going-to-the-Sun Rd., mid-May-mid-Sept., $23) anchor the east side.

On the park's east side, three separate entrance roads terminate at **Two Medicine** (100 sites, late May-late Sept., $20), **Cut Bank** (off MT 49 and US 89, 14 sites, early June-early Sept., $10), and the coveted **Many Glacier** (109 sites, Many Glacier Rd., late May-mid-Sept., $23).

In the remote North Fork Valley, small campgrounds are accessible only via rough dirt roads: **Kintla Lake** (13 sites, June-mid-Sept., $15), **Bowman Lake** (late May-early Sept., $15), **Quartz Creek** (7 sites, July-Nov., $10), and **Logging Creek** (7 sites, July-Sept., $10).

OUTSIDE THE PARK

On the west side of Glacier, lodgings, camping, and services are in **West Glacier, Coram, Hungry Horse,** and the **Flathead Valley** (Columbia Falls, Whitefish, Kalispell). On the east side, **St. Mary** and **East Glacier** have visitor services.

BLACK BEAR CUB

GETTING THERE

AIR

The closest airport to Glacier National Park is **Glacier Park International Airport** (FCA, www.iflyglacier.com). Some routes are open winter or summer only. It's a short drive of 30 minutes via US 2. Many travelers go directly into the park when they arrive. The airport has car rentals.

TRAIN

Amtrak's daily **Empire Builder** (800/872-7245, www.amtrak.com) stops at several park perimeter locations: East Glacier, Essex, and West Glacier. High summer travel volumes make reservations imperative, and riders may need to contend with delays.

CAR

From I-90 west of Missoula, Montana, take exit 96 onto US 93 North, which leads to West Entrance of the park (145 mi./233 km, 3 hrs.).

GETTING AROUND

DRIVING

Driving in Glacier National Park is not easy. Narrow roads built for cars in the 1930s barely fit today's SUVs, much less RVs and trailers. With no shoulders and sharp curves, roads require reduced speeds and shifting into second gear on extended descents to avoid burning brakes.

Two roads cross the Continental Divide: **Going-to-the-Sun Road** (mid-June-mid-Oct., no RVs over 21 ft/6.4 m) bisects the park, while **US 2** (open year-round) hugs Glacier's southern border. Both are two-lane roads. The Going-to-the-Sun Road is the more difficult drive, climbing 1,500 feet (457 m) higher on a skinnier, snakier road than US 2.

BUS SHUTTLES

The **Going-to-the-Sun Road shuttles** (7am-7pm July-Labor Day, free) stop between Apgar and St. Mary, including Logan Pass, lodges, campgrounds,

THE EXTINCTION OF GLACIERS

Glaciers are moving ice. As snow piles on a glacier's upper end, it compresses into ice that moves. In order to have the mass to move, a glacier must be 100 feet (30 m) deep and 25 acres (10 ha) large. Glacier's small glaciers move only inches per year, and scientists from the U.S. Geological Survey (USGS) estimate many will cease moving in the next couple decades. They monitor the glaciers as climate barometers, using surface measurements, aerial photography, and repeat photography. Follow the ongoing study of these glaciers at www.usgs.gov.

How Many Glaciers Remain?

Around two dozen glaciers remain, relics from a mini ice age that peaked around 1850 with more than 150 glaciers. Since then, the glaciers have thinned, split in two, shrunk, broken into pieces, formed lakes which sped up melting, or melted entirely.

Why Are the Glaciers Melting?

The park's higher elevations have warmed at three times the rate of the overall planet. Average temperatures now run 2°F (1°C) hotter than they did in the mid-1900s, and the park now sees 30 fewer days with below-freezing temperatures. Warmer summers and less snow have triggered rapid melting.

What Will Happen When the Glaciers Melt?

Forest elevations are already growing higher, taking over alpine meadows. Animals and birds, especially those on the fringes of their habitat, may seek food elsewhere. Water, now seemingly so abundant, may not shed from the mountains in sustained runoff from glaciers or at temperatures kept cool by the ice, affecting cold-loving trout, salmon runs, and irrigation.

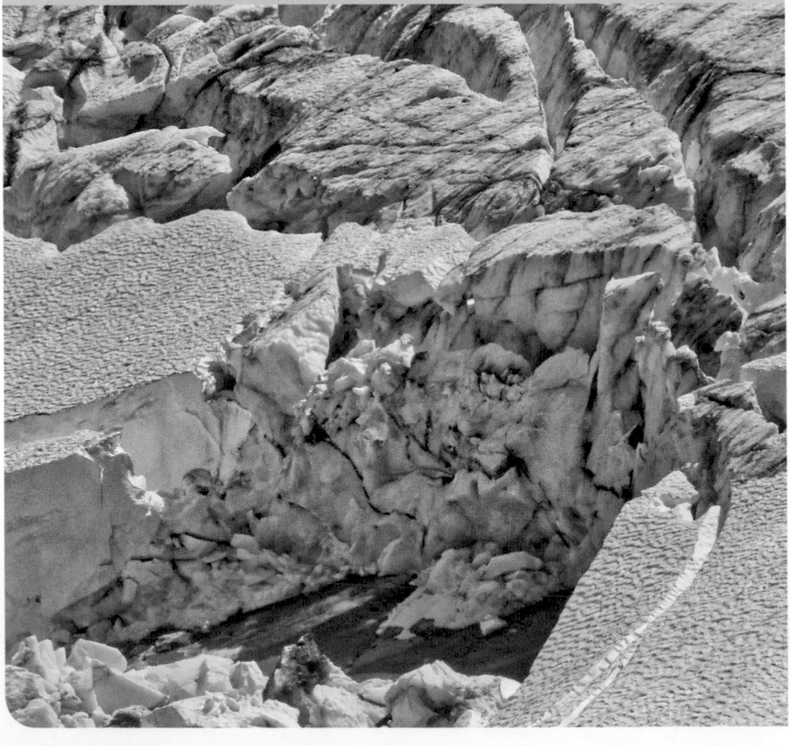

HISTORIC RED BUS ON GOING-TO-THE-SUN ROAD

and trailheads. They depart every 15-30 minutes from signed shuttle stops.

Xanterra (855/733-4522, www.glaciernationalparklodges.com, July-Labor Day) operates shuttles from Many Glacier to St. Mary.

BUS TOURS

Departing from all park lodges for Going-to-the-Sun Road, historic **red jammer buses** with rollback canvas tops are operated by **Xanterra** (855/733-4522, www.glaciernationalparklodges.com, east tours daily late June-Sept., west tours daily mid-May-Oct.).

Launching from East Glacier, St. Mary, and West Glacier, **Sun Tours** (406/732-9220 or 800/786-9220, www.glaciersuntours.com, daily mid-June-mid-Sept.) leads four- and seven-hour tours over Going-to-the-Sun Road with Blackfeet cultural history emphasis.

BOAT TOURS

Glacier Park Boat Company (406/257-2426, www.glacierparkboats.com) runs tours from four locations on historic wooden boats. Buy tickets at the boat docks or make advance reservations by phone, especially for July-August. Tours depart from **Lake McDonald Lodge** (late May-late Sept), **Rising Sun** (mid-June-early Sept.) on St. Mary Lake, **Two Medicine Lake** (early June-mid-Sept.), and **Many Glacier Hotel** (mid-June-mid-Sept.) for a two-boat tour on Swiftcurrent Lake and Josephine Lake.

◄ JACKSON GLACIER

BOAT TOURS

▲ BADLANDS PEAKS

BADLANDS NATIONAL PARK

South Dakota

WEBSITE:
www.nps.gov/badl

PHONE NUMBER:
605/433-5361

VISITATION RANK:
27

WHY GO:
Experience the prairie badlands.

KEEPSAKE STAMPS ▼▼▼

THE BADLANDS are an eerie place. In daylight, the twisted spires and pinnacles look gray and faded, but at dawn or dusk, pale yellow, deep burgundy, and light pinks emerge. A visit to here is like a visit to another planet, one that is starkly forbidding and strikingly beautiful.

Part of its geology includes an ancient seabed containing where the Lakota people first discovered fossils of marine reptiles, turtle shells, fish bones, and seashells. More recent layers buried early mammals, including horses, camels, and birds. Today, Badlands is a wildlife wonderland, filled with everything from the rare black-footed ferret to bison.

PLANNING YOUR TIME

Once you get to South Dakota, Badlands is an easy park to access, due to its location just south of I-90. Because of their close proximity, many visitors combine Badlands with a visit to Wind Cave National Park two hours the west. If you are not staying overnight, try to spend at least **3-4 hours** in the park. Overnight visitors, especially photographers, should plan to catch a **sunset** or **sunrise** due to the impressive lighting on the craggy peaks.

While **May-September** is high season, **April-June** is the best time to visit. The grasses are still a luscious green early in the year and the daytime temperatures are mild. June is the wettest month. July and August have very hot days, sometime in triple digits. Occasional storms bring lightning, hail, or even tornadoes. By fall, brown grasses remove color from the view, but the spires, buttes, and tables of the area are no less beautiful. While the park is open year-round, winter is less hospitable with strong winds and cold temperatures below freezing. While December and January see the least amount of precipitation, intermittent snow that can temporarily close roads and trails.

ENTRANCES AND FEES

Badlands National Park is divided into two units. The **North Unit** is an easy day trip from Rapid City and has three year-round entrances: **Pinnacles Entrance** (SD 240, south of Wall), **Interior Entrance** (SD 44/377, north of Interior), and **Northeast Entrance** (SD 240, south of I-90). The remoter **South Unit,** or the Stronghold District, has one road and no hiking trails.

The entrance fee is $30 per vehicle ($25 motorcycle, $15 individual) and good for seven days.

VISITORS CENTERS

The **Ben Reifel Visitor Center** (25216 Ben Reifel Rd., SD 240, 605/433-5361, 8am-5pm daily mid-Apr.-May and Sept.-late Oct., 7am-7pm daily June-mid-Aug., 8am-4pm daily Nov.-mid-Apr.) is at Park Headquarters on the south edge of the Badlands Loop Road. Paleontologists are on-site June-August working to uncover additional fossils. Visitors can tour the **Fossil Prep Lab** (9am-4:30pm daily late May-mid-Sept.), which is used to prepare fossils for display.

At the South Unit, the remote **White River Visitor Center** (SD 27, Porcupine, 605/455-2878, 9am-5pm daily June-Aug.) is 20 miles (32 km) south of the town of Scenic, off Bombing Range Road (SD 27) on the Pine Ridge Reservation. The visitors center serves those visiting Pine Ridge or backcountry camping and hiking.

SCENIC DRIVE

South of the Pinnacles Entrance, the gravel **Sage Creek Rim Road** (23 mi./37 km) travels north and west to circle the Badlands Wilderness Area. Look for the **Hay Butte Overlook** and the **Badlands**

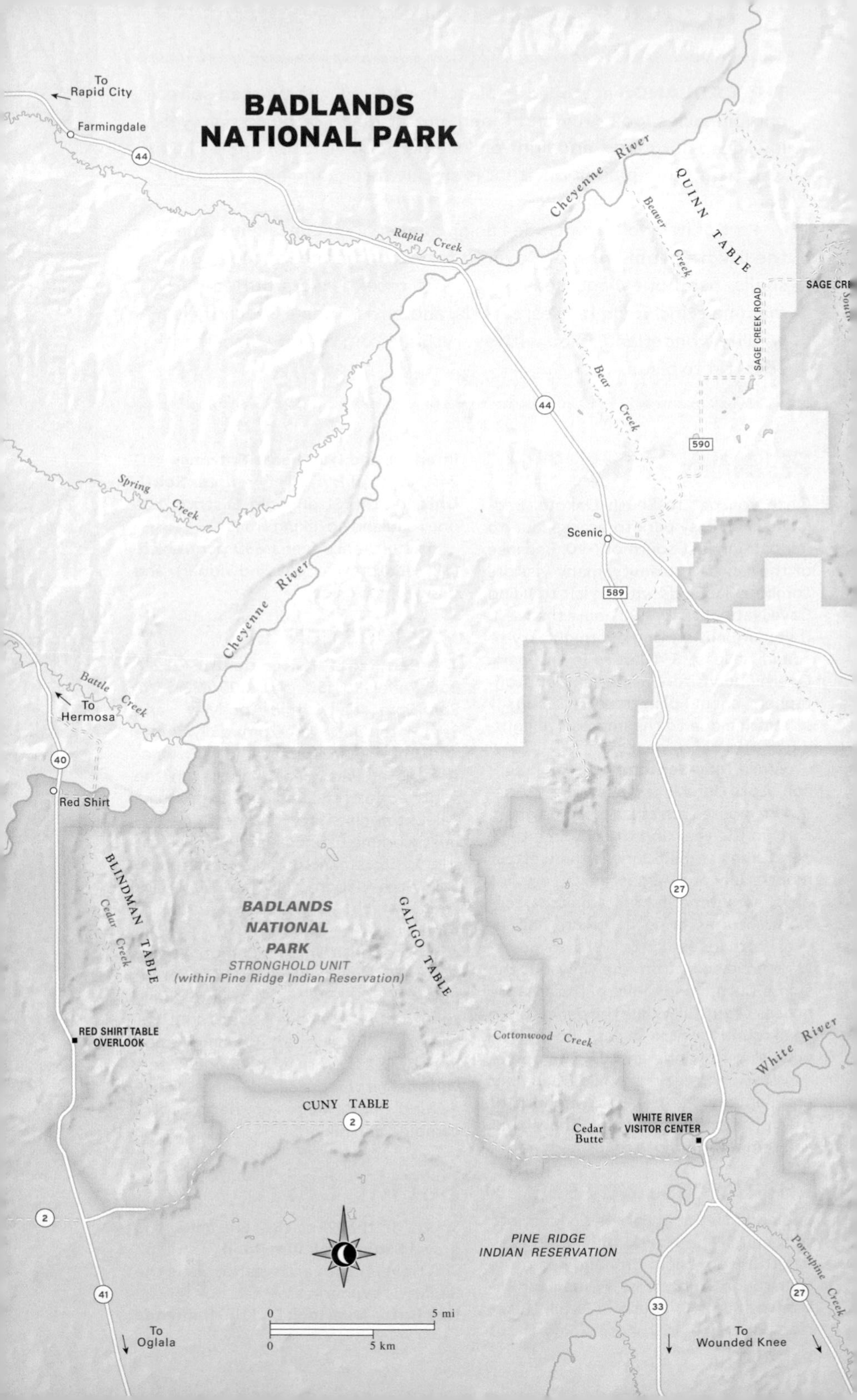

BADLANDS NATIONAL PARK
To Rapid City
Farmingdale
44
Cheyenne River
Rapid Creek
QUINN TABLE
Beaver Creek
SAGE CREEK ROAD
SAGE CR
Bear Creek
590
Spring Creek
Scenic
589
Cheyenne River
Battle Creek
To Hermosa
40
Red Shirt
BLINDMAN TABLE
Cedar Creek
BADLANDS NATIONAL PARK
STRONGHOLD UNIT
(within Pine Ridge Indian Reservation)
GALIGO TABLE
27
RED SHIRT TABLE OVERLOOK
Cottonwood Creek
White River
CUNY TABLE
2
Cedar Butte
WHITE RIVER VISITOR CENTER
2
PINE RIDGE INDIAN RESERVATION
Porcupine Creek
41
33
27
0
5 mi
0
5 km
To Oglala
To Wounded Knee

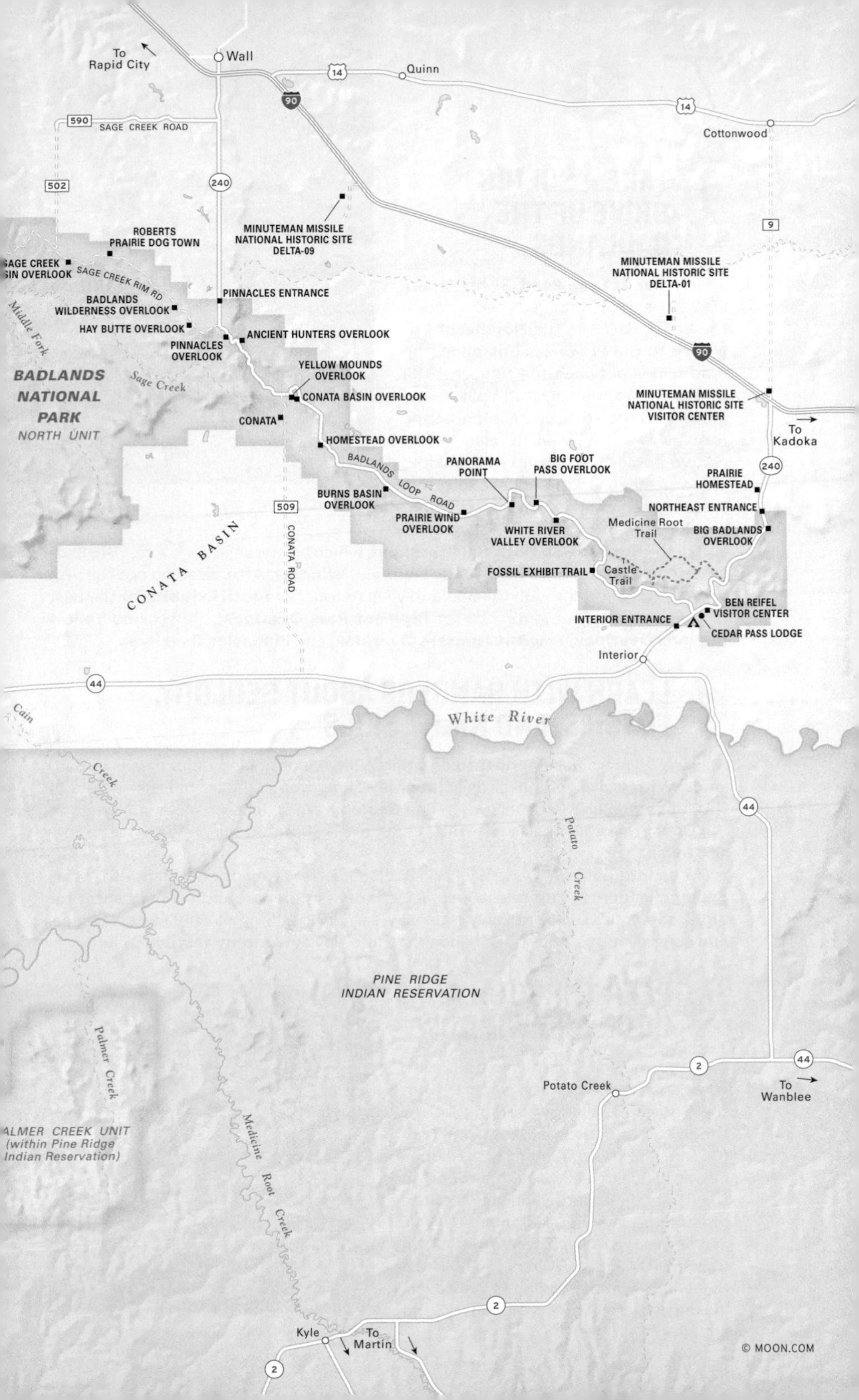

To Rapid City
Wall
14
Quinn
90
590
SAGE CREEK ROAD
14
Cottonwood
502
240
MINUTEMAN MISSILE NATIONAL HISTORIC SITE DELTA-09
9
ROBERTS PRAIRIE DOG TOWN
SAGE CREEK BASIN OVERLOOK
SAGE CREEK RIM RD
MINUTEMAN MISSILE NATIONAL HISTORIC SITE DELTA-01
PINNACLES ENTRANCE
BADLANDS WILDERNESS OVERLOOK
Middle Fork
HAY BUTTE OVERLOOK
ANCIENT HUNTERS OVERLOOK
PINNACLES OVERLOOK
90
YELLOW MOUNDS OVERLOOK
BADLANDS NATIONAL PARK
NORTH UNIT
Sage Creek
CONATA BASIN OVERLOOK
MINUTEMAN MISSILE NATIONAL HISTORIC SITE VISITOR CENTER
CONATA
To Kadoka
HOMESTEAD OVERLOOK
240
BADLANDS LOOP ROAD
PANORAMA POINT
BIG FOOT PASS OVERLOOK
PRAIRIE HOMESTEAD
BURNS BASIN OVERLOOK
509
NORTHEAST ENTRANCE
PRAIRIE WIND OVERLOOK
WHITE RIVER VALLEY OVERLOOK
Medicine Root Trail
BIG BADLANDS OVERLOOK
CONATA BASIN
CONATA ROAD
FOSSIL EXHIBIT TRAIL
Castle Trail
BEN REIFEL VISITOR CENTER
INTERIOR ENTRANCE
CEDAR PASS LODGE
Interior
44
Cain
White River
Creek
44
Potato Creek
PINE RIDGE INDIAN RESERVATION
Palmer Creek
2
44
Potato Creek
To Wanblee
PALMER CREEK UNIT (within Pine Ridge Indian Reservation)
Medicine Root Creek
2
Kyle
To Martin
2
© MOON.COM

Top 3

1 TAKE A SCENIC DRIVE OF THE BADLANDS

BADLANDS SCENIC DRIVE

The **Badlands Loop Road** (39 mi./63 km, SD 240) is the only paved road through the Badlands. From the **Northeast Entrance** to the **Pinnacles Entrance,** the road winds between the ridges of the **Badlands Wall,** a serrated split in the grasslands that looks like the landscape tore away from itself. It also crosses two passes: Cedar and Dillon. Amid bighorn sheep, prairie dogs, and bison, a dozen scenic turnouts along the road provide dramatic vistas of the Badlands and of the **Buffalo Gap National Grassland,** which borders the park. After **Big Badlands Overlook,** stop to walk to the **Door** and **Window.** After scoping out the visitors center, climb through the Badland Wall to tour the **Fossil Exhibit.** For the best of the remaining turnouts, opt for **Big Foot Pass Overlook,** the striking **Yellow Mounds Overlook, Ancient Hunters Overlook,** and **Pinnacles Overlook.**

2 LEARN WITH RANGERS ABOUT GEOLOGY, FOSSILS, AND NIGHT SKIES

Millions of years have gone into creating a legacy of geology and fossils in Badlands. With walks and talks (daily late May-Sept., free), rangers tell the secrets of this landscape and what's hidden. The **Geology Walk** (8:30am, 45 min.) meets at the Door Trailhead. The **Fossil Talk** (10:30am & 1:30pm, 30 min.) meets at the Fossil Exhibit shelter.

As an International Dark Sky Park, Badlands offers exceptional clarity for **stargazing.** Rangers set up telescopes at Cedar Pass Campground Amphitheater for **night sky tours** (9:45pm, daily late May-early Aug., 45 min.) of planets, nebulae, and constellations, and the park hosts a three-day **astronomy festival** in July.

3 PEER THROUGH A DOOR AND WINDOW

OVERLOOK ON DOOR TRAIL

Two short scenic boardwalk trails with wheelchair accessibility depart from the Door and Window parking lot. At the end of the boardwalk, the **Door Trail** (0.75 mi./1.2 km rt., 30 min., easy) slopes upward and travels through a "door" in the Badlands Wall to yield views of the grasslands, the outer Badlands Wall, and an eroded maze. The **Window Trail** (0.25 mi./0.4 km rt., 20 min., easy) leads to a window in the Badlands Wall overlooking an erosion-carved canyon and spires.

Best Hike

THE NOTCH

DISTANCE: 1.5 miles (2.4 km) round-trip
DURATION: 2 hours
ELEVATION CHANGE: 126 feet (38 m)
EFFORT: moderately strenuous
TRAILHEAD: south end of Door, Window, Notch parking lot

The **Notch Trail** ramps up the fun with two challenges. The route starts up a dead-end canyon that requires climbing a rope-and-log ladder to get above. Then, it tiptoes along a narrow ledge. After regaining more solid footing, it follows a draw up to the "notch," through which a sweeping view of the White River valley is revealed.

Wilderness Overlook. The formations here are a little softer and less craggy than the spires along the Badlands Loop Road, but wildlife is more abundant. The park's bison herd is usually seen in this area. Look for the **Roberts Prairie Dog Town,** where a large colony of black-tailed prairie dogs entertain with barking and social antics. At dusk, keep an eye out for the rare black-footed ferret. Just past Roberts Prairie Dog Town is the **Sage Creek Basin Overlook.** Head south and cross a bridge over Sage Creek where you can examine the riverbank to see the Pierre Shale—the oldest visible sedimentary layer in the park, dating back more than 70 million years. Seven miles (11 km) past Roberts Prairie Dog Town, a left-hand turn on a gravel road brings you to **Sage Creek Campground.**

SIGHTS

BADLANDS WALL

An escarpment of spindly spires, pinnacles, and severe gullies, the Badlands Wall once was the northern bank of the White River. Today, the 60-mile-long (97-km) Wall, which looks as if it should wash away in the next rain, exposes the handiwork of erosion. Drive below it, above it, and through it on Badlands Loop Road. All hiking trails in the park explore its bowels or high points.

WILDLIFE-WATCHING

Badlands is full of wildlife that is easy to spot due to very few trees. So where can you see some of the animals? For one, look on the grasslands and prairies where food is more abundant

SAGE CREED RIM ROAD

rather than in the eroded features. Drive Sage Creek Rim Road to see **bison herds.** On the same road, stop at **Roberts Prairie Dog Town** to watch prairie dogs skitter around, chattering at each other.

Look around the higher Cedar Pass and Dillon Pass (Pinnacles area) to find **bighorn sheep.** Along the Badlands Loop Road, watch for foxes, deer, coyotes, pronghorn, burrowing owls, and the black-footed ferret, a rare sight.

FOSSIL EXHIBIT

The Fossil Exhibit (0.25 mi./0.4 km rt., 30 min., easy) tours a wheelchair-accessible **boardwalk** between interpretive displays that tell a 75-million-year-old story of the fossils found in Badlands. No real fossils are here, but you can touch the fossil replicas of an early dog, horse, and alligator or bronze casts of larger fossils of Titanothere teeth and Oreodont bones.

RECREATION

HIKING

From the trailhead a 0.5 miles (0.8 km) east of the visitors center, **Cliff Shelf** (0.5 mi./0.8 km rt., 20 min., moderate) loops below the Badlands Wall. Stairs and boardwalk climb and descend through the juniper forest and take in the prairie views.

A steep ascent juts up through colorful rock formations to the natural flat platform of **Saddle Pass** (0.5 mi./0.8 km rt., 30 min., strenuous) in the Badlands Wall. Find the trailhead on Badlands Loop Road about 2 miles (3.2 km) northwest of the visitors center.

From the north end across from the Fossil Exhibit Trail, the mostly level **Castle Trail** (10 mi./16.1 km rt., 5 hr., moderate) winds through spires and mounds. Portions cross grasslands with views of the Badlands formations to the west and south; watch for cacti and rattlesnakes. The trail ends on the west side across from the Door and Window parking lot.

BIKING

Badlands Loop Road (39 mi./63 km) can be an exhilarating, downhill ride from Pinnacles Overlook to the visitors center. But be ready for narrow, curvy roads with cars and RVs zipping past.

Mountain bikers prefer the gravel **Sage Creek Rim Road** (23 mi./37 km) but may eat dust from cars. The dead-end dirt **Sheep Mountain Table Road** (14 mi./23 km rt.) about 4 miles (6.4 km) south of the town of Scenic off BIA 27/County Road 589 has spectacular views of the South Unit of the park and the Black Hills 70 miles (113 km) to the west.

Bring your own bicycles; rentals are not available. A brochure detailing loop trips on combined park and county roads is available at the visitors center. The visitors center also has a bike pump and repair station.

WHERE TO STAY

INSIDE THE PARK

If you're looking to experience a park sunrise or sunset, stay at **Cedar Pass Lodge** (20681 SD 240, 605/433-5460 or 877/386-4383, www.cedarpasslodge.com, mid-Apr.-mid-Oct., from $179). The cabins have air-conditioning, modern amenities, small decks, and lodgepole pine furnishings. The **lodge restaurant** (daily 8am-6:30pm May-Sept.,

CEDAR PASS CAMPGROUND

ONE DAY IN THE BADLANDS

Spend your one day in the park by entering through the **Northeast Entrance.** Stop to walk the **Door** and **Window Trails** before crossing Cedar Pass to the visitors center to get oriented. Take a drive north along the **Badlands Loop Road** and tour the short **Fossil Exhibit.** Finish your day trip by exiting via the **Pinnacles Entrance** on the north side of the park.

8am-4:30pm daily Apr. and Oct.) has a soup and salad bar, some vegetarian selections, and a limited dinner menu.

With 96 first-come, first-served sites, **Cedar Pass Campground** (20681 SD 240, 605/433-5460 or 877/386-4383, www.cedarpasslodge.com, $25-40 Apr.-Oct., $10 in winter with no services) is near the Ben Reifel Visitor Center. In summer, the campground has cold running water, flush toilets, and pay showers.

The **Sage Creek Wilderness Campground** (Sage Creek Rim Rd., North Unit, year-round, free) offers primitive camping with pit toilets (but no water) and equestrian facilities.

OUTSIDE THE PARK

The town of **Interior,** located at the southern edge of the North Unit of the park, has limited accommodations. The town of **Wall** 8 miles (13 km) north of the Pinnacles Entrance on the north side of the park has several accommodations and restaurants.

GETTING THERE AND AROUND

Badlands has no park shuttles or public transportation. You'll need to take a tour, drive, hike, or bicycle to see the park. In winter, check road conditions because severe snowstorms may close roads.

AIR

The nearest airport is **Rapid City Regional Airport** (RAP, 4550 Terminal Rd., 605/393-9924, www.rapairport.com), 11 miles (18 km) from downtown Rapid City off SD 44. Shuttle service between the airport and downtown is provided by **Airport Express Shuttle** (605/399-9999 or 800/357-9998). Car rental companies are at the airport.

CAR

From Rapid City, two routes go to Badlands National Park. SD 44 skirts the southern edge of the North Unit, entering through the **Interior Entrance.** It's about a 75-mile (121-km) drive (1.5 hrs.).

The second route to the park is I-90. It is the fastest route between Rapid City and the park: just 73 miles (118 km) of 80 mph (129 kph) driving. If you are planning on spending the night in or near the park, this is the best route. Travelers headed west on I-90 will take exit 131 at Cactus Flat and go south on SD 240 to the **Northeast Entrance.** It is about 10 miles (16 km) from the Northeast Entrance to the Ben Reifel Visitor Center. If traveling east on I-90, take exit 110 for Wall and drive 7 miles (11 km) south to the **Pinnacles Entrance.**

TOURS

Several tour companies make day trips to the Badlands from Rapid City. **Affordable Adventures** (5542 Meteor St., Rapid City, 605/342-7691, www.affordableadventuresbh.com) provides narrated seven-hour tours.

Black Hills Adventure Tours (4131 Pleasant Dr., Rapid City, 605/209-7817, www.blackhillsadventuretours.com) has narrated driving tours of the Badlands and hiking tours in the park.

GeoFunTrek (605/430-1531, www.geofuntrek.com) has two tours to the Badlands: one classic and one that includes a daylight/sunset/stargazing tour.

Black Hills Aerial Adventures (21020 SD 240, Interior, 605/673-2163, http://coptertours.com, May-Sept.) offers five different flying tours over the Badlands.

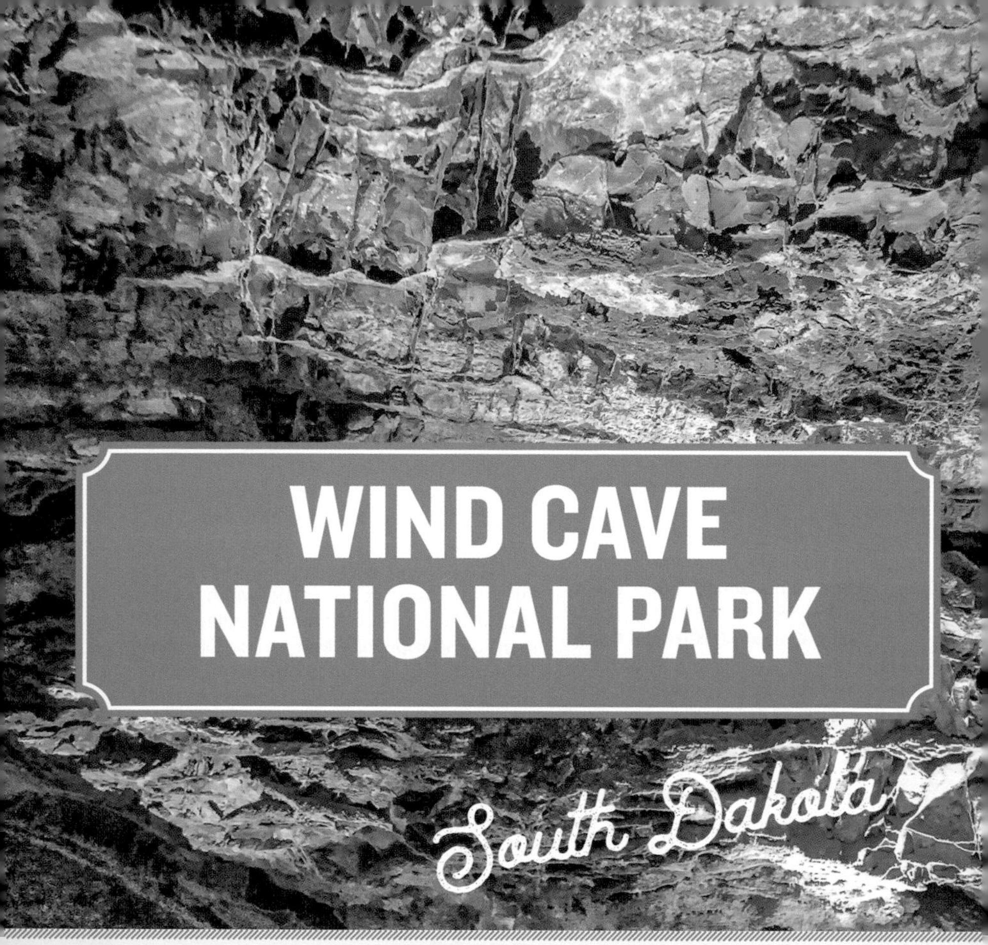

WEBSITE:
www.nps.gov/wica

PHONE NUMBER:
605/745-4600

VISITATION RANK:
35

WHY GO:
Explore underground caves.

▲ WIND CAVE NATIONAL PARK

KEEPSAKE STAMPS ▼▼▼

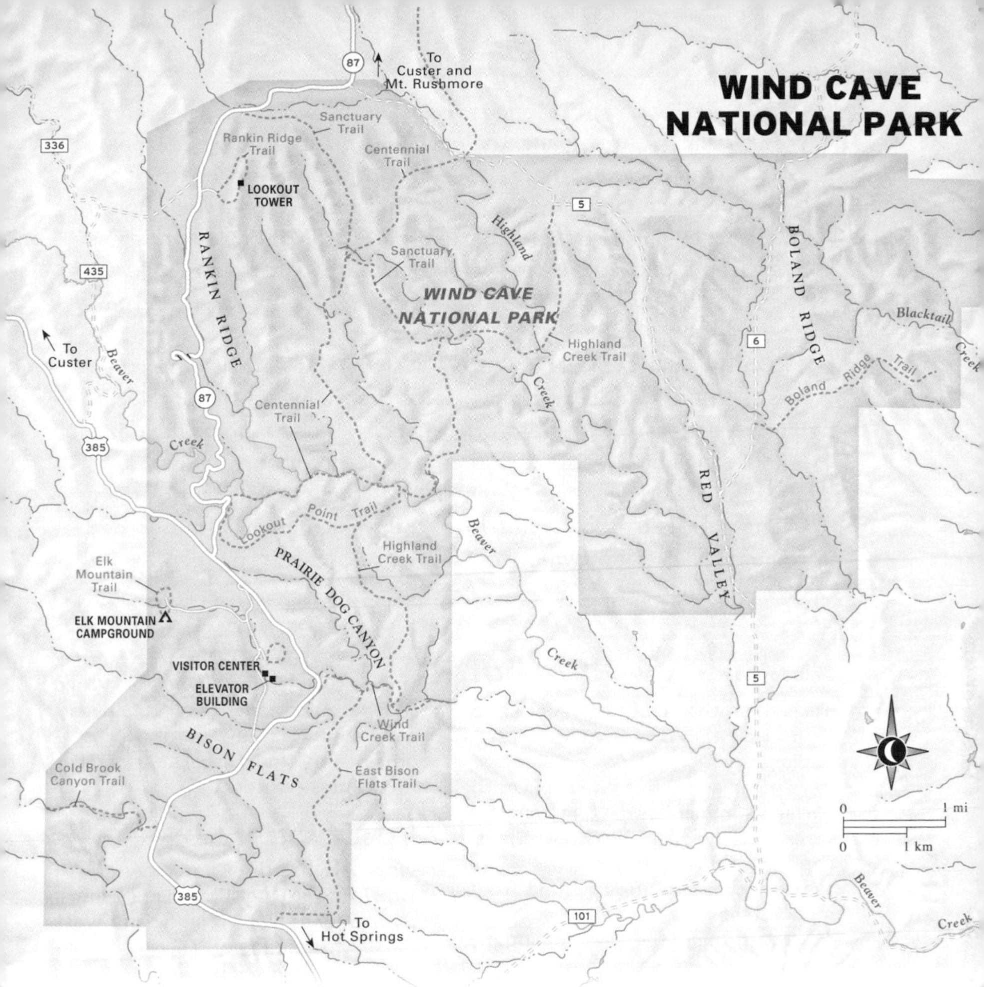
WIND CAVE NATIONAL PARK
87
To Custer and Mt. Rushmore
336
435
To Custer
Beaver
Creek
Sanctuary Trail
Rankin Ridge Trail
Centennial Trail
LOOKOUT TOWER
RANKIN RIDGE
5
Highland
Sanctuary Trail
WIND CAVE NATIONAL PARK
Highland Creek Trail
Creek
BOLAND RIDGE
6
Blacktail
Creek
Boland Ridge Trail
87
Centennial Trail
385
RED VALLEY
Lookout Point Trail
Beaver
Creek
PRAIRIE DOG CANYON
Highland Creek Trail
Elk Mountain Trail
ELK MOUNTAIN CAMPGROUND
VISITOR CENTER
ELEVATOR BUILDING
5
Wind Creek Trail
BISON FLATS
Cold Brook Canyon Trail
East Bison Flats Trail
0
1 mi
0
1 km
385
101
To Hot Springs
Beaver
Creek

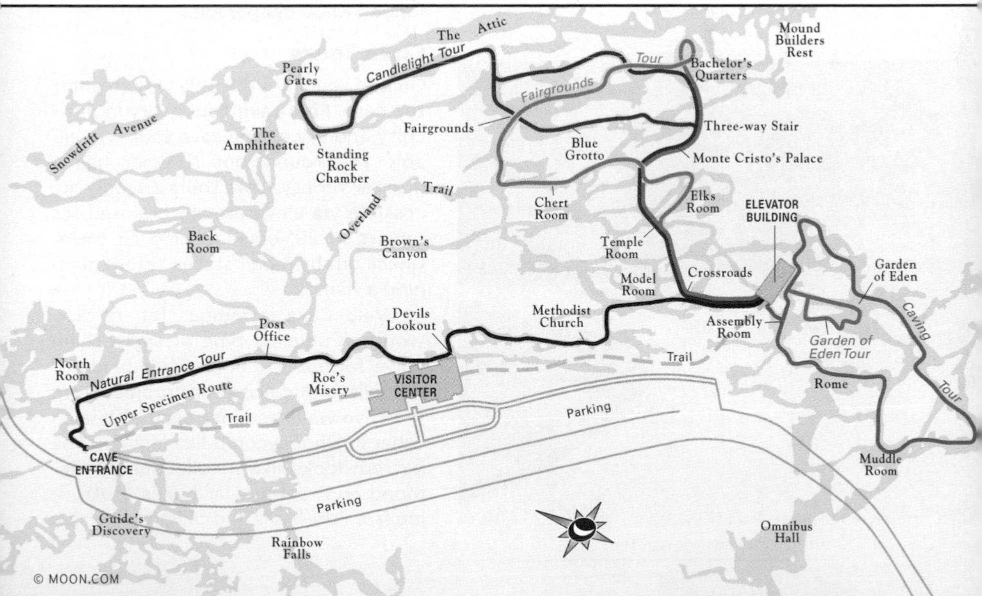
The Attic
Candlelight Tour
Pearly Gates
Tour
Bachelor's Quarters
Mound Builders Rest
Fairgrounds
Fairgrounds
Three-way Stair
Snowdrift Avenue
The Amphitheater
Standing Rock Chamber
Blue Grotto
Monte Cristo's Palace
Overland Trail
Chert Room
Elks Room
ELEVATOR BUILDING
Back Room
Brown's Canyon
Temple Room
Crossroads
Model Room
Garden of Eden
Caving Tour
Methodist Church
Devils Lookout
Post Office
Assembly Room
Garden of Eden Tour
Trail
North Room
Natural Entrance Tour
Roe's Misery
VISITOR CENTER
Rome
Upper Specimen Route
Trail
Parking
CAVE ENTRANCE
Muddle Room
Parking
Guide's Discovery
Omnibus Hall
Rainbow Falls

Wind Cave is one of the longest caves in the world. Considered sacred by Native Americans, the cave was discovered by Europeans in 1881 when two brothers, Jesse and Tom Bingham, heard a loud whistling noise. Upon investigation, they discovered a small hole in the ground. This is the only natural entrance to the cave that has ever been found. Below the surface, beneath just 1 square mile (2.6 sq km) of the park, is a maze of 143 miles (230 km) of explored cave passages.

On the surface, **WIND CAVE NATIONAL PARK** is where East meets West—where the Great Plains prairie meets the ponderosa pine forest. Its mixed-grass prairie ecosystem supports abundant wildlife, including bison, deer, prairie dogs, pronghorn, wild turkeys, and elk. Historically, these animals provided sustenance for many of the park's 26 associated tribes. Today, hiking trails tour eroded, rounded hills that provide scenic views as far as the eye can see.

PLANNING YOUR TIME

Tucked in the southwest corner of South Dakota, Wind Cave lies west of Badlands National Park, and many visitors combine both in one trip. On the surface, summer has daytime temperatures usually 80-90°F (27-32°C) and can bring thunderstorms, while winter temperatures are often around freezing with snow.

Underground, the caves maintain a stable temperature that hovers around 53°F (12°C), despite surface weather. Bring a sweatshirt or sweater. While rangers guide one cave tour year-round, **summer** (May-Sept.) is high season, with the most cave tour choices and the most visitors.

WIND CAVE VISITOR CENTER

ENTRANCES AND FEES

Wind Cave has three entrances: **north** (SD 87 from Custer State Park), **south** (US 385 from Hot Springs), and **west** (US 385 from Pringle). There is no entrance fee; however, guided cave tours range $10-30 per person.

Cave Tours

Guided tours are the only way to enter the cave. **Five cave tours** vary in difficulty and price. One cave tour is available year-round, but summer has a greater variety. Cave tours are only accessible via elevator, which closed for repairs in 2019, suspending all tours. Check on the repair status before planning a visit.

Wind Cave is famous for its boxwork, an unusual type of speleothem (cave formation). Boxwork is made of thin slices of calcite that project from the cave walls and intersect with each other in a honeycomb-like fashion. The pattern looks like a collection of diamond and rectangular boxes protruding from the walls and ceilings.

Top 3

1 TAKE IT EASY WITH THE GARDEN OF EDEN TOUR

The **Garden of Eden Tour** (3-4 tours daily year-round, adults $10, children ages 6-16 $5, children under 6 free) goes by intricate formations of cave popcorn, boxwork, and flowstone (a calcite formation that looks as if it is flowing over the rocks). Of all the cave tours, this one is the shortest and least strenuous (0.3 mi./0.5 km, 150 stairs, 1 hr.). Entry and exit to the cave is by elevator.

BOXWORK FORMATIONS

2 PICK UP THE PACE WITH THE NATURAL ENTRANCE TOUR

The **Natural Entrance Tour** (6-12 tours daily Apr.-Oct., adults $12, children ages 6-16 $6, children under 6 free) starts at the only natural entrance to the cave to discover why the cave got its name. However, entry is via an artificially constructed entrance that descends to the middle level of the cave, famous for its extensive boxwork formations. This tour is moderately strenuous (0.6 mi./1 km, 300 stairs mostly downhill, 1.25 hrs.). Exit from the cave is via elevator.

SMALL NATURAL CAVE ENTRANCE

3 WORK UP A SWEAT WITH THE FAIRGROUNDS TOUR

The **Fairgrounds Tour** (3-8 tours daily Memorial Day-Labor Day, adults $12, children ages 6-16 $6, children under 6 free) visits the upper and middle levels of the cave. Boxwork is abundant in the middle section, and the upper level of the cave features large rooms decorated with popcorn and frostwork. This tour is the most strenuous of the walking tours (0.6 mi./1 km, 450 total stairs climbing up, 1.5 hrs.) with a single staircase of more than 90 stairs.

Best Hike

LOOKOUT POINT-CENTENNIAL LOOP

DISTANCE: 4.5 miles (7.2 km) round-trip
DURATION: 2.5-3 hours
ELEVATION CHANGE: 240 feet (73 m)
EFFORT: moderate
TRAILHEAD: Centennial Trailhead

The **Lookout Point-Centennial Trail Loop** combines all of the diversity of the park: a stream ecosystem, prairie grasslands, pine forests, and rolling hills. From the trailhead, the hike begins in a stand of ridgetop pines and then descends rapidly to the valley floor to meander along Beaver Creek, winding between low hills. About 2 miles (3.2 km) in, the Centennial Trail takes a fairly sharp left. Continue straight at this point, and you will be on a short stretch of the Highland Creek Trail. This trail will loop around to join the Lookout Point Trail. Where the Highland Creek Trail veers south, continue heading west along the Lookout Point Trail; it will return you to the Centennial Trailhead.

From the visitors center, head north on US 385 and take an immediate right on SD 87; the trailhead is 0.7 mile (1.1 km) down the road on the east side.

VISITORS CENTER

The **Wind Cave Visitor Center** (26611 US 385, 605/745-4600, 8am-4:30pm daily, extended hours in summer) has maps and information, **cave tour tickets,** free backcountry camping permits, or a bookstore. Several **ranger-led programs** are available during the summer months; most begin at the campground amphitheater.

SPECIALTY CAVE TOURS

Cave tours are only accessible via elevator, which closed for repairs in 2019, suspending all tours. Check on the repair status before planning a visit.

HISTORIC CANDLELIGHT TOUR

The **Historic Candlelight Tour** (1-2 tours daily Memorial Day-Labor Day, adults $12, children ages 8-16 $6) takes place in a less developed area of the cave along a fairly rugged trail and explores Wind Cave much the way early cavers did—without the benefit of electricity. Each participant carries a candle bucket, which is the only lighting for the tour. Cave walls loom into the light and shadows dance along the walls, heightening the sensation of visiting another world. This is a strenuous tour (0.6 mi./1 km, 2 hrs.).

Participation is limited to 10 people per tour, and the minimum age is eight. Participants are required to wear shoes with nonslip soles; no sandals are permitted. Advance reservations are recommended.

CAVE COLORS

BRIDGE IN WIND CAVE NATIONAL PARK

MOUNT RUSHMORE

Four hundred people toiled for 14 years to create Mount Rushmore National Memorial. Workers used pneumatic drills, jackhammers, chisels, and dynamite. After hiking 700 stairs to the top of the mountain every morning, they climbed into sling chairs to be lowered down its face to their carving position for the day. The resulting mountainside sculpture is huge. George Washington's head is 60 feet (18 m) tall. His eye alone is 11 feet (3 m) wide, and his mouth is 18 feet (5 m) wide.

The Mount Rushmore grounds are open daily year-round (5am-11pm mid-Mar.-Oct., 5am-9pm Nov.-mid-Mar.). In summer, park buildings are open daily 8am-10pm, with shorter hours or closures in winter. The presidents' faces are illuminated nightly from sunset until closing; during summer, the illumination is preceded by the evening lighting ceremony. A café near the monument entrance is the only dining facility.

MOUNT RUSHMORE

Sights

At the **Information Center,** find maps to the grounds, schedules for ranger-guided programs, and a park newspaper. The *Mount Rushmore Audio Tour: Living Memorial* (2 hrs.) is available at the **Audio Tour Building.**

The **Avenue of Flags** lines the pedestrian walkway, forming a colorful frame for the presidential faces. These 56 flags, representing each state, district, commonwealth, and territory of the United States, end at the **Grand View Terrace,** which serves as one of the best viewpoints for photographs.

The **Lincoln Borglum Visitor Center & Museum,** on the lower level of Grand View Terrace, has interactive exhibits. See a timeline of American history and learn about Rushmore's sculptor Gutzon Borglum. Two small theaters show films.

From Grand View Terrace, follow the concrete pathway on the Lincoln side of the monument to the **Borglum Viewing Terrace,** the site of the artist's

WILD CAVE TOUR

For the adventurous soul, the **Wild Cave Tour** (Memorial Day-Labor Day, once daily, $30) requires crawling through some very narrow spaces while learning the basics of safe caving. Be prepared to get dirty. The tour is ultrastrenuous (0.5 mi./0.8 km, 4 hrs.), much of it spent crawling, and not for the claustrophobic!

The park provides kneepads, hard hats, and lights; participants should wear long pants, long sleeves, and sturdy, lace-up boots or shoes with nonslip soles. Note that participants must be at least 16 years old (those age 16-17 must have a signed parental consent form). Advance reservations are required.

HIKING

On the surface, hiking trails range from easy to strenuous. For a short hike, **nature trails** offer interpretive signage and displays. The **Elk Mountain Trail** (1 mi./1.6 km rt., 30 min., easy) begins at the end of the Elk Mountain Campground road and circles up through the forest near the park's boundary. From the visitors center or nearby picnic area, the **Prairie Vista Trail** (1 mi./1.6 km rt., 30 min. easy) focuses on information about the prairie grasses.

RANKIN RIDGE

With a bit of uphill climbing that yields the rewards of large landscape views

first temporary studio. Below, his **Sculptor's Studio** (summer only) contains the working model for Rushmore, a collection of tools, and before-and-after photographs of the carving. Rangers host 15-minute talks.

The Presidential Loop (0.5 mi./0.8 km rt., 20 min., easy) brings visitors to the closest viewpoints under the monument. The paved trail is wheelchair-accessible from the Washington side of Grand View Terrace to the base of the mountain. From that point, 450 wooden stairs climb partially up the mountain and then down to the Sculptor's Studio.

The **Lakota, Nakota, and Dakota Heritage Village** (summer only) has a collection of tepees, where interpreters talk about the traditional Native American lifestyle and customs.

AVENUE OF FLAGS WITH MOUNT RUSHMORE

Getting There and Around

Mount Rushmore National Memorial (13000 Hwy. 244, Bldg. 31, Ste. 1, 605/574-2523, www.nps.gov/moru, $10 parking) is north of Wind Cave National Park (40 mi./64 km, 1 hr.) and west of Badlands National Park (83 mi./134 km, 1.5 hrs.).

From Rapid City Airport, the fastest road to Mount Rushmore (32 mi./52 km) is US 16, also called Mount Rushmore Road. Once at Rushmore, moving from site to site is all by foot. No shuttles are available.

Several companies lead tours: **Mount Rushmore Tours** (2255 Fort Hayes Dr., Rapid City, 605/343-3113, www.mountrushmoretours.com), **ABS Travel Group** (945 Enchantment Rd., Rapid City, 888/788-6777, www.abstravelgroup.com), and **Golden Circle Tours** (12021 US 16, 605/673-4349, www.goldencircletours.com).

Black Hills Aerial Adventures (313 Speck Center Rd., Keystone, 605/646-4801, http://coptertours.com) offers flying tours.

from the park's highest point, the **Rankin Ridge Trail** (1 mi./1.6 km rt., 45 min., moderate) begins and ends at the parking lot of the Rankin Ridge Lookout Tower off SD 87 in the northwest corner of the park. Pick up an interpretive trail guide at the trailhead, and hike uphill on the dirt road to the lookout tower and loop back on a single-track through pine forest.

WIND CAVE CANYON

Wind Cave Canyon (3.6 mi./5.8 km rt., 2 hrs., easy) follows a former service road into Wind Cave Canyon at the park's boundary. This is one of the best places in the park for bird-watching; look along limestone walls to spot cliff swallows and great horned owls. Stands of dead trees make great nesting places for several varieties of woodpeckers.

The trailhead is on the east side of the road, 1 mile (1.6 km) north of the junction of the south entrance and US 385.

WHERE TO STAY

INSIDE THE PARK

The only accommodation is **Elk Mountain Campground** (75 sites, $18 summer, $9 winter; first come, first served), 1 mile (1.6 km) north of the visitors center. Facilities include restrooms with flush toilets and cold running water (in summer), but no hookups.

PRAIRIE DOGS

Backcountry camping is allowed in the northwestern part of the park. Campers must have a **permit,** which is free from the visitors center.

OUTSIDE THE PARK

Located 7 miles (11 km) south of the park, the city of **Hot Springs** has accommodations for park visitors.

GETTING THERE AND AROUND

AIR

The **Rapid City Regional Airport** (RAP, 4550 Terminal Rd., 605/393-9924, www.rapairport.com) is about 11 miles (18 km) from downtown Rapid City, off SD 44 East. The airport has car rentals.

CAR

For the most direct route (57 mi./92 km, 1.2 hr.) from I-90 and Rapid City, take SD 79 south to US 385, turning right to Hot Springs. The park entrance is 7 miles (11 km) north on US 385. To reach Wind Cave from the south, aim for Hot Springs on US 385.

For drivers coming from Mount Rushmore, drive 4.6 miles (7.4 km) west to US 385 to go south through Hill City, Custer, and Pringle to reach the west entrance of the park (57 mi./92 km, 1.2 hrs.).

Inside the park, the visitors center sits on a signed side road about 0.5 mile (0.8 km) off US 385. From the south entrance, go 4.5 miles (7.2 km) to the turnoff on the left. From the north and west entrance roads, the visitors center turnoff is on the right just south of the junction of US 385 and SD 87.

There is no public transit within the park. Driving or bicycling is the only way to travel the main paved road. Two dirt roads (#5 and #6) tour the eastern portion of the badlands.

SIGHTS NEARBY

Roughly 23 miles (37 km) north of the park on US 385, **Crazy Horse Memorial** (12151 Avenue of the Chiefs, Crazy Horse, 605/673-4681, www.crazyhorsememorial.org, summer daily 7am until after the laser light show, winter daily 8am-5pm) is a mountainside sculpture still under construction.

Jewel Cave National Monument (13 mi./18 km west of Custer via US 16, 605/673-8300, www.nps.gov/jeca, summer daily 8am-6pm, shorter hours fall-spring) has ranger-led tours through the third-longest cave in the world.

Just north of Wind Cave via SD 87, **Custer State Park** (13329 US 16A, 605/255-4515, https://gfp.sd.gov) is home to 1,300 free-roaming bison and other wildlife. The bison can often be seen from Wildlife Loop Road. Scenic drives go through Needles Highway (SD 87) with impressive rock spires and single-lane tunnels and Iron Mountain Road (US 16A) with tunnels framing Mount Rushmore and pig-tail curves. Campgrounds are available.

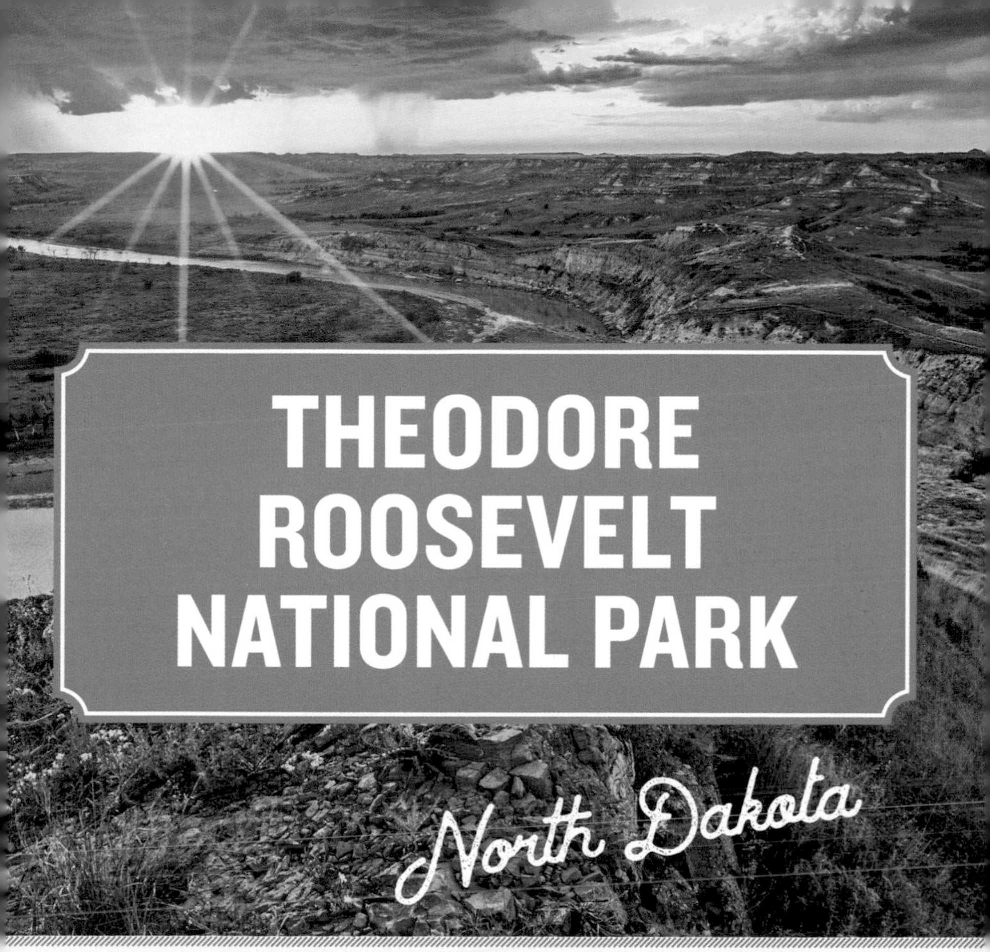

THEODORE ROOSEVELT NATIONAL PARK

North Dakota

KEEPSAKE STAMPS ▼▼▼

WEBSITE:
www.nps.gov/thro

PHONE NUMBER:
701/623-4466

VISITATION RANK:
31

WHY GO:
See wild horses, bison, and badlands.

▲ THEODORE ROOSEVELT NATIONAL PARK

THEODORE ROOSEVELT NATIONAL PARK (SOUTH)

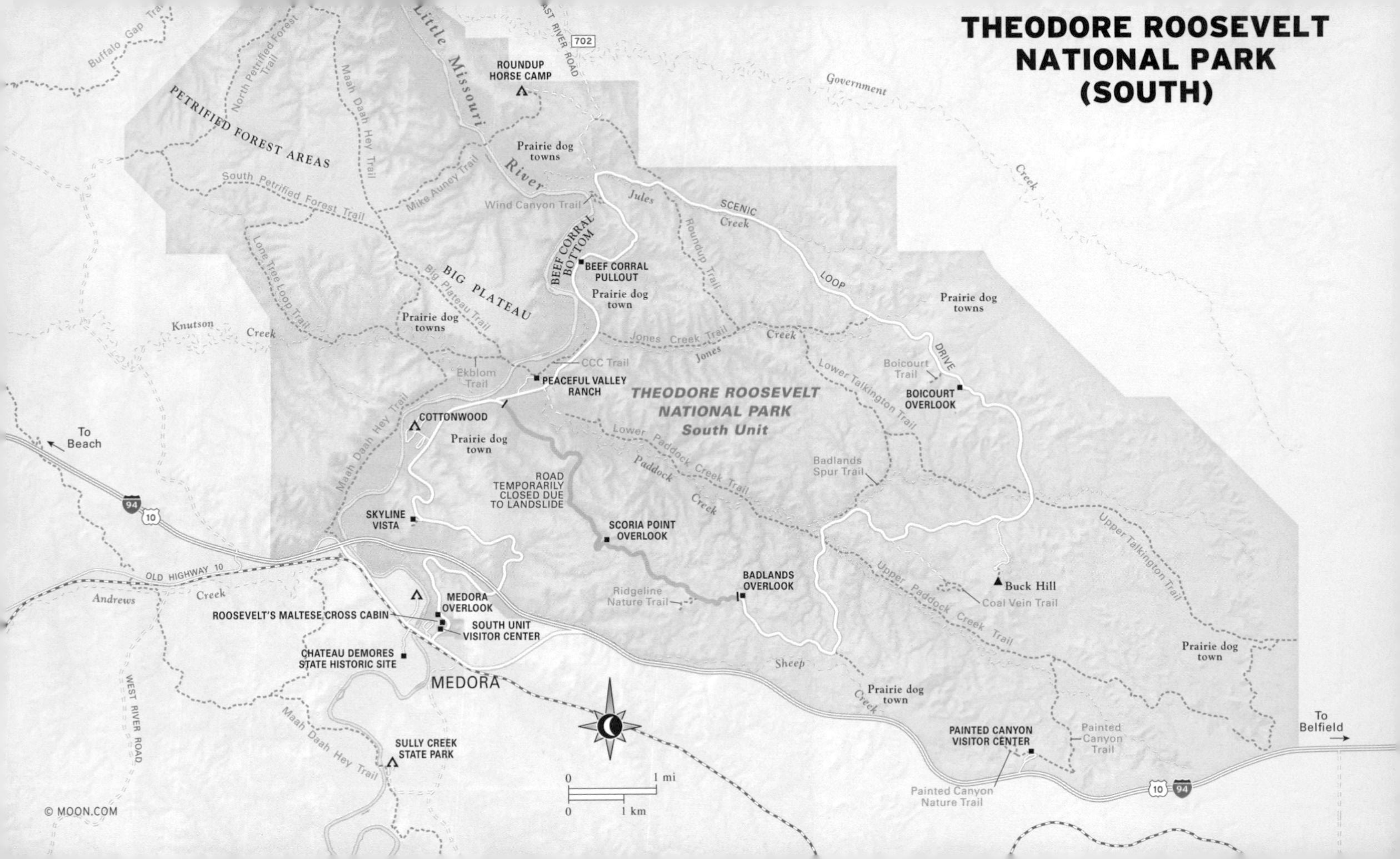

THEODORE ROOSEVELT NATIONAL PARK
South Unit
PETRIFIED FOREST AREAS
North Petrified Forest Trail
South Petrified Forest Trail
Buffalo Gap Trail
Maah Daah Hey Trail
Mike Auney Trail
Little Missouri River
ROUNDUP HORSE CAMP
EAST RIVER ROAD
702
Government Creek
Prairie dog towns
Wind Canyon Trail
BEEF CORRAL BOTTOM
BEEF CORRAL PULLOUT
Prairie dog town
Jules Creek
SCENIC LOOP DRIVE
Roundup Trail
Lone Tree Loop Trail
BIG PLATEAU
Big Plateau Trail
Knutson Creek
Jones Creek Trail
Jones Creek
CCC Trail
Ekblom Trail
PEACEFUL VALLEY RANCH
Boicourt Trail
BOICOURT OVERLOOK
Lower Talkington Trail
COTTONWOOD
Lower Paddock Creek Trail
Paddock Creek
Badlands Spur Trail
To Beach
ROAD TEMPORARILY CLOSED DUE TO LANDSLIDE
SKYLINE VISTA
SCORIA POINT OVERLOOK
Upper Talkington Trail
94
10
OLD HIGHWAY 10
Andrews Creek
MEDORA OVERLOOK
BADLANDS OVERLOOK
Ridgeline Nature Trail
Buck Hill
Coal Vein Trail
Upper Paddock Creek Trail
ROOSEVELT'S MALTESE CROSS CABIN
SOUTH UNIT VISITOR CENTER
CHATEAU DEMORES STATE HISTORIC SITE
MEDORA
Sheep Creek
WEST RIVER ROAD
SULLY CREEK STATE PARK
PAINTED CANYON VISITOR CENTER
Painted Canyon Trail
Painted Canyon Nature Trail
To Belfield
0
1 mi
1 km
© MOON.COM

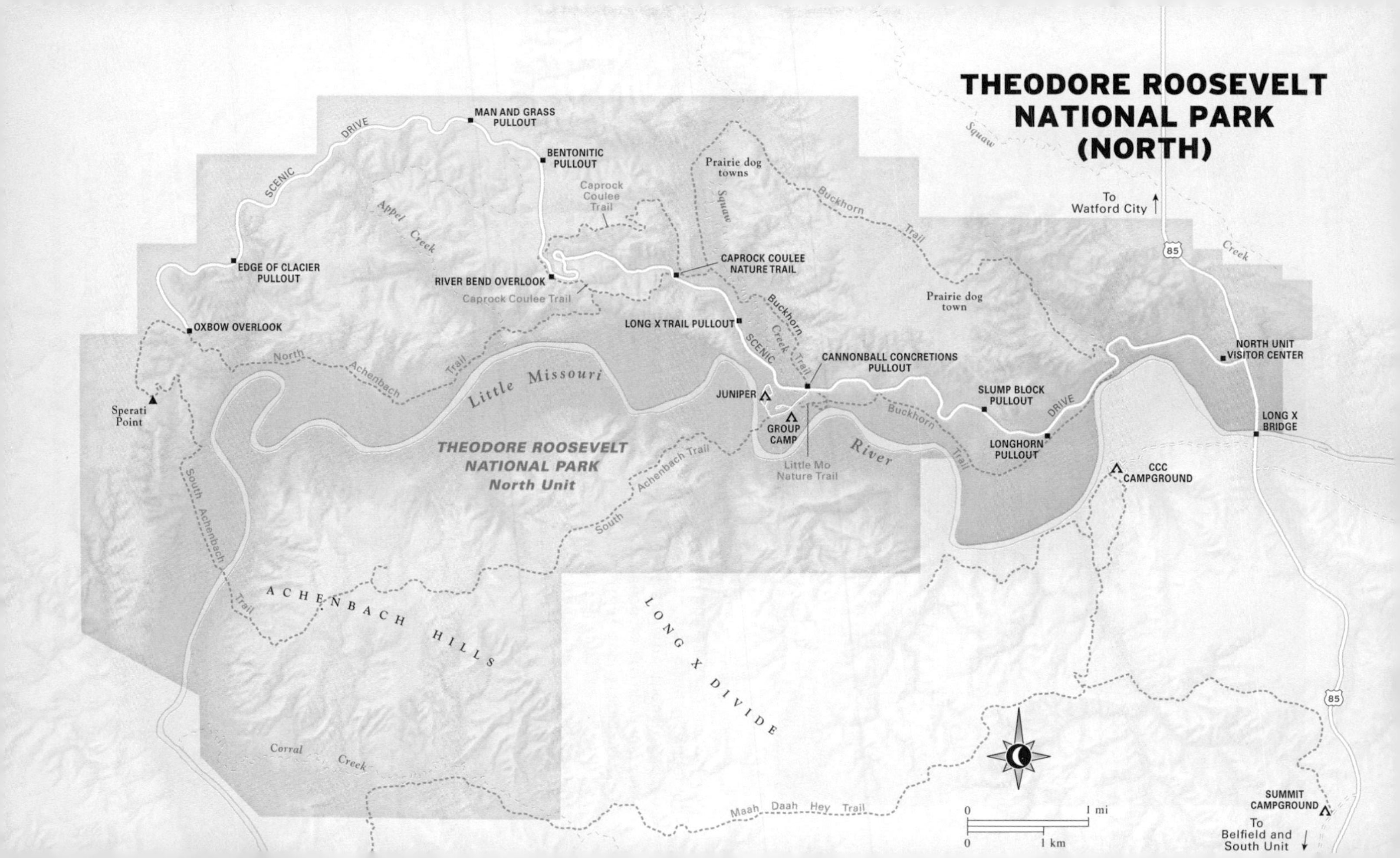
THEODORE ROOSEVELT NATIONAL PARK (NORTH)
To Watford City
85
MAN AND GRASS PULLOUT
BENTONITIC PULLOUT
SCENIC DRIVE
Caprock Coulee Trail
Appel Creek
EDGE OF CLACIER PULLOUT
RIVER BEND OVERLOOK
Caprock Coulee Trail
OXBOW OVERLOOK
Prairie dog towns
Squaw
Buckhorn Trail
Creek
CAPROCK COULEE NATURE TRAIL
Buckhorn Creek Trail
LONG X TRAIL PULLOUT
SCENIC
Prairie dog town
NORTH UNIT VISITOR CENTER
CANNONBALL CONCRETIONS PULLOUT
North Achenbach Trail
Little Missouri River
Sperati Point
JUNIPER
GROUP CAMP
SLUMP BLOCK PULLOUT
DRIVE
LONG X BRIDGE
Buckhorn Trail
LONGHORN PULLOUT
THEODORE ROOSEVELT NATIONAL PARK North Unit
Little Mo Nature Trail
CCC CAMPGROUND
South Achenbach Trail
ACHENBACH HILLS
LONG X DIVIDE
Corral Creek
Maah Daah Hey Trail
0 1 mi
0 1 km
SUMMIT CAMPGROUND
To Belfield and South Unit

In **THEODORE ROOSEVELT NATIONAL PARK**, grasslands and badlands collide around the Little Missouri River. This otherworldly park might appear barren at first glance, but it contains the kind of raw beauty favored by its namesake president.

These wild lands of the Great Plains still harbor bison, much like they did in the days when the Mandan and Hidatsa hunted here. The wind carries the alarm calls of prairie dogs, broken patches of junipers hide elk, and feral horses thrive on the native grasses. Sandstone and soft clay erode into fantastical formations—hoodoos and pillars with capstones—while mud layers lend pastel colors to bluffs rising from the river.

PLANNING YOUR TIME

Theodore Roosevelt National Park is part of the North Dakota badlands. Three separate parcels make up the park and are linked by the Little Missouri River and the Maah Daah Hey Trail.

The **South Unit** is the most visited and easily accessible, located adjacent to I-94 near the town of Medora. The **North Unit** is 70 miles (113 km) north. The **Elkhorn Ranch Unit** sits between the North and South Units and requires a high-clearance vehicle for its remote access.

The North and South Units observe different time zones: the South Unit observes Mountain Time, while the North Unit is in Central Time.

Summer (May-Sept.) is high season, when park services are open and temperatures are warm, though sudden thunderstorms can bring downpours. Winters are bitingly cold and windy. Snow can close park roads.

THEODORE ROOSEVELT'S MALTESE CROSS CABIN

Top 3

1 SEE PAINTED CANYON

PAINTED CANYON

A colorful canyon full of badland erosion is the centerpiece of the South Unit. At Painted Canyon Visitor Center, a paved wheelchair-accessible sidewalk arcs around the rim, garnering panoramic views into the canyon. Lighting for the colors is best in early morning or evening. The **Painted Canyon Nature Trail** (0.9 mi./1.4 km rt., 45 min., moderate) drops into the canyon to see the colorful layers up close. The gated road is open May through October, but you can walk in even when the road is gated.

2 WATCH WILDLIFE

COYOTE

Wildlife-watching in Theodore Roosevelt National Park can rival some of the best parks with bison, pronghorn, deer, and elk. Prairie dog towns provide places to see the burrowing rodents socialize, scurry for grasses, and chase each other. Since they are the bottom of the food chain, you may also see coyotes or foxes hunting them. Feral or wild horses are one of the biggest attractions, especially in May when you can look at young foals. The North Unit has a herd of longhorn steers as a reminder of the cattle drives that passed through the area in Roosevelt's day. Driving the park roads is the best way to see wildlife; use pullouts for watching rather than stopping in the middle of the road.

3 TOUR THE SOUTH UNIT SCENIC DRIVE

For the best way to see the badlands, tour the paved South Unit Scenic Drive. Due to a landslide that tore up roadway in 2019, the route is now an out-and-back tour (48 mi./77 km rt., 2 hrs.) rather than a loop. It passes multiple interpretive stops with several overlooks of dramatic badlands. Views from **Skyline Vista** span the Little Missouri River. Then, the road passes several **prairie dog towns** that can be noisy with alarm call barks. Farther along, **Peaceful Valley Ranch** is the only original remaining ranch house in the South Unit. At **Boicourt Overlook**, peer down on rugged eroded waterways that feed the Little Missouri. A spur road goes to the steep trail up **Buck Hill** (0.2 mi./0.3 km rt., 15 min., moderate) to stand at the top of the South Unit. Watch for pronghorn, wild horses, and bison on the narrow road with steep, sharp curves.

Best Hike

PETRIFIED FOREST LOOP

DISTANCE: 9.6 miles (15.4 km) round-trip
DURATION: 5-6 hours
ELEVATION CHANGE: 600 feet (183 m)
EFFORT: moderate
TRAILHEAD: Petrified Forest Trailhead

A romp through a badlands wilderness of flat prairie grasslands visits an ancient petrified forest by incorporating several trails in the remote northwest corner of the South Unit. Start the loop on the **North Petrified Forest Trail** to get the tough drops and climbs done early. This trail also has the larger collection of petrified stumps and log chunks on the route. When you meet up with the **Maah Daah Hey Trail** (www.mdhta.com, 144 mi./232 km), turn right to traverse grasslands on a short section of this lengthy National Recreation Trail that connects all three units of the park. At the **South Forest Trail,** turn right to see more petrified trees and return to the trailhead. Check with the visitors center for road conditions and drive west on I-94 to exit 23 and follow the signs to Petrified Forest.

ENTRANCES AND FEES

The **South Unit** has two entrances. The main entrance next to the town of Medora off I-94 launches the paved road into the interior badlands. Seven miles (11 km) east is the other entrance at Painted Canyon on I-94, exit 32. The **North Unit** entrance is on ND 85 south of Watford City.

The entrance fee is $30 per vehicle ($25 motorcycle, $15 individual) and good for seven days. You can **buy your pass online** (www.yourpassnow.com) from home to speed through entrance stations faster. You can also pay fees at entrance stations during summer or at visitors centers in fall, winter, and spring.

▼ WIND CANYON TRAIL IN THE SOUTH UNIT

THEODORE ROOSEVELT

Theodore Roosevelt came to the badlands to work as a cowboy almost two decades before becoming president of the United States. His experience here shaped him into one of the United States' earliest conservationists.

Roosevelt traveled to the Dakota Territory in 1883 to hunt bison for two weeks. These rugged badlands took root in his mind and the landscape captivated him. Before returning to New York, he bought Chimney Butte Ranch (called the Maltese Cross Ranch) and a herd of cattle. The ponderosa-pine Maltese Cabin (reconstructed near the South Unit Visitor Center) was part of this ranch and Roosevelt's part-time home as he bounced between New York and the Dakotas. After the death of his wife and mother, followed by a heavy political loss, he returned to the ranch intending to quit politics and become a cattle rancher.

Roosevelt then purchased Elkhorn Ranch, dubbed the "home ranch," to expand his cattle business. In 1884-1885, he hired two men to build the house, barn, and outbuildings. Within two years, a drought coupled with a wickedly cold winter nearly killed off his herd, prompting him to abandon the ranch and move back to New York and into politics.

Eleven years later, Roosevelt became the 26th president of the United States, attributing his election win to his experiences in North Dakota. He wrote three books on his cowboy life there, which formed the backbone for his push for conservation. Roosevelt's legacy includes the establishment of the U.S. Forest Service, the creation of five national parks, and numerous proclamations preserving wildlife reserves, national forests, national monuments, and antiquities.

This park honors Roosevelt for his vision and his efforts.

VISITORS CENTERS

The **South Unit Visitor Center** (8am-6pm daily in summer, 8am-4:30pm daily fall-spring) has a museum with exhibits on geology and history, a bookstore, and restrooms. Ranger-led talks, walks, hikes, and campfire programs are scheduled in June-mid-September. Moved here from its original location is Theodore Roosevelt's **Maltese Cross Cabin,** a restored icon from his years in the badlands. Rangers lead tours of the cabin daily in summer. The **Dakota Nights Astronomy Festival** takes place in early September and offers stargazing with astronomers and rangers.

Farther east in the South Unit is the **Painted Canyon Visitor Center** (8:30am-5:30pm daily May-Oct., closed winter), which has indoor exhibits, a bookstore, hiking trails, and an outdoor overlook with panoramic views of the badlands. Bison frequent the area. The center is off exit 32 of I-94.

The **North Unit Contact Station** (9am-5pm daily in summer) is housed in temporary trailers at the North Unit entrance. The information desk can advise on current trail conditions. Restrooms and a gift shop are available.

SCENIC DRIVES

ELKHORN RANCH

Theodore Roosevelt had the **Elkhorn Ranch** built in 1884-1885 on land sliced by the Little Missouri River. He abandoned the dwelling two years later after losing nearly all his livestock to brutal weather. Today, only stones marking the foundations remain, yet you can still get a sense of the quietude the president enjoyed while ranching in the Dakota Territory.

The Elkhorn Ranch Unit sits between the North and South Units. To get there, take exit 23 off I-94 and drive 35 miles (56 km, 90 min.) along the rough gravel road. A high-clearance 4WD vehicle is required. Stop first at the visitors center for road conditions and directions.

NORTH UNIT

From the North Unit entrance station, cruise along the 28-mile (45-km) paved and scenic drive with interpretive stops at several overlooks of the Little Missouri. **River Bend,** at the halfway point, and **Oxbow Overlook,** at the road's terminus, are the best places to soak in the views. En route, watch for the herd of **longhorn steers,** maintained by the park, and other wildlife. For a geologic oddity, stop at **Cannonball Concretions Pullout,** where large round rocks are exposed by erosion.

HIKING

SOUTH UNIT

Three trails take off from the South Unit Scenic Drive. The **Wind Canyon Trail** (0.4 mi./0.6 km rt., 20 min., easy) ascends past a wind-sculpted canyon for views of the Little Missouri.

The **Coal Vein Trail** (0.8 mi./1.3 km rt., 30-45 min., moderate) is the best way to learn the geology of the badlands—you'll see clay layers, caprocks, slumping, and chimneys. Pick up an interpretive brochure at the trailhead.

Short but steep, the **Ridgeline Trail** (0.6 mi./1 km rt., 30 min., moderate) takes in colorful badlands, grasslands, and bison, with birds and wildflowers in spring. Pick up a nature guide at the trailhead.

NORTH UNIT

Little Mo Nature Trail (0.7-1.1 mi./1.1-1.8 km, 30-45 min., easy) explores the river habitat along the Little Missouri River.

The **Caprock Coulee Nature Trail** (1.5 mi./2.4 km rt., 1 hr., moderate) explores badlands features such as coulees, erosions, and petrified wood. Pick up an interpretive brochure at the trailhead. From the same trailhead, follow a portion of the **Buckhorn Trail** (1.5 mi./2.4 km rt., 1 hr., moderate) to a prairie dog town where you can watch the antics of these furry ground dwellers.

WHERE TO STAY

INSIDE THE PARK

There are no accommodations or restaurants in the park. Camping is the only overnight option.

Two year-round campgrounds flanking the Little Missouri River have

▼ CANNONBALL CONCRETIONS

OXBOW OVERLOOK WITH LITTLE MISSOURI RIVER

drinking water and flush toilets in summer with reduced services and fees in winter. Reservations are accepted six months in advance for May through September camping at the South Unit's **Cottonwood Campground** (701/623-4466 or 877/444-6777, www.recreation.gov, 66 sites, $14); it is first come, first served for the rest of the year. The North Unit's **Juniper Campground** (701/842-2333, year-round, 50 sites, $14) has first-come, first-served sites.

Backcountry camping is allowed with a free permit available from the visitors centers. There are no established backcountry campsites.

OUTSIDE THE PARK

The closest accommodations and services are located near the South Unit in **Medora.**

GETTING THERE AND AROUND

AIR

The nearest airport is in **Bismarck** (BIS, 2301 University Dr., 701/355-1800, www.bismarckairport.com), 134 miles (216 km) east of the South Unit via I-94. The airport has rental cars.

CAR

There is no public transportation to or within the park. Visiting the park will require a car with long drives between the three units.

To reach the **South Unit,** take I-94 (exit 24 or 27) to the town of Medora and the South Unit Visitor Center. Use exit 32 (7 mi./11 km east of Medora) to reach the Painted Canyon Visitor Center.

From Medora, it's a 70-mile (113-km) drive to the **North Unit.** From I-94 at Belfield, take exit 42 to ND 85.

To reach the **Elkhorn Ranch Unit**, you'll need a high-clearance, 4WD vehicle for the rough gravel road. Obtain road conditions and directions from the visitors centers. From Medora, the drive takes 1.5 hours.

SIGHTS NEARBY

Knife River Indian Villages National Historic Site (564 County Rd. 37, Stanton, 701/745-3300, www.nps.gov/knri, 9am-6pm daily late May-early Sept., 8am-4:30pm daily mid-Sept.-mid-May) is home to a reconstructed earthen lodge, with trails through the Mandan and Hidatsa village site.

GREAT LAKES AND NORTHEAST

Along the boulder-strewn shores of Maine lies the only national park in the northeastern United States: Acadia National Park. Watch the sun rise from Cadillac Mountain, stroll the Park Loop Road, and ride the carriage roads at this East Coast gem.

The Great Lakes region is home to three national parks. In Ohio, Cuyahoga Valley National Park contains river canals of historic import. In Indiana, the southern shore of Lake Michigan is home to Indiana Dunes National Park. In Michigan, a cluster of islands in Lake Superior forms Isle Royale National Park. Tucked into a corner of Minnesota is the remote Voyageurs National Park, a haven for boaters.

◂ BASS HARBOR LIGHT, ACADIA NATIONAL PARK

GREAT LAKES AND NORTHEAST
CANADA
Voyageurs NP
Isle Royale NP
Lake Superior
MINNESOTA
MICHIGAN
WISCONSIN
Lake Michigan
Lake Huron
MICHIGAN
Lake Ontario
NEW YORK
Buffalo
Detroit
Lake Erie
Cleveland
Cuyahoga Valley NP
Chicago
Indiana Dunes NP
IOWA
ILLINOIS
INDIANA
OHIO
PENNSYLVANIA
MAINE
Acadia NP
VT
NH
MA
CT
RI
New York City
NJ
DE
MD
Washington DC
WV
VA
ATLANTIC OCEAN
0
100 mi
0
100 km
© MOON.COM

The National Parks of THE GREAT LAKES AND NORTHEAST

ACADIA, ME

Drama comes from mountains tumbling to the sea and ocean waves crashing upon granite ledges, while serene lakes provide pastoral alternatives (page 544).

CUYAHOGA VALLEY, OH

Canals and a scenic railway cut through a lush countryside of forests, wetlands, and prairies (page 560).

INDIANA DUNES, IN

Sand dunes flanking the southern beaches of Lake Michigan collide with forest, prairie, and marsh habitats for huge diversity (page 569).

ISLE ROYALE, MI

Seasonal boat tours guide visitors around this isolated archipelago (page 577).

VOYAGEURS, MN

Remote forests, 660 miles (1,060 km) of wild shoreline, and more than 500 islands are found in this water-filled park (page 584).

1: JORDAN POND, ACADIA
2: SCHOODIC PENINSULA, ACADIA
3: VIRGINIA KENDALL LEDGES, CUYAHOGA VALLEY

Best OF THE PARKS

Jordan Pond House: Sip afternoon tea at this rustic 19th-century teahouse (page 549).

Kettle Falls Hotel: Grab a meal or a drink at this historic lodge 16 miles (26 km) from the nearest road (page 588).

Canoeing and Kayaking: Paddle miles of shoreline waters at Voyageurs and Isle Royale (pages 589 and 581).

Wildlife-Watching: Spy moose at Hidden Lake (page 582).

Ohio and Erie Canal Towpath Trail: Bike along the Cuyahoga River on this historic path (page 564).

Everett Road Covered Bridge: Pose for pics on the only remaining covered bridge in Summit County, Ohio (page 564).

PLANNING YOUR TRIP

Plan at least **one weekend** in Acadia and **another week or two** to tour the national parks of the Great Lakes. Make lodging and campground **reservations** up to one year in advance.

September-mid-October is the best time to travel in Maine. Days are warm and mostly dry, nights are cool, fog is rare, bugs are gone, and crowds are few. Foliage turns by early October, usually reaching peak colors mid-month.

Summer (May-Oct.) is the most popular time to visit the Great Lakes, for beach fun, kayaking, and boating. The weather is temperate with long, lingering evenings. July is typically the warmest month, but it's also the buggiest. Time a camping trip in mid-June or after mid-August, when the mosquitoes and blackflies are less bothersome.

Fall is the best time to visit Cuyahoga, when one can savor the vibrant fall foliage and crisp, dry air. Hiking and biking trails are available spring through fall.

▲ PADDLE VOYAGEURS' WATERS.

Touring the Great Lakes

LAKE, VOYAGEURS NATIONAL PARK

VOYAGEURS AND ISLE ROYALE

You can hit these two remote national parks in **one week.** Fly into **Minneapolis-St. Paul International Airport** and then rent a car for the drive to the parks. You will also need to travel by boat to explore these gems, which are prime destinations for paddlers.

Voyageurs

310 miles (500 km) / 5 hours

From Minneapolis-St. Paul, drive north on I-35 to reach the **Rainy Lake Visitor Center.** Spend three days in **Voyageurs National Park**. Take a boat tour to either **Little American Island** or **Kettle Falls,** then get out on the water yourself in a canoe or kayak.

Isle Royale

275 miles (445 km) / 5 hours

From Voyageurs, drive southeast on US 53 to **Grand Portage** on Lake Superior, the back door to **Isle Royale.** Catch the passenger ferry to **Rock Harbor** and rent a kayak to spend three days paddling the waters around Isle Royale.

From Grand Portage, paddlers can extend their adventures with a side trip to tour the remote **Boundary Waters Canoe Area Wilderness.** This paddling paradise sits 66 miles (106 km, 1.75 hrs.) southwest from Grand Portage. Take I-35 south to head back to Minneapolis-St. Paul.

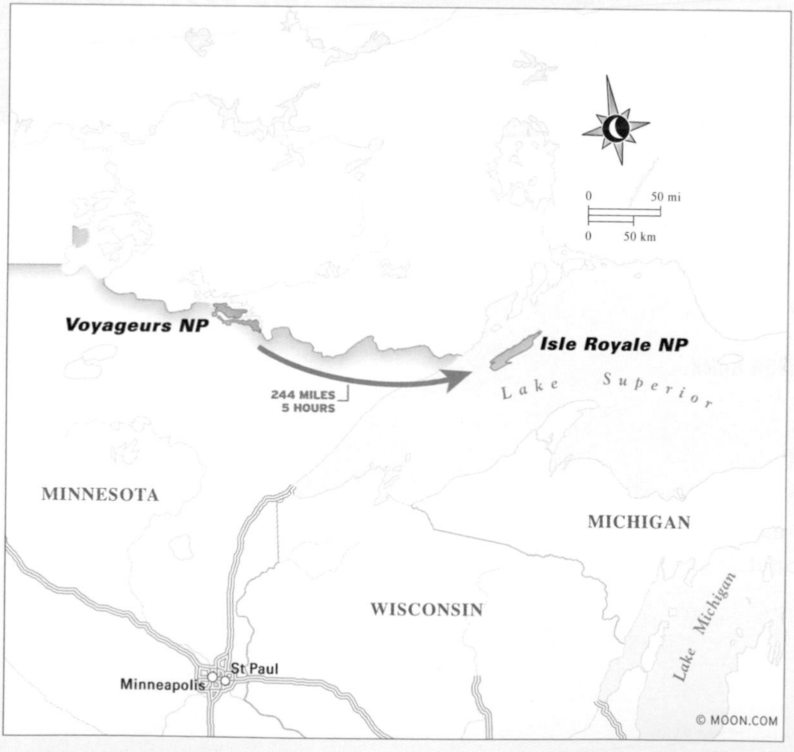

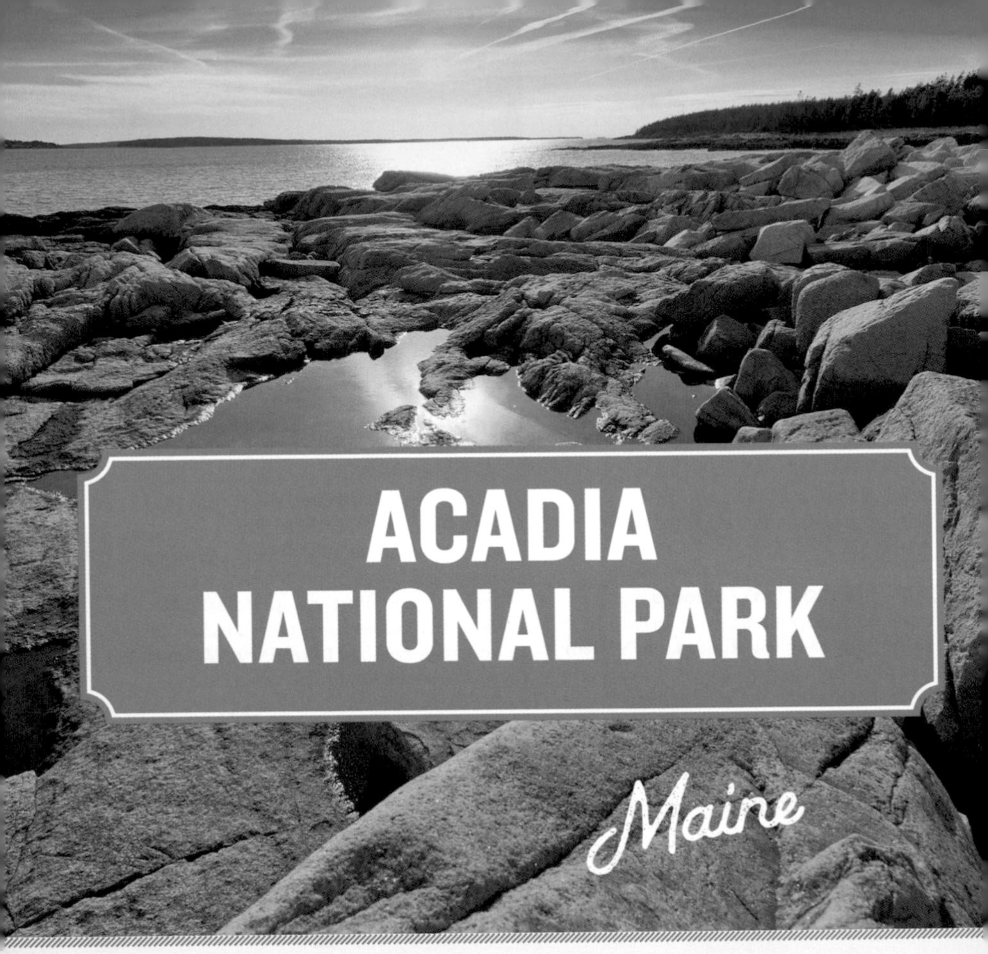

WEBSITE:
www.nps.gov/acad

PHONE NUMBER:
207/288-3338

VISITATION RANK:
7

WHY GO:
Travel the rugged northeast island seacoast.

▲ ACADIA NATIONAL PARK

KEEPSAKE STAMPS ▼▼▼

ACADIA NATIONAL PARK extends its reach here and there, like an octopus (or perhaps an amoeba), sprawling over roughly half of Mount Desert Island. The first national park east of the Mississippi River and the only national park in the northeastern United States, it was created from donated parcels—a big chunk here, a tiny piece there—and slowly fused into its present-day shape.

This park tops out at the pink granite of Cadillac Mountain, the highest point on the East Coast, which is sacred to the Wabanaki people who have called this region home for thousands of years—as are the park's mountains, lakes, ponds, and tidepools. Today, even at the height of summer, when the whole world seems to have arrived, it's possible to find peaceful niches and less trodden paths in this sacred place.

PLANNING YOUR TIME

Acadia National Park sits on the Maine coast south of Bangor. Mount Desert Island is the most accessible of the park's watery isles; the Schoodic Peninsula and Isle au Haut require time to explore and are best reached via boat or ferry.

You can circumnavigate Mount Desert Island in one day, hitting the highlights along the Park Loop Road with just enough time to *ooh* and *aah* at each. But to truly appreciate Acadia, you must hike the trails, ride the carriage roads, get afloat on a whale-watching cruise or a sea kayak, visit museums, and explore an offshore island or two. A week or longer is best, but you can get a taste of Acadia in 3-4 days.

The region is very seasonal, with most restaurants, accommodations, and shops open **mid-May-mid-October.** May and June bring spring, but also mosquitoes, blackflies, and temperamental weather—sunny and hot one day, damp and cold the next. July and August are summer at its best, but also bring the biggest crowds. September is a gem of a time to visit: few bugs, fewer people, less fog, and autumn's golden light.

Foliage usually begins turning in **early October,** making it an especially beautiful time to visit (the Columbus Day holiday weekend brings a spike in visitors). Winter is Acadia's silent season, with several roads closed due to snow.

ENTRANCES AND FEES

The main park entrance is **ME 3** through Ellsworth to Mount Desert Island. ME 3 continues southeast, passing through the **Hulls Cove Entrance** to the gateway town of Bar Harbor and the **Cadillac Mountain Entrance.**

The entrance fee is $30 per vehicle ($25 motorcycle, $15 individual) and good for seven days. You can **buy your pass online** (www.yourpassnow.com) from home to speed through entrance stations faster.

VISITORS CENTERS

Hulls Cove Visitor Center

Reached by climbing 52 steps (and with accessible access, too), the modern **Hulls Cove Visitor Center** (25 Visitor Center Rd., Bar Harbor, 8:30am-4:30pm daily mid-Apr.-late June and Sept.-Oct., 8am-6pm daily late June-early Sept.) has park passes, digital information kiosks, ranger-guided programs, a park film, a large relief map of the park, and a bookstore. Pick up schedules for ranger programs and the Island Explorer shuttle bus. You can also enroll your kids in the park's Junior Ranger Program (fee).

In winter, when the Hulls Cove Visitor Center is closed, National Park Service rangers move visitor information services to the **Bar Harbor Chamber**

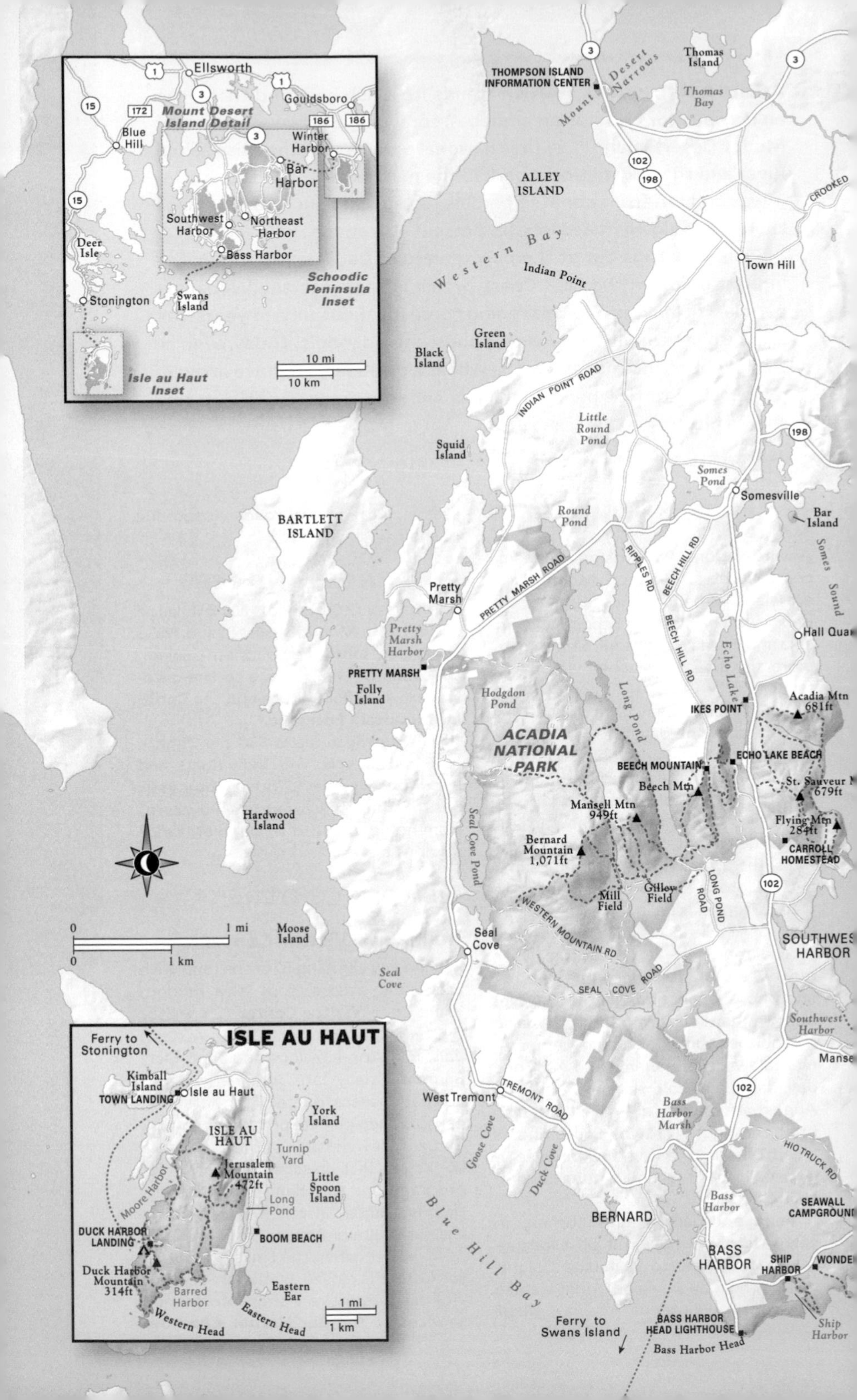

Ellsworth
Gouldsboro
Mount Desert Island Detail
Blue Hill
Winter Harbor
Bar Harbor
Southwest Harbor
Northeast Harbor
Deer Isle
Bass Harbor
Schoodic Peninsula Inset
Stonington
Swans Island
Isle au Haut Inset
10 mi
10 km
THOMPSON ISLAND INFORMATION CENTER
Mount Desert Narrows
Thomas Island
Thomas Bay
ALLEY ISLAND
CROOKED
Western Bay
Indian Point
Town Hill
Green Island
Black Island
INDIAN POINT ROAD
Little Round Pond
Squid Island
Somes Pond
Somesville
BARTLETT ISLAND
Round Pond
Bar Island
RIPPLES RD
BEECH HILL RD
Somes Sound
Pretty Marsh
PRETTY MARSH ROAD
Pretty Marsh Harbor
Hall Qua
Echo Lake
PRETTY MARSH
Folly Island
Hodgdon Pond
Long Pond
IKES POINT
Acadia Mtn 681ft
ACADIA NATIONAL PARK
BEECH MOUNTAIN
ECHO LAKE BEACH
Beech Mtn
St. Sauveur 679ft
Mansell Mtn 949ft
Hardwood Island
Seal Cove Pond
Flying Mtn 284ft
Bernard Mountain 1,071ft
CARROLL HOMESTEAD
Mill Field
Gilley Field
LONG POND ROAD
WESTERN MOUNTAIN RD
0
1 mi
1 km
Moose Island
Seal Cove
SOUTHWEST HARBOR
Seal Cove
SEAL COVE ROAD
Southwest Harbor
Manse
ISLE AU HAUT
Ferry to Stonington
Kimball Island
TOWN LANDING
Isle au Haut
York Island
ISLE AU HAUT
Turnip Yard
Jerusalem Mountain 472ft
Little Spoon Island
Moore Harbor
Long Pond
DUCK HARBOR LANDING
BOOM BEACH
Duck Harbor Mountain 314ft
Eastern Ear
Barred Harbor
Western Head
Eastern Head
1 mi
1 km
West Tremont
TREMONT ROAD
Bass Harbor Marsh
Goose Cove
Duck Cove
HIO TRUCK RD
Blue Hill Bay
Bass Harbor
BERNARD
SEAWALL CAMPGROUNI
BASS HARBOR
SHIP HARBOR
WONDE
Ferry to Swans Island
BASS HARBOR HEAD LIGHTHOUSE
Bass Harbor Head
Ship Harbor

ACADIA NATIONAL PARK
Salsbury Cove
Eastern Bay
Parker Point
Frenchman Bay
Lookout Point
Hulls Cove
Hulls Cove
START OF PARK LOOP ROAD
HULLS COVE ENTRANCE
HULLS COVE VISITOR CENTER
Lake Wood
PARK LOOP ROAD
Bar Island
Burnt Porcupine Island
Long Porcupine Island
Jordan Island
Sheep Porcupine Island
3
BAR HARBOR
VILLAGE GREEN
IRONBOUND ISLAND
Breakneck Ponds
DUCK BROOK RD
CADILLAC MOUNTAIN ENTRANCE
Breakwater
Bald Porcupine Island
PARK HEADQUARTERS
233
233
Aunt Betty Pond
PARK LOOP ROAD
Eagle Lake
CARRIAGE ROADS
SIEUR DE MONTS
WILD GARDENS OF ACADIA
NATURE CENTER
BEAR BROOK
ABBE MUSEUM
The Thrumcap
Ferry To Winter Harbor
Connors Nubble 588ft
CADILLAC MTN ROAD
SIEUR DE MONTS ENTRANCE
SCHOONER HEAD RD
The Tarn
Cadillac Mountain 1,530ft
Champlain Mountain 1,058ft
PARK LOOP ROAD
Egg Rock
CARRIAGE ROADS
North Bubble 872ft
Schooner Head
Gilmore Peak 1,036ft
Bubble Pond
The Bowl
OVERLOOK
SAND BEACH ENTRANCE STATION
Pemetic Mountain 1248ft
ACADIA NATIONAL PARK
Jordan Pond
Penobscot Mountain 1,194ft
The Beehive 520ft
OTTER CLIFF RD
SAND BEACH
Great Head
Old Soaker
JORDAN POND HOUSE
GATEHOUSE
THUNDER HOLE
PARK LOOP ROAD
FABBRI
WILDWOOD STABLES
Otter Cove
Otter Cliff
CARRIAGE ROADS
Day Mtn 583ft
Lower Hadlock Pond
Long Pond
BLACKWOODS CAMPGROUND
Otter Point
Atlantic Ocean
STANLEY BROOK ENTRANCE
SEAL HARBOR
LITTLE HUNTERS BEACH
Northeast Harbor
Seal Harbor
Hunters Head
3
Ingraham Point
Bear Island
Eastern Way
Greening Island
PASSENGER FERRY
Sutton Island
PASSENGER FERRY
ISLESFORD HISTORICAL MUSEUM
PASSENGER FERRY
Islesford
Cranberry Isles
Western Way
LITTLE CRANBERRY ISLAND
BAKER ISLAND
The Pool
GREAT CRANBERRY ISLAND
BAKER ISLAND LIGHT
SCHOODIC PENINSULA
Winter Harbor
186
Winter Harbor
SCHOODIC WOODS CAMPGROUND
Birch Harbor
FRAZER POINT
Bunker Harbor
SCHOODIC PENINSULA
Ferry to Bar Harbor
PARK LOOP ROAD
Schoodic Head
Schoodic Harbor
Spruce Point
The Anvil
SCHOODIC EDUCATION AND RESEARCH CENTER
BLUEBERRY HILL
Schoodic Island
Little Moose Island
SCHOODIC POINT
1 mi
1 km
OON.COM

of Commerce Information Center (2 Cottage St., Bar Harbor, 207/288-3338, 8am-4pm daily Nov.-mid-Apr.).

Information Centers

Tiny **Thompson Island Information Center** (8:30am-5:30pm daily mid-May-mid-Oct.) sits across the bridge from Trenton en route to Mount Desert Island. A park ranger is usually available to answer questions and give advice on hiking trails and park activities.

The park maintains the small **Village Green Information Center** (19 Firefly Ln., Bar Harbor, daily 8am-5pm late June-mid-Oct.) in downtown Bar Harbor, adjacent to the Island Explorer bus stop. Park and bus information, as well as visitor passes, are available.

AVOID THE CROWDS

During midsummer, Acadia seems to be loved to death. Long lines of cars clog the entrances, and parking lots overflow. In fact, at congested times, rangers temporarily restrict access. Try these tactics to avoid the congestion:

Go early morning or late in the afternoon for fewer crowds and more enjoyment. Most visitors fill the park roads 10am-4pm.

Visit in **spring, late fall,** or **winter** when visitation is lower.

Skip the parking headache and take an off-the-beaten path adventure such as **hiking, bicycling,** or **paddling.**

Leave your vehicle behind and take the free **Island Explorer shuttle bus** into the park.

Bicycle the carriage roads, where cars are not permitted.

Go after dark for **stargazing.**

Instead of heading to Cadillac Mountain for sunrise or sunset, catch **sunrise on Ocean Drive** or sunset from a boat.

Buy your **entrance pass online** to pass through the entrance station quickly.

SIGHTS

MOUNT DESERT ISLAND

Abbe Museum

The **Abbe Museum** (Most Island Explorer Rts., 26 Mount Desert St., Bar Harbor, 207/288-3519, www.abbemuseum.org) is a superb introduction to prehistoric, historic, and contemporary Native American tools, crafts, and other cultural artifacts, with an emphasis on Maine's Wabanaki peoples.

The **main campus** (26 Mount Desert St., Bar Harbor, 207/288-3519, www.abbemuseum.org, 10am-5pm daily May-Oct., 10am-4pm Thurs.-Sat. Nov.-Apr., $8 adults, $4 children ages 11-17) is home to a collection spanning nearly 12,000 years. Admission to the main campus also includes admission to the **museum's original site** (2.5 mi./4 km south of Bar Harbor at Sieur de Monts Spring, 9am-5pm daily May-Oct., closed winter), a small but handsome building that displays a 50,000-item collection.

Take the time to wander the paths in the adjacent **Wild Gardens of Acadia,** a 0.75-acre (0.3-ha) microcosm of more than 400 plant species native to Mount Desert Island.

Somes Sound

From the northern end of Mount Desert Island heading south toward Northeast Harbor on ME 198, cliff-lined Somes Sound appears on your right. The glacier-sculpted fjard (not as deep or as steeply walled as a fjord) juts 5 miles (8 km) into the interior of Mount Desert Island from its mouth between Northeast Harbor and Southwest Harbor. Watch for the right-hand turn for **Sargent Drive,** and follow the lovely, granite-lined route along the east side of the sound. Halfway along, a marker at one of the few pullouts explains the geology of this natural inlet. Traffic can be thick in midsummer.

Suminsby Park, off Sargent Drive (400 ft./122 m from ME 3), has rocky shore access, a hand-carry boat launch, picnic tables, grills, and a pit toilet. An ideal way to appreciate Somes Sound is from the water—sign up for an excursion departing from Northeast Harbor or Southwest Harbor.

Southwest Harbor (Island Explorer Rt. 7) is the hub of Mount Desert

Top 3

ACADIA'S PARK LOOP ROAD

1 DRIVE THE PARK LOOP ROAD

On Desert Island, the 27-mile (43-km) **Park Loop Road** (mid-Apr.-Nov., Island Explorer Rts. 3 & 4) takes in most of the big-ticket sites. Part of the route is one-way, so you'll drive the loop clockwise. From the **Hulls Cove Visitor Center,** the road winds past several of the park's scenic highlights, ascending to the summit of **Cadillac Mountain** with overlooks to magnificent vistas. Along the way are trailheads and overlooks: **Sieur de Monts Spring, Sand Beach, Thunder Hole, Otter Cliff, Fabbri Picnic Area, Jordan Pond House, Bubble Pond,** and **Eagle Lake.**

2 SIP AFTERNOON TEA AT JORDAN POND HOUSE

The **Jordan Pond House** (Island Explorer Rt. 5, 2928 Park Loop Rd., 207/276-3316, www.jordanpondhouse.com, 11am-9pm daily) is a modern facility in an idyllic waterside setting. Jordan Pond House began life as a rustic 19th-century teahouse; old photos still line the walls of the current incarnation, which was built after a disastrous fire in 1979. Afternoon tea is still a tradition, with tea, popovers, and strawberry jam served on the lawn until 5pm daily in summer, weather permitting. Expect to wait for seats at the height of summer.

3 TOUR THE CARRIAGE ROADS ON MOUNT DESERT ISLAND

RIDE A HORSE-DRAWN CARRIAGE ON ACADIA'S CARRIAGE ROADS.

In 1913, John D. Rockefeller Jr. began laying out what eventually became a 57-mile (92-km) carriage road system. Motorized vehicles have never been allowed on these lovely graded byways, making them real escapes from the auto world. Devoted now to multiple uses, the "Rockefeller roads" see hikers, bikers, baby strollers, wheelchairs, and even horse-drawn carriages. Rangers guide summer biking and walking tours on the carriage roads, which you can reach via the Island Explorer Rt. 5 & 6.

To recapture the early carriage roads era, take one of the horse-drawn open-carriage tours from **Carriages of Acadia** (Wildwood Stables, Park Loop Rd., Seal Harbor, 877/276-3622, www.acadiahorses.com), south of Jordan Pond House. Four one- and two-hour tours run daily (mid-June-mid-Oct.). Make reservations, especially in summer.

ONE DAY IN ACADIA

Drive or take the Island Explorer Rt. 4 to tour the **Park Loop Road.** To get a broad view of the mountain-and-island environment, stop at the summit of **Cadillac Mountain.** Stroll the nature trail at **Jordan Pond,** and enjoy afternoon tea at **Jordan Pond House.** Then, tour the museum and paths at **Sieur de Monts Spring.**

With more time, you can hike the Beehive Trail or Precipice Trail, take a boat tour, bike the carriage roads, and explore remote Schoodic Point.

Island's "quiet side." In summer, its tiny downtown district is the island's busiest spot west of Somes Sound.

Bass Harbor Head Lighthouse

At the southern end of Mount Desert, follow ME 102A to the turnoff toward Bass Harbor Head. Drive or bike to the end of Lighthouse Road, walk down a steep wooden stairway, and look up and to the right. **Bass Harbor Head Lighthouse**—its red glow automated since 1974—stands sentinel at the eastern entrance to Blue Hill Bay. Built in 1858, the 26-foot (8-m) tower and lightkeeper's house are privately owned, but the dramatic setting captivates photographers.

Cadillac Mountain

The sunrise awaits those who can drive predawn to the summit of **Cadillac Mountain**. It's a tradition, albeit an overcrowded one in summer, to catch the first rays to hit the eastern United States from Acadia's highest point. (You can also watch the sunrise from Ocean Drive and other locations.) Sunset aficionados also nab colors across the western horizon. Cadillac Mountain also hosts the annual **Acadia Night Sky Festival** (late Sept.) for telescope-viewing of stars and celestial wonders.

SCHOODIC PENINSULA

On the mainland, the **Schoodic Peninsula** (Island Explorer Rt. 8) is separated from Mount Desert Island by a two-hour drive. The lack of congestion, even at the height of summer, is the main appeal for a visit to the eastern side of Frenchman Bay. The Schoodic Peninsula also has abundant opportunities

BASS HARBOR HEAD LIGHTHOUSE

SCHOODIC PENINSULA

for outdoor recreation, two scenic byways, and dozens of artist and artisan studios. But the biggest attractions are the spectacular vignettes and vistas—of offshore lighthouses, distant mountains, and close-in islands—and the unchanged villages.

To reach the park boundary from ME 1 in Gouldsboro, take ME 186 south to Winter Harbor. Continue through town, heading east, and then turn right and continue to the park.

Winter Harbor

Winter Harbor, known best as the gateway to Schoodic, is home to an old-money, low-profile, Philadelphia-linked summer colony on exclusive Grindstone Neck. The landscape of the smaller and far less touristed Schoodic isn't as awe-inspiring as that on Mount Desert, but it has a remoter, rawer edge. Too-frequent fog rolls in to shroud the stunted, scraggly spruce clinging to its pink granite shores. There's a **campground** and visitors center, along with 8 miles (13 km) of **carriage roads** for foot or bicycle exploration.

Scenic Drive

The **Schoodic Peninsula Loop** (6 mi./10 km, one-way) meanders counterclockwise around the tip of the Schoodic Peninsula. You'll discover picnic areas, trailheads, offshore lighthouses, a welcome center with exhibits, and small turnouts with scenic vistas. Do this loop early in the morning or later in the afternoon. The gorgeous late September-early October foliage increases traffic. If you see a viewpoint you like with room to pull off, stop; it's a long way around to return.

Near the southern end of the loop, a short, two-way road goes to **Schoodic Point,** the highlight of the drive where surf crashes onto big slabs of pink granite. The **Schoodic Institute** campus (207/288-1310, www.schoodicinstitute.org), on the site of a former top-secret U.S. Navy base, is housed in the restored **Rockefeller Hall** (9 Atterbury Circle, 10am-4pm daily late May-mid-Oct., weekdays only in winter). It has a small info center staffed by volunteers and park rangers. Exhibits highlight Schoodic's ecology and history, the former navy base's radio and cryptologic operations, and current research programs. The institute offers ranger-led activities, lectures, and other programs and events.

On the south end of the loop, you'll spot **Little Moose Island,** accessible at low tide. At **Blueberry Hill,** a moorlike setting with low growth allows almost 180-degree views of the bay and islands.

ISLE AU HAUT

The Isle au Haut section of the park sees 5,000-7,500 visitors annually, with a daily cap of 128. The limited boat service, the remoteness of the island, and the scarcity of campsites contribute to the low count, leaving the trails and views for only a few hardy souls. The **ranger station** (207/288-3338) has trail maps, information, and the only public facilities.

HIKING

MOUNT DESERT ISLAND

Jordan Pond

The **Jordan Pond Nature Trail** (3.3 mi./5.3 km rt., 1.5 hr., easy) starts from the Jordan Pond parking area and leads through woods and down to the pond to follow the shore before looping back.

Champlain Mountain

Near Sieur de Monts Spring, the **Champlain North Ridge Trail** (Bear Brook Trail, 1.9 mi./3.1 km rt., 2-3 hr., strenuous) bolts up a steep ascent through pines and granite to Champlain Mountain. The summit yields views of the ocean, islands, Schoodic Peninsula, and Bar Harbor. (Combine this trail with the Precipice and Beechcroft Trails for more distance.)

From the Park Loop Road, the **Precipice Trail** (3.2-mi./5.2-km loop, 3 hrs., strenuous, closed mid-Apr.-mid-Aug.) lures hordes of wannabe climbers to its steep but nontechnical 1,072-foot (327-m) ascent of switchbacks, ladders, and exposed ledges to reach the summit. Return via the Champlain North Ridge Trail and Orange and Black Path.

The **Beachcroft Trail** (2.4 mi./3.9 km rt., 2-3 hrs., moderately strenuous) is known for its 1,500 beautifully engineered granite steps. The route gains 1,100 feet (335 m) over Huguenot Head to the summit of Champlain Mountain.

Sand Beach

From the east end of Sand Beach, the **Great Head Trail** (1.7-mi./2.7-km loop, 1 hr., moderate) circles a headland with views of the ocean, tidepools, and the Beehive.

▼ VIEW OVER JORDAN POND

Best Hike

BEEHIVE LOOP

DISTANCE: 3.2 miles/5.2 km round-trip
DURATION: 1-2 hours
ELEVATION CHANGE: 450 feet (137 m)
DIFFICULTY: moderately strenuous
TRAILHEAD: Bowl Trailhead on Park Loop Road across from Sand Beach

The sometimes-crowded Beehive Trail starts and ends on the Bowl Trail, which those needing less of a challenge can use to reach the beehive-shaped summit, minus the climbing option. Not for acrophobes or tiny kids, the climbing option is a fun scramble (no technical rock climbing skills needed) with switchbacks, stone steps, handrails, and iron ladders. Ascending the Beehive's southern face, the exposed, steep route picks its way up smoothed granite to Beehive summit for views of beaches and bays. When the route crowds with hikers, you may have to wait at the obstacles. From the summit, return via the Bowl Trail, which descends past Bowl Lake.

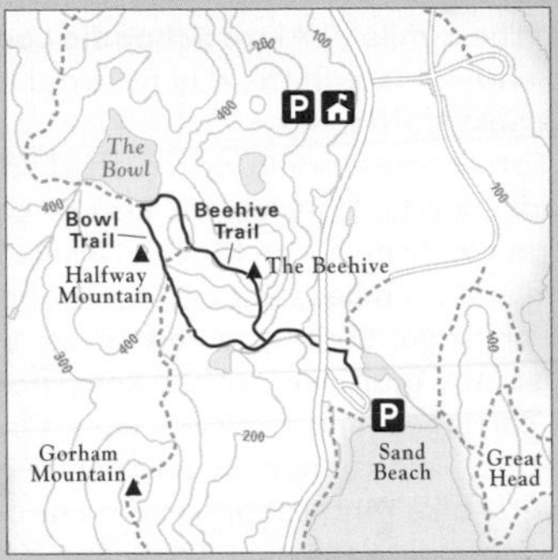

Gorham Mountain

From Gorham Mountain Trailhead, the **Gorham Mountain Trail** (3.5 mi./5.6 km rt., 2 hrs., moderate) shoots up a mountainside to follow cairns across rock ledges to the summit of Acadia's third-highest mountain, with big terrestrial and ocean views.

For an added challenge, detour via **Cadillac Cliffs,** an alternate route paralleling a portion of the Gorham Mountain Trail. Climb the granite stairs and walk under two rock slab tunnels before linking up with the main trail again. For a longer hike, combine this trail with the Bowl Trail and Ocean Path to return to your car.

Bass Harbor

From the Ship Harbor Trailhead, a figure-eight loop makes up the **Ship Harbor Nature Trail** (1.3 mi./2.1 km rt., 45 min., easy). The trail tours the forest to the ocean, where low tides beg for exploring tidepools.

From a mile west of Seawall Campground, the **Wonderland Trail** (1.4 mi./2.3 km rt., 45 min., easy) follows a fire road through a forest of mossy, wind-gnarled trees to a small cobble beach.

Beech Mountain

From the end of Beech Hill Road, climb **Beech Mountain** (2.3 mi./3.7 km rt., 1 hr., moderate) for to a fire tower overlooking Echo Lake and the Blue Hill Peninsula.

SCHOODIC PENINSULA

From Blueberry Hill parking lot, trails go to the open ledges on 440-foot-high (134-m) **Schoodic Head** (2.4 mi./3.9 km rt., 1 hr., moderate). Start on the easy Alder Trail to climb through a forest with outstanding bird habitat to reach the Schoodic Trailhead. Turn right to hike the rocky trail to the summit. An alternate route to Schoodic Head goes up the steep and rocky Alder Trail to make a loop (2.3 mi./3.7 km rt., 1 hr., moderate).

ISLE AU HAUT

The most-used park trail is **Duck Harbor Trail** (7.6 mi./12.2 km rt., 4 hrs., moderate), which connects the town landing with Duck Harbor. Though the summit is low, **Duck Harbor Mountain**

(2.4 mi./3.9 km rt., 3-4 hrs., strenuous) is the island's toughest trail loaded with rocks and roots, but rewards with a 360-degree view.

RECREATION

BICYCLING

The best choices for cycling on pavement are the 27-mile (43-km) **Park Loop Road** on Mount Desert Island and the 6-mile (9.7-km) **Schoodic Loop.** Go early or late in the day to avoid the heaviest traffic.

For car-free riding on crushed-rock roads, nearly 45 miles (72 km) of **carriage roads** await on Mount Desert Island and 8.3 miles (13.4 km) on Schoodic Peninsula. Some prohibit bikes, but most are multiuse with hikers, horses, carriages, and bicycles. Only Class I e-bikes are permitted on them. Find several bike rental shops in Bar Harbor. On Schoodic Peninsula, **SeaScape Kayak and Bike** (8 Duck Pond Rd., Winter Harbor, 908/723-0426, www.seascapekayaking.com) rents bicycles. For riding the Mount Desert Island carriage roads, the **Bicycle Express** (late June-Sept., free) runs a bike shuttle between Bar Harbor Village Green and Eagle Lake, and rangers lead frequent summer bike tours.

SWIMMING

Mount Desert Island

Sand Beach (Island Explorer Rt. 3) is Mount Desert Island's biggest sandy beach. Lifeguards are on duty during the summer—and even then, the biggest threat can be hypothermia. The saltwater is terminally glacial—in mid-July it still might not reach 60°F (15°C). Avoid the parking lot scramble by taking the shuttle.

The park's most popular freshwater swimming site is **Echo Lake** (Island Explorer Rt. 7)**,** south of Somesville on ME 102. The site is staffed with a lifeguard and can be crowded on hot days.

The eastern shore of **Hodgdon Pond** (also on the western side of the island) is accessible by car via Hodgdon Road and Long Pond Fire Road. **Lake Wood,** at the northern end of Mount Desert, has a tiny beach and restrooms. To get to Lake Wood from ME 3, head west on Crooked Road to the unpaved Park Road. Turn left and continue to the parking area, which will be crowded on a hot day. Arrive early.

Schoodic Peninsula

The best freshwater swimming on the Schoodic Peninsula is at **Jones Beach** (sunrise-sunset daily), a

▼ SAND BEACH

EXPLORE LONG POND BY CANOE OR KAYAK.

community-owned recreation area on Jones Pond in West Gouldsboro. It has restrooms, a playground, picnic facilities, a boat launch, a swim area with a float, and a small beach. The beach is located at the end of Recreation Road, off ME 195, which is 0.3 mile (0.5 km) south of ME 1.

Isle au Haut

For freshwater swimming on Isle au Haut, head for **Long Pond,** a skinny, 1.5-mile-long (2.4-km) swimming hole on the east side of the island, abutting national parkland. There's a minuscule beach-like area on the southern end with a picnic table and a float.

CANOEING AND KAYAKING

Long Pond (Pretty Marsh Rd.) is the largest lake on Mount Desert Island. Bring a canoe or kayak to launch at **Pond's End,** to paddle 4 miles (6.4 km) to the southern end of the lake. Another option is to launch your canoe on the quieter, cliff-lined southern end of the lake. To find the put-in, take Seal Cove Road (on the east end of downtown Southwest Harbor) to Long Cove Road. Turn right to enter the small parking area near the pumping station. Almost the entire west side of Long Pond is in Acadia National Park.

If you have a canoe, kayak, or rowboat, you can reach swimming holes in **Seal Cove Pond** and **Round Pond,** both on the western side of Mount Desert.

National Park Canoe & Kayak Rental (145 Pretty Marsh Rd./Rte. 102, Mount Desert, 207/244-5854, www.nationalparkcanoerental.com, mid-May-mid-Oct.) rents the boat; just carry it across the road to Pond's End, and launch it. Reservations are essential July-August.

Experienced sea kayakers can explore the coastline throughout the **Schoodic Peninsula,** while canoeists can paddle the placid waters of **Jones Pond. SeaScape Kayak and Bike** (8 Duck Pond Rd., Winter Harbor, 908/723-0426, www.seascapekayaking.com) has freshwater rental kayaks on Jones Pond.

ROCK CLIMBING

Acadia has splendid sites prized by technical rock climbers: the sea cliffs at Otter Cliff and Great Head, South Bubble Mountain, Canada Cliff (on the island's western side), and the South Wall and the Central Slabs on Champlain Mountain. If you haven't tried climbing with ropes, harnesses, and protection, never do it yourself without instruction. **Acadia Mountain Guides Climbing School** (228 Main St.,

CLIMBERS PREPARE TO SCALE ACADIA'S GRANITE CLIFFS.

Bar Harbor, 207/288-8186, www.acadiamountainguides.com) and **Atlantic Climbing School** (ACS, 67 Main St., 2nd fl., Bar Harbor, 207/288-2521, www.climbacadia.com) both provide instruction and guided climbs.

WHERE TO STAY

INSIDE THE PARK

Mount Desert Island has at least a dozen commercial campgrounds, but only two are within park boundaries. There are no other accommodations inside the park. Make **reservations** (877/444-6777, www.recreation.gov) six months in advance for all park campgrounds. For first-come, first-served campsites, arrive by 8:30am.

Mount Desert Island

Blackwoods Campground (May-mid-Oct., 306 sites, $30) is popular thanks to its location on the east side of the island. It has drive-in tent and RV sites (no hookups). A trail connects the campground to the Ocean Drive trail system. The campground is off ME 3, 6 miles (10 km) south of Bar Harbor.

Seawall Campground (late May-mid-Oct., 214 sites, $22-40) has walk-in tent sites and drive-in sites for tents and RVs (no hookups). On ME 102A, the campground is 4 miles (6.4 km) south of Southwest Harbor.

Schoodic Peninsula

Schoodic Woods Campground (late May-mid-Oct., 96 sites, $22-30) has walk-in or drive-in tent sites and RV sites with electricity and water, a welcome center, and an amphitheater. Hiking trails connect to Schoodic Head; nonmotorized paths link the east and west sides of the peninsula. The campground is off Park Loop Road 3 miles (4.8 km) south of Winter Harbor.

Isle au Haut

On Isle au Haut, reservations are mandatory for one of the lean-tos at **Duck Harbor Campground** (mid-May-mid-Oct., 5 sites, $20). The three-sided lean-tos (8 by 12 ft./2.4 by 3.7 m, 8 ft./2.4 m high) must fit all tents or tarps for up to six people. Call the **Isle au Haut Boat Company** (207/367-5193) for the current ferry schedule before choosing reservation dates.

OUTSIDE THE PARK

Bar Harbor is the largest and best known of the park's communities. It offers lodgings, restaurants, campgrounds, and services. **Ellsworth** and **Trenton** have inexpensive lodgings.

GETTING THERE

AIR

Bangor International Airport (BGR, 287 Godfrey Blvd., 207/992-4600, www.flybangor.com) is served by major U.S. carriers and is located one hour north of the park. Flying into **Boston Logan International Airport** (BOS, Boston, MA, 800/235-6426, www.massport.com) puts you within a five-hour drive of the park going north via I-95. Both airports have rental cars.

Cape Air (866/227-3247, www.capeair.com) flies from Boston to **Hancock County-Bar Harbor Airport** (BHB, 207/667-7329, www.bhbairport.com), 10 miles (16 km) from the park. The free Island Explorer Rt. 1 bus connects the Hancock County-Bar Harbor Airport in Trenton with downtown Bar Harbor.

CAR

You can't get to Acadia without going through Ellsworth and Trenton: The only way onto Mount Desert Island is **ME 3** (expect traffic 8am-9am and 3pm-4pm weekdays). **Bar Harbor** is about 20 miles (32 km, 35-45 min.) via ME 3 from Ellsworth; about 48 miles (77 km, 75 min.) via Routes 1A and 3 from Bangor; and about 280 miles (450 km, 5 hrs.) via I-95 and ME 3 from Boston. It's about 12 miles (19 km, 20 min.) via ME 233 and ME 198 or 20 miles (32 km, 35 min.) via ME 3 to Northeast Harbor.

BUS

Concord Coach (800/639-3317, https://concordcoachlines.com) runs from Boston to Bangor. The **Bar Harbor-Bangor shuttle** (207/479-5911, https://barharborshuttle.net) connects Bangor with Bar Harbor by advance reservation only.

If you're day-tripping to Mount Desert Island, you can leave your car in Trenton and hop aboard the free **Island Explorer** (www.exploreacadia.com) bus. Once on the island, continue to use the Island Explorer bus system to avoid parking hassles.

GETTING AROUND

DRIVING

Traffic gets heavy at midday in midsummer, so aim for an early morning start. The maximum speed limit on the Park Loop Road is 35 mph (56 kph), but be alert for gawkers and photographers stopping without warning, and pedestrians dashing across the road from stopped cars or tour buses. Some roads and parking areas are closed to RVs and trailers; take the Island Explorer shuttle.

▼ VIEW FROM CADILLAC MOUNTAIN

SUNRISE WAVES ON OTTER CLIFF

Be aware that Acadia will begin implementing a long-term transportation plan in 2020, which will include a peak season time-entry reservation system for congested roads and parking lots at popular destinations, including the Ocean Drive corridor, Cadillac Mountain Road, and Jordan Pond House North. Get current details online.

SHUTTLE BUS

On Mount Desert Island, use the **Island Explorer** (207/667-5796, www.exploreacadia.com, daily late June-mid-Oct., free) bus system to avoid parking hassles. The shuttle bus has nine routes that link multiple destinations within the park. Although the Island Explorer buses do reach a number of key park sights, they are not tour buses. There is no narration, the bus cuts off the Park Loop Road at Otter Cliff, and it excludes the summit of Cadillac Mountain.

GETTING TO SCHOODIC PENINSULA

Winter Harbor is about 25 miles (40 km) via US 1 and ME 186 from Ellsworth. Although Winter Harbor is roughly 41 miles (66 km, 1 hr.) from Bar Harbor by car, it's only 7 miles (11 km) by water. You can get here by passenger ferry via **Downeast Windjammer Cruise Lines** (207/288-4585, Bar Harbor, www.downeastwindjammer.com, daily mid-June-late Sept.) or the bus from Ellsworth, but you'll need a vehicle or bicycle to explore beyond the part of the Schoodic Peninsula that's served by the Island Explorer bus.

GETTING TO ISLE AU HAUT

Two companies offer transportation to Isle au Haut's town landing. The **Isle au Haut Boat Company** (Seabreeze Ave., Stonington, 207/367-5193, www.isleauhautferry.com) runs a passenger ferry daily year-round with twice daily service in peak season to Duck Harbor near the campground and trailheads. Kayaks, canoes, and bicycles can go for an extra fee.

Offering seasonal service, **Old Quarry Ocean Adventures** (Stonington, 207/367-8977, www.oldquarry.com) transports passengers from Old Quarry at 9am and arrives at the island's town landing at 9:45am, departing from the same point at 5pm.

DAY TRIP TO FRENCHBORO, LONG ISLAND

The island officially known as Long Island, but more commonly known as Frenchboro, makes for a delightful day trip. One of only 15 Maine coastal islands that still support a year-round population, Frenchboro is a very quiet place where islanders live as islanders always have—making a living from the sea and being proud of it. A good way to get a sense of the place is to take the 3.5-hour lunch cruise run by Captain Kim Strauss of **Island Cruises** (Little Island Marine, Shore Rd., Bass Harbor, 207/244-5785, www.bassharborcruises.com). For an even longer day trip to Frenchboro, plan to take the passenger ferry *R. L. Gott* during her weekly run for the Maine State Ferry Service. Each Friday early April-late October, the *R. L. Gott* departs Bass Harbor at 8am, arriving in Frenchboro at 9am. The return trip to Bass Harbor is at 6pm, allowing nine hours on the island.

The **Frenchboro Historical Society Museum** (207/334-2924, www.frenchboro.lib.me.us, afternoons Memorial Day-Labor Day, free), just up from the dock, has interesting old tools, other local artifacts, and a small gift shop. The island has a network of easy and not-so-easy maintained trails through the woods and along the shore. The trails are rustic, and most are unmarked, so proceed carefully. In the center of the island is a beaver pond.

When you go, stop at **Lunt's Dockside Deli** (207/334-2902, http://luntsdeli.com, 11am-7:30pm Mon.-Sat. July-Aug.). Lobster rolls and fish chowder are the specialties, but there are sandwiches, hot dogs, and even vegetable wraps. The view is wonderful, and you might even get to watch lobsters being unloaded from a boat.

TOURS

Bus Tours

Scenic **bus tours** (207/288-0300, www.acadiatours.com, daily early May-Oct., 2.5 hr.) soak up the sights of Park Loop Road while someone else does the driving. From Bar Harbor, these narrated tours stop at Cadillac Mountain, Thunder Hole, and either Sieur de Monts Spring or Jordan Pond House for 15 minutes at each. **Oli's Trolley** (207/288-9899, http://olistrolley.com, daily late Apr.-Oct., 1-4 hrs.) guides tours to various locations including Cadillac Mountain and downtown Bar Harbor.

TAKE A BOAT TOUR TO BAKER ISLAND.

Boat Cruises

Rangers join boat cruises offering interpretive details on the park sights. The **Baker Island Tour** is booked through **Bar Harbor Whale Watch Co.** (1 West St., Bar Harbor, 207/288-2386 or 888/942-5374, www.barharborwhales.com, mid-June-mid-Sept., 4.5 hrs.) and visits history-rich Baker Island. The tour includes skiff access to the island's farmstead, lighthouse, and intriguing rock formations. The return trip provides a view from the water of Otter Cliff (bring binoculars), Thunder Hole, Sand Beach, and Great Head. Make reservations to guarantee a space.

Other tours include the **Frenchman Bay Cruise** (207/288-4585, www.downeastwindjammer.com, daily mid-May-early Oct., 2 hrs.), on a 151-foot (46-m), four-mast schooner, and the **Islesford Historical Cruise** (207/276-5352, www.cruiseacadia.com, daily mid-May-early Oct., 2.5 hrs.), which visits Little Cranberry Island to see the Islesford Historical Museum and Somes Sound.

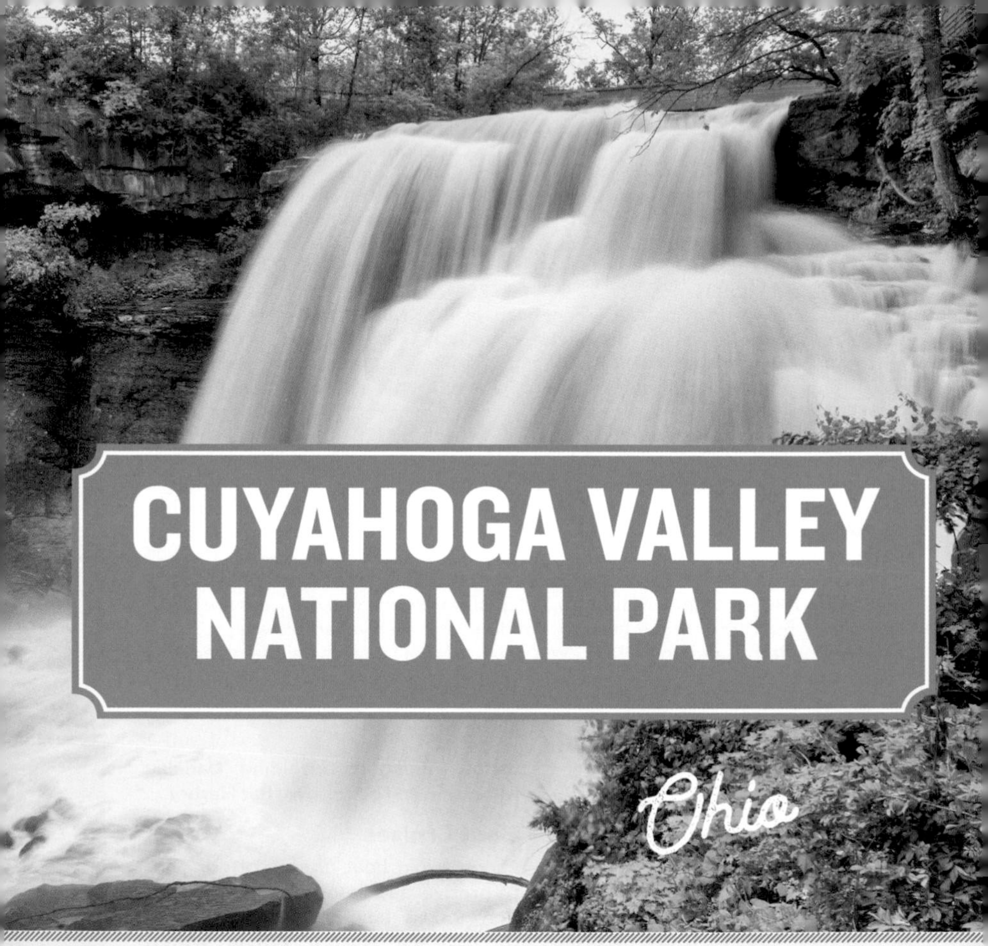

WEBSITE:
www.nps.gov/cuva

PHONE NUMBER:
330/657-2752

VISITATION RANK:
13

WHY GO:
Absorb nature with a slice of Midwest history.

▲ BRANDYWINE FALLS, CUYAHOGA VALLEY NATIONAL PARK

KEEPSAKE STAMPS ▼▼▼

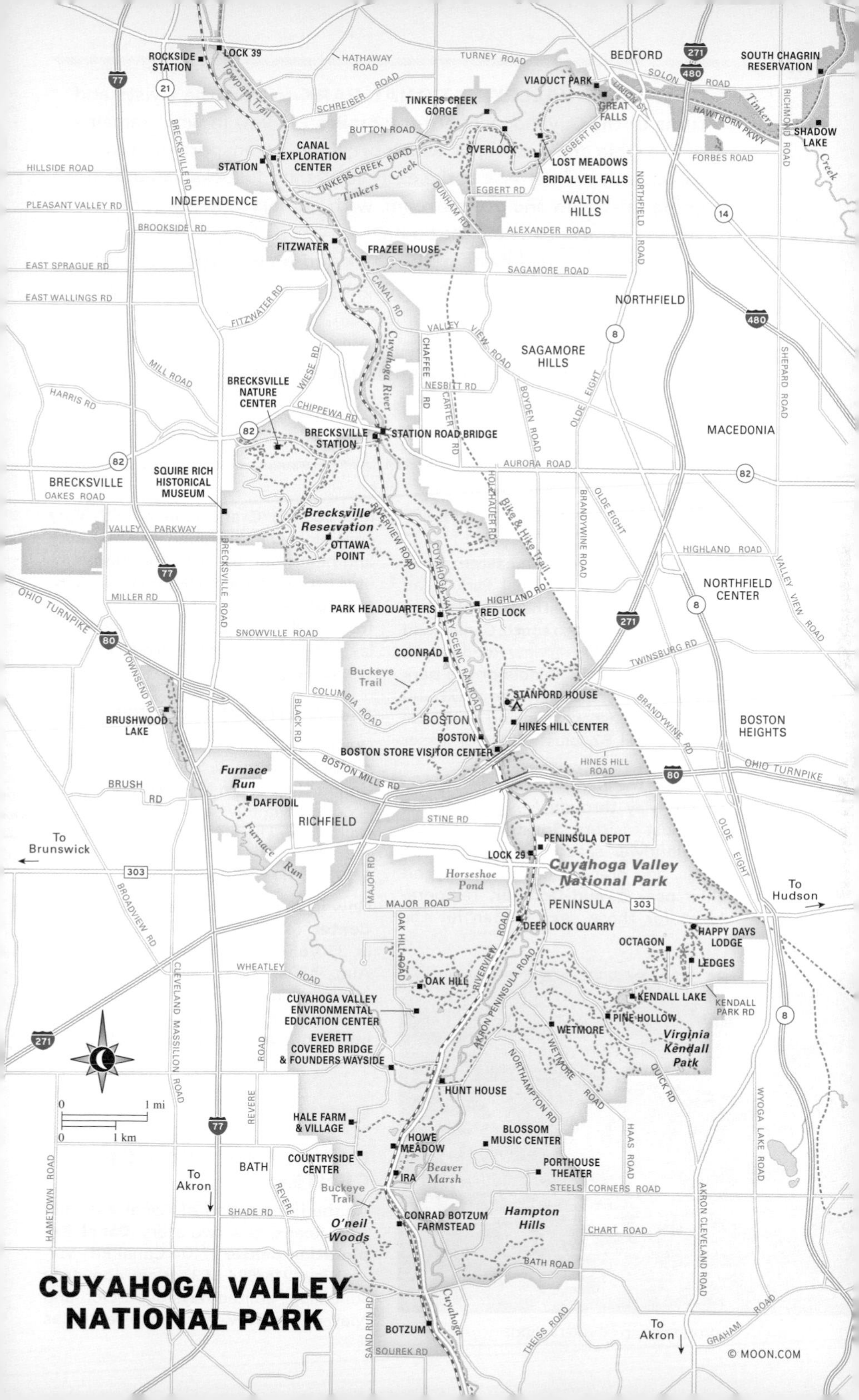
CUYAHOGA VALLEY NATIONAL PARK
ROCKSIDE STATION
LOCK 39
HATHAWAY ROAD
TURNEY ROAD
BEDFORD
SOUTH CHAGRIN RESERVATION
Towpath Trail
VIADUCT PARK
SOLON ROAD
UNION ST
GREAT FALLS
TINKERS CREEK GORGE
SCHREIBER ROAD
HAWTHORN PKWY
Tinkers Creek
SHADOW LAKE
RICHMOND ROAD
BUTTON ROAD
OVERLOOK
EGBERT RD
CANAL EXPLORATION CENTER
STATION
LOST MEADOWS
FORBES ROAD
HILLSIDE ROAD
TINKERS CREEK ROAD
BRIDAL VEIL FALLS
BRECKSVILLE RD
DUNHAM RD
INDEPENDENCE
WALTON HILLS
PLEASANT VALLEY RD
NORTHFIELD ROAD
BROOKSIDE RD
ALEXANDER ROAD
FITZWATER
FRAZEE HOUSE
EAST SPRAGUE RD
SAGAMORE ROAD
CANAL RD
EAST WALLINGS RD
NORTHFIELD
FITZWATER RD
VALLEY VIEW ROAD
Cuyahoga River
CHAFFEE RD
SAGAMORE HILLS
WIESE RD
MILL ROAD
BRECKSVILLE NATURE CENTER
NESBITT RD
HARRIS RD
CHIPPEWA RD
CARTER RD
BOYDEN ROAD
OLDE EIGHT
SHEPARD ROAD
MACEDONIA
BRECKSVILLE STATION
STATION ROAD BRIDGE
AURORA ROAD
BRECKSVILLE
SQUIRE RICH HISTORICAL MUSEUM
HOLZHAUER RD
Bike & Hike Trail
BRANDYWINE ROAD
OAKES ROAD
Brecksville Reservation
RIVERVIEW ROAD
VALLEY PARKWAY
OTTAWA POINT
CUYAHOGA VALLEY SCENIC RAILROAD
HIGHLAND ROAD
NORTHFIELD CENTER
OHIO TURNPIKE
MILLER RD
PARK HEADQUARTERS
HIGHLAND RD
RED LOCK
VALLEY VIEW ROAD
SNOWVILLE ROAD
COONRAD
TWINSBURG RD
Buckeye Trail
TOWNSEND RD
COLUMBIA ROAD
STANFORD HOUSE
BLACK RD
BRUSHWOOD LAKE
BOSTON
HINES HILL CENTER
BOSTON HEIGHTS
BOSTON STORE VISITOR CENTER
HINES HILL ROAD
BOSTON MILLS RD
Furnace Run
BRUSH RD
DAFFODIL
RICHFIELD
STINE RD
To Brunswick
PENINSULA DEPOT
LOCK 29
Cuyahoga Valley National Park
Horseshoe Pond
MAJOR RD
MAJOR ROAD
PENINSULA
To Hudson
BROADVIEW RD
DEEP LOCK QUARRY
OAK HILL ROAD
HAPPY DAYS LODGE
OCTAGON
LEDGES
WHEATLEY ROAD
AKRON PENINSULA ROAD
OAK HILL
KENDALL LAKE
KENDALL PARK RD
CUYAHOGA VALLEY ENVIRONMENTAL EDUCATION CENTER
PINE HOLLOW
WETMORE
Virginia Kendall Park
CLEVELAND MASSILLON ROAD
EVERETT COVERED BRIDGE & FOUNDERS WAYSIDE
NORTHAMPTON RD
WETMORE ROAD
QUICK RD
HUNT HOUSE
0 1 mi
0 1 km
REVERE ROAD
HALE FARM & VILLAGE
BLOSSOM MUSIC CENTER
WYOGA LAKE ROAD
HOWE MEADOW
HAAS ROAD
COUNTRYSIDE CENTER
PORTHOUSE THEATER
BATH
To Akron
Beaver Marsh
IRA
STEELS CORNERS ROAD
HAMETOWN ROAD
SHADE RD
CONRAD BOTZUM FARMSTEAD
Hampton Hills
O'neil Woods
CHART ROAD
AKRON CLEVELAND ROAD
BATH ROAD
Cuyahoga
THEISS ROAD
GRAHAM ROAD
SAND RUN RD
BOTZUM
SOUREK RD
© MOON.COM

CUYAHOGA VALLEY NATIONAL PARK follows the twists and turns of the Cuyahoga River for 22 miles (35 km) in what remains of the Ohio and Erie Canal, which provided a transportation route through the wilderness in the early 1800s. Its 15 locks aided boats going upstream and downstream, with an adjacent towpath providing the means to haul the boats.

Before the canal system, this parkland housed the Whittlesey people, who never encounter Europeans, and later the Ottawa, Ojibwe, and Mingo.

Deer, coyote, and fish occupy a wide range of habitats here—deep ravines and wetlands, open prairie and grasslands. Keep your eyes open for great blue herons, short-eared owls, bobolinks, and bald eagles, while spring peepers provide the evening soundtrack.

PLANNING YOUR TIME

Tucked as a greenbelt in eastern Ohio, Cuyahoga Valley National Park is an easy day trip from either Cleveland or Akron. From north to south, Canal Road (north end) and Riverview Road (south end) cut down the middle of the park along the rivers; meanwhile, I-271 and I-80 cross east-west, along with OH 303 and OH 82, plus a host of lesser roads.

While the park is open daily year-round, May through November draw the most visitors. **Spring** (Mar.-May) is wildflower season, while the reds, golds, and oranges of fall usually hit their peak in **mid-October.** Temperatures for those seasons can hit the low 70s (21°C and higher) with very cool nights. In **summer,** the humidity and heat ramp up, with the thermometer often hitting 95°F (35°C). In **winter,** temperatures plunge, yo-yoing from 35°F (1°C) to below freezing, as lake-effect snow rolls in from Lake Erie to the delight of skiers.

EVERETT ROAD COVERED BRIDGE

ENTRANCES AND FEES

Cuyahoga Valley National Park has multiple entrances. Start your exploration at the Boston Mills Visitor Center, accessed via I-271 and I-80 on Boston Mills Road. There is no entrance fee.

VISITORS CENTER

New in 2019, the **Boston Mills Visitor Center** (6947 Riverview Rd., Peninsula, 330/657-2752, 8am-6pm daily June-Aug., 9:30am-5pm daily Sept.-May) has information, ranger program schedules, brochures, exhibits, a short park video, bookstore, and a deck overlooking the river.

SIGHTS

CANAL EXPLORATION CENTER

At the intersection of Canal and Hillside Roads, the two-story **Canal Exploration Center** (7104 Canal Rd., Valley View, 216/524-3537, 10am-4pm daily June-Aug., limited days Sept.-Oct. and May, closed Nov.-Apr.) once served as

Top 3

CUYAHOGA VALLEY SCENIC RAILROAD

1 RIDE THE SCENIC RAILROAD

One of the longest scenic railroads in the nation, the **Cuyahoga Valley Scenic Railroad** (7900 Old Rockside Rd., 800/468-4070, www.cvsr.com, Wed.-Sun. Apr.-Oct., fee) stretches a full 51 miles (82 km), from just south of Cleveland all the way down to Canton—and "scenic" is the operative word. For much of the journey, the tracks bisect Cuyahoga Valley National Park while hugging the Cuyahoga River and paralleling the Towpath Trail. Passengers ride in authentic climate-controlled coaches built in the 1950s. More than just a tour train, the railroad is a key resource for visitors to the valley. A round-trip takes about three hours. First-class seats on the second level have more legroom and bigger windows.

2 DRIVE THE NATIONAL SCENIC BYWAY

Paralleling the Cuyahoga River, the **Ohio and Erie Canalway National Scenic Byway** (www.ohioanderiecanalway.com) bisects Cuyahoga Valley National Park from the north end of the park at Rockside Road to the south. The route travels Canal Road, Chaffee Road, Chippewa Road, and Riverview Road until it becomes Merriman Road after exiting the park's south boundary. The park's 20-mile (32-km) segment of the byway is part of a larger 110-mile (177-km) route that extends from Cleveland to Schoenbrunn Village, New Philadelphia. Inside the park, the road follows the same route as the Towpath Trail and Cuyahoga Valley Scenic Railroad. Stop to take a hike or visit the restored buildings and living museums that celebrate the canal era and its impact on Ohio's economy.

3 BIKE THE TOWPATH TRAIL

The **Towpath Trail** follows the Cuyahoga River, soaking up historic sites and exhibits. You can bicycle a total of 20 miles (32 km) from north to south; seven access points allow you to shorten the distance. For one-way biking on the towpath, you and your bike can hop on the **Cuyahoga Valley Scenic Railroad** (7900 Old Rockside Rd., 800/468-4070, www.cvsr.com, Wed.-Sun. Apr.-Oct., fee) and then cycle back to your starting point. In addition to regular depot stops, the train has several bike-aboard pickup/drop-off flagstops. Simply flag down the train by waving both hands over your head (a one-hand wave just salutes the engineer). Pay the fee when you board.

TOWPATH TRAIL

Best Hike

BRANDYWINE FALLS

DISTANCE: 1.5 miles/2.4 km round-trip
DURATION: 1 hour
ELEVATION CHANGE: 180 feet (54 m)
DIFFICULTY: easy
TRAILHEAD: 8176 Brandywine Rd., Sagamore Hills

The trail to **Brandywine Falls** follows a boardwalk through a mossy hemlock forest and gorge to reach a viewing platform facing the falls. The 65-foot (29-m) falls fans out across rock ledges creating a misty veil. Fall colors come on strong in the gorge in mid-October. Plan to go early or late in the day, as parking can fill 10am-2pm.

a tavern and a general store. Today, the historic building hosts exhibits on the canal era with interactive displays that appeal to kids and adults.

HUNT HOUSE

Kids will love the children's nature exhibits at the **Hunt House** (2054 Bolanz Rd., Peninsula, 10am-4pm daily June-Aug., Sat.-Sun. Apr.-May and Sept.-Oct.). Find it between Riverview Road and Akron Peninsula Road or via the Towpath Trail.

LEDGES LOOP

OHIO AND ERIE CANAL TOWPATH TRAIL

The crushed-limestone **Towpath Trail** attracts hikers, runners, bicycles, strollers, and wheelchairs on the 20-mile (32 km) in the park. The park segment is only a portion of the historic **Ohio and Erie Canal Towpath Trail,** more than 80 miles (129 km) long from Cleveland to Zoar. The path hugs and at times crosses the Cuyahoga River and passes old canal locks, mile markers, wayside exhibits, dense forests, fertile wetlands, and wildlife. Stop off at numerous visitors centers and historic sites along the way. With seven access points, you can go as little or as far as you want.

BLOSSOM MUSIC CENTER

Built in the late 1960s as the summer home of the Cleveland Orchestra, **Blossom Music Center** (1145 W. Steels Corners Rd., Cuyahoga Falls, 800/686-1141, www.clevelandorchestra.com) sees a full range of live-music action from spring until fall. Tucked into Cuyahoga Valley National Park, its setting is one of dense forests, leafy hillsides, and wide-open skies. On a warm summer evening, toss down a blanket to enjoy a picnic under the stars while the orchestra or your favorite band performs. Then again, that night can sour quickly if the clouds darken and the rain falls; be prepared with tarps, rain gear, and an extra set of dry clothes for the drive home. Or do what many regulars do: Spring for seats in the covered pavilion as insurance. Traffic in and out of

ONE DAY IN THE PARK

Start your visit by driving along the Ohio and Erie Canalway National Scenic Byway. Stop at the **Canal Exploration Center,** then continue south on Riverview Road to the **Boston Mills Visitor Center.** Stretch your legs by walking a little of the **Towpath Trail** south to Lock 29. Continue south on Riverview Road to see the **Everett Road Covered Bridge** and sink into history at the **Hale Farm & Village.**

the park can be brutal, so leave plenty of extra travel time.

HALE FARM & VILLAGE

Want to show your children what life was like before cell phones, computers, and refrigerators? **Hale Farm & Village** (2686 Oak Hill Rd., Bath, 330/666-3711, www.wrhs.org, 10am-5pm Wed.-Sun. June-Aug., Sat.-Sun. Sept.-Oct.) is a town trapped in the mid-1800s, when things like electricity, automobiles, and iPhones were still a few years down the road. This living-history museum employs historic interpreters dressed in period costume to recount the story of the Western Reserve, the Civil War years, and life in the middle of the 19th century.

EVERETT ROAD COVERED BRIDGE

The striking red **Everett Road Covered Bridge** (2370 Everett Rd., Peninsula) spans Furnace Run, which looks like a placid, rock-strewn stream much of the year. But in 1975, a torrent of water gushed through the ravine and destroyed the original bridge. Located 0.5 mile (0.8 km) west of Riverview Road, the reconstructed one-lane bridge is one of the most photographed locations in Cuyahoga and a tribute to Ohio's legacy of 19th-century covered

BLUE HEN FALLS

BRIDAL VEIL FALLS

bridges. Cars can no longer drive on the bridge, but you can walk through it.

RECREATION

HIKING

Twenty miles (32 km) of the **Towpath Trail** are inside the park with seven access points. From the Ira Trailhead, take the Towpath Trail to the **Beaver Marsh** (3801 Riverview Rd., Cuyahoga Falls, 0.8 mi./1.3 km rt., 30 min., easy), which the National Audubon Society has designated an Important Bird Area. For point-to-point hiking on the towpath, hop on the **Cuyahoga Valley Scenic Railroad** (7900 Old Rockside Rd., 800/468-4070, www.cvsr.com, Wed.-Sun. Apr.-Oct., fee) and hike back to your starting point.

The **Blue Hen Falls** (2001 Boston Mills Rd., Peninsula, 0.5 mi./0.8 km rt., 30 min., easy) trail crosses Spring Creek on a wooden bridge. At the junction, turn right to reach the 15-foot (4.6-m) Blue Hen Falls. Plan to go early or late in the day, as parking can pack out 10am-2pm.

Bridal Veil Falls (Gorge Pkwy., Walton Hills, 0.5 mi./0.8 km rt., 30 min., easy) is accessed by a short boardwalk that leads to a viewing platform.

The **Ledges Loop** (701 Truxell Rd., Peninsula, 2.2 mi./3.5 km rt., 1.5 hr., moderate) starts on a spur; at the loop, head in either direction. On the east side, Ice Box Cave is closed to protect bats; the west side includes an overlook of the area. Many hikers park at Kendall Lake instead of the Ledges Trailhead to add on a 1-mile (1.6-km) loop around the lake. After hiking around Kendall Lake, connect to the Ledges by crossing Kendall Park Road to the Pine Grove Trail and then heading west, after which you will link up with the Ledges Loop. Adding on the lake and connection via Pine Grove ups the distance to 4.8 miles (7.7 km) round-trip.

WINTER RECREATION

With six inches (15 cm) or more of snow, you can check out snowshoes and cross-country skis at the **Winter Sports Center at M.D. Garage** (1550 Boston Mills Rd., 330/657-2752, 10am-4pm Sat.-Sun. late Dec.-Feb., free) to tour park trails, including the Towpath

VIRGINIA KENDALL LEDGES

Trail. A sliding hill is at **Kendall Hills** for sleds and toboggans (bring your own gear) with three parking lots on Quick Road in Peninsula. For downhill skiing and snowboarding, **Peak Resorts** (800-U-Ski-241, www.bmbw.com) operates two lift-accessed hills on weekends and holidays located five minutes apart: **Brandywine Ski Resort** (1146 West Highland Rd., Sagamore Hills) and **Boston Mills Ski Resort** (7100 Riverview Rd., Peninsula). Brandywine also has a tubing hill.

WHERE TO STAY

INSIDE THE PARK

The 165-year-old **Inn at Brandywine Falls** (8230 Brandywine Rd., Sagamore Hills, 330/467-1812, www.innatbrandywinefalls.com, open year-round, from $158) is a bed-and-breakfast tucked into the park, literally steps from scenic Brandywine Falls. The six bedrooms are furnished with antiques, plus a living room, dining room, and porches. The gourmet breakfast is a candlelit affair.

The historic **Stanford House** (6093 Stanford Rd., Peninsula, 330/657-2909, www.conservancyforcvnp.org, open year-round, entire house from $600, two-night min., rooms from $50) has nine bedrooms, plus a dining room, living room, commercial kitchen, outdoor fire circle, and beautiful grounds. The entire house is available for rent.

For Towpath Trail users, the **Stanford Campsites** (near Stanford House, late May-Oct., $25) provide a place to camp on the route. Each of the five campsites can fit two tents and six campers and has picnic tables. Shared facilities include a portable toilet, potable water, and a communal firepit (firewood provided). **Reservations** (www.reserveamerica.com) for the campsites are accepted on May 1 for the season. Campers without reservations can check with the Stanford House (4pm-7pm daily) for availability.

OUTSIDE THE PARK

Lodging options are plentiful in the surrounding area, which includes **Independence, Akron,** and **Cleveland.**

GETTING THERE

AIR

Cleveland Hopkins International Airport (CLE, 5300 Riverside Dr., 216/265-6000, www.clevelandairport.com) is 25 miles (40 km) northwest of the national park, a quick drive via I-480 and I-77. It has car rentals.

TRAIN AND BUS

Amtrak (www.amtrak.com) trains and **Greyhound** (www.greyhound.com) buses stop in Cleveland. **Greater Cleveland Transit** (www.riderta.org) runs a rapid transit system and buses around the greater Cleveland area.

CAR

From Cleveland, take I-77 south for 16 miles (26 km) to exit 147 and turn left onto Miller Road. Drive 0.6 mile (1 km) and turn right onto OH 21 (Brecksville Rd.) for 0.4 mile (0.6 km). Turn left onto Snowville Road and continue 2.8 miles (4.5 km). Turn right onto Riverview Road and drive 1.7 miles (2.7 km) to reach the visitors center on the left. The drive should take about 30 minutes.

CYCLISTS RIDE ALONG THE TOWPATH TRAIL.

From Akron, drive north on OH 18 (Market St.) for 1.1 miles (1.7 km) and veer right onto Merriman Road for 4.1 miles (6.6 km) to a roundabout. Take the first exit onto Riverview Road for 4.3 miles (6.9 km) to the visitors center on your right. The drive should take about 20 minutes.

GETTING AROUND

The **Cuyahoga Valley Scenic Railroad** (7900 Old Rockside Rd., 800/468-4070, www.cvsr.com, Wed.-Sun. Apr.-Oct.) stops at two stations inside the park: Rockside and Peninsula. The train makes 2-3 round-trip journeys through the park with five flag stops where you can board or debark.

During weekends and in summer, **parking** can be difficult. The parking lots at popular trailheads fill 10am-2pm. To access the Towpath Trail, park at Canal Exploration Center, Station Road, or Rockside Rock rather than the busy locations of Boston Store, Hunt House, Ira Trailhead, and Lock 29 in Peninsula.

SIGHTS NEARBY

First Ladies National Historic Site (205 S. Market Ave., Canton, 330/452-0876, www.nps.gov/fila) celebrates U.S. first ladies with tours by costumed guides of the restored 1841 Victorian mansion of Ida Saxton, wife of William McKinley, 25th president of the United States. It's a 40-minute drive south of the park via I-77.

INDIANA DUNES NATIONAL PARK

KEEPSAKE STAMPS ▼▼▼

WEBSITE:
www.nps.gov/indu

PHONE NUMBER:
219/395-1882

VISITATION RANK:
14

WHY GO:
Explore miles of sand dunes.

▲ INDIANA DUNES NATIONAL PARK

INDIANA DUNES NATIONAL PARK

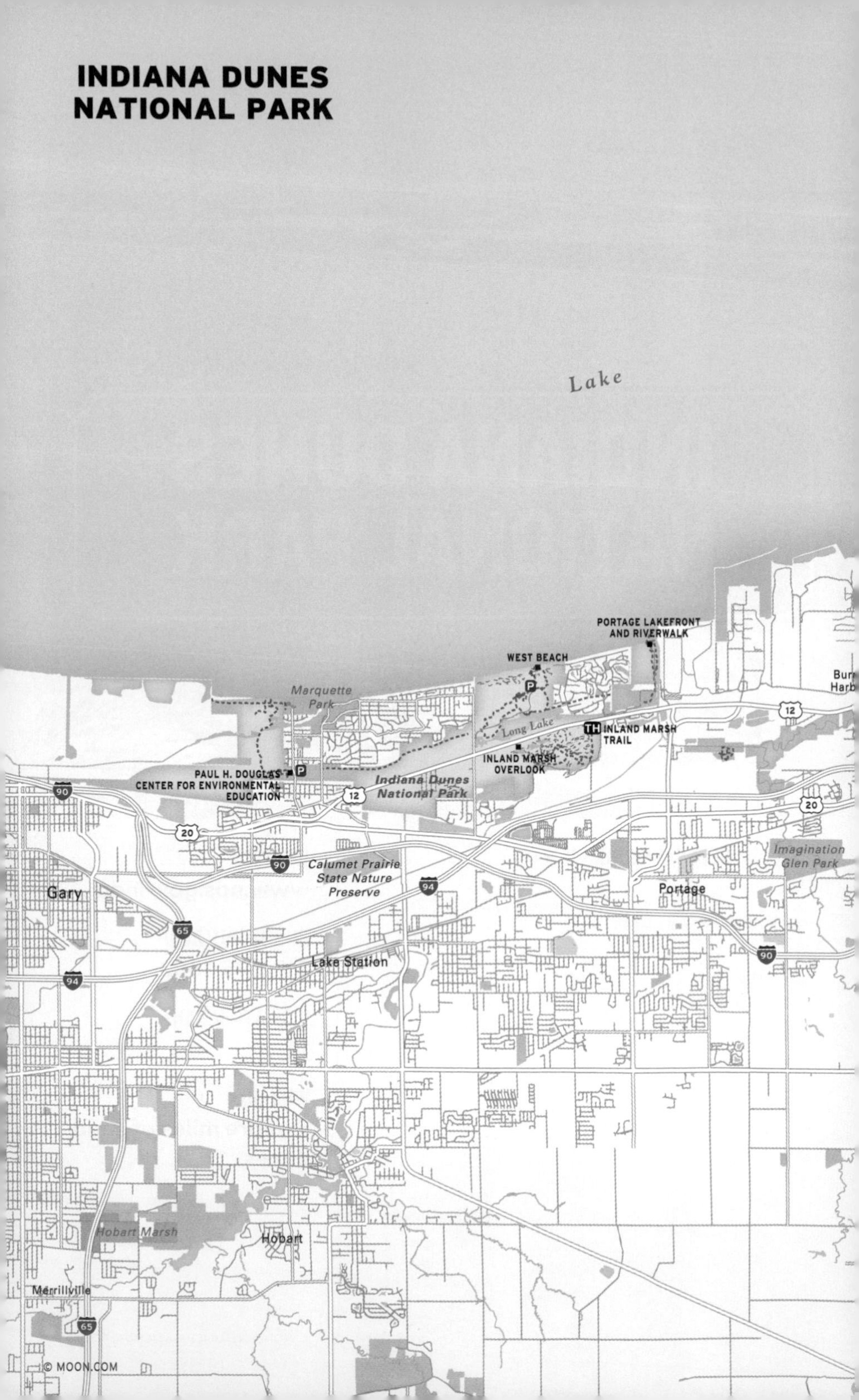
Lake
PORTAGE LAKEFRONT AND RIVERWALK
WEST BEACH
Marquette Park
Long Lake
INLAND MARSH TRAIL
INLAND MARSH OVERLOOK
PAUL H. DOUGLAS CENTER FOR ENVIRONMENTAL EDUCATION
Indiana Dunes National Park
12
90
20
Calumet Prairie State Nature Preserve
94
Gary
65
Portage
Imagination Glen Park
Lake Station
Hobart Marsh
Hobart
Merrillville
© MOON.COM

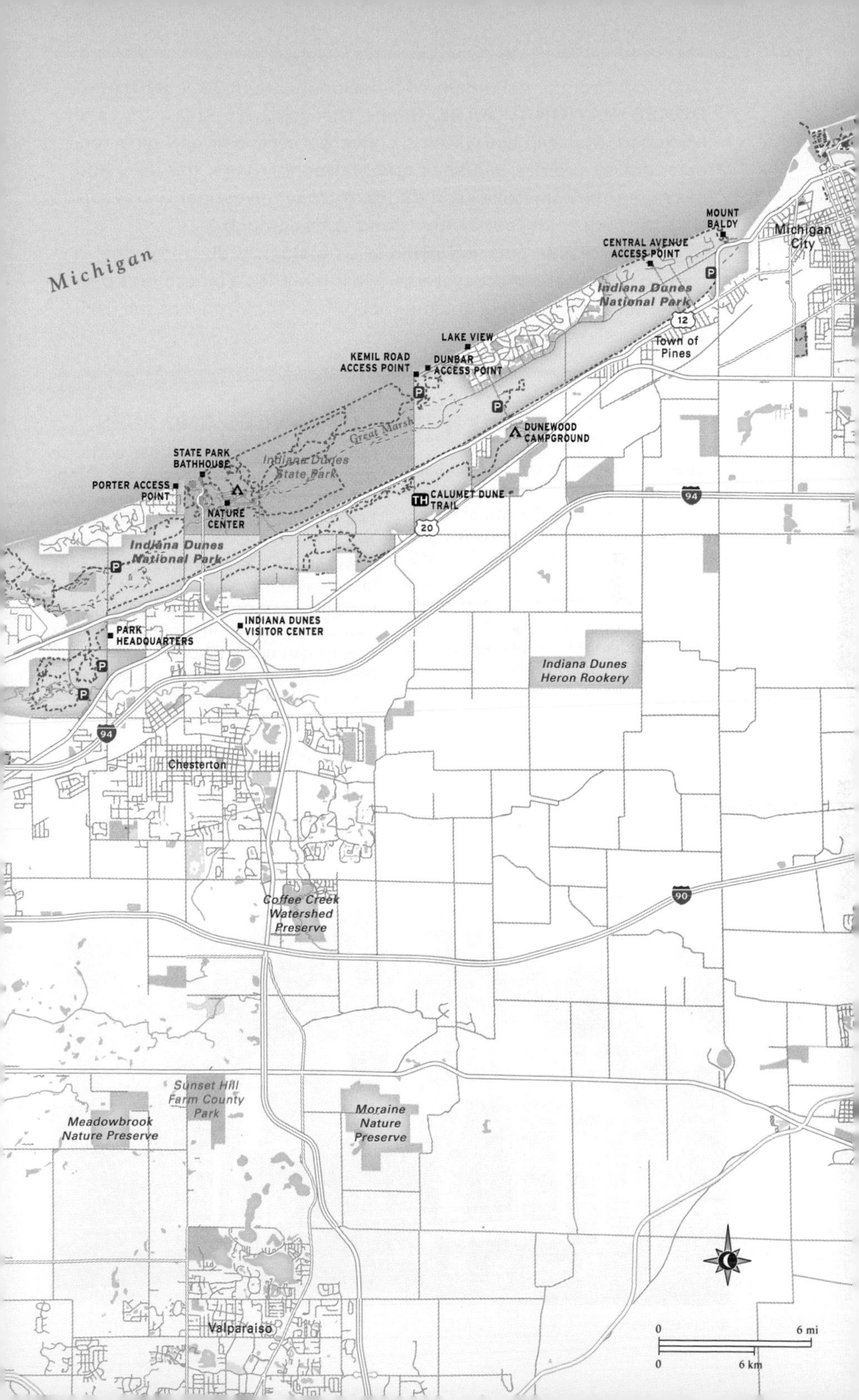

Michigan
MOUNT BALDY
Michigan City
CENTRAL AVENUE ACCESS POINT
Indiana Dunes National Park
12
Town of Pines
LAKE VIEW
KEMIL ROAD ACCESS POINT
DUNBAR ACCESS POINT
Great Marsh
DUNEWOOD CAMPGROUND
STATE PARK BATHHOUSE
Indiana Dunes State Park
PORTER ACCESS POINT
NATURE CENTER
CALUMET DUNE TRAIL
94
20
Indiana Dunes National Park
INDIANA DUNES VISITOR CENTER
PARK HEADQUARTERS
Indiana Dunes Heron Rookery
94
Chesterton
Coffee Creek Watershed Preserve
90
Sunset Hill Farm County Park
Meadowbrook Nature Preserve
Moraine Nature Preserve
Valparaiso
0
6 mi
0
6 km

Upgraded from a monument to a national park in 2019, **INDIANA DUNES NATIONAL PARK** flanks the southern shore of Lake Michigan. Multiple ecosystems converge here: oak and pine forests, grassy prairies, marshes and wetlands, rivers, the lake, and of course, it's namesake sand dunes. A closer investigation reveals that the park holds four distinct sand dune complexes.

This all-season park is loaded with biological diversity, due in part to the variety of ecosystems. Most of all, it's a bird-lover's paradise, filled with nesters and migratory fowl that frequent the Lake Michigan shoreline.

PLANNING YOUR TIME

Located southeast of Chicago on Lake Michigan's southern shore, Indiana Dunes covers 15 miles (24 km) of beach. Most of the park sits between the shore and I-94, with US 12 running east-west through the park to access more than 12 roads to beaches and other sites. The park is broken up by private lands and Indiana Dunes State Park. It is open 6am-11pm daily year-round.

Lake effects encourage weather fluctuations in the park. Summer temperatures hang around 85°F (29°C). June receives the most rain, but there are often sunny summer skies amid high humidity. Winters see temperatures in the mid-30s (around 1.6°C) and snow on the ground.

ENTRANCES AND FEES

Indiana Dunes has multiple entrance roads that access trailheads, the campground, historic sights, dunes, and beaches. But only one has an entrance fee.

West Beach Entrance (8am-7pm, late May-early Sept.) charges $6 per vehicle or motorcycle per day. Only senior annual, senior lifetime, and Access passes can get a 50 percent discount; holders of annual, fourth grade, volunteer, and military passes must pay the full fee.

VISITORS CENTERS

Located south and outside the park, **Indiana Dunes Visitor Center** (1215 N. IN 49, Porter, 219/395-1882, daily 8am-6pm summer or 8:30am-4:30pm winter) has

BAILLY HOMESTEAD

Top 3

WEST BEACH

1 SWIM ON A BEACH

Cool off, sunbathe, or play in the sand. Water temperatures usually reach 65-68°F (18-20°C) in July and August. Bring beach toys and floaties to amp up the fun, but beware of big waves and rip currents. Eight beaches have parking lots (6am-11pm) with restrooms and drinking water; **West Beach** and Lake View have accessible parking lots. All have free entrance except for West Beach (daily 8am-7pm fee station, $6 per car), which has summer lifeguards, lockers, showers, and covered picnic shelters (reservations 877/444-6777, www.recreation.gov, $25). To get a parking spot, arrive at Lake View, Dunbar, Kemil, Porter, or Portage Lakefront and Riverwalk beaches by midmorning. West Beach fills on holidays.

2 CATCH THE SUNSET

When the sun sets over Lake Michigan, the glow spreads across the water. All of the park beaches provide good locations for enjoying the view. Join a ranger for **Sunset around the Fire** (Portage Lakefront & Riverwalk pavilion, 100 Riverwalk Rd., Portage, 8pm early summer, 7:30pm midsummer, 7pm late summer Wed., 1 hr., free) and marshmallow roasting in the pavilion fireplace. Rangers also lead a **sunset hike on the Dunes Succession Trail** (Ranger Contact Station at West Beach Parking Lot, 376 North County Line Rd., Gary, 7pm Sat., 1 hr., $6/car entry), up the 250 stairs to the top of the dune to watch the setting sun reflecting on the Chicago skyline on the horizon.

3 GO BIRDING

Impressive migrations in spring and fall pack the dunes with waterfowl, songbirds, and raptors. Particularly during the fall migration, birds fly south along Lake Michigan's shorelines, which converge at the park. Go to the **Great Marsh** to see egrets, green herons, red-winged blackbirds, and kingfishers. Climb a dune to watch hawks. Go to the shore of the lake to see waterfowl. Expert guides are available for birding expeditions during the annual **Indiana Dunes Birding Festival** over four days over the third weekend in May.

HERON

Best Hike

WEST BEACH TRAIL

DISTANCE: 0.9-3.5 miles (1.4-5.6 km) round-tr
DURATION: 0.5-3 hours
ELEVATION CHANGE: 114 feet (34 m)
EFFORT: moderate
TRAILHEAD: West Beach Road parking lot

The West Beach Trail can be a quick one-loop hike or a longer two- or three-loop route. Start by walking the paved trail to the beach, across the sand, and up the boardwalk of the **Dune Succession Trail.** It climbs 250 stairs up a high dune for expansive views. Continue south along the stairs to loop back to the parking lot or connect with the flat **West Beach Loop** that tours past prickly pear cactus in an oak and prairie ecosystem. From that loop, return to the south end of the parking lot or intersect with the **Long Lake Loop** to explore wetlands and enjoy platforms for bird-watching. Use caution; trails cross the road in several places.

information, short videos, exhibits, and a bookstore.

The **Paul H. Douglas Center for Environmental Education** (100 North Lake St., Gary, 219/395-1824, daily 9am-5pm summer or 9am-4pm winter) has a Nature Play Zone for families and interactive exhibits.

SIGHTS

FALL COLOR

Hardwood trees turn brilliant colors in fall. Leaf-peeping starts in late September, with colors usually hitting their prime in mid-October and fading through the end of the month. Catch the color in the maple and oak forests on the Calumet Dunes Trail and Dune Ridge Trail. The Glenwood Dunes also yields outstanding fall colors.

BAILLY HOMESTEAD & CHELLBERG FARM

A National Historic Landmark, the **Bailly Homestead** is a survivor that got its start as a fur trading post in 1822. The main house has detailing from

CHELLBERG FARM

19th-century architecture, while the interior has been restored to its 1917 appearance. The 20th-century **Chellberg Farm** was home to three generations of immigrants. A trail (0.8 mi./1.3 km rt., 45 min., easy) goes out and back to both historic locations. Rangers guide a **history hike** (1 pm Sun. June-Aug., 2 hrs., free) from the Chellberg-Bailly Parking Lot (Mineral Springs Rd. between US 20 and IN 12, Porter).

RECREATION

HIKING

Rangers lead several guided walks in summer, including up the loose sand of the **Mt. Baldy Summit Trail** (0.8 mi./1.3 km, 1 hr., strenuous) which may only be hiked with a ranger. Consult the visitors center for the current schedule.

The accessible paved **Calumet Dunes Trail** (1596 North Kemil Rd., 0.5 mi./0.8 km, 20 min., easy) explores a forested dune ridge that remains from the shoreline of Lake Chicago, an ancient ancestor that was larger than Lake Michigan 12,000 years ago.

Tucked south of a giant forested dune, the **Dune Ridge Trail** (Kemil Beach Parking Lot, East State Park Rd., Beverly Shores, 0.7 mi./1.1 km, 30 min., moderate) tours wetlands and hardwood forest with views of Great Marsh and Kemil Beach.

MT. BALDY

Pick up a map at the trailhead kiosk to navigate the 13 junctions in loops on the **Glenwood Dunes Trail** (1475 North Brummitt Rd., Chesterton, 1-15 mi./1.6-24 km, 0.5-8 hrs., moderate). Spurs also connect with Dunewood Campground, Dune Park Railroad Station, and Calumet Dunes Trail.

The **Great Marsh** (South Trailhead Parking Lot on Broadway Ave., Beverly Shores, 1.4 mi./2.6 km rt., 1 hr., easy) tours the largest wetland in the park, the best place to see waterfowl, songbirds, and beavers. The trail trots north and loops around the east side of the wetland, and a spur paved trail goes west to the observation deck. The North Trailhead Parking Lot has accessible parking for wheelchairs to use the paved trail (0.4 mi./0.6 km) to the observation deck.

The **Heron Rookery** (1336 600 E., Michigan City, 3.3 mi./5.3 km rt., 2 hrs., easy) follows the Little Calumet River ablaze with wildflowers in spring and a birding paradise. The 100 great blue heron nests are now abandoned.

A National Natural Landmark, the **Cowles Bog** (1450 N. Mineral Springs Rd., Dune Acres, 4.7 mi./7.6 km rt., 4 hrs., moderate) is known for its plant diversity with black oak savannas, swamps, marshes, and beaches.

The **Portage Lakefront and River** (100 Riverwalk Rd., Portage, 1.5 mi./2.4 km rt., 45 min., easy) is a paved, accessible walk along Lake Michigan, good for watching lake storms, migrating birds in spring, and winter lake ice.

BICYCLING

The park contains 37 miles (60 km) of bicycle trails. Most are open year-round and allow e-bikes. Between the town of Pine and Dune Acres, the **Calumet Trail** (19 mi./30.6 km rt.) is a gravel road. The paved **Porter Brickyard Trail** (7 mi./11.3 km rt.) has a few hills between Dune Acres and Chesterton. The paved **Prairie Duneland** (22.4 mi./36 km rt.) is a flat rail trail between Chesterton and Hobart. Bike rentals are available near the visitors center from **Pedal Power** (1215 IN 49, Porter, 219/921-3085, pedalpowerrentals.com).

PADDLING

Waves, big winds, and fast-changing conditions make padding on Lake Michigan a challenge. It's best to take your kayaks, canoes, or paddleboards to the sheltered Little Calumet River and Burns Waterway. To try the lake when it is calm, you can launch from any beach except the swimming area at West Beach.

CROSS-COUNTRY SKIING & SNOWSHOEING

In winter, many trails become cross-country skiing and snowshoeing routes. The Glenwood Dunes trail system is the best for ungroomed conditions. Bring your own gear.

WHERE TO STAY

INSIDE THE PARK

The park has no lodges and only one campground. **Dunewood Campground** (645 Broadway, Beverly Shores, Apr.-Oct., 67 sites, $25) has tent, RV, and accessible campsites. Amenities include showers, restrooms, and drinking water. Make reservations (877/444-6777, www.recreation.gov) six months in advance.

OUTSIDE THE PARK

Accommodations, campgrounds, and dining options can be found in **Porter, Portage, Chesterton,** and a campground at **Indiana Dunes State Park.**

GETTING THERE

AIR

Chicago Midway International Airport (MDW, 5700 S. Cicero Ave., 773/838-0600, www.flychicago.com) to the west and **South Bend International Airport** (SBN, 4477 Progress Dr., 574/282-4590, https://flysbn.com) to the east are equidistance from Indiana Dunes (48 mi./77 km, 1.2 hrs.). Both have car rentals.

CAR

Just south of Indiana Dunes, I-94 crosses east-west across Indiana. From South Bend, drive IN 20 to I-94 West. From Chicago, follow I-94 East. From both directions, take IN 49 (exit 26) north to the park or to intersect with US 12 that accesses all roads into the park. From Valparaiso, drive IN 49 north.

TRAIN

The electric South Shore Line runs almost hourly every day between Chicago and South Bend with four stops inside the park. The **Beverly Shores Station** (US 12 and Broadway St. on the north side) is 0.5 mile (0.8 km) north of the park campground. From the west end of **Dune Park Station,** you can walk or bike to Indiana Dunes Visitor Center on the **Dunes Kankakee Trail** (1.3 mi./2.1 km, 30 min., easy). Select weekend trains allows bikes to Dunes Park Station.

BUS

From Gary, Indiana, you can catch the Oak/County Line bus run by **Gary Public Transportation Corp** (219/885-7555, www.gptcbus.com) which goes near the entrance of West Beach but no farther east into the park.

GETTING AROUND

CAR

US 12 goes east-west through the inside of the park to access more than 12 roads to beaches and other sites.

SHUTTLES

A free accessible **shuttle** (10am-6pm Sat.-Sun. Memorial Day Weekend-Labor Day) cruises two routes. The Western Park Shuttle (check schedule for times) connects Miller Train Station, Marquette Park, Douglas Center, 5th Avenue and Lake Street, and Lake Street Bridge. The **Eastern Park Shuttle** (every 20-30 min.) runs between Dunewood Campground, USGS Great Lakes Research Center, and Kemil Beach Parking Lot.

ISLE ROYALE NATIONAL PARK

Michigan

KEEPSAKE STAMPS ▼▼▼

WEBSITE:
www.nps.gov/isro

PHONE NUMBER:
906/482-0984

VISITATION RANK:
59

WHY GO:
Explore a unique freshwater island.

▲ ISLE ROYALE NATIONAL PARK

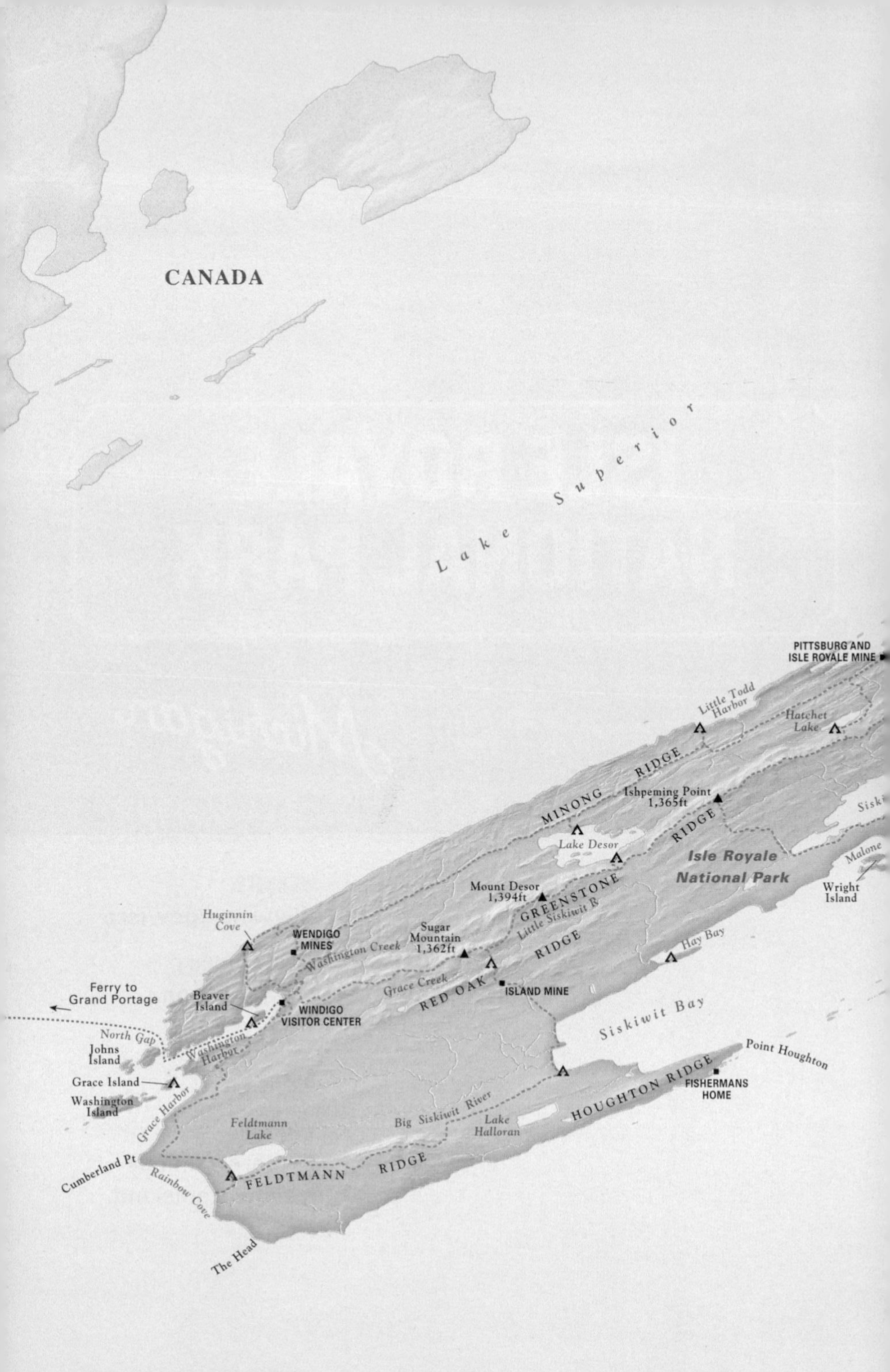

CANADA
Lake Superior
PITTSBURG AND
ISLE ROYALE MINE
Little Todd
Harbor
Hatchet
Lake
MINONG RIDGE
Ishpeming Point
1,365ft
RIDGE
Lake Desor
Isle Royale
National Park
Malone
Wright
Island
Mount Desor
1,394ft
GREENSTONE
Little Siskiwit R
Huginnin
Cove
WENDIGO
MINES
Sugar
Mountain
1,362ft
Washington Creek
RIDGE
Hay Bay
Ferry to
Grand Portage
Beaver
Island
Grace Creek
RED OAK
ISLAND MINE
WINDIGO
VISITOR CENTER
Siskiwit Bay
North Gap
Johns
Island
Washington
Harbor
Point Houghton
Grace Island
HOUGHTON RIDGE
FISHERMANS
HOME
Washington
Island
Grace Harbor
Big Siskiwit River
Lake
Halloran
Feldtmann
Lake
RIDGE
Cumberland Pt
FELDTMANN
Rainbow Cove
The Head

ISLE ROYALE NATIONAL PARK

Remote **ISLE ROYALE NATIONAL PARK** is the largest island in frigid Lake Superior, located near the border with Canada. The park encompasses an archipelago of the 45-mile-long (72-km) Isle Royale and about 400 tiny islands, with more than 80 percent of it lying underwater. This upthrust of land consisting of folded rock layers is now host to a rich mixed forest that provides habitat for moose, beavers, foxes, and wolves.

For the Ojibwe, the island provided a place to fish and hunt. Today, those who make the trek by boat or seaplane to Isle Royale come to hike rails, paddle the saw-toothed shoreline, and see the moose that swam here from Ontario several decades back. It's a place for those who like the feel of wilderness and water, where solitude offers a chance to soak up the sights, sounds, and smells below a starlit sky or the northern lights.

PLANNING YOUR TIME

Isle Royale sits in Lake Superior, north of Michigan's Upper Peninsula near the Canadian border. No roads reach the island, and its only contact with the outside world is ship-to-shore radio. All access is by boat or seaplane.

Civilization on Isle Royale is concentrated in two small developments at opposite ends of the island. **Windigo,** on the south end, has a visitors center, grocery, and marina. **Rock Harbor,** on the north end, offers the same, plus a lodge, restaurant, and cabins. The rest of the island is backcountry wilderness.

Isle Royale is open daily **mid-April-October** and closed November-mid-April, with most visitation June-September. Summer is the warmest time to visit, but plan for it to be buggy June-July. The island bans dogs and wheeled vehicles (mountain bikes or canoe carts), except for wheelchairs.

ENTRANCES AND FEES

Most boats and seaplanes land in **Rock Harbor** at the northeast tip of the island. Boats from Minnesota dock in **Windigo,** at the southern tip. The entrance fee is $7 per person per day, or $60 per season, which is collected by ferry or seaplane concessionaires. Private boaters can pay at the visitors centers.

VISITORS CENTERS

Houghton Visitor Center (800 E. Lakeshore Dr., 906/482-0984, 8am-6pm Mon.-Fri., 10am-6pm Sat. June-mid-Sept., 8am-4pm Mon.-Fri. mid-Sept.-May) is on the mainland in Houghton, where the Ranger III passenger ferry docks. The visitors center has boating permits, a park orientation video, a Junior Ranger Program, and a park store.

The **Rock Harbor Visitor Center** (8am-6pm daily July-Aug., hours vary May-June and Sept.) is on the northeast end of Isle Royale where ferries and seaplanes land from Houghton or Copper Harbor. The center has exhibits, backcountry permits, ranger-led programs, field guides, and maps.

The **Windigo Visitor Center** (8am-6pm daily July-Aug., hours vary May-June and Sept.-Oct.) is on the southwest end of the island where ferries arrive from Grand Portage, Minnesota. The center has exhibits, backcountry permits, and ranger programs, plus maps and field guides.

RECREATION

HIKING

The islands' wildlife, especially the **moose** and **wolf** populations, is a draw. Hikers have a decent chance of

Top 3

FOGGY TRAIL ON ISLE ROYALE

1 HIKE TO SCOVILLE POINT

East of Rock Harbor, the **Scoville Point Trail** (4.2 mi./6.8 km rt., 2 hrs., moderate) traces a rocky finger of forested land in a figure-eight loop to a point surrounded by Lake Superior. The route begins on the Stoll Memorial Loop which links to the smaller Scoville Point Loop. Go either way around both loops. The bluffs of the rocky point yield outstanding views of the rugged Isle Royale shoreline and islands.

2 PADDLE THE ISLAND WATERS

For paddlers, Isle Royale is a dream destination, a nook-and-cranny wilderness of rocky islands, secluded coves, and quiet bays interrupted only by the low call of a loon. Rental kayaks and canoes are available in Windigo and Rock Harbor.

First-time visitors should aim for the **Five Fingers,** the collection of fjord-like harbors and rocky promontories on the east end of the island. The area is well protected (except from northeasterly winds) and offers some of the finest scenery and solitude. Isle Royale is generally better suited to **kayaks,** though canoes can handle these waters in calm weather.

A paddle-hike destination, **Lookout Louise** (2 mi./3.2 km rt., 1 hr., moderate) has spectacular views of the island's ragged northeastern shoreline. To get there from Rock Harbor, paddle for 20-minute to the trailhead in Tobin Harbor and then hike to the overlook.

3 CAMP IN THE BACKCOUNTRY

Isle Royale has 36 **campsites** that offer a chance for solitude, wildlife-watching, and soaking up the stars. They are accessible by foot or boat and some only by canoe or kayak. These first-come, first-served sites include drinking water and vault toilets. A free camping permit, available from visitors centers, is required for all overnight stays. Group sites (7-10 people) require advance reservations.

ONE DAY IN ISLE ROYALE

If you only have one day, take the ***MV Isle Royale Queen*** ferry from Copper Harbor to Rock Harbor, which gives you three hours to explore. Hike to **Suzy's Cave** or rent a canoe from **Rock Harbor Lodge** to explore the bay.

spotting moose in ponds, lowlands, inland lakes, and especially the mineral licks at **Hidden Lake.**

Near Rock Harbor Visitor Center, interpretive signs on the Rock Harbor Trail lead to **Suzy's Cave** (3.8 mi./6.1 km rt., 2 hrs., moderate), formed by wave action of a once-deeper Lake Superior. Follow the Lake Superior shoreline to Daisy Farm campground and the **Ojibway Trail** to go to the **Ojibway Fire Tower** (3.5 mi./5.6 km rt., 2 hrs., moderate) for an unmatched view of the island's interior lakes and bays.

From Windigo Visitor Center, head uphill on the **Windigo Nature Trail** (1.2 mi./1.9 km rt., 40 min., easy) as it rolls through forests of cedar, maple, and birch. From the Feldtmann Lake Trailhead, **Grace Creek Overlook** (3.6 mi./5.8 km rt., 2 hrs., moderate) climbs to a rocky outcrop for views of the island.

BACKPACKING

Along the spine of Greenstone Ridge, the **Greenstone Ridge Trail** (42 mi./68 km, 4 days) runs the length of the island through the highest points. The route goes between Rock Harbor and Windigo; use the boat to return to your starting end. Pick up free permits at visitors centers.

BOATING AND FISHING

Isle Royale's scenic waterways beckon private boaters. Boats that dock overnight need a backcountry **permit** (even for anchoring). Pick up free backcountry permits at the island visitors centers or on board the Ranger III. The docks in **Rock Harbor** and **Windigo** have pump-out services, fuel, and potable water. Rock Harbor has seasonal dockage with power and water.

A **Michigan fishing license** (24-hour cash-only, available in island stores, longer licenses on mainland) is required to fish Lake Superior. No license is needed to fish the island's inland lakes.

WHERE TO STAY

INSIDE THE PARK

Rock Harbor Lodge (800 E. Lakeshore Dr., 906/337-4993 May-Sept. or 866/644-2003 Oct.-Apr., http://rockharborlodge.com, from $250, includes canoe rental and meals) has 60 basic motel-style lodge rooms with glorious views of nearby islands and Lake Superior. Nearby, 20 housekeeping cottages

ROCK HARBOR

include small kitchens, one double bed, and one bunk bed. Reservations are a must.

Rock Harbor has the **Lighthouse Restaurant** and **Greenstone Grill** (7am-10am, noon-1:30pm, and 5:30pm-7:30pm daily late May-early Sept.). The **Marina Store** (8am-6pm daily) carries food and camping supplies.

Two rustic, one-room **Windigo Camper Cabins** (906/337-4993 May-Sept. or 866/644-2003 Oct.-Apr., http://rockharborlodge.com, from $52) are located in Washington Harbor, 45 miles (72 km) from Rock Harbor.

OUTSIDE THE PARK

Houghton and **Hancock** are the gateways to Isle Royale, with lodgings and restaurants.

GETTING THERE

AIR

Grand Portage, Minnesota, is the gateway to the park. There are several international airports within driving distance.

Thunder Bay International Airport (YQT, 100 Princess St., Thunder Bay, ON, Canada, 807/473-2600, www.tbairport.on.ca) is 42 miles (68 km) northeast of Grand Portage, an hour drive via MN 61.

Duluth International Airport (DLH, 4701 Grinden Dr., Duluth, MN, 218/727-2968, http://duluthairport.com) is 149 miles (240 km) south of Grand Portage, a three-hour drive via MN 61.

Green Bay-Austin Straubel International Airport (GRB, 2077 Airport Dr., Green Bay, WI, 920/498-4800, www.flygrb.com) is 250 miles (405 km) south of Houghton, Michigan, a 7- to 8-hour drive.

All three airports have rental cars.

A pricey service, **Isle Royale Seaplanes** (21125 Royce Rd., Hancock, 906/483-4991, https://isleroyaleseaplanes.com, mid-May-mid-Sept., 35 min.) fly from Houghton County Memorial Airport to Windigo and Rock Harbor. Reservations are required.

BOAT AND FERRY

Boats and ferries are for passengers only; cars are not permitted. Make reservations for all ferries at least three months in advance, although last-minute spots can be available. Canoes and kayaks are allowed for a fee.

ISLE ROYALE COVE

From Houghton, Michigan: The National Park Service operates the 165-foot (50-m) ***MV Ranger III*** (800 E. Lakeshore Dr., 906/482-0984, late May-Sept., 6 hrs., $55 adults) for the 73-mile passage to Rock Harbor. Departures go from Houghton (9am Tues. & Fri.) and Rock Harbor (9am Wed. & Sat.).

From Copper Harbor, Michigan: The ***MV Isle Royale Queen IV*** (14 Waterfront Landing, 906/289-4437, www.isleroyale.com, daily early May-Sept., 3 hrs., $136) passenger ferry departs at 8am for Rock Harbor; the return trip departs Rock Harbor at 2:45pm.

From Grand Portage, Minnesota: ***MV Voyageur II*** (218/475-0024, www.isleroyaleboats.com, May-early Oct., schedule varies) travels to Windigo (2 hrs.) and Rock Harbor (8.5 hrs.) every other day and returns on opposite days. Other drop-off and pickup locations are available.

BUS

Indian Trails (800/292-3831, www.indiantrails.com) operates bus service from Green Bay, Wisconsin, to Houghton, Michigan.

GETTING AROUND

Hiking or kayaking are the best modes for getting around the islands. The park service offers boat tours on its 25-passenger ***MV Sandy*** (906/482-0984, June-early Sept., times and rates vary) from Rock Harbor. ***MV Voyageur II*** (4.5-5 hrs.) circles each half of the island on different days with additional stops.

VOYAGEURS NATIONAL PARK

WEBSITE:
www.nps.gov/voya

PHONE NUMBER:
218/283-6600

VISITATION RANK:
48

WHY GO:
Soak up a watery wilderness.

▲ VOYAGEURS NATIONAL PARK

KEEPSAKE STAMPS ▼▼▼

Befitting the Land of 10,000 Lakes, **VOYAGEURS NATIONAL PARK** is defined by water. The park is centered on four large lakes—Rainy, Kabetogama, Namakan, and Sand Point. Hundreds of lopsided islands, peninsulas, and slender bays comprise this wilderness park, formed in the footprint of an ancient glacial lake. Water, which covers more than 40 percent of the park, isn't just part of the scenery; it's the primary means of transportation. Most people tour the park from a fishing boat, houseboat, kayak, or pontoon.

This is Ojibwe country, but the park is named for early French Canadian fur traders called *voyageurs*. It shares its waters with Canada. Its remote northern location makes it one of the least visited national parks. You'll find space to find solitude and commune with nature, especially if you head out to the Kabetogama Peninsula or spend a night under brilliant stars or the northern lights.

PLANNING YOUR TIME

Voyageurs National Park follows the northern Minnesota-Ontario border for 55 meandering miles (89 km). Access for most visitors is through one of the four resort areas on the park's periphery. **Rainy Lake** is at the northwest corner, not far from International Falls, while **Crane Lake** is outside the park on the far southeast end. **Kabetogama** and **Ash River** sit in between. Each gateway offers lodgings, food, fishing guides, water taxis, and just about anything else you could need during your trip.

Most visitors arrive in **summer** (May-Sept.) for the warmest weather. Mosquitoes arrive June-July. Snow covers the park November-early April when it becomes a playground for snowmobiling, cross-country skiing, and snowshoeing. Lake ice usually lasts until early May.

ENTRANCES AND FEES

The park has three main entrances. East of International Falls, access **Rainy Lake** off MN 11. **Kabetogama** is north of US 53. To reach **Ash River,** drive 12 miles (19 km) northeast of US 53 on the Ash River Trail to Mead Wood Road. Except for roads leading to these entry points, there are no roads inside the park.

There is no entrance fee; however, all overnight visitors must have a **free permit,** available from the park visitors centers or self-registration stations at most boat launches.

VISITORS CENTERS

Roads go to three visitors centers that have exhibits, films, bookstores, and backcountry permits. **Rainy Lake Visitor Center** (1797 Town Rd. 342, 218/286-5258, 9am-5pm daily late May-Sept., 10am-4:30pm Thurs.-Sun. Jan.-late May) offers boat tours and ranger-led programs. **Ash River Visitor Center** (9899 Mead Wood Rd., 218/374-3221, 10am-4pm Thurs.-Sun. late May-Sept.) is housed in the historic Meadwood Lodge, a 1935 log building. **Kabetogama Lake Visitor Center** (9940 Cedar Ln., 218/875-2111, 9am-5pm daily late May-Sept.) has boat tours and ranger-led programs. Crane Lake has a ranger station, which may be unstaffed.

SIGHTS

NIGHT SKIES

When the weather is clear, the dark skies at Voyageurs light up at night with brilliant stars and the Milky Way. In August, shooting stars streak across the sky in the **Perseid meteor shower** (50-75 meteors per hour). Stargazing

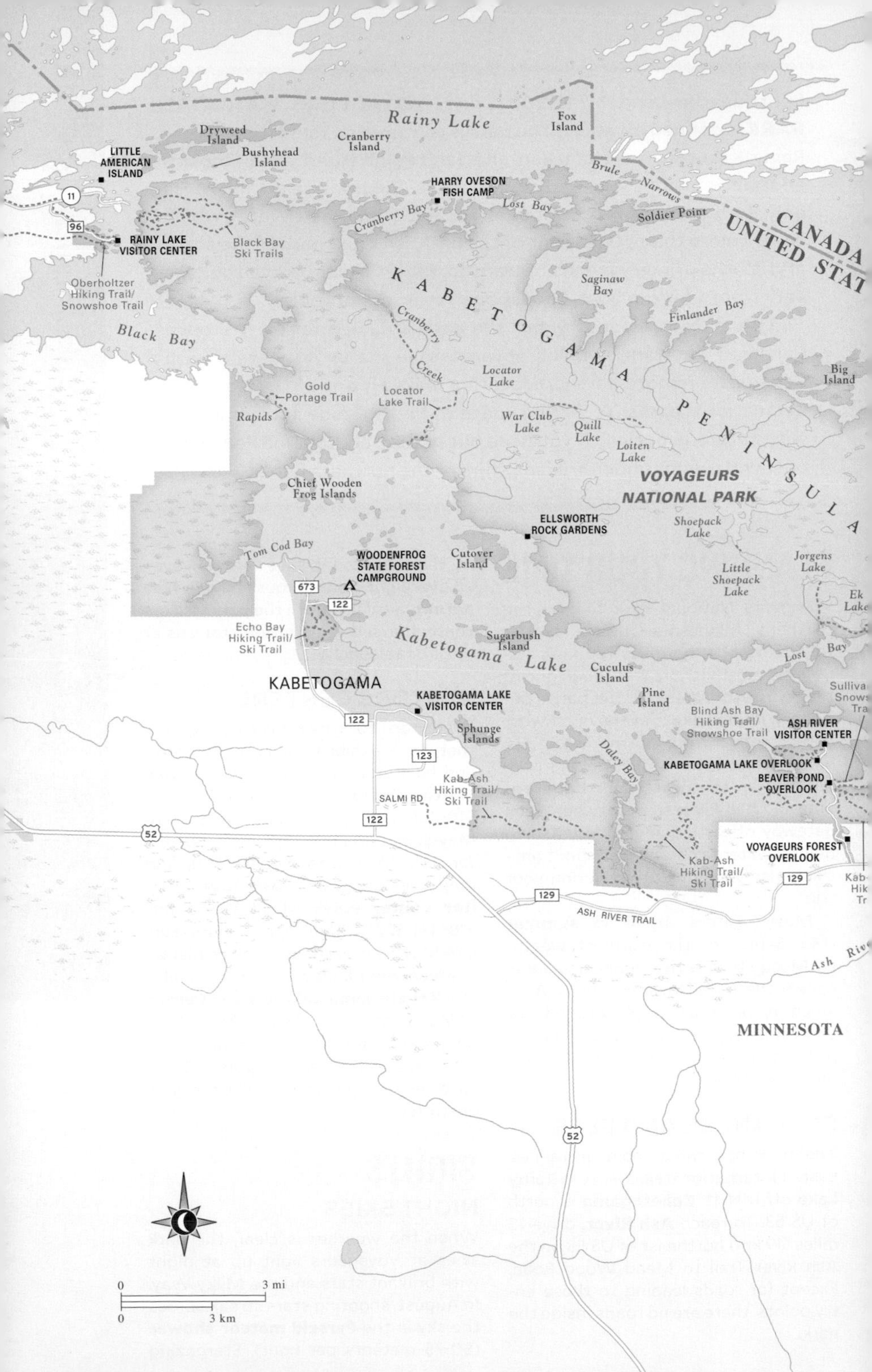
Rainy Lake
Dryweed Island
Cranberry Island
Fox Island
LITTLE AMERICAN ISLAND
Bushyhead Island
Brule Narrows
HARRY OVESON FISH CAMP
Lost Bay
Soldier Point
CANADA
UNITED STAT
11
96
RAINY LAKE VISITOR CENTER
Black Bay Ski Trails
Cranberry Bay
Oberholtzer Hiking Trail/ Snowshoe Trail
K A B E T O G A M A P E N I N S U L A
Saginaw Bay
Finlander Bay
Cranberry Creek
Black Bay
Locator Lake
Big Island
Gold Portage Trail
Locator Lake Trail
Rapids
War Club Lake
Quill Lake
Loiten Lake
VOYAGEURS NATIONAL PARK
Chief Wooden Frog Islands
ELLSWORTH ROCK GARDENS
Shoepack Lake
Tom Cod Bay
WOODENFROG STATE FOREST CAMPGROUND
Cutover Island
Little Shoepack Lake
Jorgens Lake
673
122
Ek Lake
Echo Bay Hiking Trail/ Ski Trail
Kabetogama Lake
Sugarbush Island
Lost Bay
KABETOGAMA
Cuculus Island
Pine Island
KABETOGAMA LAKE VISITOR CENTER
Blind Ash Bay Hiking Trail/ Snowshoe Trail
ASH RIVER VISITOR CENTER
Sulliva Snows Tra
122
Sphunge Islands
Daley Bay
123
KABETOGAMA LAKE OVERLOOK
BEAVER POND OVERLOOK
Kab-Ash Hiking Trail/ Ski Trail
SALMI RD
122
52
VOYAGEURS FOREST OVERLOOK
Kab-Ash Hiking Trail/ Ski Trail
129
Kab- Hik Tr
129
ASH RIVER TRAIL
Ash River
MINNESOTA
52
0
3 mi
0
3 km

VOYAGEURS NATIONAL PARK

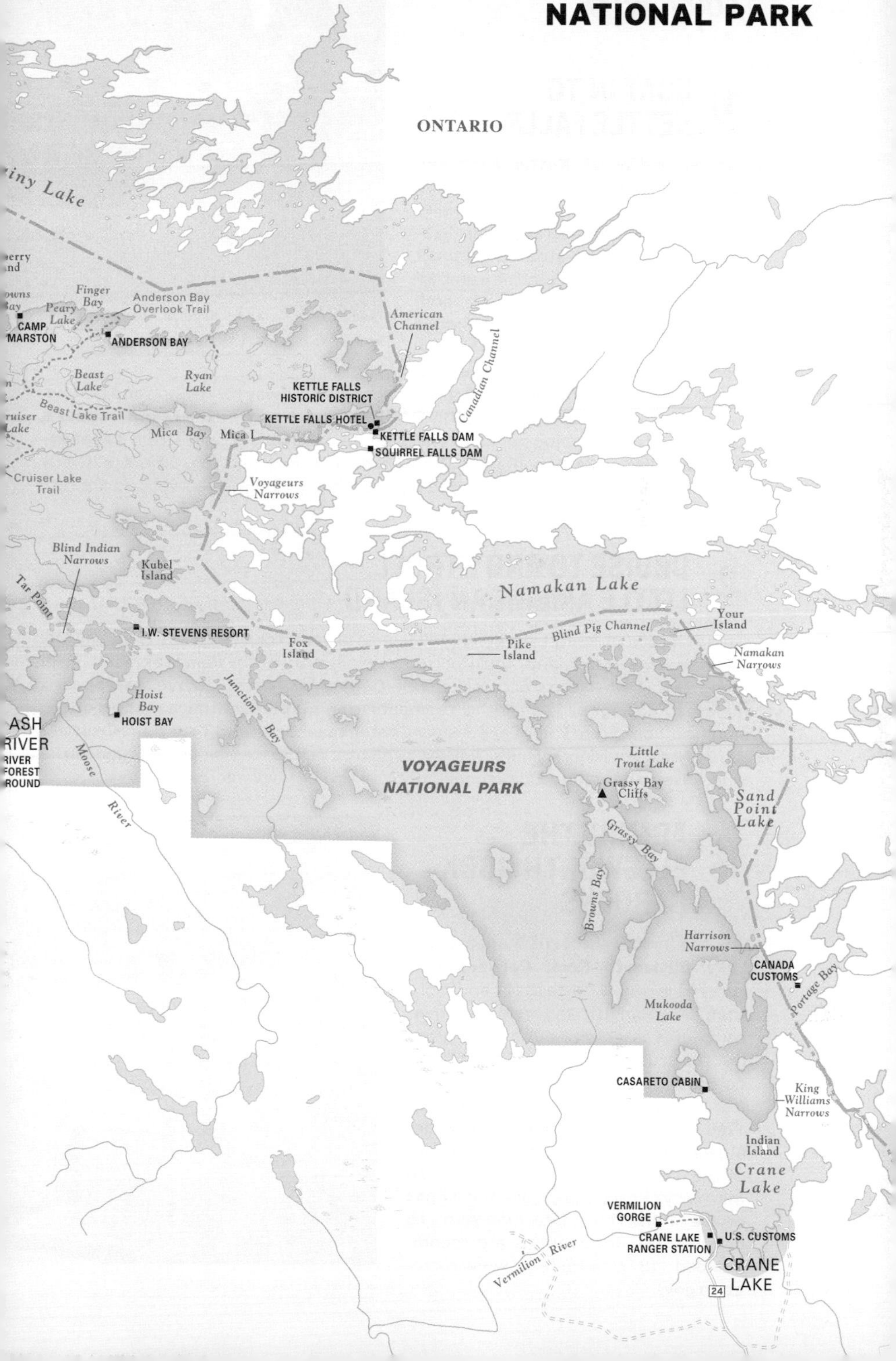
ONTARIO
Finger Bay
Peary Lake
Anderson Bay Overlook Trail
CAMP MARSTON
ANDERSON BAY
American Channel
Canadian Channel
Beast Lake
Ryan Lake
Beast Lake Trail
KETTLE FALLS HISTORIC DISTRICT
KETTLE FALLS HOTEL
KETTLE FALLS DAM
SQUIRREL FALLS DAM
Mica Bay
Mica I.
Cruiser Lake Trail
Voyageurs Narrows
Blind Indian Narrows
Kubel Island
Tar Point
Namakan Lake
I.W. STEVENS RESORT
Fox Island
Pike Island
Blind Pig Channel
Your Island
Namakan Narrows
Junction Bay
Hoist Bay
HOIST BAY
Moose River
VOYAGEURS NATIONAL PARK
Little Trout Lake
Grassy Bay Cliffs
Grassy Bay
Sand Point Lake
Browns Bay
Harrison Narrows
CANADA CUSTOMS
Portage Bay
Mukooda Lake
CASARETO CABIN
King Williams Narrows
Indian Island
Crane Lake
VERMILION GORGE
CRANE LAKE RANGER STATION
U.S. CUSTOMS
Vermilion River
CRANE LAKE
24

Top 3

1 BOAT IN TO KETTLE FALLS

KETTLE FALLS HOTEL

The red-and-white **Kettle Falls Hotel** (12977 Chippewa Tr., 218/240-1724, www.kettlefallshotel.com) sits 16 miles (26 km) from the nearest road. Visitors arrive by boat to stroll its grounds, enjoy a meal or a drink in the Lumberjack Saloon, or just relax on the endless veranda. The antiques-filled lodge is rumored to have started as a brothel around 1910 and did a thriving business during Prohibition, but then became a fashionable getaway for the rich and famous such as Charles Lindbergh and John D. Rockefeller. Nearby is the **Dam Tender's Cabin,** a restored 1912 log home. To visit the site, catch boat cruises from **Kabetogama Lake Visitor Center** (10am-3:30pm Mon., Tues., Fri., July-Aug., 5.5 hrs., $20-40) or **Rainy Lake Visitor Center** (varied days, 6.5 hrs., $23-45). Reservations are recommended (877/444-6777, www.recreation.gov).

2 CRUISE TO AND STROLL LITTLE AMERICAN ISLAND

Gold fever struck Rainy Lake in July 1893 when prospector George Davis hit pay dirt on **Little American Island.** You'll learn the whole story of the Rainy Lake Gold Rush along a short wheelchair-accessible **trail** (0.25 mi./ 0.4 km rt., 20 min., easy) past a mineshaft, tailings piles, and other remnants from the only area mine that produced significant ore. From Rainy Lake Visitor Center, take the **Grand Tour Boat Cruise** (2 pm daily, except Mon. & Thurs., July-Aug., 2.5 hrs., $15-30) to visit Little American Island. Reservations are recommended (877/444-6777, www.recreation.gov).

3 ADMIRE THE ELLSWORTH ROCK GARDENS

ELLSWORTH ROCK GARDENS

On the north shore of Kabetogama Lake, **Ellsworth Rock Gardens** features 52 terraced flower beds and more than 150 geometric and animal-themed sculptures assembled out of local granite. The sculptures were built by Chicago contractor and regular summer visitor Jack Ellsworth between 1944 and 1965 and make this singular spot an ideal picnic ground. A ranger leads a tour of the gardens (0.25 mi./ 0.4 km rt., 20 min., easy). Reach the gardens on a **boat cruise** (1 pm Thurs. late June-Aug., 1.5 hrs., $13-25). Reservations are recommended (877/444-6777, www.recreation.gov).

ONE DAY IN VOYAGEURS

If you only have one day in the park, take a narrated **boat tour** from Rainy Lake to **Little American Island** or **Kettle Falls**.

is best 1am-3am from lakeside camps. At visitors centers, pick up the Junior Ranger Night Explorer booklet for kids. The park aims to become certified as an International Dark Sky Park in 2020.

Due to its northern latitude, Voyageurs also sees the **northern lights,** most often on moonless nights in spring and fall. Look at them from lakeside camps, Rainy Lake Visitor Center, and Ash River Visitor Center.

RECREATION

HIKING

Voyageurs may be all about the water, but hikers will not be disappointed. These trails do not require boat access.

Rainy Lake's **Oberholtzer Interpretive Trail** (1.7 mi./2.7 km rt., 1 hr., easy) covers a cattail marsh, pine forest, and scenic views of Black Bay; the first half of the trail is wheelchair-accessible.

The hilly path of Ash River's **Blind Ash Bay Trail** (2.5 mi./4 km rt., 1.5 hrs., moderate) follows a rocky ridge to great views of Kabetogama Lake and the narrow namesake bay.

A few miles northwest of the Kabetogama Lake Visitor Center, the slightly hilly **Echo Bay Trail** (2.5 mi./4 km rt., 1.5 hrs. moderate) loops through aspen and conifer stands. The trail passes beaver ponds, and you may spot wolf tracks.

The **Kab-Ash Trail** (27.9 mi./44.9 km one-way, strenuous) links the Kabetogama Lake and Ash River gateways. The path travels through a variety of forest types and over wetland boardwalks for wildlife-viewing.

CANOEING AND KAYAKING

Canoes and kayaks can navigate to 33 day-use sites. Most paddlers start at Ash River because it has the easiest access to quiet back bays, though the north end of Kabetogama Lake (accessible from the private Woodenfrog Campground) has loads of small islands

SERENE LAKES AWAIT EXPLORATION.

WATER COVERS NEARLY 40 PERCENT OF THE PARK.

with few boaters. From Ash River, paddle along the waterway to view wildlife. Rentals are available at each of the four gateway towns.

Ranger-led canoe tours (1.5-2 hr., summer only, reservations, free) launch from **Rainy Lake** (218/286-5258) and **Kabetogama Lake Visitor Centers** (218/875-2111). The historic North Canoe Tours are aboard 26-foot (7.9-m) canoes that you help paddle. Rainy Lake also guides the Beaver Lodge Tour through Black Bay. Make reservations by calling the visitors centers.

BOATING AND FISHING

Boaters can launch from all visitors centers as well as the Crane Lake Ranger Station. **Permits** (877/444-6777, www.recreation.gov) are required to overnight on houseboats ($10 per night May-Oct.) or camp ($12-35 per night May-Sept.). Reservations for permits become available mid-November for the following summer. A Minnesota fishing license (available in gateway towns) is needed for angling. The gateway towns have marinas, rentals, and free public boat ramps. Boaters should understand the U.S. Coast Guard buoy system and be able to read navigation maps, which are available at visitors centers.

WINTER RECREATION

Snow blankets Voyageurs in winter and the lakes freeze. That's when the groomed trails in the park call to snowmobilers, cross-country skiers, and snowshoers. Winter ice roads are maintained on frozen **Rainy Lake,** around the Kabetogama Peninsula's north end, and on **Kabetogama Lake.** It's the one season when you can drive a (snow) vehicle into the park! Accessed via an ice road, a sledding hill is on **Sphunge Island.**

WHERE TO STAY

INSIDE THE PARK

A night in the historic **Kettle Falls Hotel** (12977 Chippewa Tr., Kabetogama, 218/240-1724 or 218/875-2070 in winter, www.kettlefallshotel.com, May-Sept., from $90) is a highlight for many visitors. The 12 antiques-filled rooms in the main lodge share three baths; more modern cabins sleep up to six. The hotel rents canoes, kayaks, and boats and provides a shuttle service (fee) from the mainland.

There are more than 270 **boat-in campsites** ($12-35 per night). Sites have fire rings, picnic tables, privies, tent pads, and bear-proof food lockers, and some have canoe rentals. Advance

VIEW OF THE NORTHERN LIGHTS FROM THE ASH RIVER VISITOR CENTER

reservations (877/444-6777, www.recreation.gov) for a permit are required.

HOUSEBOATS

A houseboat is a popular means for exploring Voyageurs—it lets you enjoy the wilderness with all the comforts of home. No experience (or license) is needed; rental companies set you up with everything from food to maps. The National Park Service maintains designated mooring sites with fire rings throughout the park, or you can overnight at one of the resort areas. Overnight stays on a houseboat require a **permit reservation** (877/444-6777, www.recreation.gov, available Nov. 15 for following year, $10 per night). Park-authorized rentals include **Northernaire Houseboats** (2690 County Rd. 94, 218/286-5221, www.northernairehouseboats.com) and **Rainy Lake Houseboats** (800/554-9188, www.rainylakehouseboats.com) in the Rainy Lake area and **Ebel's Voyageur Houseboats** (888/883-2357, www.ebels.com) in Ash River.

OUTSIDE THE PARK

Dozens of lodging and campground options sit on the periphery of the park in **International Falls, Rainy Lake, Ranier, Kabetogama Lake, Crane Lake, Ash River,** and **Orr.**

GETTING THERE AND AROUND

The park has no public transit. Most visitors get around in a motorboat, sailboat, canoe, or kayak.

AIR

The nearest airport is **Falls International Airport** (INL, 3214 2nd Ave. E., 218/373-1073, www.internationalfallsairport.com), which has car rentals. The Rainy Lake Visitor Center is 14 miles (23 km) east along MN 11; the Kabetogama Lake Visitor Center is 26 miles (42 km) southeast on US 53.

BOAT

Narrated **boat tours** (June-Sept., 1.5-6.5 hrs., $25-45) go out on national park vessels from visitors centers at Rainy Lake, Kabetogama Lake, and Ash River. Starting in spring, make advanced **reservations** (877/444-6777, www.recreation.gov) until midnight prior to the tour. You can also make reservations at the three visitors centers.

THE SOUTH

Virginia's Shenandoah straddles the cultural border between East and South. The park's scenic Skyline Drive links to the Blue Ridge Parkway to reach the Smoky Mountains, home to Great Smoky Mountains National Park. Here, crystal clear trout streams and white-water rivers cut through rounded balds and jagged mountaintops.

Tiny, singular national parks are scattered throughout the South. Kentucky houses the immense underground Mammoth Cave. Arkansas harbors historic hot springs. Missouri celebrates the westward expansion with Gateway Arch, and South Carolina supports ancient stands of old-growth cypress in Congaree National Park.

Florida's languid lushness is captured in Everglades National Park, home to birds, alligators, and crocodiles. Coral reefs surround the offshore islands of Biscayne and Dry Tortugas.

◄ UPPER ROSE RIVER FALLS

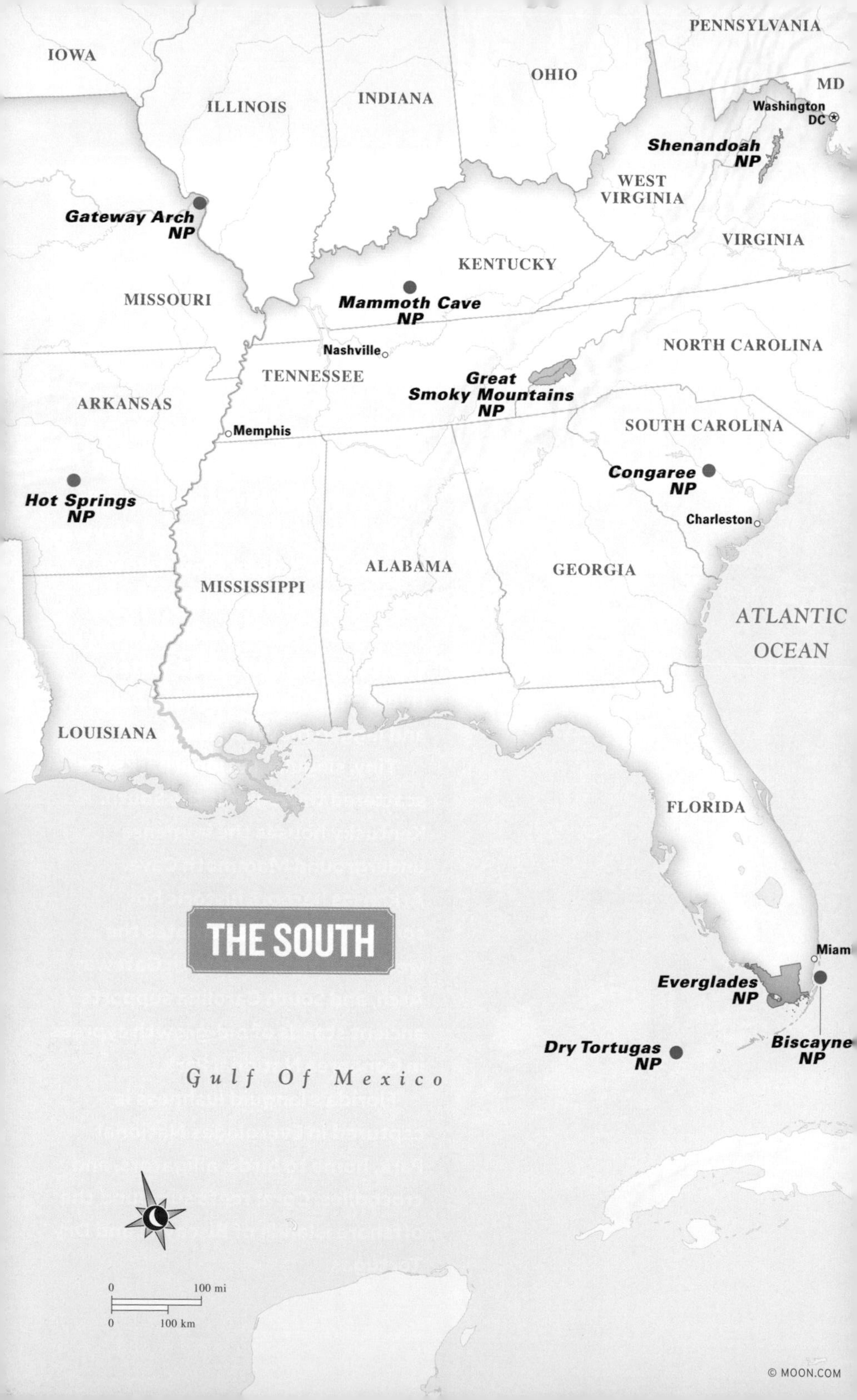
THE SOUTH
IOWA
ILLINOIS
INDIANA
OHIO
PENNSYLVANIA
MD
Washington DC
Shenandoah NP
WEST VIRGINIA
VIRGINIA
Gateway Arch NP
KENTUCKY
MISSOURI
Mammoth Cave NP
Nashville
NORTH CAROLINA
TENNESSEE
Great Smoky Mountains NP
ARKANSAS
Memphis
SOUTH CAROLINA
Congaree NP
Hot Springs NP
Charleston
ALABAMA
GEORGIA
MISSISSIPPI
ATLANTIC OCEAN
LOUISIANA
FLORIDA
Miam
Everglades NP
Biscayne NP
Dry Tortugas NP
Gulf Of Mexico
0
100 mi
0
100 km
© MOON.COM

The National Parks of THE SOUTH

GREAT SMOKY MOUNTAINS, NC/TN

The most visited national park has big reason for its popularity: scenic drives, historic early settlements, hikes to high viewpoints, and evening firefly shows (page 599).

SHENANDOAH, VA

This long, narrow park is home to Skyline Drive, hiking trails, and a hardwood forest that blazes with fall colors (page 616).

MAMMOTH CAVE, KY

The world's longest cave system features flowstones, columns, stalactites, and bottomless pits (page 626).

GATEWAY ARCH, MO

The world's biggest freestanding arch pays tribute to the westward expansion of the United States (page 634).

HOT SPRINGS, AK

This historic landmark houses one of the most sumptuous clusters of natural hot spring bathhouses in North America (page 640).

CONGAREE, SC

The ancient cypress swamp contains what may be the tallest old-growth canopy remaining on earth (page 649).

EVERGLADES, FL

Guided trams, bike routes, and water trails offer access to this fragile, swampy ecosystem where alligators and crocodiles coexist (page 654).

BISCAYNE, FL

This largely underwater park features coral reefs, shipwrecks, and mangrove forests on islands (page 668).

DRY TORTUGAS, FL

Reached by boat or seaplane, the park's seven islands combine diverse wildlife, remarkable coral reefs, shipwrecks, pirate legends, and a military fort (page 674).

1: ROARING FORK MOTOR NATURE TRAIL, GREAT SMOKY MOUNTAINS
2: STALACTITES, MAMMOTH CAVE
3: SUNSET OVER THE EVERGLADES

Best OF THE PARKS

Newfound Gap Road: Drive this scenic road through multiple types of forests and over the lowest pass in the Smokies (page 603).

Bathhouse Row: Soak in historic hot springs (page 641).

Skyline Drive: Cruise the curves on Shenandoah's scenic ridgetop road with 75 overlooks (page 620).

Mammoth Cave: Explore the most extensive cave system in the world (page 626).

PLANNING YOUR TRIP

Plan at least **two weeks** to tour the national parks of the South. Make lodging and campground **reservations** for Great Smoky Mountains, Shenandoah, and Everglades in advance. Tickets for tours of Mammoth Cave frequently sell out; make advance reservations to guarantee slots. Snow sometimes closes Newfound Gap Road in the Great Smoky Mountains in winter.

May-October is high season in most of the southern U.S. parks, with July and August the busiest months. Expect peak-season rates, congested roads, and difficulty getting reservations. Although summer is the prime tourist season, unless your plans involve some beach time or a stay in a mountain retreat, the humidity in the southern parks can be oppressive.

Accompanied by pleasant weather and fewer tourists, late spring **(May-June)** and fall **(September-October)** are the best times to explore the parks of Virginia and Tennessee. Fall foliage in the region is some of the most spectacular in the country. South Carolina is best in spring, **mid-March to mid-May,** when natural beauty hits its apex and lodging is at a premium.

Late December-April is high season in Florida, when lodging rates are usually higher. Accommodations often cost less midseason (May-July, late Oct.-mid-Dec.). Summer is the least crowded time to visit Florida: temperatures and humidity are fairly high, and the Atlantic **hurricane season** (June-September) can bring storms.

1: SKYLINE DRIVE, SHENANDOAH
2: FROZEN NIAGARA FORMATION, MAMMOTH CAVE

Road Trip

GREAT SMOKY MOUNTAINS, SHENANDOAH, AND MAMMOTH CAVE

Connecting two Appalachian national parks, the **Blue Ridge Parkway** links Shenandoah with Great Smoky Mountains. Fly into Dulles International Airport outside **Washington DC** and rent a car to start your journey.

Shenandoah

109 miles (175 km) / 4 hours

From Dulles, drive 56 miles (90 km, 1 hr.) on I-66 to **Front Royal,** the north entrance to **Shenandoah National Park.** Follow **Skyline Drive** at a leisurely pace to enjoy the scenery, multiple overlooks, and spectacular fall colors on the 105-mile drive (169 km, 3 hrs.). Spend the night at **Lewis Mountain Cabins,** 58 miles (93 km) into the drive. The next morning continue south on Skyline

SKYLINE DRIVE, SHENANDOAH

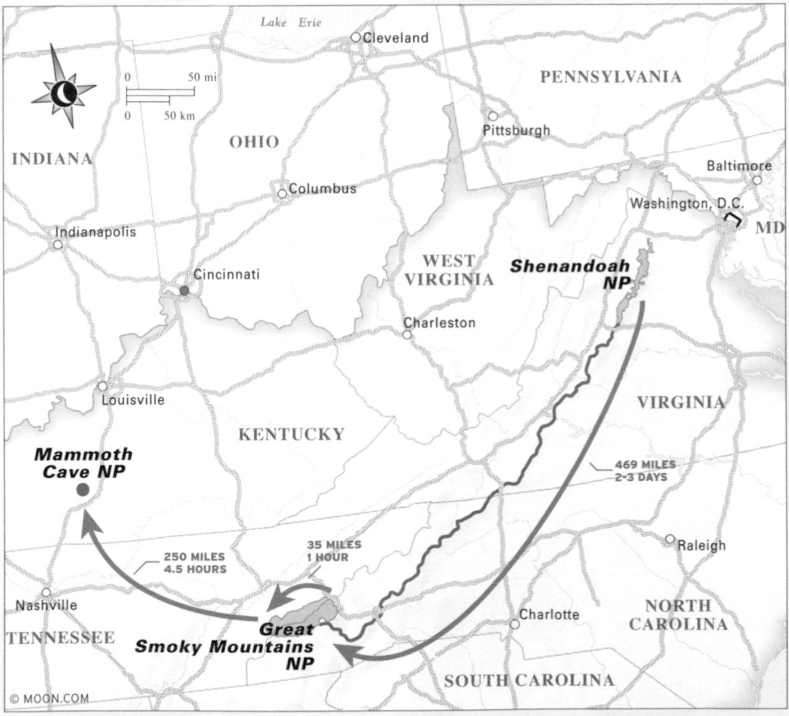

Drive to exit the park at Rockfish Gap near **Waynesboro.**

Blue Ridge Parkway

470 miles (755 km) / 2-3 days

After crossing I-64, Skyline Drive continues south as the **Blue Ridge Parkway.** Follow the parkway for 470 winding miles (755 km) from I-64 southwest to **Great Smoky Mountains National Park.** The drive from Floyd to the North Carolina state line is one of the most beautiful on the parkway. You'll want to break the drive into a couple of days to stop at parks, museums, and sights. Overnight in Roanoke, Virginia, or Asheville, North Carolina. The parkway ends at Newfound Gap Road near **Cherokee, North Carolina,** where your journey into the Smokies begins.

Great Smoky Mountains

35 miles (56 km) / 1 hour

Begin your cross-park route heading north via **Newfound Gap Road** (31 mi./50 km, 1 hr.). The twisting road is popular for motorcycle touring, autumn foliage, and wildlife, such as black bears and white-tailed deer. Stop along the way at any of the multiple overlooks. Add on a detour to **Cades Cove** (68 mi./109 km rt., 3 hrs.), a onetime mountain community where you might spy bears lounging in the remnants of an apple orchard. Wrap up this segment at **Gatlinburg, Tennessee.**

Mammoth Cave

235 miles (380 km) / 4.5 hours

From Gatlinburg, go northwest to **Mammoth Cave National Park,** where you can spend the night in the **Lodge at Mammoth Cave.** The following day, go underground with a ranger-led tour, with options ranging from 1.25 to 6 hours.

1: LINN COVE VIADUCT ON THE BLUE RIDGE PARKWAY
2: CADES COVE ROAD, GREAT SMOKY MOUNTAINS
3: MAMMOTH CAVE NATIONAL PARK ENTRANCE

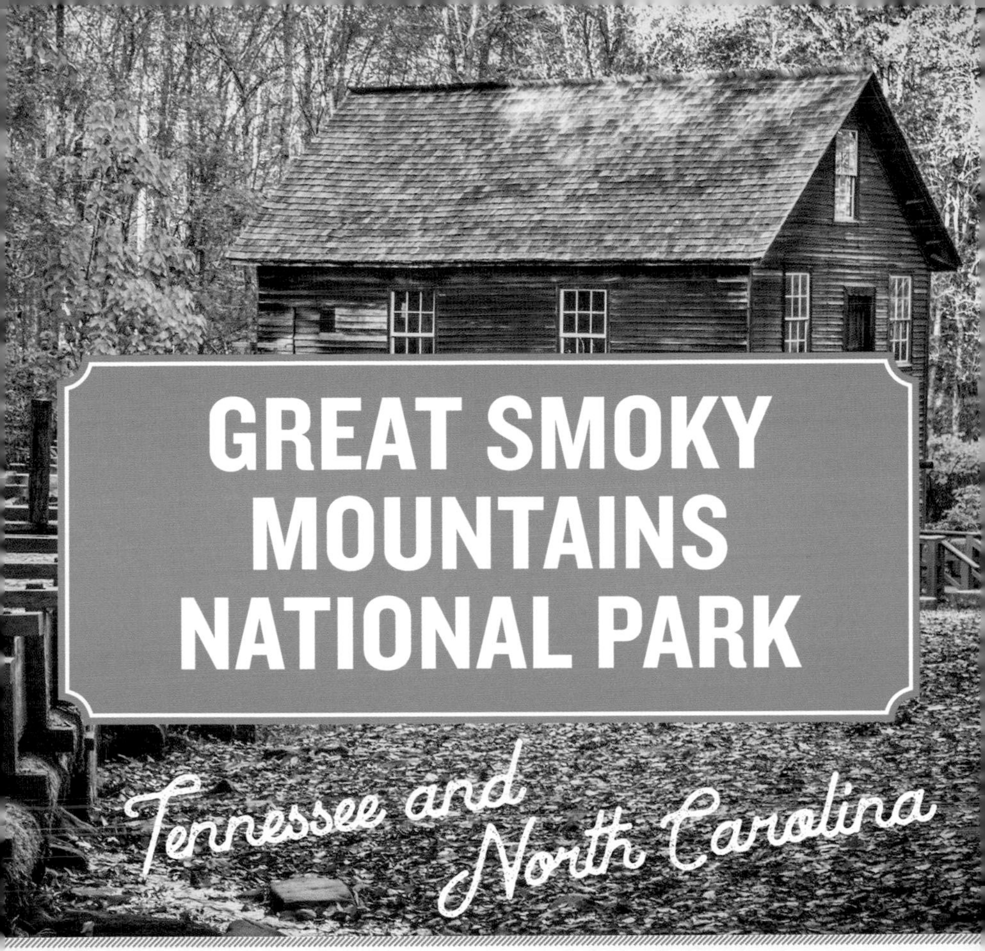

GREAT SMOKY MOUNTAINS NATIONAL PARK

Tennessee and North Carolina

KEEPSAKE STAMPS ▾▾▾

WEBSITE:
www.nps.gov/grsm

PHONE NUMBER:
865/436-1200

VISITATION RANK:
1

WHY GO:
See the country's oldest mountains.

▲ GREAT SMOKY MOUNTAINS NATIONAL PARK

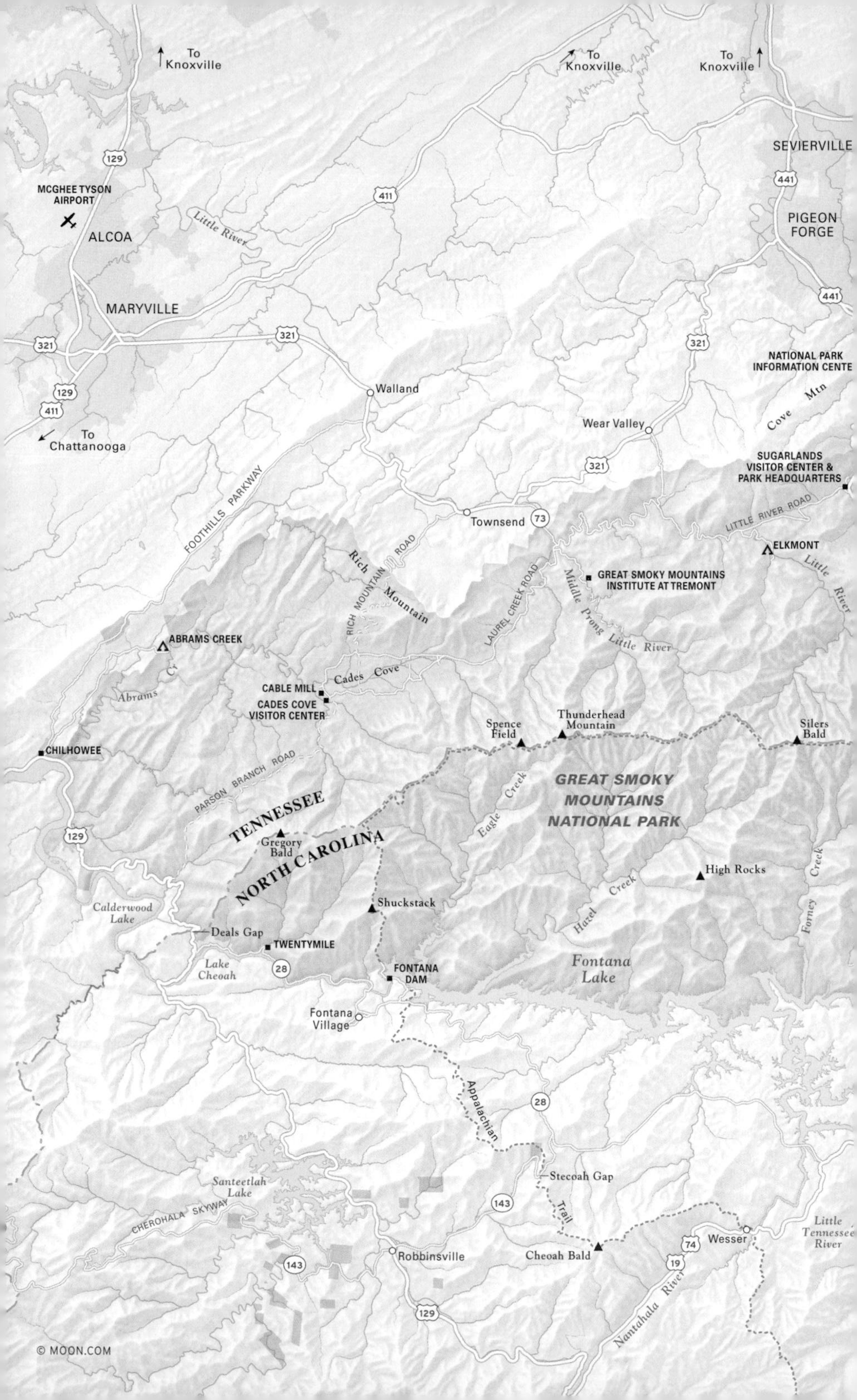
To Knoxville
To Knoxville
To Knoxville
129
MCGHEE TYSON AIRPORT
ALCOA
Little River
411
SEVIERVILLE
441
PIGEON FORGE
441
MARYVILLE
321
321
321
NATIONAL PARK INFORMATION CENTE
129
411
To Chattanooga
Walland
Wear Valley
Cove Mtn
321
SUGARLANDS VISITOR CENTER & PARK HEADQUARTERS
FOOTHILLS PARKWAY
Townsend
73
LITTLE RIVER ROAD
ELKMONT
Rich Mountain
RICH MOUNTAIN ROAD
LAUREL CREEK ROAD
Middle Prong Little River
GREAT SMOKY MOUNTAINS INSTITUTE AT TREMONT
Little River
ABRAMS CREEK
Abrams Cr
Cades Cove
CABLE MILL
CADES COVE VISITOR CENTER
Spence Field
Thunderhead Mountain
Silers Bald
CHILHOWEE
PARSON BRANCH ROAD
GREAT SMOKY MOUNTAINS NATIONAL PARK
Eagle Creek
TENNESSEE
NORTH CAROLINA
Gregory Bald
129
High Rocks
Forney Creek
Hazel Creek
Shuckstack
Calderwood Lake
Deals Gap
TWENTYMILE
Lake Cheoah
28
FONTANA DAM
Fontana Lake
Fontana Village
Appalachian Trail
28
Stecoah Gap
Santeetlah Lake
CHEROHALA SKYWAY
143
143
Robbinsville
Cheoah Bald
74
19
Wesser
Little Tennessee River
Nantahala River
129
© MOON.COM

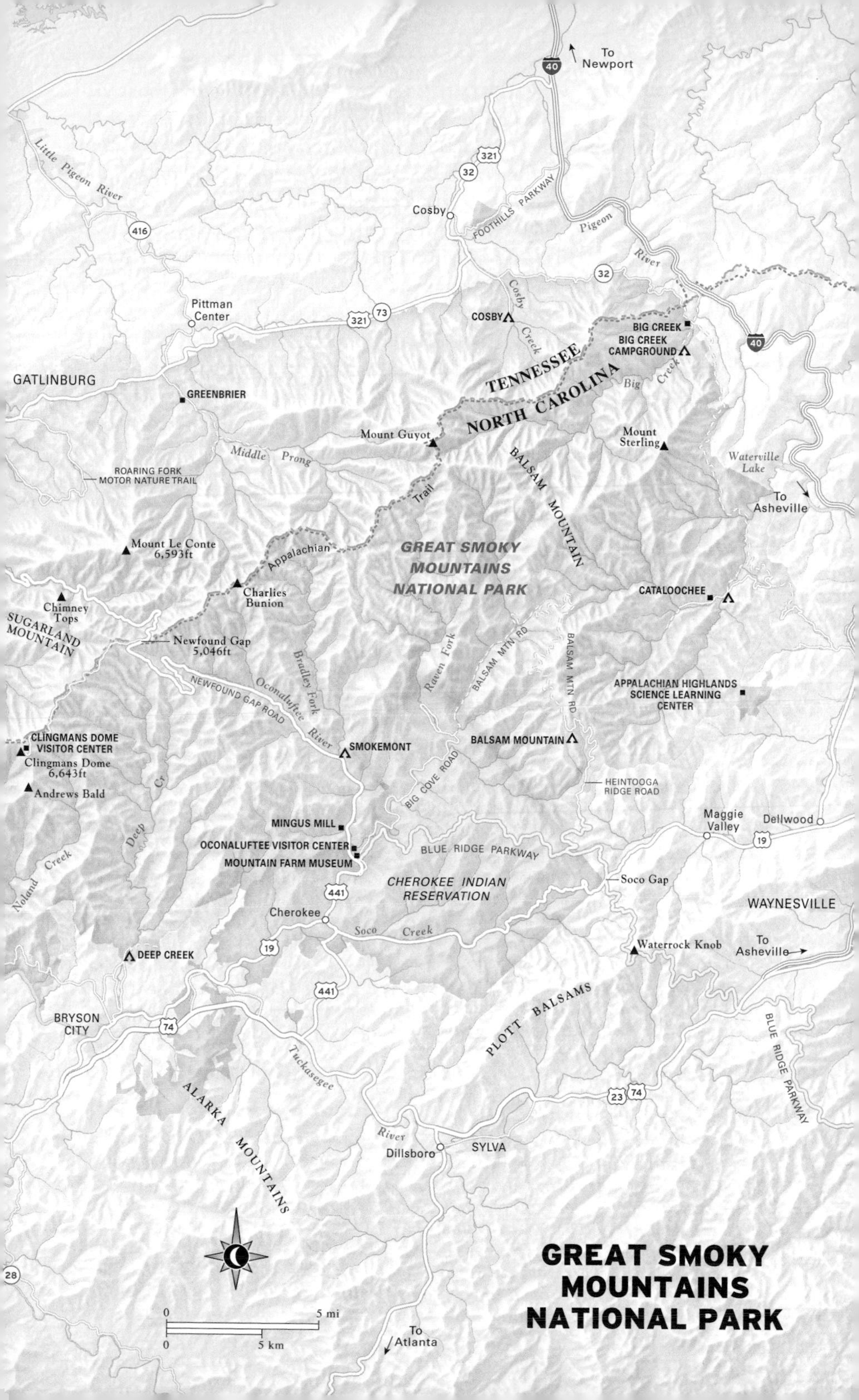
To Newport
Little Pigeon River
Cosby
Foothills Parkway
Pigeon River
Pittman Center
Cosby Creek
COSBY
BIG CREEK
BIG CREEK CAMPGROUND
Big Creek
TENNESSEE
NORTH CAROLINA
GATLINBURG
GREENBRIER
Mount Guyot
Middle Prong
Mount Sterling
Waterville Lake
ROARING FORK MOTOR NATURE TRAIL
BALSAM MOUNTAIN
Appalachian Trail
To Asheville
Mount Le Conte 6,593ft
GREAT SMOKY MOUNTAINS NATIONAL PARK
Charlies Bunion
Chimney Tops
SUGARLAND MOUNTAIN
CATALOOCHEE
Newfound Gap 5,046ft
Bradley Fork
Raven Fork
BALSAM MTN RD
NEWFOUND GAP ROAD
Oconaluftee River
APPALACHIAN HIGHLANDS SCIENCE LEARNING CENTER
CLINGMANS DOME VISITOR CENTER
Clingmans Dome 6,643ft
SMOKEMONT
BALSAM MOUNTAIN
Andrews Bald
Deep Cr
BIG COVE ROAD
HEINTOOGA RIDGE ROAD
MINGUS MILL
Maggie Valley
Dellwood
OCONALUFTEE VISITOR CENTER
BLUE RIDGE PARKWAY
MOUNTAIN FARM MUSEUM
Noland Creek
Soco Gap
CHEROKEE INDIAN RESERVATION
WAYNESVILLE
Cherokee
Soco Creek
To Asheville
Waterrock Knob
DEEP CREEK
PLOTT BALSAMS
BRYSON CITY
BLUE RIDGE PARKWAY
Tuckasegee River
ALARKA MOUNTAINS
Dillsboro
SYLVA
0 5 mi
0 5 km
To Atlanta
GREAT SMOKY MOUNTAINS NATIONAL PARK

GREAT SMOKY MOUNTAINS NATIONAL PARK is the most visited national park in the country, with visitor numbers around 11-12 million annually. The park is nearly equally split between two states, straddling the North Carolina-Tennessee state line. On the wild, sparsely populated North Carolina side, the mountains pile up against one another, making for tall peaks, steep slopes, and deep coves. You'll find places so remote and so isolated they've remained undisturbed by humans since the Cherokee first lived here—or at least they feel that way.

The Tennessee side is more developed. Cades Cove is a sightseer's delight, with its preserved historic churches, schools, and homesteads. In the fall, when hardwood trees turn gold, red, and orange, droves of visitors come for one of the most impressive color shows in the eastern United States.

PLANNING YOUR TIME

Great Smoky Mountains National Park straddles the border between Tennessee and North Carolina. Most visitors devote a single day to the park, driving **Newfound Gap Road** from Gatlinburg, Tennessee, south to the North Carolina town of Cherokee. To give the park a fair shake, spend at least **three days** here.

Summer (mid-June-mid-Aug.) and **fall** (Oct.) constitute the park's high season but May through October sees crowds. Seasonal considerations have a big influence on park visitation. Crowds arrive for the blooming of spring wildflowers. Each autumn the park is crawling with visitors for a look at the mountains blazing with red, yellow, and burgundy leaves. Summer brings hikers for the cool mountain air, while winter finds the park more empty than full, but no less beautiful.

Within the park, make **camping reservations** six months in advance and reservations at LeConte Lodge **one year in advance.**

Due to a vast difference in elevation (5,700 ft./1,737 m) between the park's lowest and highest point, weather can vary wildly. Clingmans Dome, the highest point in the park, has an average high temperature of only 65°F (18°C) in July; the only time you're guaranteed *not* to see snow flurries is June-August. While Clingmans Dome has cool temperatures, it can be in the low 90s (32°C) and humid in Cades Cove.

Park roads close in winter, though dates vary. **Newfound Gap Road** remains open in all but the most serious of weather. In winter, check current conditions (865/436-1200).

ENTRANCES AND FEES

Great Smoky Mountains National Park has three main entrances. **From Gatlinburg, Tennessee,** at the north end of Newfound Gap Road, US 441 leads south 2 miles (3.2 km) into the park. The southern entrance of Newfound Gap Road is in **Cherokee, North Carolina,** 2 miles (3.2 km) north along US 441. From **Townsend, Tennessee,** TN 73 heads 3 miles (4.8 km) east into the park at Cades Cove.

There is no entrance fee.

VISITORS CENTERS

Sugarlands Visitor Center

From Tennessee, **Sugarlands Visitor Center and Park Headquarters** (107 Park Headquarters Rd., 865/436-1291, 8am-7pm daily June-Aug., closes at 6pm Apr.-May and Sept.-Oct., 5pm Mar. and Nov., 4:30pm Dec.-Feb.) is just inside the park about 2 miles (3.2 km) from Gatlinburg. The center has natural history exhibits, a bookstore,

Top 3

COLORFUL FALL VISTAS ALONG CADES COVE ROAD

1 DRIVE NEWFOUND GAP ROAD

Easily the most heavily traveled route in the Smokies, **Newfound Gap Road** (US 441, 33 mi./53 km, 1-1.5 hrs.) connects Cherokee with Gatlinburg. Newfound Gap Road is the perfect introduction to Great Smoky Mountains National Park: Contour-hugging curves, overlooks with million-dollar views, easy hikes right off the roadway, and a 3,000-foot (914 m) elevation change give you a great overview of these mountains and this spectacular park. During peak times in the summer and fall, you'll encounter traffic jams along this scenic route.

2 TOUR CADES COVE

Fields, forests, high peaks, wildlife, and historic structures are just some of the highlights of the **Cades Cove Loop** (11 mi./18 km, 2 hrs., open to bicycles but closed to vehicles Wednesdays May-Sept.). This one-way paved road circles the valley floor. Wildlife is especially active in the hours around dawn and dusk. Due to its popularity, expect crowds, especially in the fall. Two shortcuts cross the valley to shorten the drive or circle back for one more look.

In 1850, nearly 700 people called this valley home. Today, a number of historic structures remain: churches, a few barns, log houses, and smaller buildings. Among them is the most photographed structure in the park, the **Methodist Church.** From time to time a wedding is held here, though it's more common for visitors to leave handwritten prayers on scraps of paper at the altar. The **Cable Mill Area** is the busiest section of the loop, where an actual mill still operates, and you can even buy cornmeal or flour ground on-site. Hikes include gentle strolls to homesteads, cabins, and churches, or longer walks to **Abrams Falls.**

3 LOOK OVER THE MOUNTAINS FROM CLINGMANS DOME

At 6,643 feet (2,025 m), **Clingmans Dome** is the third-highest mountain in the eastern United States, and the highest in the Great Smoky Mountains. A flying saucer-like observation tower at the end of a long, steep walkway gives 360-degree views of the surrounding mountains. To get to Clingmans Dome, turn off Newfound Gap Road 0.1 mile (0.2 km) south of Newfound Gap, and then take Clingmans Dome Road (closed Dec.-Mar.), which leads 7 miles (11 km) to the parking lot. The peak is near the center of the park, due north from Bryson City, North Carolina. In winter when the road is closed, the observation tower remains open for those willing to hike.

ONE DAY IN GREAT SMOKY

From either entrance, drive the **Newfound Gap Road,** stopping at sights along the way. En route from Clingmans Dome, hike **Andrews Bald** to take in the 360-degree view of the Great Smokies. Finish by circling **Cades Cove** to soak up the pastoral countryside.

backcountry office, and a 20-minute film introducing the park.

Oconaluftee Visitor Center

From North Carolina, **Oconaluftee Visitor Center** (1194 Newfound Gap Rd., 828/497-1904, 8am-7pm daily June-Aug., closes at 6pm Apr.-May and Sept.-Oct., 5pm Mar. and Nov., 4:30pm Dec.-Feb.) is 2 miles (3.2 km) north of Cherokee on US 441/Newfound Gap Road. It has history exhibits, ranger programs, a bookstore, and the Mountain Farm Museum outside.

Clingmans Dome Visitor Contact Station

Along Newfound Gap Road is the turnoff to Clingmans Dome and the **Clingmans Dome Visitor Contact Station** (Clingmans Dome Rd., 865/436-1200, 10am-6:30pm daily June-Aug., 10am-6pm daily Apr.-May and Sept.-Oct., 9:30am-5pm daily Nov.). It has park information and a bookstore.

Cades Cove Visitor Center

In Cades Cove, the **Cades Cove Visitor Center** (Cades Cove Loop Rd., 865/436-1200, 9am-4:30pm daily Dec.-Jan., except Dec. 25, 9am-5pm daily Feb., 9am-6:30pm daily Mar. and Sept.-Oct., 9am-7pm daily Apr.-Aug., 9am-5:30pm daily Nov.). It has ranger programs and a bookstore plus indoor and outdoor exhibits, including historic structures illustrating southern mountain life and culture.

SIGHTS

NEWFOUND GAP ROAD

Mountain Farm Museum

The **Mountain Farm Museum** (Oconaluftee Visitor Center, sunrise-sunset daily year-round, free) showcases some of the finest farm buildings of the park. Most date to the early 1900s. Among them are a barn, an apple house, and the Davis House, a log home built from chestnut wood and constructed before the American chestnut blight decimated the species. During peak times, costumed living-history interpreters

▼ CLINGMANS DOME

AVOID THE CROWDS

The most crowded months are July-August and October. In summer, road congestion peaks 10am-5pm on **Newfound Gap Road** and **Cades Cove Loop;** early morning and evening drives will have less traffic. For October leaf-peeping, roads tend to clog in late afternoon and evening; take your driving tour earlier in the day for more breathing room.

demonstrate the day-to-day chores that would've occurred.

Mingus Mill

North of the Oconaluftee Visitor Center you'll find **Mingus Mill** (9am-5pm daily mid-Mar.-Oct. and Fri.-Sun. Nov.). This historic gristmill was built in 1886; rather than use a waterwheel to power the machinery and mill in the building, it uses a water-powered turbine to generate power. The cast-iron turbine still works!

Deep Creek Valley Overlook

The **Deep Creek Valley Overlook** (14 mi./23 km north of Oconaluftee Visitor Center and 16 mi./26 km south of Sugarlands Visitor Center) yields a long view of the mountains, which roll away into the horizon.

Oconaluftee River Valley Overlook

Midway along Newfound Gap Road is the **Oconaluftee River Valley Overlook,** where you can spy the deep cut of the valley formed by the Oconaluftee River.

Newfound Gap

At 5,046 feet (1,538 m), **Newfound Gap** is the highest elevation on Newfound Gap Road with impressive views. The Rockefeller Memorial, a simple stone terrace that straddles the Tennessee-North Carolina state line, commemorates a $5 million gift made by the Rockefeller Foundation to acquire land for the park. To avoid the crowds, go early in the morning or near sunset.

Campbell Overlook

Named after one of the founding members of the Smoky Mountains Hiking Club, the **Carlos Campbell Overlook** (2 mi./3.2 km south of Sugarlands Visitor Center) is home to one of the best views of Mount LeConte. At 6,593 feet (2,009 m), LeConte is the third-highest peak in the Smokies.

GREENBRIER COVE

Greenbrier Cove was once home to a mountain community. This area was settled in the early 1800s, and families farmed, trapped, and hunted the land until the establishment of the national park. This cove has an interesting footnote: Dolly Parton's ancestors, Benjamin C. and Margaret Parton, moved here in the 1850s and their descendants left when the park was formed. Greenbrier is stunning, especially in the spring. The cove is known as a wildflower hot spot, but don't underestimate the beauty of this place in any season.

MINGUS MILL

COSBY

For the first half of the 20th century, **Cosby** was known as the moonshine capital of the world. Today, it is a friendly town with a few restaurants and a handful of cabin rentals at one of the lesser-used park entrances. The real attraction is spring wildflowers and hiking trails such as Hen Wallow Falls.

CATALOOCHEE VALLEY

This isolated valley on the northeastern edge of the park was home in 1910 to more than 1,200 people in the communities of Big and Little Cataloochee. By the 1940s all but a few were gone. Today, a few **historic structures** are all that remain of the communities that thrived here.

The most prominent building is the **Palmer Chapel.** Built in 1898, it still sees sporadic use. Across the road is the **Beech Grove School,** the last of three schools to serve the children of the valley. Just up the road is the **Caldwell House,** a frame-built home with paneling on the interior walls. The final structure is the **Palmer House** (off Big Creek Rd.), an 1800s log home with a 20th-century addition. Surrounding the historic structures are good locations for wildlife-watching, especially for elk. Pick up a self-guided tour booklet at the valley entrance.

ELKMONT

Elkmont Historic District, now listed on the National Register of Historic Places, started as the little logging town of Elkmont in 1908, adding in subsequent years the Wonderland Park Hotel and cottages. Once the park was established, cottage owners were granted lifetime leases on their property, and family members continued to renew the leases at 20-year intervals until the early 1990s. The hotel collapsed in the early 2000s. Restoration of the few remaining cottages has yet to happen.

Fireflies

The **synchronous fireflies** may have been one of the reasons the Wonderland Park Hotel was built in Elkmont. For a two-week window in early summer (late May-early June), their nightly light show delights crowds as drifts of male fireflies rise from the grass to flash their mating signal—blinking in coordination.

Viewing the synchronous fireflies has become so popular that a **lottery** (877/444-6777, www.recreation.gov) controls access to limit traffic congestion. The lottery opens for three days in late April with applicants choosing two dates; results become available by mid-May. Winners receive a parking pass for Sugarlands Visitor Center, where they board a shuttle to Elkmont and back for the firefly show.

FONTANA LAKE

At the southern edge of Great Smoky Mountains National Park lies Fontana Lake, a long reservoir created in the 1940s by **Fontana Dam,** the tallest dam in the eastern United States. It provided much-needed electricity to the factories churning out materials for World War II, including Oak Ridge, Tennessee, where research leading to the atomic bomb was conducted.

The exhibits at the **Fontana Dam Visitor Center** (Fontana Dam Rd., www.tva.gov, 9am-7pm daily Apr.-Aug., closes 6pm Sept.-Oct., free) tell the story of the region and the construction of the dam. There's also a small gift shop and a viewing platform overlooking the dam.

DEEP CREEK

Just south of Cherokee and north of Bryson City, **Deep Creek** is a spot more popular with locals than tourists, but it's worth a stop. Deep Creek is relatively placid, aside from a couple of waterfalls upstream. It's a good place for wading, tubing, picnicking, and hiking.

SCENIC DRIVES

ROARING FORK

The **Roaring Fork Motor Nature Trail** (5.5 mi./8.8 km, 2 hrs., open Mar.-Nov., no RVs or trailers) used to be one of the most beautiful drives in Great Smoky Mountains National Park. This narrow **one-way loop,** which follows the old curvy roadbed of the Roaring Fork Community, passes through what were lush rhododendron thickets and dense hardwood forests. A 2016 wildfire left

ROARING FORK CREEK

a landscape of charred tree stands and fewer rhodies and laurel, but the greenery will flourish again in time.

To start, turn onto Historic Nature Trail (Old Airport Road) at traffic light #8 in Gatlinburg and follow the signs. Drive a short distance on Cherokee Orchard Road, which runs through what was an 800-acre (324 ha) commercial orchard in the 1920s and 1930s. Shortly after the orchard, you'll be at the head of the trail.

RICH MOUNTAIN ROAD

Rich Mountain Road (7 mi./11 km, 30 min., open mid-Apr.-mid-Nov., no RVs or trailers) is a photographer's dream. Running north from Cades Cove over Rich Mountain to **Tuckaleechee Cove** and **Townsend,** this primitive **one-way gravel road** provides a few stunning views of Cades and Tuckaleechee Coves. Bear, deer, turkeys, and other wildlife make frequent appearances. The narrow, twisting, and sometimes steep road is typically in good condition, but it's not for low-clearance vehicles or economy rental cars; trucks or SUVs (no 4WD necessary) are best.

BALSAM MOUNTAIN ROAD

Balsam Mountain Road (14 mi./23 km, 1.5 hrs., open mid-May-Oct., no RVs or trailers) is a secluded drive where you may be lucky to see 10 other cars. Accessible only from the Blue Ridge Parkway near Soco Gap, the curvy, narrow road traverses a ridgeline. To reach Balsam Mountain Road, turn off the Parkway at milepost 458 and follow Heintooga Ridge Road to the Heintooga Overlook and Picnic Area; here the road changes names to Balsam Mountain Road and turns to gravel. As soon as it turns into Balsam Mountain Road, it becomes **one-way,** so you're committed to follow it to its end.

FOOTHILLS PARKWAY

Separated from the main body of the national park, the paved **Foothills Parkway** (open year-round, weather permitting) delivers vibrant fall foliage in October. It is in two segments in Tennessee. **Foothills Parkway West** (33 mi./53 km, 1 hr.) goes from US 129 at Chilhowee, crosses US 321 near Walland, and ends at US 321 at Wears Valley.

Best Hike

ANDREWS BALD

DISTANCE: 3.6 miles (5.8 km) round-trip
DURATION: 3 hours
ELEVATION GAIN: 1,200 feet (366 m)
DIFFICULTY: moderate
TRAILHEAD: Clingmans Dome parking area at the end of Clingmans Dome Road (closed in winter)

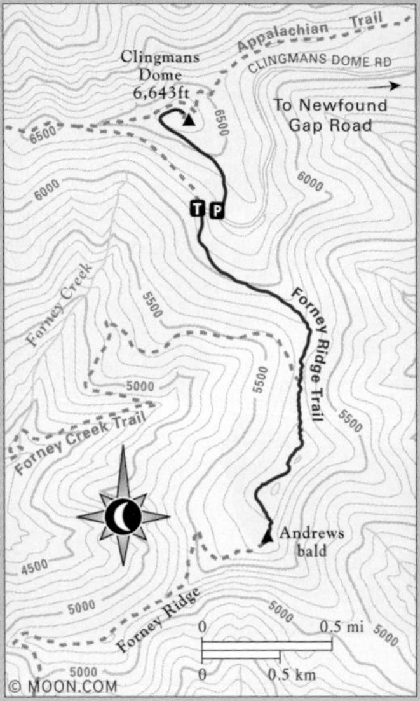

The highest grassy bald in Great Smoky Mountains National Park, Andrews Bald is a beautiful sight. Balds are meadows found higher up on the mountain, and this one is colorful with wildflowers, flame azalea, and rhododendron blooms in the summer.

The **Forney Ridge Trail** starts in a spruce-fir forest that was once beautiful, but is now dead or dying due to a tiny bug—the balsam woolly adelgid—that devours Fraser firs. However, there is a certain beauty in the white bones of the tree trunks jutting up from the land. But the views get considerably better at the edge of **Andrews Bald,** where the forest opens up into a broad panorama.

From Chilhowee to Walland, the route hugs the spine of Chilhowee Mountain with more than 15 overlooks including an observation tower at Look Rock. From Walland to Wears Valley, the new curvy route that opened in December 2018 has about 10 overlooks and spans multiple bridges as it arcs past Rocky Mountain. **Foothills Parkway East** (6 mi./10 km, 20 min.) goes from I-40, exit 443, over Green Mountain with three scenic pullouts to Cosby.

HIKING

NEWFOUND GAP ROAD

Kephart Prong Trail

Begin by crossing the Oconaluftee River via a footbridge to follow the wide, nearly flat **Kephart Prong Trail** (4 mi./6.4 km rt., 2 hrs., easy). The route passes a 1930s Civilian Conservation Corps camp containing ruins of foundations and chimneys, the remains of a fish hatchery, and narrow-gauge railroad tracks from a long-gone logging operation. The route terminates at Kephart Shelter.

Charlies Bunion

From the Newfound Gap parking lot, the **Charlies Bunion Trail** (8 mi./12.9 km rt., 7-8 hrs., strenuous) follows the Appalachian Trail and the Boulevard to Mount LeConte. In a little more than an hour, the Boulevard forks off to the left; continue straight to the Icewater Spring Shelter. From the spring, continue to a short spur trail on the left that leads to the rock outcrop known as Charlies Bunion where the views spread out.

Alum Cave Bluffs to Mount LeConte

Arrive early to get a parking spot for the popular **Alum Cave Bluffs to Mount LeConte** Trail (10 mi./16.1 km rt., 5 hrs., moderate). From Alum Cave Trailhead, it starts off gently climbing alongside Alum Cave Creek amid rhododendrons.

MOUNTAINS LINED WITH COLORFUL AUTUMN FOLIAGE

After reaching Arch Rock, a natural tunnel at Alum Cave Bluffs, climb stone steps to Inspiration Point for a territorial view, the halfway point where many hikers turn around. Then, the path steepens and narrows onto precipitous rock ledges with steel cables bolted into the mountain for handholds. Soon, the trail intersects with Rainbow Falls Trail, leading to the summit of Mount LeConte. This is the shortest trail to Mount LeConte Lodge.

Chimney Tops

Chimney Tops (4 mi./6.4 km rt., 3.5 hrs., strenuous) leads to an outstanding view from its namesake pinnacles. The route climbs along picturesque cascades, pools, and boulders on **Walker Camp Prong** before crossing **Road Prong** twice. At a fork, the right trail steepens and narrows on the ridge and up a steep rock scramble to the summit the first of the **Chimney Tops.**

CADES COVE

Abrams Falls Trail

Abrams Falls Trail (5 mi./8 km rt., 3 hrs., moderate) follows **Abrams Creek** all the way to the waterfall. The only real elevation gains come when you leave the creek three times to climb up and around a ridge to drop to the falls.

Rich Mountain Loop

At the beginning of Cades Cove Loop Road, **Rich Mountain Loop** (8.5 mi./13.7 km rt., 4.5 hrs., moderate) makes a circle around Rich Mountain via several trails: Rich Mountain Loop, Indian Grave Gap, Crooked Arm Ridge, and back to Rich Mountain Loop. The trail links up one of the classic Cades Cove meadows with higher views overlooking Cades Cove. On the Indian Gap Trail, take the side spur to Cerulean Knob, the highest point on Rich Mountain.

CATALOOCHEE VALLEY

Boogerman Trail

Starting from Cataloochee Campground, the **Boogerman Trail** (7.4 mi./11.9 km rt., 3.5-4 hrs., moderate) combines with the **Caldwell Fork Trail** to make a loop. The Boogerman Trail climbs, drops, and climbs to reach signs of human settlement, **stone walls** and a **cabin,** before turning right onto the Caldwell Fork Trail. Cross Caldwell Fork several times before connecting back to the trailhead.

Laurel Falls Trail

As the shortest waterfall hike in the park, **Laurel Falls** (2.3 mi./3.7 km rt., 1.5-2 hrs., easy) lures scads of hikers. From Little River Road, a short, steep start on

A SMALL WATERFALL IN THE SMOKIES

the paved trail assumes a gentle grade to the waterfall.

ROARING FORK

Rainbow Falls

On Cherokee Orchard Loop Road, **Rainbow Falls Trail** (5.4 mi./8.7 km rt., 3-4 hrs., moderate) is the most popular waterfall hike. The route climbs alongside LeConte Creek through a couple of switchbacks and across the creek on a **log bridge.** At another crossing, you can see 80-foot-high (24-m) **Rainbow Falls** above but the trail continues to a spot just below the falls.

GREENBRIER COVE AND COSBY

Ramsey Cascades Trail

Ramsey Cascades (8 mi./12.9 km rt., 5.5 hrs., strenuous) is the park's tallest waterfall, spilling 100 feet (30 m) in a series of steps before collecting in a pool at the base. From Greenbrier Road, the route starts on an easy jeep trail prolific with wildflowers in early summer. Then, trail steepens and crosses **Ramsey Prong.** When you hear the waterfall, be cautious on the final rocky and slick approach.

BLACK BEAR IN CADES COVE

Porters Creek Trail

On Greenbrier Road, **Porters Creek Trail** (4 mi./6.4 km rt., 2 hrs., moderate) goes to **Fern Branch Falls** at 60 feet (18 m) high. In spring, the path is thick with moss and wildflowers.

Hen Wallow Falls Trail

From the Gabes Mountain Trailhead, take the steady climb up the sometimes rugged **Gabes Mountain Trail** to a signed steep side spur. This side trail goes to **Hen Wallow Falls** (4.4 mi./7.1 km rt., 2-3.5 hrs., moderate) which tumbles 90 feet (27 m) in a fan into a small pool that is full of salamanders. During dry months, they are still pretty, but less wow-inducing.

RECREATION

BACKPACKING

Backpacking in the Smokies requires **permits** ($4 pp per night) with options to stay in tent sites or backcountry shelters both with bear cable systems for hanging food. Reservations are available 30 days in advance with the **Backcountry Information Office** (Sugarlands Visitor Center, 865/436-1297, https://smokiespermits.nps.gov, 8am-5pm). Backpacking to **Mount LeConte from Grotto Falls** (13.9 mi./22.4 km rt., 2 days, strenuous) has the option to overnight in LeConte Shelter, but the most coveted trip is the **Appalachian Trail** (71.6 mi./115.2 km, 7-8 days).

BIKING

Due to popularity of cycling the **Cades Cove Loop Road,** the NPS is implementing a trial program closing the road to vehicles on Wednesdays (May-Sept.) for car-free cycling. Check online for its current status. The **Cades Cove Store** (near Cades Cove Campground, 865/448-9034) rents bicycles in summer and fall.

FISHING

Smallmouth bass and rock bass are fairly abundant in the Smokies' streams. Anglers go to **Cosby Creek** year-round, fishing along the creek in spring and in the headwaters in summer. Other top fishing creeks include **Cataloochee Creek, Little Pigeon**

River, and **Little River. Fontana Lake** contains largemouth, smallmouth, and rock bass plus deeper water has walleye and muskies. Anglers use boats and kayaks on the lake. Regardless of where you fish in the park, you'll need a license from either Tennessee or North Carolina.

HORSEBACK RIDING

Three commercial stables in the park offer "rental" horses. **Smokemont** (828/497-2373, www.smokemontridingstable.com) is near Cherokee, North Carolina. Two are in Tennessee: **Smoky Mountain** (865/436-5634, Gatlinburg, TN, www.smokymountainridingstables.com) and **Cades Cove** (10018 Campground Dr., Townsend, TN, 865/448-9009, www.cadescovestables.com).

WHERE TO STAY

INSIDE THE PARK

LeConte Lodge (865/429-5704, www.lecontelodge.com, late Mar.-Nov., from $152) offers the only true lodgings in the park, accessible via a 5.5- to 8-mile (8.8-12.9 km) hike on the easier Trilium Gap Trail, shorter Alum Cave Trail, or more difficult Boulevard Trail. Meals and bedding are included. Even though there is no running water or electricity, the lodge books quickly. Reservations are via lottery **one year in advance.**

The park has nine campgrounds (plus group and horse camps), equipped with flush toilets, fire rings, and picnic tables. On the park's south side, **Deep Creek Campground** (Bryson City, NC, 92 tent and RV sites, late Apr.-late Oct., $21) is first come, first served. **Reservations** (877/444-6777, www.recreation.gov, $17-27) are accepted up to six months in advance for part or all of the remaining campgrounds.

Four campgrounds offer reservations and first-come, first-served tent and RV sites. **Smokemont** (Cherokee, NC, 142 sites, year-round) is the only campground on Newfound Gap Road. **Cades Cove** (Townsend, TN, 159 sites, year-round), **Elkmont** (Gatlinburg, TN, 220 sites, year-round), and **Cosby** (Cosby, TN, 157 sites, late Apr.-late Oct.) are on the park's north side.

Reservations are required for four campgrounds: **Balsam Mountain** (Cherokee, NC, 46 tent and RV sites, mid-May-early Oct.) on the south, **Cataloochee** (Waynesville, NC, 27 tent and RV sites, late Apr.-late Oct.) and **Big**

▼ RAMSEY CASCADES

MIDDLE PRONG OF THE LITTLE RIVER

Creek (Waterville, NC, 12 walk-in tents sites, Apr.-Oct.) on the east side, and **Abrams Creek** (Walland, TN, 16 tent and small RV sites, late Apr.-mid-Oct.) on the west side.

OUTSIDE THE PARK

Most accommodations, dining options, and services are found in **Gatlinburg, Tennessee,** or **Cherokee, North Carolina. Cosby, Tennessee,** has a few accommodations and dining options, but selections are limited. For spring, summer, and fall, make reservations at least six months in advance.

GETTING THERE

AIR

Asheville Regional Airport (AVL, 61 Terminal Dr., Asheville, NC, 828/684-2226, www.flyavl.com) is about one hour east of Cherokee. **McGhee Tyson Airport** (TYS, 2055 Alcoa Hwy., Alcoa, TN, 865/342-3000, www.flyknoxville.com) is about one hour west of Gatlinburg. Car rentals are available at the airports.

CAR

There are three main entrances to Great Smoky Mountains National Park. From **Cherokee, North Carolina,** drive 2 miles (3.2 km) north along US 441 into the park on Newfound Gap Road.

From **Gatlinburg, Tennessee,** follow US 441 south 2 miles (3.2 km) into the park along Newfound Gap Road.

Townsend, Tennessee, provides access to Cades Cove via TN 73, 3 miles (4.8 km) east.

There are 17 additional points of entry into the park via automobile. The majority are gravel roads in varying states of maintenance that require different degrees of driving confidence and skill. If you're up for an adventure, these roads can lead to some beautiful corners of the park that few others experience.

GETTING AROUND

The park has no park shuttles or public transportation—you will need **your own vehicle.** It also has **no gas stations;** fill up first in Cherokee, North Carolina, or in Tennessee at Gatlinburg or Townsend.

APPALACHIAN TRAIL

Cutting through the heart of Great Smoky Mountains National Park, the **Appalachian Trail** runs along the high ridgeline that forms the border between North Carolina and Tennessee. There are 71.6 miles (115.2 km) of the Appalachian Trail in Great Smoky Mountains National Park, and it's a highlight for thru-hikers (those taking the Appalachian Trail north to Maine or south to Georgia, all in one enormous hike), segment hikers (those hiking the whole thing one piece at a time), and day hikers (those just out for a taste). For the lowdown on the Appalachian Trail, contact the **Appalachian Trail Conservancy** (www.appalachiantrail.org) or visit the **National Park Service** (www.nps.gov/appa), where you'll find trip-planning information, maps, trail reports, and more.

Permits

Though there are no fees required to hike the Appalachian Trail outside the national parks, hiking it in Great Smoky Mountains National Park requires a permit. Thru-hikers are eligible for a **thru-hiker permit** (www.smokiespermits.nps.gov, $20); thru-hikers must begin and end their hike at least 50 miles (81 km) from the border of the park and only travel on the Appalachian Trail while in the park. Segment hikers and backpackers need a permit from the **Backcountry Information Office** (Sugarlands Visitor Center, 865/436-1297, https://smokiespermits.nps.gov, 8am-5pm daily, $4 pp/night), available 30 days in advance. A permit is not required for day hikers.

Trail Shelters

For AT thru-hikers there's only one choice for where to stay in Great Smoky Mountains National Park: **Appalachian Trail shelters.** Of the 12 sites at each shelter, four spots are reserved for thru-hikers only and they're first come, first served. If you're thru-hiking and find a shelter full, you are permitted to pitch your tent next to the shelters. Segment hikers and backpackers can reserve spots in these Appalachian Trail shelters or at any of the numerous backcountry campsites along and near the Appalachian Trail. For a complete list of shelters and backcountry campsites, consult a park trail map (www.nps.gov/grsm).

Day Hikes

Day hikers are drawn to the Appalachian Trail's fantastic balds (high natural and agricultural meadows), like Andrews Bald; nobs like Charlies Bunion; peaks like Mount Cammerer and Rocky Top (yes, the one from the song); and just to say they've hiked part of the Appalachian Trail. The route through the park is always high and at times rocky, steep, or both, but the views are worth it.

Day hikers who want to log a few miles of the Appalachian Trail will find a few opportunities to get their boots muddy. Notable day hikes include:

THE APPALACHIAN TRAIL

Mount Cammerer (11.1 mi./17.9 km rt., 6 hrs., strenuous): Take the Low Gap Trail at the Cosby Campground to the Appalachian Trail, then proceed to the summit and a stone fire tower. Note: Only 4.2 miles (6.8 km) are on the Appalachian Trail.

Rocky Top (13.9 mi./22.4 km rt., 7 hrs., strenuous): Follow the Anthony Creek Trailhead from the Cades Cove picnic area to Bote Mountain Trail. At Spence Field, you'll meet up with the Appalachian Trail; follow it to Rocky Top and spectacular views.

WHERE TO CAMP IN GREAT SMOKY MOUNTAINS

NAME	LOCATION	PRICE	SEASON	SITES	AMENITIES
Abrams Creek	Foothills Pkwy.	$17.50	Apr-Oct.	16	tent and RV sites
Balsam Mountain	Balsam Mountain Rd.	$17.50	May-Oct.	46	tent sites
Big Creek	off Hwy. 284	$17.50	Mar.-Oct.	12	tent, RV, group, and horse sites
Cades Cove	Cades Cove	$21-25	year-round	159	tent and RV sites; camp store
Cataloochee	Cataloochee	$25	Mar.-Oct	27	tent and RV sites
Cosby	Cosby	$17.50	Mar.-Oct	157	tent and RV sites
Deep Creek	north of Bryson City	$21	Apr.-Oct.	92	tent and RV sites; dump station
Elkmont	Sugarlands Visitor Center	$21-27	Mar.-Nov.	220	tents and RV sites; dump station
Smokemont	Newfound Gap Road	$21-25	year-round	142	tent and RV sites; dump station

DRIVING

In Great Smoky, **Newfound Gap Road** (US 441, 33 mi./53 km) bisects the park from north to south. It's the most heavily traveled route in the park and provides a good introduction for first-time visitors. But the full length of Newfound Gap Road (70 mi./113 km) starts at the southern terminus of the Blue Ridge Parkway, just outside Cherokee, North Carolina, and ends in Knoxville, Tennessee, 32 miles (52 km) to the northwest of the park. It's easy to make the trip from one end to the other in an afternoon, though it may take a little longer in peak seasons.

To reach **Cataloochee Valley** from I-40, take exit 20 onto US 276. Take an immediate right onto Cove Creek Road. Zigzag up the gravel and paved road following the narrow, winding route for about 12 miles (19 km). It will suddenly open up into the wide, grassy expanse that is Cataloochee Valley. The valley is open to vehicle traffic 8am-sunset.

HISTORIC CABIN ON MOUNT LECONTE

WEBSITE:
www.nps.gov/shen

PHONE NUMBER:
540/999-3500

VISITATION RANK:
20

WHY GO:
Tour the Blue Ridge Mountains.

▲ DARK HOLLOW FALLS

KEEPSAKE STAMPS ▼▼▼

Amid the thick forest of **SHENANDOAH NATIONAL PARK**, both rare and common species thrive: big brown bats and black bears, white-tailed deer and bald eagles, and the endangered Shenandoah salamander. But it's the vast forests of Shenandoah that lend the park its beauty. About 95 percent of the park is covered in trees that change color with the season, flowering in spring, greening in summer, and turning gold and red in fall. Those trees emit organic compounds into the air that give the Blue Ridge Mountains their name.

This ridgetop land has hollows once used by Native Americans for hunting and foraging. Skyline Drive winds through lush forests with trails departing to a dozen waterfalls and multiple summits. Paralleling Skyline Drive, a 101-mile (163-km) segment of the Appalachian Trail crosses and recrosses the road. Remnants of former homesites are visible in crumbling walls and chimneys and mossy cemeteries hidden in the underbrush.

PLANNING YOUR TIME

Located only 70 miles (113 km) west of Washington DC, Shenandoah National Park is a popular escape. The park follows the ridge of Virginia's Blue Ridge Mountains for 105 miles (169 km) and is divided into three sections, designated by roads bisecting Skyline Drive.

- The **Northern District** stretches from Front Royal (US 340, MP 0) to Thornton Gap (US 211, MP 31.5).
- The **Central District** continues south to Swift Run Gap (US 33, MP 62.7).
- Rockfish Gap (I-64, US 250, MP 104.6) marks the southern boundary of the **Southern District.**

The most popular time to visit is May-October. Cruising Skyline Drive is especially popular in **autumn** (Sept.-Oct.), when the leaves turn and the broad, green valleys become a riot of color. This can mean long lines at entrance stations and slow traffic along Skyline Drive; expect a lot of leaf-peeping companions, especially on weekends.

Inclement weather can close the road at any time of year, and spring and summer storms can bring heavy rain, lightning, and hail to the area. Fog can pop up in any season. During deer-hunting season (mid-Nov.-early Jan.), Skyline is closed at night to give the deer a break.

Though the park and Skyline Drive remains open year-round, sometimes winter snow accumulation outpaces the park's ability to maintain roadways, forcing temporary closures, and some sections may close for the season. However, many people hike in or drive a short way up Skyline to take in the snowy views.

ENTRANCES AND FEES

There are entrance stations at four points along Skyline Drive:

- **Front Royal** (MP 0) off US 340 near Front Royal
- **Thornton Gap** (MP 31.5) off US 211 east of Luray
- **Swift Run Gap** (MP 62.7) off US 33 east of Elkton
- **Rockfish Gap** (MP 104.6) off US 250 east of Waynesboro

The entrance fee is $30 per vehicle ($25 motorcycle, $15 individual) and good for seven days.

VISITORS CENTERS

Shenandoah National Park has two visitors centers. The historic, stone **Dickey Ridge Visitor Center** (MP 4.6, 8:30am-5pm daily Apr.-mid-Nov., 9am-5pm daily Nov.-Apr.) is the first stop when traveling southbound along Skyline Drive. It

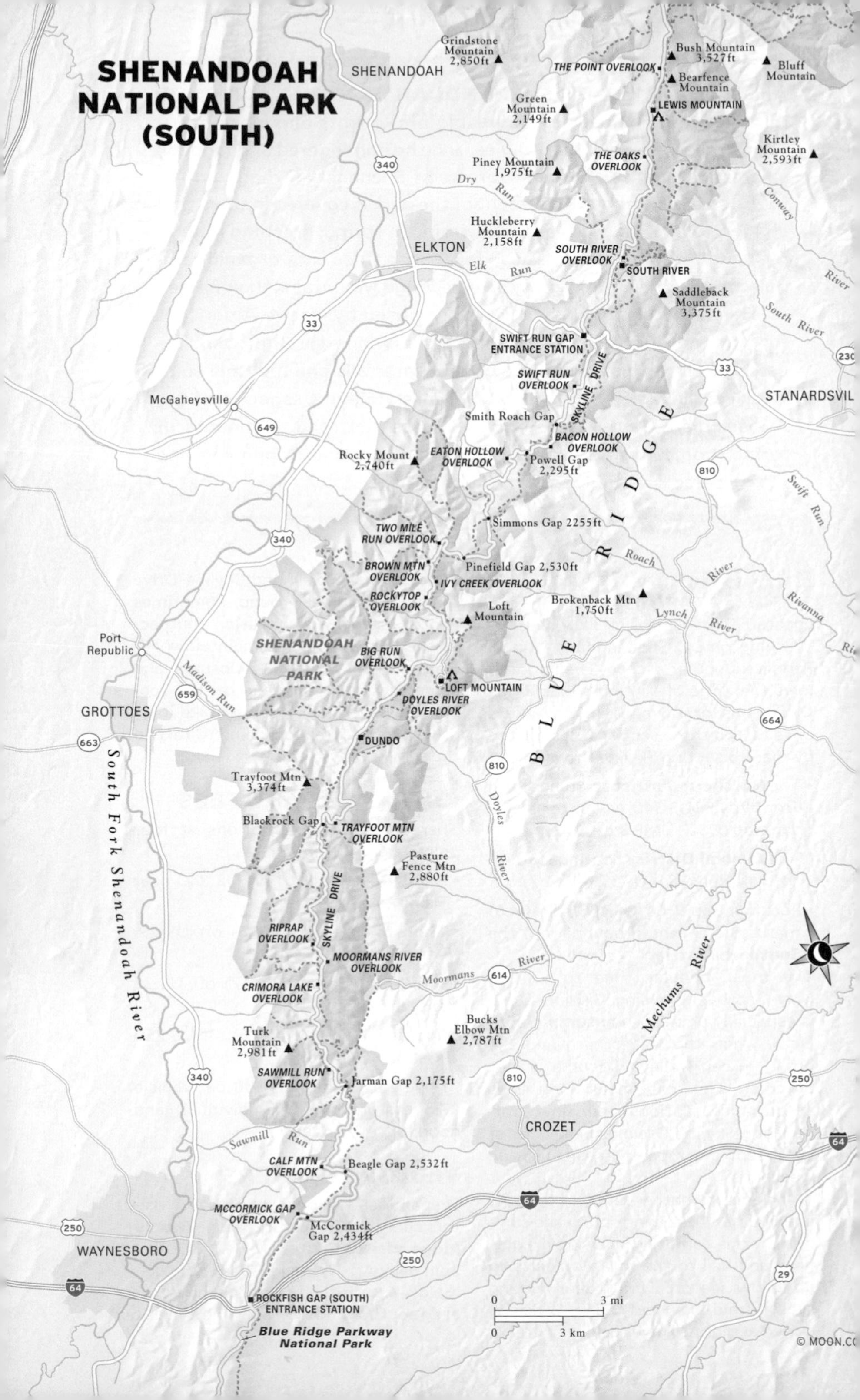
SHENANDOAH NATIONAL PARK (SOUTH)
SHENANDOAH
Grindstone Mountain 2,850ft
Bush Mountain 3,527ft
Bluff Mountain
THE POINT OVERLOOK
Bearfence Mountain
Green Mountain 2,149ft
LEWIS MOUNTAIN
Kirtley Mountain 2,593ft
Piney Mountain 1,975ft
THE OAKS OVERLOOK
340
Dry Run
Conway River
Huckleberry Mountain 2,158ft
ELKTON
SOUTH RIVER OVERLOOK
SOUTH RIVER
Elk Run
Saddleback Mountain 3,375ft
South River
33
SWIFT RUN GAP ENTRANCE STATION
230
SWIFT RUN OVERLOOK
SKYLINE DRIVE
STANARDSVIL
McGaheysville
649
Smith Roach Gap
BACON HOLLOW OVERLOOK
Rocky Mount 2,740ft
EATON HOLLOW OVERLOOK
Powell Gap 2,295ft
810
Swift Run
Simmons Gap 2255ft
TWO MILE RUN OVERLOOK
BLUE RIDGE
Roach River
BROWN MTN OVERLOOK
Pinefield Gap 2,530ft
IVY CREEK OVERLOOK
Rivanna Ri
ROCKYTOP OVERLOOK
Brokenback Mtn 1,750ft
Loft Mountain
Lynch River
Port Republic
SHENANDOAH NATIONAL PARK
BIG RUN OVERLOOK
LOFT MOUNTAIN
Madison Run
659
DOYLES RIVER OVERLOOK
GROTTOES
664
663
DUNDO
South Fork Shenandoah River
Trayfoot Mtn 3,374ft
Doyles River
Blackrock Gap
TRAYFOOT MTN OVERLOOK
Pasture Fence Mtn 2,880ft
RIPRAP OVERLOOK
MOORMANS RIVER OVERLOOK
Moormans River
614
Mechums River
CRIMORA LAKE OVERLOOK
Bucks Elbow Mtn 2,787ft
Turk Mountain 2,981ft
SAWMILL RUN OVERLOOK
Jarman Gap 2,175ft
250
CROZET
Sawmill Run
64
CALF MTN OVERLOOK
Beagle Gap 2,532ft
MCCORMICK GAP OVERLOOK
McCormick Gap 2,434ft
WAYNESBORO
29
ROCKFISH GAP (SOUTH) ENTRANCE STATION
0 3 mi
0 3 km
Blue Ridge Parkway National Park
© MOON.CO

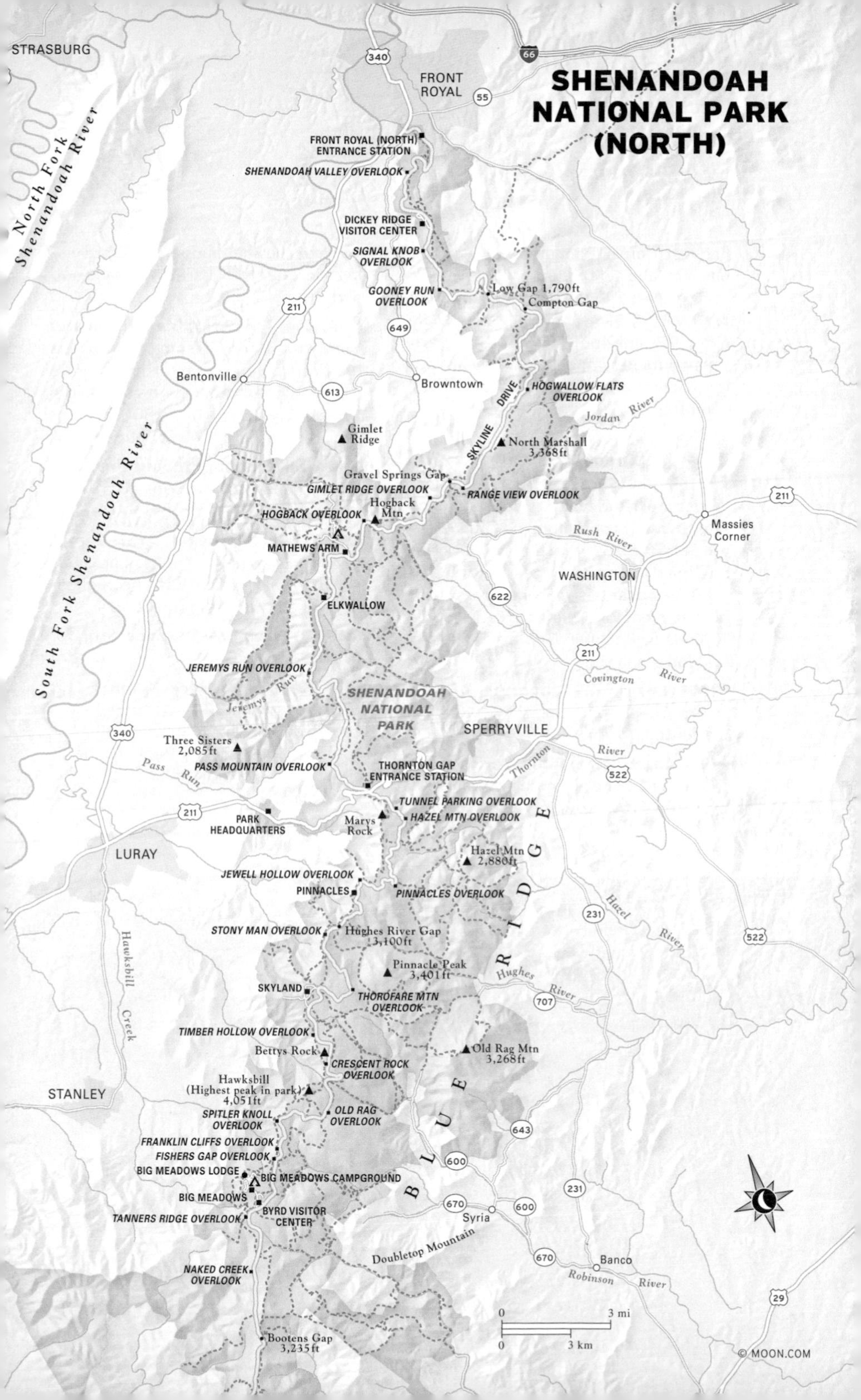
SHENANDOAH NATIONAL PARK (NORTH)
STRASBURG
340
66
FRONT ROYAL
55
North Fork Shenandoah River
FRONT ROYAL (NORTH) ENTRANCE STATION
SHENANDOAH VALLEY OVERLOOK
DICKEY RIDGE VISITOR CENTER
SIGNAL KNOB OVERLOOK
GOONEY RUN OVERLOOK
Low Gap 1,790ft
Compton Gap
211
649
Bentonville
Browntown
613
HOGWALLOW FLATS OVERLOOK
SKYLINE DRIVE
Jordan River
Gimlet Ridge
North Marshall 3,368ft
Gravel Springs Gap
GIMLET RIDGE OVERLOOK
RANGE VIEW OVERLOOK
Hogback Mtn
HOGBACK OVERLOOK
MATHEWS ARM
211
Massies Corner
Rush River
WASHINGTON
622
ELKWALLOW
South Fork Shenandoah River
211
Covington River
JEREMYS RUN OVERLOOK
Jeremys Run
SHENANDOAH NATIONAL PARK
SPERRYVILLE
340
Three Sisters 2,085ft
PASS MOUNTAIN OVERLOOK
THORNTON GAP ENTRANCE STATION
Thornton River
522
Pass Run
211
PARK HEADQUARTERS
TUNNEL PARKING OVERLOOK
HAZEL MTN OVERLOOK
Marys Rock
LURAY
Hazel Mtn 2,880ft
JEWELL HOLLOW OVERLOOK
PINNACLES
PINNACLES OVERLOOK
231
Hazel River
522
STONY MAN OVERLOOK
Hughes River Gap 3,100ft
Hawksbill Creek
Pinnacle Peak 3,401ft
Hughes River
SKYLAND
THOROFARE MTN OVERLOOK
707
TIMBER HOLLOW OVERLOOK
Bettys Rock
Old Rag Mtn 3,268ft
CRESCENT ROCK OVERLOOK
Hawksbill (Highest peak in park) 4,051ft
STANLEY
SPITLER KNOLL OVERLOOK
OLD RAG OVERLOOK
BLUE RIDGE
643
FRANKLIN CLIFFS OVERLOOK
FISHERS GAP OVERLOOK
600
BIG MEADOWS LODGE
BIG MEADOWS CAMPGROUND
231
BIG MEADOWS
BYRD VISITOR CENTER
670
Syria
600
TANNERS RIDGE OVERLOOK
Doubletop Mountain
670
Banco
Robinson River
NAKED CREEK OVERLOOK
29
0 3 mi
0 3 km
Bootens Gap 3,235ft
© MOON.COM

ONE DAY IN SHENANDOAH

Skyline Drive traverses the entire length of the park from north to south. A scenic drive along its twisting corridor should be on your one-day agenda. If you have time, add a short day hike along the way.

has restrooms, brochures, backcountry permits, and a gift shop.

The **Harry F. Byrd Sr. Visitor Center** (MP 51, 9am-5pm daily late Mar.-Nov., 9:30am-4pm Fri.-Sun. Dec.-early Jan., hours vary mid-Jan.-late Mar.) has restrooms, an information desk, and exhibits.

SIGHTS

Sights are listed north to south on **Skyline Drive.** Stops along Skyline Drive are referred to by milepost (MP), and milepost markers appear along the road. Milepost 0 is at Front Royal, at the northern end of Skyline Drive. Milepost 104.6 is at Rockfish Gap at the southern end.

- **(MP 4.6) Dickey Ridge Visitor Center:** Check out the view and get oriented.
- **(MP 6.8) Gooney Run Overlook:** You can see Gooney Run, the stream that drains Browntown Valley. Several turns of the Shenandoah River are visible here as well, as are Signal Knob and Dickey Ridge.
- **(MP 10.4) Fort Windham Rocks and Compton Gap:** Carson Mountain is unremarkable except for its summit, a geologic feature known as the Fort Windham Rocks, 600- to 800-million-year-old Catoctin lava formations.
- **(MP 20.8) Hogback Mountain Overlook:** The largest overlook area in the park.
- **(MP 22.2) Mathews Arm Campground:** Matthews Arm is near Overall Run Falls, which has the highest drop of all the falls in the park.
- **(MP 24) Elkwallow Wayside:** Stop for food or services.
- **(MP 32) Mary's Rock Tunnel:** This 670-foot-long (204-m) tunnel was cut through Mary's Rock in 1932. Narrow in width, Mary's Rock Tunnel is tight for RVs or trailers.

▼ MARY'S ROCK TUNNEL

Top 3

1 TOUR SKYLINE DRIVE

Skyline Drive (105 mi./169 km, 3 hrs.) curves through Shenandoah National Park from Front Royal to Rockfish Gap, just outside of Waynesboro. Along the narrow, ridgetop route, 70 overlooks offer views of the Shenandoah Valley to the west and the piedmont of Virginia to the east. The drive is lovely in any season but most colorful in the fall. Spring buds and wildflowers and jewel-green summer mountains are other seasonal attractions. Constructed in the 1930s by the Civilian Conservation Corps, this touring road was designed for scenic driving and bicycling.

SKYLINE DRIVE IN SPRING

2 EXPLORE DARK HOLLOW FALLS

One of the most popular waterfall hikes in Shenandoah, **Dark Hollow Falls** (MP 50.7; 1.4 mi./2.3 km rt., 2 hrs., strenuous) descends and follows Hogcamp Branch. As the trail works downhill, you'll get your first overlook of the 70-foot (21-m) falls before it breaks into several shorter drops. Continue on the trail to the base of the falls at a bridge over the creek before climbing back up.

DARK HOLLOW FALLS

3 CLIMB HAWKSBILL MOUNTAIN

The highest peak in the park, 4,051-foot (1,235 m), **Hawksbill Mountain** tops with a stone-and-mortar platform that contains peak identifiers along the walls. Just to its south is a stone trail shelter. While you can hike from several trailheads, the two shortest routes reach the summit the fastest. Be sure to return down your same trail.

Upper Hawksbill Parking (MP 46.5, 2.1 mi./3.4 km rt., 1.5 hrs., moderate) has a pleasant less-steep ascent with less elevation gain because it starts from a higher trailhead. **Hawksbill Gap Parking** (MP 45.5, 1.7 mi./2.7 km rt., 1.25 hrs., moderate) is a rockier, steeper trail, although shorter.

FIRE FINDER AT HAWKSBILL SUMMIT OVERLOOK

Best Hike

OLD RAG

DISTANCE: 9.2 miles (14.8 km) round-trip
DURATION: 6-7 hours
ELEVATION GAIN: 2,380 feet (725 m)
DIFFICULTY: strenuous
TRAILHEAD: Exit east from Thornton Gap (MP 31.5) to Sperryville, then take US 522, VA 321, VA 707 and VA 600/Nether Road to the trailhead

Hiking **Old Rag Mountain** is a rite of passage for many visitors. It's harsh, rocky, and exposed near the summit, so if there's the chance of bad weather (especially lightning), keep an eye on the sky. From the parking lot, walk up Nethers Road about 0.8 mile (1.3 km) to the trailhead. The blue-blazed trail climbs steadily, canting steeper toward the ridge. At the ridgetop, you'll emerge onto the outcrop with a sweeping view. This is where the fun scramble begins, climbing over granite boulders and down cracks, using your hands and feet. After several false summits, the real summit is marked with a concrete post.

To complete the loop, descend via the Saddle Trail (blue blazes) switchbacks which widen into a fire road after Old Rag Shelter. At a large intersection of fire roads, turn right onto Weakley Hollow Fire Road (yellow blazes) for a forested saunter along creeks to return to the trailhead.

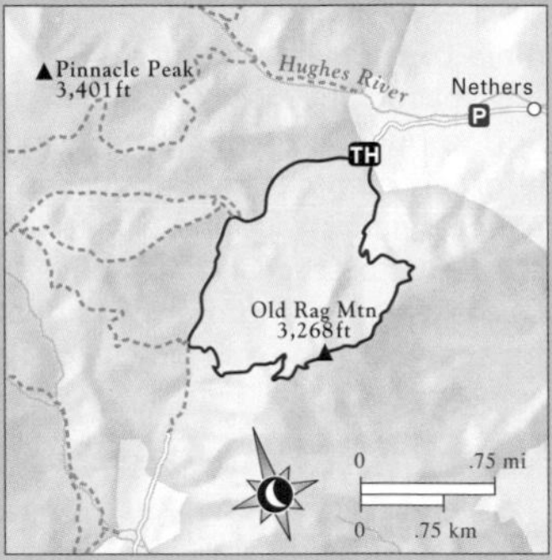

- **(MP 35.1) Pinnacles Overlook:** Look eastward for Old Rag Mountain.
- **(MP 41.7) Skyland Resort:** At the northern entrance to Skyland Resort, the road reaches 3,680 feet (1,122 m) in elevation, Skyline Drive's highest point.
- **(MP 51) Big Meadows:** Big Meadows is home to the largest open meadow in the park, the Harry F. Byrd Sr. Visitor Center, and Big Meadows Wayside for snacks.
- **(MP 76.9) Brown Mountain Overlook:** Ridges descend to the valley floor in stacked waves; at their head is a mountain with rocky protrusions that in autumn is ablaze with color.
- **(MP 79.5) Loft Mountain:** Grab a bite to eat from Loft Mountain Wayside.
- **(MP 84.8) Blackrock Summit:** This is a beautiful spot to stop and take in the scenery.
- **(MP 92.6) Crimora Lake Overlook:** This is one of the top vistas primarily because of Crimora Lake forming the centerpiece.
- **(MP 98.9) Calf Mountain Overlook:** This viewpoint provides some dizzying scenery. As you round the bend, the road seems to continue right out into the air (but it really just makes a tight turn). The long overlook has near-360-degree views.
- **(MP 105) Rockfish Gap:** The south entrance station marks the end of Skyline Drive and the beginning of the Blue Ridge Parkway.

RECREATION

HIKING

The second-highest peak in the park, **Stony Man** (MP 41.7, 1.6 mi./2.6 km rt., 1 hr., moderate) overlooks Shenandoah Valley from a rocky promontory. From Skyland's Stony Man Parking, go north on the Appalachian Trail to the blue-blazed Stony Man loops. Circle the overlook and return via the Appalachian Trail.

Whiteoak Canyon-Cedar Run Loop (7.3 mi./11.7 km rt., 6.5 hrs., strenuous) features eight waterfalls and a few

HISTORIC ROCK WALL ALONG SKYLINE DRIVE

pools to soak your feet. From Hawksbill Gap Parking (MP 45.5), make a loop by descending Cedar Run Trail, taking the Link Trail, climbing Whiteoak Canyon Trail, and returning to the start via the Whiteoak Canyon Fire Road.

From Big Meadows amphitheater, the **Lewis Falls Trail** (MP 51, 3.3 mi./5.3 km rt., 2.5 hrs., moderate) descends a rocky trail to an observation point of the 81-foot (25-m) falls before circling back to the trailhead via the Appalachian Trail.

The **Bearfence Mountain Trail** (MP 56.5, 1.4 mi./2.3 km rt., 1 hr., moderate) offers a rocky hand-and-foot scramble to a summit with 360-degree views, a rarity with most of Shenandoah's vegetated mountains. Cross the Appalachian Trail to climb to the top. Continue south, taking two right turns to walk the Appalachian Trail north to your starting point.

CLIMBING OLD RAG

The blue-blazed trail to **South River Falls** (MP 62.8, 4.4 mi./7.1 km rt., 3 hrs., strenuous) descends several switchbacks to reach an overlook where the river plunges into the falls and a deep grotto. Then, the route joins an old road, which connects with a short spur trail to the base of the falls and its large pool.

In the Southern District, **Riprap Hollow Trail** (MP 90, 9.8 mi./15.8 km rt., 7 hrs., strenuous) makes a loop via the Appalachian Trail north, Riprap Hollow Trail southwest, Wildcat Ridge Trail east, and the Appalachian Trail north. On Riprap Hollow Trail, vistas including Chimney Rock appear descending into Cold Springs Hollow, where a stream cuts through a small gorge to a waterfall and large swimming hole.

BACKPACKING

The **Appalachian Trail** passes through Shenandoah for 101 miles (163 km),

BICYCLING SKYLINE DRIVE

mostly paralleling Skyline Drive. Contrary to other wilderness sections of the trail outside the park, this portion of the trail crosses the road many times. The route has minimal water and a couple of shelters.

Backcountry camping **permits** (free) are required and available from entrance stations, park headquarters, and visitors centers. **Appalachian Trail permits** (for long-distance AT hikers) are available by self-registration on the AT near park entry points.

BICYCLING

Skyline Drive is favored by road cyclists for its ups, downs, and curves. But it has minimal shoulders. Ride single file, and wear bright colors. If possible, avoid weekends and fall when traffic is heavy.

WHERE TO STAY

INSIDE THE PARK

Make **reservations** (DNC Parks & Resorts, 877/847-1919, www.goshenandoah.com) for park lodges and cabins.

Skyland Resort (MP 41.7 and 42.5, early Apr.-late Nov., from $128) has traditional motel-style rooms overlooking the valley as well as older cabins and a full-service dining room (7:30am-10:30am, noon-2:30pm, 5:30pm-9pm), adjoining taproom, and grab-and-go items in the lobby.

Big Meadows Lodge (MP 51.2, early May-Oct., from $130) accommodations range from lodge rooms to small, rustic cabins. It also has a dining room (7:30am-10am, noon-2pm, 5:30pm-9pm) with indoor or terrace seating and a taproom.

Lewis Mountain Cabins (MP 57.5, early Apr.-early Nov., from $133) are cozy and rustic, with no phone or Internet. Each cabin has electricity, a private bathroom, linens, and an outdoor grill.

For a quick bite, stop by one of three Wayside Food Stops: the **Elkwallow Wayside** (MP 24.1), **Big Meadows Wayside** (MP 51.2), and **Loft Mountain Wayside** (MP 79.5). Camping supplies are also available.

Shenandoah also has four **campgrounds** (early spring-late fall) on Skyline Drive. Make **reservations**

SKYLAND RESORT

(877/444-6777, www.recreation.gov) six months in advance. Campgrounds have picnic tables, fire rings, restrooms, and potable water, but no hookups.

- **Mathews Arm Campground** (MP 22.1, 166 sites, $15, groups $50) is nearest the north entrance.
- **Big Meadows Campground** (MP 51.2, 200 sites, $20, groups $45) has showers, walk-in tent sites, and back-in and pull-through RV sites.
- **Loft Mountain Campground** (MP 79.5, 219 sites, $15, groups $35-50) has showers, a dump station, camp store, walk-in tent sites, pull-through RV sites, and views.
- **Lewis Mountain Campground** (MP 57.5, 31 sites, $15) is first come, first served only and has showers.

OUTSIDE THE PARK

The northern gateway of **Front Royal** has accommodations and restaurants. The town of **Luray** is the western gateway to Shenandoah National Park and has rental cabins, a few inns and motels, and eateries. For the greatest variety and choices, stay in **Washington DC.**

GETTING THERE AND AROUND

Skyline Drive is the main access through the park. There is no public transit. Inside the park, **gasoline** is only available at the **Big Meadows Wayside** (MP 51.2).

AIR

Several major regional airports serve the region, but **Dulles International Airport** (IAD, 1 Saarinen Circle, Dulles, VA, 703/572-2700, www.flydulles.com) has the most flights. Car rentals are available at the Washington DC airports.

CAR

Front Royal, Virginia, and the entrance to Shenandoah National Park is just a few miles east of where I-66 meets I-81 (18 mi./29 km west). US 340 and US 522 also go through Front Royal. On Skyline Drive, there are only two points where roads intersect the route. US 211 crosses Skyline Drive at Thornton Gap (MP 31.5); from here, the town of **Luray** is 10 miles (16 km) west. Farther south, US 33 intersects Skyline at Swift Run Gap (MP 62.7); the town of **Elkton** is 7 miles (11 km) west. There are entrance stations to Shenandoah National Park at both Thornton Gap and Swift Run Gap.

TOURS

Advance reservations are required for the ranger-led tour to **Rapidan Camp** (877/444-6777, www.recreation.gov, Thurs.-Sun. May-Oct., 2.5 hrs., $10), the former summer camp of President Herbert Hoover and a National Historic Landmark. Two restored cabins—the President's Cabin and the Prime Minister's Cabin—are included on the tour. Tours depart on national park vans from Harry F. Byrd Sr. Visitor Center.

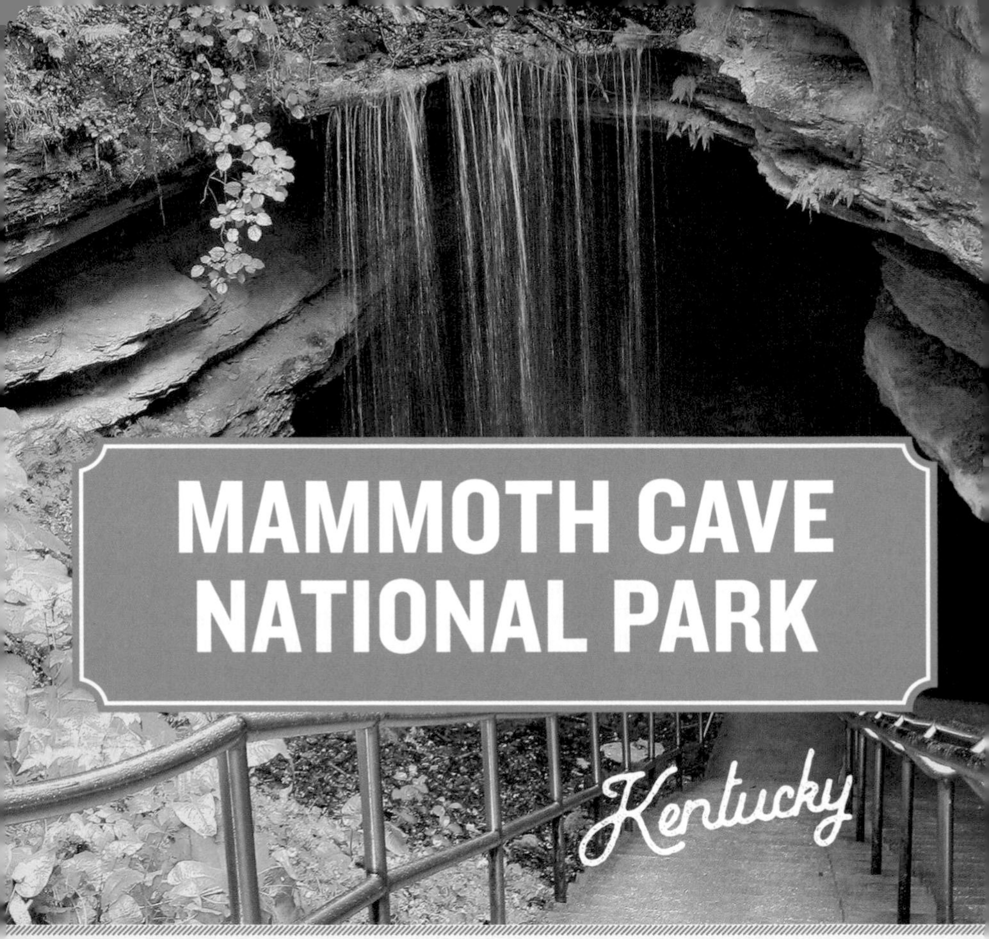

WEBSITE:
www.nps.gov/maca

PHONE NUMBER:
270/758-2180

VISITATION RANK:
39

WHY GO:
Explore the world's longest cave system.

▲ MAMMOTH CAVE NATIONAL PARK

KEEPSAKE STAMPS ▼▼▼

Upon entering **MAMMOTH CAVE NATIONAL PARK,** visitors first see dense stands of eastern hardwood forest that are home to large populations of deer and wild turkeys. But beneath this forest lies the park's main attraction: the most extensive cave system in the world. Mammoth Cave is massive, with more than 400 miles (645 km) of mapped passageways through limestone caverns and perhaps hundreds of miles still undiscovered routes. No known cave in the world is even half as long. It's also a surprisingly diverse ecosystem, supporting approximately 130 life-forms. Evidence indicates that humans explored Mammoth Cave 4,000 years ago, although it wasn't until 1798 that the cave was "rediscovered." It became a tourist attraction as early as 1816, making it the second-oldest tourist site in the United States after Niagara Falls.

PLANNING YOUR TIME

Mammoth Cave sits 90 miles (145 km) south of Louisville, close to the border with Tennessee. The national park is split into two regions: "aboveground" and "belowground." Above the ground you'll find hiking trails, campgrounds, and rivers for fishing, floating, and paddling. Belowground are the tours that enter the cave. Only one cave tour route is self-guided; all the others are guided. Tour reservations are accepted six months in advance.

The park is open year-round, with peak visits April-August. Underground, the cave stays a cool 54°F (12°C) year-round. Aboveground, **summer** (May-Sept.) temperatures warm into the 80s (27°C and above), while winters keep it cool in the 40s (4°C), with possible snow and ice. Winter sees limited operations, including limited cave tours.

ENTRANCES AND FEES

The park has multiple entrances; most visitors will enter via **Cave City** or **Park City** to reach the Historic Entrance and visitors center. There is no entrance fee to the park, but underground tours require fees.

VISITORS CENTER

Mammoth Cave National Park Visitor Center (8am-6:30pm daily mid-Mar.-Aug., 8am-6pm daily Sept.-Oct., 8:30am-4:30pm daily Nov.-mid-Mar.) is where to go for all park tours—options, schedules, tickets, and departures. The center has exhibits, permits, and information on ranger-led walks, evening presentations, and the Junior Ranger Program.

CAVE TOURS

There are more than a dozen **cave tours** (adults $14-60) offered daily. Tours range in distance (0.25 mi./0.4 km-5.5 mi./8.8 km) and time (1.25-6.5 hrs.). Introductory and general tours give an overview of the cave, its history, and its formation. Mammoth Cave also offers specialty tours, such as lantern-lit and photography- or geology-focused tours. Review tour details (distance, length, difficulty, and number of stairs) carefully—some tours depart multiple times daily, while others enter the cave elsewhere than the visitors center. **Tour reservations** (877/444-6777, www.recreation.gov) are highly recommended in summer. In addition to the Top 3 tours already described, these are some of the options...

To be wowed by large cave rooms like the Rotunda, take the **Historic Tour** (2 mi./3.2 km, 440 stairs, 2 hrs., moderate). First though, you'll need to enter Fat Man's Misery, a serpentine slot that requires squeezing through sideways. You may need to stoop or squat to

728
Bylew Creek
Whistle Mountain
695 ft
Sweeden
259
OLLIE RIDGE ROAD
OLLIE ROAD
LINCOLN
1827
GREAT ONYX
JOB CORPS CENTER
Second Creek
Stables Trail
FIRST CREEK
FERGUSON
Collie Ridge Trail
Nolin River
SECOND CREEK
First Creek Trail
Wet Prong Trail
Blair Spring Hollow Trail
RAYMER HOLLOW
Raymer Hollow Trail
First Creek
FIRST CREEK 1
FIRST CREEK 2
First Creek Lake
Mill Branch Trail
HOUCHIN FERRY ROAD
TEMPLE HILL
COLLIE RIDGE
McCoy Hollow Trail
Buffalo Creek Trail
THREE SPRINGS
MCCOY HOLLOW
HOMESTEAD
GOOD SPRING CHURCH
BLUFFS
Dry Prong Trail
MAPLE SPRINGS TRAILHEAD
Crump Island
HOUCHIN FERRY
MILES-DAVIS CEMETERY
MAPLE SPRINGS GROUP CAMPGROUND
Indian Hill
740 ft
HOUCHIN FERRY CAMPGROUND
SAL HOLLOW
Crumps Knob
835 ft
Sal Hollow Trail
Brooks Knob
852 ft
Green River
BROWNSVILLE
BROWNSVILLE ROAD
70
Stice Island
Turnhole Bend Trail
Boardcut Island
TURNHOLE BEND
Sand Cave Island
Turnhole Bend Nature Trail
Rhoda
Cedar Sink Trail
CEDAR SINK
101
CEDAR SINK ROAD
Pig
Chalybeate
422
Cedar Spring
CHAUMONT
743
0
1 mi
1 km
To Bowling Green
31W
© MOON.COM

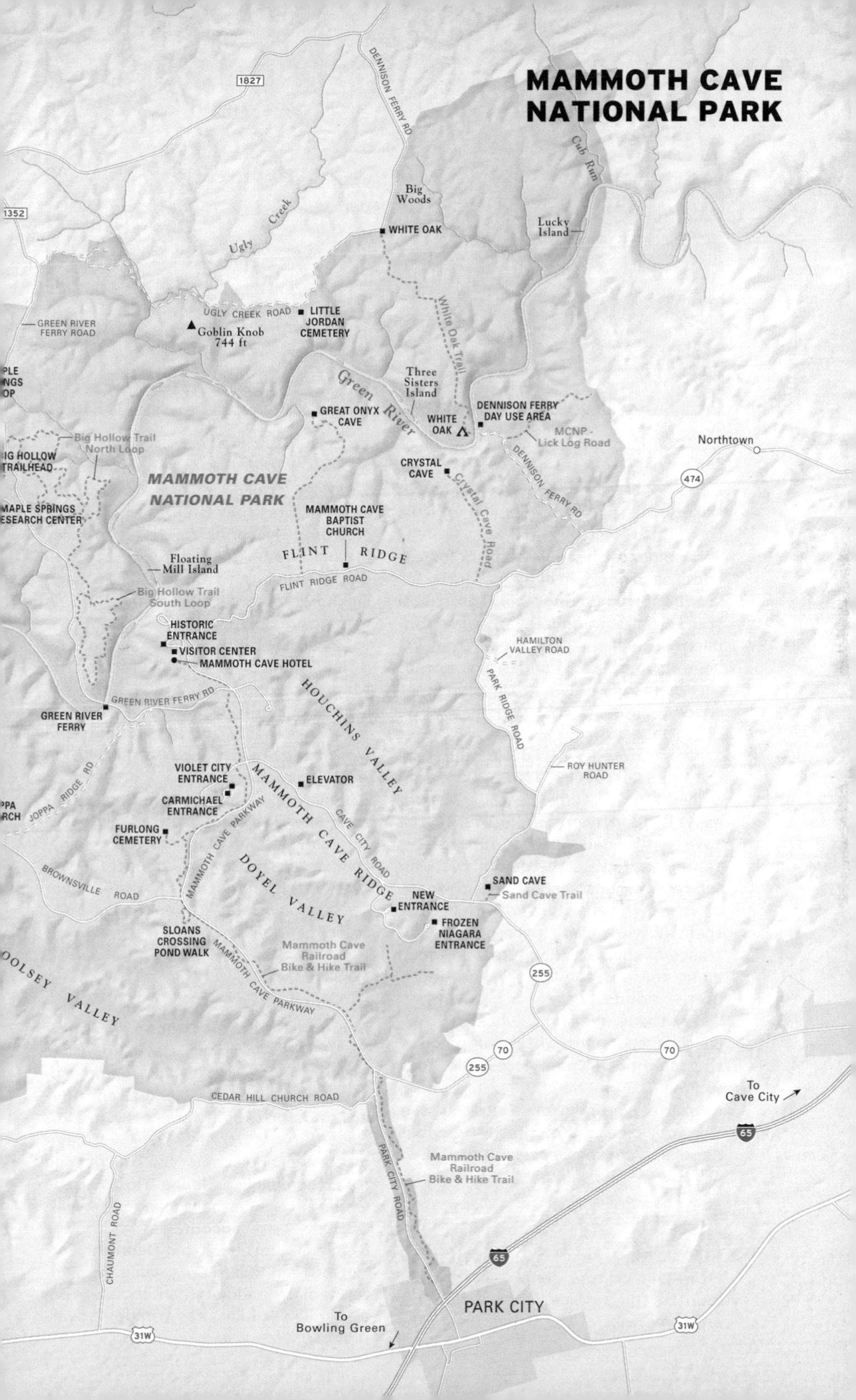

MAMMOTH CAVE NATIONAL PARK
1827
1352
DENNISON FERRY RD
Cub Run
Big Woods
Lucky Island
Ugly Creek
WHITE OAK
White Oak Trail
GREEN RIVER FERRY ROAD
UGLY CREEK ROAD
LITTLE JORDAN CEMETERY
Goblin Knob 744 ft
Three Sisters Island
Green River
GREAT ONYX CAVE
WHITE OAK
DENNISON FERRY DAY USE AREA
MCNP - Lick Log Road
Northtown
474
Big Hollow Trail North Loop
BIG HOLLOW TRAILHEAD
MAPLE SPRINGS RESEARCH CENTER
MAMMOTH CAVE NATIONAL PARK
CRYSTAL CAVE
Crystal Cave Road
DENNISON FERRY RD
MAMMOTH CAVE BAPTIST CHURCH
FLINT RIDGE
FLINT RIDGE ROAD
Floating Mill Island
Big Hollow Trail South Loop
HISTORIC ENTRANCE
VISITOR CENTER
MAMMOTH CAVE HOTEL
HAMILTON VALLEY ROAD
PARK RIDGE ROAD
HOUCHINS VALLEY
GREEN RIVER FERRY RD
GREEN RIVER FERRY
JOPPA RIDGE RD
VIOLET CITY ENTRANCE
CARMICHAEL ENTRANCE
ELEVATOR
ROY HUNTER ROAD
MAMMOTH CAVE RIDGE
CAVE CITY ROAD
MAMMOTH CAVE PARKWAY
FURLONG CEMETERY
DOYEL VALLEY
BROWNSVILLE ROAD
SAND CAVE
Sand Cave Trail
NEW ENTRANCE
FROZEN NIAGARA ENTRANCE
SLOANS CROSSING POND WALK
MAMMOTH CAVE PARKWAY
Mammoth Cave Railroad Bike & Hike Trail
255
WOOLSEY VALLEY
70
255
70
CEDAR HILL CHURCH ROAD
To Cave City
65
PARK CITY ROAD
Mammoth Cave Railroad Bike & Hike Trail
CHAUMONT ROAD
65
PARK CITY
To Bowling Green
31W
31W

CAVE TOUR

avoid bonking your head on Tall Man's Misery. An extended version of this tour is also available.

To dip into the more challenging aspects of caving, join a ranger for the **Introduction to Caving** (1 mi./1.6 km, 300 stairs, 3.5 hrs., strenuous). You'll be supplied with all the caving gear, but will need to wear sturdy shoes. The adventure demands crawling through tight spaces, climbing, and working around obstacles.

Only offered when other tours sell out, the **Discovery Tour** (10am-2pm daily, 0.75 mi./1.2 km, 125 stairs, 30 min., easy) is the only option for touring the cave self-guided. Stop at the visitors center for tickets the day of the tour (no reservations), and explore the cave at your own pace starting with the descent down a trail to the historic entrance of the cave. Rangers are staged along the passageway to share interpretive tidbits.

For those needing a wheelchair-accessible tour with their companions, the **Mammoth Cave Accessible Tour** (0.5 mi./0.8 km, no stairs, 2 hrs., easy) uses an elevator entrance into the cave. The tour passes through the Snowball Room and part of Cleaveland Avenue.

RECREATION

HIKING AND BIKING

From the visitors center, short trails loop to the surface of cave features and overlooks of the Green River. The **Sinkhole Trail** (2 mi./3.2 km rt., 1 hr., easy) starts from the paved Heritage Trail and descends to the Echo River Springs Trail. Along the way, the trail passes Mammoth Dome Sink, a huge sinkhole that created Mammoth Dome in the cave.

For spring bird-watching and fall color, hikers and bikers can head out on the **Maple Springs Trail** (2 mi./3.2 km rt., 1 hr., easy), **White Oak Trail** (5 mi./8 km rt., 2.5 hrs., easy), and **Big Hollow Trail North and South Loops** (9.1 mi./14.6 km rt., 5 hrs., moderate).

The gravel **Mammoth Cave Railroad Bike and Hike Trail** (18 mi./29 km rt., easy) follows parts of the original train route that once connected Park City with Mammoth Cave Visitor Center. At the visitors center, the trailhead starts at Engine No. 4.

CANOEING AND KAYAKING

Mammoth Cave Canoe & Kayak (1240 Old Mammoth Cave Rd., Cave City, 270/773-3366, http://mammoth-cave-adventures.com) and **Green River Canoeing** (3057 Mammoth Cave Rd., Cave City, 270/773-5712, www.mammothcavecanoe.com) can outfit you for an enjoyable paddling trip down the Green River in either a canoe or kayak. Beginners are encouraged to try the 8-mile (13-km) trip from Dennison Ferry to Green River Ferry, while more intermediate paddlers can choose from a 12-mile (19.3-km) day trip or an overnight trip.

Top 3

1 ADMIRE FROZEN NIAGARA

Frozen Niagara Falls is one of the most artistic collections of dripstones and the most famous feature in Mammoth Cave. The **Frozen Niagara Tour** (0.25 mi./0.4 km, 12 stairs, 75 min., easy, $7-14) is best for families with kids. Frozen Niagara is also included on four longer and more difficult tours: Domes and Dripstones, Grand Avenue, Introduction to Caving, and Wild Cave. Make advance **reservations** (877/444-6777, www.recreation.gov).

FROZEN NIAGARA

2 GAZE AT DOMES AND DRIPSTONES

Beginning at a sinkhole, the **Domes and Dripstones Tour** (0.75 mi./1.2 km, 500 stairs, 120 min., moderate, $9-17) shows off dramatic cave features: large-domed rooms, stalactites, stalagmites, and Frozen Niagara. It is more of a workout with several steep sections. Rangers share the science of cave formations. Make advance **reservations** (877/444-6777, www.recreation.gov).

3 WRIGGLE THROUGH CRAWLSPACES

For a real spelunking adventure, you can crawl, slither, and duckwalk the less accessible cave features. Spring through fall, the **Wild Cave Tour** (5 mi./8 km, 500 steps, 6 hrs., strenuous, $60) is not for claustrophobes or acrophobes. Hiking boots with ankle support are required, but you'll be provided with coveralls, kneepads, gloves, and lamp helmets. Participants must be 16 years or older; make advance **reservations** (877/444-6777, www.recreation.gov).

CRAWL THROUGH ONE OF MAMMOTH'S SMALLER CAVES

STALACTITES

HIKING TRAILS OFFER ABOVE-GROUND VIEWS.

WHERE TO STAY

INSIDE THE PARK

Rooms at the **Lodge at Mammoth Cave** (171 Hotel Rd., 844/760-2283, http://mammothcavelodge.com, from $71) may be small and a bit dated, but they have a central location near the visitors center. (Request a room on the ravine side to enjoy a view from your balcony.) Quaint cottages and cabins offer a more private retreat. Make reservations a year in advance. The lodge has two eateries: **Green River Grill** (7am-10am, 11am-3pm, 5pm-8pm daily summer, winter hours shorten) for dining and **Spelunkers Café** (8am-5pm daily, closed winter) for light meals, ice cream, and to-go fare.

The **Mammoth Cave Campground** (877/444-6777, www.recreation.gov, Mar.-Nov., 11 sites, $20-50), a five-minute walk from the visitors center, has flush toilets and hot showers. Half the sites are available by reservation six months in advance; remaining sites are first come, first served. **Maple Springs Group Campground** (Mar-Nov., $25-35) has seven group sites. **Houchin Ferry Campground** (first come, first served, year-round, $15) has 12 primitive sites on the banks of the Green River.

OUTSIDE THE PARK

Cave City is the gateway to Mammoth Cave National Park and provides accommodations, dining, and services.

GETTING THERE AND AROUND

The park has no shuttle system or public transportation. Driving is the only way to get around. Do not rely on GPS mobile navigation systems—bring a map instead.

AIR

Two international airports sit within 100 miles (161 km) of Mammoth Cave. To the north is **Louisville International Airport** (SDF, 600 Terminal Dr., Louisville, KY, www.flylouisville.com, 502/367-4636), a 90-minute drive via I-65. To the south is **Nashville International Airport** (BNA, 1 Terminal Dr., Nashville, TN, 615/275-1675, www.flynashville.com), two hours' drive via I-65. Both airports have car rentals.

CAR

Mammoth Cave National Park is west of I-65, between Elizabethtown and Bowling Green. From the north, take exit 53 for Cave City and turn right onto KY 70 to reach the park entrance. From the south, take exit 48 to Park City. Turn left onto KY 255 to the park entrance.

GATEWAY ARCH NATIONAL PARK

Missouri

WEBSITE:
www.nps.gov/jeff

PHONE NUMBER:
314/655-1600

VISITATION RANK:
15

WHY GO:
Learn about how U.S. westward expansion began.

KEEPSAKE STAMPS ▼▼▼

▲ GATEWAY ARCH

GATEWAY ARCH NATIONAL PARK
METROLINK STATION
M
WASHINGTON AVE
LUCAS AVE
N 2ND ST
N 1ST ST
COMMERCIAL ST
METROLINK STATION
EADS BRIDGE
NORTH ENTRANCES
S LEONOR K. SULLIVAN BLVD
LOCUST ST
44
OLIVE ST
PINE ST
MEMORIAL DR
N BROADWAY
N 4TH ST
CHESTNUT ST
Gateway Arch National Park
HELICOPTER TOURS
Kiener Plaza
Old Courthouse
Luther Ely Smith Square
WEST ENTRANCE
MARKET ST
THE GATEWAY ARCH
VISITORS CENTER AND MUSEUM
EAST ENTRANCE
WALNUT ST
Riverfront Trail
GATEWAY ARCH RIVERBOATS
Mississippi River
CLARK AVE
S BROADWAY
S 4TH ST
MEMORIAL DR
S LEONOR K. SULLIVAN BLVD
64
40
64
55
55
44
0
100 yds
0
100 m
© MOON.COM

Rather than a park of natural wonders, **GATEWAY ARCH NATIONAL PARK** is a historical landmark in an urban setting. The 630-foot (192-m) silver arch on the west bank of the Mississippi River commemorates one of the main routes for westward expansion during the 19th century. From Missouri, Lewis and Clark launched their Corps of Discovery upriver, opening the gateway for the riverboats, pioneers, and homesteaders who followed them west into the frontier.

The park is also a memorial to Thomas Jefferson, who initiated the Corps of Discovery. It also includes the historic courthouse where Dred and Harriet Scott sued for emancipation from slavery. The court upheld the racist institution, continuing along the path to the Civil War.

PLANNING YOUR TIME

Gateway Arch is open daily year-round. The grounds are accessible 5am-11pm, but various attractions have shorter hours. Summer and school holidays draw the biggest crowds (Mar., May-Aug.); visit in early morning or evening for fewer people. Spring and fall have lighter visitation, and winter is the best time to avoid crowds.

To get around waiting in lines, purchase tickets for the Arch Tram, riverboat cruises, and/or the documentary movie up to two hours in advance (877/982-1410, www.gatewayarch.com). Combo tickets will save you a few dollars.

Daytime temperatures range 80-90°F (27-32°C) in summer, usually accompanied with high humidity and mugginess. Winter dips to hover around freezing with a few inches of snow that melts off quickly.

ENTRANCES AND FEES

Entry to the park costs $3 per person. Kids 15 years and younger are free. Entry fees are waived for park passholders. Attractions and tours in the park have additional fees, which vary by activity.

The main entry to the park is through the **West Entrance** (11 N. 4th St.). Visitors coming from riverboats or Leonor K. Sullivan Boulevard use the sloped cobbled pathways on either side of the Grand Staircase below the Arch as the **East Entrances.** From Laclede's Landing, the **North Entrances** are on 1st and 2nd Streets.

Entry to the Arch itself is via a secure checkpoint, with the same rules in place as airport checkpoints. Be sure to arrive a half hour before you need to get on the tram with a prepurchased ticket.

VISITORS CENTERS

Gateway Arch Visitor Center (11 N. 4th St., 877/982-1410, www.gatewayarch.com, 8am-10pm daily summer, 9am-6pm daily winter) contains the ticket office, a movie theater, the Arch Café, park store, and gift shop.

SIGHTS

THE ARCH

Completed in 1965, the Arch is the tallest human-made monument in the

PARK GROUNDS IN SPRING

United States. Each leg is 54 feet (16.5 m) wide, with its base buried 60 feet (18 m) into the ground. The legs are the same distance apart as the arch is high (630 ft./192 m). The stainless-steel exterior hides cement and structural steel. You can admire the immense Arch from various locales in the park. Stroll the grounds (5am-11pm daily year-round) on paved tree-lined pathways to see it close up and at a distance. Trails with interpretive signs loop past ponds north and south of the Arch and run the length of the riverfront just west of Leonor K. Sullivan Boulevard.

A 35-minute **documentary** (Tucker Theater, 877/982-1410, www.gatewayarch.com, on the hour, 9am-9pm summer, 9am-5pm winter, $7 adults, $3 kids, $4 for America the Beautiful passholders), called Monument to the Dream, narrates how the Arch was built.

HIKING

The paved **Riverfront Trail** (0.7 mi./1.1 km, 20 min., easy) along the Mississippi River is shared with bicycles. It's more of a walk than a hike, but you can admire the riverboats and the city skyline.

WHERE TO STAY

INSIDE THE PARK

No lodgings are available inside the park, but two cafés are on-site. On the riverboat dock, the **Paddlewheel Café** (50 S. Leonor K. Sullivan Blvd., 877/982-1410, www.gatewayarch.com, 11am-3pm Thurs.-Sun. summer, hours and days shorten Apr.-Oct.) serves sandwiches, shrimp, and ice cream. In Gateway Arch Visitor Center, the **Arch Café** (314/300-8710, www.cafearch.com, 9am-5pm daily) serves farm-to-table and organic meals.

OUTSIDE THE PARK

Plentiful accommodations and dining options are available in **St. Louis.**

GETTING THERE

AIR

St. Louis Lambert International Airport (STL, 10701 Lambert International Blvd., 314/890-1333, www.flystl.com) is 14 miles (23 km) from Gateway Arch. Car rentals are available.

CAR

From Missouri

To get to Gateway Arch National Park, follow I-44, I-55, I-64, or I-70 into downtown St. Louis. Once downtown, use the following exits and directions to reach the park:

From I-44 East and I-55 North, use exit 292 (Lumiere Place Blvd., Washington Ave., Eads Bridge). From the left lane, make a U-turn to reach Pine Street.

From I-64 East, take exit 40 (last Missouri exit). Turn left turns onto Gratiot and then 4th Street.

From I-70 East, use exit 249B (Tucker Blvd.) and go left onto Market Street.

From Illinois

From Illinois, take I-55, I-64, or US 40 to cross the Mississippi River on the Poplar Street Bridge. After crossing, stay on I-64/US 40 West to turn off at exit 40A (Stadium/Tucker Blvd.), going straight and then right onto Walnut Street.

RAIL

The **MetroLink Lightrail** (www.metrostlouis.org) goes every 15-20 minutes from St. Louis Lambert International Airport to the Gateway Arch (28 min.). Debark at 8th and Pine or use Laclede's Landing and walk less than 10 minutes to the park entrances.

BUS

The **MetroBus** (www.metrostlouis.org) has multiple routes downtown with stops near the park. The #99 Downtown Trolley, which is actually one of the buses in the downtown core, has a stop on 4th Street and Pine near the park entrance.

TAXIS

St. Louis has taxis, ride-sharing, and car services.

BICYCLES

Part of the **Great Rivers Greenway** (https://greatriversgreenway.org), a paved bicycle trail (12.5 mi./20 km one-way), hugs the west bank of the Mississippi River and levee wall. Less than 1

Top 3

ARCH

1 RIDE TO TOP OF THE ARCH

The only way to go up into the Arch is via the **Arch Tram** (877/982-1410, www.gatewayarch.com, 8am-10pm daily summer, 9am-6pm daily winter, $12-16 adults, $8-12 kids 3-15 years, discounts with America the Beautiful passes). Tours usually take 45-60 minutes, depending on how much time you spend at the top on the observation platform looking out the small windows. Tours start with a multimedia presentation before loading onto the tram. Trams run every 10 minutes, taking four minutes to go up and three minutes to come down. Getting from the top of the tram to the observation platform requires walking up six flights of stairs, and no seating is available in the observation area. Views from the top take in St. Louis and the two states of Missouri and Illinois. Exit from the Arch via its legs.

2 SEE THE OLD COURTHOUSE

Built in 1839, the **Old Courthouse** (11 N. 4th St., 8am-4:30pm daily, free) is a tribute to classic government buildings of the era, with three tiers of balconies overlooking the rotunda inside. Rangers lead daily free tours (times vary), but you can tour the building and three exhibit galleries on your own.

Two landmark court cases decided here were central to determining the course of U.S. history. In 1847, Dred Scott and his wife sued for freedom from slavery, but the U.S. Supreme Court ultimately ruled that African Americans were not citizens and therefore could not sue, ultimately leading to the Civil War. One exhibit details Scott's struggle for freedom. In 1873, Virginia Minor and her husband sued for women's right to vote, which finally came to fruition 47 years later.

OLD COURTHOUSE

3 TOUR THE MUSEUM

The museum under the Arch features six themed galleries with exhibits you can touch. Kids enjoy hands-on activities, and computerized simulations give insight into history. Exhibits focus on the indigenous and Creole cultures, colonial St. Louis, Thomas Jefferson, explorers and pioneers, the Riverfront Era, and building the Arch.

RIVERFRONT TRAIL

mile (1.6 km) follows the Riverside Trail through Gateway Arch National Park, but you can use the route to ride to the park from North Riverside Park near Old Chain of Rocks Bridge. You can also access the route at multiple locations in between.

PARKING

Gateway Arch has no on-site parking. Near the entrances, there is **metered accessible parking** on Memorial Drive between Walnut Street and Market Street and between Chestnut Street and Pine Street. Multiple **parking garages and surface lots** (http://getaroundsl.com) are within a few blocks of the entrances. You can also drop off or pick up passengers in two locations on 4th Street between Market Street and Chestnut Street in front of the Old Courthouse. Find parking for RVs and cars on Leonor K. Sullivan Boulevard between the Poplar Street Bridge and the levee.

GETTING AROUND

The only way to get around is on foot. No shuttles operate on the grounds, which are around 0.7 miles (1.1 km) long by 0.2 miles (0.3 km) wide. Electric-powered mobility assistance devices are allowed, and wheelchairs are available to borrow from the information desk inside Gateway Arch or the Old Courthouse.

TOURS

One-hour **riverboat cruises** (877/982-1410, www.gatewayarch.com, times vary, daily Mar.-early Dec., $19-32 adults, $8-11 kids age 3-15) tour the Mississippi on replica historic paddlewheel steamboats. A National Park Service ranger or the captain narrates the tour. A variety of themed riverboat tours (prices, dates, and times vary) offer different ways to enjoy the cruise: dinner, brunch, lunch, holidays, music, theatrical, and drag shows.

For a unique way to see Gateway Arch and the riverfront, you can fly above in a **helicopter** (www.gatewayhelicoptertours.com, 11am-5pm daily Apr.-Nov., starts at $43 pp, 2-person min.) that fits 2-3 passengers. Flights are weather-dependent and super-short—about three minutes. No reservations are needed, just go below the Arch to the helipad on the riverfront to buy tickets.

HOT SPRINGS NATIONAL PARK

Arkansas

WEBSITE:
www.nps.gov/hosp

PHONE NUMBER:
501/620-6715

VISITATION RANK:
19

WHY GO:
Soak in historic hot springs.

▲ HOT SPRINGS FOUNTAIN, HOT SPRINGS NATIONAL PARK

KEEPSAKE STAMPS ▼▼▼

More than 4,400 years ago, rainwater soaked deep into the earth here, more than 1 mile (1.6 km) down. Coming into contact with a hot fault, the water heated, boiling to the surface again. In today's **HOT SPRINGS NATIONAL PARK,** this hot water gushes at 700,000 gallons (2.6 million) per day, a unique phenomenon in the eastern United States.

In the heyday of the Edwardian era, this once luxurious spot attracted the rich and famous to Arkansas to enjoy the health benefits of the minerals in these waters—and the most sumptuous cluster of natural hot spring bathhouses in North America. The historic architecture, with buildings of marble surrounded by fountains, speaks to the affluence of those times. Today, the buildings house museums, the visitors center, and even a brewery, but are still lauded for their architectural distinction.

PLANNING YOUR TIME

This urban park is just an hour's drive from Little Rock. The small park has two sections. **Bathhouse Row** covers a few downtown blocks at the base of Hot Springs Mountain and can be toured on foot. **Hot Springs Mountain** contains scenic drives, hiking trails, and a campground.

The bathhouses are open year-round with peak visits March-November. Soaking in hot springs loses its appeal during the hot, humid summer with triple-digit heat outdoors. However, that is when visitor services are in full swing and outdoor tours are available.

September-May offers a more tempting and less crowded time to plunge into the hot water. In winter, when the thermometer plummets below freezing, the baths offer a cozy respite.

ENTRANCE AND FEES

The national park is in the town of **Hot Springs** and has no official entrance. There is no entrance fee.

VISITORS CENTER

Located on Bathhouse Row, **Fordyce Bathhouse Visitor Center** (369 Central Ave., 501/620-6715, 9am-5pm daily year-round, free) claims the most elegant bathhouse from the early 1900s. It even had a bowling alley in the basement and a third-floor music room with a grand piano and a gym.

Rangers lead **guided tours** (daily, free) of the restored building, pointing out stained-glass ceilings and a ceramic fountain. The tour takes in 23 rooms replicated with furniture of the period, including treatment rooms that featured massage and electrotherapy. The history museum has exhibits, films (one shows what the bathing routine entailed), and pictures of its operation from 1915 to 1962.

SIGHTS

BATHHOUSE ROW ENVIRONS

The minerals in the hot springs were believed to have health benefits, thus many **drinking fountains** line Bathhouse Row and the Grand Promenade. Many visitors bring water bottles to fill and take home. **Whittington Spring** (Whittington Ave.) and **Happy Hollow Spring** (Fountain Ave.) are cold-water springs treated with ozone filtration.

North of Bathhouse Row, a cluster of paths connects a gazebo and lawns. **Hot Water Cascade** tumbles into a collection pool, where you can dip your hand in to check the temperature. **Tufa Rock,** a large gray rock, was created from the buildup of minerals brought to the surface in thermal waters, which

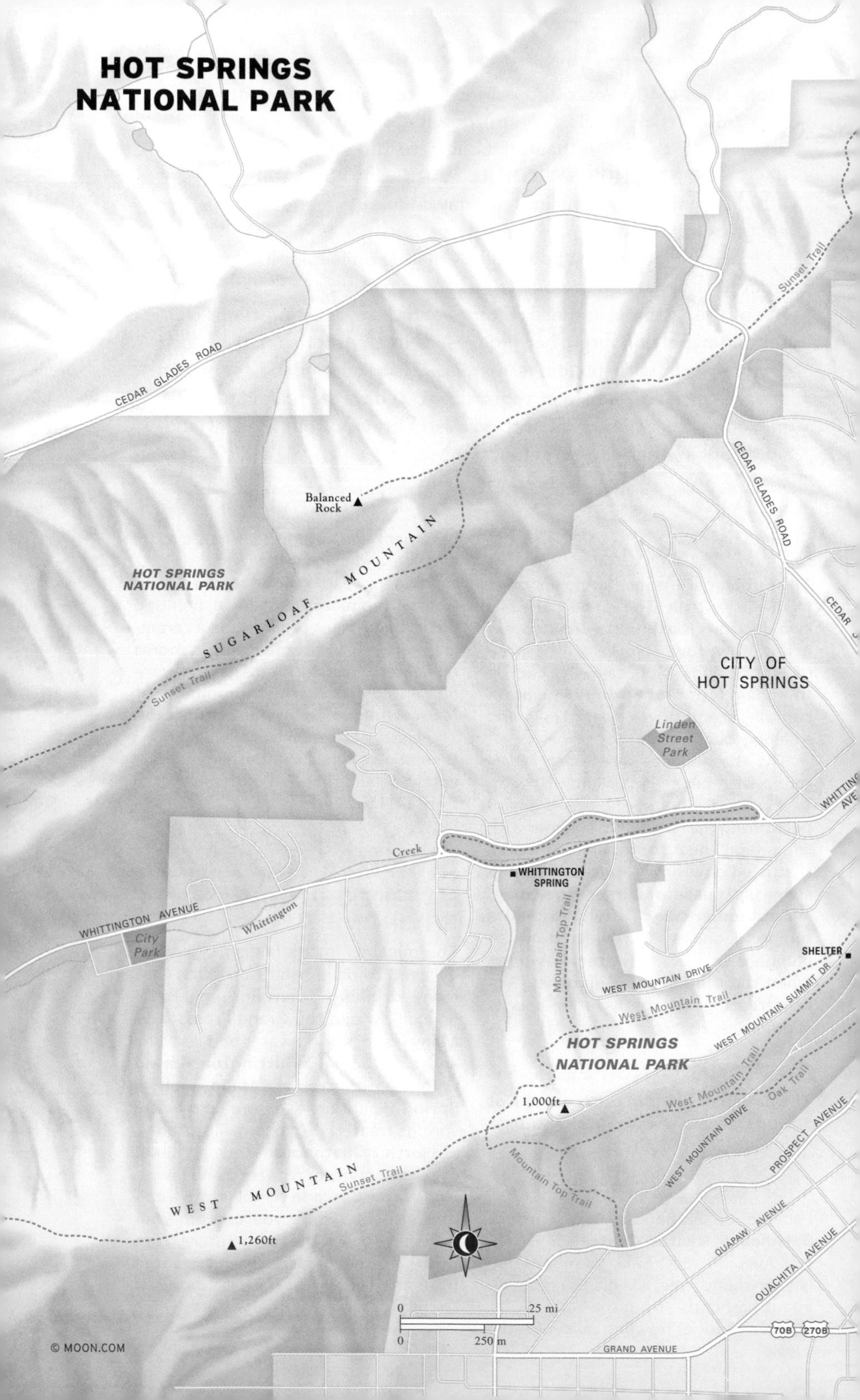

HOT SPRINGS NATIONAL PARK
CEDAR GLADES ROAD
Sunset Trail
Balanced Rock
HOT SPRINGS NATIONAL PARK
SUGARLOAF MOUNTAIN
CEDAR GLADES ROAD
CITY OF HOT SPRINGS
Linden Street Park
Creek
WHITTINGTON SPRING
WHITTINGTON AVENUE
Whittington
City Park
Mountain Top Trail
SHELTER
WEST MOUNTAIN DRIVE
West Mountain Trail
WEST MOUNTAIN SUMMIT DR
HOT SPRINGS NATIONAL PARK
1,000ft
Oak Trail
PROSPECT AVENUE
WEST MOUNTAIN DRIVE
WEST MOUNTAIN
Mountain Top Trail
QUAPAW AVENUE
1,260ft
OUACHITA AVENUE
0
.25 mi
0
250 m
70B
270B
GRAND AVENUE
© MOON.COM

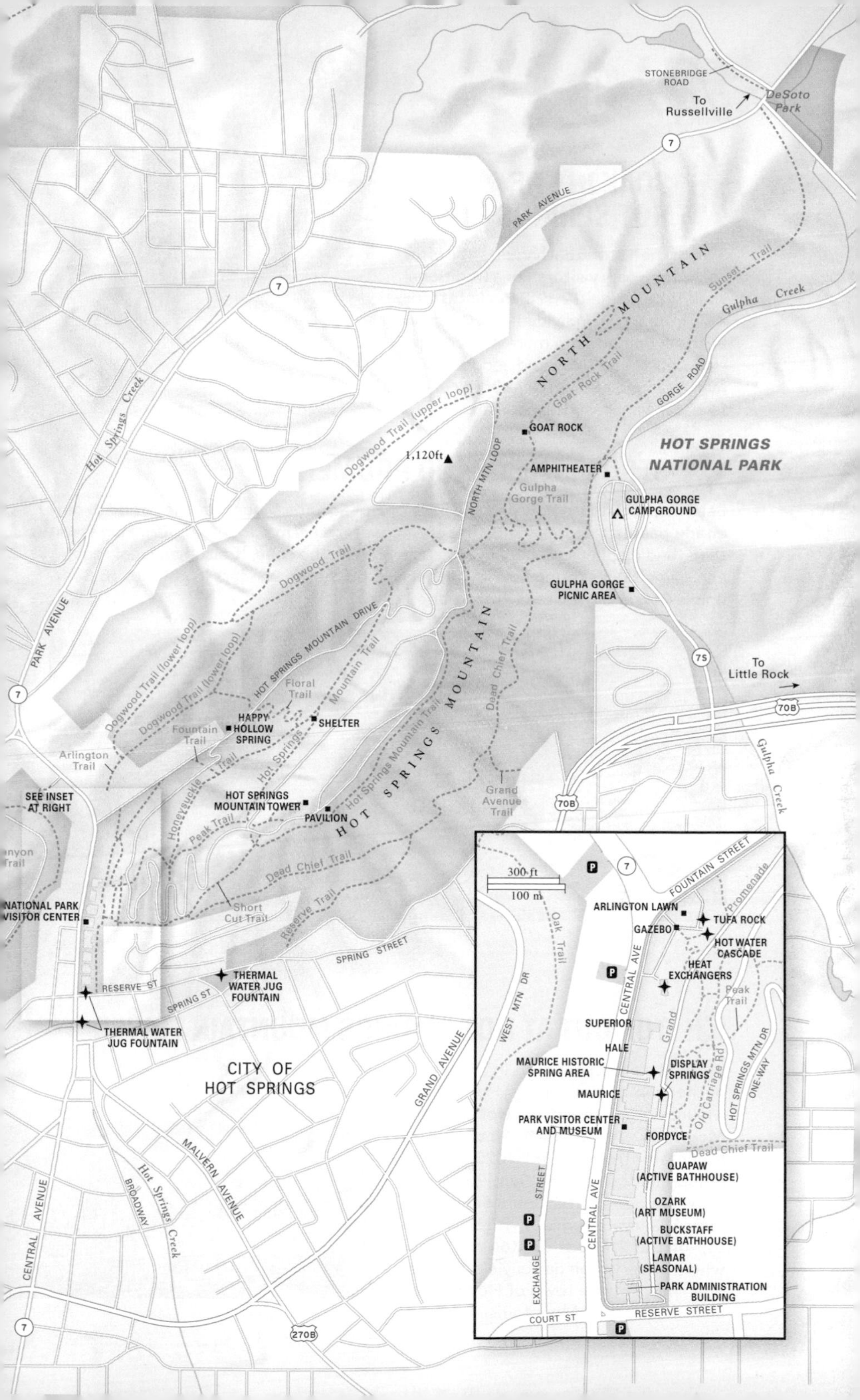

STONEBRIDGE ROAD
To Russellville
DeSoto Park
7
PARK AVENUE
NORTH MOUNTAIN
Sunset Trail
Gulpha Creek
Goat Rock Trail
GORGE ROAD
Hot Springs Creek
Dogwood Trail (upper loop)
GOAT ROCK
HOT SPRINGS NATIONAL PARK
1,120ft
NORTH MTN LOOP
AMPHITHEATER
Gulpha Gorge Trail
GULPHA GORGE CAMPGROUND
Dogwood Trail
GULPHA GORGE PICNIC AREA
HOT SPRINGS MOUNTAIN DRIVE
Dead Chief Trail
7S
To Little Rock
70B
Dogwood Trail (lower loop)
Floral Trail
Mountain Trail
HAPPY HOLLOW SPRING
SHELTER
Fountain Trail
Hot Springs Mountain Trail
HOT SPRINGS MOUNTAIN
Arlington Trail
Honeysuckle Trail
Hot Springs
Gulpha Creek
SEE INSET AT RIGHT
HOT SPRINGS MOUNTAIN TOWER
PAVILION
Grand Avenue Trail
Peak Trail
Dead Chief Trail
NATIONAL PARK VISITOR CENTER
Short Cut Trail
Reserve Trail
SPRING STREET
THERMAL WATER JUG FOUNTAIN
RESERVE ST
SPRING ST
THERMAL WATER JUG FOUNTAIN
CITY OF HOT SPRINGS
GRAND AVENUE
MALVERN AVENUE
BROADWAY
Hot Springs Creek
CENTRAL AVENUE
270B
300 ft
100 m
P
FOUNTAIN STREET
Promenade
Oak Trail
ARLINGTON LAWN
TUFA ROCK
GAZEBO
HOT WATER CASCADE
WEST MTN DR
CENTRAL AVE
HEAT EXCHANGERS
Peak Trail
SUPERIOR
Grand
HALE
HOT SPRINGS MTN DR
ONE-WAY
MAURICE HISTORIC SPRING AREA
DISPLAY SPRINGS
MAURICE
Old Carriage Rd
PARK VISITOR CENTER AND MUSEUM
FORDYCE
Dead Chief Trail
EXCHANGE STREET
QUAPAW (ACTIVE BATHHOUSE)
OZARK (ART MUSEUM)
BUCKSTAFF (ACTIVE BATHHOUSE)
LAMAR (SEASONAL)
PARK ADMINISTRATION BUILDING
COURT ST
RESERVE STREET

Top 3

1 SOAK IN THE HOT SPRINGS

Two of the historic bathhouses still offer soaks for weary visitors. For a traditional soak, walk inside the 1912 **Buckstaff** for a dip in your own individual tub. **Quapaw Baths & Spa** offers a more modern spa experience with covered indoor thermal pools and a steam cave. Both charge fees that vary based on services.

QUAPAW BATHS & SPA

2 STROLL THE GRAND PROMENADE

Between Bathhouse Row and the base of Hot Springs Mountain, the **Grand Promenade** passes features fed by hot spring water: thermal fountains, drinking fountains, and display springs. This was the place to be seen. It also has picnic tables and game tables (bring your own checkers or chess). Rangers lead tours on Bathhouse Row and the Grand Promenade.

GRAND PROMENADE

3 TOP OUT AT HOT SPRINGS MOUNTAIN TOWER

Rising like a forested oasis in the middle of the town of Hot Springs, Hot Springs Mountain is topped by **Hot Springs Mountain Tower** (401 Hot Springs Mountain Dr., 501/881-4020, http://hotspringstower.com, 9am-9pm daily in summer, shorter hours Sept.-June, fee). An elevator whisks visitors to the top of the 216-foot-tall (66-m) tower where observation decks yield 360-degree views of the town of Hot Springs and the Ouachita Mountains.

BEAUTIFUL VIEW FROM HOT SPRINGS MOUNTAIN TOWER

ONE DAY IN HOT SPRINGS

Thanks to its small size, you can easily experience the park in one day. Start at the **Fordyce Bathhouse Visitor Center** to get oriented and take a tour. Then walk the National Historic District of **Bathhouse Row** and the **Grand Promenade** and go for a soak in one of the bathhouses. Afterward, drive to the top of Hot Springs Mountain and climb the **Hot Springs Mountain Tower** to take in the views. Return to Bathhouse Row and relax at the **Superior Bathhouse Brewery**.

then evaporated to leave the hardened mass behind. **Tufa terraces** also line the hillside, where you can depart for a side trail (0.2 mi./0.3 km one-way) that takes off at Stevens Balustrade and returns to Grand Promenade at Hot Water Cascade.

BATHHOUSE ROW

A National Historic Landmark, **Bathhouse Row** has eight bathhouses, leftover hallmarks of 20th-century opulence. The actual row is about 0.25 mile (0.4 km) long, an easy walk along Central Avenue. All are open to the public. From north to south, the bathhouses include:

Superior is the smallest bathhouse, built in 1916, with a sunporch and brick pilasters. Its services—massage, hydrotherapy, and mercury—were the least expensive. Today it houses a brewery and pub.

Hale, the oldest bathhouse on the row, was built in 1892. Two subsequent remodels changed its architecture to Mission Revival style, with its original red brick covered in white stucco. Today, it is a hotel with two restaurants.

Maurice opened in 1912 with a roof garden and basement pool. It is not open to the public.

Fordyce, the largest and most elegant bathhouse, opened in 1915 with the most services—from chiropody to ice thermal water and electrotherapy. It now serves as the visitors center.

Quapaw, which opened in 1922, is the longest bathhouse on the row. Topped with a mosaic tile dome, the Spanish Colonial Revival building now

BATHHOUSE ROW

OZARK BATHHOUSE

houses modern spa services where visitors can bathe in water from the hot springs.

Ozark, built in Spanish Colonial Revival architecture, opened shortly after Quapaw with less extravagant services for the middle class.

Buckstaff is the best-preserved traditional bathhouse. Built in 1912 with a marble interior, it is fronted by Doric columns and classical architecture. Today, visitors soak in individual tubs and get massages.

Lamar, which opened in 1923, reflects Spanish-style architecture with stucco trimmed with brick and stone. It contains **Bathhouse Row Emporium** (501/620-6740, 9am-5pm daily Apr.-Sept., 10am-5pm Mon.-Fri. and 9am-5pm Sat.-Sun. Oct.-Mar.), which sells books, bath souvenirs, bottles to fill with water from the hot springs, and hot beverages made with spring water

SCENIC DRIVES

NORTH MOUNTAIN DRIVE

North of Bathhouse Row on Central Avenue, follow Fountain Street northeast for **North Mountain Drive.** The short yet scenic drive travels 3 miles (4.8 km) to Hot Springs Mountain. In 0.25 mile (0.4 km), turn right to begin the one-way climb along seven hairpin switchbacks to reach the summit loop. A right turn immediately reveals a picnic area, restrooms, an overlook, and a pavilion. Turn left onto a side spur to the parking lot for **Hot Springs Mountain Tower,** the main attraction. To return to Fountain Drive, leave the summit loop at its northeast end and descend 1 mile (1.6 km, one-way) for fewer switchbacks.

WEST MOUNTAIN DRIVE

West Mountain Drive offers a scenic tour with access to nearby trails. From Bathhouse Row, drive north for 0.25 mile (0.4 km) and turn left onto Whittington Avenue. A left turn follows West Mountain Drive along a one-way loop around the east flank of the mountain and past three overlooks to its tiny summit. Exit the loop by heading south on West Mountain Drive, which ends at Prospect Avenue, south of Bathhouse Row.

RECREATION

HIKING

Sunset Trail (10 mi./16.1 km one-way, 4-5 hrs.) leads from Gulpha Gorge Campground to the summit of West Mountain Summit Overlook. The trail crosses several roads that break it into shorter hiking segments and connect it with other hiking trails. The most popular section is the 2.9 miles (4.5 km) from

Black Snake Road to West Mountain Summit Overlook, which has the best sunset-viewing location.

On West Mountain, the **West Mountain Trail** (2.3 mi./3.7 km rt., 1.5 hrs.) features stone steps and a stone footbridge with ironwork rather than a dramatic destination. Catch it from the Mountain Top Trailhead above Prospect Avenue to return on the Mountain Top Trail.

From the north overlook on Hot Springs Mountain, the **Goat Rock Trail** (2.2 mi./3.5 km rt., 1.5 hrs.) drops down switchbacks to small meadows that lead to a stone stairway. The trail climbs 40 feet (12 m) to the novaculite Goat Rock Overlook with views of Indian Mountain.

HOT SPRINGS

Quapaw Baths & Spa

For a modern-day spa experience, **Quapaw Baths & Spa** (413 Central Ave., 501/609-9822, http://quapawbaths.com, 10am-6pm Wed.-Mon., fees vary) offers four large indoor hot pools covered by a stained-glass ceiling. Private baths (individuals or couples) include hydrotherapy plus a variety of herbal additions to enhance your relaxation. After soaking, unwind further in a small steam cave. The spa has a full menu of facials, massages, and body treatments. Proper swim attire is required, and visitors are provided with a robe and slippers. Reservations are requested; guests age 14-18 must be with an adult.

Buckstaff

For a traditional Hot Springs soak, **Buckstaff** (509 Central Ave., 501/623-2308, www.buckstaffbaths.com, 8am-11:45am and 1:30pm-3pm Mon.-Sat., 8am-11:45am Sun. Mar.-Nov.; 8am-11:45am and 1:30pm-3pm Mon.-Fri. and 8am-11:45am Sat. Dec.-Feb., fees vary) has individual tubs in separate men's and women's facilities. Add on a Swedish massage, loofah mitt, or paraffin hand treatment. Reservations are not accepted for the baths and massages. Manicures, pedicures, and facials require reservations. Kids must be at least 10 years old.

WHERE TO STAY

INSIDE THE PARK

In the historic Hale Bathhouse, **Hotel Hale** (341 Central Ave., 501/760-9010, www.hotelhale.com, from $150) opened a nine-room boutique inn in 2019. Rooms are modern with thermal mineral soaking baths. Two restaurants offer meals: fine dining is in **Eden** (5pm-10pm Fri.-Sat., 10am-2pm Sun.) and lighter meals in **Zest** (breakfast: 7am-11am Fri.-Sat.; lunch: 11am-3pm Tues.-Sat.; dinner: 5pm-10pm Wed.-Thurs.).

In the Superior Bathhouse, **Superior Bathhouse Brewery** (329 Central Ave., 501/624-2337, www.

HOT SPRINGS NATIONAL PARK

THE TRADITIONAL BATHING ROUTINE

At Hot Springs, the traditional bathing routine followed the protocols of European spas.

1. In the bath hall, soak in a private tub for 20 minutes in 100°F (38°C) water. Optionally, scrub with a loofah.
2. Climb into a steam cabinet, with head inside for two minutes or head outside for five minutes.
3. In a sitting tub, soak in 108°F (42°C) water for 10 minutes.
4. Apply heat packs for 4-20 minutes on any achy spots.
5. Cool down with a two-minute shower of cold water.
6. Finish with a full-body Swedish massage.
7. Leave refreshed.

superiorbathhouse.com, 11am-9pm Sun.-Thurs., 11am-11pm Fri.-Sat.) turns hot spring water into thirst-quenching adult beverages and serves pub-style food.

Gulpha Gorge Campground (305 Gorge Rd., first come, first served, 40 sites, $30, credit and debit cards only) can accommodate tents and RVs. All campsites have picnic tables, pedestal grills, full hookups, and fire rings. Facilities include restrooms with flush toilets, potable water, and a dump station.

OUTSIDE THE PARK

The town of **Hot Springs** has chain and independent motels, B&Bs, and inns that surround the national park. The vicinity also has several campgrounds.

GETTING THERE

AIR

Six airlines service Little Rock National Airport, known as the **Bill and Hillary Clinton National Airport** (LIT, 1 Airport Dr., 501/372-3439, www.clintonairport.com). It's just an hour drive west to the park via I-30 and US 7. Car rentals are at the airport.

TRAIN

Amtrak (LRK, 1400 W. Markham St., 800/872-7245, www.amtrak.com) services Little Rock.

BUSES

Intercity Transportation (501/960-5162, http://intercitytransportation.com) runs **buses** from the Little Rock airport to Hot Springs National Park. City buses service the town and the national park of Hot Springs. Routes begin and end at the Transportation Plaza downtown.

CAR

From Little Rock, go west on I-30 to exit 111. Take US 70 west to reach the town of Hot Springs. In town, US 70 becomes East Grand Avenue. Turn right onto Spring Street, which becomes Reserve Street in about 0.5 mile (0.8 km). At Central Avenue, turn right to reach the visitors center. The total distance is 56 miles (90 km), and it takes one hour to drive.

GETTING AROUND

Parking is limited on Central Avenue along Bathhouse Row. You'll find easier parking for free in the city lot on Exchange Street. To get there, drive south on Central Avenue to Court Street (also called Reserve St.) and turn right. Continue one block west and turn right onto Exchange Street (one-way). Off-street parking is available on the right and in a parking garage on the left.

KEEPSAKE STAMPS ▼▼▼

WEBSITE:
www.nps.gov/cong

PHONE NUMBER:
803/776-4396

VISITATION RANK:
51

WHY GO:
See the largest intact old-growth hardwood forest.

▲ CONGAREE NATIONAL PARK

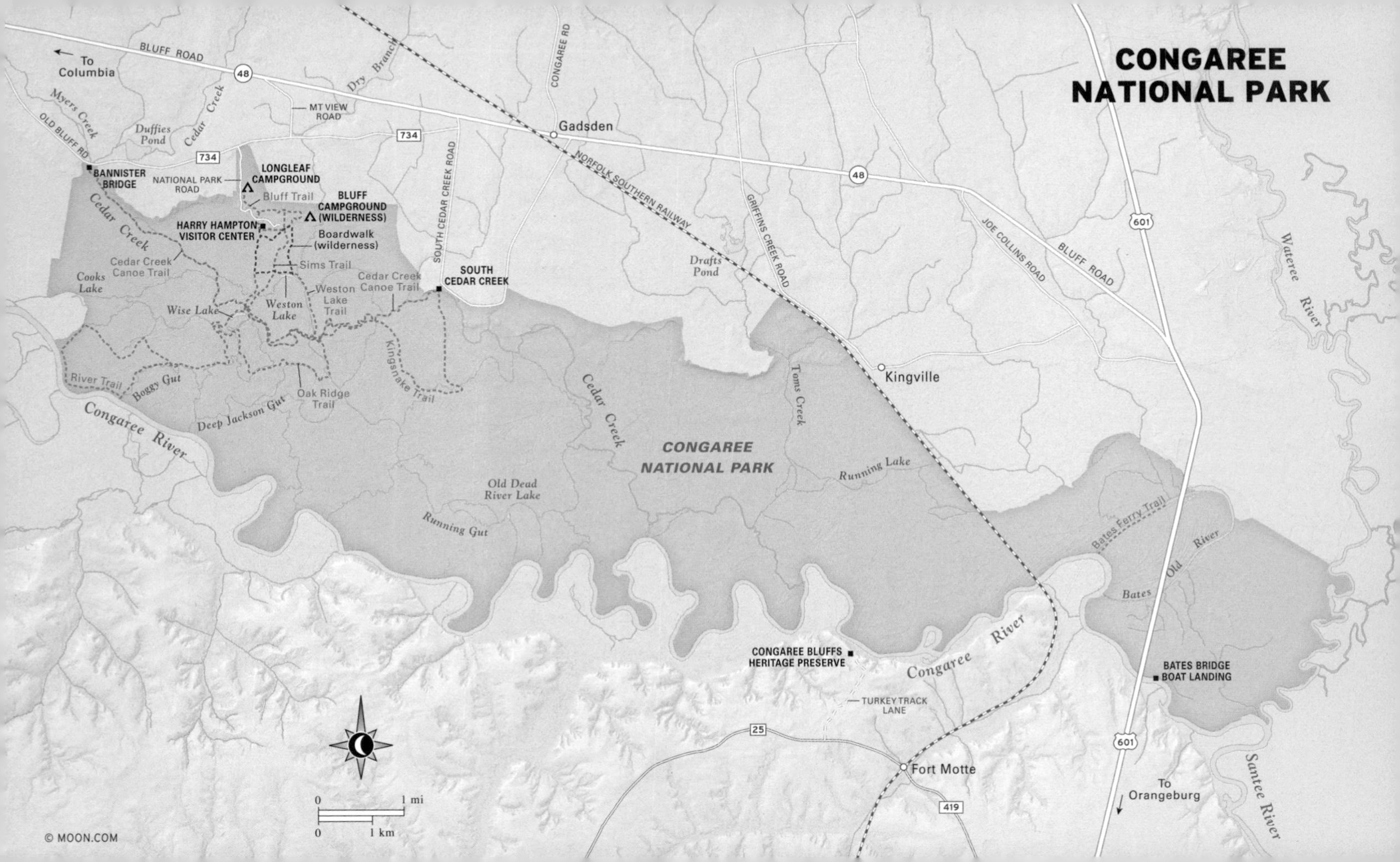

CONGAREE NATIONAL PARK
To Columbia
BLUFF ROAD
48
Myers Creek
OLD BLUFF RD
Duffies Pond
Cedar Creek
734
MT VIEW ROAD
Dry Branch
CONGAREE RD
Gadsden
NORFOLK SOUTHERN RAILWAY
BANNISTER BRIDGE
NATIONAL PARK ROAD
LONGLEAF CAMPGROUND
Bluff Trail
BLUFF CAMPGROUND (WILDERNESS)
HARRY HAMPTON VISITOR CENTER
Boardwalk (wilderness)
Sims Trail
Cedar Creek Canoe Trail
Cooks Lake
Weston Lake
Weston Lake Trail
SOUTH CEDAR CREEK ROAD
SOUTH CEDAR CREEK
Wise Lake
River Trail
Boggy Gut
Oak Ridge Trail
Kingsnake Trail
Deep Jackson Gut
Congaree River
Drafts Pond
GRIFFINS CREEK ROAD
JOE COLLINS ROAD
601
Wateree River
Kingville
Toms Creek
CONGAREE NATIONAL PARK
Running Lake
Old Dead River Lake
Running Gut
Bates Ferry Trail
Bates Old River
CONGAREE BLUFFS HERITAGE PRESERVE
BATES BRIDGE BOAT LANDING
TURKEY TRACK LANE
25
Fort Motte
419
To Orangeburg
Santee River
0
1 mi
1 km
© MOON.COM

There's nothing like it on the planet. **CONGAREE NATIONAL PARK** contains the most ancient stands of old-growth cypress left in the world. The forest populates a floodplain of the Congaree and Wateree Rivers, which swell with water several times each year to overflow their banks. In doing so, they deposit a nutrient-rich silt that helps sustain the immensely tall trees—loblolly pine, tulip trees, sweet gum, bald cypress, white pine, sycamore, and laurel oak. The park contains the tallest of 15 species of trees, plus six national champion trees for their overall size.

Swamps are one of the hallmarks of the bottomlands that support the forest. The wetlands nurse birds galore, as well as otters, turtles, alligators, snakes, frogs, and catfish. While the rivers served as travel routes for the Congaree people, it's the swamps that saved this habitat from several centuries of plunder for timber and ranching. The result is a unique national park that is also a National Natural Landmark and an International Biosphere Reserve.

PLANNING YOUR TIME

Congaree sits smack in the middle of South Carolina, about a 30-minute drive south of Columbia. Despite its relatively urban locale, this park is wilderness—swamps mean no roads. To see the old-growth forest requires hiking or paddling. Flooding may occur without warning, especially in Cedar Creek and the Congaree River. Check weather and conditions before entering the park.

While visitors come year-round, **spring** (Mar.-June) and October see the most people. Spring can be wet, and summers are hot and humid, fraught with frequent thunderstorms, and a general bug-fest with swarms of 21 species of mosquitoes.

Fall (Sept.-Nov.) is a favorite time to visit—the air is crisp, and the foliage stunning. Autumn colors peak late October-early November. Winter (Nov.-Feb.) brings unpredictable floods that can submerge trails.

ENTRANCE AND FEES

The main entrance to the park is on Old Bluff Road, 1 mile (1.6 km) before the visitors center. There is no entrance fee.

VISITORS CENTER

The **Harry Hampton Visitor Center** (Old Bluff Rd., 9am-5pm daily) is the place to get oriented in the park, with exhibits, a film, information, backcountry permits, and a gift shop. Ranger-led programs depart from the visitors center.

RECREATION

HIKING

Trails in Congaree are marked with brown blazes and numbers. Due to frequent flooding, be prepared for trails to be muddy with standing water and have downed trees. Most trails are a series of stacked loops.

Departing the Boardwalk Loop at Weston Lake, the **Weston Lake Loop** (#3, 4.4 mi./7.1 km rt., 2-3 hrs., easy) passes cypress knees and waterbirds along Cedar Creek. Crossing Cedar Creek, the **Oakridge Trail** (#4, 7 mi./11.3 km rt., 3-4 hrs., easy) loops through large oaks where you might see wild turkeys. From the west end of the Oakridge Trail, the **River Trail** (#5, 10.4 mi./16.7 km rt., 5 hrs., moderate) goes to loop along the Congaree River (check flood status). Departing from the east

Top 3

1 TOUR THE BOARDWALK

BOARDWALK LOOP

Adjacent to the visitors center, elevated and low boardwalks loop through old-growth forest. The **Boardwalk Loop** (2.4 mi./3.9 km, 1.5 hrs., easy) is a flat trail great for wheelchairs, strollers, and small kids. A self-guided brochure explains the fascinating aspects of this unique environment. Along the trail, cypresses tower more than 130 feet (40 m) into the air. At ground level, hundreds of cypress "knees" (parts of their root system) jut aboveground, and you'll see unbelievably massive loblolly pines.

Because the canopy shuts off so much light, there is almost no understory, appearing like a scene from *Lord of the Rings*. The boardwalk goes to Weston Lake, once an oxbow of the Congaree River, but now isolated as the river has changed course. You'll see—and more often, hear—a wide range of wildlife, including owls, waterfowl, and several species of woodpecker, including the rare red-cockaded woodpecker.

2 PADDLE CEDAR CREEK CANOE TRAIL

Paddlers can float the **Cedar Creek Canoe Trail** (15 mi./24.2 km) from Bannister's Bridge to the Congaree River. You must bring your own boat or rent gear in Columbia. Be aware of fluctuating water levels. In spring and fall, rangers guide **canoe tours** (4 hrs., limited schedule, free) with canoes, PFDs, and paddles provided. **Reservations** (877/444-6777, www.recreation.gov) are required and open on the first day of the previous month.

3 WATCH SYNCHRONOUS FIREFLY LIGHT SHOW

In May, synchronous fireflies light up the forest in tandem during mating. Exact dates are always a last-minute calculation based on weather and other conditions, but the annual Firefly Festival usually runs for two weeks during mid-May. The park designates one trail as the Firefly Trail, and the boardwalk is open only for visitors with mobility needs. The visitors center stays open until 10pm. With limited parking, a shuttle (7:30pm-10:30pm, $2 each way) runs from Columbia to the park on select nights.

BALD CYPRESS KNEES

end of the Oakridge Trail, the out-and-back **Kingsnake Trail** (#6, 11.7 mi./18.8 km rt., 6 hrs., moderate) attracts birders to habitat along Cedar Creek.

CANOEING AND KAYAKING

Recognized as the first Blue Trail for paddling in the country, the Congaree River Blue Trail (50 mi./81 km) flows from Columbia to Congaree National Park. This multiday paddler route spends the last 20 river miles (32 km) winding through the old-growth forest of the park. Before launching, call for a permit (803/776-4396, free) for camping on sandbars and check river gauges.

WHERE TO STAY

INSIDE THE PARK

There are no lodges or restaurants inside the park. The only accommodations are two walk-in, tent-only campgrounds where your vehicle stays in the parking lot. **Longleaf Campground** (year-round, $10-20) has 14 walk-in campsites and a restroom. **Bluff Campground** (year-round, $5) has six campsites that require a 1-mile (1.6-km) hike from the parking lot; there is no restroom.

Reservations (877/444-6777, www.recreation.gov) are required up to six months in advance. Both campgrounds have picnic tables and fire rings, but no water (bring your own).

OUTSIDE THE PARK

Twenty miles (32 km) northwest, **Columbia** has the closest lodgings and the most restaurants. A few dining options are nearby in **Gadsden,** but there are no lodgings.

GETTING THERE AND AROUND

AIR

Charlotte Douglas International Airport (CLT, 5501 Josh Birmingham Pkwy., Charlotte, NC, 704/359-4013, www.cltairport.com) is located in North Carolina, just two hours north via I-77. **Charleston International Airport** (CHS, 5500 International Blvd., Charleston, SC, 843/767-7000, www.iflychs.com) is in South Carolina, two hours southeast via I-26. Both airports have rental cars.

CAR

From Charlotte, drive south on I-77 for 95 miles (153 km) to Columbia. Take exit 5 to SC 48 East (Bluff Rd.) and continue 8 miles (13 km). Veer right onto Old Bluff Road and go 4.5 miles (7.2 km) to the park entrance.

From Charleston, drive northwest on I-26 to exit 145B. Continue north on US 601 to SC 48 (Bluff Rd.), where the road heads west. Turn left onto South Cedar Creek Road, then turn right onto Old Bluff Road to the park entrance.

The nearest town of Columbia has no public transportation to the park, but does have rental cars and taxis.

WEBSITE:
www.nps.gov/ever

PHONE NUMBER:
305/242-7700

VISITATION RANK:
24

WHY GO:
See the largest subtropical wetland in the United States.

▲ EVERGLADES NATIONAL PARK

KEEPSAKE STAMPS ▼▼▼

Shingle Creek, a small and inconspicuous stream behind an elementary school in Orlando, is the humble origin of one of the world's most-treasured wetland ecosystems. Those headwaters merge into the Kissimmee River, which flows into Lake Okeechobee to discharge into **EVERGLADES NATIONAL PARK**—a vast expanse of marshes, swamps, islands, forests, and waterways encompassing mainland Florida's southernmost points. Despite the best efforts of voracious real estate developers, most of the Everglades remain wild—although decades of attempts at "taming" the land, along with nearby population growth, have dramatically (and in some cases, permanently) altered the ecosystems for the worse. Rising sea levels associated with climate change are endangering this unique landscape.

Traditional lands of the Miccosukee and Seminole tribes, the swamps, forests, and waterways of the Everglades teem with diversity, which is one of the reasons it's been named an International Biosphere Reserve and World Heritage Site.

PLANNING YOUR TIME

The Everglades are a relatively undisturbed swamp that sprawls across three counties at the southern tip of Florida, with three entrances in three different cities. You'll need a car for the long drives between, as no roads connect the entrances, and facilities are few and far between.

Miami accesses the northeast part of the Everglades for Shark Valley and is often the only part that many visitors see. **Homestead** is the gateway to the southern Everglades, with a scenic drive and abundant outdoor activities: hiking, canoeing, kayaking, camping, and boating. On the west coast, **Everglades City** is the launch point for the remote Ten Thousand Islands.

You can see one section of the park in one day. But to immerse into the Everglades demands 5-7 days. Driving between the south entrance and Shark Valley takes about 1.25 hours (49 mi./79 km), and another hour further (58 mi./93 km) brings you to the Gulf Coast Visitor Center.

The best time to visit is **December-March** (the dry season) with visitors peaking November-April. Temperatures linger in the mid-70s (around 24°C), the bugs are less overwhelming, and the skies and trees are filled with scores of migratory bird species.

In summer (the wet season), the heat amps up into the 90s (32°C and above) with a sweltering humidity of 90 percent. Hurricane season is mid-May to November. July is peak season for voracious mosquitoes and biting flies; bring repellent, long-sleeve shirts, and long pants.

ENTRANCES AND FEES

The park's main entrance is the southern gateway near Ernest F. Coe Visitor Center on the Main Park Road (SR 9336). Shark Valley Visitor Center (Tamiami Trail, US 41), west of **Miami,** serves as the park's north entrance. A remote entrance at **Everglades City** goes to the Gulf Coast Visitor Center.

The entrance fee is $35 per vehicle ($30 motorcycle, $20 individual) and good for seven days. You can **buy your pass online** (www.yourpassnow.com), which works best for those who plan to boat into the park.

VISITORS CENTERS

Shark Valley Visitor Center

The **Shark Valley Visitor Center** (36000 SW 8th St., 305/221-8776, 8:30am-5pm daily Dec.-Apr., 9am-5pm

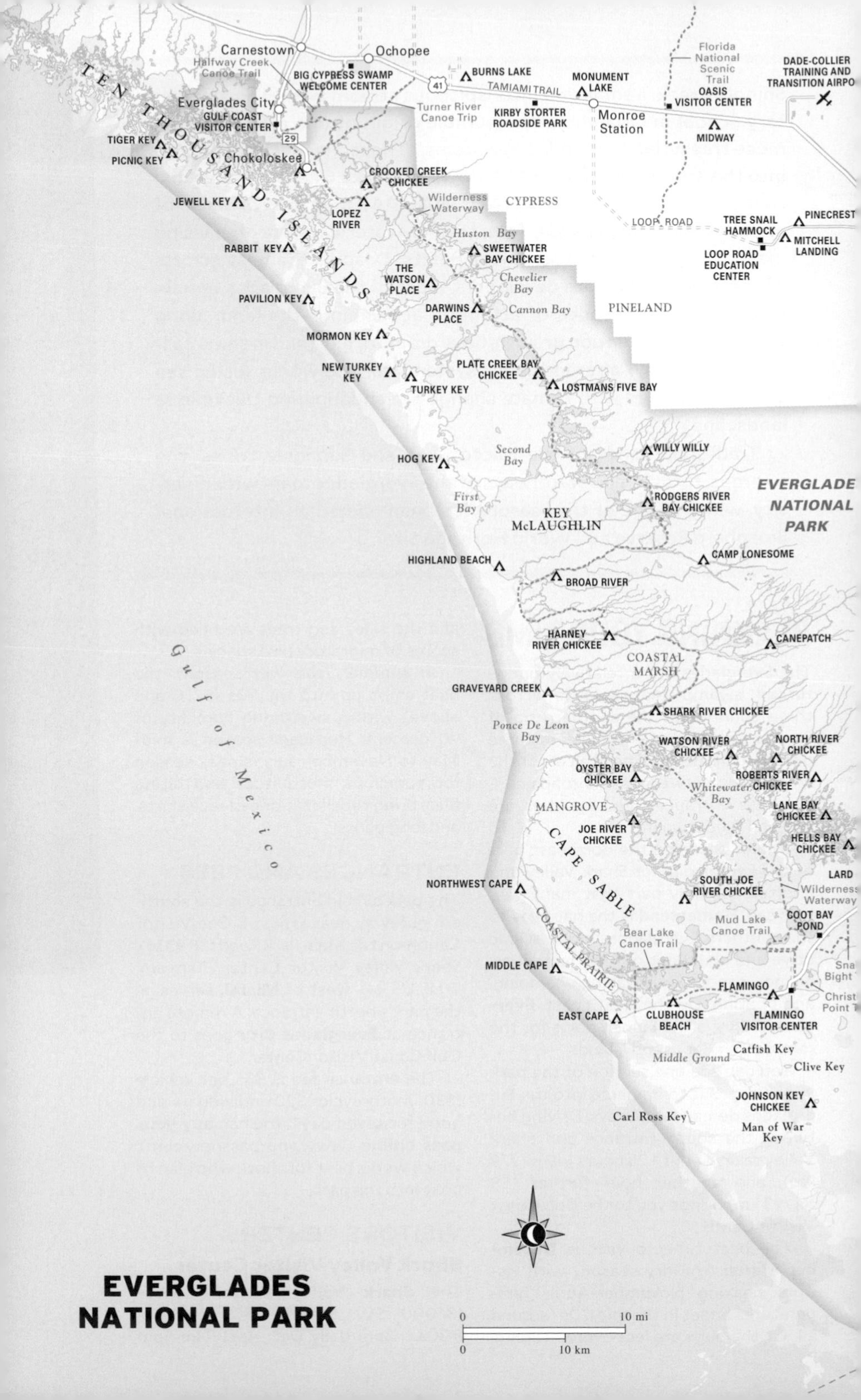

EVERGLADES NATIONAL PARK
TEN THOUSAND ISLANDS
Carnestown
Ochopee
Halfway Creek Canoe Trail
BIG CYPRESS SWAMP WELCOME CENTER
BURNS LAKE
41
TAMIAMI TRAIL
MONUMENT LAKE
Florida National Scenic Trail
OASIS VISITOR CENTER
DADE-COLLIER TRAINING AND TRANSITION AIRPO
Everglades City
GULF COAST VISITOR CENTER
29
Turner River Canoe Trip
KIRBY STORTER ROADSIDE PARK
Monroe Station
MIDWAY
TIGER KEY
PICNIC KEY
Chokoloskee
CROOKED CREEK CHICKEE
JEWELL KEY
LOPEZ RIVER
Wilderness Waterway
CYPRESS
LOOP ROAD
TREE SNAIL HAMMOCK
PINECREST
MITCHELL LANDING
LOOP ROAD EDUCATION CENTER
Huston Bay
RABBIT KEY
SWEETWATER BAY CHICKEE
THE WATSON PLACE
Chevelier Bay
PAVILION KEY
DARWINS PLACE
Cannon Bay
PINELAND
MORMON KEY
NEW TURKEY KEY
TURKEY KEY
PLATE CREEK BAY CHICKEE
LOSTMANS FIVE BAY
Second Bay
WILLY WILLY
HOG KEY
First Bay
EVERGLADE NATIONAL PARK
RODGERS RIVER BAY CHICKEE
KEY McLAUGHLIN
HIGHLAND BEACH
CAMP LONESOME
BROAD RIVER
Gulf of Mexico
HARNEY RIVER CHICKEE
CANEPATCH
COASTAL MARSH
GRAVEYARD CREEK
SHARK RIVER CHICKEE
Ponce De Leon Bay
WATSON RIVER CHICKEE
NORTH RIVER CHICKEE
OYSTER BAY CHICKEE
ROBERTS RIVER CHICKEE
Whitewater Bay
MANGROVE
LANE BAY CHICKEE
JOE RIVER CHICKEE
CAPE SABLE
HELLS BAY CHICKEE
LARD
NORTHWEST CAPE
SOUTH JOE RIVER CHICKEE
Wilderness Waterway
COASTAL PRAIRIE
Mud Lake Canoe Trail
COOT BAY POND
Bear Lake Canoe Trail
MIDDLE CAPE
FLAMINGO
EAST CAPE
CLUBHOUSE BEACH
FLAMINGO VISITOR CENTER
Catfish Key
Middle Ground
Clive Key
JOHNSON KEY CHICKEE
Carl Ross Key
Man of War Key
0
10 mi
0
10 km

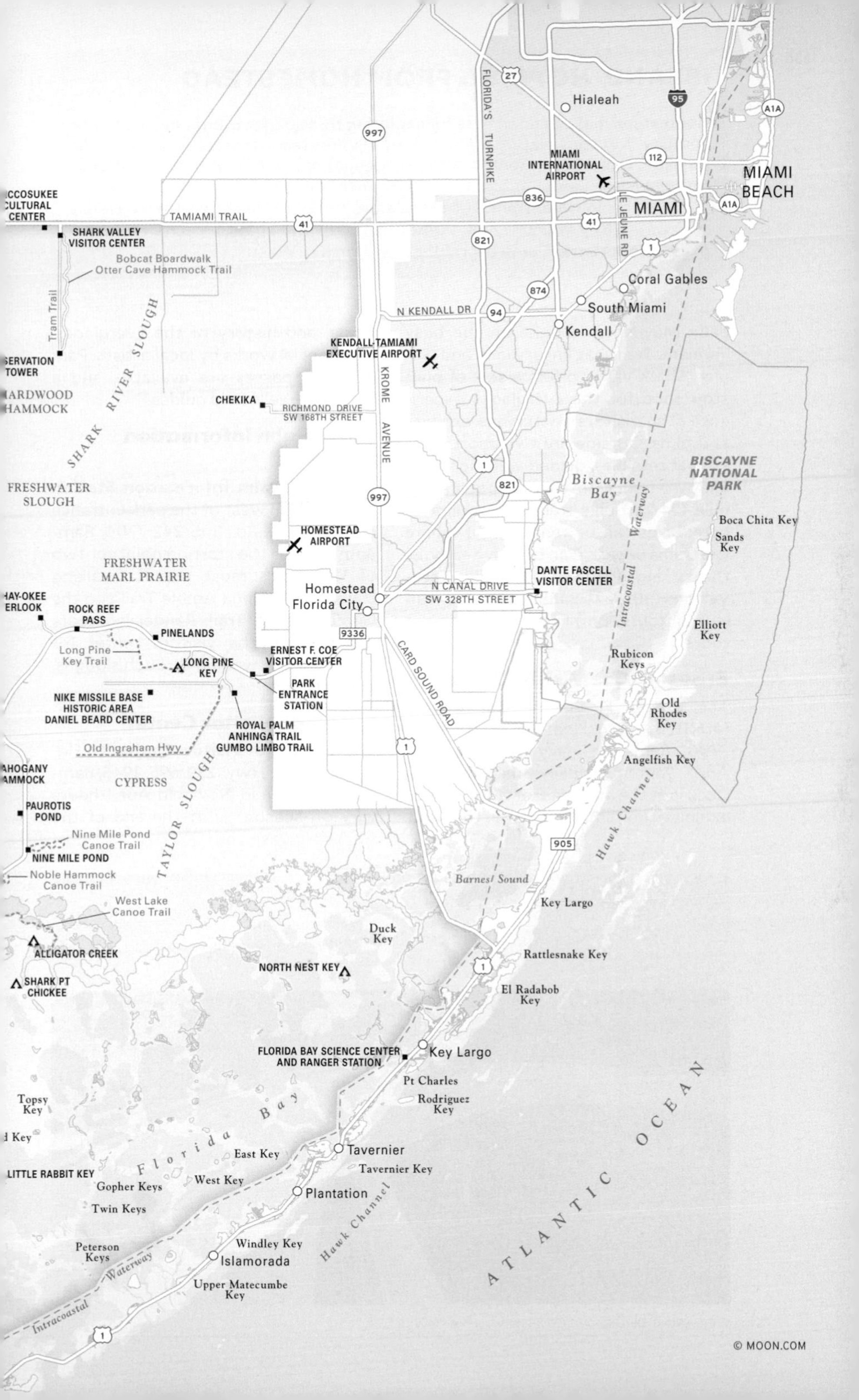

Hialeah
MIAMI INTERNATIONAL AIRPORT
MIAMI BEACH
MIAMI
FLORIDA'S TURNPIKE
LE JEUNE RD
TAMIAMI TRAIL
SHARK VALLEY VISITOR CENTER
Bobcat Boardwalk
Otter Cave Hammock Trail
Tram Trail
SHARK RIVER SLOUGH
Coral Gables
South Miami
Kendall
N KENDALL DR
KENDALL-TAMIAMI EXECUTIVE AIRPORT
CHEKIKA
RICHMOND DRIVE SW 168TH STREET
KROME AVENUE
FRESHWATER SLOUGH
Biscayne Bay
BISCAYNE NATIONAL PARK
Intracoastal Waterway
Boca Chita Key
Sands Key
HOMESTEAD AIRPORT
FRESHWATER MARL PRAIRIE
Homestead
Florida City
N CANAL DRIVE SW 328TH STREET
DANTE FASCELL VISITOR CENTER
ROCK REEF PASS
PINELANDS
Long Pine Key Trail
LONG PINE KEY
ERNEST F. COE VISITOR CENTER
PARK ENTRANCE STATION
CARD SOUND ROAD
Elliott Key
Rubicon Keys
Old Rhodes Key
Angelfish Key
NIKE MISSILE BASE HISTORIC AREA
DANIEL BEARD CENTER
ROYAL PALM
ANHINGA TRAIL
GUMBO LIMBO TRAIL
Old Ingraham Hwy
CYPRESS
TAYLOR SLOUGH
PAUROTIS POND
Nine Mile Pond Canoe Trail
NINE MILE POND
Noble Hammock Canoe Trail
West Lake Canoe Trail
ALLIGATOR CREEK
SHARK PT CHICKEE
Hawk Channel
Barnes Sound
Key Largo
Duck Key
Rattlesnake Key
NORTH NEST KEY
El Radabob Key
FLORIDA BAY SCIENCE CENTER AND RANGER STATION
Key Largo
Pt Charles
Rodriguez Key
Florida Bay
Topsy Key
East Key
Tavernier
Tavernier Key
LITTLE RABBIT KEY
Gopher Keys
West Key
Plantation
Twin Keys
Windley Key
Peterson Keys
Islamorada
Upper Matecumbe Key
Intracoastal Waterway
ATLANTIC OCEAN
© MOON.COM

ISLAND-HOPPING FROM HOMESTEAD

Homestead makes a good base for exploring three parks: Everglades, Biscayne, and Dry Tortugas National Parks. From Homestead, short drives go to the Ernest F. Coe Visitor Center in Everglades (11 mi./18 km, 18 min.) and Dante Fascell Visitor Center at Biscayne (10 mi./16 km, 21 min.).

From the south entrance of Everglades, drive southeast on the Overseas Highway to **Key West** (127 mi./204 km, 3 hrs.). Hop a boat to reach **Dry Tortugas National Park.** Camp overnight or stay in Key West.

daily May-Nov.) is right on the busy Tamiami Trail that links Miami and Naples. Shark Valley offers a sort of one-stop shop for the Everglades experience. The visitors center has exhibits and films. Outside are two short trails (one accessible), guided walking tours, and two-hour tram tours. A popular 15-mile (24-km) bike trail loop originates here; bikes can be rented right where the trams depart. Plan to arrive early, as the parking lots fill quickly. Make **reservations** (305/221-8455, www.sharkvalleytramtours.com) in advance for tram tours.

Ernest F. Coe Visitor Center

The **Ernest F. Coe Visitor Center** (40001 SR 9336, Homestead, 305/242-7700, 8am-5pm daily mid-Dec.-mid-Apr., 9am-5pm daily mid-Apr.-mid-Dec.) is at the main park entrance. It has exhibits and films that detail the flora, fauna, and history of the Everglades, plus special works by local artists. Park entrance passes are available, and a bookstore sells field guides.

Royal Palm Information Station

The **Royal Palm Information Station** (4 mi./6.4 km west of the park entrance on Main Park Rd., 305/242-7700, 8am-4pm daily) is the starting point for two of the park's most popular walking trails: the Anhinga Amble Trail and the Gumbo Limbo Trail. Ranger-led tours depart from the visitors center for walking trails, wading through sloughs, or bicycling.

Flamingo Visitor Center

The **Flamingo Visitor Center** (1 Flamingo Lodge Hwy., 239/695-2945, 8am-4pm daily mid-Nov.-mid-Apr., hours vary off-season) is at the end of the

VIEW FROM SHARK VALLEY OBSERVATION TOWER

Top 3

AMERICAN CROCODILE

1 WATCH WILDLIFE

The one animal instantly associated with the Everglades is the **American alligator,** a stealthy predator growing up to 16 feet (5 m). Backwater paddlers are frequently surprised when they discover that they've come within inches of one of these prehistoric marvels. Gators tend to hug the shoreline and prefer the tree cover. Look on the Anhinga Trail below mangroves.

American crocodiles tend to be found in the park's southern area around Flamingo. These carnivorous relics headline the park's endangered species, along with **manatees, Florida panthers, wood storks,** and **snail kites.**

The most abundant wildlife are **birds.** Dozens of species call the Glades home, including **spoonbills, egrets, flamingos,** and **bald eagles.** During migration season, hoards more nonnative species can be seen as well. Spot them best on wetland hiking trails and paddling trips. Free ranger-led bird-watching programs depart from Flamingo Visitor Center.

2 CANOE AND KAYAK THE GLADES

The best way to experience the Everglades is in a canoe or kayak. Kayaks are better suited to the narrow waterways, and you'll appreciate the navigational flexibility when paddling through mangrove tunnels. You can go self-guided on paddle trips or join **ranger-led tours** via the visitors centers at Flamingo, Shark Valley, and Gulf Coast (daily, winter, reservations required). **Rentals** are available at Flamingo Marina, Gulf Coast Visitor Center, and Everglades City. Winter is the best time to canoe and kayak, when the waters are calmer and the weather mild.

Beginner paddlers can explore calm backwater sloughs and lakes on several canoe trails located on Main Park Road near Flamingo. Advanced paddlers have options there, too. But the king of paddle trips is spending 7-10 days touring **Ten Thousand Islands** on the western coast. Several Seminole-style **"chickees"** (backcountry permit required) are located throughout the park, providing an elevated and roofed camping area right on the water.

SHARK VALLEY TRAIL TO THE OBSERVATION TOWER

3 BIKE SHARK VALLEY

Pedal along the utterly flat paved loop of the **Shark Valley Trail** (15 mi./24.2 km, 2-3 hrs.), where you can encounter wildlife, including alligators. At the south end, climb the observation tower to view the flat swampy expanse from the highest point in the Everglades. Rent bikes (first come, first served) from **Shark Valley Tram Tour** (305/221-8455, www.sharkvalleytramtours.com, 9 am-4pm daily).

Best Hike

ANHINGA TRAIL

DISTANCE: 0.8 miles (1.3 km) round-trip
DURATION: 30 minutes
ELEVATION GAIN: 3 feet (1 m)
DIFFICULTY: easy
TRAILHEAD: Royal Palm Visitor Center

The paved and boardwalk **Anhinga Trail** strolls through a classic Everglades sawgrass marsh. The flat wheelchair-accessible trail goes from the visitors center to loop through lush wetlands with overlooks, interpretive signs, and two short spurs. Even during the hottest summer months, you're likely to see a decent array of wildlife, especially alligators. During the winter months, bird-watching is incredible, with egrets, herons, cormorants, and anhingas. Abundant winter wildlife includes turtles, fish, and snakes. Rangers guide walks daily on this trail.

park's main paved road, about an hour south of Ernest Coe. Inside, it has educational displays and backcountry permits. Outside are short trails and a marina with boat tours and rentals of canoes, kayaks, boats, and bicycles.

Gulf Coast Visitor Center

On the park's remote northwest coast, the **Gulf Coast Visitor Center** (815 Oyster Bar Ln., Everglades City, 239/695-3311, 8am-4:30pm daily mid-Nov.-mid-Apr., 9am-4:30pm daily mid-Apr.-mid-Nov., free) gives visitors access to the waterways and tiny islands of the Ten Thousand Islands. The center's main building has nature exhibits, films, and backcountry permits.

SCENIC DRIVE

MAIN PARK ROAD

There's only one road in and out of Everglades National Park, so dedicate a full day to the journey from the park entrance and **Ernest F. Coe Visitor Center** to the far reaches of the **Flamingo Visitor Center.** A handful of pullovers along the **Main Park Road** (38 mi./61 km) offer stops to walk along a boardwalk,

▼ SUNSET OVER THE EVERGLADES

ONE DAY IN THE EVERGLADES

Start at the **Ernest F. Coe Visitor Center** to get oriented, and then drive the **Main Park Road** through the Everglades, taking in the sights and boardwalk trails through wetlands. Then cruise down to the **Flamingo Marina** for a **boat tour** through the backwaters of Florida Bay.

have a picnic, or just stare off into the vast expanse of the Everglades.

Long Pine Key

At **Long Pine Key** (4 mi./6.4 km along Main Park Rd.), walk the unnamed 0.5-mile (0.8-km) multipurpose trail, which offers a diverse look at the area's ecology.

Rock Reef Pass

The sign just before **Rock Reef Pass** (11 mi./18 km along Main Park Rd.) reminds you just how flat and near-swampy this part of the state is. It states, "Elevation: Three Feet." This is practically mountainous for the Everglades, as much of the area is actually at or below sea level. The high altitude of Rock Reef Pass makes for a unique ecological combination of pine forest and marshes filled with dwarf cypress trees. A short **boardwalk** allows you to get out into areas that alternate between a dry tinderbox in winter and foot-deep swamp in the summer rainy season.

Pa-hay-okee Overlook

The elevated wheelchair-accessible boardwalk at **Pa-hay-okee Overlook** (12.5 mi./20 km along Main Park Rd.) offers expansive vistas onto the grassy infinity of the Everglades. In the busy season, the parking lot packs full and crowds on the boardwalk create cattle-chute movement. For the best chance of having these beautiful views to yourself, visit before 9am.

Mahogany Hammock

Mahogany Hammock (20 mi./32 km along Main Park Rd.) is a boardwalk-through-the-Glades experience. The self-guided loop trail (0.5 mi./0.8 km rt., 15 min., easy) tours dense mahogany trees that provide shade from the canopy, usually full of migratory birds.

ANHINGA TRAIL

GUMBO LIMBO TRAIL

You'll also see the largest mahogany tree in the United States.

RECREATION

HIKING

Due to seasonal flooding and wetland environments, many trails in the Everglades are paved or boardwalks. Those that are not may be muddy and, in some places, flooded in summer.

Located 2 miles (3.2 km) west of Long Pine Key, **Pineland Trail** (0.4 mi./0.6 km rt., 15 min., easy) is a paved trail through slash pine and palmettos. Although the trail is wheelchair-accessible, roots have heaved up the pavement in places.

From the Royal Palm Visitor Center, the wheelchair-accessible **Gumbo Limbo Trail** (0.4 mi./0.6 km rt., 20 min., easy) tours under the shade of gumbo-limbo trees and royal palms. Amid ferns and air plants, you might also spot birds and wildlife on this interpretive path.

The mangrove-lined, waterfront **Bayshore Trail** (2 mi./3.2 km rt., 1 hr., easy) that launches from the Flamingo Campground jaunts along Florida Bay with interpretive signs. Check on trail status first at a visitors center. From the Flamingo Visitor Center, the **Eco-Pond Trail** (0.5 mi./0.8 km rt., 20 min., easy) loops with interpretive signs around a freshwater pond full of waterfowl and songbirds.

From Shark Valley Visitor Center, the wheelchair-accessible **Bobcat Boardwalk** (0.4 mi./0.6 km one-way, 15 min., easy) loops through classic Shark Valley sawgrass fields and swamp trees

MANGROVE AT NINE MILE POND

KAYAK THE GULF COAST

thick with migrating and nesting birds December through May.

BIKING

Off the Main Park Road, the **Long Pine Key Nature Trail** (13 mi./21 km rt., 2-3 hrs.) is a loop that goes on double-track through palmettos and pines from the campground to Pine Glades Lake. It connects with the paved (and trafficked) Main Park Road to return. The **Snake Bight Trail** (3.2 mi./5.2 km rt.) goes to a boardwalk (dismount here) to see a small bay known as a bight within Florida Bay. Check on maintenance status before riding either of these trails.

Five miles (8 km) east of Shark Valley, a grassy gravel **canal road** (6.4 mi./10.3 km rt.) parallels Shark Valley Slough where you can see alligators, turtles, and in winter birds.

For biking, bring water for the heat. Ride in the morning to avoid afternoon lightning in summer. Rangers lead several bicycle tours, including a nighttime meteor shower ride and moonlight rides, plus daytime rides; some require reservations. Bicycle rentals are available at **Shark Valley Tram Tours** (305/221-8455, www.sharkvalleytramtours.com) and **Flamingo Marina** (352/701-6581 or 855/708-2207, www.flamingoeverglades.com).

CANOEING AND KAYAKING

Everglades was made for paddlers! Mangrove tunnels, freshwater sloughs, bays, and islands offer a breadth of habitats to explore, often loaded with birds and wildlife. Rangers guide multiple canoe trips from the visitors centers at Flamingo, Shark Valley, and the Gulf Coast. For some, you must bring your own canoe or kayak; others tours provide canoes. Make required reservations by calling the visitors centers.

For self-guided trips, inquire about water levels at visitors centers before launching, especially during the winter dry season.

Flamingo

Experienced paddlers can explore the twists and turns of the popular **Hell's Bay Canoe Trail** (3-6 mi./4.8-9.7 km), a challenging run that announces its intentions with a comically difficult put-in and a trail that can take up to six hours to navigate completely. The difficult **West Lake Canoe Trail** (8 mi./12.9 km) runs mainly through open waters but also squeezes through some impressive mangrove tunnels that are occasionally claustrophobic.

Beginners options include the **Nine-Mile Pond Canoe Trail** (3.5 mi./5.6 km) through mangrove tunnels and several wider marshes. It's best explored during the summer when water levels are high. **Noble Hammock Canoe Trail** (2 mi./3.2 km) is a short loop through mangroves. From Flamingo Marina, paddlers can also explore the waters of **Florida Bay** and its numerous keys.

Ten Thousand Islands

The massive **Ten Thousand Islands** covers an extensive coastline in southwestern Florida. It contains mangrove swamps, tiny keys, grassy marshes, sandy beaches, mud bars, and tropical hardwood hammocks, nearly all of which are undeveloped. Running along Cape Sable and the western edge of the Glades, this region includes the **Ten Thousand Islands National Wildlife Refuge** (239/657-8001, www.fws.gov/refuge/ten_thousand_islands) and Everglades National Park.

Serious canoers and kayakers go for the **Wilderness Waterway** (99 mi./159 km, 7-10 days), which gets paddlers into some of the most isolated fringes of the Everglades. Launch at Everglades City in Chocoloskee Bay to finish at Flamingo Marina to have prevailing winds aid paddling. Winter is best for this adventure, and permits are required ($15 fee plus $2 pp/day). Pick them up in person at Gulf Coast Visitor Center or Flamingo Visitor Center.

Rentals and Tours

Flamingo Marina (352/701-6581 or 855/708-2207, www.flamingoeverglades.com) rents kayaks and canoes. Canoe rentals are also available at the Gulf Coast Visitor Center, but you may have better luck at private operators, as these rentals run out quickly during winter.

Everglades Adventures (605 Buckner Ave. N., Everglades City, 877/567-0679, www.iveyhouse.com) operates out of the Ivey House Inn. Its daytime, sunset, and overnight tours have a decidedly ecofriendly bent and can be done in either kayaks or canoes. Rentals are also available, and the company runs shuttle services for Wilderness Waterway route kayakers and their boats between Everglades City and Flamingo.

Shurr Adventures (32016 Tamiami Trail, Miami, 239/300-3004, www.schurradventures.com) leads kayak tours through Ten Thousand Islands.

▼ TAYLOR SLOUGH

FLAMINGO AREA

It also offers a backcountry mangrove tour.

BOATING

In such a water-filled park, boating is the way to tour much of the southern and western parts of the park. Boaters entering Florida Bay waters within the national park must have a permit (free), obtainable after completing an online education course.

Flamingo Marina (352/701-6581 or 855/708-2207, www.flamingoeverglades.com, year-round) has a boat launch, overnight slips for boats with power and water hookups, pump-out services, fuel, showers, and rentals of fishing pontoons, skiffs, and houseboats. Boat rentals are also available in Everglades City.

FISHING

Numerous fishing charters are available in the area. Most charters are essentially the same, offering anglers the opportunity to choose between flats and deepwater fishing excursions, and most are geared toward small groups (2-5 people).

Everglades Kayak Fishing (239/682-9920, www.evergladeskayakfishing.com) and **Capt. Tony Polizos** (239/695-2608) operate out of Everglades City.

WHERE TO STAY

INSIDE THE PARK

There are no accommodations. But overnight options on the Main Park Road include camping and unique solutions where you don't need to bring a tent.

Flamingo Adventures (855-708-2207, www.flamingoeverglades) has **eco-tents** (from $60) with queen or two double beds on a platform; restrooms are communal. It's all set up for you with bed linens, electricity, and storage bins and picnic table and grills outside. If you'd rather sleep on water, you can rent a fully-equipped, two-bedroom **houseboat** (from $350) with bed and bath linens, shower, and outfitted galley; you bring food and personal items. You can stay in the marina, which has electrical and water hookups.

Two traditional campgrounds welcome tent campers and RVs. Facilities include solar-heated showers, RV dump stations, picnic tables, grills, drinking water, and amphitheaters for evening ranger programs. Near Flamingo Visitor Center, **Flamingo Campground** (877/444-6777, www.recreation.gov, year-round, $20-30) has 234 drive-up sites, 40 walk-in single sites, 41 RV sites, and 3 walk-in group sites. Reservations are accepted up to six months in advance for stays in November-April. Nearest the southern entrance, **Long Pine Key Campground** (mid-Nov.-Apr., $20-30) has 108 drive-up sites and one group site. Sites are available first come, first served.

A food truck visits the Flamingo Marina (11:30am-5pm, Wed.-Sun), and the Flamingo Marina store (7am-7:30pm daily) has convenience foods.

Backcountry Camping

Backcountry campsites range from chickees along the Wilderness Waterway and in Florida Bay to "beach" sites in Cape Sable to standard ground sites. All are only accessible by boat. The three beach sites at **Cape Sable** are the largest, accommodating around 150 people. They're as beautiful as they are rustic and often uncrowded.

Backcountry permits ($15 processing fee, $2 pp/day) are required for

BIG CYPRESS NATIONAL PRESERVE

You can get a taste of Big Cypress National Preserve when driving from Shark Valley to Everglades City. This immense freshwater swamp supports diverse wildlife: alligators, crocodiles, fish, turtles, birds, and the elusive Florida panther.

Big Cypress has two visitors centers for maps, information, permits, and bookstores. Ask about schedules for ranger-led programs that include walks, talks, and paddle trips. The **Big Cypress Swamp Welcome Center** (33000 Tamiami Trail, 9am-4:30pm daily) has indoor and outdoor exhibits. The **Oasis Visitor Center** (52105 Tamiami Trail E., 9am-4:30pm daily) has small educational and art exhibits.

Scenic Drives

Depart the Tamiami Trail (US 41) and drive the well-marked **Loop Road** (27 mi./43 km) through dense forests of dwarf cypress, slash pine, and wildlife. Starting at H. P. Williams Roadside Park, **Turner River Loop** (16 mi./26 km) is a great option for bird-watchers.

BIG CYPRESS NATIONAL PRESERVE

Recreation

At **Kirby Storter Roadside Park** (US 41/Tamiami Trail, sunrise-sunset daily, free), an interpretive boardwalk trail (1 mi./1.6 km rt., 30 min. easy) provides views of the swamp and vast expanses of marshlands. Bird-watching is excellent.

Launch canoes and kayaks from the **Turner River Canoe Access** (entry point at US 41 west of Turner River Rd.). Paddling season is November-March.

Where to Stay

Big Cypress National Preserve campgrounds (877/444-6777, www.recreation.gov, from $24) near Ochopee take reservations. **Midway Campground** (52870 Tamiami Trail E.) is open year-round. **Monument Lake Campground** (50215 Tamiami Trail E.) and the primitive **Burns Lake Campground & Backcountry Access** (18495 Burns Rd.) are open mid-August-mid-April.

On Tamiami Trail, Ochopee has a couple restaurants and lodging options.

Getting There

The **Tamiami Trail** (US 41), east of Naples (36 mi./58 km, 45 min.), bisects southern Big Cypress National Preserve. From Shark Valley Visitor Center in Everglades, drive 20 miles (32 km, 25 min.) east to Oasis Visitor Center. From Everglades City, drive 6 miles (10 km, 8 min.) northwest to Big Cypress Swamp Welcome Center.

overnight trips and are first come, first served. Campsites that only fit 1-2 people go fast. Pick up permits at the Gulf Coast Visitor Center or Flamingo Visitor Center.

OUTSIDE THE PARK

Accommodations, restaurants, and services are in **Miami, Homestead,** and **Everglades City.** Camping is available in Big Cypress National Preserve.

GETTING THERE

AIR

The nearest airport is **Miami International Airport** (MIA, 2100 NW 42nd Ave., 305/876-7000, www.miami-airport.com), about an hour drive north. It is also the primary point of entry for travelers entering the United States from South America and the Caribbean. Car rentals are available at the airport.

CAR

From Miami, a 40-mile (64-km, 1 hr.) drive goes to the Tamiami Trail (US 41) to reach the Shark Valley Visitor Center, a busy spot that's the northwest entry to the Everglades. About 36 miles (58 km, 45 min.) southwest of Naples via the Tamiami Trail (US 41) is the town of Everglades City, home to the Gulf Coast Visitor Center. This visitors center is the best starting point for exploring the western half of the Everglades, including the Ten Thousand Islands area.

From Miami, it's 50 miles (81 km, 1 hr.) south via FL 997 or FL 821 to reach Ernest F. Coe Visitor Center at the southern entrance to Everglades.

From Key West, take the Overseas Highway (US 1) through Florida City before dropping into Homestead. The 127-mile (204-km) drive takes three hours.

GETTING AROUND

There is no public transportation within the park.

TOURS

From Homestead, the **Homestead Trolley** (www.cityofhomestead.com, weekends and holidays late Nov.-Apr., free) runs guided tours to the Everglades.

Tram Tours

The most popular tour is the **Shark Valley Tram Tour** (305/221-8455, www.sharkvalleytramtours.com, 9am-4pm daily mid-Dec.-Apr., 9:30am-4pm daily May-mid-Dec., fee) departing from the Shark Valley Visitor Center. Park naturalists guide two-hour tours in covered, open-air buses with pull-behind cars. Midway through the tour, you'll stop at a 45-foot-high (14-m) observation platform to see the Everglades from above. Guides point out sharks and gators. Reservations are highly recommended in winter.

Ranger Tours

Ranger-led tours (daily, free) depart the visitors centers for short walks that vary from easy trails (some wheelchair-accessible) to "Slough Slogs," bird-watching, or nighttime starlight tours. Other tours travel by bicycle, canoe, or boat. Tour schedules change seasonally; winters run full schedules of programs while summers have reduced tours.

Boat Tours

Two 90-minute narrated boat tours depart **Flamingo Marina** (352/701-6581 or 855/708-2207, www.flamingoeverglades.com, fee), adjacent to Flamingo Visitor Center. The Everglades Backcountry Whitewater Bay Tour (four times daily late Nov.-mid-Apr.) motors up a canal, creek, and two bays on a pontoon boat. The **Florida Bay Boat Tour** (1-3 times daily, late Nov.-early May) circles Florida Bay on a double-deck catamaran. Purchase tickets for both online or at the marina store.

Everglades National Park Boat Tours (www.evergladesnationalparkboattoursgulfcoast.com, daily year-round, rates and times vary) take in the Ten Thousand Islands, mangrove wilderness, and wildlife, with narration by national park-trained naturalists. Tours depart from the Gulf Coast marina. Purchase tickets at the Gulf Coast Visitor Center (905 S. Copeland Ave., 239/695-2591) in Everglades City.

Airboat Tours

Airboat tours are a controversial way to speed through an Everglades' sea of grass. Damage to fragile ecosystems and boat noise disturbing wildlife are two of the reasons the national park is evaluating whether to continue allowing them. They are already banned in most of the park, except for a tiny portion near Everglades City. Check on the status first. Airboat tours into this area are operated by **Coopertown** (305/226-6048, www.coopertownairboats.com), **Gator Park** (305/559-2255, www.gatorpark.com), and **Everglades Safari Park** (305/226-6923, www.evergladessafaripark.com). Plenty of other airboat tours go to locations outside the national park.

BISCAYNE NATIONAL PARK

Florida

WEBSITE:
www.nps.gov/bisc

PHONE NUMBER:
305/230-1144

VISITATION RANK:
29

WHY GO:
Explore a national park that is 95 percent water.

▲ BISCAYNE NATIONAL PARK

KEEPSAKE STAMPS ▼▼▼

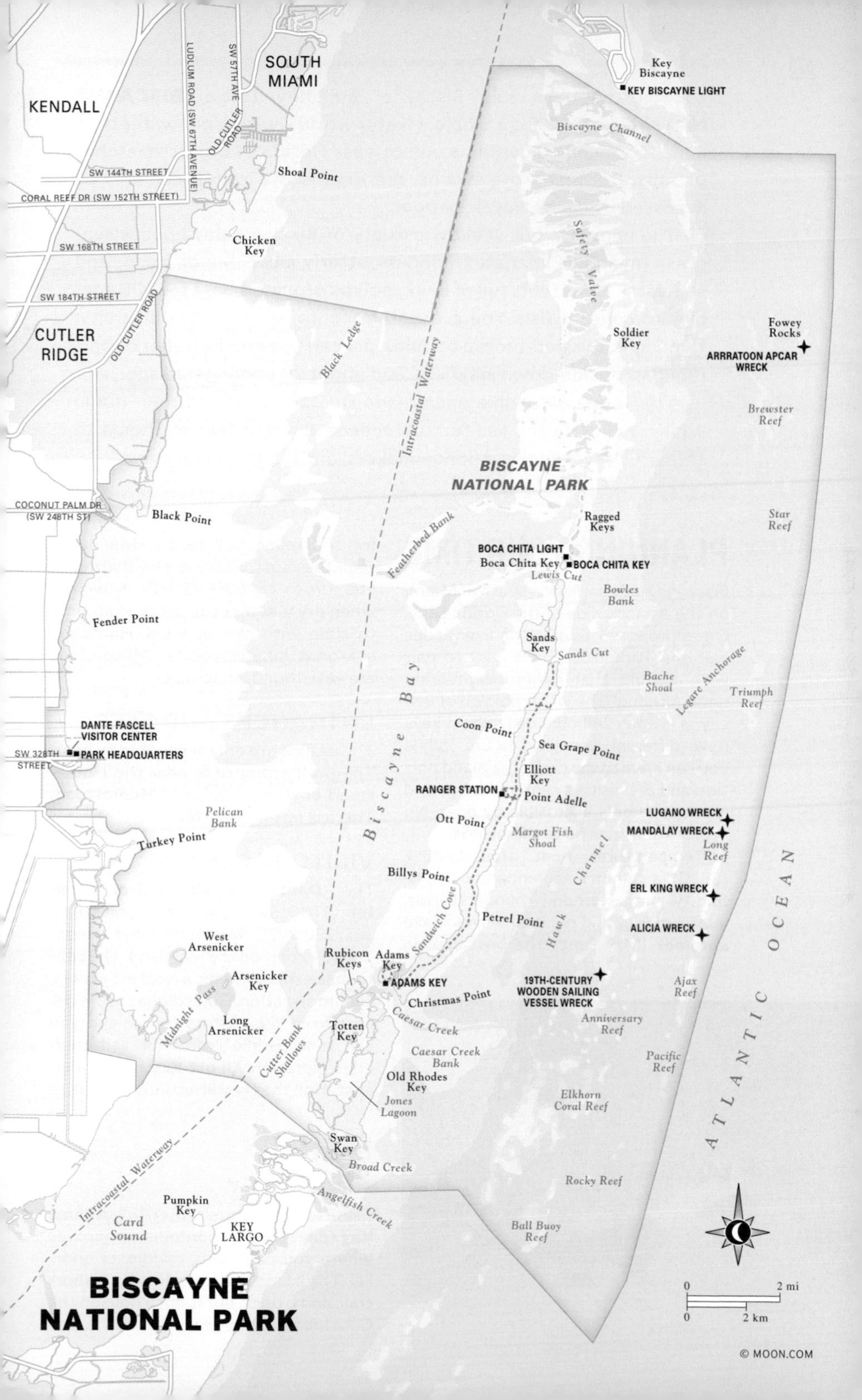

BISCAYNE NATIONAL PARK
KENDALL
SOUTH MIAMI
CUTLER RIDGE
SW 57TH AVE
LUDLUM ROAD (SW 67TH AVENUE)
OLD CUTLER ROAD
SW 144TH STREET
CORAL REEF DR (SW 152TH STREET)
SW 168TH STREET
SW 184TH STREET
OLD CUTLER ROAD
COCONUT PALM DR (SW 248TH ST)
SW 328TH STREET
DANTE FASCELL VISITOR CENTER
PARK HEADQUARTERS
Shoal Point
Chicken Key
Black Point
Fender Point
Pelican Bank
Turkey Point
West Arsenicker
Arsenicker Key
Long Arsenicker
Midnight Pass
Cutter Bank Shallows
Intracoastal Waterway
Pumpkin Key
Card Sound
KEY LARGO
Key Biscayne
KEY BISCAYNE LIGHT
Biscayne Channel
Safety Valve
Soldier Key
Fowey Rocks
ARRRATOON APCAR WRECK
Brewster Reef
Black Ledge
Intracoastal Waterway
BISCAYNE NATIONAL PARK
Star Reef
Ragged Keys
Featherbed Bank
BOCA CHITA LIGHT
Boca Chita Key
BOCA CHITA KEY
Lewis Cut
Bowles Bank
Sands Key
Sands Cut
Bache Shoal
Legare Anchorage
Triumph Reef
Biscayne Bay
Coon Point
Sea Grape Point
Elliott Key
RANGER STATION
Point Adelle
Ott Point
Margot Fish Shoal
LUGANO WRECK
MANDALAY WRECK
Long Reef
Billys Point
Sandwich Cove
Hawk Channel
ERL KING WRECK
Petrel Point
ALICIA WRECK
Rubicon Keys
Adams Key
ADAMS KEY
19TH-CENTURY WOODEN SAILING VESSEL WRECK
Christmas Point
Caesar Creek
Ajax Reef
Anniversary Reef
Totten Key
Caesar Creek Bank
Old Rhodes Key
Pacific Reef
Jones Lagoon
Elkhorn Coral Reef
ATLANTIC OCEAN
Swan Key
Broad Creek
Angelfish Creek
Rocky Reef
Ball Buoy Reef
0
2 mi
0
2 km
© MOON.COM

Located between Key Biscayne and Key Largo, **BISCAYNE NATIONAL PARK** is a tropical water world—with more water than land. Its mainland contains one of east Florida's longest stretches of saltwater mangrove swamp, but most of its islands can only be accessed by canoe, kayak, or boat.

The immense but shallow estuary of Biscayne Bay houses seagrass meadows, manatees, and an utterly clear mix of fresh- and seawater. Coral reefs full of living polyps provide a base for 500 species of colorful fish. The ecosystem contains incredible diversity: flamingos, ibis, red-footed boobies, pelicans, sea turtles, sharks, barracudas, upside-down jellyfish... and about 20 endangered species.

The Tequesta people once made the largest island their home while relying on the sea for sustenance. Later, it became home to shipwreck scavengers, sponge makers, and pineapple farmers.

PLANNING YOUR TIME

Biscayne National Park is south of Miami on the Atlantic side of the Florida cape. Once proposed as part of Everglades National Park, Biscayne is easy to pair with visiting that larger neighboring park. Although the water portion of Biscayne is open 24 hours daily, some keys have different operating hours. While you can drive to the park's mainland portion and the visitors center, the bay and islands are only accessible by boat. No bridges or ferries go to the islands.

Temperatures float around 82°F (28°C) in summer, accompanied by humidity and afternoon thunderstorms. Water clarity and minimal waves make **summer** (May-Sept.) the best season for snorkeling but spring (Mar-June) sees the most visitors.. The thermometer drops to 68°F (20°C) in winter, when dry weather can break from time to time with rain or wind. Hurricane season is June-November. Mosquitoes are year-round inhabitants.

SEA TURTLE

ENTRANCES AND FEES

The islands are only accessible by boat. The park entrance is near the Homestead Bayfront Marina in **Homestead.** There is no entrance fee.

VISITORS CENTER

The **Dante Fascell Visitor Center** (9700 SW 328th St., Homestead, 305/230-7275, 9am-5pm daily) is near Convoy Point on the mainland. The center has exhibits, films, a local art gallery, and information. Guided boat tours depart from the visitors center and you can rent paddle crafts for self-guided exploration. **Elliott Key** has a ranger station that is staffed intermittently.

SIGHTS

ADAMS KEY

Close to the visitors center, tiny **Adams Key** (day use only) contains mangroves where you can swim, paddle, or snorkel. The island has a picnic area, a short trail, and a dock, but it once housed the Cocolobo Club, a getaway for the rich

Top 3

1 SNORKEL SHIPWRECKS

Accessible only by boat, Biscayne is lined with shallow-water shipwrecks to the delight of snorkelers and divers. Six shipwrecks line the **Maritime Heritage Trail** on the Atlantic side of the park. Looking more like skeletons than ships, the wrecks date mostly from the late 1800s and early 1900s. Pick up maps at the visitors center to locate the shipwrecks and their mooring buoys. **Biscayne National Park Institute** (786/335-3644, www.biscaynenationalparkinstitute.org) guides tours.

SNORKELERS EXPLORE ELKHORN REEF

2 PADDLE MANGROVES

Biscayne Bay is rimmed with mangroves in one of the longest mangrove forests on Florida's east coast. These unique forests thrive in saltwater and in turn keep the water clean while creating a rich habitat for birds and aquatic life, including manatees. Paddling a kayak, canoe, or paddleboard into the mangroves is the best way to explore these wonders, even for beginners who should stick to the rim of the bay. Rent paddle craft at the visitors center or take a guided paddle tour with **Biscayne National Park Institute** (786/335-3644, www.biscaynenationalparkinstitute.org).

3 VISIT BOCA CHITA KEY

The most visited island, small **Boca Chita Key** has an idyllic harbor and a lighthouse that dates from the 1930s. If a park ranger is available, you can access the observation deck for big views full of water, islands, and Miami. Reach this island on the north end of the keys by boat, and camp overnight. **Biscayne National Park Institute** (786/335-3644, www.biscaynenationalparkinstitute.org) guides daily tours to the island.

BOCA CHITA KEY

TOTTEN KEY

and famous. Reach this island on the south end of the keys by boat.

ELLIOTT KEY

North of Key Largo, **Elliott Key** is the largest island at about 7 miles (11 km) long. It offers swimming, paddling, camping, picnicking, and a hiking trail. Historically, the Tequesta Indians used it periodically, but its early settlers grew pineapples, collected sponges, and sought spoils from wrecked ships.

RECREATION

HIKING

From the visitors center, cross a bridge to reach the jetty to **Convoy Point** (open 7am-5:30pm daily, 0.6 mi./1 km rt., 20 min., easy) to see the bay.

On Elliott Key, the **Spite Highway Nature Trail** (6 mi./9.7 km one-way, 3 hrs., easy) travels the length of the island, crossing through subtropical forest that harbors butterflies. Access to the key is by boat; camping is available.

CANOEING, KAYAKING, AND PADDLEBOARDING

Beginner paddlers should stick to the mangrove fringes around Biscayne Bay, but experienced paddlers can tackle the 7-mile (11 km) crossing to the keys to camp on Boca Chita Key and Elliott Key.

Secluded **Jones Lagoon**, a shallow waterway with tiny islets between Totten and Old Rhodes Keys, offers sheltered paddling routes to see fish, sharks, and birds. **Hurricane Creek** is a paddling destination that has snorkeling in mangroves on Old Rhodes Key. Consult with the visitors center on paddle routes before launching. Winter is the best time for these two trips.

SPADE FISH

Dante Fascell Visitor Center (9700 SW 328th St., Homestead, 305/230-7275) rents canoes, kayaks, and paddleboards. By reservation only, rangers guide full-day paddling trips to Jones Lagoon. **Biscayne National Park Institute** (786/335-3644, www.biscaynenationalparkinstitute.org) also guides kayaking and paddleboarding trips.

DIVING AND SNORKELING

If you have a boat, you can snorkel shallow coral reefs and shipwrecks on your own or go on deeper dives. Otherwise, board a guided snorkeling trip with **Biscayne National Park Institute** (786/335-3644, www.biscaynenationalparkinstitute.org) around Biscayne Bay and the offshore coral reefs and shipwrecks on the Atlantic side of the park. **Tropic Scuba** (305/669-1645, http://tropicscuba.com) has charter snorkeling and scuba diving trips.

BOATING AND FISHING

Anglers must bring their own boat into Biscayne National Park to go after tarpon, grouper, snapper, and bonefish. For boaters, **Miami County Parks** (www.miamidade.gov) operates two launching marinas that go directly into the park: **Homestead Bayfront Park** (9698 N. Canal Dr., Homestead, 305/230-3033) and **Black Point Marina** (24775 SW 87th Ave., Miami, 305/258-4092). A Florida fishing license is required.

WHERE TO STAY

INSIDE THE PARK

The park has no lodgings or services. **Camping** (tents only, first come, first served, $25) is available on two islands, and boaters can overnight in the two harbors (fee).

Popular **Boca Chita Key** features a grassy waterside camping area with picnic tables, grills, and toilets. Spacious **Elliott Key** offers waterside and forested camping areas, picnic tables, grills, drinking water, and restrooms with cold showers. Contact **Biscayne National Park Institute** (786/335-3644, www.biscaynenationalparkinstitute.org) for transportation to the islands. For paddlers, overnight parking by permit (free) is at the visitors center.

OUTSIDE THE PARK

The closest accommodations and restaurants are in **Homestead** and **Florida City.** Just over 30 miles (48 km) away, **Miami** adds plentiful options.

GETTING THERE AND AROUND

The nearest international airport is **Miami International Airport** (MIA, 2100 NW 42nd Ave., 305/876-7000, www.miami-airport.com), which also has car rentals.

To reach the Dante Fascell Visitor Center in Homestead, drivers have three options:

From the Florida Turnpike: Take exit 6 (Speedway Blvd.) and turn left onto SW 328th Street (North Canal Drive). Turn left and drive 4 miles (6.4 km) to the park entrance.

From the north on US 1: At Homestead, turn east onto SW 137th Avenue (Speedway Blvd.) and continue 5 miles (8 km). At SW 328th Street (North Canal Dr.), turn left and drive 4 miles (6.4 km) to the park entrance.

From the south on US 1: At Homestead, turn right onto SW 344th Street (Palm Dr.) and continue 4 miles (6.4 km). Turn right on SW 328th Street (North Canal Dr.) and drive east for 4 miles (6.4 km) to the park entrance.

The **Homestead National Parks Trolley** (www.cityofhomestead.com, late Nov.-Apr., free) provides guided tours from Homestead to Biscayne and Everglades National Parks.

BOAT TOURS

Biscayne National Park Institute (786/335-3644, www.biscaynenationalparkinstitute.org, reservations recommended) guides interpretive boat or sailing tours. Three-hour trips go to Boca Chita Key. The institute also guides higher-activity, full-day tours that combine sightseeing the islands with snorkeling and paddling. Several other companies operate boat or sailing charters; consult with the visitors center for licensed concessionaires.

DRY TORTUGAS NATIONAL PARK

Florida

WEBSITE:
www.nps.gov/drto

PHONE NUMBER:
305/242-7700

VISITATION RANK:
55

WHY GO:
Explore the underwater habitat of coral and sand islands.

▲ DRY TORTUGAS NATIONAL PARK

KEEPSAKE STAMPS ▼▼▼

DRY TORTUGAS NATIONAL PARK

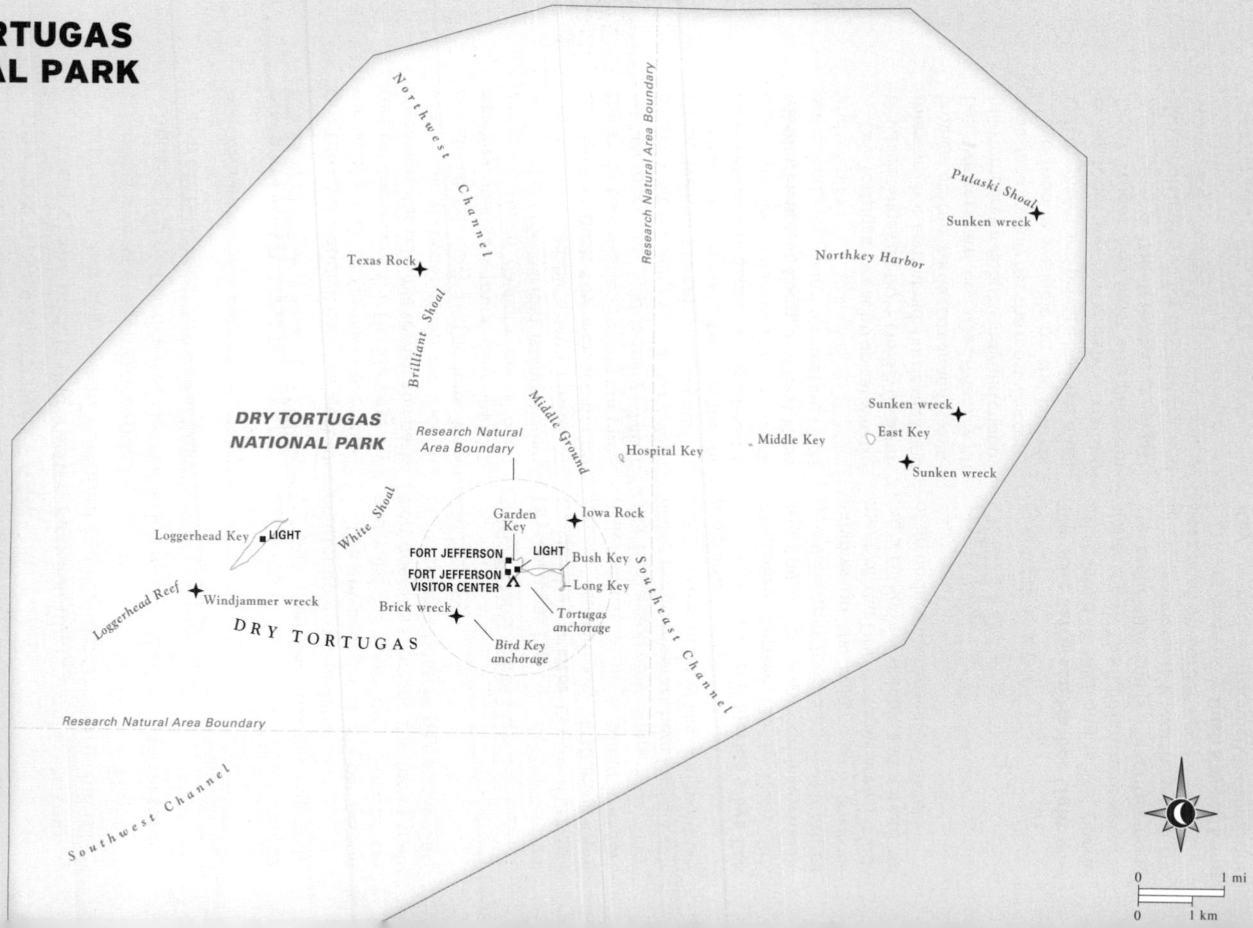

Northwest Channel
Texas Rock
Brilliant Shoal
Research Natural Area Boundary
Pulaski Shoal
Sunken wreck
Northkey Harbor
DRY TORTUGAS NATIONAL PARK
Research Natural Area Boundary
Middle Ground
Hospital Key
Middle Key
Sunken wreck
East Key
Sunken wreck
White Shoal
Garden Key
Iowa Rock
Loggerhead Key
LIGHT
FORT JEFFERSON
LIGHT
Bush Key
FORT JEFFERSON VISITOR CENTER
Long Key
Southeast Channel
Loggerhead Reef
Windjammer wreck
Brick wreck
Tortugas anchorage
DRY TORTUGAS
Bird Key anchorage
Research Natural Area Boundary
Southwest Channel
0
1 mi
0
1 km

West of Key West lies a cluster of seven islands, composed of coral and sand. Originally named Las Tortugas ("the Turtles") by Spanish explorers, they eventually became the Dry Tortugas on mariners' navigational charts to indicate the lack of freshwater. Today, these islands, in addition to the surrounding shoals and waters, comprise **DRY TORTUGAS NATIONAL PARK.**

Most of the park is underwater. Rich abundant sealife, striking coral reefs, and shipwrecks surround the islands. On shore, the islands serve as breeding grounds for rare birds. They also hold lighthouses and on Garden Key the red-bricked, six-sided Fort Jefferson, one of the largest forts ever built.

PLANNING YOUR TIME

Dry Tortugas National Park lies west of the southern tip of Florida in open waters off the end of the Florida Keys archipelago. It is possible to visit the park year-round via boat or seaplane, though certain islands have restrictions. **Garden Key,** open year-round, contains Fort Jefferson (open daylight hours only) and is the most visited island. Sometimes connected by a land bridge to Garden Key, **Bush Key** is closed during the sooty tern nesting season but open mid-October to mid-January. Most people visit Garden Key via ferry, with about five hours to enjoy the island.

Other islands require private or charter boats for access. **Loggerhead** is open year-round during daylight hours. **Middle, Hospital, Long,** and **East Keys** are closed year-round for nesting birds and wildlife.

Dry Tortugas has subtropical weather, which ranges 60-90°F (16-32°C). **Summers** are hot and humid; hurricanes and tropical storms can occur June-November. **Winters** are dry (Dec.-Mar.) with mild temperatures, but windy and choppy seas. January-July has the most visitors.

No food is available on the islands. Overnighters and private boaters must bring food and water when visiting Dry Tortugas. You must also pack out your garbage. The ferry has breakfast and lunch included for day visitors, and snacks are available.

ENTRANCES AND FEES

No roads access the park. A ferry from **Key West** travels to Garden Key daily. You can also reach Dry Tortugas via your own boat (permit required), charter boat, or seaplane.

The entrance fee is $15 per person and valid for seven days. Transportation operators include the fee in their rates; private boaters pay at the Garden Key dock.

VISITORS CENTERS

Dry Tortugas has two visitors centers. **Garden Key Visitor Center** (Fort Jefferson, Garden Key, 8:30am-4:30pm daily) shows a movie about the fort and has a souvenir shop. Free ranger-led programs start here for Fort Jefferson tours, moat walks, and night sky programs.

In Key West, the **Florida Keys Eco Discovery Center** (35 E. Quay Rd., 305/809-4750, www.floridakeys.noaa.gov, 9am-4pm Tues.-Sat., free) features exhibits on the wildlife and environment of the Dry Tortugas area, including a living reef exhibit and a mock-up of an underwater research vessel.

SIGHTS

GARDEN KEY

The **Fort Jefferson Harbor Light** was established in 1825 and is still operational today. The lighthouse tower was erected in 1876 and is a favorite among photographers. It is northeast of the boat dock on Garden Key.

Near Garden Key, **Bush Key** and **Long Key** are both surrounded by tempting white-sand beaches. You can walk the beaches around Bush Key mid-October

Top 3

1 SNORKEL CORAL REEFS

Dry Tortugas has one of the richest coral communities in the Florida Keys. The warm, shallow waters boast a cornucopia of kaleidoscopic tropical fish, conch shells, lobster, sponges, sea fans, sea anemones, staghorn coral clusters, and the occasional sea turtle. On Garden Key, you can snorkel directly off **Fort Jefferson Beach,** in reef-protected waters, near the moat walls, and around the coaling dock ruins. Snorkeling gear is included for ferry riders; otherwise, bring your own.

FORT JEFFERSON

2 TOUR FORT JEFFERSON

Fort Jefferson (open daylight hours), the well-preserved six-sided fort on Garden Key, is the centerpiece of these remote islands. Nicknamed the "American Gibraltar," it was built in 1846 to control navigation strategically in the Gulf of Mexico, though construction was never completed. During and after the Civil War, it served as a Union-affiliated military prison. By the 1880s, the U.S. Army had abandoned the facility.

Within the fortified walls of the historic citadel are the officers' quarters, soldiers' barracks, cistern, magazines, and cannons. From November to May, parts of Fort Jefferson are closed to the public while mason crews work on much-needed preservation projects. An estimated 16 million red bricks were handmade for the fort. You can do a self-guided stroll through the fort or take a ranger tour.

MOAT AROUND FORT JEFFERSON

3 EXPLORE THE MOAT WALL

Built as added protection, 0.5 mile (0.8 km) of moat and moat wall surrounds Fort Jefferson. You can stroll portions of the moat wall for views of the water and the fort exterior or take a ranger tour on the moat wall. While no swimming is permitted in the moat, you can snorkel around outside portions of the moat wall. For a unique underwater experience, overnighters on the island snorkel the Moat Wall after dark to see nocturnal sea creatures (bring a light).

to mid-January, when they may be accessible via a land bridge. During the rest of the year, this key is closed to protect nesting sooty terns. Long Key is closed year-round for nesting birds and wildlife. With binoculars, you can view birds and wildlife on both even during closures.

LOGGERHEAD KEY

Accessible only by private boat or charter, **Loggerhead Key** features the **Loggerhead Lighthouse,** with the existing tower erected in 1858. The park is day use only with public pathways open to visitors, but all buildings are closed.

RECREATION

BIRD-WATCHING

Garden Key has excellent bird-watching. More than 200 varieties of birds are spotted annually, especially March-September when nearby **Bush Key** serves as the nesting ground for migratory birds (bring binoculars for viewing). April-May, more than 85,000 brown noddies and sooty terns nest on Bush Key. In spring, look for herons, raptors, and shorebirds; in summer, look for frigatebirds and mourning doves. The fall and winter months bring hawks, merlins, peregrine falcons, gulls, terns, American kestrels, and belted kingfishers. Other birds might include cormorants, masked boobies, black noddies, mangrove cuckoos, and white-crowned pigeons.

Sea-Clusive Charters (1107 Key Plaza, Ste. 315, Key West, 305/744-9928, www.seaclusive.com) features tailored excursions led by professional bird guide Larry Manfredi (www.southfloridabirding.com). While on board, you might also spot sharks, dolphins, and if you're lucky, gigantic sea turtles. The cruises can accommodate 8-11 passengers.

BOATING AND KAYAKING

Kayaking can be a wonderful way to experience the islands; however, the area is only suitable for experienced sea kayakers, as the currents can be very strong. By advanced reservation, you can bring kayaks aboard the ***Yankee Freedom*** (800/634-0939, www.drytortugas.com) ferry. Also bring a life vest, an anchor, a bailer, extra paddles, drinking water, waterproof bags for gear, and required safety equipment.

Garden Key and **Loggerhead Key** are both accessible by private boat, though docking on Garden Key can be problematic. It's best to anchor in the harbor and use a dinghy to reach the island's dinghy beach. Overnight anchoring is allowed between sunset and sunrise in the designated anchorage area with a sand-and-rubble bottom. On Loggerhead Key, the dock is only open to government vessels, but visitors are allowed to land south of the boathouse.

FISHING

Anglers can fish from the public dock on Garden Key and the beach west of the dock. (Fishing from a boat is only permitted within a 1-mile (1.6-km) radius of Garden Key.) Several local fishing charters operate multiday trips to the area; guides are allowed to fish in and around Dry Tortugas.

Contact charter companies for trips: **Andy Griffiths Charters** (6810 Front St., Stock Island, 305/296-2639, www.fishandy.com), **Dream Catcher Charters** (5555 College Rd., Key West, 305/292-7702 or 888/362-3474, www.dreamcatchercharters.com), or **Lethal**

CORAL

DIVING CORAL REEFS

Weapon Charters (245 Front St., Key West, 305/744-8225).

DIVING AND SNORKELING

Reefs and shipwrecks await snorkelers and divers. Off Loggerhead Island, snorkelers can see fish and coral in **Little Africa Reef** while divers can explore early 20th-century **Windjammer Wreck** (check with the park for current status of the mooring ball). Off Bird Key is the 19th-century **Bird Key Wreck** in 4-9 feet (1.2-2.7 m) of water. **Sea-Clusive Charters** (1107 Key Plaza, Ste. 315, Key West, 305/744-9928, www.seaclusive.com) offers multiday diving excursions.

WHERE TO STAY

INSIDE THE PARK

Dry Tortugas National Park has no public lodgings. Camping is the only option for overnighting on Garden Key. A short walk from the public dock leads to a primitive **campground** (10 sites and a shared overflow area, $15, first come, first served, 3 nights max.) with picnic tables, barbecue grills, and composting toilets. Campers must bring their own water, pack out all garbage, and make ferry reservations.

OUTSIDE THE PARK

Accommodations, restaurants, and services are available in **Key West.**

GETTING THERE AND AROUND

Travelers can reach Key West by flying into the **Key West International Airport** (EYW, 3491 S. Roosevelt Blvd., 305/809-5200, www.eyw.com). Dry Tortugas National Park lies approximately 70 miles (113 km) west of Key West and is only accessible by ferry or private boat from Key West.

Ferries and seaplanes access Garden Key, but not the other islands (personal boat, kayak, or canoe only). To reach Garden Key by ferry, schedule a day trip on the 100-foot (30-m) catamaran ***Yankee Freedom II*** (100 Grinnell St., 800/634-0939, www.drytortugas.com, 8am-5:30pm daily), which docks in the Historic Seaport at Key West Bight. Reservations are recommended and required for overnighting on Garden Key.

If traveling to Garden Key by private vessel (permit required), docking restrictions limit use of the public dock (closed 10am-3pm and sunset-sunrise). On Loggerhead Key, you can only land vessels south of the dock and boathouse.

ISLANDS

A handful of national parks lie isolated on remote U.S. islands. The Hawaiian Islands offer the easiest access for visitors. On the Big Island, lava leaps from the Kīlauea Crater at Hawai'i Volcanoes National Park. Maui's upcountry is the place to watch the day begin over the 10,023-foot (3,055-m) summit of Haleakalā Crater.

East of Puerto Rico, Virgin Islands National Park sits nestled in the Caribbean Sea. More than 60 percent of the island of St. John is national park, with sandy beaches, coral gardens, and peaceful hiking paths.

Hidden deep in the South Pacific, the National Park of American Samoa comprises a handful of tiny islands in the Samoan archipelago. Tenacious visitors can discover its treasures—unique rainforests, coral communities, and a traditional Samoan culture.

◂ HALEAKALĀ NATIONAL PARK, HAWAII

ISLANDS

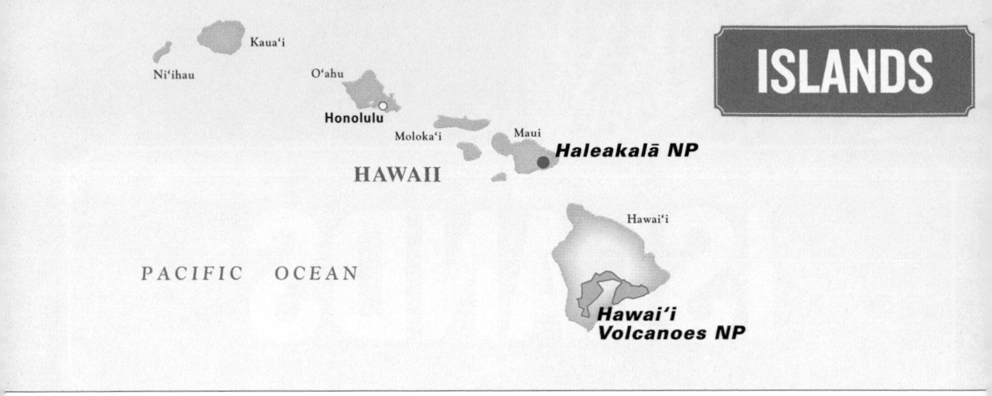

Kaua'i
Ni'ihau
O'ahu
Honolulu
Moloka'i
Maui
Haleakalā NP
HAWAII
Hawai'i
PACIFIC OCEAN
Hawai'i Volcanoes NP

National Park of American Samoa
Tutuila
Ofu
Ta'ü
Pago Pago
AMERICAN SAMOA
PACIFIC OCEAN

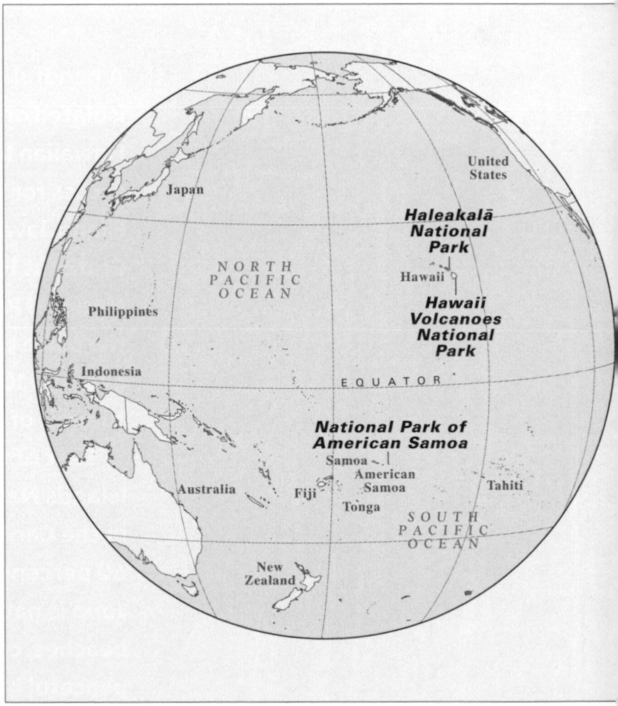

United States
Japan
Haleakalā National Park
NORTH PACIFIC OCEAN
Hawaii
Hawaii Volcanoes National Park
Philippines
Indonesia
EQUATOR
National Park of American Samoa
Samoa
American Samoa
Australia
Fiji
Tonga
Tahiti
SOUTH PACIFIC OCEAN
New Zealand

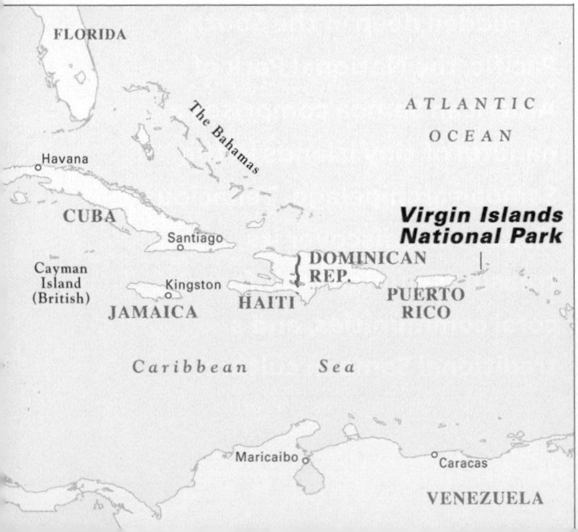

FLORIDA
The Bahamas
ATLANTIC OCEAN
Havana
CUBA
Santiago
Virgin Islands National Park
Cayman Island (British)
Kingston
DOMINICAN REP.
JAMAICA
HAITI
PUERTO RICO
Caribbean Sea
Maricaibo
Caracas
VENEZUELA

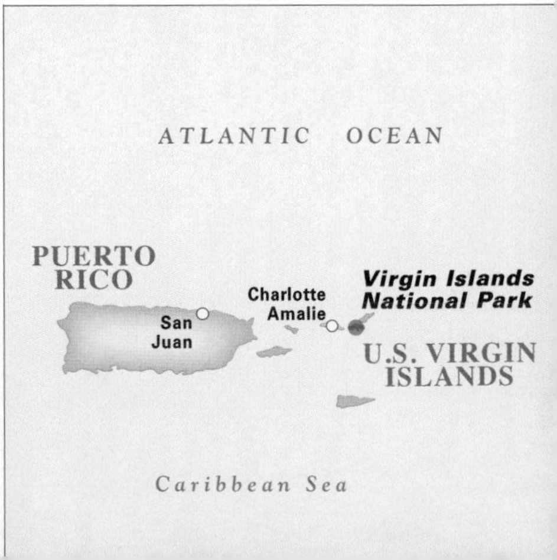

ATLANTIC OCEAN
PUERTO RICO
Virgin Islands National Park
Charlotte Amalie
San Juan
U.S. VIRGIN ISLANDS
Caribbean Sea

The National Park ISLANDS

HALEAKALĀ, MAUI

Most visitors go to Haleakalā for sunrise, but there are also trails that tour the colorful crater and a portion of the park that spills to the coast at Kīpahulu (page 685).

HAWAI'I VOLCANOES, HAWAI'I

The 13,679-foot (4,169-m) summit of Mauna Loa looms above the shorter Kīlauea, an active volcano in the process of building new land (page 695).

VIRGIN ISLANDS

Surrounded by turquoise seas, the island of St. John includes historic plantations, snorkeling beaches, boating, and opportunities for hiking amid tropical forests (page 705).

AMERICAN SAMOA

This tropical paradise has rainforest hiking trails, sandy beaches, coral reefs for snorkeling, and the customs of the 3,000-year-old Samoan culture (page 714).

1: THE SUMMIT AREA, HALEAKALĀ, MAUI
2: HIKING IN HAWAI'I VOLCANOES, HAWAI'I
3: FOUREYE BUTTERFLYFISH, VIRGIN ISLANDS

Best OF THE ISLANDS

Sunrise over Haleakalā: Watch the sun come up and then spend the day hiking across the crater floor (page 689).

Crater Rim Drive: See the volcanic forces that created the Hawaiian archipelago (pages 699 and 704).

Trunk Bay: Lounge under coconut palms on this white-sand beach flanking clear, turquoise water for snorkeling (page 709).

Vai'ava Strait: One of American Samoa's National Natural Landmarks was created by volcanoes (page 718).

PLANNING YOUR TRIP

HAWAI'I

Hawai'i Volcanoes is located on the Big Island of Hawai'i, while Haleakalā is on the island of Maui. Both islands have airports.

The prime tourist season for the Hawaiian Islands starts two weeks before **Christmas** and lasts until **Easter.** It picks up again in early June and ends in late August. Everything is heavily booked, and prices are higher. Hotel, airline, and car reservations are a must. You can generally save money and avoid a lot of hassle if you travel in the off-season (September-early December and late-April-late May). Hurricane season is June-November.

VIRGIN ISLANDS

There are no airports on St. John. Travelers must fly into St. Thomas Cyril E. King Airport on Charlotte Amalie and then take a car barge or ferry to St. John.

December-March is the dry season with the best sailing winds and most comfortable temperatures. However, the island sees its highest number of visitors April-June, August, and October-December.

Hurricane season runs June-November with the peak from August to October.

AMERICAN SAMOA

Tutuila Island has the only international airport. All visitors must have a valid passport, a return ticket, and confirmation of funds. A visa may be required. **October-May** is the monsoon season with tropical storms, but that's also when there are the most visitors (Mar.-May, Oct.-Nov.). Go June-September for cooler, drier weather.

▲ TRUNK BAY, VIRGIN ISLANDS

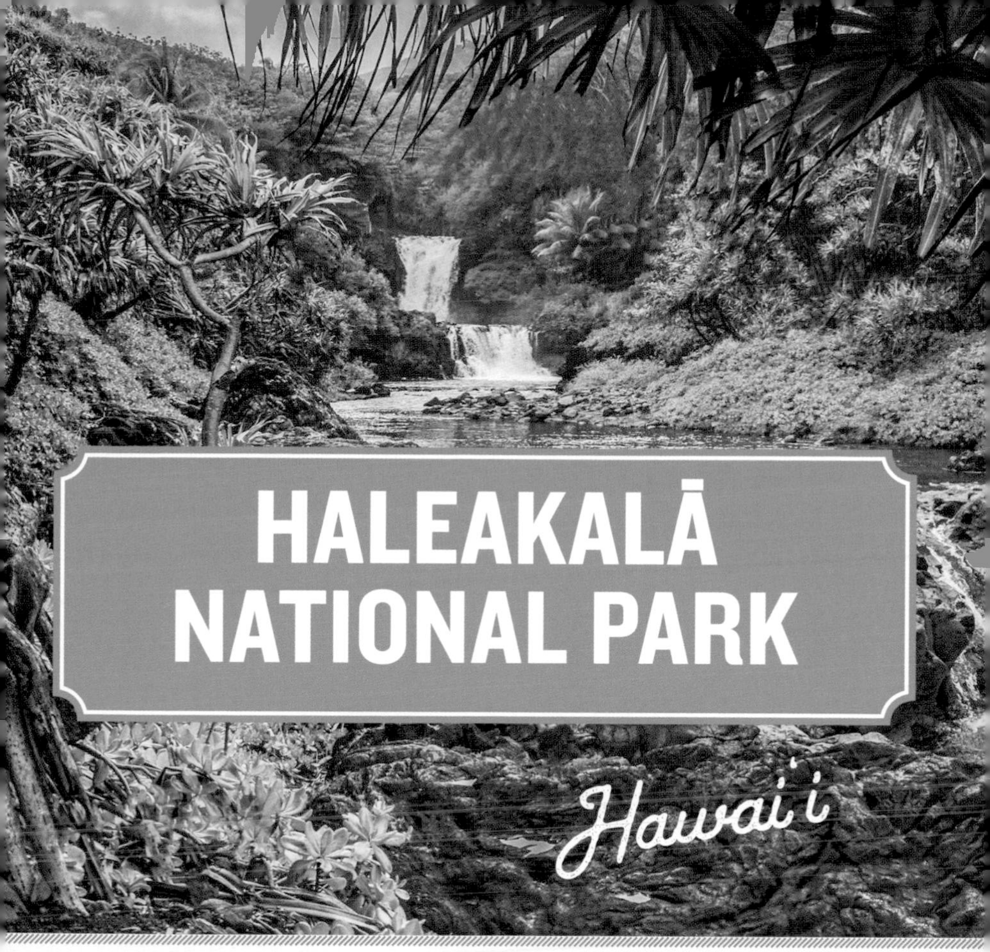

HALEAKALĀ NATIONAL PARK

Hawai'i

KEEPSAKE STAMPS ▼▼▼

WEBSITE:
www.nps.gov/hale

PHONE NUMBER:
808/572-4400

VISITATION RANK:
26

WHY GO:
Watch the sun rise over a volcanic summit.

▲ OHÈO IN HANA, HALEAKALĀ NATIONAL PARK

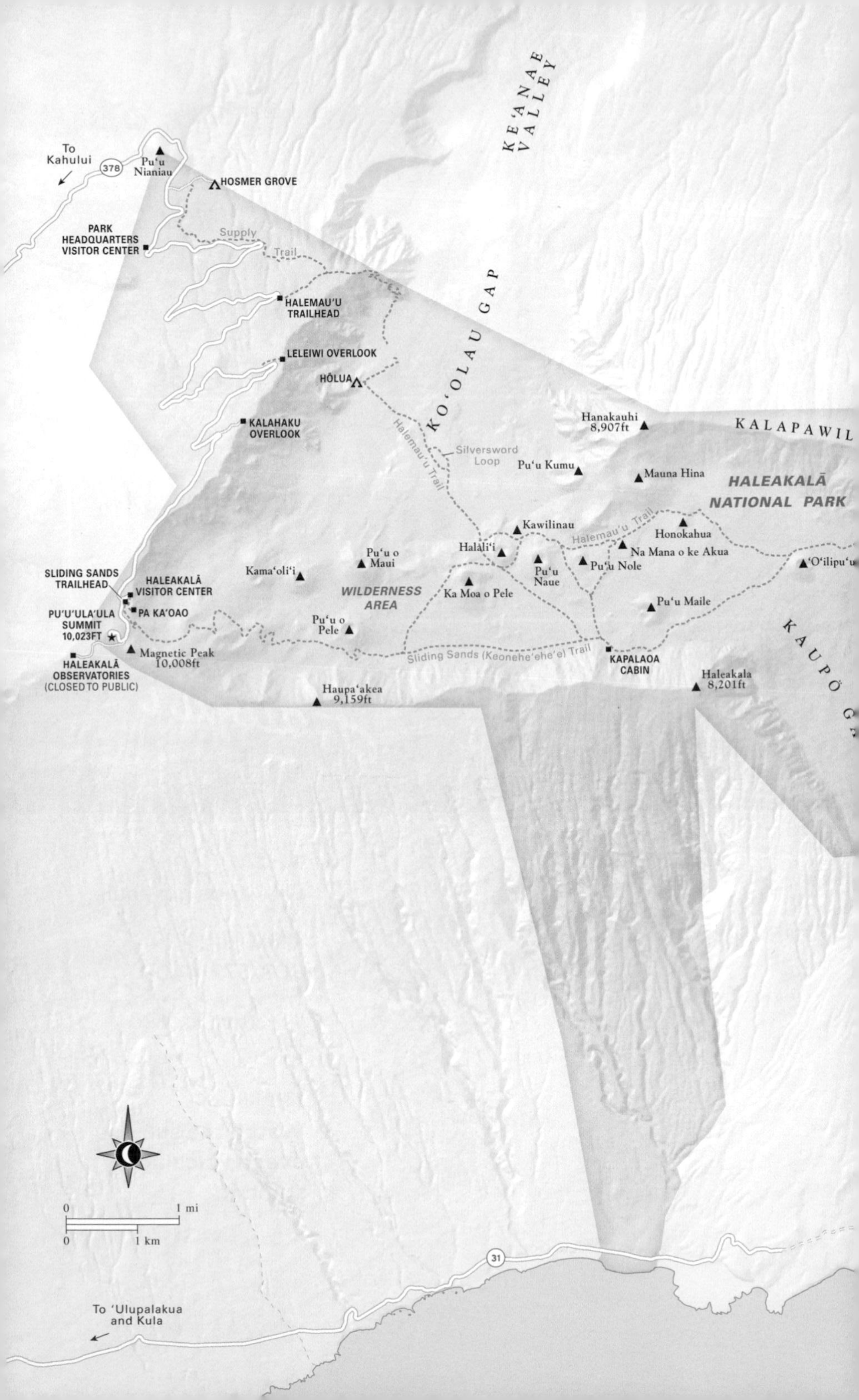

KE'ANAE VALLEY
To Kahului
378
Pu'u Nianiau
HOSMER GROVE
PARK HEADQUARTERS VISITOR CENTER
Supply Trail
HALEMAU'U TRAILHEAD
KO'OLAU GAP
LELEIWI OVERLOOK
HŌLUA
KALAHAKU OVERLOOK
Halemau'u Trail
Silversword Loop
Hanakauhi 8,907ft
KALAPAWIL
Pu'u Kumu
Mauna Hina
HALEAKALĀ NATIONAL PARK
Kawilinau
Halemau'u Trail
Honokahua
Halāli'i
Na Mana o ke Akua
Pu'u o Maui
Pu'u Naue
Pu'u Nole
'O'ilipu'u
Kama'oli'i
SLIDING SANDS TRAILHEAD
HALEAKALĀ VISITOR CENTER
WILDERNESS AREA
Ka Moa o Pele
PA KA'OAO
PU'U'ULA'ULA SUMMIT 10,023FT
Pu'u Maile
KAUPŌ G
Pu'u o Pele
Magnetic Peak 10,008ft
Sliding Sands (Keonehe'ehe'e) Trail
KAPALAOA CABIN
HALEAKALĀ OBSERVATORIES (CLOSED TO PUBLIC)
Haleakala 8,201ft
Haupa'akea 9,159ft
0
1 mi
0
1 km
31
To 'Ulupalakua and Kula

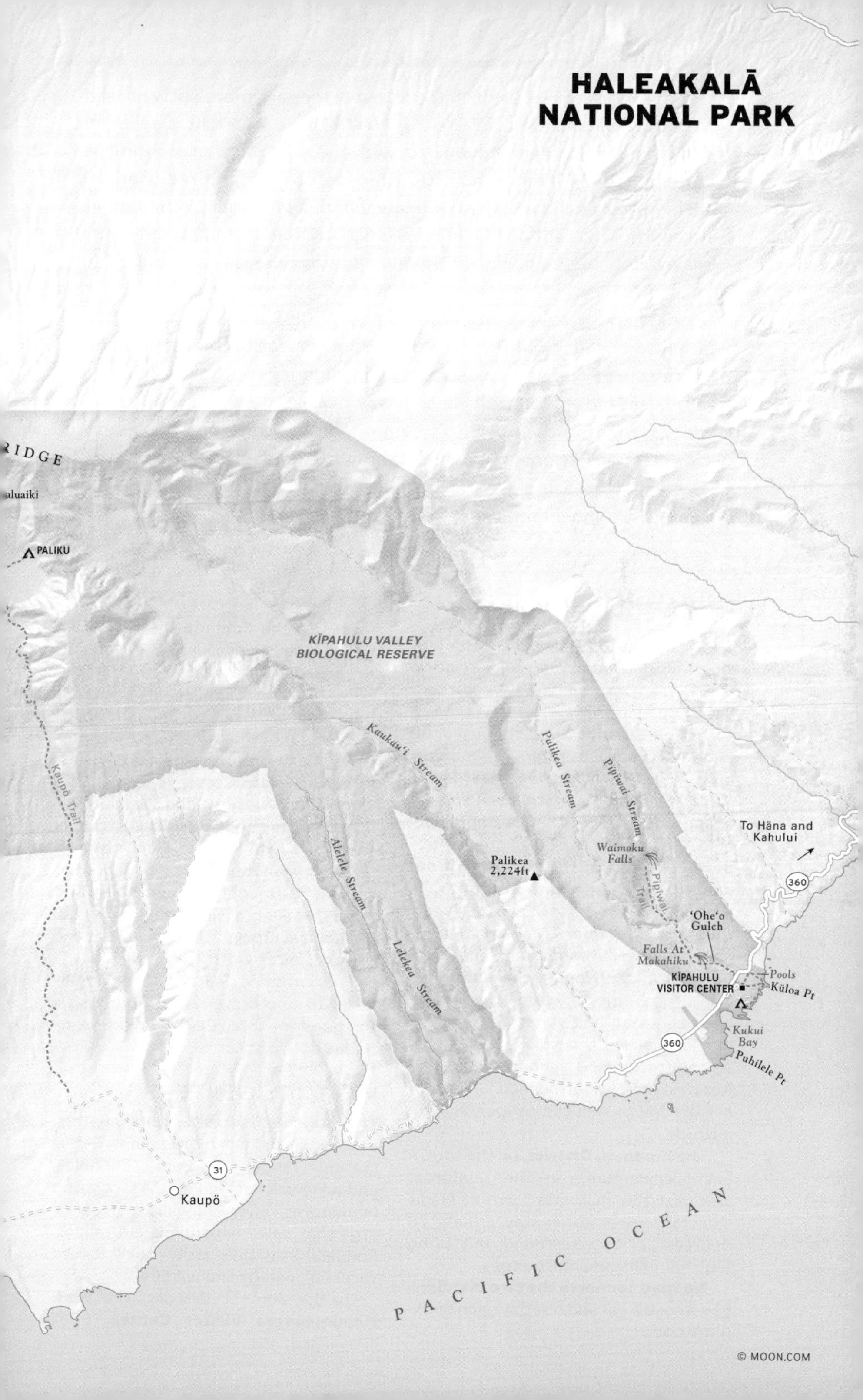

HALEAKALĀ NATIONAL PARK
RIDGE
aluaiki
PALIKU
KĪPAHULU VALLEY BIOLOGICAL RESERVE
Kaukau'i Stream
Palikea Stream
Pīpīwai Stream
Kaupō Trail
Alelele Stream
Lelekea Stream
Palikea 2,224ft
Waimoku Falls
Pīpīwai Trail
To Hāna and Kahului
360
'Ohe'o Gulch
Falls At Makahiku
Pools
KĪPAHULU VISITOR CENTER
Kūloa Pt
Kukui Bay
Puhilele Pt
31
Kaupō
PACIFIC OCEAN
© MOON.COM

"Hale-a-ka-la..." House of the Sun: few places are more aptly named than this volcano in **HALEAKALĀ NATIONAL PARK.** It is believed to have been dormant since 1790, with the summit area around the crater inactive for more than 300 years before that, yet radiocarbon dating recorded use by Native Hawaiians even earlier. When measured from the seafloor, Haleakalā is 30,000 feet (9,144 m) tall—surpassed only by the peaks on the Big Island as the tallest mountains on earth.

Views plunge from the crater's seemingly barren volcanic rock down to the lush rainforest. On the high-elevation pumice slopes, graceful and fragile silversword maintains its foothold while the rainforest hides waterfalls and glassy pools. The most popular activity is visiting the volcano's summit for sunrise—but there's far more to this national park than simply the light of dawn. The sunsets and stargazing are just as spectacular. Any time of day, the mountain's sheer immensity provokes awe.

PLANNING YOUR TIME

Two sections of Haleakalā commandeer Maui's southesast. Peak visitation (Feb.-Sept., Dec.) splits between them based on seasonal weather. The more accessible **Summit District** houses the famous Haleakalā Crater. The summit of Haleakalā is 20-30 degrees cooler (12-18°C) than the warm and tropical coast, and the weather is unpredictable. You can leave an 80-degree (27°C) beach to arrive at the crater in 50-degree (10°C) weather with wind and rain.

Rain and even snow can fall year-round, but **summer** (May-Sept.) typically sees better conditions. There are **no visitor services at the summit**—bring food, drinks, warm layers, sunglasses, a hat, and sunscreen. At this high elevation, the solar radiation is strong, prompting sunburns, and visitors may feel light-headed or out of breath due to reduced oxygen at high altitude.

The **Kīpahulu District,** on the southeast coast, tucks in the rainforest just past the charming town of Hana. Coastal temperatures stay around 70 degrees (21°C) year-round, but bring high humidity and mosquitoes.

No road connects the two districts; you'll need a car and one day each to explore both.

ENTRANCES AND FEES

Access to the **Summit District** is via HI 378 (open year-round), a paved and curvy road; severe weather may temporarily close the road. The entrance station is located prior to the park headquarters and the turnoff to Hosmer Grove Campground. The Park Headquarters Visitor Center is less than 1 mile (1.6 km) farther along the road.

Access to the **Kīpahulu District** is via HI 360 (the Road to Hana) and HI 31 (open year-round). The paved Road to Hana is fraught with potholes and bumps, making it very rough to drive. The official Kīpahulu entrance is at the visitors center.

The entrance fee is $30 per vehicle ($25 motorcycle, $15 individual) and good for three days. Admission includes both districts.

VISITORS CENTERS

The park has three visitors centers. They each have exhibits, maps, information, ranger program schedules, and a Hawaii Pacific Parks Association bookstore (www.hawaiipacificparks.org) that sells maps and field guides. Rangers also give daily talks (times vary) on geology and wildlife.

In the Summit District, the **Park Headquarters Visitor Center** (808/

Top 3

SUNRISE PEEKING UP OVER THE CRATER WALLS OF HALEAKALĀ NATIONAL PARK

1 WATCH SUNRISE FROM HALEAKALĀ CRATER

A Haleakalā sunrise is a unique experience. But it requires advance planning, **reservations** (877/444-6777, www.recreation.gov, $1 per vehicle), and waking up at 2-3am.

The biggest crowds go for the highest point at **Pu'u 'Ula'ula** (Red Hill) at a glass-sided observation area (open 24/7) on the official summit of Haleakalā (10,023 ft./3,055 m). **Haleakalā Visitor Center** (9,740 ft./2,969 m) is the second-highest viewing point. Two lower-elevation viewpoints offer less crowded alternatives: **Leleiwi Overlook** (8,840 ft./2,694 m) and **Kalahaku Overlook** (9,324 ft./2,842 m, only accessible downhill).

Most mornings are clear enough to see the sunrise over the crater. But call the **Hotline for Haleakalā Summit** (808/944-5025, ext. 4) for current conditions. Bring warm clothes for the near or below freezing temperatures and beach chairs for sitting. The reservation allows Summit District access between 3am and 7am. Reservations are not required after 7am.

2 DRIVE UP THE VOLCANO

The sheer climb up **Haleakalā Road** (HI 378, 10 mi./16.1 km) wows with each curve from the park entrance to the summit as the air thins with elevation. At **Leleiwi Overlook** (mile marker 17.5, 8,840 ft./2,694 m), walk to see the massive crater from this vantage point (0.5 mi./0.8 km rt., 20 min., moderate). You'll peer down at the huge floor and sheer multihued cliffs. At **Kalahaku Overlook** (mile marker 18.7, 9,324 ft./2,842 m), view the crater from the interpretive observation platform. The road terminates at the summit and **Haleakalā Visitor Center,** where a slow meander at altitude is needed to climb to the highest point in the park at 10,023 feet (3,055 m).

3 FIND PARADISE AT THE POOLS OF 'OHE'O

The **Pools of 'Ohe'o** (near the Kīpahulu Visitor Center) in 'Ohe'o Gulch are the stuff of a dreamy paradise. Tucked in the rainforest, waterfalls drop into placid pools. Also called the Seven Sacred Pools (there are actually more), they are closed to swimming, but you can still enjoy their serenity.

Walk the **Kuloa Point Trail** (0.5 mi./0.8 km rt., 30 min., easy) that loops past the famed pools, taking in the ocean views and archaeological sites. Access to the pools may close periodically. Stop at the visitors center first for updates.

THE POOLS OF 'OHE'O

THE KIPAHULU COAST

572-4459, 8am-4pm daily), located at an elevation of 7,000 feet (2,134 m), has backcountry camping permits and is the place to inquire about sunrise-viewing reservations at the summit.

Also in the Summit District, the **Haleakalā Visitor Center** (sunrise-noon daily) is located at 9,740 feet (2,969 m), 10 miles (16.1 km) up the park road from the Park Headquarters Visitor Center. Geology exhibits detail the history of the volcano. A ranger-guided walk takes place most days (10am and 11am). From the parking lot, take in the short **Pa Ka'oao Trail** (0.4 mi./0.6 km rt, 20 min., moderate) with views toward the crater.

AVOID THE CROWDS

Sunset at Haleakalā is nearly as colorful as sunrise, but without all the crowds: There are often only 20 people instead of 400, and it isn't as cold. The lava rock ridge just in front of the parking area is the best place to watch the sunset. If you can't see the mountain from below, don't bother driving up.

The **Kīpahulu Visitor Center** (808/248-7375, 9:30am-5pm daily) is on the coast in the southeast portion of the park. Exhibits offer insights into the Hawaiian culture.

RECREATION

HIKING

Hike Maui (808/784-7982, www.hikemaui.com) is the only company that offers commercially guided hiking tours in the park, both at the summit and at Kīpahulu.

Summit District

The **Hosmer Grove Nature Trail** (0.5 mi./0.8 km rt., 30 min., easy) is at the park's lower boundary just after the entrance. The short trail loops through a dense grove of sweet-smelling pine and fir. To extend the trip, hike the **Supply Trail** (4.6 mi./7.4 km rt., 3 hrs., strenuous) to the crater rim. To reach the trailhead, turn left on the road toward the campground.

The Haleakalā Crater is a vast wilderness with Maui's best hiking. Temperatures can range 30-80°F (-1-27°C) over the course of a single day and the high elevation (7,000-10,000 ft./2,134-3,048 m) can tax lungs.

TRAILS CROSS VOLCANIC CINDER VALLEYS.

For a more oxygenated excursion at 7,990 feet (2,435 m), the **Halemau'u Trail** (7.5 mi./12.1 km rt., 4-5 hrs., strenuous) meanders through scrub brush before reaching the edge of a giant cliff. The view down into the Ko'olau Gap, where the volcano exploded outward, is better than from the summit. Although the 1,000-foot (305-m) descent on the switchbacked trail is well defined, the drop-offs can be disconcerting. The trail reaches Holua Cabin, where you need a permit to camp overnight before climbing out.

In the thin air of 9,800 feet (2,987 m) at the summit visitors center, the **Keonehe'ehe'e Trail** (8 mi./12.9 km rt., 4-5 hrs., strenuous) descends to the crater floor. This barren and windswept trail is without shade, and with a 2,500-foot (762 m) elevation loss, but it's a stunning conduit to the cinder cones. The rough part comes with the grunt at altitude back up to the visitors center.

Kīpahulu District

The **Pipiwai Trail** (4 mi./6.4 km rt., 2 hrs., moderate) follows boardwalks and footbridges through the rainforest, lending an adventurous feel. The last 0.5 mile (0.8 km) winds through bamboo so thick it blocks out the sun. Just when you think it couldn't get any more tropical, the path emerges at the base of ribbonlike 400-foot (122-m) Waimoku Falls. Plan to camp overnight at the Kīpahulu Campground to hit the trail before the day-trippers arrive. The trailhead is at mile marker 41.7 on the Road to Hana.

SILVERSWORD

Best Hike

SLIDING SANDS SWITCHBACK LOOP

DISTANCE: 12.2 miles (19.6 km) round-trip
DURATION: 7-8 hours
ELEVATION CHANGE: 1,000-2,500 feet (305-762 m)
EFFORT: strenuous
TRAILHEAD: Halemauʻu

The **Sliding Sands Switchback Loop** combines the best segments of hiking inside the crater of Haleakalā. Park at the Halemauʻu trailhead, then hitch a ride to the top to hike down to the crater floor on the Sliding Sands Trail. Follow the signs toward Holua Cabin and the Halemauʻu Trail, where a leg-burning, switchbacking, 1,000-foot (305-m) grind ascends back to the car.

Native Hawaiian guides lead cultural interpretive hikes through the **Kipahula ʻOhana** (Hana, 808/281-2021, http://kipahulu.org, 2 hrs. $49, 3.5 hrs. $79, reservations required), a living farm and traditional wetland growing taro inside the park. Sample foods such as poi, breadfruit, and bananas. The hike also takes in historic sites and the Pools of ʻOhe'o.

BACKPACKING

Backcountry campsites require a permit (free) from the Park Headquarters Visitor Center. The Holua campsite is accessible via a 3.7-mile (6-km) hike down Halemauʻu Trail, while the Paliku campsite requires hiking 9.3 miles (15 km) from the Sliding Sands Trail at the summit. The Holua campsite is cold and dry; the Paliku campsite is a few degrees warmer and set in a lush forest.

Three **backcountry cabins** are available at Holua, Kapalaoa, and Paliku and have basic cooking facilities and bunk beds. Reservations (877/444-6777, www.recreation.gov, $75) are required about six months in advance.

WATERFALLS ALONG THE PIPIWAI TRAIL

BIKING

Watching the day begin from Haleakalā Crater, followed by feeling the crisp air in your face as you weave through cow-speckled pastures via bicycle, is full of adrenaline magic. To bike from the summit, you must make **advance reservations** for sunrise access and provide **your own bicycle and transportation.**

Bike tours down Haleakalā start at 6,500 feet (1,981 m), outside the national park. If you want to include sunrise at Haleakalā Crater, that means waking up early, with pickups at 2am. (After watching the sun rise, it's back in the van for the drive down to the bike start.) Tours without sunrise usually visit the summit at around 10am and then descend to the start of the bike tour.

To rent a bike or book a tour, contact **Maui Sunriders** (71 Baldwin Ave., Paiʻa, 808/579-8970, www.mauisunriders.com) or **Haleakalā Bike Company** (810

ONE DAY IN HALEAKALĀ

With only one day, aim to drive to the **summit of Haleakalā**. On the road between the Park Headquarters and Haleakalā Summit Visitor Centers, stop to admire the views from roadside overlooks. At the summit, you can stroll to the highest point in the park at 10,023 feet. With advance planning, you can book a reservation to **watch the sunrise** from the summit.

Ha'iku Rd., Ste. 120, Haiku, 808/575-9575, www.bikemaui.com).

STARGAZING

Haleakalā's elevation and lack of light pollution make the summit a prime location for stargazing. Bring a pair of binoculars or rent them from a local dive shop. Star maps, available at the Haleakalā visitors centers, can help you identify the constellations. Nights can be cold on the summit; bring layers to stay warm.

To observe the night sky through big telescopes with astronomy experts, book a tour with **Maui Stargazing** (808/298-8245, www.mauistargazing.com). The four-hour tour starts at sunset. Their scopes are big enough to see deep-space celestial objects. As a bonus, they bring outerwear and hot chocolate to keep you warm.

BIRD-WATCHING

One of the best bird-watching places is at **Hosmer Grove** on the loop trail. Even if you don't see native honeycreepers (birds whose bills have adapted to extract nectar from native plant species), the treetops chirp with birdsong different from anywhere else on the planet.

Higher up toward the summit, bird-watchers should look for two endangered species: the 'u'au (Hawaiian petrel), which burrows in areas near the **summit visitors center**, and the

VIEW FROM HALEAKALĀ SUMMIT

nene (Hawaiian goose), which can be spotted along park roadways and the valley floor. The nene is Hawaii's state bird, and one of the best places to spot it is in the grasslands surrounding **Paliku Cabin.**

WHERE TO STAY

INSIDE THE PARK

The park has two first-come, first-served campgrounds. Each has picnic tables, barbecue grills, and pit toilets. Camping fees are included in the park entrance fee.

The more accessible is **Hosmer Grove Campground** (drinking water available) at 6,800 feet (2,072 m) in the Summit District. Its grassy sites can pack in up to 50 campers. Nights can get close to freezing, but it makes a great staging ground for driving to the summit for sunrise.

Some of Maui's best camping is on the coast at the **Kīpahulu Campground** (drinking water available at the visitors center). The grassy campsites can fit up to 100 people; the best sites are hidden beneath lauhala trees on the trail leading toward the pools.

OUTSIDE THE PARK

Most accommodations in **Makawao, Pai'a,** and **Kula** are conveniently located within an hour's drive of Haleakalā summit. Near the Kīpahulu coast, the closest services are in **Hana.**

GETTING THERE AND AROUND

AIR

Kahului Airport (OGG, 1 Kahului Airport Rd., 808/872-3830, www.airports.hawaii.gov) has direct flights from a host of mainland cities. Car rentals are at the airport.

CAR

To reach the Summit District from Kahului, take HI 37 to HI 377 where it meets HI 378. The Summit District of Haleakalā National Park is located at the end of HI 378. The curvy drive has multiple switchbacks and will take

WILDFLOWERS

about 2.5-3 hours to reach the summit. The last gas en route is in Pukalani.

To reach the coastal Kīpahulu District, you'll have to drive the Road to Hana. From Kahului, take HI 36 to HI 37, then to HI 31. Kīpahulu is 11 miles (18 km) past Hana. The narrow, curvy, and partially unpaved drive will take approximately four hours one-way. Fill up on gas before you go; the last gas on the way to Hana is in Pai'a. Plan to depart Hana early in the day so that you won't be driving the rough road in the dark.

There is no public transit—and no gas station—within the park.

TOURS

Several tour companies guide trips to Haleakalā summit for sunrise, sunset, or daytime visits, as well as excursions on the Road to Hana and to Kīpahulu. Vehicles range from buses to minivans, and all tours include narration. The following guide companies are licensed in the park: **Polynesian Adventures** (888/206-4531, www.polyad.com), **Temptation Tours** (800/817-1234 or 808/877-8888, www.temptationtours.com), **Roberts Hawaii** (808/425-9861, www.robertshawaii.com), and **Valley Isle Excursions** (808/871-5224, www.tourmaui.com).

HAWAI'I VOLCANOES NATIONAL PARK

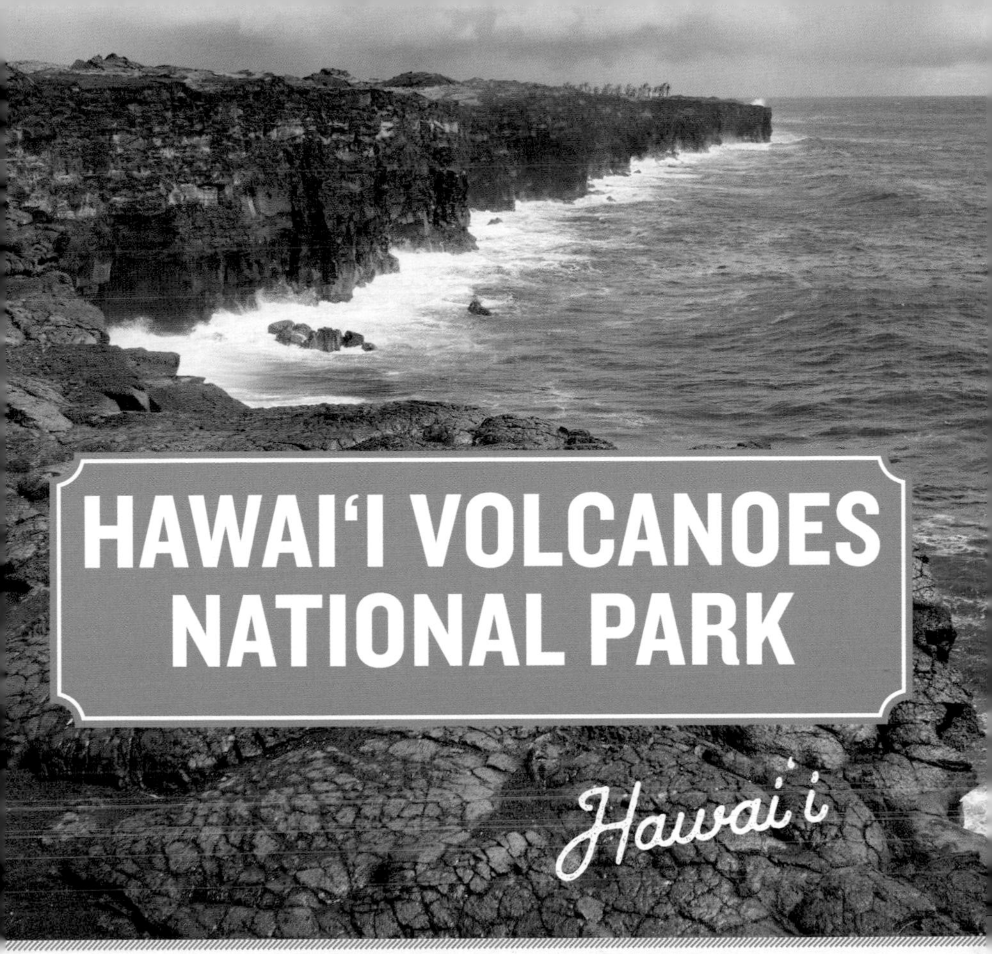

KEEPSAKE STAMPS ▼▼▼

WEBSITE:
www.nps.gov/havo

PHONE NUMBER:
808/985-6101

VISITATION RANK:
21

WHY GO:
Watch a volcano in action.

▲ HAWAI'I VOLCANOES NATIONAL PARK

HAWAI'I VOLCANOES NATIONAL PARK

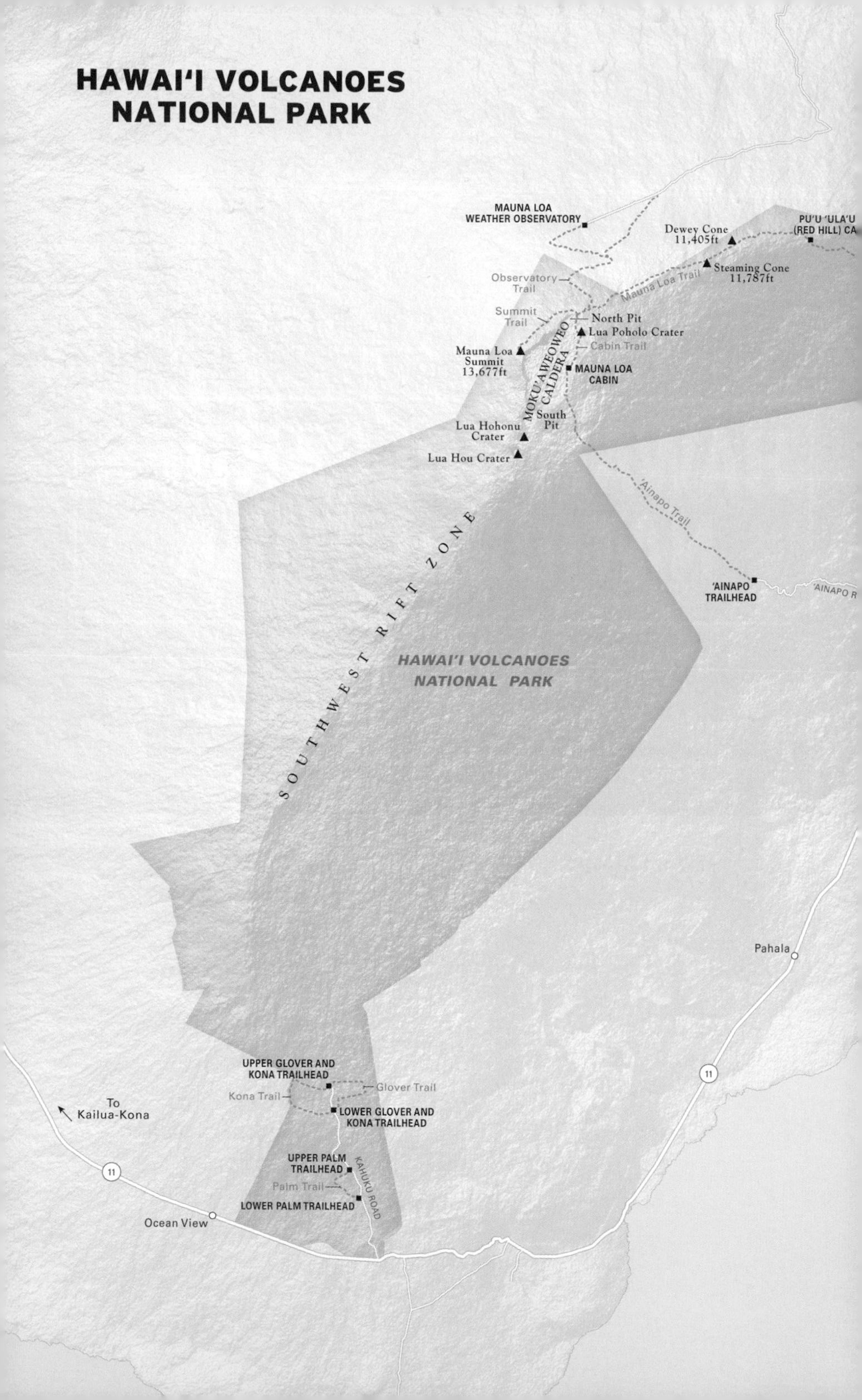

MAUNA LOA WEATHER OBSERVATORY
Dewey Cone 11,405ft
PU'U 'ULA'U (RED HILL) CA
Steaming Cone 11,787ft
Mauna Loa Trail
Observatory Trail
Summit Trail
North Pit
Lua Poholo Crater
Cabin Trail
Mauna Loa Summit 13,677ft
MOKU'AWEOWEO CALDERA
MAUNA LOA CABIN
South Pit
Lua Hohonu Crater
Lua Hou Crater
'Ainapo Trail
'AINAPO TRAILHEAD
'AINAPO R
SOUTHWEST RIFT ZONE
HAWAI'I VOLCANOES NATIONAL PARK
Pahala
11
UPPER GLOVER AND KONA TRAILHEAD
Glover Trail
Kona Trail
LOWER GLOVER AND KONA TRAILHEAD
To Kailua-Kona
UPPER PALM TRAILHEAD
KAHUKU ROAD
Palm Trail
LOWER PALM TRAILHEAD
11
Ocean View

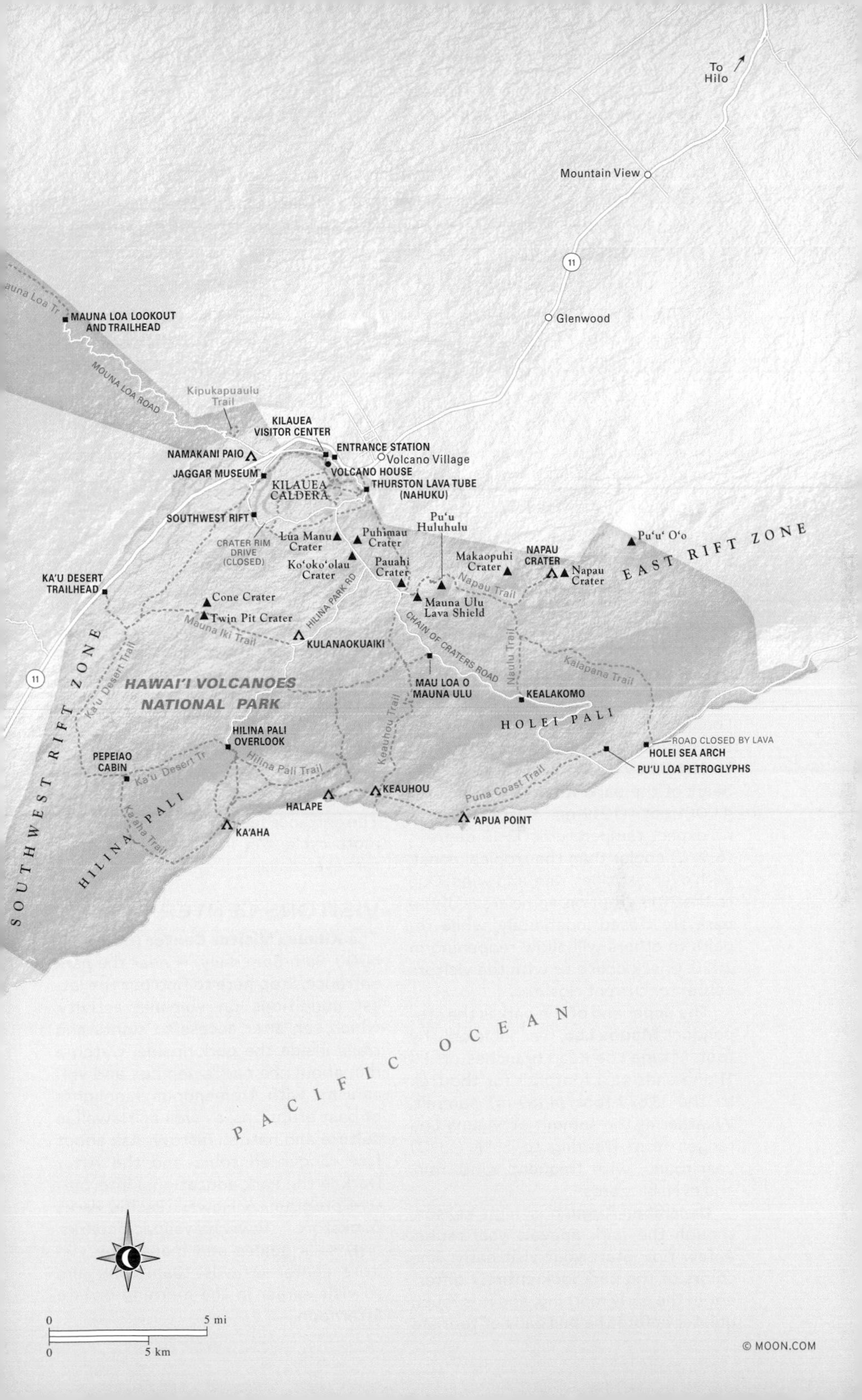

To Hilo
Mountain View
11
Glenwood
Mauna Loa Tr
MAUNA LOA LOOKOUT AND TRAILHEAD
MOUNA LOA ROAD
Kipukapuaulu Trail
KILAUEA VISITOR CENTER
ENTRANCE STATION
NAMAKANI PAIO
Volcano Village
VOLCANO HOUSE
JAGGAR MUSEUM
KILAUEA CALDERA
THURSTON LAVA TUBE (NAHUKU)
SOUTHWEST RIFT
CRATER RIM DRIVE (CLOSED)
Lua Manu Crater
Puhimau Crater
Pu'u Huluhulu
Pu'u' O'o
EAST RIFT ZONE
Ko'oko'olau Crater
Pauahi Crater
Makaopuhi Crater
NAPAU CRATER
Napau Crater
Napau Trail
KA'U DESERT TRAILHEAD
Cone Crater
Twin Pit Crater
HILINA PARK RD
Mauna Ulu Lava Shield
Mauna Iki Trail
KULANAOKUAIKI
CHAIN OF CRATERS ROAD
Naulu Trail
Kalapana Trail
SOUTHWEST RIFT ZONE
Ka'u Desert Trail
HAWAI'I VOLCANOES NATIONAL PARK
MAU LOA O MAUNA ULU
KEALAKOMO
HOLEI PALI
Keauhou Trail
HILINA PALI OVERLOOK
ROAD CLOSED BY LAVA
HOLEI SEA ARCH
PEPEIAO CABIN
Hilina Pali Trail
PU'U LOA PETROGLYPHS
Ka'u Desert Tr
Puna Coast Trail
KEAUHOU
HALAPE
HILINA PALI
Ka'aha Trail
KA'AHA
'APUA POINT
PACIFIC OCEAN
0
5 mi
0
5 km
© MOON.COM

This volcanic landscape fumes steam, pumps sulfur, seethes lava, and lights up a fiery display like something out of Dante's *Inferno.* Viewed from the crater's rim, Kīlauea's volcanic activity shows the birthing process of the still-growing Hawaiian Islands. High above Kīlauea, the behemoth Mauna Loa is the largest active volcano on earth. Together, they make up **HAWAI'I VOLCANOES NATIONAL PARK.**

Because of its scientific and scenic value, the park has also been named an International Biosphere Reserve and a World Heritage Site, giving it international prestige. It became newsworthy as well in 2018, when Kīlauea erupted, ramping up its activity to historically devastating levels. Molten lava broke free from fresh cracks in the earth and flowed into local neighborhoods, destroying more than 700 homes. Accompanying earthquakes ravaged park roads, buildings, and trails. Today, many of these have been repaired and reopened, but the landscape of the park has changed forever. For many Native Hawaiians, this was not a surprising development. Living with Pele, the primordial force of the volcanoes, is part of their lives, their culture, and their history.

PLANNING YOUR TIME

Located on the Big Island of Hawaii, the park extends north and south off HI 11. Most visitors head south for the heart of the park: **Kīlauea Caldera.** At 4,000-foot (1,219-m) Kīlauea Caldera, expect temperatures 12-15 degrees (6-9°C) cooler than the tropical coast, with overcast skies, rain, and wind. Due to the 2018 eruption, some areas of the park are closed indefinitely, while repairs to others will allow reopening in 2020. Check online or with the visitors center for current closures.

The upper end of the park is the stupendous **Mauna Loa,** reachable only by foot. Mauna Loa Road branches off HI 11 and ends at a footpath for the trek to the 13,679-foot (4,169-m) summit. Weather at the summit of Mauna Loa ranges from freezing to 55°F (13°C) year-round, with frequent wind, rain, and even blizzards.

December-August is high season, though the park appeals year-round. A few tips: Start your visit early. The colors of the park look entirely different in the early morning, and it is much quieter before the busloads of tourists arrive. Also, pack a lunch; services within the park are minimal.

ENTRANCE AND FEES

The park entrance is on **HI 11** (near mile marker 28), west of Volcano Village. The entrance fee is $30 per vehicle ($25 motorcycle, $15 individual) and good for seven days.

VISITORS CENTER

The **Kīlauea Visitor Center** (808/985-6000, 9am-5pm daily) is near the park entrance. Stop here to find out the latest conditions on volcanic activity, which can alter access to sights and trails inside the park. Inside, watch a film about the park's geology and volcanism, with tremendous highlights of past eruptions, as well as Hawaiian culture and natural history. Ask about free ranger-led tours and the After Dark in the Park educational interpretive program. A Hawai'i Pacific Parks bookstore (www.hawaiipacificparks.org) sells guides and maps. The visitors center crowds 10am-2pm; aim to visit earlier in the morning or late afternoon.

Top 3

1 VIEW KĪLAUEA CALDERA

KĪLAUEA CRATER PLUMES

Continuously active since 1983, the huge **Kīlauea Caldera** and its collection of smaller craters dominate the heart of the park. It's an ever-changing otherworldly landscape. During the 2018 eruption, Halema'uma'u Crater changed: its lava lake drained, the crater collapsed, and now it is refilling with water. While the 2018 eruption has subsided, the rumbling volcano still steams and sputters lava, which is best viewed at night from Steaming Bluff on the Crater Rim Trail just east of Steam Vents. See the caldera from overlooks on Crater Rim Drive or the Crater Rim Trail.

2 GAZE OUT FROM MAUNA LOA

At 60 miles (97 km) long and 30 miles (48 km) wide, snowcapped Mauna Loa (13,679 ft./4,169 m) occupies the entire southern half of the Big Island. The summit of Mauna Loa contains the giant **Moku'aweoweo Caldera.** Visitors can drive up the 11-mile (18 km) **Mauna Loa Road** to a lookout at 6,600 feet (2,012 m), but only hikers can reach the summit. This remote mountaintop bastion is the least-visited part of the park but visible from many locations.

3 TOUR CRATER RIM DRIVE

Crater Rim Drive (11 mi./18 km, 2-3 hrs.) arcs around Kīlauea Caldera past steam vents, sulfur springs, and tortured fault lines that always seem on the verge of swallowing the landscape. Along the way, peer into the mouth of Halema'uma'u Crater, home of the fire goddess Pele.

Start at the **Kīlauea Visitor Center** to get oriented. On the north rim, the **Kīlauea Overlook** offers views into the caldera. Afterward, stop at the **steaming vents** pullout, where even the parking lot steams. As of early 2020, the road here was still under repair; check the status at the visitors center.

To explore the south portion of Crater Rim Dive, return past the visitors center and turn south just before the park entrance. At **Kīlauea Iki Overlook**, the steaming crater floor resembles a desolate desert landscape. Next, stop to walk through the **Nāhuku-Thurston Lava Tube.** Finish at the overlook of the brownish-red cinder cone **Pu'u Pua'i** (Gushing Hill).

KĪLAUEA IKI VOLCANIC CRATER

ONE DAY IN HAWAI'I VOLCANOES

You can see the park's "greatest hits" in one long day by driving **Crater Rim Road** and **Chain of Craters Road.** Stop at the visitors center and then walk along the **Crater Rim Trail.** Visit the **Thurston Lava Tube** and hike the **Kīlauea Iki Trail.**

SIGHTS

VOLCANO ART CENTER GALLERY

Located in the original 1877 Volcano House, the **Volcano Art Center Gallery** (808/967-7565, http://volcanoartcenter.org, 9am-5pm daily) contains one of the finest art galleries in the state. Featured artists exhibit in a variety of mediums: metal, painting, sculpture, jewelry, photography, and mixed media.

Join **Aloha Fridays** (11am-1pm, free) for demonstrations of traditional Hawaiian ukulele, hula, language, chants, and lei-making. Other programs including cultural forest walks, hula performances, and "talk stories" at the center's **Niaulani Campus** (19-4074 Old Volcano Rd., Volcano, 808/967-8222, volcanocenter.org), located five minutes east of the gallery outside the park entrance.

NĀHUKU-THURSTON LAVA TUBE

South of the Kīlauea Iki Overlook is the remarkable **Nāhuku-Thurston Lava Tube.** A paved path starts as a steep incline that quickly enters a vibrantly green fern forest filled with native birds. The lighted lava tube tunnel takes about 10 minutes to walk through. At the other end, a fantasy world of ferns and moss reappears, and the trail climbs back to the parking lot.

SCENIC DRIVES

CHAIN OF CRATERS ROAD

At the south end of Crater Rim Drive, the **Chain of Craters Road** (38 mi./61 km rt., 1.5 hrs.) drops 3,700 feet (1,128 m) in elevation down the *pali* (cliff) to

▼ HAWAI'I VOLCANOES NATIONAL PARK

VIEW FROM CHAIN OF CRATERS ROAD

the coast. En route, the road traverses lava that was laid down about 40 years ago; remnants of the old road can still be seen in spots. The road sustained damage during the 2018 eruption; check on repair status before driving.

Several craters line the road. **Lua Manu Crater** is a deep depression lined with green vegetation. At **Puhimau Crater,** walk to the viewing stand to peer over the crater's edge. Next, you'll pass **Ko'oko'olau Crater, Hi'iaka Crater,** and **Pauahi Crater.** At 9.9 miles (15.9 km) is **Kealakomo Lookout,** a picnic area with unobstructed views of the coast. The road then heads over the edge of the *pali* and diagonally down to the flats. The last section of road runs close to the sea, where cliffs rise up from the pounding surf. Near the end of the road is the **Holei Sea Arch.**

HILINA PALI ROAD

Two miles (3.2 km) down Chain of Craters Road, **Hilina Pali Road** (18 mi./29 km rt., 2 hrs.) shoots southwest over a narrow, roughly paved road to **Hilina Pali Overlook,** on the edge of the rift. Expansive views stretch over the benched coastline. As of 2019, this rough, but passable road was reopened for car access only as far as Kulanaokuaiki Campground. You can still walk or bicycle beyond that point while the road is repaired for vehicle travel.

MAUNA LOA ROAD

Mauna Loa Road (22 mi./35 km rt., 1.5 hrs.) is a narrow, curvy, and potholed one-lane road that leads to the **Tree Molds** (scattered potholes of entombed tree trunks) and the **Kipuka Puaulu** bird sanctuary, as well as the trailhead for Mauna Loa summit. From its terminus at 6,662 feet (2,030 m), you can overlook Kīlauea below on a clear day. Traveling this road leaves 99 percent of the tourists behind. Find the road 2.5 miles (4 km) south of the park entrance on HI 11.

RECREATION

HIKING

Kīlauea Summit

With multiple trailheads, the **Crater Rim Trail** is a long trail arcing around the north, east, and south rims of Kīlauea Caldera. Check on trail repair status before hiking. The most popular sections explore westward and eastward routes (5 mi./8 km rt., 2.5 hrs., easy) from the visitors center or Volcano House. Begin with unparalleled views of the vast Kīlauea Caldera before heading west to **Steam Vents** and **Steaming Bluff** (1.2 mi./2 km rt) where

Best Hike

KĪLAUEA IKI TRAIL

DISTANCE: 4.8 miles (7.7 km) round-trip
DURATION: 3 hours
ELEVATION CHANGE: 400 feet (122 m)
EFFORT: moderate
TRAILHEAD: Kīlauea Iki Overlook

In 1959, lava spewed 1,900 feet (579 m) into the air from a 0.5-mile (0.8-km) crack in the Kīlauea crater wall. Within weeks, 17 separate lava flow episodes occurred, creating a lake of lava now known as **Kīlauea Iki** (Little Kīlauea). From the Kīlauea Iki Overlook, the **Kīlauea Iki Trail** drops from the rim into the crater where lush tropical rainforest fills part of the floor and the solidified lake (you can walk on it!) has heaved into cracks. Due to crowded parking lots, plan to hike at 7am. You can also park at the Devastation Trailhead to hike via the Byron Ledge Trail to connect with Kīlauea Iki Trail (adds 2.2 mi./3.5 km rt.).

water heated by the volcano rises from cracks in the earth, and farther to **Kīlauea Overlook** (3.2 mi./5.2 km rt) before returning. Or instead, go eastward to tiptoe along the **Waldron Ledge** before cruising the rim of **Kīlauea Iki** to the Kīlauea Iki Trailhead (3.4 mi./5.5 km rt.) and back

From the visitors center, the paved and boardwalk **Ha'akulamanu Trail** (1.2 mi./2 km rt., 1 hr. min., easy), also called **Sulphur Banks,** explores smelly fumaroles surrounded by red-brown earth covered in yellow-green sulfur.

Behind Volcano House, the wheelchair-accessible paved **Earthquake Trail** (0.8 mi./1.3 km rt., 30 min., easy) leads to the **Waldron Ledge** for superb views of Kīlauea Caldera. Nearby, the **Halema'uma'u Trail** (1.6 mi./2.6 km rt, 1 hr., moderate) descends through lush mosses and rainforest to the crater floor, but then you must climb back up! Pick up a trail guide for interpretive stops.

From the Pu'u Pua'i Overlook, the paved **Devastation Trail** (1 mi./1.6 km rt., 30 min., easy) heads across a field ravaged by the Kīlauea Iki eruption and one of the most photographed areas in the park.

Chain of Craters Road

The **Pu'u Huluhulu Trail** (2.5 mi./4 km rt., 2 hrs., moderate) climbs 210 feet (64 m) to the summit of a steaming volcanic crater with 360-degree panoramic views. Start the hike from the Mauna Ulu Trailhead.

The **Pu'u Loa Petroglyphs** (1.4 mi./2.3 km rt., 1 hr., easy) trail follows a boardwalk encircling most of the petroglyphs, ensuring protection for the designs. Some rocks are entirely covered with designs, while others have only a symbolic scratch or two.

Guides

Friends of Hawaii Volcanoes National Park (808/985-7373, http://fhvnp.org) tour guides are retired park rangers and wildlife biologists. Tours are on demand, and transportation is not provided. Other guided hikes are led by **Native Guide Hawaii** (808/982-7575, www.nativeguidehawaii.com).

BACKPACKING

A **permit** ($10) is required for most trails outside the Crater Rim Drive area and the coastal stretch beyond the end of Chain of Craters Road. Obtain permits in person from the Backcountry Office at the **Visitor Emergency Operations Center** (Crater Rim Dr., daily 8am-4pm) the day prior to your hike, or reserve up to a week in advance.

Halapē

From the Hilina Pali Overlook on Hilina Pali Road, the **Hilina Pali Trail** (9.8 mi./15.8 km rt., 2-3 days) descends across hot, dry, rugged terrain. It drops straight down the *pali* with multiple switchbacks to a junction, where the hot, steep left fork yo-yos up and down to **Halapē**. The reward is a sugary beach and a sheltered lagoon with backcountry campsites and bathroom facilities.

Mauna Loa

It's a grueling climb to the 13,679-foot (4,169-m) summit of the island's largest volcano. Be prepared for altitude sickness and changes in weather—rain or even snow. Staying hydrated is imperative. There are two trail options.

From the terminus of Mauna Loa Road, the **Mauna Loa Road Trail** (36 mi./58 km rt., 6,600 ft./2,012 m elevation gain, 3-4 days) ascends to the **Pu'u 'Ula'ula cabin** (Red Hill, 4-6 hrs., 7.5 mi./12.1 km one-way). The next day, climb 11.5 miles (18.5 km) to the **Mauna Loa summit cabin** (8-12 hrs. one-way) on the caldera's rim. Both cabins, available first come, first served, have bunks and pit toilets.

A shorter but still ultra-strenuous trail to the summit goes from Mauna Loa Observatory trailhead outside the park, a two-hour drive via Saddle Road. The **Mauna Loa Observatory Trail** (7.6 mi./12.2 km rt., 1,975 ft./602 m elevation gain, 7-9 hrs.) climbs up the volcano's north slope to the rim of the Moku'aweoweo Caldera (the summit). The Mauna Loa summit cabin is at 2.1 miles (3.4 km).

BIKING

Bring your bike along to cruise the paved **Crater Rim Drive** (11 mi./17.7 km), the moderate **Hilina Pali Road** (18 mi./29 km rt.), or the challenging **Mauna Loa Road** (22 mi./35 km rt.). The classic challenge follows the **Summit to Sea** (36 mi./58 km rt.)—the path of the Mauna Ulu eruption on the Chain of Craters Road. Biking maps are available from the visitors center.

You can also take a guided bike tour with **Bike Volcano** (808/934-9199, www.bikevolcano.com) or **Nui Pohaku Adventure Tours** (808/937-0644, www.nuipohaku.com).

WHERE TO STAY

INSIDE THE PARK

Volcano House (1 Crater Rim Dr., 808/756-9625 or 844/569-8849, www.hawaiivolcanohouse.com, from $250) is the only hotel inside the park. Dating from the 1940s, it has the feel of a country inn, but with updated decor and facilities. From its rim location, you can see the glow of the crater from your window. Inside, **Uncle George's Lounge** (11am-10pm daily) and **The Rim Restaurant** (breakfast 7am-10:30am, lunch 11am-2pm, dinner 5pm-8:30pm daily) have priceless views of the crater.

North of the caldera, **Nāmakanipaio Campground and Cabins** (HI 11, 808/756-9625 or 866/536-7972, www.hawaiivolcanohouse.com, reservations recommended) has spartan A-frame cabins (from $80) that sleep up to four people with a double bed and two single bunks. Linens, soap, towels, a

THE TRAIL TO THE PU'U LOA PETROGLYPHS

blanket, and an electric light are provided, but there are no electrical outlets. The campground is a large grassy area surrounded by trees. Rent a tent ($55) or bring your own ($15, no hookups). Cabins and campsites have picnic tables, firepits, and communal restrooms with showers.

South of the caldera off the Chain of Craters Road, **Kulanaokuaiki Campground** (Hilina Pali Rd., $10) has nine first-come, first-served sites. Facilities include picnic tables and a vault toilet, but no drinking water.

Kīlauea Military Camp (Hilina Pali Rd., 808/967-8333, http://kilaueamilitarycamp.com) is where military families vacation. Two eateries are open to the public: **Crater Rim Café** (6:30am-1pm Mon.-Fri., 6:30am-11am Sat.-Sun., and 5pm-8pm daily).

OUTSIDE THE PARK

Volcano Village has accommodations and restaurants. Most are on Old Volcano Road, the inner road that parallels HI 11 through town.

GETTING THERE AND AROUND

AIR

Most direct mainland-Big Island flights land at the **Ellison Onizuka Kona International Airport** (KOA, Keahole Airport Rd., 808/327-9520, http://airports.hawaii.gov/koa) on the island's west side. It's a two hour drive to the park via HI 11. Some planes land on the east side at **Hilo International Airport** (ITO, 808/961-9300, Kekuanaoa St., http://airports.hawaii.gov/ito). From Hilo, the park is roughly 40 miles (64 km) south via HI 11. Both airports have car rentals.

LAVA FLOWING INTO THE OCEAN

CAR

From Kailua-Kona, drive southeast on HI 11 for 96 miles (155 km, 2.5 hrs.) to the park entrance. From Hilo, take HI 11 southwest for 29 miles (47 km, 45 min.).

Once inside the park, the caldera is encircled by 11 miles (18 km) of the paved **Crater Rim Drive.** From Crater Rim Drive, the paved **Chain of Craters Road** leads through lava flows down the *pali* to the coast.

Due to overcrowded parking lots, plan to arrive by 7am. The park updates online the status of popular parking lots (visitors center, Kīlauea Iki, Pu'u Pua'i, Devastation Trailhead, and end of Chain of Craters Road) so you can plan your itinerary accordingly. Always have alternatives in mind.

BUS

Hele-On Bus (808/961-8744, www.heleonbus.org) connects Hilo with the Kīlauea Visitor Center and Volcano Village. Once inside the park, there is no public transit.

TOURS

Bus Tours

Bus tours depart from Big Island locations to tour the national park. Hilo-based tours include **Roberts Hawaii** (808/966-5483, www.robertshawaii.com) and **Kapoho Kine Adventures** (25 Waianuenue Ave., Hilo, 808/964-1000, www.kapohokine.com). From the Kona side, **Hawaii Forest and Trails** (808/201-2329, www.hawaii-forest.com) offers a 12-hour round-trip adventure of the main park sights.

Helicopter Tours

A dramatic way to experience the volcano's power is via a helicopter. **Sunshine Helicopters** (808/270-3999 or 866/501-7738, www.sunshinehelicopters.com) fly from the island's north end. **Blue Hawaiian Helicopters** (808/886-1768 in Waikoloa, 800/745-2583, www.bluehawaiian.com) operates tours from the Kona and Hilo sides.

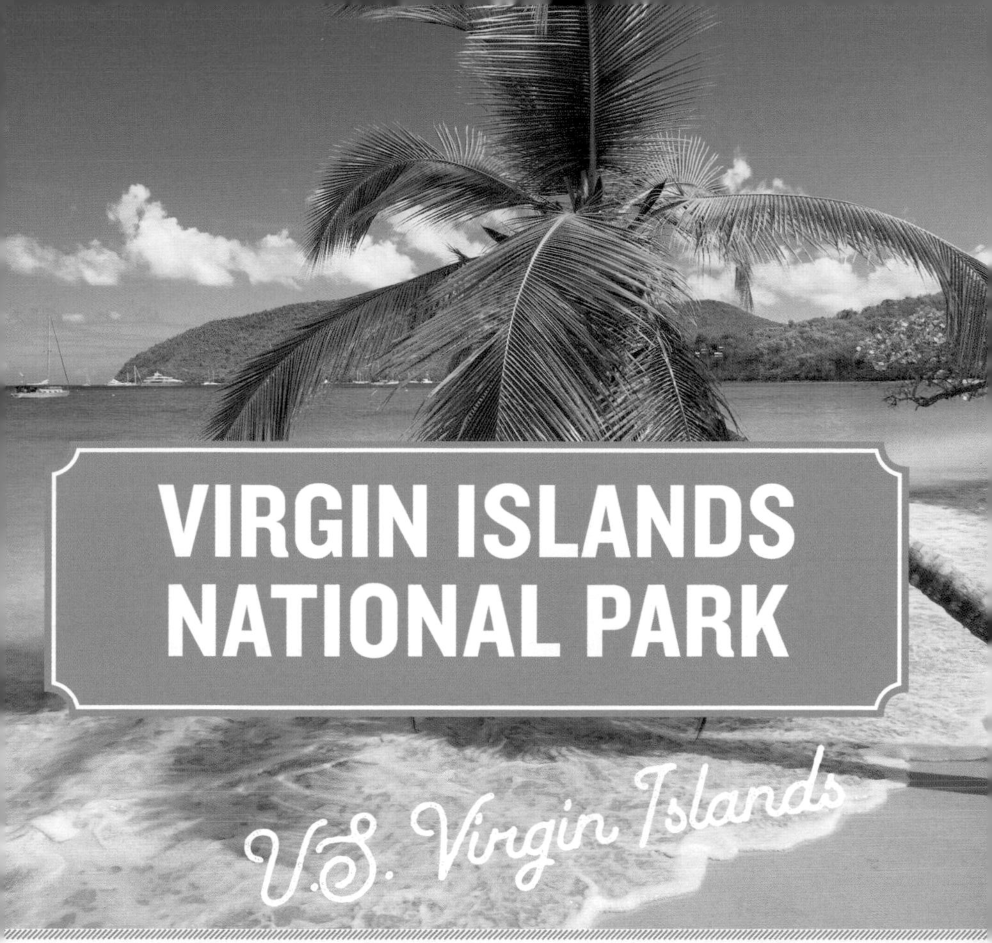

VIRGIN ISLANDS NATIONAL PARK

U.S. Virgin Islands

KEEPSAKE STAMPS ▼▼▼

WEBSITE:
www.nps.gov/viis

PHONE NUMBER:
340/776-6201,
ext. 238

VISITATION RANK:
52

WHY GO:
Snorkel and dive amid coral reefs.

▲ MAHO BEACH, SAINT MARTIN

VIRGIN ISLANDS NATIONAL PARK

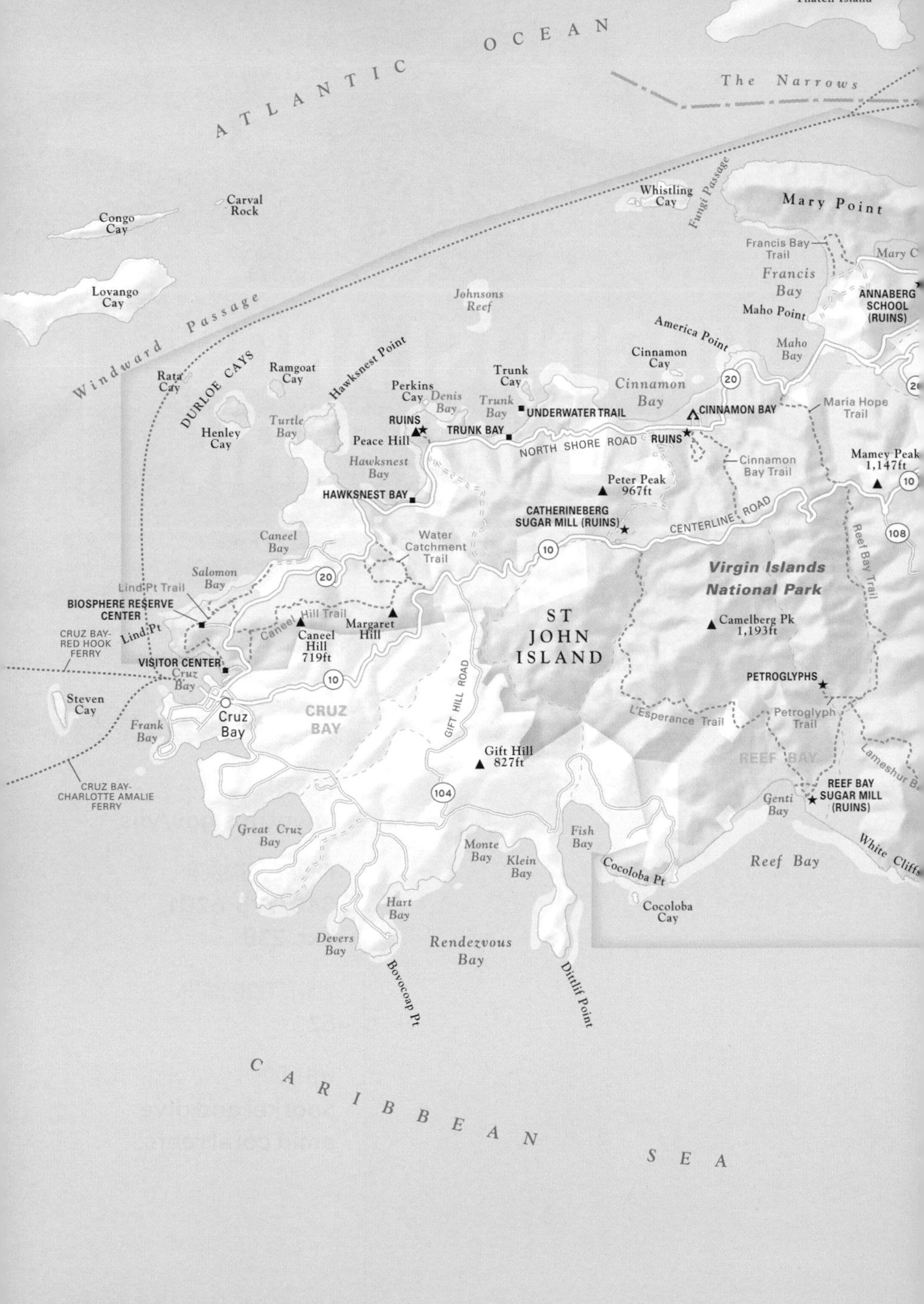

Great Thatch Island
ATLANTIC OCEAN
The Narrows
Whistling Cay
Fungi Passage
Mary Point
Carval Rock
Congo Cay
Lovango Cay
Windward Passage
Francis Bay Trail
Mary C
Francis Bay
ANNABERG SCHOOL (RUINS)
Maho Point
Johnsons Reef
America Point
Maho Bay
Cinnamon Cay
Rata Cay
DURLOE CAYS
Ramgoat Cay
Hawksnest Point
Trunk Cay
Cinnamon Bay
20
Perkins Cay
Denis Bay
Trunk Bay
UNDERWATER TRAIL
CINNAMON BAY
Maria Hope Trail
Henley Cay
Turtle Bay
RUINS
Peace Hill
TRUNK BAY
NORTH SHORE ROAD
RUINS
Cinnamon Bay Trail
Mamey Peak 1,147ft
Hawksnest Bay
Peter Peak 967ft
10
HAWKSNEST BAY
CATHERINEBERG SUGAR MILL (RUINS)
CENTERLINE ROAD
108
Caneel Bay
Water Catchment Trail
10
Reef Bay Trail
Virgin Islands National Park
Salomon Bay
20
Lind Pt Trail
BIOSPHERE RESERVE CENTER
ST JOHN ISLAND
Camelberg Pk 1,193ft
Caneel Hill Trail
Margaret Hill
CRUZ BAY-RED HOOK FERRY
Lind Pt
Caneel Hill 719ft
VISITOR CENTER
Cruz Bay
10
GIFT HILL ROAD
PETROGLYPHS
Steven Cay
Cruz Bay
CRUZ BAY
Frank Bay
L'Esperance Trail
Petroglyph Trail
REEF BAY
Lameshur B
Gift Hill 827ft
CRUZ BAY-CHARLOTTE AMALIE FERRY
104
REEF BAY SUGAR MILL (RUINS)
Genti Bay
Great Cruz Bay
Fish Bay
White Cliffs
Monte Bay
Klein Bay
Reef Bay
Cocoloba Pt
Cocoloba Cay
Hart Bay
Devers Bay
Rendezvous Bay
Bovocoap Pt
Ditlif Point
CARIBBEAN SEA

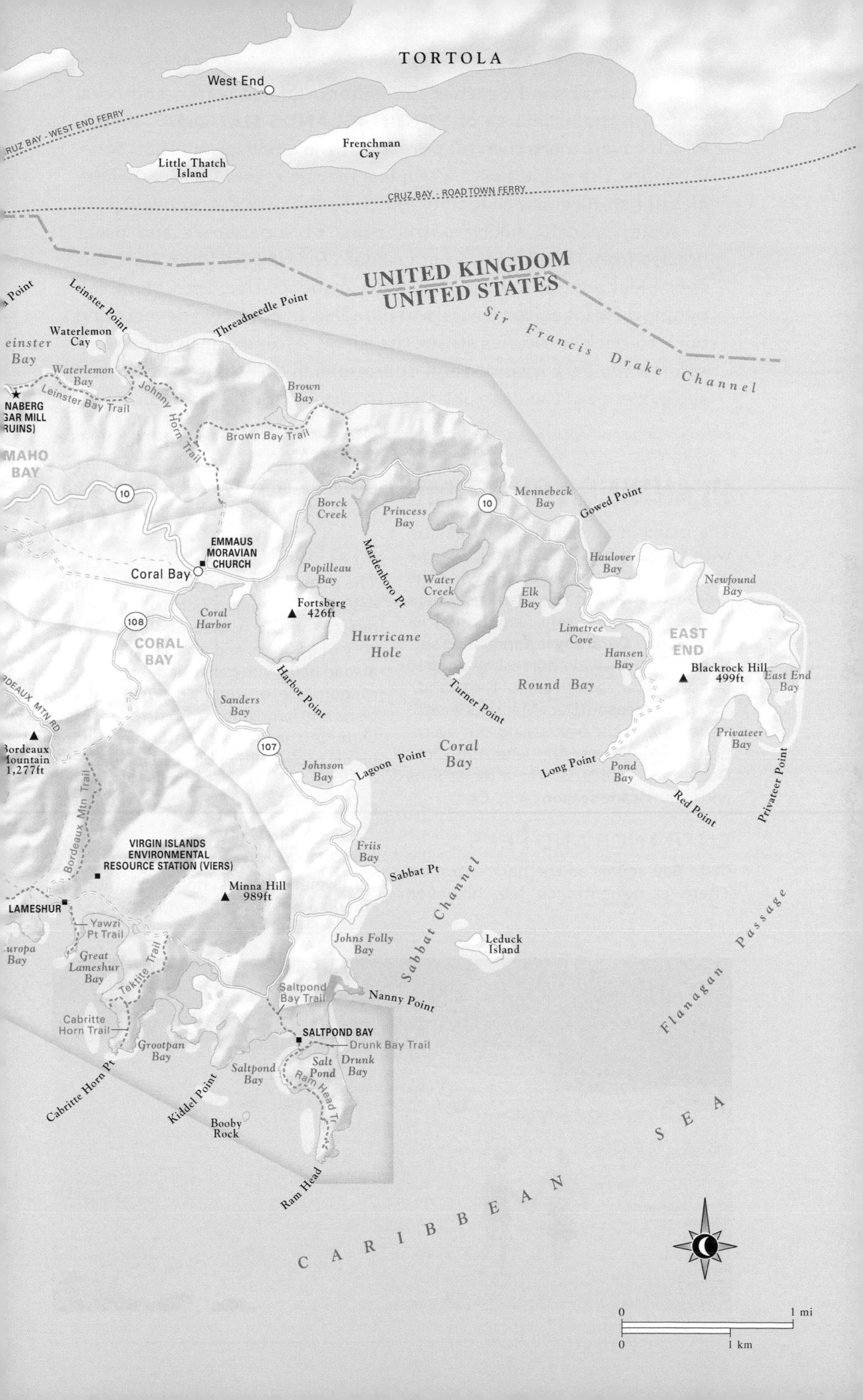
TORTOLA
West End
CRUZ BAY - WEST END FERRY
Frenchman Cay
Little Thatch Island
CRUZ BAY - ROAD TOWN FERRY
UNITED KINGDOM
UNITED STATES
Sir Francis Drake Channel
Leinster Point
Threadneedle Point
Waterlemon Cay
Leinster Bay
Waterlemon Bay
Leinster Bay Trail
Johnny Horn Trail
Brown Bay
Brown Bay Trail
MAHO BAY
Borck Creek
Princess Bay
Mennebeck Bay
Gowed Point
EMMAUS MORAVIAN CHURCH
Coral Bay
Popilleau Bay
Mardenboro Pt
Water Creek
Haulover Bay
Newfound Bay
Fortsberg 426ft
Elk Bay
Coral Harbor
CORAL BAY
Hurricane Hole
Limetree Cove
EAST END
Hansen Bay
Blackrock Hill 499ft
East End Bay
Round Bay
Harbor Point
Turner Point
Sanders Bay
Bordeaux Mountain 1,277ft
Privateer Bay
Coral Bay
Johnson Bay
Lagoon Point
Long Point
Pond Bay
Red Point
Privateer Point
Bordeaux Mtn Trail
VIRGIN ISLANDS ENVIRONMENTAL RESOURCE STATION (VIERS)
Friis Bay
Sabbat Pt
Minna Hill 989ft
LAMESHUR
Yawzi Pt Trail
Sabbat Channel
Johns Folly Bay
Leduck Island
Great Lameshur Bay
Tektite Trail
Saltpond Bay Trail
Nanny Point
Flanagan Passage
Cabritte Horn Trail
SALTPOND BAY
Drunk Bay Trail
Grootpan Bay
Salt Pond
Drunk Bay
Saltpond Bay
Ram Head Tr
Cabritte Horn Pt
Kiddel Point
Booby Rock
Ram Head
CARIBBEAN SEA
0
1 mi
0
1 km

Dreamy white-sand beaches, brilliant turquoise water, and coral reefs are the hallmarks of **VIRGIN ISLANDS NATIONAL PARK,** which covers more than 60 percent of the small island of St. John. Offshore, the island hosts a tropical marine reserve with 302 species of fish, diversity that contributes to the park's utter beauty.

Along peaceful hiking paths, ruins of sugarworks and great houses from the plantation era remain for visitors to explore. But even older are the Taino petroglyphs, evidence that pre-Columbian people once inhabited this island paradise. In 2017, two devastating back-to-back hurricanes struck the island. After extensive recovery efforts, the park resumed full operations in 2019, but you will still see evidence of the destruction both on land and underwater.

PLANNING YOUR TIME

The island of St. John is mountainous, with two laid-back hamlets outside the national park boundary. **Cruz Bay,** on the far western end of the island, is where ferries and boats from neighboring islands arrive. **Coral Bay** is a sprawling settlement along a wide, horseshoe-shaped bay on the far eastern end of the island.

The **dry season** (Dec.-Mar.) has weather perks with the best sailing, but visitation peaks in waves (Apr.-June, Aug., Oct.-Dec.). Mosquitoes swarm after storms and in **hurricane season** (Aug.-Oct.).

ENTRANCE AND FEES

Cruz Bay serves as the park entrance. There is no entrance fee; however, there are amenity fees for **Trunk Bay** ($5) and for overnight mooring ($26).

VISITORS CENTER

The **Cruz Bay Visitor Center** (8am-4:30pm daily) has a permanent exhibit describing the human and natural history of St. John, and a three-dimensional map helps you get your bearings. Park rangers are on duty to answer questions and hand out maps and brochures. Outside, the visitors center has shaded picnic tables and public restrooms.

SIGHTS

HAWKSNEST BEACH

Hawksnest Bay is home to glorious **Hawksnest Beach,** a wide, long strip

CINNAMON BEACH

Top 3

1 SWIM IN TRUNK BAY

Trunk Bay (8am-4pm daily, $5 pp) is St. John's most magnificent beach and its most popular, a vision of fluffy white sand, sea grape trees, and coconut palms. Named for the leatherback turtles that nest here, Trunk Bay is a long beach—even at its most crowded you will find some quiet. Facilities include a snack bar and restrooms. An underwater snorkel trail lies along Trunk Cay, just offshore.

TRUNK BAY

2 SNORKEL WATERLEMON CAY

Waterlemon Cay is home to the best coral reef snorkeling in St. John, but it is not for beginners. To reach the tiny offshore islet requires a walk (1.6 mi./2.6 km rt., 1 hr., easy) from **Leinster Bay Beach** east on an old Danish road to **Waterlemon Bay** and then a 0.2-mile (0.3 km) swim. A shallow reef fringes the protected side of the cay, deepening to 20 feet (6.1 m) with an intricate diversity of coral life.

3 TOUR THE NORTH SHORE SCENIC DRIVE

From Cruz Bay, the **North Shore Road** (Rte. 20, 6.8 mi./10.9 km one-way, 20 min.) enters Virgin Islands National Park in a few minutes. Then, the road curves in and out along the north coastline of the park. This is quintessential St. John: powder-white beaches, pristine coral reefs, hiking trails, and awesome overlooks. You'll pass **Hawksnest Beach, Trunk Bay, Cinnamon Bay,** and **Maho Bay.** The route terminates at **Leinster Bay** and the **Annaberg ruins.**

of pale sand fringed by a canopy of mature trees and sandwiched between rock promontories. Hawksnest is the closest beach you can drive to from Cruz Bay.

At the top of the headland between Hawksnest and Trunk Bays is **Peace Hill,** a grassy knoll and windmill ruin with beautiful views.

CINNAMON BAY

Cinnamon Bay is home to an excellent beach, extensive ruins, a hiking trail, and some of St. John's best water sports. The long and winding shore gives way to expansive **Cinnamon Beach,** where the fine white sand creates a wide, shallow bank ideal for snorkeling on the reef about 100 yards (91 m) from shore.

Explore the remains of the bay's 1680 colonial settlement at the **Cinnamon Bay ruins,** across the street from the beach. A self-guided walk (0.5 mi./0.8 km, 20 min., easy) leads through the ruins of a sugar factory, an estate house, bay rum stills, and a small Danish cemetery.

MAHO BAY BEACH

Maho Bay is a long, narrow beach well protected from surf, which makes it a good destination for stand-up paddleboarding and swimming. Facilities include three new pavilion and restrooms.

Best Hike

REEF BAY

DISTANCE: 5.2 miles (8.4 km) round-trip
DURATION: 3.5 hours
ELEVATION CHANGE: 900 feet (274 m)
EFFORT: strenuous
TRAILHEAD: Reef Bay Trailhead on Centerline Road

The **Reef Bay Trail** descends steeply to the shore at Reef Bay. At about halfway on the rocky and sometimes slippery forested trail, a spur visits the Taino **petroglyphs** that date to about 1300-1450 CE. On the main trail, you'll also pass the remains of four different sugar factories, including the extensive Reef Bay ruins, and some of the oldest and tallest trees in the park. **Reef Bay** was the site of one of the most productive sugar plantations on St. John. The remains of the **Reef Bay Sugar Mill,** now home to bats, consist of a well-preserved mill building, handsome stone smokestack, and cattle round. Large copper pots used in the manufacture of sugar lie on the ground outside of the building. At Reef Bay, you can swim or snorkel (bring your own gear). The tough part is the climb back up to the trailhead.

FRANCIS BAY

Francis Bay is a great place for swimming and home to the best bird-watching on St. John, especially at **Francis Bay Pond.** A small coral reef at the western end of **Francis Bay Beach** is perfect for beginning snorkelers. The **Francis Bay Trail** (1 mi./1.6 km rt., 30 min., easy) passes through a crumbling great house "ruin" before reaching an overlook with a view of the pond before ending at the beach.

ANNABERG RUINS

In 1844, two government schools were constructed on St. John (then called the Danish West Indies). The **Annaberg School ruins** are a short distance from the road to the Annaberg Plantation. Climb the steps for the best views. A display describes the history of the school.

The ruins of the **Annaberg Sugar Mill** are the best place to learn about the colonial-era life of both planters and slaves on St. John. The site includes the ruins of a windmill, a sugar factory, a mill round, a rum still, and slave quarters. An 0.25-mile (0.4 km, one-way) paved trail meanders through the grounds past interpretive signs that describe the ruins.

LEINSTER BAY

Calm **Leinster Bay Beach** is covered with packed, coarse yellow sand and fringed by shade trees. It's a decent place to swim and snorkel. From the beach, hike 0.25 mile (0.4 km, one-way) up the **Johnny Horn Trail** to reach great house ruins once associated with the Annaberg estate.

SALTPOND BAY

Remote and uncrowded**, Saltpond Bay** is located near the end of Route 107. After a 10-minute hike to the beach, you can snorkel the underwater landscape around the jagged rocks in the middle of the bay. The site offers picnic tables and pit toilets and is accessible by public transportation.

RECREATION

HIKING

The **Cinnamon Bay Trail** (2 mi./3.2 km, 1 hr., strenuous) is an uphill trek that follows an old Danish road all the way to Centerline Road. The trail passes through ruins and land that would have been cultivated with sugarcane during the plantation era, now all secondary forest.

The **Yawzi Point Trail** (0.6 mi./1 km, 30 min., easy) follows the headland separating Little Lameshur and Great Lameshur Bays. The trail cuts through a dry forest before reaching the point. People suffering from a tropical skin disease were sent to a quarantine camp here in the 18th and 19th centuries.

RUINS OF THE ANNABERG SUGAR MILL

The extreme southeastern tip of St. John is a narrow finger of land called **Ram Head** (2.4 mi./3.8 km rt., 1.5 hrs., moderate) a dramatic place with views of the Caribbean Sea and the irregular foothills of southern St. John. The trail starts from the Saltpond Bay parking lot.

From behind the Cruz Bay Visitor Center, the **Lind Point Trail** (1.7 mi./2.7 km rt., 1 hr., moderate), a forested loop, is the only way to reach secluded **Honeymoon Beach.** Enjoy the powdery white sand for pleasant views of Lovango, Mingo, and Henley Cays.

SNORKELING

Snorkeling is the most popular activity on St. John. On the north shore, the **Trunk Bay Underwater Trail** is a good reef for beginners. The 225-yard (206-m) underwater snorkel trail lies between a series of buoys off the southwestern tip of Trunk Cay. It's a short swim out to the trail, and the area is normally protected from currents and wind.

Jumbie Beach has a shallow, maze-like reef along the eastern side, where you may see lobsters and nurse sharks.

On the south shore, **Saltpond Bay** has good reef snorkeling around the two jagged rocks that break the surface of the bay. At **Great Lameshur Bay,** the snorkeling is best along the eastern shore. **Little Lameshur Bay** has snorkeling for beginners just off the western end of the beach.

Maho Bay has offshore seagrass beds that provide food for green turtles, especially in the early morning and late afternoon. **Leinster Bay,** near Annaberg, has nice seagrass beds where you may see sea stars, conchs, and turtles. **Brown Bay,** accessible only on foot, has a seagrass bed just offshore.

Mangroves provide a fascinating glimpse into an important marine habitat. The best place for mangrove snorkeling is **Princess Bay,** along Route 10 (East End Road).

Rent snorkel gear from **Crabby's Watersports** (Cocoloba Shopping Center, Coral Bay, 340/626-1570), **Concordia Eco-Resort** (Concordia, 340/693-5855); **Arawak Expeditions** (Mongoose Junction, 340/693-8312, www.arawakexp.com), and **Low Key Watersports** (1 Bay St., Cruz Bay, 340/693-8999, http://divelowkey.com). **Virgin Islands Ecotours** (Honeymoon Beach, 340/779-2155, www.viecotours.com) offers a three-hour hike and snorkel on the grounds of Caneel Bay Resort.

ANCIENT PETROGLYPHS ALONG THE REEF BAY TRAIL

DIVING

St. John has several dive sites, including two off Cruz Bay. The **Maj. Gen. Rogers,** a 1940 army freighter, was sunk in 1972 to become an artificial reef. The excellent reefs around **Grass Cay** and **Mingo Cay** are good for beginning divers. There is a dizzying array of sealife at **Witch's Hat** on the southern tip of Steven's Cay, just off Cruz Bay.

South shore dives include **Cocoloba,** an easy, sandy reef dive, and **Maple Leaf,** a large offshore reef east of Reef Bay. The most famous east-end dive site is **Eagle Shoal,** between Ram Head and Leduck Island. Access to Eagle Shoal is limited.

Low Key Watersports (Cruz Bay, 340/693-8999, http://divelowkey.com) offers daily dive trips.

KAYAKING

Kayaking is popular off St. John's north shore, where you can paddle up to beaches or out to offshore islets, like Whistling Cay, Waterlemon Cay, or the Durloe Cays.

Hurricane Hole (Borck Creek, Princess Bay, and Water Creek) is a critical mangrove ecosystem best explored by kayak or stand-up paddleboard. From Coral Bay, it takes about an hour to paddle into it. Check on status first as the U.S. Coast Guard may still be removing some 50 boats sunk or washed into the mangroves from the hurricanes. Bring a snorkel to explore the enchanting world amid the knobbed knees and underwater roots of the mangrove trees.

On the north shore, rent kayaks at **Virgin Islands Ecotours** (Honeymoon Beach, 340/779-2155, www.viecotours.com). For Coral Bay, **Crabby's Watersports** (Cocoloba Plaza, 340/626-1570, www.crabbyswatersports.com) rents single and two-seater kayaks.

THE REFLECTING POOL ON THE REEF BAY TRAIL

NUMEROUS BEACHES OFFER RELAXATION.

Outfitters guiding paddle trips include **Arawak Expeditions** (Mongoose Junction, 340/693-8312, www.arawak-exp.com) and **Virgin Islands Ecotours** (Honeymoon Beach, 340/779-2155, www.viecotours.com).

WHERE TO STAY

INSIDE THE PARK

Recovery from the hurricanes is ongoing. As of early 2020, **Cinnamon Bay Resort** (1 Great Cinnamon Bay, St. John, 669/999-8784, https://cinnamonbayresort.com) is still undergoing an extensive rebuild to have cottages, camping, food service, and water sports rentals once again.

A handful of beaches have outdoor cafés or food stands: Honeymoon Beach, Trunk Bay, and Cinnamon Bay.

OUTSIDE THE PARK

St. John's hotels and villas are among the priciest in the Virgin Islands. A few moderate hotels in **Cruz Bay** offer affordable options.

GETTING THERE AND AROUND

AIR

There is no airport on St. John. The closest airport is on **St. Thomas** (SST, Cyril E. King Airport, Airport Rd., Charlotte Amalie West, 340/774-5100, www.viport.com). **Varlack Ventures** (340/776-6412) operates ferries between St. Thomas and Cruz Bay. Ferries leave Charlotte Amalie daily (10am, 1pm, and 5:30pm, $12 one-way).

TAXIS

Taxis are widely available on St. John, especially in Cruz Bay and at the popular north shore beaches. Try **C&C Taxi Service** (340/693-8164) or **St. John Taxi Services** (340/693-7530).

CAR RENTALS

Rental companies based on St. John only rent 4WD sport-utility vehicles suitable for the island's roads. Numerous rental companies are located in or around Cruz Bay. There are two gas stations on St. John, both on the road between Cruz Bay and the Westin Resort.

BUSES

The air-conditioned **VITRAN buses** (340/774-4844, $1) run hourly from Cruz Bay to Coral Bay and Saltpond Bay, along Centerline Road.

TOURS

Cruz Bay Watersports (340/776-6234, http://cruisebaywatersports.com) offers catamaran trips for sunsets, snorkeling, and beach visits. A number of day-sail operators offer sailing trips around St. John. Contact the activity desks around St. John for sailing operators, availability, and pricing.

NATIONAL PARK OF AMERICAN SAMOA

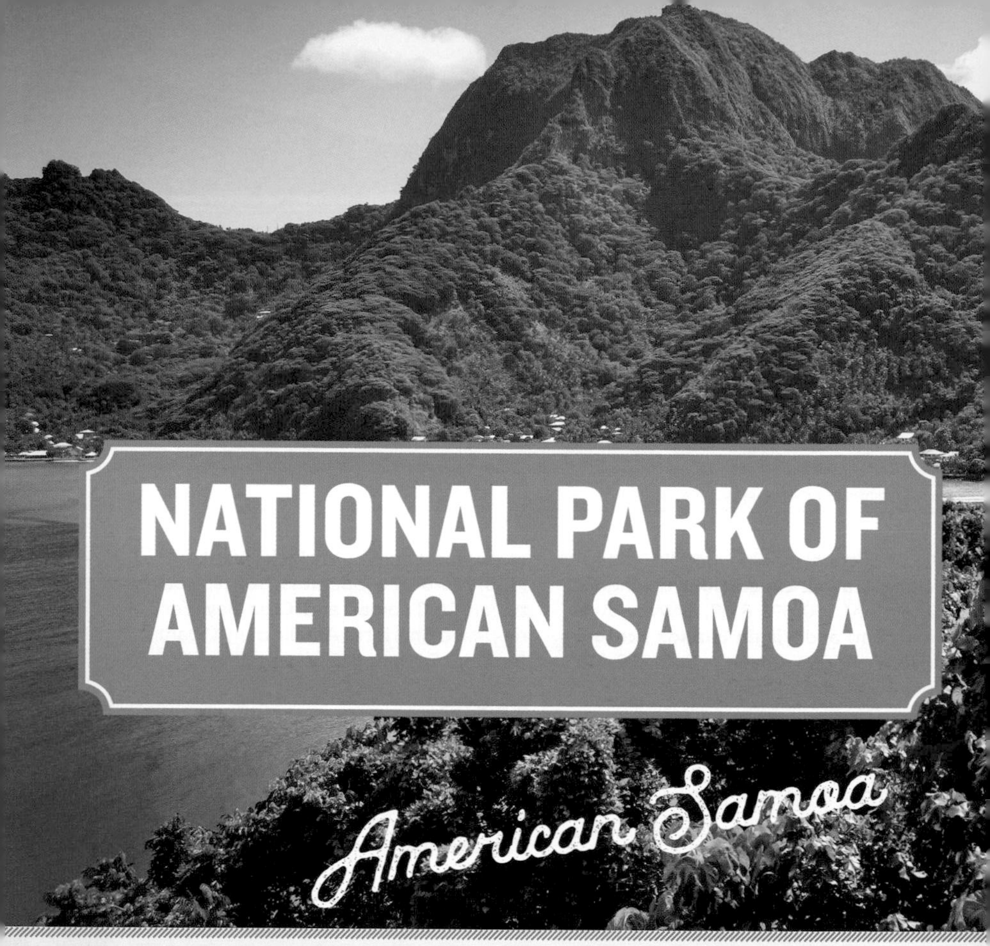

WEBSITE:
www.nps.gov/npsa

PHONE NUMBER:
684/633-7082, ext. 22

VISITATION RANK:
57

WHY GO:
Explore a tropical rain forest and coral reefs.

▲ PAGO PAGO

KEEPSAKE STAMPS ▼▼▼

Located south of the equator, the remote **NATIONAL PARK OF AMERICAN SAMOA** is the southernmost national park in the United States. It's anchored by three islands in the Samoan archipelago, where lush mountain rainforests cling to the volcanic landscape, tapering down to tropical beaches. Underwater, a prolific marine ecosystem contains 950 species of fish and 250 species of coral in one of the planet's largest living coral communities.

The National Park of American Samoa also preserves historic military sites from World Wars I and II, when Tutuila Island served as a base for U.S. troops. But more important, it pays tribute to traditional Samoan culture, which has endured here for 3,000 years. Contrary to other U.S. national parks, which are owned by the federal government, the National Park of American Samoa leases land from the local people.

PLANNING YOUR TIME

Located in the South Pacific (north of Fiji, Tonga, and Tahiti), American Samoa sits just east of the international date line, far south of the equator. The national park is split across three of the Samoan Islands.

Tutuila Island has the largest national park tract and is the most visited due to its easier access. **Pago Pago** serves as the main base for the park; Pago Pago International Airport is at the south end of the island. Most of the island is composed of villages rather than towns, and roads can be rough. The village of Vatia is inside the park, while Fagasa and Afono are also close to the park boundaries. Bring a sense of adventure and a good dose of self-sufficiency (for snorkeling, bring your own gear), as services are few.

Sixty miles (97 km) east are the tiny Manu'a Islands of **Ta'ū** and **Ofu,** reachable by boat and air. On **Ta'ū Island,** the main access points are the boat harbor at Faleasao and Fiti'uta Airport. The village of **Ofu** is the main access point for Ofu.

The most popular time to visit splits between **spring** (Mar.-May) and **fall** (Oct.-Nov.). October-May is the monsoon season, which sees tropical storms. Temperatures range 75-85°F (24-29°C), but oppressive humidity can make it feel much hotter. Rain is frequent, the mosquitoes are ubiquitous, and acute solar radiation can intensify sunburns. Humpback whales migrate to the islands in September and October.

The Samoan people follow fa'asamoa, a distinct set of cultural mores. In villages, plan to ask permission to take photos and use beaches, observe evening prayer time with silence, and respect Sundays with quiet and in some locations no swimming or hiking. Swimwear should be modest.

ENTRANCES AND FEES

For entry into American Samoa, visitors must have a passport, return ticket, and confirmation of funds. Upon arrival, nationals from the UK, Australia, and 14 European Union countries may receive 30-day entry permits. Visas are required for all other international travelers.

There is no national park entrance fee and no official entrance station.

VISITORS CENTER

The **national park visitors center** (8am-4:30pm Mon.-Fri.) is in Pago Pago across from the Pago Way Service Station. Exhibits explore the island's natural history and Samoan culture and rangers advise on trip planning. Field guides and natural history books are sold in the **Hawaii Pacific Parks Association** (www.hawaiipacificparks.

NATIONAL PARK OF AMERICAN SAMOA

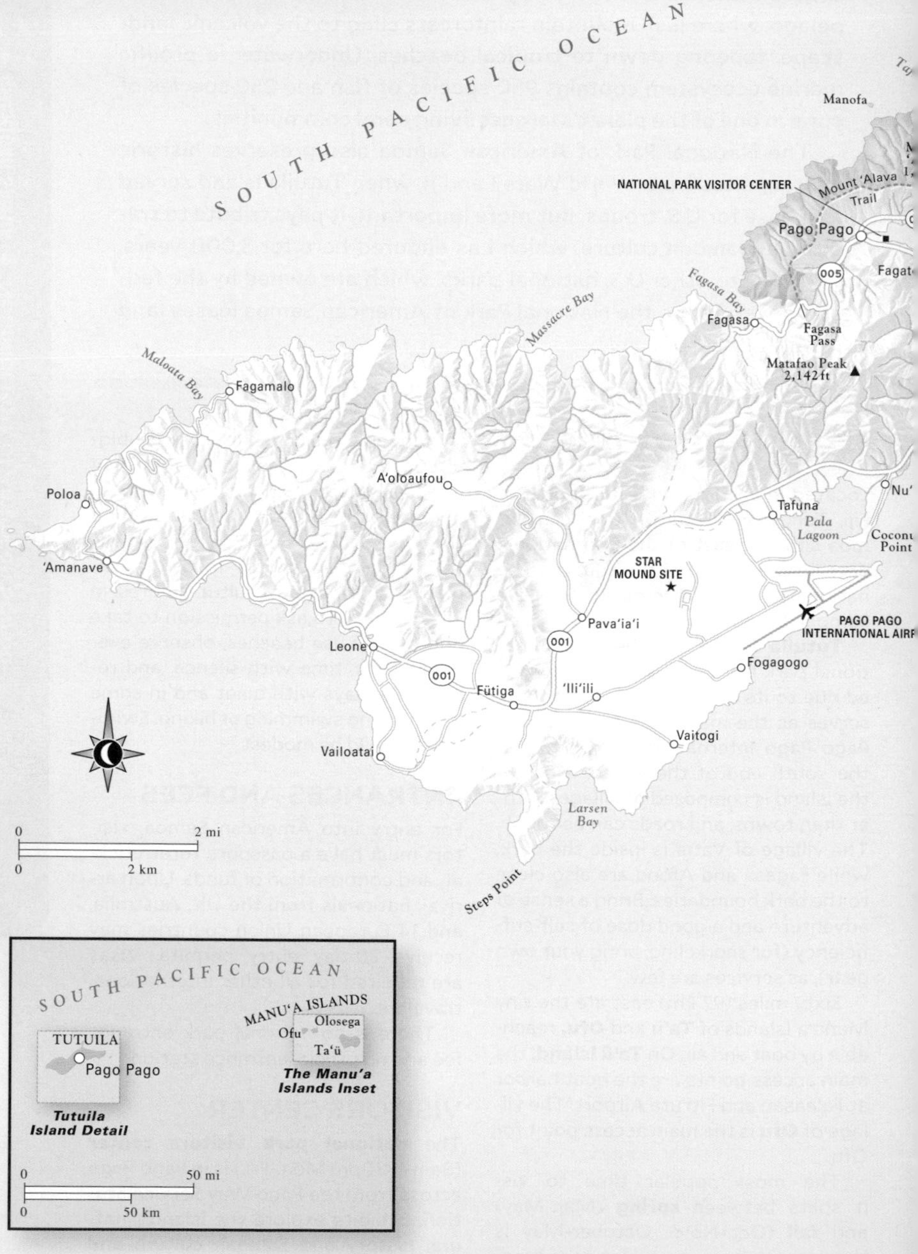
SOUTH PACIFIC OCEAN
Manofa
NATIONAL PARK VISITOR CENTER
Mount 'Alava Trail
Pago Pago
005
Fagasa Bay
Fagasa
Fagasa Pass
Matafao Peak 2,142 ft
Massacre Bay
Maloata Bay
Fagamalo
A'oloaufou
Poloa
'Amanave
Tafuna
Pala Lagoon
STAR MOUND SITE
PAGO PAGO
Pava'ia'i
001
Leone
Fogagogo
Fütiga
'Ili'ili
Vaitogi
Vailoatai
Larsen Bay
Steps Point
0
2 mi
0
2 km
SOUTH PACIFIC OCEAN
MANU'A ISLANDS
Olosega
Ofu
Ta'ū
TUTUILA
Pago Pago
The Manu'a Islands Inset
Tutuila Island Detail
0
50 mi
0
50 km

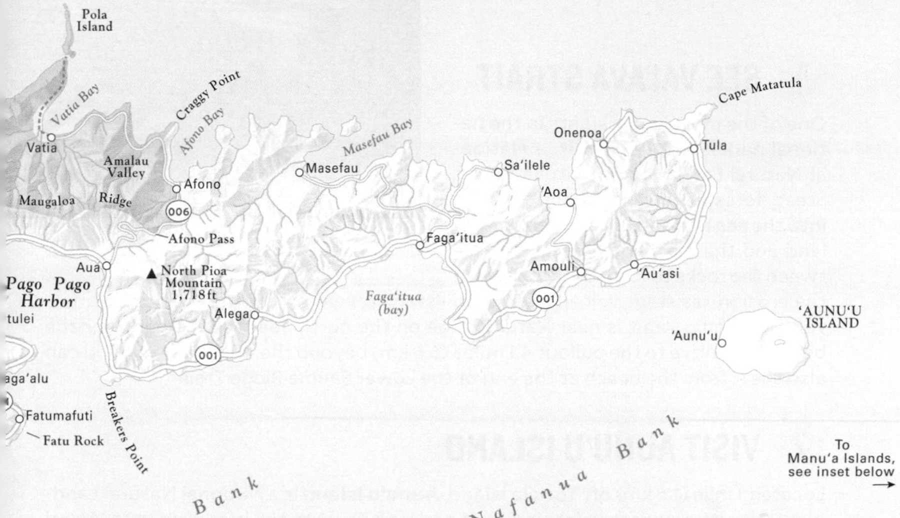

Pola Island
Vatia Bay
Craggy Point
Afono Bay
Masefau Bay
Cape Matatula
Onenoa
Tula
Vatia
Amalau Valley
Afono
Masefau
Sa'ilele
'Aoa
Maugaloa Ridge
006
Afono Pass
Faga'itua
Aua
North Pioa Mountain 1,718 ft
Amouli
'Au'asi
Pago Pago Harbor
Faga'itua (bay)
001
Alega
'AUNU'U ISLAND
'Aunu'u
001
Fatumafuti
Fatu Rock
Breakers Point
Taema Bank
Nafanua Bank
To Manu'a Islands, see inset below

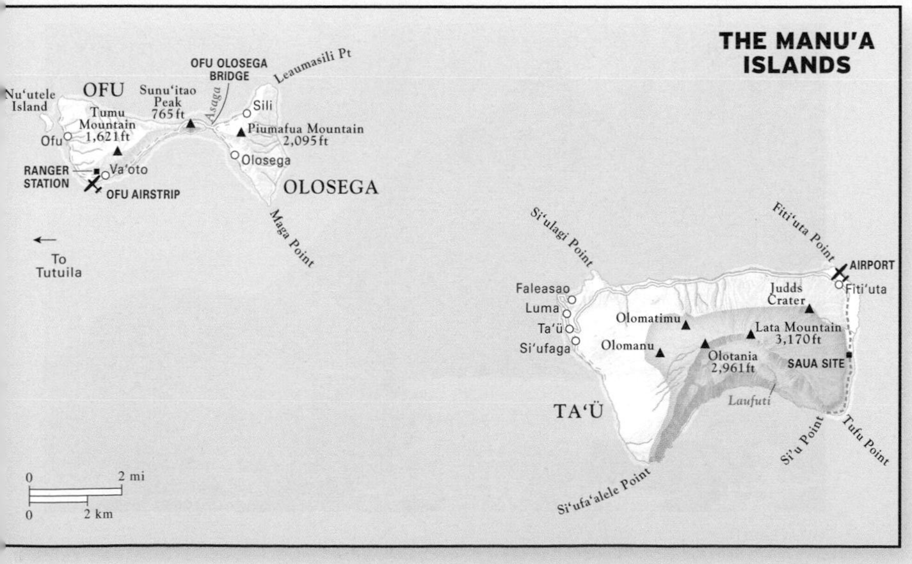

THE MANU'A ISLANDS
OFU OLOSEGA BRIDGE
Leaumasili Pt
Nu'utele Island
OFU
Sunu'itao Peak 765 ft
Asaga
Sili
Tumu Mountain 1,621 ft
Piumafua Mountain 2,095 ft
Ofu
Olosega
RANGER STATION
Va'oto
OFU AIRSTRIP
OLOSEGA
Maga Point
To Tutuila
Si'ulagi Point
Fiti'uta Point
AIRPORT
Fiti'uta
Faleasao
Judds Crater
Luma
Olomatimu
Ta'ū
Lata Mountain 3,170 ft
Si'ufaga
Olomanu
Olotania 2,961 ft
SAUA SITE
Laufuti
TA'Ū
Si'u Point
Tufu Point
Si'ufa'alele Point
0 2 mi
0 2 km

Top 3

ROCKY CLIFFS OF TUTUILA

1 SEE VAI'AVA STRAIT

One of the most iconic sights in the national park is **Vai'ava Strait,** a National Natural Landmark on Tutuila Island. Steep, forested, and rocky cliffs plunge into the sea at a gap in between Pola Island and the mainland. Waves cut between the rocks to form the strait while the erosion-resistant volcanic rocks still stand on either side as a geological marvel. The scenic strait is near Vatia Village on the north coast of the park. For the best views, drive to the pullout 4.1 miles (6.6 km) beyond the village of Aüa. You can also see it from the beach at the end of the Lower Sauma Ridge Trail.

2 VISIT AUNU'U ISLAND

Located 1 mile (1.6 km) off Tutuila Island, **Aunu'u Island** is a National Natural Landmark with its origins in volcanic basalt and tuff. To go to the island, drive to 'Au'asi on the eastern end of Tutuila Island and take the Aunu'u Island ferry. Aunu'u Beach has outstanding snorkeling (bring your own gear) in protected coral reefs with a white-sand beach. The island is small enough that you can walk from the dock to the beach.

3 SNORKEL OFU BEACH

On remote Ofu Island, the long white-sand **Ofu Beach** is one of the best places for snorkeling in American Samoa. Its protected reef lies in easily accessible shallow water, with a diverse range of coral and fish. Clear water yields outstanding visibility for spotting tropical fish and brilliant coral. Bring your own snorkel gear.

OFU BEACH

Best Hike

MOUNT 'ALAVA ADVENTURE TRAIL

DISTANCE: 5.6 miles (9 km) round-trip
DURATION: 3.5 hours
ELEVATION CHANGE: 400 feet (122 m)
EFFORT: strenuous
TRAILHEAD: in Vatia, park at Lower Sauma Overlook

For hikers who enjoy challenges, the **Mount 'Alava Adventure Trail** navigates a steep ascent of a ridge via 56 ladders with ropes and 783 stairs. The reward is reaching the summit of the tallest peak in the park and a Samoan fale (pavilion). Views include Pago Pago and Vai'ava Strait. Return down the same way.

org) bookstore. Kids can pick up Junior Ranger activity books to complete for a certificate and badge.

TUTUILA ISLAND

NATIONAL NATURAL LANDMARKS

Tutuila Island has several National Natural Landmarks. Even though most are outside the national park boundary, they are part of the national park system for their unique geology and flora. Many are on private land; you can view them but they may not be accessible. **Vai'ava Strait** and **Aunu'u Island** are the two most easily recognized geological marvels.

MATAFAO PEAK

Two rainforest-draped landmarks stand on either side of Pago Pago Harbor, both created from molten magma. **Matafao Peak** (2,164 ft./660 m) is the highest mountain on Tutuila. Opposite the harbor sits **Rainmaker Mountain.** Driving Route 001 around the west side of the harbor arcs around the base of Matafao, while driving to Äfono Pass from the village of Aüa yields a good view of Rainmaker.

South of Pago Pago International Airport on Route 001, a side trip from Leone Village down Taputima Road leads across private land (ask permission) to **Le'ala Shoreline.** It contains tropical flora, rock sculpted by wave action, and two types of volcanic layers.

HIKING

Many trails are primitive or unimproved and cross private land; request permission before hiking. Look for large fruit bats in trees or flying, even in daytime.

The **Lower Sauma Ridge Trail** (0.4 mi./0.6 km rt., 30 min., moderate) visits archaeological sites. The short trail with interpretive signs cuts through rainforest until it reaches a beach. At the beach, look across Vatia Bay for views of Vai'ava Strait **National Natural Landmark** and try to spot Pola Island, where seabirds nest.

The **World War II Heritage Trail** (1.7 mi./2.7 km rt., 1 hr., moderate) passes several World War II historic sites before entering a rainforest loaded with birds. Near the end of the trail, you'll encounter steep steps with rope

OFU ISLAND

NORTH COAST, TUTUILA

handrails. The trailhead is between Faga'alu and Utulei on the coast road; a sign next to the IBM Laundromat denotes the path. Park at the nearby public parking lot next to the harbor.

MANU'A ISLANDS

The remote islands of **Ta'ū** and **Ofu** are 60 miles (97 km) east of Tutuila Island. The islands contain half of the National Park of American Samoa, which lines their southern shores. These small, undeveloped islands are home to traditional Samoans who live on farms or in tiny villages. There are no amenities or services.

HIKING

Island trails are rugged, primitive, and undeveloped. Consider hiring a local guide, or check with the park service for options.

On Ta'ū, the **Si'u Point Trail** (5.7 mi./9.2 km rt., 3 hrs., moderate) tours a coastal tropical forest on an old dirt roadbed—an extension of the main paved road in Fiti'uta—and passes a cultural history site.

Ofu Island is home to the **Tumu Mountain Trail** (5.5 mi./8.8 km rt., 3 hrs., strenuous), which climbs an old road to the top of the highest point on the island at 1,621 feet (494 m). From the summit, it follows another trail 0.25 mile (0.4 km) to Leolo Ridge where a rocky outcrop overlooks coral lagoons and the three Manu'a Islands. Look for the trailhead near the Ofu Harbor. Though the trail is outside the national park boundary, it is park-maintained and yields views inside the national park.

WHERE TO STAY

INSIDE THE PARK

The National Park Service runs a **homestay program** for those who want to immerse themselves in Samoan life. Guests live in a Samoan village, learn local customs, and participate in traditional village activities, such as gardening, collecting fruit, and fishing. Activities vary by location and host family. Each host sets an independent fee for your stay (the transaction is between you and the host, with no park service involvement).

OUTSIDE THE PARK

For lodging outside the park, **Pago Pago** has the most options. Lodging options on the **Manu'a Islands** are extremely limited: homestays are best for Ta'ū; Ofu has **Vaoto Lodge** (684/655-1120, www.vaotolodge.com).

GETTING THERE AND AROUND

The most accessible airport is **Pago Pago International Airport** (PPG, Pago Pago, http://americansamoaport.as.gov) on Tutuila Island. Car rentals are available. From Pago Pago, **Samoa Airways** (684/699-9126 or 684/699-9127, http://samoaairways.com) offers several flights per week to **Fiti'uta Airport** (FAQ) on the island of Ta'ū or a twice weekly flight to **Ofu Airport** (Z08) on the island of Ofu.

To get around **Tutuila Island,** take a taxi or the independently operated **Aiga buses** (Mon.-Sat.), which run often though not on any set schedule. From Fagatogo market, buses travel to Vatia Village within the national park and to the island's remote corners. Simply flag one down for pickup. The islands of Ta'ū and Ofu have no public transportation or taxis, but Ofu is small enough that you can walk most everywhere.

ESSENTIALS

THE HISTORY OF THE NATIONAL PARKS

THE FIRST NATIONAL PARK

No country in the world recognized any land as a national park until President Ulysses S. Grant signed a bill in 1872 to create **Yellowstone National Park.** Some countries had nature preserves and lands with national protection, as did the United States, but none set aside national parks for the preservation of unique features and enjoyment by the people.

Yellowstone benefited from champions of preservation such as John Muir and George Bird Grinnell, who laid the groundwork, while artists and photographers documented its features. Expedition leader Ferdinand Hayden in 1871 recommended a national park, an idea suggested to him by Northern Pacific Railway lobbyist A. B. Nettleton, who saw the benefit to train ridership. Hayden's report to Congress included details of Yellowstone's uniqueness, but also pointed out that the land was unsuitable for farming or mining, rendering it useless for development. With Hayden's recommendations also came a warning: to avoid the fate of Niagara Falls, a national treasure surrounded by private development.

In part, the creation of the first national park was a function of bureaucracy. When Yellowstone was created in 1872, the states in which it now resides—Wyoming and Montana—did not yet exist. So, the federal government designated it—a big square on the map with no accommodation for topographical features that would later be included.

But the federal vision fell far short of launching a national park by failing to provide funding or an agency to run Yellowstone. No one really knew what a national park was, except that it was for people to enjoy rather than develop. No legislation protected its natural features and wildlife, and the park's first superintendent—who was unpaid—visited it only twice. Several expeditions surveyed Yellowstone for science, mapping, and exploration, but the park floundered, unfunded and directionless.

Six years after the park's inception, Congress finally appropriated money to "protect, preserve, and improve" Yellowstone. The park's second superintendent, Philetus Norris, built a few primitive roads and constructed a rudimentary station at Mammoth Hot Springs. He hired the park's first gamekeeper to battle poachers. But after Norris, political machinations swapped in a series of useless superintendents, and in its second decade, Yellowstone ran wild. Vandals destroyed natural features, poachers slaughtered wildlife, loggers harvested timber, squatters threw up shelters and camps for tourists, and hot springs facilities were erected as laundries and baths.

The public loved the idea of Yellowstone, but Congress trashed its annual funding in 1886 due to ineffective management. The solution to Yellowstone's lack of oversight turned out to be the **U.S. Army,** already operating out of several forts in the territories of Montana, Idaho, and Wyoming. That year, the army erected Fort Yellowstone in the park to enforce regulations.

Outside the park, bison slaughters fed the booming fur and meat business. The federal government even encouraged them, especially as a means to subdue Native American tribes that relied on bison for food and to force them to move onto reservations. Inside Yellowstone, poachers likewise jeopardized the survival of bison. With eviction from the park as the maximum punishment, the army had no strong clout. After a journalistic outcry at one bison slaughter in Pelican Valley, Congress passed the **National Park Protection Act** in 1894 to protect birds, animals, and natural features in Yellowstone. Guilty violators faced fines and jail.

As the first national park, Yellowstone eventually paved the way for other U.S. national parks. Yosemite and Sequoia National Parks followed in 1890, and Mount Rainier gained parkhood in 1899. With the idea of national parks taking off, the first two decades of the 1900s saw the frenzied addition of 12 more national parks—Crater Lake, Wind Cave, Mesa Verde, Glacier, Rocky Mountain, Lassen Volcanic, Hawai'i Volcanoes, Haleakalā, Denali, Grand Canyon, Zion, and Acadia.

THE NATIONAL PARK SERVICE

Managing the growing number of national parks became problematic. While the U.S. Army units managed Yellowstone and Yosemite, other parks relied on various agencies for oversight. The addition of national monuments, mineral springs, memorials, military parks, and historical sites compounded the problem by taking the total number of federal preservation lands to 35.

By 1910, several national organizations, including the Sierra Club, were lobbying for a new federal agency to take over the national parks and monuments. The U.S. Forest Service opposed the concept, arguing in favor of the timber industry that relied on public lands. Stephen Mather, a conservationist and industrialist, and Horace Albright, a young lawyer, launched a campaign in support of creating the National Park Service, spreading the word via journalist Robert Yard.

Finally, 44 years following the creation of Yellowstone National Park, President Woodrow Wilson put his signature on the 1916 **Organic Act** to establish the **National Park Service.** The act directed the agency to preserve the scenery, natural and historic objects, and wildlife. The act also required the agency provide for the enjoyment of those things in a way that preserved them for future generations.

The new agency was placed under the Department of the Interior, an entirely different branch of the federal government from the Department of Agriculture that oversaw the U.S. Forest Service. To this day, that differentiation in federal management separates the purpose of the national parks and national forests and the way they can be used.

THE PARKS TODAY

National parks were steadily added to the system over the century following the creation of the National Park Service. Today, the NPS oversees 62 national parks and more than 400 public lands. Most recently, since 2018 the system added Gateway Arch, Indiana Dunes, and White Sands.

Many of our parks have gained recognition beyond the country's boundaries. UNESCO (United Nations Educational, Scientific and Cultural Organization) has named 15 of the parks as World Heritage Sites and 19 as Biosphere Reserves.

Our national parks protect some of the country's most scenic and unique places. From the first rays of sunlight to hit the country in Acadia to the ice-draped highest peak on the continent in Denali, these national prizes yield visions of raw, uncontrolled beauty. Glacier's ice-scoured mountains, Grand Canyon's deep chasm, and Yosemite's vertical walls remind us of the earth-shaping forces that wrought our landscape. Bison herds wandering in Yellowstone let us connect with our roots, as do the cliff dwellings in Mesa Verde. For those where city lights drown out the stars, the parks are places where the Milky Way still sparkles in the night sky. These parks offer renewal for the human spirit and a regeneration of that deep connection to how we, as humans, fit in the world.

ROAD RULES

CAR AND RV RENTAL

Most car rental companies have locations in major international airports. To reserve a car in advance, contact **Budget** (U.S. 800/218-7992, outside U.S. 800/472-3325, www.budget.com), **Dollar Rent A Car** (866/434-2226, www.dollar.com), **Enterprise** (855/266-9289, www.enterprise.com), or **Hertz** (U.S. and Canada 800/654-3131, international 800/654-3001, www.hertz.com).

To rent a car, most companies require drivers to be at least 21 years old and have a valid driver's license. Companies may also tack on additional fees for those under age 25. You will also need liability insurance, which you can purchase through the rental company. Private auto insurance also tends to cover rental cars, but check with your insurance company to verify.

The **average cost** of a rental car is $50 per day or $210 per week; however, rates vary greatly based on the time of year and distance traveled. Weekend and summer rentals cost significantly more. Generally, it is more expensive to rent from car rental agencies at an airport because of added fees. To avoid excessive rates, first plan travel to areas where a car is not required, then rent a car from an agency branch in town to further explore more rural areas. Rental agencies occasionally allow vehicle drop-off at a different location from where it was picked up for an additional fee.

Another option is to rent an **RV.** You won't have to worry about camping or lodging options, and many facilities, particularly farther north, accommodate RVs. However, RVs are difficult to maneuver and park, limiting your access to some trailheads and sights in national parks. Be aware that some national park roads ban RVs or restrict length. They are also expensive, both in terms of gas and the rental rates. Rates during the summer average $1,300 per week and $570 for three days, the standard minimal rental. **Cruise America** (800/671-8042, www.cruiseamerica.com) has branches throughout the United States.

ROAD CONDITIONS

Road closures are not uncommon, especially in winter in mountain parks. Traffic jams, accidents, mudslides, fires, and snow can affect interstates and local highways at any time. Before heading out on your adventure, check road conditions online with the state highway department.

In an emergency, **dial 911** from any phone. The American Automobile Association, better known as **AAA** (800/222-4357, www.aaa.com), offers roadside assistance free to members; others pay a fee.

Be aware of your car's maintenance needs while on the road. The most frequent issues result from **summer heat.** If the car gets hot or overheats, stop for a while to cool it off. Never open the radiator cap if the engine is steaming. After the engine cools, squeeze the top radiator hose to see if there's any pressure in it; if there isn't, it's safe to open. Never pour water into a hot radiator because it could crack the engine block. If you start to smell rubber, your tires are overheating, and that's a good way to have a blowout. Stop and let them cool off. When descending steep mountain roads, use lower gears for the engine to force a slowdown rather than riding your brakes and wearing them down. During **winter**, a can of silicone lubricant such as WD-40 will unfreeze door locks, dry off humid wiring, and keep your hinges in shape. Mountain parks may require chains or traction devices for winter access.

MAPS AND GPS NAVIGATION

Always travel with a printed map or guide; do *not* rely solely on GPS navigation, which is notoriously unreliable inside the national parks. Some park travelers relying on GPS get led to the wrong location, into dead ends, or onto closed roads, snowbound passes, or defunct roads. Carry printed, up-to-date road maps and learn how to read them. Check seasonal access and weather conditions for all driving routes prior to travel.

Upon entering any national park and paying the park entrance fee, you'll be offered a free park map. These maps are good for paved road navigation and locating services, but they are not detailed enough for backcountry trails or rough, 4WD roads. For topographical maps, download maps from **National Geographic** (www.natgeomaps.com) or order them from the **USGS** (http://store.usgs.gov).

INTERNATIONAL DRIVERS LICENSES

If you are visiting the United States from another country and planning to drive, you need to secure an International Driving Permit from your home country before your arrival. (You won't be able to get one once you're here.) You must also bring your government-issued driving permit.

Visitors from outside the United States should check the driving rules of the states they will visit at www.usa.gov. Among the most important rules is that traffic runs on the right side of the road in the United States. Note that many states have bans on using handheld cell phones while driving. If caught, expect to pay a hefty fine.

HEALTH AND SAFETY

HOSPITALS AND EMERGENCIES

Most national parks are tucked into remote locations where emergency services take longer to respond. Often, hospitals, emergency rooms, and urgent care facilities are located outside the national parks in nearby towns several hours away. The larger parks with huge visitation numbers may have an urgent care clinic.

If you are injured in a park, **dial 911** (if you have phone service) or the park phone number for emergencies. If phone service is not available, flag down a ranger or passing motorist to get help instead. Due to the remote locations of many national parks, do not rely on having cell phone service to call for help.

WILDERNESS SAFETY

For hikers, backpackers, mountain bikers, climbers, and river travelers, be prepared to handle emergencies on your own. Be competent in administering first aid, self-rescuing, and providing your own evacuation. Rely only on calling for help in life-threatening situations or where severe injuries prevent you from being able to get out on your own.

HEAT EXHAUSTION AND HEATSTROKE

Being out in the elements can present its own set of challenges. Heat exhaustion and heatstroke can affect anyone during the hot summer months, particularly during a long strenuous hike in the sun. Common symptoms include nausea, light-headedness, headache, or muscle cramps.

DEHYDRATION

Many first-time hikers to high-mountain or arid parks are surprised to find they drink more water than at home. Wind, sun, altitude, and lower humidity can add up to a fast case of dehydration. It manifests first as a headache. While hiking, drink lots of water, even more than you normally would. With children, monitor their fluid intake. For hiking desert parks, plan to carry and drink 1 gallon (3.8 l) of water per person per day. Before launching at a trailhead, consult with rangers about current reliable water sources.

HYPOTHERMIA

Exhausted and physically unprepared hikers are at risk for insidious and subtle hypothermia. The body's inner core loses heat, reducing mental and physical functions. Watch for uncontrolled shivering, incoherence, poor judgment, fumbling, mumbling, and slurred speech. Avoid becoming hypothermic by staying dry. Don rain gear and warm moisture-wicking layers, rather than cottons that won't dry and fail to retain heat. Get hypothermic hikers into dry clothing and shelter. Give them warm nonalcoholic and non-caffeinated liquids. If the victim cannot regain body heat, get into a sleeping bag with the victim, both stripped for skin-to-skin contact.

HYPERNATREMIA

Often occurring in hotter, arid parks, hypernatremia is an imbalance of sodium. Taking electrolytes with fluids prevents the onset of nausea, weakness, and loss of appetite that accompanies hypernatremia. More severe symptoms may include confusion and twitching muscles.

POISON OAK, IVY, AND SUMAC

Poison oak, ivy, and sumac are vines or shrubs that inhabit forests. Common in western states, poison oak has three scalloped leaves. Found across the United States except for tropical islands and Alaska, poison ivy has three spoon-shaped leaves and grows along rivers, lakes, and oceans. With 7-13 leaflets, poison sumac grows in wet, swampy zones in the north and Florida. Contact with these plants may cause a rash and itching, which can be transferred to your eyes or face via touch. Your best protection is to wear long sleeves and long pants when hiking, no matter how hot it is. Tecnu can protect your skin from poison oak and ivy. Calamine lotion can help ease the rash and itching.

GIARDIA

Lakes and streams can carry parasites like *Giardia lamblia*. If ingested, it causes cramping, nausea, and severe diarrhea for up to six weeks. Avoid giardia by boiling water (for one minute, plus one minute for each 1,000 ft./305 m of elevation above sea level) or using a one-micron filter. Bleach also works (add two drops per quart and wait 30 minutes). Tap water in campgrounds, hotels, and picnic areas has been treated; you'll taste the chlorine.

ALTITUDE

Some visitors from sea-level locales feel the effects of altitude at high elevations in mountain parks of the Rockies and the Sierra. Watch for light-headedness, headaches, or shortness of breath. To acclimate, slow down the pace of hiking and drink lots of fluids. If symptoms spike, descend in elevation as soon as possible. Altitude also increases UV radiation exposure: To prevent sunburn, use a strong sunscreen and wear sunglasses and a hat.

WILDLIFE

BEARS

Many of the national parks are home to **black bears** and **grizzly bears.** Food is the biggest bear attractant. Bears are dangerous around food, be it a carcass in the woods, pack on a trail, or cooler in a campsite. Proper use, storage, and handling of food and garbage prevent bears from being conditioned to look for food around humans and turning aggressive.

On the trail, pick up any dropped food, including wrappers and crumbs, and pack out all garbage. When camping, use low-odor foods, keep food and cooking gear out of sleeping sites in the backcountry, and store them inside your vehicle in front-country campgrounds.

Bear Bells vs. Pepper Spray

On trails in grizzly country (Alaska, Washington, Idaho, Montana, and Wyoming), you'll hear jingle bells, sold in gift shops as **bear bells.** While making noise on the trail does prevent

▸ BLACK BEAR, YELLOWSTONE

WILDLIFE SAFETY TIPS

While you may see bison, elk, moose, deer, pronghorn, wolves, coyotes, or bears, remember that wildlife is just that . . . *wild*. Though bison, elk, or even bears may appear tame, they are not and gorings are common. Here are a few tips to remain safe.

Do not approach wildlife. Crowding wildlife puts you at risk and endangers the animal, often scaring it off. Seemingly docile bison and elk have suddenly gored people crowding too close. Stay at least **100 yards away** (91 m, the length of a football field) from bears and wolves. For all other wildlife, stay at least **25 yards (23 m) away.**

For spying wildlife up close, use a good pair of **binoculars** or a **spotting scope.** Use telephoto lenses for photography.

Take safe selfies. Bison gorings are more prevalent now, and many are related to people trying to take selfie photos with tablets or cell phones. Avoid getting too close to these large creatures and maintain a distance of 25-100 yards (23-91 m) between yourself and all wildlife.

Do not feed any animal. Because human food is not part of their natural diet, they may suffer at foraging on their own. As they rely on people for handouts, they become aggressive, endangering both human visitors and themselves.

Follow instructions for food storage. Bears, wolves, and coyotes may become more aggressive when acquiring food, and ravens can strew food and garbage, making it more available to other wildlife.

Let the animal's behavior guide your behavior. If an animal appears twitchy, nervous, or points eyes and ears directly at you, back off: You're too close. If you behave like a predator stalking an animal, the creature will assume you are one.

If you see **wildlife along a road,** use pullouts or broad shoulders to drive completely off the road. Use the car as a blind to watch wildlife, and keep pets inside. Watch for cars, as visitors can be injured by inattentive drivers whenever a wildlife jam occurs.

surprising a bear, bear bells are not a substitute for human noise on the trail in the form of talking, singing, hooting, and hollering.

Most hikers in grizzly country carry an 8-ounce (237-ml) can of **pepper spray,** which deters bear attacks without injuring the bears or humans. Spray it directly into a bear's face, aiming for the eyes and nose. Carry it on the front of your pack where it is easily reached. (If confronted with a bear, you won't have time to dig it out of your pack.)

MOUNTAIN LIONS

Because of their solitary nature, it is unlikely you will see a mountain lion, even on long trips in the backcountry. These large cats rarely prey on humans, but they can—especially small kids. Hike with others, keep kids close, and make noise on the trail. If you do stumble upon a cougar, do not run: Remain calm and gather your group together to appear bigger. Look at the cat with peripheral vision, rather than staring straight on, and back away slowly. If the lion attacks, fight back with rocks, sticks, or by kicking.

HANTAVIRUS

Hantavirus infection is contracted by inhaling dust from deer mice droppings. When camping, store food in rodent-proof containers. If you find rodent dust in your gear, disinfect the gear with water and bleach (1.5 cups bleach to 1 g water/240 ml to 3.8 l). If you contract the virus, which results in flu-like symptoms, seek immediate medical attention.

SPIDERS, MOSQUITOES, AND TICKS

Spiders, mosquitoes, and ticks can carry diseases such as West Nile virus and Rocky Mountain spotted fever. Protect yourself by wearing long sleeves and pants and use insect repellent in spring-summer, when mosquitoes and ticks are common. If you are bitten by a tick, carefully remove it by the head with tweezers, disinfect the bite, and then see a doctor. Some spiders, such as the brown recluse, carry poison in their bites. If symptoms are severe (breathing difficulty, nausea, sweating, and vomiting), seek medical attention immediately.

SNAKES

Rattlesnakes are ubiquitous in prairie and desert parks across the West. When hiking, keep your eyes on the ground and an ear out for the telltale rattle—a warning to keep away. Should you be bitten, seek immediate medical help.

TRAVEL TIPS

ENTERING THE UNITED STATES

PASSPORTS AND VISAS

If you are visiting from another country, you must have a **valid passport** and a **visa** to enter the United States. You may qualify for the **Visa Waiver Program** if you hold a current passport from one of the following countries: Andorra, Australia, Austria, Belgium, Brunei, Chile, Czech Republic, Denmark, Estonia, Finland, France, Germany, Greece, Hungary, Iceland, Ireland, Italy, Japan, Latvia, Liechtenstein, Lithuania, Luxembourg, Malta, Monaco, the Netherlands, New Zealand, Norway, Portugal, San Marino, Singapore, Slovakia, Slovenia, South Korea, Spain, Sweden, Switzerland, Taiwan, and the United Kingdom. To qualify, you must apply online with the Electronic System for Travel Authorization at www.cbp.gov and hold a **return plane or cruise ticket** to your country of origin dated less than **90 days** from your date of entry. Holders of Canadian passports don't need visas or visa waivers.

In most other countries, the local U.S. embassy should be able to provide a **tourist visa.** The application fee for a visa is US$160, plus you'll need to pay an issuance fee. While a visa may be processed in as little as 24 hours on request, plan for at least a couple of weeks, as there can be unexpected delays, particularly during the busy summer season (June-Aug.). For information, visit https://travel.state.gov.

Travelers from Canada and countries in the Western Hemisphere Travel Initiative may use a U.S. passport card, enhanced driver's license, or NEXUS card instead of a passport. Except Canadians, international travelers entering the United States must have a current I-94 form ($6).

MONEY AND CURRENCY EXCHANGE

International travelers should exchange currency at their major port of entry. As you travel, use ATM cards to get more cash. Smaller denominations ($50 and under) work best. Using a credit card while traveling will give you the best exchange rates.

EMBASSIES AND CONSULATES

If you should lose your passport or find yourself in some other trouble while visiting the United States, contact your country's offices for assistance. The website of the **U.S. State Department** (www.state.gov) lists the websites for all foreign embassies and consulates within the United States. Also, a representative can direct you to the nearest embassy or consulate.

CUSTOMS

Before you enter the United States from another country by sea or by air, you'll be required to fill out a customs form. Those driving into the country will make verbal declarations at their point of entry. Check with the U.S. embassy in your country or the **Customs and Border Protection** website (www.cbp.gov) for an updated list of items you must declare.

In general, the United States does not allow plants, drugs, firewood, or live bait to cross borders. Some fresh meats, poultry products, fruits, and vegetables are restricted, as are firearms. Pets are permitted to cross the border with a certificate of rabies vaccination dated within 30 days prior to crossing. Bear sprays are not allowed on airplanes in checked or carry-on luggage and are considered firearms in Canada; they must have a U.S. Environmental Protection Agency-approved label to go across the border.

If you require medication administered by injection, you must pack your syringes in a checked bag; syringes are not permitted in carry-ons coming into the United States. Also, pack documentation describing your need for any narcotic medications you've brought with you. Failure to produce documentation for narcotics on request can result in severe penalties in the United States.

PASSES, PERMITS, AND FEES

Many national park passes are available for purchase online at **https://store.usgs.gov/pass.** Entrance fees must be paid in person at the individual park entrances; some unstaffed entrances may be cash-only.

ENTRY FEES

Entrance fees range from free to $35 or more per vehicle; entry fees for motorcycles, bicyclists, and individuals on foot are slightly reduced. Once paid, most entrance fees are good for seven days.

ANNUAL PASSES

The **Annual Pass** ($80) admits entrance to all national parks and federal fee areas for up to one year. Most national parks also offer their own **Annual Pass** ($50-70) granting access to the one park for up to one year. All U.S. fourth graders are eligible to receive a free annual pass.

SENIOR PASS

U.S. citizens or permanent residents age 62 and older have two pass options: an **Annual Senior Pass** ($20, $10 processing fee), good for one year, or a **Lifetime**

Senior Pass ($80, $10 processing fee), which is valid for life. To purchase either pass, apply online (https://yourpassnow.com) or bring proof of age (state driver's license, birth certificate, or passport) in person to any national park entrance station (processing fee waived at park entrances). In a private vehicle, the card admits four adults, plus all children under age 16. Four annual senior passes can be traded in for the lifetime senior pass.

Both senior passes grant the passholder discounts on fees for federally run tours and campgrounds; however, discounts do not apply to park concessionaire services like hotels, boat tours, and bus tours.

ACCESS PASS

Blind or permanently disabled U.S. citizens or permanent residents can request a lifetime **National Parks and Federal Recreational Lands Access Pass** (free, $10 processing fee) for access to all national parks and other federal sites. The pass admits the passholder plus three other adults in the same vehicle; children under age 16 are free. Passholders also receive a 50 percent discount on federally run tours and campgrounds. Proof of medical disability or eligibility is required for receiving federal benefits.

MILITARY PASS

U.S. military personnel can get a lifetime **National Parks and Federal Recreational Lands Access Pass** (free) for access to all national parks and other federal sites. The pass admits the passholder plus three other adults in the same vehicle; children under age 16 are free. Passholders also get 50 percent discounts on federally run tours and campgrounds. Passes must be acquired in person at entrance stations; proof of service is required.

FEE-FREE DAYS

Admission is free on Fee-Free Days: Martin Luther King Jr. Day (Jan.), the first day of National Park Week (Apr.), National Park Service Anniversary (Aug.), National Public Lands Day (Sept.), and Veterans Day (Nov. 11).

VOLUNTEER PASS

Those volunteering in national parks or other federal lands can get an annual pass to all national parks by reaching 250 service hours. Service hours may be accrued in one year or across several years.

WILDERNESS PERMITS

If you're planning a backcountry excursion, follow all rules and guidelines for obtaining **wilderness permits** for specific parks (www.nps.gov). Rules vary between parks, especially regarding fees, reservations, and procedures for picking up permits. Park-specific backcountry offices will have information on any health, trail, bear, or other alerts in the area. For your safety, let someone outside your party know your route and expected date of return.

TRAVELING WITHOUT RESERVATIONS

During the busy summer months, accommodations can be hard to come by. It's common for national park lodgings and campgrounds to be full days, weeks, and even months in advance. While it may be possible to find a last-minute campsite at one of the nearby national forests, savvy travelers book lodgings, some campsites, and wilderness permits **up to 13 months in advance.** Most campground reservations are handled by www.recreation.gov.

Don't have reservations for camping? Here are a few tips to snagging a campsite in summer.

Make a base camp and stay put rather than shuffling campgrounds every day or so. You'll spend a little more time driving to some destinations, but you'll experience the park more with the time you save from searching campground after campground only to be confronted with Full signs.

On any day you plan to move camp, change locations in early morning to get a campsite before campgrounds fill up. Make getting your next campsite the first priority rather than sightseeing.

At campgrounds that allow self-selection of campsites, plan to begin prowling to nab a site when someone departs an hour or more before the fill times mentioned on the park's website.

TRAVELING WITH CHILDREN

The National Park Service has designed ways to pique the interest of kids through educational activities online (www.nps.gov, under "Learn About the Park"), in-park activities, and visitors center hands-on exhibits.

Hiking with kids can either be a nightmare or a hoot. To make it more fun, take water and snacks along to prevent hunger and thirst from zapping their energy. Take extra layers to keep kids warm if the weather turns. Help them connect with the environment while hiking by asking them about what they see and why things are the way they are. If you make hiking a fun experience for them, they'll want to do it again.

JUNIOR RANGER PROGRAMS

Junior Ranger Programs (www.nps.gov/kids/jrRangers.cfm) mix educational activities with experiences for families to do in the park. Most activities target ages 6-12. Pick up Junior Ranger activity guides ($3-5 or free) at any visitors center. Kids complete the self-guided activities and receive a Junior Ranger badge after stopping at a visitors center to get sworn in.

TRAVELING WITH PETS

Pets are allowed inside national parks, but only in limited areas: campgrounds, parking lots, and roadsides. They are not allowed on most trails and beaches, in the backcountry, or at most park lodges or motor inns. When outside a vehicle or in a campground, pets must be on a leash or caged. Be kind enough to avoid leaving them unattended in a car anywhere. Be considerate of wildlife and other visitors by keeping your pet under control and disposing of waste in garbage cans. Some national parks (such as Grand Canyon) provide kennel services for a fee.

ACCESSIBILITY

While some national park structures have been fitted with ramps and wider doors, many historic or remote structures remain inaccessible. Many short hiking trails are accessible to wheelchairs and most campgrounds designate specific campsites that meet the Americans with Disabilities Act standards.

If you are traveling with a disability, there are many resources to help you plan your trip. Check on the specific park's website (www.nps.gov) for services pertinent to that park. Many parks have facilities, programs, and trails designed for those with physical or mobility challenges. Most park brochures are also available in large print or braille. With enough notice, some parks can provide services for those with hearing impairments, and park videos often have captioned versions. Trained service dogs are permitted in many parks, but check on requirements; some parks with prevalent grizzly bear populations discourage them in the backcountry.

FIREARMS

Federal law allows people that can legally carry firearms under federal, state, and local laws to bring their guns into the national parks. However, federal law prohibits firearms in government offices, visitors centers, ranger stations, fee-collection buildings, and maintenance facilities. Those places are marked with signs at all public entrances. Discharging firearms in the park is illegal except when presented with "imminent danger."

WI-FI AND CELL SERVICE

Cellular service and Internet connectivity within the national parks tend to be limited. In general, plan to be out of reach while you travel in the parks, where service is unavailable on many roads, trails, campgrounds, picnic areas, and lodges. National park visitors centers, ranger stations, and campgrounds rarely have Wi-Fi. Some park lodges may offer limited Wi-Fi for overnight guests, but connectivity will often be very slow.

MOBILE APPS

The National Park Service has **mobile phone apps** for individual parks that contain information on visitors centers, hikes, geyser predictions, road construction, ranger programs, and interactive park maps. **Download the apps before** you begin your trip because Internet is limited inside the parks.

Be aware that you will have dead zones for phones and that mobile phone apps don't account for seasonal road or trail closures. Your first stop for accurate, up-to-date information should always be a national park visitors center and the national park website.

LEAVE NO TRACE

To keep the national parks pristine, visitors to these parks need to take an active role in maintaining them.

Plan ahead and prepare. Hiking in the backcountry is inherently risky. Three miles (4.8 km) hiking at the high elevations in Wyoming may be much harder than the same distance through your neighborhood park back home. Choose appropriate routes for mileage and elevation gain with this in mind, and carry hiking essentials.

RESPECT WILDLIFE.

Travel and camp on durable surfaces. In front-country and backcountry campgrounds, camp in designated sites. Protect fragile plants by staying on trails even in mud, refusing to cut switchbacks, and walking single file. If you must walk off the trail, step on rocks, snow, or dry grasses rather than wet soil and delicate plants.

Leave what you find. Flowers, rocks, and fur tufts on shrubs are protected park resources, as are historical and cultural items. For lunch stops and camping, sit on rocks or logs where you find them rather than moving them to accommodate comfort.

Properly dispose of waste. Pack out whatever you bring, including all garbage. If toilets are not available, pack out toilet paper. Urinate on rocks, logs, gravel, or snow to protect soils and plants from salt-starved wildlife, and bury feces 6-8 inches (15-20 cm) deep at least 200 feet (61 m) from water.

Minimize campfire impacts. Make fires in designated firepits only, not on beaches. Use small wrist-size dead and downed wood, not live branches. Be aware: Fires and collecting firewood are not permitted in some places in the parks.

Respect wildlife. Bring along binoculars, spotting scopes, and telephoto lenses to aid in watching wildlife. Keep your distance. Do not feed any wildlife, even ground squirrels. Once fed, they become more aggressive.

Be considerate of other visitors. Particularly be aware of cell phones and how their use or noise cuts into the natural soundscapes of the parks.

For more Leave No Trace information, visit www.LNT.org.

INDEX

I

JK

S

TUV

WXYZ

LIST OF MAPS

Great Lakes and Northeast

The South

Islands

PHOTO CREDITS

Photo/Shaina Niehans; 186: © Photog_67 | Dreamstime.com (top), ©Trevor Ducken | Dreamstime.com (bottom); 187: © NPS; 188: © NPS/S. Olson; 191: © Cheri Alguire | Dreamstime.com; 195: © Becky Lomax; 196: © Randy Vavra | Dreamstime.com; 198: © Jay Beiler | Dreamstime.com; 199: © Stevehymon | Dreamstime.com; 202: © Trekandshoot | Dreamstime.com (top), ©Rick Moulton | Dreamstime.com (bottom); 204: © Stevehymon | Dreamstime.com; 205: © Jay Beiler | Dreamstime.com; 206: © Sean Pavone | Dreamstime.com; 209: © NPS/D. Archuleta (top), ©Becky Lomax (middle), ©Becky Lomax (bottom); 210: © Curtis Smith | Dreamstime.com (top), ©Matthew Lombardi (bottom); 211: © Becky Lomax; 212: © NPS/B. Baccus (top), ©Blueenayim | Dreamstime.com (middle), ©Matthew Lombardi (bottom); 213: © Craig Hanson | Dreamstime.com; 217: © Becky Lomax; 218: © Becky Lomax; 219: © Judy Jewell; 220: © Becky Lomax; 221: © Becky Lomax (top), ©Judy Jewell (bottom); 223: © Sean Pavone | Dreamstime.com; 227: © NPS/J. Preston (top), ©NPS/D Archuleta (bottom); 228: © NPS/C Bubar; 229: © Justek16 | Dreamstime.com (top), ©NPS (bottom); 230: © Gregg Brekke | Dreamstime.com; 232: © Pete Zaidel; 233: © Stanislav Moroz | Dreamstime.com; 234: © NPS/B. Baccus; 235: © Nat693 | Dreamstime.com; 236: © NPS; 237: © NPS/D. Archuleta; 238: © NPS/B. Baccus; 239: © Pierre Leclerc | Dreamstime.com; 240: © Becky Lomax; 244: © Becky Lomax (top), ©Becky Lomax (bottom); 246: © Becky Lomax; 247: © Becky Lomax; 248: © Becky Lomax; 249: © Becky Lomax; 251: © Edmund Lowe | Dreamstime.com; 255: © Galyna Andrushko | Dreamstime.com; 256: © NPS Photo/Deby Dixon (top), ©Matthew Lombardi (bottom); 257: © NPS Photo/Deby Dixon; 258: © Amadeustx | Dreamstime.com; 259: © Matthew Lombardi; 260: © Kan1234 | Dreamstime.com; 263: © Becky Lomax (left), ©Becky Lomax (middle), ©Becky Lomax (right); 264: © NPS/Michael Quinn; 265: © Philip Bird | Dreamstime.com; 266: © Jason P. Ross | Dreamstime.com (top), ©Josep Miquel Ubalde Baulo | Dreamstime.com (middle), ©NPS/Michael Quinn (bottom); 267: © Thin Air Photography | Dreamstime.com; 271: © NPS/Kristen M. Caldon (top), © Becky Lomax (bottom); 272: © NPS/Michael Quinn; 273: © NPS/Michael Quinn; 276: © NPS/Kristen M. Caldon (top), © NPS/Michael Quinn (bottom); 277: © NPS/Michael Quinn; 278: © NPS/Michael Quinn; 279: © NPS/Michael Quinn (top), ©NPS/W. Tyson Joye (bottom); 281: © NPS/Michael Quinn (top), ©Becky Lomax (bottom); 282: © NPS/Michael Quinn; 283: © NPS/Michael Quinn; 284: © NPS/Michael Quinn (top), ©NPS/Michael Quinn (bottom); 285: © NPS/Michael Quinn; 287: © NPS/Michael Quinn; 292: © Becky Lomax; 293: © Becky Lomax (top), ©Becky Lomax (bottom); 294: © NPS/Hallie Larsen; 295: © Becky Lomax; 299: © Crackerclips | Dreamstime.com (top), ©Becky Lomax (bottom); 300: © Becky Lomax (top), ©Becky Lomax (bottom); 302: © Arlene Hochman Waller | Dreamstime.com; 303: © Sandra Foyt | Dreamstime.com; 304: © NPS (top), © Rinus Baak | Dreamstime.com (bottom); 307: © Arlene Hochman Waller | Dreamstime.comi; 308: © NPS; 309: © Chris Sargent | Dreamstime.com; 313: © NPS/Rebecca Alfafara (top), © NPS/Marc Neidig (bottom); 314: © NPS/Rendall Seely; 315: © NPS/Caitlin Ceci; 317: © NPS/Rebecca Alfafara; 318: © NPS/Sarah Stio; 319: © NPS/Marc Neidig (top), ©NPS/Sarah Stio (bottom); 321: © Anna Dudko | Dreamstime.com (top), ©NPS/Caitlin Ceci (bottom); 322: © NPS/Rendall Seely; 323: © NPS/Rendall Seely; 324: © NPS/Caitlin Ceci; 325: © NPS; 326: © Sergiyn | Dreamstime.com; 327: © NPS/Brian B. Roanhorse; 330: © Assignments | Dreamstime.com (top), ©Hasan Can Balcioglu | Dreamstime.com (middle), ©Brucemacdonald | Dreamstime.com (bottom); 331: © NPS/Brian B. Roanhorse; 332: © Ekaterina Pokrovsky | Dreamstime.com; 333: © Jason Busa | Dreamstime.com (top), ©Venemama | Dreamstime.com (bottom); 334: © Jason Busa | Dreamstime.com; 335: © Scott Prokop | Dreamstime.com; 336: © Sergio Boccardo | Dreamstime.com; 337: © Alyssand | Dreamstime.com; 338: © Larry Gevert | Dreamstime.com; 342: © JJamie Frattarelli | Dreamstime.com (top), ©Larry Gevert | Dreamstime.com (bottom); 343: © Paul Brady | Dreamstime.com; 344: © Kwiktor | Dreamstime.com; 345: © Frank Bach | Dreamstime.com; 346: © James Phelps Jr | Dreamstime.com (top), © Scott Prokop | Dreamstime.com (bottom); 347: © Björn Alberts | Dreamstime.com; 348: © Maciejbledowski | Dreamstime.com (top), ©Pierre Leclerc | Dreamstime.com (bottom); 349: © Philip Kononuk | Dreamstime.com; 350: © NPS/Neal Herbert; 353: © NPS/Jacob W. Frank (top), ©NPS/Neal Herbert (bottom); 354: © NPS/Neal Herbert (top), ©NPS/Casey Hodnett (bottom); 355: © NPS/Kait Thomas (top), ©NPS/Neal Herbert (bottom); 356: © NPS/Neal Herbert (left), ©NPS/Jacob W. Frank (right); 359: © Sandra Foyt | Dreamstime.com; 360: © Arlene Hochman Waller | Dreamstime.com; 364: © Edwin Verin | Dreamstime.com; 365: © NPS/Kirsten Kearse (top), ©Peng Ge | Dreamstime.com (middle), ©Sumikophoto | Dreamstime.com (bottom); 366: © NPS/Neal Herbert; 367: © Becky Lomax; 368: © NPS/Neal Herbert; 369:

© NPS/Emily Ogden; 370: © Twildlife | Dreamstime.com; 372: © Kojihirano | Dreamstime.com; 376: © Bill Kennedy | Dreamstime.com; 377: © Josep Miquel Ubalde Baulo | Dreamstime.com (top), ©Gnagel | Dreamstime.com (bottom); 379: © NPS; 381: © NPS/Patrick Myers; 384: © NPS/Patrick Myers (top), ©NPS/Patrick Myers (bottom); 385: © NPS/Patrick Myers (left), ©NPS/Patrick Myers (right); 386: © NPS/Patrick Myers; 387: © NPS/Patrick Myers; 388: © NPS/Scott Hansen; 389: © Becky Lomax; 392: © Becky Lomax; 393: © Becky Lomax (top), © Becky Lomax (bottom); 394: © Becky Lomax; 395: © Becky Lomax (top), © Becky Lomax (bottom); 396: © Becky Lomax; 397: © Becky Lomax; 399: © Becky Lomax; 400: © Sandra Foyt | Dreamstime.com (top), ©Becky Lomax (bottom); 401: © Glenn Nagel | Dreamstime.com; 402: © Becky Lomax; 403: © Anton Foltin | Dreamstime.com; 406: © Becky Lomax; 407: © Becky Lomax (top), ©Wilsilver77 | Dreamstime.com (bottom); 412: © Becky Lomax; 413: © Becky Lomax (top), © Jody Wissing | Dreamstime.com (bottom); 414: © Becky Lomax; 415: © Becky Lomax; 416: © Becky Lomax; 417: © Becky Lomax; 418: © Becky Lomax; 421: © Becky Lomax (left), ©Becky Lomax (middle), ©Becky Lomax (right); 422: © Becky Lomax; 423: © Becky Lomax; 424: © Becky Lomax (top), ©Becky Lomax (middle), ©Becky Lomax (bottom); 425: © RIRFStock | Dreamstime.com; 428: © Becky Lomax; 429: © Becky Lomax (top), ©NPS (bottom); 432: © Becky Lomax; 433: © Becky Lomax; 434: © Becky Lomax; 435: © Becky Lomax; 436: © Jzehnder1 | Dreamstime.com; 437: © Becky Lomax; 438: © Jruffa | Dreamstime.com; 439: © Tupungato | Dreamstime.com; 440: © Becky Lomax; 441: © Steve Lagreca | Dreamstime.com; 442: © NPS/Zach Schierl; 446: © Anna Dudko | Dreamstime.com; 447: © Zrfphoto | Dreamstime.com (top), © Sdbower | Dreamstime.com (bottom); 449: © Becky Lomax; 453: © Becky Lomax; 454: © Becky Lomax; 455: © Becky Lomax (top), © Becky Lomax (bottom); 456: © Becky Lomax (top), © Becky Lomax (bottom); 457: © Becky Lomax (top), © Becky Lomax (bottom); 458: © Becky Lomax; 459: © Becky Lomax; 460: © Becky Lomax (top), © Becky Lomax (bottom); 461: © Becky Lomax; 462: © Becky Lomax; 463: © Becky Lomax; 464: © Becky Lomax; 466: © Becky Lomax (top), © Becky Lomax (bottom); 468: © Becky Lomax; 469: © Becky Lomax; 470: © Becky Lomax; 472: © Becky Lomax; 476: © Becky Lomax; 477: © Becky Lomax (top), © Becky Lomax (bottom); 478: © Becky Lomax; 480: © Becky Lomax; 481: © Becky Lomax; 482: © Becky Lomax (top), © Becky Lomax (bottom); 483: © Becky Lomax; 485: © Becky Lomax; 486: © Becky Lomax; 487: © Becky Lomax; 488: © Becky Lomax; 490: © Becky Lomax; 491: © Becky Lomax; 494: © Becky Lomax; 495: © Becky Lomax (top), © Becky Lomax (middle), © Becky Lomax (bottom); 496: © Becky Lomax; 499: © Becky Lomax (top), © Becky Lomax (bottom); 500: © Becky Lomax; 501: © Becky Lomax (top), © Becky Lomax (bottom); 503: © Becky Lomax (top), © Becky Lomax (bottom); 504: © Becky Lomax (top), © Becky Lomax (bottom); 505: © Becky Lomax (top), © Becky Lomax (bottom); 506: © Becky Lomax; 507: © Becky Lomax; 509: © Becky Lomax; 510: © Becky Lomax; 511: © Becky Lomax (top), © Becky Lomax (bottom); 512: © Becky Lomax; 516: © Becky Lomax (top), © Becky Lomax (bottom); 517: © Becky Lomax; 518: © Becky Lomax; 520: © Becky Lomax; 522: © Becky Lomax; 523: © Becky Lomax (top), © Becky Lomax (bottom); 524: © Becky Lomax; 525: © Zrfphoto | Dreamstime.com; 526: © Becky Lomax; 527: © Becky Lomax; 528: © Becky Lomax; 529: © NPS/Dave Bruner; 532: © Becky Lomax; 533: © Becky Lomax (top), © Becky Lomax (bottom); 534: © NPS/Kim Wehner; 536: © Becky Lomax; 537: © Becky Lomax; 538: © Paul Lemke | Dreamstime.com; 541: © Hilary Nangle (top), © Jon Bilous | Dreamstime.com (middle), © Kenneth Keifer | Dreamstime.com (bottom); 542: © George Burba | Dreamstime.com; 543: © George Burba | Dreamstime.com; 544: © Christian Delbert | Dreamstime.com; 549: © Hilary Nangle (top), © Hilary Nangle (bottom); 550: © F11photo | Dreamstime.com; 551: © Hilary Nangle; 552: © Hilary Nangle; 554: © Colin Young | Dreamstime.com; 555: © Hilary Nangle; 556: © Hilary Nangle; 557: © Chris Hill | Dreamstime.com; 558: © NPS/Matthew Lambert; 559: © Hilary Nangle; 560: © Kenneth Sponsler | Dreamstime.com; 562: © Zrfphoto | Dreamstime.com; 563: © Kenneth Sponsler | Dreamstime.com (top), © Stechouse | Dreamstime.com (bottom); 564: © Sandrafoyt | Dreamstime.com; 565: © Michael Shake | Dreamstime.com; 566: © Sandrafoyt | Dreamstime.com; 567: © Michael Shake | Dreamstime.com; 568: © NPS; 569: © NPS/Katrina George; 572: © NPS/Jeff Manuszak; 573: © Darren Dwayne Frazier | Dreamstime.com (top), © NPS/Katrina George (bottom); 574: © NPS/Katrina George; 575: © NPS/Jeff Manuszak; 577: © Mikhail Semenov | Dreamstime.com; 581: © kgcphoto / istockphoto.com; 582: © Posnov / istockphoto.com; 583: © Daniel Hosie / istockphoto.com; 584: © Jacob Boomsma | Dreamstime.com; 588: © NPS (top), © NPS (bottom); 589: © George Burba | Dreamstime.com; 590: © George Burba | Dreamstime.com; 591: © Patrick Barron | Dreamstime.com;

592: © NPS/Brett Raeburn; 595: © Dndavis | Dreamstime.com (left), © NPS (middle), © NPS/G.Gardner (right); 596: © Becky Lomax (top), © Wangkun Jia | Dreamstime.com (bottom); 597: © Becky Lomax; 598: © Pierre Leclerc | Dreamstime.com (top), © Daveallenphoto | Dreamstime.com (middle), © Kottapsm | Dreamstime.com (bottom); 599: © Teri Virbickis | Dreamstime.com; 603: © NPS; 604: © Sean Pavone | Dreamstime.com; 605: © Lightscribe | Dreamstime.com; 607: © Cvandyke | Dreamstime.com; 609: © Teri Virbickis | Dreamstime.com; 610: © Donald Fink | Dreamstime.com; 611: © Anthony Heflin | Dreamstime.com; 612: © Anton Foltin | Dreamstime.com; 613: © Anthony Heflin | Dreamstime.com; 614: © Alex Grichenko | Dreamstime.com; 615: © Melinda Fawver | Dreamstime.com; 616: © Becky Lomax; 620: © Becky Lomax; 621: © Becky Lomax (top), © Becky Lomax (middle), © Becky Lomax (bottom); 623: © Becky Lomax (top), © Becky Lomax (bottom); 624: © Becky Lomax; 625: © Becky Lomax; 626: © NPS; 630: © NPS; 631: © Wangkun Jia | Dreamstime.com (top), © Wangkun Jia | Dreamstime.com (bottom); 632: © NPS; 633: © Zrfphoto | Dreamstime.com; 636: © NPS; 638: © Paul Brady | Dreamstime.com (top), © NPS (bottom); 639: © Legacy1995 | Dreamstime.com; 640: © Sandra Foyt | Dreamstime.com; 644: © Sandra Foyt | Dreamstime.com (top), © Josh Kroese | Dreamstime.com (middle), © Itsadream | Dreamstime.com (bottom); 645: © NPS; 646: © Sandra Foyt | Dreamstime.com; 647: © Zrfphoto | Dreamstime.com; 649: © Alex Grichenko | Dreamstime.com; 652: © Tashka | Dreamstime.com; 653: © Pierre Leclerc | Dreamstime.com; 654: © NPS; 658: © Typhoonski | Dreamstime.com; 659: © NPS/R. Cammauf (top), © Dietmar Rauscher | Dreamstime.com (bottom); 660: © John Anderson | Dreamstime.com; 661: © Peter Etchells | Dreamstime.com; 662: © NPS/R. Cammauf (top), © NPS (bottom); 663: © NPS/R. Cammauf; 664: © Sandra Foyt | Dreamstime.com; 665: © NPS/T.Taylor; 666: © Chiyacat | Dreamstime.com; 668: © NPS/Shaun Wolfe; 671: © NPS (top), © NPS/Judd Patterson (bottom); 672: © NPS (top), © NPS/Rob Waara (bottom); 674: © NPS/Glenn Gardner; 677: © Varina and Jay Patel | Dreamstime.com (top), © NPS/Brett Seymour (bottom); 678: © NPS/John Dengler; 679: © NPS/Brett Seymour; 680: © MNStudio | Dreamstime.com; 683: © Mikko Ryynänen | Dreamstime.com (top), © MNStudio | Dreamstime.com (middle), © NPS/Susan Pershern (bottom); 684: © Susanna Henighan Potter; 685: © Gilney Lima | Dreamstime.com; 689: © Estabienn | Dreamstime.com (top), © Dayton344 | Dreamstime.com (bottom); 690: © Fairytaleportraits | Dreamstime.com; 691: © Anne M. Fearon-wood | Dreamstime.com (top), © Mike7777777 | Dreamstime.com (bottom); 692: © MNStudio | Dreamstime.com; 693: © MNStudio | Dreamstime.com; 694: © Anne M. Fearon-wood | Dreamstime.com; 695: © Birdiegal717 | Dreamstime.com; 699: © Chee-onn Leong | Dreamstime.com (top), © MNStudio | Dreamstime.com (bottom); 700: © Alexander Demyanenko | Dreamstime.com; 701: © NPS/J. Wei; 703: © NPS/J. Wei; 704: © NPS; 705: © Jimschw1 | Dreamstime.com; 708: © Susanna Henighan Potter; 709: © Susanna Henighan Potter; 711: © Susanna Henighan Potter; 712: © Susanna Henighan Potter (top), © Susanna Henighan Potter (bottom); 713: © Svecchiotti | Dreamstime.com; 714: © Kevin Berry | Dreamstime.com; 718: © NPS (top), © NPS (bottom); 719: © NPS; 720: © NPS; 721: © NPS; 722: © NPS/Neal Herbert; 729: © Becky Lomax; 734: © NPS/Penny Knuckles

TEXT CREDITS

Alaska

Text for the Alaska national parks adapted from *Moon Alaska,* first edition, by Lisa Maloney.

California

Text for Death Valley National Park adapted from *Moon Death Valley National Park,* first edition, by Jenna Bough

Text for Joshua Tree National Park adapted from *Moon Palm Springs & Joshua Tree,* first edition, by Jenna Bough

Text for Redwoods National and State Parks and for Channel Island National Park adapted from *Moon Coastal California,* fifth edition, by Stuart Thornton

Text for Pinnacles National Park adapted from *Moon Northern California,* seventh edition, by Elizabeth Linhart Veneman & Christopher Arns, and from *Moon Monterey & Carmel,* fifth edition, by Stuart Thornton

Pacific Northwest

Text for Crater Lake National Park adapted from *Moon Oregon,* 11th edition, by Judy Jewell & W. C. McRae

Text for the Washington national parks adapted from *Moon Washington,* 10th edition, by Matthew Lombardi

Southwest

Text for the Arizona national parks adapted from *Moon Arizona & the Grand Canyon,* 13th edition, by Tim Hull

Text for the Colorado national parks adapted from *Moon Colorado,* ninth edition, by Terri Cook

Text for Great Basin National Park adapted from *Moon Nevada,* eighth edition, by Scott Smith

Text for the Texas national parks adapted from *Moon Texas,* ninth edition, by Andy Rhodes

Text for the Utah national parks adapted from *Moon Utah,* 12th edition, by W. C. McRae & Judy Jewell

Rocky Mountains

Text for the Colorado national parks adapted from *Moon Colorado,* ninth edition, by Terri Cook

Text for the South Dakota national parks adapted from *Moon Mount Rushmore & the Black Hills,* third edition, by Laural A. Bidwell

Great Lakes and Northeast

Text for Acadia National Park adapted from *Moon Maine,* seventh edition, by Hilary Nangle

Text for Cuyahoga Valley National Park adapted from *Moon Cleveland,* second edition, by Douglas Trattner

Text for Isle Royale National Park adapted from *Moon Michigan,* sixth edition, by Paul Vachon

Text for Voyageurs National Park adapted from *Moon Minnesota,* fourth edition, by Tricia Cornell

South

Text for Great Smoky Mountains National Park adapted from *Moon Great Smoky Mountains National Park,* first edition, by Jason Frye

Text for Shenandoah National Park adapted from *Moon Blue Ridge Parkway Road Trip,* first edition, by Jason Frye

Text for Mammoth Cave National Park adapted from *Moon Kentucky,* second edition, by Theresa Dowell Blackinton

Text for Congaree National Park adapted from *Moon South Carolina,* sixth edition, by Jim Morekis

Text for Everglades National Park adapted from *Moon Sarasota & Naples,* second edition, by Jason Ferguson

Text for Biscayne National Park and Dry Tortugas National Park adapted from *Moon Florida Keys,* third edition, by Joshua Lawrence Kinser

Islands

Text for Hawai'i Volcanoes National Park adapted from *Moon Big Island of Hawai'i,* eighth edition, by Bree Kessler

Text for Virgin Islands National Park adapted from *Moon U.S. & British Virgin Islands,* sixth edition, by Susanna Henighan Potter

ACKNOWLEDGMENTS

A huge thank-you goes out to all past and present members of the National Park Service. It's through their labors that we have access to such treasures. For many in the park service, their work is a devotion to the park they love.

I thank my parents for introducing me to the national parks. Before I was born, my father worked summers at Mount Rainier National Park. On one of my parents' first dates, he took my mom bushwhacking to see a secret cluster of ancient trees. After they were married, my parents led us kids to the giant trees, which later became known as Grove of the Patriarchs (after the trail and bridge were installed). As grandparents, my folks took their small grandchildren to hug the no-longer-secret trees. After my father passed away, my mother, along with all of the kids and grandkids, returned to our grove to honor his memory amid those sacred trees. Experiencing the national parks is one of the greatest gifts parents can give their children.

I thank the regional writers who contributed mounds of their expertise. Their valuable insight into their "home" parks provided the backbone of this project; without it, this book could not be. Cheers also go to my editor, Kevin McLain, for his outstanding shepherding of the project, Mike Morgenfeld who handled the maps, and Darren Alessi who wrangled the photos.

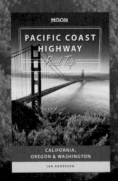

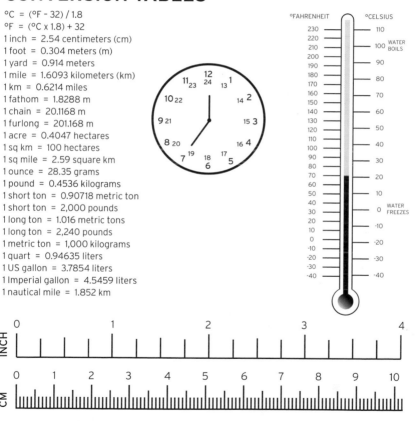

MAP SYMBOLS

- Expressway
- Primary Road
- Secondary Road
- Unpaved Road
- Feature Trail
- Other Trail
- Ferry
- Pedestrian Walkway
- Stairs

- ○ City/Town
- ◉ State Capital
- ⊛ National Capital
- ★ Point of Interest
- ● Accommodation
- ▼ Restaurant/Bar
- ■ Other Location
- Λ Campground

- Airport
- Airfield
- ▲ Mountain
- ✦ Unique Natural Feature
- Waterfall
- Park
- T Trailhead
- Skiing Area

- Golf Course
- P Parking Area
- Archaeological Site
- Church
- Gas Station
- Glacier
- Mangrove
- Reef
- Swamp

CONVERSION TABLES

°C = (°F - 32) / 1.8
°F = (°C x 1.8) + 32
1 inch = 2.54 centimeters (cm)
1 foot = 0.304 meters (m)
1 yard = 0.914 meters
1 mile = 1.6093 kilometers (km)
1 km = 0.6214 miles
1 fathom = 1.8288 m
1 chain = 20.1168 m
1 furlong = 201.168 m
1 acre = 0.4047 hectares
1 sq km = 100 hectares
1 sq mile = 2.59 square km
1 ounce = 28.35 grams
1 pound = 0.4536 kilograms
1 short ton = 0.90718 metric ton
1 short ton = 2,000 pounds
1 long ton = 1.016 metric tons
1 long ton = 2,240 pounds
1 metric ton = 1,000 kilograms
1 quart = 0.94635 liters
1 US gallon = 3.7854 liters
1 Imperial gallon = 4.5459 liters
1 nautical mile = 1.852 km

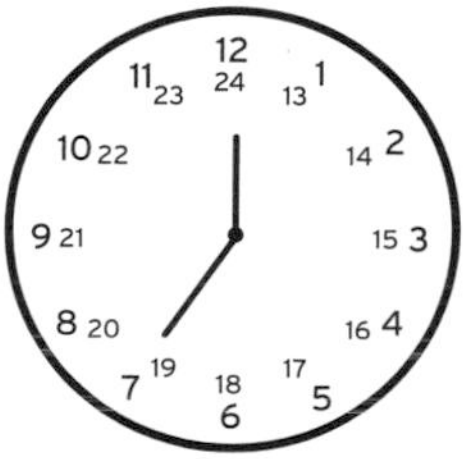

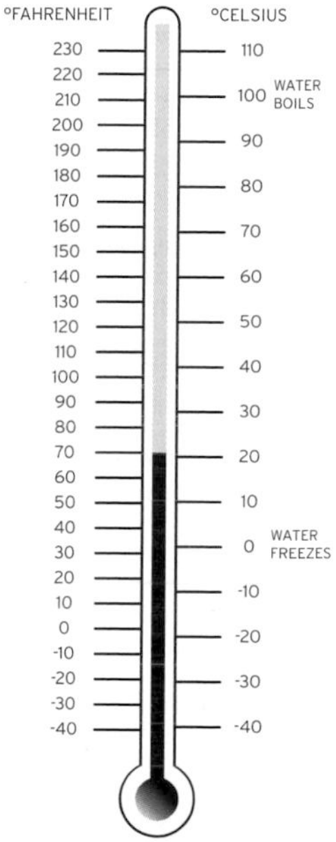

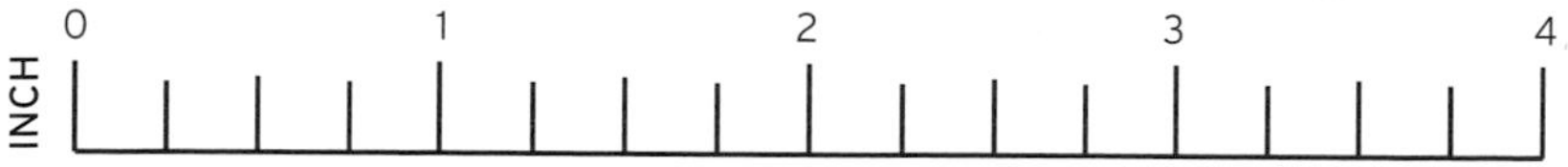

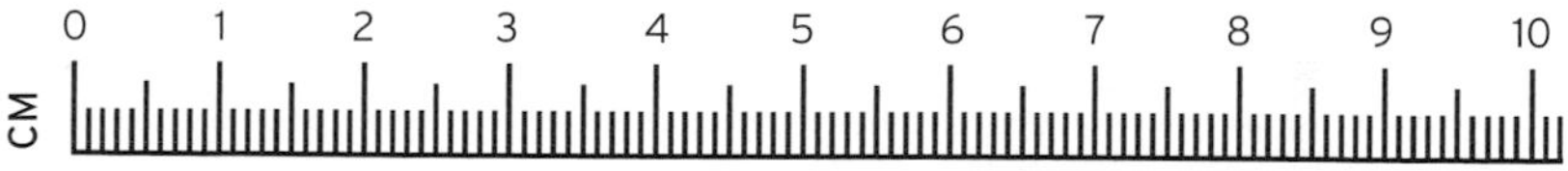

MOON USA NATIONAL PARKS

Avalon Travel
Hachette Book Group
1700 Fourth Street
Berkeley, CA 94710, USA
www.moon.com

Editor: Kevin McLain
Acquiring Editor: Nikki Ioakimedes
Series Manager: Sabrina Young
Fact checker: Ashley M. Biggers
Copy Editor: Ashley Benning
Graphics and Production Coordinator: Darren Alessi
Cover Design: Kimberly Glyder Design
Interior Design: Megan Jones Design
Moon Logo: Tim McGrath
Map Editor: Mike Morgenfeld
Cartographers: Moon Street Cartography, Mike Morgenfeld, John Culp
Proofreader: Kelly Lydick
Indexer: Greg Jewett

ISBN-13: 978-1-64049-918-8

Printing History
1st Edition — 2018
2nd Edition — October 2020
5 4 3 2 1

Front cover photo: Turret Arch seen through North Window at first light in Arches National Park, Utah © Larry Geddis / Alamy Stock Photo
Back cover photos (top to bottom): Kenai National Park, Alaska © Galyna Andrushko | Dreamstime.com; Joshua Tree National Park, California © Lunamarina | Dreamstime.com; Virgin Islands National Park, U.S. Virgin Islands © Fairytaleportraits | Dreamstime.com

Printed in China by R.R. Donnelley